ABOUT FACE
ACT
ALOHA
AMAZON QUARTERLY
amex-canada
AMPO
it aint me babe
kaleidoscope
THE LIBERATOR
FREE PRESS
MASSES
ANN ARBOR SUN
APPEAL TO REASON
AVATAR
Berkeley Tribe
BIAFRA
MODERN UTOPIAN
MOTHER EARTH
sds new left notes
NOLA EXPRESS
Notes from Cuba
off our backs
BLACK MASK
THE BOND
BREAD AND PUPPET NEWSPAPER
Clear Creek
OLD MOLE
ORACLE
THE ORGAN
OTHER SCENES
OZ
PAC·O·LIES
come out!
COMMON SENSE
COUNTERPOINT
distant drummer
DOCK of the BAY
Observer
The Pentagon Paper
People's Computer Company
RADICAL SOFTWARE
THE RAG
The Realist
REVOLUTION
DOMEBOOK
EL MALCRIADO
FATEH
FATIGUE PRESS
FED UP!
THE FIFTH ESTATE
San Francisco Express Times
THE SECOND FRONT
SEED
SHAKEDOWN
SMALL ARMS
FREEDOM'S JOURNAL
the furies
gay liberator
Gay Sunshine
UP AGAINST THE WALL
UP FRONT
VECTOR
VIETNAM COURIER
Vietnam GI
vocations for social change
GOOD TIMES
BLIMP
The BIRD
inner-city VOICE
The International Times it
VOICE of the LUMPEN
WALKER'S APPEAL
WHERE IT'S AT
Whole Earth Catalog
WHOLE EARTH Review
WIN
Yipster Times

ABOUT FACE
ACT
ALOHA
AMAZON QUARTERLY
amex-canada
AMPO
it ain't me babe
kaleidoscope
THE LIBERATOR
FREE PRESS
MASSES
ANN ARBOR SUN
APPEAL TO REASON
AVATAR
Barb
Berkeley Tribe
BIAFRA
MODERN UTOPIAN
MOTHER EARTH
sds new left notes
NOLA EXPRESS
Notes from Cuba
off our backs
BLACK MASK
THE BOND
BREAD AND PUPPET NEWSPAPER
Clear Creek
OLD MOLE
ORACLE
THE ORGAN
OTHER SCENES
OZ
PAC·O·LIES
come out!
COMMON SENSE
COUNTERPOINT
distant drummer
DOCK of the BAY
Observer
The Pentagon Paper
People's Computer Company
RADICAL SOFTWARE
THE RAG
The Realist
DOMEBOOK
EL MALCRIADO
FATEH
FATIGUE PRESS
FED UP!
THE FIFTH ESTATE
San Francisco Express Times
THE SECOND FRONT
SEED
SHAKEDOWN
SMALL ARMS
FREEDOM'S JOURNAL
the furies
gay liberator
Gay Sunshine
UP AGAINST THE WALL!
UP FRONT
VECTOR
VIETNAM COURIER
Vietnam GI
vocations for social change
GOOD TIMES
BLIMP
THE BIRD
inner-city VOICE
The International Times it
VOICE of the LUMPEN
WALKER'S APPEAL
WHERE IT'S AT
Whole Earth Catalog
WHOLE EARTH Review
WIN
Yipster Times

POWER TO THE PEOPLE

THE GRAPHIC DESIGN OF THE RADICAL PRESS
AND THE RISE OF THE
COUNTER-CULTURE, 1964–1974

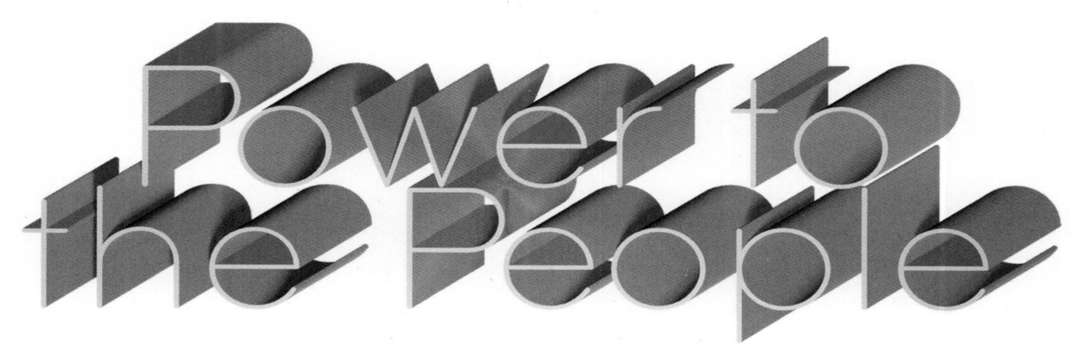

The Graphic Design of the Radical Press and the Rise of the Counter-Culture, 1964–1974

EDITED
BY
GEOFF KAPLAN

UNIVERSITY OF CHICAGO
PRESS

CHICAGO and LONDON

Geoff Kaplan has produced projects for a range of academic and cultural institutions, and his work is included in the permanent collections of the San Francisco Museum of Modern Art and MoMA. He teaches in the Graduate Program of Design at the California College of Art.

The University of Chicago Press, Chicago 60637
The University of Chicago Press, Ltd., London

Printed in China

22 21 20 19 18 17 16 15 14 13   1 2 3 4 5

Publication of this book has been aided by a grant from the Neil Harris Endowment fund, which honors the innovative scholarship of Neil Harris, the Preston and Sterling Morton Professor Emeritus of History at the University of Chicago. The Fund is supported by contributions from the students, colleagues, and friends of Neil Harris.

ISBN-13: 978-0-226-42435-4 (cloth)
ISBN-13: 978-0-226-42437-8 (e-book)
ISBN-10: 0-226-42435-9 (cloth)
ISBN-10: 0-226-42437-5 (e-book)

Library of Congress Cataloging-in-Publication Data
Power to the people : the graphic design of the radical press and the rise of the counter-culture, 1964–1974 / edited by Geoff Kaplan.
pages. color illustrations cm
Includes bibliographical references and index.
ISBN-13: 978-0-226-42435-4 (hardcover : alkaline paper)
ISBN-10: 0-226-42435-9 (hardcover : alkaline paper)
ISBN-13: 978-0-226-42437-8 (e-book)
ISBN-10: 0-226-42437-5 (e-book) 1. Underground press publications—United States—History—20th century. 2. Underground press publications—United States—History—20th century—Pictorial works. 3. Graphic design (Typography)—United States—History—20th century. 4. Counterculture—United States—Bibliography. 5. Youth—Books and reading—United States—History—20th century. I. Kaplan, Geoff.
Z1033.U58P69 2013
741.6'5097309046—dc23

2012024547

♾ This paper meets the requirements of ANSI/NISO Z39.48-1992 (Permanence of Paper).

CONTENTS

INTRODUCTION

Geoff Kaplan

In the 1960s, a media revolution was afoot as explosive as the revolutions taking place in the streets of Chicago and Paris, Prague and Mexico City. With the increased availability of cheap offset printing, countless groups linked to the antiwar, civil rights, and various liberation movements were able to spread their messages through both elaborately designed newspapers and visually plainspoken broadsheets. Ranging from the psychedelic pages of the ***San Francisco Oracle***, Haight-Ashbury's paper of choice, to the fiery editorials of the ***Black Panther Party Paper***, these papers were remarkable for their do-it-yourself ethos, their fervent belief in freedom of expression, and their staunch advocacy of both a politically radical and countercultural lifestyle. In keeping with such convictions, the publications were also remarkable for their graphic innovations. Experimental typography and wildly inventive layouts gave shape to an alternative media culture as much informed by the space age, television, the computer era, and socialism as by the holy trinity of the sixties underground: sex, drugs, and rock 'n' roll.

Power of the People examines the role of alternative and underground media in the formation of social movements in the United States, with a particular focus on design. It documents the ways in which such collective practices graphically fashioned the image of a culture undergoing pronounced and systemic change. Recalling an era in which Marshall McLuhan could proclaim, "The Medium Is the Message," ***Power of the People*** treats the design practices of this period as continuous with a range of activist strategies: as a vehement challenge to the dominance of official media and a critical form of self-representation. Considering the publications linked to a diverse body of social and political interests (black power, women's liberation, gay rights, environmentalism, the antiwar movement, etc.) the book explores these graphic innovations relative to the context of sixties visual culture at large. And it poses the question of the implications of such work today, at a moment when corporate media has exerted even more decisive control over the public sphere even as there has been an unprecedented explosion of self-publishing and blogging.

Indeed, the history of the underground press at this time reveals an interest in graphic design not conventionally discussed in the narrative of sixties social movements. Yet technical advances in printing were critical to the proliferation of this media revolution—and the messages disseminated by extension. While acknowledging the methodological pitfalls of technological determinism, one does need to acknowledge the following developments: typesetting machines were progressively automated so that production costs were lower; press-on lettering Letraset afforded a quick and dirty way to produce eye-catching headlines; and cold-type setters, which required no training to use, replaced expensive and complicated typesetting machines. Such processes are extraordinarily crude compared to today's forms of graphic mediation—not to mention digital technology—but these strides in media enabled previously untrained individuals to produce their own publications, wildly diverse in visual style.

Of course, many of these papers were established and staffed largely by affluent white college graduates, many of whom came to social consciousness through the impact of the civil rights movement in the early 1960s. As this volume amply shows, there were notable exceptions to this rule—consider the work of Black Panther artist Emory Douglas as a signal example—but the graphic style typically associated with the Hippies has indeed been seen as synonymous with the counterculture. And while one needs to stress the mostly collective and anonymous nature of such endeavors, produced by untrained "professionals," it is also the case that several important figures emerged in this period who are now household names within the era's visual culture, including R. Crumb, Rick Griffin, Steven Heller, Martin Sharp, and Stewart Brand.

Yet it is the largely anonymous efforts of amateurs that are of the greatest importance here: the work of those media pioneers who threw off the yoke of the proper name—the singular Author—to embrace the DIY spirit of the era. It's for this reason that I've reprinted in full a three-part article from ***Amazon Quarterly***, the groundbreaking lesbian magazine published in Northern California, as the most eloquent—because direct—statement of this ideal. Written by one "Laurel," the essay "How to Make a Magazine" is to the point in the political and cultural motivations of its maker. Not only has "Laurel" rejected her last name as a symbol of patriarchal authority, she has given her community of readers the tools to reproduce the medium itself (fig. 1.1).

"How to Make a Magazine" is the only text from the period reproduced in this book; all the other contributions are contemporary. Let me say here that it's a great privilege to feature essays of scholars Gwen Allen, Bob Ostertag and Fred Turner, not to mention the many recollections of that period from a wide range of artists, critics, and activists. Yet "How to Make a Magazine" is reprinted not merely as a period piece, inspiring nostalgia for a utopian moment that by definition could never exist, but as an object lesson for the interests of independent and alternative media today. Indeed, this book takes its motivation in part from the battles waged over media in the last decade, not to mention the sense of weary resignation, or even outright hostility, expressed toward the role of graphic design in the enabling of global spectacle. Names such as Rupert Murdoch and Roger Ailes are virtually synonymous with the most dispiriting aspects of mainstream media: the ways in which the public sphere has been irredeemably compromised by corporate interests. Likewise, there is little doubt that design has played a central role in the manufacture of the "experience economy," to say little of the relentless branding of culture, nations, and commerce that comes with the territory.

HOW TO MAKE A MAGAZINE

BY LAUREL

When we started Amazon Quarterly *we knew almost nothing about what was involved in publishing a magazine, which was a good thing, since we assumed it was fun and easy and that helped make it so. We've just blundered through and learned from our mistakes . . . but often we've muttered "Why didn't somebody tell us!" as we realized we'd taken the long way around once again. We thought some of you might want to share some of what we've picked up, whether you think you might want to start a magazine, print a book of poetry or photographs, or just help out with the newsletter from your women's center.*

Because of new advances in printing technology, small runs (less than 2,000 copies, say) can be printed for much less than it would cost to xerox the material -- and, of course, the quality is much better. So, even if you have to pay a printer, it shouldn't be more than 3¢ per sheet (or 1 1/2 ¢ per page since there are 2 pages per sheet), and the more copies you print the cheaper each one will be.

The first step is to typeset your copy. Professional typesetting on a machine that "justifies" the length of lines so that they come out even on the right hand side is very expensive. It could cost you as much or more than what you pay the printer. Even margins aren't all that important, so we decided to use an IBM Selectric and type the manuscripts ourselves, saving about $350 per issue. A Selectric can be rented for @$30 per month or purchased for $490 new. It is preferable to other electrics because the style of type can easily be changed from this to this *to this, but whatever electric typewriter you decide on, you should use a carbon ribbon which you type on only once and throw away.*

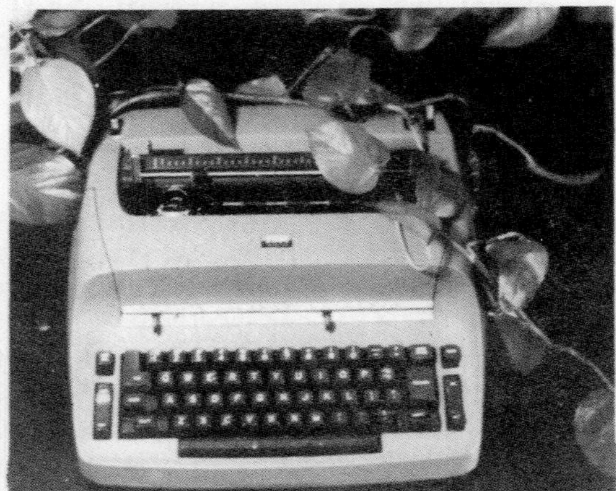

What comes out of the typewriter will be exactly what the printed copy will look like unless you decide to have the printer reduce it when she/he prints it. We reduce everything by 10% in order to fit more into

66

Fig. 1.1. "How to Make a Magazine, Part 1," **Amazon Quarterly** (March 1974), vol. 2, no. 3, pp. 66–70; "Part 2," July 1974, vol. 2, no. 4, pp. 63–66; and "Part 3," November 1974, vol. 3, no. 1, pp. 71–72

AQ's pages. When we type the copy we set the margins so that what is typed will be 10% larger than we want it to be when it's printed.

After everything is typeset you're ready to start puzzling over what will fit where. We use a chart like the one below to help us visualize what pages are opposite each other. If you'll open this issue up all the way and flatten it out, you'll find that its 72 pages are printed on 18 legal size sheets (8½ x 14). There are 36 sides. Now except for the centerfold (pp. 36 and 37 in AQ) none of the consecutive pages are on the same sheet: page 1 and page 72 are on the same sheet, page 2 and page 71 are on the same sheet, etc. At first this was mind boggling, so we made up a dummy--that is, a mock-up with the number of pages we wanted (72) all numbered and stapled like the finished-product-to-be. This is a work-book for planning your layout. You'll undoubtedly need to reshuffle things, so use a pencil, and don't panic -- everything is fixable.

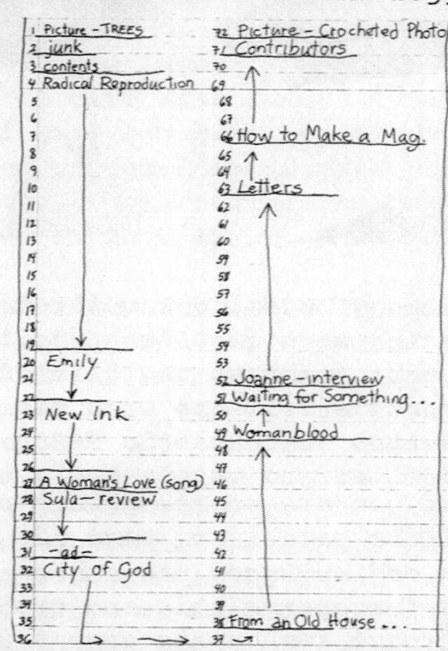

O.K., when you know where all the copy will go and have measured carefully to insure it will really fit, you're ready to do layout, or paste up as some people say. Only DON'T USE PASTE and don't use that old standby rubber cement unless it's really an emergency. Paste will ruin your fine typing job with blisters and bubbles, and rubber cement is a pain in the ass.

One of the tools you really owe it to yourself to get is an Electro-Stik Hand Waxer like the one pictured here:

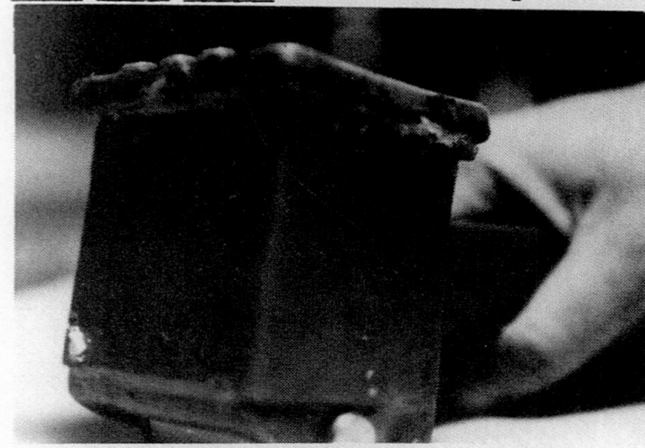

This little gizmo rolls warm wax onto the back of your copy. It dries and hardens, but it will be sticky forever--no rush like with rubber cement, and you can peel up the copy 3 or 4 different times if you have to without ruining it. The waxer costs around \$30 new, but we got ours for \$10 used (good photo-supply stores carry them). The Electro-Stik wax costs around \$2 per box, but it goes a long way.

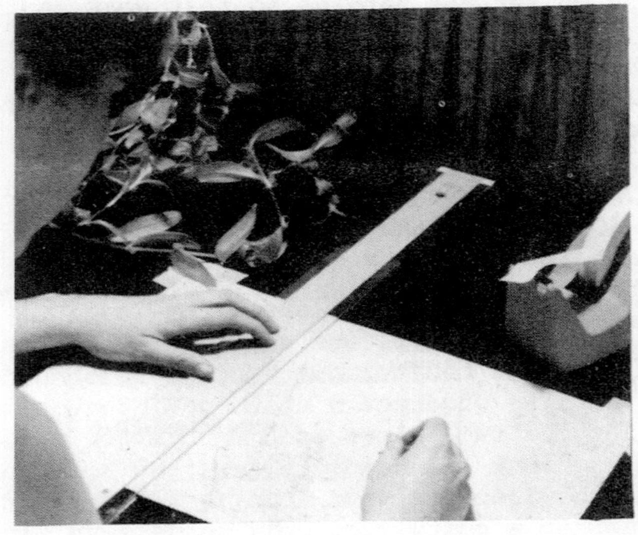

After you've waxed your copy, you're ready to make your layout sheets. Some people use blue-lined commercial graph paper and some printers can furnish layout sheets to you free. We've never found just the right size, so we make our own using a T-square and a non-photographic light blue pencil.

You need a large flat surface to work on -- we use an old door atop concrete blocks for a layout table. It should be smooth and have some reliable right angles (check with your T-square). If you make a "frame" for your layout sheets on the table with strips of tape, you won't have to keep measuring when you draw in your margins with the blue pencil. If you use the side of the table next to your tummy as the base of your frame, you'll just need to make two corners at the top with masking tape. Mark the margins on the table and then just use the T-Square to blue pencil them onto the layout sheets as you go.

If you are starting with page 1, what you'll have in front of you will be page 1 and page 72. Even numbered pages are always on the left and odd numbered pages are always on the right. Our most common mistake was forgetting this and trying to put page two on the same layout sheet as page one, for example. So, remember, after you've layed down page one, you've got to get out another sheet and make page 2 and page 71.

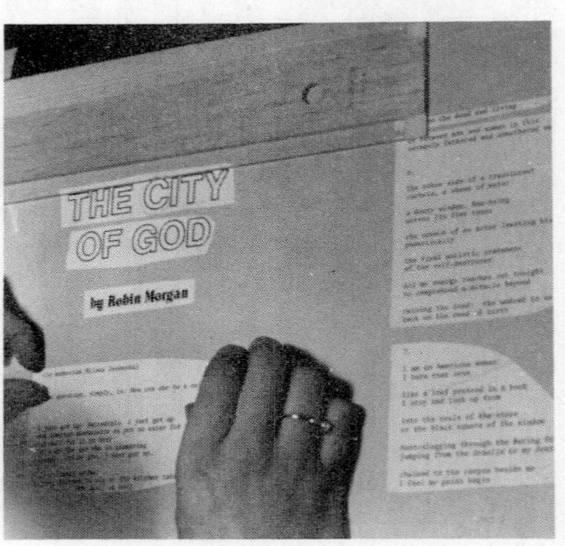

Check the placement of each strip of copy you lay down both top to bottom and across with the T-square. The wax will allow you to slide things into place. A pair of tweezers will be helpful for placing small chunks--use the point of an X-acto knife to adjust things.

Tap the copy gently into place, now you're ready to roll it down.

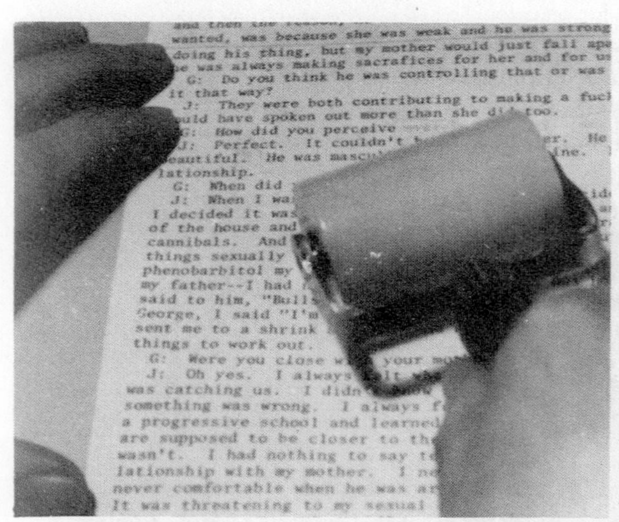

For this you'll need another gizmo which you shouldn't try to do without--a porcelain hand roller. Roll from the center outward, like making a pie shell. Even after you've rolled down the copy, you should be able to pull it up if you've made a mistake, but unless you really work at it, the copy is permanently put.

Be careful not to get wax anywhere on the layout sheet -- it picks up dirt like a magnet, and you'll have big blotches on your printed copies. Use liquid paper typing correction fluid to cover any finger prints or spills you've incurred during layout. This will cover stray wax too.

Usually, at this point, we put down our headlines which we've saved room for at the beginning of each article. This is a slow and painstaking process unless you have access to a headliner machine. Most small magazines don't and, like us, they use press type lettering. This comes in alphabet sheets--as many as 50 or 60 different styles depending on the company. Many styles and sizes should be available at your local architectural supply store. Choose whatever you like, but keeping the mood of your articles in mind, you'll have some idea of what is most appropriate. For our splashy Double Issue layout we used outrageously baroque lettering. Last issue we wanted things quiet and understated--and we used completely different kinds of press type.

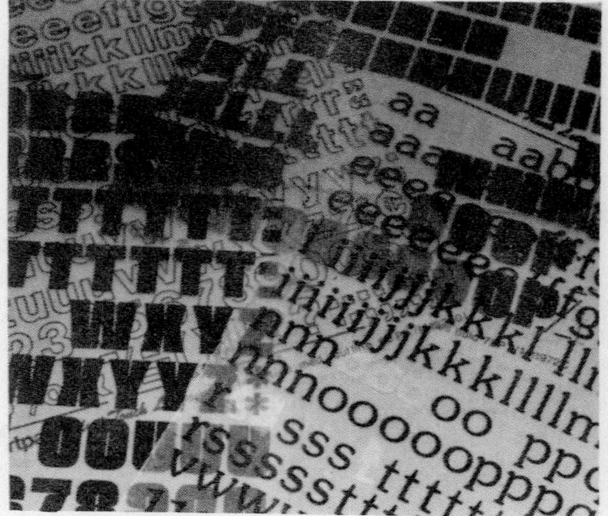

They'll probably try to sell you a stylus for rubbing on the press type, but all you really need is the rounded end of your X-acto knife. Don't be discouraged if letters tend to break apart and peel off at first. It takes a little practice. Be sure to line the letters up straight with your T-square and to make them equidistant. Note that some letters like "L" have lots of "open space" on one side and can be placed closer to the next letter than a letter like "H" which is *solid on both sides.*

Once you think everything including the headlines is in the right place, you're ready for several proofreadings. Try to get people to proof who've never read the stuff before and who aren't immune to the errors. Each error should be circled with the blue pencil--the marks will not be picked up by the printer's camera, so you can make them as big and bad as you like. Make a list of the corrections that go on each page. Type them along with their page number, wax the correction sheet, and simply cut them out and stick them over the goofs. Use the T-square to help you keep things in line. Unless you've been a perfect typist, expect to spend some time on this proofing process. Make sure that you check to see a sentence which carries over from say p. 13 to p. 14 makes sense, and really read each paragraph to make sure you haven't accidentally left something out.

So far, I've been talking about only the typed copy. Next issue we'll pick up with graphics and half tones, show you how the printer photographs the copy, burns the metal plates, and runs the press. Drop us a note if you have any questions about the process so far.

SPRING/1974 AMAZON QUARTERLY AWARDS

The first quarterly $50 award will be divided and given to: Pat Emmerson for "Emily" and Frances Rooney for "Womanblood." A generous sister has given us a grant for the 1974 year so we can continue to offer this incentive to new writers and artists. We especially would like to encourage women to send us in-depth essays and visual art, as our need is greatest in these areas. See page 62 for details.

SAVING THE TREES

In the Fall 1973 Special Issue, we asked for women to help us with the extra cost of using recycled paper. We were especially concerned since the trees AQ is printed on are cut down in Canada for use in the U.S. A very kind sister from Canada has made this issue possible by sending the $300 extra necessary to buy recycled paper. We hope that her example will lead other women's publications to want to save the trees, and that you will want to send a contribution (however small) to:

TREES
Amazon Quarterly
554 Valle Vista
Oakland, CA 94610

HOW TO MAKE A MAGAZINE

PART TWO == BY LAUREL

Last issue we covered the basics of typesetting and layout. Now we can go on to the mysteries of the print shop.

Depending on the number of copies you intend to run, the quality desired, and how much you can spend, you will choose either a paper/plastic plate process or a metal plate process. As there's nothing to the former, I'll concentrate here on metal plates. These must be used for any page you want to print with a half-tone photo.

The Copy Camera

Most commercial printers have a huge wall-model camera that takes pictures (later to be transferred onto metal plates) of both straight-line copy and half-toned graphics. This piece of equipment is at least a $2000 investment, so many people who have small presses go to big printers to use the camera and plate-making facilities.

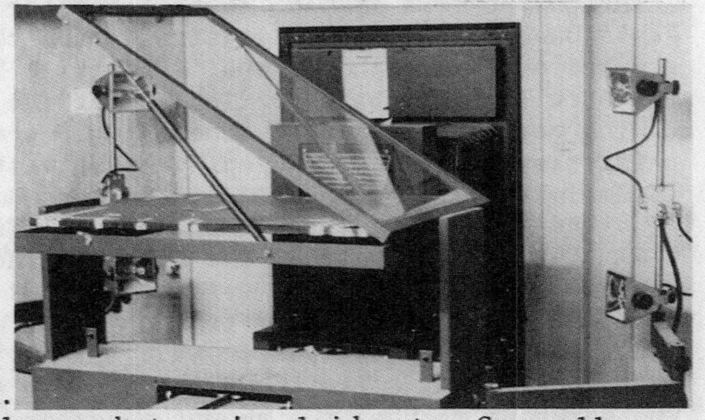

The camera pictured here is a Brown 2000. There are many different kinds of copy cameras with various handy features, but, basically, it is just a very large model of your own hand camera. Half of the camera, where the controls are (shutter, lens focus, exposure timer, half-tone screen rack, etc), has to be in a darkroom and the other half should be outside, in another room.

The copy camera can reduce or enlarge what you've laid out. Generally we reduce by 10%-15% depending on how many good submissions we want to fit in. This issue is reduced to 85% of the original size.

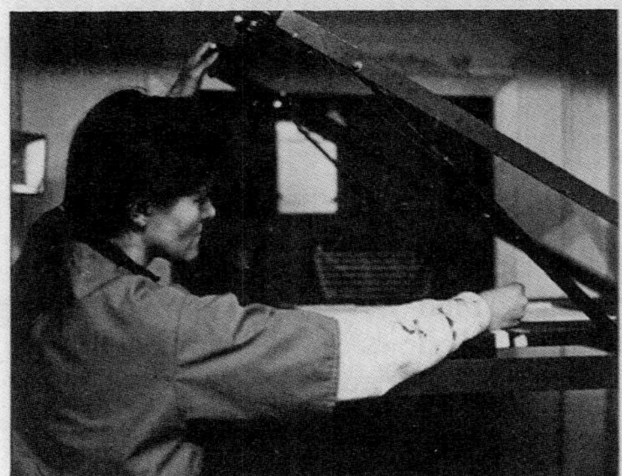

Graphics

Reductions and enlargements are especially necessary for graphics since you rarely find a picture just the size you need. Your printer should give you a reduction wheel (or pick one up at a photo supply) which will make it easier to calculate how much a picture needs to be reduced or enlarged.

Once you've calculated the to-be-printed size of your graphic (to the nearest 16th of an inch), you make a "window" for it on the appropriate layout page.

The "window" is made with Rubilith, a red translucent film that can be cut with a cleaner edge than something like construction paper. It is very expensive, so we use red construction paper and border it with red lithographer's tape to get a clean edge. Your window material must be either red or black in order to leave a clear window on the negative produced by the copy camera.

Negatives -- Regular and Half-toned

The copy camera exposes film just like any other, but the objective is to make a negative only, not a print. The negatives will be used for the next step, burning the metal plates. Line negatives are shot where only words and line drawings are on the layout page, or a "window" for a to-be-reduced (or enlarged) photo. Half-tone negatives must be shot for any graphics with shading (all except line drawings). If you look at any magazine picture, you'll see that the image is made of tiny dots -- the larger the dots, the darker the image. (We like to use a very fine screen for most of our photos, so that the dots are less obvious.)

The copy camera is made so the operator can easily slip the screen (a glass panel with dots on it) inside the camera where the dots will be photographed over your photograph. They will be larger or smaller depending on how much light is being reflected off the photo you have on the easel.

Line negatives and half-tone negatives are essentially treated alike after this: they go into a developing bath, a stop bath, fixer, and a final wash. It definitely takes practice to do good half-tones though, as there is magic required in getting the right exposure, developing time, chemical strength, etc. The next step after the developed negatives have dried (they're just hung up with clothes pins to drip dry) is the opaquing and stripping process.

Though you wouldn't have to know about opaquing with most commercial printers, some small press people will ask if you want to do it yourself to save money. Any monkey could do it with a little practice. Extra care in the darkroom reduces the amount necessary, but there is always some opaquing to do. Essentially, you brush on red or black fluid to cover any scratches or bubble spots on the negatives. This almost has to be done on a light table. It's time consuming and a certain pain in the neck, but you may be saving $10 an hour if you do it yourself.

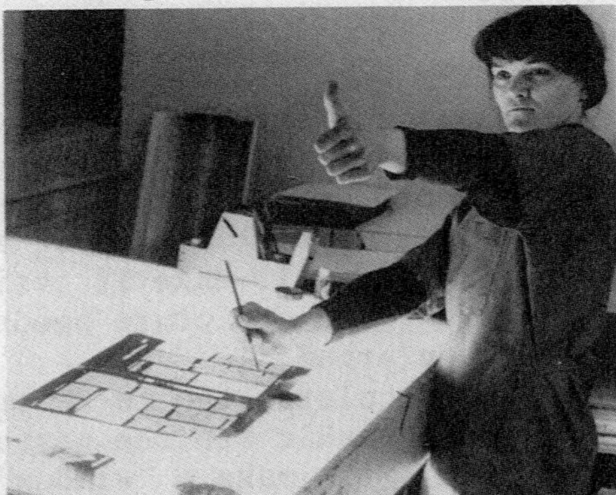

Opaquing

Similarly, some press shops will allow you to do your own stripping. This is a little more difficult than it sounds, but basically, this is fitting your half-toned negatives into the appropriate "windows" and taping them into place with red or black litho tape. There's an art to this--ask for instructions at the print shop.

Making the Metal Plates

The next step in the process is burning the plates. The negatives are laid on top of what looks to be a sheet of heavy aluminum foil (the metal plate) and put into a vacuum suction glass compartment. The vacuum assures perfect contact of the negative with the metal plate (no air bubbles, slips or slides). The vacuum easel tilts to face an extremely powerful arc lamp which is some distance across the room. For me, visions of the electric chair and shock treatments accompany the extremely high voltage zap necessary to burn the metal plate. It's frightening at first. There's a timer which allows you to leave the room, or at least to turn away while the blinding light is on.

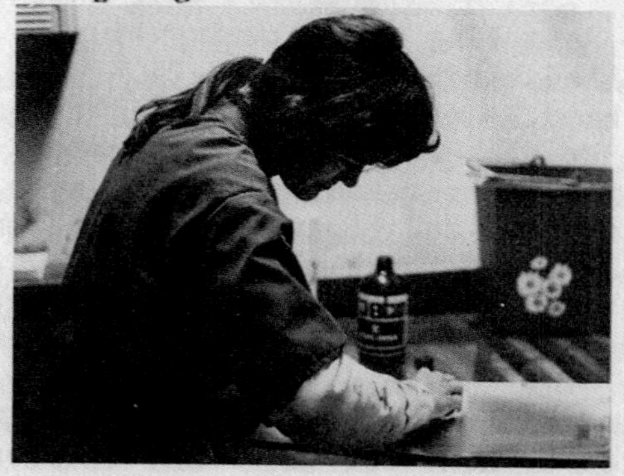

Next the burned plates are developed and fixed, a very simple process which anyone can do with a bit of practice. It doesn't require a darkroom as developing the negatives does, just a couple of chemicals and a flowing water tank for rinse. The metal plates are hung to dry, awaiting the next step, going onto the press. Your original copy or pictures are readily visible, exactly as they will print, on the metal plates now.

The Press

If you've ever used a mimeo machine you have a simplified but helpful picture of how the press works. The metal plate clamps on like a stencil and curves around a roller. Sections of the metal plate (depending on your image) are water soluble and others repel anything water-based. The water-based ink slides off the parts of the plate which are to be clear white space on your finished page, and sticks to the type and image area in photos.

A really big offset press can print both sides of 8-10 of your pages at once. I don't want to get into the presses here--there's too much to learn --but, if possible, you should find a printer with the most economical press for your needs. The more press operator's time you can save, the better. We've been paying about $14 per hour, so it is an important consideration.

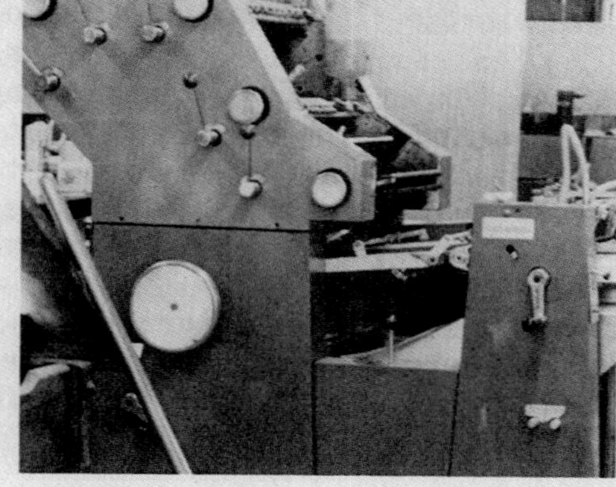

Another consideration will be ink color. Generally your inside print will be black. If you want a color ink on the cover you'll have to pay for a washup charge on the press. It takes a half hour or so to clean up the mess whenever the pressperson changes the ink color on a press.

Some large presses can run 2 or more colors at once, but, of course, this adds to your cost.

Before the presses start to roll, you must have decided the quality, color, and weight (thickness) of paper you want. Your printer usually can order in bulk, so unless you spot a super deal, it's best to order through them. Same with the cover stock. Choose your color and weight from the printer's samples. Coated stock is usually the most expensive, and it is also more difficult to fold if you're planning to do that part by hand.

Your book will roll off the press either on precut sheets or parent sheets which will later be folded into signatures and collated.

BINDING

There are many different ways of collating, stapling and trimming your books -- all of which, taken together, is called bindery.

We collated the first two issues of AQ by hand...an incredible thing to do, but our only financial choice at that time. We picked up the 18 separate bundles of pages and the printed cover from the printer and brought it home to a waiting band of women who licked their fingers and began the production-line strut. It took 6 women about 5 hours--30 women hours altogether--to collate 1000 copies. Then we had to staple, fold, and trim them.

When we began printing 3,000 copies we made an arrangement with the printer to let us use the print shop's automatic collator. With a little training and a lot of trial and error, we were able to collate 3,000 in 30 woman-hours.

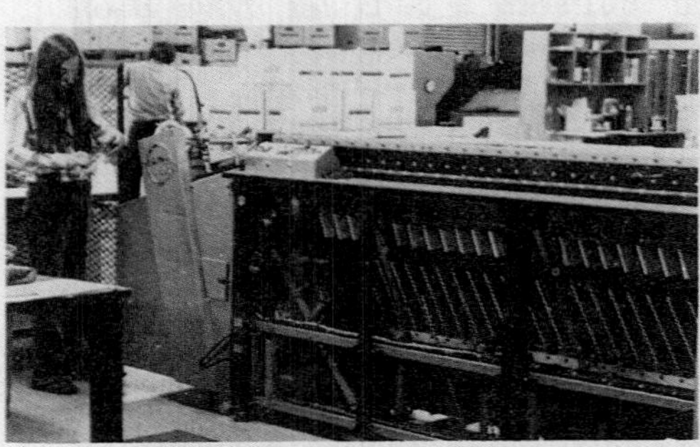

Automatic Collator

We stapled by hand for the first 4 issues --not really by hand, but one copy at a time on an electric saddle stitcher. Easy enough--but boring! Then we had to use real elbow grease to fold each issue flat.

There is another kind of binding, perfect binding, which is much more expensive. This provides a "spine" on your book. The pages are cut and glued together instead of stapled.

AQ grew and the printer's facilities too. We learned how to use new machinery as it came, particularly the automatic stitcher and folder. Now, since moving to Boston and going up to 5,000 copies per issue, we are using a mammoth commercial printer and bindery with automatic everything. It's expensive, but it's a relief to turn over at least part of making the magazine to someone else now. Their super machinery can collate, fold, and trim all in one graceful motion...an elegance we're willing to pay for.

After trimming off the uneven edges caused by folding, your books are ready to spread to your sisters. Next issue we'll finish up with some advice on distribution, the long finger of the IRS and the U.S. Post Office, applying for grants, etc.

HOW TO MAKE A MAGAZINE

PART THREE==============================BY LAUREL

In the first 2 parts of this article we've shown how to typeset, lay out, and print your own magazine, book, or newspaper. All that remains is how to distribute it. There are generally 5 major outlets: 1)subscriptions or single issues sent to individuals, 2)library and other institutional orders, 3) bookstores, 4)wholesale distributors, 5)feminist distributors.

Subscriptions: To build up your subscription list you'll have to advertise either by exchanging free ads with other magazines and newspapers or by purchasing space. Off Our Backs, Majority Report, and, of course, Ms. reach a larger audience than the other women's publications and are usually the best places for ads.

As the subs roll in you'll want to set up an efficient system so you can tell when they have expired and track down change of addresses. Before we changed over to a computer system, we typed the subscription information on carbon set addressing labels (4 or 5 copy sets are available.) Usually it's best to say with what volume and what issue the sub expires (Vol.1, issue 4 for example) since you may get behind sometime and a date might be confusing. We clipped our sub labels to 3 x 5 cards and filed them under states, alphabetically by last name. Eventually, when you have enough, you'll want to file by zip code order (if you mail 2nd or 3rd class).

The post office will give you booklets on how to wrap, address, label, and bundle the books for mailing. Be sure to apply for 2nd class status--it may take a year for it to come through, but it saves tremendously on postage. Meanwhile, you can use either special 4th class book rate or 3rd class, depending on the weight of your publication. The PO is an ironclad bureaucracy. Save yourself a lot of grief by doing everything exactly as they specify...and remember the tolerance level of the gentry in your town when you design the cover. AQ has not been censored in Oakland or Boston, but you may have problems in a small town.

Library subscriptions are a substantial source of income because there are so many libraries and because they usually renew automatically. Try college and university libraries and major city's public libraries remembering to address your inquiry to serials or periodicals as the case may be. Most women's magazines charge an institutional rate higher than regular subscriptions.

Bookstores: Building a bookstore list takes time. Try to get lists of likely bookstores from other women's, gay, radical publications, and visit the stores in person whenever possible. Almost all our bookstores work on consignment, i.e. we send the books and wait till they're sold to get payed for them. The bookstores can return unsold copies for full credit. (We give a 25% discount, 75¢ to us and 25¢ to them, but some stores demand a 40% standard large-publisher discount.)

Non-payers will always crop up. Since most women's publications have similar bookstore outlets, we can work together to blacklist a store until it pays. At the moment we have only one definite candidate: we're asking that our sisters not buy anything at Oscar Wilde Bookstore in New York City until they've paid all the women's publications they owe, and particularly the $155 they've owed us for almost a year.

Wholesale distributors usually aren't interested in small press ventures, but there are a few who are trying to be alternatives. Write women's publications around the country for the addresses. Our cut with these folks doesn't even break even (50¢ to them and 50¢ to us) but more women see the magazines and some may subscribe.

Feminist distributors: We long for the day when there will be a widespread women's distribution system. There is First Things First, a national fe-mail order house, and there are a few local networks, but this fantastic opportunity to both create jobs for women and spread women's culture has not been explored very thoroughly to date. Anyone seriously interested in this should contact us for further details.

In addition to distribution there will be paper work similar to any small business. You'll have to buy city (county, state) licenses and set up your bookkeeping to meet IRS approval. Consult a feminist lawyer about the advantages of incorporation, non-profit status, and the best ways to get around fattening this country's "defense" budget. Get whatever pamphlets you can on starting a small business from the small business administration (or ask your librarian). Remember to check with other women's groups in your area: you may be able to "use" their non-profit status to funnel a grant or to pull off a mailing using their permit. Don't forget that N.O.W. and the more conservative women's rights organizations can be very helpful too since they may know more about "the system" than our more radical sisters.

We'll be happy to answer specific questions about publishing a women's magazine if you'll send us a stamped self-addressed envelope. Good luck, and let us know how your venture goes so we can include yours in our next directory of women's publications.

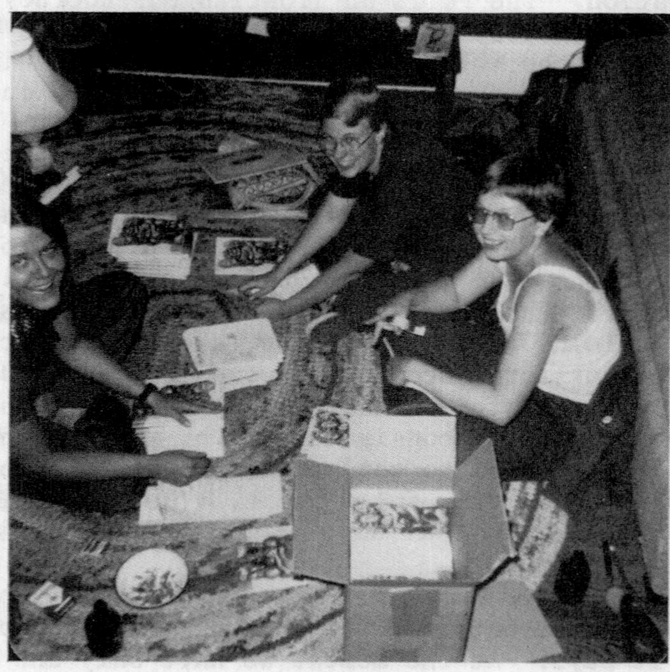

Distributing AQ*--A scene from an all-you-can-drink mailing party to which all Boston area subscribers are invited quarterly.*

Nonetheless, in the last few years alone, there have been countless examples of the transformative powers of media, in spite or because of governmental or corporate regulation. We need barely mention the recent use of social media in the Middle East in the toppling of decades-old dictatorships. Or consider the role of the cell phone in the consolidation of "flash mobs," whether in the Battle in Seattle in 1999, or the overthrowing of the Philippine government in 2001. If in a far less radical vein, the presidential campaign of Barack Obama merged the most novel forms of social media with more traditional graphic arts in a way that has repeatedly been described through the language of grassroots activism.

Although there's much that one would want to unpack in this last characterization, the larger lesson drawn from this example rests with the power of graphic media to effect productive change at the ground level. ***Power of the People*** stands as a testament to that change. Focusing on the diverse and instructive ways in which design met the political, social, and cultural interests of that period, it documents the historical and aesthetic innovations of the past as it points forward to its progressive potential in the present.

Goldwater Says He'll Run To Give Nation A 'Choice'

He Joins G.O.P. Presidential Race With Vow to Hew to His Conservatism

SEES A HARD CONTEST

Arizonan Planning to Enter New Hampshire Primary—He Chides Johnson

PARADISE CITY, Ariz., Jan. 3—Senator Barry Goldwater of Arizona announced today that he would seek the Republican nomination for the Presidency to give the American people a "clear choice"—an opportunity to choose conservative leadership.

POPE AND ORTHODOX LEADER MEET AND OPEN 'DOOR' TO COOPERATION PONTIFF CALLS FOR UNITED CHURCH

Accord is Sought

2 CHURCH HEADS BEGIN TALKS IN JERUSALEM WITH EMBRACE

JERUSALEM (Jordanian Sector) Jan. 5—Pope Paul VI and Ecumenical Patriarch Athenagoras I of Constantinople met here tonight in a spirit of reconciliation between the Roman Catholic and Orthodox Churches.

JOHNSON STATE OF UNION ADDRESS PROVIDES BUDGET OF $97.9 BILLION WAR ON POVERTY ATOMIC CUTBACK

Urges Rights Bill

DROP OF $500 MILLION INFEDERALSPENDINGSEEN BY PRESIDENT

WASHINGTON, Jan. 8—President Johnson, reporting for the first time on the State of the Union, announced today a surprising reduction of the next Federal budget to $97.9 billion.

The President also called for a wide-ranging program to end poverty and discrimination at home and the threat of war abroad.

24TH AMENDMENT BANNING POLL TAX HAS BEEN RATIFIED

Vote in South Dakota Senate Completes the Process of Adding to Constitution

PIERRE, S.D., Jan. 23—The South Dakota Legislature, beating out Georgia legislators in a race to make history, wrote the anti-poll tax amendment into the United States Constitution today.

50 CYPRIOTES DIE IN STRIFE AT PORT

Fighting at Limassol Defies British Cease-Fire Bid

LIMASSOL, Cyprus, Feb. 13—At least 50 Cypriotes have been slain and 100 wounded in two days of renewed communal fighting here. An unofficial count of the casualties was made today, but it was incomplete because many were still missing.

MALCOLM X SPLITS WITH MUHAMMAD

SUSPENDED MUSLIM LEADER PLANS BLACK NATIONALIST POLITICAL MOVEMENT

March 9—Malcolm X broke last night with Elijah Muhammad's Chicago-based Black Muslim movement and announced that he was organizing a politically oriented "black nationalist party."

He said the party would seek to convert the Negro population from nonviolence to active self-defense against white supremacists in all parts of the country.

"I remain a Muslim," Malcolm said, "but the main emphasis of the new movement will be black nationalism as a political concept and form of social action against the oppressors."

"I have reached the conclusion," he said, "that I can best spread Mr. Muhammad's message

LEADERS OF COUP PRESS FOR PURGE OF BRAZIL'S REDS

Accord on Military Leader to Serve Out Goulart's Term is Indicated

VOTE UP TO CONGRESS

RIO DE JANEIRO, April 4—Brazil's military leaders pressed today for the complete elimination of Communist influence in the Government.

SENATE INVOKES CLOSURE ON RIGHTS BILL 71 TO 29 ENDING 75-DAY FILIBUSTER

4 VOTES TO SPARE

WASHINGTON, June 10—The Senate of the United States invoked closure on the civil rights bill today by a vote of 71 to 29, thus ending a 75-day filibuster.

Crisis In South Africa

Seriousness of Confrontation Between Blacks and Whites Indicated by African Leaders' Trial

JOHANNESBURG, April 24—A tall, drawn-looking African rose from the prisoners dock here in the knowledge that he faced the death penalty and explained the meaning of his life.

SEOUL AREA PUT UNDER ARMY RULE WHEN 10,000 RIOT

Police Force in Capital is Overpowered by Mob of Marching Students

U.S. ENVOY CONSULTED

Gen. Park Confers With Him and U.N. Aide—Violence Erupts in Provinces

SEOUL, South Korea, June 3—President Chung Hee Park proclaimed martial law in the Seoul area tonight as mob rule threatened his Government.

EIGHT CONVICTED IN SOUTH AFRICA

9thClearedinSabotageTrial—

PRETORIA, South Africa, June 11—Nelson R. Mandela, Walter M.E. Sisulu and six other men were convicted today of having planned a "violent revolution against South Africa's racial poli-

Pope Says Church Is Making 'Profound' Birth Control Study

ROME, June 23—Pope Paul VI said today that the Roman Catholic Church was giving "wide and profound" study to the problem of birth control. But the Pontiff cautioned against public statements deviating from the church's opposition to the practice of birth control.

PRESIDENT SIGNS CIVIL RIGHTS BILL; BIDS ALL BACK IT

APPROVES SWEEPING MEASURE 5 HOURS AFTER PASSAGE IN HOUSE BY 289-126 VOTE

WASHINGTON, July 2—President Johnson signed the Civil Rights Act of 1964 tonight.

It is the most far-reaching civil rights law since Reconstruction days. The President announced steps to implement it and called on all Americans to help "elimi-

CONVENTION ENDS

SAN FRANCISCO, July 16—Senator Barry Goldwater of Arizona accepted the Republican Presidential nomination tonight with a call to his party "to free our people and light the way for liberty throughout the world."

Night of Riots Began With Calm Rally

July 20—A few minutes before 7 o'clock Saturday night a young woman from the Congress of Racial Equality set up a rickety blue cafe chair and a child's American flag on the southwest corner of 125th Street and Seventh Avenue.

CONGRESS EXPECTED TO APPROVE TODAY JOHNSON'S RESOLUTION ON VIETNAM ACTION

WASHINGTON, Aug. 6—Congress moved swiftly today toward overwhelming approval of President Johnson's Vietnam resolution despite the doubts and apprehensions expressed by several members in debate. Final action, originally expected today, was deferred until tomorrow.

F.B.I. FINDS 3 BODIES BELIEVED TO BE RIGHTS WORKERS

GRAVES AT A DAM

DISCOVERY IS MADE IN NEW EARTH MOUND IN MISSISSIPPI

JACKSON, Miss., Aug. 4—Bodies believed to be those of three civil rights workers missing since June 21 were found early tonight near Philadelphia, Miss.

Federal Bureau of Investigation agents recovered the bodies from a newly erected earthen dam in a thickly wooded area about six miles southwest of Philadelphia.

REDS DRIVEN OFF

TWO TORPEDO VESSELS BELIEVED SUNK IN GULF OF TONKIN

WASHINGTON, Aug. 4—The Defense Department announced tonight that North Vietnamese PT boats made a "deliberate attack" today on two United States destroyers patrolling international waters in the Gulf of Tonkin off North Vietnam.

JOYOUS WELCOME

HALL ERUPTS IN SOUND AS SUSPENSE OVER TICKET IS ENDED

Johnson and Humphrey

ATLANTIC CITY, Thursday, Aug. 27—Lyndon Baines Johnson of Texas, the man who took over the Presidency last Nov. 22 in the shattering hour of John F. Kennedy's assassination, was nominated for a term of his own last night by the 34th Democratic National Convention.

FALL OF KHRUSHCHEV

EVIDENCE INDICATES CAREFUL MANEUVERING AND MILITARY BACKING TO OUST PREMIER

October 17—Evidence of what went on in the Soviet Union in the last 72 hours suggests that Nikita S. Khrushchev was removed from office in a virtual coup d'etat by a group of close associates with the aid and support of the Soviet armed forces.

SLIM EDGE LIKELY

Wilson Aide Defeated in Campaign Marred by a Racial Issue

LONDON, Friday, Oct. 16—Britain apparently elected a Labor Government in yesterday's general election and sent the Conservatives, who have governed for 13 years, into opposition.

BERKELEY STUDENTS STAGE SIT-IN TO PROTEST CURB ON FREE SPEECH

BERKELEY, Calif., Dec. 2—Demonstrating students took possession of the University of California administration building today.

President Terms Strength Of U.S. The Key To Peace

He Assesses Shift in Soviet and Chinese Atom Blast— Warns Against Blackmail

WASHINGTON, Oct. 18—President Johnson told the people of the United States tonight that despite the Chinese Communists' nuclear explosion and the change of Government in the Soviet Union, "the key to peace is to be found in the strength and the good sense of the United States."

TURNOUT IS HEAVY

President Expected to Get 60% of Vote With 44 States

Nov. 4,—Lyndon Baines Johnson of Texas compiled one of the greatest landslide victories in American history yesterday to win a four-year term of his own as the 36th President of the United States.

PRESIDENT OF BOLIVIA FLEES; MILITARY JUNTA TAKES OVER

OBANDO NEW CHIEF AFTER PAZ GOES INTO EXILE—DEATH TOLL IS PUT AT 7

LA PAZ, Bolivia, Nov. 4—President Victor Paz Estenssoro fled into exile today as a one-day military rebellion succeeded in taking control of the Government.

DR. KING ACCEPTS NOBEL PEACE PRIZE AS 'TRUSTEE'

OSLO, Norway, Dec. 10—The Rev. Dr. Martin Luther King Jr. accepted the Nobel Peace Prize today on behalf of the civil rights movement and "all men who love peace and brotherhood." The Baptist minister, in a ceremony at Oslo University, said the award came "at a moment when 22 million Negroes of the United States are engaged in a creative battle to end the long night of racial injustice." Nevertheless, he said that he had an "abiding faith in America" and refused to believe that mankind was "so tragically bound to the starless midnight of racism and war that the bright daybreak of peace and brotherhood can never become a reality." Dr. King's sermon was delivered before an audience that included King Olav V of Norway, Government and diplomatic leaders, members of Dr. King's family and his associates in the civil rights movement. He spoke in English and the ceremony was televised throughout Europe. The award carried a money prize equivalent to about $54,000.

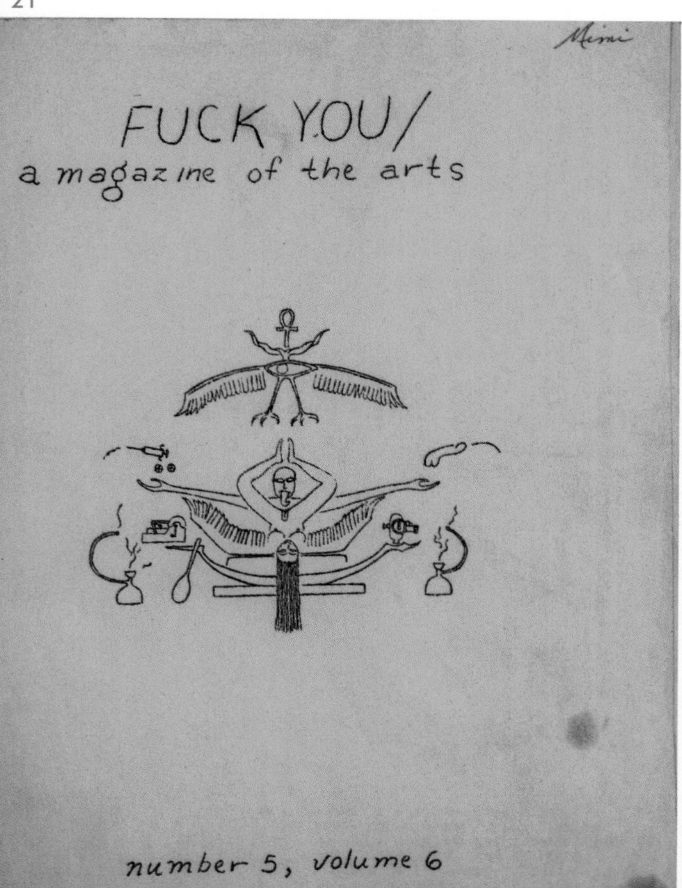

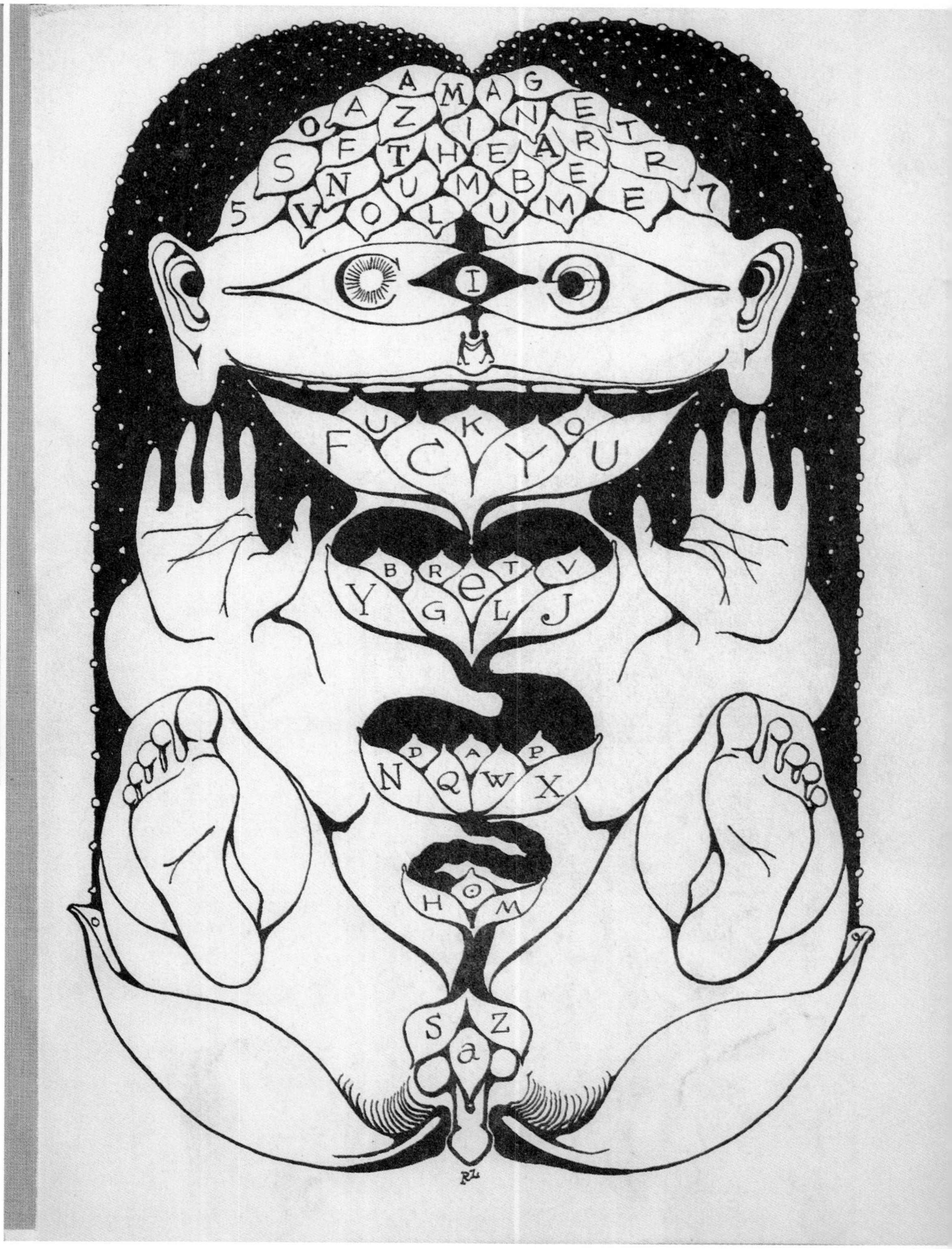

Fuck You (New York), April 1964, vol. 5, no. 6, cover
Fuck You (New York), September 1964, vol. 5, no. 7, cover

FUCK YOU/
a magazine of the arts

OUR THIRD ANNIVERSARY

MAD MOTHERFUCKER

ISSUE!

COVER BY

ANDY WARHOL!!

from his evil
COUCH movie

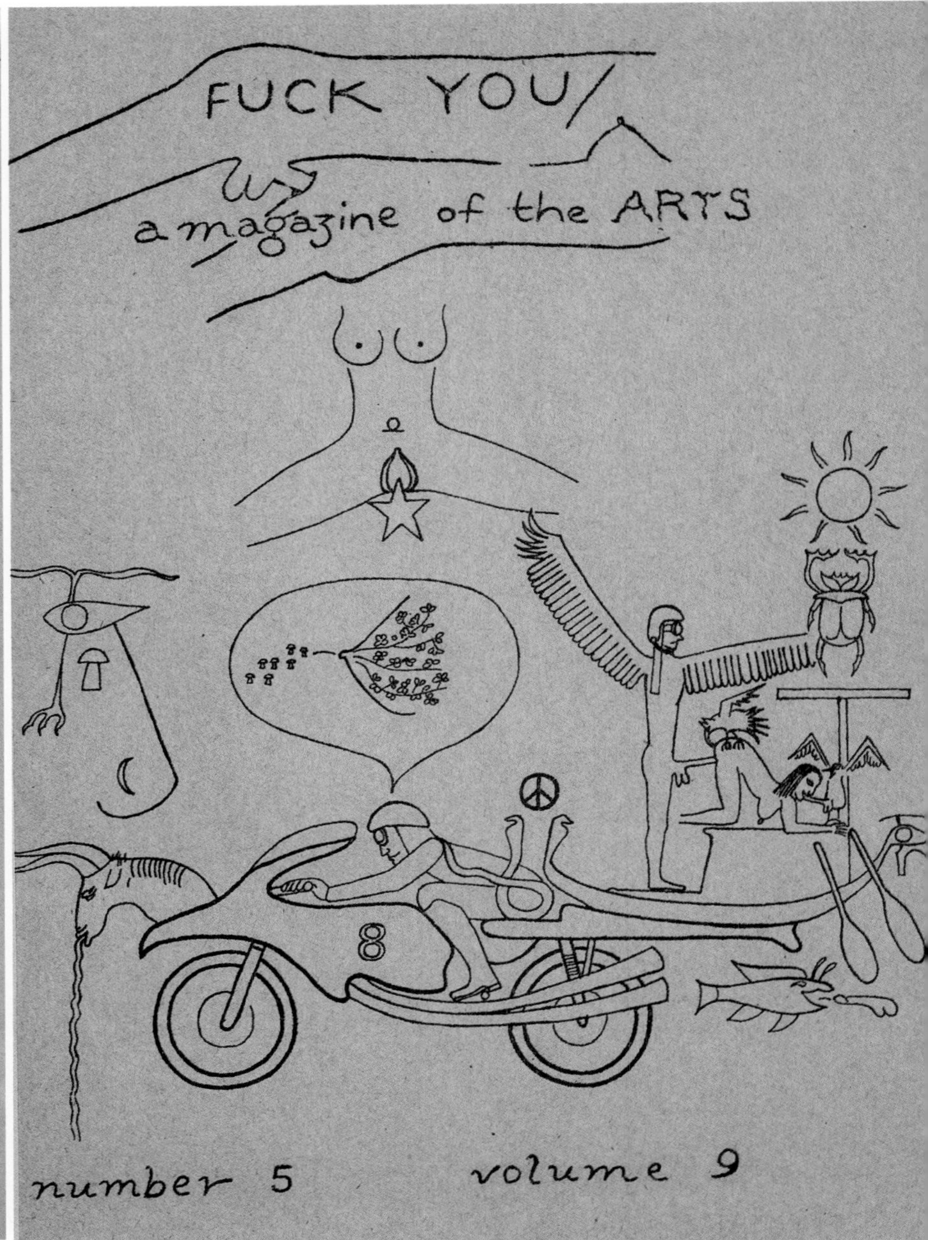

Fuck You (New York), February 1965, vol. 5, no. 8, p. 1 (Warhol cover is missing)
Fuck You (New York), June 1965, vol. 5, no. 9, cover

He Envisions Steps for U.S. Progress and World Peace

WASHINGTON, Jan. 16—Lyndon Baines Johnson of Texas will be sworn in at noon Wednesday for a four-year Presidential term that he believes offers the greatest opportunities in a generation for progress at home and more peaceful relations abroad.

MALCOLM X SHOT TO DEATH AT RALLY HERE

THREE OTHER NEGROES WOUNDED—ONE IS HELD IN KILLING MALCOLM X

Feb. 26—Malcolm X, the 39-year-old leader of a militant black nationalist movement, was shot to death yesterday afternoon at a rally of his followers in a ballroom in Washington Heights.

Force 'Strictly Defensive'—Arrival Is Protested By Hanoi And Peking

U.S. Marine Units Arrive In Danang

SAIGON, South Vietnam, Monday, March 8—United States marines began landing this morning at the bay north of Danang to take up security duties around the large United States jet airfield there.

INDIA, PAKISTAN DISPUTE ENCLAVE

Trade Charges on Tiny Area—Expulsion Is Reported

KARACHI, Pakistan, March 20—A dispute over ancient enclaves in Bengal has flared up this week to add to the strain in relations between India and Pakistan.

The Unfinished Business of the Civil War; 100 Years After Appomattox

April 4—ROBERT E. LEE surrendered the Army of Northern Virginia to U.S. Grant at Appomattox Court House on April 9, 1865, one century ago, and although the last Confederate troops did not lay down their arms until June 2, the Appomattox date is the one we remember.

FREEDOM MARCH BEGINS AT SELMA; TROOPS ON GUARD

3,200 TAKE PART IN PROTEST AS 54-MILE RIGHTS WALK TO MONTGOMERY STARTS

DR. ENVISIONS 'A NEW ALABAMA' AND 'A NEW AMERICA'—CROWD'S MOOD FESTIVE

SELMA, Ala., March 21—Backed by the armed might of the United States, 3,200 persons marched out of Selma today on the first leg of a historic venture in nonviolent protest.

RUMANIAN LEADER PICKED SUCCESSOR

Ceausescu, New Party Head, Backs Independent Stand

BUCHAREST, March 23—Reliable sources said today that Gheorghe Gheorghiu-Dej chose Nicolae Ceausescu to succeed him as First Secretary of the Rumanian Workers' (Communist) party.

BERKELEY STUDENTS PROTEST 'INVASION'

BERKELEY, Calif., May 5—Hundreds of University of California students marched on the Berkeley draft board headquarters today and presented the board coordinator with a black coffin. Forty students burned their draft cards.

15,000 White House Pickets Denounce Vietnam War

Students Picket At White House

WASHINGTON, April 17—More than 15,000 students and a number of their elders picketed the White House in spring sunshine today, calling for an end of the fighting in Vietnam. Walking three and four abreast in orderly rows and carrying printed white signs, the students clogged the sidewalk.

MICHIGAN FACULTY CREATED TEACH-IN

49 at University Staged the First Vietnam Protest

DETROIT, May 8—The idea for university "teach-in" demonstrations that have spread across the nation in protest of United States policies in Vietnam was developed by 49 University of Michigan professors, sharply divided over what form the protest should take.

INDIAN ARMY UNITS GO INTO PAKISTAN IN AREA OF LAHORE

NEW DELHI, Monday, Sept. 6—Indian troops in the Punjab have moved across the border with Pakistan in the vicinity of Lahore "for the protection of the Indian border," India's Defense Minister, Yashwantrao Chavan, told the House of the People (lower house) here today.

U.S. to Increase Military Forces by 330,000 Men

Rise in Draft and Enlisting to Push Total to 3 Million for First Time in 10 Years

WASHINGTON, July 29—The Administration plans to increase its active-duty military forces by about 330,000 men, official sources said today.

POPE PAUL PROMULGATES FIVE COUNCIL DOCUMENTS, ONE ABSOLVING THE JEWS

Changing Church

DECREES REVISE POLICY AND OFFER AMITY TO OTHER FAITHS

ROME, Oct. 28—Pope Paul VI formally promulgated as church teaching today five documents embodying significant changes in Roman Catholic policies and structures and offering friendship and respect to other great world religions.

President Signs Medicare Bill; Praises Truman

Social Security is Expanded to Provide Medical Care for Americans Over 65

INDEPENDENCE, Mo., July 30—President Johnson flew to Independence today and signed the Medicare-Social Security bill in a moving tribute to former President Harry S. Truman.

DECEMBER DRAFT OF 45,224 BIGGEST SINCE KOREAN WAR

CALL ISSUED AS THE PENTAGON BUILDS UP FORCES FOR U.S. COMMITMENT IN VIETNAM

WASHINGTON, Oct. 14—The Defense Department announced today a military draft call of 45,224 men for December, the biggest quota since the Korean War.

Johnson Signs Voting Rights Bill, Orders Immediate Enforcement

4 Suits Will Challenge Poll Tax

WASHINGTON, Aug. 6—President Johnson signed today the Voting Rights Act of 1965 and announced steps to bring about its quick and vigorous enforcement.

PAKISTANI THRUST CHARGED BY INDIA

'Infiltrators' Said to Be Near Srinagar in Kashmir

NEW DELHI, Aug. 9—Pakistani "infiltrators" were reported tonight to have penetrated to within a few miles of Srinagar, the summer capital of the Indian-controlled sector of Kashmir.

Reports by telephone from Srinagar said three Pakistani groups of undetermined size were believed to have clashed with Indian troops at a village near the city.

British Abolish Death Penalties

Parliament Finishes Action on Bill Ending Hangings

LONDON, Oct. 28—Capital punishment was brought to an end in Britain today.

Parliament completed action on an abolition bill after 11 months of intermittent debate and years of public controversy. The bill was sponsored by Sydney Silverman, a Labor Member who has crusaded since World War II to end hanging.

2,000 TROOPS ENTER LOS ANGELES ON THIRD DAY OF NEGRO RIOTING

4 DIE AS FIRES AND LOOTING GROW

YOUTHS RUN WILD

VIOLENCE SPREADS TO CITY'S WHITE AREAS—SHOTS EXCHANGED

LOS ANGELES, Saturday, Aug. 14—Two thousand heavily armed National Guardsmen moved into Los Angeles last night to battle rioters in the burning and looted Negro area.

The Guardsmen were under orders to use rifles, machine guns, tear gas and bayonets in support of a battered contingent of 900 policemen and deputy sheriffs.

Four persons were killed in the rioting yesterday, including three Negroes and a police officer. Thirty-three police officers had been injured, 75 civilians seriously injured, and 249 rioters had been arrested. This morning violence spread to white areas.

WAR CRITIC BURNS HIMSELF TO DEATH OUTSIDE PENTAGON

Baby of Quaker Escapes Unharmed—Wife Says He Was Protesting Loss of Life and Suffering in Vietnam

VIETNAM WAR FOE BURNS TO DEATH

WASHINGTON, Nov. 2—A Quaker official described by friends as upset over Administration policy in Vietnam, burned himself to death in front of the Pentagon late this afternoon.

Rabbi Hails Shift In Vatican Views; Calls Council A Landmark In Religious History

November 7—A leading New York rabbi told his congregation yesterday that Ecumenical Council Vatican II must be viewed as one of the most significant landmarks in religious history. The Council is expected to complete its three-year work in Rome on Dec. 8.

PHILIPPINE 'NO. 1'; FERDINAND EDRALIN MARCOS

MANILA, Nov. 12—Senator Ferdinand Edralin Marcos, the apparent winner of the Philippines Presidency, was "No. 1" to his countrymen long before they voted him into the highest Government office.

Alabama Negroes Protest At School

EUTAW, Ala., Nov. 11—About 70 Negro pupils left their classes today for a civil rights meeting at a nearby church, and when they tried to return to the school they were blocked by police officers.

U.S. BEGINS SEALIFT OF CUBAN REFUGES TO KEY WEST HAVEN

KEY WEST, Fla., Nov. 13—A United States excursion boat, escorted by a Coast Guard cutter put in here late tonight and landed 108 Cuban refugees, the first of about 2,000 awaiting evacuation from Premier Fidel Castro's island in Operation Sealift.

DE GAULLE WINS FRENCH RUNOFF WITH 54.7% VOTE

Candidate of the Left Never Ran Ahead—Concedes Early

PARIS, Monday, Dec. 20—General de Gaulle won the runoff election yesterday for the French presidency.

U.S. TROOPS RENEW SEARCH FOR ENEMY IN VIETNAM VALLEY

AIRMOBILE UNITS, IN 6TH DAY OF IADRANG DRIVE, EXPECT ANOTHER MAJOR BATTLE

FOES' TACTICS ALTERED

AMERICAN OFFICERS SUSPECT THEIR TENACITY INDICATES PRESENCE OF BIG BASE

G.I.'S RENEW SEARCH IN VIETNAM VALLEY

PLEIKU, South Vietnam, Nov. 19—United States troops pushed through the Iadrang River valley again today in search of North Vietnamese regulars after five days of sustained fighting that has altered the character of the war in South Vietnam's central highlands.

Nixon Views Vietnam War As Major Issue in '68 Vote

Nov. 22—Former Vice President Richard M. Nixon said yesterday that the Vietnam war could become a major issue next year and in the 1968 Presidential election if the Johnson Administration failed to take steps "to win the war in Vietnam" and to end it."

DIVERSE GROUPS JOIN IN PROTEST

Participants Range From Pacifists to Far Leftists

Nov. 28—The groups participating in the Washington march protesting United States policy in Vietnam ranged from several old-line peace organizations to a radical group set up a few months ago to raise money to buy medical supplies for the Vietcong.

SOVIET ACCORD GIVES MORE HELP TO HANOI

MOSCOW, Dec. 21—The Soviet Union agreed today to give North Vietnam more technical and economic aid. The agreement could also involve increased military assistance.

A brief official announcement made no mention of military aid, but the Deputy Premiers of the countries who signed the aid pact spoke of it during an exchange of speeches.

Antiwar Leaflet Annoys Marines

Troops in Vietnam Exhorted by Mail to Oppose Fighting

DANANG, South Vietnam. Nov. 28—American servicemen in Vietnam are receiving printed leaflets calling them to "oppose the war." Some of the servicemen are sore about it: others think it's a joke.

U.S. AIDES DOUBT TRUCE IN VIETNAM WILL BRING TALKS

Officials Believe 30-Hour Pause Ordered by Allies Won't Lead to Long Halt

ADMINISTRATION SILENT

WASHINGTON, Dec. 23—Johnson Administration officials were highly doubtful today that the Christmas time truce agreed to by the United States and South Vietnam would provide an opening wedge for a prolonged cease-fire or negotiations in the Vietnamese war.

U.S. AND MOSCOW PLAN ARMS TALKS

Agree to Try in January for Pact to Limit A-Weapons

WASHINGTON, Dec. 4—The United States and the Soviet Union have agreed to resume disarmament negotiations in Geneva in late January in a renewed effort to draft a treaty to prevent the spread of atomic weapons, State Department officials disclosed

15 Divers Working To Save Drill Rig

LONDON, Dec. 28—Fifteen divers worked in 85 feet of water 42 miles off the Yorkshire coast today to try to save the British Petroleum Company's drilling rig, Sea Gem, which collapsed yesterday.

A TROOP ACCORD

India and Pakistan Will Give Up Areas Won in Border War

TASHKENT, U.S.S.R., Tuesday, Jan. 11—India and Pakistan agreed yesterday to withdraw their armed personnel to positions they held before last fall's fighting. They pledged to complete the withdrawals by Feb. 25.

SPEECH SWEEPING

$112.8-Billion Budget Disclosed in State of Union Message

WASHINGTON, Jan. 12—President Johnson pledged soberly tonight to stay in Vietnam "until aggression has stopped" but also promised to continue and expand the Great Society at home.

PRESIDENT NAMES WEAVER TO HEAD HOUSING AGENCY

Negro Chosen to Run New Department is First of His Race Picked for Cabinet

DEPUTY ALSO APPOINTED

Johnson Calls Top Nominee Best of 300 Considered—Confirmation Expected

WASHINGTON, Jan. 13—Robert C. Weaver was named by President Johnson today to be the Secretary of the new Cabinet-level Department of Housing and Urban Development.

MRS. GANDHI, NEHRU'S DAUGHTER, IS CHOSEN INDIA'S THIRD PRIME MINISTER

NEW DELHI, Jan. 19—Mrs. Indira Gandhi became India's third Prime Minister today. Her father, Jawaharlal Nehru, was the country's first, and held the job for 17 years. In the first direct contest ever held for the post, Mrs. Gandhi was elected by legislators of the Congress party gathered in the great teak and green plush central hall of Parliament.

POWER STRUGGLE RAGES IN NIGERIA

50 Officers Reported Slain Since Saturday's Coup

LAGOS, Nigeria, Jan. 18—A bloody power struggle has set in among the leaders of Nigeria's two-day-old military Government.

PICTURE FROM MOON: CRUST SEEMS FIRM

Porous Surface is Dotted By Oddly Shaped Rocks

Feb. 5—The Soviet Union's Luna 9, from its location on the moon, has sent to earth pictures showing a moonscape covered with peculiar porous material and scattered with oddly shaped rocks.

Luna 10 May Send Vital Moon Data

Moscow Tells of Devices on Craft in Lunar Orbit

April 6—The Soviet Union's Luna 10, in orbit around the moon since Sunday, may be making several vitally important observations, American specialists believe.

SYRIAN STRONGMAN IS REPORTED OUSTED IN DAMASCUS COUP

BEIRUT, Lebanon, Wednesday, Feb. 23—A political crisis in Syria erupted into a coup d'etat today and the Damascus radio announced that Lieut. Gen. Amin el-Hafez had been overthrown as head of the Socialist state.

U.S. STRENGTH RISES TO 250,000

VUNGTAU, South Vietnam, Friday, April 29—More than 4,000 fresh United States troops landed in Vietnam today, bringing the total American strength in the Vietnamese war to nearly 250,000.

Gemini 8 Crew Is Forced Down In Pacific After Successful Linkup with Satellite; Spacemen Picked up After 3 Hours in Sea

Flight Unstable

Tumbling Forced Use of Thruster Fuel in Re-entry System

CAPE KENNEDY, Fla., Thursday, March 17—The Gemini 8 astronauts suddenly lost maneuverability of their craft last night after making the first docking in space.

THOUSANDS ON FIFTH AVE. MARCH IN VIETNAM PROTEST

March 27—Thousands of antiwar demonstrators paraded down Fifth Avenue yesterday as part of an international protest against the war in Vietnam and the role played by American troops.

BREZHNEV OPENS SOVIET CONGRESS

BIDS U.S. END WAR

PARTY CHIEF SAYS BETTER TIES HINGE ON HALT OF 'POLICY OF AGGRESSION' IN VIETNAM

CHINESE ARE CRITICIZED

COMMUNIST LINE IS AFFIRMED IN THE ARTS—OVER-ALL TONE OF SPEECH IS MODERATE

MOSCOW, March 29—The Communist party leadership declared today that the Soviet Union stood ready to improve relations with the United States, but only after the United States Government "ends its policy of aggression" against Vietnam

8,000 IN CAPITAL PICKET FOR PEACE

Demonstrators Circle White House for Two Hours

WASHINGTON, May 15—The moderate wing of the American peace movement staged a large demonstration here today in an effort to increase Congressional opposition to President Johnson's policies in Vietnam.

PARIS AND MOSCOW MAP COOPERATION

DeGaulle and Podgorny Sign a Declaration of Principle—General Leaves Today

MOSCOW, June 30—France and the Soviet Union declared today their intent to collaborate with each other as a catalyst around which all Europe would refashion itself in confidence and peace.

Castro Decrees a State of Alert

Sees War Threat in Rusk's Guantanamo Statement

HAVANA, May 27—Premier Fidel Castro ordered a state of alert tonight for the Cuban armed forces "and all the Cuban people" as a result of what he called provocations by the United States against his country.

MEREDITH IS SHOT IN BACK ON WALK INTO MISSISSIPPI

AMBUSHED NEGRO REPORTED IN SATISFACTORY CONDITION—JOHNSON DENOUNCES ACT

WHITE SUSPECT IS HELD

CORE PLANS TO FINISH MARCH TO SPUR VOTER REGISTRATION AND END FEAR OF RACISTS

HERNANDO, Miss., June 6—James H. Meredith, the Negro who desegregated the University of Mississippi in 1962, was shot in the back from ambush today as he walked along United States Highway 51 two miles south of here.

High Court Puts New Curb on Powers of the Police to Interrogate Suspects

Dissenters Bitter

Four View Limitation on Confessions as Aid to Criminals

WASHINGTON, June 13—The Supreme Court announced today sweeping limitations on the power of the police to question suspects in their custody.

Catholics Warned on 'Index' of Books

ROME, June 14—The Roman Catholic Church's "index" of forbidden books and related sanctions have no juridical effect upon Catholics, but it is still a sin to read them and other publications "contrary to faith and morals."

INFORMATION BILL SENT TO JOHNSON

House Votes, 307-0, to Open Federal Records to Public

WASHINGTON, June 20—A bill to grant Americans the right of access to Federal records cleared Congress today and was sent to President Johnson.

ONE DEAD IN OHIO

Riot By Negroes Hits Cleveland

CLEVELAND, Tuesday, July 19—Rioting broke out last night in the all-Negro Hough area of Cleveland. A woman was shot and killed and four policemen were injured by bricks and bottles.

VIETNAM DAY GROUP BANNED IN BERKELEY CAMPUS DISPUTE

BERKELEY, Calif., Aug. 14—The University of California has banned the Vietnam Day Committee, a militant antiwar group, from the Berkeley campus for allegedly violating campus rules.

ROCK HITS DR. KING AS WHITES ATTACK MARCH IN CHICAGO

FELLED RIGHTS LEADER RISES AND CONTINUES PROTEST AS CROWD OF 4,000 RIOTS

CHICAGO, Saturday, Aug. 6—The Rev. Dr. Martin Luther King Jr. was struck by a stone yesterday as a crowd of whites raged out of control and battled policemen in a white residential area of Chicago.

A special force of 960 policemen succeeded in preventing Dr. King and about 600 civil rights demonstrators from being critically injured during a march to protest segregated housing.

LANSING POLICE QUELL MOB OF NEGRO YOUTH AFTER NEW VIOLENCE

LANSING, Mich., Aug. 8—Policemen firing tear gas broke up a mob of 200 Negro youths at a downtown intersection here tonight and then said this city's second night of racial violence "definitely was contained."

CHINA'S PURGE PUZZLES U.S.

August 13—For the experts in the State Department and observers at widespread listening posts, the purge-ridden "proletarian cultural revolution" sweeping Communist China presents a dizzying puzzlement.

FUEDING LEADERS OF YEMEN CONFER

But Conflict Over Egyptian Aid Is Not Resolved

CAIRO, Aug. 17—President Abdullah al-Salal and Premier Hassan al Amri, who are engaged in a struggle for control of Yemen's republican Government, met today for the first time since Field Marshal al-Salal returned to Yemen last Friday after a nine-month stay in Egypt.

A.F.L.-C.I.O. BACKS COAST FARM UNIT

Merged Group Gets Charter in Fight With Teamsters

CHICAGO, Aug. 23—The Executive Council of the American Federation of Labor and Congress of Industrial Organizations threw its strength and prestige today behind two merged California farm labor groups engaged in a bitter representation election battle with the Teamsters Union.

RED LEADERS SIGN DECLARATION ON EUROPEAN SECURITY

RED BLOC ASSAILS U.S. OVER VIETNAM

WARSAW PACT PARLEY ENDS—BOMBINGS CONDEMNED AS 'CRIMINAL ACTION'

BUCHAREST, July 6—The leaders of the Warsaw Pact nations ended their conference tonight by signing a communique that said they had drafted a statement about the Vietnamese war "in the light of the new criminal action by the American armed forces."

The new action to which they referred was undoubtedly the bombing of oil depots in Hanoi and Haiphong.

BROOKE'S VICTORY HAILED IN BOSTON

First Elected Negro Senator Scored Smashing Victory

BOSTON, Nov. 9—The Commonwealth of Massachusetts, which gave the nation its first Roman Catholic President, today hailed the first Negro to be elected to the Senate directly by the voters.

Despite the efforts of men who once surrounded President Kennedy, a Massachusetts native, Edward W. Brooke, a Negro who was born in Washington, D.C. 46 years ago, overcame a series of obstacles to retain a seat in the Senate for the Republicans.

REAGAN ELECTED BY A WIDE MARGIN

Governor Brown Fails to Win Third Term in California—Turnout Is Heavy

LOS ANGELES, Nov. 8—Republican Ronald Reagan was elected Governor of California tonight, defeating Gov. Edmund G. Brown, a two-term Democrat.

The Republican nominee, a movie and television actor seeking office for the first time, took an early lead, which grew to commanding proportions as the vote was counted.

Gemini 12 Nearing Splashdown Today Southeast of Miami

Flight by Gemini Ends Series Today

CAPE KENNEDY, Fla., Nov. 14—For the third time in three days, Maj. Edwin E. Aldrin Jr. of the Air Force braved the void of space outside Gemini 12 today as it orbited toward the completion of its four-day mission.

In a joint scientific experiment with France earlier in the day, the American astronauts also attempted to photograph yellow vapor trails released over the Sahara by two French sounding rockets, which were launched as Gemini 12 passed over. The pictures could help scientists learn more about the velocity and direction of winds in the upper atmosphere.

Major Aldrin and Capt. James A. Lovell Jr. of the Navy, the Gemini 12 command pilot, are scheduled to splash down at 2:21 P.M. Eastern standard time tomorrow.

Verwoerd is Slain by An Assassin in the South African Parliament; Killer, White, is Subdued by M.P.'S

Knife is Weapon

Doctors are Unable to Save Prime Minister, Stabbed 4 Times

CAPETOWN, Sept. 6—Dr. Hendrik F. Verwoerd, Prime Minister of South Africa and architect of apartheid, was stabbed to death on the front bench in the South African Parliament today.

The Changing Times in Lowndes County: An All-Negro Ticket

HAYNEVILLE, Ala., Oct. 27—There are seven candidates from the Lowndes County Freedom Organization in the election on Nov. 8. They are Negroes, and their symbol is a toothy, crouching black panther. They probably will not win the county offices they seek, but it may not matter. What matters is that they are running.

BLACK MASK

No. 1 NOV. 1966 5 Cents

A new spirit is rising. Like the streets of Watts we burn with revolution. We assault your Gods - - We sing of your death. DESTROY THE MUSEUMS - - our struggle cannot be hung on walls. Let the past fall under the blows of revolt. The guerilla, the blacks, the men of the future, we are all at your heels. Goddamn your culture, your science, your art. What purpose do they serve? Your mass-murder cannot be concealed. The industrialist, the banker, the bourgeoisie, with their unlimited pretense and vulgarity, continue to stockpile art while they slaughter humanity. Your lie has failed. The world is rising against your oppression. There are men at the gates seeking a new world. The machine, the rocket, the conquering of space and time, these are the seeds of the future which, freed from your barbarism, will carry us forward. We are ready - -

LET THE STRUGGLE BEGIN.

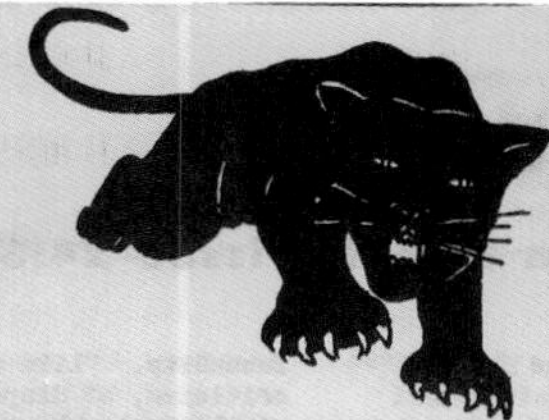

POWER CONCEDES NOTHING WITHOUT A DEMAND

'Find out just what any people will quietly submit to and you have found out the exact measure of injustice and wrong which will be imposed upon them, and these will continue till they are resisted with either words or blows, or with both.'

For many years black people in hte black belt of Alabama have been the victims of a vicious system of political, economic and social exclusion. Political exclusion is maintained in many ways-- the denial of the right to vote, service on juries, access to political offices, and by naked brutality acting under color of law or just a plain white sheet.

Although black people are a numerical majority of Lowndes County, Alabama the Democratic Party only provides them with white candidates who will adhere to a policy of white supremacy. The Lowndes County Freedom Organization wants a politics that is responsive to the needs of the poor--responsive to the need for education, decent law enforcement, paved roads, decent housing, good medical facilities, and all the things they hope for themselves and their children.

On November 8th, black people in Lowndes County will have a chance to cast ballots for candidates representing these interests. These candidates running under the symbol of the Black Panther, if elected, will be in positions of control. These will be black people in control, seeking to use the county governing mechanism for the benefit of all persons in Lowndes County. **THIS POLITICAL EFFORT IS SIGNIFICANT FOR BLACK PEOPLE AROUND THE COUNTRY, AND NOT JUST IN LOWNDES COUNTY. THIS EFFORT NEEDS THE SUPPORT OF ALL BLACK PEOPLE.**

WHAT YOU CAN DO TO HELP

The Lowndes County Freedom Organization will need money for gasoline to make sure that everyone gets out to vote on November 8th. Candidates need money to help in the canvassing of the county between now and November 8th.

The word needs to be spread about whats happening in Lowndes County.

On election day support rallies should be held for the people of Lowndes County.

Vote fraud, or violent assult against the Lowndes County Freedom Organization on election day is a real possibility. Some form of action may be neccessary. You may be called on to help.

A VICTORY FOR THE LOWNDES COUNTY FREEDOM ORGANIZATION IS A VICTORY FOR US.

'The whole history of the progress of human liberty shows that all concessions yet made to her.......have been born or earnest struggle.

If there is no struggle there is no progress. Those who profess to favor feeedom yet deprecate agitation, are men who want crops without plowing up the ground they want rain without thundet and lightning. They want the ocean without the roar of it's many waters.

This struggle may be a moral one, or it may be a physical one, and it may be both moral and physical, but it must be a struggle.

SNCC
360 Nelson St. S.W.
Atlanta, Georgia30313
Phone--404 688-0331

LOWNDES COUNTY
FREEDOM ORGANIZATION
Rte. 1, Box 191
Hayneville, Alabama

Black Mask (Alabama), November 1966, no. 1, cover
Black Mask (Alabama), November 1966, no. 1, back cover

Man's Ancestor Found to Be More Than 19 Million Years Old

NAIROBI, Kenya, Jan. 14—The family of man is more than 19 million years old, according to paleontological evidence gathered over the last 18 years in Kenya that was presented in Nairobi today by Dr. Louis S. B. Leakey.

11 SEIZED IN BERLIN IN A REPORTED PLOT TO KILL HUMPHREY

BERLIN, April 5—The West Berlin police said tonight that they had arrested 11 persons on charges of having plotted to assassinate Vice President Humphrey.

3 APOLLO ASTRONAUTS DIE IN FIRE; GRISSOM, WHITE, CHAFFEE CAUGHT IN CAPSULE DURING A TEST ON PAD

TRAGEDY AT CAPE

RESCUERS ARE BLOCKED BY DENSE SMOKE

CAUSE IS STUDIED

CAPE KENNEDY, Fla., Jan. 27—The three-man crew of astronauts for the Apollo 1 mission were killed tonight in a flash fire aboard the huge spacecraft designed to take man to the moon.

WHERE THE ACTION IS

Feb. 19—SAN FRANCISCO ranks high in alcoholism, divorce, tennis, fresh air, suicide, egg rolls, seafood, free verse and experimental prose. It has turbulent rock-and-roll bands, an erratic police force and a population that can be aroused to the pitch of stopping the slicing up of the town by freeways. It is hay-fever free. It is famous for its fleas.

ISRAEL REPORTS HER JETS DOWNED 6 SYRIAN MIG-21'S

Damascus Says 5 of Foe's Mirages Were Destroyed in Series of Battles

Troop Clash at Border

Tanks and Mortars Used in Buffer Zone Fight That Led to Action in Air

JERUSALEM (Israel), April 7—Israel reported that six MIG-21's of the Syrian Air Force were shot down today by Israeli Mirage fighter planes in a series of air battles east of the Sea of Galilee.

SUKARNO HANDS AUTHORITY TO SUHARTO BUT KEEPS TITLE

BJAKARTA, Indonesia, Feb. 22—President Sukarno has turned over all governmental authority to General Suharto but has retained the title he has held since 1949.

10,000 CHANT 'L-O-V-E'

March 27—"L-O-V-E, L-O-V-E, L-O-V-E." They circled policemen and shrieked it. They strummed guitars and sang of it. They painted their foreheads pink with it. And they jumped up and down and hollered it.

50,000 AT SAN FRANCISCO—PEACE RALLY

SAN FRANCISCO, April 15—A throng estimated by the police at 50,000 persons, mostly young people, attended a rally at Kezar Stadium today to protest the war in Vietnam.

DR. KING PROPOSES A BOYCOTT OF WAR

Calls for Nationwide Drive of Conscientious Objectors

April 5—The Rev. Dr. Martin Luther King Jr. called yesterday on Negroes and "all white people of goodwill" to boycott the Vietnam war by becoming conscientious objectors to military service.

CLAY REFUSES ARMY OATH; STRIPPED OF BOXING CROWN

HOUSTON, April 28—Cassius Clay refused today, as expected, to take the one step forward that would have constituted induction into the armed forces. There was no immediate Government action.

'Draft Caravans' Visit City Schools

Peace Groups Urge Pupils to Be Conscientious Objectors

April, 6—"End the Draft Caravans" visited high schools throughout the city yesterday, urging students to register as conscientious objectors in protest against the war in Vietnam.

LEFTISTS DISRUPT HONG KONG LABOR

Big Cement Factory Closed After Pro-Mao Rallies

HONG KONG, May 5—The Hong Kong industrial scene has been marked by a number of Leftist-inspired labor disputes that have culminated in the closing of one of the British colony's top 10 industrial concerns.

A NEW PRESIDENT IS CHOSEN IN INDIA

Hussain Held Likely Winner —Vice President Elected

NEW DELHI, May 6—An electoral college made up of the Members of Parliament and the 17 state legislatures voted today for a new President of India. The results will not be known until Tuesday.

SYRIA REINFORCES TROOPS NEAR ISRAEL

DAMASCUS, Syria, May 17—Syria announced today that her armed forces and militia had been brought to "maximum preparedness" in light of "information about the Israeli build-up along the Syrian border and threatening statements made by Israeli officials."

JUSTICES UPSET ALL BANS ON INTERRACIAL MARRIAGE

9-TO-0 DECISION RULES OUT VIRGINIA LAW—15 OTHER STATES ARE AFFECTED

WASHINGTON, June 12—The Supreme Court ruled unanimously today that states cannot outlaw marriages between whites and nonwhites.

MARSHALL NAMED FOR HIGH COURT, ITS FIRST NEGRO

JOHNSON CALLS NOMINEE 'BEST QUALIFIED,' AND RIGHTS LEADERS ARE JUBILANT

SOUTHERNERS SILENT ON CONFIRMATION

WASHINGTON, June 13—President Johnson named Solicitor General Thurgood Marshall to the Supreme Court today.

Soviet Ratifies Pact to Bar Nuclear Weapons in Space

Soviet Ratifies Treaty On Space

MOSCOW, May 19—The Soviet Union, after waiting four months, ratified today the treaty banning nuclear weapons in outer space. The treaty was signed here Jan. 27 by the United States, the Soviet Union and Britain. Dozens of other nations signed later, and the United States ratified it.

EASTERN REGION QUITS NIGERIA; LAGOS VOWS TO FIGHT SECESSION

LAGOS, Nigeria, May 30—Nigeria's Eastern Region seceded early today, declaring itself an independent republic, Biafra. The Federal Government immediately ordered a mobilization and said it would use force to thwart the secession.

JOHNSON IS TOLD OF MIDEAST CLASH

Outbreak Follows Capital's Report That High Cairo Official Is Due in U.S.

WASHINGTON, Monday, June 5—President Johnson was alerted today to reports that war had begun between Israel and the United Arab Republic.

FIGHTING IS RAGING IN GAZA AND SINAI; ACTION IN AIR HEAVY

MajorMideastDevelopments on the Battlefronts

June 6—Israel and the Arab nations were locked in full-scale war yesterday along the borders of Israel and in the skies.

BLAST HAILED IN CHINA

PEKING, June 18—China's first hydrogen bomb blast was hailed by the entire Peking press today as a victory for Chairman Mao and his thought.

Commons Adopts a Bill to Modify Penalty for Adult Homosexuality

LONDON, July 4—The House of Commons, after sitting through the night to overcome a threatened filibuster, voted today to approve the long-argued bill to reform British law on homosexual conduct.

PEKING BOLSTERS TIES TO ASIAN REDS

Openly Sponsors Parties in Indonesia and Burma

HONG KONG, July 10—Communist China has emerged openly during the last week as the sponsor of two of Southeast Asia's most important Communist parties, the Indonesian and the Burmese.

Wisconsin Village 'Seceding'

WINNECONNE, Wis., July 13—Winneconne announced today that it was seceding from the State of Wisconsin.

Student Bill of Rights Drafted; Education Groups to Vote on it

WASHINGTON, July 20—A proposed bill of rights for the nation's college and university students has been drawn up by representatives of five major education organizations from New York.

U.S. TROOPS SENT INTO DETROIT; 19 DEAD; JOHNSON DECRIES RIOTS; NEW OUTBREAK IN EAST HARLEM

TANKS IN DETROIT

800 ARE INJURED AND 2,000 ARRESTED—BUSINESS AT HALT

DETROIT, Tuesday, July 25—President Johnson rushed 4,700 Army paratroopers into Detroit at midnight last night as Negro snipers besieged two police stations in rioting that brought near-paralysis to the nation's fifth largest city.

Racial Violence Erupts In Newark

Bands of Negroes Smash Windows and Stone the Police in Ghetto Area

NEWARK, Thursday, July 13—Bands of Negroes went through a heavily Negro neighborhood in South Newark last night and early today smashing windows and looting stores. Several policemen were struck by stones.

Shots Fired in Washington As Negro Youths Rampage

WASHINGTON, Tuesday, Aug. 1—Policemen were fired upon early today, the police said, as two Negro gangs of about 50 persons each roamed a predominantly Negro district of Washington amid six or seven fires.

PEKING SIGNS PACT GIVING AID TO HANOI

HANOI, North Vietnam, Aug. 7—China has signed an agreement to give North Vietnam an undisclosed amount of free aid, the official Communist party newspaper Nhan Dan reported today.

THE PRESIDENT-ELECT

Nguyen Van Thieu

SAIGON, South Vietnam, Sept. 3—After 20 years of war, countless intrigues in which the penalty for misjudgment was death, jail or exile, two years as chief of state of a nation with a history of short-lived governments, and a political campaign that led today to his

BOLIVIA CONFIRMS GUEVARA'S DEATH; BODY DISPLAYED

Army Reports Fingerprints Prove Rebel Leader Was Killed in Sunday Clash

CONFESSION DESCRIBED

He Made Himself Known and Admitted Failure Before He Died,General Says

VALLE GRANDE, Bolivia, Oct. 10—The army high command officially confirmed today that Ernesto Che Guevara, the Latin revolutionary leader, was killed in a clash between guerrillas and Bolivian troops in southeastern Bolivia last Sunday.

Abortion Reforms Adopted in Britain

LONDON, Oct. 25—Abortions will soon be available without cost in Britain on broad social and medical grounds.

IRAN'S SHAH CROWNS HIMSELF AND QUEEN

TEHERAN, Iran, Oct. 26—The Shah of Iran crowned himself and his young Empress today in a blaze of pomp and splendor. Under the arabesque arches of the Golestan Palace, the 48-year-old Shah pledged his life "to bring the Iranian nation up to the level of the most progressive and prosperous societies of the world."

FOE HANDS 3 G.I.'S TO ANTIWAR GROUP

Two Displayed to Newsmen in Cambodia—3rd Ailing

PNOMPENH, Cambodia, Saturday, Nov. 12—The National Liberation Front, political arm of the Vietcong, handed three captive over a representative of an American peace committee today. Two of the American prisoners appeared at a news conference in the Front's headquarters here. The third was reported to be ill.

MAJOR SHIFT IN CAPITAL

McNamara Has Been an Influential Force in Policies of Two Presidents

WASHINGTON, Nov. 27—President Johnson's willingness—or desire—to have Robert S. McNamara move from the Pentagon to the World Bank has raised many important questions of policy and politics, but there were no reliable answers to any of them here today.

264 SEIZED HERE IN DRAFT PROTEST

Dr. Spock and Ginsberg Are Among Those Arrested at Induction Center

Dec. 6—The police arrested 264 persons, including Dr. Benjamin Spock and the poet Allen Ginsberg, during a demonstration yesterday between 5 A.M. and 6 A.M. by more than 2,500 anti-draft, anti-war protesters at the armed forces induction center at 39 Whitehall Street.

7 MEN SENTENCED IN RIGHTS KILLINGS

TWO GET 10-YEAR MAXIMUM IN MISSISSIPPI KLAN PLOT

JACKSON, Miss., Dec. 29—Seven men convicted of taking part in a Ku Klux Klan plot to kill three young civil rights workers in Neshoba County were sentenced today to Federal prison terms ranging from 3 to 10 years.

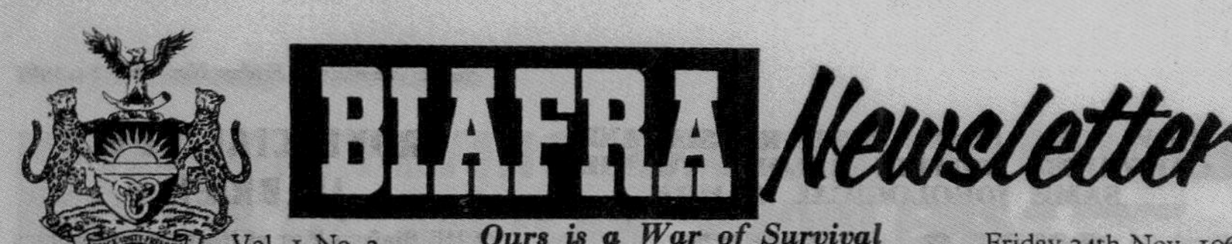

BIAFRA Newsletter

Vol. 1 No. 3 — *Ours is a War of Survival* — Friday 24th Nov. 1967

HEAD OF STATE ASSURES THE NATION—

BIAFRA WILL BE MODERN WELFARE STATE

THE Head of State and Commander-in-Chief of the Armed Forces, Colonel Odumegwu Ojukwu, has assured Biafrans that post-war Biafra would be a stable, modern, welfare state in which all ophans and women who lost their husbands during the war would benefit from the welfare activities of the Government.

He urged all Biafrans to continue to rally to the support of the fighting forces who did not give up the struggle after the wicked betrayal in Benin.

Colonel Ojukwu gave the assurance while addressing thousands of Owerri people who assembled at Owerri town to welcome him to their Province.

Backward North

The Head of State reviewed the contributions and sacrifices made by Biafrans to evolve the greatness that was Nigeria, especially the efforts made by Biafrans to enlighten the backward and indolent Northern Nigerians, but regretted that these ungrateful Northerners, led by the overbearing Emirs, later "turned round to bite the fingers that fed them".

Commenting on the military situation, Colonel Odumegwu Ojukwu reaffirmed that the morale of Biafran soldiers is very high.

He then assured the people that the enemy in all the war fronts would suffer the same crushing defeat as they met in their recent invasion of Onitsha in which more than two thousand Nigerian soldiers were wiped out by Biafran Forces.

West Niger Ibos

Recounting the atrocities committed by the Nigerian soldiers when they arrived at Asaba, the Head of State appealed to the West Niger Ibos not to be disheartened by their sad experiences, adding, "our future is woven together with yours; if we sink, you will sink, if we float, you will float".

Earlier in their address of welcome, the Owerri War Committee pledged the unswerving loyalty of the entire Owerri people to the Head of State and his Government.

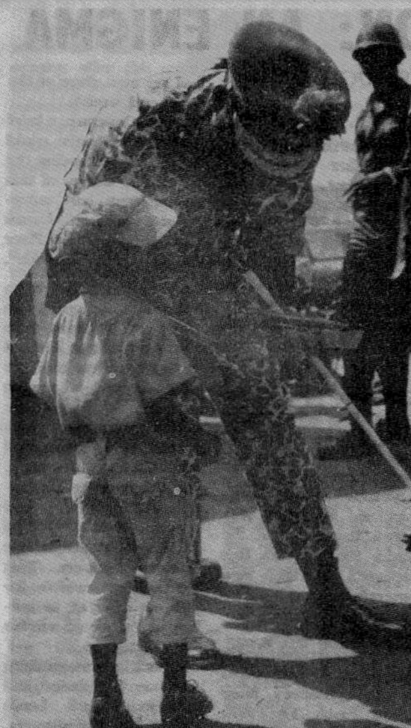

His Excellency Lt. Col. Odumegwu Ojukwu inspects a young Biafran militia impatient to contribute to Biafra's war of liberation.

A BASELESS WAR
— DR. IBIAM

THE Adviser to the Biafran Head of State, Dr. Akanu Ibiam, has severely criticised the role of the British Broadcasting Corporation in the present Nigerian-Biafra War.

In a strongly worded letter to the BBC, Dr. Ibiam said the Corporation has lost all sense of proportion in what he called this vexing and baseless Nigeria-Biafra war by dishing out to the world deliberate falsehood.

Atheists

This is because, unlike the past, the present breed of authorities of the Corporation are atheists with no regard for uprightness, and who take delight in intrigues and uncharitable acts.

Dr. Ibiam observed that from all indications, the BBC would like the Republic of Biafra to revert to its old status of Eastern Nigeria, adding that if such is the aspiration of the BBC, then it is asking for the moon.

Dr Ibiam recalled the Kano riot and last year's incidents in the North during which over thirty thousand Biafrans were brutally killed for no reason, and noted that the strange silence of the BBC to the inhuman crimes gave the impression that the BBC was gloating over and enjoying the wicked drama.

Conspiracy of Silence

He observed that when these atrocities and unconstitutional acts were being committed, the BBC was strangely silent.

Dr. Ibiam re-affirmed that Nigeria in collusion with Britain and Russia, cannot subdue Biafra. They will have to kill all

(Continued on page 8)

Letter From Biafra p. 3.

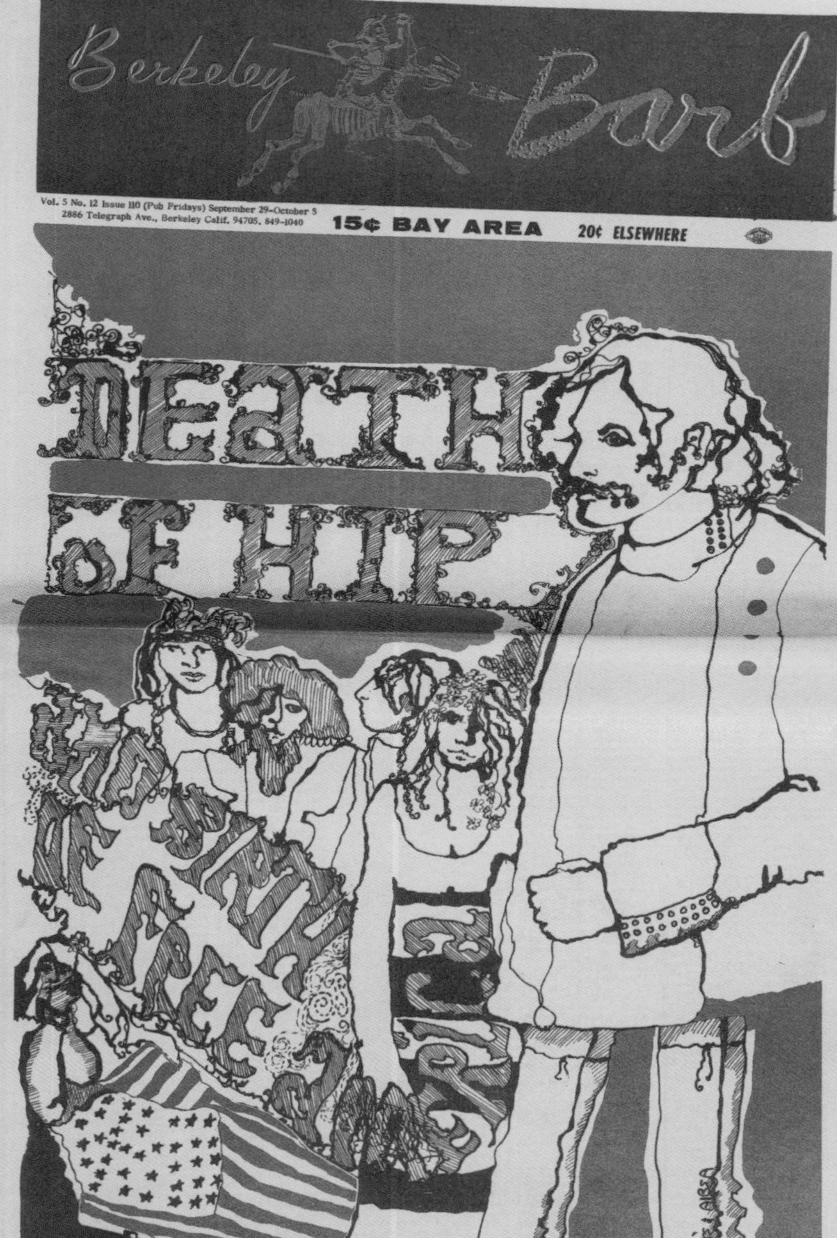

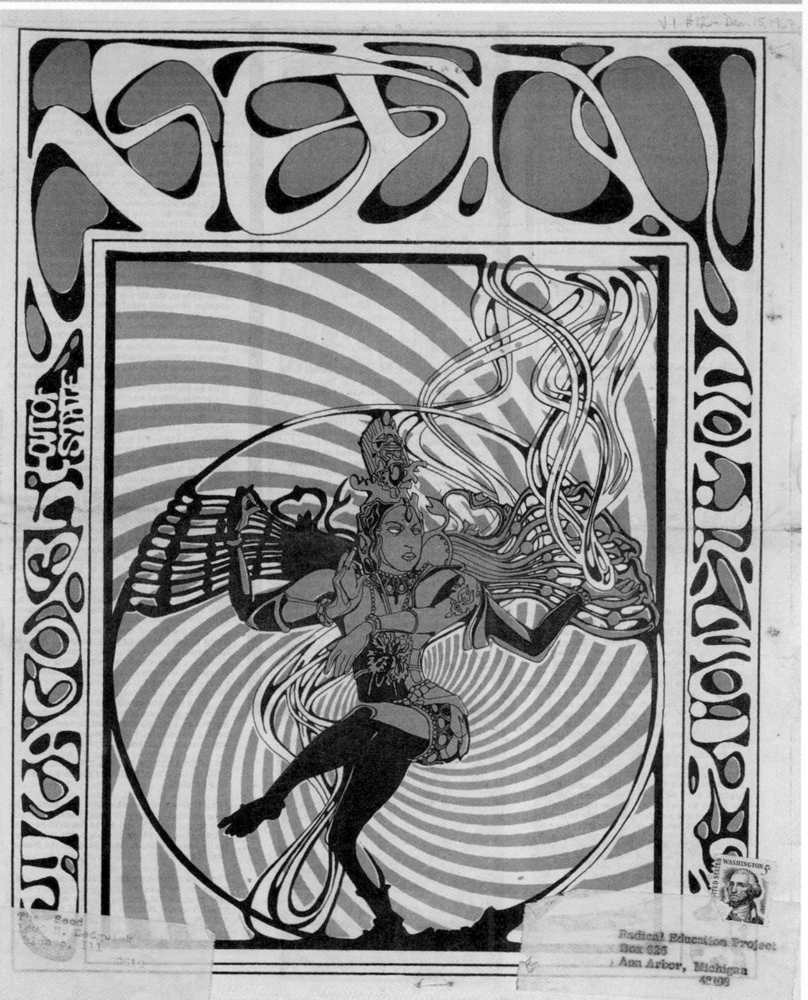

Biafra Newsletter (Republic of Biafra), November 24, 1967, vol. 1, no. 3, cover
The Berkeley Barb, September 29–October 5, 1967, vol. 5, no. 12, cover
The Chicago Seed, December 15, 1967, vol. 1, no. 12, cover

A NEW PRAGUE LEADER; ALEXANDER DUBCEK

Jan. 6—The new First Secretary of the Communist party in Czechoslovakia, Alexander Dubcek, is the son of a dedicated Marxist-Leninist worker and thus a "noble Communist" in the tradition of party aristocracy.

100 Held in Danang in Anti-U.S. Protest

DANANG, South Vietnam, Jan. 8—South Vietnamese national policemen arrested about 100 peasants in the Danang produce market today for protesting against United States bombing and the American military presence in this country.

HE WANTS GOLD RESERVE FREED

Congress Asked to End Gold Cover

WASHINGTON, Jan. 17—President Johnson asked Congress tonight to repeal the last remaining "gold cover" behind the nation's currency so that all the $12-billion in gold remaining in the Treasury would be freed for international settlements.

EARTHA KITT DENOUNCES WAR POLICY TO MRS. JOHNSON

WASHINGTON, Jan. 18—Eartha Kitt, the singer, stunned other guests at a White House luncheon today when she angrily told Mrs. Lyndon B. Johnson that American youth was rebelling because of the Vietnam war.

3 NEGRO STUDENTS SHOT IN NEW VIOLENCE AT ORANGEBURG, S.C.

ORANGEBURG, S. C., Feb. 7—Three Negro students were wounded superficially by shotgun fire here late tonight as violence growing out of a racial protest flared for the second day.

WARSAW QUELLS STUDENT PROTEST

Militia Disperses 4,000 in Campus Demonstration

WARSAW, March 8—About 4,000 chanting students marched on the grounds of Warsaw University today demanding the reinstatement of two students who had demonstrated against the Government-directed closing of a classic Polish play.

M'CARTHY GETS ABOUT 40%, JOHNSON AND NIXON ON TOP IN NEW HAMPSHIRE VOTING

Rockefeller Lags

SENATOR EXCEEDS TOP PRIMARY PREDICTIONS ON PEACE CAMPAIGN

March 12—President Johnson turned back a strong challenge by Senator Eugene J. McCarthy in the first 1968 Democratic primary tonight, but not before the Minnesotan had won about 40 per cent of the vote.

North Korea Seizes Navy Ship, Holds 83 on Board as U.S. Spies; Enterprise is Ordered to Area

4 Crewmen Hurt

Rusk Says Efforts Are Under Way to Obtain Vessel's Release

WASHINGTON, Jan. 23—North Korean patrol boats seized a United States Navy intelligence ship off Wonsan today and took the vessel and her 83 crew members into the North Korean port.

The Defense Department, reporting the incident, said the ship had been in international waters about 25 miles off the eastern coast of North Korea when she was boarded by armed North Korean sailors at 1:45 P.M.

Vietcong Attack 7 Cities

Allies Call Off Tet Truce

Rockets Destroy 6 U.S. Planes at Danang—Prisoners Freed

SAIGON, South Vietnam, Tuesday, Jan. 30—Vietcong raiders drove into the center of seven major Vietnamese cities early today, burning Government buildings, freeing prisoners from provincial jails and blasting military installations and airfields with rockets and mortars.

ANTIWAR BOYCOTT SET AT COLUMBIA

University Vice President to Take Part in Protest

March 12—Student leaders at Columbia University have called for a campus-wide boycott of classes tomorrow to protest the draft and the war in Vietnam.

BANKERS HOPEFUL ON FATE OF DOLLAR

But They Emphasize Need for Long-Range Reforms and Strict Enforcement

March 18—American bankers and economists were cautiously hopeful last night that the agreement reached in Washington to effect a two-price system for gold would end the run on the dollar.

HOWARD STUDENTS END CAMPUS SIT-IN

After 4 Days They Report They Won Concessions

WASHINGTON, March 23—About 1,000 Howard University students ended a four-day sit-in and sleep-in occupation of the campus administration building this afternoon, asserting they had won important concessions from university officials.

JOHNSON SAYS HE WON'T RUN

Surprise Decision

PRESIDENT STEPS ASIDE IN UNITY BID—SAYS 'HOUSE' IS DIVIDED

WASHINGTON, March 31—Lyndon Baines Johnson announced tonight: "I shall not seek and I will not accept the nomination of my party as your President."

KENNEDY MESSAGE REACHES MILLIONS

Senator Speaks to 250,000 and Uses Mass Media

WASHINGTON, March 30—In the first two weeks of his Presidential campaign, Senator Robert F. Kennedy has spoken to perhaps 250,000 persons in 15 states, had physical contact with several thousands and reached millions through the mass media.

MARTIN LUTHER KING IS SLAIN IN MEMPHIS; A WHITE IS SUSPECTED; JOHNSON URGES CALM

GUARD CALLED OUT; CURFEW IS ORDERED IN MEMPHIS, BUT FIRES AND LOOTING ERUPT

MEMPHIS, Friday, April 5—The Rev. Dr. Martin Luther King Jr., who preached nonviolence and racial brotherhood, was fatally shot here last night by a distant gunman who then raced away and escaped.

WEST BERLIN GUNMAN WOUNDS LEADER OF LEFT-WING STUDENTS

STUDENT RADICAL IS SHOT IN BERLIN

BERLIN, April 11— A gunman fired three shots at Rudi Dutschke on Kurfurstendamm, Berlin's main shopping street, today, critically injuring the 27-year-old left-wing student leader.

FRANCE EXPLODES HER FIRST H-BOMB IN SOUTH PACIFIC

Device, Tested on an Atoll, Adds Fifth Power to Thermonuclear Group

PARIS, Aug. 24—France exploded her first hydrogen bomb today and became the world's fifth thermonuclear power.

PRESIDENT SIGNS CIVIL RIGHTS BILL

PLEADS FOR CALM

ACTS A DAY AFTER FINAL VOTE ON MEASURE THAT STRESSES OPEN HOUSING IN NATION

FINDS MUCH TO BE DONE IN WHITE HOUSE CEREMONY, HE CALLS FOR ENACTMENT OF REST OF HIS PROGRAM

WASHINGTON, April 11—With another plea against violence and for the legal redress of injustice, President Johnson signed today the Civil Rights Act of 1968.

STUDENT RAMPAGE IN WEST GERMANY FOLLOWS SHOOTING

Youth Says He Shot Leftist After Reading of Killing of Martin Luther King

BERLIN, April 12—The young West German who shot Rudi Dutschke, the radical student leader, said today that his murder attempt had been prompted by the assassination of Dr. Martin Luther King Jr.

COLUMBIA CLOSES CAMPUS AFTER DISORDERS

Office of President is Seized — Dean Freed but Protest Widens

April 25—Columbia University students expanded their protest early today, invading two more buildings after the Morningside Heights campus was closed following a second day of tumultuous demonstrations.

Police Shooting of Oakland Negro

May 6—Recent actions by Oakland, Calif., police, in particular the killing of seventeen-year-old Bobby James Hutton and the wounding of two other blacks, including Eldridge Cleaver (Times April 8 and 13), are cause for grave concern to all.

Police In Madrid Battle Students

MADRID, May 16—Eight hundred University of Madrid students, shouting slogans against the Government, stoned the police today during a demonstration that left the campus littered with burned furniture and broken glass.

9 SEIZE AND BURN 600 DRAFT FILES

2 Priests Among War Foes Arrested Near Baltimore

BALTIMORE, May 17—Nine opponents of the Vietnam war, six of them present or former members of Roman Catholic religious orders, stormed a draft board office in suburban Catonsville today and seized about 600 individual

PARISIAN YOUTHS AND POLICE CLASH IN LATIN QUARTER

Hundreds Hurt as Students Throw Paving Blocks and Set Fires in Streets

MASS PROTESTS URGED

Labor Leader Calls for Them to be Held When de Gaulle Addresses Nation Today

PARIS, Friday, May 24—Rebellious students and other youths clashed with riot policemen last night in the Latin Quarter of Paris as France remained in the grip of nationwide strikes.

Kaleidoscope (Milwaukee, Wisconsin), November 22-December 5, 1968, vol. 2, no. 1, cover
Kaleidoscope (Milwaukee, Wisconsin), November 22-December 5, 1968, vol. 2, no. 1, second section cover

U.S. CONFIRMS CALL FOR ALL-OUT FIGHT

But the Command in Saigon Denies 3-Month Target

SAIGON, South Vietnam, May 26—The United States military command confirmed today that it had called for an "all-out" effort against the enemy in a secret directive sent to all field commanders just before the Paris talks began.

STUDENTS REJOICE AT DANNY'S FEAT

Sorbonne's Occupiers Hail Return of Cohn-Bendit

PARIS, May 29—"We're out to destroy capitalism, to change governments—this isn't just a fight for pretty classrooms and different kinds of exams," said Alain, a 19-year-old who stood today, with thousands of others, chatting in the great open-air courtyard of the Sorbonne. The stronghold of the student revolt, the university has been occupied since May 14 by students.

"Its what Danny said last night—we want to overthrow capitalism and if a government of this kind uses force, we'll do the same," the boy said, in a voice that no longer seemed adolescent.

WARHOL GRAVELY WOUNDED IN STUDIO

Actress is Held

WOMAN SAYS SHE SHOT ARTIST, WHO IS GIVEN A 50-50 CHANCE TO LIVE

June 4—Andy Warhol, the artist who brought a bewildering new dimension to American pop culture through his films, sculptures and paintings, was shot and critically wounded in his film studio yesterday afternoon.

Suspect in Assassination of Dr. King Is Seized in London

Ray Found Armed—Arrested at the Airport by Scotland Yard on Way From Lisbon

WASHINGTON, June 8—James Earl Ray, accused of the assassination of the Rev. Dr. Martin Luther King Jr., was arrested this morning at London Airport, Attorney General Ramsey Clark announced here today.

BAN ON ATOM ARMS SPREAD SIGNED

9-Point Disarmament Plan Is Proposed by Kosygin

MOSCOW, July 1—The treaty to prevent the spread of nuclear weapons was signed by 36 countries in Moscow today and the Soviet Union took occasion to issue a new appeal to the world for urgent measures to stop the arms race and achieve disarmament.

CHURCHES UPHOLD RIGHT TO OPPOSE 'PARTICULAR WARS'

World Council's Statement Backs Stand of Selective Conscientious Objection

UPPSALA, Sweden, July 16—The World Council of Churches declared today that the legal right of the individual to refrain from participation in "particular wars" on grounds of conscience must be regarded now as essential to the protection of fundamental human rights.

OUSTER OF REGIME IN IRAQ REPORTED

Radio Says Arif Has Been Sent Abroad — Council Set Up to Run the Country

BEIRUT, Lebanon, Wednesday, July 17—The Baghdad radio reported today that the Iraqi Government had been overthrown and that President Abdel Rahman Arif had been stripped of his powers and pensioned off.

Paris Police Break Up Student Demonstration

PARIS, July 19—Policemen with clubs charged a group of several hundred students demonstrating against the Government tonight in front of the Comedie Francaise theater.

8 IN CLEVELAND SLAIN IN FIGHTING BEGUN BY SNIPERS

Gunmen Kill 3 Policemen in Attack in Negro Slum—Ohio Guard Mobilized

CLEVELAND, Wednesday, July 24—The police used Brink's armored cars last night to seal off an East Side Negro area after eight persons were killed—three of them policemen hit by bursts of automatic gunfire from snipers in an apartment building.

POPE BARS BIRTH CONTROL BY ANY ARTIFICIAL MEANS

Tone Forthright

ENCYCLICAL BINDING ON CATHOLICS BUT IS NOT IMMUTABLE DOGMA

ROME, July 29—Five years of uncertainty over how the Roman Catholic Church would view modern methods of birth control ended today with the official presentation of a papal encyclical letter that upheld the prohibition on all artificial means of contraception.

KENNEDY SHOT AND GRAVELY WOUNDED AFTER WINNING CALIFORNIA PRIMARY; SUSPECT SEIZED IN LOS ANGELES HOTEL

CONDITION 'STABLE'

AIDE REPORTS SENATOR IS 'BREATHING WELL'—LAST RITES GIVEN

LOS ANGELES, Wednesday, June 5—Senator Robert F. Kennedy was shot and critically wounded by an unidentified gunman this morning just after he made his victory speech in the California primary election.

NIXON IS NOMINATED ON THE FIRST BALLOT

Original Vote 692

BUT CONVENTION THEN MAKES IT UNANIMOUS ON PLEA BY REAGAN

MIAMI BEACH, Thursday, Aug. 8—Richard Milhous Nixon, the "old pro" of American politics, was nominated for President today on the first ballot at the Republican National Convention.

Miss America Pageant Is Picketed by 100 Women

ATLANTIC CITY, Sept. 7—Women armed with a giant bathing beauty puppet and a "freedom trash can" in which they threw girdles, bras, hair curlers, false eyelashes, and anything else that smacked of "enslavement," picketed the Miss America Pageant here today.

The women pickets marched around the Boardwalk outside Convention Hall, singing anti-Miss America songs in three-part harmony, carrying posters deploring "the degrading mindless-boob-girlie symbol," and insisting that the only "free" woman is "the woman who is no longer enslaved by ludicrous beauty standards."

Czechoslovakia Invaded By Russians and Four Other Warsaw Pact Forces

Tanks Enter City

Deaths Are Reported—Troops Surround Offices of Party

Aug. 21—Czechoslovakia was occupied early today by troops of the Soviet Union and four of its Warsaw Pact allies in a series of swift land and air movements. Airborne Soviet troops and paratroopers surrounded the building of the Communist party Central Committee.

HUNDREDS OF PROTESTERS BLOCK TRAFFIC IN CHICAGO

Anti-War and Anti Humphrey Groups Clash With Police After Ouster From Park

CHICAGO, Monday, Aug. 26—Hundreds of antiwar and anti-Humphrey demonstrators, driven out of a park on the shores of Lake Michigan here last night staged a series of hit-and-run protests today that blocked traffic and triggered angry shoving matches with heavily armed police.

HUMPHREY NOMINATED ON THE FIRST BALLOT AFTER HIS PLANK ON VIETNAM IS APPROVED

Victor Gets 1,761

CHICAGO, Thursday Aug. 29—While a pitched battle between the police and thousands of young antiwar demonstrators raged in the streets of Chicago, the Democratic National Convention nominated Hubert H. Humphrey for President last night, on a platform reflecting his and President Johnson's views on the war in Vietnam.

ARMY COUP OUSTS PERUVIAN REGIME

President Belaunde Exiled to Argentina—Students Battle Troops in Lima

ARMY COUP OUSTS PERUVIAN REGIME

LIMA, Peru, Oct. 3—Military leaders overthrew the Government of President Fernando Belaunde Terry before dawn today in a coup-d'etat that encountered stiffening resistance as the day wore on. Students fought troops and policemen in the streets.

JAMAICAN IS KILLED IN PROTEST ON BAN

KINGSTON, Jamaica, Oct. 17—One man was killed and another wounded last night after demonstrations by students at the University of the West Indies in Kingston.

The students were protesting a Government order preventing Dr. Walter Rodney from entering the country Tuesday. Dr. Rodney, a 26-year-old university lecturer from Guyana, was returning from a black writers' conference at McGill University in Canada.

NIXON WINS BY A THIN MARGIN, PLEADS FOR REUNITED NATION

Nixon's Election Expected To Slow Paris Negotiation

ALLIED DIPLOMATS SUGGEST ALL SIDES MAY ADOPT A WAIT-AND-SEE STANCE

PARIS, Nov. 6—Allied diplomats suggested tonight that Richard M. Nixon's election victory would add, at least temporarily, to the delays and complications of getting meaningful Vietnam peace negotiations under way.

The American, the North Vietnamese and the National Liberation Front delegations here had no comment on the election results.

But allied diplomats close to the talks suggested that the Republican victory would probably bring eventual changes in the American negotiating team, encourage delays by the South Vietnamese Government, and induce a wait-and-see attitude by all sides until Mr. Nixon's own approach to the talk became clearer.

3 On Apollo 7 Circling Earth in 11-Day Test For Moon Trip; Nasa Hails 'Perfect Mission'

Lift-Off Smooth

Astronauts Carry Out Early Maneuvers on 163-Orbit Journey

CAPE KENNEDY, Fla., Oct. 11—Three American astronauts rocketed into orbit today for the first manned test flight of the Apollo spacecraft, which may some day fly men to the moon.

2 ACCEPT MEDALS WEARING BLACK GLOVES

MEXICO CITY, Oct. 16—Tommie Smith wore a black glove on his right hand tonight to receive his gold medal for winning the final of the Olympic 200-meter dash in the world-record time of 19.8 seconds.

Yale Going Coed Next September; 500 Undergraduate Girls to Be Admitted as a Start

NEW HAVEN, Nov. 14—For the first time in its 265-year history Yale University will admit undergraduate women next fall to "enhance its contribution to the generations ahead."

NOLA EXPRESS

muckraker

no.5

15c

15 c

Let's put the power suckers up against the wall.

TULANE: SCAB UNIVERSITY

No. 16

NOLA EXPRESS

Nola Express (New Orleans), 1968, vol. 1, no. 5, cover
Nola Express (New Orleans), 1968, vol. 1, no. 16, cover

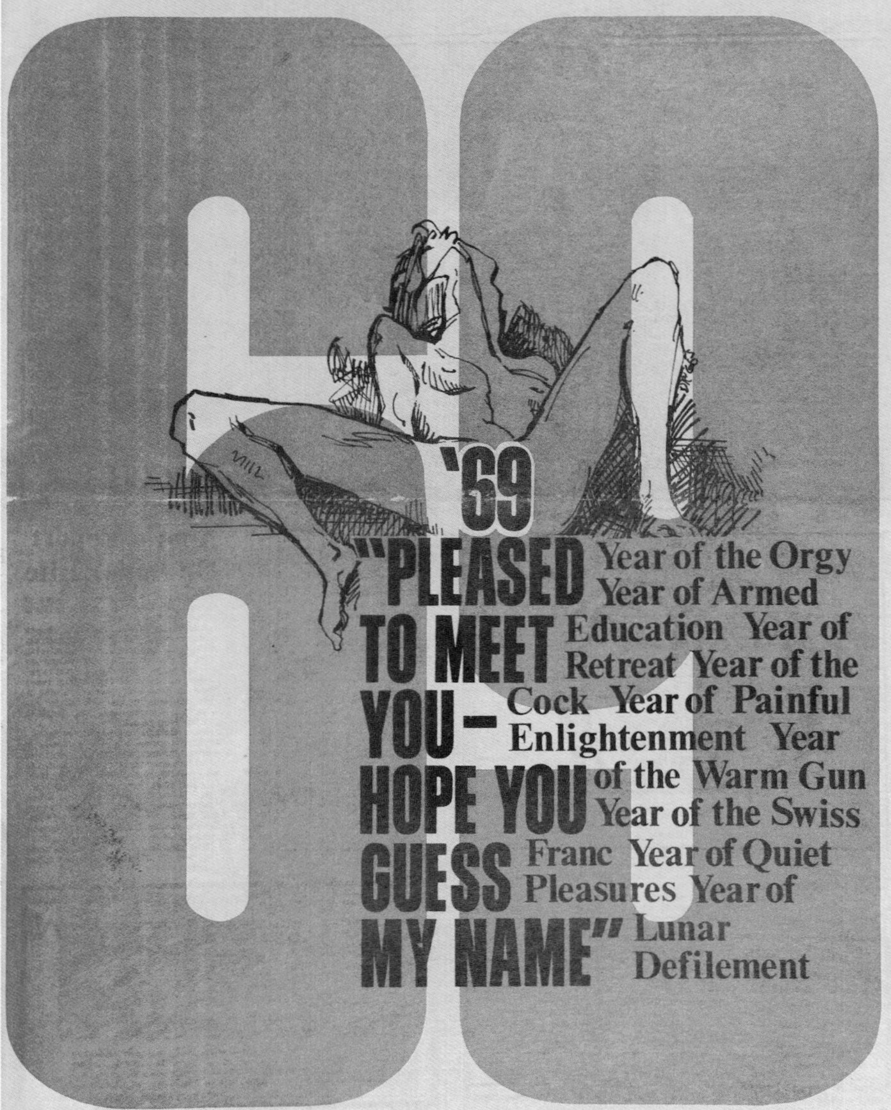
San Francisco Express Times
Vol 2, No 1 January 7, 1969, 15¢ Bay Area, 25¢ Elsewhere
'69
"PLEASED TO MEET YOU– HOPE YOU GUESS MY NAME"
Year of the Orgy Year of Armed Education Year of Retreat Year of the Cock Year of Painful Enlightenment Year of the Warm Gun Year of the Swiss Franc Year of Quiet Pleasures Year of Lunar Defilement

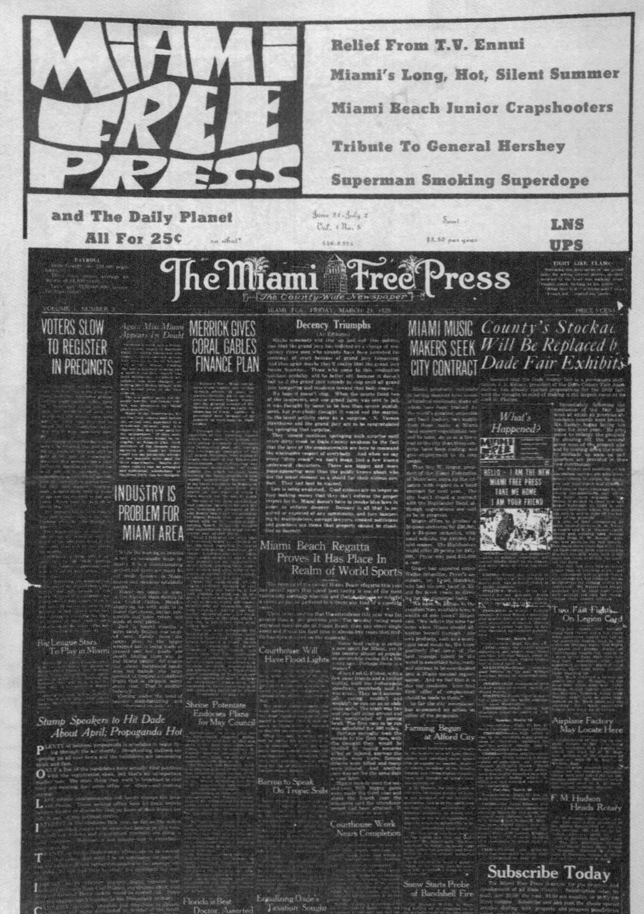
MIAMI FREE PRESS
Relief From T.V. Ennui
Miami's Long, Hot, Silent Summer
Miami Beach Junior Crapshooters
Tribute To General Hershey
Superman Smoking Superdope
and The Daily Planet
All For 25¢
LNS
UPS
The Miami Free Press
VOTERS SLOW TO REGISTER IN PRECINCTS
MERRICK GIVES CORAL GABLES FINANCE PLAN
Decency Triumphs
MIAMI MUSIC MAKERS SEEK CITY CONTRACT
County's Stockade Will Be Replaced by Dade Fair Exhibits
INDUSTRY IS PROBLEM FOR MIAMI AREA
Miami Beach Regatta Proves It Has Place In Realm of World Sports
Subscribe Today

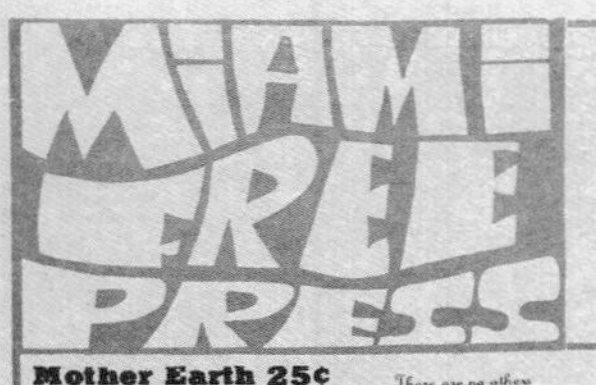

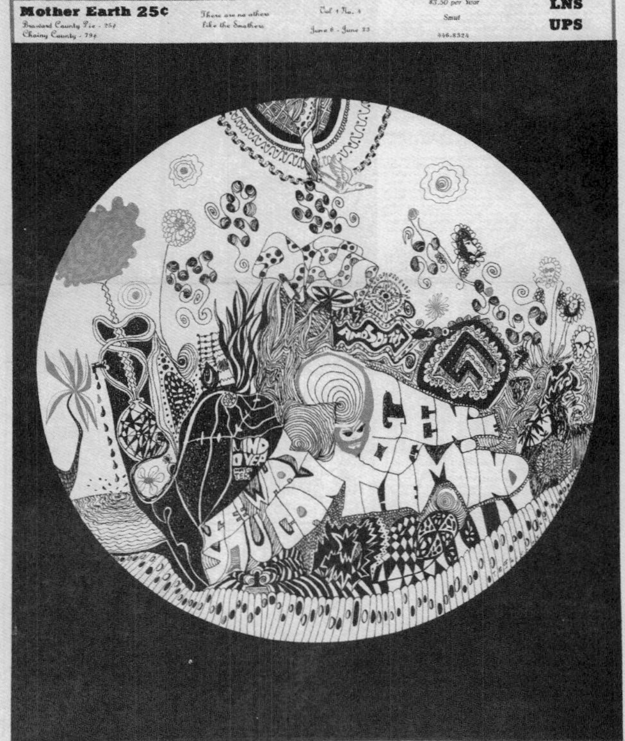
MIAMI FREE PRESS
Something For Everyone
Libel, Slander, And Sex
Miss U.S.A. Today
Dirty Words And Unrelated Filth
Nothing For Anyone
Tribute To Wometco Enterprises
Mother Earth 25¢
LNS
UPS

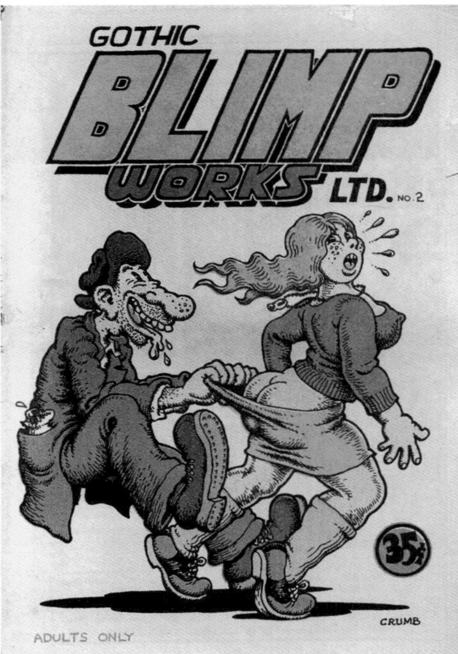
GOTHIC
BLIMP
WORKS
LTD. NO. 2
35¢
CRUMB
ADULTS ONLY

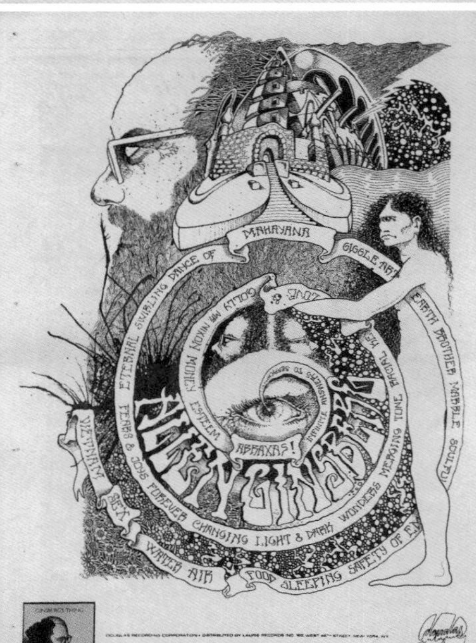
MAHAYANA
ABRAXAS!

Two Sides In Paris Maintain Contact

U.S. and North Vietnam Are Expected to End the Long Delay in the Talks Soon

PARIS, Jan. 1—The united States and North Vietnamese delegations to the talks here are maintaining "some sort of contact" despite an unusually long interval between more formal exchanges, an American source said today.

Rupert Murdoch

Jan. 17—Once the boy wonder of Australian newspaper publishing and now, at 37, managing director of the world's biggest-selling newspaper (six million plus), London's News of the World.

When his father, Sir Keith Murdoch, head of The Melbourne Herald, died early in 1950, he returned from Britain with a master of arts degree from Oxford and Socialist

Santa Barbara Harbor Closed; Oil Fouls Beaches, Fire Hazard Feared

SANTA BARBARA, Calif., Feb. 5—Cleanup crews toiled along 16 miles of oil-smeared beaches tonight as the contamination of this resort community by an oil slick worsened. The Coast Guard, coordinating the effort to plug a leaking underseas oil well, reported that shoreward winds over the next 24 hours threatened to aggravate contamination of the coast.

CZECH PROTESTER DIES OF HIS BURNS

Student Pleads to Others to Shun Self-Immolation

PRAGUE, Jan. 19—Jan Palach, the 21-year-old student who set himself afire Thursday in a protest for freedom, died today after having told a colleague, "My act has fulfilled its purpose."

U.S. AIDES OPPOSE RAIDS IN CAMBODIA

March 25— High State Department officials were reported today to be strongly opposed to any military proposals for air or ground raids against North Vietnamese and Vietcong bases in Cambodia.

NIXON, SWORN, DEDICATES OFFICE TO PEACE

OFFERS A ROLE TO YOUNG AND DISAFFECTED AND A CHANCE TO 'BLACK AS WELL AS WHITE'

HAILED BY PARADE

CHEERED BY 250,000 ON ROUTE—AGNEW ALSO TAKES OATH

WASHINGTON, Jan. 20—In sober pageantry, Richard M. Nixon became the 37th President of the United States today and vowed to "consecrate" himself to the cause of world peace.

MADRID SUSPENDS LIBERTIES TO CURB RISING OPPOSITION

Student Disorder is Blamed as the Regime Declares a State of Emergency

3-MONTH LIMIT IS SET

But Officials Make it Clear Restrictions Won't End if Incidents Continue

MADRID, Jan. 24—The Spanish Government, hitting back hard at signs of growing opposition, announced today that the country was being placed under a "state of exception," under which five articles of the Constitution were being suspended.

300 STUDENTS SEIZE BUILDING AT HARVARD AND EJECT 9 DEANS

CAMBRIDGE, Mass., Thursday, April 10—The main administration building at Harvard University was seized shortly after noon yesterday by about 300 militant students, who ejected nine deans and locked the doors with bicycle chains.

ARGENTINE CITY RIOT-TORN AS UNIONS DEFY STRIKE BAN

BUENOS AIRES, May 29—Street battles broke out between rioters and police forces in the central Argentine city of Cordoba today as the Government braced itself for nationwide strikes and violence.

STRIKERS ON CURACAO LOOT RESORT PORT

Dutch Troops Used

WILLEMSTAD, Curacao, May 30—About 5,000 striking oil refinery workers went on a rampage in this Caribbean resort city today, burning and looting stores and gasoline stations and threatening whites.

4 POLICEMEN HURT IN 'VILLAGE' RAID

Melee Near Sheridan Square Follows Action at Bar

June 29—Hundreds of young men went on a rampage in Greenwich Village shortly after 3 A.M. yesterday after a force of plainclothes men raided a bar that the police said was wellknown for its homosexual clientele. Thirteen persons were arrested and four policemen injured.

FIRST G.I.'S IN PULL-OUT LEAVE SAIGON

SAIGON, South Vietnam, Tuesday, July 8—Draped in flower leis and grinning broadly, a battalion of 814 infantrymen left Saigon today in the initial withdrawal of American combat troops from Vietnam.

ACTRESS IS AMONG 5 SLAIN AT HOME IN BEVERLY HILLS

Sharon Tate, 2 Woman and 3 Men Victims—Suspect Is Seized

LOS ANGELES, Aug. 9—Five persons, including the actress Sharon Tate, were found this morning brutally murdered in a home in a secluded area of Beverly Hills.

SOVIET AND CHINA FIGHT NEW BATTLE IN CENTRAL ASIA

Outbreak Appears the Most Serious Since Clashes on the Ussuri in March

PROTESTS ARE TRADED

Each Charges Intrusion and Says the Other Fired First—2 Chinese Captured

MOSCOW, Aug. 13—The Soviet Union and Communist China today disclosed a new and apparently bloody clash along their Central Asian frontier. Each side blamed the other, and no casualty figures were made known by either side.

Nixon To Reduce Vietnam Force, Pulling Out 25,000 G.I.'S By Aug. 31

A Midway Accord

Leaders Agree First Cutbacks Will Begin Within 30 Days

MIDWAY ISLAND, June 8—President Nixon met with President Nguyen Van Thieu of South Vietnam today and announced that 25,000 American soldiers would be withdrawn from Vietnam before the end of August.

After the first two hours of five hours of talks on this Pacific island, Mr. Nixon emerged to declare that the Presidents had agreed that troop withdrawals would begin within 30 days.

A JUNTA IN LIBYA OUSTS MONARCHY, SETS UP REPUBLIC

Military Council Proclaims Socialist State After Coup Without Bloodshed

RECOGNITION BY CAIRO

New Regime Says It Plans an Arab Nationalist Policy—King Is in Turkey

BEIRUT, Lebanon, Tuesday, Sept. 2—A revolutionary council took control of Libya yesterday after overthrowing the conservative regime of the 79-year-old King Idris I, according to reports from Tripoli.

8 GO ON TRIAL TODAY IN ANOTHER ROUND IN CHICAGO CONVENTION STRIFE

CHICAGO, Wednesday, Sept. 24—More than a year has passed. The grass has grown over the scuffle marks in Grant Park. The tear gas and stink bombs have been flushed from the Conrad Hilton's lobby. But there is still no truce in the Battle of Chicago.

WAR VETERAN SAYS HE KILLED 35 TO 40 IN SONGMY SWEEP

November 25—A 22-year-old disabled Army veteran said yesterday that he killed 35 to 40 men, women and children during an attack on the village of Songmy in South Vietnam in March, 1968.

INDIANS RALLY BEHIND THE SEIZURE OF ALCATRAZ ISLAND

SAN FRANCISCO, Nov. 29—When a band of Indians boated through the foggy dark to Alcatraz Island, their invasion was seen as a delightful stunt. Now the event is portrayed by many Indians as perhaps their most important exploit since the end of the Indian wars.

LOTTERY IS HELD TO SET THE ORDER OF DRAFT IN 1970

FIRST BIRTH DATES SELECTED ARE SEPT. 14, APRIL 24, DEC. 30 AND FEB. 14

850,000 ARE AFFECTED

EACH IS ASSIGNED A NUMBER—TOP THIRD OF THE LIST IS LIKELY TO BE CALLED

WASHINGTON, Dec. 1—The futures of young men across the country were decided tonight as, one by one, the dates of their births were drawn in the first draft lottery in a generation.

POMPIDOU CHOSEN AS FRENCH LEADER WITH 57% OF VOTE

He Succeeds de Gaulle as President—Poher Weakened as 31% Abstain in Drive Led by Communists

PARIS, Monday, June 16—France yesterday elected Georges Pompidou, a Gaullist, to succeed Charles de Gaulle as President of the Republic for the next seven years. Mr. Pompidou defeated Alain Poher, the Interim President, after a short and bitter campaign. He won nearly 58 per cent of the

TV: AN AWESOME EVENT

LIVE PICTURES OF ASTRONAUTS ON THE MOON LEAVE LITTLE ROOM FOR WORDS

July 21—A day of unparalleled uncertainty, marked by minutes of breathless suspense, culminated in the majestic event of live television pictures of Neil A. Armstrong becoming the first human being to place a foot on a planet other than the earth.

Even in Hostile Nations, the Feat Inspires Awe

All the World's in the Moon's Grip, Even Countries Usually Hostile to the U.S.

July 22—From Wollongong, Australia, where a local judge brought in a television set to watch while hearing cases, to Norwegian Lapland, where shepherds tended their reindeer with transistor radios pressed to their ears, the people of the world were looking to the moon yesterday.

A TAKE-OVER BID CONFRONTS S.D.S.

Progressive Labor Faction Strong at Chicago Parley

CHICAGO, June 19—The Students for a Democratic Society convention settled down to factional infighting, caucuses and heated debate today, with a strong bid for a takeover by members of the Progressive Labor party.

NIXON PLANS CUT IN MILITARY ROLE FOR U.S. IN ASIA

Starting Tour, He Promises Respect for Commitments, but Under New Forms

ARRIVES IN PHILIPPINES

President, at Guam, Asserts Nation Won't Be Drawn Into More Vietnams

MANILA, Saturday, July 26—President Nixon declared yesterday that the United States would not be enticed into future wars like the one in Vietnam and would redesign and reduce its military commitments throughout non-Communist Asia.

PROTESTANT PARADE SPARKS ULSTER RIOT

LONDONDERRY, Northern Ireland, Wednesday, Aug. 13—The police used tear gas against a rioting Roman Catholic mob last night in an effort to break up savage sectarian fighting after nearly eight hours.

300,000 AT FOLK-ROCK FAIR CAMP OUT IN A SEA OF MUD

BETHEL, N.Y., Aug. 16—Despite massive traffic jams, drenching rainstorms and shortages of food, water and medical facilities, about 300,000 young people swarmed over this rural area today for the Woodstock Music and Art Fair.

De Gaulle Quits After Losing Referendum; Senate Leader To Serve Pending Election

Vote Weeks Away

President, in Office a Decade, Will Leave at Noon Today

PARIS, Monday, April 28—Charles de Gaulle stepped down early today after more than 10 years as President of France. He acted after his regime suffered a numbing defeat in a referendum.

Nixon Calls For Public Support As He Pursues His Vietnam Plan On A Secret Pullout Timetable

Policy Unchanged

President Says Hasty Withdrawal Would Be a 'Disaster' Nixon Calls for Support Of Vietnam Pullout Plan

WASHINGTON, Nov. 3—President Nixon pleaded tonight for domestic support as he persisted in his effort to find peace in Vietnam and as he unfolded what he said was a plan to bring home all United States ground combat forces on an orderly but secret timetable.

250,000 War Protesters Stage Peaceful Rally In Washington; A Record Throng

WASHINGTON, Nov. 15—A vast throng of Americans, predominantly youthful and constituting the largest mass march in the nation's capital, demonstrated peacefully in the heart of the city today, demanding a rapid withdrawal of United States troops from Vietnam.

U.S. FACES PERIOD OF LABOR UNREST

Unions Are Seeking Higher Wages to Offset Sharp Rise in Cost of Living

LABOR UNREST LOOMS AS UNIONS ARE SEEKING WAGE GAINS TO OFFSET INFLATION

Dec. 1—The nation is facing a period of tough and perhaps abrasive collective bargaining in the months ahead as unions attempt to offset sharply rising living costs and to make new gains for their

POLICE IN CHICAGO SLAY 2 PANTHERS

Illinois Chairman of Party Is Killed in Shoot-Out

CHICAGO, Dec. 4—Fred Hampton, the Illinois chairman of the Black Panther party, and another Panther leader were killed today in a pre-dawn shoot-out with a police raiding party.

NUCLEAR ACCORD SIGNED BY NIXON AND BY PODGORNY

U.S. AND SOVIET VIRTUALLY COMPLETE RATIFICATION OF PACT TO PREVENT SPREAD

NEW CABINET MORE POSITIVE—PRESIDENT SAYS TREATY ADDS TO WORLD'S SAFETY

WASHINGTON, Nov., 24—President Nixon signed the treaty to halt the spread of nuclear weapons today, all but completing formal ratification some seven years after negotiations began on

200,000 Attend Coast Rock Fete

Free Concert Causes Huge Jam Near San Francisco

TRACY, Calif., Dec. 6—Thousands of fans of the Rolling Stones rock group converged on the hillsides around the Altamont Speedway here today, turning pastures into parking lots and campsites.

San Francisco Express Times, January 7, 1969, vol. 2, no. 1, cover
Miami Free Press (Miami), June 21–July 2, 1969, vol. 1, no. 5, cover
Gothic Blimp Works Ltd. (New York), 1969, no. 2, cover
Gothic Blimp Works Ltd. (New York), 1969, no. 2, back cover
Miami Free Press (Miami), June 6–23, 1969, vol. 1, no. 4, cover

LEADER PROCLAIMS BIAFRA'S LOYALTY TO LAGOS REGIME

Effiong Says the Republic is Ended and People Accept Structure of Federation

BIG RELIEF DRIVE VOWED

Government Acts as Britain Begins to Send Trucks; Officials are Reinstated

LAGOS, Nigeria, Jan. 14—Lieut. Col. Philip Effiong, who was the leader of secessionist Biafra in the final hours before it fell last week-end, came to Lagos today and made a formal declaration of surrender.

SIHANOUK REPORTED OUT IN A COUP BY HIS PREMIER

Cambodia Airports Shut

PRINCE IS ABROAD

He Hints at Forming an Exile Regime—Reaches Peking

BANGKOK, Thailand, March 18—Prince Norodom Sihanouk, Chief of State of Cambodia, was overthrown today in his absence, the Pnompenh radio announced.

The Southeast Asia country was cut off from the world, except for the broadcasts. The nation's two commercial airports were closed to all traffic.

Chicago 7 Cleared of Plot

5 Guilty on Second Count; Dellinger, Davis, Hayden, Hoffman and Rubin are Convicted Individually

CHICAGO, Feb. 18—All seven defendants in the Chicago conspiracy trial were acquitted today of plotting to incite a riot here during the 1968 Democratic National Convention, but five of them were convicted of seeking to promote a riot through individual acts.

WHITE RHODESIA OFFICIALLY TAKES REPUBLIC STATUS

The Proclamation Severing Last Ties With Britain Dissolves Parliament

SALISBURY, Rhodesia, Monday, March 2—Rhodesia's white minority Government formally severed its last tie with the British Crown last midnight, dissolving Parliament and declaring a racially segregated republic.

Postal Anarchy

March 19—Defiance of law and court injunction by postal workers in New York and elsewhere constitutes the most serious threat to orderly governmental process in the history of the Federal civil service.

Millions Join Earth Day Observances Across the Nation

NEW YORK, April 23—Huge, light-hearted throngs ambled down autoless streets here yesterday as the city heeded Earth Day's call for a regeneration of a polluted environment by celebrating an exuberant rite of spring.

If the environment had any enemies they did not make themselves known. Political leaders, governmental departments and corporations hastened to line up in the ranks of those yearning for a clean, quiet, fume-free city.

For two hours, except for crosstown traffic, the internal combustion engine was barred from Fifth Avenue between 59th and 14th Streets.

NUCLEAR-WEAPONS PACT TAKES EFFECT THURSDAY

WASHINGTON, March 3—The White House announced today that President Nixon would officially declare the treaty to prevent the spread of nuclear weapons in effect at a State Department ceremony Thursday.

TWO FIGURES IN 'VILLAGE' BLAST LINKED TO POLITICS OF NEW LEFT

March 11—Two of the individuals involved in the mysterious explosion that demolished a Greenwich Village townhouse last Friday have been linked by sources close to the investigation with the world of New Left politics.

NIXON SENDS COMBAT FORCES TO CAMBODIA

'NOT AN INVASION'

PRESIDENT CALLS STEP AN EXTENSION OF WAR TO SAVE G.I. LIVES

WASHINGTON, April 30—In a sharp departure from the previous conduct of war in Southeast Asia, President Nixon announced tonight that he was sending United States combat troops into Cambodia for the first time.

U.S. Troops Flown In for Panther Rally

New Haven Braces for Protest by 20,000

4,000 Will Be on Duty in New England Today—Dempsey Asks Aid

Store Windows Boarded Up—Yale Moves its Files From Campus

NEW HAVEN, April 30—Federal troops were flown to New England today to stand by in the event of violence at a massive demonstration planned for here tomorrow to protest the murder trial of the Black Panther national chairman, Bobby Seale.

4 KENT STATE STUDENTS KILLED BY TROOPS

8 HURT AS SHOOTING FOLLOWS REPORTED SNIPING AT RALLY

KENT, Ohio, May 4—Four students at Kent State University, two of them women, were shot to death this afternoon by a volley of National Guard gunfire. At least 8 other students were wounded.

The burst of gunfire came about 20 minutes after the guardsmen broke up a noon rally on the Commons, a grassy campus gathering spot, by lobbing tear gas at a crowd of about 1,000 young people.

PROTESTS ON CAMBODIA AND KENT STATE ARE JOINED BY MANY LOCAL SCHOOLS

May 6—Tens of thousands of students in dozens of educational institutions here and in adjoining states halted their studies yesterday to show their bitterness and anguish over the invasion of Cambodia and the killing of four Kent State University students.

Peaceful protests ranged from the occupation of buildings at New York University and Niagara University to a solemn memorial service for the slain students at the Princeton University Chapel, where the congregation expressed its sense of crisis by reciting this verse from a poem by James Russell Lowell...

WAR FOES HERE ATTACKED BY CONSTRUCTION WORKERS

City Hall Is Stormed

May 9—Helmeted construction workers broke up a student antiwar demonstration in Wall Street yesterday, chasing youths through the canyons of the financial district in a wild noontime melee that left about 70 persons injured.

JACKSON POLICE FIRE ON STUDENTS

2 Killed and 12 Injured at Women's Dormitory

JACKSON, Miss., Friday, May 15—Two persons were killed and 12 wounded early today after the police opened fire on a women's dormitory at Jackson State College here.

ARGENTINA: AGAIN THE COUP

June 9—President Organia never really regained his political grip on Argentina after the bloody rioting and popular upheaval of May and June, 1969. From then on it was mostly downhill for the shy, taciturn Army general who did not seek the presidency but came to enjoy political power and tried clumsily to build a popular base in order to retain it. His attempts to woo the Peronists in and outside the trade unions infuriated key military leaders who had suffered under General Peron or had helped oust the dictator in 1955.

BILL TO LOWER VOTING AGE TO 18 BY THE '71 ELECTIONS APPROVED IN HOUSE, 272-132

NIXON MAY SIGN IT

MEASURE ALSO EXTENDS VOTING RIGHTS ACT FOR FIVE YEARS

WASHINGTON, June 17—The House approved and sent to President Nixon today a bill to lower the voting age from 21 to 18 in all Federal, state and local elections beginning in 1971. The measure would open the political process to about 11 million young people.

Senators, 81 to 10, Vote For Repeal Of Tonkin Action

G.O.P. Seizes Initiative on Resolution Johnson Used as Basis for Wider War

House Backing Needed

Doves Accuse Republicans of Indulging in Crude and Cynical Partisanship

WASHINGTON, June 24—The Senate voted today in favor of repeal of the 1964 Gulf of Tonkin resolution, once interpreted as the statutory equivalent of a declaration of war in Vietnam.

Ground Operation By U.S. in Cambodia to End Tomorrow

As Pullout of G.I.'s Goes on, Enemy Soldiers Step Up Action in South Vietnam

Lon Nol Hopes for Aid

He Wants Nixon to Send the Troops Back if Situation Continues to Deteriorate

SAIGON, South Vietnam, June 28—As American troops continued their withdrawal from Cambodia, scheduled to be completed by Tuesday, a slight increase in enemy activity was reported throughout South Vietnam in the last 48 hours.

WOMEN MARCH DOWN FIFTH AVENUE TO A RALLY IN BRYANT PARK IN DRIVE FOR EQUALITY

10,000 in Parade Flood the Street

August 27—Celebrating the 50th anniversary of American women's right to vote and the start of a new crusade for equality a crowd of more than 10,000 people, mostly women of all ages, occupations and viewpoints, marched down Fifth Avenue to an enthusiastic rally in Bryant Park last night.

Isle of Wight Festival Turns Slightly Discordant

ISLE OF WIGHT, England, Aug. 30—Carrying rucksacks and bedrolls, thousands of young men and women engulfed this normally sedate island of chalk cliffs and cricket fields this weekend for an outdoor pop festival that reached a peak today in a surge of dust, music and litter.

4 Jets Hijacked; One, a 747, is Blown Up

Arab Group Says it Took Planes—El Al Foils Move

4 Jets Bound for New York Hijacked Over Europe

LONDON, Monday, Sept. 7—Four jets bound for New York with more than 600 persons aboard were hijacked over Europe yesterday, apparently by members of an Arab guerrilla group. Three of the flights were diverted to the Middle East; the fourth landed at London after a gunfight in which a hijacker was killed.

ISRAELIS GET ASSURANCES FROM CONGRESS THAT THEY CAN BUY MISSILES AND TANKS AS WELL AS PLANES

WASHINGTON, Sept. 28—Israel received explicit assurances from Congress today that the arms she might buy on favorable credit terms in the United States would include missiles and tanks as well as aircraft.

Schoolgirls Stitch Hastily Improvised Flag for New Cambodian Republic

PNOMPENH, Cambodia, Oct. 8—At 2 o'clock this morning Mrs. Sim Song Lung received a telephone call telling her what the new flag of the Khmer Republic, to be proclaimed tomorrow, was to look like. Parliament had just decided.

SEPARATISTS' EARLIER WEAPONS: BOMBS, DYNAMITE AND ROBBERY

MONTREAL, Oct. 11—The Front for the Liberation of Quebec, the organization responsible for two political kidnappings in Montreal this week, has been terrorizing this city intermittently for seven years.

SADAT TAKES OATH OF OFFICE AS PRESIDENT OF EGYPT

Pledges Are Given to Follow Nasser's Policies Including Recovery of Arab Lands

CAIRO, Oct. 17—Anwar Sadat was sworn in today as the President of the United Arab Republic, succeeding the late Gamal Abdel Nasser, his revolutionary colleague and friend for more than 30 years.

Mr. Sadat took the oath of office during a brief special session of the National Assembly. He received a 90.04 per cent affirmation vote in a Presidential plebiscite held Thursday.

ALLENDE, MARXIST LEADER, ELECTED CHILE'S PRESIDENT

SANTIAGO, Chile, Oct. 24—Dr. Salvador Allende, a Marxist, was elected President of Chile by a joint session of congress today.

CALLEY RETURNS TO AREA OF THE ALLEGED MASSACRE

SONMY, South Vietnam, Oct. 29—The Vietnamese of Sonmy say that 570 civilians were massacred here on March 16 1968, when an American infantry company entered the area but none of them know the name of Lieut. William L. Calley Jr., nor what he looks like nor do they understand why he was in Quangngai Province today.

The 27-year-old American lieutenant—the first man to be accused by the Army in the alleged massacre—arrived shortly after 5 P.M. in Chulai, headquarters of the Americal Division, 335 miles northeast of Saigon.

Senate Confirms Ruckelshaus to Head Environment Agency

WASHINGTON, Dec. 2—The Senate approved today, by unanimous voice vote, the nomination of William D. Ruckelshaus as director of the new Environmental Protection Agency.

NIXON SIGNS JOB SAFETY BILL, ENDING LONG STRUGGLE

WASHINGTON, Dec. 29—President Nixon signed today an occupational health and safety bill giving the Secretary of Labor authority to set safety standards for factories, farms and construction sites and creating a three-member panel to enforce the standards.

FRANCO COMMUTES DEATH SENTENCES FOR SIX BASQUES

Decision, Following Many Clemency Appeals, Eases the Tension in Spain

TERMS TO BE 30 YEARS

Announcement Comes After Cabinet Meeting—General Speaks to Nation on TV

MADRID, Dec. 30—Generalissimo Francisco Franco today commuted all the death sentences imposed in the Burgos court-martial of 15 Basque guerrillas charged with banditry and the killing of a police inspector.

Inner-City Voice (Detroit), October–December 1970, vol. 2, no. 9, cover
Inner-City Voice (Detroit), October–December 1970, vol. 2, no. 9, back cover
Come Out! (New York), September–October 1970, vol. 1, no. 5, cover
Come Out! (New York), September–October 1970, vol. 1, no. 5, back cover

THE LEAGUE OF REVOLUTIONARY BLACK WORKERS REPRESENTS THE HIGHEST FORM OF STRUGGLE WHICH THE CONSCIOUS INSURGENT MOVEMENT OF BLACK LABOR HAS REACHED. BEING GUIDED BY REVOLUTIONARY PRINCIPLES AND STRIVING TO UNITE ALL BLACK WORKERS, WE WILL CERTAINLY BE VICTORIOUS.

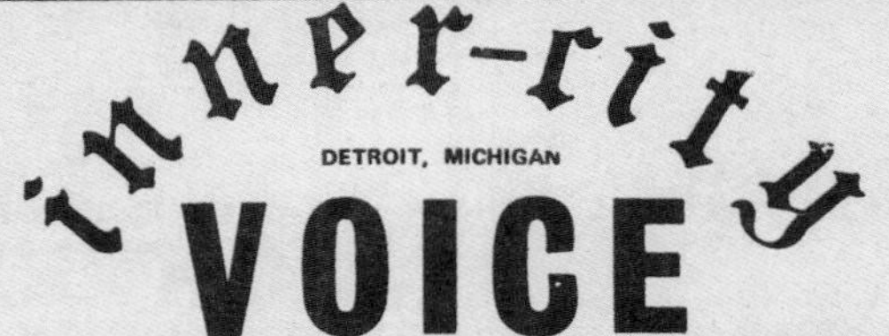

25¢

VOLUME 2 NUMBER 9 OFFICIAL ORGAN OF THE LEAGUE OF REVOLUTIONARY BLACK WORKERS NOVEMBER—DECEMBER, 1970

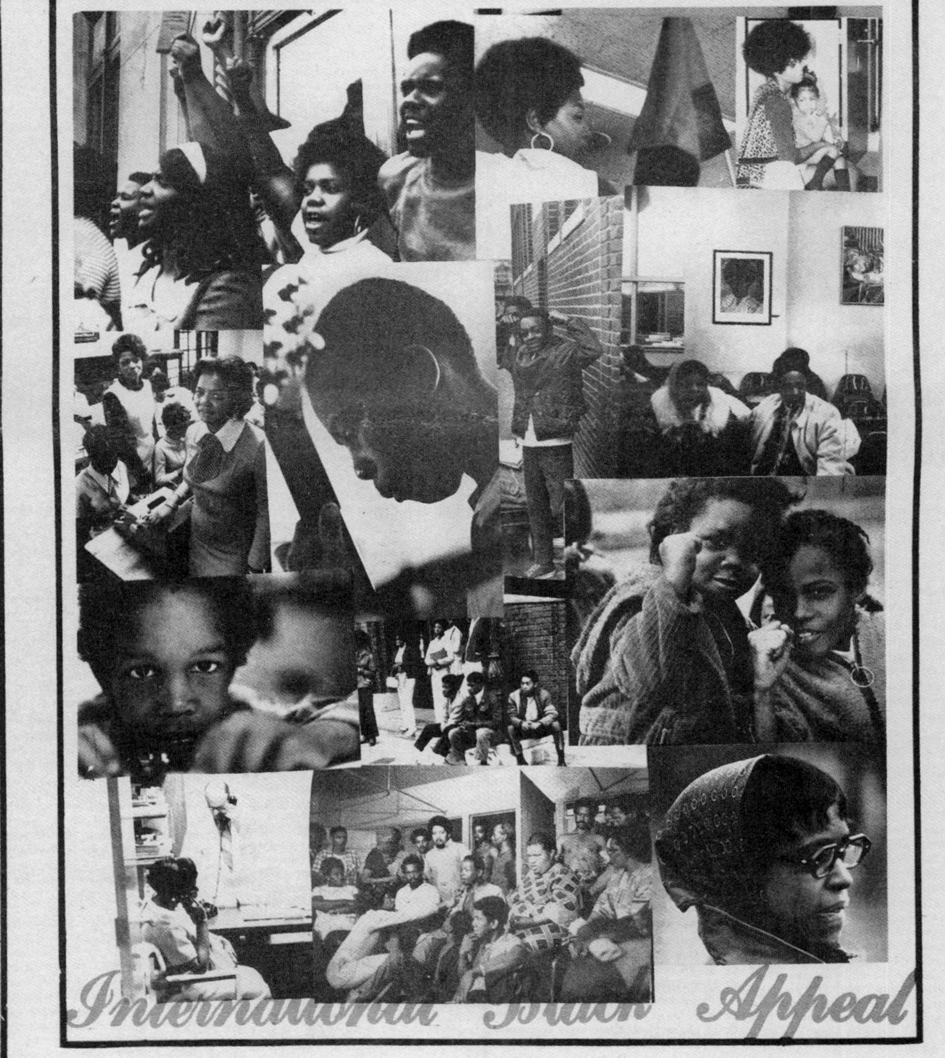

JOIN the League of Revolutionary Black Workers

inner-city VOICE

Subscribe Now!

Inner City Voice
Box 464
Detroit, Michigan 48232

—4 issues $1.00 —8 issues $2.00
—12 issues $3.00

NAME ________
ADDRESS ________
CITY ________
STATE ________ ZIP ____
NATION ________

(Please Pay With Money Order)

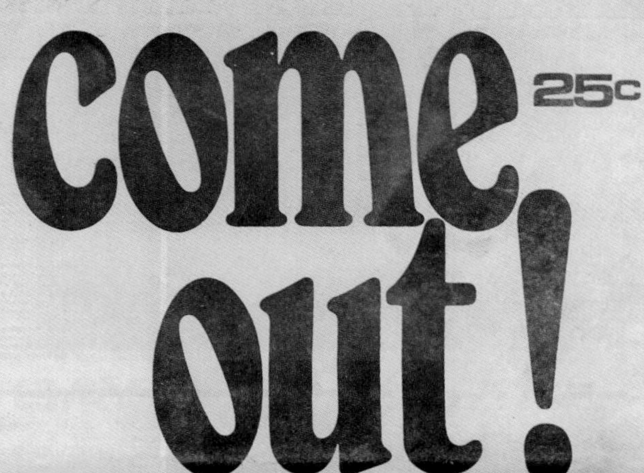

a liberation forum for the gay community

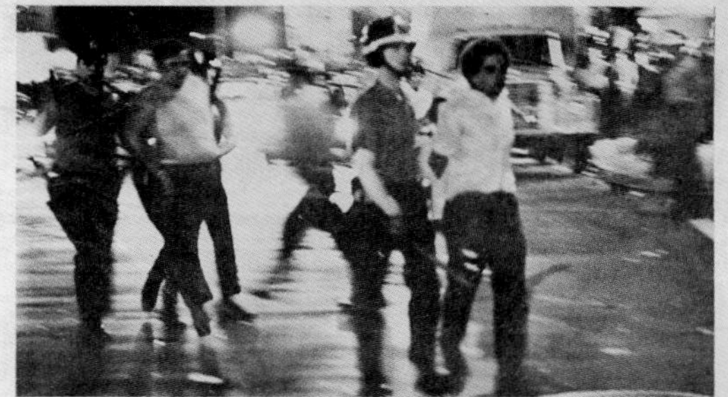

GAY LIBERATION FRONT

VOL1 NO 5 NEW YORK SEPT OCT 1970 35c OUTSIDE NYC

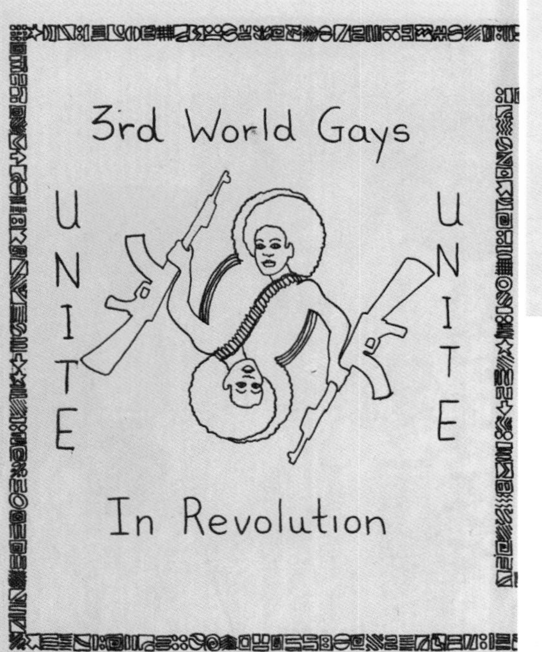

Manson and 3 Women Found Guilty

State to Ask Death Penalty

LOS ANGELES, Jan. 25—Charles M. Manson and three young women who were members of his hippie family were found guilty today of the Tate-LaBianca murders.

UGANDA'S NEW RULER RELEASES 55 POLITICAL PRISONERS

KAMPALA, Uganda, Jan. 28—Uganda's new ruler, Maj. Gen. Idi Amin, today freed 55 political prisoners, dismissed the Cabinet of the ousted President, Milton Obote, and imposed a temporary ban on political activities.

BOMB IN CAPITOL CAUSES WIDE DAMAGE

WASHINGTON, March 1—A bomb, apparently planted by a group or person protesting against the Vietnam war, exploded early this morning in the Senate wing of the Capitol, causing extensive damage but no injuries.

COUNTER MARKET ACTIVATES NEW QUOTE UNIT

Issues End Day Up in Widened Trading—Amex Advances Counter Market Activates Unit to Speed Stock-Price Quotations

Feb. 9—The most revolutionary innovation in the history of the over-the-counter market, an automated-quotation system, went into operation yesterday as most counter issues finished higher in stepped-up trading.

SYRIAN VOTERS BACK ASSAD AS PRESIDENT

BEIRUT, Lebanon, March 13—Lieut. Gen. Hafez al-Assad was today proclaimed the President of Syria after having received overwhelming approval from voters in yesterday's referendum.

ARGENTINE JUNTA OUSTS PRESIDENT IN POST 9 MONTHS

Levingston Removed After He Dismisses Army Chief—9th Shift Since Peron

BUENOS AIRES, Tuesday, March 23—The commanders of Argentina's three armed services early today announced the dismissal of Roberto Marcelo Levingston from the presidency.

BAN ON ATOM ARMS ON SEABED SIGNED IN THREE CAPITALS

At Ceremony in Washington, Nixon Expresses the Hope for Wider Accords

AT LEAST 63 NATIONS ACT

In Moscow, Kosygin Says Soviet Will Do Utmost to Curb Arms Race

WASHINGTON, Feb. 11—The United States and the Soviet Union today signed the new treaty barring nuclear weapons from the ocean floor. The area covers about 70 per cent of the earth's surface.

EAST PAKISTANIS UNVEIL NEW FLAG

President, Heavily Guarded, Takes Ride in Hostile City

DACCA, Pakistan, March 23—The President of Pakistan, who has spent eight days in the eastern wing of his country under heavy protection, came out of his walled compound for the first time today for a heavily protected drive to the military cantonment on the edge of the city.

SOUTH VIETNAMESE DRIVE INTO LAOS PUT AT 14 MILES

FIELD REPORT PUTS SAIGON TROOPS 14 MILES INSIDE LAOS

KHESANH, South Vietnam, Feb. 13—South Vietnamese troops were reported today to have advanced about 14 miles into Laos in their six-day-old drive to cut the enemy supply network there.

For the third day, however, no supply convoys traveled over the bumpy road, Route 9, from South Vietnam to the forward elements in Laos

CALLEY GUILTY OF MURDER OF 22 CIVILIANS AT MYLAI; SENTENCE EXPECTED TODAY

APPEAL IS CERTAIN

ARMY JURY MUST SET PENALTY OF DEATH OR LIFE IMPRISONMENT

CALLEY IS GUILTY OF MURDER OF 22 CIVILIANS

FORT BENNING, Ga., March 29—First Lieut. William L. Calley Jr. was found guilty today of the premeditated murder of at least 22 South Vietnamese civilians at Mylai three years ago.

OPINION BY BURGER

Segregation in North Based on Housing is Not Affected

SUPREME COURT BACKS BUSING TO COMBAT DUAL SCHOOLS IN SOUTH

WASHINGTON, April 20—The Supreme Court unanimously upheld today the constitutionality of busing as a means to "dismantle the dual school systems" of the South.

PRESIDENT DUVALIER OF HAITI DIES

19-Year-Old Son Succeeds Him

PORT-AU-PRINCE, Haiti, April 22—President Francois Duvalier, dictator of Haiti for 13 and a half years, died last night. His death was announced this morning by the Government radio several hours after his son, Jean-Claude, was sworn in as the new "President for Life" of the world's oldest black republic.

200,000 RALLY IN CAPITAL TO END WAR

WASHINGTON, April 24—Antiwar marchers massed today at a new rallying point, the Capitol, to urge Congress to assume the leadership they seek to bring the Indochina war to an immediate end.

LAWYERS STAGE RALLY TO PROTEST WAR

May 1—Hundreds of lawyers took to the streets here yesterday in an uncharacteristic protest against the war in Vietnam.

GUERRILLAS STEP UP RAIDS, CEYLON SAYS

GALLE, Ceylon, May 3—The Ceylonese Government today reported a sharp increase in raids by insurgents as policemen searched the alleys of this old fortress town for guerrillas.

"Terrorist attacks on villages and public buildings have increased," the Government announced. Today was the third day of the four-day amnesty period for insurgents who surrender, and more than 900 were reported to have turned themselves in so far.

PRESIDENT ENDS 21-YEAR EMBARGO ON PEKING TRADE

Authorizes Export of Many Nonstrategic Items—Lifts Controls on All Imports

SHIPPING CURB DROPPED

White House List Includes Farm Goods, Appliances and Basic Metals

WASHINGTON, June 10—President Nixon ended a 21-year embargo on trade with Communist China today. He authorized the export of a wide range of nonstrategic items and he lifted all controls on imports from China.

THE COVERT WAR

June 13—The Pentagon papers disclose that in this phase the United States had been mounting clandestine military attacks against North Vietnam and planning to obtain a Congressional resolution that the Administration regarded as the equivalent of a declaration of war. The papers make it clear that these far-reaching measures were not improvised in the heat of the Tonkin crisis.

PRESIDENT ORDERS WIDER DRUG FIGHT; ASKS $155-MILLION

Message Opens Addiction Drive—Illinois Aide to Head Special Office

NIXON SEES 'EMERGENCY'

Presses for Rehabilitation, Research, Education and Tighter Enforcement

WASHINGTON, June 17—President Nixon said today that drug abuse had "assumed the dimensions of a national emergency," and he asked Congress for $155-million more for a campaign of rehabilitation, research, education, enforcement and international control of drug traffic.

SEVERS LINK BETWEEN DOLLAR AND GOLD

A World Effect

UNILATERAL U.S. MOVE MEANS OTHERS FACE PARITY DECISIONS

U.S. to End Dollar Conversion to Gold

WASHINGTON, Aug. 15—President Nixon announced tonight that henceforth the United States would cease to convert foreign-held dollars into gold—unilaterally changing the 25-year-old international monetary system.

How many pounds, marks, yen and francs the dollar will buy tomorrow will depend on decisions of other countries. In some countries, the value of the dollar may "float," moving up and down in

NIXON HAILS YOUTH VOTE AS 26TH AMENDMENT IS CERTIFIED AT THE WHITE HOUSE

WASHINGTON, July 5—The 26th Amendment to the Constitution, which lowers to 18 the minimum voting age in all elections, was officially certified today in a ceremony conducted by President Nixon.

More than 500 members of a singing group, Young Americans in Concert, witnessed the event in the East Room of the White House.

Mr. Nixon arrived by helicopter shortly after 3 P.M. after a weekend at Camp David, Md.

He told the young people that it was "particularly appropriate" that the ceremony which marked the addition of 11 million potential voters to the electorate, had fallen on the official observance of the nation's 195th birthday.

200 Women Organize for Political Power and Vote to Disavow Any Racist Candidate of Either Sex

WASHINGTON, July 10—More than 200 women—Republicans, Democrats and independents—met today to inaugurate a new organization aimed at increasing the number of women holding public office.

BRITISH SHIFTING MORE ARMY UNITS TO IRISH BORDER

Patrols Will be Reinforced to Cut Down Movement of Terrorists and Arms

ARMOR WILL BE SENT

Soldier Is Slain in Belfast as New Rioting Erupts—Death Toll Now 26

BELFAST, Northern Ireland, Aug. 14—British troops seeking to prevent terrorist infiltration moved toward the Irish border today following a battle between

MINERS AND PEASANTS MOVE AGAINST REBELS IN BOLIVIA

Bolivia Loyalists March On Rebels

LA PAZ, Bolivia, Aug. 20—More than 35,000 peasants and armed miners were reported marching tonight against rightist army rebels who had earlier proclaimed Gen. Hugo Banzir president of Bolivia in place of President Juan Jose Torres Gonzales, a leftist.

ATTICA RIOTERS, HOLDING OUT, ASK FOREIGN ASYLUM

ATTICA, N.Y., Saturday, Sept. 11—Groups of angry prisoners holding 33 guards as hostages at the Attica State Correctional Facility continued negotiations into this morning with State Correction Commissioner Russell G. Oswald.

BUDDHISTS URGE ELECTION BOYCOTT

Militant Vietnamese Group Protests One-Man Race—Street Fighting Erupts

SAIGON, South Vietnam, Sept. 16—The powerful anti-Government An Quang Buddhists today called on South Vietnam's Buddhist majority and "all other freedom and democracy loving people" to boycott the one-man presidential election on Oct. 3.

A Persian Night of Kings, Queens, Sheiks, Sultans and Diamonds

PERSEPOLIS, Iran, Oct. 14—The Shah of Iran established himself tonight as one of the world's great party givers. For sheer grandeur, his gala in a silk tent will be hard for any nation to surpass.

CAMBODIA'S DRIVE COLLAPSES IN FACE OF ENEMY ATTACK

Half of 20,000-Man Force is Termed all but Wrecked as a Fighting Unit

A DISORDERLY RETREAT

25 Miles of Key Highway in Foe's Hands—Rest May Have to Be Abandoned

PNOMPENH, Cambodia, Dec. 2—Thousands of Cambodian Government troops were reported in disorderly retreat today as a major military campaign north of the capital collapsed in the face of heavy North Vietnamese attacks.

QUICK FULL SURRENDER OF EAST PAKISTAN IS SET AS OBJECTIVE OF INDIA'S INVADERS

A Unified Command With Rebels Is Sought

CALCUTTA, India, Dec. 4—The objective of India's land-and-air invasion of East Pakistan is the full surrender of the Pakistani forces there and the establishment of the insurgent Bangla Desh (Bengal Nation) Government, Indian officials made clear today.

BOMBING IS HALTED

Suspension of Attacks Followed a Plea by City Commander

NEW DELHI, Thursday, Dec. 16—Pakistan's army commander in East Pakistan surrendered to India today, and a military spokesman said the formal capitulation ceremony could take place in Dacca in he next few hours.

Voice of the Lumpen (Germany), January 1971, no. 1, cover
Small Arms (Springfield, MA), vol. 1, no. 4, cover
Voice of the Lumpen (Germany), January 1971, no. 1, back cover
Small Arms (Springfield, MA), April 1971, vol. 1, no. 5, cover

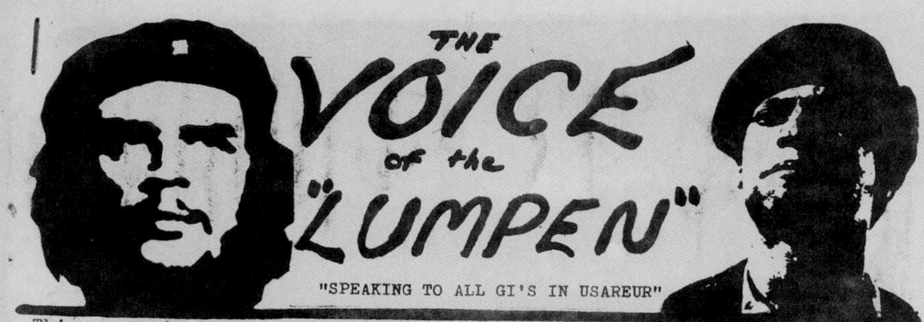

This paper is legal,but the PIGS will probably bust anyone caught reading it So be cool!!!Check out AR 381-135(D) in case they do happen to vamp on you.

FIRST EDITION

The nature of a panther is that he never attacks. But if anyone attacks him or backs him into a corner,the panther comes up to wipe that agressor or that attacker out, absolutely,resolutely,wholly,thoroghly,and completely.

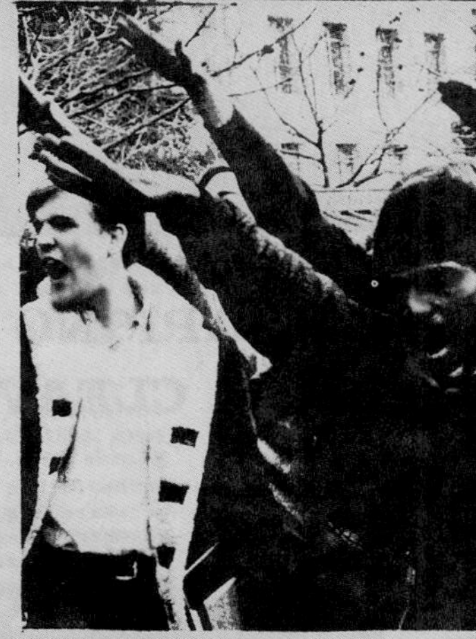

"THE TIME WHEN PEOPLE CAN SIT BACK AND VIEW PROCESSES OF INJUSTICE AND INEQUALITY HAS COME TO AN END"

TABLE OF CONTENTS

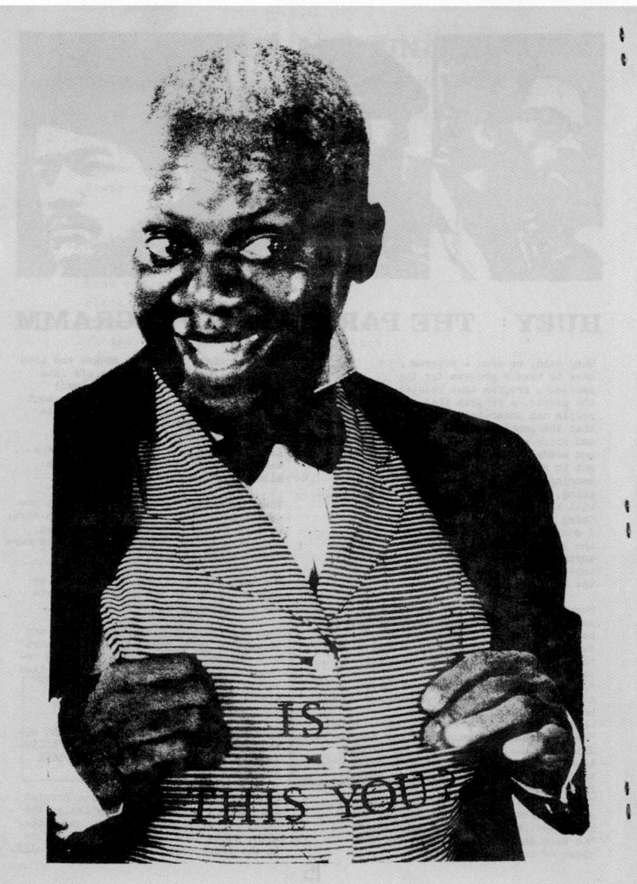

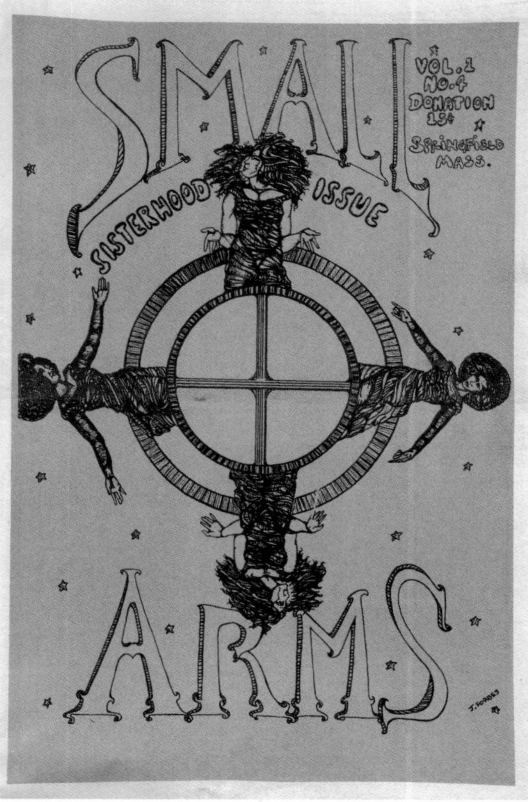

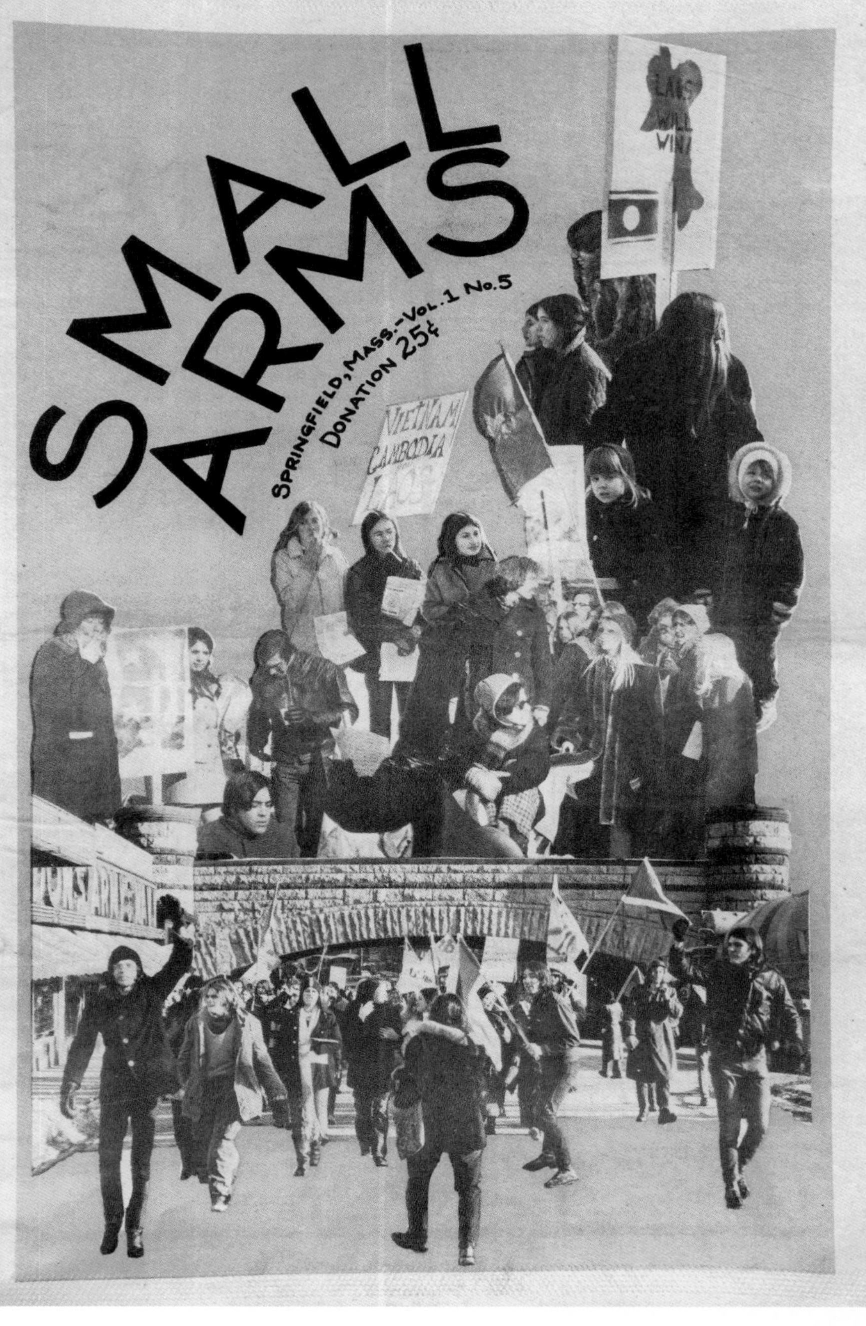

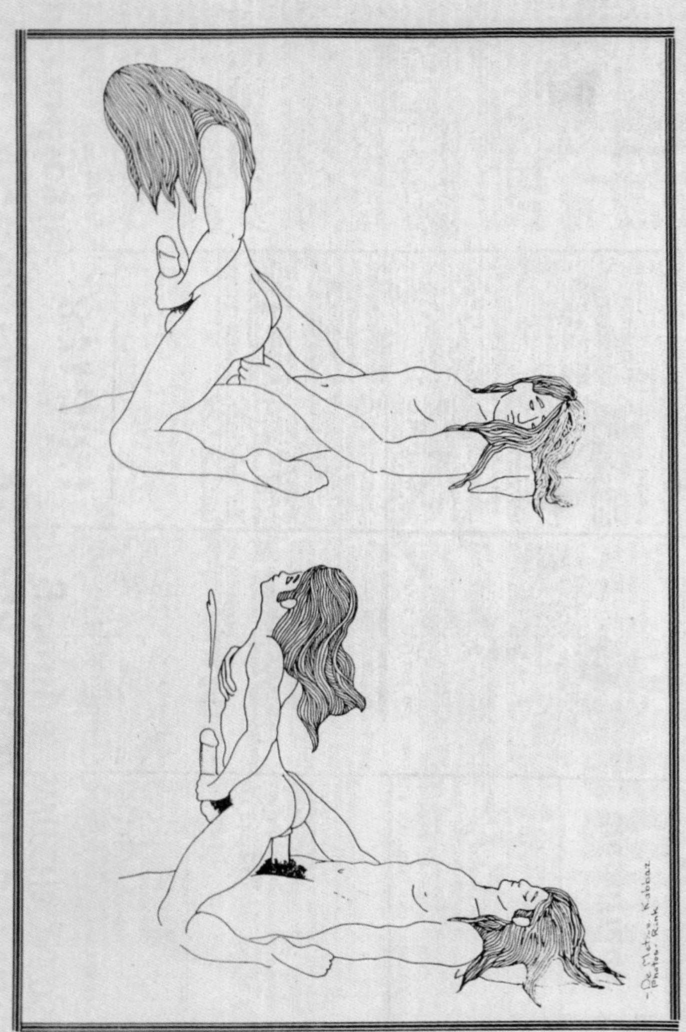

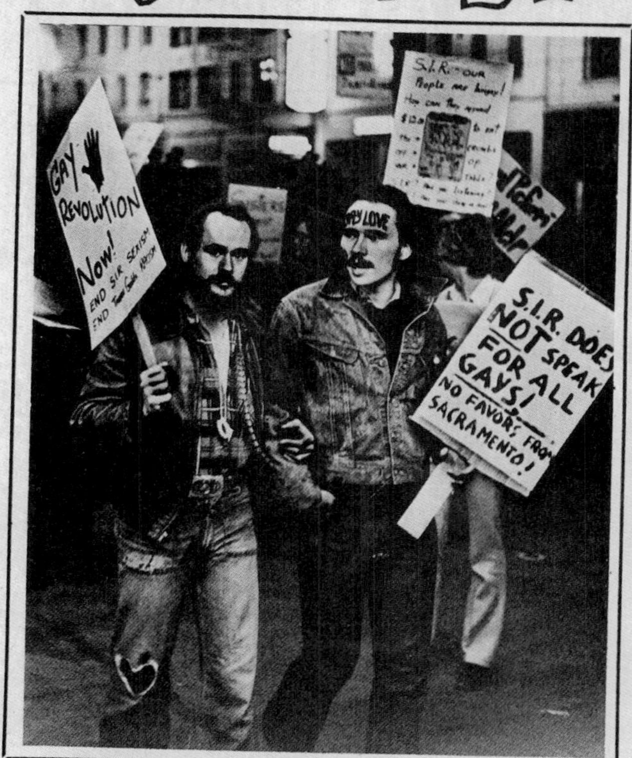

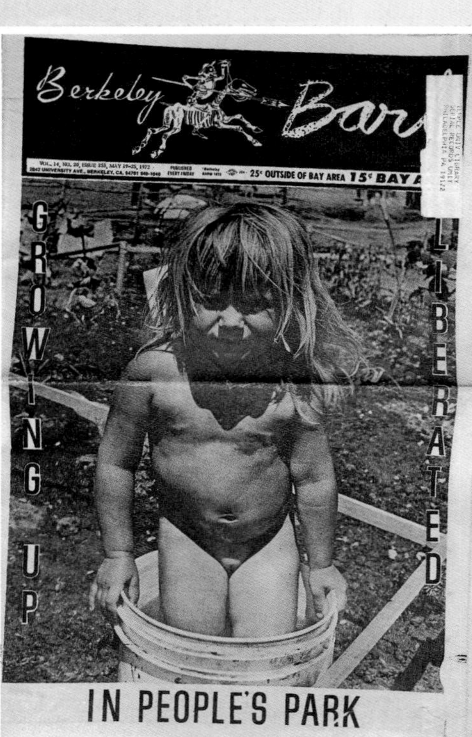

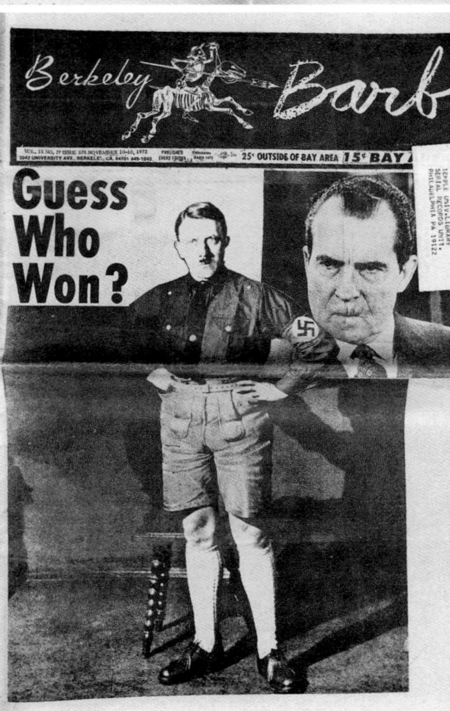

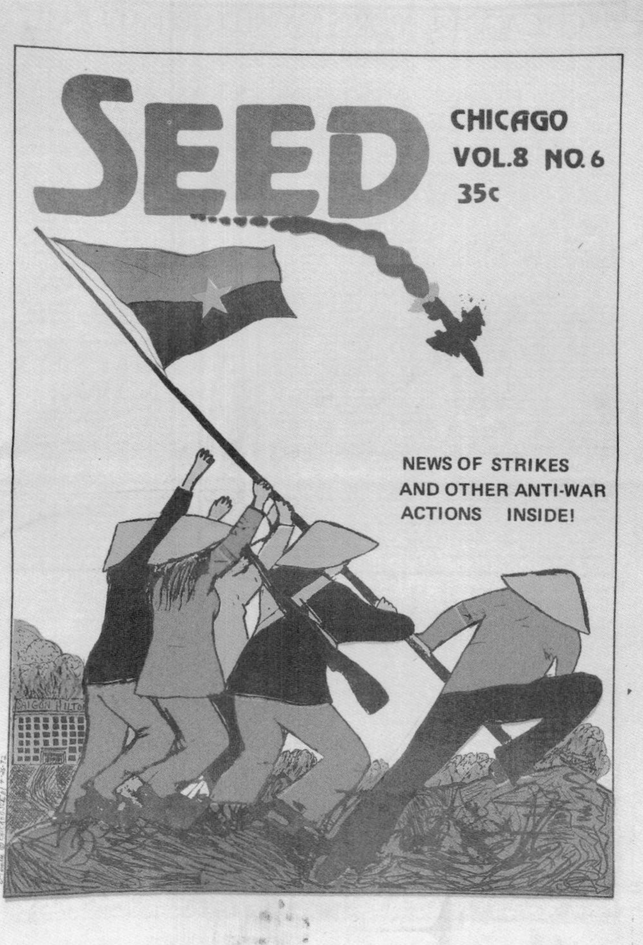

Gay Sunshine, February–March 1972, no. 11, front and back covers
The Berkeley Barb, May 19–25, 1972, vol. 14, no. 20, cover
The Berkeley Barb, November 10–16, 1972, vol. 15, no. 19, cover
The Chicago Seed, April 26, 1972, vol. 8, no. 6, cover

2,000 IN BELFAST PROTEST INTERNMENT OF SUSPECTS

BELFAST, Northern Ireland, Jan. 2—Two thousand people protesting the internment of suspected Irish Republican Army guerrillas marched, sang and demonstrated in Belfast today without violence.

NEW HAT IN RING: MRS. CHISHOLM'S

Representative Is Seeking Presidency as Democrat Mrs. Chisholm Joins Presidential Race

Jan. 26—Representative Shirley Chisholm announced her candidacy yesterday for the Democratic Presidential nomination— the first black woman to seek a major-party

BRITISH SOLDIERS KILL 13 AS RIOTING ERUPTS IN ULSTER

Deaths Come as Catholics Defy Ban on Londonderry March

BELFAST, Northern Ireland, Jan. 30—At least 13 persons were shot dead by British troops in Londonderry today when rioting broke out after a civil rights march held in defiance of a Government ban.

BASKETBALL HALL OF FAME ELECTS ITS FIRST BLACK: DOUGLAS OF RENS

Feb. 6—Six men, including the first black, have been elected to the Naismith Basketball Hall of Fame on the campus of Springfield College in Massachusetts. They were Bob Douglas, Eddie Gottlieb, Cliff Wells, Ed Diddle, Paul Endacott and Max (Marty) Friedman.

ALL U.S. AIRLINES SET UP A MANDATORY SCREEN TO CATCH HIJACKERS

Feb. 7—Trans World Airlines flight 41 was about to leave for San Francisco yesterday morning when a ticket agent whispered to a security officer, "I've got two."

A young couple—the boy was black, the girl was white—advanced to a T.W.A. boarding gate at Kennedy International Airport, and a uniformed officer of the Bureau of the Customs watched for the flash of a small blue light as the pair walked between two upright steel poles.

Britain Enforces Wide Power Cuts

Factories to Work a 3-Day Week as the Coal Strike Reduces Fuel Supplies

LONDON, Feb. 11—The British Government ordered industry today to reduce its use of electricity drastically because of the national coal strike. The move will mean a three-day week for most factories.

MISS DAVIS FREED ON $102,500 BAIL

Judge in California Releases Her Under Ruling Ending Death Penalty in State

PALO ALTO, Calif., Feb. 23—Angela Davis, jailed for 16 months while facing murder charges, was released on $102,500 bail here tonight.

COMMUNISTS WALK OUT OF PARIS SESSION

PARIS, Feb. 24—The Communist delegations walked out of a session of the Vietnam peace talks today in protest against American bombing of North Vietnam. This is the first time that one side has walked out on the other.

Only a few minutes after the talks had been convened, the North Vietnamese and Vietcong delegations headed for the door, leaving the Americans and the South Vietnamese to register their protest on a tape recorder.

70 States Reject Biological Arms

U.S., Soviet Among Those Signing Accord That Also Calls for Destruction

MOSCOW, April 10—More than 70 nations, including the United States, the Soviet Union and Britain, signed a convention today that outlaws biological weapons and, for the first time under a modern arms-control measure, requires states to destroy their stocks of such weapons.

HEAVY ATTACKS ENDANGER SAIGON'S DEFENSE OF ANLOC

SAIGON, South Vietnam, Sunday, April 16—The South Vietnamese defenses in the provincial capital of Anloc, 60 miles north of Saigon, appeared to be gravely endangered last night after North Vietnamese troops, with tanks and artillery, pounded the town from all sides and hit hard at reinforcements trying to move up Route 13.

[South Vietnamese officers in Lailke said Sunday that enemy forces on the northern fringes of Anloc had hoisted the Vietcong flag, Reuters reported.]

OKINAWA ISLANDS RETURNED BY U.S. TO JAPANESE RULE

Agnew, in Tokyo, Declares 'Last Major Issue' of the Pacific War Is Resolved; U.S. Returns Okinawa to Japanese Rule

TOKYO, Monday, May 15—The return of Okinawa to Japan after 27 years of American rule was celebrated at colorful ceremonies here this morning and hailed as marking a new phase in the friendly relations between Japan

Equal Rights Amendment is Approved by Congress

WASHINGTON, March 22—The Senate passed the Equal Rights Amendment today, thus completing Congressional action on the amendment, which would prohibit discrimination based on sex by any law or action of any government — Federal, state or

California Court, In 6-1 Vote, Bars Death Sentences

Holds Penalty Is Cruel and Unusual—Bases View on the State Constitution

107 In Prisons Spared; Sirhan and Manson Among Them—Life Sentences Ordered by Justices

SAN FRANCISCO, Feb., 18—Capital punishment was declared unconstitutional today in the State of California.

Currency Futures Due; Trading to Start Tuesday In Chicago

May 14—A unit of the Chicago Mercantile Exchange is about to offer futures contracts in what many consider the basic commodity — currency.

NIXON IN CHINA— A POLITICAL PILGRIM

Feb. 19—Some incurable optimists would have us see Mr. Nixon in Peking as an American Moses confronting Mao, the Chinese Pharaoh, with a divine mandate to convert at once and return to the "family of nations." Needless to say, this religious analogy, projected and enhanced with moralistic rhetoric, is an impious fraud.

ULSTER'S STATUS TO MATCH THAT OF SCOTLAND, WALES

LONDON, March 24 (Reuters)—The British Government's decision to assume direct rule of Northern Ireland will leave the province largely on the same constitutional footing as Scotland and Wales.

GUNMAN'S ATTACK CLOUDS CAMPAIGN

Uncertainty Created Both by Wallace's Status and Impact of Shooting

WASHINGTON, May 15—The bullets that felled George C. Wallace on the eve of his greatest achievements in national politics will also upset both the conduct and the calculations of the 1972 Presidential campaign.

TERRORIST LEADER SEIZED IN GERMANY

BONN, June 16—The state police in Hanover today announced the capture of Ulrike Meinhof, a founding member of a leftist terrorist group known popularly as the Baader-Meinhof gang.

Last American Ground Combat Unit is Deactivated in South Vietnam

SAIGON, South Vietnam, Aug. 11—The last American ground-combat unit in Vietnam was deactivated today, a day after one of its companies returned from a four-day mission during which two men were wounded by booby traps. The unit, the Third Battalion of the 21st Infantry, with supporting artillery and a medical detachment, guarded the big Unites States air base at Danang. The battalion has 1,043 men. The United States command said that most would be going home in the next few days.

DEMOCRATIC RAID TIED TO REALTOR

ALLEGED LEADER SAID TO HAVE G.O.P. LINKS AND TO HAVE AIDED C.I.A. ON CUBA

WASHINGTON, June 18—The apparent leader of five men arrested yesterday for breaking into the headquarters of the Democratic National Committee here was identified today as an affluent Miami real estate man with important Republican party links in Florida.

INDIANS RIPPED UP FEDERAL BUILDING

Bureau is Found Littered by Debris After Protest

WASHINGTON, Nov. 9—Militant American Indians left behind them today a battered Bureau of Indian Affairs Building that may take months to restore to usefulness.

130 Refuse to Join Ship; Most Reassigned by Navy

SAN DIEGO, Nov. 9—One hundred thirty men attached to the aircraft carrier Constellation refused for hours today to obey an order to board their ship in the latest incident of racial conflict involving warships of the Pacific Fleet.

Soviet Underground Urges Strikes to Raise Standards

MOSCOW, June 19—An underground appeal circulating in Moscow calls on Russians to strike and to demonstrate for better living conditions, as the Poles successfully did in 1970.

CEILINGS ARE SET

NIXON AND BREZHNEV PLEDGE TO ABIDE BY TREATY AT ONCE

May 27—President Nixon and the Soviet Communist party leader, Leonid I. Brezhnev, signed two historic agreements last night that for the first time put limits on the growth of American and Soviet strategic nuclear arsenals.

In a brief televised ceremony in the Great Hall of the Kremlin, the two leaders put their signatures to a treaty that establishes a ceiling of 200 launchers for each side's defensive missile systems and commits them not to try to build nationwide antimissile defenses. The treaty, which is to run indefinitely, requires ratification by the Senate in Washington, but both sides pledged to abide by it at once.

They signed an interim accord on offensive systems that freezes land-based and submarine-based intercontinental missles at the level now in operation or under construction.

A 23-Hour Drama

2 Others are Slain in Their Quarters in Guerrilla Raid

2 Other Athletes Killed in Rooms During Attack

MUNICH, West Germany, Wednesday, Sept. 6—Eleven members of Israel's Olympic team and four Arab terrorists were killed yesterday in a 23-hour drama that began with an invasion of the Olympic Village by the Arabs. It ended in a shootout at a military airport some 15 miles away as the Arabs were preparing to fly to Cairo with their Israeli hostages.

ANGELA DAVIS ACQUITTED ON ALL CHARGES

Angela Davis Found Not Guilty By White Jury on All Charges

SAN JOSE, Calif., June 4—After just 13 hours of deliberations, an all-white jury found Angela Davis not guilty today of murder, kidnapping and criminal conspiracy charges.

4 BEING HUNTED IN INQUIRY INTO RAID ON DEMOCRATS

WASHINGTON, June 21—The authorities are searching for four men who rented rooms at Washington's Watergate Hotel with four other men who have been accused of breaking into the headquarters of the Democratic National Committee last Saturday.

NIXON ISSUES CALL TO 'GREAT TASKS'

AT VICTORY CELEBRATION, HE VOWS TO MAKE HIMSELF 'WORTHY' OF VICTORY

WASHINGTON, Wednesday, Nov. 8—President Nixon summoned the nation last night "to get on with the great tasks that lie before us" and, in a later statement to a crowd of cheering supporters, pledged to make himself "worthy of this victory."

OUT OF THE QUAGMIRE?

Jan. 16—President Nixon's decision to halt all offensive military action against North Vietnam is a promising gesture. It reinforces the cautious optimism voiced by both sides after six days of marathon peace talks in Paris last week between Presidential aide Henry A. Kissinger and North Vietnam's chief negotiator, Le Duc Tho.

U.S. Forces out of Vietnam; Hanoi Frees the Last P.O.W.

War Role Is Ended After Decade of Controversy

March 30—The last American troops left South Vietnam today, leaving behind an unfinished war that has deeply scarred this country and the United States.

There was little emotion or joy as they brought to a close almost a decade of American military intervention.

Remaining after the final jet transport lifted off from Tan son Nhut air base at 5:53 P.M. were about 800 Americans on the truce observation force who will leave tomorrow and Saturday. A contingent of 159 Marine guards and about 50 military attachés also stayed behind.

Mrs. King Defeats Riggs, 6-4, 6-3, 6-3, Amid a Circus Atmosphere

Mrs. King Trounces Mr. Riggs

Sept. 21—Mrs. Billie Jean King struck a proud blow for herself and women around the world with a crushing 6-4, 6-3, 6-3 rout of Bobby Riggs tonight in their $100,000 winner-take-all tennis match at the Astrodome.

House And Senate Override Veto By Nixon On Curb Of War Powers; Backers Of Bill Win 3-Year Fight

Troop Use Limited

Vote Asserts Control of Congress Over Combat Abroad

Nov. 8—The House and the Senate, dealing President Nixon what appeared to be the worst legislative setback of his five years in office, today overrode his veto of a measure aimed at limiting Presidential power to commit the armed forces to hostilities abroad without Congressional approval.

Nixon Takes Oath Today for 2nd Term

Jan. 20—President Nixon will be sworn into office for a second term tomorrow, emboldened by his sweeping electoral triumph of last November and a Vietnam peace settlement apparently within his grasp.

National Guidelines Set by 7-to-2 Vote; High Court Backs Abortions in First Three

Jan. 23—The Supreme Court overruled today all state laws that prohibit or restrict a woman's right to obtain an abortion during her first three months of pregnancy. The vote was 7 to 2.

CAMPORA BECOMES ARGENTINA'S CHIEF

New President is the First Civilian in Post in 7 Years; Pledges Peronist Regime

CAMPORA, A CIVILIAN AND PERONIST, SWORN IN AS ARGENTINE PRESIDENT

May 26—Dr. Hector J. Campora, a loyal follower of former President Juan Domingo Peron, was inaugurated today as the president of a popularly elected government, ending seven years of military rule in Argentina.

SYRIA ASSERTS HER FORCES HAVE TAKEN MT. HERMON

Oct. 7—Syrian forces today struck across the cease-fire line with Israel in the Golan heights in their first offensive since the six-day war six years ago, and a military spokesman in Damascus said the forces had succeeded in occupying a number of positions formerly held by Israel, including Mount Hermon.

NIXON DECLARES HE DIDN'T PROFIT FROM PUBLIC LIFE

TELLS A.P. MANAGING EDITORS 'I'VE EARNED EVERY CENT, I'M NOT A CROOK'

DISCUSSES MILK DEAL

PREDICTS BOTH HALDEMAN AND EHRLICHMAN WILL EVENTUALLY 'COME OUT ALL RIGHT'

Nov. 18—President Nixon told a group of newspaper executives tonight that he had never "profited from public service." He added: "I've earned every cent. I'm not a crook."

CAPITAL BRIEFING

Goals 'Substantially Achieved,' Kissinger Says of Efforts

SERIES OF KEY POINTS

U.S. Expects Cease-Fire Taking Effect in Vietnam Saturday Will Soon Extend to Laos and Cambodia

Jan. 25—Henry A. Kissinger said today, that the United States had "a firm expectation" that the Vietnam cease-fire that goes into effect on Saturday would soon extend to both Laos and Cambodia as well.

Governors Dedicate Trade Center Here; World Pole is Cited

The Trade Center Is Dedicated Here

Rockefeller and Cahill Hail Port as Major Capital of World Commerce

April 5—The $700-million World Trade Center, its two 1,350-foot towers the largest buildings in the world, was dedicated formally yesterday by Governors Rockefeller and Cahill.

SURPRISE WITNESS

BUTTERFIELD, EX-AIDE AT WHITE HOUSE, TELLS OF LISTENING DEVICES

NIXON WIRED PHONE AND OFFICES TO RECORD CONVERSATIONS

SENATORS TO SEEK TAPES; BUTTERFIELD, FORMER AIDE, IS A SURPRISE WITNESS

July 17—President Nixon had listening devices in the White House that would have automatically tape-recorded his conversations with John W. Dean 3d and other key figures in the Watergate case, a former White House aide disclosed today.

Ford Sworn as Vice President After House Approves, 387-35; He Vows Equal Justice for All

Loyalty to Nixon

1,500 Hear Ford Give His Full Support to President

Dec. 6—Gerald R. Ford, pledging "equal justice for all Americans," took office just after dusk tonight as the 40th Vice President of the United States.

VIETNAM PEACE PACTS SIGNED; AMERICA'S LONGEST WAR HALTS

BUILT ON COMPROMISES

Jan. 28—The Vietnam cease-fire agreement was signed here today in eerie silence, without a word or a gesture to express the world's relief that the years of war were officially ending.

4 NATIONS CHARGED IN REPORT AS USERS OF TORTURE

U.S. is Cited

PARIS, Dec. 15—Amnesty International, the organization dedicated to assisting political prisoners, has charged that torture as a systematic weapon of control is being used by almost half the world's governments and is spreading rapidly.

AFGHAN KING OVERTHROWN; A REPUBLIC IS PROCLAIMED

NEW DELHI, July 17—The mountainous kingdom of Afghanistan was proclaimed a republic today in a coup d'etat led by a brother-in-law of King Mohammad Zahir Shah, who is on a visit to Italy.

Evidence Shows Gifts To Agnew in 3 Elective Offices, of More Than $100,000

Data are Entered in District Court

Become Permanent Part of Record Along With Denial by Ex-Vice President

Oct. 11—Spiro T. Agnew, in three elective offices including the Vice-Presidency, asked for and accepted cash payments totaling more than $100,000, according to the evidence gathered against him by the United States Attorneys in Baltimore.

Long Wait Is Ended for 27, Set Free in South Vietnam

Long Wait Ends as 27 Arrive at Saigon; One Asks to Remain

Feb. 13—After 12 hours of debate and anguishing delay, 27 American prisoners of war held in South Vietnam were freed last night by the Vietcong, flown to Saigon and then rushed to Clark Air Base in the Philippines.

MIDEAST PARLEY BEGINS TODAY

Early Accord is Held Unlikely

ARABS AND ISRAEL OPEN TALKS TODAY

Security Precautions

ROLE OF UNITED NATIONS

GENEVA, Dec. 20—Israel and the Arabs open a conference here tomorrow designed to bring peace to the Middle East after four wars and 25 years of hostility.

There is little optimism on either side about the chances of any early agreement, apart from a possible military accord next month on the separation of forces along the Suez front.

NO CHAMPAGNE OR CHEERS AS LAST PLANE COMES IN FROM CAMBODIA; NOT 'ENTHUSIASTIC'

Aug. 16—The last United States fighter-bomber to strike in Cambodia touched down here at 11:32 this morning.

OIL AS AN ARAB WEAPON

Cautious Action at Parley in Kuwait Reflects Dangers of Embargo Policy

Oct. 18—An oil embargo is a double-edged sword, which is why the Arab oil states meeting in Kuwait have had trouble agreeing on ways to use it.

Psychiatrists, in a Shift, Declare Homosexuality No Mental Illness

Dec. 16—The American Psychiatric Association, altering a position it has held for nearly a century, decided today that homosexuality is not a mental disorder.

ARMED INDIANS SEIZE WOUNDED KNEE, HOLD HOSTAGES

Dakota Indians Hold 10 Hostages

PLEDGE BY ABOUREZK

March 1—Militant Indians held at least 10 persons hostage in the historic settlement of Wounded Knee today, exchanging gunfire with Federal officers and, firing on cars and low-flying planes that came within rifle range.

OCCUPATION OF WOUNDED KNEE IS ENDED

Seizure of Town; Delay in Settlement

May 9—The second Battle of Wounded Knee ended today. After 70 days, two deaths, numerous injuries, countless meetings, bureaucratic bickering and a last-minute gunfight, more than 100 militants lay down their arms and surrendered this occupied reservation town to wary Federal officials.

TRAGEDY IN CHILE

Sept. 12—Any military coup is a tragedy, representing a breakdown of civilian authority and usually the collapse of government by consent.

Bork Takes Over

Events Listed Duties of Prosecutor are Shifted Back to Justice Dept.

Nixon Ousts Cox for Defiance; Richardson and Ruckelshaus Out; No Official Reaction

Oct. 21—President Nixon, reacting angrily tonight to refusals to obey his orders, dismissed the special Watergate prosecutor, Archibald Cox, abolished Mr. Cox's office, accepted the resignation of Elliot L. Richardson, the Attorney General, and dis-

The Great Speckled Bird (Atlanta), October 29, 1973, vol. 6, no. 42, cover

LIBERATION NEWS SERVICE APR.74
160 CLAREMONT AVENUE
NEW YORK, NEW YORK 10027

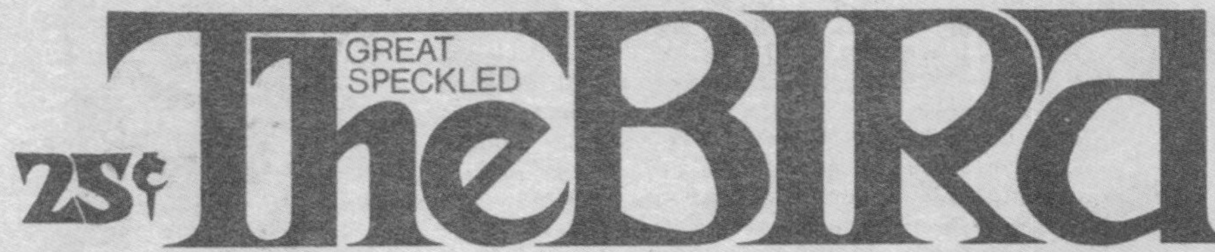

ALTERNATIVE MEDIA SHARED BY 50,000 PEOPLE IN ATLANTA, THE SOUTH AND THE NATION

Volume Six Number Forty-Two October 29, 1973

IMPEACH NIXON

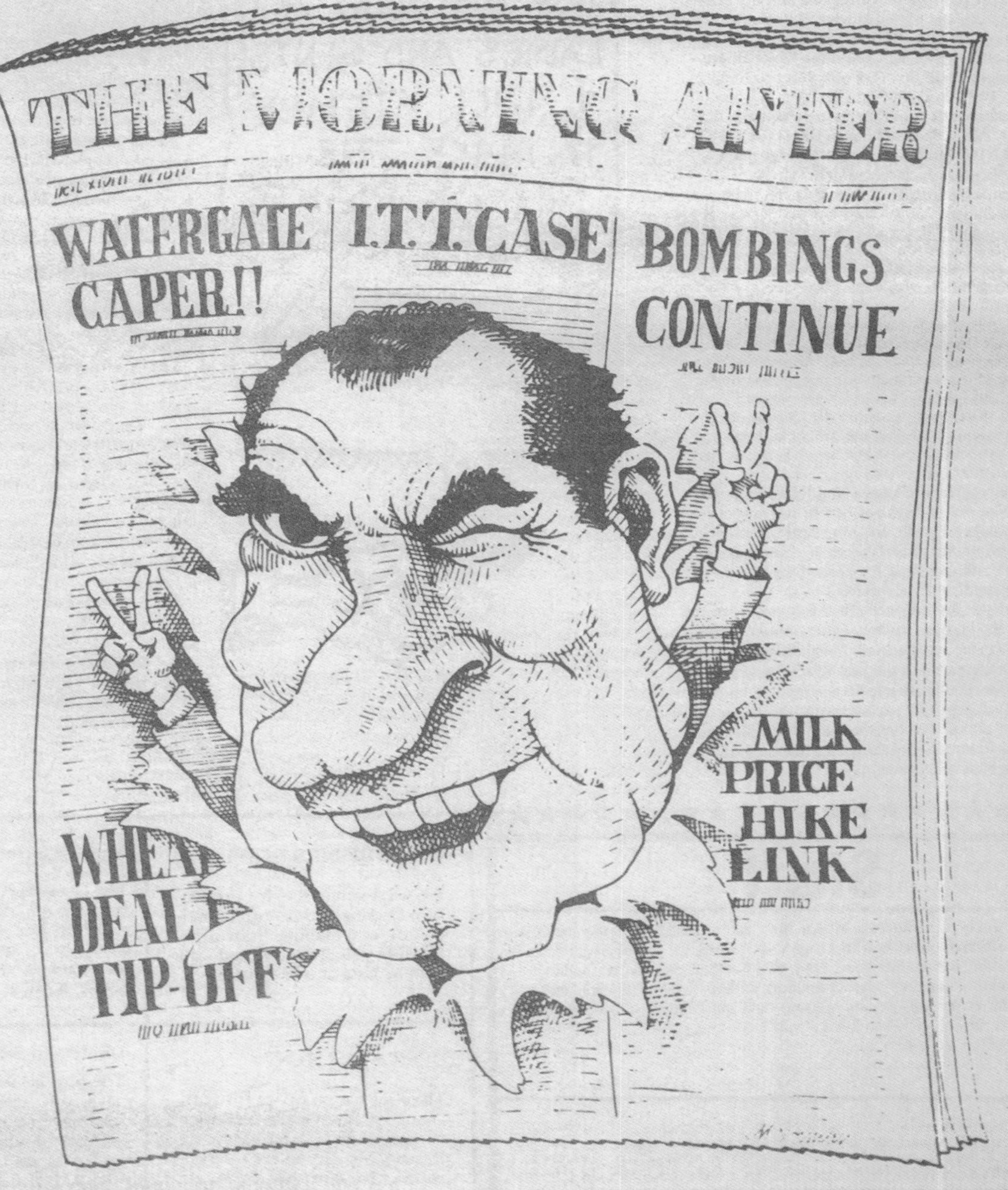

Nixon Rejects Subpoenas from Senate Committee For 500 Tapes and Papers

Staff Shaken Up

Buzhardt and Garment Are Off Watergate Defense Team

Jan. 5—President Nixon rejected today the Senate Watergate committee's subpoenas seeking more than 500 tape recordings and documents, and simultaneously overhauled his Watergate defense staff.

REBEL PRESSURE ON PHNOM PENH GROWING

Hundreds of Civilians Flee

Jan. 10—Communist-led insurgents intensified pressure on Phnom Penh's defensive perimeters yesterday, striking from north and south, according to reports from the field.

Mantle and Ford Voted Into Hall of Fame

Jan. 17— The New York Yankees received a dramatic reminder of their long lost past yesterday when Mickey Mantle and Whitey Ford were voted into baseball's Hall of Fame.

EGYPT AND ISRAEL REACH ACCORD ON SEPARATION OF CANAL FORCES; A PACT TO OPEN SUEZ IS REPORTED

Signing Set Today

GENEVA PARLEY TO TAKE UP LARGER ISSUES WHEN IT RESUMES

Jan. 17—Egypt and Israel reached agreement today on separating their forces along the Suez Canal and limiting the arms each is to have in the area.

WHITE HOUSE DENIES NIXON ERASED PART OF KEY TAPE

Jan. 17—The White House denied today that President Nixon had personally erased part of a key Watergate tape, but otherwise refused to discuss yesterday's testimony by technical experts suggesting that the tape may have been tampered with.

Supreme Court Rules Pregnant Teachers Cannot Be Forced to Take Long Leaves

Jan. 22—Public school systems cannot force female teachers to take maternity leave months before they expect to give birth, the Supreme Court ruled today.

EX-CAMPAIGN AIDE MAY ADMIT GUILT

Porter, Charged With Lying to F.B.I., Waives Formal Indictment Before Sirica

Jan. 22—Herbert L. Porter, former scheduling director for the Committee for the Re-election of the President, waived today a formal indictment on a charge of lying to the F.B.I. and is apparently prepared to admit his guilt.

Mr. Porter, who said he was thought of as a "team player" and who wore his first Nixon button when he was 8 years old, was the subject of a criminal information filed today by the Watergate special prosecutor's office.

Wobbly Skylab Astronauts End 84-Day Orbital Flight

Feb. 8—Wobbly-legged but cheerful, the Skylab 3 astronauts returned this morning from 84 days in orbit around the earth, man's longest space flight. Except for a link-up between United States and Soviet spacecraft planned for next year, the Skylab mission that ended today was the last scheduled flight by American astronauts until a two-stage shuttle rocket now being developed begins operations in 1979 or later.

NEW CULTURAL REVOLUTION IS PROCLAIMED BY PEKING

Feb. 4—In a loud and insistent chorus, broadcasts and editorials in China are proclaiming a largescale renewal of the Cultural Revolution under the active direction of the nation's aging leader, Mao Tse-tung.

SOVIET SPACECRAFT FAILS TO ORBIT MARS, BUT A SECOND SUCCEEDS

Feb. 14—The latest Soviet campaign to explore the planet Mars with four unmanned spacecraft suffered a setback this week when the first of two craft apparently designed for an orbital mission failed to go into orbit. The second succeeded.

Soldier Lands a Stolen Copter on White House Lawn

Feb. 18—A soldier landed a stolen Army helicopter in a hail of shotgun buckshot on the South Lawn of the White House at 2 A.M. today. He was wrestled to the ground by officers of the Executive Protection Service after bouncing the helicopter to a rough landing about 100 yards short of the White House.

House, 410-4, Gives Subpoena Power in Nixon Inquiry

Judiciary Panel is Authorized to Summon Anyone, Including President, With Evidence

Feb. 7—The House of Representatives voted 410 to 4 today to grant the Judiciary Committee broad constitutional power to investigate President Nixon's conduct. The House thus formally ratified the impeachment inquiry begun by the committee last October and subpoened anyone, including the President, with evidence pertinent to the investigation.

SOLZHENITSYN EXILED TO WEST GERMANY AND STRIPPED OF HIS SOVIET CITIZENSHIP

Told of His Safety, Wife Says Family Will Join Him

Feb. 13—The Soviet Union deported Aleksandr I. Solzhenitsyn to West Germany today and issued a decree stripping him of his citizenship for "performing systematically actions that are incompatible with being a citizen."

CHAVEZ CALLS 2-DAY STRIKE; HIS MEN CLASH WITH POLICE

Feb. 22—Cesar Chavez today called a two-day strike against Imperial County lettuce growers holding contracts with the teamsters union. Clashes were reported almost immediately between sheriff's deputies and about 350 members of the United Farm Workers of America.

PAKISTAN ADMITS THAT BANGLADESH EXISTS AS NATION

Prime Minister Bhutto, at Islamic Parley, Accords Recognition of '71 Foe

Feb. 23—Pakistan yesterday recognized Bangladesh, her former eastern wing, in a sudden move preceding the opening here of a major conference of Moslem nations.

Prime Minister Zulfikar Ali Bhutto, speaking in an emotional tone to legislators and chief ministers, said, in Urdu: "In the name of Allah and on behalf of the peoples of this country, I declare that we are recognizing Bangladesh.

345 KILLED AS JUMBO JET DIVES INTO FRENCH FOREST IN HISTORY'S WORST CRASH

Turkish Airliner Falls Soon After Leaving Paris for London

March 4—A Turkish jumbo jet plunged into a forest 26 miles northeast of herd today, killing all 345 persons aboard. It was the worst air disaster in history.

Hearst Captors Offered 4-Million

Corporation Vows To Meet New Demands—

Violence Mars Food Distribution

Feb. 23—The Hearst Corporation offered today to meet demands for $4-million more for free food for the needy, if the Symbionese Liberation Army releases Patricia Hearst unharmed.

FEDERAL GRAND JURY INDICTS 7 NIXON AIDES ON CHARGES OF CONSPIRACY ON WATERGATE

HALDEMAN, EHRLICHMAN, MITCHELL ON LIST

COLSON IS NAMED

A QUESTION OF VERACITY OF THE PRESIDENT IS INDIRECTLY RAISED

March 1—A Federal grand jury today indicted seven men, all former officials of President Nixon's Administration or of his 1972 re-election campaign, on charges of covering up the Watergate scandal.

WILSON IS PRIME MINISTER AS HEATH FAILS IN EFFORT TO WIN LIBERALS' SUPPORT

Both Visit Queen

LABOR TO FORM FIRST MINORITY CABINET IN 45 YEARS

LONDON, March 4—Edward Heath, his party defeated last week by Britain's voters, tonight gave up his effort to hold onto power, and Harold Wilson took over as Prime Minister.

GENERAL GEISEL IS SWORN IN AS PRESIDENT OF BRAZIL AS HOPES RISE FOR SOME POLITICAL LIBERALIZATION

BRASILIA, March 16—Gen. Ernesto Geisel was ceremoniously sworn in as Brazil's new President today amid cautious hopes for some liberalization after a decade of authoritarian military rule.

Wreck of the Monitor Is Reported Found

Feb. 18—The long-sought wreck of the U.S.S. Monitor, the Union vessel in history's first duel between ironclads, during the Civil War, has been found on the bottom of the Atlantic off Cape Hatteras, N. C., an oceanographic researcher at Duke University reported today.

The ship, which fought the Confederacy's Virginia—popularly known as the Merrimack—to a standoff during their historic encounter in Hampton Roads on March 9, 1862, sank in a gale off Hatteras less than 10 months later.

FAG RAG
GAY SUNSHINE
Stonewall 5th Anniversary Issue

SUMMER 1974 · ONE DOLLAR

Gay Sunshine, Summer 1974, cover

Next page
Win Peace and Freedom through Nonviolent Action (New York), June 20, 1974, vol. 10, no. 22, cover
Win Peace and Freedom through Nonviolent Action (New York), June 27, 1974, vol. 10, no. 23, cover

Most Arab Lands End Ban on Oil Shipments for U.S.

Saudis Plan Output Rise; 2 Countries Balk; Libya and Syria Fail to Join 7 Others in Vienna Decision

March 19—Most of the Arab oil countries announced officially today that they would lift the embargo against shipments to the United States that they had imposed during the Middle East war of last October.

Vietcong Offer a Detailed Plan For Vote in South

U.S. Deems Proposal Most Specific Since Paris Pact—New Cease-Fire Asked

March 23—The Vietcong proposed today a six-point plan that included detailed provisions for a new cease-fire and the holding of general elections in South Vietnam.

House Subpoena Bids President Turn Over Tapes, Other Material; White House May Yield Some Data

Panel's Vote 33-3

April 25 Deadline Set After Rejection of a Compromise

April 12—The House Judiciary Committee today subpoenaed President Nixon to produce all tape recordings and other materials requested by the committee in its impeachment inquiry, The vote was 33 to 3.

Rejecting a last-minute offer of compromise, after 45 days of negotiations and delay, the committee decided to subpoena the material and set April 25 as the deadline for compliance. That will be three days after Congress returns from its Easter recess, which begins tomorrow.

The final vote on the subpoena came shortly after the committee returned from a recess at 1:30 P.M. It was preceded by nearly an hour and a half of partisan debate touched off when the motion to subpoena was introduced at 10:30 A.M. by Representative Harold D. Donohue, Massachusetts Democrat.

Photos of Mercury Sent by Mariner 10 Are Clearest Ever

March 24—The clearest photographs ever taken of the tiny planet Mercury began coming back to earth today from the Mariner 10 space probe. However, they were

U.S. JURY INDICTS 8 IN CAMPUS DEATHS AT KENT STATE

ONE PRESENT AND 7 FORMER MEMBERS OF GUARD CHARGED IN MAY 4, 1970, KILLINGS

NO CONSPIRACY FOUND

20-MAN PANEL DOES NOT CITE ANY OFFICERS OR OFFICIALS OF GOVERNMENT FOR ROLES

March 29—A Federal grand jury today indicted one present member and seven former members of the National Guard of Ohio on charges of violating the civil rights of four Kent State University students who were shot to death and nine others who were wounded.

CEAUSESCU IS PRESIDENT

BUCHAREST, March 28—The Rumanian National Assembly elected Nicolae Ceausescu, the Communist party leader, to the post of President today, giving him absolute power. In his acceptance speech, Mr. Ceausescu said that he would do all he could to keep Stalinist "illegalities" out of Rumanian socialism.

Appeals Court Sends Evidence on Nixon Back to Sirica

March 23—The Watergate grand jury's secret report on President Nixon, locked in its briefcase, was carried back today from the Court of Appeals to Federal District Judge John J. Sirica's chambers to be ready Monday for delivery to the House of Representatives.

Aaron Ties Babe Ruth With 714th Homer

First-Inning Drive in Season Opener Equals Record

April 5—With the unobtrusive grace that has symbolized his career, Henry Aaron tied Babe Ruth's record today with his 714th home run—a 400-foot, three-run line drive over the fence in left-center field at Riverfront Stadium on his first swing of the major league baseball season.

GISCARD APPOINTS CHIRAC, GAULLIST, FRANCE'S PREMIER

Interior Minister, 41, Picked by President for Support During the Campaign

May 28—Jacques Chirac, the 41-year-old Minister of the Interior, was named Premier of France today.

The announcement was made a few hours after the inauguration of President Valery Giscard d'Estaing.

STATE PROSECUTOR KIDNAPPED IN ITALY IS REPORTED FREED

May 21—A state prosecutor kidnapped by leftist terrorists five weeks ago was released tonight, his wife reported.

A court earlier this week had agreed to the demands of the "Red Brigade" that eight imprisoned leftists be released in exchange for the freedom of the prosecutor, Mario Sossi, who was known for his investigations of extremists. The court specified, however, that Mr. Sossi, 38 years old, must be freed first.

There was no immediate word tonight on the release of the prisoners, who were members of the Maoist "October 22" organization.

STRIKE IN ULSTER ENDED IN 15TH DAY; LONDON WILL RULE

Protestant Group Calls for Return to Work—Britain Suspends Assembly

May 29—The general strike that brought the economy of Northern Ireland almost to a standstill and toppled the coalition government of the province was called off today by its organizers.

A few hours later in London, the British Government announced that a form of direct rule was being imposed on the province.

INDIA BECOMES 6TH NATION TO SET OFF NUCLEAR DEVICE

ANNOUNCES BLAST

AIDES SAY EXPLOSION UNDERGROUND DIDN'T VIOLATE TREATY BAN

May 19—Secretary of State Kissinger returned to Israel tonight from Damascus after achieving an apparent breakthrough in his efforts to bring about a troop-separation agreement between Syria and Israel on the Golan Heights.

ISRAEL AND SYRIA ACCEPT ACCORD FOR DISENGAGING ON GOLAN FRONT; LONG KISSINGER EFFORT SUCCEEDS

A 32-Day Mission

MILITARY CHIEFS ARE TO SIGN AGREEMENT IN GENEVA TOMORROW

May 30—Israel and Syria agreed today on an accord to separate their forces on the Golan Heights.

NIXON, IN MOSCOW, MET BY BREZHNEV; FIRST TALKS HELD

Leaders Pledge Effort to Bolster Peace—Voice Hope for Arms Gain

June 28—President Nixon arrived here today to a warm welcome and began his third summit meeting with Leonid I. Brezhnev, the Soviet party chief.

EHRLICHMAN CONVICTED OF PLOT AND PERJURY IN ELLSBERG BREAK-IN; LIDDY AND 2 OTHERS ALSO GUILTY

July 12—John D. Ehrlichman, former chief domestic adviser to President Nixon, and three others were found guilty by a jury today of conspiring to violate the civil rights of Dr. Daniel Ellsberg's former psychiatrist.

PERON DEAD AT 78; WIFE TAKES OVER A DIVIDED NATION

A Mood of Uncertainty Prevails Among Argentines—Roles of Leader's Aides in Doubt

July 2—President Juan Domingo Peron of Argentina, one of the most remarkable and controversial political figures in Latin American history, died today at the age of 78.

ARMY TAKES OVER CYPRUS IN A COUP LED BY GREEKS; MAKARIOS'S FATE IN DOUBT

Successor Named

July 16—Cypriote troops led by Greek Army officers overthrew the Government of Cyprus yesterday.

The Failure of Mr. Ford

Sep. 9—In giving former President Nixon an inappropriate and premature grant of clemency, President Ford has affronted the Constitution and the American system of justice. It is a profoundly unwise, divisive and unjust act. Like many lesser public figures who have commented at various stages of the long Watergate controversy, President Ford has sadly confused his responsibilities to the Republic and his understandable sentiments toward one who has inflicted grave damage upon the body politic.

FLEXIBLE AMNESTY PLAN IS REPORTED SET BY FORD

Sep. 16—Administration sources said today that President Ford's conditional amnesty plan would require repatriated war resisters to spend between six and 24 months in alternative service.

Mr. Ford will issue his amnesty program next week, these sources said.

The flexible formula was said to have been substituted for an earlier proposed 18-month service plan. Military desertions and draft evaders would be dealt with on a case-by-case basis, with their period of alternative service depending on part on their military record.

House Panel Moves Toward Vote on First Article of Impeachment

Move To Delete A Charge Beaten

Ballot Is 27 To 11

Committee, by Same Majority, Rejects Effort at Delay

WASHINGTON, July 26—The House Judiciary Committee formally refused to delay impeachment proceedings today and moved fitfully but inexorably toward adoption of a charge that President Nixon had obstructed justice in the Watergate case.

THE NIXON RESIGNATION

August 9—The resignation of Richard M. Nixon, 37th President of the United States and the first to leave office under threat of impeachment, comes as a tragic climax to the sordid history of misuse of the Presidential office that has been unfolding before the eyes of a shocked American public for the last two years.

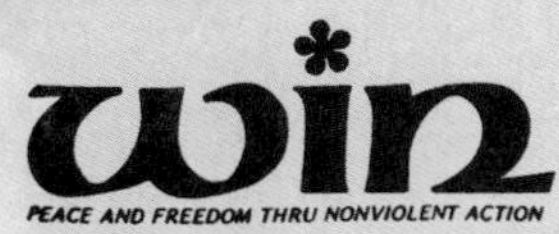

MINERS STRUGGLE IN KENTUCKY
NEW HAMPSHIRE TRIES ANTI-INFLATION MONEY
NEW POEMS BY BORIA SAX

June 20, 1974/30¢

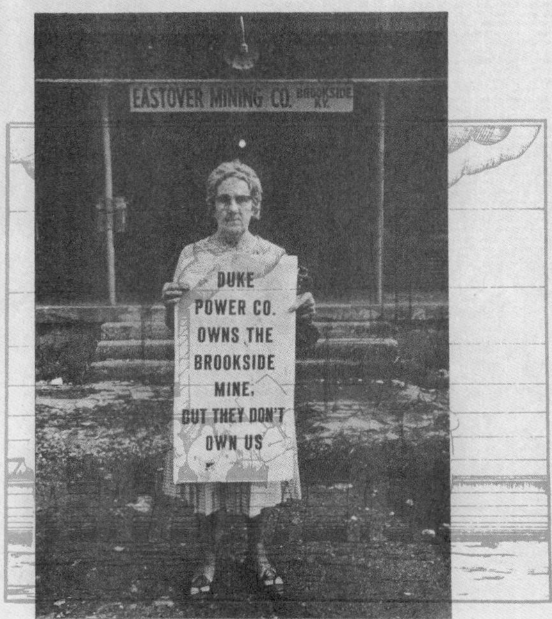

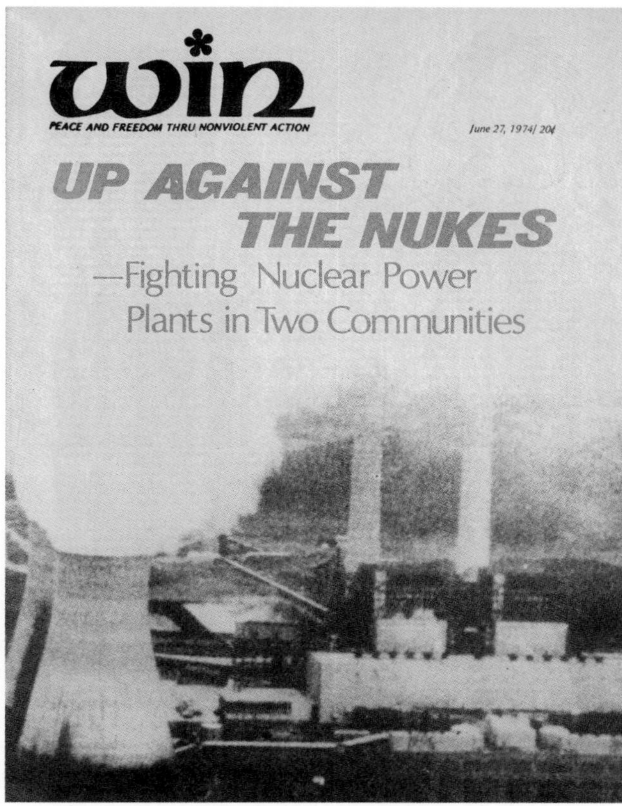

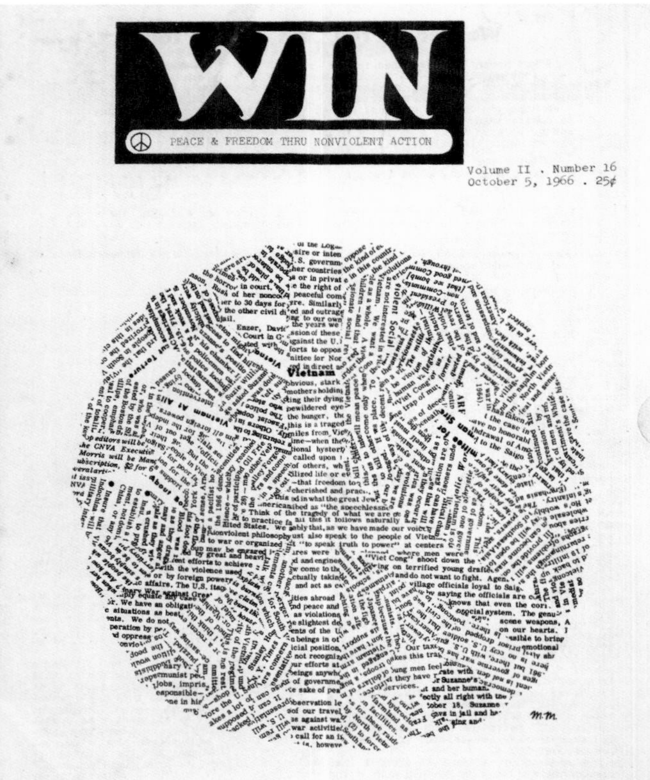

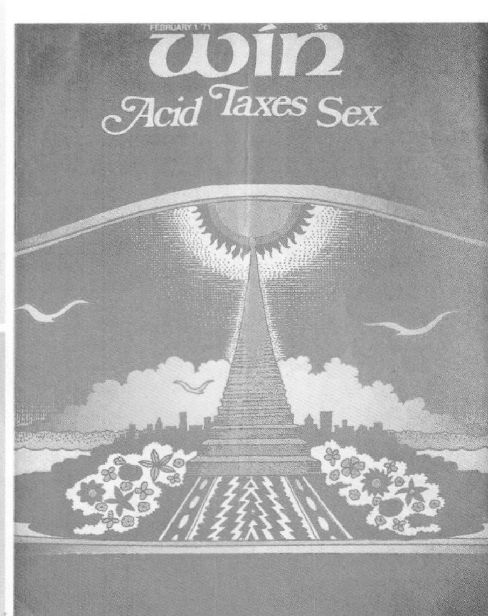

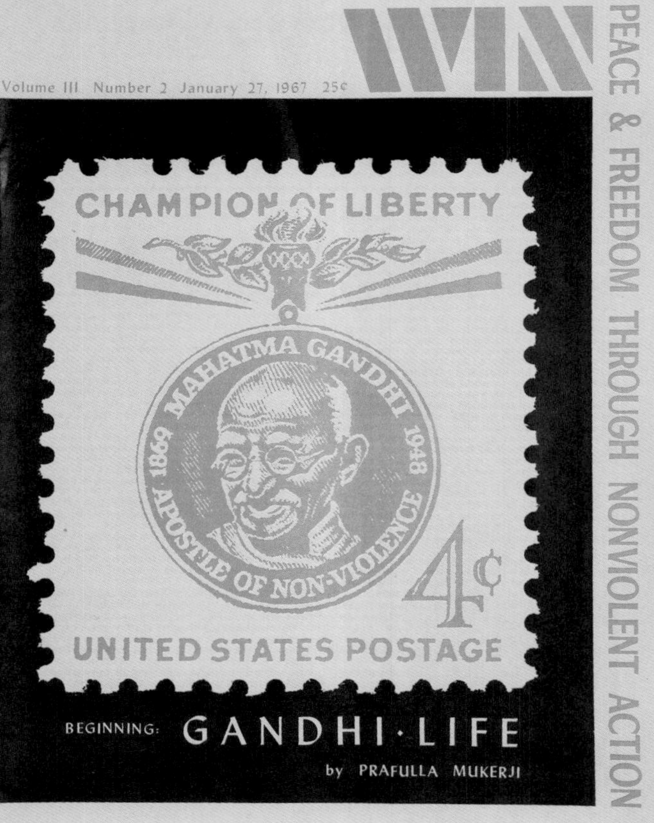

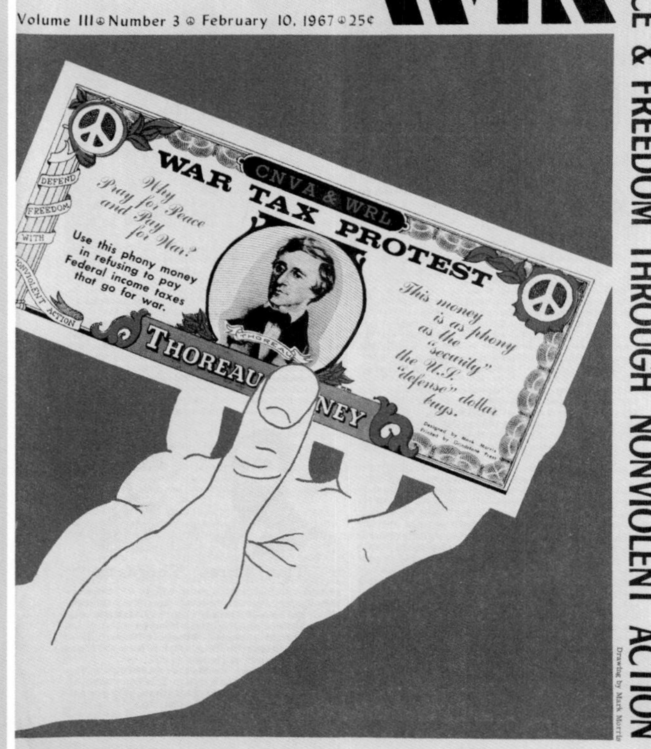

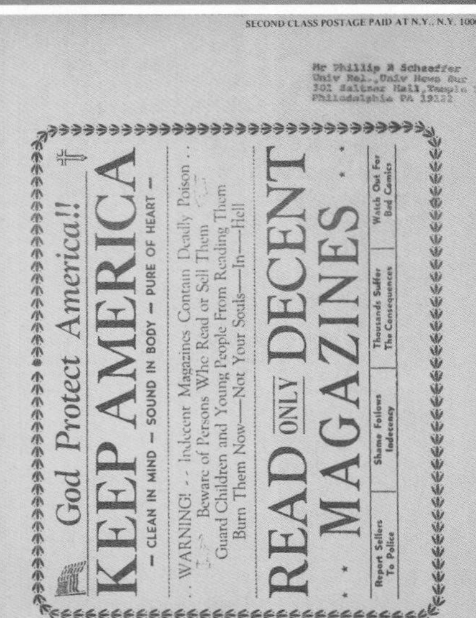

Win Peace and Freedom through Nonviolent Action (New York), April 29, 1966, vol. 2, no. 8, cover
Win Peace and Freedom through Nonviolent Action (New York), October 5, 1966, vol. 2, no. 16, cover
Win Peace and Freedom through Nonviolent Action (New York), February 1, 1971, vol. 7, no. 2, cover
Win Peace and Freedom through Nonviolent Action (New York), January 27, 1967, vol. 3, no. 2, cover
Win Peace and Freedom through Nonviolent Action (New York), February 10, 1967, vol. 3, no. 3, cover
Win Peace and Freedom through Nonviolent Action (New York), April 1, 1970, vol. 6, no. 6, back cover

Next page
Win Peace and Freedom through Nonviolent Action (New York), September 15, 1967, vol. 3, no. 15, cover
Win Peace and Freedom through Nonviolent Action (New York), March 31, 1968, vol. 4, no. 6, back cover
Win Peace and Freedom through Nonviolent Action (New York), March 15, 1970, vol. 6, no. 5, cover
Win Peace and Freedom through Nonviolent Action (New York), December 15, 1969, vol. 5, no. 22, back cover

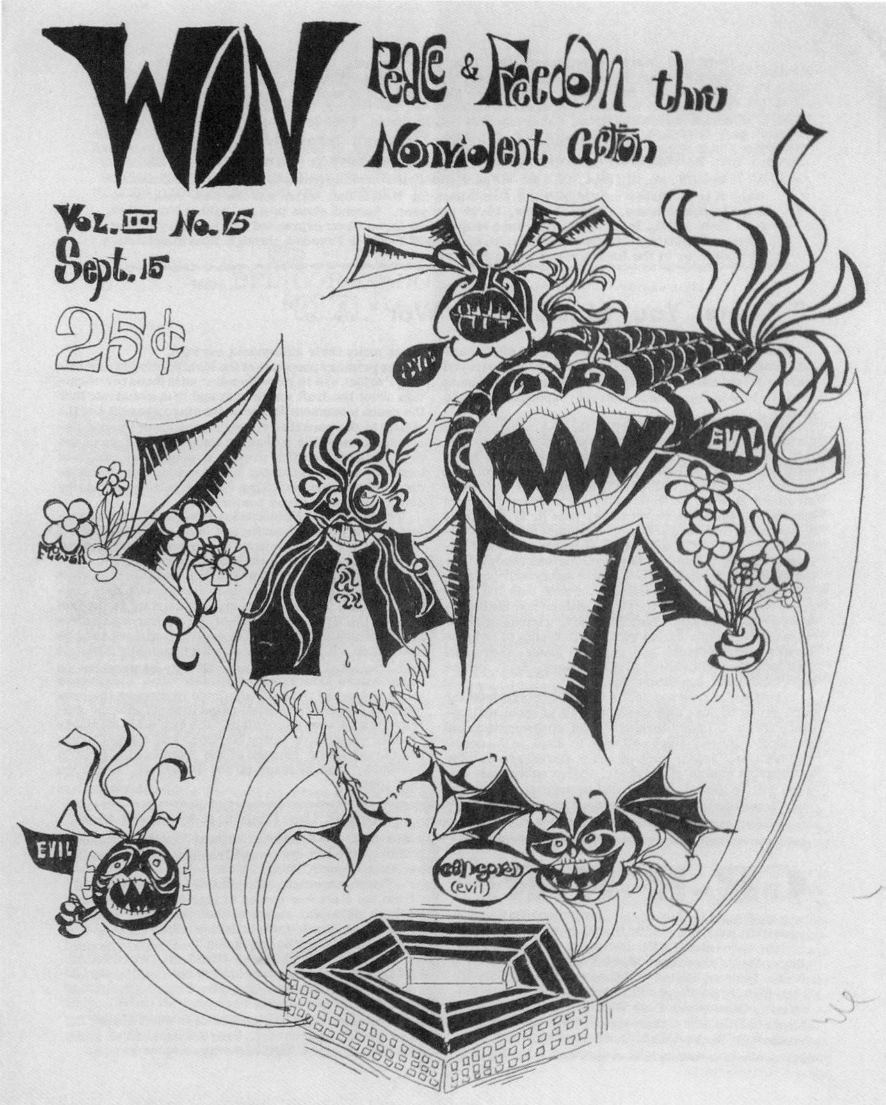

WEEKLY VIGILS *for peace*

Albany, N.Y., Capitol Park, State St. Hill, Wed., noon - 1:00 p.m.
Amherst, Mass., Amherst Center, Sun., noon - 1:00 p.m.
Atlanta, Ga., Agnes Scott College, Winthrop Hall, Fri., 12-1 p.m.
Atlanta, Ga., Emory University, Cox Hall, Fri., 12-1 p.m.
Atlanta, Ga., Five Points, Fri., noon - 1:00 p.m.
Babylon, N.Y., Argyle Sq., Sat., noon - 1:00 p.m.
Bedford Village, N.Y., Village Green, Sun., 10:45 a.m. - 12:15 p.m.
Bellingham, Wash., Federal Bldg., Fri., 3:30 - 4:30 p.m.
Bennington, Vt., Main & N. Smith Sts., Fri., 5:00 - 6:00 p.m.
Berkeley, Calif., City Hall, Sun., 12:30 - 1:30 p.m.
Bethesda, Md., Wisconsin Ave. bet. Elm & Willow Sts., Sat., 11—12 p.m.
Boston, Old State House, Wed., noon - 1:00 p.m.
Brooklyn, N.Y., Pierpont St. & Columbia Hdqts., Sun., 12:30 - 1:30 p.m.
Brunswick, Maine, Mall, Sun., noon - 1:00 p.m.
Bryn Mawr, Pa., Post Office, Tues., 11:00 a.m. - noon
Carbondale, Ill., Student Union (north entrance), Wed., noon - 1:00 p.m.
Champaign-Urbana, Ill., Green and Wright Sts., Thurs., 11:45 a.m. - 12:15 p.m.
Chapel Hill, N.C., opposite Post Office, Wed., noon - 1:00 p.m.
Charlotte, N.C., Post Office, Wed., noon - 1:00 p.m.
Chicago, Civic Center Plaza (Picasso statue), Wed., noon - 1:00 p.m.
Chicago, Hutchinson Court, U. of Chicago, Wed., 12:15 - 12:45 p.m.
Chicago, State St., Madison & Washington, Sat., 11:00 a.m. - 1:00 p.m.
Claremont, Cal., Pomona College, Thur., 12:30 - 1:00 p.m.
Cleveland, Soldier and Sailor Monument, Sat., 12:15 - 1:15 p.m.
College Park, Md., Main Library, U. of Md., Wed., noon - 1:00 p.m.
Columbia, Mo., Student Union, Wed., noon - 1:00 p.m.
Columbus, O., Student Union, Ohio State U., Wed., noon - 1:00 p.m.
Cortland, N.Y., Post Office, Wed., noon - 1:00 p.m.
Corvallis, Oreg., Oreg. State U., Wed., noon - 1:00 p.m.
Dayton, O., 2nd & Ludlow, Wed., noon - 1:00 p.m.
Denver, Cherry Creek shopping center, Sat., noon - 1:00 p.m.
Del-Mar, Calif., Post Office, Sat., 11:00 - noon
Denver, Colo., 16th & Court Pl., Wed., noon - 1:00 p.m.
Duluth, Minn., Federal Building, Wed., 12-12:30 p.m.
Duluth, Minn., Civic Center, Wed., 12-1:00 p.m.
East Hartford, Conn., Pratt & Whitney, Thur., noon - 1:00 p.m.
Easton, Pa., Center Square, Sat., 11:00 a.m. - noon
Eugene, Oreg., City Park, Sat., noon - 1:00 p.m.
Everett, Wash., Federal Bldg., Wed., 12:30 - 1:30 p.m.
Fair Lawn, N.J., Sat., 11:00 a.m. - noon
Fayettesville, Ark., Maple & Campus Dr., Wed., noon - 1:00 p.m.
Flushing, N.Y., Quaker Meeting House, Sat., 1:00 - 3:00 p.m.
Flushing, N.Y., Queens College, Wed., noon - 1:00 p.m.
Freeport, N.Y., Post Office, Sun., 1:00 - 2:00 p.m.
Greensboro,N.C., Post Office, Wed., noon - 1:00 p.m.
Hanover, N.H., on the green, Wed., noon - 1:00 p.m.
Hartford, Conn., Old State House, Wed. & Sat., noon - 1:00 p.m.
Hemet, Calif., Post Office, Sat., 11:00 a.m. - noon
Hempstead, N.Y., bet. Hofstra hall & library, Mon., 11:30 a.m. - 1:30 p.m.
Highland Park, Ill., public library, Sat., 12:30 - 1:00 p.m.
Honolulu, Hawaii, Varney Circle, Wed., noon - 1:00 p.m.
Hudson, N.Y. Court House Square, Thurs., 12-1 p.m.
Huntington, L.I., Village Green at Park Ave. & Main St., Sun., 11:30 a.m.-12:30 p.m.
Ithaca, N.Y., downtown Post Office, Sat., 11:00 - noon
Iowa City, Iowa, Washington & Clinton St., Wed., noon - 12:30 p.m.
Irvine, Calif., lower plaza coffee shop, U. of C., Mon., noon - 1:00 p.m.
Jenkintown, Pa., York Rd. & West Ave., Sat., 1:00 - 2:00 p.m.;
Kensington, Cal, Sun., 11:30 a.m. - 12:30 p.m.
La Jolla, Calif., Post Office, Sat., 11:00 a.m. - noon
Lancaster, Pa., Penn Square, Sat., 11:00 a.m. - noon
Laguna Beach, Calif., public library, Sat., noon - 1:00 p.m.
Lewisburg, Pa., Post Office, Sat., 11:00 a.m. - noon
Little Rock, Ark., Federal Bldg., Fri., 4:00 - 5:00 p.m.
Louisville, Ky., Gutherie Green, Mon., 4:30 - 5:30 p.m.
Los Angeles, Calif., Los Angeles Music Center, Fri., 7:45-8:35 p.m.
Los Angeles, New Federal Bldg., 300 N. Los Angeles, Wed., noon - 1:00 p.m.
Los Angeles, UCLA Campus, election walk, Wed., noon - 1:00 p.m.
Los Angeles, Calif., Veterans Administration Cemetery, corner of Wilshire & Veteran, Sat., 12-1 p.m.
Madison, N.J., Madison Borough Hall, Sun., 12:15 - 12:45 p.m.
Media, Pa., Old Post Office, Tues., 11:15-12:15 p.m.
Miami, Public Library, Biscayne & Flagler, Wed., noon - 1:00 p.m.
Miami Beach, Lincoln Mall & Washington Ave., noon - 1:00 p.m.
Middletown, Conn., Episcopal Church, Main St., noon - 1:00 p.m.
Milwaukee, Wisc., Fed. Bldg./Post Office, Sat., noon - 1:00 p.m.
Minneapolis, University & 17th St., S.E., Wed., noon - 1:00 p.m.
Monterey, Cal., Colton Hall, Sat., noon - 1:00 p.m.
Montpelier, Vt., Wed., noon - 2:00 p.m
Mt. Kisco, N.Y., Bedford U., Sun., 10:45 a.m. - 12:15 p.m.
Nanuet, N.Y., Rt. 59 & Middletown Rd., Sat., noon - 1:00 p.m.
New Haven, Conn., Church & Elm Sts., Wed., noon - 1:00 p.m.
New Orleans, Elk Pl. & Canal, Sat., noon - 12:30 p.m.
New York, 86 St. & East End Ave., Sun., 10:15 a.m. - 10:45 a.m.
New York, Times Square, Sat., 12:30 - 2:30 p.m.
New York, 20 St. & First Ave., Sat., 11:00 a.m. - noon.
New York, women only, 6th Ave. & 8th St., Sat., 11:30 a.m. - 1:00 p.m.
New York, Washington Square Arch, Sun., 10:15 - 10:45 a.m.
New York, 162nd & Amsterdam, 1st. & 3rd. Sat. each month, 11:00 a.m.
Norman, Okla., Student Bldg., Wed., noon - 1:00 p.m.
Northampton, Mass., on the Green, Sun., noon - 1:00 p.m.
Oakland, Calif., 15th & San Pablo, Sat., noon - 1:00 p.m.
Oakland, Calif., Oakland Memorial Plaza, Sat., noon - 1:00 p.m.
Oberlin, O., Tappan Square, Wed., noon - 1:00 p.m.
Oklahoma City, Okla., County Court House, Fri., noon - 1:00 p.m.
Palo Alto, Calif., Stanford shopping center, Sat., noon - 1:00 p.m.
Pasadena, Post Office, Wed., noon - 1:00 p.m.
Peoria, Ill., Bradley Hall, Bradley U., Wed., noon - 1:00 p.m.
Phoenix, Ariz., Federal Bldg., Wed., noon - 1:00 p.m.
Pittsburgh, Stanwix St. at Liberty Ave., Wed., noon - 1:00 p.m.
Pittsburgh, Stephen Foster Hall, U. of Pittsburgh, Wed., noon - 1:00 p.m.
Pittsburgh, Pa., Walnut & S. Aiken (Shadyside), Sat., 1:00 - 2:00 p.m.
Pittsfield, Mass., Park Square, Sat., noon - 1:00 p.m.
Pomona, Calif., Sat., 11:00 a.m. - noon
Port Chicago, Calif., waterfront entrance, every day, 9:00 a.m. - 5:00 p.m.
Port Washington, N.Y., Post Office, Mon., 3:45 - 4:45 p.m.
Portland, Ore., park next to Portland State College, Wed., noon - 1:00 p.m.
Princeton, N.J., Nassau St., Sun., 10:00 a.m. - 11:00 a.m.
Providence, R.I., Westminster Mall, Thurs., noon - 1:00 p.m.
Raleigh, N.C., Main Post Office, Wed., noon - 1:00 p.m.
Redding, Calif., Butte & Market Sts., Sat., noon - 1:00 p.m.
Richmond, Calif., Civic Center, Sat., 11:30 a.m. - 12:30 p.m.
Richmond, Ind., Earlham College, Wed., 12:15 - 1:00 p.m.
Ridgewood, N.J., Van Neste Sq., Sat., 11:00 a.m. - noon
Riverhead, N.Y., 1300 Ostrander (Rep. Pike's office) Sat., 11:00 a.m.
Riverside, Calif., on the Mall., Sat., 1:00 - 2:00 p.m.
Sacramento, Calif., Capitol Mall, weekdays, 9:00 a.m. - 5:00 p.m.
St. Louis, Mo., Olin Library, Washington U., Wed., 12:30 - 1:30 p.m.
St. Paul, Minn., Grand & Snelling Aves., Thur., noon - 1:00 p.m.
San Antonio, Tex., at the Alamo, Sat., 2:00 - 3:00 p.m.
San Francisco, Federal Bldg., weekdays, 8:00 a.m. - 5:00 p.m.
San Francisco, Union Sq., Sat., 1:00 - 3:00 p.m.
San Jose, Cal., 1st & Clara Sts., Thurs., noon - 1:00 p.m.
Santa Ana, Calif., Prentice Park at 1st St., Sun., 1:00 - 2:00 p.m.
Santa Barbara, Art Museum, Wed., noon - 1:00 p.m.
Santa Maria, Calif., B'way & Main Sts., Wed., noon-1:00 p.m.
Santa Maria, Calif., Allan Hancock campus, Wed., 12:30 p.m.
Seattle Wash., public library, Wed., 12:30 - 1:30 p.m.
Seattle, Wash., the Hub, U. of Wash., Wed., 12:30 - 1:30 p.m.
Springfield, Mass., Court Sq., Sat., noon - 1:00 p.m.
Stamford, Conn., City Hall, Sat., noon - 1:00 p.m.
Stephens Point, Wisc., Post Office, Sat., 11:30 a.m. - 12:30 p.m.
Syracuse, N.Y., South Saline & Washington Sts., Wed., noon - 1:45 p.m.
Tacoma, Wash., Univ. of Puget Sound, Wed., noon - 1:00 p.m.
Tucson, Ariz., main Post Office, Wed., noon - 1:00 p.m.
Tulsa, Okla., McFarlin Library, Wed., 11:30 a.m. - 12:30 p.m.
Vancouver B.C., Georgia & Granville Sts., Sat., 12:30 - 1:30 p.m.
Victoria, B.C., Douglas & View, Sat., 1-2 p.m.
Washington, D.C., 11th St. near F, N.W., Wed., noon - 1:30 p.m.
Washington, D.C., "The Mall," Catholic U., Thurs., noon - 1:00 p.m.
Waterbury, Conn., The Green, Wed., noon - 1:00 p.m.
Westport, Conn., Town Hall, 11:00 a.m. - noon
White Plains, N.Y., County Courthouse, Sat., noon - 1:00 p.m.
Whittier, Calif., Greenleaf & Philadelphia, Sat., noon - 1:00 p.m.
Wilmington, Del., Federal Bldg., Wed., 11:30 a.m. - 12:30 p.m.
Wilmington, O., Wilmington College carillon, Wed., 11:50 a.m. - 1:00 p.m.
Winona, Minn., Post Office, Sat., 11:00 a.m. - noon
Winston-Salem, N.C., Post Office, Sat., 1 - 2 p.m.
Worcester, Mass., City Hall, sat, noon - 1:00 p.m.

KEEP US HONEST!

This list is only as complete and up to date as we are able to make it with your help. If you know of any vigils which have been changed in time or location or discontinued, or for which we have no listing, please send us that information now. If there is no vigil in your vicinity, and you would like to start one, let us know that also, and we will do whatever we can to help you.—Eds.

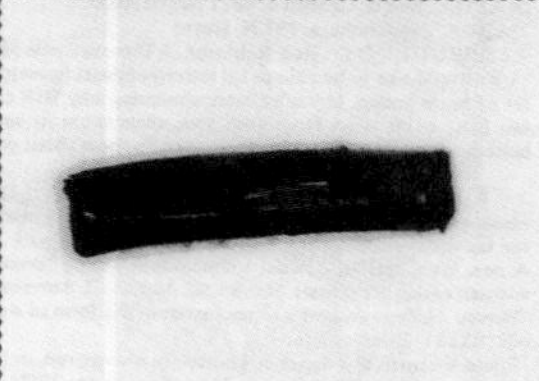

SECOND CLASS POSTAGE PAID AT N.Y., N.Y. 10001

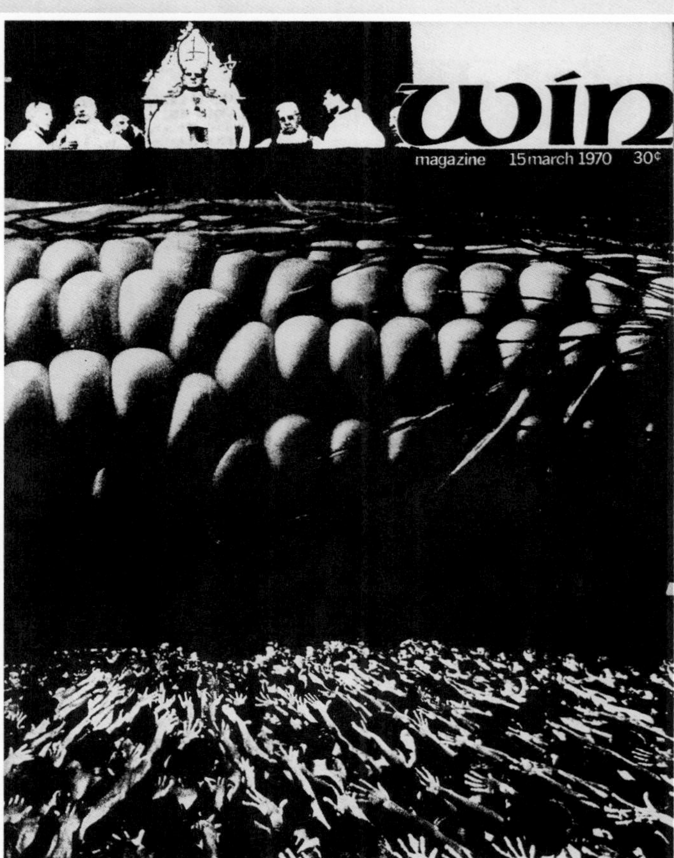

SECOND CLASS POSTAGE PAID AT N.Y., N.Y. 10001

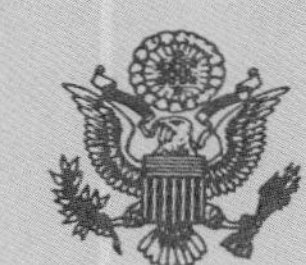

UNDESIRABLE DISCHARGE

FROM THE ARMED FORCES OF THE
UNITED STATES OF AMERICA

THIS IS TO CERTIFY THAT

KENNETH CHRISTOPHER CROSS 11 843 754 PRIVATE E-1 REGULAR ARMY

WAS DISCHARGED FROM THE
ARMY OF THE UNITED STATES
ON THE 7TH DAY OF NOVEMBER 1969
AS UNDESIRABLE

William H Criswell
WILLIAM H CRISWELL
CW4 USA

Dock of the Bay (San Francisco), October 13, 1969, vol. 1, no. 11, cover
Dock of the Bay (San Francisco), November 18, 1969, vol. 1, no. 16, center spread
Dock of the Bay (San Francisco), October 28, 1969, vol. 1, no. 13, center spread
Dock of the Bay (San Francisco), November 11, 1969, vol. 1, no. 15, center spread

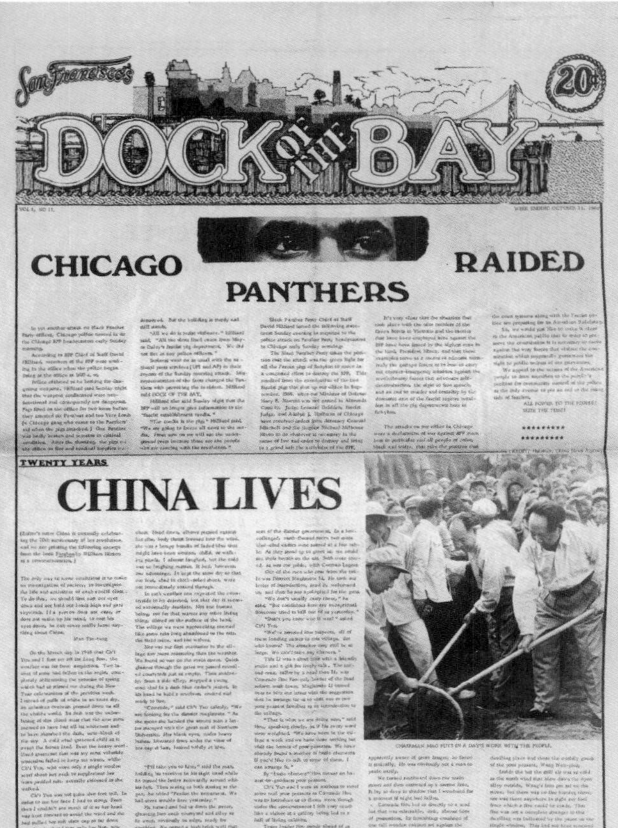

San Francisco's DOCK OF THE BAY 20¢

CHICAGO PANTHERS RAIDED

TWENTY YEARS

CHINA LIVES

CHAIRMAN MAO PUTS IN A DAY'S WORK WITH THE PEOPLE

we will win

DOCK of the BAY

COMMUNITY CONTROL OF POLICE

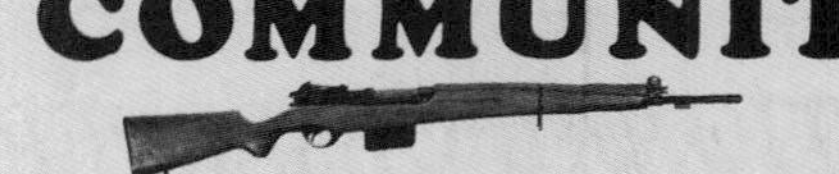

MAP OF PROPOSED SAN FRANCISCO POLICE DEPARTMENTS

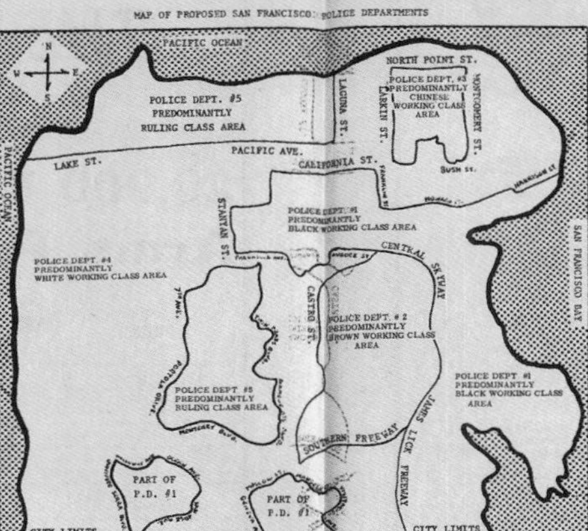

THE POWER MUST RETURN TO THE PEOPLE

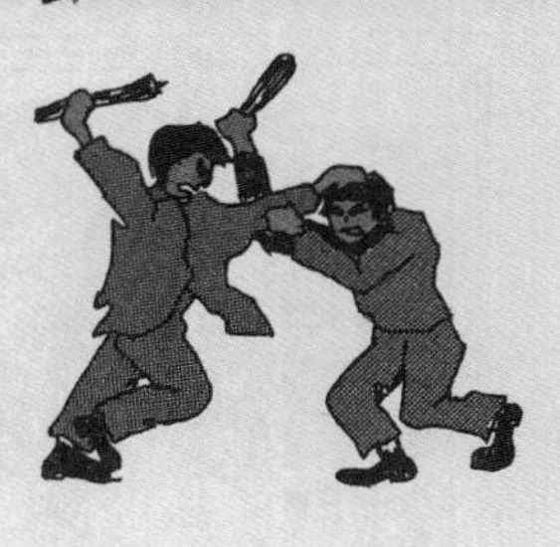

A LOT OF PEOPLE GROW UP TO BECOME PIGS BECAUSE THIS SYSTEM TEACHES EXPLOITATION; TEACHES US TO FORGET OUR SISTERS AND BROTHERS

THE PEOPLE HAVE TO CHANGE THE SYSTEM -- GET RID OF THE PIGGISHNESS IN OUR SOCIETY

Fascist Police Force San Francisco

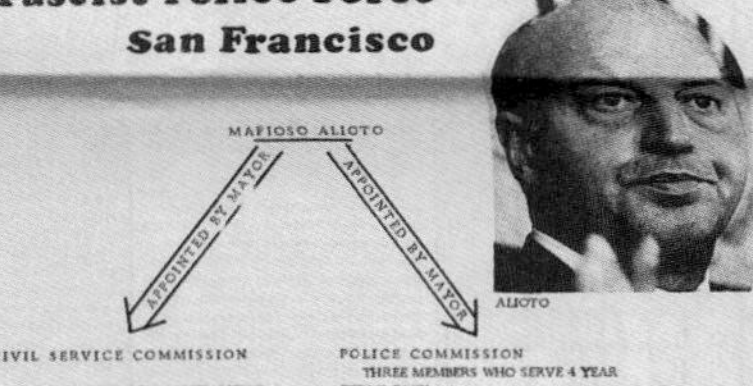

ALIOTO

CIVIL SERVICE COMMISSION

THREE MEMBERS WHO SERVE 6 YEAR TERMS EACH.

THEY GIVE PROMOTION EXAMS AND ENTRANCE EXAMS FOR POLICEMEN AND MANY OTHER CITY EMPLOYEES.

THEY ALSO DISCIPLINE THE PEOPLE THEY HIRE EXCEPT FOR:

THE PIGS, WHO "DISCIPLINE" THEMSELVES!

THE FIRE DEPT. ALSO PIGS WHO DO THEIR OWN "DISCIPLINING."

POLICE COMMISSION

THREE MEMBERS WHO SERVE 4 YEAR TERMS EACH.

APPOINTS

POLICE CHIEF WHOSE TERM "IS AT THE PLEASURE OF THE POLICE COMMISSION." (SF CITY CHARTER)

APPOINTS

POLICEMEN FOR:
BUREAU OF INSPECTORS
JUVENILE BUREAU
BUREAU OF ACCIDENT INVESTIGATION
BUREAU OF SPECIAL SERVICES
TAC SQUAD
INTELLIGENCE BUREAU

ALL "DISCIPLINED" BY THE POLICE CHIEF.

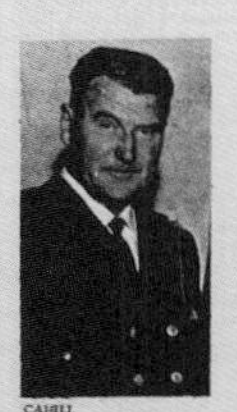

CAHILL

PEOPLE'S POLICE DEPARTMENTS

THE ACTION BEGINS WITH EACH POLICE COUNCIL PRECINCT (15 TO 30 BLOCK AREA) ... THAT AREA. THIS COUNCILMAN IS ONE OF 15 ON THE POLICE COUNCIL OF EACH NEIGHBORHOOD DIVISION:

POLICE DEPARTMENT #1: BLACK WORKING CLASS COMMUNITY
7 NEIGHBORHOOD DIVISIONS

POLICE DEPARTMENT #2: BROWN WORKING CLASS COMMUNITY
5 NEIGHBORHOOD DIVISIONS

POLICE DEPARTMENT #3: CHINESE WORKING CLASS COMMUNITY
2 NEIGHBORHOOD DIVISIONS

POLICE DEPARTMENT #4: WHITE WORKING CLASS COMMUNITY
7 NEIGHBORHOOD DIVISIONS

POLICE DEPARTMENT #5: RULING CLASS COMMUNITY
3 NEIGHBORHOOD DIVISIONS

EACH POLICE DEPT. LOOKS LIKE THIS:

THE PEOPLE OF EACH PRECINCT ELECT ONE COUNCILMAN

THE PEOPLE

ELECT

POLICE COUNCIL FOR ONE NEIGHBORHOOD DIVISION (15 COUNCILMEN)

15 15 15 15 15 15 15 POLICE COUNCILMEN

ELECT

SELECT POLICEMEN

7 POLICE COMMISSIONERS

PEOPLE'S POLICE DEPARTMENT
DIAGRAMMED FOR ONE OF OUR CITY'S POLICE DEPARTMENTS
EXAMPLE: A PEOPLE'S POLICE DEPT. WITH 7 NEIGHBORHOOD DIVISIONS.

THE PEOPLE OF THE PRECINCTS:
15 PRECINCTS PER NEIGHBORHOOD DIVISION.
THE PEOPLE IN EACH PRECINCT ELECT A POLICE COUNCILMAN.
QUALIFICATIONS FOR POLICE COUNCILMEN ARE: →

QUALIFICATIONS FOR POLICE COUNCILMEN:
1. RESIDENCE IN HIS PRECINCT FOR SIX MONTHS PRIOR TO THE UPCOMING ELECTION.
2. MUST BE OF VOTING AGE.

ELECTED

POLICE COUNCILS FOR THE NEIGHBORHOOD DIVISIONS:
THE 7 NEIGHBORHOOD DIVISIONS EACH HAVE A 15 MAN POLICE COUNCIL. THE DUTIES OF THE POLICE COUNCIL ARE: →

DUTIES OF POLICE COUNCILMEN:
1. SET QUALIFICATIONS FOR SELECTION OF POLICEMEN.
2. HEAR AND ACT ON COMPLAINTS OF PEOPLE AGAINST POLICEMEN.
3. DISCIPLINE POLICEMEN WHO BREAK LAWS OR POLICIES WITHIN THE DISTRICT.
4. SELECT ONE COMMISSIONER TO REPRESENT THE PEOPLE ON THE BOARD OF COMMISSIONERS. THEY CAN FIRE HIM, TOO, IF THEY'RE NOT SATISFIED WITH HIS ACTIONS.
5. MAKE POLICY DECISIONS. THE COMMISSIONER FOR THAT POLICE COUNCIL IS BOUND TO BRING UP THESE DECISIONS AT COMMISSIONERS' MEETINGS AND VOTE ACCORDING TO THE POLICE COUNCIL'S INSTRUCTIONS.

THE POLICE COMMISSIONERS FORM THE POLICE COMMISSION FOR EACH POLICE DEPARTMENT IN THE CITY.

ELECTED

POLICE COMMISSIONERS: SEVEN
ONE COMMISSIONER FOR EACH NEIGHBORHOOD DIVISION.
THE DUTIES OF THE COMMISSIONERS ARE: →

DUTIES OF POLICE COMMISSIONERS:
1. SELECT POLICEMEN.
2. DISCIPLINE POLICEMEN.
3. SET QUALIFICATIONS FOR POLICEMEN.
4. SET POLICIES WITHIN THE POLICE DEPARTMENT.
5. FIX SALARIES OF POLICE COUNCILMEN AND POLICEMEN.
6. MAKE NECESSARY AGREEMENTS WITH OTHER POLICE DEPARTMENTS AND GOVERNMENT AGENCIES.

THE POWER IS RETURNED TO THE PEOPLE

THIS IS A REVOLUTIONARY PROGRAM:

THE COMMUNITY CONTROL OF POLICE PETITION PROVIDES THAT ALL WEAPONS, VEHICLES, EQUIPMENT, FUNDS AND FILES OF THE PRESENT FASCIST POLICE FORCE WILL BE DISTRIBUTED TO THE PEOPLE'S COMMUNITY POLICE DEPARTMENTS. (Section 35.1-A of petition)

POLICE BECOME COMMUNITY PEOPLE

ALL POLICE OFFICERS MUST LIVE IN THE POLICE DEPARTMENT AREAS THEY WORK IN. (Section 35.1-B)

THE YOUTH HAVE A STRONG VOICE

COUNCILMEN CAN BE RECALLED BY A PETITION BEARING THE SIGNATURES OF RESIDENTS EQUALLING 20% OF THE NUMBER OF PEOPLE VOTING IN THAT PRECINCT. THE 20% SIGNING DO NOT HAVE TO BE REGISTERED VOTERS AND THEY CAN BE OF ANY AGE.

COMMISSIONERS CAN BE RECALLED (through a petition) BY 20% OF THE REGISTERED VOTERS IN THAT PRECINCT.

COMMUNITY CONTROL OF POLICE MEANS

CONTROL OF OUR DESTINIES: SELF DETERMINATION FOR ALL PEOPLES.

AN END TO THE RACIST HARRASSMENT BY POLICE. HUEY NEWTON, BOBBY SEALE, LOS SIETE AND MANY OTHER POLITICAL PRISONERS WOULD NOT BE IN JAIL TODAY IF WE HAD COMMUNITY CONTROL OF POLICE.

POLICE COULD NOT BE USED AS STRIKE BREAKERS BY THE RULING CLASS, BECAUSE IF THEY DO NOT REPRESENT THE INTEREST OF THE PEOPLE THEY WILL BE EXPELLED FROM THE DEPARTMENT.

FULLER EMPLOYMENT IN LOW INCOME COMMUNITIES BECAUSE RESIDENTS OF THE COMMUNITY WOULD BE EMPLOYED AS POLICEMEN.

POWER TO THE PEOPLE

POWER TO THE PEOPLE!

N.C.C.F. COMMITTEE

DOCK OF THE BAY

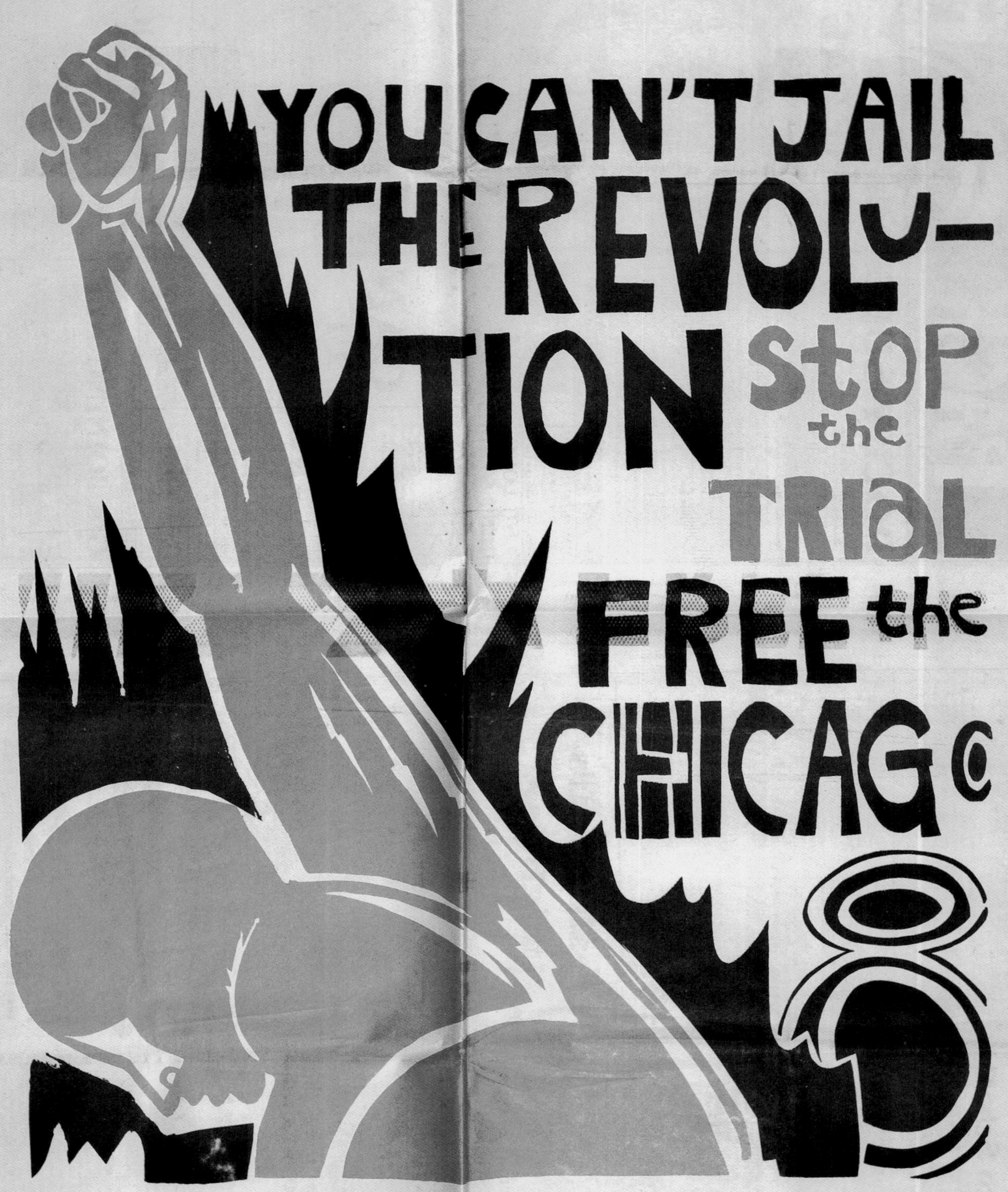

DOCK OF THE BAY

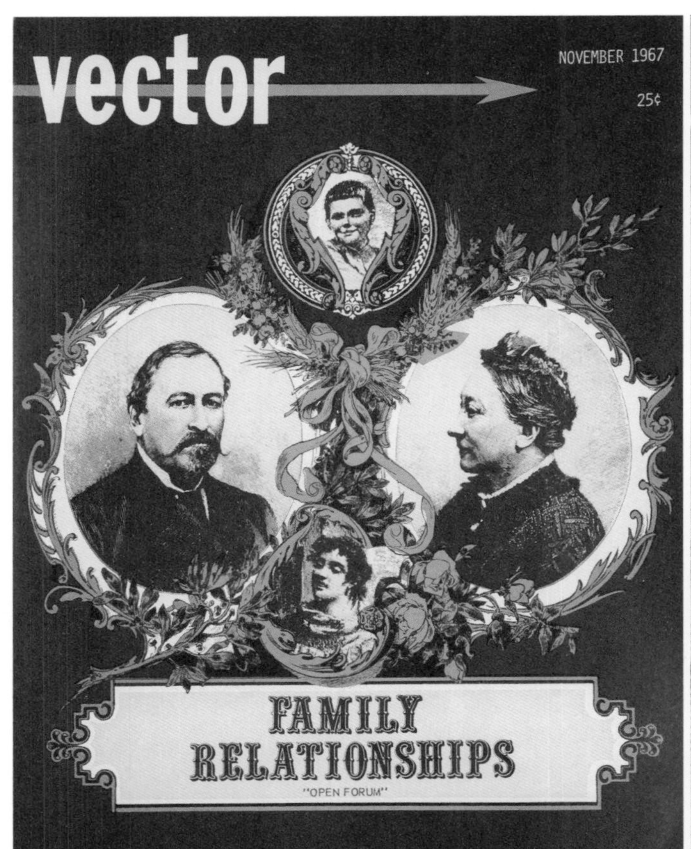
vector
NOVEMBER 1967
25¢
FAMILY
RELATIONSHIPS
"OPEN FORUM"

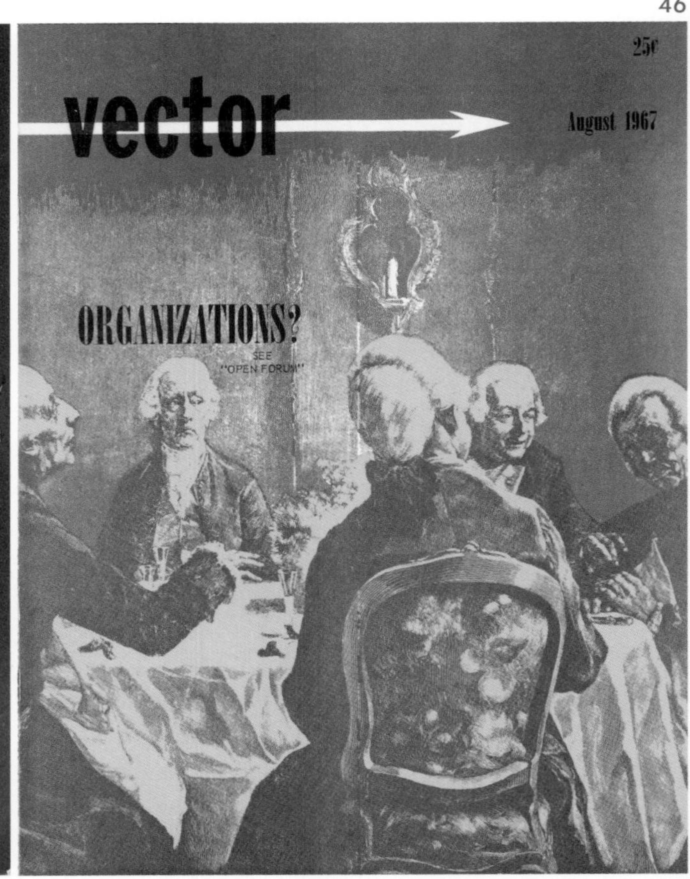
25¢
vector
August 1967
ORGANIZATIONS?
SEE
"OPEN FORUM"

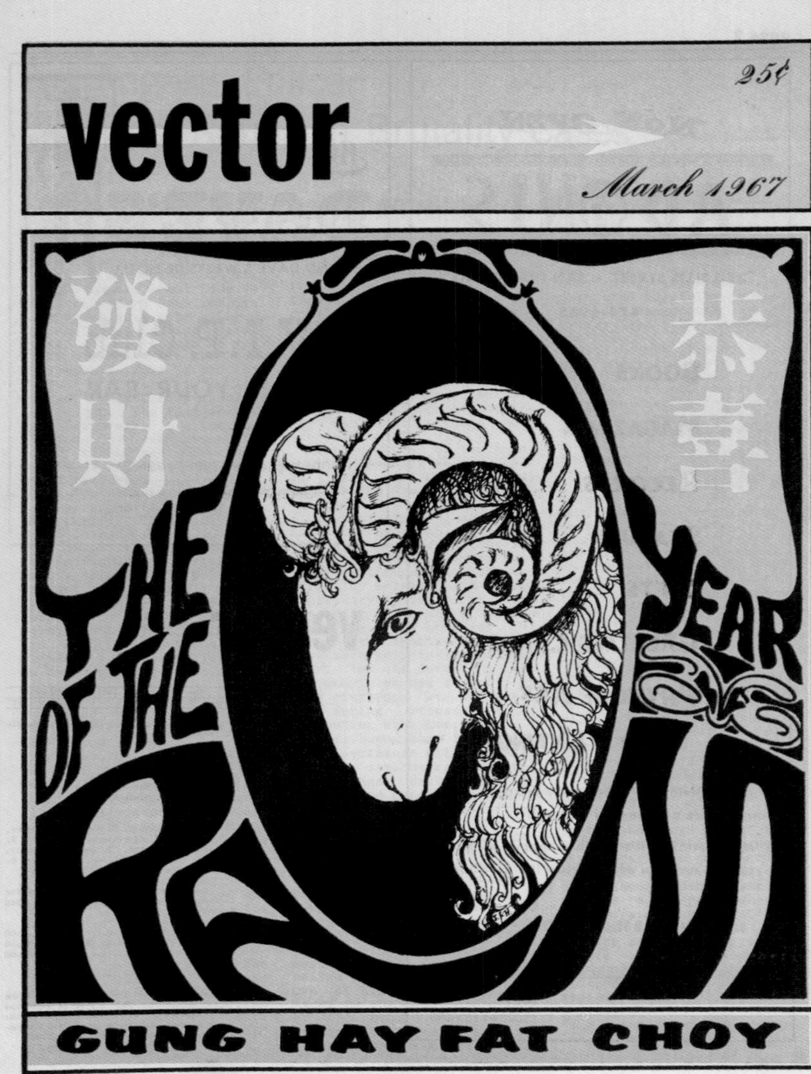
25¢
vector
March 1967
發財
恭喜
THE YEAR OF THE RAM
GUNG HAY FAT CHOY

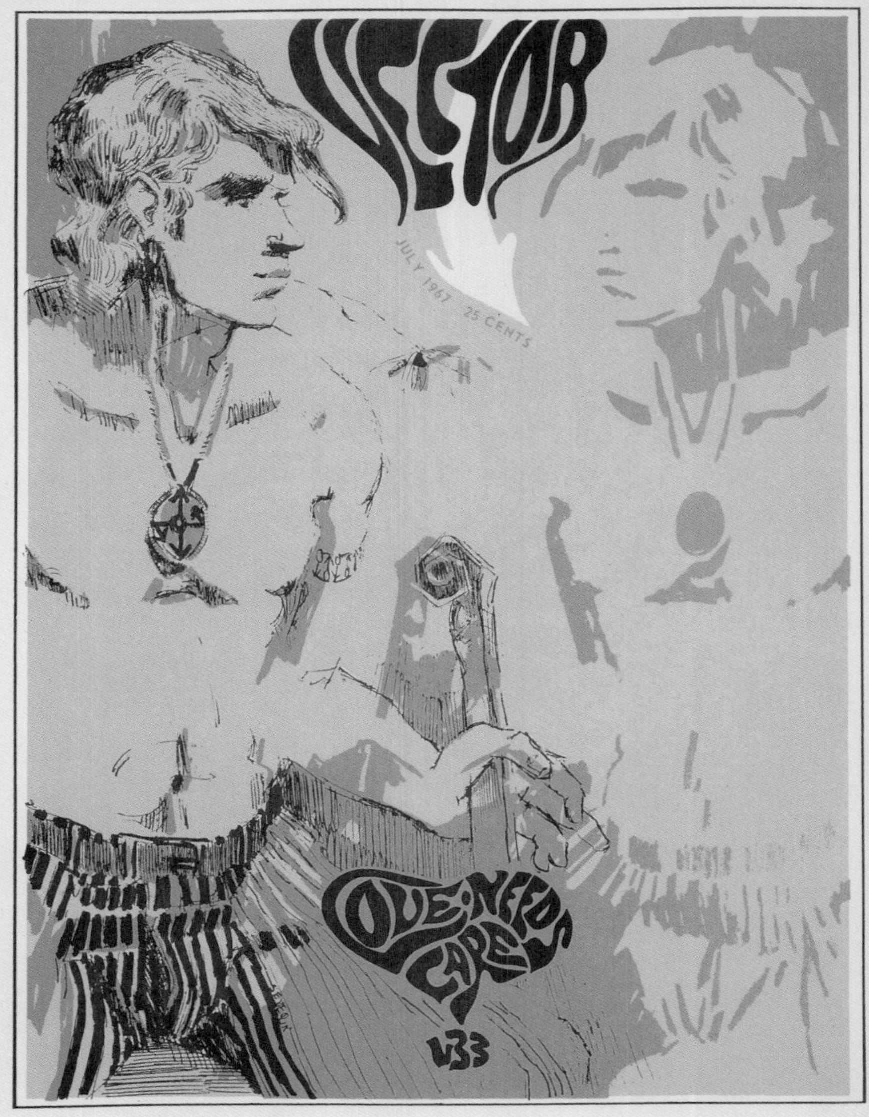
VECTOR
JULY 1967 25 CENTS
LOVE NEEDS CARE

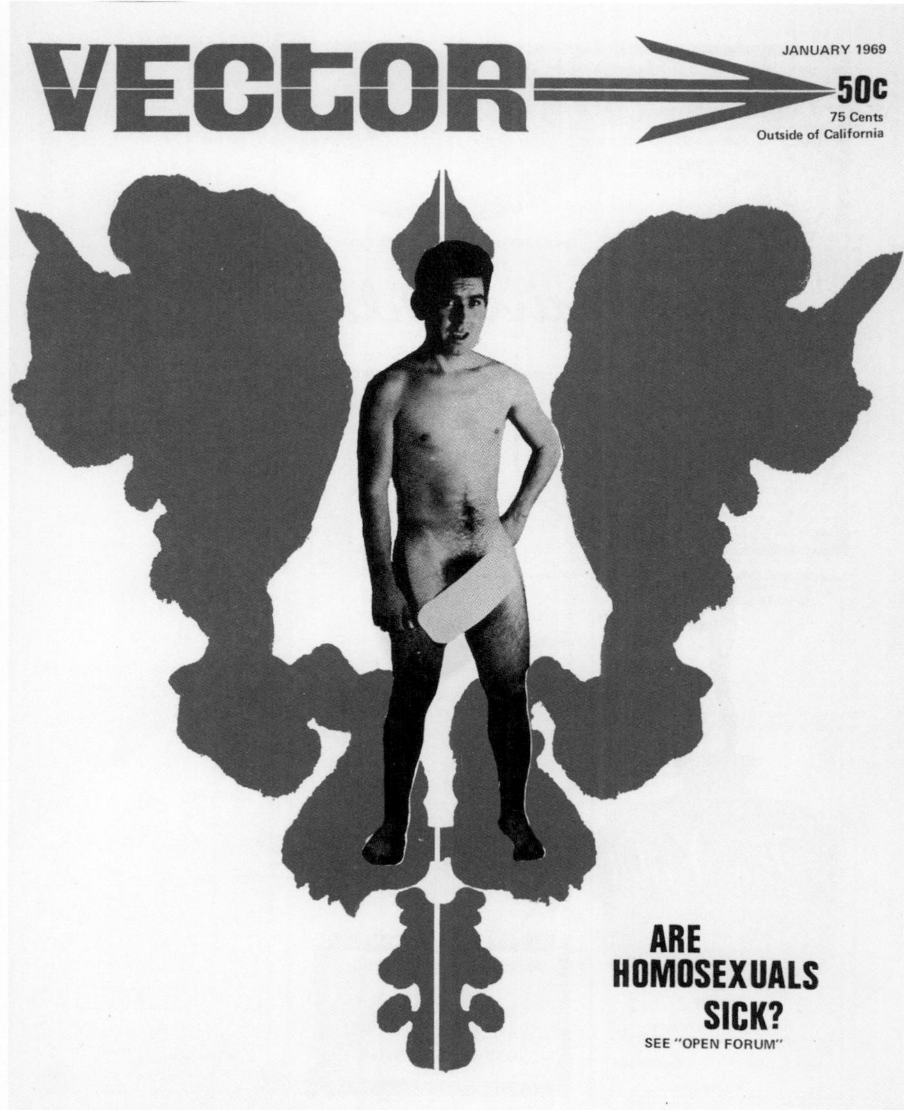

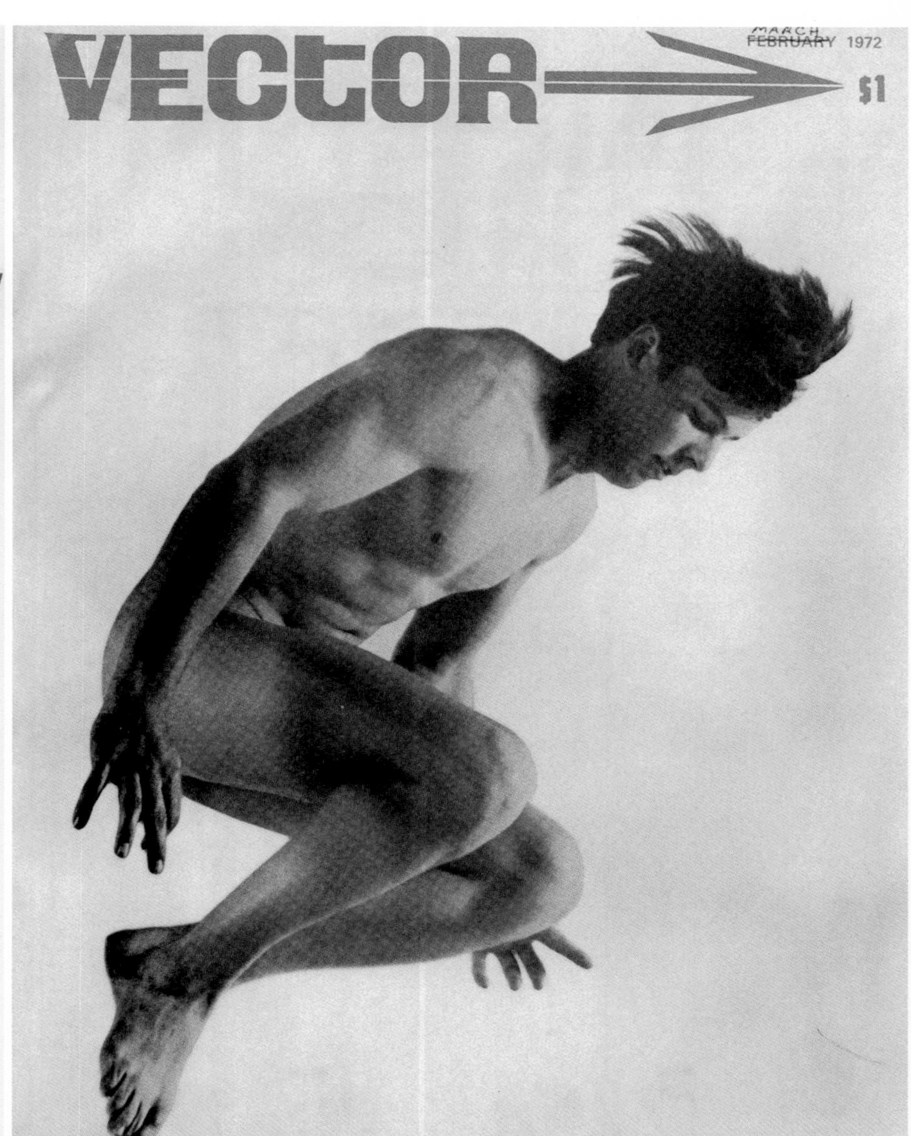

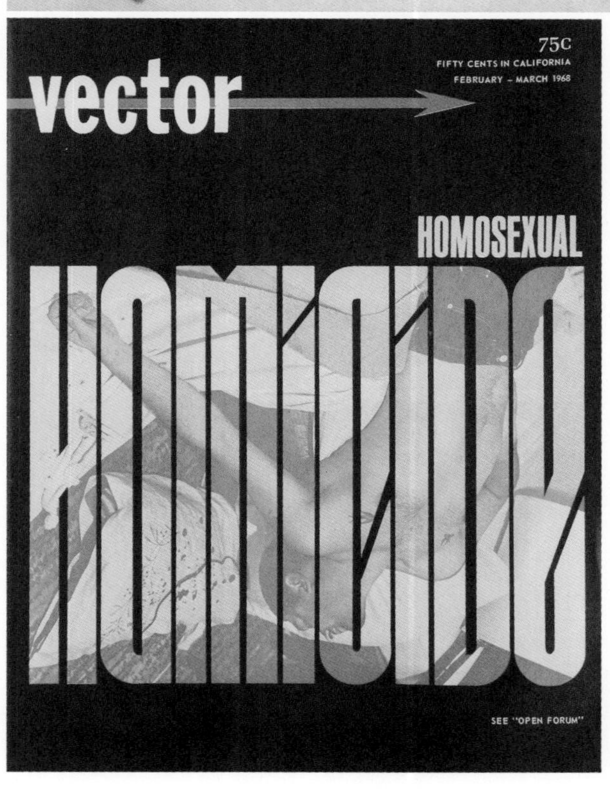

Previous page
Vector (San Francisco), November 1967, vol. 3, no. 12, cover
Vector (San Francisco), August 1967, vol. 3, no. 9, cover
Vector (San Francisco), March 1967, vol. 2, no. 4, cover
Vector (San Francisco), July 1967, vol. 3, no. 8, cover

Vector (San Francisco), January 1969, vol. 5, no. 1, cover
Vector (San Francisco), March 1972, vol. 8, no. 3, cover
Vector (San Francisco), February–March 1968, vol. 4, no. 3, cover

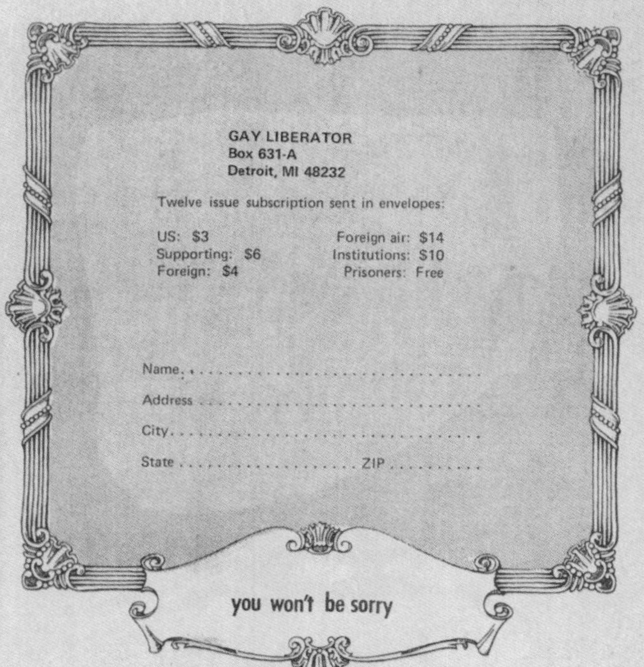

gay liberator

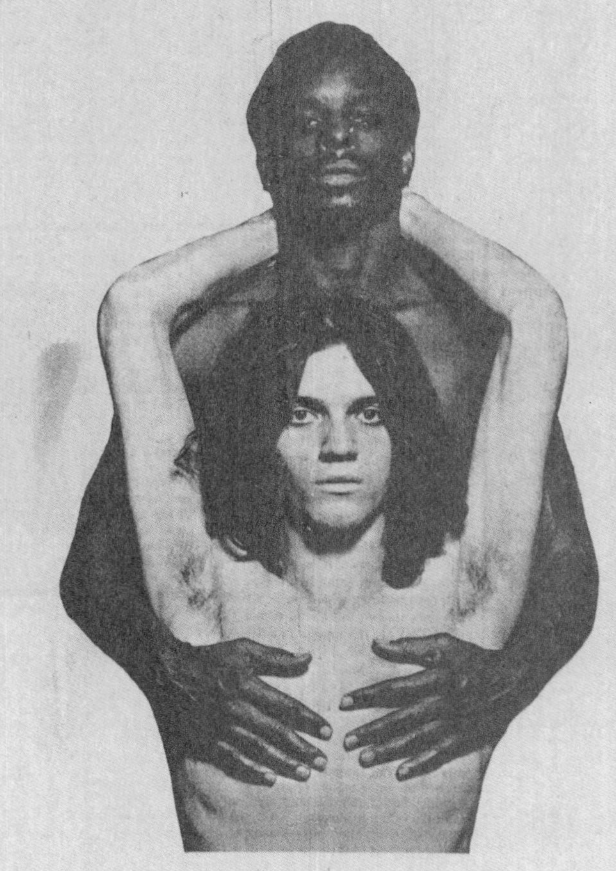

November 1973 Detroit No. 32

25c
30¢ outside Michigan

THE
GAY LIBERATOR
IS QUEER AS A...

25¢
no. 15

GAYS OF AMERICA UNITE!
GAY POWER TO THE GAY PEOPLE
OUT OF THE CLOSETS! INTO THE STREETS!
WHITMAN
IN GAY WE TRUST
THREE DOLLARS
LOVE

directory

read this!

we can be bought

HEY! WE'RE BEAUTIFUL!

The Gay Liberator (Detroit), November 1973, no. 32, front and back covers
The Gay Liberator (Detroit), February 1972, no. 15, front and back covers

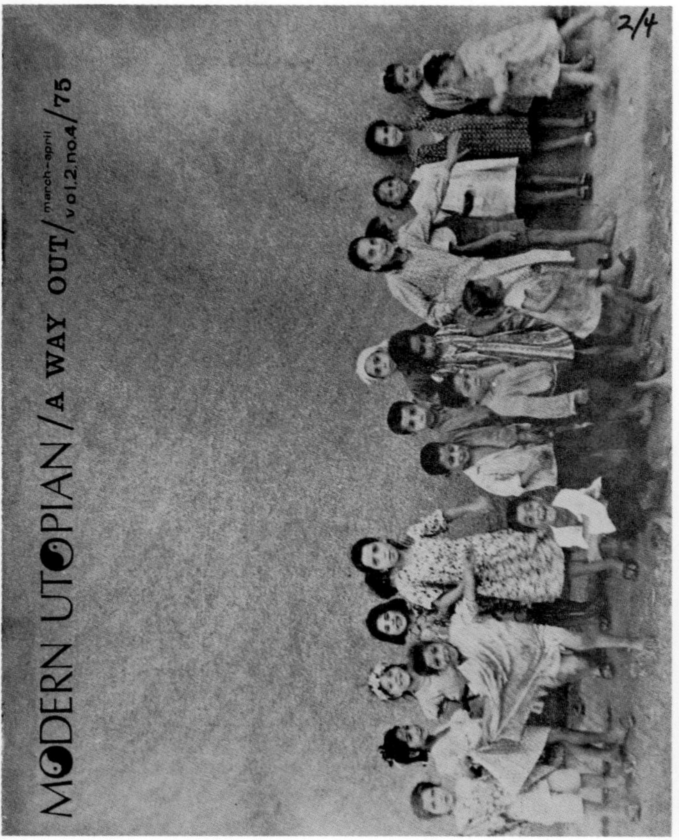

Gestalt Training Institute, Lake Cowichan, Box 39, Vancouver, B.C.
Shalal, 750 West Broadway, Vancouver, B.C.
Strathmere, North Gower, Ontario.
Synergia, P.O. Box 1685, Station B, Montreal 2, Quebec.

Outside U.S. & Canada

Australian Institute of Human Relations, 12 Webb St., Altona, Australia.
Center House, 10-A Airlie Gardens, Kensington, London W8, England.
Centre for Applied Social Research, Belzise Lane, London NW 3, England.
Esalen-In-Chile, 1413 Allston Way, Berkeley, California 94702.
Human Interaction Seminars, Box 4984, G.P.O. Sydney 2001 NSW, Australia.
Quawsitor, Vernon Road, Sutton, Surrey, England.
Yoloti, Sierra Vertientes 365, Mexico D.F. 10, Mexico.

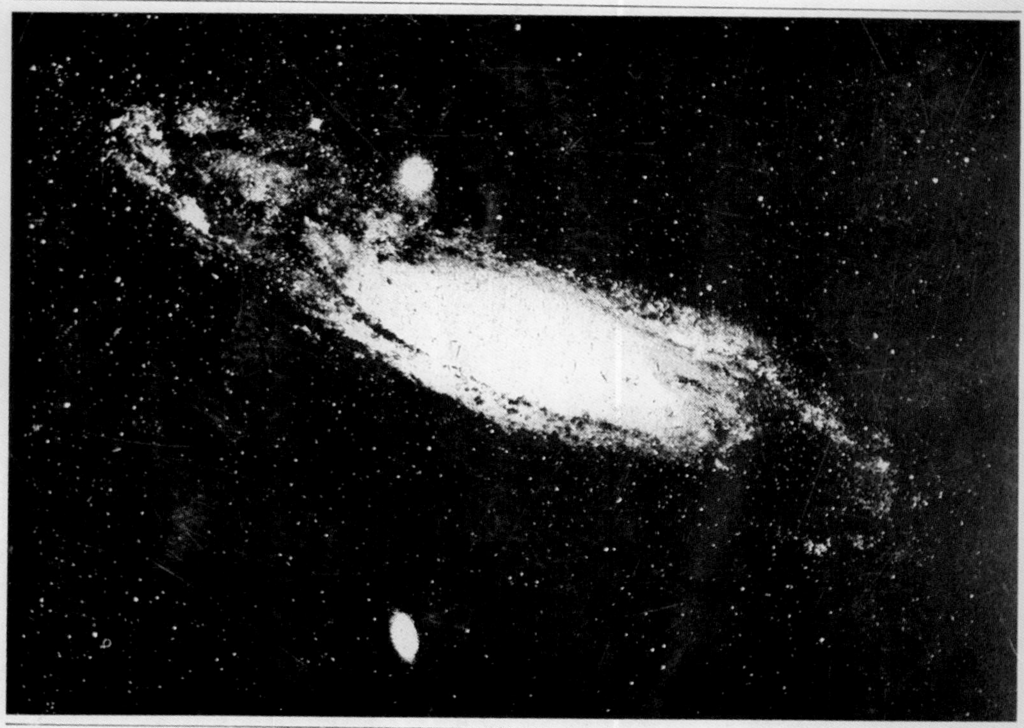

DIRECTORY of FREE SCHOOLS,
SOCIAL CHANGE, PERSONAL GROWTH

Modern Utopian (Berkeley), March–April 1968, vol. 2, no. 4, cover
Modern Utopian (Berkeley), 1971, vol. 5, nos. 4–6, cover

San Francisco
Express Times

god nose
comix - p.8

MARCUSE: 'THE OLD MODEL WON'T DO' p.3

IF YA GOT SOMETHIN'
IT'S CAUSE YOU'RE GOOD
IF YA GOT NOTHIN'
IT'S CAUSE YOU'RE
BAD...
ASK SANTA
CLAUS

©1968 R. COBB ALL RIGHTS RESERVED

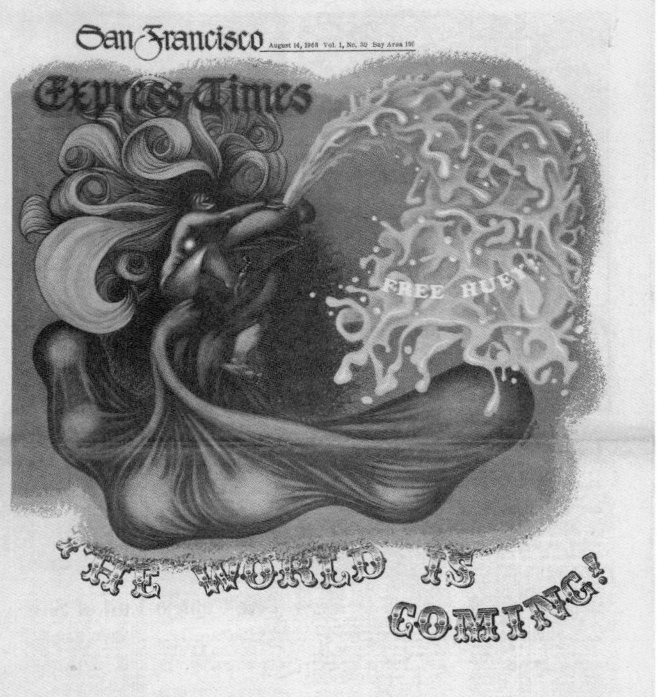
San Francisco
August 14, 1968 Vol. 1, No. 30 Bay Area 15¢
Express Times

PRESIDIO UPRISING

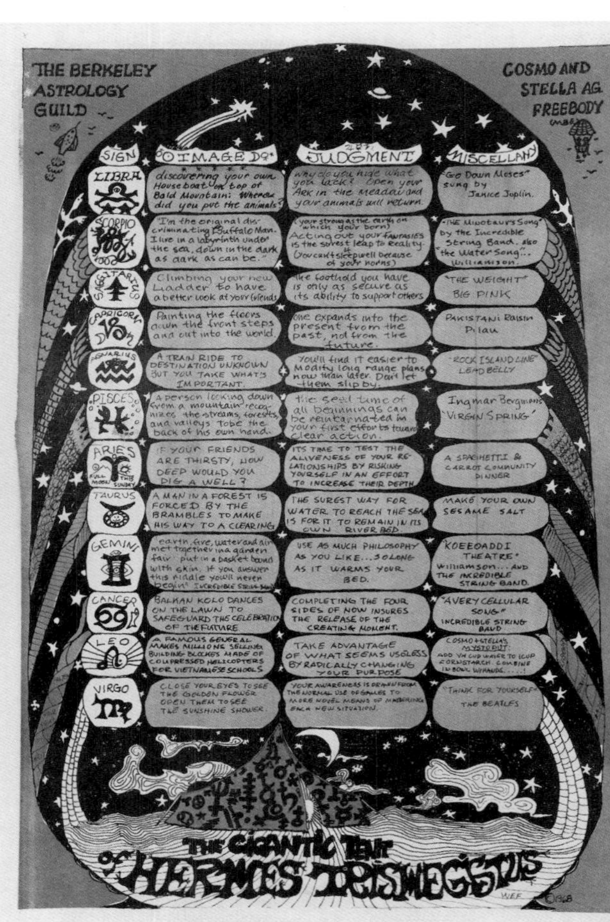
THE BERKELEY ASTROLOGY GUILD

COSMO AND STELLA AG FREEBODY

SIGN	IMAGE	JUDGMENT	MISCELLANY
LIBRA	discovering your own Houseboat on top of Bald Mountain: Where did you put the animals?	why do you hide what you lack? Open your Ark in the meadow and your animals will return.	"Go Down Moses" sung by Janice Joplin.
SCORPIO	"I'm the original discriminating Buffalo Man. I live in a labyrinth under the sea, down in the dark as dark as can be."	(your strong as the earth on which your born) Acting out your fantasies is the surest leap to reality. (You can't sleep well because of your horns)	"THE Minotaur's Song" by the Incredible String Band. also "the Water Song"... Williamson.
SAGGITARIUS	Climbing your new Ladder to have a better look at your friends	the foothold you have is only as secure as its ability to support others	"THE WEIGHT" BIG PINK
CAPRICORN	Painting the floors down the front steps and out into the world.	one expands into the present from the past, not from the future.	PAKISTANI Raisin Pilau
AQUARIUS	A TRAIN RIDE TO DESTINATION UNKNOWN BUT YOU TAKE WHAT'S IMPORTANT.	You'll find it easier to Modify long range plans now than later. Don't let them slip by.	"ROCK ISLAND LINE" LEAD BELLY
PISCES	A person looking down from a mountain recognizes the streams, forests, and valleys to be the back of his own hand.	the seed time of all beginnings can be reincarnated in your first efforts toward clear action.	Ingmar Bergman's 'VIRGIN SPRING'
ARIES	IF YOUR FRIENDS ARE THIRSTY, HOW DEEP WOULD YOU DIG A WELL?	ITS TIME TO TEST THE ALIVENESS OF YOUR RELATIONSHIPS BY RISKING YOURSELF IN AN EFFORT TO INCREASE THEIR DEPTH	A SPAGHETTI & CARROT COMMUNITY DINNER
TAURUS	A MAN IN A FOREST IS FORCED BY THE BRAMBLES TO MAKE HIS WAY TO A CLEARING	THE SUREST WAY FOR WATER TO REACH THE SEA IS FOR IT TO REMAIN IN ITS OWN RIVER BED.	MAKE YOUR OWN SESAME SALT
GEMINI	"earth, fire, water and air met together in a garden fair put in a basket bound with skin. If you answer this riddle you'll never begin" INCREDIBLE STRING BAND	USE AS MUCH PHILOSOPHY AS YOU LIKE... SO LONG AS IT WARMS YOUR BED.	"KOEEOADDI THEATRE" Williamson... AND THE INCREDIBLE STRING BAND.
CANCER	BALKAN KOLO DANCES ON THE LAWN TO SAFEGUARD THE CELEBRATION OF THE FUTURE	COMPLETING THE FOUR SIDES OF NOW INSURES THE RELEASE OF THE CREATING MOMENT.	"A VERY CELLULAR SONG" INCREDIBLE STRING BAND
LEO	A FAMOUS GENERAL MAKES MILLIONS SELLING BUILDING BLOCKS MADE OF COMPRESSED HELICOPTERS FOR VIETNAMESE SCHOOLS	TAKE ADVANTAGE OF WHAT SEEMS USELESS BY RADICALLY CHANGING YOUR PURPOSE	COSMO+STELLA'S MYSTOPUT: ADD 1/4 CUP WATER TO 1 CUP CORNSTARCH. COMBINE IN BOWL W/HANDS.....!
VIRGO	CLOSE YOUR EYES TO SEE THE GOLDEN FLOWER OPEN THEM TO SEE THE SUNSHINE SHOWER.	YOUR AWARENESS IS DRAWN FROM THE NORMAL USE OF GAMES TO MORE NOVEL MEANS OF MASTERING EACH NEW SITUATION.	"THINK FOR YOURSELF" THE BEATLES

THE GIGANTIC TENT OF HERMES TRISMEGISTUS

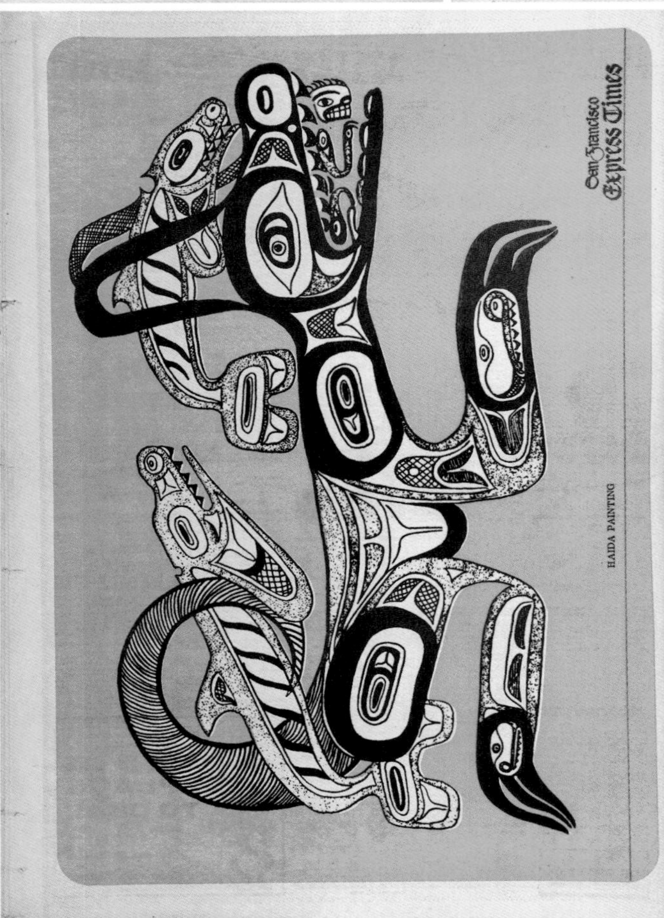
San Francisco
Express Times

HAIDA PAINTING

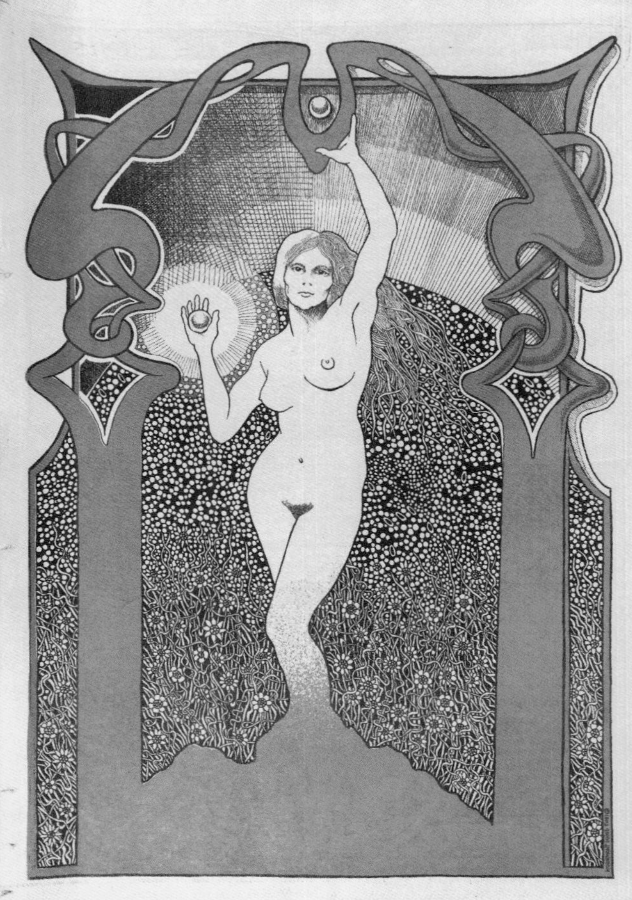

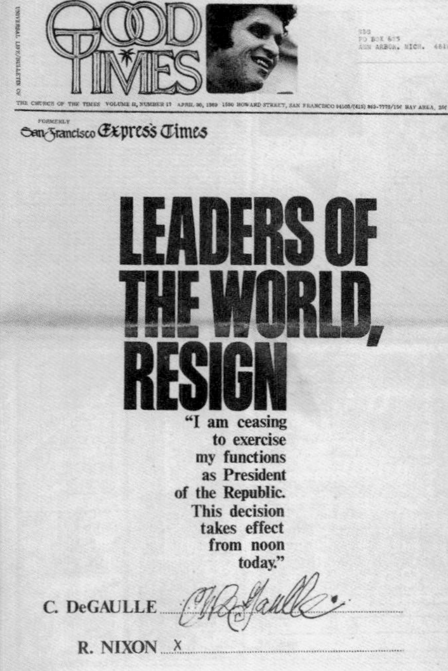
GOOD TIMES

FORMERLY San Francisco Express Times

LEADERS OF THE WORLD, RESIGN

"I am ceasing to exercise my functions as President of the Republic. This decision takes effect from noon today."

C. DeGAULLE

R. NIXON X

San Francisco Express Times, December 18, 1968, vol. 1, no. 48, cover
San Francisco Express Times, August 14, 1968, vol. 1, no. 30, cover
San Francisco Express Times, October 2, 1968, vol. 1, no. 37, cover
San Francisco Express Times, June 26, 1968, vol. 1, no. 23, back cover
San Francisco Express Times, June 19, 1968, vol. 1, no. 22, back cover
Good Times (San Francisco), April 30, 1969, vol. 2, no. 15, cover

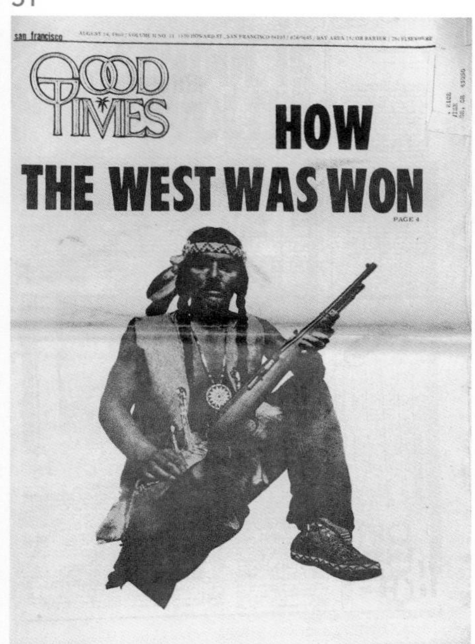

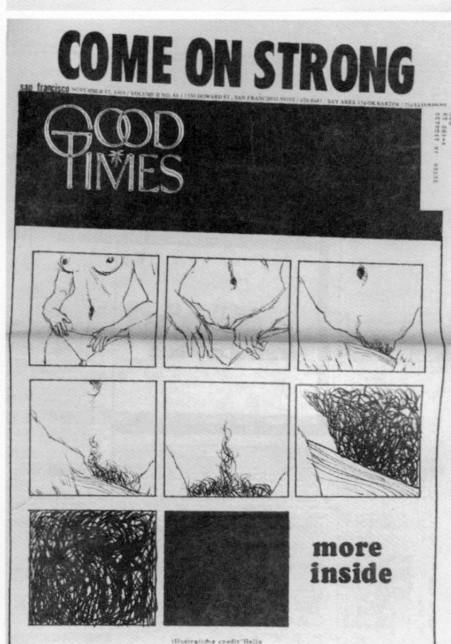

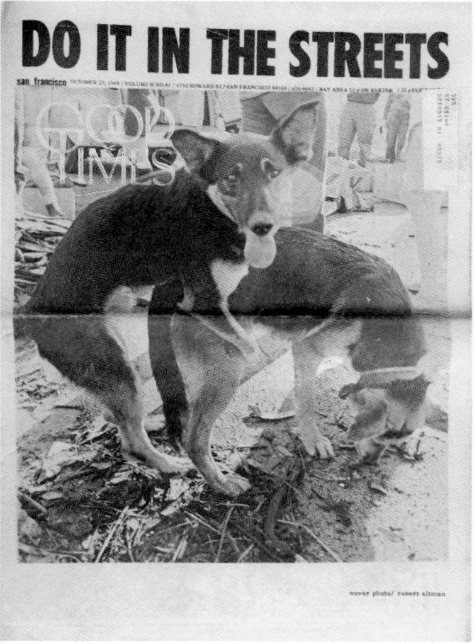

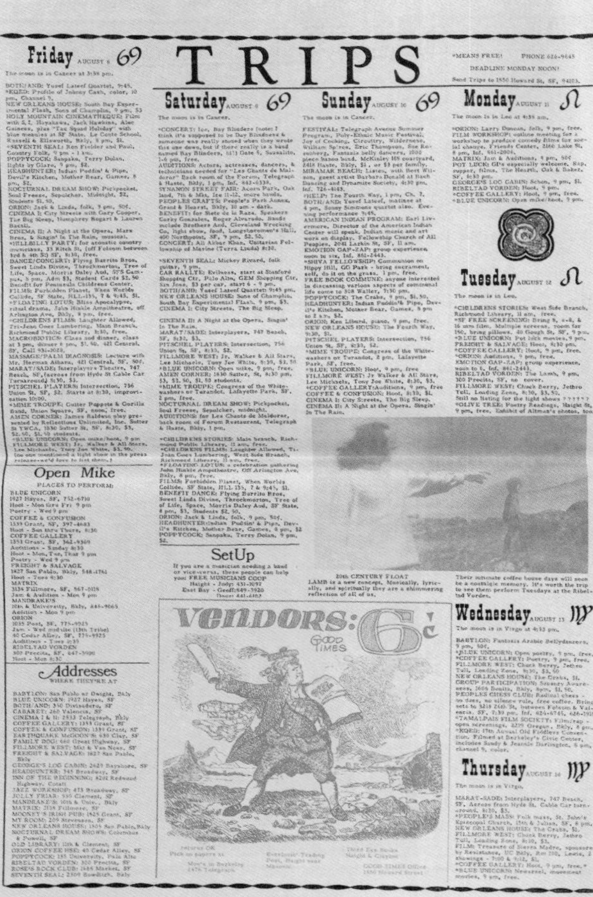

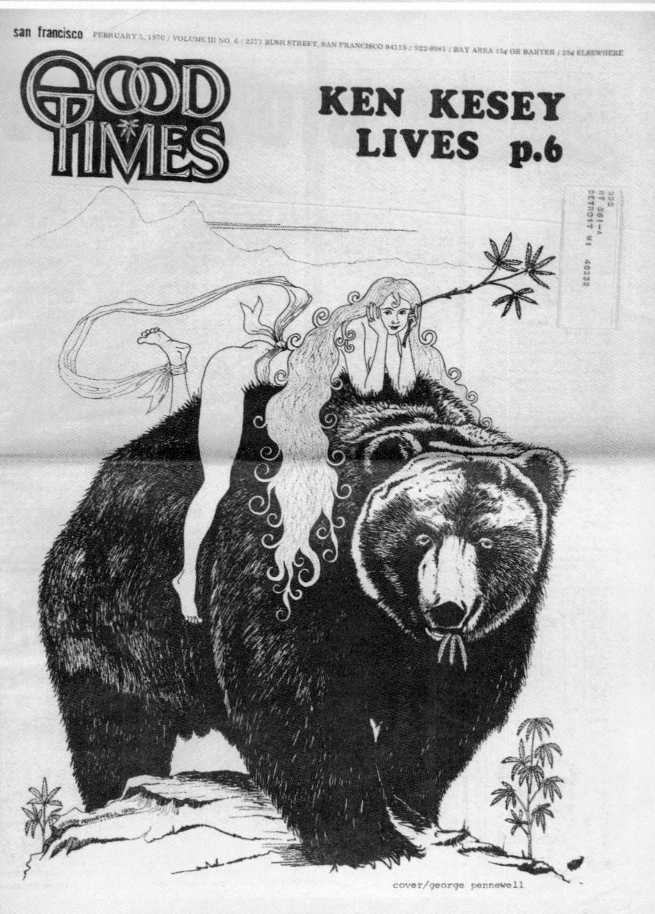

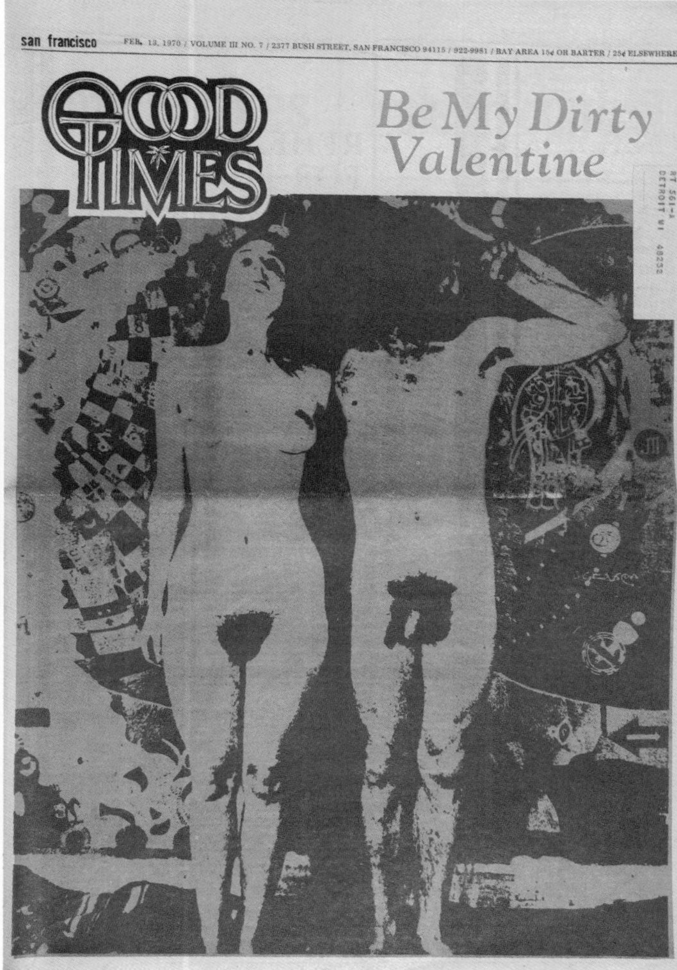

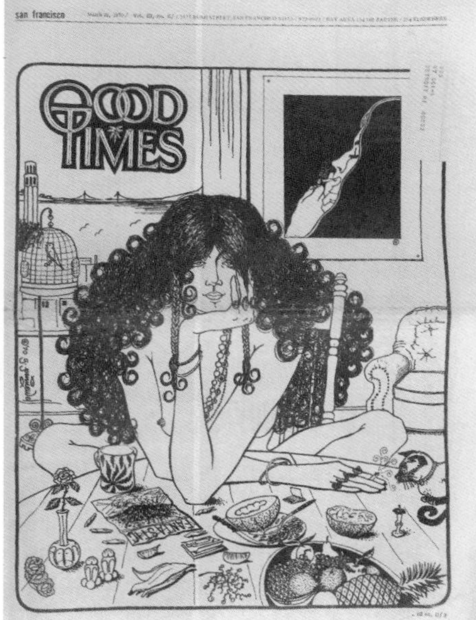

Good Times (San Francisco), August 14, 1969, vol. 2, no. 31, cover
Good Times (San Francisco), August 7, 1969, vol. 2, no. 30, back cover
Good Times (San Francisco), February 13, 1970, vol. 3, no. 7, cover
Good Times (San Francisco), November 13, 1969, vol. 2, no. 44, cover
Good Times (San Francisco), October 23, 1969, vol. 2, no. 41, cover
Good Times (San Francisco), February 5, 1970, vol. 3, no. 6, cover
Good Times (San Francisco), March 13, 1970, vol. 3, no. 11, cover

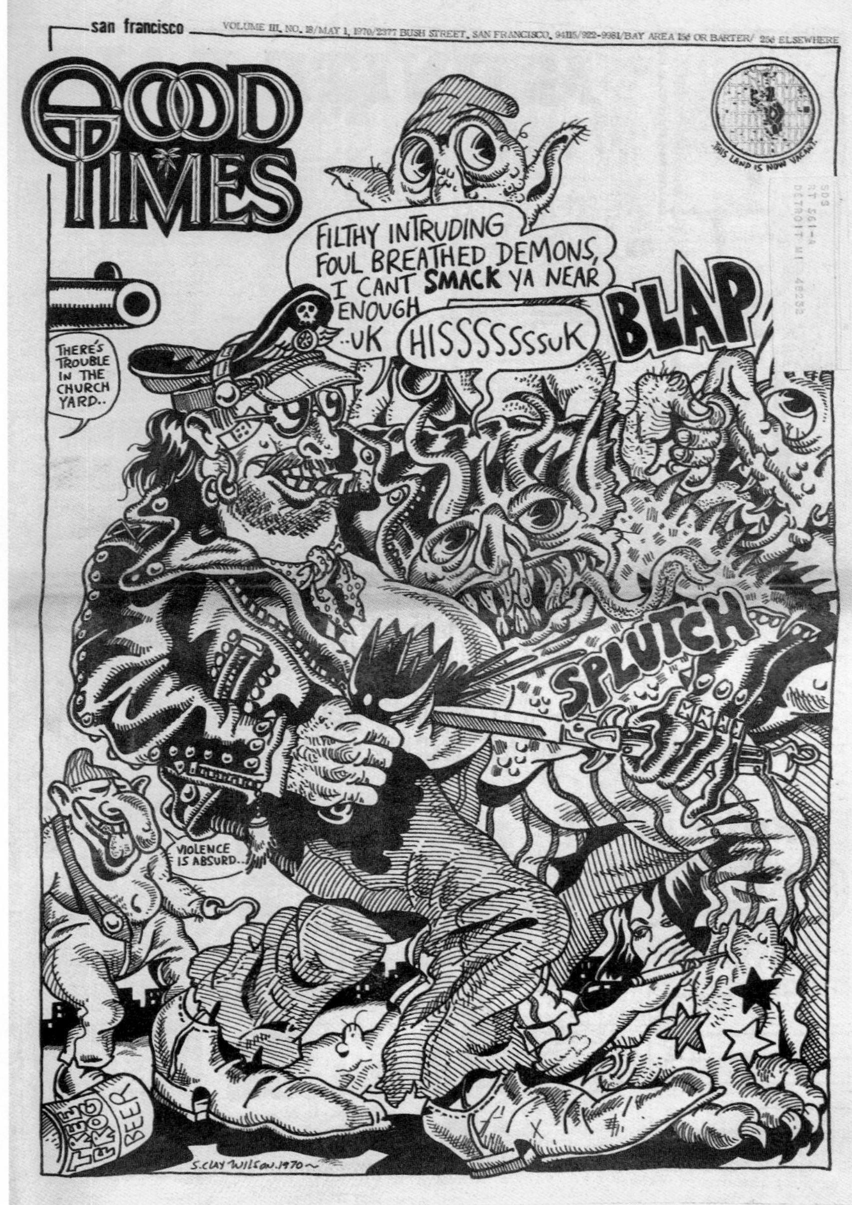

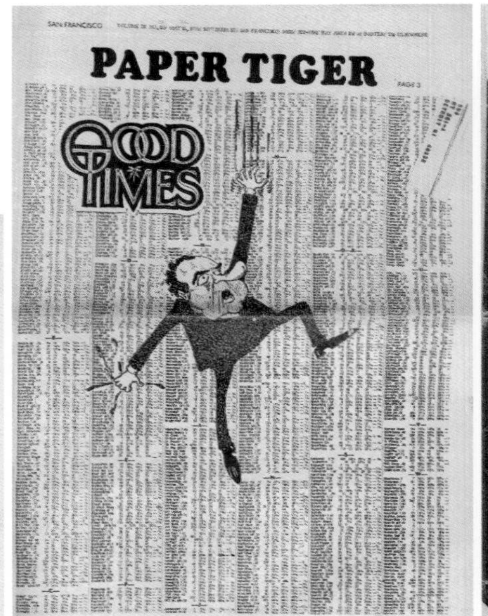

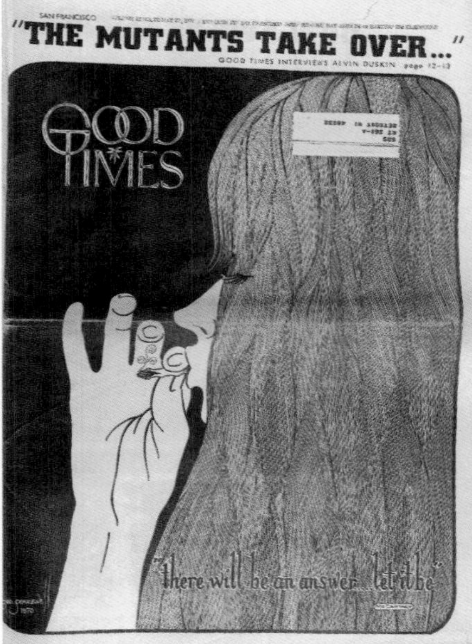

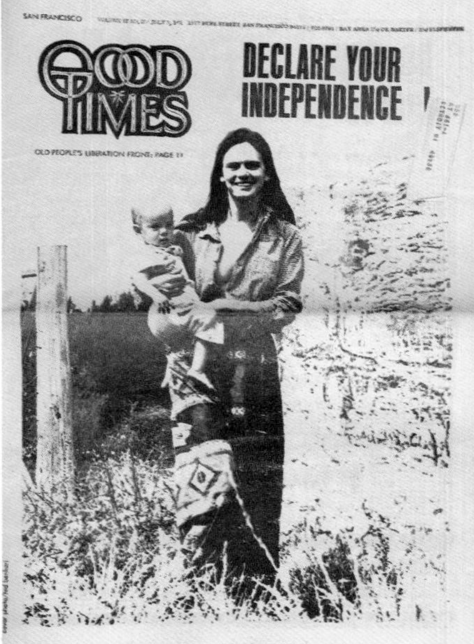

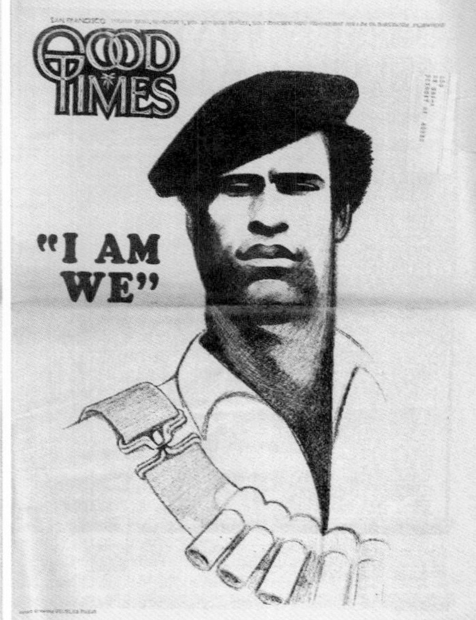

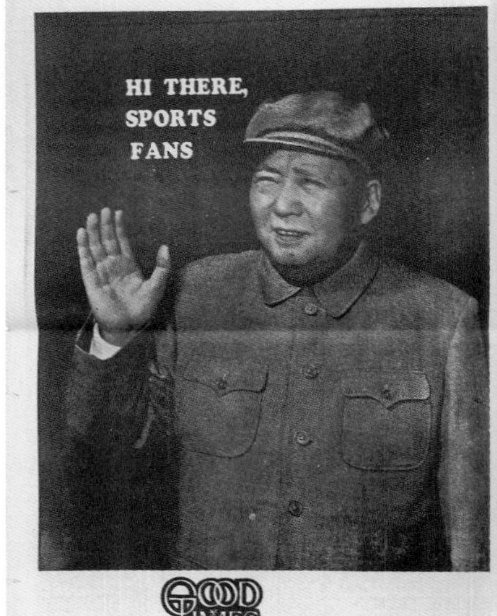

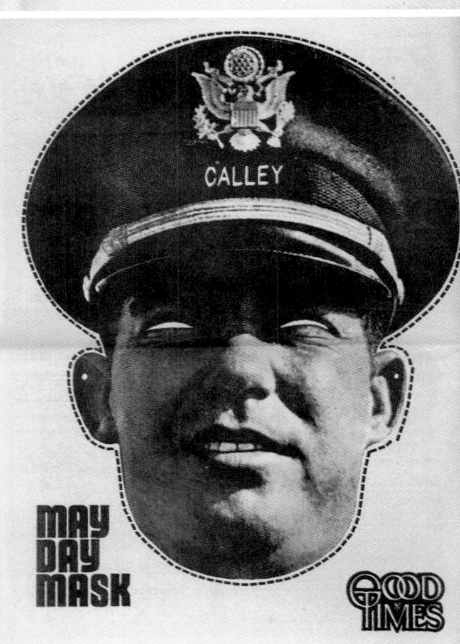

Good Times (San Francisco), May 1, 1970, vol. 3, no. 18, cover
Good Times (San Francisco), May 22, 1970, vol. 3, no. 21, cover
Good Times (San Francisco), May 29, 1970, vol. 3, no. 22, cover
Good Times (San Francisco), July 3, 1970, vol. 3, no. 27, cover
Good Times (San Francisco), August 7, 1970, vol. 3, no. 31, cover
Good Times (San Francisco), April 16, 1971, vol. 4, no. 15, back cover
Good Times (San Francisco), April 30, 1971, vol. 4, no. 17, back cover

unchained

When the jury came into the New Haven, Conn., courtroom and announced they couldn't reach a verdict, Bobby Seale, Black Panther Party Chairman merely sighed. Ericka Huggins, his co-defendant, smiled faintly. The trial had taken seven months and it looked like they were going to have to go through the whole thing again.

But on Tuesday, after the judge dismissed the murder-kidnap charges against them, they both smiled broadly and embraced. Judge Harold V. Mulvey ruled that it would be impossible to get an unbiased jury for a re-trial. The judge was not being kind. It took four months to select the jury which heard the case and then couldn't decide on their innocence or guilt.

Even for those who cling to the fiction that justice is possible in America, the judge had some sobering words. He said that it was impossible to find 12 unbiased people in the state of Connecticut for a retrial. Over 1,000 Connecticut citizens were rejected before a jury was finally selected last March.

The prosecution claimed Seale ordered the slaying of Alex Rackley, a suspected police informer, and that Ericka had participated in the murder. But the only witness of any consequince produced by the prosecution was, George Sams, the confessed killer.

The jury deliberated for five days on the fate of Seale and Ericka before giving up. The jury voted almost immediately to acquit Seale and all but two voted to acquit Ericka. When the rest of the jury refused to trade Seale's acquittal for Ericka's conviction, the two changed their vote on Seale, voted for his conviction, and deadlocked the jury.

Ericka was set free immediately but Seale was forced to stay behind bars until bail could be obtained on his four year contempt conviction in the Chicago conspiracy trial. It doesn't matter that the government dropped the conspiracy charges against him. They still want him to do time because he demanded to have the attorney of his choice, Charles Garry, who was ill at the time. The contempt conviction is being appealed.

And, if Seale beats the Chicago rap, he may have to do time in Alameda County. His probation was revoked after he was charged in the Chicago conspiracy case. He was convicted and placed on probation for carrying a weapon too close to the Alameda County Jail, back in 1967.

It's also not known how many trumped up charges the government has waiting to slap him with. Someone has gone to a lot of trouble to try to put Bobby Seale behind bars and it's doubtful they're about to give up.

The Panthers won another victory in New York, May 13, when 13 party members were found not quilty for allegedly conspiring to blow up department stores and police stations.

The jury, which sat for seven months hearing the case, took only 90 minutes to reach their decision. This was after Judge Murtagh had carefully reminded the jury that they could consider the flight of Richard Moore and Michael Tabor to Algeria as evidence of consciousness of guilt. He also told the jury that the flight of two other defendants, William King and Lee Roper, arrested later in Ohio, could also be considered evidence of guilt.

It's not known how many thousands of dollars the Panthers were forced to spend on these cases. Both in the case of Seale and Ericka and the New York 13, the defendants were forced to spend two years in jail waiting for "justice".

The Panthers were also forced to divert a lot of energy that would have gone into community organizing into defense. So, the government won even if they failed to secure convictions.

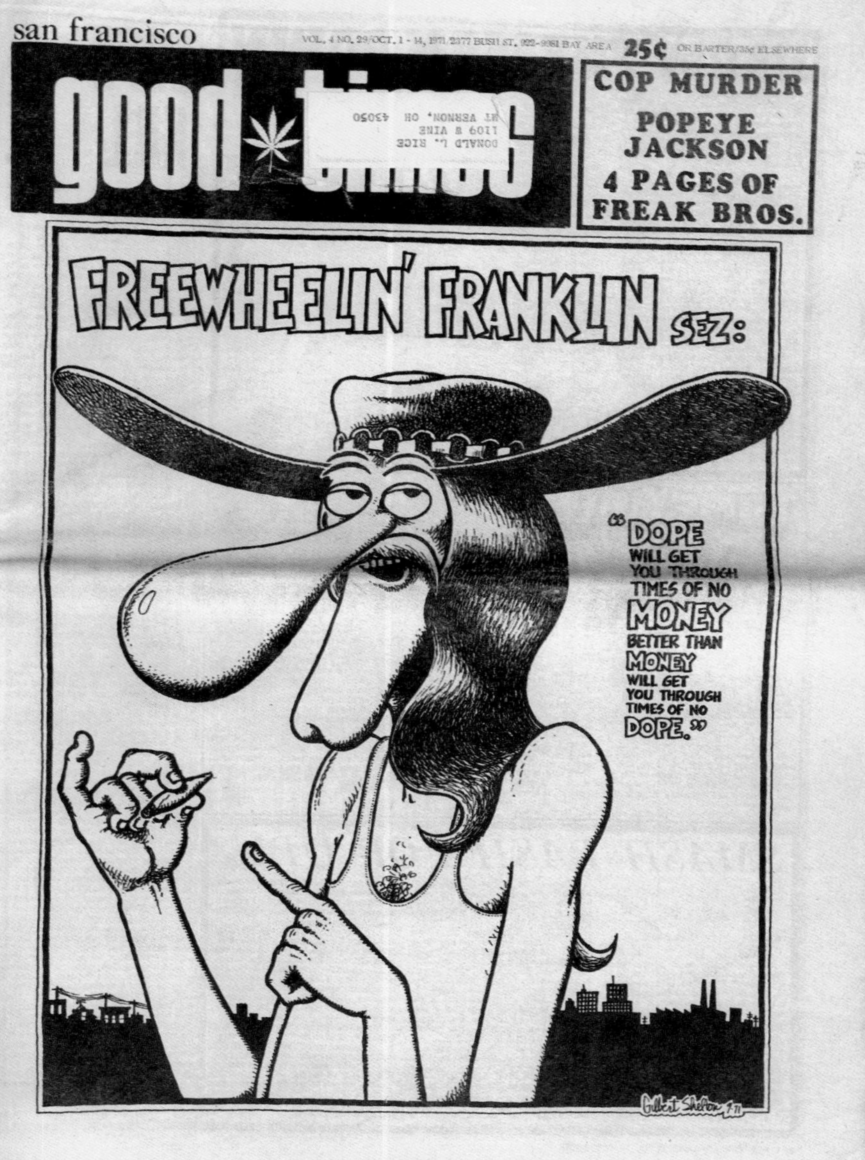

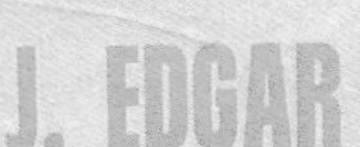

And I hope that you die
And your death'll come soon
I will follow your casket
On a pale afternoon
And I'll watch while you're lowered
Down to your death bed
And I'll stand o'er your grave
Till I'm sure that you're dead.

Masters Of War- Bob Dylan.

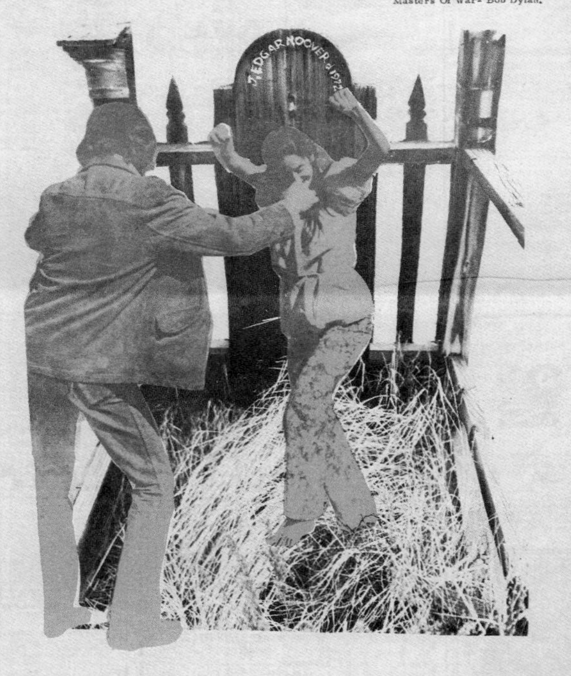

GOOD TIMES/ VOL 5 NO 10/ MAY 5, 1972

Good Times (San Francisco), May 28, 1971, vol. 4, no. 20, back cover
Good Times (San Francisco), October 1-14, 1971, vol. 4, no. 29, cover
Good Times (San Francisco), May 5-18, 1972, vol. 5, no. 10, back cover

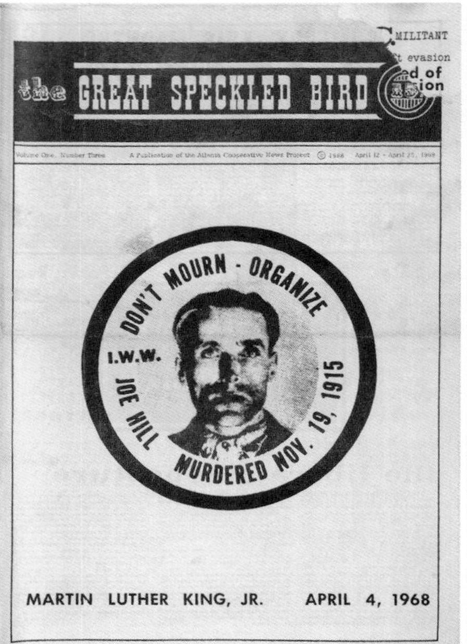

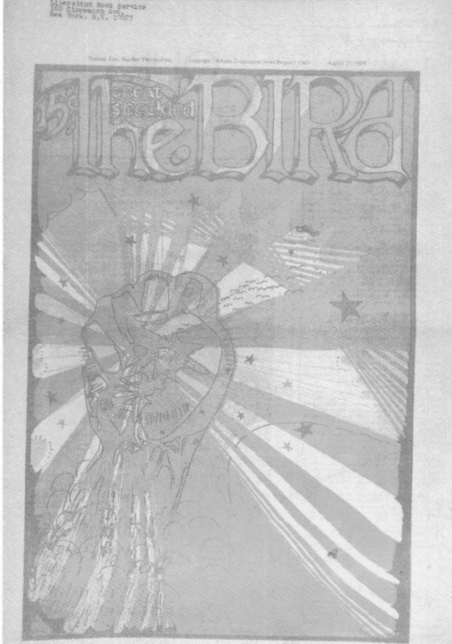

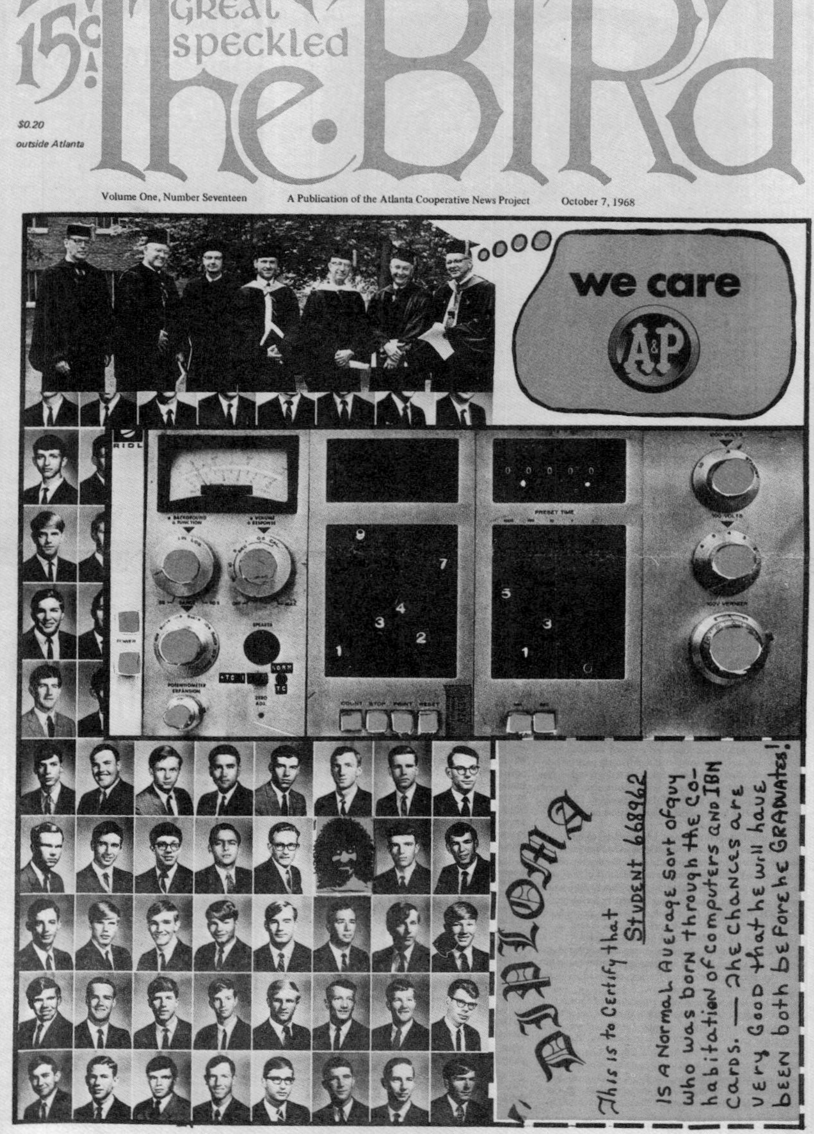

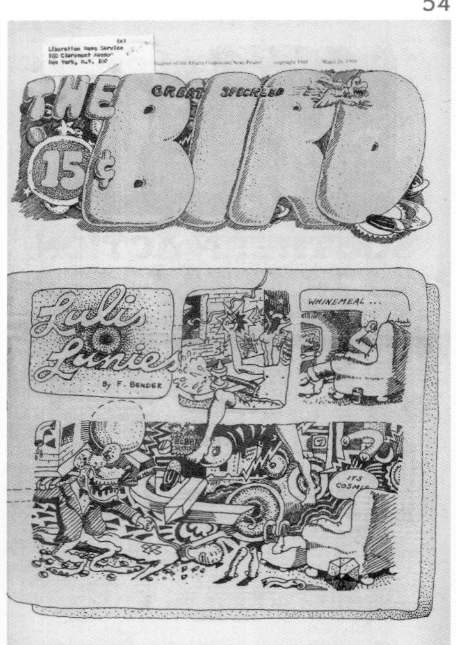

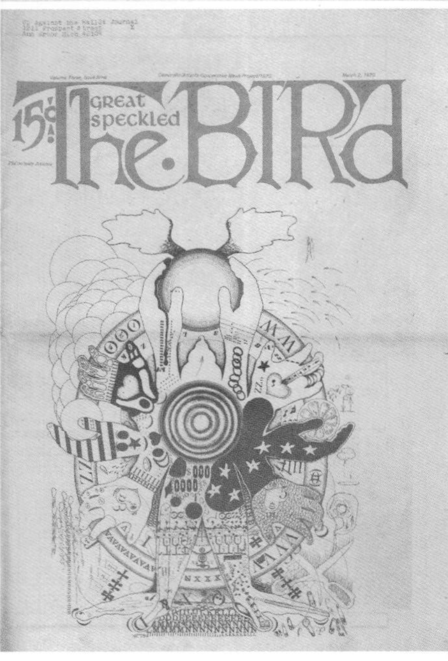

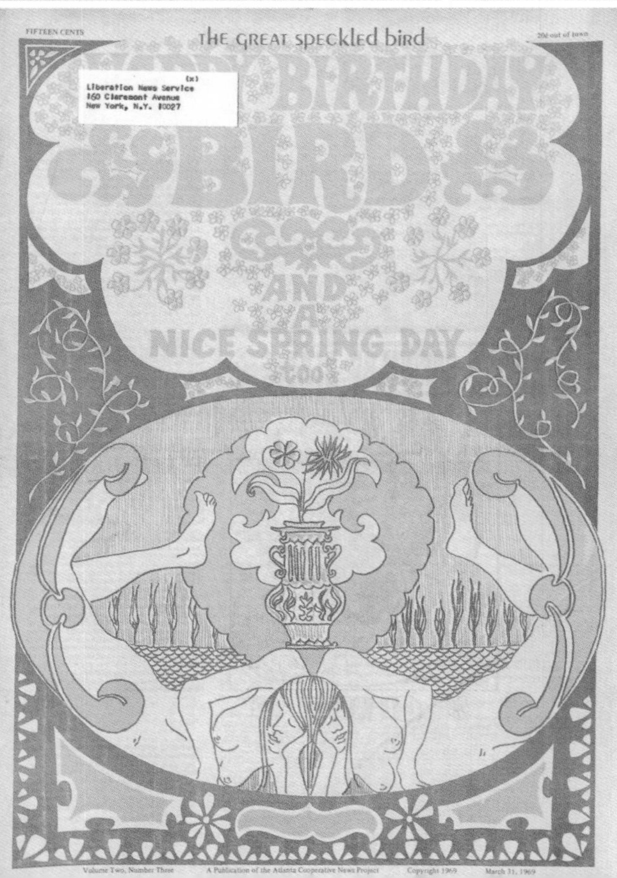

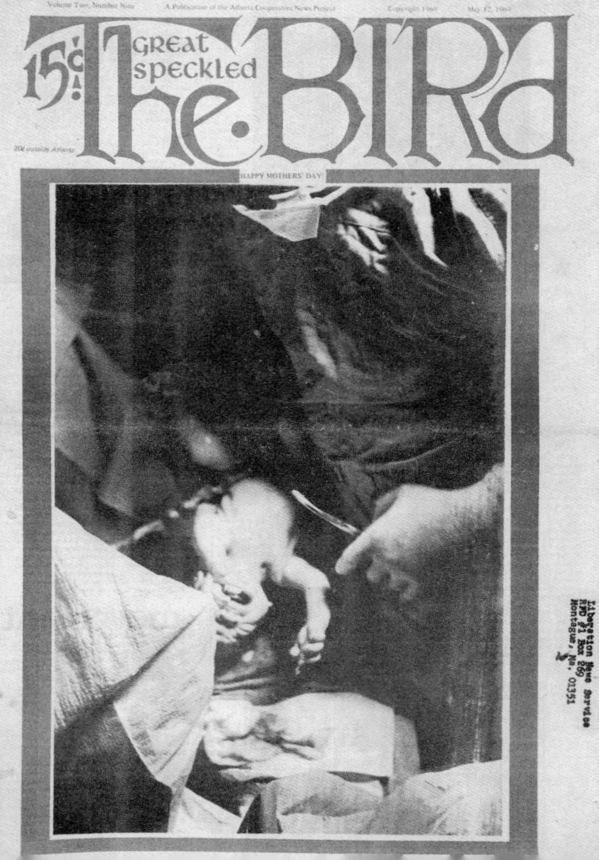

The Great Speckled Bird (Atlanta), April 12–25, 1968, vol. 1, no. 3, cover
The Great Speckled Bird (Atlanta), October 7, 1968, vol. 1, no. 17, cover
The Great Speckled Bird (Atlanta), March 24, 1969, vol. 2, no. 2, cover
The Great Speckled Bird (Atlanta), August 25, 1969, vol. 2, no. 24, cover
The Great Speckled Bird (Atlanta), March 2, 1970, vol. 3, no. 9, cover
The Great Speckled Bird (Atlanta), March 31, 1969, vol. 2, no. 3, cover
The Great Speckled Bird (Atlanta), May 12, 1969, vol. 2, no. 9, cover

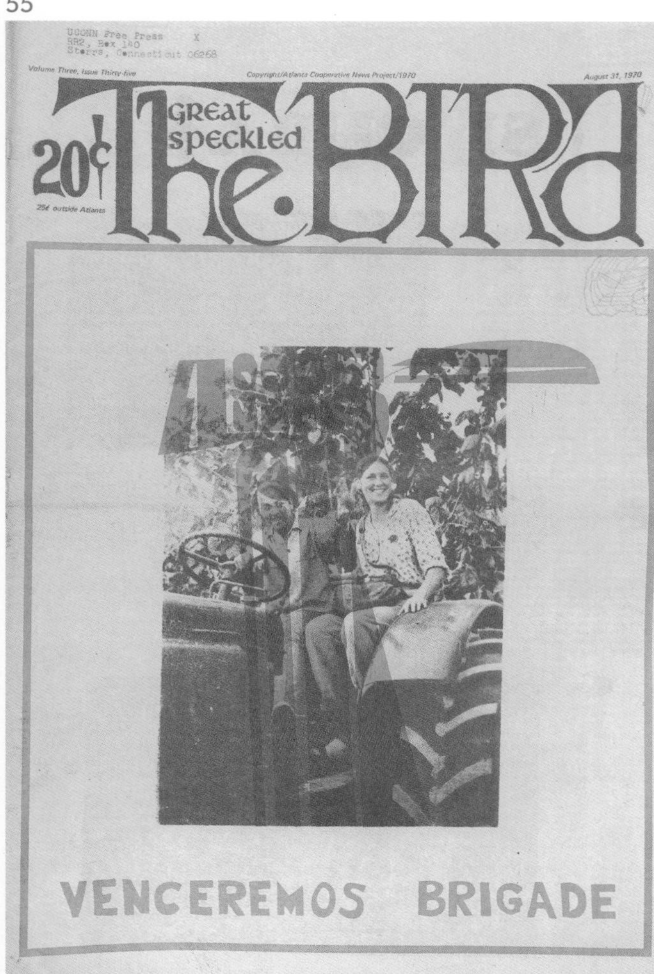

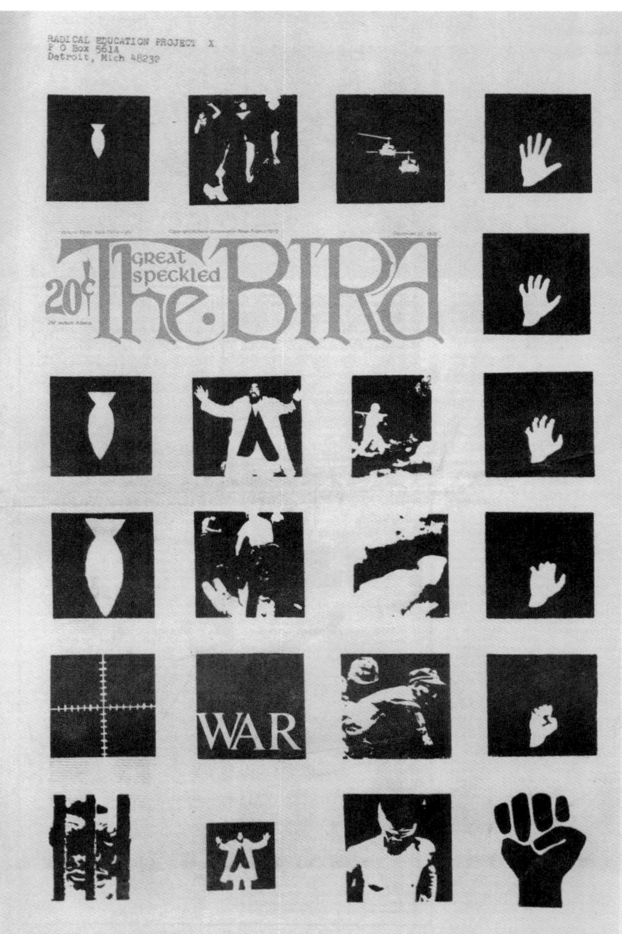

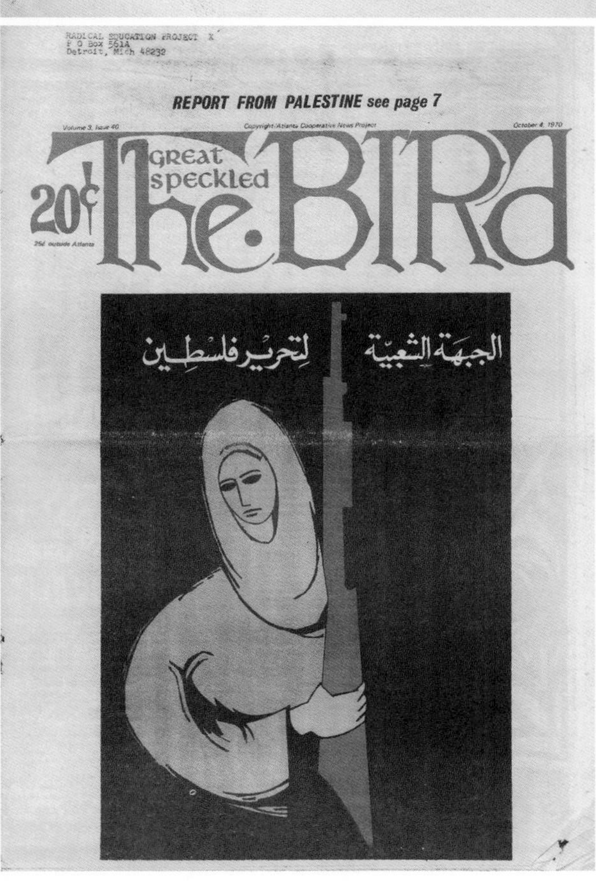

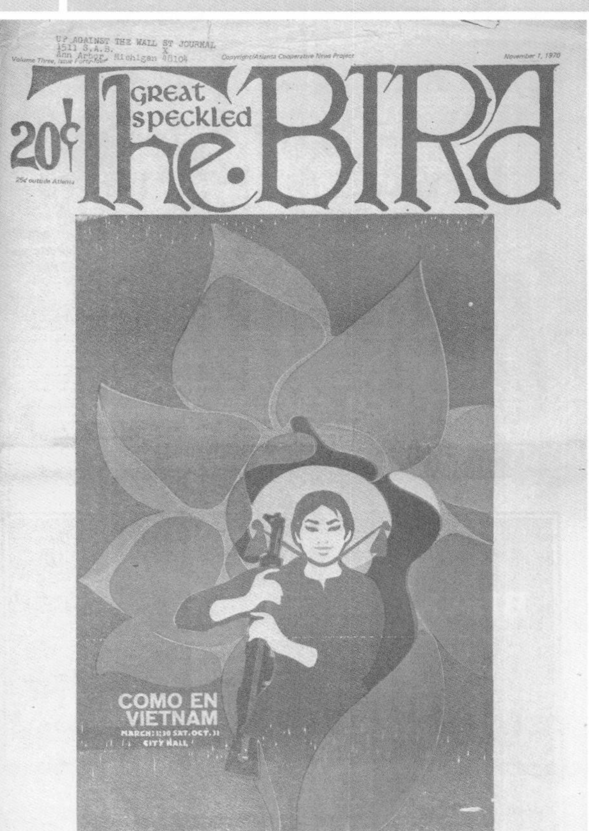

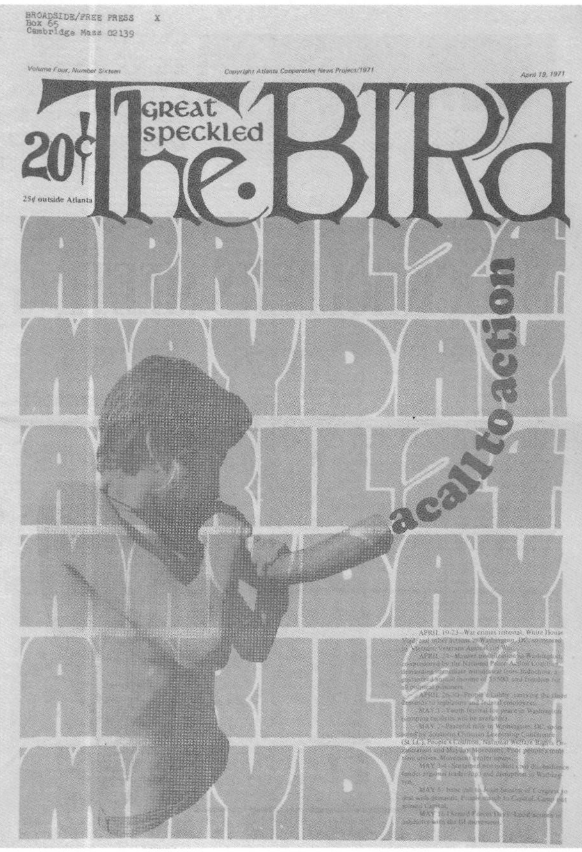

The Great Speckled Bird (Atlanta), August 31, 1970, vol. 3, no. 35, cover
The Great Speckled Bird (Atlanta), September 21, 1970, vol. 3, no. 38, cover
The Great Speckled Bird (Atlanta), October 4, 1970, vol. 3, no. 40, cover
The Great Speckled Bird (Atlanta), November 1, 1970, vol. 3, no. 44, cover
The Great Speckled Bird (Atlanta), April 19, 1971, vol. 4, no. 16, cover

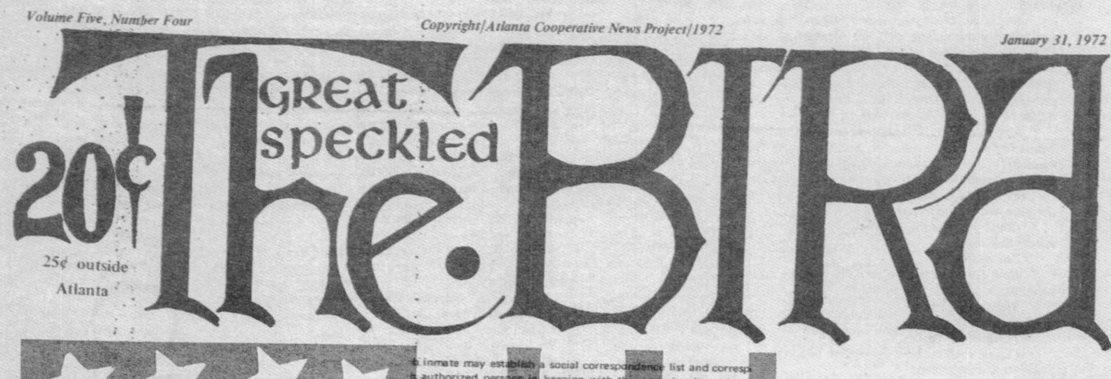

inmate may establish a social correspondence list and corresp
authorized persons in keeping with the general policy relatec
matter.
1. The authorized correspondence list may list no more than
ons; normally all correspondents must be members of the inma
ediate family. The Classification Committee may approve char
his list to include persons outside the immediate family.
2. Each inmate is permitted to mail only two letters per week
ons on his authorized correspondence list.
3. Each inmate is permitted to receive two letters per week f
person listed as an authorized correspondent.
4. Letters, outgoing or incoming, are to be written on paper
than letter-size, 8½" x 11", written on one side only, and
of no more then two pages. Letters must be written in Englis
5. All outgoing letters should be addressed in the following man
8. Business letters may be forwarded and received by inmates,
they are not logged against the social correspondent list. The
ness" should appear in the lower left hand corner of all Busi
ters.
9. The institution will furnish postage for the authorized numbe
letters (2) forwarded to persons on an inmate's authorized co
dence list. Inmates will be required to furnish postage for all
g Business Letters.
10. Correspondants are not permitted to forward newpaper c
s, letters from other people, stamps or stationary in their let
11. Inmates housed in a Punitive Segregation Status will no
itted to correspond on a social basis while in that status. They
ever, be permitted to write one letter to a social correspondе
y them of their assignment to that status.
12. Each inmate is responsible for notifying his correspond
these rules and regulations.

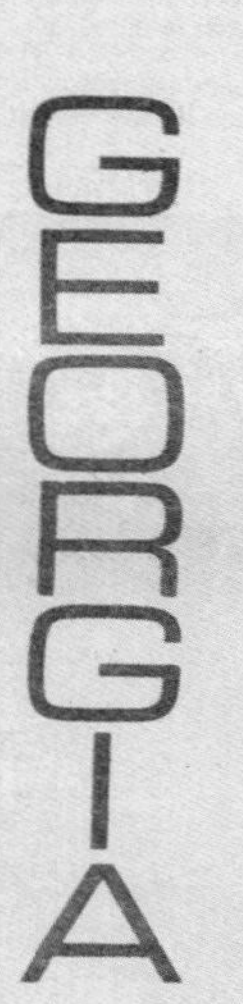

PRISONS

SEE P. 12

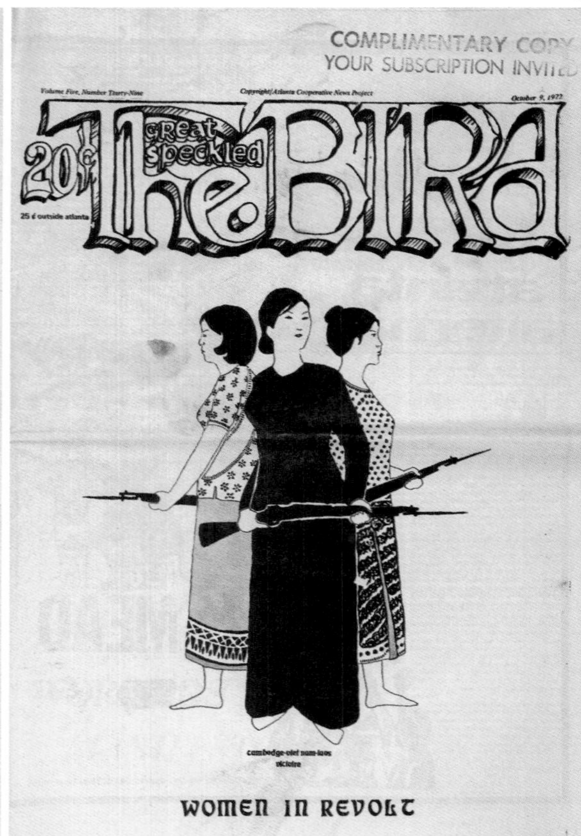

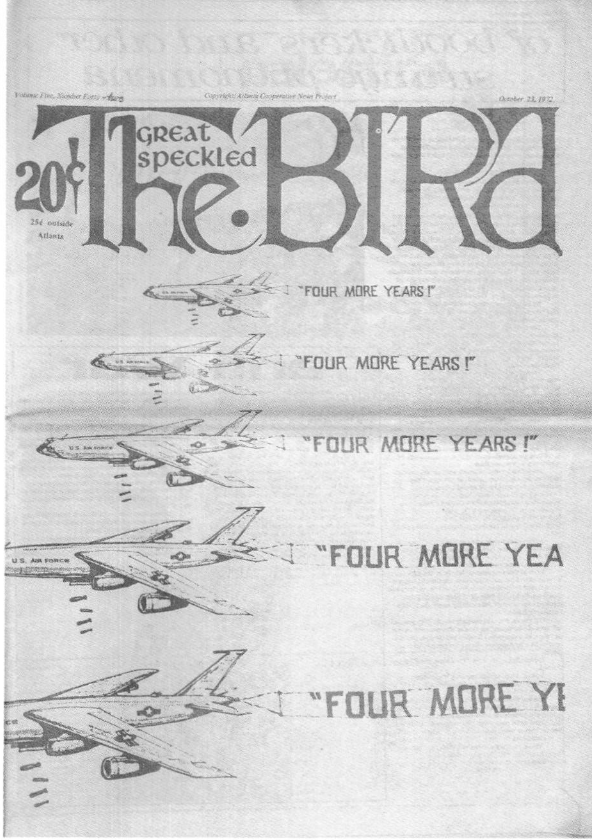

The Great Speckled Bird (Atlanta), January 31, 1972, vol. 5, no. 4, cover
The Great Speckled Bird (Atlanta), October 9, 1972, vol. 5, no. 39, cover
The Great Speckled Bird (Atlanta), October 23, 1972, vol. 5, no. 42, cover

PAGE SIX FATEH MONDAY APRIL 12 1971

IN PALESTINE
WE HAVE
A PAST,
A FUTURE

FATEH

PAGE SEVEN FATEH MONDAY APRIL 12 1971

ISRAEL'S RULING LABOR PARTY WANTS BIG BORDER CHANGES

TEL AVIV -The 3-day Convention of the ruling Israeli Labor Party beamed April 7 a very loud and clear message of expansionism and annexation:

1. No withdrawal to the 1967 borders, and

2. "Substantial changes" in frontiers should be made if a settlement is reached.

The tough talk heard at the Convention -from party hawks and doves alike - was embodied in the party resolution adopted by an overwhelming share of hands at 1.30 a.m.

The resolution said "substantial changes will have to be made in these former border lines." The decision has considerable significance since the Labor Party controls 14 of the 18 seats in the Israeli cabinet.

Speaker after speaker at the Convention affirmed Israel's expansionist and annexationist designs.

It was written into the resolution with no opposition that Israel must retain Syria's Golan Heights, Egypt's Sharmelsheikh, East Jerusalem and the Gaza Strip. It was also said clearly in the resolution that no Arab Armed Forces will be allowed to cross the River Jordan again into the occupied West Bank.

Oil Tankers

TEL AVIV -- Six new oil tankers were commissioned recently on the Eilat oil run at Israel's port on the Gulf of Aqaba. Another six will go into service this month.

This will double the number of tankers feeding Israel's 42-inch pipeline linking the Red Sea with the Mediterranean the line with the Mediterranean. The line is fed with crude from Iran.

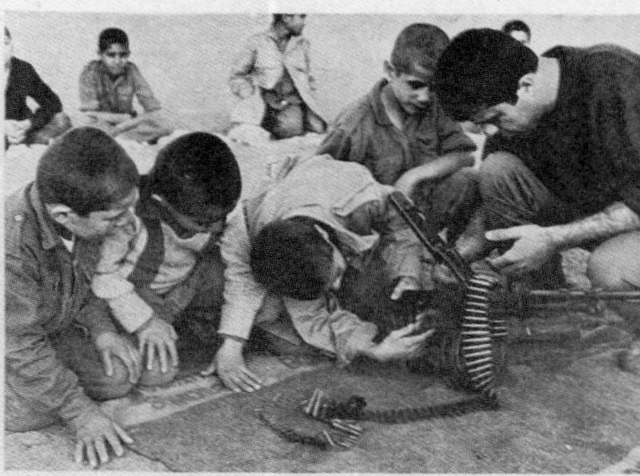

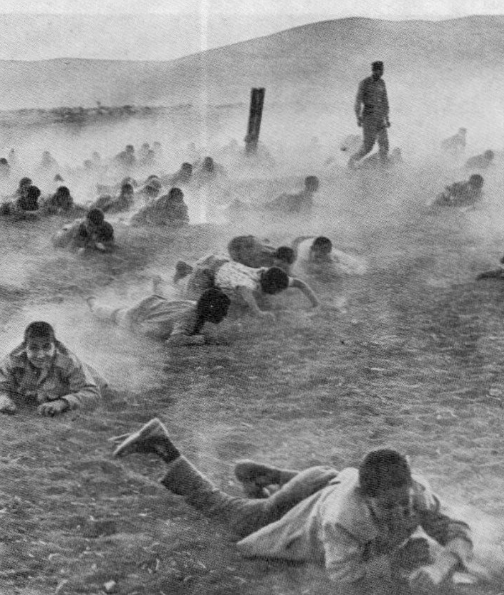

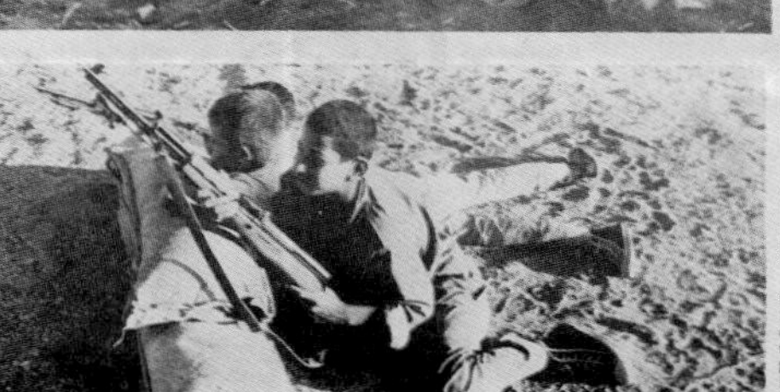

MOBIL OIL LIFTS BOYCOTT OF ISRAELI GOODS

NEW YORK -- Mobil Oil Company has lifted its boycott of Israeli goods for its tankers.

This was revealed by the company's executive vice-president, Hermann J. Schmidt, to Arnold Forster, of the B'nai B'rith Anti-Defamation League.

Mobil's only considerations now "are that products meet our traditionally high requirements of quality, availability and reasonableness of cost." In other words, Schmidt told Forster, ships' chandlers were now authorised to buy Israeli products.

Schmidt announced that the company would advertise in some 100 Zionist newspapers, stating that "there is no Mobil 'boycott.'"

Mobil's move follows the publication of numerous reports in the British and world press, after the Jewish Chronicle had highlighted the boycott.

Ex-UN Officials Rap Settler State

LONDON -- Two former United Nations officials charged Israel March 23 of perpetuating a cruel and intolerable policy by refusing to allow Palestinian Arab to return to their homeland.

John Davis, former commissioner general of the U.N. Relief and Works Agency for Palestinian Arab (UNRWA) and John Reddaway, former UNRWA deputy commissioner general, made their charge in a letter published in the March 23 issue of the "Times" newspaper.

The letter said: "The U.N. formula... declares that all the refugees should have the choice either of returning to their homes to live at peace... or of receiving compensation for their property and help in settling themselves elsewhere.

"By denying the refugees the right to return to their homes Israel has frustrated the choice envisaged in the U.N. formula and so blocked both repatriation and compensation."

The letter continued: "If ever there is to be peace in the Middle East, the world must extract from Israel some substantial relaxation of the cruel policy she has pursued since 1948 of denying the Arabs of Palestine the right to return to their homes."

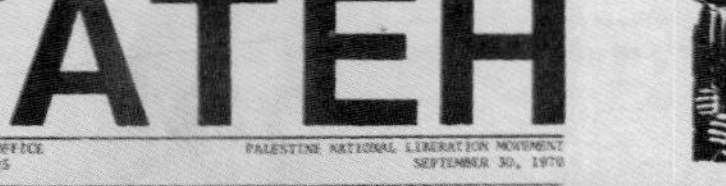

INFORMATION OFFICE
Vol. II No. 15
PALESTINE NATIONAL LIBERATION MOVEMENT
SEPTEMBER 30, 1970

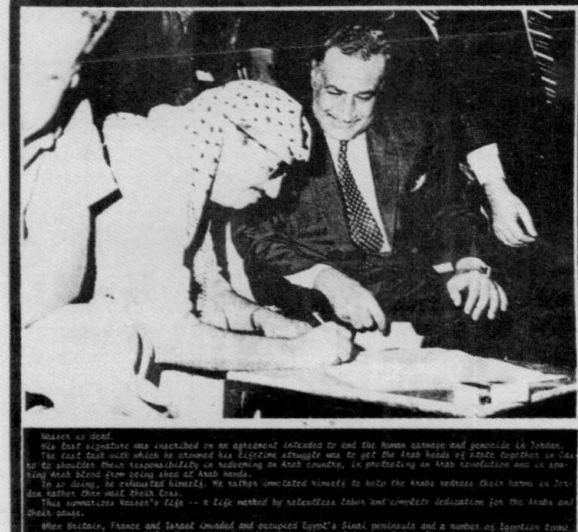

Nasser is dead.

His last signature was inscribed on an agreement intended to end the human carnage and genocide in Jordan.

The last task with which he crowned his lifetime struggle was to get the Arab heads of state together in Cairo to shoulder their responsibility in redeeming an Arab country, in protecting an Arab revolution and in sparing Arab blood from being shed at Arab hands.

In so doing, he exhausted himself. He rather immolated himself to help the Arabs redress their harm in Jordan rather than mull their loss.

This summarizes Nasser's life -- a life marked by relentless labor and complete dedication for the Arabs and their cause.

When Britain, France and Israel invaded and occupied Egypt's Sinai peninsula and a number of Egyptian towns along the Suez Canal in 1956, Nasser stood amidst the masses in Cairo to pledge: "We shall not surrender...we shall resist from house to house... from street to street."

Evacuation of the Tripartite Aggression troops from Egypt spurred Nasser to continue leading the masses in their struggle against exploitation and colonialism. He sought to liberate and protect an area which world imperialism had beset with fragmentation, capitalist interests and a military base.

The confrontation task was too formidable to be assumed by a leader alone, by one movement only, and even by one generation. Nasser paid the price of this struggle from his nerves, his health and his life-span.

From the setbacks and defeats sustained by the Arab nation in its bitter struggle against world imperialism and its base in the area emerged new revolutionary trends, with the Palestinian Revolution in the vanguard.

The Palestinian Revolution set forth with the avowed intention of rejecting capitulation and with the unflinching conviction that if the onslaught of the strong against the weak is tantamount to oppression and if the onslaught of two equals against each others engenders struggle, the onslaught of the weak against the strong alone constitutes a revolution.

No doubt, differences of opinion and over the means of struggle emerged lately between the new revolutionary trends and the Nasserite leadership, particularly in the wake of the latter's acceptance of the Rogers Plan.

But even then, Nasser was perhaps the only Arab leader to realize fully why the adolescents who heard him vow in 1956: "We shall not surrender...we shall resist from house to house...from street to street" have found it their right and their duty to struggle for this pledge in their adulthood.

Who, then, said Nasser is dead?

And who, then, said the Arabs should condole one another?

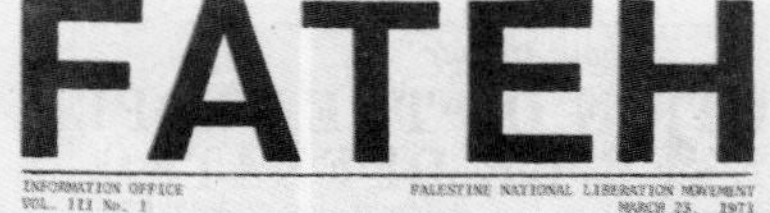

INFORMATION OFFICE
VOL. III No. 1
PALESTINE NATIONAL LIBERATION MOVEMENT
MARCH 23, 1971

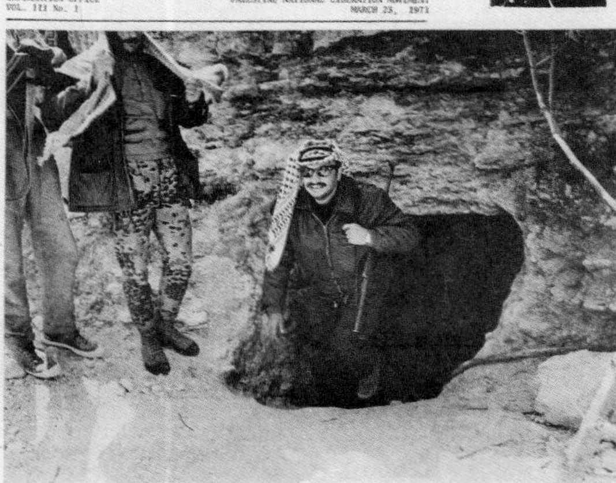

ABOU AMMAR IN EXCLUSIVE INTERVIEW:

- The Year 1971 Will Be that of Epics
- The Answer to the Peace Plan Lies In the Survival of the Revolution
- The Eighth National Assembly Has Endorsed the Democratic State Idea
- We Had to Prevent Genocide And the Creation of "Two Yemens"

Fateh (Beirut, Lebanon), April 12, 1971, vol. 3, no. 2, pp. 6-7
Fateh (Beirut, Lebanon), September 30, 1970, vol. 2, no. 15, cover
Fateh (Beirut, Lebanon), March 23, 1971, vol. 3, no. 1, cover

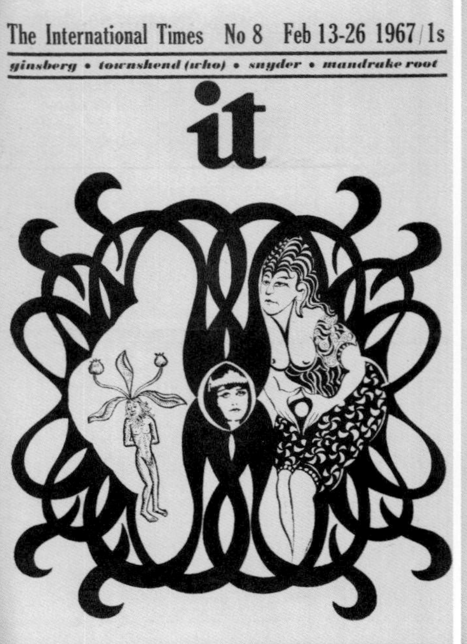

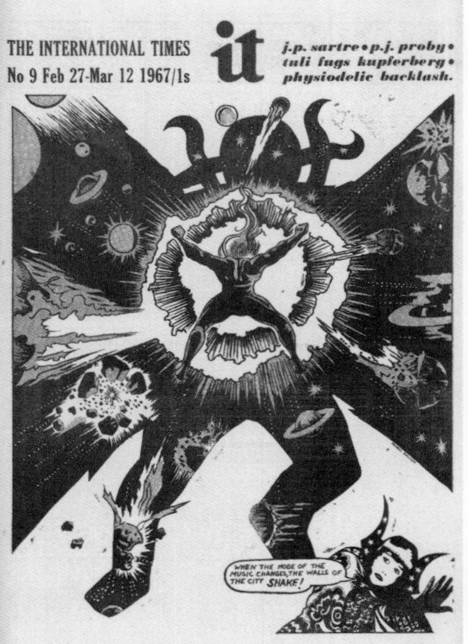

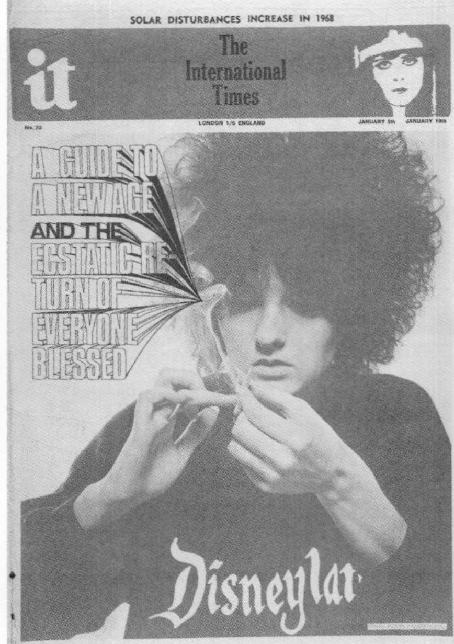

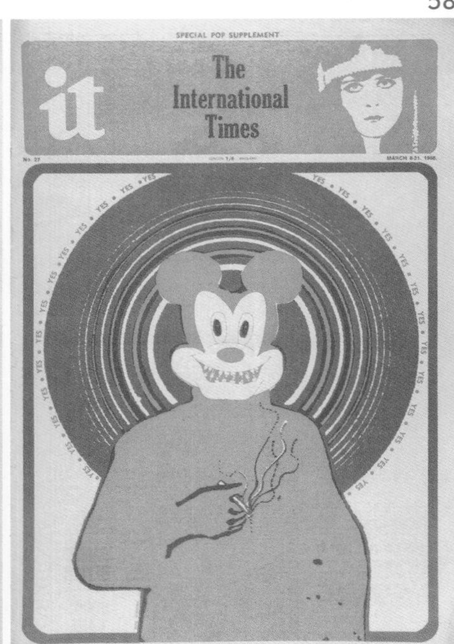

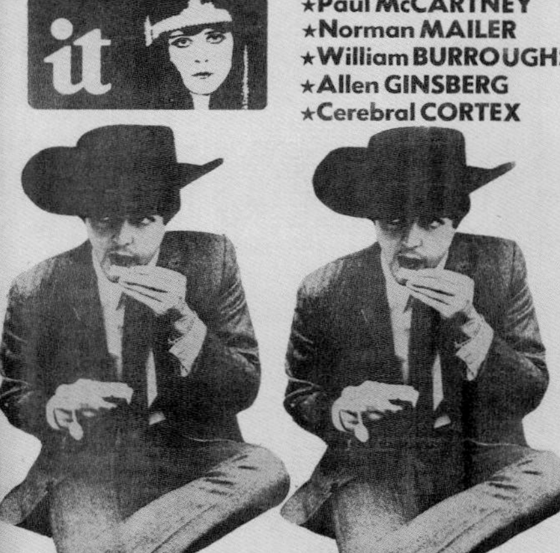

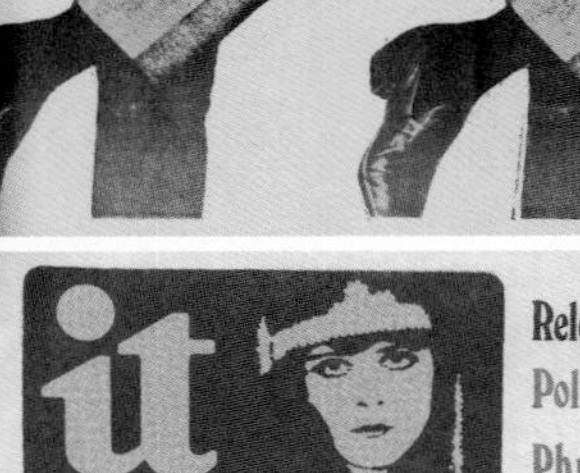

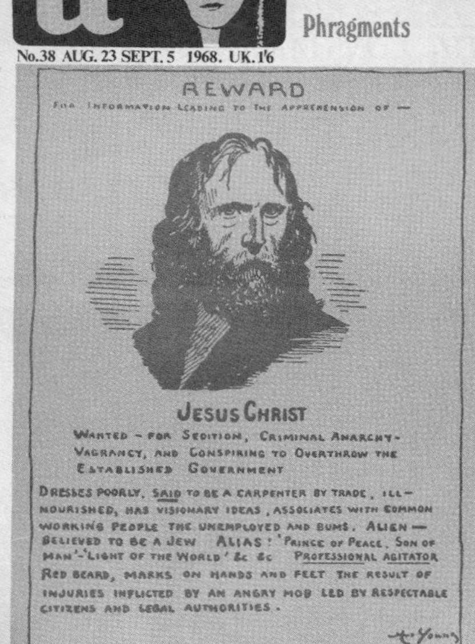

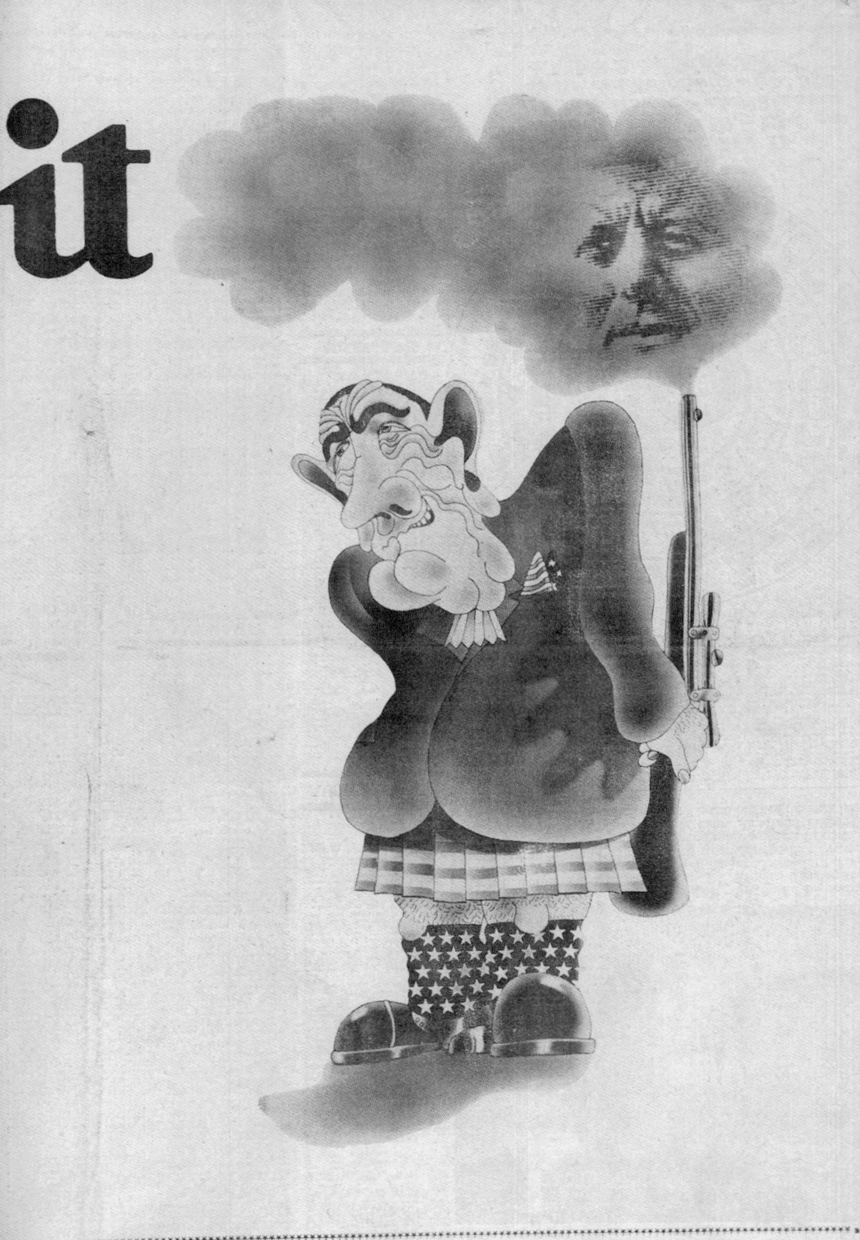

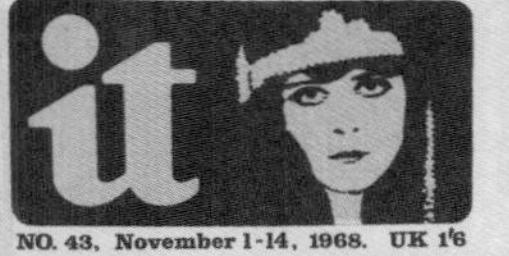

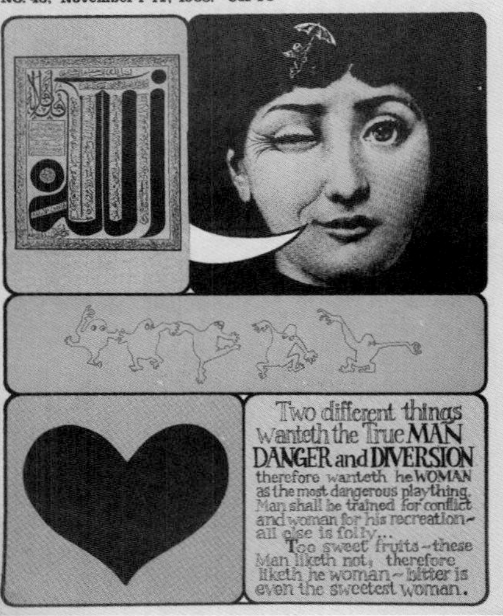

The International Times (London), February 13-26, 1967, no. 8, cover
The International Times (London), February 27-March 12, 1967, no. 9, cover
The International Times (London), January 5-19, 1968, no. 23, cover
The International Times (London), March 8-21, 1968, no. 27, cover
The International Times (London), January 16-29, 1967, no. 6, cover
The International Times (London), March 13-26, 1967, no. 10, back cover
The International Times (London), November 1-14, 1968, no. 43, cover
The International Times (London), August 23-September 5, 1968, no. 38, cover

Next page
The International Times (London), February 16-29, 1968, no. 26, cover
The International Times (London), April 5-18, 1968, no. 28, cover
The International Times (London), June 28-July 11, 1968, no. 34, cover
The International Times (London), August 9-22, 1968, no. 37, cover
The International Times (London), January 1-16, 1969, no. 47, cover

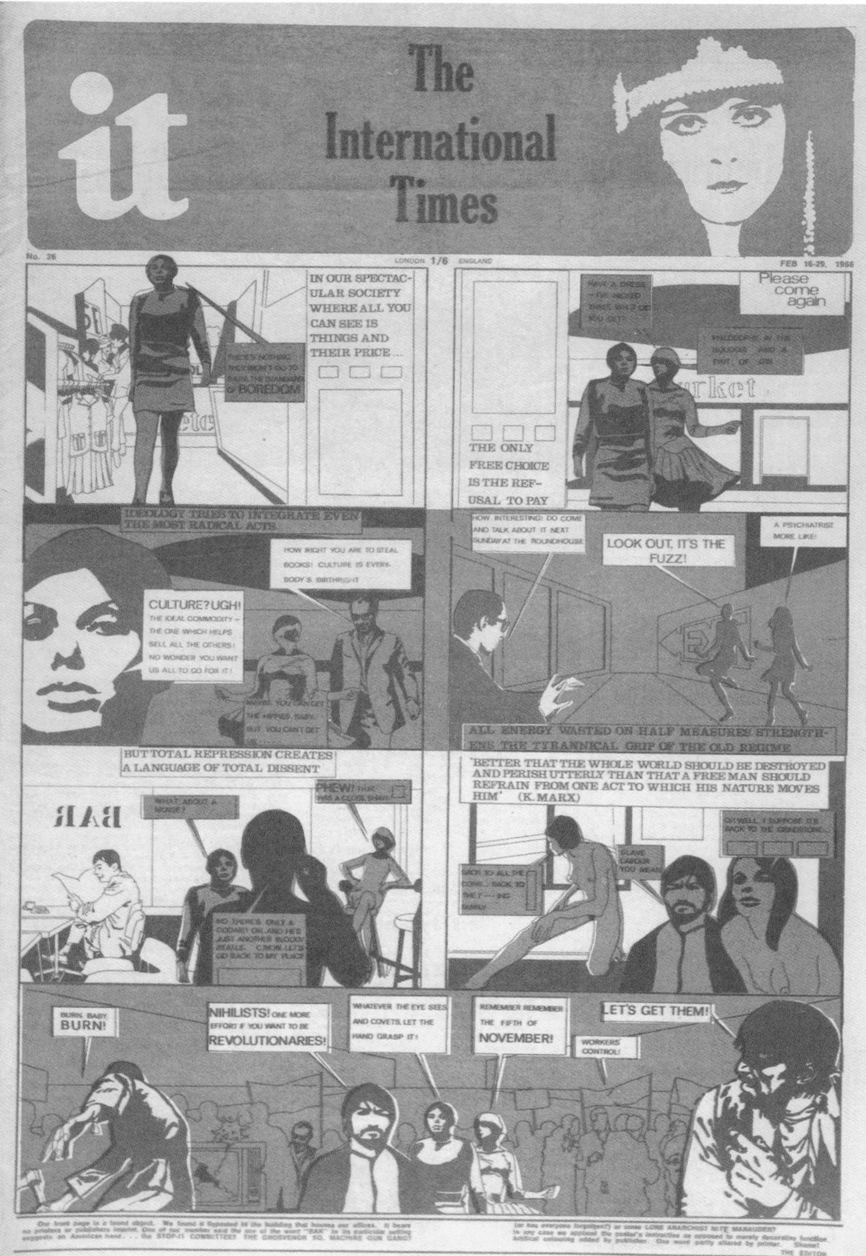

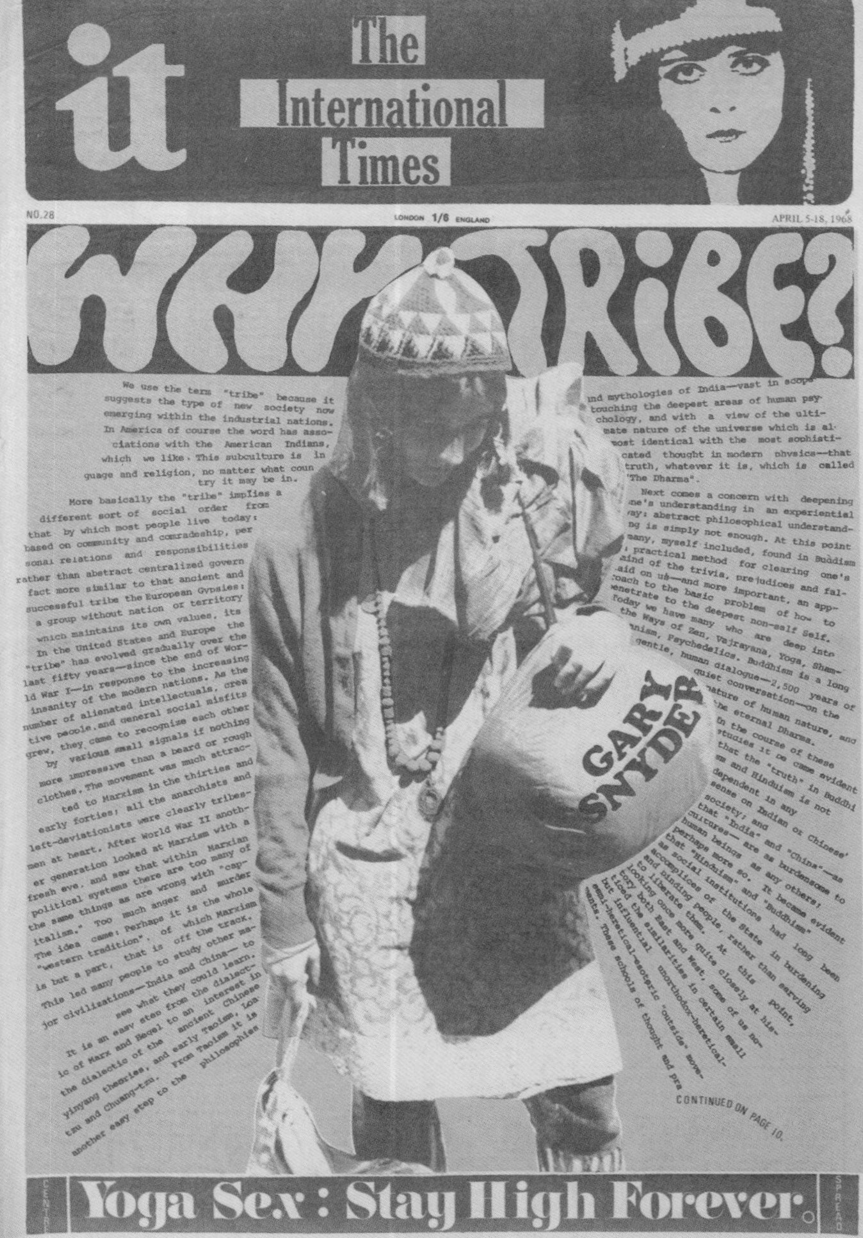

We use the term "tribe" because it suggests the type of new society now emerging within the industrial nations. In America of course the word has associations with the American Indians, which we like. This subculture is in quage and religion, no matter what coun try it may be in.

More basically the "tribe" implies a different sort of social order from that by which most people live today: based on community and comradeship, personal relations and responsibilities rather than abstract centralized govern fact more similar to that ancient and successful tribe the European Gypsies: a group without nation or territory which maintains its own values, its In the United States and Europe the "tribe" has evolved gradually over the last fifty years—since the end of World War I—in response to the increasing insanity of the modern nations. As the number of alienated intellectuals, creative people, and general social misfits grew, they came to recognize each other by various small signals if nothing more impressive than a beard or rough clothes. The movement was much attracted to Marxism in the thirties and early forties; all the anarchists and left-deviationists were clearly tribesmen at heart. After World War II another generation looked at Marxism with a fresh eye, and saw that within Marxian political systems there are too many of the same things as are wrong with "capitalism." Too much anger and murder. The idea came: Perhaps it is the whole "western tradition", of which Marxism is but a part, that is off the track. This led many people to study other major civilizations—India and China— to see what they could learn.

It is an easy step from the dialectic of Marx and Hegel to an interest in the dialectic of the ancient Chinese yinyang theories, and early Taoism, Lao tzu and Chuang-tzu. From Taoism it is another easy step to the philosophies and mythologies of India—vast in scope touching the deepest areas of human psychology, and with a view of the ultimate nature of the universe which is almost identical with the most sophisticated thought in modern physics—that truth, whatever it is, which is called "The Dharma".

Next comes a concern with deepening one's understanding in an experiential way: abstract philosophical understanding is simply not enough. At this point many, myself included, found in Buddhism a practical method for clearing one's mind of the trivia, prejudices and falsehoods laid on us—and more important, an approach to the basic problem of how to penetrate to the deepest non-self Self. Today we have many who are deep into the Ways of Zen, Vajrayana, Yoga, Shamanism, Psychedelics. Buddhism is a long gentle, human dialogue—2,500 years of quiet conversation—on the nature of human nature, and the eternal Dharma. In the course of these studies it be came evident that the "truth" in Buddhism and Hinduism is not dependent in any sense on Indian or Chinese society; and that "India" and "China"—as cultures— are as burdensome to human beings as any others; perhaps more so. It became evident that "Hinduism" and "Buddhism" as social institutions had long been accomplices of the State in burdening and binding people, rather than serving to liberate them. At this point, looking once more quite closely at history both East and West, some of us noticed the similarities in certain small but influential unorthodox-heretical-semi-heretical-esoteric "outside" movements. These schools of thought and pra

CONTINUED ON PAGE 10.

Yoga Sex : Stay High Forever.

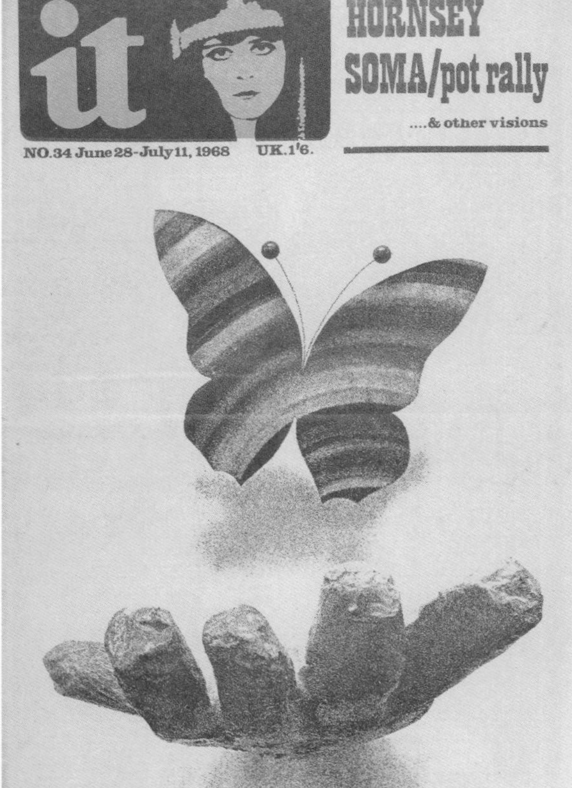

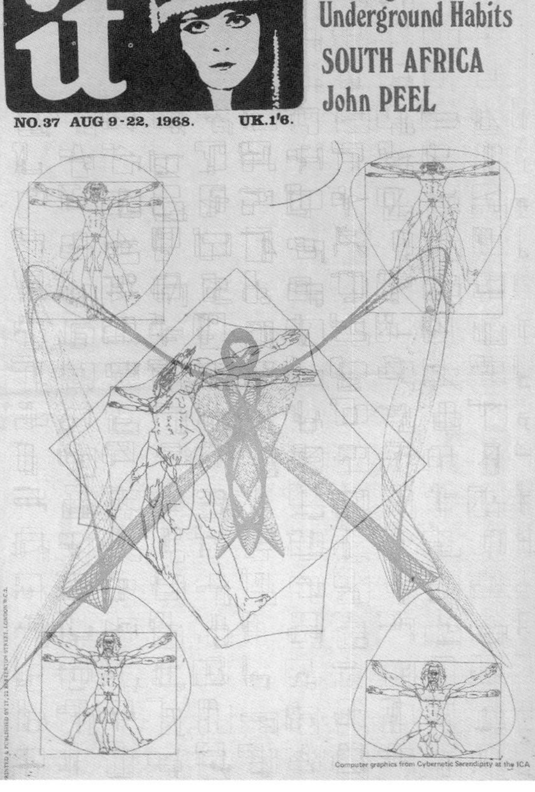

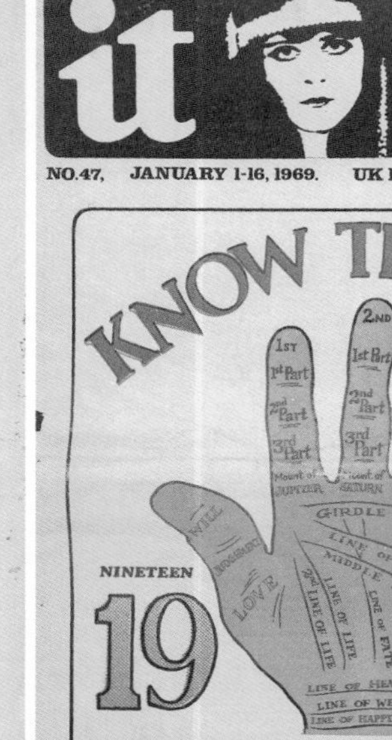

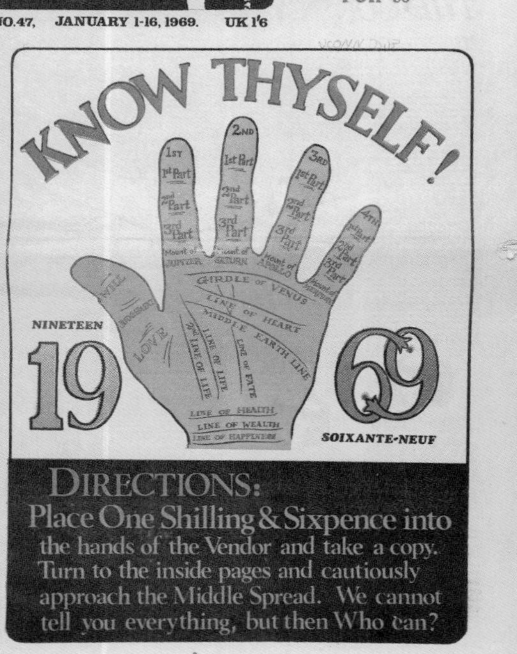

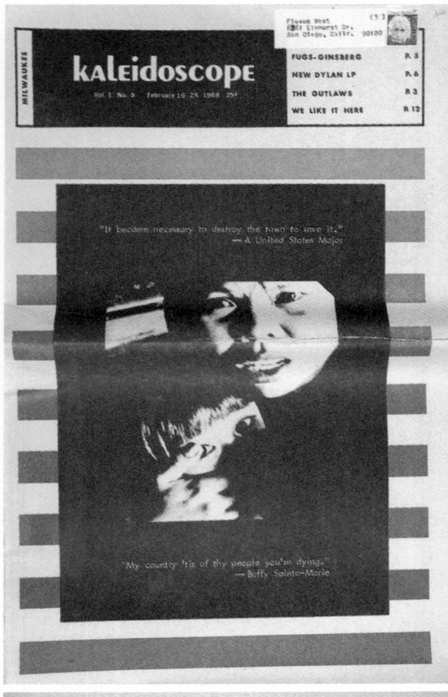

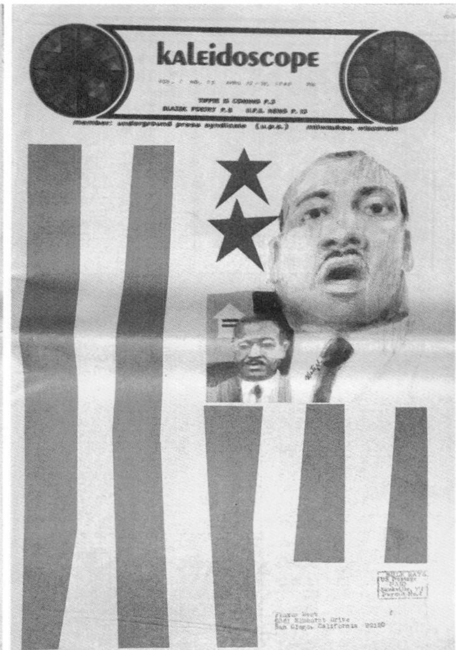

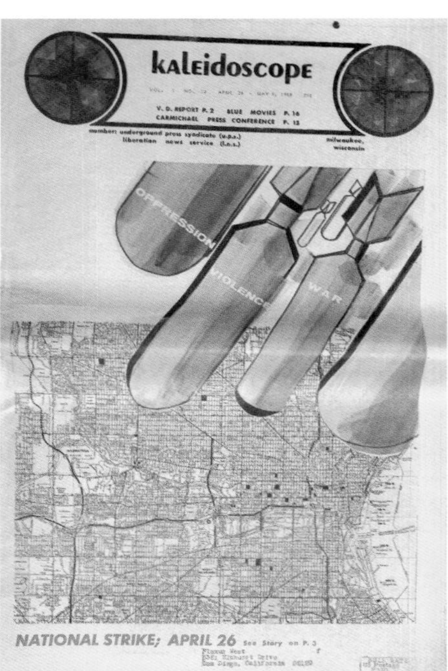

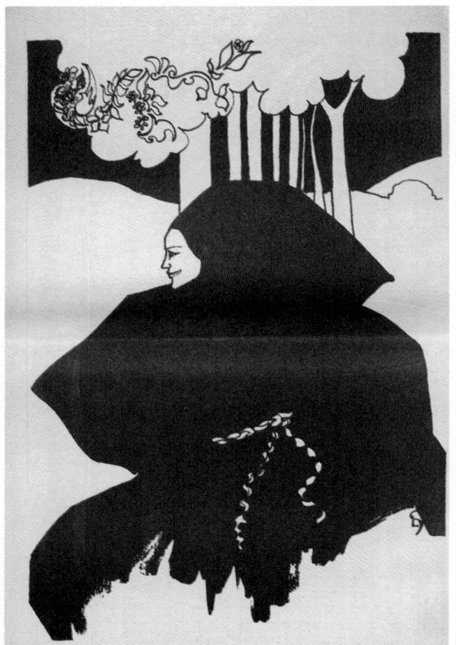

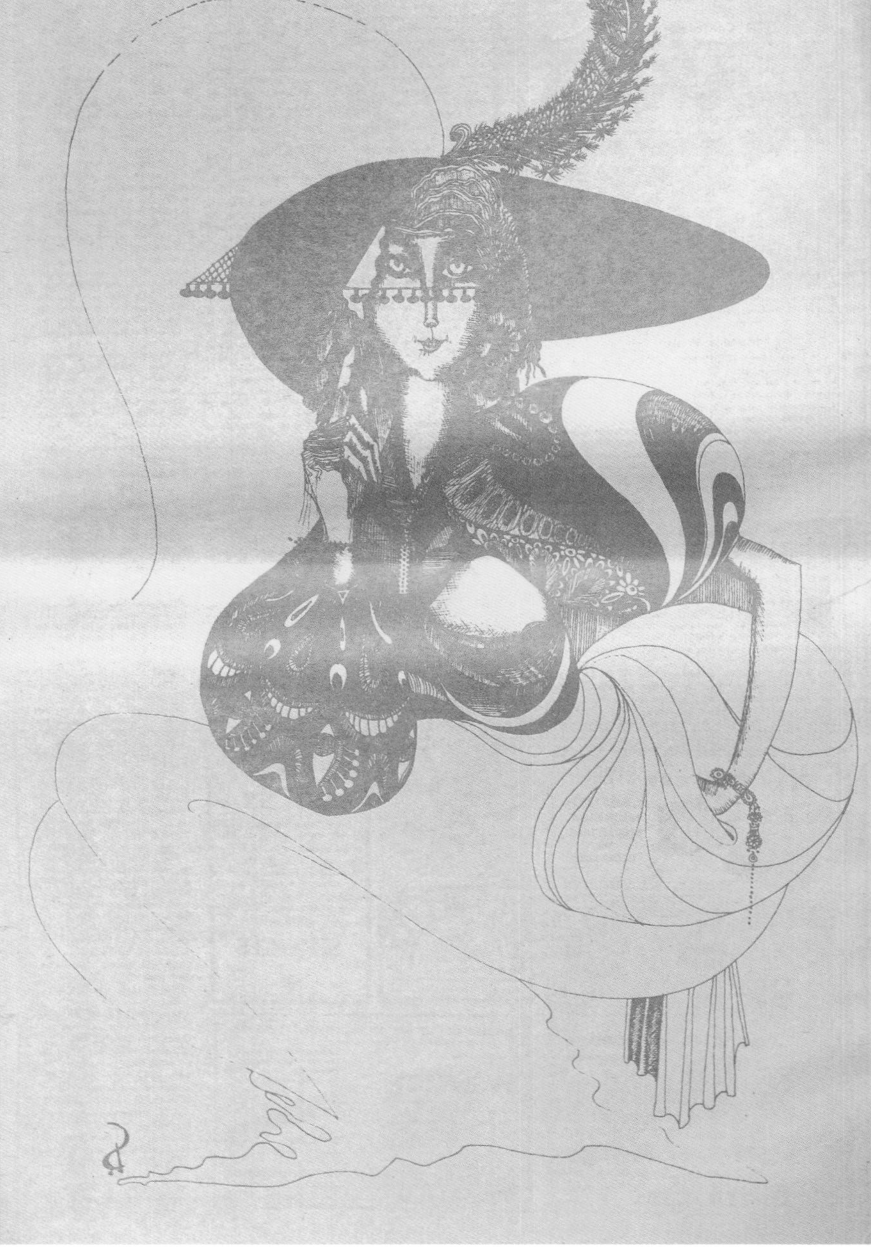

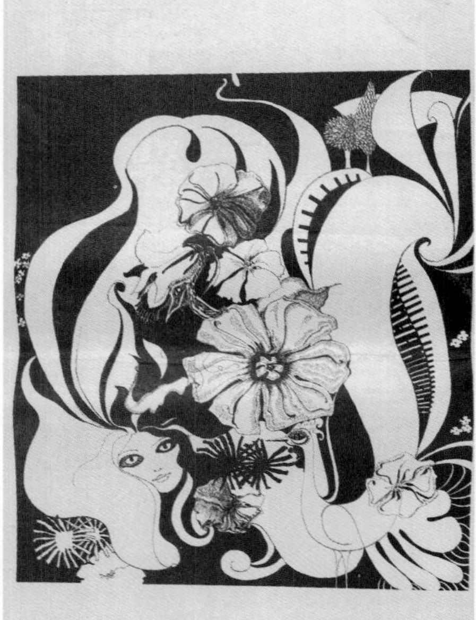

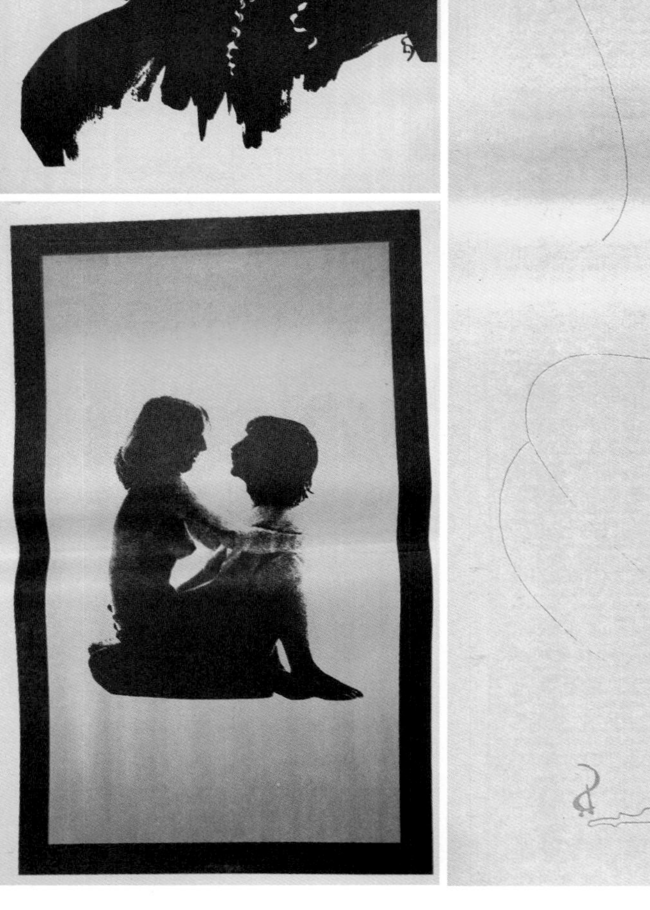

Kaleidoscope (Milwaukee, Wisconsin), February 16–29, 1968, vol. 1, no. 8, cover
Kaleidoscope (Milwaukee, Wisconsin), April 12–25, 1968, vol. 1, no. 12, cover
Kaleidoscope (Milwaukee, Wisconsin), April 26–May 9, 1968, vol. 1, no. 13, cover
Kaleidoscope (Milwaukee, Wisconsin), February 16–29, 1968, vol. 1, no. 8, back cover
Kaleidoscope (Milwaukee, Wisconsin), April 12–25, 1968, vol. 1, no. 12, back cover
Kaleidoscope (Milwaukee, Wisconsin), July 26–August 8, 1968, vol. 1, no. 19, back cover
Kaleidoscope (Milwaukee, Wisconsin), March 1–4, 1968, vol. 1, no. 9, back cover

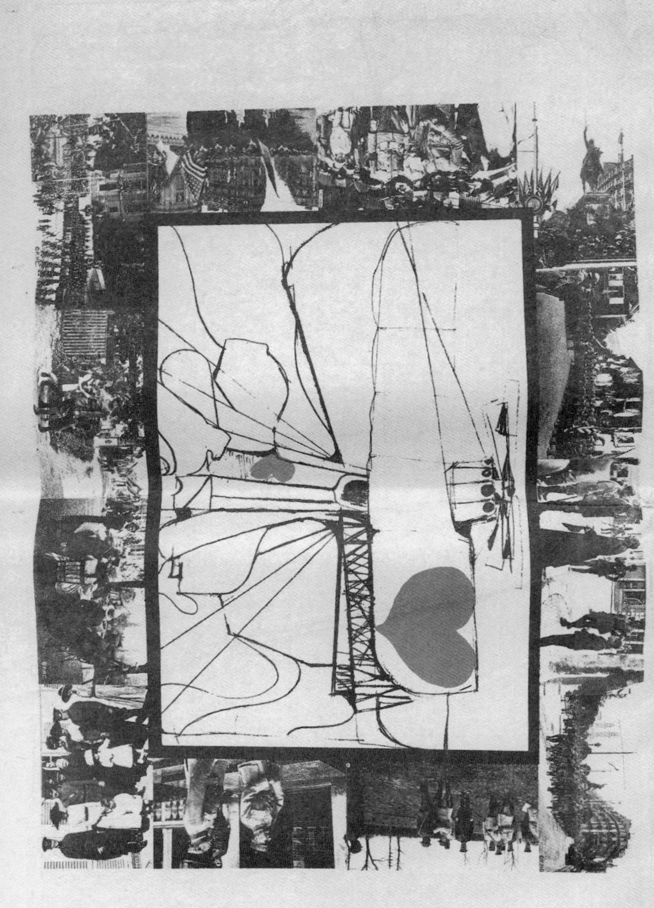

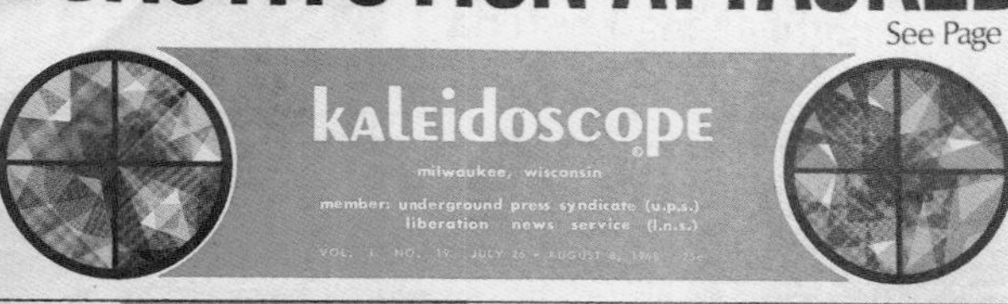

CONSTITUTION ATTACKED

See Page 3

kaleidoscope

milwaukee, wisconsin

member: underground press syndicate (u.p.s.) liberation news service (l.n.s.)

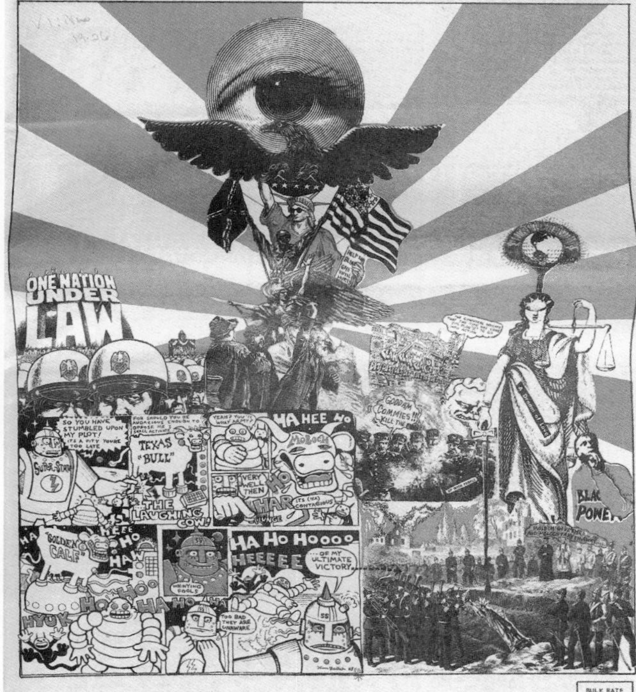

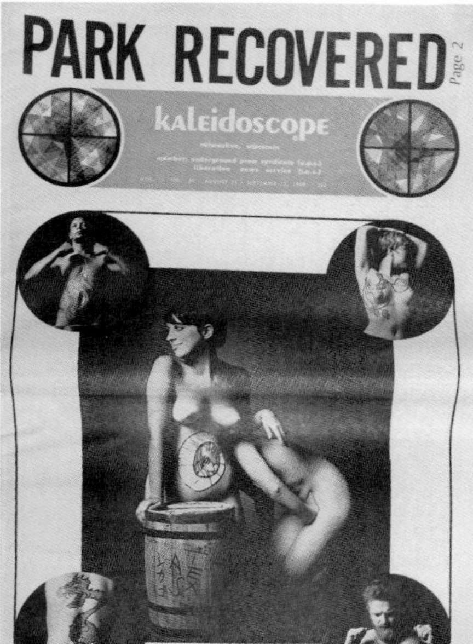

PARK RECOVERED

Page 2

kaleidoscope

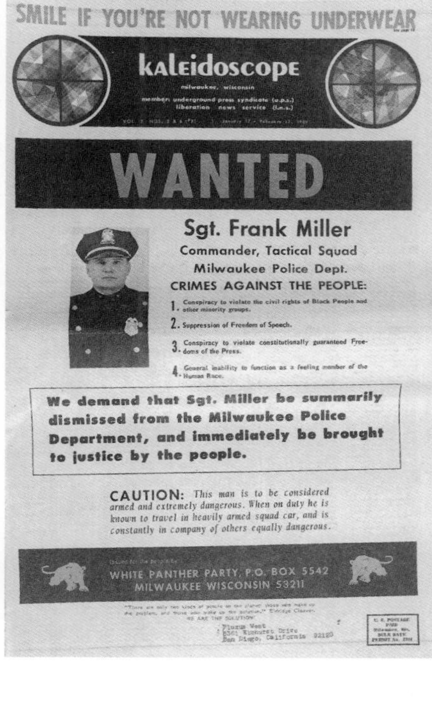

SMILE IF YOU'RE NOT WEARING UNDERWEAR

kaleidoscope

milwaukee, wisconsin

member: underground press syndicate (u.p.s.) liberation news service (l.n.s.)

WANTED

Sgt. Frank Miller

Commander, Tactical Squad

Milwaukee Police Dept.

CRIMES AGAINST THE PEOPLE:

1. Conspiracy to violate the civil rights of Black People and other minority groups.
2. Suppression of Freedom of Speech.
3. Conspiracy to violate constitutionally guaranteed Freedoms of the Press.
4. General inability to function as a feeling member of the Human Race.

We demand that Sgt. Miller be summarily dismissed from the Milwaukee Police Department, and immediately be brought to justice by the people.

CAUTION: *This man is to be considered armed and extremely dangerous. When on duty he is known to travel in heavily armed squad car, and is constantly in company of others equally dangerous.*

WHITE PANTHER PARTY, P.O. BOX 5542
MILWAUKEE WISCONSIN 53211

Fluxus West
8361 Elmhurst Drive
San Diego, California 92120

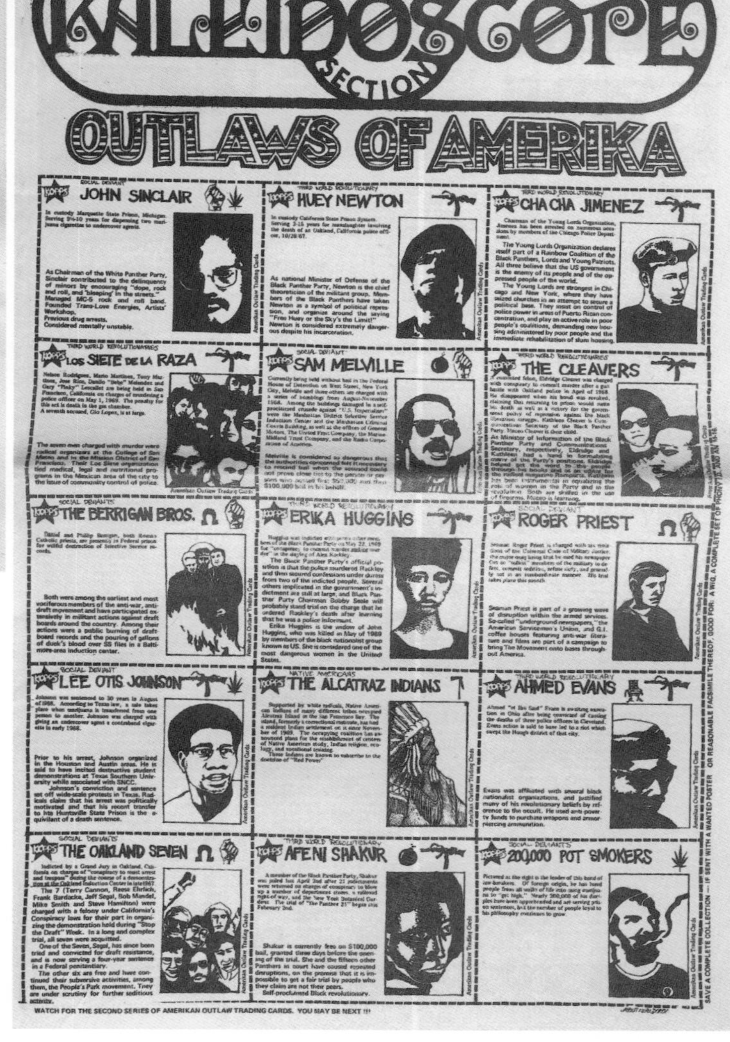

Kaleidoscope (Milwaukee, Wisconsin), April 26–May 9, 1968, vol. 1, no. 13, back cover
Kaleidoscope (Milwaukee, Wisconsin), July 26–August 8, 1968, vol. 1, no. 19, cover
Kaleidoscope (Milwaukee, Wisconsin), August 23–September 12, 1968, vol. 1, no. 21, cover
Kaleidoscope (Milwaukee, Wisconsin), January 17–February 13, 1969, vol. 2, nos. 5 and 6, cover
Kaleidoscope (Milwaukee, Wisconsin), March 1, 1970, vol. 3, second section cover

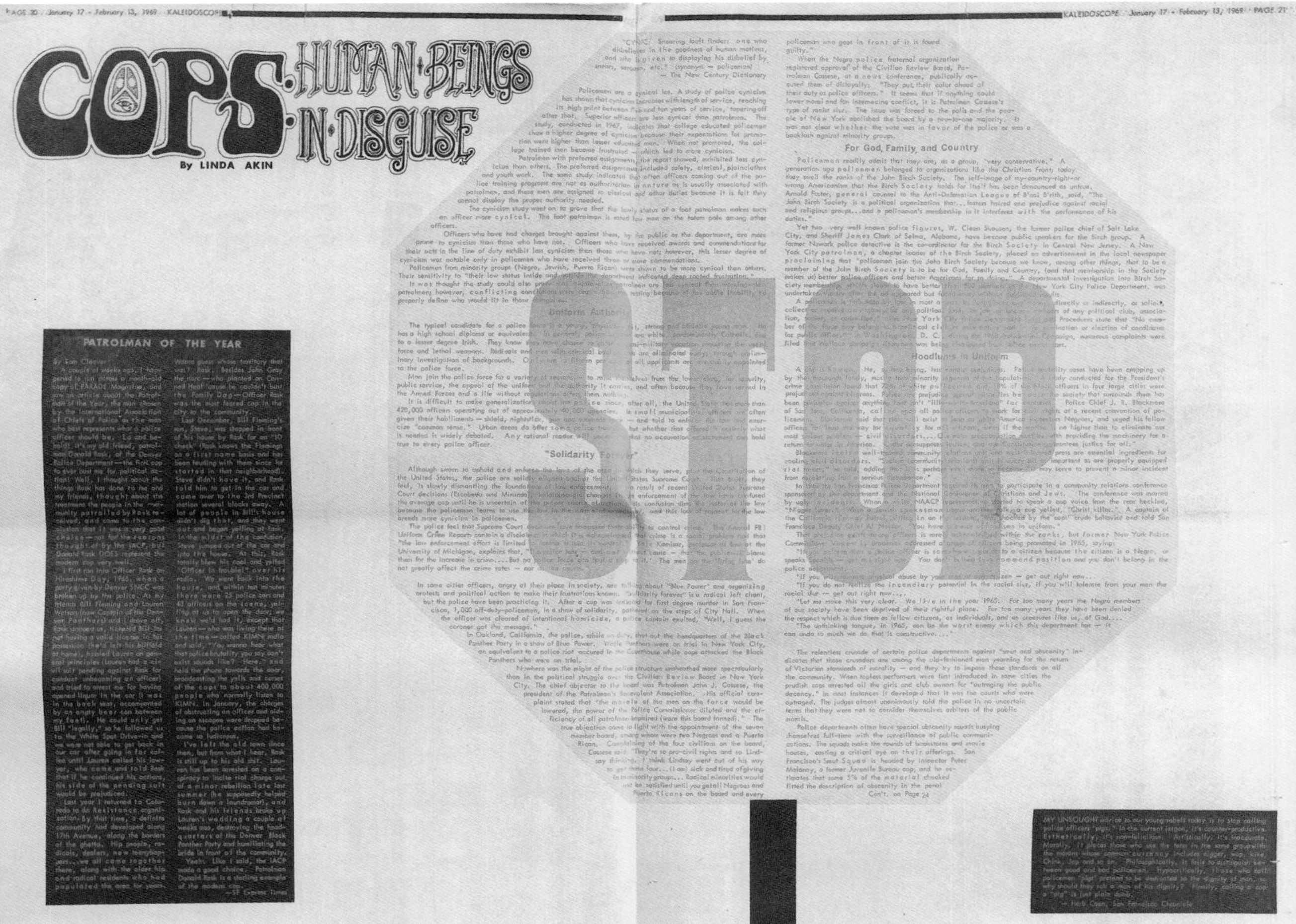

PAGE 20 · January 17 – February 13, 1969 · KALEIDOSCOPE

COPS: HUMAN BEINGS IN DISGUISE

By LINDA AKIN

PATROLMAN OF THE YEAR

STOP

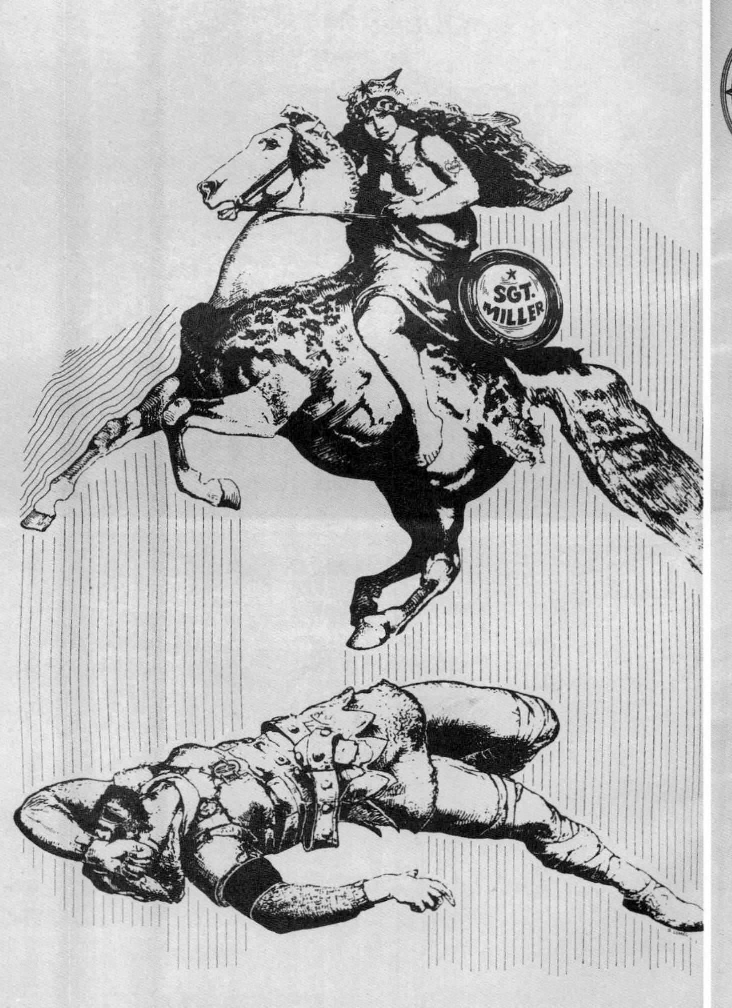

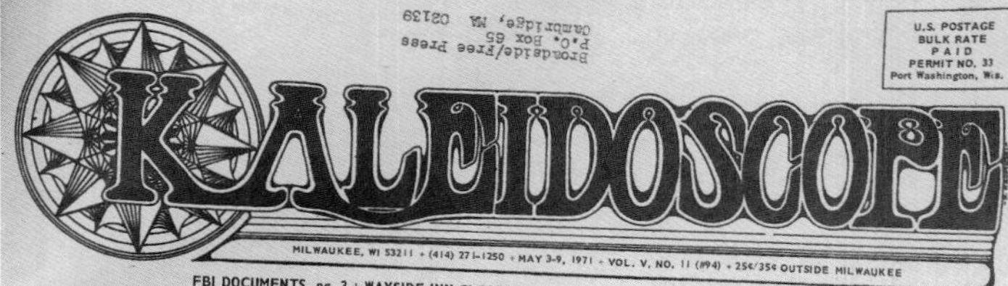

THE FAMOUS REVOLUTIONARIES SCHOOL

Are you one of the angry ones who bangs his head against the wall while all your friends talk about "peace and love" and "reforming the system"? Then why not send away for our simple aptitude test and see if you might not have the potential to become a real revolutionary. FAMOUS REVOLUTIONARIES SCHOOL is the only correspondance school of revolution actually taught by real revolutionaries. You'll receive personal attention in your attempts to off the pig and relate through Marxist-Leninist dialectics to the oppreseed masses. Write in today. If you are one of the first 500 people to answer this ad, you'll receive a free AK-47 and 2000 rounds of ammunition.

SAMPLE QUESTIONS FROM THE FAMOUS REVOLUTIONARIES SCHOOL APTITUDE TEST:

Fill in the blanks:	Multiple choise:
1. "Right__" 2. "Ho, Ho, Ho Chi Mihn/ NLF will surely__" 3. "1 . . . 2 . . . 3 . . . 4 . . ./ We don't want your fucking__"	The chairman of the standing committee of the Chinese People's Communist Party is: 1. Blaze Starr 2. Gregory Peck 3. Tina Turner 4. All of the above

FACULTY

Enver Hoxha Alexander Karensky Kin Agnew
Mario Savio Charles Manson Maharishi Mahesh Yogi
Nikita Khrushchev Adam Clayton Powell Tim Leary
Vance Packard Bo Bolinski Amelia Earhart
William Burroughs John Dos Passos

FAMOUS REVOLUTIONARIES SCHOOL
233 E. 25th Street, Baltimore, Md. 21218

YES I want to crush the state! Rush me my aptitude test and the free AK-47 while the supply lasts.

name ________________

st. add ________________ state ________ zip ________

preferred country of exile ________________

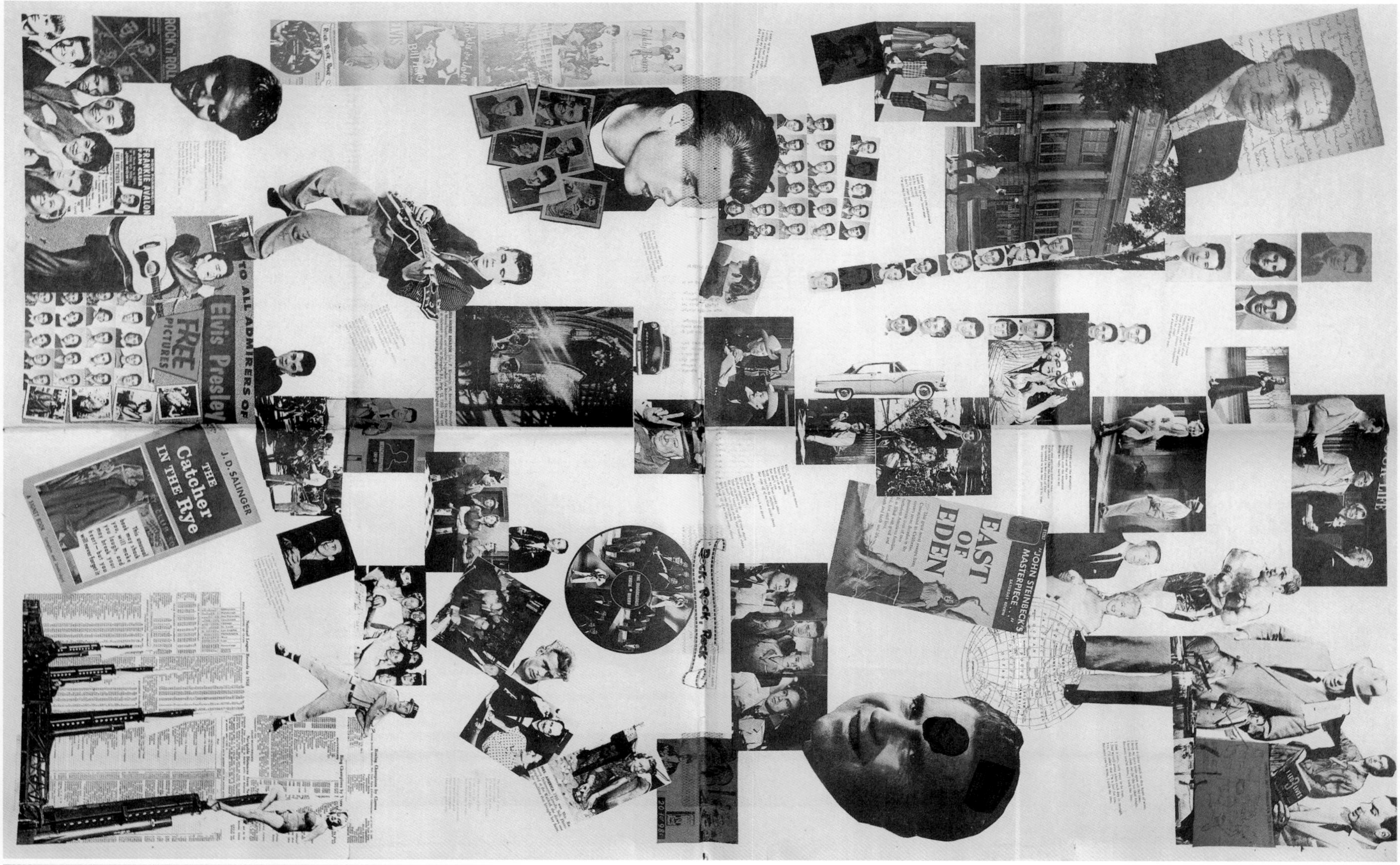

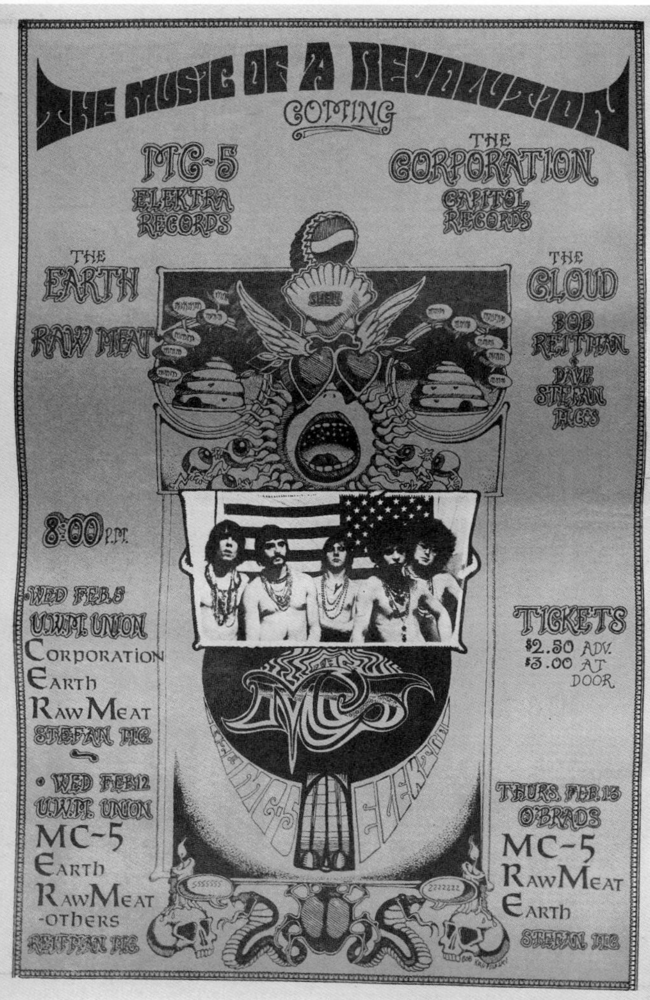

Previous page
Kaleidoscope (Milwaukee, Wisconsin), January 17–February 13, 1969, vol. 2, nos. 5 and 6, second section center spread
Kaleidoscope (Milwaukee, Wisconsin), February 28–March 13, 1969, vol. 2, no. 8, back cover
Kaleidoscope (Milwaukee, Wisconsin), May 3–9, 1971, vol. 5, no. 11, cover

Kaleidoscope (Milwaukee, Wisconsin), January 17–February 13, 1969, vol. 2, nos. 5 and 6 second section center spread
Kaleidoscope (Milwaukee, Wisconsin), January 17–February 13, 1969, vol. 2, nos. 5 and 6, back cover

NOLA EXPRESS

15¢

Vol. 1 #1 APRIL 1968

(Mark Lane Interview continued from page 9)

L - No one has confessed and I don't think you can expect many confessions in this case because if you're convicted without confessing all you can get in a conspiracy to kill the president is 20 years and you don't serve 20 years, you may just serve 1/3 of them. And if you confessed you'd probably be "permanently terminated" by the sponsor.

F - What kind of support has Garrison received from the press or say a "movement"?

L - Well almost none from the press as you know. The press is almost unanimous. NBC had a historically unprecedented program which was the trial of Clay Shaw. It took place on television before it took place in real life. Shaw was found not guilty and Garrison was found guilty. CBS did four, 1-hour programs on the Warren Report defending the Report from its critics and at one point Walter Cronkite said "Garrison has made many charges but he hasn't proven any of them in court." In fact Garrison has made two charges, one against Dean Andrews for perjury in a case closely related to the assassination investigation and the other against Clay Shaw. It's true he hasn't proven the guilt of Shaw because for over a year now Shaw has been doing everything to prevent that case from coming to trial. About Dean Andrews - 3 days after Cronkite said Garrison had not proven anything in court, Dean Andrews was convicted of perjury. I watched television the next night to see how Cronkite was going to explain this but he never did. The only movement which has supported Garrison has been the Citizens Committee of Inquiry on various college campuses and cities which were established early after the assassination for the purpose of making the facts known. Of course RAMPARTS magazine has been very helpful in terms of publishing new material but one of the things that dismays me, that while one would expect attacks from the right, one would expect the left to have a more sophisticated view, a knowledgeable view of what takes place in this society. One would expect the left to support Garrison but the left seems to be sitting back watching, waiting very cautiously. That's not the position the left should be taking at the present time it seems to me. One of the problems is the atmosphere around to convince us that Garrison is some kind of nut. One listens long enough and tends to believe it and gives that as an excuse for not participating. I think that's unforgiveable.

F - I think one of the problems is that even assuming everything Garrison says is true, what happens is that as you say you have to get three new letters for the agency and everything is the same again. There have been heads of states assassinated in other countries and nothing changes. Why should it be different here?

L - Well that's a very cynical view by those who are sitting back and taking no position right now and saying that the truth is not sufficient, the truth must do that which we want it to do; the abstract truth is not sufficient. But I think things will change - comes the conclusion that the CIA, an agency of the federal govt, killed President Kennedy, things can never again be exactly the same in America. I don't think a revolution will take place the next day. I don't think there'll be rioting in the streets either, but I think there'll be a change in America and a healthy change.

F - I know your position on the war in Vietnam. What is Garrison's view on the war?

L - I spoke at the La. Polytechnic Institute about 4 months ago. Garrison had been there just a year ago, that was before his investigation began, and they asked if he'd go back to discuss the assassination and I said I'd raise the issue with him. I saw him the next day and told him I was there. He said "I was there a year ago. Did they tell you." I said yes they told me. He said "Did they tell you what I talked about there." I said no. He said "I was a lieutenant colonel in the active reserve. I spoke in favor of the war in Vietnam." He blushed. He said that in his 40's when he came across the Warren Commission report and the contradictions and he began his investigation, he realized for the first time that honorable men had issued this false report. It brought a great change in his thinking. He is now wholeheartedly against the war in Vietnam and has resigned as a lieutenant colonel in the active reserve and he believes in the very near future there will be an American Dienbienphu. He says the American people probably don't realize that those in this country and outside this country who oppose our policy in Vietnam are the only ones today defending Americas freedom.

NOLA EXPRESS c/o SDS-DRU
Box 2497, New Orleans La 70116

3rd class / return requested

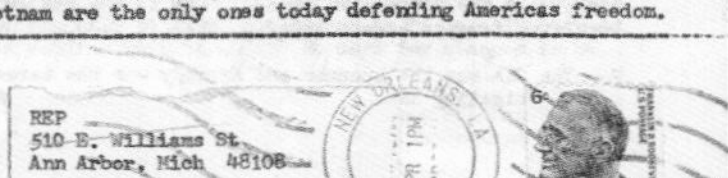

No. 3 NOLA EXPRESS

15¢

Tulane University Placement Office had been referring students in need of temporary employment to the Southern Bell Office. On Monday, Tulane SDS went in and had a talk with the Placement Office. A while later, another student went in looking for work. There was no mention made of Southern Bell.

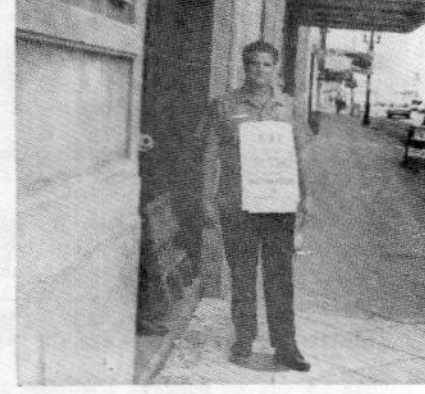

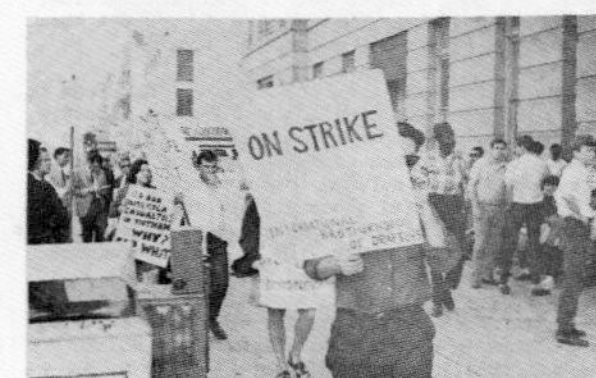

Communication Workers of America on strike against the Western Electric Co., a wholly-owned subsidiary of A.T. & T.

Tulane SDS, Student Liberal Federation (LSUNO), MDS, Spartacist, and Draft Resisters Union Local #3 picket New Orleans Customhouse Induction Center at Joe Verret's pre-induction physical - April 23,6:30 AM

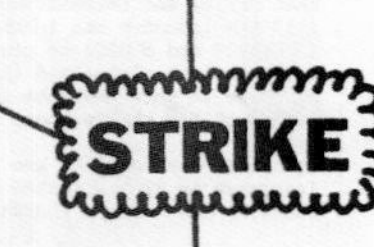

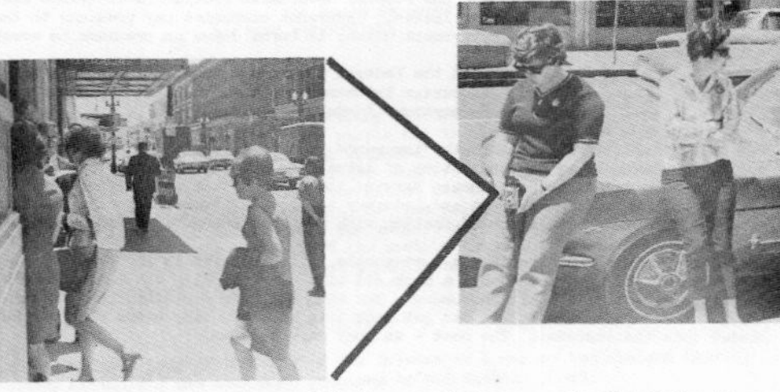

"There's the women. They're the worst!" A group of five women hesitated when they saw another group of women leaning against a car parked in front of the Southern Bell office at Poydras and Baronne. They hesitated for a few seconds and then walked past the other women and into the building. As they passed, one said,"we have to eat." The other group of women watched. One took pictures as they entered the building. One commented, "They must be the new trainees." Another said,"JUST PLAIN SCABS."

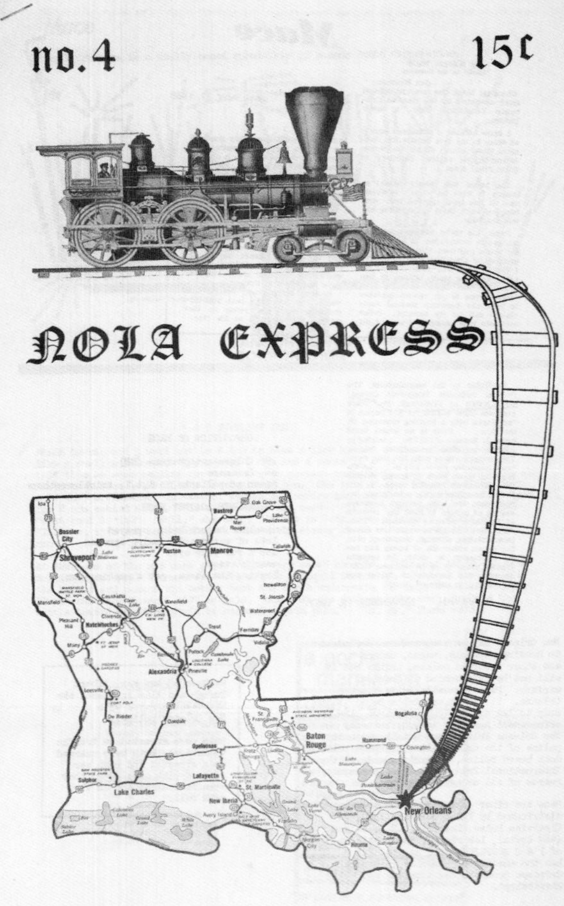

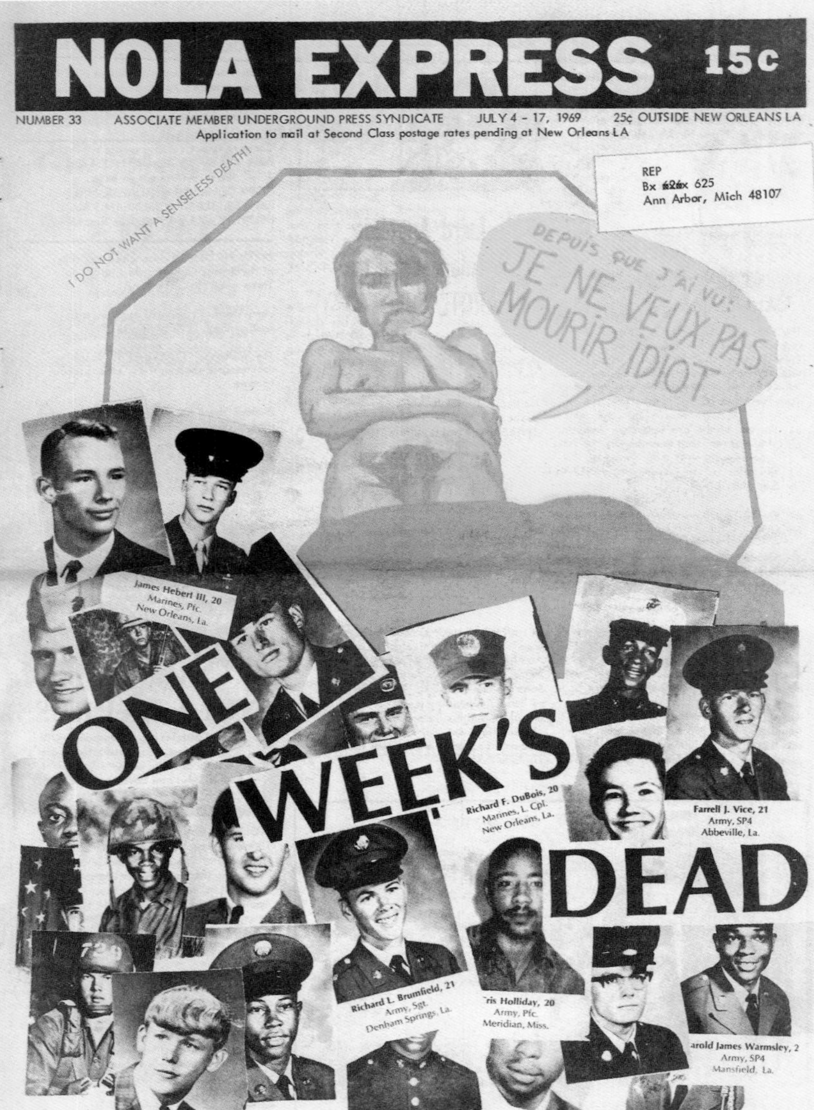

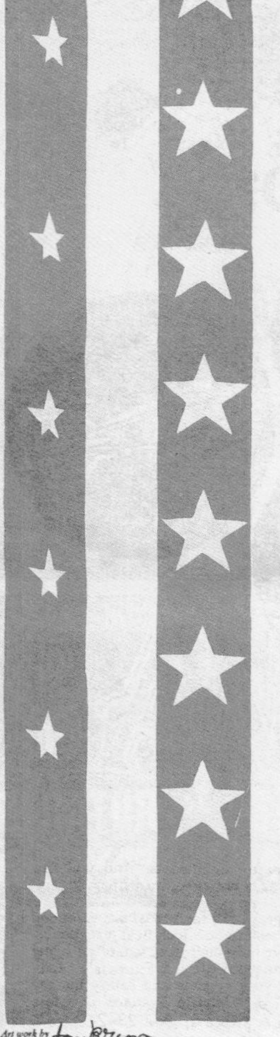

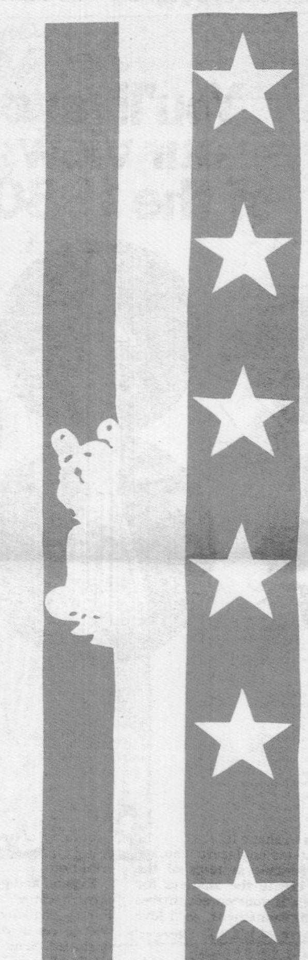

THE PROFESSIONAL SOLDIER'S PRAYER

Lord God of Hosts
I thank Thee
That Thou hast given me
Strength in battle and courage.

Grant me this my prayer,
That I may persevere
In this most difficult way
That I have chosen
To serve Thee and my country.

Vouchsafe to me that I may always
Have skill and cunning in the ambush
So that I may see mine enemy
Before he sees me.
And when I have seen him
Drive out from my heart
All those feminine weaknesses
Of mercy, pity and lovingkindness,
Clothe me in the armor of salutary cruelty,
And remind me, Almighty Father,
That this creature in my sights
Is not man
But enemy
So that I may squeeze gently the trigger
And drive the bullet home
With scientific accuracy
Into that vital spot
That Thou in Thine infinite mercy
Hast exposed to my gaze.
And when he falls,
Grant that I may feel no remorse.
Let me observe his death
With triumphant exultation
And let me not forget
That sudden death is kind
And that I have done this deed
For the sake of democracy
And for those freedoms that we rightly hold
To be more precious than life itself,
Even his and even mine.

And in the fulness of time
Saturate me from top to toe with poisonous wrath
So that I may be an unforgiving vessel of hate.
Harden me with a holy imperviousness
To all feelings of compassion
To the end that some day
I may be a perfectly functioning machine of destruction
For my country and my mother,
My wife and my children,
For Thou knowest my love for them.

I confess in the secrecy of my prayer, O God,
That I am often afraid
When I go into combat.
The good soldier has no fear.
Teach me so that I shall not anticipate
That his bullet may find me
Before mine finds him
And that it may one day be me
Who falls slowly sideways
Into the arms of Death
With a spot of blood marking the place
Where the bullet entered in
And sought out my life.
Grant me, O Lord,
That I may be free of this paralyzing fear
That causes the trigger finger to tremble
And makes me hesitate even when most needful
To call in our planes with their bombs and napalm.

And if my moment should some day come upon me,
Let it be with quick mercy
On the field of battle
With the sounds of war in my ears,
The roar of engines,
The screams of shells and of men,
The explosion of bombs
And the crackling of flames in house and tree.
And when cold death shall close mine eyes,
Grant that I may drag with me many of the foe,
So that my comrades will say of me
That I lived and died the perfect soldier,
And Thine will be the power
And the honor
And the glory
Forever and ever.
Amen.

Art work by

Poem by

Published by nevada/tatoo press
bx 27263 west portal station
san francisco, ca 94127

Edition limited to 300 Copies, signed by illustrator & poet

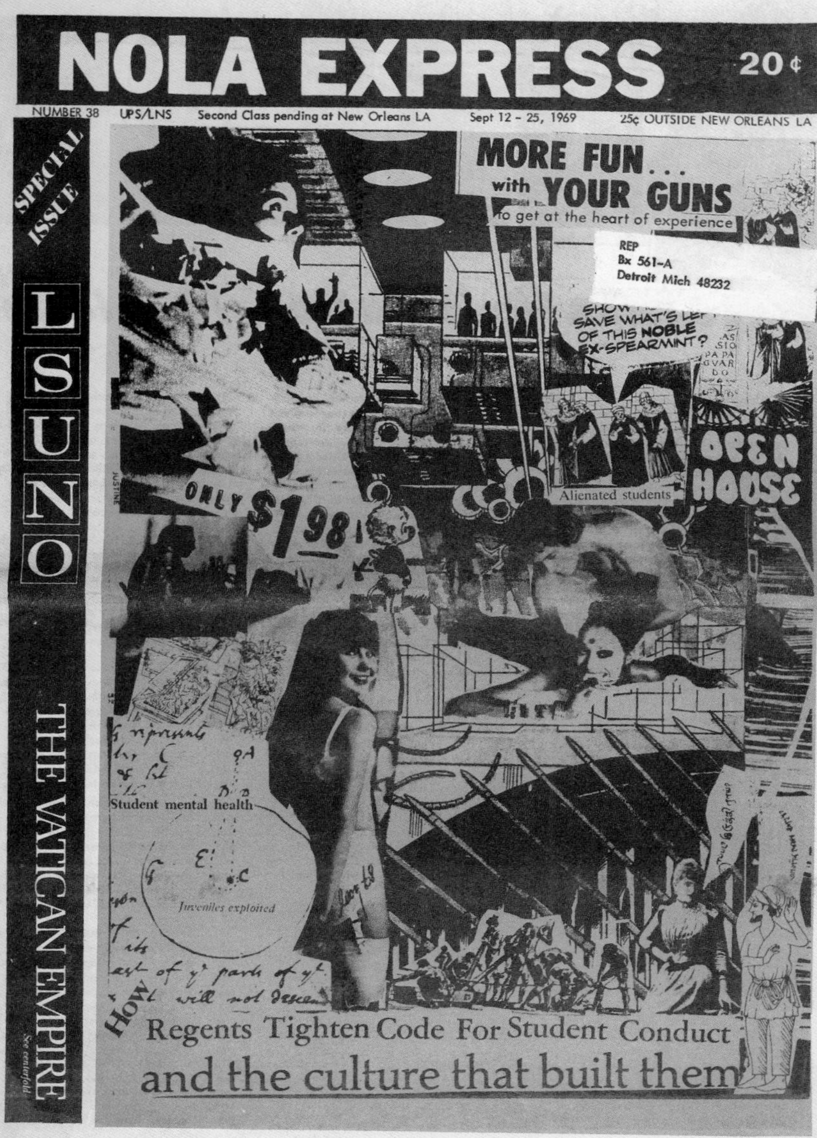

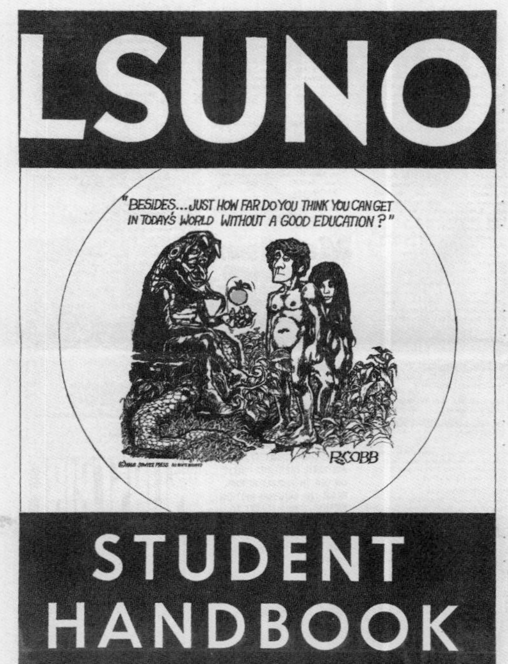

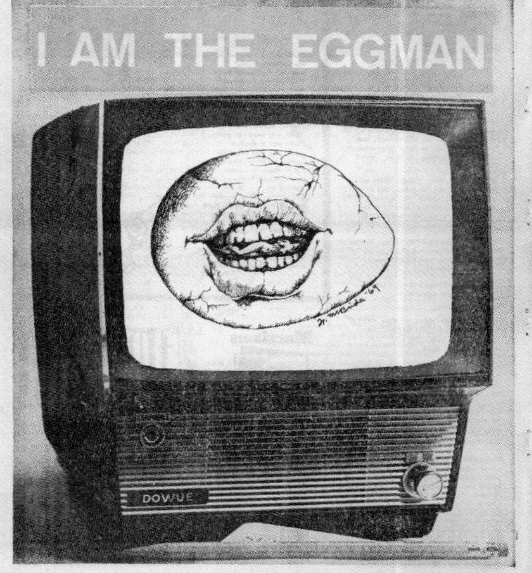

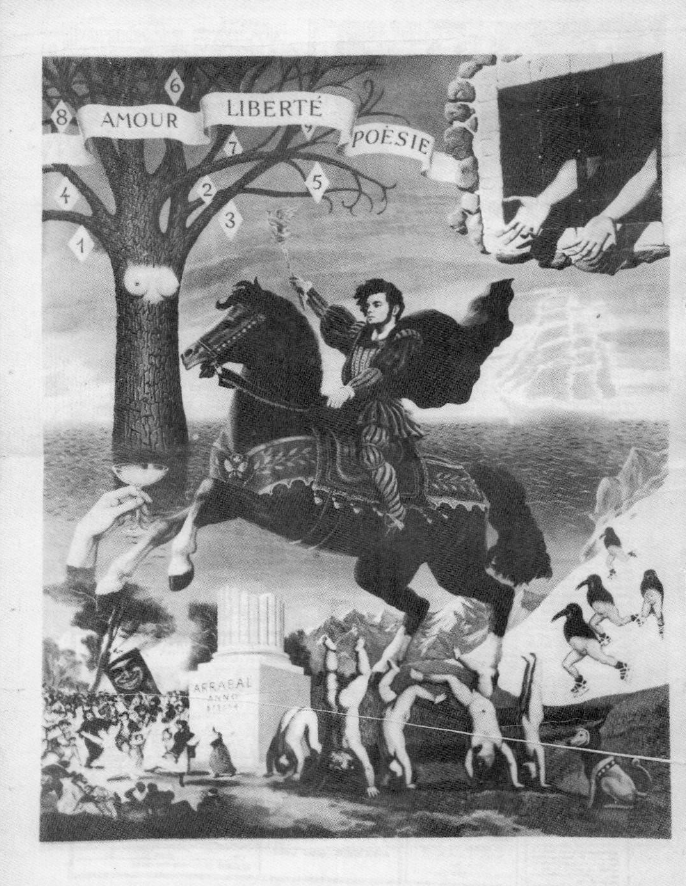

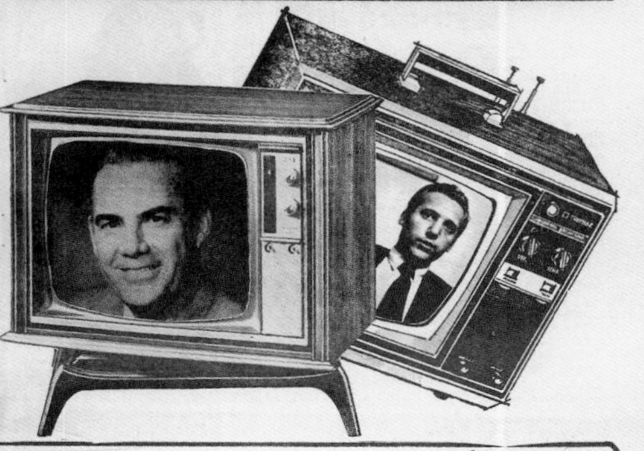

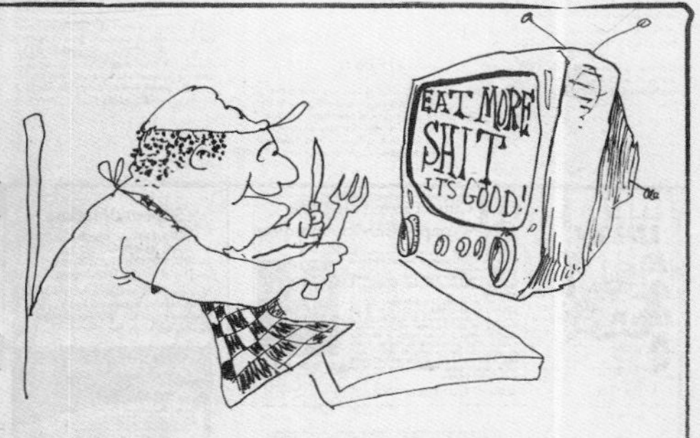

Previous page
Nola Express (New Orleans), April 1968, vol. 1, no. 1, cover
Nola Express (New Orleans), 1968, vol. 1, no. 3, cover
Nola Express (New Orleans), May 9, 1968, vol. 1, no. 4, cover
Nola Express (New Orleans), July 4–17, 1969, vol. 1, no. 33, cover
Nola Express (New Orleans), July 4–17, 1969, vol. 1, no. 33, back cover

Nola Express (New Orleans), September 12–25, 1969, vol. 1, no. 38, cover
Nola Express (New Orleans), September 12–25, 1969, vol. 1, no. 38, back cover
Nola Express (New Orleans), October 24–November 6, 1969, vol. 1, no. 41, back cover
Nola Express (New Orleans), December 5–18, 1969, vol. 1, no. 42, back cover
Nola Express (New Orleans), December 5–18, 1969, vol. 1, no. 44, back cover

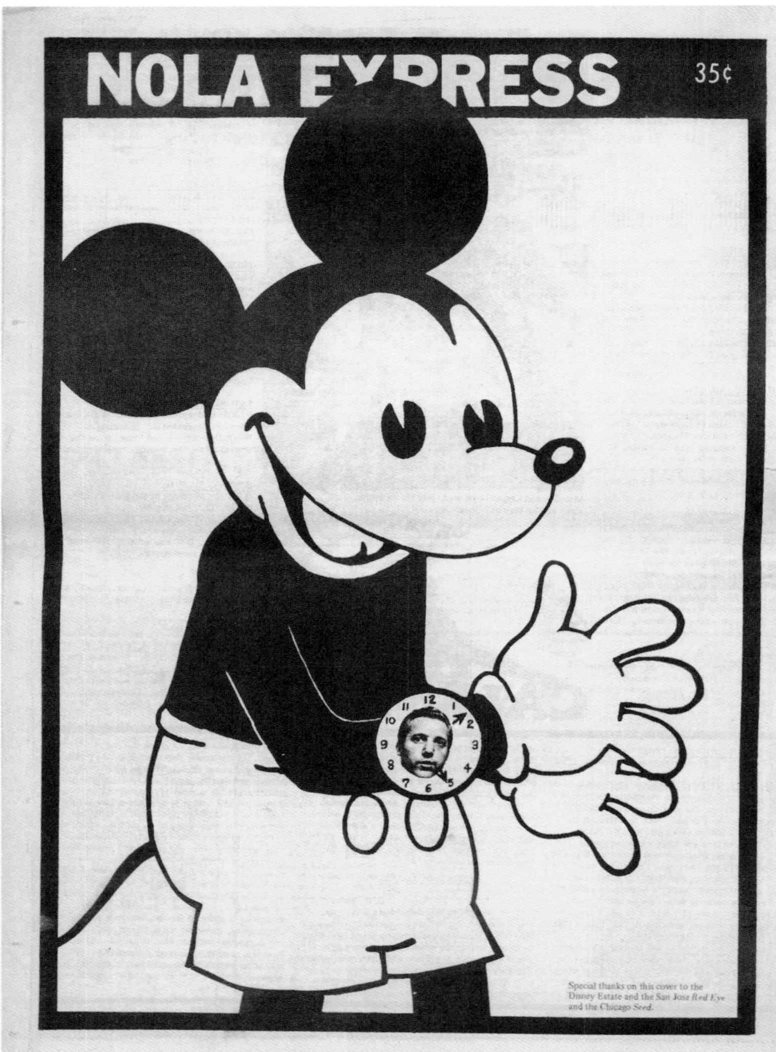

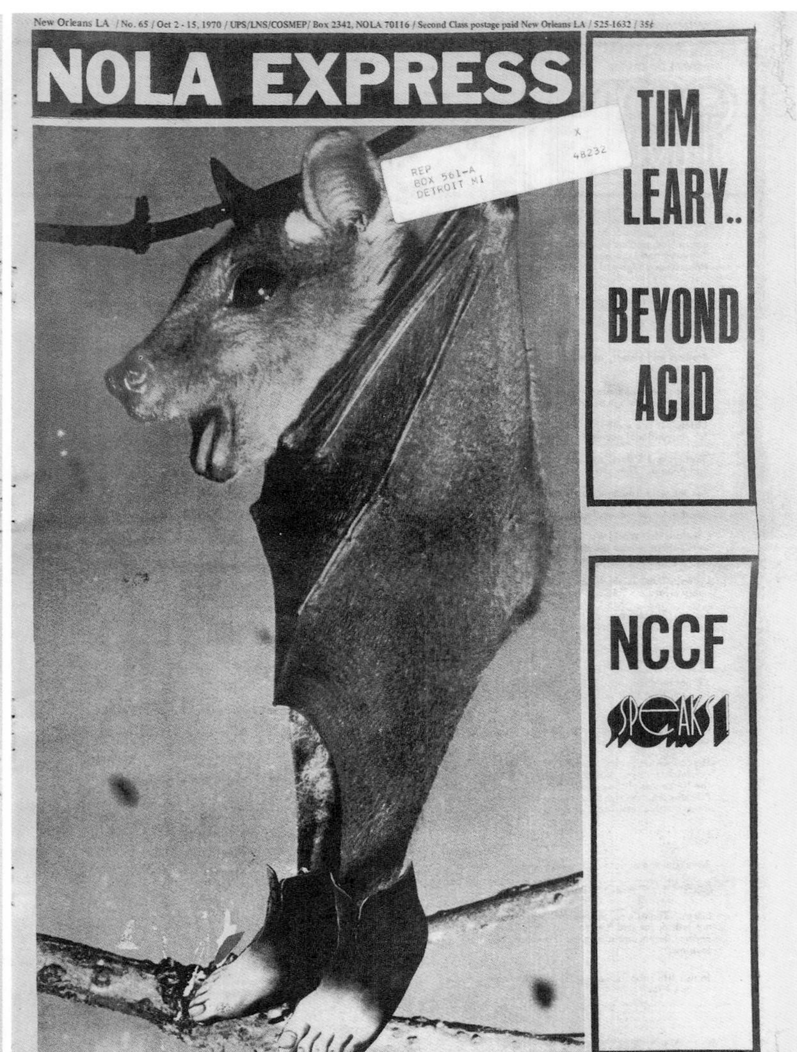

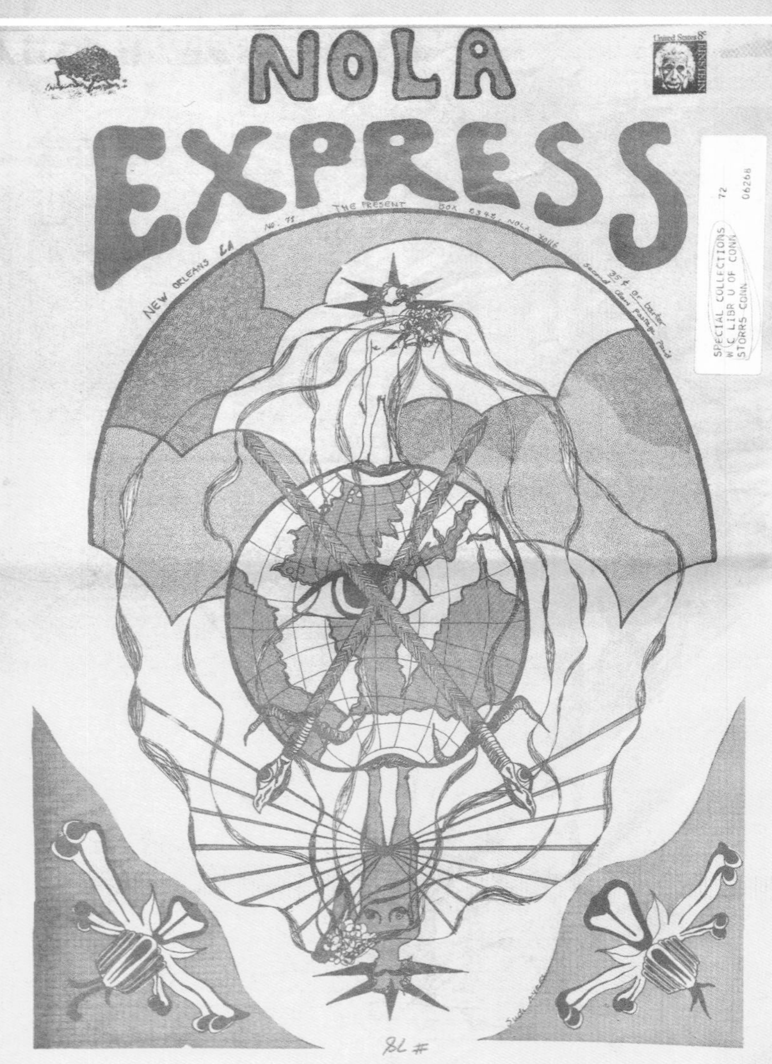

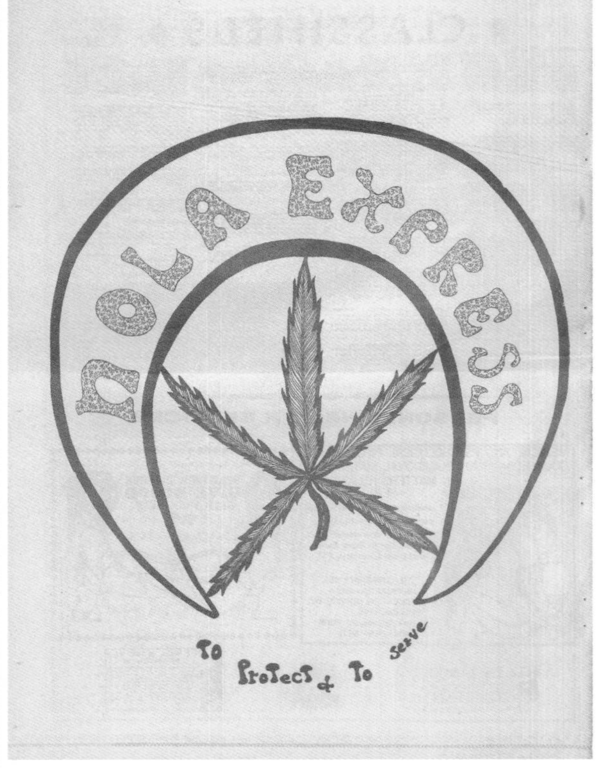

Nola Express (New Orleans), July 10–23, 1970, vol. 1, no. 59, back cover
Nola Express (New Orleans), October 2–15, 1970, vol. 1, no. 65, cover
Nola Express (New Orleans), April 1–15, 1971, vol. 1, no. 78, cover
Nola Express (New Orleans), April 16–29, 1971, vol. 1, no. 79, back cover

SCHOOLS SQUELCH SMUT

BY RACHEL MAINES

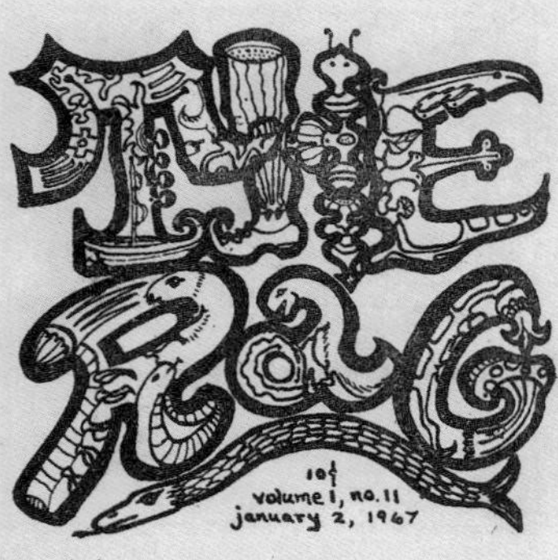

Austin and Travis High Ragamuffins were recently called into the offices of their respective principals for Rag-selling, or, as the Austin High Dean of Girls called it, "selling that trash."

At Austin High, Marie (no last name - high school principals have a nasty habit of expelling people) was called before the Lord Principal Mr. Robbins, in his office, where he sat glowering at a copy of Rag #10, open to page 11. The principal then proceeded to extol the glories of the Ben Hur Masons [Bad Trip #5 parodies a giant tin Mason fez--fun.] It seems he's a member.

He was outraged at the statement on page one--to wit: "And think of Jesus, the first anarchist, who is now the center of the greatest commercial enterprise on earth." This, says he, is disgraceful. According to Marie, Mr. Robbins also took issue with words in the "Buy a War Toy" article, including it in his general summary of The Rag as "pornography". On rereading this article, I have failed to find any words that could possible be construed as "pornography"unless Mr. Robbins thinks "ad nauseum" is dirty Latin.

He asked Marie whether she was a member of the Students for a Democratic Society and questioned her carefully about the nature and location of the SDS office. Even when she denied any knowledge or affiliation with the group, he deplored her lack of patriotism and proudly informed her that he had spend two years in Korea.

Shortly afterwards, the Dean of Girls came

Continued on 4

AND MORE. MUCH MORE. OH, SO MUCH MORE. ALL THIS GOODNESS FOR ONLY A DIME. YES, YOU HAVE INDEED MADE A WISE PURCHASE, SIR OR MADAM.

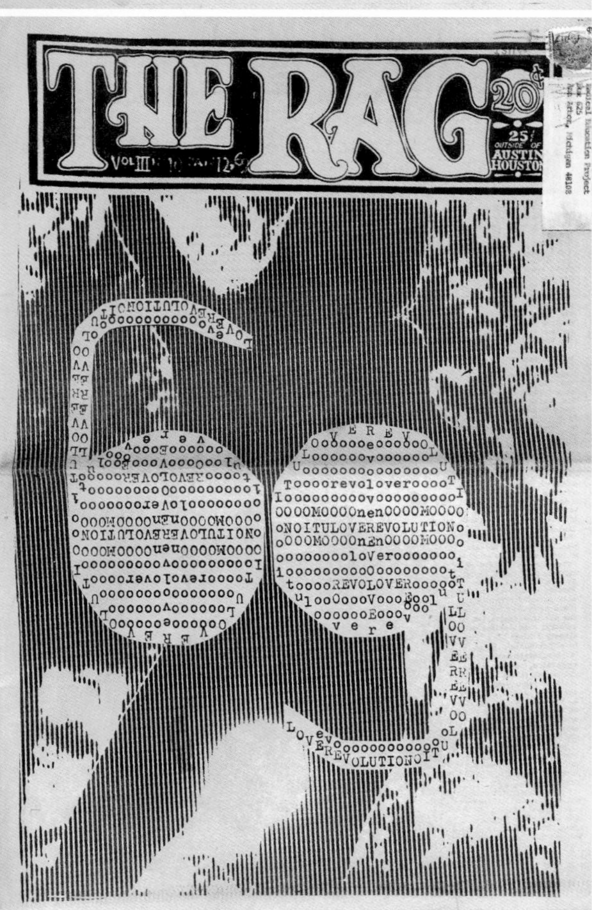

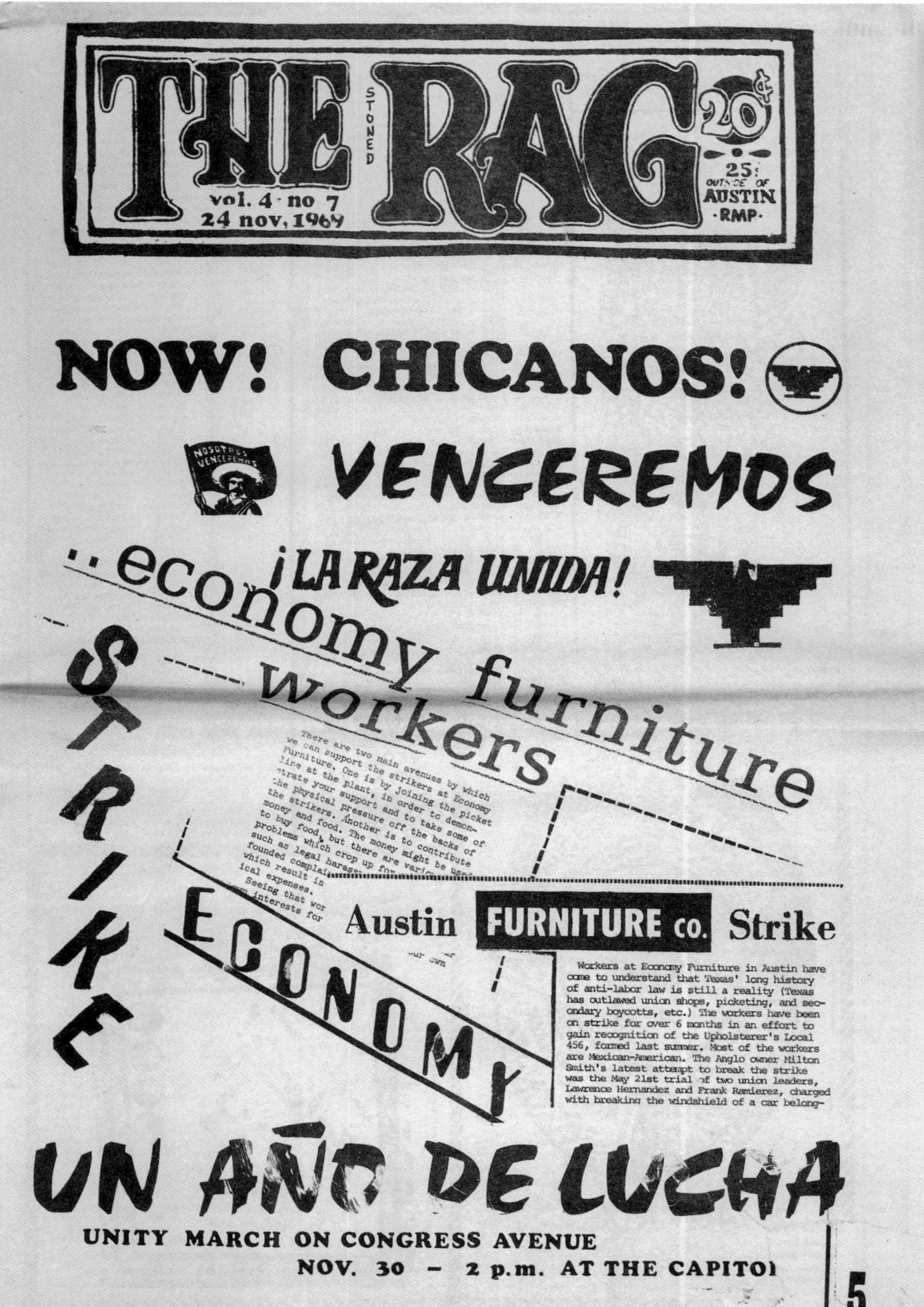

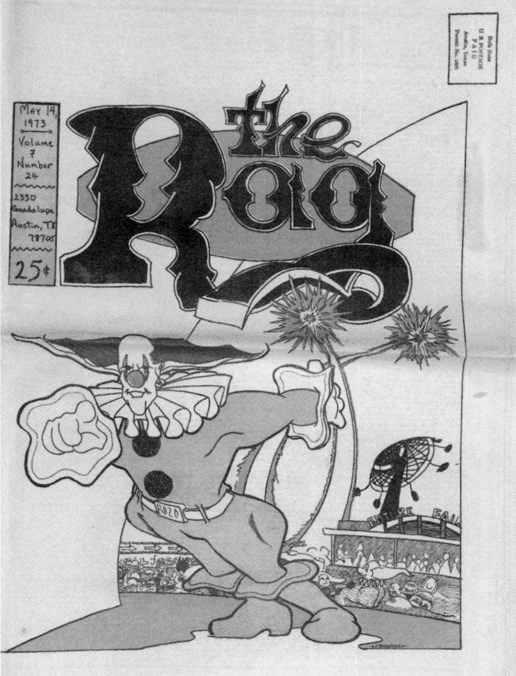

The Rag (Austin, Texas), January 2, 1967, vol. 1, no. 11, cover
The Rag (Austin, Texas), November 24, 1969, vol. 4, no. 7, cover
The Rag (Austin, Texas), January 12, 1969, vol. 3, no. 10, cover
The Rag (Austjn, Texas), May 14, 1973, vol. 7, no. 24, cover

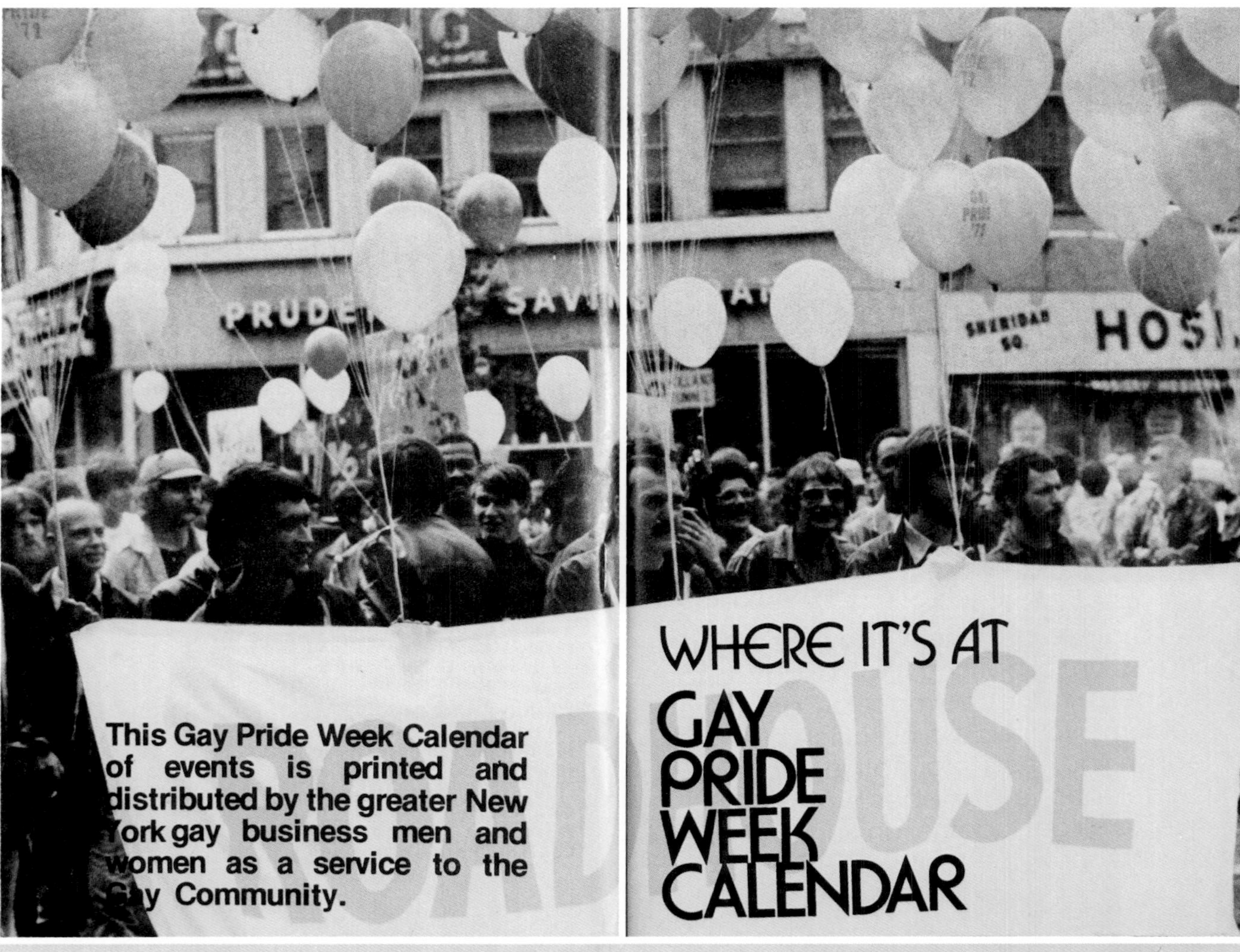
PRUDE
SAVIN
SHERIDAN SQ.
HOS
WHERE IT'S AT
GAY PRIDE WEEK CALENDAR
This Gay Pride Week Calendar of events is printed and distributed by the greater New York gay business men and women as a service to the Gay Community.

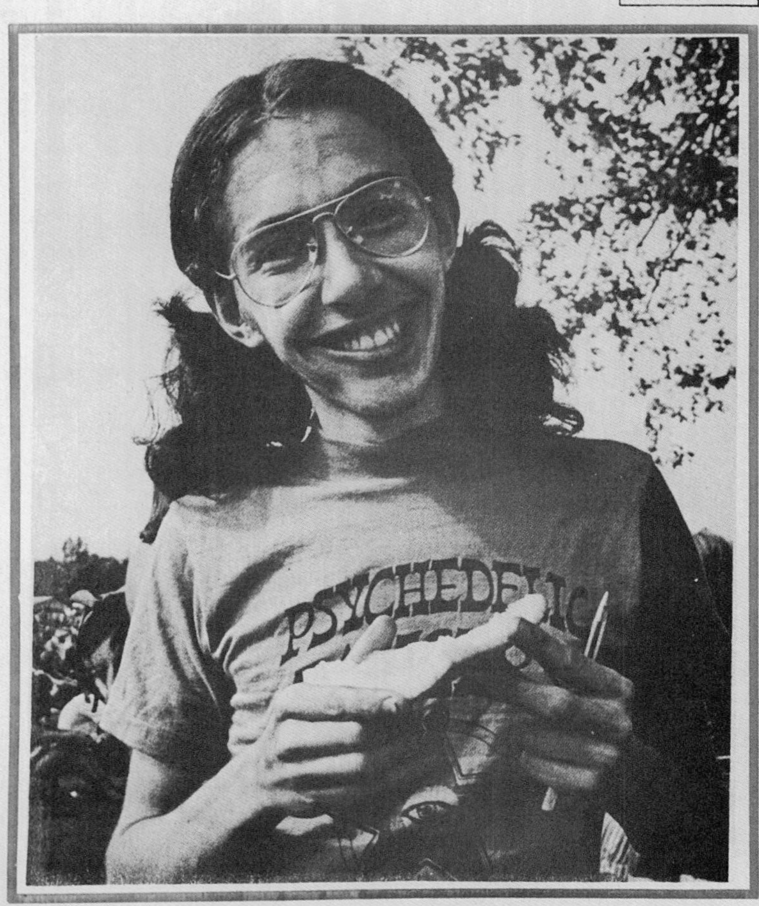
WILBUR CROSS LIBRARY52
UNIV OF CONN /SERIALS
STORRS CT 06268
BULK RATE
U.S. Postage
PAID
Permit No. 4433
Chicago, Ill.
PSYCHEDELIC

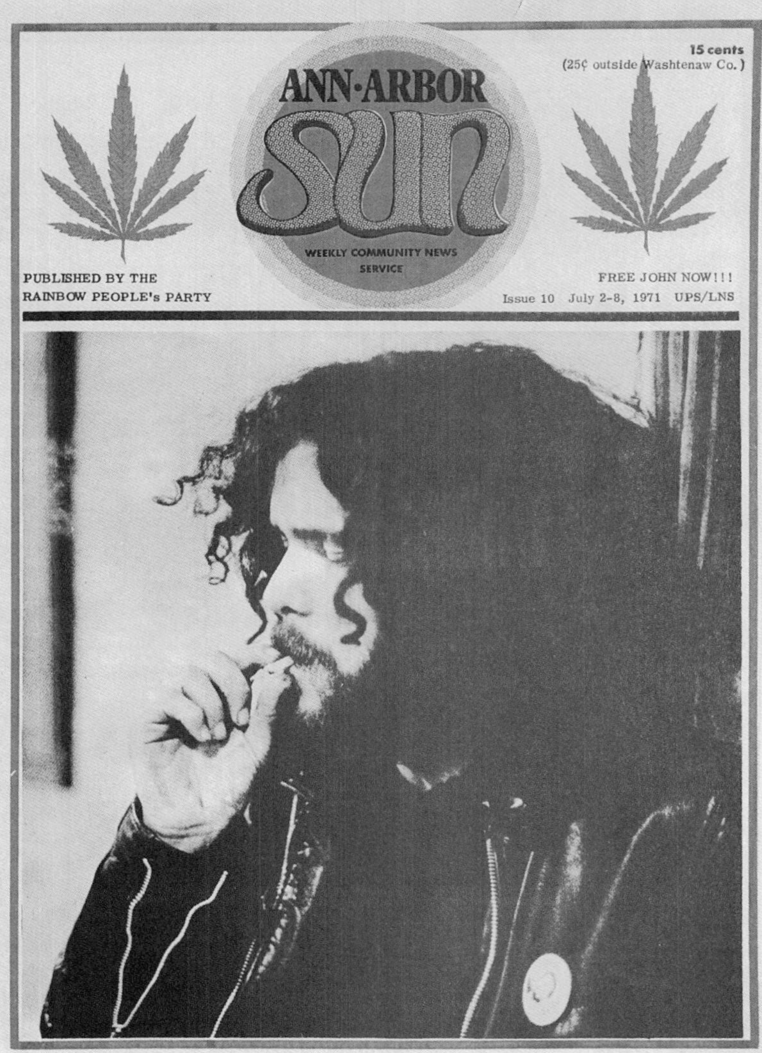
15 cents
(25¢ outside Washtenaw Co.)
ANN·ARBOR
SUN
WEEKLY COMMUNITY NEWS SERVICE
PUBLISHED BY THE
RAINBOW PEOPLE's PARTY
FREE JOHN NOW!!!
Issue 10 July 2-8, 1971 UPS/LNS

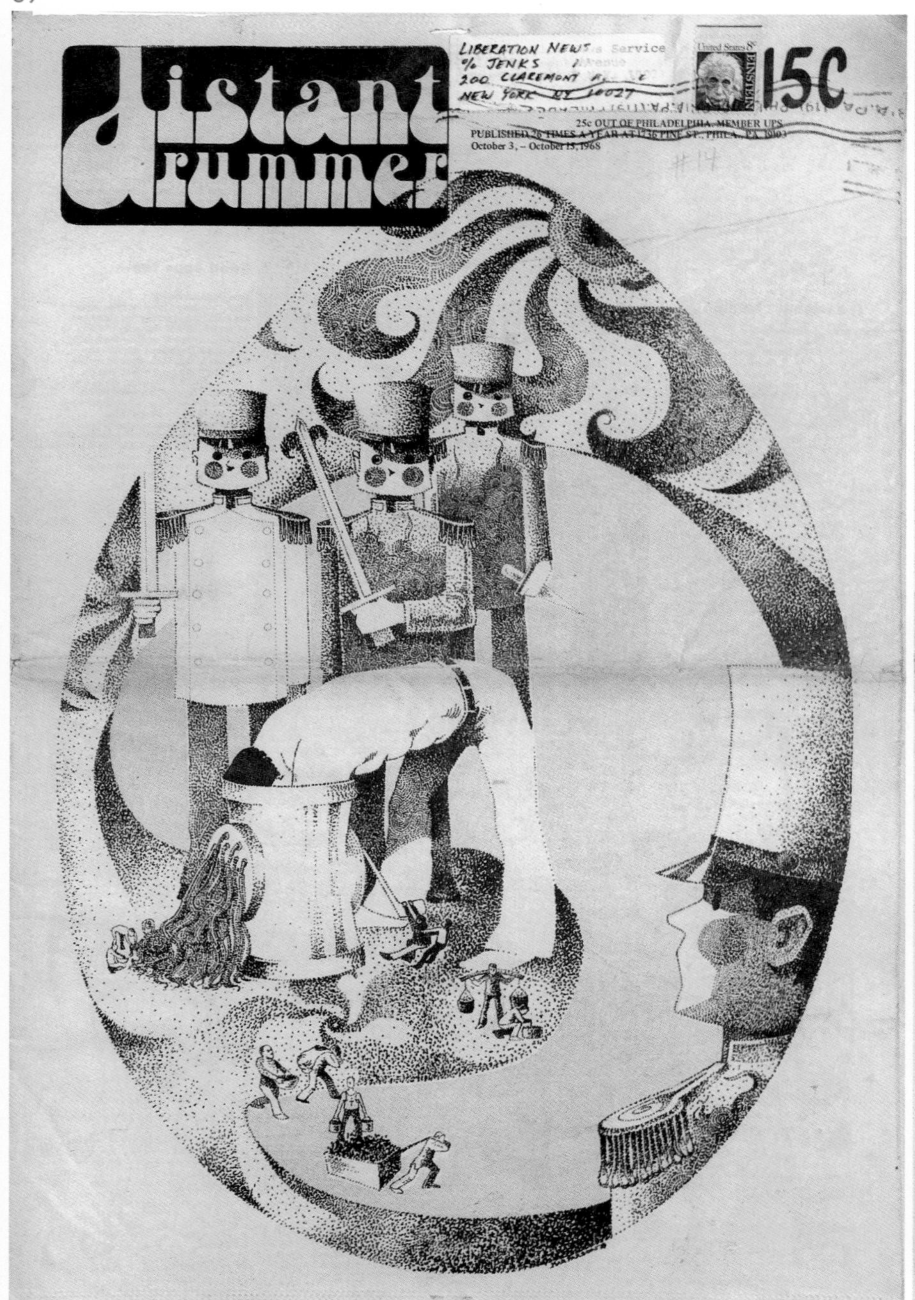

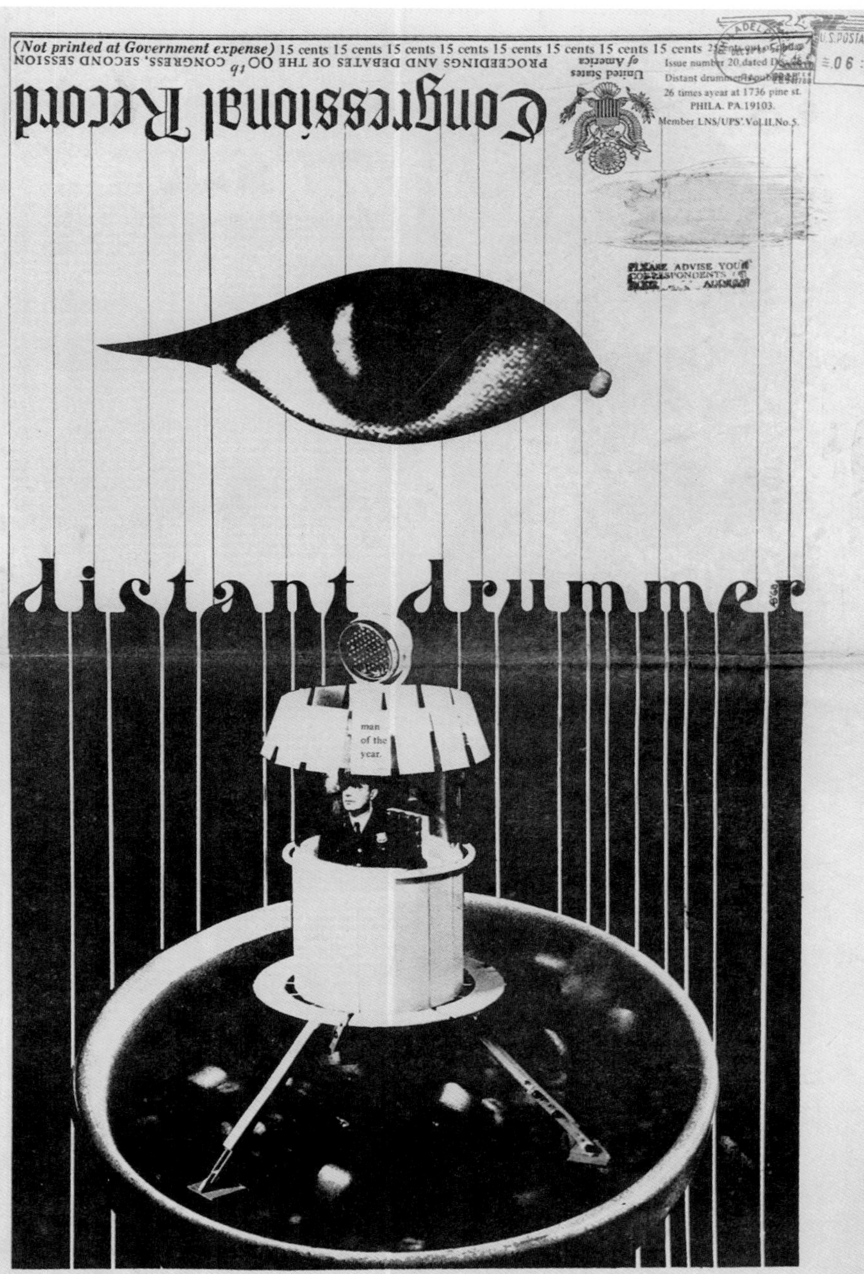

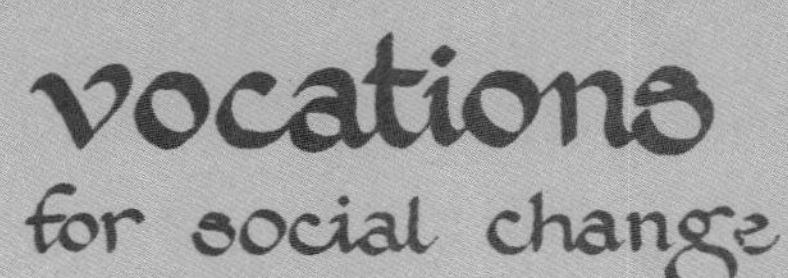

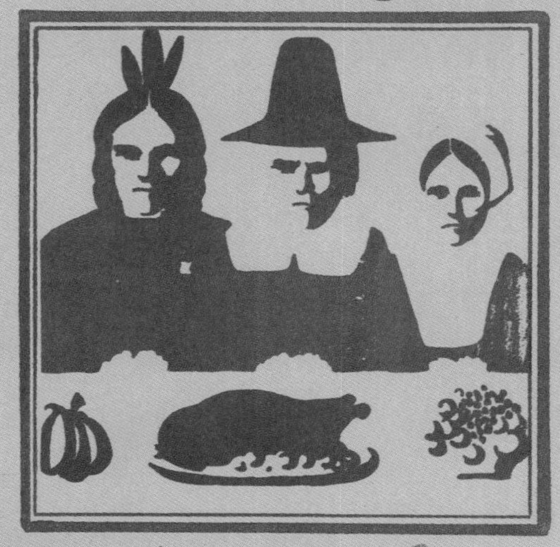

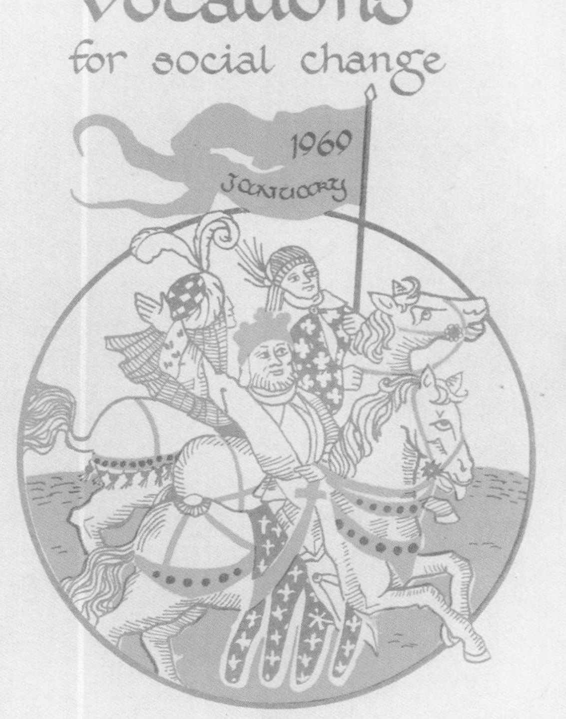

Previous page
Where It's At, June 1973, vol. 2, no. 5, back cover
Where It's At, June 1973, vol. 2, no. 5, cover
Ann Arbor Sun (Ann Arbor, Michigan), July 2–8, 1971, no. 10, front and back covers

Distant Drummer (Philadelphia), October 3–15, 1968, issue 14, cover
Distant Drummer (Philadelphia), December 26, 1968, issue 20, cover
Vocations for Social Change (Hayward, California), November 1968, cover
Vocations for Social Change (Hayward, California), January 1969, cover

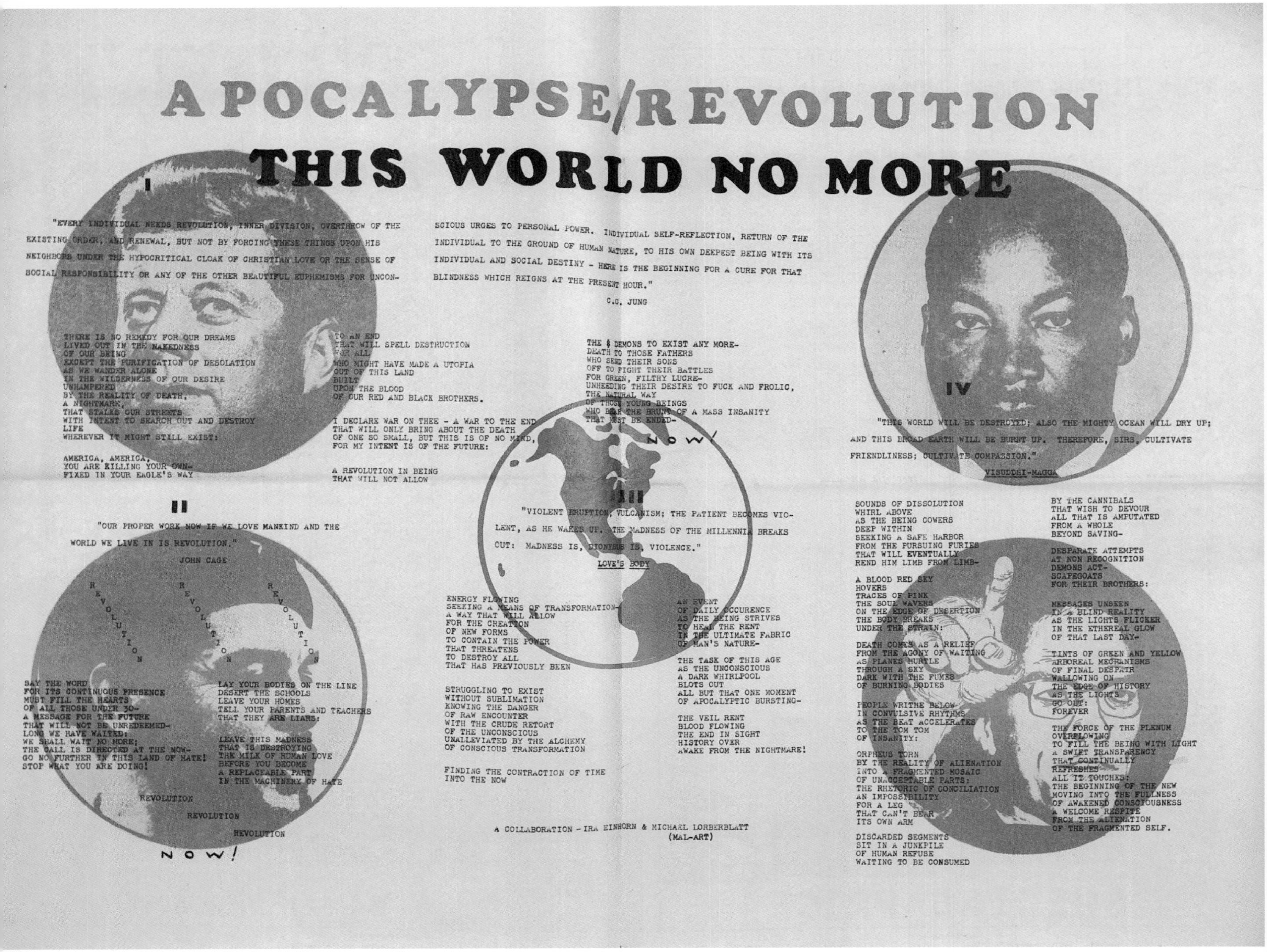

APOCALYPSE/REVOLUTION

THIS WORLD NO MORE

I

"EVERY INDIVIDUAL NEEDS REVOLUTION, INNER DIVISION, OVERTHROW OF THE EXISTING ORDER, AND RENEWAL, BUT NOT BY FORCING THESE THINGS UPON HIS NEIGHBORS UNDER THE HYPOCRITICAL CLOAK OF CHRISTIAN LOVE OR THE SENSE OF SOCIAL RESPONSIBILITY OR ANY OF THE OTHER BEAUTIFUL EUPHEMISMS FOR UNCONSCIOUS URGES TO PERSONAL POWER. INDIVIDUAL SELF-REFLECTION, RETURN OF THE INDIVIDUAL TO THE GROUND OF HUMAN NATURE, TO HIS OWN DEEPEST BEING WITH ITS INDIVIDUAL AND SOCIAL DESTINY - HERE IS THE BEGINNING FOR A CURE FOR THAT BLINDNESS WHICH REIGNS AT THE PRESENT HOUR."

C.G. JUNG

THERE IS NO REMEDY FOR OUR DREAMS
LIVED OUT IN THE NAKEDNESS
OF OUR BEING
EXCEPT THE PURIFICATION OF DESOLATION
AS WE WANDER ALONE
IN THE WILDERNESS OF OUR DESIRE
UNHAMPERED
BY THE REALITY OF DEATH,
A NIGHTMARE,
THAT STALKS OUR STREETS
WITH INTENT TO SEARCH OUT AND DESTROY
LIFE
WHEREVER IT MIGHT STILL EXIST:

AMERICA, AMERICA,
YOU ARE KILLING YOUR OWN-
FIXED IN YOUR EAGLE'S WAY
TO AN END
THAT WILL SPELL DESTRUCTION
FOR ALL
WHO MIGHT HAVE MADE A UTOPIA
OUT OF THIS LAND
BUILT
UPON THE BLOOD
OF OUR RED AND BLACK BROTHERS.

I DECLARE WAR ON THEE - A WAR TO THE END
THAT WILL ONLY BRING ABOUT THE DEATH
OF ONE SO SMALL, BUT THIS IS OF NO MIND,
FOR MY INTENT IS OF THE FUTURE:

A REVOLUTION IN BEING
THAT WILL NOT ALLOW
THE $ DEMONS TO EXIST ANY MORE-
DEATH TO THOSE FATHERS
WHO SEND THEIR SONS
OFF TO FIGHT THEIR BATTLES
FOR GREEN, FILTHY LUCRE-
UNHEEDING THEIR DESIRE TO FUCK AND FROLIC,
THE NATURAL WAY
OF THOSE YOUNG BEINGS
WHO BEAR THE BRUNT OF A MASS INSANITY
THAT MUST BE ENDED-

NOW!

II

"OUR PROPER WORK NOW IF WE LOVE MANKIND AND THE WORLD WE LIVE IN IS REVOLUTION."

JOHN CAGE

REVOLUTION REVOLUTION REVOLUTION

SAY THE WORD
FOR ITS CONTINUOUS PRESENCE
MUST FILL THE HEARTS
OF ALL THOSE UNDER 30-
A MESSAGE FOR THE FUTURE
THAT WILL NOT BE UNREDEEMED-
LONG WE HAVE WAITED:
WE SHALL WAIT NO MORE;
THE CALL IS DIRECTED AT THE NOW-
GO NO FURTHER IN THIS LAND OF HATE!
STOP WHAT YOU ARE DOING!

LAY YOUR BODIES ON THE LINE
DESERT THE SCHOOLS
LEAVE YOUR HOMES
TELL YOUR PARENTS AND TEACHERS
THAT THEY ARE LIARS:

LEAVE THIS MADNESS
THAT IS DESTROYING
THE MILK OF HUMAN LOVE
BEFORE YOU BECOME
A REPLACEABLE PART
IN THE MACHINERY OF HATE

REVOLUTION
REVOLUTION
REVOLUTION

NOW!

III

"VIOLENT ERUPTION, VULCANISM; THE PATIENT BECOMES VIOLENT, AS HE WAKES UP. THE MADNESS OF THE MILLENNIA BREAKS OUT: MADNESS IS, DIONYSUS IS, VIOLENCE."

LOVE'S BODY

ENERGY FLOWING
SEEKING A MEANS OF TRANSFORMATION-
A WAY THAT WILL ALLOW
FOR THE CREATION
OF NEW FORMS
TO CONTAIN THE POWER
THAT THREATENS
TO DESTROY ALL
THAT HAS PREVIOUSLY BEEN

STRUGGLING TO EXIST
WITHOUT SUBLIMATION
KNOWING THE DANGER
OF RAW ENCOUNTER
WITH THE CRUDE RETORT
OF THE UNCONSCIOUS
UNALLEVIATED BY THE ALCHEMY
OF CONSCIOUS TRANSFORMATION

FINDING THE CONTRACTION OF TIME
INTO THE NOW
AN EVENT
OF DAILY OCCURENCE
AS THE BEING STRIVES
TO HEAL THE RENT
IN THE ULTIMATE FABRIC
OF MAN'S NATURE-

THE TASK OF THIS AGE
AS THE UNCONSCIOUS
A DARK WHIRLPOOL
BLOTS OUT
ALL BUT THAT ONE MOMENT
OF APOCALYPTIC BURSTING-

THE VEIL RENT
BLOOD FLOWING
THE END IN SIGHT
HISTORY OVER
AWAKE FROM THE NIGHTMARE!

IV

"THIS WORLD WILL BE DESTROYED; ALSO THE MIGHTY OCEAN WILL DRY UP; AND THIS BROAD EARTH WILL BE BURNT UP. THEREFORE, SIRS, CULTIVATE FRIENDLINESS; CULTIVATE COMPASSION."

VISUDDHI-MAGGA

SOUNDS OF DISSOLUTION
WHIRL ABOVE
AS THE BEING COWERS
DEEP WITHIN
SEEKING A SAFE HARBOR
FROM THE PURSUING FURIES
THAT WILL EVENTUALLY
REND HIM LIMB FROM LIMB-

A BLOOD RED SKY
HOVERS
TRACES OF PINK
THE SOUL WAVERS
ON THE EDGE OF DESERTION
THE BODY BREAKS
UNDER THE STRAIN:

DEATH COMES AS A RELIEF
FROM THE AGONY OF WAITING
AS PLANES HURTLE
THROUGH A SKY
DARK WITH THE FUMES
OF BURNING BODIES

PEOPLE WRITHE BELOW
IN CONVULSIVE RHYTHMS
AS THE BEAT ACCELERATES
TO THE TOM TOM
OF INSANITY:

ORPHEUS TORN
BY THE REALITY OF ALIENATION
INTO A FRAGMENTED MOSAIC
OF UNACCEPTABLE PARTS:
THE RHETORIC OF CONCILIATION
AN IMPOSSIBILITY
FOR A LEG
THAT CAN'T BEAR
ITS OWN ARM

DISCARDED SEGMENTS
SIT IN A JUNKPILE
OF HUMAN REFUSE
WAITING TO BE CONSUMED
BY THE CANNIBALS
THAT WISH TO DEVOUR
ALL THAT IS AMPUTATED
FROM A WHOLE
BEYOND SAVING-

DESPARATE ATTEMPTS
AT NON RECOGNITION
DEMONS ACT-
SCAPEGOATS
FOR THEIR BROTHERS:

MESSAGES UNSEEN
IN A BLIND REALITY
AS THE LIGHTS FLICKER
IN THE ETHEREAL GLOW
OF THAT LAST DAY-

TINTS OF GREEN AND YELLOW
ARBOREAL MECHANISMS
OF FINAL DESPAIR
WALLOWING ON
THE EDGE OF HISTORY
AS THE LIGHTS
GO OUT:
FOREVER

THE FORCE OF THE PLENUM
OVERFLOWING
TO FILL THE BEING WITH LIGHT
A SWIFT TRANSPARENCY
THAT CONTINUALLY
REFRESHES
ALL IT TOUCHES:
THE BEGINNING OF THE NEW
MOVING INTO THE FULLNESS
OF AWAKENED CONSCIOUSNESS
A WELCOME RESPITE
FROM THE ALIENATION
OF THE FRAGMENTED SELF.

A COLLABORATION - IRA EINHORN & MICHAEL LORBERBLATT
(MAL-ART)

Distant Drummer (Philadelphia), May 1968, issue 6, center spread

10 11

WHO ? ? ? ? ? ? ? ? ? ? ? ? ? ? ? CARES ? ? ? ? ? ? ? ? ? ? ? ? ? ? WHAT

(THE A&P DOES)

STUDENTS SIGN UP

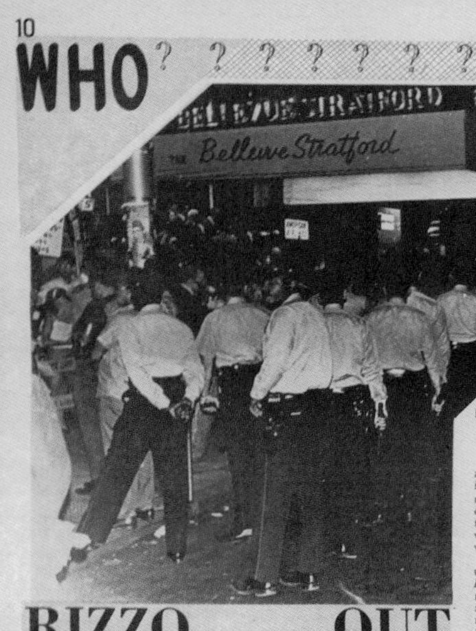

RIZZO OUT FRONT LOOKS FOR BANDAGES

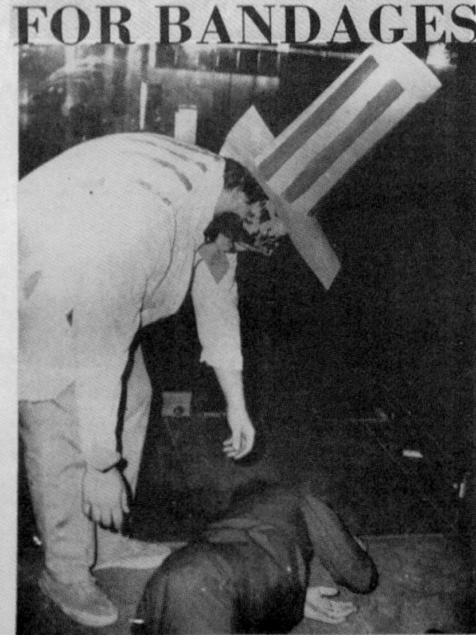

ANTI-RUSK RALLY SEPTEMBER 25 TURNED OUT TO BE A DISAPPOINTMENT FOR SUPER-COP RIZZO. HE DIDN'T SEE ANY BLOOD.

BY STEVE KUROMIYA and JOE MIKULIAK JR.

The FBI is loose on Penn campus.

This time the object of the hunt is a certain individual who placed an ad in the Oct. 18,1967 issue of the student newspaper–an ad signed by 81 men of draft age who declared their intention to refuse service in the armed forces while we are engaged in the Vietnam war.

Two agents of the FBI paid an uhannounced visit to the offices of the *Daily Pennsylvanian* to extract the name of the person who placed the ad. The agents said that the information was "vital to the security of the United States" and would be used by the Department of Justice to build conspiracy cases against the draft resisters. The agents said if the newspaper refused to comply, the information would be subpoenaed by the Justice Department.

Berl Schwartz, the managing editor of the DP, was also asked questions concerning a statement attributed to Jonathan Goldstein, a college senior. The statement–printed in the DP–concerned his wish to fail his induction physical.

Twice in the next two days, the editorial board of the newspaper voted not to divulge the name of the advertiser. It stated editorially that "The Daily Pennsylvanian will not open any of its files to outside agencies voluntarily." The editorial said it would not incriminate a fellow student because of 1) freedom of the press to protect its sources, 2) the right of privacy in business contracts, and 3) the first amendment "free speech" clause.

The editorial also questioned the presence of federal agents running loose on campus without the knowledge of the school administration. It concluded, "We personally find the FBI's activities much more a threat to the nation's security than our unnamed advertisers."

More than once in the past, investigatory agencies on campus have made their presence known. The incidents go back to when Robert Longley was Dean of Men and the object of the FBI's presence was the membership of the now defunct Student Peace Union.

At an SDS meeting on Wednesday (Sept. 18), it was decided to run another "We Won't Go" ad along with a statement of support for the DP's stand to not cooperate with the FBI. The statement also asked the administration to make clear its position vis-a-vis the FBI, especially in regard to furnishing of information and the presence of agents on the campus.

President Harnwell replied that the DP was justified in refusing to give the name of the advertiser to the FBI. However, he said if the records were subpoenaed, they should be made available to the courts.

He also said the campus is open to everyone, including the police and the FBI, and that no restrictions are made on the entrance of anyone onto the campus. This statement represents a wide departure on a stand he took about ten months ago. At that time, he sent a registered letter to several anti-war activists, including this reporter (Kuromiya). It read:

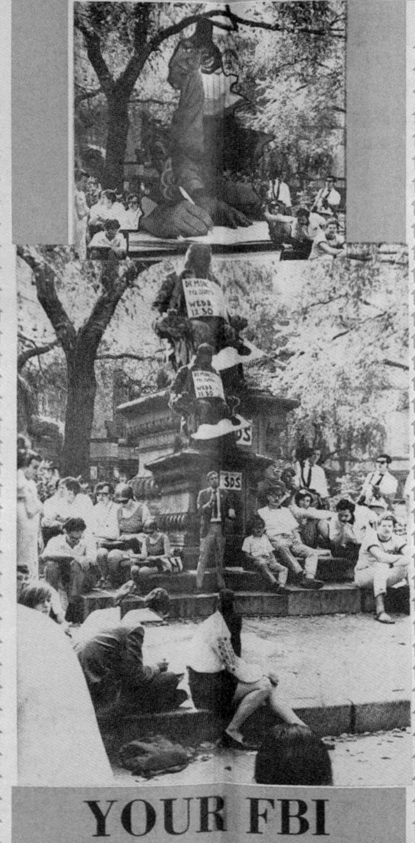

YOUR FBI ON CAMPUS

PICS: PENN RALLY – MICHAEL LORBERBLATT
RUSK RALLY – JAY STEINBRUNN
ALEX BROUWER

Dear Sir:

The campus of the University of Pennsylvania is private property. You are therefore hereby advised not to enter upon the campus, and particularly not to enter upon any of its buildings.

Trespassing on the University's private property will result in our taking legal action against you.

Very Truly Yours,
Gaylord P. Harnwell /s/

The Penn chapter of SDS and the U of P Resistance decided to make the FBI incident an issue of freedom of speech and press on the Penn campus.

A rally was called for Sept. 25 to support the DP position. People were asked to sign three petitions. After 4 days of beautiful weather and hard work, close to 200 people signed a "We Won't Go" statement, 400 people signed a "We Support Those Who Won't Go" statement, and over 2,000 signed the "DP Support" petiton.

Four hundred people showed at the rally, which was sponsored by a coalition of five anti-war groups on campus. A telegram from Paul O'Dwyer, Democratic candidate for US Senate from New York, was read. He supported the DP stand as did Richard Block, a local candidate for Congress, who spoke breifly.

Following the rally, in a move to invalidate the FBI's singling out of the lone person who submitted the first ad, a group of 200 students marched to the DP office where 135 persons signed an insertion order for the second ad and submitted the ad to Stanley Berke, business manager. Berke said that the anonymity of these 135 will be protected.

In a conversation with the *Drummer*, managing editor Schwartz said, "I feel fairly sure that we'll get a subpoena either late this week or early the next (Oct. 5–12)." He also said the university's counseling attorneys had checked into the matter and reported that there was no precedent for the FBI's action and that the newspaper might be able to "quash the subpoena on the basis of relevancy."

In other words, the advertisement was not illegal and therefore the name of the advertiser is irrelevant to the FBI.

The Daily Pennsylvanian is not a timid newspaper and perhaps that is the reason there is no underground publication on the campus, while the Free Press continues to thrive and expand on the campus of Temple University where freedom of the press is defined along the same lines as it is in Red China.

Penn students in general are behind their newspaper on this issue, Schwartz said, but have differed twice with the paper in the immediate past–once when the DP ran a story on Kuromiya's arrest for mailing a Fuck the Draft poster. The DP carried a copy of the poster, which prompted tomato throwing and other such garbage.

It also incurred some agitation when it ran–several times–an advertisement for the 13th Street Conspiracy which was headlined "We're Full of Shit."

Schwartz said the newspaper will continue to run the ad as long as the store wants it run.

RUSK DOES THE BACK DOOR THING

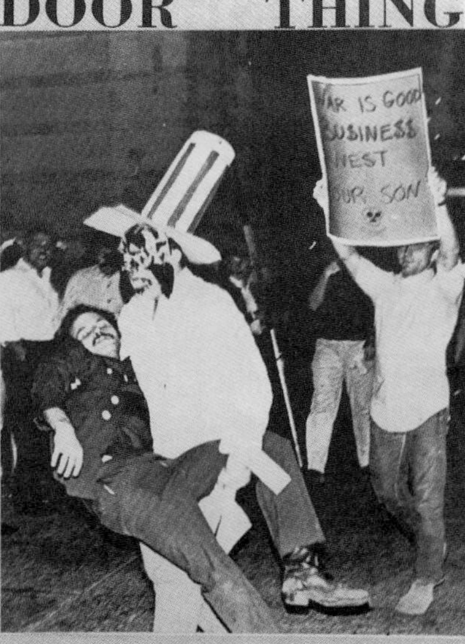

GORILLA THEATER = MAKING LIFE CLEAR TO THE SIMPLE-MINDED AMERICANS BY MEANS OF REALISTIC VISUAL TEACHING METHODS.

Distant Drummer (Philadelphia), October 3–15, 1968, issue 14, center spread

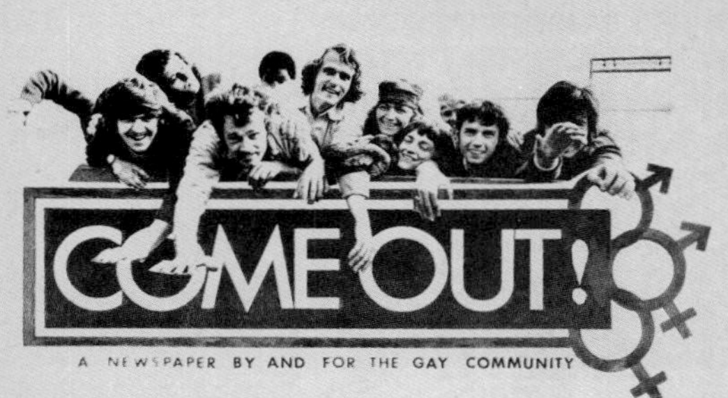

COME OUT FOR FREEDOM! COME OUT NOW! POWER TO THE PEOPLE! GAY POWER TO GAY PEOPLE! COME OUT OF THE CLOSET BEFORE THE DOOR IS NAILED SHUT!

COME-OUT, A NEWSPAPER FOR THE HOMOSEXUAL COMMUNITY, dedicates itself to the joy, the humor, and the dignity of the homosexual male and female. COME-OUT has COME OUT to fight for the freedom of the homosexual; to give voice to the rapidly growing militancy within our community; to provide a public forum for the discussion and clarification of methods and actions necessary to end our oppression. COME-OUT has COME OUT indeed for "life, liberty and the pursuit of happiness."

Make no mistake about our oppression: It is real, it is visible, it is demonstrable. IN NEW YORK A HOMOSEXUAL IS LEGITIMATE AS AN INDIVIDUAL BUT ILLEGITIMATE AS A PARTICIPANT IN A HOMOSEXUAL ACT. Hell, every homosexual and lesbian in this country survives solely by sufferance, not by law or even that cold state of grace known as tolerance. Our humanity is questioned, our choice of housing is circumscribed, our employment is tenuous, OUR FRIENDLY NEIGHBORHOOD TAVERN IS A MAFIOSO-ON-THE-JOB TRAINING SCHOOL FOR DUM-DUM HOODS. It is just such grievances as these which have sparked the revolutionary movements of history.

COME-OUT salutes militant oppressed groups, offers aid, but realizes that very often other oppressed people are also our own oppressors. THROUGH MUTUAL RESPECT, ACTION, AND EDUCATION COME-OUT HOPES TO UNIFY BOTH THE HOMOSEXUAL COMMUNITY AND OTHER OPPRESSED GROUPS INTO A COHESIVE BODY OF PEOPLE WHO DO NOT FIND THE ENEMY IN EACH OTHER.

COME-OUT will hasten the day when it becomes not only passe, but actual political suicide to speak of further repression of the homosexual. WE ARE COMING OUT IN COMMUNITY, A COMMUNITY THAT NUMBERS IN THE MILLIONS. We shall aggressively promote the use of the very real and potent economic power of Gay people throughout this land in order to further the interests of the homosexual community. We shall convince society at large of the reality of homosexual political power by the active use thereof.

We will not be gay bourgeoisie, searching for the sterile "American dream" of the ivy-covered cottage and the good corporation job, but neither will we tolerate the exclusion of homosexuals from any area of American life.

Because our oppression is based on sex and the sex roles which oppress us from infancy, we must explore these roles and their meanings. We must recognize and make others recognize that BEING HOMOSEXUAL SAYS ONLY ONE THING: EMOTIONALLY YOU PREFER YOUR OWN SEX. IT SAYS NOTHING ABOUT YOUR WORTH, YOUR VALUE AS A HUMAN BEING. Does society make a place for us. . . as a man? A woman? A homosexual or lesbian? How does the family structure affect us? What is sex, and what does it mean? What is love? As homosexuals, we are in a unique position to examine these questions from a fresh point of view. You'd better believe we are going to do so – that we are going to transform the society at large through the open realization of our own consciousness.

STEP & FETCHIT FEMALE
MARCHI & PROCACCINO
VILLAGE VOICE GOES DOWN

vol.1, no.1 new york, nov.14.1969 35c / 50c outside n.y.c.

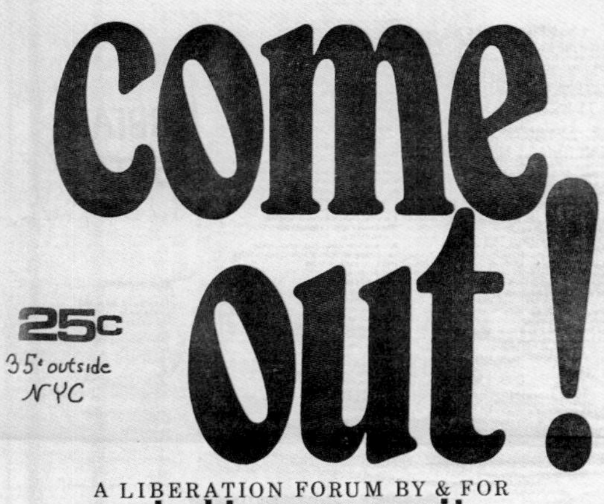

A LIBERATION FORUM BY & FOR
the **lesbian community**

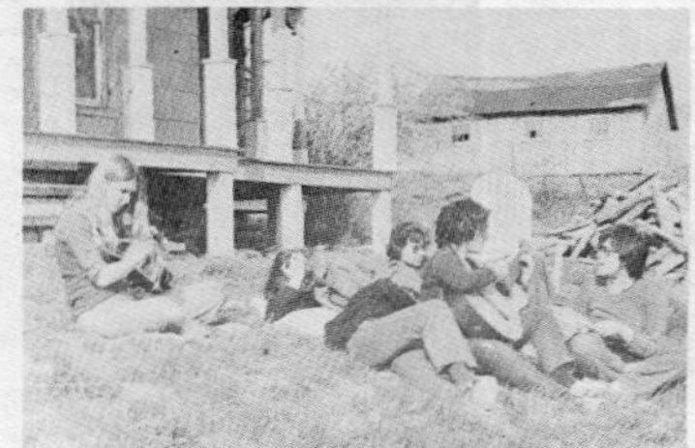

Winter 1972 issue 8
love each other love ourselves

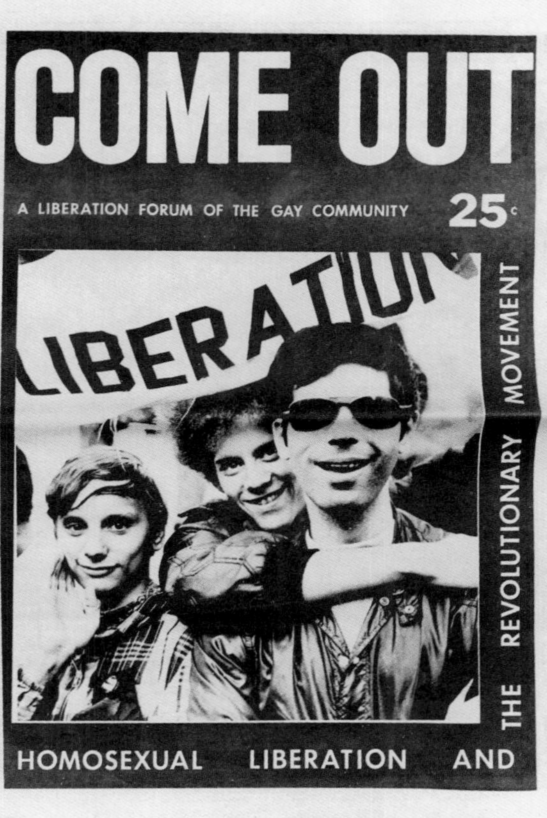

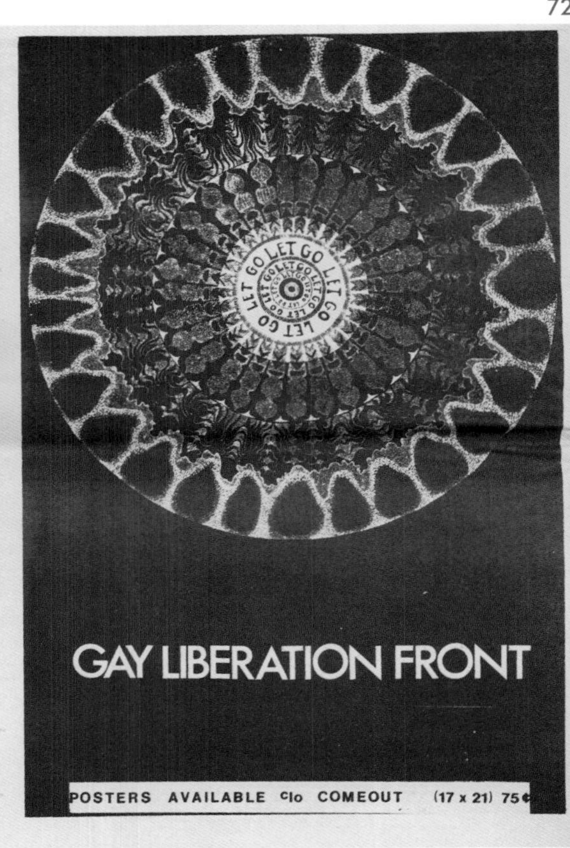

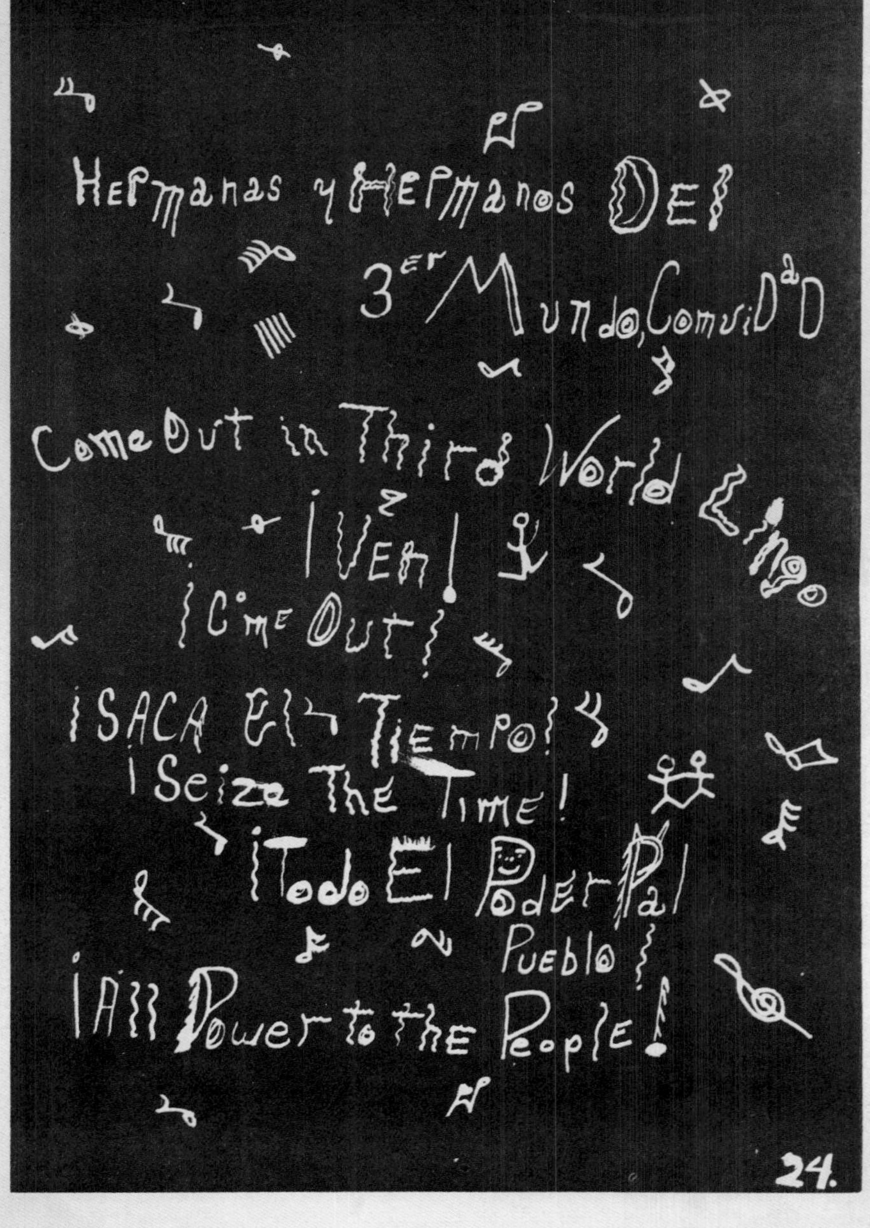

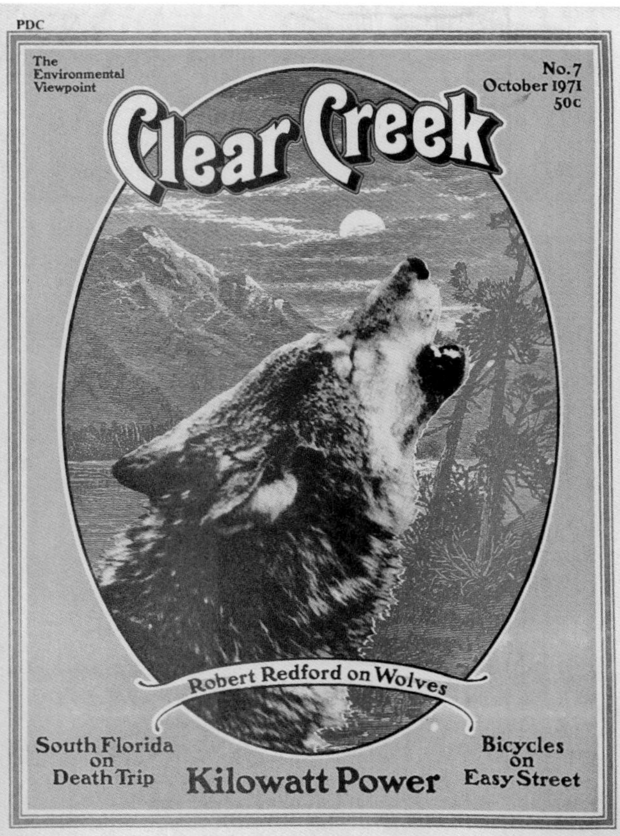
PDC

The Environmental Viewpoint

No. 7
October 1971
50¢

Clear Creek

Robert Redford on Wolves

South Florida on Death Trip

Kilowatt Power

Bicycles on Easy Street

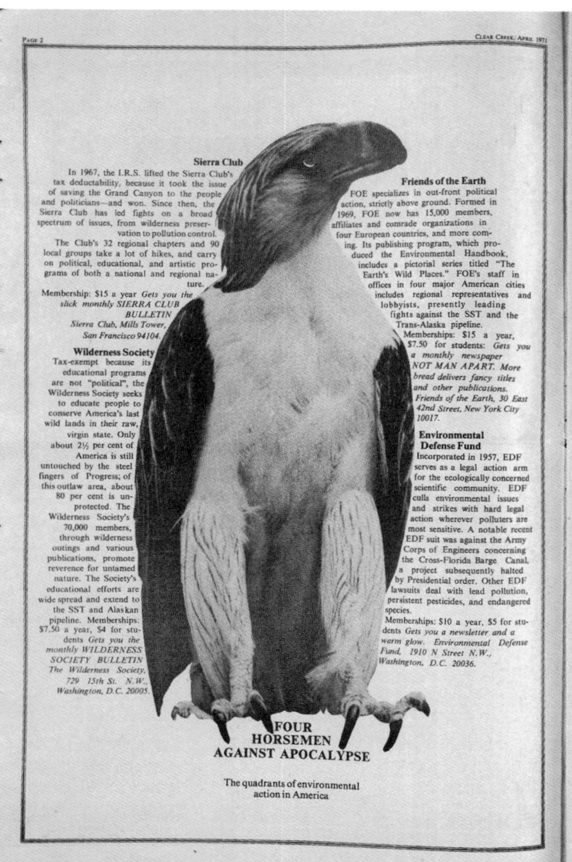

Sierra Club

In 1967, the I.R.S. lifted the Sierra Club's tax deductability, because it took the issue of saving the Grand Canyon to the people and politicians—and won. Since then, the Sierra Club has led fights on a broad spectrum of issues, from wilderness preservation to pollution control.

The Club's 32 regional chapters and 90 local groups take a lot of hikes, and carry on political, educational, and artistic programs of both a national and regional nature.

Membership: $15 a year *Gets you the slick monthly SIERRA CLUB BULLETIN Sierra Club, Mills Tower, San Francisco 94104.*

Wilderness Society

Tax-exempt because its educational programs are not "political", the Wilderness Society seeks to educate people to conserve America's last wild lands in their raw, virgin state. Only about 2½ per cent of America is still untouched by the steel fingers of Progress; of this outlaw area, about 80 per cent is unprotected. The Wilderness Society's 70,000 members, through wilderness outings and various publications, promote reverence for untamed nature. The Society's educational efforts are wide spread and extend to the SST and Alaskan pipeline. Memberships: $7.50 a year, $4 for students *Gets you the monthly WILDERNESS SOCIETY BULLETIN The Wilderness Society, 729 15th St. N.W., Washington, D.C. 20005.*

Friends of the Earth

FOE specializes in out-front political action, strictly above ground. Formed in 1969, FOE now has 15,000 members, affiliates and comrade organizations in four European countries, and more coming. Its publishing program, which produced the Environmental Handbook, includes a pictorial series titled "The Earth's Wild Places." FOE's staff in offices in four major American cities includes regional representatives and lobbyists, presently leading fights against the SST and the Trans-Alaska pipeline.

Memberships: $15 a year, $7.50 for students: *Gets you a monthly newspaper NOT MAN APART. More bread delivers fancy titles and other publications. Friends of the Earth, 30 East 42nd Street, New York City 10017.*

Environmental Defense Fund

Incorporated in 1957, EDF serves as a legal action arm for the ecologically concerned scientific community. EDF culls environmental issues and strikes with hard legal action wherever polluters are most sensitive. A notable recent EDF suit was against the Army Corps of Engineers concerning the Cross-Florida Barge Canal, a project subsequently halted by Presidential order. Other EDF lawsuits deal with lead pollution, persistent pesticides, and endangered species.

Memberships: $10 a year, $5 for students *Gets you a newsletter and a warm glow. Environmental Defense Fund, 1910 N Street N.W., Washington, D.C. 20036.*

FOUR HORSEMEN AGAINST APOCALYPSE

The quadrants of environmental action in America

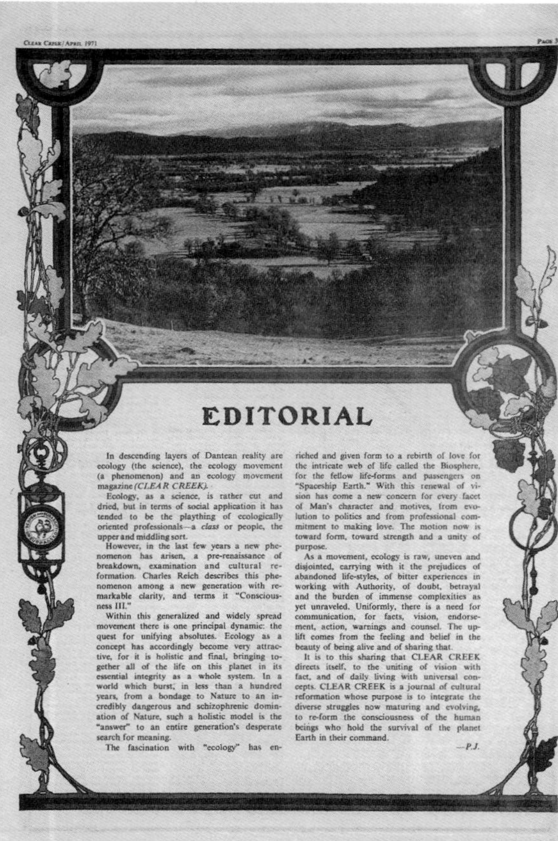

EDITORIAL

In descending layers of Dantean reality are ecology (the science), the ecology movement (a phenomenon) and an ecology movement magazine *(CLEAR CREEK)*.

Ecology, as a science, is rather cut and dried, but in terms of social application it has tended to be the plaything of ecologically oriented professionals—a *class* or people, the upper and middling sort.

However, in the last few years a new phenomenon has arisen, a pre-renaissance of breakdown, examination and cultural reformation. Charles Reich describes this phenomenon among a new generation with remarkable clarity, and terms it "Consciousness III."

Within this generalized and widely spread movement there is one principal dynamic: the quest for unifying absolutes. Ecology as a concept has accordingly become very attractive, for it is holistic and final, bringing together all of the life on this planet in its essential integrity as a whole system. In a world which burst, in less than a hundred years, from a bondage to Nature to an incredibly dangerous and schizophrenic domination of Nature, such a holistic model is the "answer" to an entire generation's desperate search for meaning.

The fascination with "ecology" has enriched and given form to a rebirth of love for the intricate web of life called the Biosphere, for the fellow life-forms and passengers on "Spaceship Earth." With this renewal of vision has come a new concern for every facet of Man's character and motives, from evolution to politics and from professional commitment to making love. The motion now is toward form, toward strength and a unity of purpose.

As a movement, ecology is raw, uneven and disjointed, carrying with it the prejudices of abandoned life-styles, of bitter experiences in working with Authority, of doubt, betrayal and the burden of immense complexities as yet unraveled. Uniformly, there is a need for communication, for facts, vision, endorsement, action, warnings and counsel. The uplift comes from the feeling and belief in the beauty of being alive and of sharing that.

It is to this sharing that CLEAR CREEK directs itself, to the uniting of vision with fact, and of daily living with universal concepts. CLEAR CREEK is a journal of cultural reformation whose purpose is to integrate the diverse struggles now maturing and evolving, to re-form the consciousness of the human beings who hold the survival of the planet Earth in their command.

—P.J.

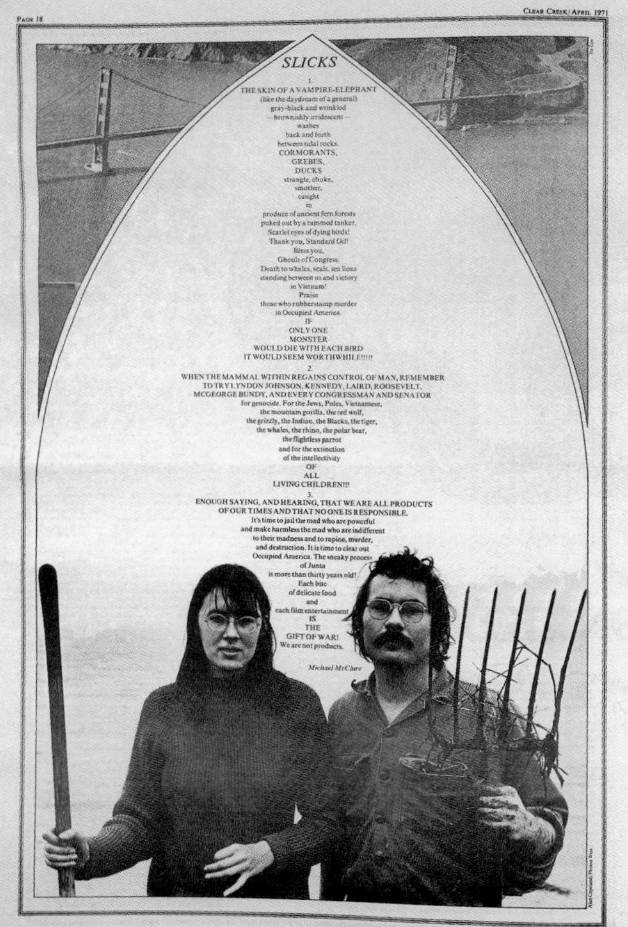

SLICKS

1.
THE SKIN OF A VAMPIRE-ELEPHANT
(like the daydream of a general)
gray-black and wrinkled
—brownishly irridescent—
washes
back and forth
between tidal rocks.
CORMORANTS,
GREBES,
DUCKS
strangle, choke,
smother,
caught
in
produce of ancient fern forests
puked out by a rammed tanker.
Scarlet eyes of dying birds!
Thank you, Standard Oil!
Bless you,
Ghouls of Congress.
Death to whales, seals, sea lions
standing between us and victory
in Vietnam!
Praise
those who rubberstamp murder
in Occupied America.
IF
ONLY ONE
MONSTER
WOULD DIE WITH EACH BIRD
IT WOULD SEEM WORTHWHILE!!!!!

2.
WHEN THE MAMMAL WITHIN REGAINS CONTROL OF MAN, REMEMBER
TO TRY LYNDON JOHNSON, KENNEDY, LAIRD, ROOSEVELT,
MCGEORGE BUNDY, AND EVERY CONGRESSMAN AND SENATOR
for genocide. For the Jews, Poles, Vietnamese,
the mountain gorilla, the red wolf,
the grizzly, the Indian, the Blacks, the tiger,
the whales, the rhino, the polar bear,
the flightless parrot
and for the extinction
of the intellectivity
OF
ALL
LIVING CHILDREN!!!

3.
ENOUGH SAYING, AND HEARING, THAT WE ARE ALL PRODUCTS
OF OUR TIMES AND THAT NO ONE IS RESPONSIBLE.
It's time to jail the mad who are powerful
and make harmless the mad who are indifferent
to their madness and to rapine, murder,
and destruction. It is time to clear out
Occupied America. The sneaky process
of Junta
is more than thirty years old!
Each bite
of delicate food
and
each film entertainment
IS
THE
GIFT OF WAR!
We are not products.

Michael McClure

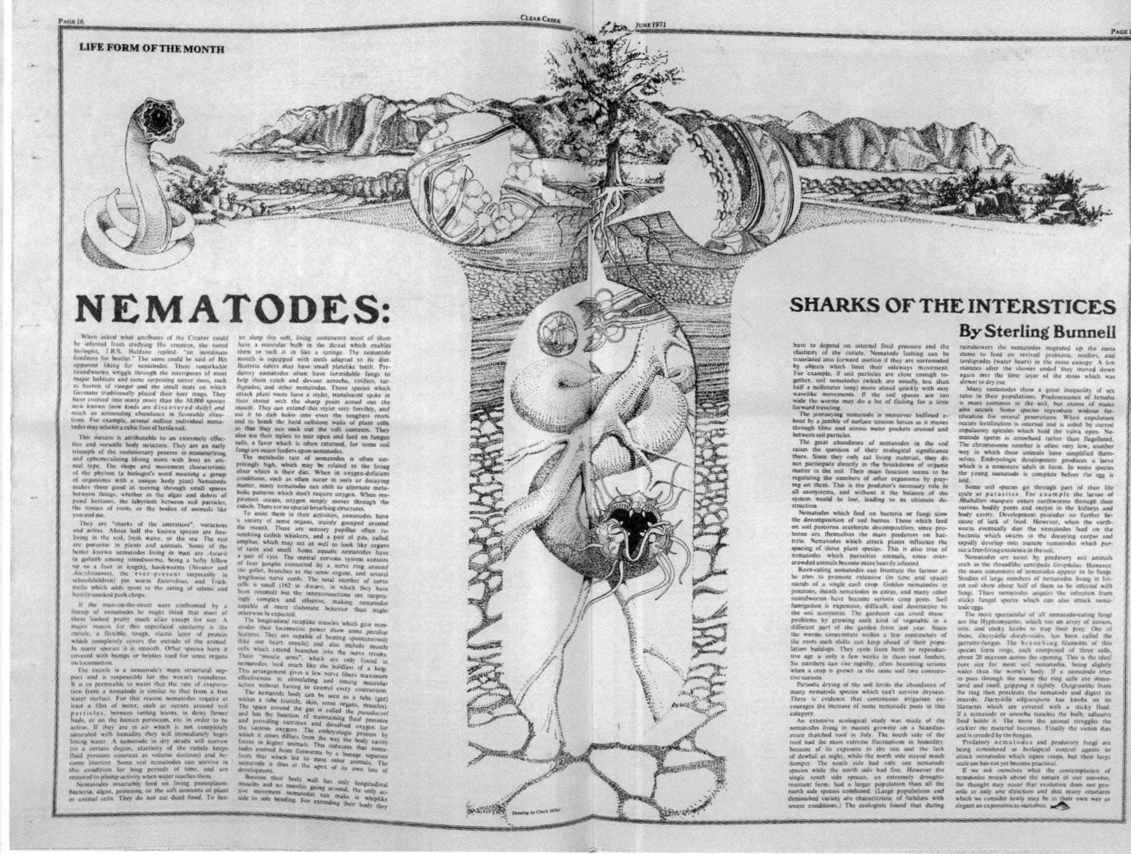

LIFE FORM OF THE MONTH

NEMATODES: SHARKS OF THE INTERSTICES

By Sterling Bunnell

Drawing by Chuck Miller

Previous page
Come Out! (New York), November 14, 1969, vol. 1, no. 1, cover
Come Out! (New York), January 10, 1970, vol. 1, no. 2, cover
Come Out! (New York), June–July 1970, vol. 1, no. 4, back cover
Come Out! (New York), Winter 1972, no. 8, cover
Come Out! (New York), December–January 1970, vol. 1, no. 7, back cover

Clear Creek (San Francisco), October 1971, no. 7, cover
Clear Creek (San Francisco), July 1971, no. 4, pp. 2–3
Clear Creek (San Francisco), July 1971, no. 4, p. 18
Clear Creek (San Francisco), July 1971, no. 4, pp. 16–17

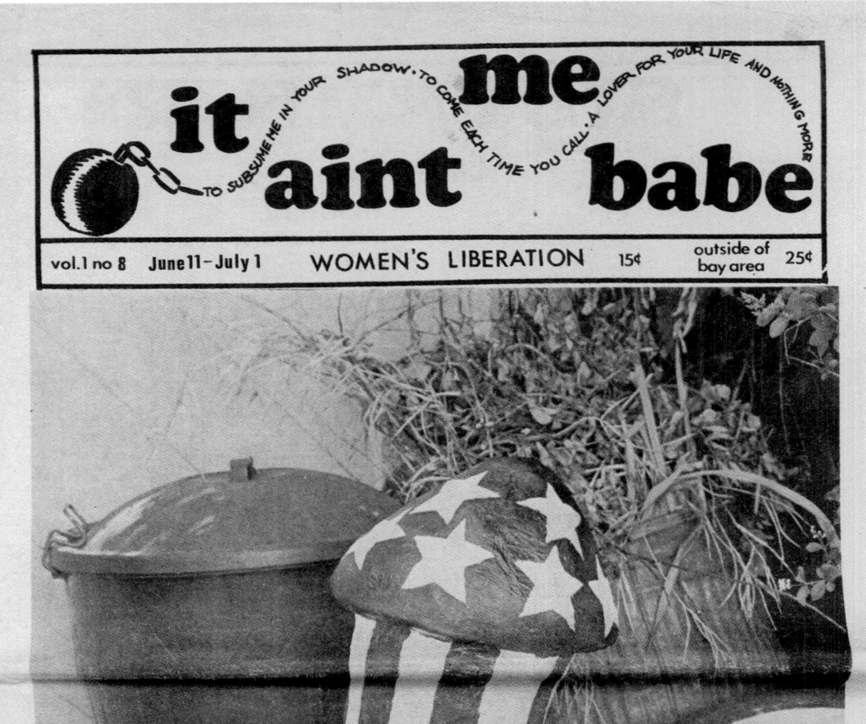

it aint me babe

TO SUBSUME ME IN YOUR SHADOW · TO COME EACH TIME YOU CALL · A LOVER FOR YOUR LIFE AND NOTHING MORE

vol.1 no 8 June 11 - July 1 WOMEN'S LIBERATION 15¢ outside of bay area 25¢

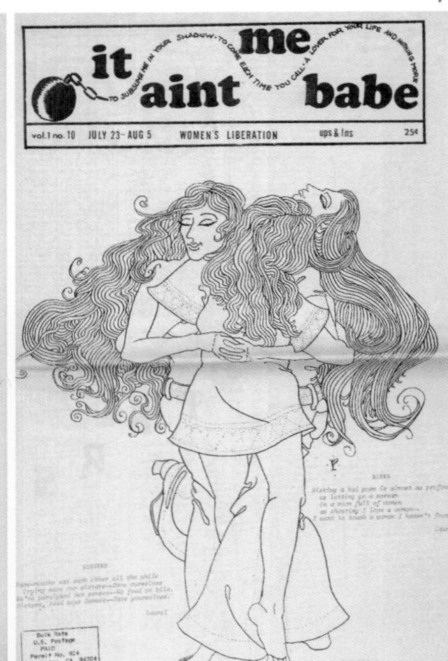

it aint me babe

vol.1 no. 10 JULY 23 - AUG 5 WOMEN'S LIBERATION 25¢

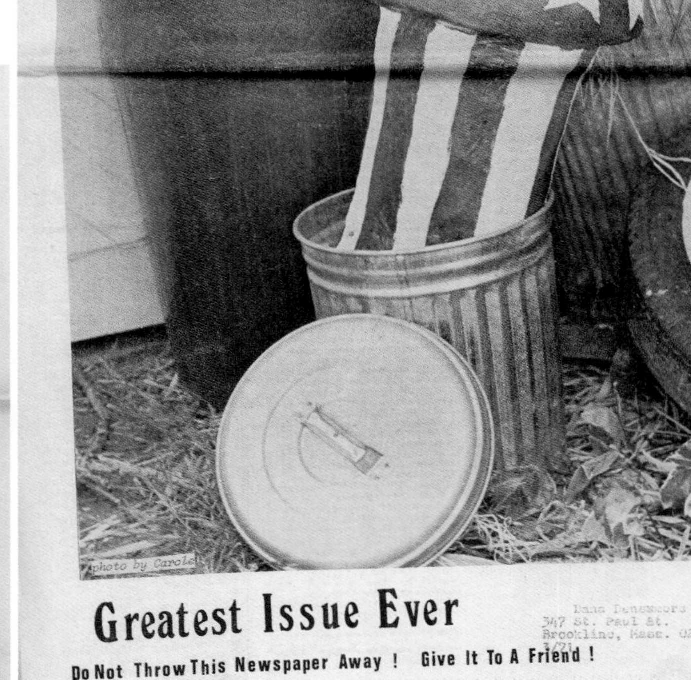

photo by Carole

Greatest Issue Ever

Do Not Throw This Newspaper Away ! Give It To A Friend !

Bulk Rate
U.S. Postage
PAID
Permit No. 924
Berkeley, CA. 94704

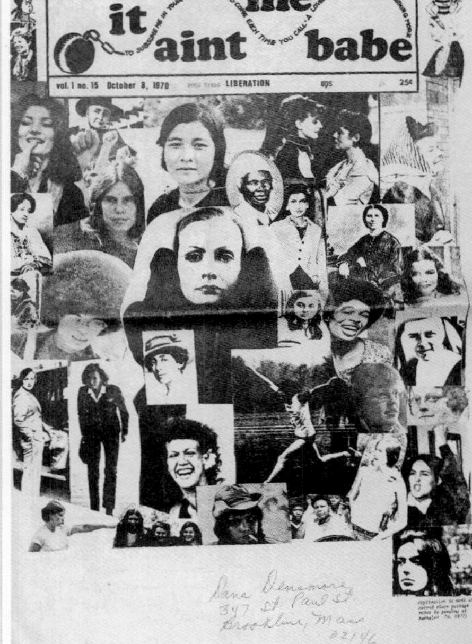

it aint me babe

vol. 1 no. 15 October 8, 1970 LIBERATION 25¢

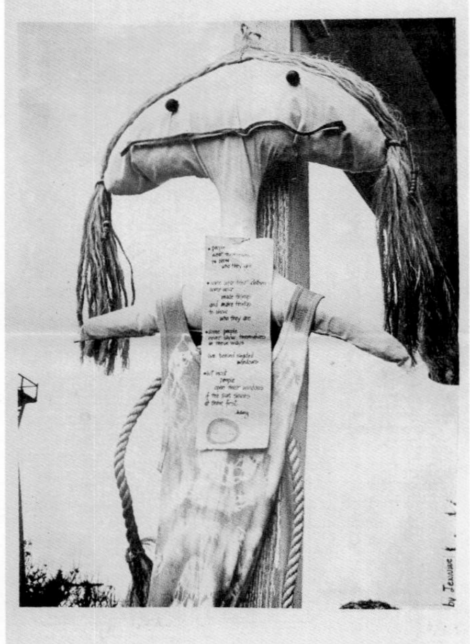

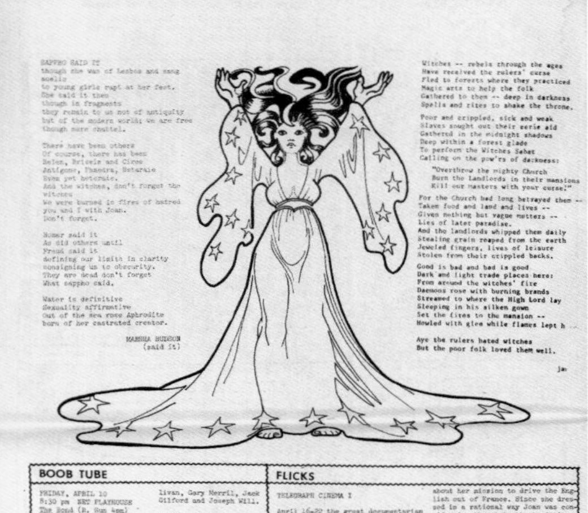

BOOB TUBE

FLICKS

16.

It Ain't Me Babe (Albany, California), April 28, 1970, vol. 1, no. 6, cover
It Ain't Me Babe (Albany, California), June 11–July 1, 1970, vol. 1, no. 8, cover
It Ain't Me Babe (Albany, California), July 23–August 5, 1970, vol. 1, no. 10, cover
It Ain't Me Babe (Albany, California), October 8, 1970, vol. 1, no. 15, cover
It Ain't Me Babe (Albany, California), October 30, 1970, vol. 1, no. 16, back cover
It Ain't Me Babe (Albany, California), April 7, 1970, vol. 1, no. 5, back cover

Next page
Gay Sunshine (San Francisco), October–November 1972, no. 15, front and back covers
Gay Sunshine (San Francisco), April 1972, no. 12, front and back covers

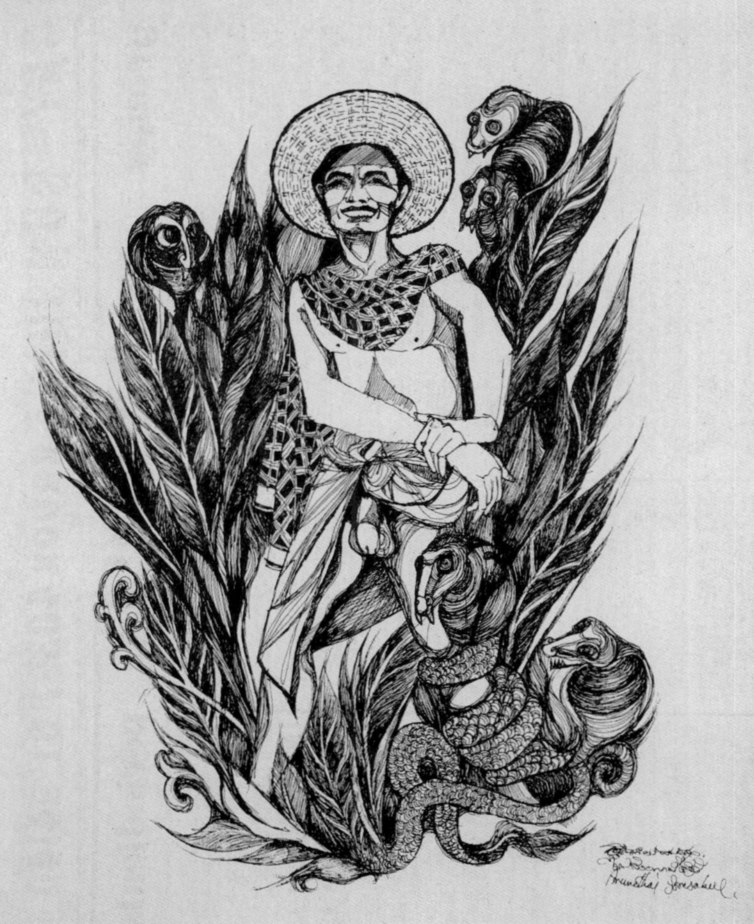

GAY SUNSHINE

A Newspaper of Gay Liberation
.35 Calif. / .50 Elsewhere
Number 15

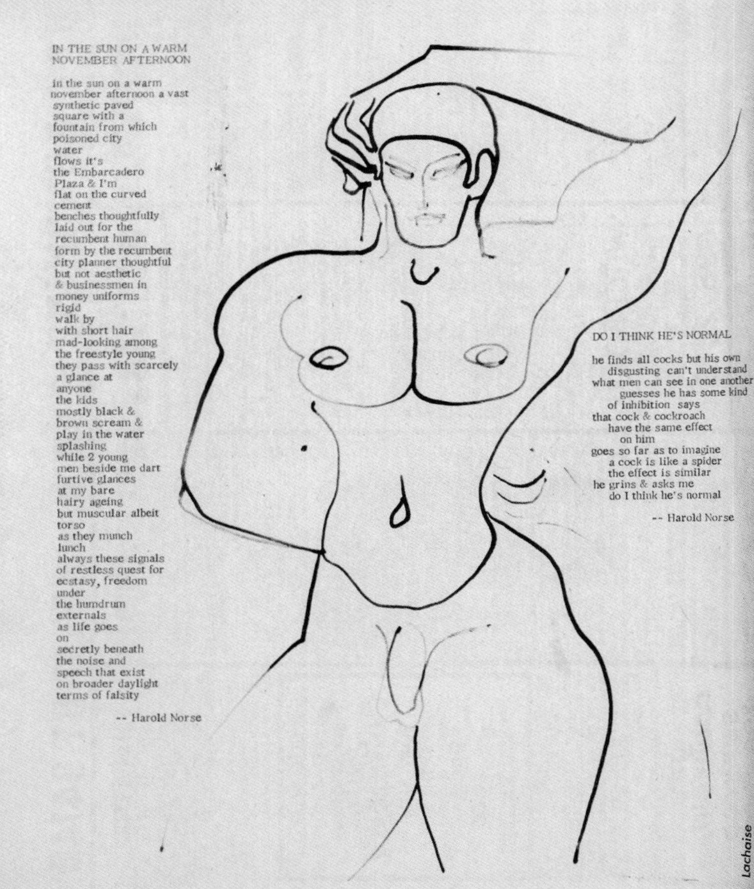

IN THE SUN ON A WARM
NOVEMBER AFTERNOON

in the sun on a warm
november afternoon a vast
synthetic paved
square with a
fountain from which
poisoned city
water
flows it's
the Embarcadero
Plaza & I'm
flat on the curved
cement
benches thoughtfully
laid out for the
recumbent human
form by the recumbent
city planner thoughtful
but not aesthetic
& businessmen in
money uniforms
rigid
walk by
with short hair
mad-looking among
the freestyle young
they pass with scarcely
a glance at
anyone
the kids
mostly black &
brown scream &
play in the water
splashing
while 2 young
men beside me dart
furtive glances
at my bare
hairy ageing
but muscular albeit
torso
as they munch
lunch
always these signals
of restless quest for
ecstasy, freedom
under
the humdrum
externals
as life goes
on
secretly beneath
the noise and
speech that exist
on broader daylight
terms of falsity

-- Harold Norse

DO I THINK HE'S NORMAL

he finds all cocks but his own
disgusting can't understand
what men can see in one another
guesses he has some kind
of inhibition says
that cock & cockroach
have the same effect
on him
goes so far as to imagine
a cock is like a spider
the effect is similar
he grins & asks me
do I think he's normal

-- Harold Norse

Lachaise

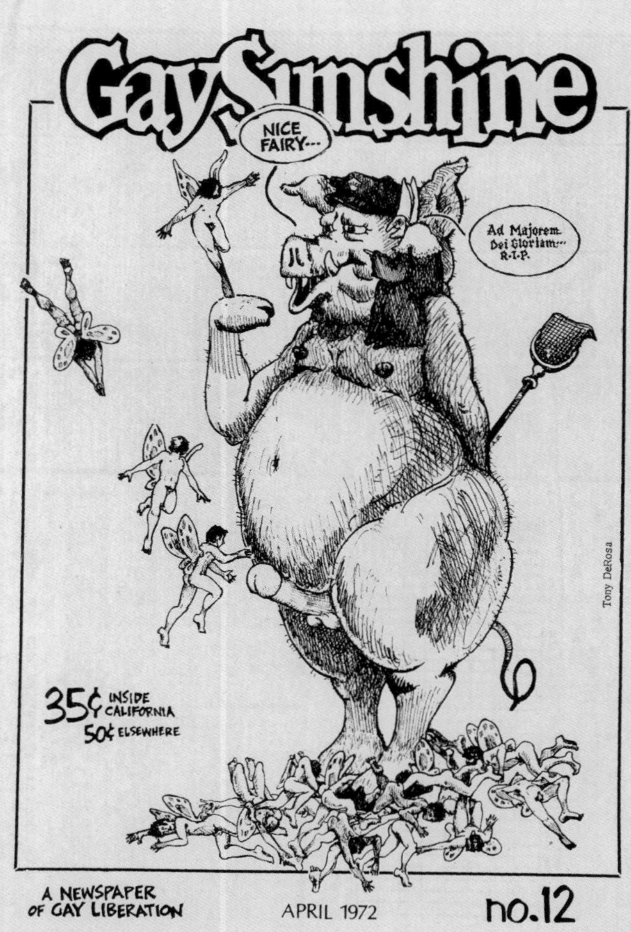

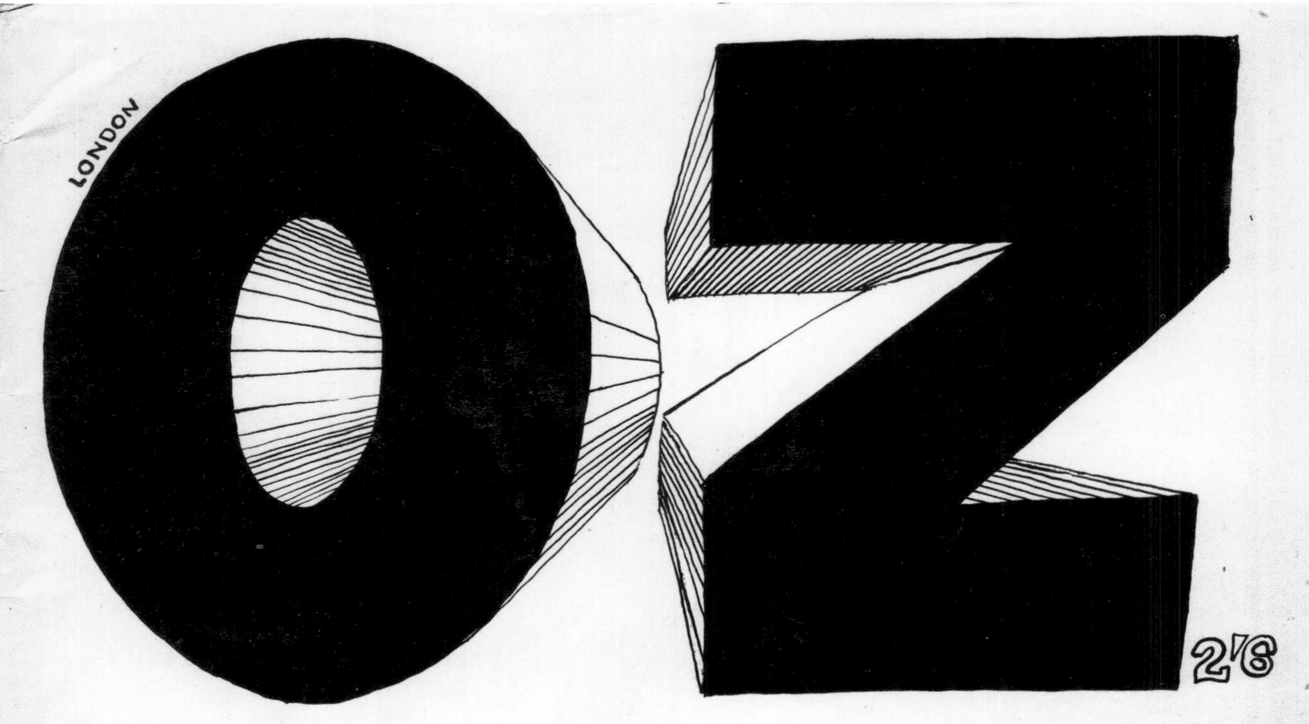

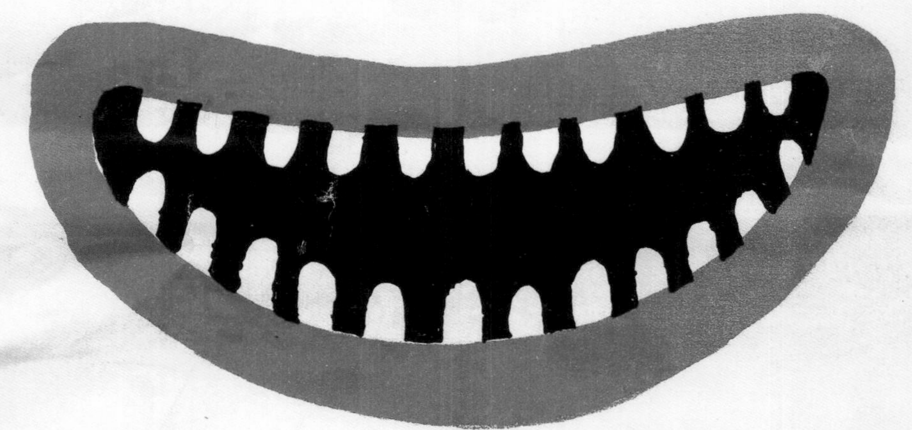

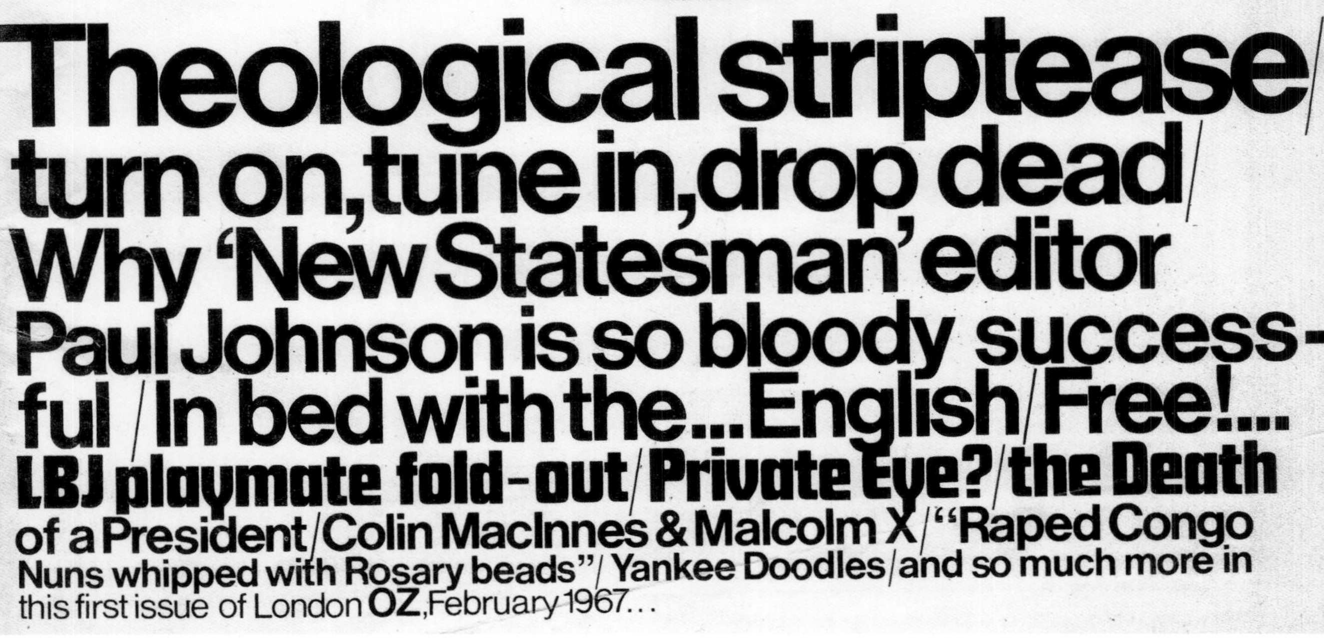

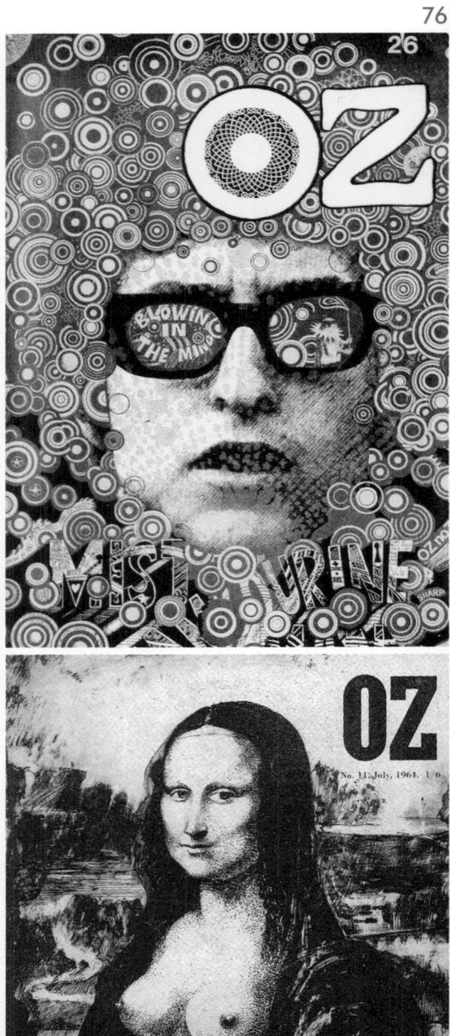

Oz (London), February 1967, no. 1, cover
Oz (London), no. 7, cover
Oz (Sydney, Australia), July 1964, no. 11, cover

Next page
Oz (London), no. 16, cover
Oz (London), no. 3, cover
Oz (London), no. 8, cover
Oz (London), no. 10, cover

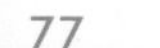

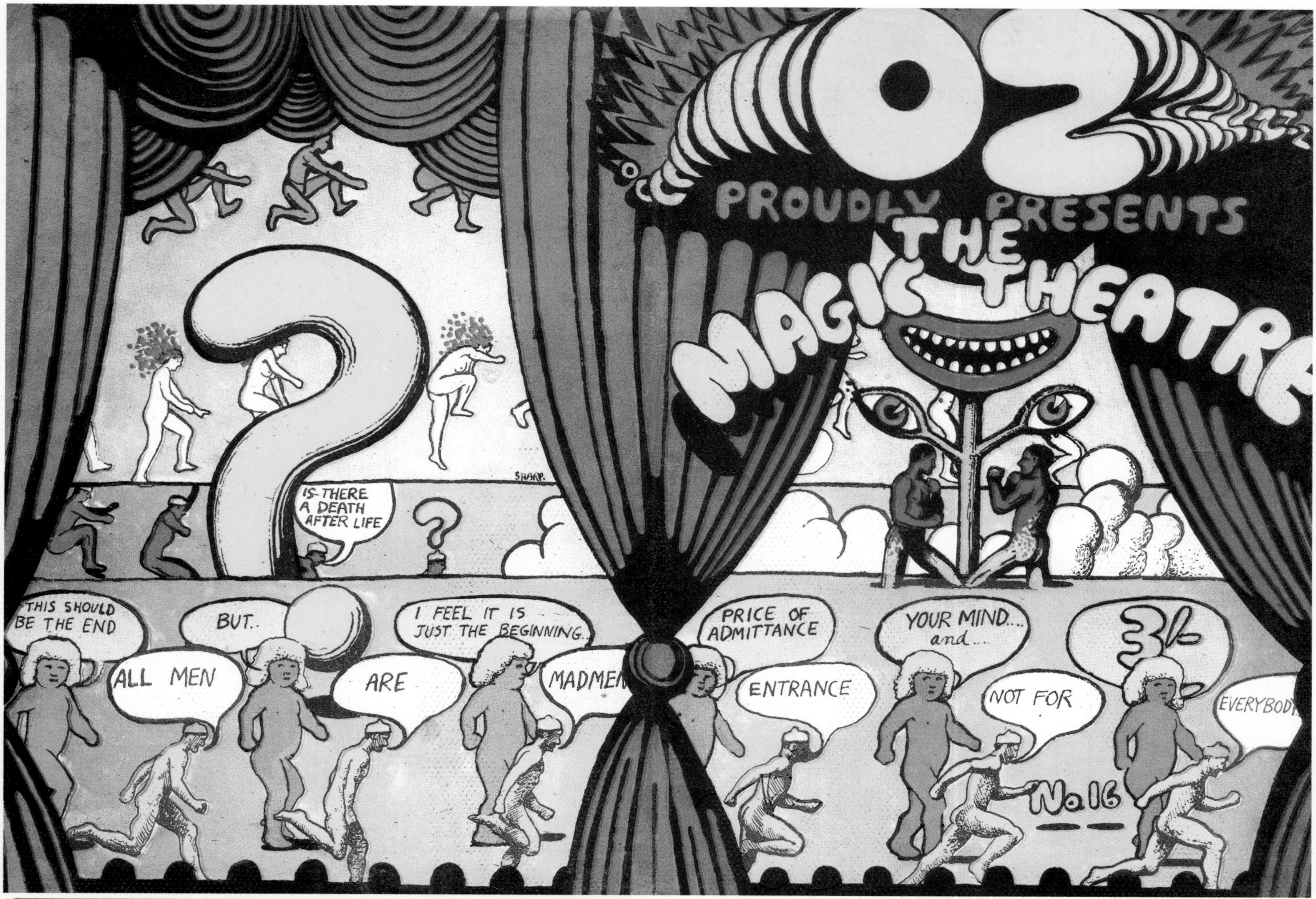

OZ
PROUDLY PRESENTS
THE MAGIC THEATRE
IS THERE A DEATH AFTER LIFE
SHARP.
THIS SHOULD BE THE END
BUT..
I FEEL IT IS JUST THE BEGINNING..
ALL MEN
ARE
MADMEN
PRICE OF ADMITTANCE
YOUR MIND.... and...
3/-
ENTRANCE
NOT FOR
EVERYBODY
No.16

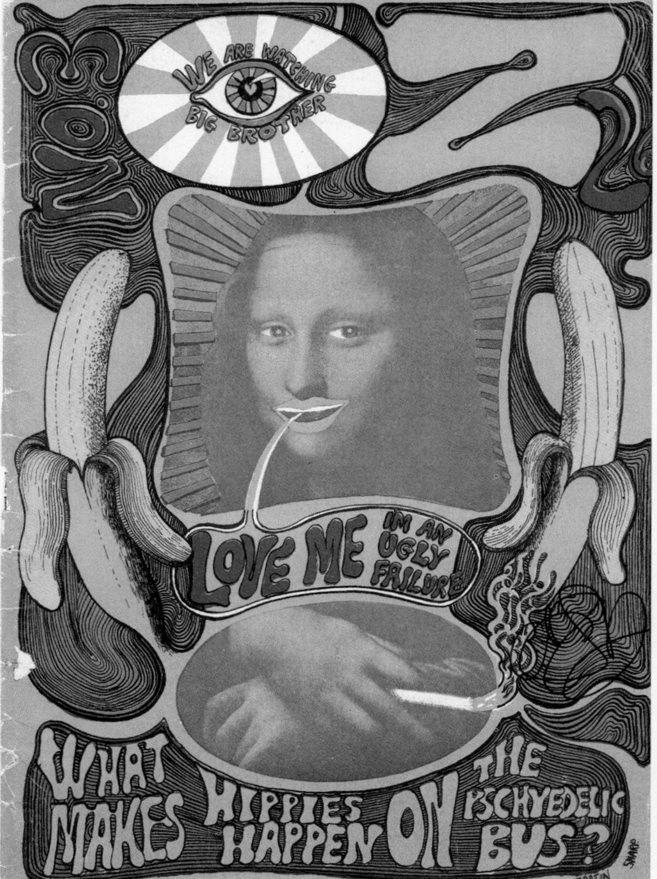
No. 3
OZ
WE ARE WATCHING BIG BROTHER
LOVE ME I'M AN UGLY FAILURE
WHAT MAKES HIPPIES HAPPEN ON THE PSCHYEDELIC BUS?
MARTIN SHARP

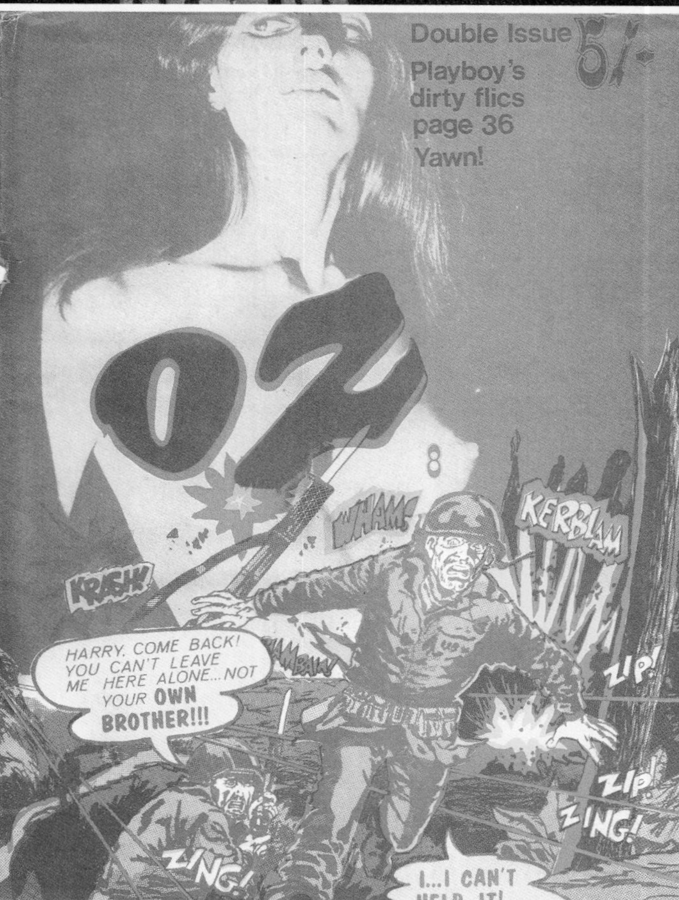
Double Issue 5/-
Playboy's dirty flics page 36
Yawn!
OZ
WHAM!
KERBLAM
KRASH!
HARRY, COME BACK! YOU CAN'T LEAVE ME HERE ALONE...NOT YOUR OWN BROTHER!!!
ZIP!
ZIP!
ZING!
ZING!
I...I CAN'T HELP IT!

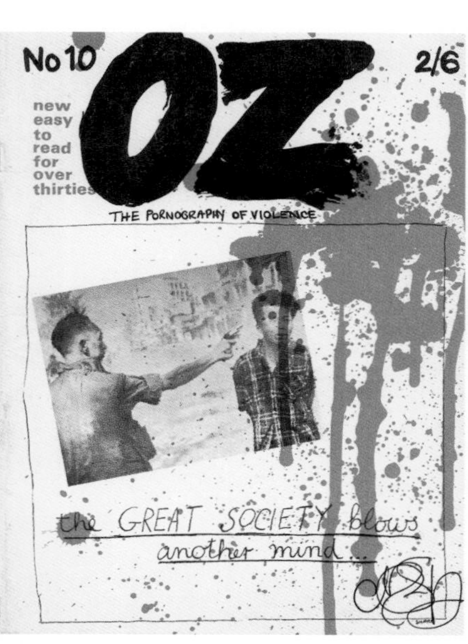
No 10
OZ
2/6
new easy to read for over thirties
THE PORNOGRAPHY OF VIOLENCE
the GREAT SOCIETY blows another mind...

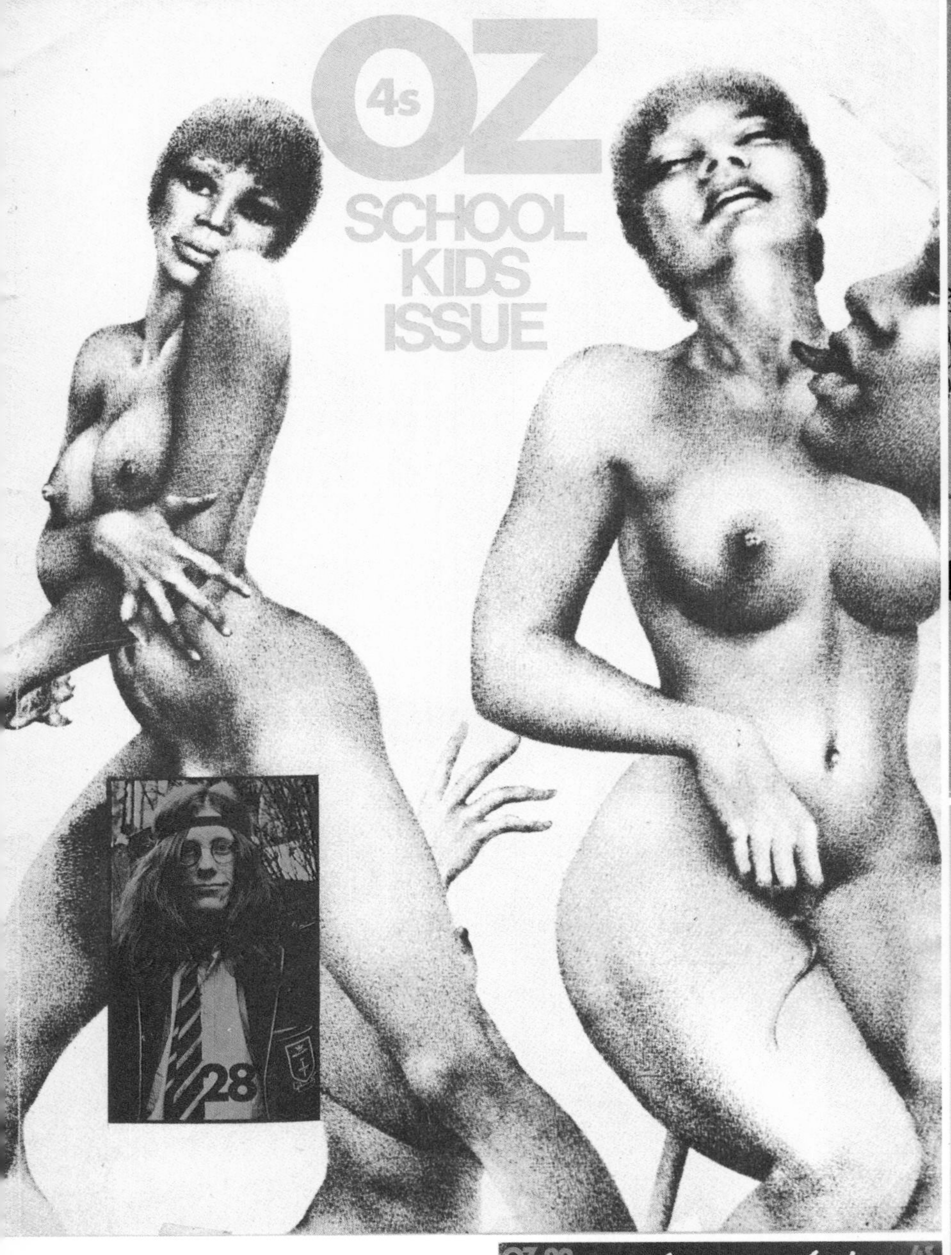

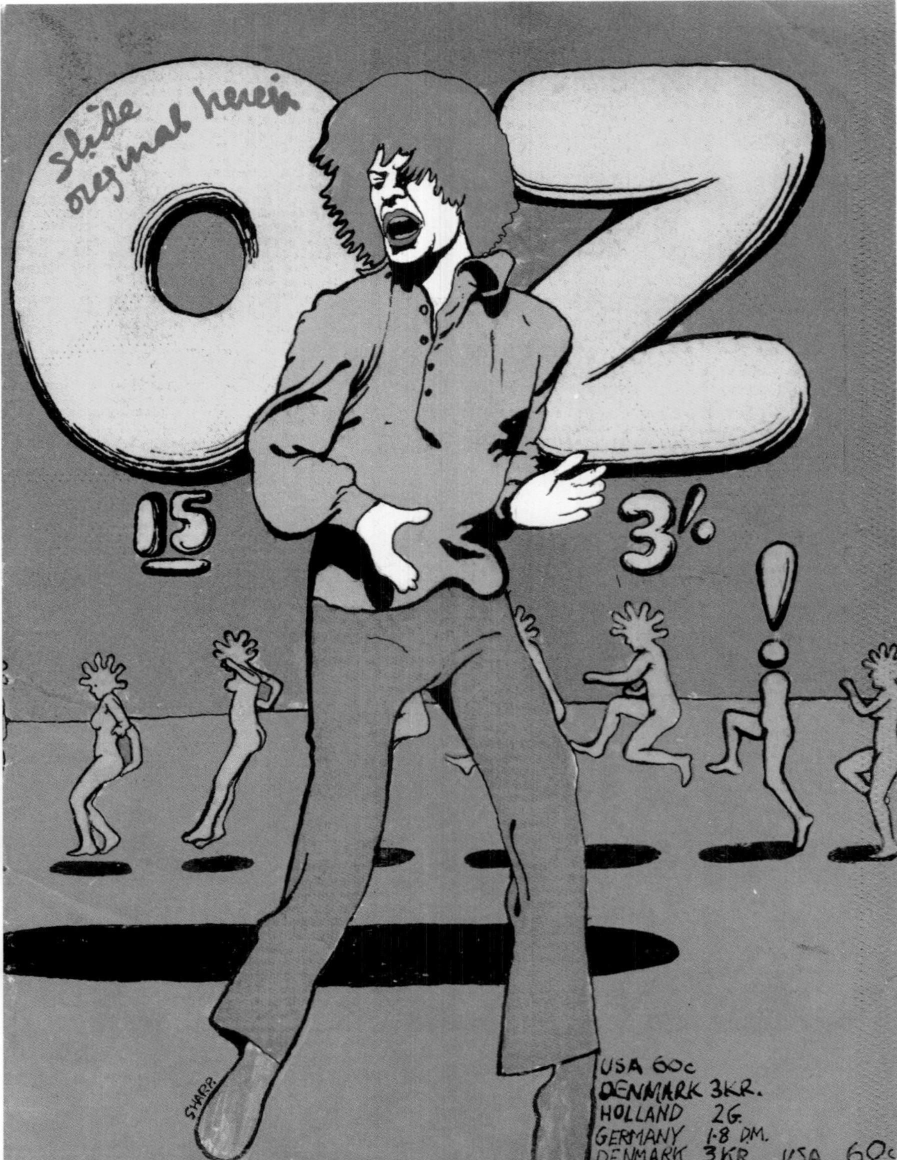

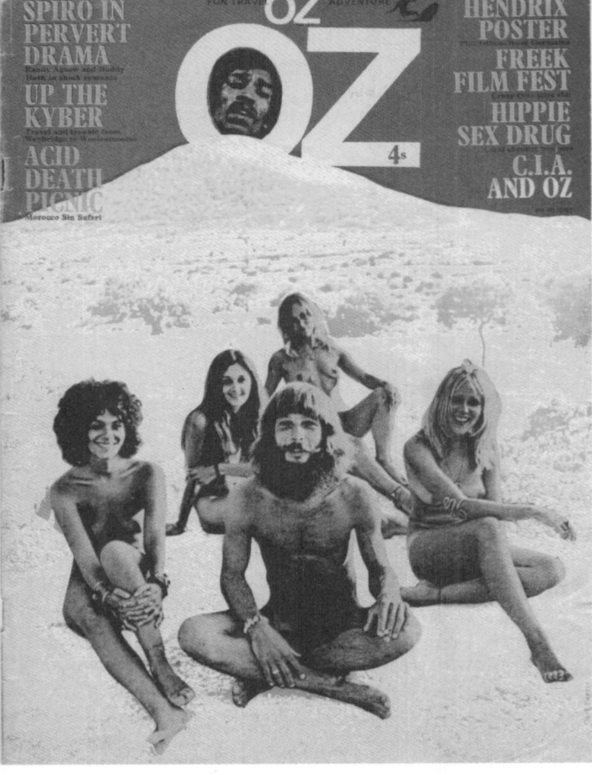

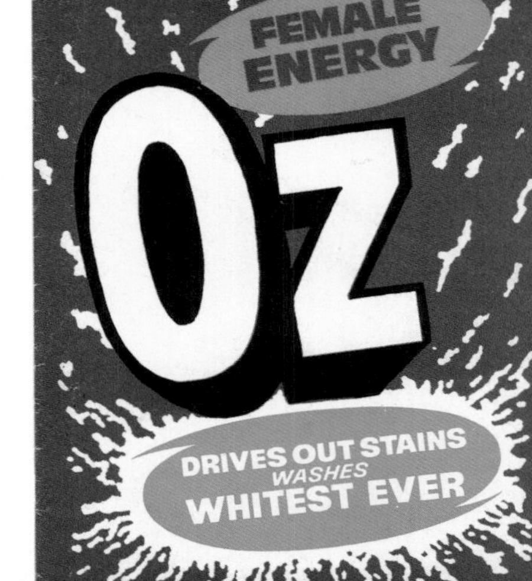

Oz (London), 1970, no. 28, cover
Oz (London), 1969, no. 15, cover
Oz (London), 1970, no. 30, cover
Oz (London), 1970, no. 29, cover

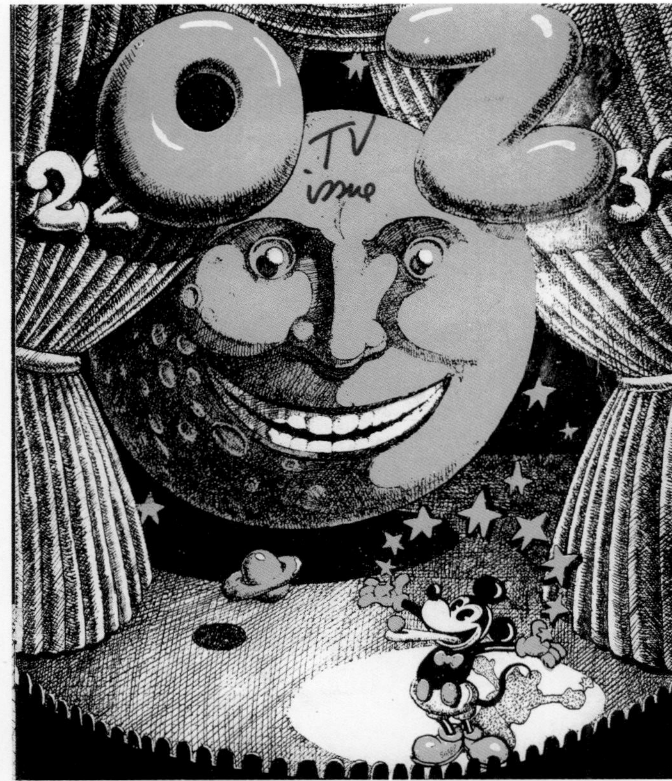

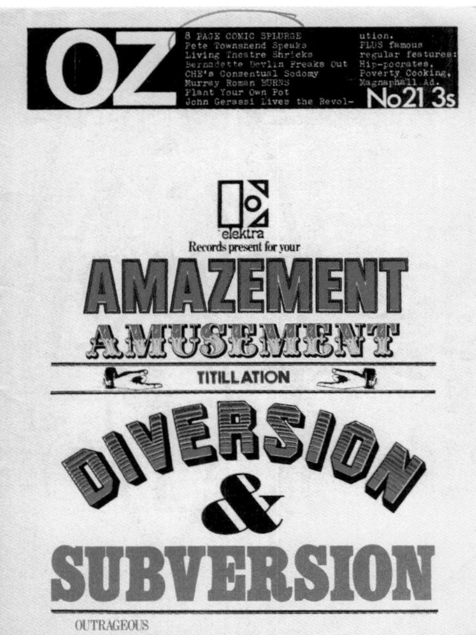

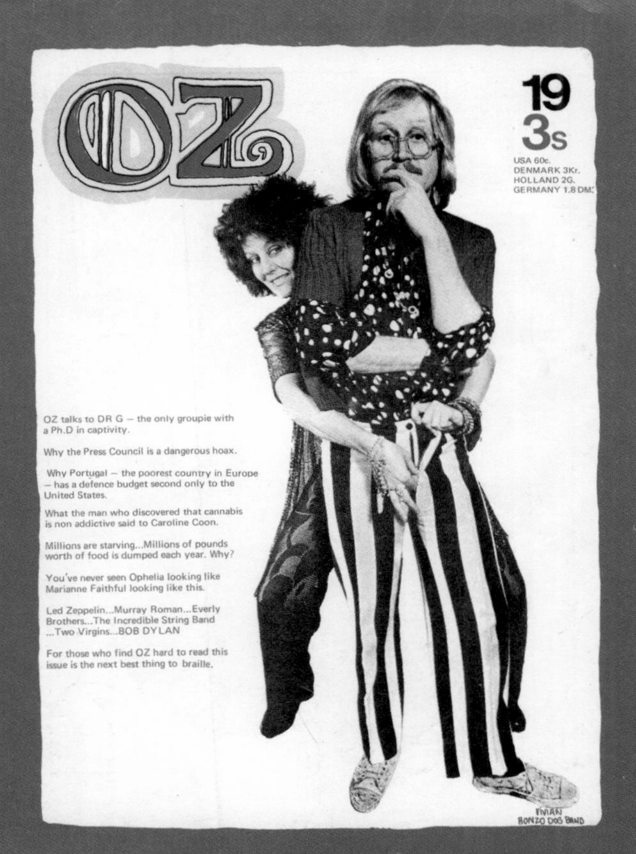

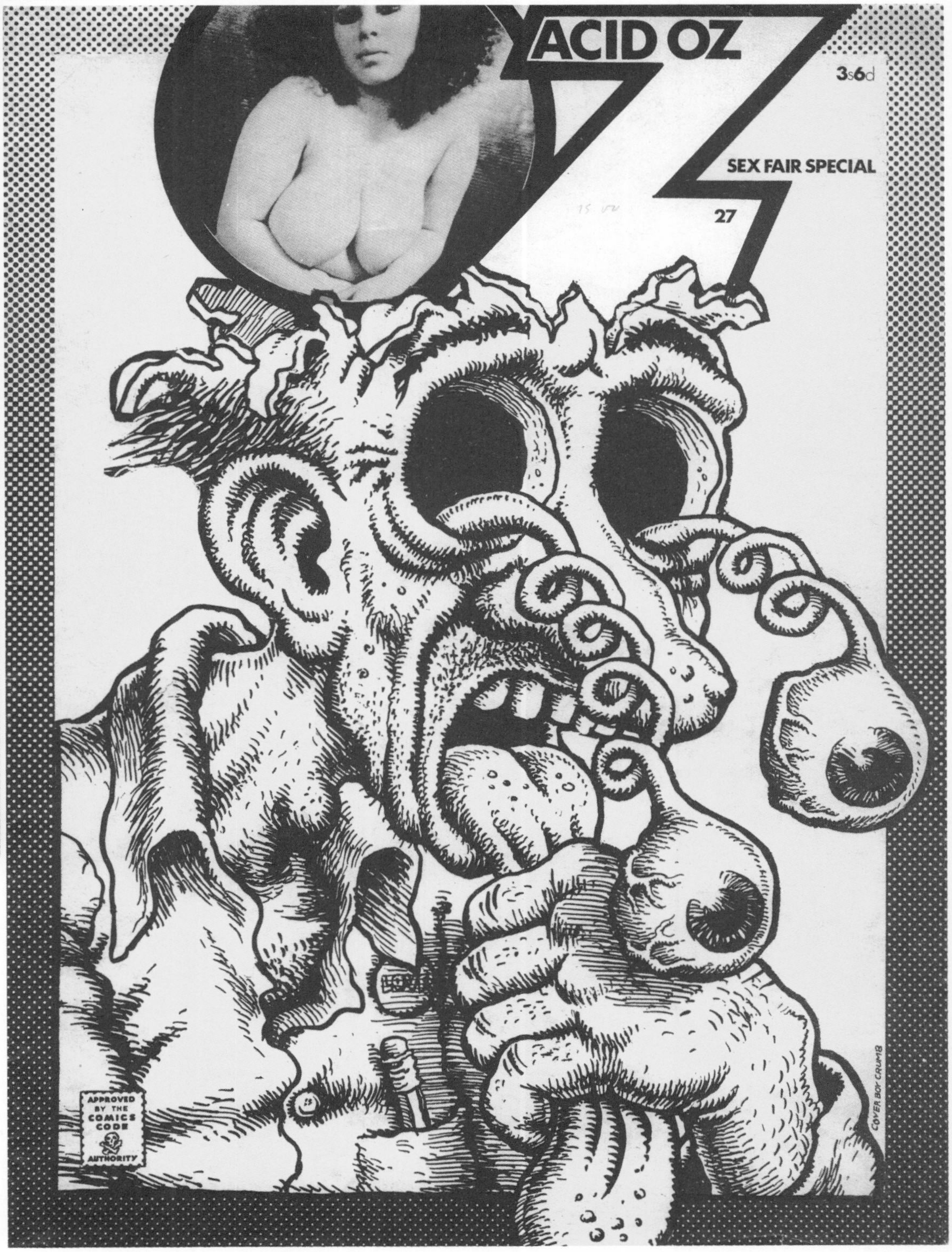

ACID OZ

3s6d

SEX FAIR SPECIAL

27

APPROVED BY THE COMICS CODE AUTHORITY

COVER BOY CRUMB

Oz (London), 1969, no. 27, cover
Oz (London), 1969, no. 21, cover
Oz (London), 1969, no. 19, cover
Oz (London), 1970, no. 27, cover

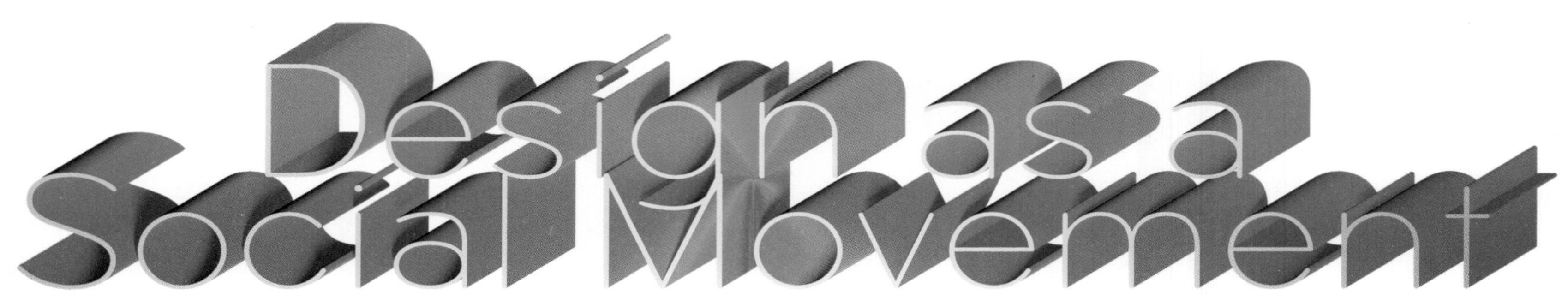

Design as a Social Movement

Gwen Allen

WHAT DOES SOCIAL REVOLUTION LOOK LIKE? This essay examines the graphic design of alternative and underground publications of the 1960s as it relates to the social and political ideals they espoused. Periodicals such as *Oz*, *Earth First*, *Off Our Backs*, the *Furies*, the *Oracle*, the *East Village Other*, the *Whole Earth Catalog*, *Radical Software*, and the *Black Panther Party Paper* were crucial tools for communicating "the movement" to a broader public. However, just as the counterculture itself was composed of the distinct and sometimes disparate agendas of the civil rights, antiwar, gay and lesbian, feminist, new communalist, and environmental movements, the underground press was deeply heterogeneous, ranging from the psychedelic style of the *Oracle* to the art nouveau–influenced pages of *Avatar* to the social realist approach of the *Black Panther Party Paper*. This essay offers a close formal analysis of these publications and historicizes their graphic innovations within the context of art history as well as in relationship to contemporary social, political, and technological transformations.

While often depicted as a group of amateurs whose hallucinogenic imagery, barely legible fonts, delirious borders, and crude layouts reflected either a lack of skill or a mind-altered state, the editors and designers of the underground press in fact strategically employed a range of sophisticated visual practices that parallel those utilized by artists during this period—even as they challenged the conventions of both official high culture and mass-produced commercial culture. Like artists, designers developed strategies of montage, ***détournement***, and deskilling to challenge official representations and to counter traditional notions of expertise and cultural authority. They investigated the materiality of language, critiqued traditions of documentary photography, and invented participatory strategies to transform the relationship between cultural producers and consumers. Here, I consider the graphic design of the underground press alongside radical artistic practices of the period not in order to collapse or conflate these two things but to demonstrate how they deeply informed one another within the wider visual culture and media politics of the 1960s and 1970s. Such comparisons affirm the similarities between artists and other kinds of cultural producers, underscoring the value of visual and creative activity outside the art world, and allow us to more fully appreciate the aesthetic significance and political stakes of both art and graphic design during this period.

IN HIS 1967 ARTICLE "Academy 23: A Deconditioning," published in the tenth issue of the *San Francisco Oracle*, William S. Burroughs heralded the benefits of mind-altering drugs such as marijuana and LSD in "deconditioning" the mind, allowing it to shed the automatic beliefs and mores imposed by mainstream American society. The implications of such a personal and perceptual reawakening—whether achieved through hallucinogens or political consciousness raising—were wide-reaching in the 1960s and 1970s, key to questioning the repressive rationality of the technocracy and its deep-seated sexist, racist, and imperialist values, or so the counterculture believed: "Take LSD and wipe the slate clean of all that Madison Avenue–Big Business–Behavioralist crap."[1]

Burroughs' article is provocative not only in its advocacy of illegal drugs but in its visual format (fig. 3.1). The first page, printed in blue, is crowded into three misshapen columns by an overgrown decorative lavender border—a teeming filigree of arabesque foliage, rays, flowers, and paisley, which does not frame the text so much as threaten to swallow it up. The article continues in the form of six neat circles of text covering the page like giant polka dots, which echo the shape of the florescent orange and purple mandala on the facing page (fig. 3.2). Reading the article is disorienting as the eye, accustomed to the regular rhythms of consistently spaced, rectangular columns of text, adjusts to the unfamiliarity and unpredictability of this altered printed reality.

Indeed, by disturbing the rules that normally govern the page, the unusual layout visually conveys the mind-altering effects of LSD, a drug known for its ability to distort perception and disrupt the brain's capacity to filter and categorize the world. This analogy—one that the editors and designers of the *Oracle* undoubtedly intended—extends beyond the obvious, however. More than just a simple exercise in eyestrain, the visual design of the *Oracle* suggests the important role that mass media promised to play in the personal and political transformation of the 1960s and 1970s. Burroughs himself alluded to this possibility, noting that deconditioning depended on the ability to "turn the word into a useful tool instead of an instrument of control in hands of a misinformed and misinforming press."[2]

This was precisely the goal of the hundreds of independently published and distributed newspapers that made up the underground press in the 1960s and 1970s. If it is a truism that these alternative papers did not report on reality but sought to transform it, Burroughs' article suggests the important role of graphic design in this endeavor. As headlines broadcast radical political views and lifestyle choices, the underground press gave rise to an equally revolutionary new visual culture through which it reimagined the meanings of gender, race, authority, technology, and the environment.

The underground press of the 1960s and 1970s fulfilled Walter Benjamin's demand for a radical media practice that would transform mass communication on the level of form as well as subject matter by altering its means of production and distribution.[3] Taking advantage of newly accessible, inexpensive printing technologies such as offset, cold-type composition, and mimeograph, individuals with little experience and negligible startup funds edited, designed, and distributed their own publications, developing "quick and dirty" layout methods that could work for anyone who had access to a typewriter, scissors, and a jar of rubber cement. This democratization of printing

1. Jay Stevens, *Storming Heaven: LSD and the American Dream* (New York: Harper & Row, 1987), p. 246, quoted in Peter Braunstein, "Forever Young: Insurgent Youth and the Sixties Culture of Rejuvenation," in *Imagine Nation: The American Counterculture of the 1960s & 70s*, ed. Peter Braunstein and Michael William Doyle (New York: Routledge, 2002), p. 254.

2. William S. Burroughs, "Academy 21: A Deconditioning," *San Francisco Oracle*, vol. 1, no. 10 (1967), p. 21.

3. Walter Benjamin, "The Author as Producer," in *Reflections*, ed. Peter Demetz, trans. Edmond Jephcott (New York: Schocken Books, 1978), p. 238.

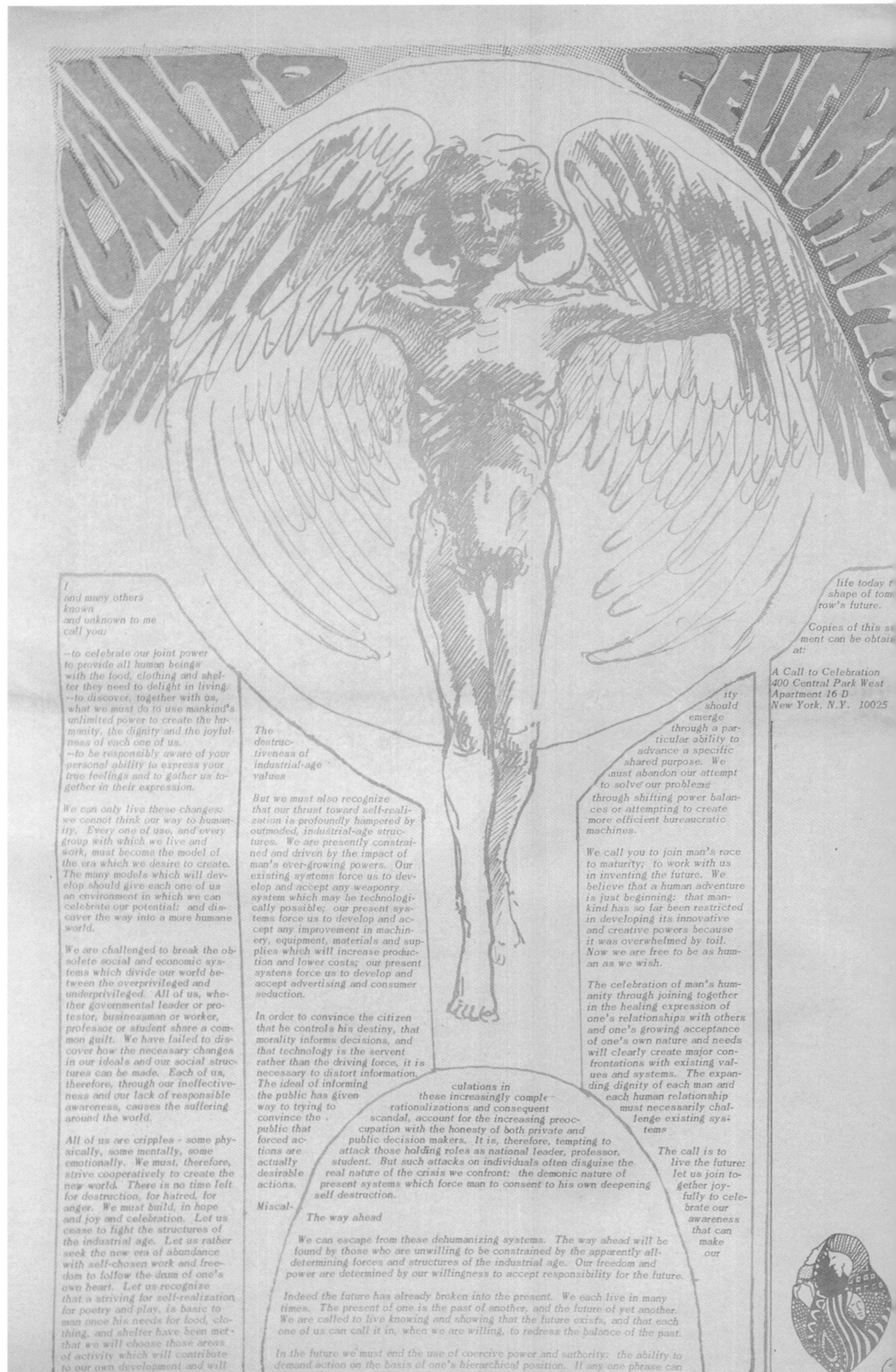

I
and many others
known
and unknown to me
call you:

--to celebrate our joint power to provide all human beings with the food, clothing and shelter they need to delight in living.
--to discover, together with us, what we must do to use mankind's unlimited power to create the humanity, the dignity and the joyfulness of each one of us.
--to be responsibly aware of your personal ability to express your true feelings and to gather us together in their expression.

We can only live these changes: we cannot think our way to humanity. Every one of use, and every group with which we live and work, must become the model of the era which we desire to create. The many models which will develop should give each one of us an environment in which we can celebrate our potential: and discover the way into a more humane world.

We are challenged to break the obsolete social and economic systems which divide our world between the overprivileged and underprivileged. All of us, whether governmental leader or protestor, businessman or worker, professor or student share a common guilt. We have failed to discover how the necessary changes in our ideals and our social structures can be made. Each of us, therefore, through our ineffectiveness and our lack of responsible awareness, causes the suffering around the world.

All of us are cripples - some physically, some mentally, some emotionally. We must, therefore, strive cooperatively to create the new world. There is no time left for destruction, for hatred, for anger. We must build, in hope and joy and celebration. Let us cease to fight the structures of the industrial age. Let us rather seek the new era of abundance with self-chosen work and freedom to follow the drum of one's own heart. Let us recognize that a striving for self-realization, for poetry and play, is basic to man once his needs for food, clothing, and shelter have been met - that we will choose those areas of activity which will contribute to our own development and will be meaningful to our society.

The destructiveness of industrial-age values

But we must also recognize that our thrust toward self-realization is profoundly hampered by outmoded, industrial-age structures. We are presently constrained and driven by the impact of man's ever-growing powers. Our existing systems force us to develop and accept any weaponry system which may be technologically possible; our present systems force us to develop and accept any improvement in machinery, equipment, materials and supplies which will increase production and lower costs; our present systens force us to develop and accept advertising and consumer seduction.

In order to convince the citizen that he controls his destiny, that morality informs decisions, and that technology is the servent rather than the driving force, it is necessary to distort information. The ideal of informing the public has given way to trying to convince the public that forced actions are actually desirable actions.

Miscalculations in these increasingly complex rationalizations and consequent scandal, account for the increasing preoccupation with the honesty of both private and public decision makers. It is, therefore, tempting to attack those holding roles as national leader, professor, student. But such attacks on individuals often disguise the real nature of the crisis we confront: the demonic nature of present systems which force man to consent to his own deepening self destruction.

The way ahead

We can escape from these dehumanizing systems. The way ahead will be found by those who are unwilling to be constrained by the apparently all-determining forces and structures of the industrial age. Our freedom and power are determined by our willingness to accept responsibility for the future.

Indeed the future has already broken into the present. We each live in many times. The present of one is the past of another, and the future of yet another. We are called to live knowing and showing that the future exists, and that each one of us can call it in, when we are willing, to redress the balance of the past.

In the future we must end the use of coercive power and authority: the ability to demand action on the basis of one's hierarchical position. If any one phrase can sum up the nature of the new era, it is the end of privilege and license. Author-

ity should emerge through a particular ability to advance a specific shared purpose. We must abandon our attempt to solve our problems through shifting power balances or attempting to create more efficient bureaucratic machines.

We call you to join man's race to maturity; to work with us in inventing the future. We believe that a human adventure is just beginning: that mankind has so far been restricted in developing its innovative and creative powers because it was overwhelmed by toil. Now we are free to be as human as we wish.

The celebration of man's humanity through joining together in the healing expression of one's relationships with others and one's growing acceptance of one's own nature and needs will clearly create major confrontations with existing values and systems. The expanding dignity of each man and each human relationship must necessarily challenge existing systems

The call is to live the future: let us join together joyfully to celebrate our awareness that can make our

life today the shape of tomorrow's future.

Copies of this statement can be obtained at:

A Call to Celebration
400 Central Park West
Apartment 16 D
New York, N.Y. 10025

Fig. 3.1. **Oracle** (San Francisco), October 1967, vol. 1, no. 10, pp. 2-3

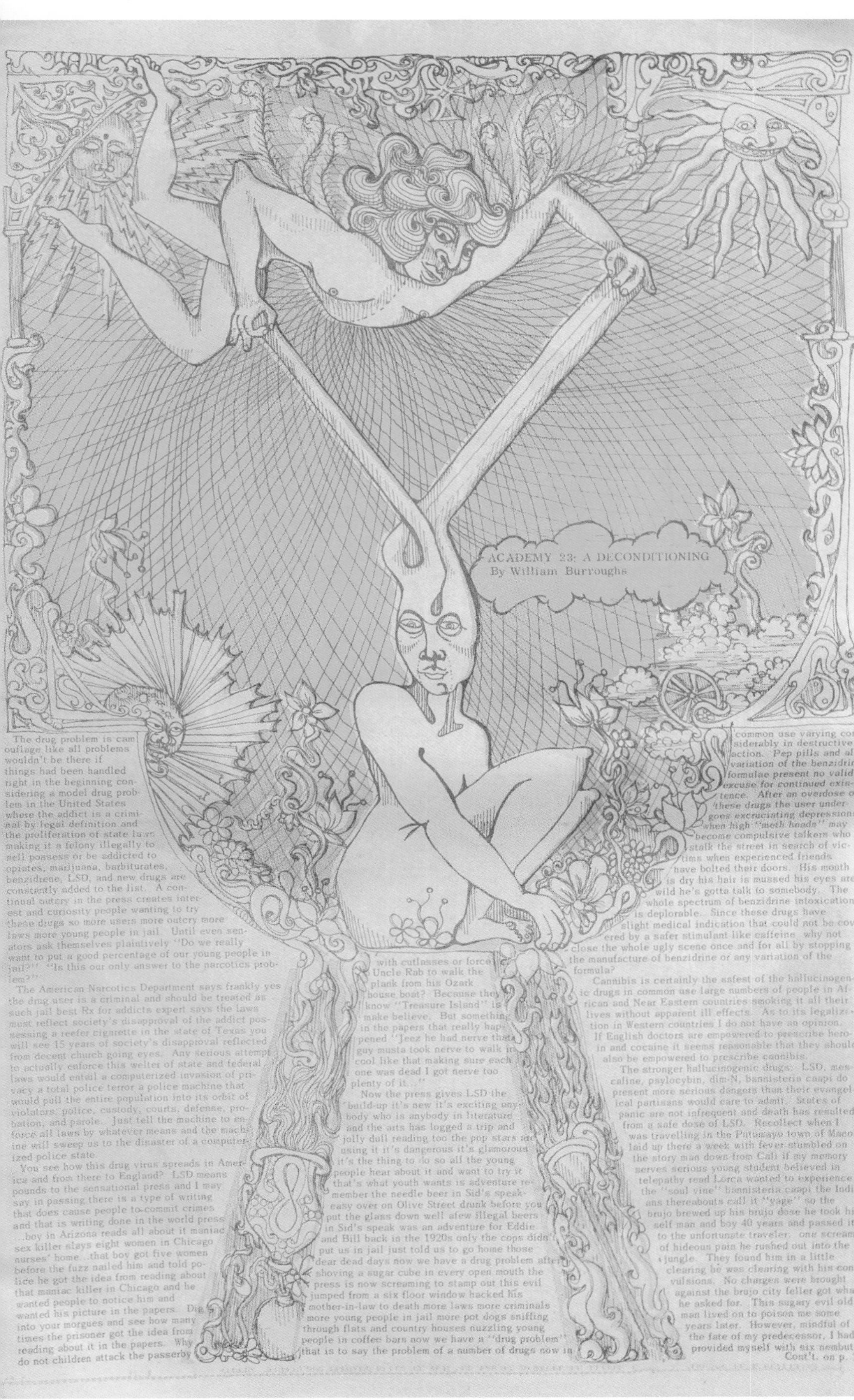

ACADEMY 23: A DECONDITIONING
By William Burroughs

The drug problem is camouflage like all problems wouldn't be there if things had been handled right in the beginning considering a model drug problem in the United States where the addict is a criminal by legal definition and the proliferation of state laws making it a felony illegally to sell possess or be addicted to opiates, marijuana, barbiturates, benzidriene, LSD, and new drugs are constantly added to the list. A continual outcry in the press creates interest and curiosity people wanting to try these drugs so more users more outcry more laws more young people in jail. Until even senators ask themselves plaintively "Do we really want to put a good percentage of our young people in jail?" "Is this our only answer to the narcotics problem?"

The American Narcotics Department says frankly yes the drug user is a criminal and should be treated as such jail best Rx for addicts expert says the laws must reflect society's disapproval of the addict possessing a reefer cigarette in the state of Texas you will see 15 years of society's disapproval reflected from decent church going eyes. Any serious attempt to actually enforce this welter of state and federal laws would entail a computerized invasion of privacy a total police terror a police machine that would pull the entire population into its orbit of violators, police, custody, courts, defense, probation, and parole. Just tell the machine to enforce all laws by whatever means and the machine will sweep us to the disaster of a computerized police state.

You see how this drug virus spreads in America and from there to England? LSD means pounds to the sensational press and I may say in passing there is a type of writing that does cause people to commit crimes and that is writing done in the world press ...boy in Arizona reads all about it maniac sex killer slays eight women in Chicago nurses' home...that boy got five women before the fuzz nailed him and told police he got the idea from reading about that maniac killer in Chicago and he wanted people to notice him and wanted his picture in the papers. Dig into your morgues and see how many times the prisoner got the idea from reading about it in the papers. Why do not children attack the passerby with cutlasses or force Uncle Rab to walk the plank from his Ozark house boat? Because they know "Treasure Island" is make believe. But something in the papers that really happened "Jeez he had nerve that guy musta took nerve to walk in cool like that making sure each one was dead I got nerve too plenty of it..."

Now the press gives LSD the "build-up it's new it's exciting anybody who is anybody in literature and the arts has logged a trip and jolly dull reading too the pop stars are using it it's dangerous it's glamorous it's the thing to do so all the young people hear about it and want to try it that's what youth wants is adventure remember the needle beer in Sid's speakeasy over on Olive Street drunk before you put the glass down well afew illegal beers in Sid's speak was an adventure for Eddie and Bill back in the 1920s only the cops didn't put us in jail just told us to go home those dear dead days now we have a drug problem after shoving a sugar cube in every open mouth the press is now screaming to stamp out this evil jumped from a six floor window hacked his mother-in-law to death more laws more criminals more young people in jail more pot dogs sniffing through flats and country houses nuzzling young people in coffee bars now we have a "drug problem" that is to say the problem of a number of drugs now in common use varying considerably in destructive action. *Pep pills and all variation of the benzidrine formulae present no valid excuse for continued existence. After an overdose of these drugs the user undergoes excruciating depressions* when high "meth heads" may become compulsive talkers who stalk the street in search of victims when experienced friends have bolted their doors. His mouth is dry his hair is mussed his eyes are wild he's gotta talk to somebody. The whole spectrum of benzidrine intoxication is deplorable. Since these drugs have slight medical indication that could not be covered by a safer stimulant like caffeine why not close the whole ugly scene once and for all by stopping the manufacture of benzidrine or any variation of the formula?

Cannibis is certainly the safest of the hallucinogenic drugs in common use large numbers of people in African and Near Eastern countries smoking it all their lives without apparent ill effects. As to its legalization in Western countries I do not have an opinion. If English doctors are empowered to prescribe heroin and cocaine it seems reasonable that they should also be empowered to prescribe cannibis.

The stronger hallucinogenic drugs: LSD, mescaline, psylocybin, dim-N, bannisteria caapi do present more serious dangers than their evangelical partisans would care to admit. States of panic are not infrequent and death has resulted from a safe dose of LSD. Recollect when I was travelling in the Putumayo town of Macoa laid up there a week with fever stumbled on the story man down from Cali if my memory serves serious young student believed in telepathy read Lorca wanted to experience the "soul vine" bannisteria caapi the Indians thereabouts call it "yage" so the brujo brewed up his brujo dose he took himself man and boy 40 years and passed it to the unfortunate traveler: one scream of hideous pain he rushed out into the jungle. They found him in a little clearing he was clearing with his convulsions. No charges were brought against the brujo city feller got what he asked for. This sugary evil old man lived on to poison me some years later. However, mindful of the fate of my predecessor, I had provided myself with six nembutal

Cont't. on p. 21

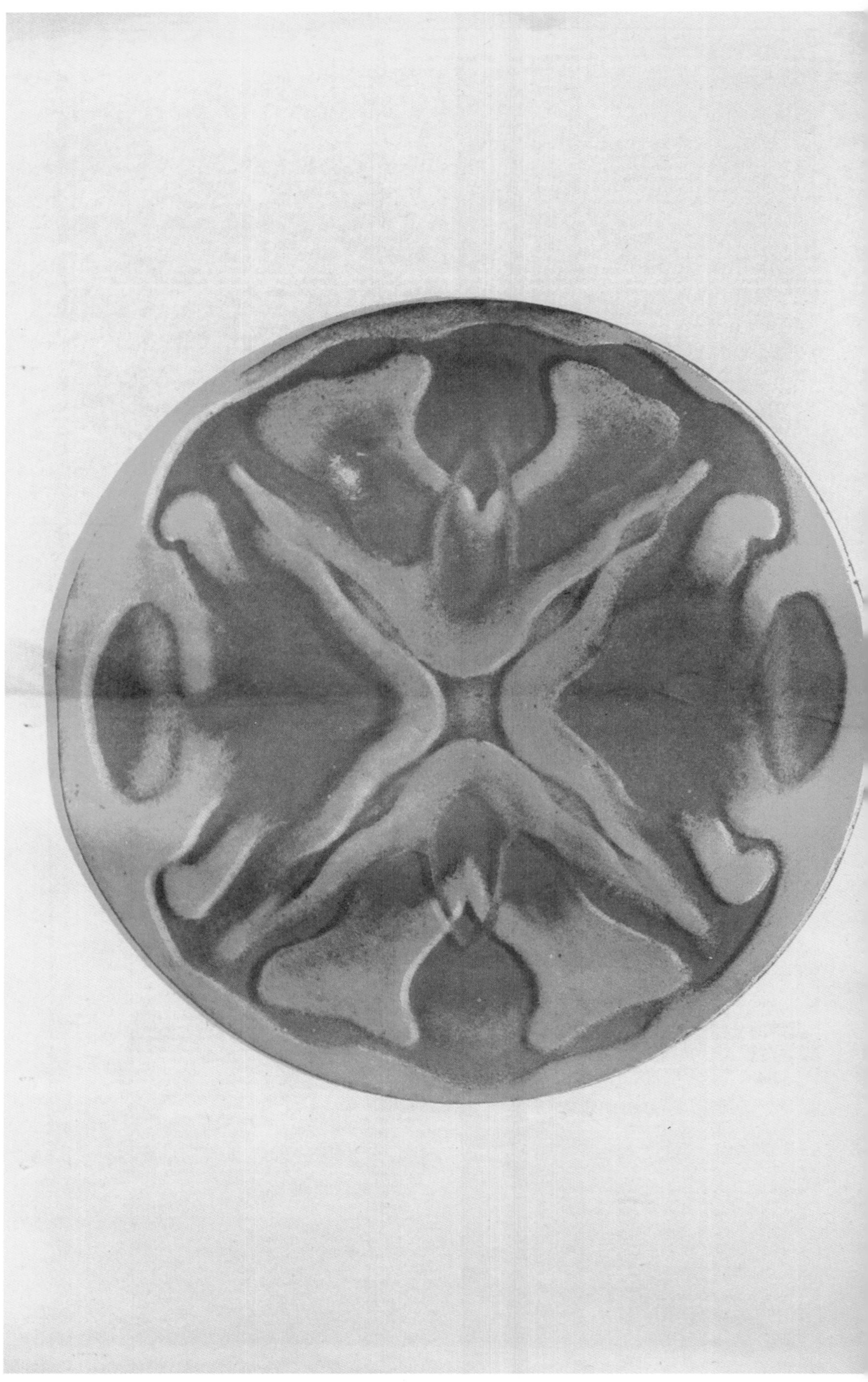

Fig. 3.2. **Oracle** (San Francisco), October 1967, vol. 1, no. 10, pp. 20–21

BURROUGHS

capsules and 20 codeine tablets a piece of foresight to which I may well owe my life. Even so I lay on the ground outside the brujo's hut for hours paralyzed in a hermetic vice of pain and fear. A high tolerance is acquired with use and the brujo's daily dose to get his power up could readily be lethal to a novice. Setting aside the factor of tolerance there is considerable variation in reaction to these drugs from one individual to another a safe dose for one tripper could be dangerous for another. The prolonged use of LSD may give rise in some cases to a crazed unwholesome benevolence the old tripster smiling into your face sees all your thoughts loving and accepting you inside out. Admittedly these drugs can be dangerous and they can give rise to deplorable states of mind. To bring the use of these drugs in perspective I would suggest that academies be established where young people will learn to get really high...high as the Zen master is high when his arrow hits a target in the dark...high as the Karate master is high when he smashes a brick with his fist...high...weightless ...in space. This is the space age. Time to look beyond this run down radioactive cop rotten planet. Time to look beyond this animal body. Remember anything that can be done chemically can be done in other ways. You don't need drugs to get high but drugs do serve as a useful short cut at certain stages of the training. The students would receive a basic course of training in the non-chemical disciplines of Yoga, Karate, prolonged sense withdrawal, stroboscopic lights, the constant use of tape recorders to break down verbal association lines. Techniques now being used for control of thought could be used instead for liberation. With computerized tape recorders and sensitive throat microphones we could attain insight into the nature of human speech and turn the word into a useful tool instead of an instrument of control in hands of a misinformed and misinforming press. Verbal techniques are now being used to achieve more reliable computer processed techniques in the direction of opinion control and manipulation the "propaganda war" it's called. The CIA does not give away money for nothing. It gives away money for opion control in certain directions. Opion control is a technical operation extending over a period of years. First a population segment – segment "preparation" is conditioned to react to words rather than word referents. Count Korzybski who formulated General Semantics used to begin a lecture by pointing to a chair and saying "Whatever that is it is not a 'chair.' "

That is the object chair is not the verbal or written label "chair." He considered the confusion between label and object the "is of identity" he called it, to be a basic flaw in Western thought this flaw is cultivated by the practitioners of opinion control. You will notice in the subsidized periodicals a curious prose without image. If I say the word "chair" you see a chair. If I say "the concommittance of societal somnolence with the ambivalent smugness of unavowed totalitarianism" you see nothing. This is pure word conditioning the reader to react to words. "Preparations" so conditioned will then react predictably to words. The conditioned preparation is quite impervious to facts.

The aim of academy training is precisely decontrol of opinion the students being conditioned to look at the facts before formulating any verbal patterns. The initial training in non-chemical methods of expanding awareness would last at least two years. During this period the student would be requested to refrain from all drugs including alcohol since bodily health is essential to minimize mental disturbance. After basic training the student would be prepared for drug trips to reach areas difficult to explore by other means in the present state of our knowledge. The program proposed is essentially a disintoxication from inner fear and inner control a liberation of thought and energy to prepare a new generation for the adventure of space. With such possibilities open to them I doubt if many young people would want the destructive drugs. Remember junk keeps you right here in junky flesh on this earth where Boot's is open all night. You can't make space in an aqualung of junk. The problem of those already addicted remains. Addicts need medical treatment not jail and not prayers. I have spoken frequently of the apo-morphine treatment as the quickest and most efficacious method of treating addicts. Variations and synthesis of the apo-morphine formula might well yield a miracle drug for disintoxication. The drug lomotil which greatly reduces the need for opiates but is not in itself addicting, might prove useful. With experimentation a painless cure would certainly emerge. What makes a cure stick is when the cured addict finds something better to do and realizes he could not do it on junk. Academies of the type described would give young people something better to do incidentally reducing the drug problem to unimportance.

GREED, con't. from p. 18

But, and this is so important, think what the rich kid is getting spiritually. We Buddhists insist that temples, and other offerings, earn us no merit. *Well, maybe that is right in some stern way. But I think this young boy's offering of this bookstore, and the 2-family faring-well bit, is meritorious. Of course, it all depends on how he takes it, or gives it.* That's his problem.

But do you know what this kid's damn fool father did? He, already slated to inherit more money than he could ever spend, stepped into Daddy's shoes and ran this huge corporation. Why?

Let's see it as the true revolution it is.

Success, Ambition, Yankee Trading, and the rest of that is jazz, just plain old horseshit jazz. It's clear to those of us who don't have money, it's clear to those of us who do, and the removal of Money-as-God from America will crack America faster than Christ cracked Rome.

Good riddance.

. . . . .

"You are all children of the Universe, you have a right to be here" the anonymous monk said. And while you are here you must:

(1) Eat and drink
(2) Sleep
(3) Piss and shit
(4) Die

(you can conceivably go without balling, though it is not recommended).

Since we have to pay money for (buy): (1) our eats (there being no land not owned, anywhere, anymore) and (2) a place to sleep or we get arrested, and (3) pay dearly for the place we shit and piss in, it appears that only a drink of water is still free, most places. For we certainly (4) have to pay dearly for death and burial, unless we are very clever indeed.

We are not free. We are slaves from the minute of birth until long after death --- we're on an eat later, work now, plan (maybe that's what is meant by Original Sin).

In order to pay for these things we cannot live without, we are expected to sell ourselves, not to the Devil (which might be a way better deal), but to a Corporation, a State System of several kinds, a husband, a rich relative, there are a variety of purchasers and the price may vary, but the fact remains we must, in order to live, die a little or a lot.

(Note that we left out breathing, and that the city of Tokyo now has a vending machine which gives you several breaths of good air, and that soon we will all wear metered masks).

Money is death. Ask yourself why banks and currency use the same images as tomb-stones.

. . . . .

But how to do it? And will it happen fast enough? Almost 15 years ago Gary Snyder had the vision: "If nobody bought a new car for just one year, the whole thing would collapse. Then maybe we could build it right this time."

This country, all countries, get younger every year. By 1970 more than half the population of the world will be under 25.

Some of these will find themselves "owning" huge amounts of money and power. I know one person who, years ago, told me he could "buy"

Cont. on p. 26

prompted, among other things, extraordinary graphic experimentation, as untrained professionals—in spite of, or more likely because of, their lack of expertise—improvised, turning the constraints of the offset medium to profound artistic and expressive effect.

So, for example, the ragged alignment of text necessitated by less sophisticated typesetting equipment evolved into distinctive wraparound columns that integrated image and text in imaginative new ways. Headlines were hand drawn or set with throwaway press-on letter sheets, which lent an idiosyncratic, homemade look to copy through a panoply of font sizes and styles. The split-fountain techniques which gave rise to the famous rainbow and kaleidoscopic color effects that were a signature feature of many underground publications were invented serendipitously by the editors of the San Francisco Oracle, who realized, as its founder Allen Cohen recalled, that they could "use the presses like a paint brush" by placing different colors of ink in the inkwells and allowing them to merge and blend in unpredictable ways.[4] Because they could only afford to pay the printer for a portion of the print run at a time, copies of the same issue of the Oracle were frequently printed in different colors.

The unorthodox visual practices of the underground press violated nearly every known convention of professional graphic design, especially the principles of objectivity and legibility associated with the so-called Swiss style (fig. 3.3), which dominated much advertising and corporate identity graphics in the 1960s. The Swiss prescription for ordering the page—which included the use of uniform, sans serif fonts; orderly, grid-based layouts; and "sparing but methodical use of color"[5]—served the functionalism of its ideology: "The rule that a text should be easily readable is unconditional,"[6] the Swiss typographer Emile Ruder insisted. By contrast, many underground papers teetered on the edge of illegibility, undermining text and image with their highly stylized fonts, crooked columns, distracting overlays, delirious borders that melted into copy, and souped-up color.

The renegade character of underground graphic design has frequently been chalked up to the amateur staff, makeshift equipment, and shoestring budgets of most papers. For example, Steven Heller attributed the "resolute sloppiness" of underground graphic design to the fact that "they did not know any better or because of the pressure of deadlines" and that they "worked under the influence of marijuana, LSD, and other drugs."[7] And in his important 1970 account of the underground press, Robert Glessing observed, "Necessity is the mother of invention, and much of the innovative graphic art in underground papers stems directly from their lack of funds."[8]

While there is certainly some truth to these claims, they reduce the relationship between economic or technological factors and cultural forms to a strictly causal, deterministic one, when in fact, the cooperative economic structures of the underground press were themselves deeply ideological: as the rock critic John Sinclair wrote in the Underground Press Syndicate ***Directory***, "Copyright is just another bullshit Western ego trip and a capitalist greed scheme. Nobody can own the fucking words."[9] Indeed, the visual formats of underground papers did not just straightforwardly or literally reflect the technological and economic circumstances under which they were produced but were the result of conscious and unconscious aesthetic choices through which these circumstances were rendered meaningful to designers and their audiences.

Consider, for example, the crude, artless appearance of many underground publications with their scrawled, hand-drawn lettering, Courier typewriter font, and rudimentary illustrations. Even as such do-it-yourself elements manifested the actual self-published nature of these papers, they also functioned metaphorically, as a powerful set of signifiers that opposed the slickness of mainstream media and helped to define a grassroots, anticonsumerist ethos. Such practices found a corollary within the more rarified realm of

4. Allen Cohen, "The *San Francisco Oracle*: A Brief History," in *Voices from the Underground*, ed. Ken Wachsberger (Ann Arbor: Azenphony Press, 1993), p. 142.

5. Josef Müller-Brockmann, *The Graphic Artist and His Design Problems* (Switzerland: Arthur Niggli), p. 48.

6. Emile Ruder, "The Typography of Order," *Graphis* vol. 15, no. 85 (September/October 1959), p. 404.

7. Steven Heller, *Merz to Émigré and Beyond: Avant-Garde Magazine Design of the Twentieth Century* (London: Phaidon Press, 2003), pp. 192, 188, 194.

8. Robert J. Glessing, *The Underground Press in America* (Bloomington: Indiana University Press, 1970), p. 45.

9. Quoted in ibid., p. 70.

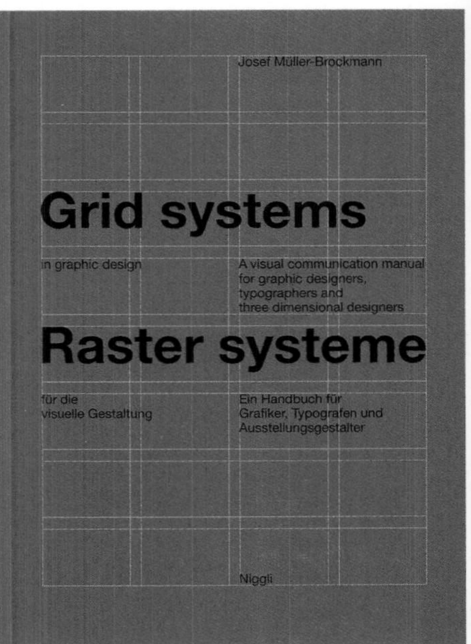

Fig. 3.3. **Grid Systems in Graphic Design,** Josef Müller-Brockmann's 1981 "manifesto" of the high modernist grid

avant-garde art in the 1960s, in the strategy of deskilling: the deliberate attempt to eliminate mastery and virtuosity from the work of art, witnessed, for example, in the task-like dance of the Judson dancers (fig. 3.4) or the industrially produced, reductive forms of minimalist sculpture. Just as part of the intended effect of such artistic practices was to foreground the spectator's own competence and ability, the DIY techniques and visual forms of the underground press corresponded to the goal of empowering readers to reject the authority of the expert and take control of their own destinies. From the *Whole Earth Catalog*, in which editor Stewart Brand advocated "the power of the individual to conduct his own education, find his own inspiration, shape his own environment, and share his adventure," to the feminist paper *Off Our Backs*, in which a regularly published column called "Survival" provided simple instructional drawings that taught readers how to change a tire, do a breast self-exam, or use a diaphragm, underground papers rejected the authority of the expert and encouraged individuals and communities to take charge of their own lives: information was a form of emancipation.

If the experimental graphic design of the underground press flouted the rules of professional design, it resonated unexpectedly with the critical investigations of language, photography, and the mass media so central to conceptual art of the 1960s and 1970s. "Language to be looked at and/or things to be read" was the title of Robert Smithson's press release for the first of four annual "Language" exhibitions at the Dwan gallery in New York between 1966 and 1970, signaling the interest of conceptual artists in language as a new kind of artistic medium. Smithson, for example, conceived of print as a quasi-sculptural material, likening it to geological formations in works such as ***A Heap of Language***, 1966 (fig. 3.5), and ***Strata: A Geophotographic Fiction***, 1970, in which words are stacked like layers of the earth. Meanwhile, in Ed Ruscha's "liquid word" paintings (fig. 3.6), letters took on the character of substances, including sweet, sticky maple syrup, oil, or

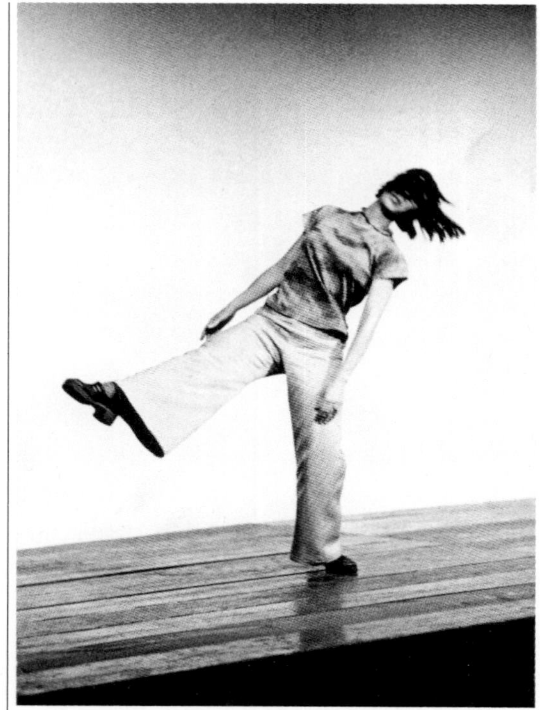

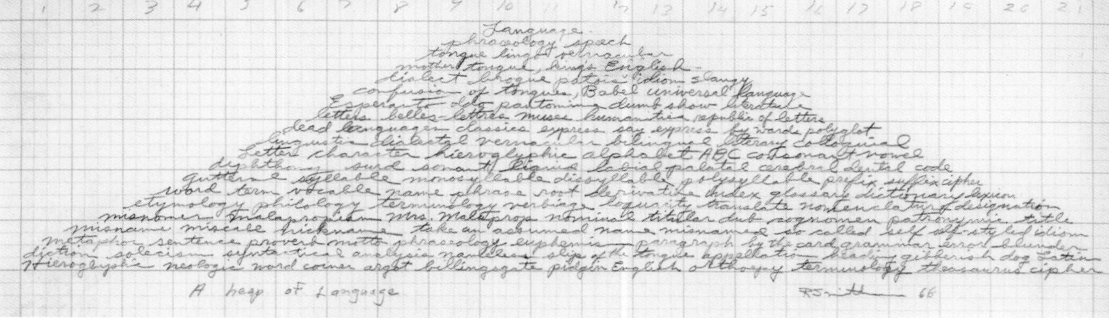

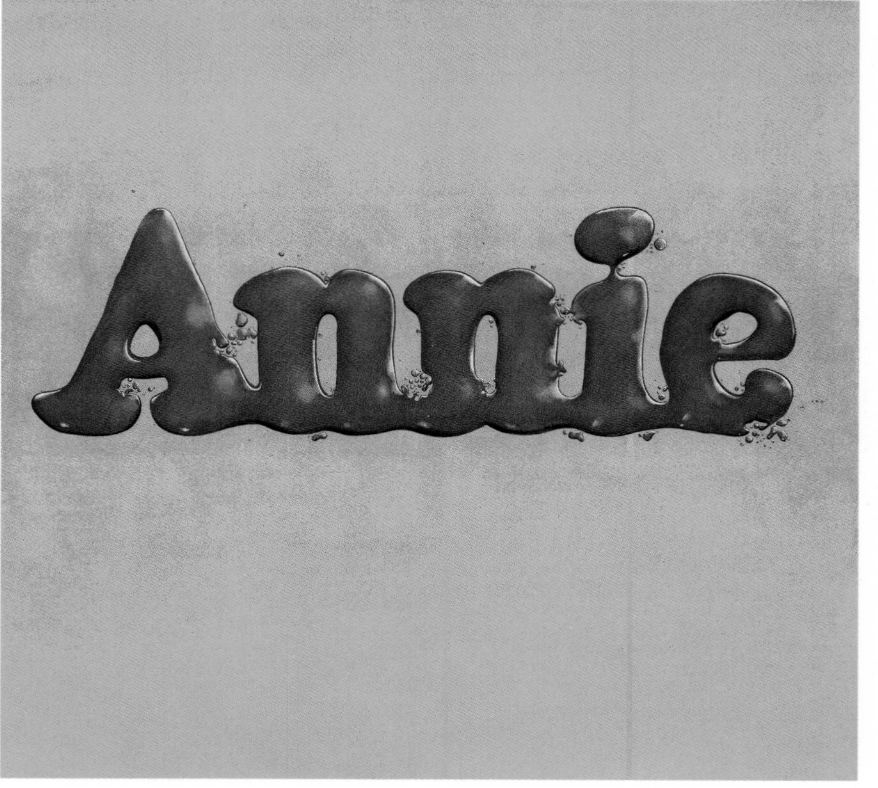

Fig. 3.4. Yvonne Rainer performing **Trio A,** video still, image from a 1973 postcard

Fig. 3.5. Robert Smithson, **A Heap of Language,** 1966

Fig. 3.6. Ed Ruscha's "liquid word" painting **Annie Poured from Maple Syrup,** 2008, 55 × 59 in.

off our backs

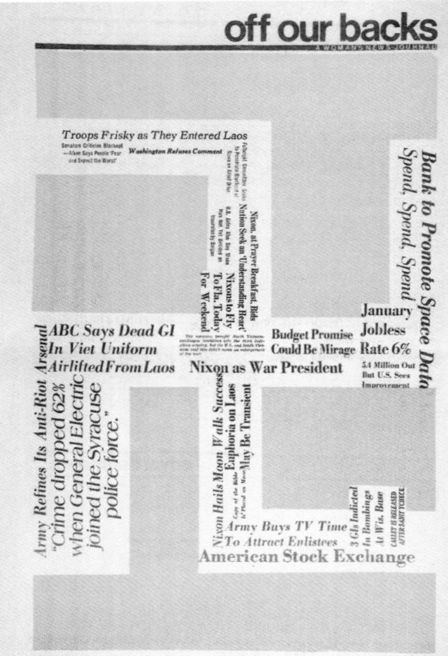

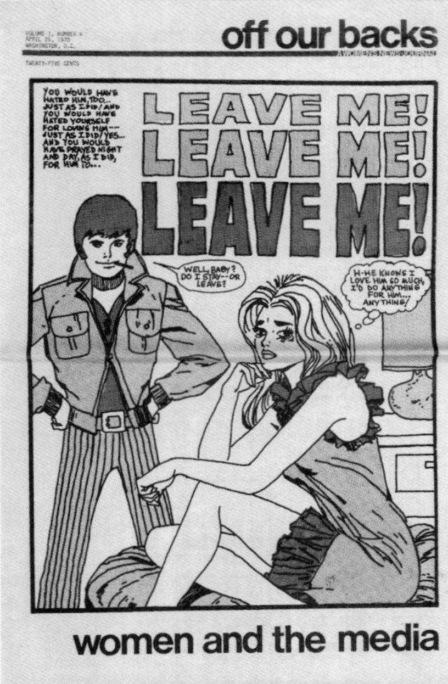

survival
the diaphragm

by Marlene Wicks

This is a serial column written to serve as a forum for our physical and mental well-being. The recent "pill" hearings have unsettled us all. We must turn to other means of birth control until we have more information regarding oral contraceptives. I'll start with the diaphragm.

The diaphragm, also called a pessary, is a birth control device and the safest in terms of the woman's health of all the devices known. It is designed to cover the opening to the uterus (cervix), and with experience will be as easy to insert as a tampon. It is made of soft rubber and looks like half a lemon peel with the rim rolled back upon itself. Inside the rim there is either a coil spring or a flat spring which may be compressed on opposite sides into the shape of a slipper for insertion.

Vaginal creams or jellies are available and should be used with the diaphragm. They come in tubes like toothpaste and are spread around the rim and inside the cup. These preparations help destroy male sperm, are impenetrable by semen and act as suction to keep the diaphragm in position.

You can insert the diaphragm standing, squatting, or lying down. Hold and compress the diaphragm between the thumb, index and third fingers. The index finger is placed inside the compressed diaphragm. Insert the diaphragm as far back as it will go behind the cervix. Then push the near part of the rim up behind the pubic bone in front. The diaphragm will have sprung into position to cover the cervix. Check this by running your forefinger around the rim and over the dome to be sure.

Mechanical inserters are sometimes prescribed as an alternate to the coil spring diaphragm. The diaphragm is placed on the introducer, which looks like a curved plastic stick, fitting the rim into the end groove, then hooking the opposite rim over the appropriate notch. Ease the introducer along the floor of the vagina, as you would a tampon, until it can no longer be pushed in. To remove the introducer after the diaphragm is in place, give it a quarter turn left or right - which disengages it from the diaphragm. Then, gently withdraw the introducer. The near rim of the diaphragm is then pushed up behind the pubic bone. Check as before to make sure the dome is covering the cervix.

When inserted properly, neither you nor your mate will be aware of the diaphragm in the vagina, and there will be no dulling of sensation. The contraceptive preparation is not harmful to the vaginal canal nor harmful if ingested orally.

It should remain in place for from six to eight hours after intercourse. Intercourse may be repeated without removing the diaphragm, however, an applicator filled with the contraceptive cream or jelly must be inserted outside the diaphragm each time.

A douche may be taken at the time of removal, half before and half after. To remove the diaphragm, a finger is hooked under its edge and it is drawn out. The douche will wash away any remaining semen and eliminate the odor which is offensive to some women. Opinions differ on the use of a douche, especially concerning whether or not to add medication to the water. Some doctors feel that douching is not necessary at all. Douches will be discussed in another column.

Diaphragms must be fitted to your cervix. This is very important; many women have just gone to a drug store, bought the wrong size and become pregnant. If the diaphragm is too small or too large, it is more likely to become dislodged. The size of your cervix will change after giving birth to a child and may change again after a few months. It must be refitted both times. The doctor will fit your diaphragm and either write a prescription for you to obtain one from a drugstore or sell you one from his office. The approximate cost is $3 to $5, and with good care lasts several years.

Rubber deteriorates with age. Prior to use, the diaphragm should be filled with water or held up to a light to detect any holes or cracks. After use, wash it with mild soap and water and dry it to prevent early deterioration. A light dusting of talc will help keep the rubber from sticking together.

When the diaphragm is properly fitted and used as directed, it is almost impossible for a woman to become pregnant. We must get over our shame of "planning for sex" if we are going to protect ourselves from unwanted pregnancies.

Readers' opinions or questions are encouraged. Let us hear from you.

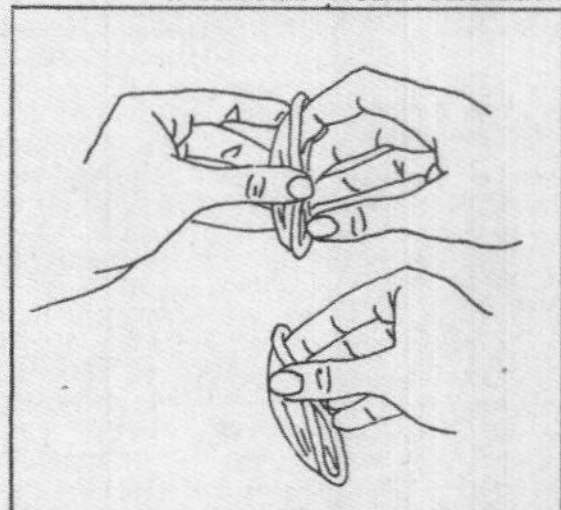

A STANDARD MODERN DIAPHRAGM

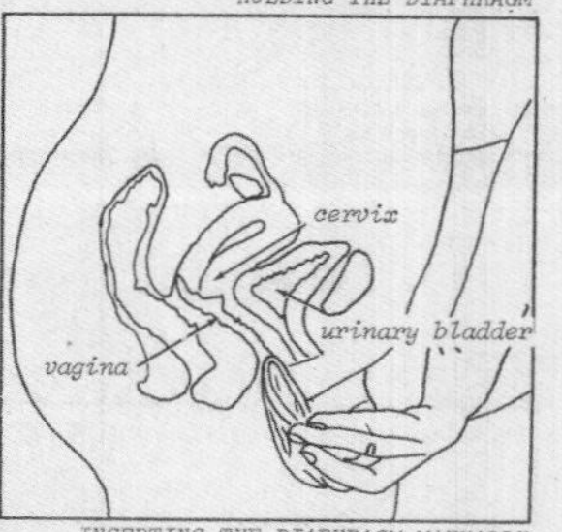

HOLDING THE DIAPHRAGM

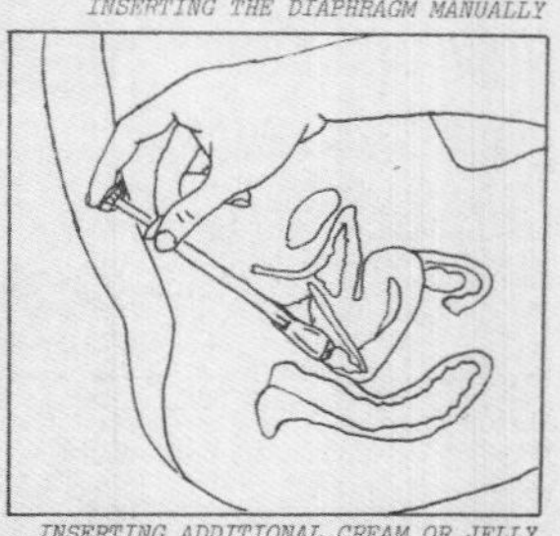

INSERTING THE DIAPHRAGM MANUALLY

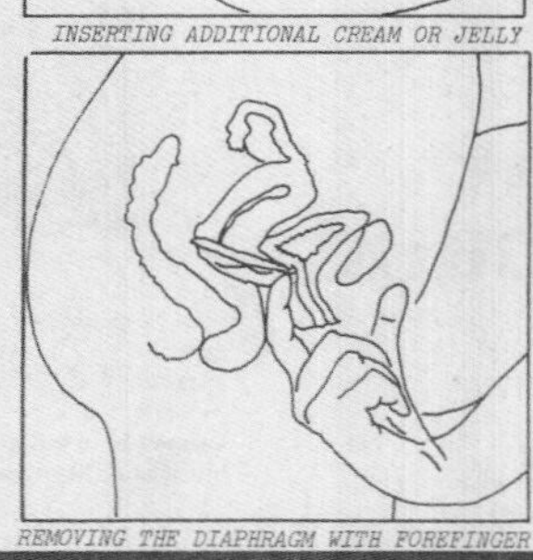

INSERTING ADDITIONAL CREAM OR JELLY

REMOVING THE DIAPHRAGM WITH FOREFINGER

psychology of the diaphragm

by Alison Sand

"My doctor told me that if using a diaphragm were a test of mental ability I'd be given a moron rating."

That quote is unique to one woman's experience with one strange gynecologist but it is, unfortunately, revealing. Most women don't receive adequate instruction or encouragement from their doctor and leave his office insecure about the device itself and about their ability to use it.

Learn to use your diaphragm before you need to use it. Make time for a thorough reading of the preceding article and the instruction pamphlet that will come with your diaphragm. Then take that written material and all the diaphragm paraphernalia into the bathroom, close the door, and practice.

Practice unabashedly. All alone you are acquiring a skill that is roughly comparable in difficulty to learning chords on a guitar, knitting, or rolling a joint, and a thousand times more crucial to your emotional and physical well being.

Check out the diagrams. Explore yourself sans guilt or embarrassment. It's perfectly all right for your fingers to be exploring your vagina in search of your cervix. In fact, it's really a turn on to locate and to recognize and be able to understand the function of those important parts of your self.

More important possibly than your confidence in your ability to use a diaphragm as a contraceptive is your matter-of-fact acceptance of your right to use it. Men should take their cues from you. Be righteous about using that diaphragm! You have assumed the major responsibility for contraception. He can be grateful for that and supportive of you.

Abortion counselors too often hear this refrain:"My old man gets angry when I interrupt our lovemaking to put in my diaphragm." If your gentle interjection of reality offends his sense of aesthetics, his interest is clearly in some sort of fantasy event and not in happy, honest lovemaking with old flesh and blood you.

12/February 27, 1970/off our backs

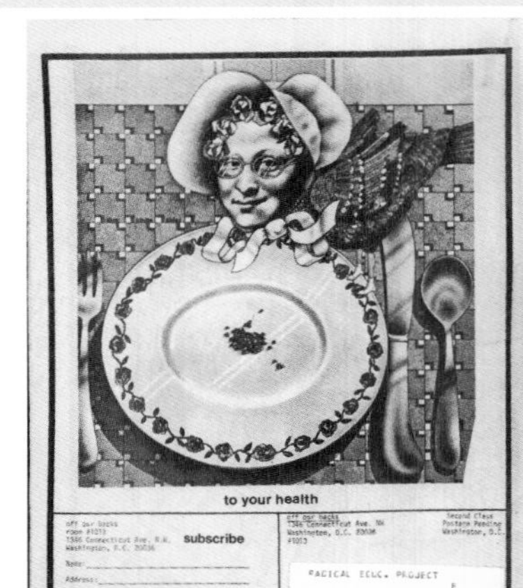

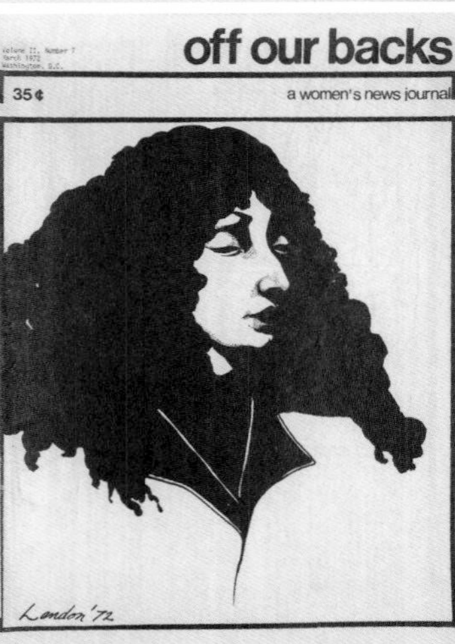

Off Our Backs: A Women's News Journal (Washington, DC), February 27, 1970, vol. 1, no. 1, cover
Off Our Backs: A Women's News Journal (Washington, DC), February 27, 1970, vol. 1, no. 1, back cover
Off Our Backs: A Women's News Journal (Washington, DC), February 26, 1971, vol. 1, no. 18, cover
Off Our Backs: A Women's News Journal (Washington, DC), April 25, 1970, vol. 1, no. 4, cover
Off Our Backs: A Women's News Journal (Washington, DC), March 25, 1972, vol. 2, no. 7, front and back covers

VOLUME I, NUMBER 2
MARCH 19, 1970
WASHINGTON, D.C.
TWENTY-FIVE CENTS

off our backs

A WOMAN'S NEWS JOURNAL

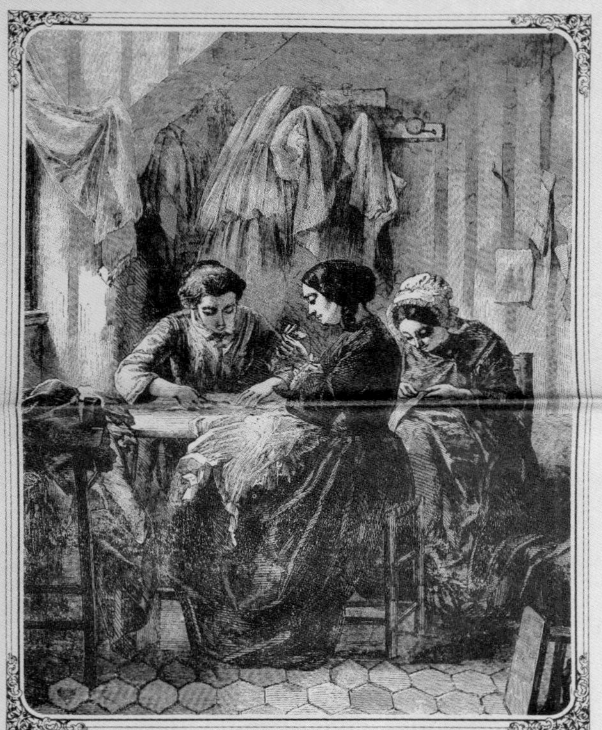

working women

off our backs

A WOMAN'S NEWS JOURNAL

jailhouse rock

On Sunday, the 13th of December, the New Haven Women's Liberation Rock Band played a concert at Niantic State Prison for Women. We played for an hour and a half to an audience of about 150 women--pre-trial detainees and prisoners. The women sat in formal rows of folding chairs in the prison gymnasium. Although they were not permitted to dance, they moved and grooved to the music. We felt that despite the fact that we played on a stage separated from the audience, warmth and sisterhood grew tremendously during the performance. It was a great sight to see the women digging the music as well as the words. By the concert we hoped to tell the women in Niantic that we out here do know, care, and want to do something about the oppression our sisters suffer in jail. As one prison sister said, "A lot of sisters left there stronger, it was one for our side."

The following poem was written by Erika Huggins, who as a pretrial detainee attended the concert. Her poem expressed better than anything else the feelings of sisterhood and strength we felt from playing there.

reflections on sunday:

sounds that come from the soul are always the
same
free
open sounds
giving the kind that reach out
and touch...
that's what our sisters did/minimum
touching maximum/sharing oppression
and the wish for its
removal...
feeling these sounds
seeing them felt on others
watching faces smile
really smile for the first time in months...
getting high--on the natural power of the
people to resist/to smile/to laugh/to sing
shout/love/give
even here...
wild hair, funky guitar
long, hairfunky voice (someone said bessie smith
came to mind)
hair--all lengths, legs, arms, smiles, music--
SISTERS - and us...
raggedy pea coats, cotton dresses, rocking
swaying
screaming
enjoying it--
crying too--even if not too many
let the tears fall free
...us--black/brown/white/poor..SISTERS-
and it was all a total exchange
of energy
communication
even if we did not share words
we all knew their soul-songs were
saying
we understand
we know
we can see what amerika is doing
to you - mother/daughter/child/woman
of oppression
we can see, they sang -
and our voices answered their guitars,
horns - flute - voice - cowbell - tambourine demand for freedom with an unspoken right or
...a feeling there that one day - soon -
all people will be free ... and
we left
stronger
able to smile
til we returned to
rules that degrade
schedules that destroy sanity
racism that they cannot see
sexism that rapes us of our womanhood...
and the locks, keys, windows, walls, doors,
threats
warnings
bribes that harden our hearts and
chain our souls...
the time
must be
seized
venceremos!

survival

on the road

Changing a tire is a simple and gratifying task which has generally been left to men for cultural, not physical reasons. It requires about the same energy output as shoveling snow, and only a little more knowledge.

You'll need two basic tools:

1) A jack comes with all cars--it's a variation on the simple lever with which an 80-pound person can lift a car with ease (see diagrams). Most jacks will fit anywhere under the car's bumper. Some newer American cars have four little flat "lips" under the bumpers near the corners of the car. To find out if your car has this just run your fingers along the underside of the bumper. This is where your jack will fit. Volkswagens, Volvos, Porsches and some other foreign cars have a special hole in the side of the car under the body. Check your owner's manual to see how this works, or just experiment.

2) A usable lug wrench may or may not be provided with your jack. This tool is used in getting the lugs (the large nuts that hold the tire to the car) off and on. The most efficient type is cross-shaped (see diagram). Your car may come supplied with a straight bar with a wrench socket (which should fit your car's lugs) at the end and a hole in the middle of the bar. Fitting your jack handle through this hole makes a cross-shaped wrench with good leverage. If, instead, your wrench is only a curved jack handle with a socket at the end you should get a better tool, as this won't give enough leverage unless your tire is on too loosely. Any tool store sells cross-shaped lug wrenches for $3 up, depending on the size. The bigger the wrench, the better the leverage. Even with a good wrench, you may have to use a sledge hammer (or a rock, whatever is handy), hitting the wrench to loosen the lug.

Now that you have your tools you'll probably never have a flat tire. But if you do, pull over to the side immediately--the tire can be repaired unless you ruin it by driving on it--if possible stopping at a flat place. Put on the emergency brake, get out your tools and your spare tire. If you think the car might roll off the jack because the ground is sloped, it's probably worth the risk to your tire to drive a little further (a few yards) to a flatter place. A couple of wedge-shaped blocks of wood are good extras to keep in your trunk--these go under the tires to keep the car from rolling. Pry off the hub-cap with your jack handle (see diagram) and you're ready to jack up the car.

First, elevate the car only 4-5 notches (or turns), just enough to take the stress off the flat tire but not enough to lift it off the ground. Stop and loosen each of the lugs half a turn or so--don't remove them yet. This will test the stability of the positions of car and jack. When loosening the lugs, try to get yourself into a position of maximum leverage and minimum strain to your back--feet wide apart, legs slightly bent. Turning sideways (parallel to the car) may help too, since you are simultaneously pushing down with one arm and pulling up with the other. After fitting the wrench socket over a lug, grab the wrench near the ends of the cross-bar and turn it counter-clockwise as hard as you can. This is the most difficult part of changing a tire, but don't get discouraged. Keep trying one lug after the other even if you don't get the first ones. The problem is psychological as well as physical. Once you loosen one lug you're sure to manage the others.

With the lugs loosened, but not all the way off the tire, you can finish jacking up the car. When the tire is just off the ground, move back and look to make sure the car is stable. Then, using your wrench as before, remove all the lugs and put them in the upturned hub-cap so they can't roll away. Have your spare tire immediately handy.

Next, remove the flat tire and roll it away or set it down--do not lean it against the car. Quickly fit the spare on the protruding bolts and screw on two or three lugs a few turns with your hands. This is important, since if the car falls off the jack when it has only three tires, it could easily break an axle. In putting on a lug, note that one end of it is slightly tapered. This end should go on first, i.e., point toward the car, as you screw on the lug clockwise.

The rest is easy. Put all the lugs on loosely, with your hands. Then tackle each with the wrench, turning clockwise until you feel some resistance against the wrench. In order for the tire to be correctly balanced, the lugs should be further tightened in an alternating order. In other words, tighten a lug on the left, then one diagonal to it on the right, one at the top, then one at the bottom.

Let the car down some, so the tire is touching the ground but not supporting full weight, before the final tightening. Again using the alternating technique, get each lug as tight as you can. If they are too loose they will get looser as you drive.

Finally, jack the car down and throw your tools in the trunk. The hub-cap will fit back on easily if you put it in place with your hands and, while you hold it there, give it a kick or a firm rap with the ball of your hand. If that doesn't work put it partially in place with your hand, let go, back up a step and kick it straight on with the whole bottom of your foot. Then drive away feeling sweaty and secure.

By Lynne Cobb

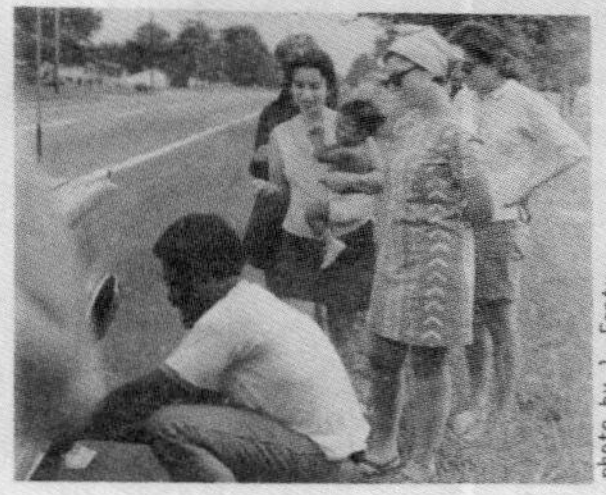

photo by J. Fenty

RACHET JACK

To position your rachet jack, pull the lifting mechanism (lifting platform and lever) up until the lifting platform is just under the bumper. There is a small switch under the lever--when it is up the jack will raise the car; when down, it will lower the car. When raising or lowering, just pump the lever. Be sure to swing it all the way up and all the way down--you will hear a click at either end of the arc.

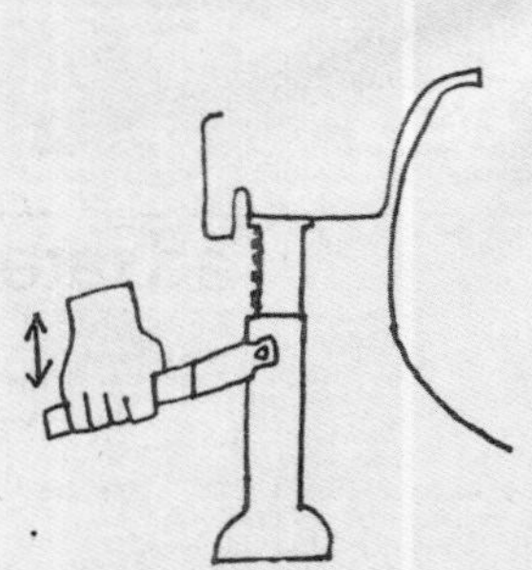

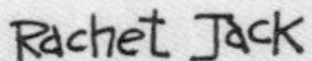

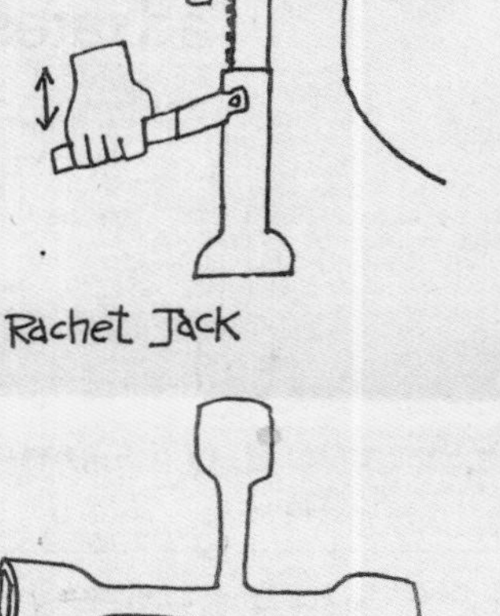

Rachet Jack

Screw Jack

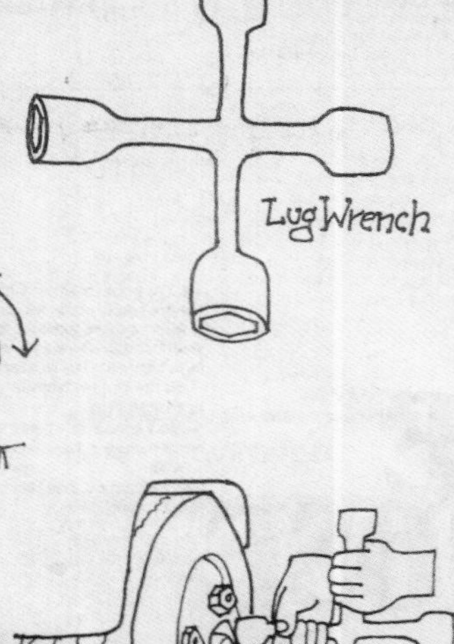

Lug Wrench

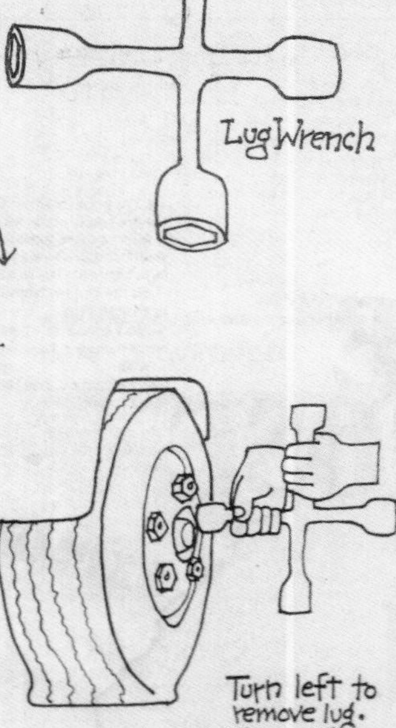

Pry off hub cap.

Turn left to remove lug. Turn right to tighten.

illustrations by Johanna Vogelsang

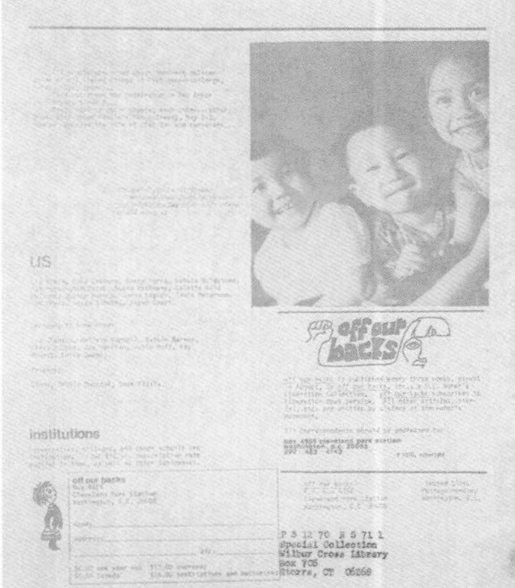

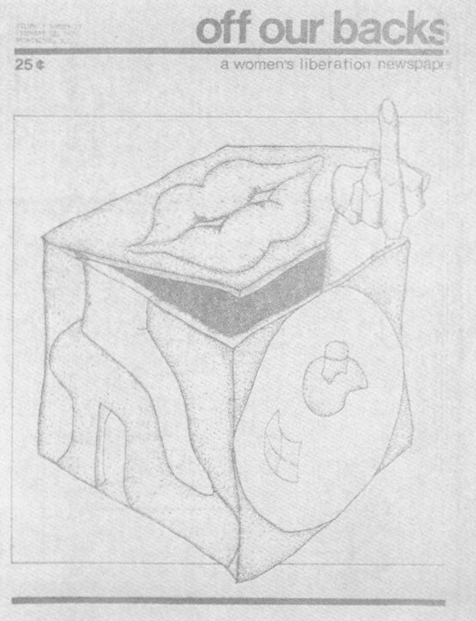

off our backs

25¢

a women's liberation newspaper

Off Our Backs: A Women's News Journal (Washington, DC), March 19, 1970, vol. 1, no. 2, cover
Off Our Backs: A Women's News Journal (Washington, DC), March 19, 1970, vol. 1, no. 2, back cover
Off Our Backs: A Women's News Journal (Washington, DC), February 12, 1971, vol. 1, no. 17, front cover
Off Our Backs: A Women's News Journal (Washington, DC), February 12, 1971, vol. 1, no. 17, inside cover spread

survival

fertility or fertilizer

estrogen component (mg.)

brand name	estrogen component (mg.)
OVRAL	0.05
OVRAL 28	
OVRAL 28+Fe Fumarate	
NORINYL-1 1mg.	
NORLESTRIN 1mg.	
ORTHO NOVUM 1mg.	
NORINYL-1 21 Day	
NORLESTRIN 21 1 mg.	
NORINYL-1 28 Day	
NORLESTRIN 28 1 mg.	
ORTHO NOVUM 1 mg. 28 Day	
NORIDAY Fe	
NORLESTRIN Fe 1 mg.	
ORTHO NOVUM Fe 28 1 mg.	
NORLESTRIN 2.5 mg.	
PROVEST	
NORINYL 10 mg.	0.06
ORTHO NOVUM 10 mg.	
ENOVID 5 mg.	0.075
NORINYL 1-80 21 Day	0.08
ORTHO NOVUM 1/80 28 Day	
ORTHO NOVUM 1/80 Fe 28	
OVULEN	0.10
OVULEN 21	
OVULEN 28	
OVULEN Fe 28	
NORINYL 2mg.	
ORTHO NOVUM 2 mg.	
ENOVID E 2.5	

Dr. Louis Hellman, now Deputy Assistant Secretary for Population Affairs in the Department of Health, Education, and Welfare, explains why some researchers fear the pill may cause cancer. "Every time you use estrogen (a pill ingredient) in experimental animals, you cause cancer. In all animals, that is, except monkeys. Now you ask yourself: Is there any reason to suppose that, biologically, human beings are going to react differently? There isn't." Every known cancer causing agent that triggers cancer in man also causes it in one or more species of animal.

Dr. Ray Hertz, a respected cancer researcher, charged that one ingredient of birth-control pills--a hormone called estrogen--is "to breast cancer what wheat fertilizer is to a wheat crop."

The above chart gives the estrogen component of brand-name birth control pills. The pills are listed in order of increasing estrogen component in milligrams per tablet.

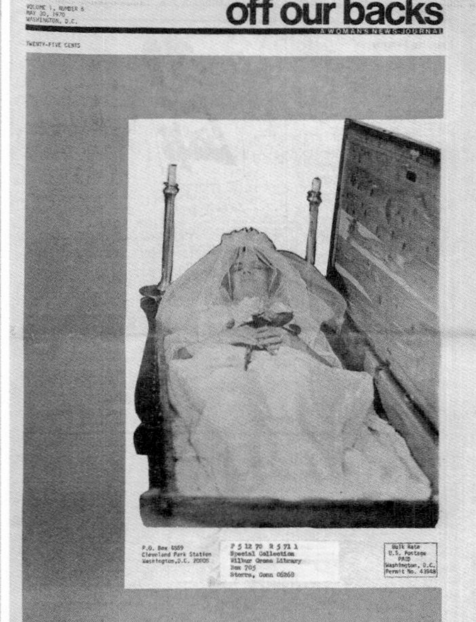

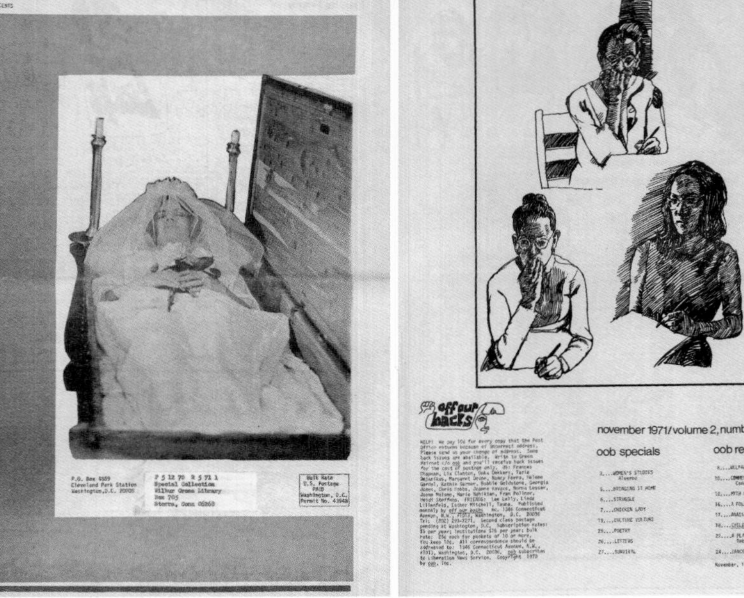

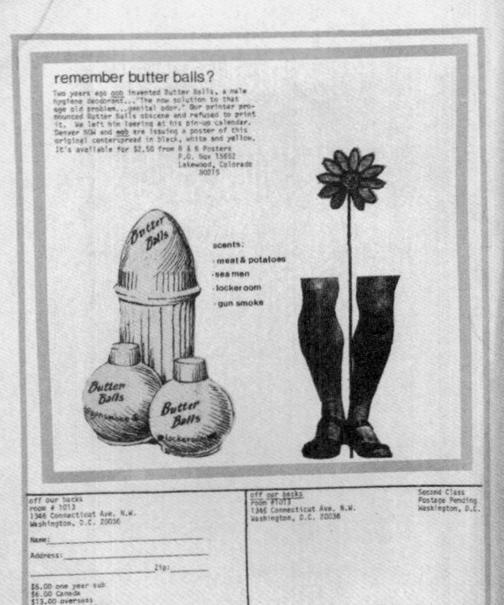

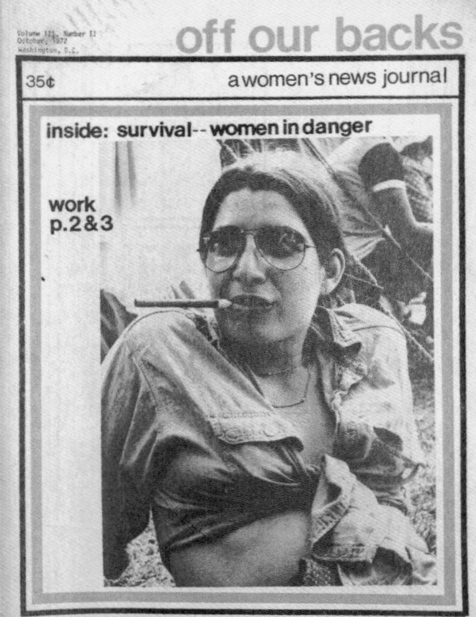

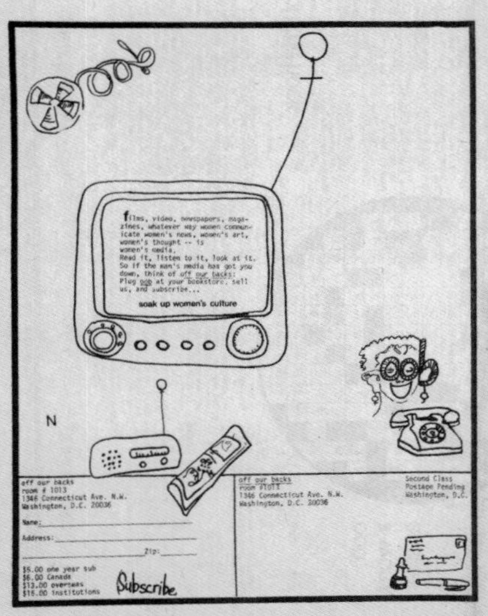

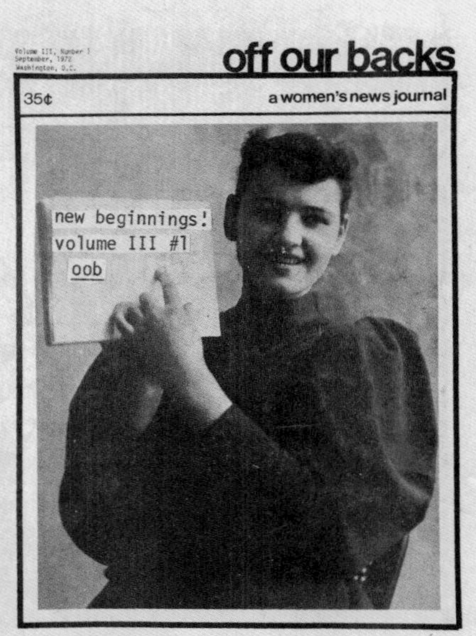

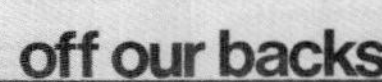

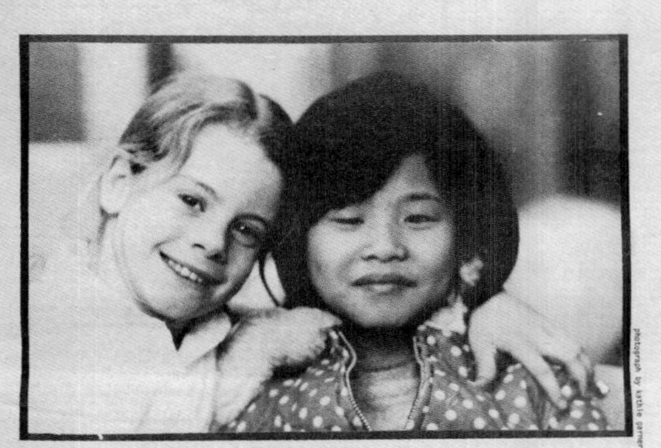

FRIENDS

march 1972/volume 2, number 7

oob specials

oob regulars

US

survival

spermicidal contraceptives

While the controversy over the comparative values of the pill and IUD rages, the vaginal spermicidal contraceptives have been overlooked.

These contraceptives do not jeopardize the health of women by causing cancer, infertility, or death.

These contraceptives, usually called jellies, creams, aerosol foams, foam tablets, and suppositories have a failure rate of about four per 100 woman years compared to zero for the pill, one for the IUD, and five for the condom. Used in conjunction with the condom this rate of four improves.

These foams have the advantage of availability without a doctor's prescription. In an emergency situation they are probably the best protection available.

Aerosal vaginal foam is rated "very effective," compared to "most effective" for the pill and "highly effective" for the diaphragm, by the "Birth Control Handbook" published by the McGill Students' Society of McGill University.

This publication, available free with postage, from the Students' Society, 3480 McTavish St., Montreal, Quebec,Canada has the blessings of the Royal Victoria Hospital (Montreal), student liberation groups, and Planned Parenthood Organization. Copies may be ordered in bulk for $35 per 1,000 copies.

DISADVANTAGES

The usual objection to a spermicidal contraceptive is that it must be used immediately preceding coitus, thus interrupting sexual foreplay. Some people term the spermicidal contraceptive "messy" although this objection has been greatly overcome by the introduction of aerosol foams used with an applicator.

Another objection is that after the spermicidal contraceptive is applied the woman is advised not to urinate or walk around. Also, use of a douche must be delayed at least 6 hours following coitus since it dilutes or removes the spermicidal protection without effectively removing any remaining living sperm.

METHOD

Instructions come with the products which can be purchased in the feminine hygiene section of a drug store for two to three dollars.

The aerosol foams are packaged in a container under pressure. The plastic applicator is attached to the container and pressure on the tip of the container releases the foam into the applicator (see diagram).

The applicator is then inserted into the vagina in the same way a tampon is applied. Pressure on the plunger releases the foam to cover the cervix.(see diagram)

Compared to jellies, the foams deliver a smaller amount of weight, the cost per application is less, and the non-reactive base, similar to vanishing cream, reduces "messiness" and leakage from the vagina after coitus.

Following use, the applicator should be washed with warm water and soap.

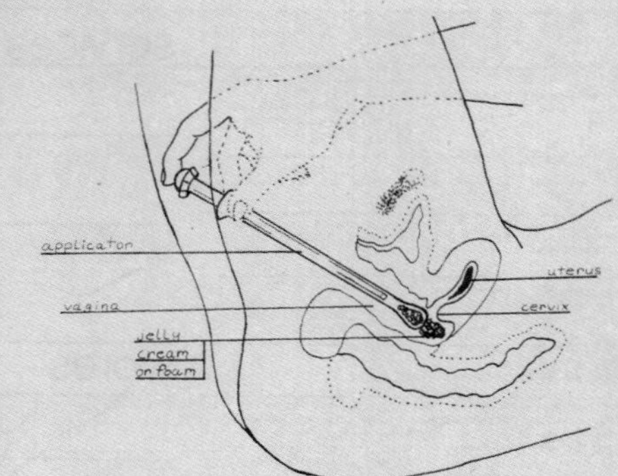

How To Apply...

DESCRIPTION

The chemicals which make up the spermicidal preparations are usually an analogue of ethanol (to kill sperm) and a non-reactive base which mechanically blocks the cervix.

These chemicals are, relatively speaking, not very potent. Very rarely are there any side effects or reactions. Occasionally there is some slight allergic irritation: however consultation with a doctor can determine the allergy and irritation can usually be avoided by changing brands. They are not harmful if ingested.

The woman should be careful that the agent is not diluted either by skimpy use to begin with or by vaginal secretions and leakage. The foam must be applied preceeding each act of sexual intercourse.

All spermicidal preparations must be applied within the hour (and some the half hour) immediately preceding coitus.

SUPPOSITORIES

Only suppositories approved for contraceptive use can be depended upon. Those advertised for "femine hygiene" may not have strong enough sperm killing qualities to give good protection. Also, these non-foaming suppositories may not completely block the entrance to the womb or they may fail to melt sufficiently. Clinicians advise against their use for birth control.

The vaginal foam tablets (foaming suppositories) are flat, round, white, one gram tablets, usually packaged twelve per vial.

The foam producing spermatocidal materials are tantaric acid and sodium bicarbonate which, when moistened, produce carbon dioxide to form the foam.

With proper packaging, foam tablets keep under most adverse conditions. However, it is recommended they be kept tightly closed in a cool place. They must be used within six months of purchase.

METHOD

The tablet is moistened slightly and immediately inserted in the vagina and pushed as deep as possible in the vaginal canal. This is easiest in a reclining position. After insertion at least five minutes must be allowed before intercourse. No more than one hour should elapse.

A new tablet should be applied if there is a delay of more than one hour, if the woman gets up to walk around or urinate, and before intercourse is repeated.

ORDINARY SUPPOSITORIES

Ordinary suppositories are small cones designed to melt at slightly below body temperature. The two commercial types used containing cocoa-butter and glycero-gelatin are not very good.

These suppositories, containing quinine derivatives, salicyclic acid and carbolic-mercurial are difficult to keep in hot weather because of their low melting point.

OBSERVATIONS

There have been no reports of cancer related to use of spermicidal preparations. Although the possibility of side effects while using spermicidal preparations is low compared to other birth control devices they are not as reliable as pills or IUDs.

However, they can be obtained without a prescription. To the young woman without access to medical facilities, spermicidal preparations may be the best chance available to avoid an unwanted pregnancy.

It should be again noted that the use of a condom in conjunction with spermicidal preparations gives more protection.

By Mary Dresser

Illustrations by Susan Abts

survival

a poke in time...

Every woman should be aware of her body, how it functions and what to be aware of if something should go wrong.

Breast self-examination is important for women of all ages since nearly all breast changes or lumps are first found by the woman herself. If you find any changes go to a clinic or a doctor at once. Remember, most breast lumps are not cancer. Early breast cancer does not hurt and is curable.

The breasts should be examined every month, just after you menstruate. Women who have passed menopause should continue this monthly habit.

Remember, a poke in time...

FOLLOW THESE STEPS...

1

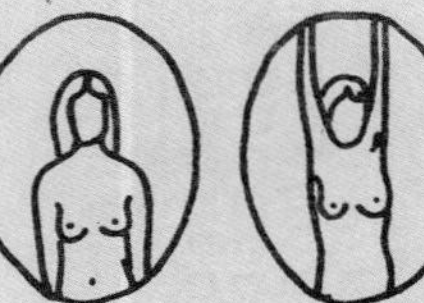

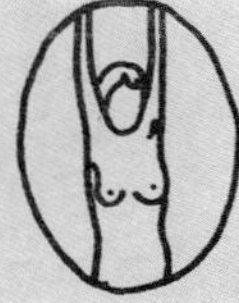

In front of mirror with arms down, then overhead.
Look for: changes in shape, size and dimpling of skin.

2

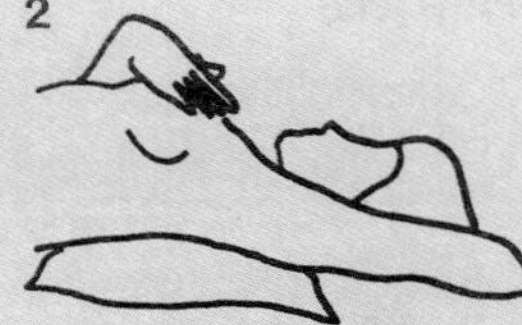

Lie down flat; put pillow or folded bath towel under left shoulder; place left hand under head.

3

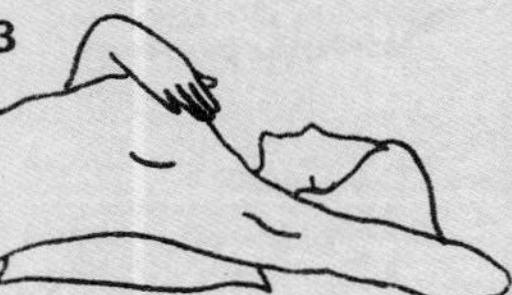

With right hand, fingers out flat, gently feel left breast.
(Do not squeeze or pinch!)

4

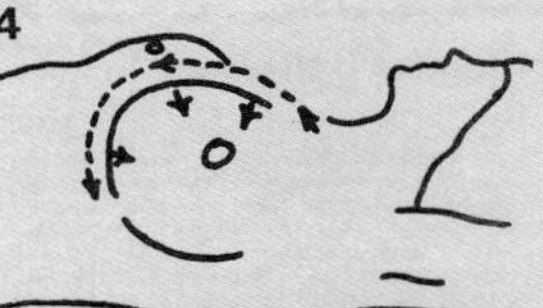

Feel inner half carefully, from nipple line to breast bone, and from top to bottom, as shown by arrows.
Feel for: Lumps or any other changes.

5

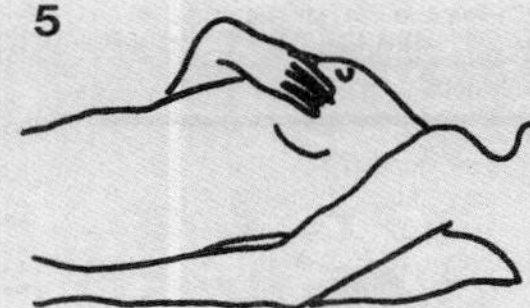

Lower arm to side. Feel outer half gently from nipple line to side where arm is resting, from bottom to top.
Feel for: Lumps or any other changes.

6

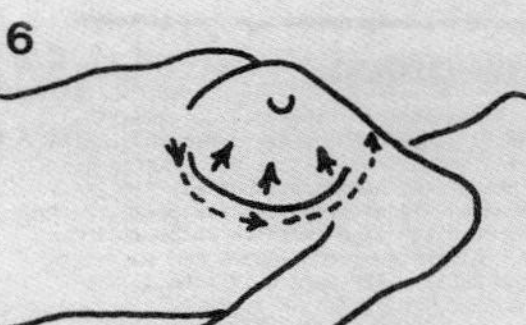

Feel outer half carefully, from edge of breast to nipple line, and from bottom to top, as shown by arrows.

7

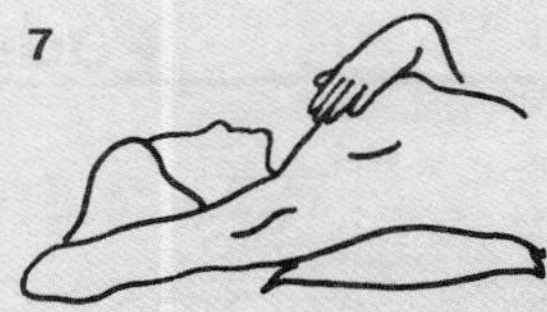

Now put pillow or folded bath towel under your right shoulder, place right hand under head. With fingers of left hand, gently feel right breast.
Repeat steps 4, 5, and 6.

8

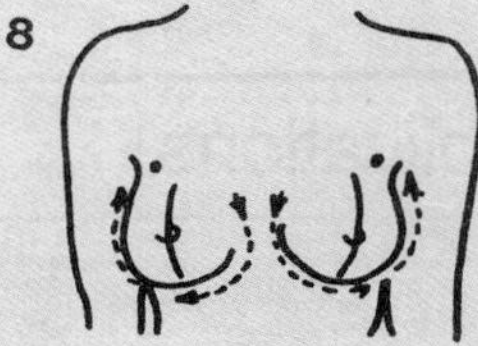

Follow arrows; pay special attention to the part shown by circle.

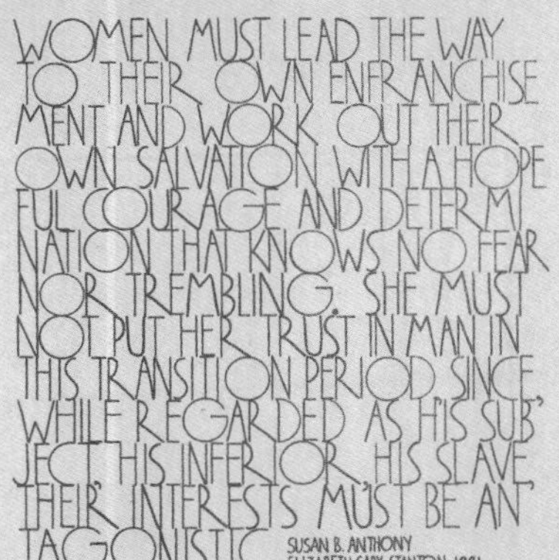

SPECIAL SUMMER EDITION
Volume 1, Numbers 9 & 10
WASHINGTON, D.C.

THIRTY-FIVE CENTS

off our backs
a women's liberation bi-weekly

WOMEN MUST LEAD THE WAY TO THEIR OWN ENFRANCHISEMENT AND WORK OUT THEIR OWN SALVATION WITH A HOPEFUL COURAGE AND DETERMINATION THAT KNOWS NO FEAR NOR TREMBLING. SHE MUST NOT PUT HER TRUST IN MAN IN THIS TRANSITION PERIOD SINCE, WHILE REGARDED AS HIS SUBJECT, HIS INFERIOR, HIS SLAVE, THEIR INTERESTS MUST BE ANTAGONISTIC.

SUSAN B. ANTHONY
ELIZABETH CADY STANTON 1881

special summer edition

Previous page
Off Our Backs: A Women's News Journal (Washington, DC), May 30, 1970, vol. 1, no. 6, back cover
Off Our Backs: A Women's News Journal (Washington, DC), May 30, 1970, vol. 1, no. 6, cover
Off Our Backs: A Women's News Journal (Washington, DC), November 1971, vol. 2, no. 3, back cover
Off Our Backs: A Women's News Journal (Washington, DC), October 1972, vol. 3, no. 2, front and back covers
Off Our Backs: A Women's News Journal (Washington, DC), September 1972, vol. 3, no. 1, front and back covers
Off Our Backs: A Women's News Journal (Washington, DC), March 1972, vol. 2, no. 7, back cover

Off Our Backs: A Women's News Journal (Washington, DC), March 19, 1970, vol. 1, no. 3, back cover
Off Our Backs: A Women's News Journal (Washington, DC), June 26, 1970, vol. 1, no. 7, back cover
Off Our Backs: A Women's News Journal (Washington, DC), July 31, 1970, vol. 1, nos. 9 and 10, cover

evanescent soap bubbles. Other artists cultivated an indifference to the appearance of language, choosing the cheapest, most run-of-the-mill formats to suggest their antielitist leanings, as was the case with Lawrence Weiner, whose ***Statements***, a nondescript paperback compiling a series of declarative sentences indicating acts that the viewer/reader could carry out, sold for two dollars.

Like the designers of underground papers, conceptual artists often seemed less concerned with legibility of words than with their corporeality—Smithson once dedicated a work to flies, citing the insect's distorted eyesight, akin, according to the artist, to looking at newsprint through a magnifying glass[10]—succinctly expressed by the title of Mel Bochner's 1969 work, ***Language Is Not Transparent*** (fig. 3.7). Consisting of four standard note cards on which the artist used a rubber stamp to print the phrase LANGUAGE IS NOT TRANSPARENT—first once, then multiple times until it becomes an unreadable smudge of ink—the piece underscored the opacity of language as a material substance in its own right. If such investigations of language had radical aesthetic implications, challenging the received definitions and categories of art and altering the possibilities for making and viewing it, they also had profound social and political implications. Indeed the use of language as a medium was deeply tied to the egalitarian potential of new forms of distribution, such as books and magazines, which promised to deprivilege art by circumventing the gallery space and allowing artists to reach different kinds of audiences. Artists seized upon these accessible formats, manipulating the form, content, and distribution of the media in order to express alternative artistic ideas and criteria, and to forge artistic communities and counterpublics.

In doing so, they not only reveled in the materiality of language for its own sake but developed a heightened awareness of its ideological dimensions, as it circulated through various media and institutions. For example, Dan Graham explored the site-specificity of the printed page in ***Schema (March 1966)***, 1966 (fig. 3.8), which consisted of a template—a

10. Robert Smithson, "Incidents of Mirror-Travel in the Yucatan," in *Robert Smithson: The Collected Writings*, ed. Jack Flam (Berkeley: University of California Press, 1996), p. 129.

Fig. 3.7. Mel Bochner, **Language Is Not Transparent,** 1969, rubber stamp on four notecards, 5 × 8 in. each

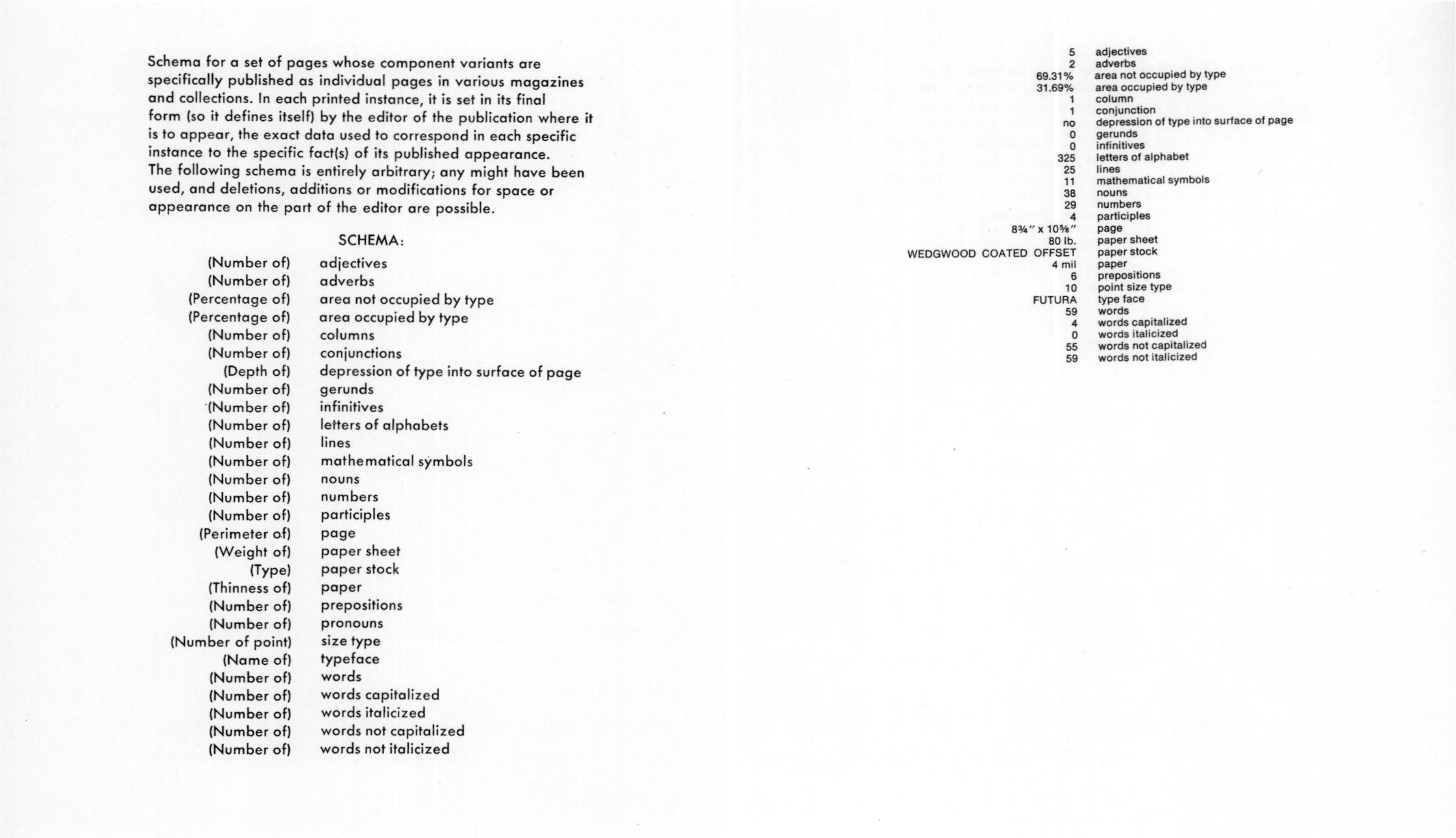

Schema for a set of pages whose component variants are specifically published as individual pages in various magazines and collections. In each printed instance, it is set in its final form (so it defines itself) by the editor of the publication where it is to appear, the exact data used to correspond in each specific instance to the specific fact(s) of its published appearance. The following schema is entirely arbitrary; any might have been used, and deletions, additions or modifications for space or appearance on the part of the editor are possible.

SCHEMA:

(Number of)	adjectives
(Number of)	adverbs
(Percentage of)	area not occupied by type
(Percentage of)	area occupied by type
(Number of)	columns
(Number of)	conjunctions
(Depth of)	depression of type into surface of page
(Number of)	gerunds
(Number of)	infinitives
(Number of)	letters of alphabets
(Number of)	lines
(Number of)	mathematical symbols
(Number of)	nouns
(Number of)	numbers
(Number of)	participles
(Perimeter of)	page
(Weight of)	paper sheet
(Type)	paper stock
(Thinness of)	paper
(Number of)	prepositions
(Number of)	pronouns
(Number of point)	size type
(Name of)	typeface
(Number of)	words
(Number of)	words capitalized
(Number of)	words italicized
(Number of)	words not capitalized
(Number of)	words not italicized

5	adjectives
2	adverbs
69.31%	area not occupied by type
31.69%	area occupied by type
1	column
1	conjunction
no	depression of type into surface of page
0	gerunds
0	infinitives
325	letters of alphabet
25	lines
11	mathematical symbols
38	nouns
29	numbers
4	participles
8¾" x 10⅝"	page
80 lb.	paper sheet
WEDGWOOD COATED OFFSET	paper stock
4 mil	paper
6	prepositions
10	point size type
FUTURA	type face
59	words
4	words capitalized
0	words italicized
55	words not capitalized
59	words not italicized

Fig. 3.8. Dan Graham, **Schema (March 1966)**, 1966

self-referential list of variables about the typography and format of the magazine page (such as paper stock, typeface, number of columns, number of words, point size of type) that was published in various magazines and was completed by the editor according to the design and layout of the particular publication in which it appeared. *Schema* provides a model of language whose content is inflected by both its form and its context. To come across it is to be momentarily distracted from the meaning of words by the shapes of letters and numbers, and even by the density and pliability of the paper. In this sense, Graham conceived of the printed page as a physical and socioeconomic "site," which modulates the process of communication.

It seems impossible to fully understand and appreciate conceptual art's radical investigations of language and the printed page in isolation from the revolutionary media practices of the underground press. Indeed, the idea that language was not transparent—that it was not merely a neutral conduit for meaning, but could affect and interfere with meaning—was also central to the counterculture's ideological challenge to the supposed transparency and neutrality of mainstream media. As underground papers chronicled events and experiences that were omitted from established media venues and expressed alternative political views and lifestyles, they insisted that communication was not only a matter of what was said, but how something was said. Like artists, the editors and designers of the underground press used the media as a vehicle to disseminate their ideas but also paid attention to the materiality of language, experimented with the graphic form of the printed page, and invented participatory strategies to transform the relationship between producers and consumers of media. The civil rights, feminist, gay and lesbian, and anticolonial movements depended crucially on reclaiming and reinventing discourse, as previously marginalized groups and individuals asserted the right to speak publically—a process in which alternative and underground publications played a pivotal role. As these counter publics seized

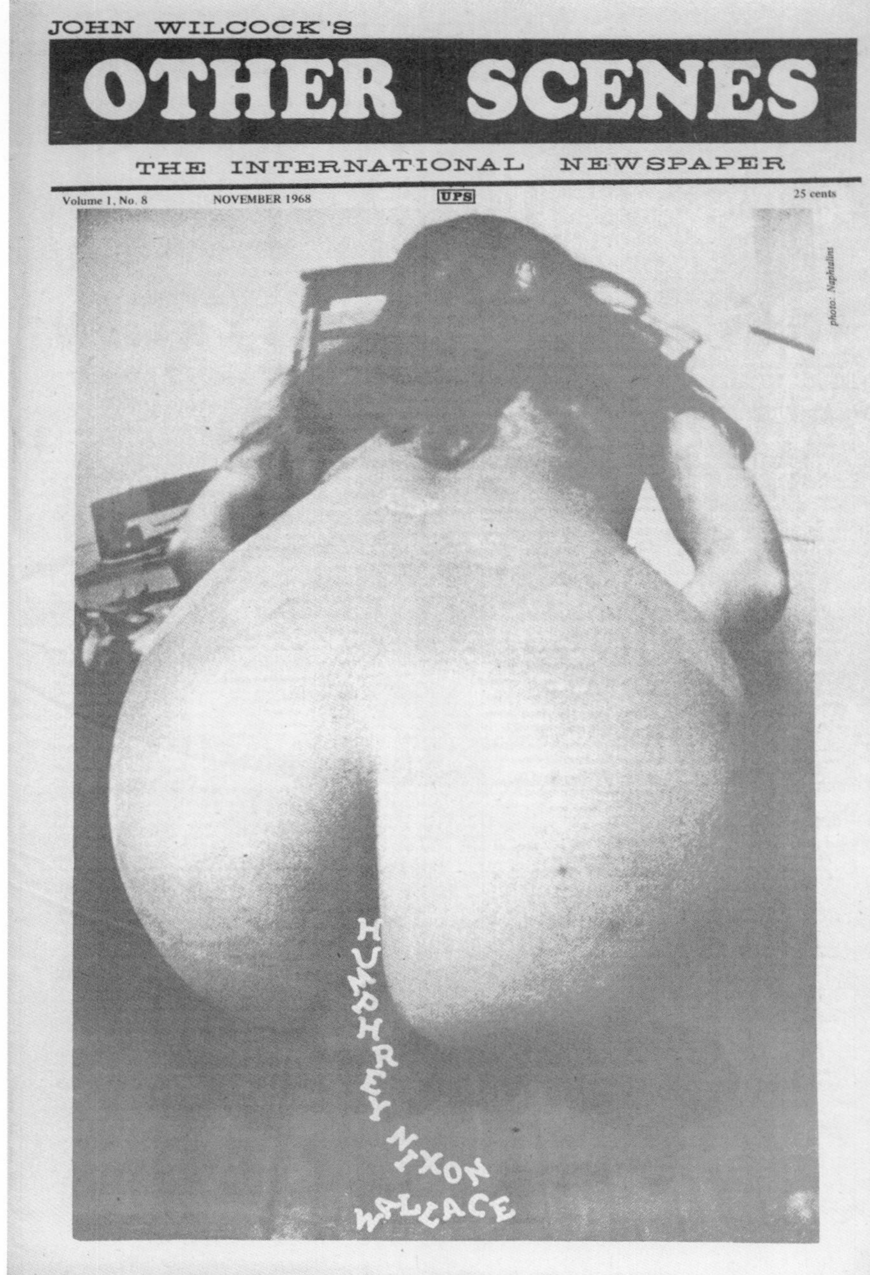

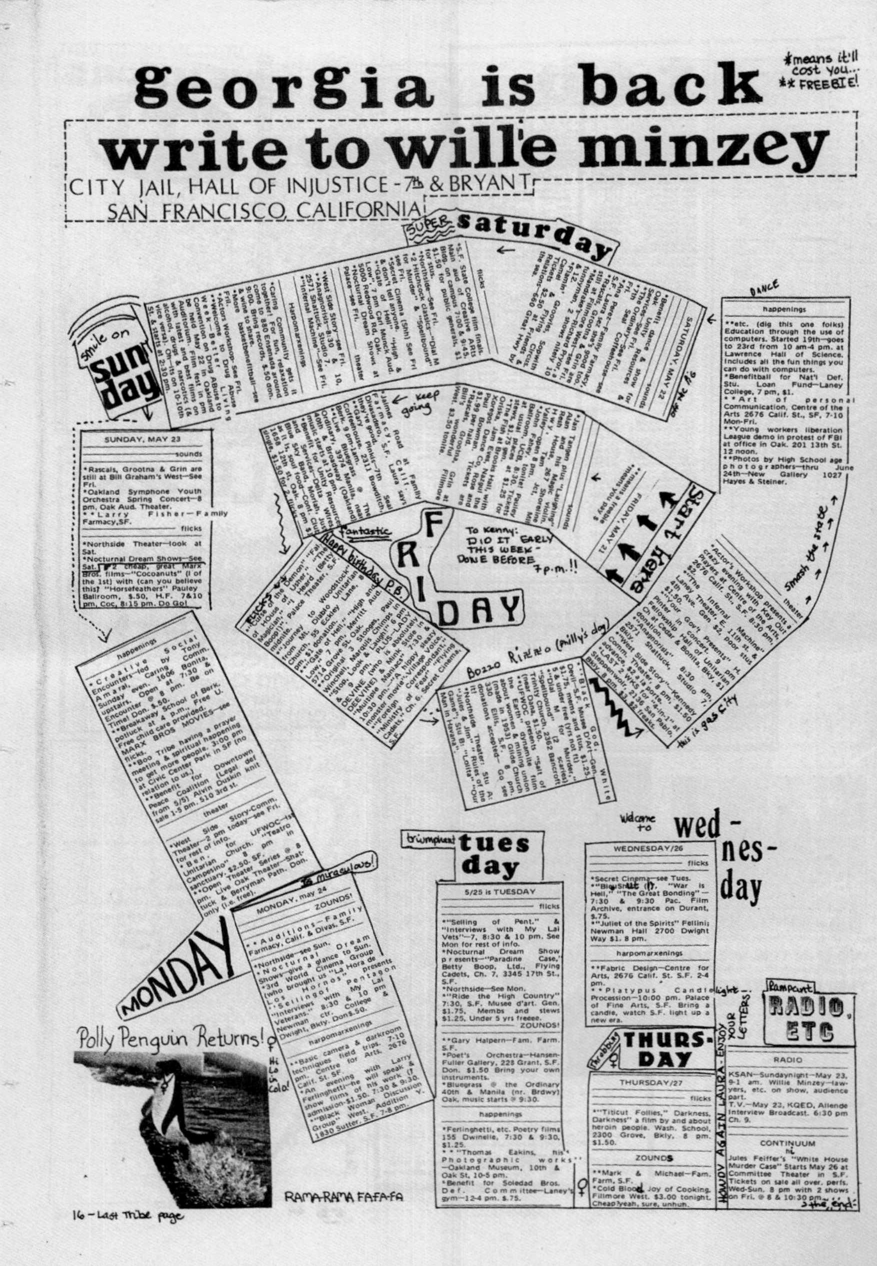

control of the media and used it as a vehicle to disseminate their ideas, they also altered the very form of communication in order to express new social and political identities.

Against the modernist notion of the page as a universal, hierarchical, and highly rational space, underground papers embodied new countercultural models of information and communication. They exploited the materiality of language in order to connote alternative attitudes and lifestyles: psychedelic fonts and op-art patterning simulated the effects of mind-altering pharmaceuticals; art nouveau lettering and patterns harkened back to the antiindustrial aesthetic of the late nineteenth century while capturing the ironic retrosensibility that Susan Sontag dubbed "camp";[11] "primitivist" motifs referenced the "retribalization" of communal living; woodblock and stenciled designs cited political protest posters of the 1920s and 1930s. Freed from the perpendicular coordinates of the modernist grid, columns of text zigzagged and snaked around borders and illustrations, or formed shapes and Smithsonesque stacks. Typographical arrangement was used not to enhance legibility but to inflect the meaning of words and create graphological puns, as when the editors of *Other Scenes* expressed their frustration with the limited choices of the 1968 presidential election by depicting the names of the candidates Humphrey, Nixon, and Wallace dropping from the shapely derriere of a woman (fig. 3.9).

11. Sontag defines "camp" as "an aesthetic in-joke" that functioned as "a desirable and even rebellious counterpoint to 'good taste.'" "Notes on Camp," in *Against Interpretation and Other Essays* (New York: Macmillan, 1966), pp. 275-292.

Fig. 3.9. **Other Scenes,** November 1968, vol. 1, no. 8, cover

Fig. 3.10. **Berkeley Tribe,** May 21-27, 1971, vol. 5, no. 16, back cover

More than just stylistic affectations or amateur efforts at concrete poetry, such graphics rejected the repressive mores and conventions of "straight" society. The barely legible fonts and serpentine layouts disturbed the rational, gridded hierarchy of the modernist page ("the lockstep military-industrial rigidity of the column form," as one editor described it)[12] and by extension, repudiated the repressive rationality of technocratic society to which such forms correlated. Indeed, underground graphic design questioned the rational basis of modern communication itself, envisioning the printed page as a very different kind of interface—one that was deeply antiauthoritarian in nature. Even the calendars and free events listings (often titled "Happenings" or "Trips") that were a staple of many underground publications, announcing antiwar protests, feminist consciousness-raising groups, be-ins, potlucks, free concerts, draft resistance counseling, and vague, exotic-sounding gatherings like "All Day Pleasure Festivals," conveyed, through their meandering, board-game-like layouts and cluttered overlays, an alternative attitude toward time, one that prized immediacy and spontaneity over the rigid scheduling of days into commodifiable blocks (fig. 3.10).

Rejecting the disinterested, detached tone of mainstream journalism, the underground press developed more personal, subjective styles of writing and used slang and profanity to challenge the propriety of established cultural conventions—a practice that prompted criminal charges to be filed against several publications. When Boston city officials arrested the publishers of the *Avatar* on obscenity charges (charges likely provoked less by the paper's liberal use of certain four-letter words than by its sharp criticism of the city government and police department) the publishers fought back, taunting authorities with a centerfold that shouted "FUCK SHIT PISS CUNT" (fig. 3.11). Printed in large, yellow ornamental letters against a busily patterned background, the partially obscured text merely piques the reader's curiosity, suggesting how the quality of illegibility can be used, paradoxically, to render a text more noticeable and prominent.

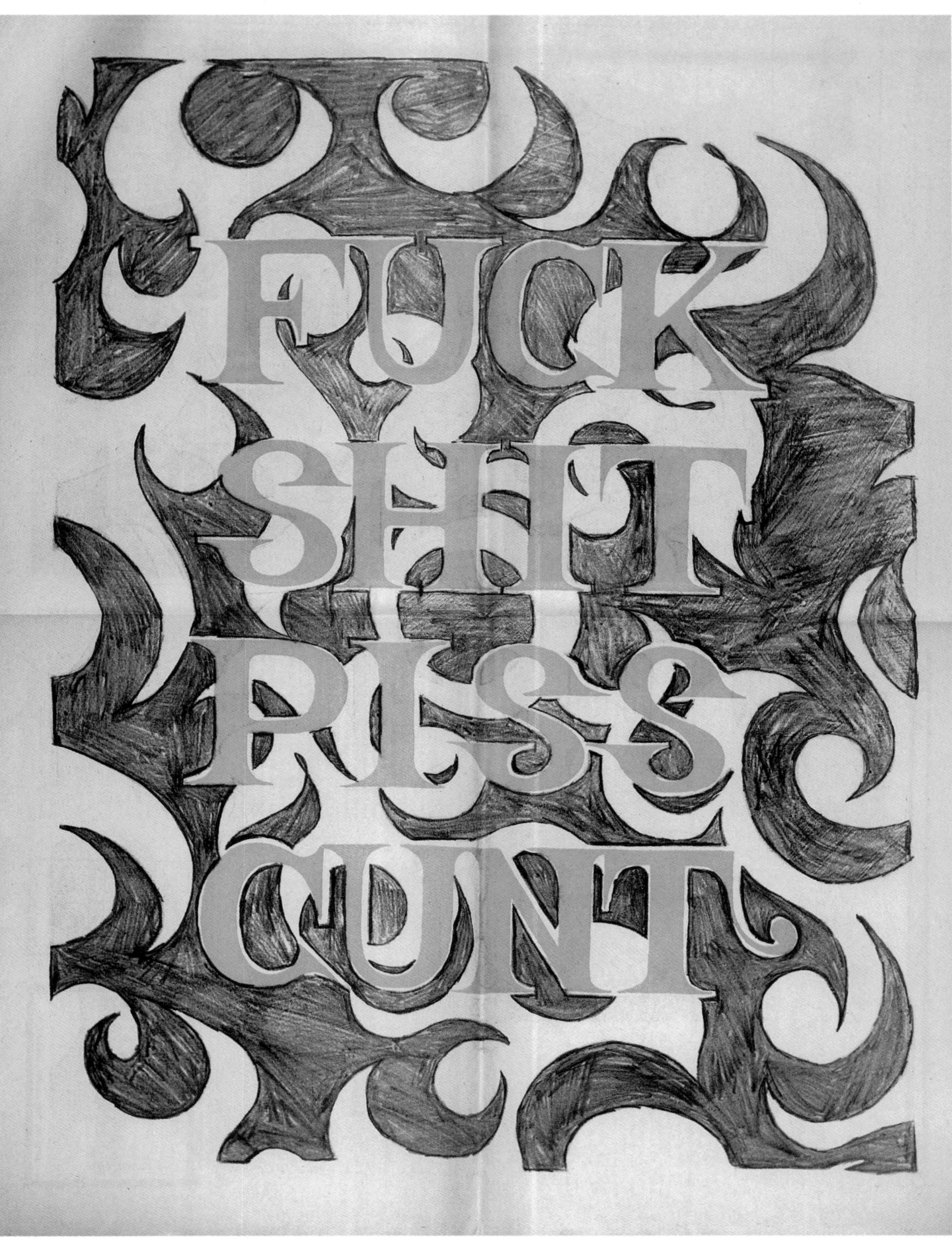

12. Cohen, "The *San Francisco Oracle*," 133.

Fig. 3.11. **Avatar** (Boston), 1967, no. 13, inside spread

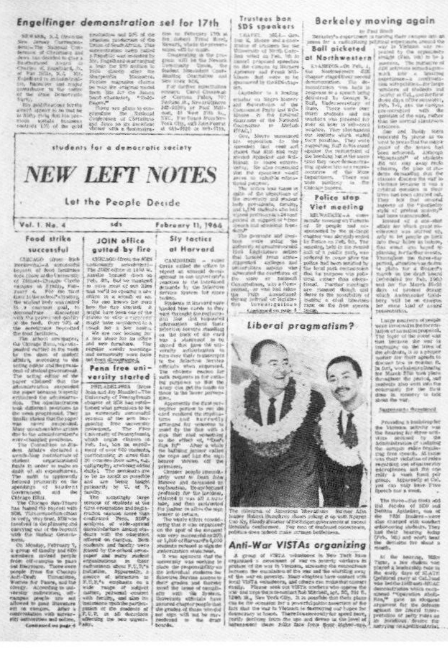

Italians Cheer New Left

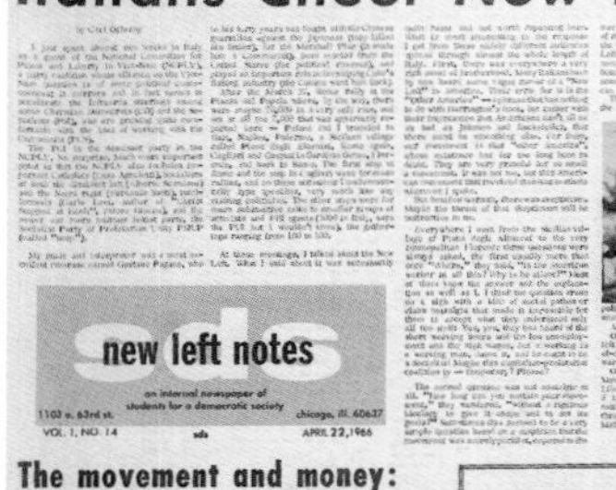

The movement and money: Kissinger asks contribution

EDITOR NEEDED!!

New Left Notes needs an editor.

No experience is required

Apply: 1103 E. 63rd Chicago, Ill., or call 312-667-6050

Urge political action

Poor tell it 'like it is'

join gets rent strike contract

sds new left notes

Vol. 1, No. 19 let the people decide May 27, 1966

chicago public aid workers on strike

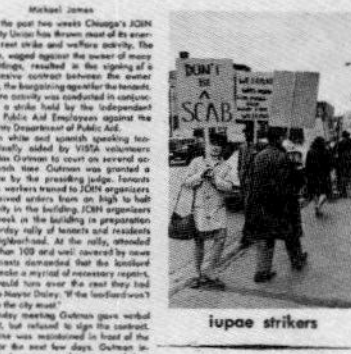

iupae strikers

oglesby replies to criticism

nac minutes

NATIONAL CONVENTION

Clear Lake, Iowa August 27--Sept. 1

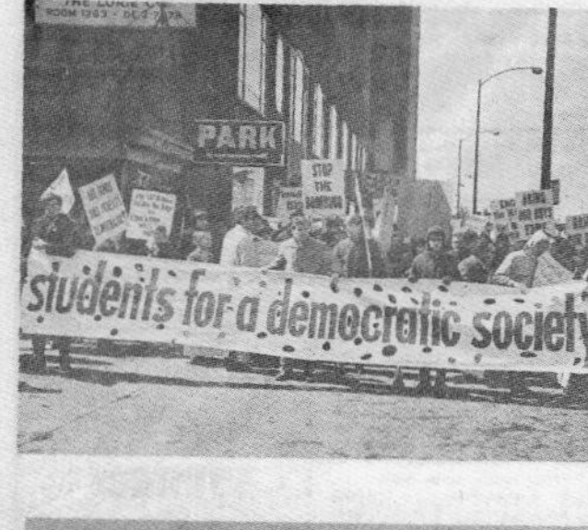

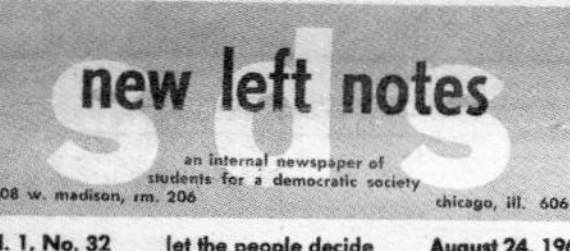

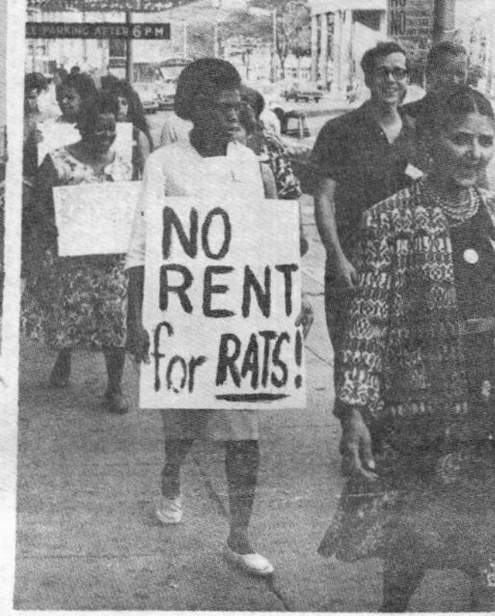

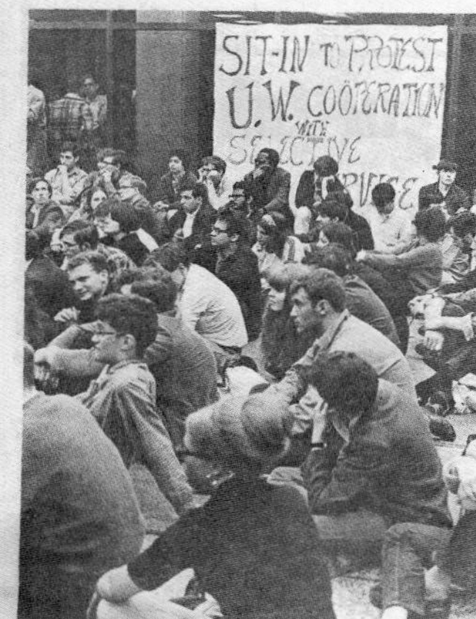

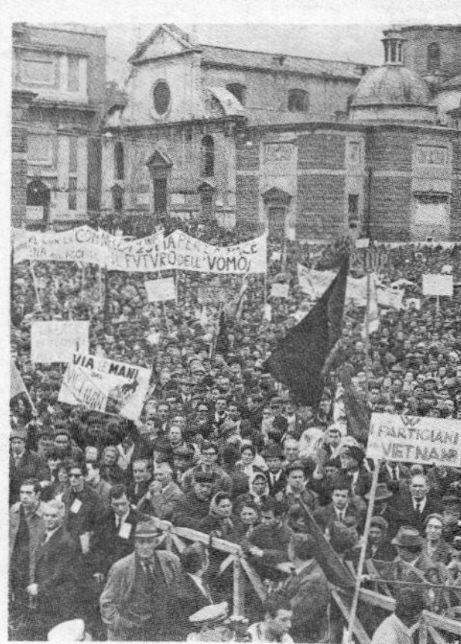

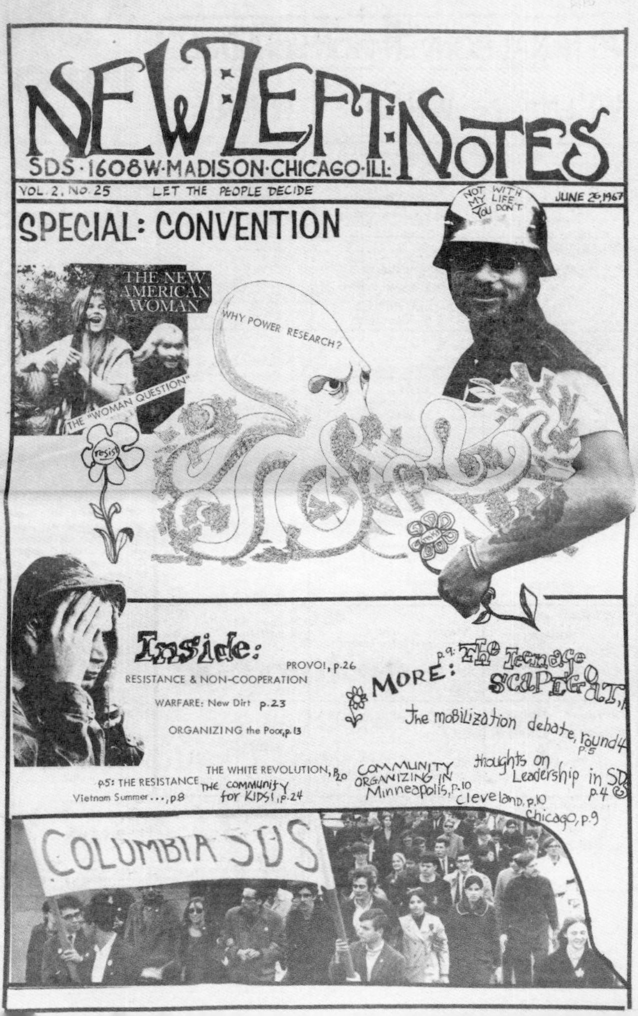

WORKERS & STUDENTS OF THE WORLD UNITE !! COME TO MAY 1st page

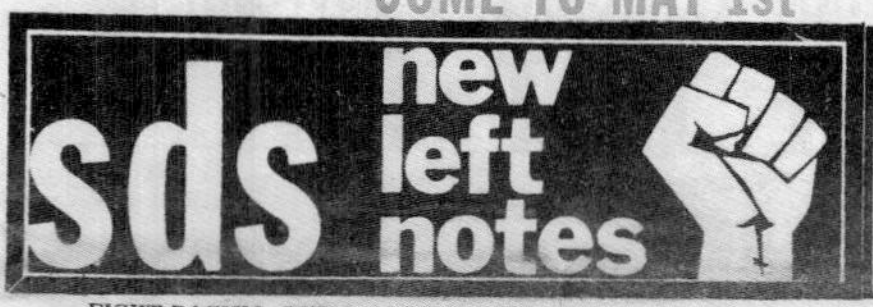

IN THIS ISSUE
INTERNATIONAL SOLIDARITY page 6
CALLEY & ALL RACIST BOSSES GUILTY OF MURDER page 8
JUNIOR COLLEGE STRUGGLES page 10
PALO ALTO SIT-IN page 4
MAYTAG STRIKE SUPPORT page 5

FIGHT RACISM - BUILD THE WORKER-STUDENT ALLIANCE

Vol. 6, No. 5 April 21, 19

WELFARE MOTHERS & STUDENTS FIGHT GOV'T CUTBACKS page

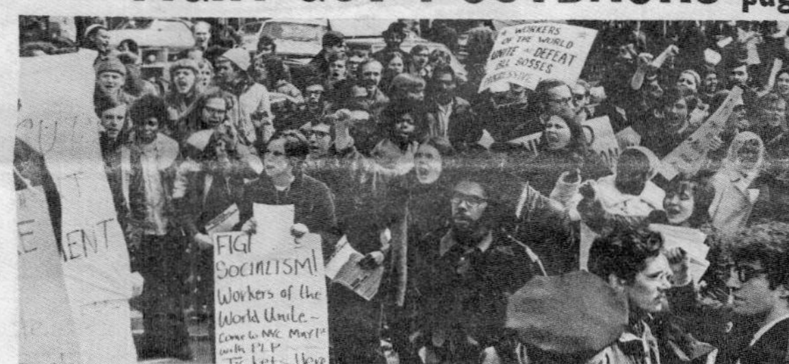

DON'T BE MISLED ON APRIL 24 BY RACIST SELLOUTS

ALLY WITH WORKERS

SUPPORT SDS BREAK-AWAY page

NEW LEFT NOTES

SDS · 1608 W. MADISON · CHICAGO · ILL.

VOLUME 2, NUMBER 21 LET THE PEOPLE DECIDE MAY 22

MISSOURI REPORT

ANTIOCH CANCELS

vietnam work–in

co spokesmen:

Fig. 3.12. **New Left Notes** (Chicago), covers: February 11, 1966, vol. 1, no. 4; August 24, 1966, vol. 1, no. 32; April 21, 1971, vol. 6, no. 5; April 22, 1966, vol. 1, no. 14; May 27, 1966, vol. 1, no. 16; June 26, 1967, vol. 2, no. 25; May 29, 1967, vol. 2, no. 21

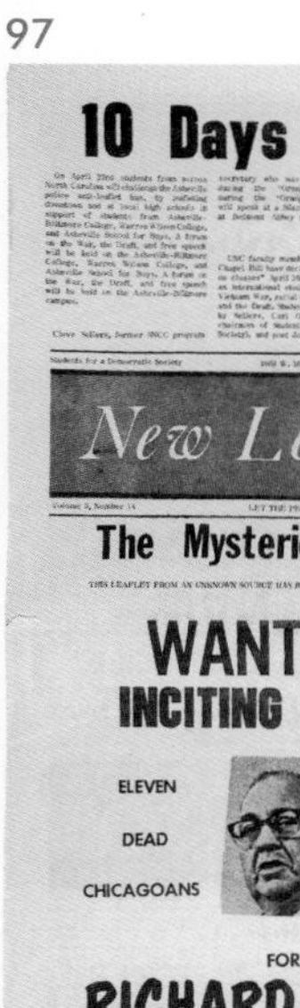

10 Days of Secession

New Left Notes

Information on Mass Anti-Draft Suit

The Mysterious Leaflet

WANTED : INCITING TO RIOT

ELEVEN DEAD CHICAGOANS ARE NOT ENOUGH FOR RICHARD DALEY ALLEGED MAYOR OF CHICAGO

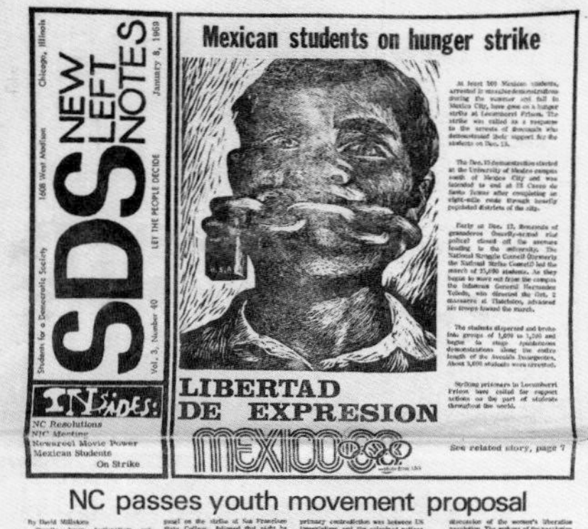

SDS NEW LEFT NOTES

Mexican students on hunger strike

LIBERTAD DE EXPRESION

MEXICO 68

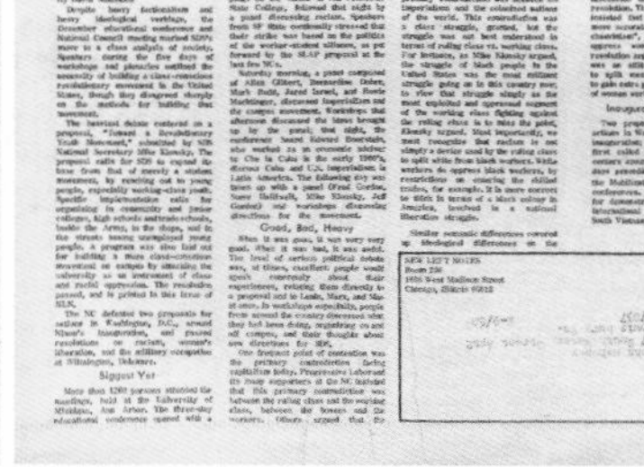

NC passes youth movement proposal

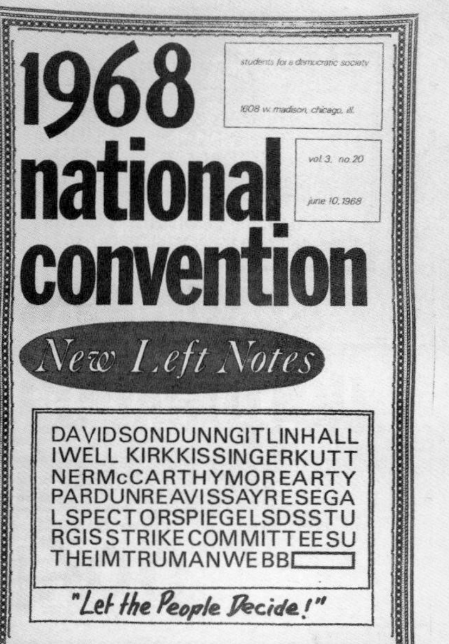

1968 national convention

students for a democratic society

1608 w. madison, chicago, ill.

vol 3, no 20

june 10, 1968

New Left Notes

DAVIDSONDUNNGITLINHALL
IWELL KIRKKISSINGERKUTT
NERMcCARTHYMOREARTY
PARDUNREAVISSAYRESEGA
LSPECTORSPIEGELSDSSTU
RGISSTRIKECOMMITTEESU
THEIMTRUMANWEBB

"Let the People Decide!"

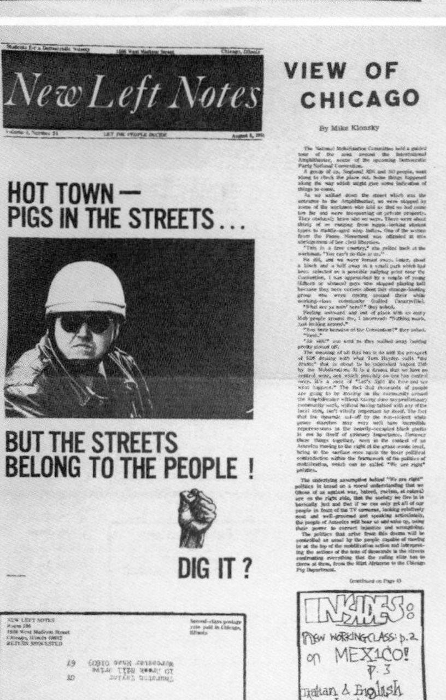

New Left Notes

VIEW OF CHICAGO

HOT TOWN — PIGS IN THE STREETS...

BUT THE STREETS BELONG TO THE PEOPLE !

DIG IT ?

INSIDE: NEW WORKING CLASS p. 2; on MEXICO! p. 3; Italian & English Students p. 8

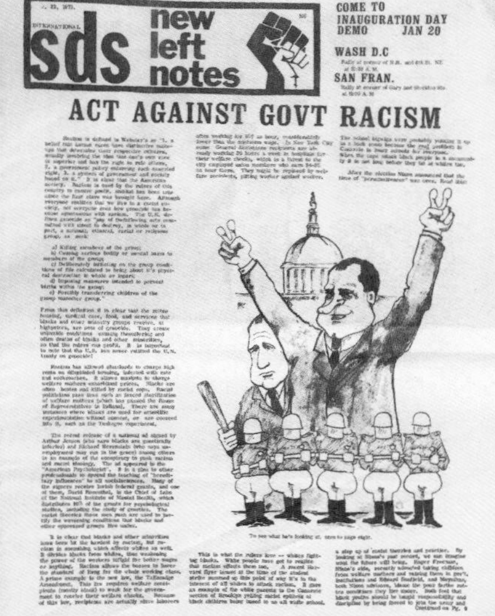

sds new left notes

COME TO INAUGURATION DAY DEMO JAN 20

WASH D.C

SAN FRAN.

ACT AGAINST GOVT RACISM

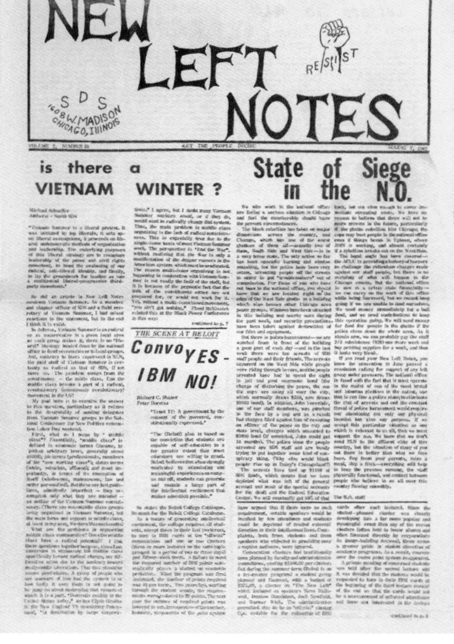

NEW LEFT NOTES

RESIST

S D S 1608 W. MADISON CHICAGO, ILLINOIS

is there a VIETNAM WINTER ?

State of Siege in the N.O.

Convoy YES - IBM NO!

Fig. 3.12 (cont'd.) **New Left Notes** (Chicago), April 22, 1968, vol. 3, no. 14; June 10, 1968, vol. 3, no. 20; December 22, 1972; August 5, 1968, vol. 3, no. 24; August 7, 1967, vol. 2, no. 28

Indeed, this tongue-in-cheek attempt to camouflage the words mimics the very effects of censorship itself—the way in which the effort to suppress meaning frequently backfires, resulting in creative new forms of visibility and expression.[13]

While many underground papers emphatically proclaimed their difference from the mainstream press through their unusual visual appearance, others took the opposite tack, mimicking more conventional publications as a form of subterfuge, like Trojan horses. Encountered fleetingly on the newsstand, papers such as the SDS's ***New Left Notes*** might slip under the radar, passing for an establishment paper with its understated design, standard roman type, and justified columns (fig. 3.12). Upon closer examination, however it shows its hand, subtly signaling its alternative status. Regular readers would have noticed, for example, the occasional hand-drawn headline, or the way the logo and format kept changing from issue to issue. Other publications produced ***tromp l'oeil*** papers within their pages indistinguishable from the ***New York Times*** or the ***Wall Street Journal***—until one read their decidedly antiestablishment headlines.

Highly rational and bureaucratic modes of information design such as charts, grids, graphs, and maps were appropriated by the underground press, not to support a positivist stance but to challenge it. For example, a graph published in ***AMPO: A Report from the Japanese New Left*** (fig. 3.13) meticulously illustrated the kinds and numbers of military vehicles observed entering and leaving a Japanese-American military base, despite the US government's downright denial such vehicles existed; a flowchart in ***Fifth Estate*** titled "Who Owns Detroit?" diagrammed the network of banks, corporations, and utilities that controlled the city's economy, with connecting lines indicating their elaborate involvement with one another (fig. 3.14); a lengthy gridded table in the ***Black Panther Party Paper*** documented countless arrests of black men, detailing the charge, bail, and disposition status of each. In these instances, the rhetoric and visual forms of objectivity constituted an "aesthetics of

13. See Richard Meyer, *Outlaw Representation: Censorship and Homosexuality in Twentieth-Century American Art* (New York: Oxford University Press, 2002).

AMPO

OKINAWA

A SPECIAL ISSUE OF AMPO

a report from the japanese new left No. 7-8

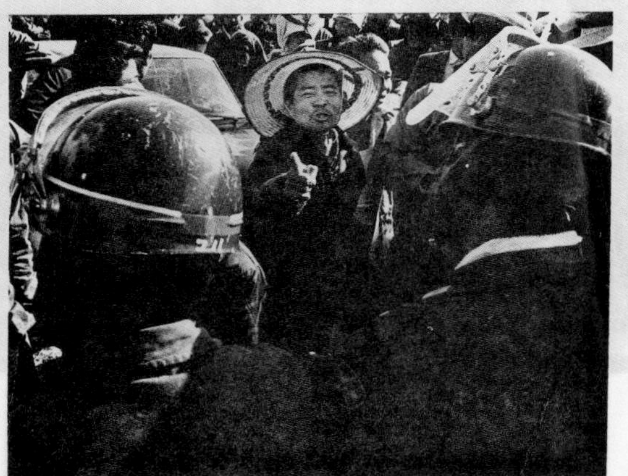

CONTENTS:

AMPO

AMPO

a report on the JAPANESE PEOPLE'S MOVEMENTS

no. 12 (march, 1972)

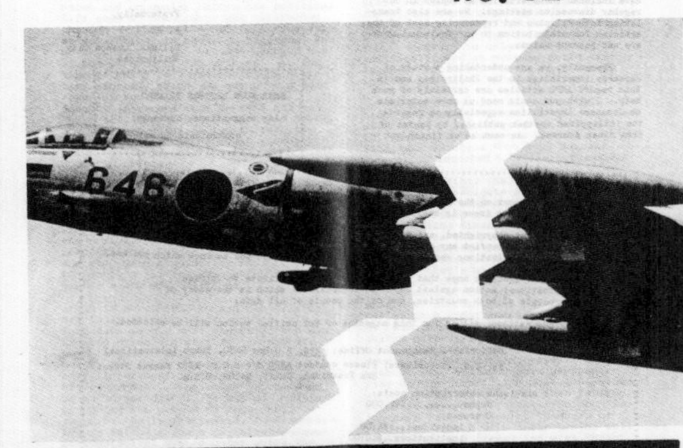

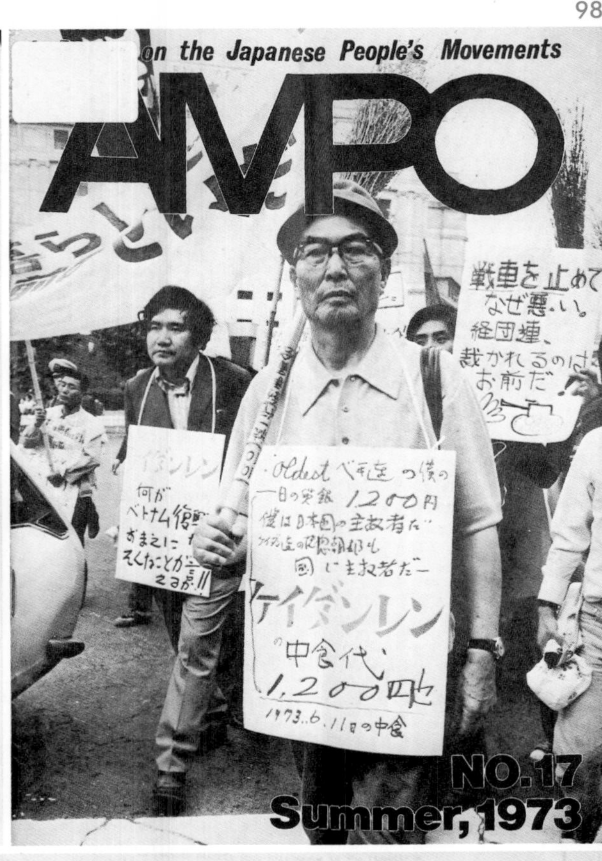

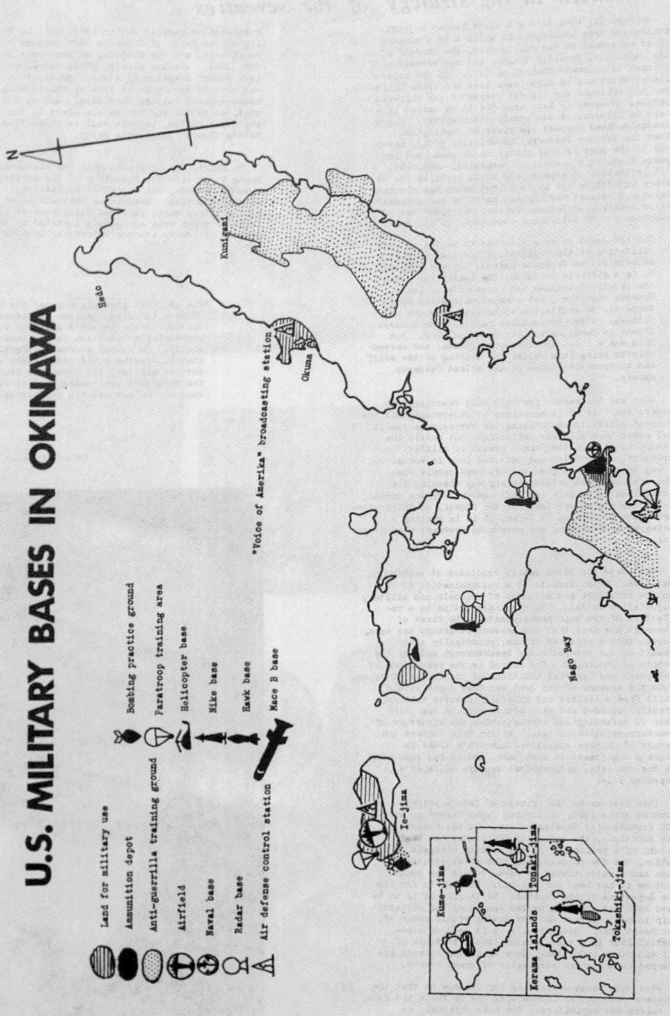

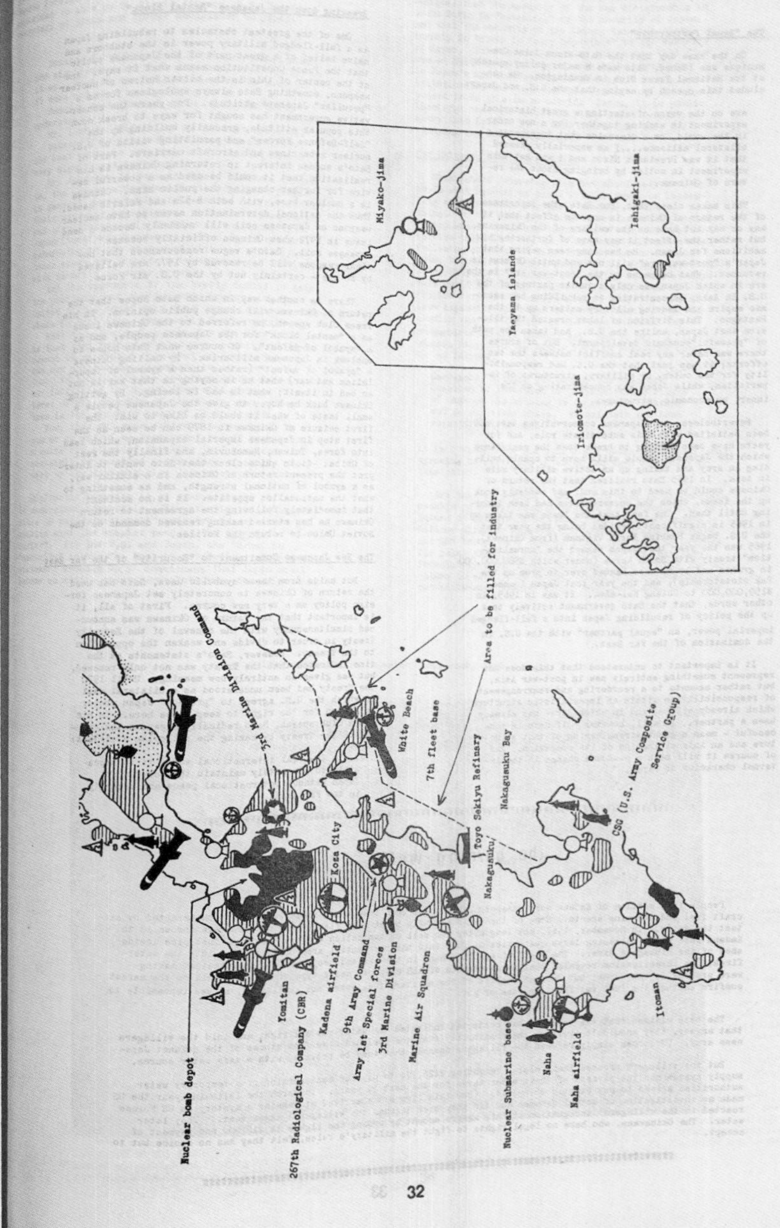

U.S. Army Paper Bares War Role of 'Sagami Maintenance' Depot

The Sagamihara Citizens' Group to Stop the Tanks has obtained a U.S. Army program for the repair of vehicles at the Sagami Maintenance Depot, which clearly indicates that the maintenance base continues to be actively employed to back U.S. military action in Asia, particularly in Vietnam and South Korea.

Titled "FY-74 Combat Vehicle Program," the U.S. document details plans to send 38 M113 and other tanks from Sagamihara to South Vietnam, 98 to the Eighth Army in south Korea, and seven to Cambodia in fiscal year 1974. (The whole program is reproduced on the opposite page.)

After receiving this document, the group immediately protested to Foreign Minister Ohira, who, at the height of the 1972 anti-tank deployment struggle, promised that in principle war vehicles would not be allowed to be sent to Vietnam and that no more damaged vehicles would be brought into the maintenance base.

The group exposed this promise as utterly false. According to their investigation (daily all-night vigils), 147 combat-destroyed tanks and other combat vehicles were brought in between January, 1973 and March, 1974. The group has calculated that since July, 1973, 29 combat vehicles have been sent to South Vietnam and nine more are scheduled to be sent there within the current fiscal year.

Representatives of the citizens' group visited the Foreign Minister on March 22 to hand over an open questionnaire seeking clarification of Ohira's breach of faith. A young official of the U.S. Bureau's Security section met them, and quibbled that the Minister did not betray his promise, because his earlier statement included the words, "in principle". "So, exceptions exist".

The group has corroborated that the Sagami Maintenance Depot's activities have intensified since the beginning of the year. Despite earlier press reports that the facilities will be returned to Japan (for use by the Japanese Self-Defense Forces), U.S. Embassy sources were quoted by the press on March 21 as stating categorically that the repair base would never be returned to Japan.

Another point the group emphasizes is that a large number of war vehicles are being sent from Sagami Maintenance Depot to South Korea for use by the U.S. Eighth Army. "We opposed the shipment of tanks and other war vehicles from Sagami to Vietnam. For the same reason we must express our grave concern about the use of the base to support one of the antagonistic parties in the Korean peninsula," the group's statement reads.

U.S. ARMY TANK REPAIR PROGRAM FOR SAGAMIHARA

Customer \ month	1973 7	8	9	10	11	12	1974 1	2	3	4	5	6	total
CONUS	47	42	43	48	29	23	1	20					253
8A			7		14	14	4		15	19	25		98
OP PROJ	7				4		4	22	24	13	5		79
RVN	2	2	1		3	6	10	5		2	7		38
Cambodia R&R						7							7
WAR RES	1				1		4						6
total	54	44	51	48	51	50	23	47	39	34	37	0	481

note:

M106 107mm Self-Propelled Gun
M113 Armored Personnel Carrier
M548 Armored Cargo Carrier
M577 Armored Commander
M125 81mm Self-Propelled Gun
M132 Flame Thrower
M578 Recovery Vehicle
M88 Armored Recovery Vehicle
XM806 Recovery Vehicle

12

27 Nov 73

FY-74 COMBAT VEHICLE PROGRAM

PRON NO.	ITEM	CUSTOMER	QTY	JUL	AUG	SEP	OCT	NOV	DEC	JAN	FEB	MAR	APR	MAY	JUN
* 8A4A1153	M106 C2 H/M	8A R&R	13					4						9	
* 8A4A1153	M106 C2 H/M	8A WAR RES	2					2							
* 8A4A1153	M106 C2 H/M	OP PROJ	4											4	
8A4A1067	M106A1 S/C	CONUS	1	1											
8A4A1088	M106A1 H/M	OP PROJ	7	7											
8A4A1088	M106A1 H/M	WAR RES	1	1											
8A4A1089	M106A1 B/D	RVN	2					1	1						
8A4A1085	M106 B/D GAS	RVN	1						1						
8A4A1025	M113A1 H/M	CONUS	46			10	9	4	2	1	20				
8A4A1025	M113A1 H/M	WAR RES	4							4					
8A4A1025	M113A1 H/M	OP PROJ	64							4	22	24	13	1	
8A4A1025	M113A1 H/M	8A R&R	27						14	4			9		
8A4A1026	M113A1 S/C	CONUS	12	12											
8A4A1033	M113A1 B/D	CONUS	45	20	16	4	5								
8A4A1154	M113A1 B/D	RVN	2							2					
8A4A1155 (LTV)	M113A1 B/D C2	RVN	1								1				
8A4A1074	M113 H/M GAS	CONUS	1						1						
8A4A1051	M548 B/D	OP PROJ	4					4							
8A4A1051	M548 B/D	CONUS	66	8	8	19	27	4							
8A4A1046	M548 B/D	RVN	12	2				2	4		1			3	
8A4A1065	M577 H/M GAS	CONUS	4				4								
8A4A1056	M577A1 H/M	CONUS	28					13	15						
8A4A1056	M577A1 H/M	8A R&R	7			7									
8A4A1060	M577A1 S/C	CONUS	15		11	4									
8A4A1061	M577A1 B/D	CONUS	7	4	3										
8A4A1059	M577A1 B/D	RVN	1								1				
8A4A1001	M125A1 H/M	WAR RES	1					1							
8A4A1001	M125A1 H/M	CONUS	9					4	5						
8A4A1001	M125A1 H/M	8A R&R	16					8				8			
8A4A1010	M125A1 B/D	CONUS	11	2	4	4		1							
8A4A1003	M125A1 B/D	RVN	11		2	1				8					
8A4A1156	M125A1 H/M	RVN	2								2				
8A4A1018	M132A1 H/M	CONUS	6				3	3							
8A4A1020	M132A1 B/D	CONUS	2			2									
8A4A1016	M132A1 B/D	RVN	4										2	2	
8A4A1092	XM806 B/D GAS	RVN	2											2	
8A4A1095	XM806E1 B/D	Cambodia R&R	1						1						
8A4A1091	XM806E1 H/M	Cambodia R&R	6						6						
	M113A1 S/C	8A	15										5	10	
	M577A1 S/C	8A	7									7			
	M578 S/C	8A	11										5	6	
		TOTAL:	481	57	44	51	48	51	50	23	47	39	34	37	

FY-74 CVAP PROGRAM

PRON NO.	ITEM	CUSTOMER	QTY	JUL	AUG	SEP	OCT	NOV	DEC	JAN	FEB	MAR	APR	MAY	JUN
8A4B1037	Eng M113A1	CONUS	95					20		22	19	34			
8A4B1037	Eng M113A1	EUSA	20						2	18					
8A4B1157	Eng M125A1	RVN	31								31				
8A4B1077	Eng M48A3	CONUS	1		1										
8A4B1077	Eng M60A1	8A R&R	21					3	10	8					
8A4B1106	Eng M48A3	RVN R&R	50		1	2	6	1			8	8	8	8	8
8A4B1150	Eng M88	RVN R&R	6						1	5					
8A4C1151	T/M M88	RVN R&R	6							3	3				
8A4C1107	T/M M48A3	RVN R&R	20				6	1			5	8			
8A4C1038	T/M M113A1	CONUS	173		23	30	30	30			60				
8A4C1040	T/F M113A1	CONUS	9	9											
8A4C1049	T/F M548	CONUS	4			4									
8A4C1039	Diff M113A1	CONUS	11	9		2									
8A4C1067	F/D M113A1	CONUS	9	6	3										
8A4E1140	Computer M48A3	RVN R&R	21								10	11			
8A4E1142	Range Finder	RVN R&R	21								10	11			
EH2B0084	Cyl/H M113A1	ASP	666												666
		TOTAL:	1164	24	28	38	42	55	13	56	146	72	8	8	674

FY-74 TVAP PROGRAM

PRON NO.	ITEM	CUSTOMER	QTY	JUL	AUG	SEP	OCT	NOV	DEC	JAN	FEB	MAR	APR	MAY	JUN
8A4B0211	7871 Eng Dsl 5T W/C	ROKFV RR	1	1											
8A4B0211	7871 Eng Dsl 5T W/C	USARBCO	21	21											
8A4B0211	7871 Eng Dsl 5T W/C	8A	1	1											
8A4B0211	7871 Eng Dsl 5T W/C	RVN II	35			1		1	10				23		
8A4B0092	7871 Eng Dsl 5T W/C	THAI-A	1	1											
8A4B0262	7407 Eng Dsl 5T W/C	USARBCO	101	49	10							42			
8A4B0262	7407 Eng Dsl 5T W/C	RVN II	3			3									
8A4B0262	7407 Eng Dsl 5T W/C	ROKFV II	10	10											
8A4B0263	7092 Eng Dsl 5T WO/C	USARBCO	81	19	8	5	20	21	8						
8A4B0264	5076 Eng Dsl 5T WO/C	USARBCO	1		1										
8A4B0265	2273 Eng Dsl 5T WO/C	USARBCO	2	2											
8A4B0084	6865 Eng Dsl 5T WO/C	RVN II	2					2							
8A4B0084	6865 Eng Dsl 5T WO/C	TMA	4				4								
8A4B0084	6865 Eng Dsl 5T WO/C	USARBCO	104	17	87										
8A4B0270	6865 Eng Dsl 5T WO/C	RVN RR	174		4	62	81	10	17						
8A4B0007	3645 Eng MF 5T	8A	90						40	27	23				
8A4B0291	364- Eng MF 5T	8A	27								27				
	4086 T/M MF 5T	8A	70								30	30	10		
	3773 T/F 5T	8A	1									1			
	2955 T/F 5T	8A	66								30	30	6		
	1280 Axle R 5T	8A	45								20	20	5		
	1350 Gears ST 5T	8A	76							16	20	20	20		
	6821 Diff 5T	8A	100									50	50		
		TOTAL:	1016	121	110	71	105	34	75	43	150	193	114		

Programs without PRON's are for Planning Purpose.

13

People's Vigil:

WATCHING THE TANKS ROLL BY

AMPO readers may recall the report in No.15 on the movement to "stop the tanks" -- tanks and other military vehicles which flow between the U.S. Army Supply and Maintenance Activities Facility in Sagamihara and America's war fronts throughout the Third World, particularly Indochina. One group of participants which has sustained that struggle for two years, the Sagamihara Citizen's Group to Stop the Tanks, has sent us news of their recent activities.

"For the past year we have been observing the movement of military vehicles (M48 tanks, M113 APCs, etc.) and vehicles carrying military supplies into and out of the Sagami Depot every night. The enclosed graph is our report on the kinds and numbers of vehicles we observed. (Since we are not free to keep watch during the day, the report is incomplete.) The reason we felt compelled to gather this information was our realization that the government's statements simply can't be believed. In the fall of 1972 Foreign Minister Ohira claimed that 'Tanks are no longer being shipped to Vietnam,' while we know that in fact they are.

"The group's watchdog activities, night-long vigils for an entire year, have revealed that the depot's activities have continued essentially unchanged since Nov. 1972. The number of vehicles shipped out has not decreased.

"At the end of September, 1973, for instance, 40 M113 APCs were shipped in, and between the November 11-12, we

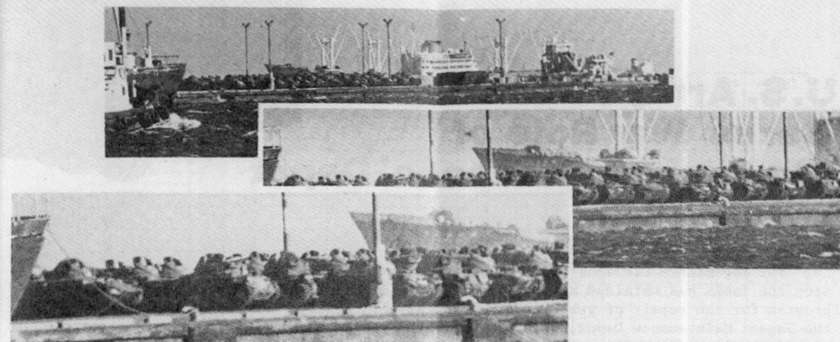

saw 30 APCs leave. We learned that vehicles which had been shipped out in the beginning of September were loaded on ships bound for Panama. Could this be completely unrelated to U.S. strategy in Latin America -- its involvement in the Chile coup included?"

The Sagamihara group has found that cooperation with anti-military activities in other areas is very important; especially fruitful has been its collaboration with a Yokohama citizens' group active at the North Pier, from which military equipment leaves Japan. It seeks cooperation with other groups in the future. ●●

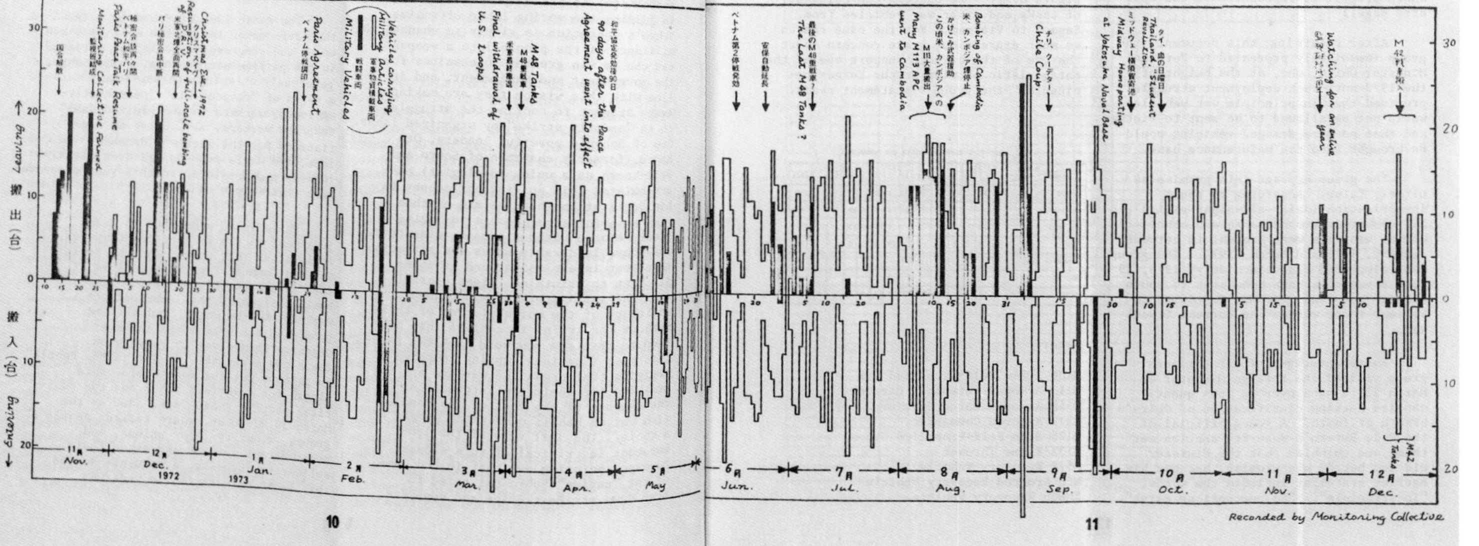

10

11

Fig. 3.13. **AMPO: A Report on the Japanese People's Movements** (Tokyo), no. 7–8, cover; March 1972, no. 12, cover; Summer 1973, no. 17, cover; no. 7–8, pp. 31–32; Spring 1974, vol. 6, no. 2, pp. 12–13; Spring 1974, vol. 6, no. 2, pp. 10–11

PAGE TWENTY FOUR/THE FIFTH ESTATE

Network of Controlling Interests in the Detroit Economy

BANKS
Detroit Bank and Trust
National Bank of Detroit

CORPORATIONS
Fruehauf
Burroughs
BUHL
Parke Davis
FORD
Wyandotte Chemicals
HANNA
Chrysler
ROCKE-

UTILITIES
Detroit Edison
Mich. Con. Gas
Mich. Bell

Connecting lines mean involvement by investment or interlocking directorships

WHO RULES DETROIT?

by Millard

The real pig is not the obvious pig. The obvious pig is the one that we see every day: the police force. These are the neanderthals who patrol our communities trying to keep us in line. Government institutions are also the overt pig. The Congress, state legislatures and city councils in Amerika direct the police and military and mouth the policies of the actual controllers.

Politicians and political institutions are the overt oppressors in Amerika. The real pigs are the people who put them in power and direct their policies: the ruling class.

The ruling class is a relatively small percentage of people who control the massive interwoven corporations in Amerika. This amounts to control over the nation's economic structure which in turn influences all other institutions.

The ruling class keeps its money and power tight within its control, passing them on from generation to generation. This means that there is a virtual aristocracy in Amerika. It remains in the background and manipulates the institutions of society from Nixon down to the local cop.

The control that the ruling class maintains over the economy is what gives them control over our lives. Rather than competing for profits from the consumer by putting out better products, they cooperate in putting out cheaply made products and fixing the prices. If a new company enters the market and refuses to cooperate in the constant conspiracy, it is undercut and forced out of business.

This cooperation also allows them to exploit workers to the maximum. They don't compete for workers by offering higher wages or better working conditions. They cooperate in keeping wages low and working conditions poor. Sellout unions serve an important function in working with the corporations making sure that the workers are given only token wage increases and improvements in working conditions. The UAW is a prime example in the Motor City.

Taxes are another way in which the people are exploited by the ruling class. It is common knowledge that they pay little or no taxes. It is the working people who bear the heavy burden of taxes. These taxes go to support an imperialistic war that protects foreign investments of the ruling class, a war that reaps huge profits for the war industry owned by the ruling class.

WHO ARE THESE PEOPLE?

We've heard the names Rockefeller, Mellon, Ford and DuPont, but many of us do not realize the ways in which these people control our lives.

Detroit has its very own ruling class composed of both national and local families who form a tight controlling network of private businesses and public institutions. Most of the controlling family elites in Detroit live in the Detroit area. One of the oldest and largest is the Buhl family of Grosse Pointe. They hold controlling interest in Parke, Davis & Co., Burrough's and are involved in the National Bank of Detroit.

The Ford family (not related to the automobile Fords) is another major Detroit dynasty. They control Wyandotte Chemical and have a large interest in Libby-Owen-Ford. Through LOF they are tied into Continental Oil Co. which links them up with the Rockefeller family. The Fords are also linked with the Buhls in Parke, Davis & Co.

A third prominent family are the Fishers of Fisher Body Co., GM, and the Fisher-New Center Realty Corporation. Through Max Fisher they are heavily into utilities (Michigan Bell and Michigan Consolidated Gas) and banks (Manufacturers' National Bank of Detroit).

The Fruehaufs, another well-known Detroit family, control Fruehauf Corporation (trailers, shipping containers and modular housing) and are into Burroughs, Detroit Edison, Michigan Consolidated Gas, Michigan Bell and Detroit Bank and Trust.

J.L. Hudson Co. (controlled by the Hudson family) is part of the Dayton-Hudson chain of retail stores in Minneapolis and is into the National Bank of Detroit and Detroit Edison.

The largest outside interest in Detroit is the Hanna dynasty of Cleveland. They control Chrysler and Great Lakes Steel. They also are involved in Consolidated Coal (now Continental Oil) and the National Bank of Detroit. Internationally, the Hannas control much of the mining in Brazil.

Also involved in the NBD are the DuPonts who control GM. The massive Mellon family is into Chrysler and GM. The Rockefellers have inroads into almost every major Detroit corporation.

Surprisingly, with the exception of Chrysler, the auto companies are not heavily involved in the Detroit economy. Ford and GM have plants in the Detroit area but they exercise little control over the Detroit economy. They have broadened their interests to a national level.

It is true that billions of dollars are pumped into the Detroit economy in wages to workers, but this money has no directive influence on the economy. It is only one element in the political-economic projections of the ruling class. The consumers and workers in Detroit have no directive influence in how the Detroit economy is run. They are merely a vast sea out of which the ruling class sucks labor and profit.

While the corporations are controlled by families, the banks and utilities are controlled jointly by the corporations in order to facilitate their manipulation of Detroit's economy. The three utilities, Detroit Edison, Michigan Consolidated Gas and Michigan Bell, are composed of a tight network of investments and people of the major corporations. Fruehauf, Chrysler and Ex-Cello Corporation virtually dominate all three utilities. In this way these "public" utilities become mere profit making extensions of the long arm of the ruling class.

The banks of Detroit, especially the National Bank of Detroit, are very key in the economic structure. They overlap with the major corporations (chiefly Fruehauf, Burrough's, Parke-Davis, and Chrysler) and are controlled by them. The National Bank of Detroit is the largest bank in Detroit and is connected with every major family elite both local and national. It serves two functions: as the chief exchange center for financial capital in Detroit and as the link between Detroit financiers and national financiers.

This is only a brief scratch on the surface of an understanding of the Detroit economic structure, but through this several things come to light. Each of the major corporations in Detroit is controlled by a family, each of which has involvements that link it with the other families. These involvements are of two kinds: by direct financial investment and, more importantly, by interlocking directorships.

In interlocking directorships, men from the Board of Directors of one company are also members of the Board of Directors of another company. The corporations, banks and utilities cooperate in this way for the maximum exploitation of workers and consumers. Thus, the capitalist ruse of "free competition for the market" is total bullshit. They don't call it a ruling class for nothing.

The ruling class is thus a tight circle of control amounting to complete monopoly of the leading sectors of the American economy. And this conspiracy overlaps onto all levels of government. Nixon and Agnew and all politicians are bought, packaged and sold by the ruling class and are little more than instruments in their grabbing for money and power.

A few of the key men in the Detroit ruling class are:

Walker Cisler: age, 73; residence, 1071 Devonshire Rd., Grosse Point Park. He is involved in Detroit Edison, Fruehauf, Burroughs, Detroit Bank and Trust and others, and is one of the key controllers of the Detroit economy.

Max Fisher: of the Fisher family. He is into Fruehauf, Michigan Bell, Michigan Consolidated Gas and Manufacturers National Bank.

Robert Surdham: age, 64; residence, 46 Lake Shore Rd., Grosse Pointe Farms. He is into the National Bank of Detroit, Cunningham Drugs, National Steel and Wyandotte Chemicals. He represents the huge interests of the Hanna family in Detroit through the National Bank of Detroit.

The next issue of the paper will discuss Detroit's civic and governmental institutions and how they are controlled by the ruling class.

Fig. 3.14. **Fifth Estate** (Detroit), July 9–22, 1970, vol. 5, no. 5, back cover

administration"[14] that functioned subversively—as it did in the practice of Institutional Critique developed by artists such as Hans Haacke and Marcel Broodthaers in the 1960s and 1970s—in order to unmask and demystify rather than collude with institutional power (fig. 3.15).

As the underground press challenged the transparency of language through which mainstream media naturalized and maintained its jurisdiction over the truth, it also challenged the objectivity of images, especially one of the most time-honored genres of photojournalism: straight photography. Against the privileged claim to present an unmediated version of reality sanctioned by the photograph's indexical status, underground papers favored images that refused such straightforward documentary ambitions. Photomontage offered a form of image making that was at once technically accessible, depending on the same cut-and-paste procedures as standard offset layout, and enormously effective at conveying the social and political turbulence of the 1960s and 1970s. As it had functioned earlier in the century for Dadaist and constructivist artists such as Hannah Hoch, John

14. See Benjamin Buchloh, "Conceptual Art 1962–1969: From the Aesthetics of Administration to the Critique of Institutions," *October* 55, Winter 1990, pp. 105–143.

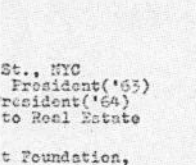
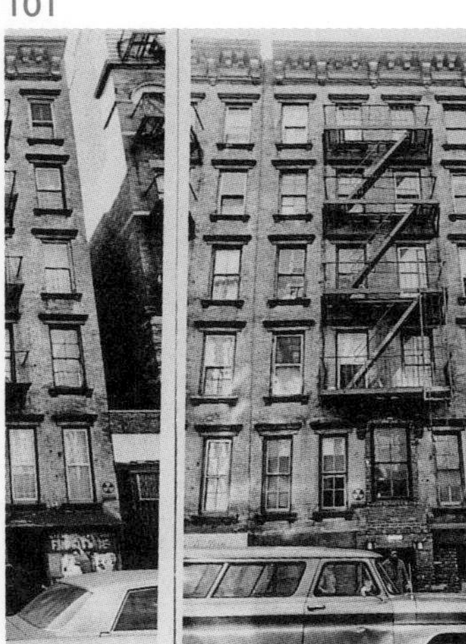
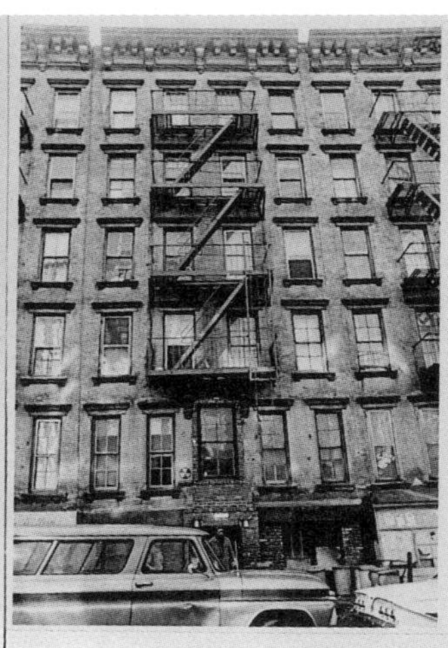
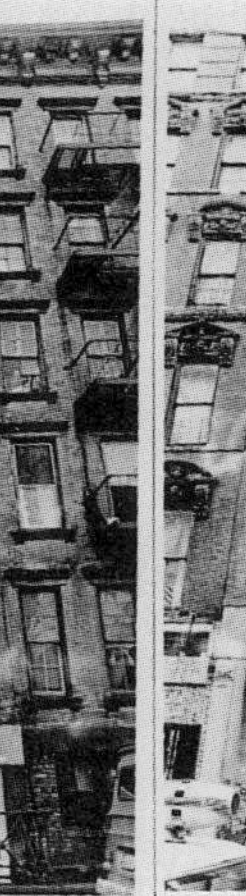
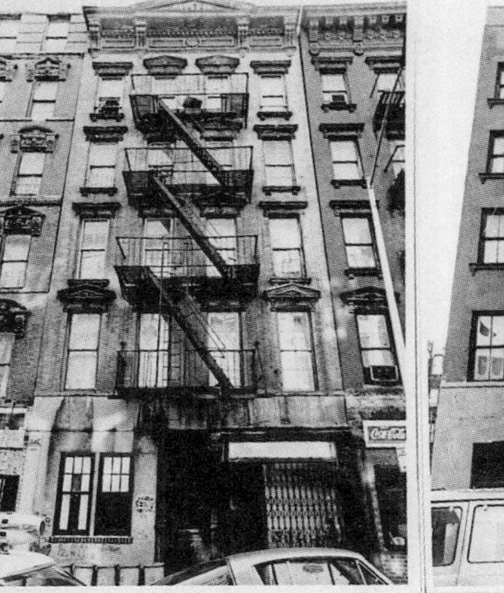
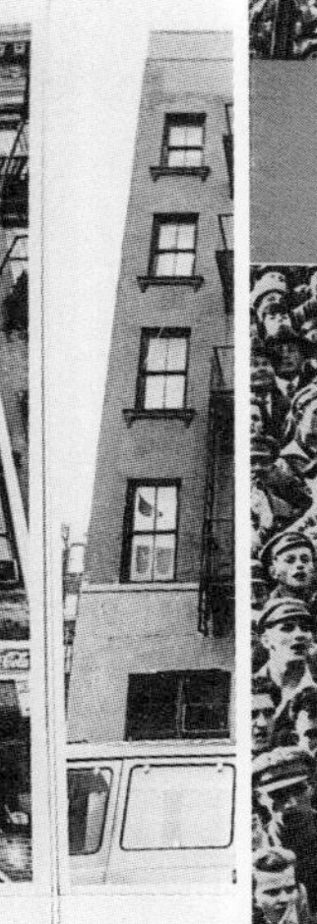

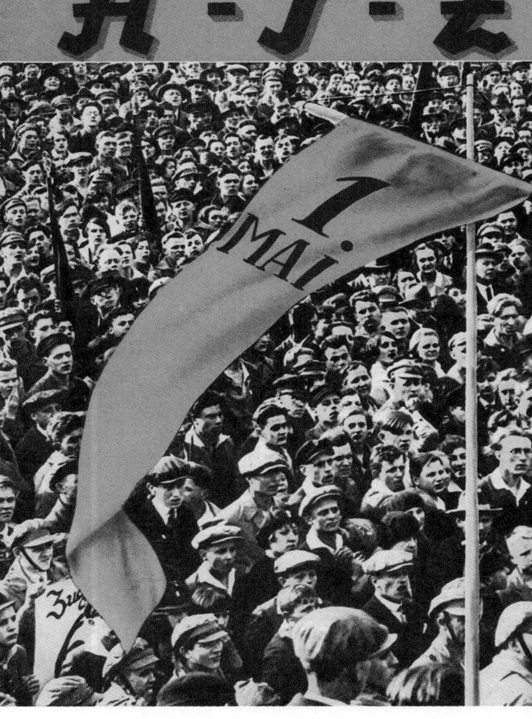

Fig. 3.15. Hans Haacke, **Shapolsky et al. Manhattan Real Estate Holdings, a Real-Time Social System, as of May 1, 1971**

Fig. 3.16. John Heartfield, **A-I-Z: Die Arbeiter-illustrierte Zeitung aller Länder,** 1930

Heartfield (fig. 3.16), and El Lissitzky, photomontage served as a critical representational strategy that operated according to the allegorical principles of appropriation, accumulation, juxtaposition, and fragmentation in order to protest contemporary conditions.[15]

The montages published in underground papers were not seamless, but announced their constructed nature through uneven, torn edges and jarring contrasts in scale and perspective. They registered a sense of crisis, of rupture and conflict, of things breaking apart: in the *Distant Drummer* a Philadelphia street decked out in campaign banners appears to be crumbling as if in a violent earthquake, as a pig at the top of the image oinks (fig. 3.17); in the Chicago paper *Rising Up Angry*, a government building is literally riven into pieces by the pressures enumerated in the accompanying caption, "Government in Trouble: The Economy, Indochina, Watergate." (fig. 3.18).

If photomontage was used to express the counterculture's disillusionment with mainstream society, it

15. See Benjamin Buchloh, "Allegorical Procedures: Appropriation and Montage in Contemporary Art," *Artforum*, September 1982, pp. 43-56.

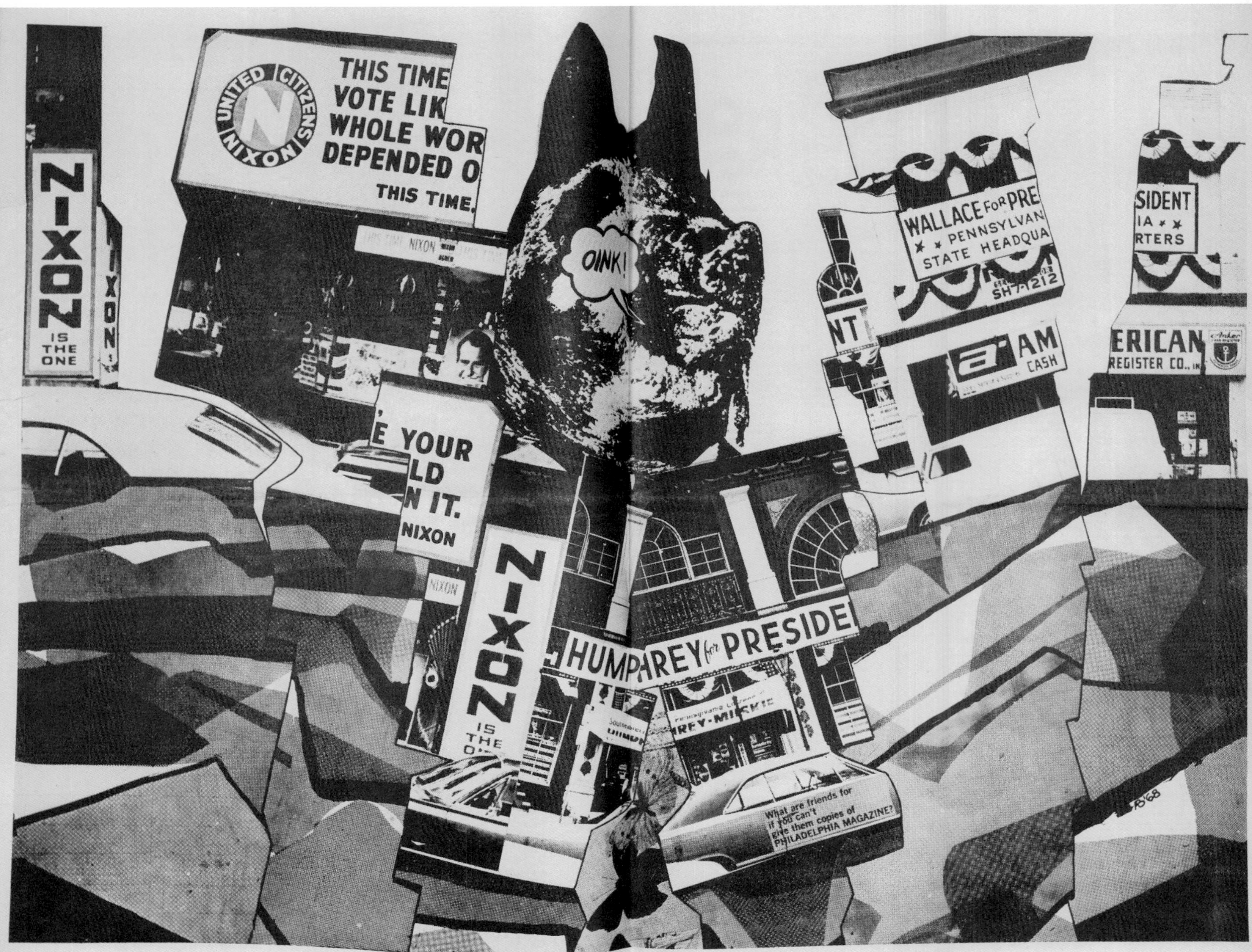

was also mobilized to imagine radical new social formations. "Be-ins" (fig. 3.19) and "love-ins," those quintessential social gatherings of the late 1960s that married the civil disobedience practice of the sit-in with a flower child sensibility, were pictured through overlapping photographs of swarms and throngs of people, conveying a sense of heterogeneity and sheer multitude that would have been impossible to capture with the focal length of a camera lens. Such images, in their obvious constructedness, also suggested the fabricated and utopian character of such gatherings, and by extension the collectivities of the counterculture in general—the fact that they were highly unstable alliances—as much about the way groups were represented and imagined as about their essential or empirical nature. Indeed, there was no consensus on exactly how many people were actually present at the first Human Be-In at Golden Gate Park, never mind precisely what this event signified.

In other montages, dissatisfaction with current social conditions was fused with hopefulness about alternative possibilities. This was the case in Emory Douglas's illustrations for the *Black Panther*

Fig. 3.17. **Distant Drummer** (Philadelphia), November 1–13, 1968, no. 16, center spread

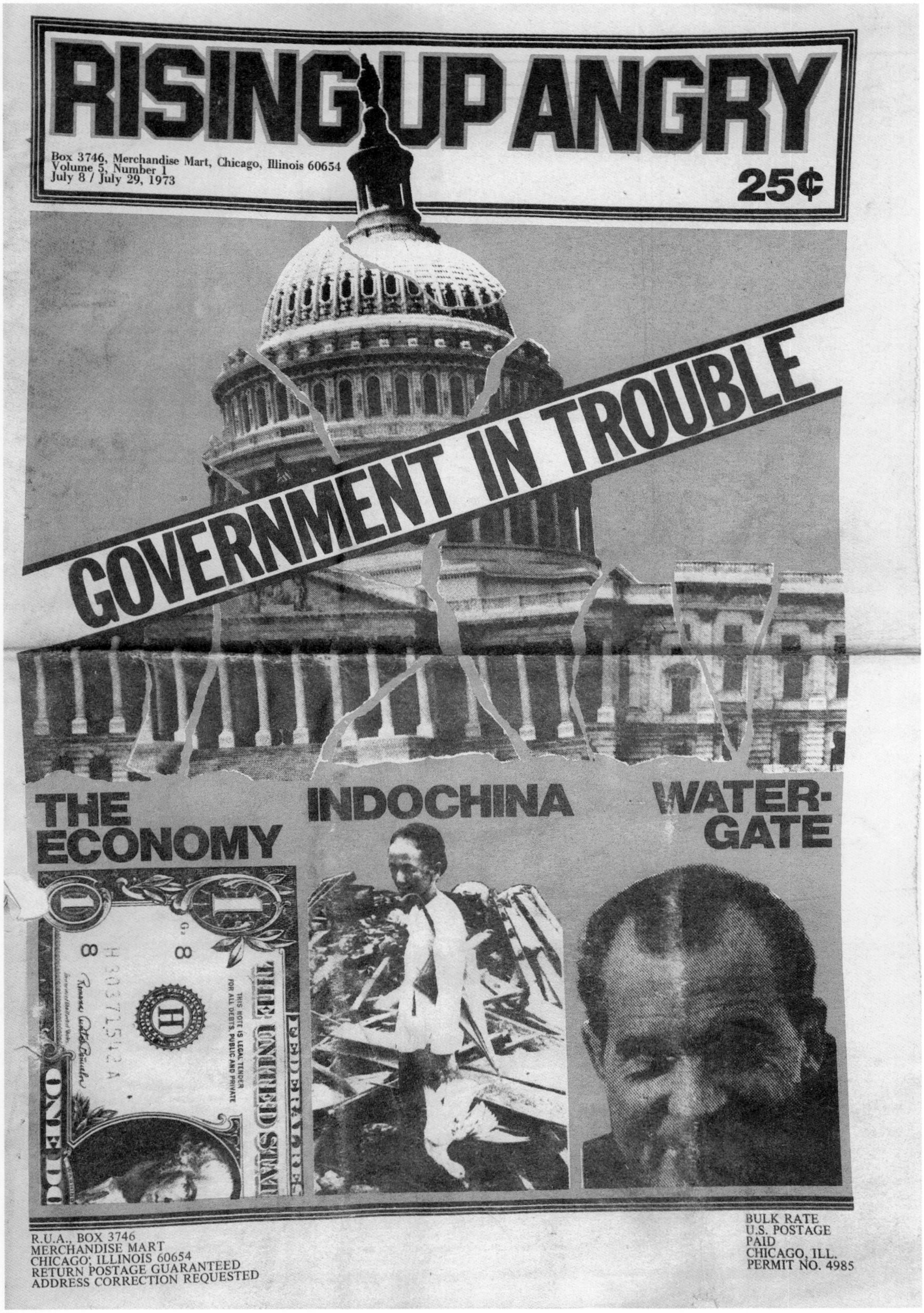

RISING UP ANGRY

Box 3746, Merchandise Mart, Chicago, Illinois 60654
Volume 5, Number 1
July 8 / July 29, 1973

25¢

GOVERNMENT IN TROUBLE

THE ECONOMY

INDOCHINA

WATER-GATE

R.U.A., BOX 3746
MERCHANDISE MART
CHICAGO, ILLINOIS 60654
RETURN POSTAGE GUARANTEED
ADDRESS CORRECTION REQUESTED

BULK RATE
U.S. POSTAGE
PAID
CHICAGO, ILL.
PERMIT NO. 4985

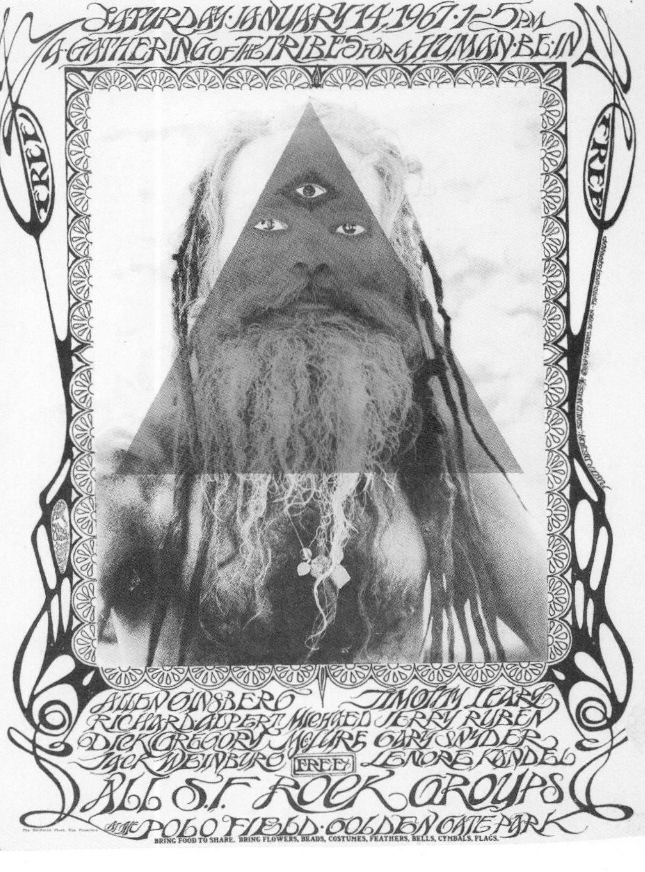

Fig. 3.18. **Rising Up Angry** (Chicago), July 8–29, 1973, vol. 5, no. 1, cover

Fig. 3.19. Stanley Mouse, Michael Bowen, Casey Sonnabend, Bindweed Press, "Gathering of the Tribes for a Human-Be-In," poster, San Francisco, 1967

Party Paper, which frequently pictured cultural oppression and disenfranchisement alongside images of resilience and empowerment (fig. 3.20). Douglas combined photomontage with drawing, quoting the experimental social realist graphics of Cuban poster art to create bold, legible designs that compressed multiple and seemingly contradictory realities and levels of representation into the space of a single image. His ability to juxtapose different issues and topics in the same picture visually paralleled the antiseparatist agenda of the Black Panther Party, which sought to demonstrate links between racial inequality and other forms of social and economic injustice, imperialism, and war.

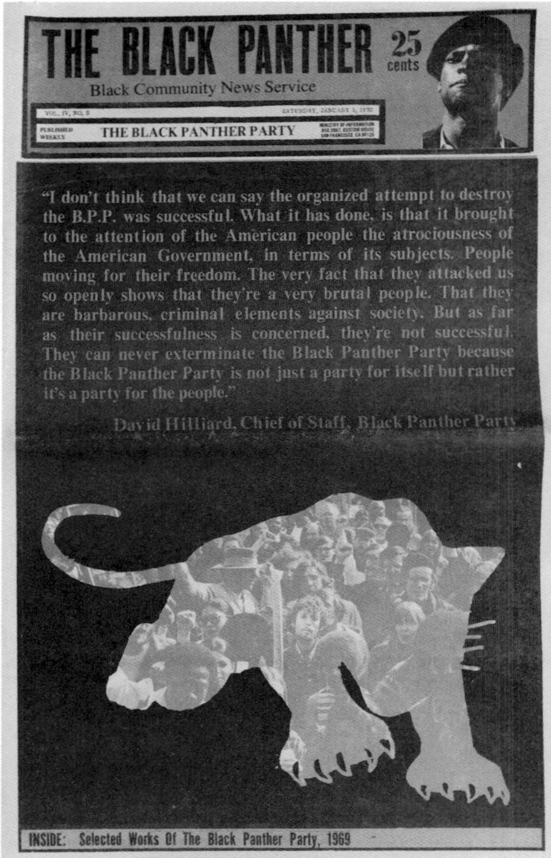

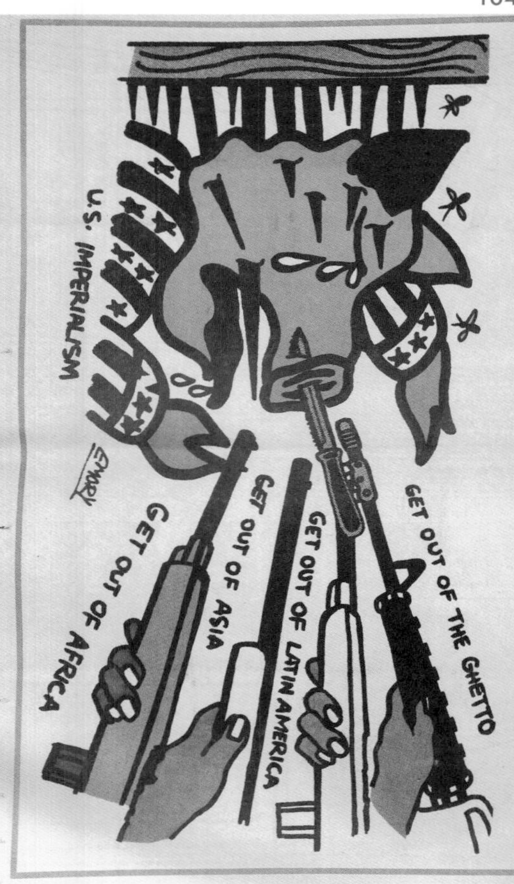

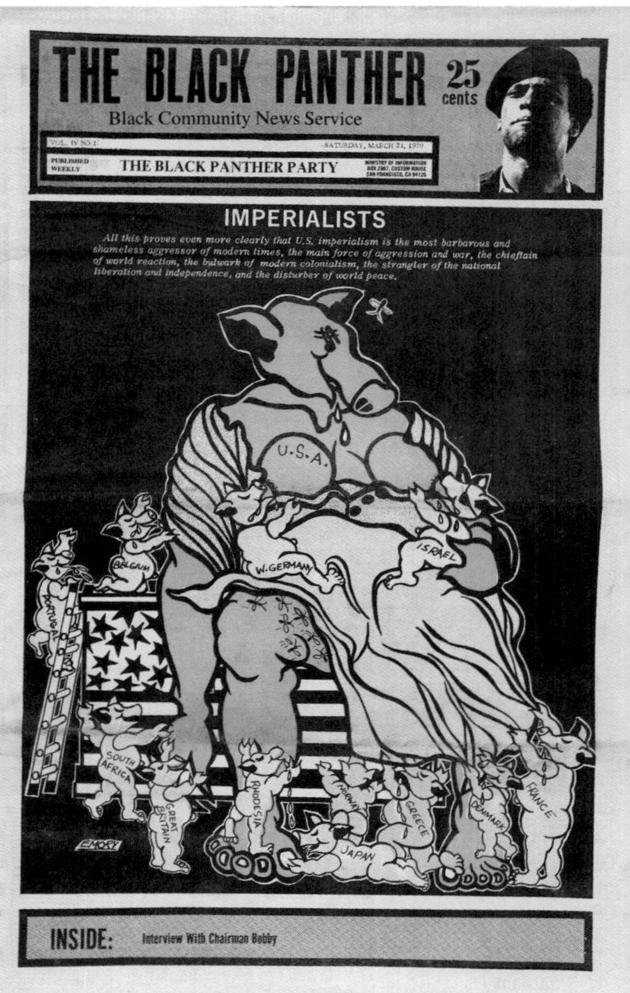

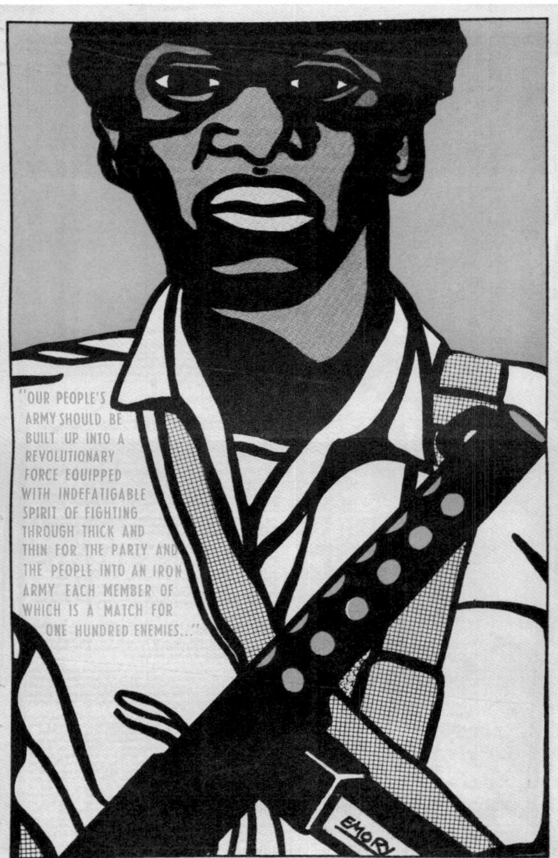

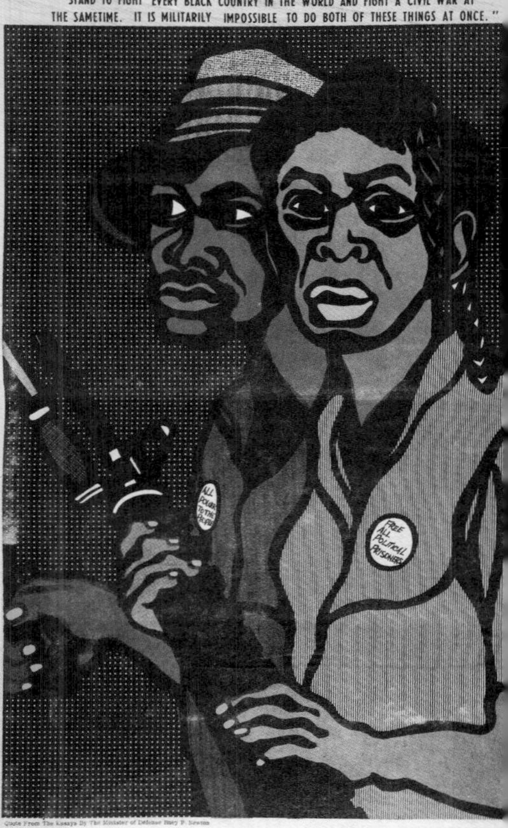

Fig. 3.20. **Black Panther** (San Francisco), January 3, 1970, vol. 4, no. 5, front and back covers; March 21, 1970, vol. 4, no. 1, front cover; May 2, 1970, vol. 4, no. 22, back cover; April 18, 1970, vol. 4, no. 20, back cover

Next page
Fig. 3.20 (cont'd.). **Black Panther** (San Francisco), January 31, 1970, vol. 4, no. 8, front and back covers; January 24, 1970, vol. 4, no. 8, back cover; April 6, 1970, vol. 4, no. 18, back cover; February 7, 1970, vol. 4, no. 10, back cover

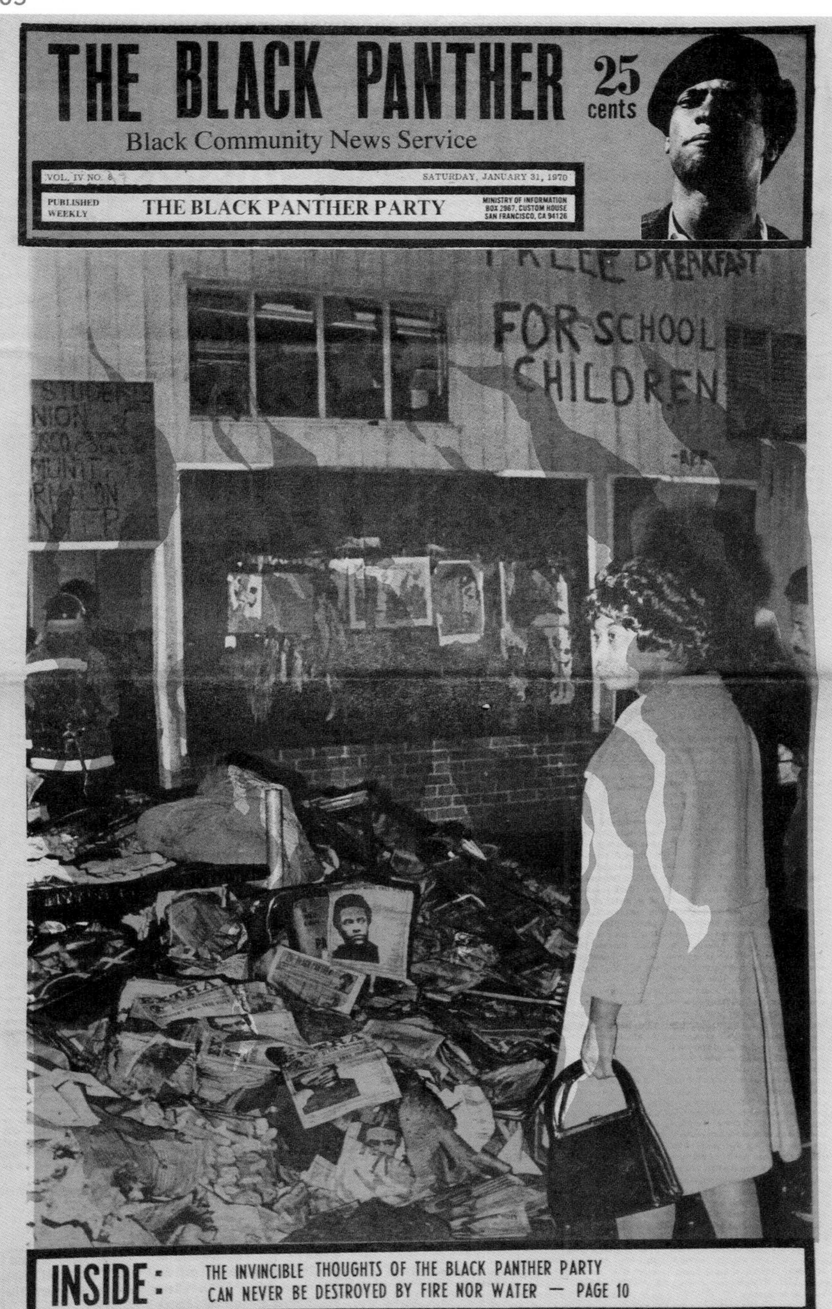

THE BLACK PANTHER 25 cents
Black Community News Service
VOL. IV NO. 8 SATURDAY, JANUARY 31, 1970
PUBLISHED WEEKLY THE BLACK PANTHER PARTY MINISTRY OF INFORMATION BOX 2967, CUSTOM HOUSE SAN FRANCISCO, CA 94126

INSIDE: THE INVINCIBLE THOUGHTS OF THE BLACK PANTHER PARTY CAN NEVER BE DESTROYED BY FIRE NOR WATER — PAGE 10

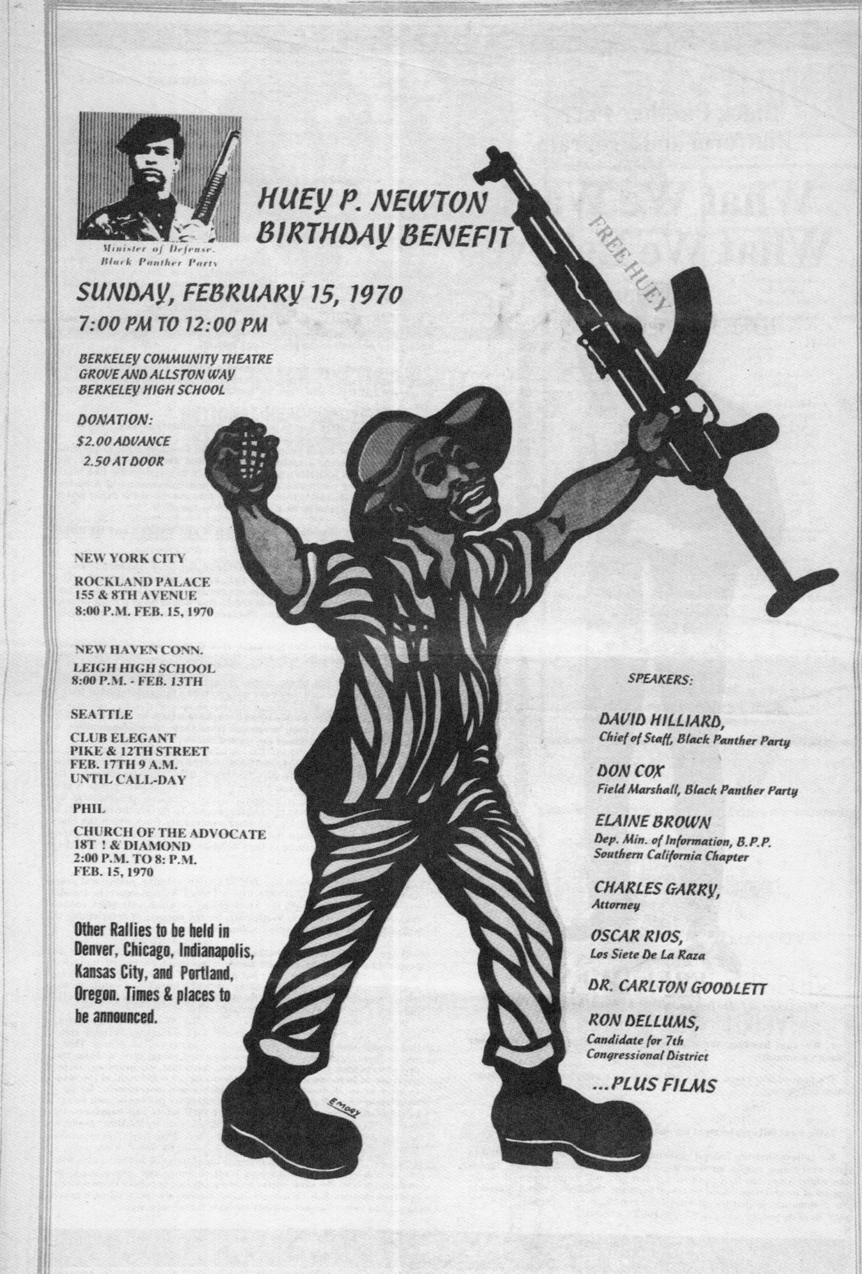

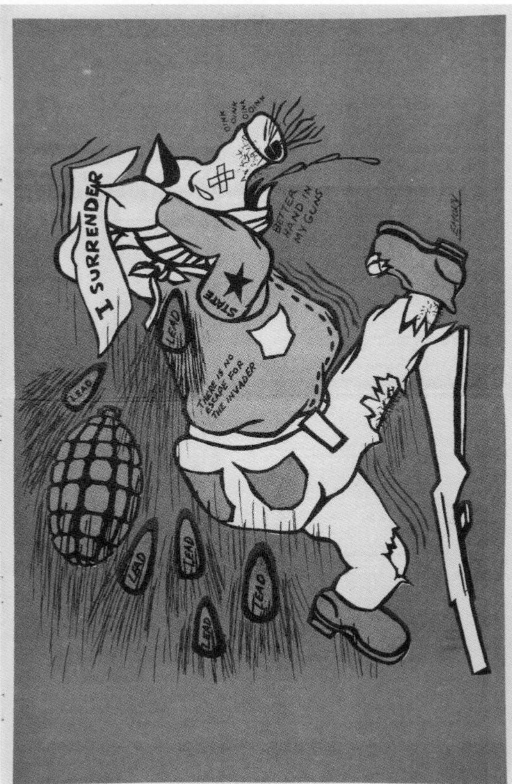

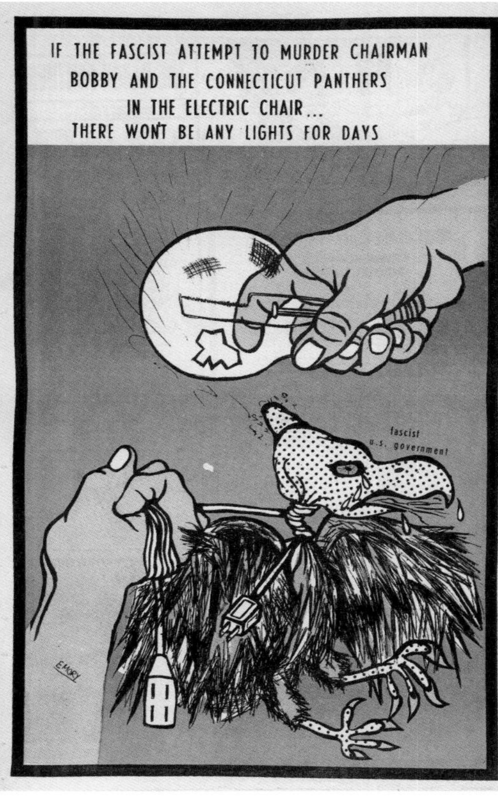

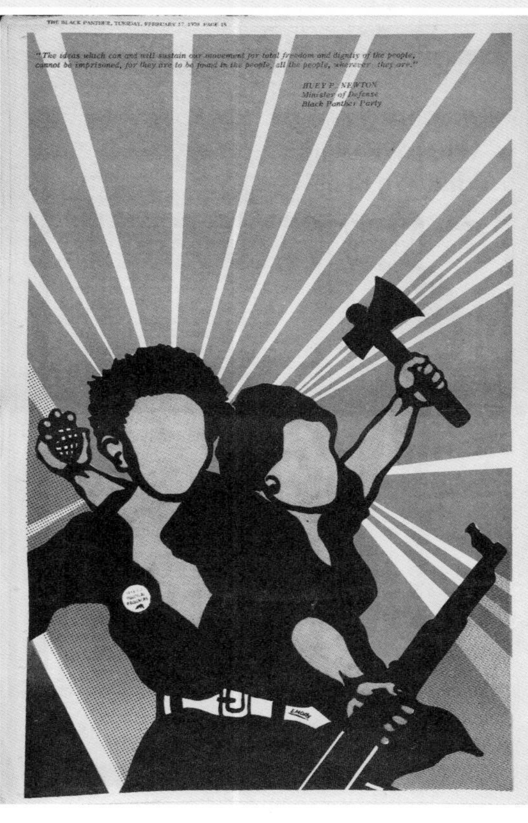

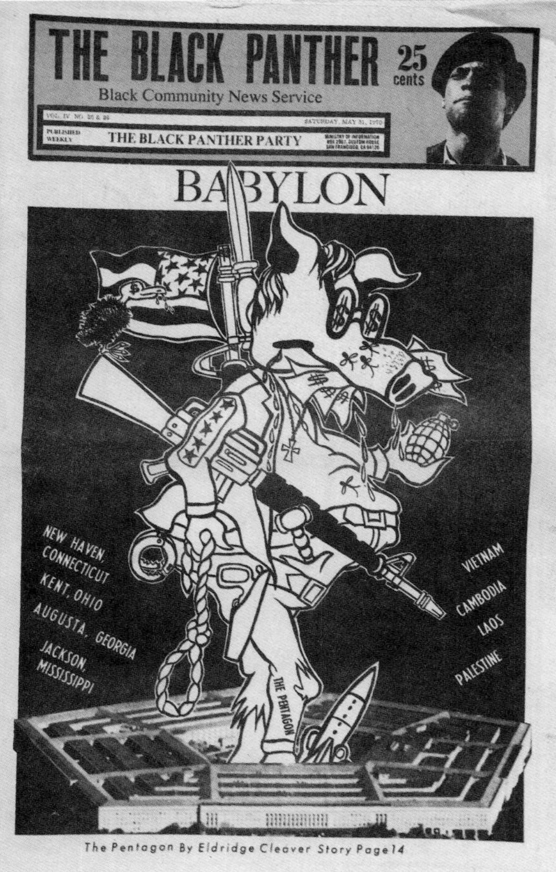

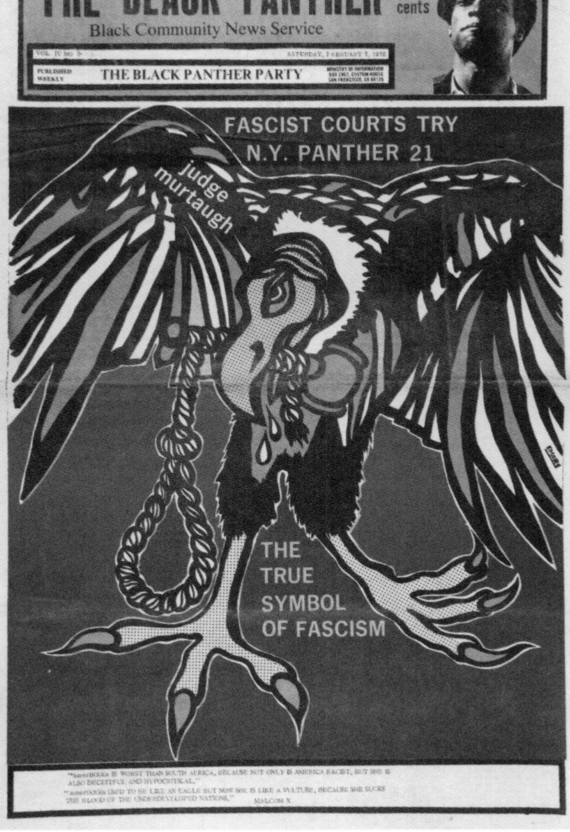

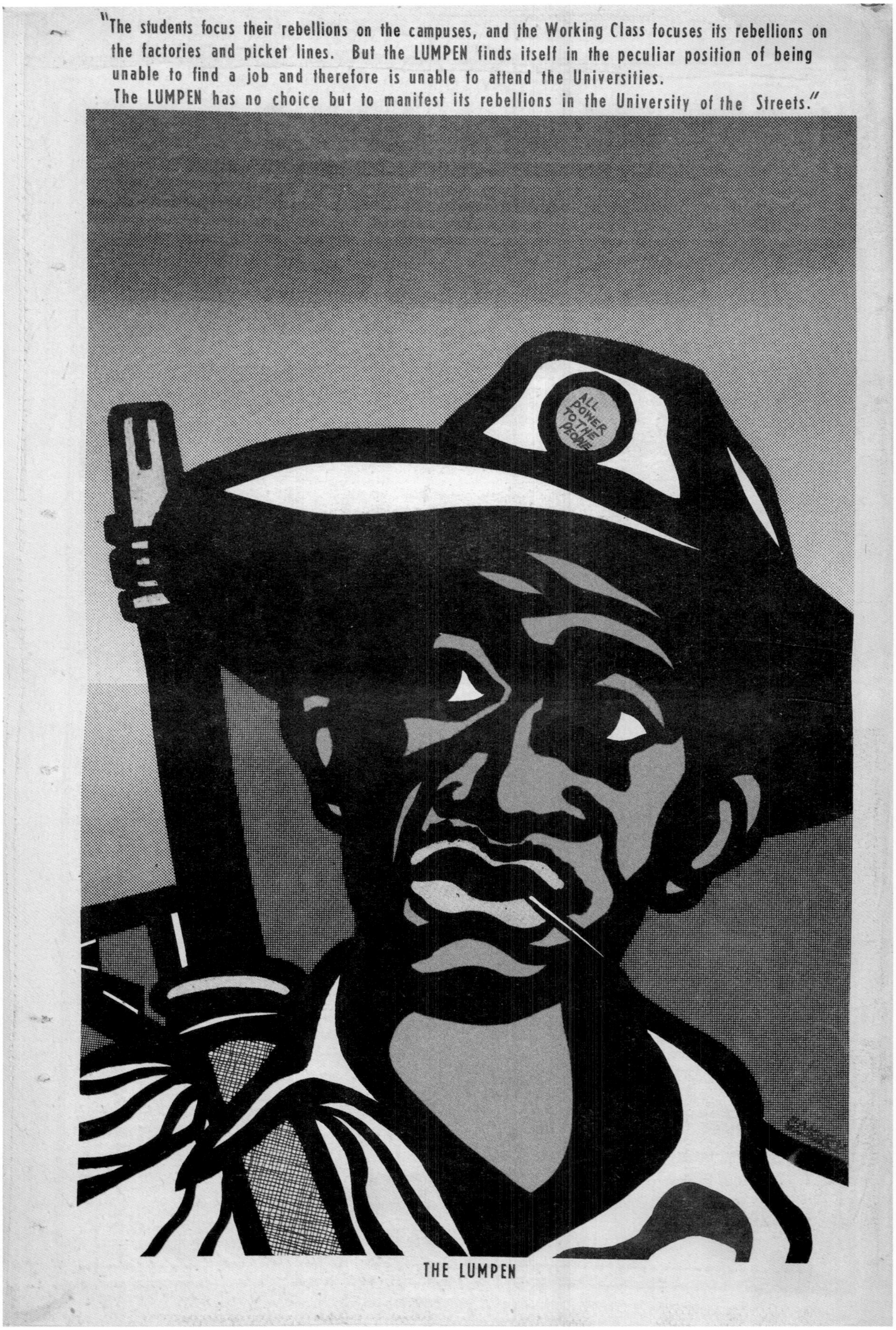

"The students focus their rebellions on the campuses, and the Working Class focuses its rebellions on the factories and picket lines. But the LUMPEN finds itself in the peculiar position of being unable to find a job and therefore is unable to attend the Universities.
The LUMPEN has no choice but to manifest its rebellions in the University of the Streets."

ALL POWER TO THE PEOPLE

THE LUMPEN

Fig. 3.20 (cont'd). **Black Panther** (San Francisco), May 31, 1970, vol. 4, no. 25, front and back covers; January 31, 1970, vol. 4, no. 9, cover

"WE ARE FROM 25 TO 30 MILLION STRONG, AND WE ARE ARMED. AND WE ARE CONSCIOUS OF OUR SITUATION. AND WE ARE DETERMINED TO CHANGE IT. AND WE ARE UNAFRAID."

SELF-DEFENSE

EMORY

WARNING TO AMERICA

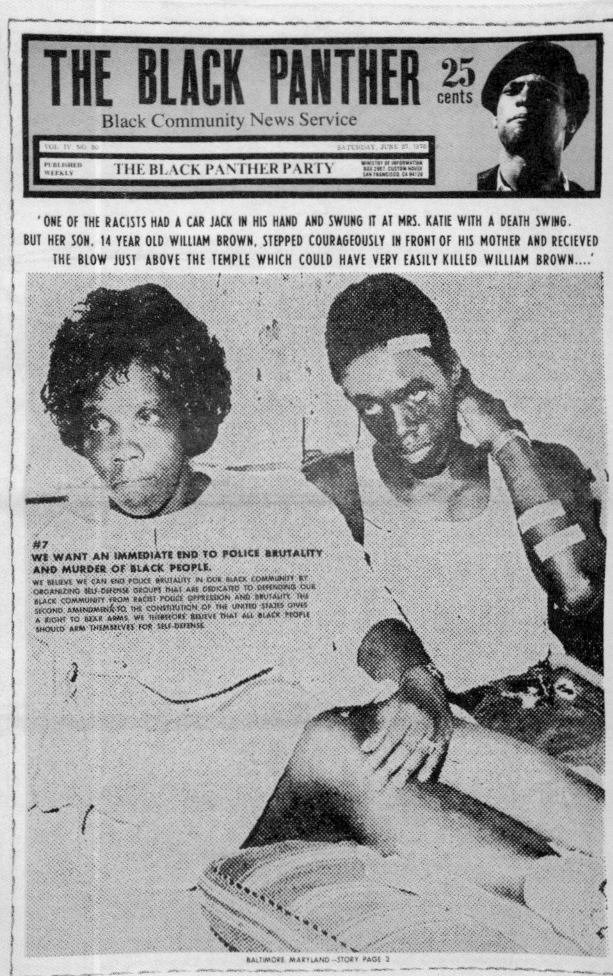

THE BLACK PANTHER 25 cents

Black Community News Service

VOL. IV NO. 30 SATURDAY, JUNE 27, 1970

PUBLISHED WEEKLY THE BLACK PANTHER PARTY MINISTRY OF INFORMATION BOX 2967, CUSTOM HOUSE SAN FRANCISCO, CA 94126

'ONE OF THE RACISTS HAD A CAR JACK IN HIS HAND AND SWUNG IT AT MRS. KATIE WITH A DEATH SWING. BUT HER SON, 14 YEAR OLD WILLIAM BROWN, STEPPED COURAGEOUSLY IN FRONT OF HIS MOTHER AND RECIEVED THE BLOW JUST ABOVE THE TEMPLE WHICH COULD HAVE VERY EASILY KILLED WILLIAM BROWN....'

#7
WE WANT AN IMMEDIATE END TO POLICE BRUTALITY AND MURDER OF BLACK PEOPLE.

WE BELIEVE WE CAN END POLICE BRUTALITY IN OUR BLACK COMMUNITY BY ORGANIZING SELF-DEFENSE GROUPS THAT ARE DEDICATED TO DEFENDING OUR BLACK COMMUNITY FROM RACIST POLICE OPPRESSION AND BRUTALITY. THE SECOND AMENDMENT TO THE CONSTITUTION OF THE UNITED STATES GIVES A RIGHT TO BEAR ARMS. WE THEREFORE BELIEVE THAT ALL BLACK PEOPLE SHOULD ARM THEMSELVES FOR SELF-DEFENSE.

BALTIMORE MARYLAND—STORY PAGE 2

Fig. 3.20 (cont'd.). **Black Panther** (San Francisco), June 27, 1970, vol. 4, no. 30, back and front covers

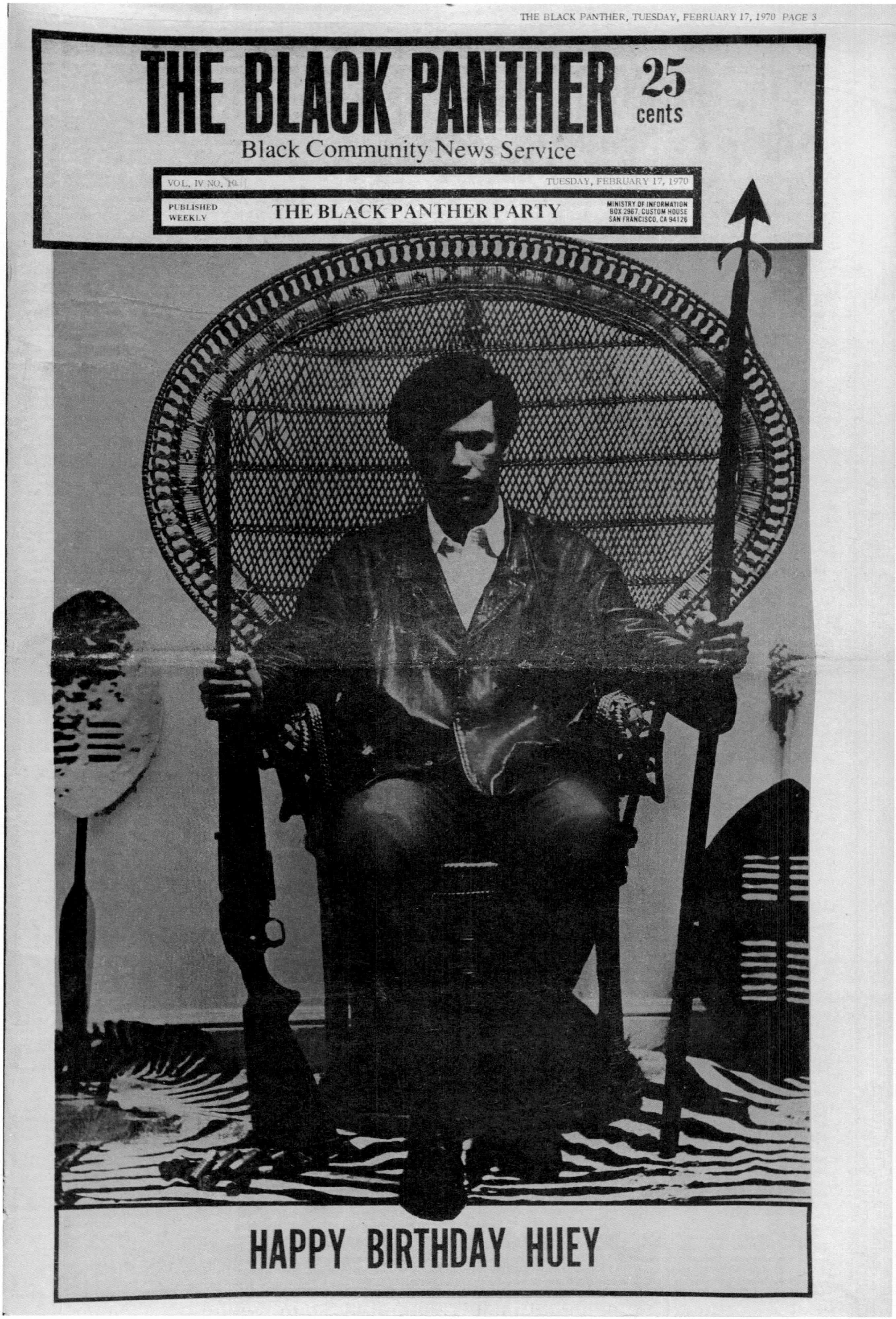

THE BLACK PANTHER, TUESDAY, FEBRUARY 17, 1970 PAGE 3

THE BLACK PANTHER

25 cents

Black Community News Service

VOL. IV NO. 10. TUESDAY, FEBRUARY 17, 1970

PUBLISHED WEEKLY THE BLACK PANTHER PARTY MINISTRY OF INFORMATION BOX 2967, CUSTOM HOUSE SAN FRANCISCO, CA 94126

HAPPY BIRTHDAY HUEY

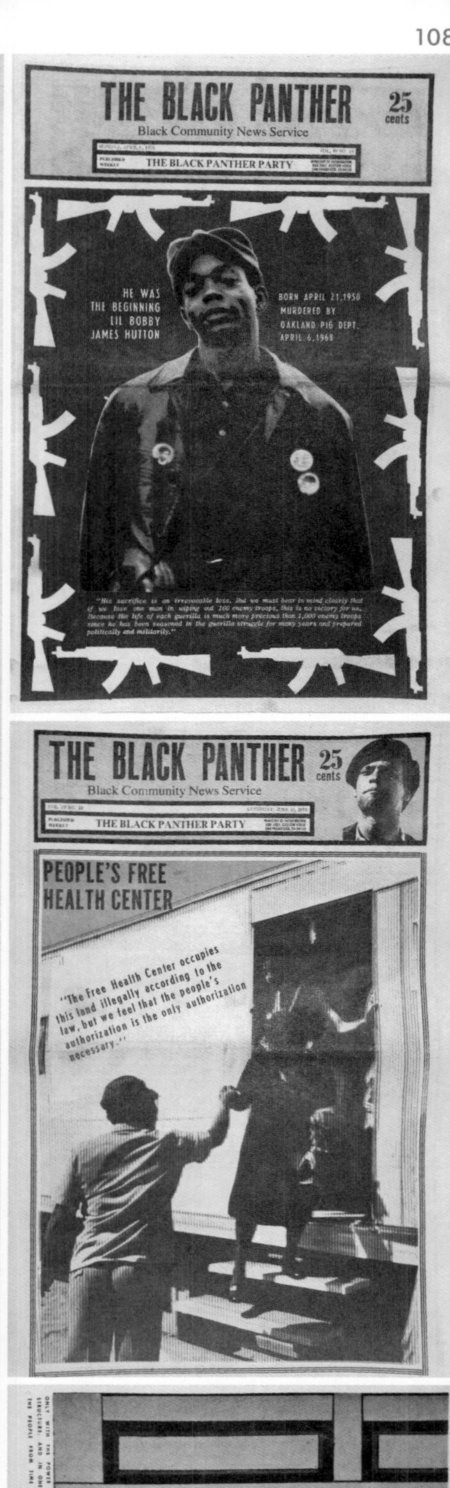

THE BLACK PANTHER 25 cents

Black Community News Service

THE BLACK PANTHER PARTY

HE WAS THE BEGINNING LIL BOBBY JAMES HUTTON

BORN APRIL 21,1950 MURDERED BY OAKLAND PIG DEPT. APRIL 6,1968

THE BLACK PANTHER 25 cents

Black Community News Service

THE BLACK PANTHER PARTY

PEOPLE'S FREE HEALTH CENTER

"The Free Health Center occupies this land illegally according to the law, but we feel that the people's authorization is the only authorization necessary."

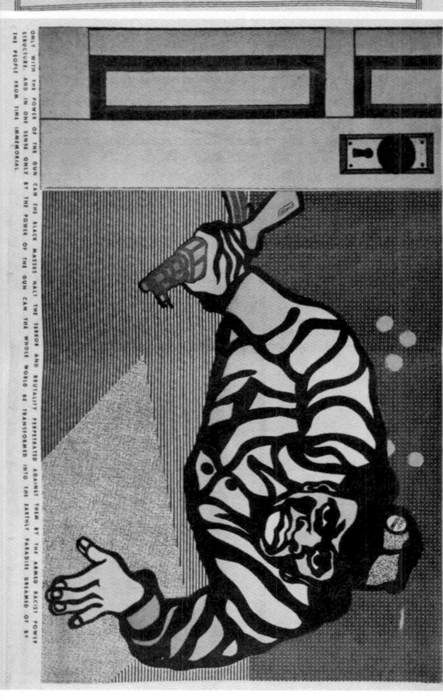

Fig. 3.20 (cont'd.) **Black Panther** (San Francisco), February 7, 1970, vol. 4, no. 10, cover; April 6, 1970, vol. 4, no. 18, cover; June 13, 1970, vol. 4, no. 28, front and back covers

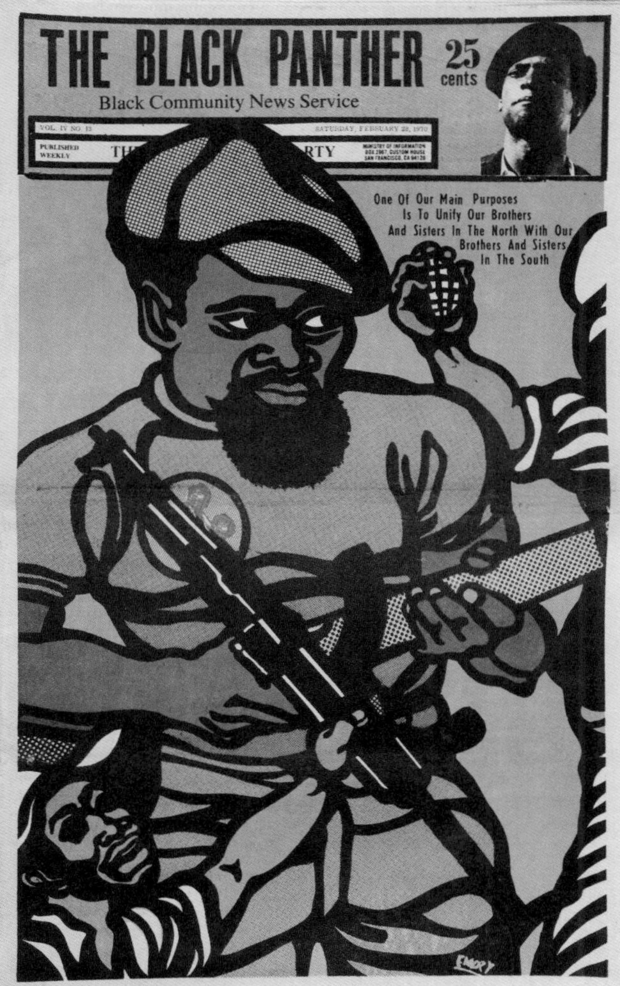
THE BLACK PANTHER 25 cents
Black Community News Service
PUBLISHED WEEKLY
One Of Our Main Purposes Is To Unify Our Brothers And Sisters In The North With Our Brothers And Sisters In The South
EMORY

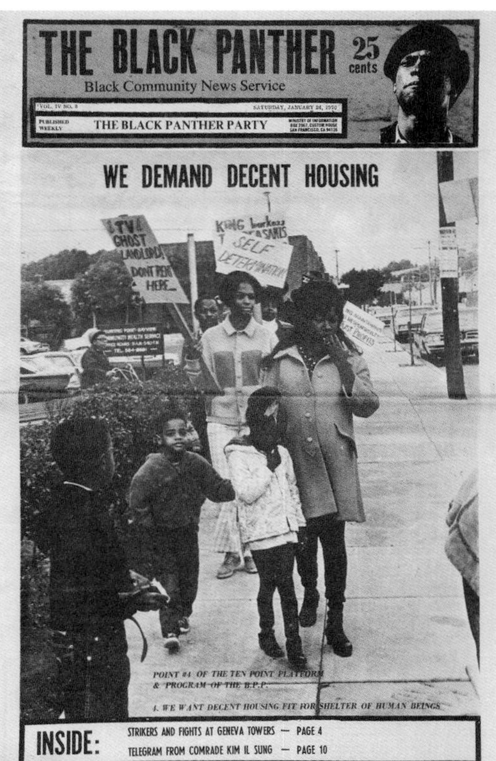
THE BLACK PANTHER 25 cents
Black Community News Service
SATURDAY, JANUARY 24, 1970
PUBLISHED WEEKLY
THE BLACK PANTHER PARTY
WE DEMAND DECENT HOUSING
POINT #4 OF THE TEN POINT PLATFORM & PROGRAM OF THE B.P.P.
4. WE WANT DECENT HOUSING FIT FOR SHELTER OF HUMAN BEINGS
INSIDE:
STRIKERS AND FIGHTS AT GENEVA TOWERS — PAGE 4
TELEGRAM FROM COMRADE KIM IL SUNG — PAGE 10

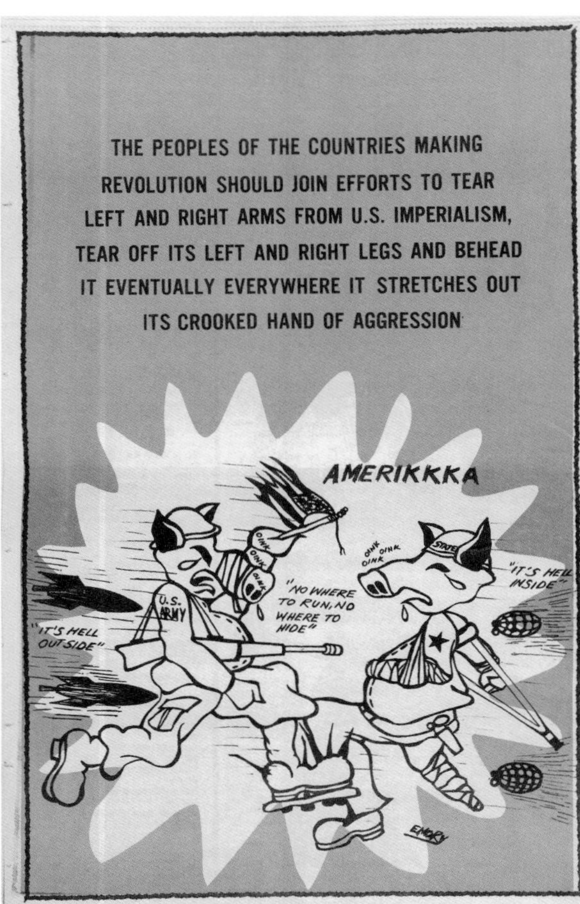
THE PEOPLES OF THE COUNTRIES MAKING REVOLUTION SHOULD JOIN EFFORTS TO TEAR LEFT AND RIGHT ARMS FROM U.S. IMPERIALISM, TEAR OFF ITS LEFT AND RIGHT LEGS AND BEHEAD IT EVENTUALLY EVERYWHERE IT STRETCHES OUT ITS CROOKED HAND OF AGGRESSION

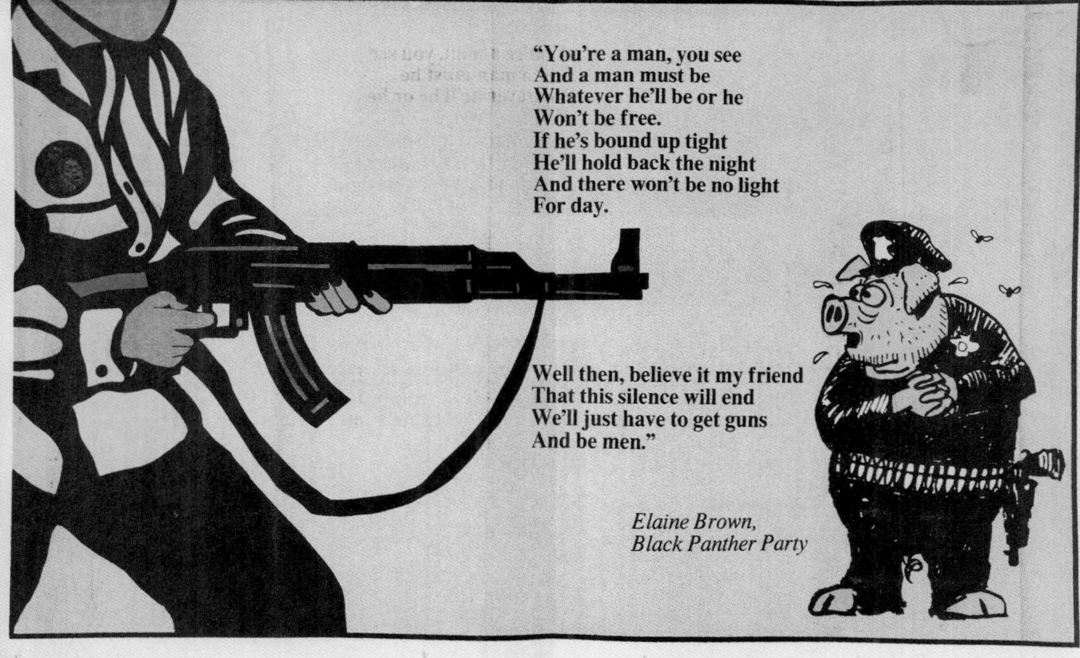
"You're a man, you see
And a man must be
Whatever he'll be or he
Won't be free.
If he's bound up tight
He'll hold back the night
And there won't be no light
For day.

Well then, believe it my friend
That this silence will end
We'll just have to get guns
And be men."

Elaine Brown,
Black Panther Party

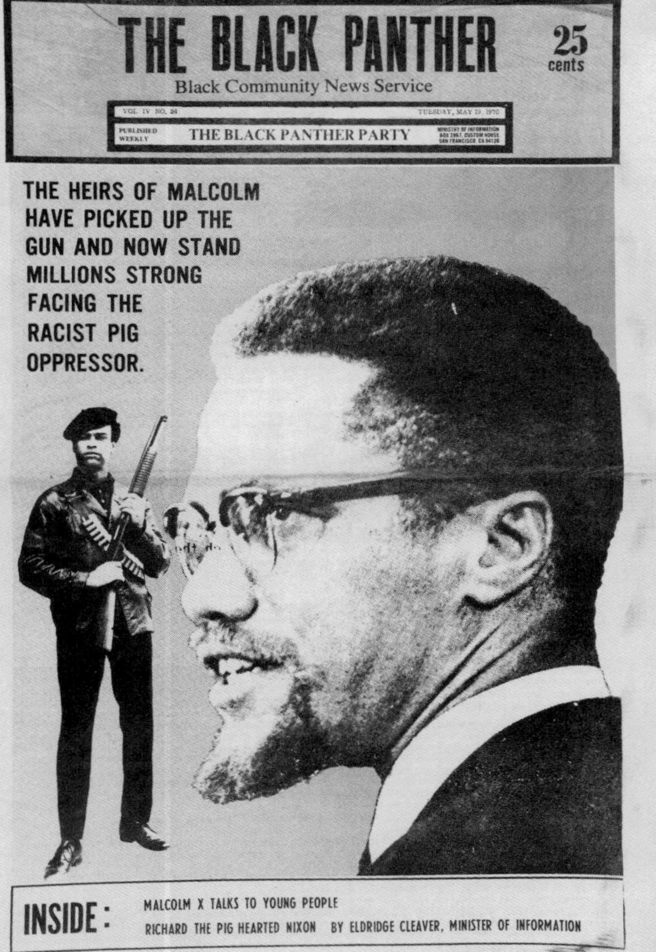
THE BLACK PANTHER 25 cents
Black Community News Service
TUESDAY, MAY 19, 1970
PUBLISHED WEEKLY
THE BLACK PANTHER PARTY
THE HEIRS OF MALCOLM HAVE PICKED UP THE GUN AND NOW STAND MILLIONS STRONG FACING THE RACIST PIG OPPRESSOR.
INSIDE:
MALCOLM X TALKS TO YOUNG PEOPLE
RICHARD THE PIG HEARTED NIXON BY ELDRIDGE CLEAVER, MINISTER OF INFORMATION

Fig. 3.20 (cont'd.) **Black Panther** (San Francisco), February 29, 1970, vol. 4, no. 13, cover; January 24, 1970, vol. 4, no. 8, cover; May 19, 1970, vol. 4, no. 24, back cover; January 10, 1970, vol. 4, no. 6, back cover; May 19, 1970, vol. 4, no. 25, back cover

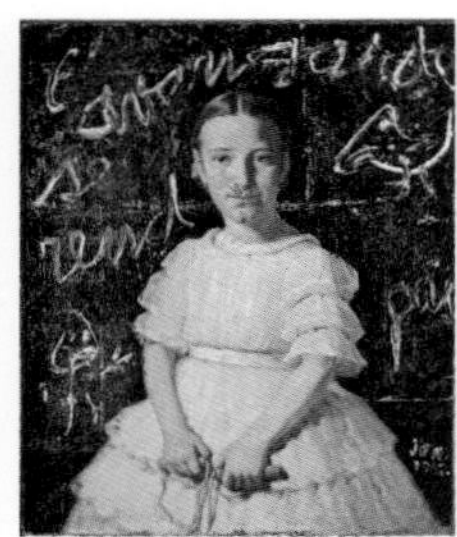

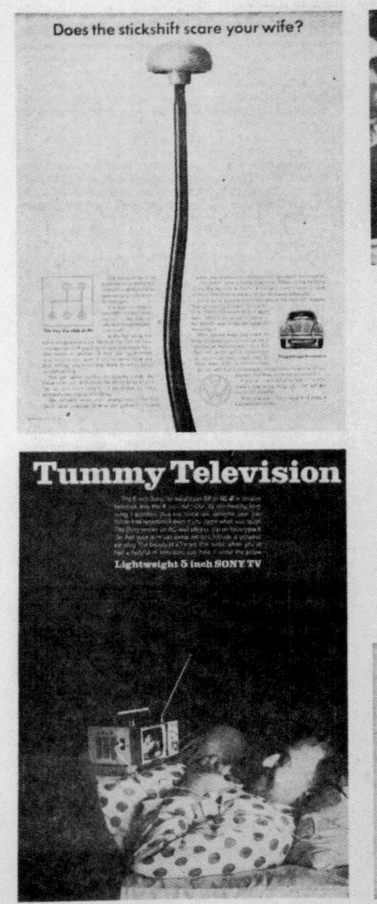

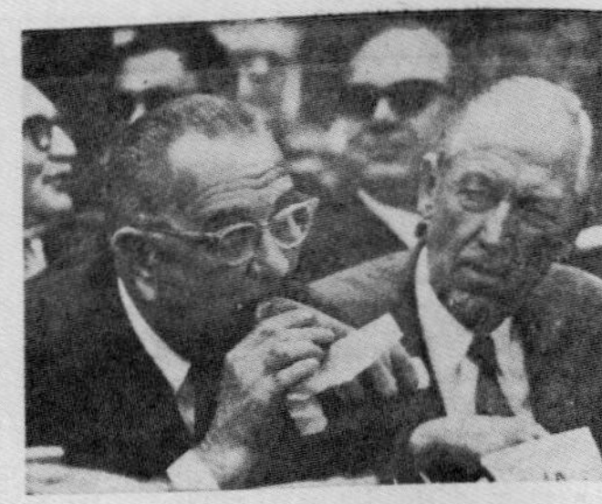

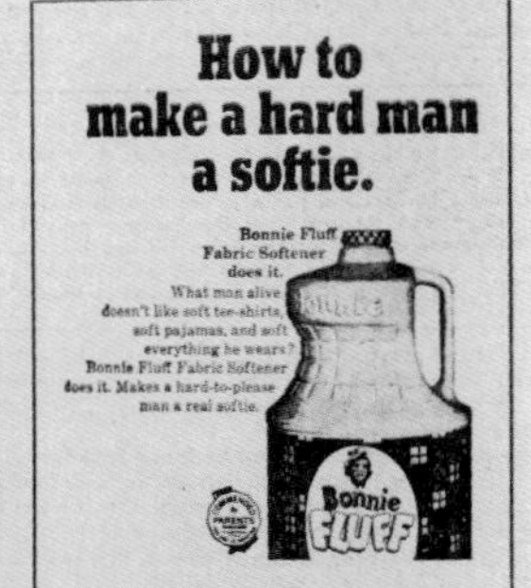

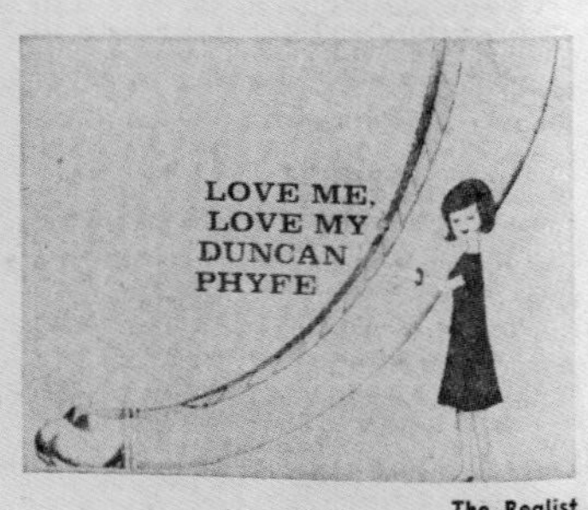

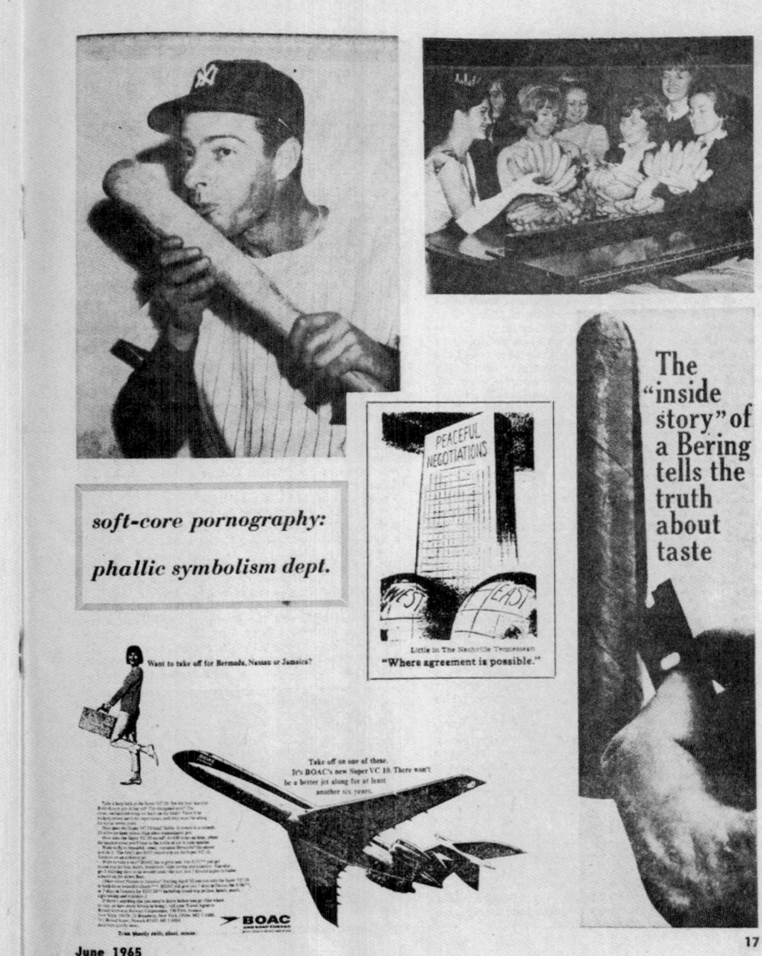

Fig. 3.21. Asger Jorn, **The Avant-Garde Doesn't Give Up,** 1962

Fig. 3.22. **Realist** (New York), June 1965, no. 60, pp. 16–17

A related representational strategy frequently employed in the underground press was ***détournement***, the practice, associated with Guy Debord and the Situationist International, of appropriating and repurposing preexisting images and texts—what the artist Jacques Villeglé called the making of "subversive speech bubbles."[16] Literally meaning "a diversion" of meaning, ***détournement*** functioned, as Tom McDonough points out, to create "a counterdiscourse through stealing, plagiarizing, and expropriating speech, through reversing dominant meanings and accepted usages,"[17] as witnessed in Asger Jorn's vandalism of found kitsch paintings such as ***The Avant-Garde Doesn't Give Up***, 1962 (fig. 3.21) (which itself recalls Duchamp's defacement of the ***Mona Lisa*** in ***L.H.O.O.Q.***, 1919). Like these artists, underground designers hijacked official symbols, such as US currency, stamps, and flags, and gave them unauthorized new captions and attributes: the stripes of the American flag become prison bars; the Statue of Liberty is portrayed variously as a dying prostitute, as a skull, and as a

16. Quoted in Tom McDonough, *The Beautiful Language of My Century: Reinventing the Language of Contestation in Postwar France, 1945–1968* (Cambridge: MIT Press, 2007), p. 15.

17. Ibid., p. 5.

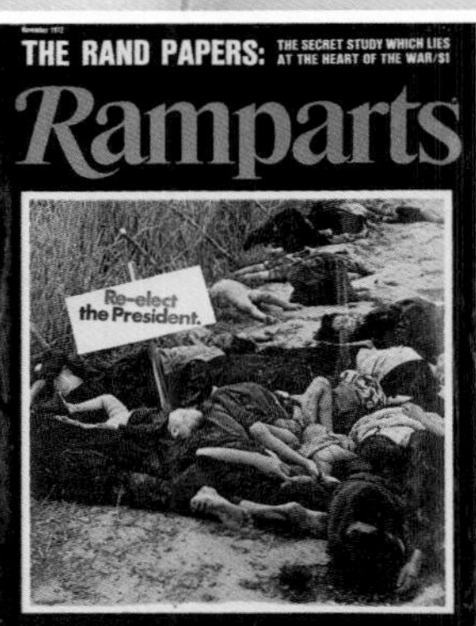

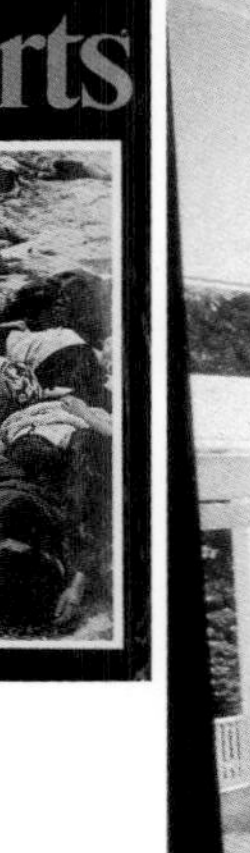

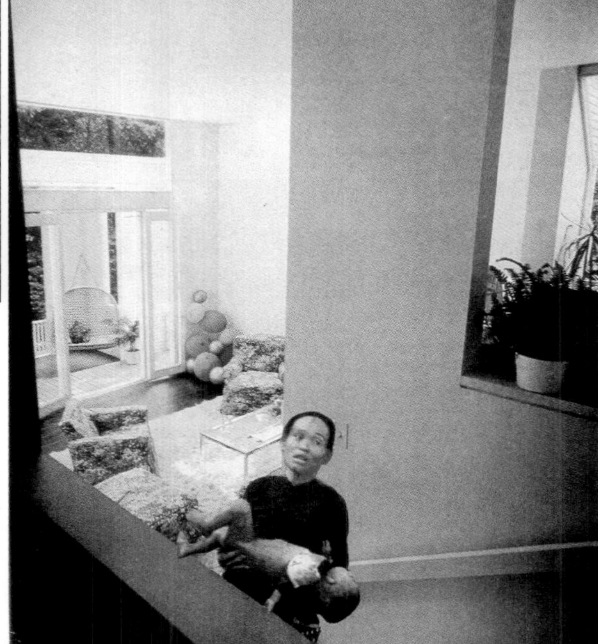

Fig. 3.23. **Ramparts** (Berkeley), November 1972, cover

Fig. 3.24 (two images). Martha Rosler, **Bringing Home the War** series, 1967–1972

Fig. 3.25. **FILE,** April 15, 1972, cover

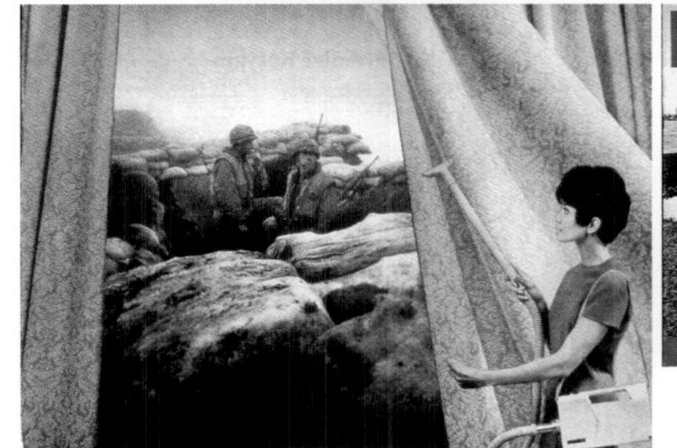

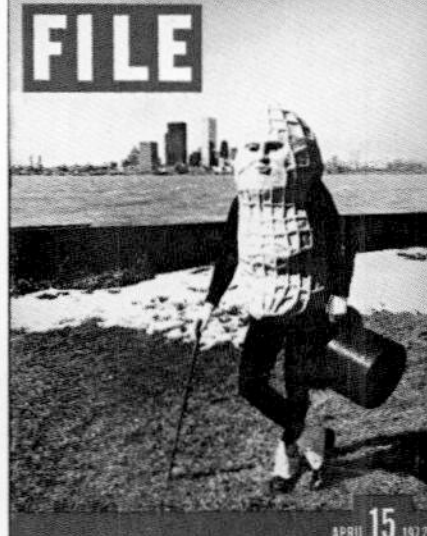

revolutionary, her torch replaced by a clenched fist. Mainstream media representations were pilfered and repurposed. The *Realist* published a regular column titled "Soft Core Pornography of the Month" (fig. 3.22) in which advertisements and other media images were imbued with sexual double entendre. The famous Ron Haeberle photograph of the My Lai massacre was printed in *Ramparts* with a sign that ironically reads "Re-elect the President," referencing Nixon's cover-up of the incident (fig. 3.23). Pictures of the moon landing were given satirical taglines—"Yankee go home" and "Whites Only"—making explicit the parallels between space exploration and cultural imperialism.

Artists also used photomontage and ***détournement*** during the 1960s and 1970s to protest contemporary social and political conditions. Martha Rosler combined photographs of dead babies and battlefields from the Vietnam War with upscale domestic interiors in her ***Bringing Home the War*** series, 1967–1972 (fig. 3.24). The General Idea collective hijacked and repurposed imagery from the mainstream media to subvert spectacular consumption of images and explore alternative and countercultural identities in their magazine ***FILE*** (fig. 3.25). By acknowledging the relationship of such works to the visual practices of the underground press we can better understand the politics of these works, and the historical context in which they gained meaning.

The visual representations of the underground press fostered solidarity both within and among various countercultural social and political movements, as iconography such as defiantly clenched fists, or cartoons of politicians and policemen as pigs, defined shared struggles and common enemies. However these images also revealed the limits of such affiliations. For example, underground comix often used carnivalesque imagery, as well as sexist and racist depictions, to offend conventional social codes, walking an exceedingly thin line between lampooning stereotypes and perpetuating them. Representations of women were an especially charged site of conflict within the underground

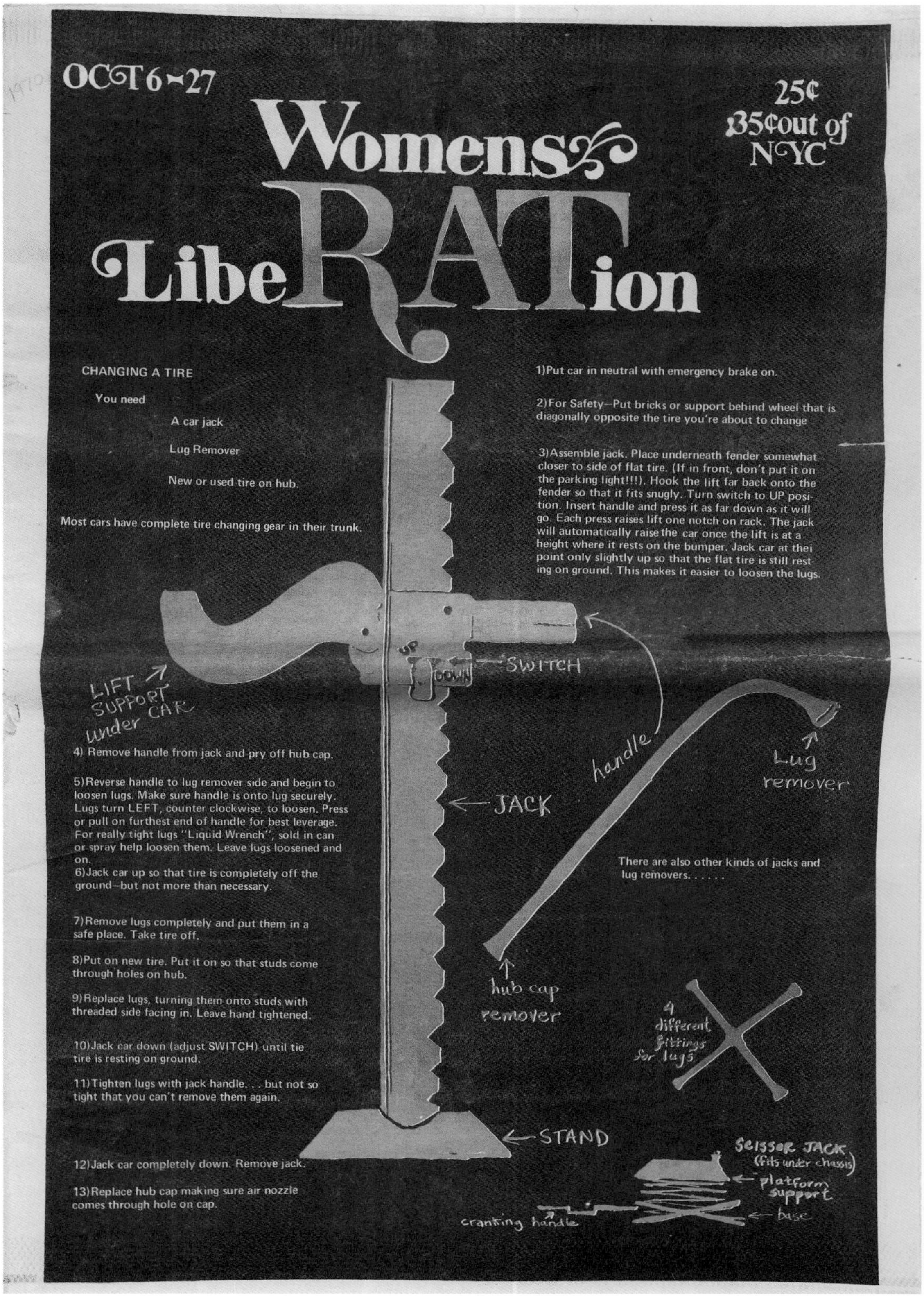

OCT 6–27

25¢
35¢ out of NYC

Womens LibeRATion

CHANGING A TIRE

You need

A car jack

Lug Remover

New or used tire on hub.

Most cars have complete tire changing gear in their trunk.

1)Put car in neutral with emergency brake on.

2)For Safety—Put bricks or support behind wheel that is diagonally opposite the tire you're about to change

3)Assemble jack. Place underneath fender somewhat closer to side of flat tire. (If in front, don't put it on the parking light!!!). Hook the lift far back onto the fender so that it fits snugly. Turn switch to UP position. Insert handle and press it as far down as it will go. Each press raises lift one notch on rack. The jack will automatically raise the car once the lift is at a height where it rests on the bumper. Jack car at thei point only slightly up so that the flat tire is still resting on ground. This makes it easier to loosen the lugs.

LIFT SUPPORT under CAR

UP DOWN

SWITCH

handle

Lug remover

JACK

4) Remove handle from jack and pry off hub cap.

5)Reverse handle to lug remover side and begin to loosen lugs. Make sure handle is onto lug securely. Lugs turn LEFT, counter clockwise, to loosen. Press or pull on furthest end of handle for best leverage. For really tight lugs "Liquid Wrench", sold in can or spray help loosen them. Leave lugs loosened and on.
6)Jack car up so that tire is completely off the ground—but not more than necessary.

7)Remove lugs completely and put them in a safe place. Take tire off.

8)Put on new tire. Put it on so that studs come through holes on hub.

9)Replace lugs, turning them onto studs with threaded side facing in. Leave hand tightened.

10)Jack car down (adjust SWITCH) until tie tire is resting on ground.

11)Tighten lugs with jack handle. . . but not so tight that you can't remove them again.

12)Jack car completely down. Remove jack.

13)Replace hub cap making sure air nozzle comes through hole on cap.

There are also other kinds of jacks and lug removers. . . . . .

hub cap remover

4 different fittings for lugs

STAND

Scissor JACK (fits under chassis)

platform support

base

cranking handle

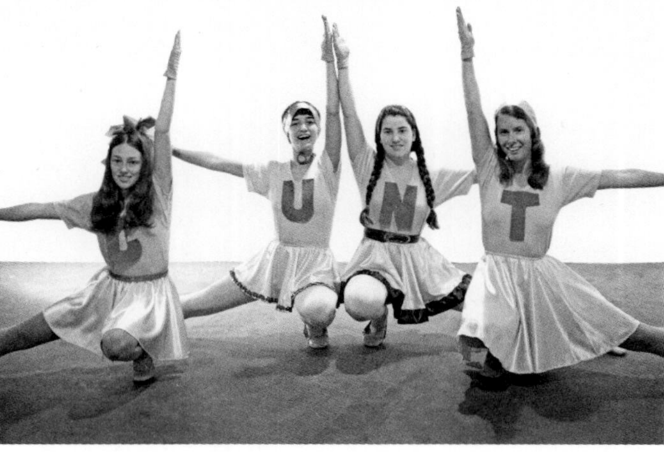

Fig. 3.26. **Rat** (New York), October 6–27, 1970, cover

Fig. 3.27. Left to right: Cay Lang, Vanalyne Green, Dori Atlantis, and Sue Boud, 1971 press. Images of nude women were omnipresent, and were often used as shorthand for sexual liberation, which was itself metonymically linked to various other kinds of freedom for which the counterculture crusaded. And yet such images suggest that sexual liberation was not always tantamount to sexual equality. Indeed, it was over what they perceived as pornographic imagery in the New York underground publication the *Rat*, that several women editors took over the publication, founding the Women's *LibeRATion* in 1970 (fig. 3.26). At the same time, sexually explicit imagery played an important role in the women's movement and the gay and lesbian movement, where it challenged patriarchal and heterosexist norms, paralleling the role of so-called "cunt art" pioneered by Judy Chicago (fig. 3.27) and others within the feminist art movement as an oppositional visual practice intended to rescue images of the female body from the control of men.[18] Whether inside or outside the art world, the role of visual representation in identity politics was complex, and, like identity itself, not essential or universal, but deeply dependent on context and reception.

Indeed, the representations of the counterculture within the pages of the underground press were not monolithic but unstable, inconsistent, and sometimes incoherent; their meaning was not a foregone conclusion but still very much in the process of being worked out. Graphic design participated deeply in this process, and encouraged readers to participate in it, too. To this end, underground papers embraced nonlinear layouts and exploited the tactile, interactive properties of printed matter in order to engage readers in new ways. For example, the *Old Mole* published a "Southeast Asian coloring page" including a map of the region, encouraging readers to "keep a red crayon handy" and a paper doll which could be dressed in three different outfits: a military uniform, prison garb, and a coffin (fig. 3.28). Several papers, including the *Old Mole* and the *Black Panther Party Paper*, published posters that could be pulled out and displayed to reach different audiences in different

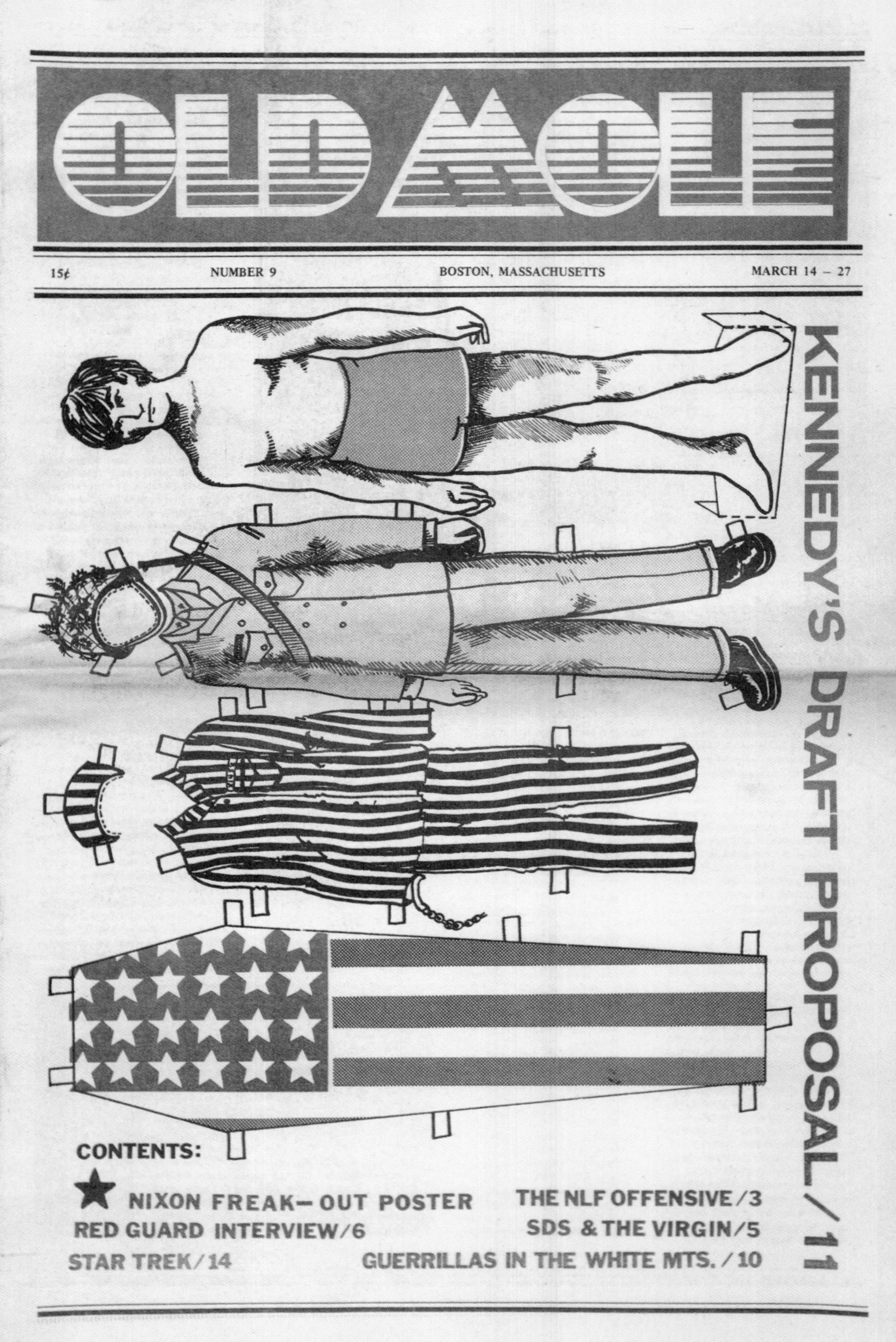

18. Judy Chicago, "Woman as Artist," in *Feminism-Art-Theory: An Anthology, 1968-2000*, ed. Hilary Robinson (New York: Wiley-Blackwell, 2001).

Fig. 3.28. **Old Mole** (Boston), March 14–27, 1969, no. 9, cover

This is your Southeast Asia coloring page.

Keep a red crayon handy.

Red means that the people in these countries are rising up Angry. They are saying, "We don't want outsiders or tyrants pushing us around. And once we get rid of them, we won't let some people inside the country push others around."

People used to think that this was only happening in South Vietnam. (It happened in North Vietnam some time ago). This week there have been signs it might happen in Laos and Cambodia.

While American newspapers talked about a "North Vietnamese invasion of Laos," French papers reported that there were only 500 North Vietnamese troops involved. Most of the fighters were Laotians who did not want the US, the CIA, and the people only the US likes running the country.

When the military ousted the sly prince Sihanouk of Cambodia last week, it looked for a while as though it might be a boon to those who are against the people. But since then there have been demonstrations and fighting. For the first time people have realised that maybe the Cambodians, too, are prepared to fight to control their country.

Right now many parts of this map need to be colored greedy black, sly prince purple, intriguing pink, and US Army green. In fact, you need to add some more army green in Laos and Cambodia, because the the US and the CIA are getting more involved as they get more scared.

After the map is red, you can, if you like, start over coloring it what the people want: peace blue, friendship orange, cooperation violet, hospital white, and countryside green.

(Anti-war demonstrations coming up. See page 10.)

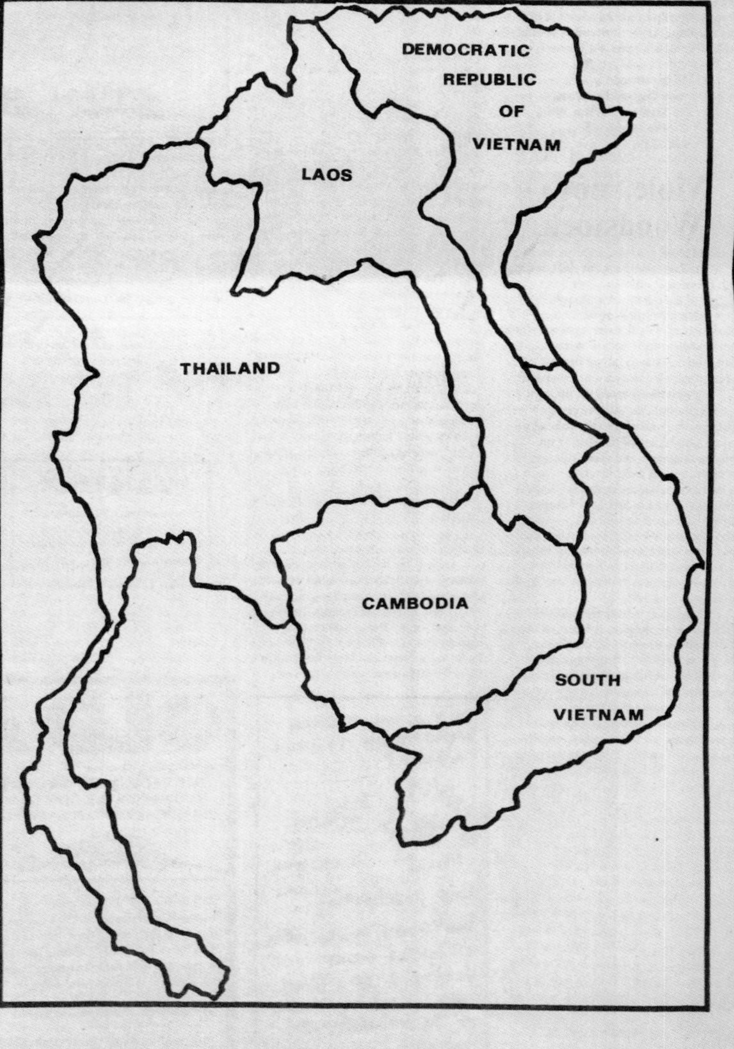

We recognize our old friend, our old mole, who knows so well how to work underground, suddenly to appear: THE REVOLUTION.

-Marx

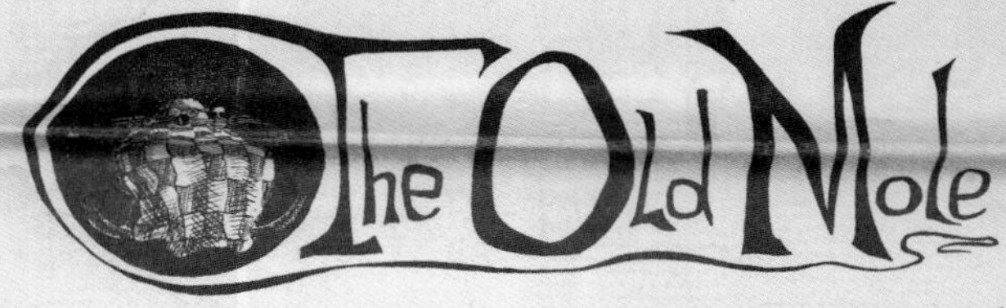

Volume I, number 1 September 13, 1968 15¢

Contents

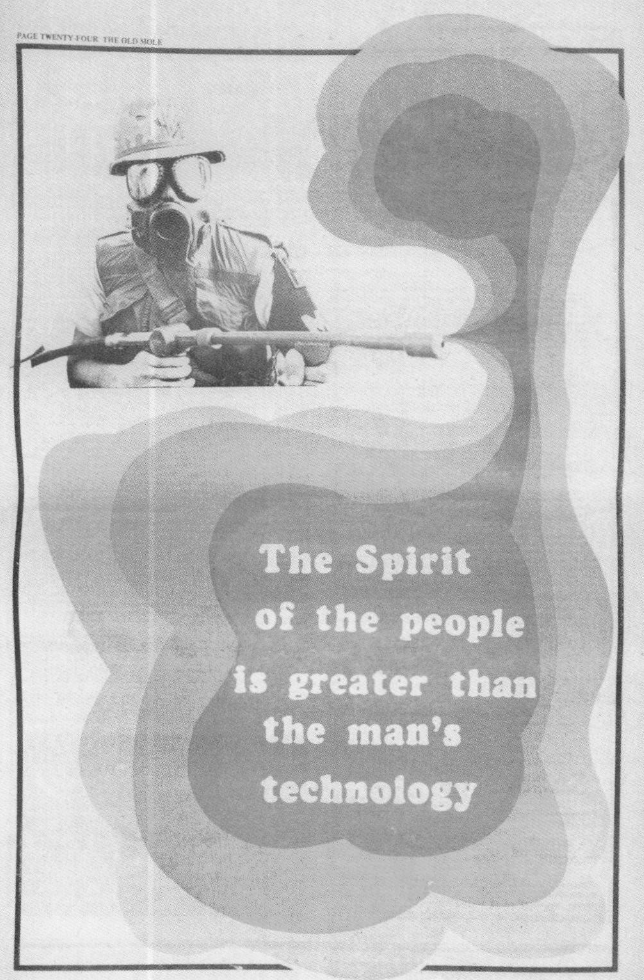

Fig. 3.28 (cont'd.). **Old Mole** (Boston), April 3-16, 1970, no. 36, back cover; September 13, 1968, vol. 1, no. 1, cover; October 24-November 6, 1969, no. 25, back cover

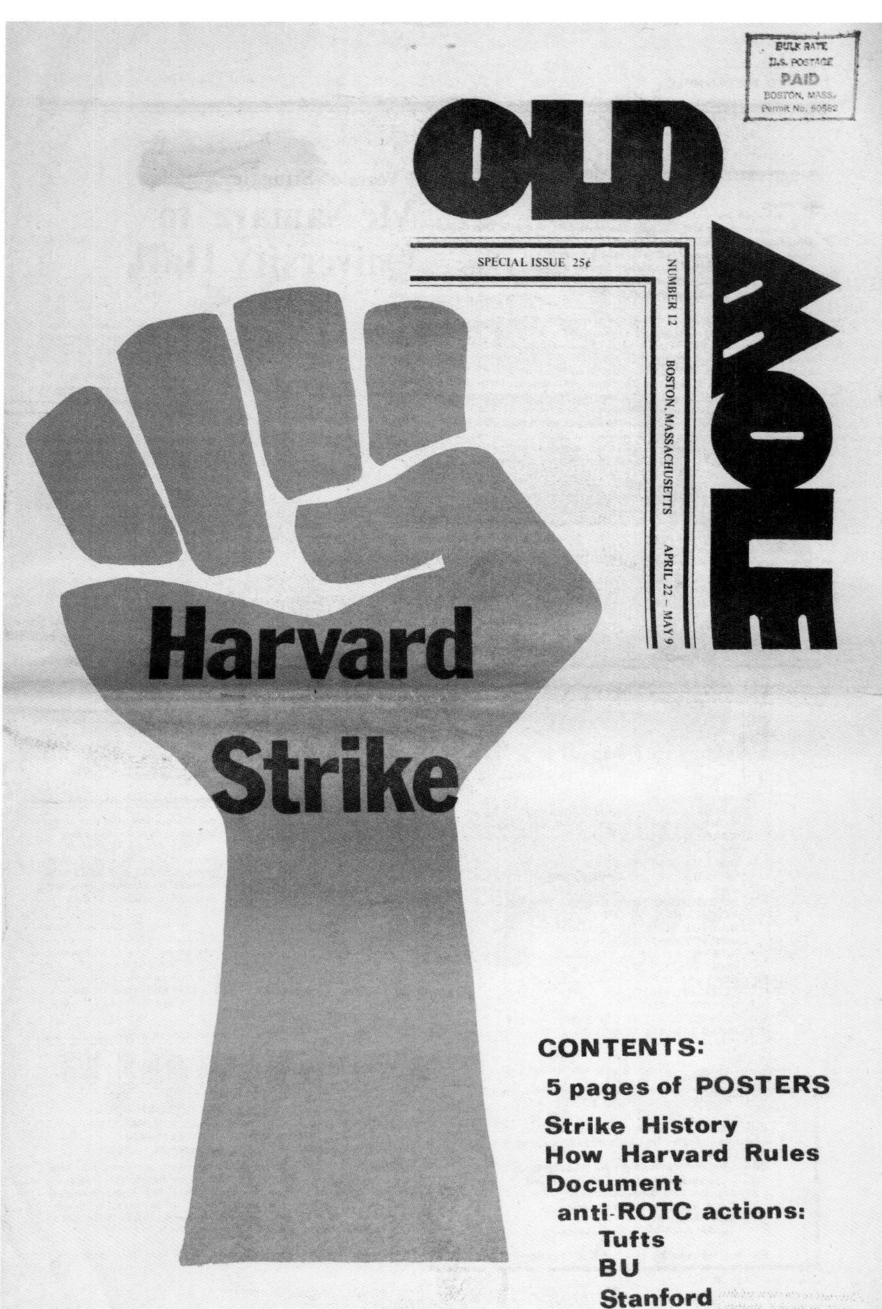

STRIKE FOR THE EIGHT
DEMANDS STRIKE BE
CAUSE YOU HATE COPS
STRIKE BECAUSE YOUR
ROOMMATE WAS CLUBBED
STRIKE TO STOP EXPANSION
STRIKE TO SEIZE CONTROL
OF YOUR LIFE STRIKE TO
BECOME MORE HUMAN STR
IKE TO RETURN PAINE HALL
SCHOLARSHIPS STRIKE BE
CAUSE THERE'S NO POETRY
IN YOUR LECTURES
STRIKE BECAUSE CLASSES
ARE A BORE STRIKE FOR
POWER STRIKE TO SMASH THE
CORPORATION STRIKE TO MAKE
YOURSELF FREE STRIKE TO
ABOLISH ROTC STRIKE BECAUSE
THEY ARE TRYING TO SQUEEZE
THE LIFE OUT OF YOU STRIKE

Created and produced by

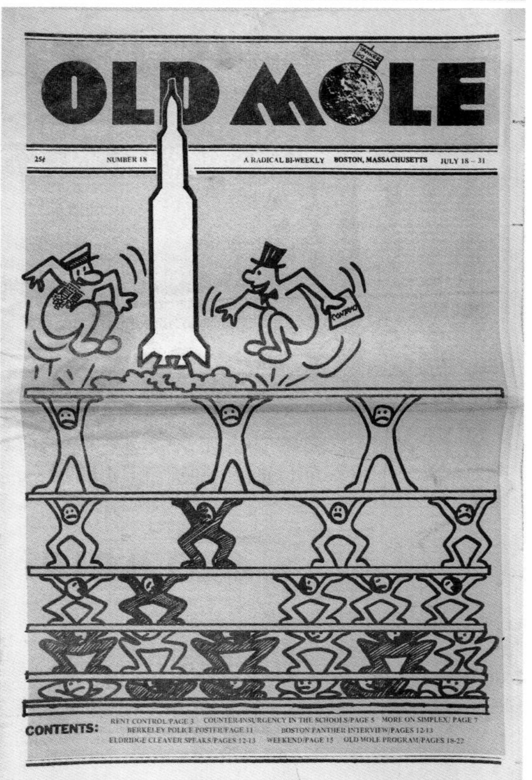

Fig. 3.28 (cont'd.) **Old Mole** (Boston), April 22–May 9, 1969, no. 12, cover and back cover; July 18, 1969, no. 18, cover

Next page
Fig. 3.28 (cont'd.) **Old Mole** (Boston), April 22–May 9, 1969, no. 12, center spread, pp. 8–9

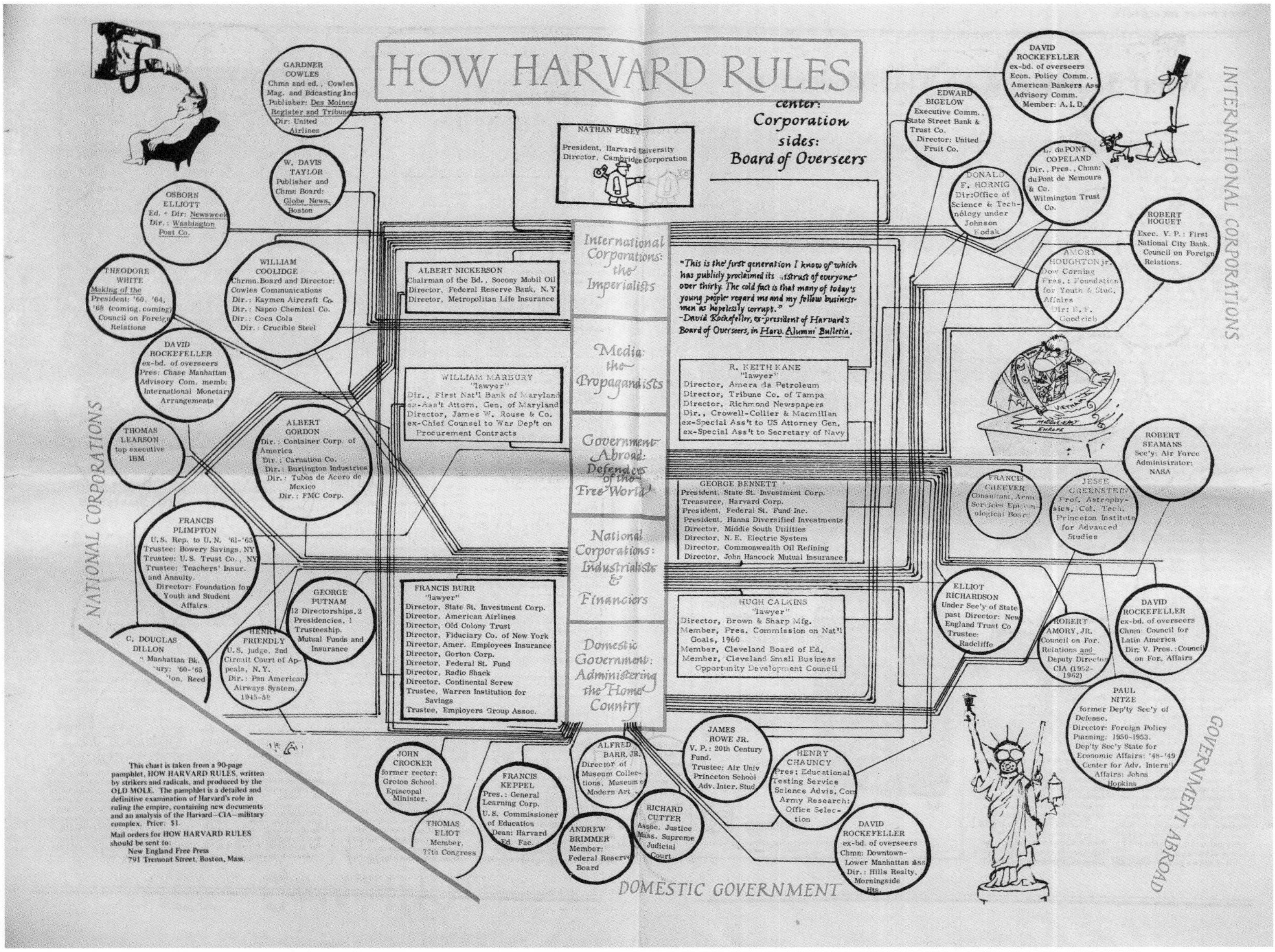

HOW HARVARD RULES

center: Corporation
sides: Board of Overseers

NATHAN PUSEY
President, Harvard University
Director, Cambridge Corporation

International Corporations: the Imperialists

Media: the Propagandists

Government Abroad: Defenders of the Free World

National Corporations: Industrialists & Financiers

Domestic Government: Administering the Home Country

INTERNATIONAL CORPORATIONS

NATIONAL CORPORATIONS

GOVERNMENT ABROAD

DOMESTIC GOVERNMENT

"This is the first generation I know of which has publicly proclaimed its distrust of everyone over thirty. The cold fact is that many of today's young people regard me and my fellow businessmen as hopelessly corrupt."
–David Rockefeller, ex-president of Harvard's Board of Overseers, in Harv. Alumni Bulletin.

GARDNER COWLES
Chmn and ed., Cowles Mag. and Bdcasting Inc
Publisher: Des Moines Register and Tribune
Dir: United Airlines

W. DAVIS TAYLOR
Publisher and Chmn Board: Globe News, Boston

OSBORN ELLIOTT
Ed. + Dir: Newsweek
Dir.: Washington Post Co.

THEODORE WHITE
Making of the President: '60, '64, '68 (coming, coming)
Council on Foreign Relations

WILLIAM COOLIDGE
Chrmn.Board and Director: Cowles Communications
Dir.: Kaymen Aircraft Co.
Dir.: Napco Chemical Co.
Dir.: Coca Cola
Dir.: Crucible Steel

DAVID ROCKEFELLER
ex-bd. of overseers
Pres: Chase Manhattan
Advisory Com. memb: International Monetary Arrangements

THOMAS LEARSON
top executive IBM

ALBERT GORDON
Dir.: Container Corp. of America
Dir.: Carnation Co.
Dir.: Burlington Industries
Dir.: Tubos de Acero de Mexico
Dir.: FMC Corp.

FRANCIS PLIMPTON
U.S. Rep. to U.N. '61-'65
Trustee: Bowery Savings, NY
Trustee: U.S. Trust Co., NY
Trustee: Teachers' Insur. and Annuity.
Director: Foundation for Youth and Student Affairs

GEORGE PUTNAM
12 Directorships, 2 Presidencies, 1 Trusteeship.
Mutual Funds and Insurance

HENRY FRIENDLY
U.S. judge, 2nd Circuit Court of Appeals, N.Y.
Dir.: Pan American Airways System, 1945-59

C. DOUGLAS DILLON
... Manhattan Bk.
...ury: '60-'65
...lon, Reed

ALBERT NICKERSON
Chairman of the Bd., Socony Mobil Oil
Director, Federal Reserve Bank, N.Y.
Director, Metropolitan Life Insurance

WILLIAM MARBURY
"lawyer"
Dir., First Nat'l Bank of Maryland
ex-Ass't Attorn. Gen. of Maryland
Director, James W. Rouse & Co.
ex-Chief Counsel to War Dep't on Procurement Contracts

FRANCIS BURR
"lawyer"
Director, State St. Investment Corp.
Director, American Airlines
Director, Old Colony Trust
Director, Fiduciary Co. of New York
Director, Amer. Employees Insurance
Director, Gorton Corp.
Director, Federal St. Fund
Director, Radio Shack
Director, Continental Screw
Trustee, Warren Institution for Savings
Trustee, Employers Group Assoc.

R. KEITH KANE
"lawyer"
Director, Amerada Petroleum
Director, Tribune Co. of Tampa
Director, Richmond Newspapers
Dir., Crowell-Collier & Macmillan
ex-Special Ass't to US Attorney Gen.
ex-Special Ass't to Secretary of Navy

GEORGE BENNETT
President, State St. Investment Corp.
Treasurer, Harvard Corp.
President, Federal St. Fund Inc.
President, Hanna Diversified Investments
Director, Middle South Utilities
Director, N.E. Electric System
Director, Commonwealth Oil Refining
Director, John Hancock Mutual Insurance

HUGH CALKINS
"lawyer"
Director, Brown & Sharp Mfg.
Member, Pres. Commission on Nat'l Goals, 1960
Member, Cleveland Board of Ed.
Member, Cleveland Small Business Opportunity Development Council

DAVID ROCKEFELLER
ex-bd. of overseers
Econ. Policy Comm., American Bankers Ass
Advisory Comm.
Member: A.I.D.

EDWARD BIGELOW
Executive Comm., State Street Bank & Trust Co.
Director: United Fruit Co.

DONALD F. HORNIG
Dir:Office of Science & Technology under Johnson
Kodak

L. duPONT COPELAND
Dir., Pres., Chmn: du Pont de Nemours & Co.
Wilmington Trust Co.

ROBERT HOGUET
Exec. V.P.: First National City Bank.
Council on Foreign Relations.

AMORY HOUGHTON jr.
Dow Corning
Pres.: Foundation for Youth & Stud. Affairs
Dir: B.F. Goodrich

ROBERT SEAMANS
Sec'y: Air Force
Administrator: NASA

FRANCIS CHEEVER
Consultant, Armed Services Epidemiological Board

JESSE GREENSTEIN
Prof. Astrophysics, Cal. Tech.
Princeton Institute for Advanced Studies

ELLIOT RICHARDSON
Under Sec'y of State
past Director: New England Trust Co
Trustee: Radcliffe

ROBERT AMORY, JR.
Council on For. Relations and Deputy Director CIA (1952-1962)

DAVID ROCKEFELLER
ex-bd. of overseers
Chmn: Council for Latin America
Dir. V. Pres.: Council on For. Affairs

PAUL NITZE
former Dep'ty Sec'y of Defense.
Director: Foreign Policy Planning: 1950-1953.
Dep'ty Sec'y State for Economic Affairs: '48-'49
Center for Adv. Intern'l Affairs: Johns Hopkins

JOHN CROCKER
former rector: Groton School.
Episcopal Minister.

THOMAS ELIOT
Member, 77th Congress

FRANCIS KEPPEL
Pres.: General Learning Corp.
U.S. Commissioner of Education
Dean: Harvard Ed. Fac.

ALFRED BARR, JR.
Director of Museum Collections, Museum of Modern Art

ANDREW BRIMMER
Member: Federal Reserve Board

RICHARD CUTTER
Assoc. Justice Mass. Supreme Judicial Court

JAMES ROWE JR.
V.P.: 20th Century Fund.
Trustee: Air Univ
Princeton School Adv. Inter. Stud.

HENRY CHAUNCY
Pres: Educational Testing Service
Science Advis. Com. Army Research Office Selection

DAVID ROCKEFELLER
ex-bd. of overseers
Chmn: Downtown-Lower Manhattan Ass
Dir.: Hills Realty, Morningside Hts.

This chart is taken from a 90-page pamphlet, HOW HARVARD RULES, written by strikers and radicals, and produced by the OLD MOLE. The pamphlet is a detailed and definitive examination of Harvard's role in ruling the empire, containing new documents and an analysis of the Harvard–CIA–military complex. Price: $1.
Mail orders for HOW HARVARD RULES should be sent to:
New England Free Press
791 Tremont Street, Boston, Mass.

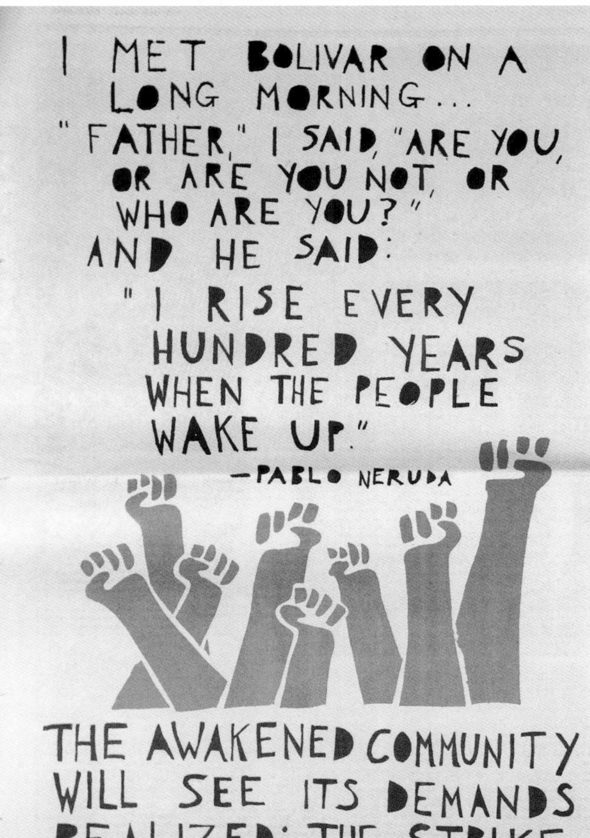

Created and produced by striking students of Harvard University's Graduate School of Design.

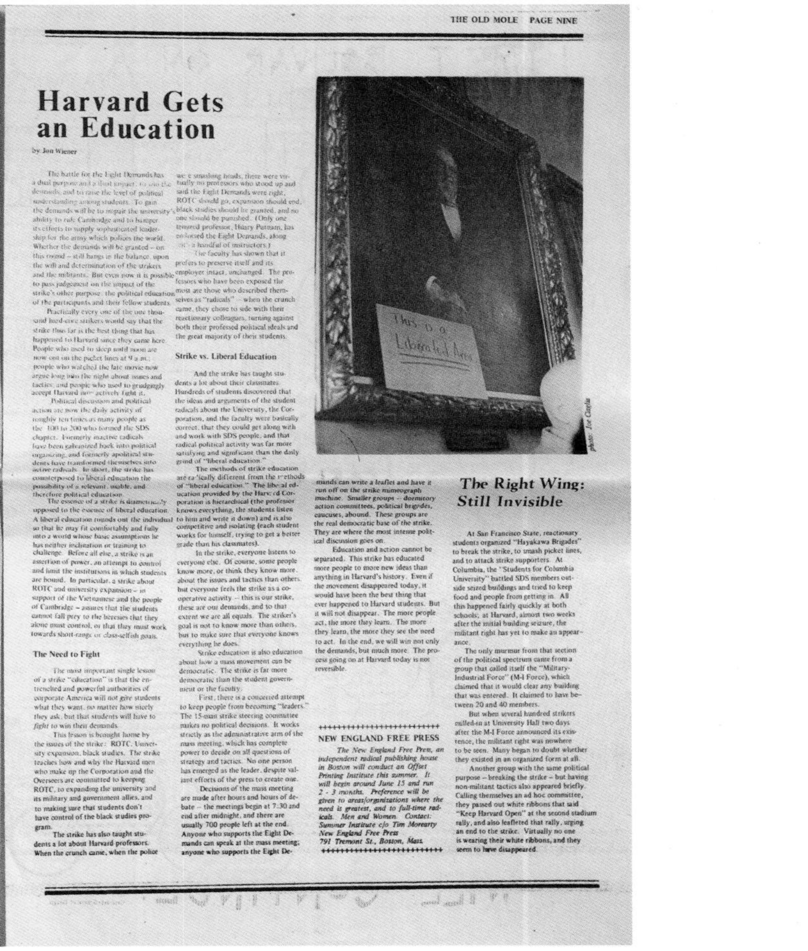

Harvard Gets an Education

by Jon Wiener

The battle for the Eight Demands has a dual purpose and a dual impact: to win the demands, and to raise the level of political understanding among students. To gain the demands will be to impair the university's ability to rule Cambridge and to hamper its efforts to supply sophisticated leadership for the army which polices the world. Whether the demands will be granted – on this round – still hangs in the balance, upon the will and determination of the strikers and the militants. But even now it is possible to pass judgement on the impact of the strike's other purpose: the political education of the participants and their fellow students.

Practically every one of the one thousand hard-core strikers would say that the strike thus far is the best thing that has happened to Harvard since they came here. People who used to sleep until noon are now out on the picket lines at 9 a.m.; people who watched the late movie now argue long into the night about issues and tactics, and people who used to grudgingly accept Harvard now actively fight it.

Political discussion and political action are now the daily activity of roughly ten times as many people as the 100 to 200 who formed the SDS chapter. Formerly inactive radicals have been galvanized back into political organizing, and formerly apolitical students have transformed themselves into active radicals. In short, the strike has counterposed to liberal education the possibility of a relevant, usable, and therefore political education.

The essence of a strike is diametrically opposed to the essence of liberal education. A liberal education rounds out the individual so that he may fit comfortably and fully into a world whose basic assumptions he has neither inclination or training to challenge. Before all else, a strike is an assertion of power, an attempt to control and limit the institutions in which students are bound. In particular, a strike about ROTC and university expansion – in support of the Vietnamese and the people of Cambridge – assures that the students cannot fall prey to the heresies that they alone must control, or that they must work towards short-range or class-selfish goals.

The Need to Fight

The most important single lesson of a strike "education" is that the entrenched and powerful authorities of corporate America will not *give* students what they want, no matter how nicely they ask, but that students will have to *fight* to win their demands.

This lesson is brought home by the issues of the strike: ROTC, University expansion, black studies. The strike teaches how and why the Harvard men who make up the Corporation and the Overseers are committed to keeping ROTC, to expanding the university and its military and government allies, and to making sure that students don't have control of the black studies program.

The strike has also taught students a lot about Harvard professors. When the crunch came, when the police were smashing heads, there were virtually no professors who stood up and said the Eight Demands were right, ROTC should go, expansion should end, black studies should be granted, and no one should be punished. (Only one tenured professor, Hilary Putnam, has endorsed the Eight Demands, along with a handful of instructors.)

The faculty has shown that it prefers to preserve itself and its employer intact, unchanged. The professors who have been exposed the most are those who described themselves as "radicals" – when the crunch came, they chose to side with their reactionary colleagues, turning against both their professed political ideals and the great majority of their students.

Strike vs. Liberal Education

And the strike has taught students a lot about their classmates. Hundreds of students discovered that the ideas and arguments of the student radicals about the University, the Corporation, and the faculty were basically correct, that they could get along with and work with SDS people, and that radical political activity was far more satisfying and significant than the daily grind of "liberal education."

The methods of strike education are radically different from the methods of "liberal education." The liberal education provided by the Harvard Corporation is hierarchical (the professor knows everything, the students listen to him and write it down) and is also competitive and isolating (each student works for himself, trying to get a better grade than his classmates).

In the strike, everyone listens to everyone else. Of course, some people know more, or think they know more, about the issues and tactics than others, but everyone feels the strike as a cooperative activity – this is our strike, these are our demands, and to that extent we are all equals. The striker's goal is not to know more than others, but to make sure that everyone knows everything he does.

Strike education is also education about how a mass movement can be democratic. The strike is far more democratic than the student government or the faculty.

First, there is a concerted attempt to keep people from becoming "leaders." The 15-man strike steering committee makes no political decisions. It works strictly as the administrative arm of the mass meeting, which has complete power to decide on all questions of strategy and tactics. No one person has emerged as the leader, despite valiant efforts of the press to create one.

Decisions of the mass meeting are made after hours and hours of debate – the meetings begin at 7:30 and end after midnight, and there are usually 700 people left at the end. Anyone who supports the Eight Demands can speak at the mass meeting; anyone who supports the Eight Demands can write a leaflet and have it run off on the strike mimeograph machine. Smaller groups – dormitory action committees, political brigades, caucuses, abound. These groups are the real democratic base of the strike. They are where the most intense political discussion goes on.

Education and action cannot be separated. This strike has educated more people to more new ideas than anything in Harvard's history. Even if the movement disappeared today, it would have been the best thing that ever happened to Harvard students. But it will not disappear. The more people act, the more they learn. The more they learn, the more they see the need to act. In the end, we will win not only the demands, but much more. The process going on at Harvard today is not reversible.

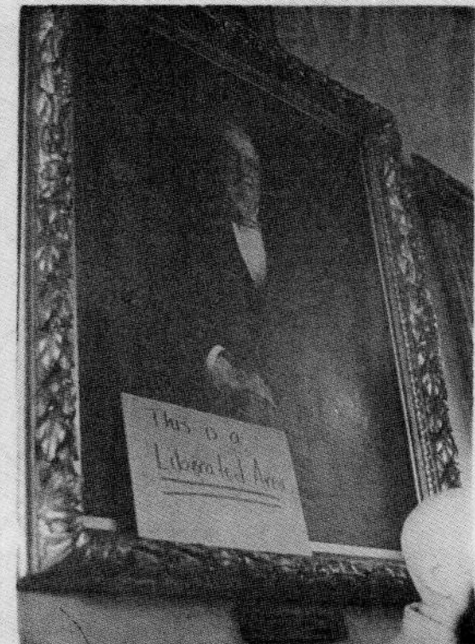

photo: Joe Carlin

The Right Wing: Still Invisible

At San Francisco State, reactionary students organized "Hayakawa Brigades" to break the strike, to smash picket lines, and to attack strike supporters. At Columbia, the "Students for Columbia University" battled SDS members outside seized buildings and tried to keep food and people from getting in. All this happened fairly quickly at both schools; at Harvard, almost two weeks after the initial building seizure, the militant right has yet to make an appearance.

The only murmur from that section of the political spectrum came from a group that called itself the "Military-Industrial Force" (M-I Force), which claimed that it would clear any building that was entered. It claimed to have between 20 and 40 members.

But when several hundred strikers milled-in at University Hall two days after the M-I Force announced its existence, the militant right was nowhere to be seen. Many began to doubt whether they existed in an organized form at all.

Another group with the same political purpose – breaking the strike – but having non-militant tactics also appeared briefly. Calling themselves an ad hoc committee, they passed out white ribbons that said "Keep Harvard Open" at the second stadium rally, and also leafleted that rally, urging an end to the strike. Virtually no one is wearing their white ribbons, and they seem to have disappeared.

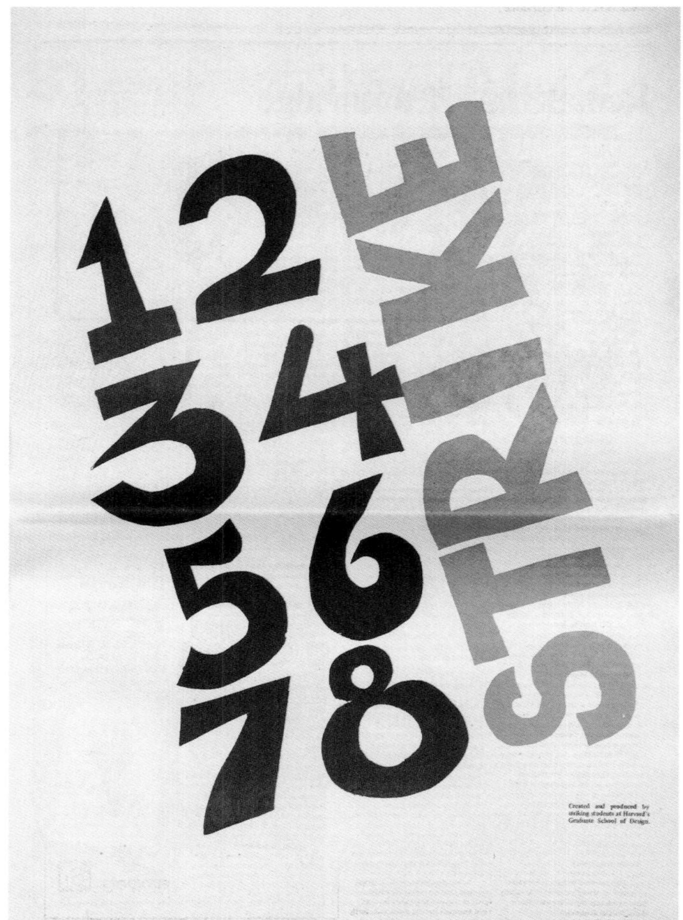

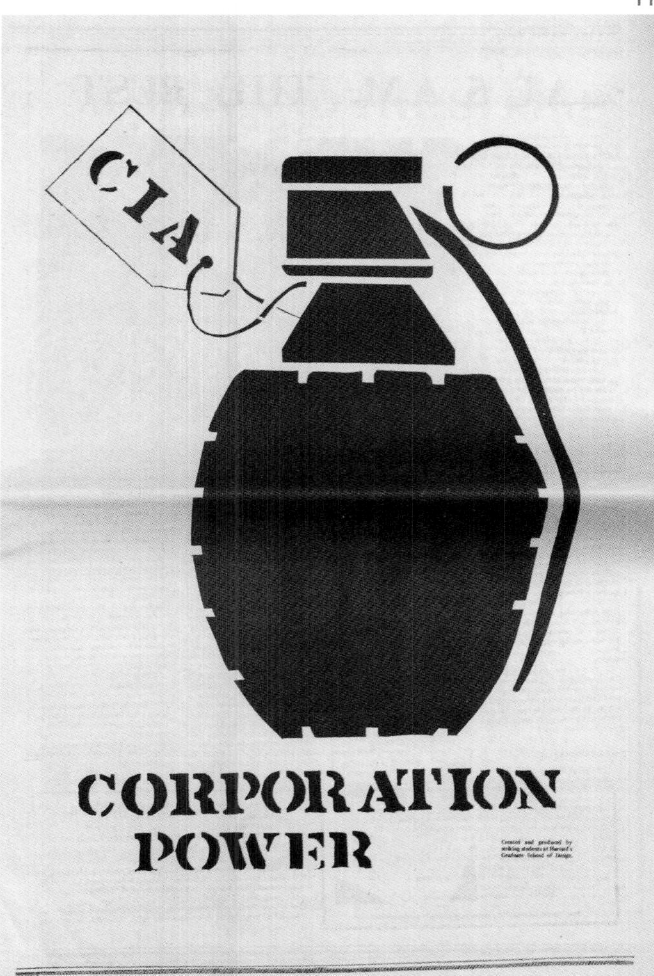

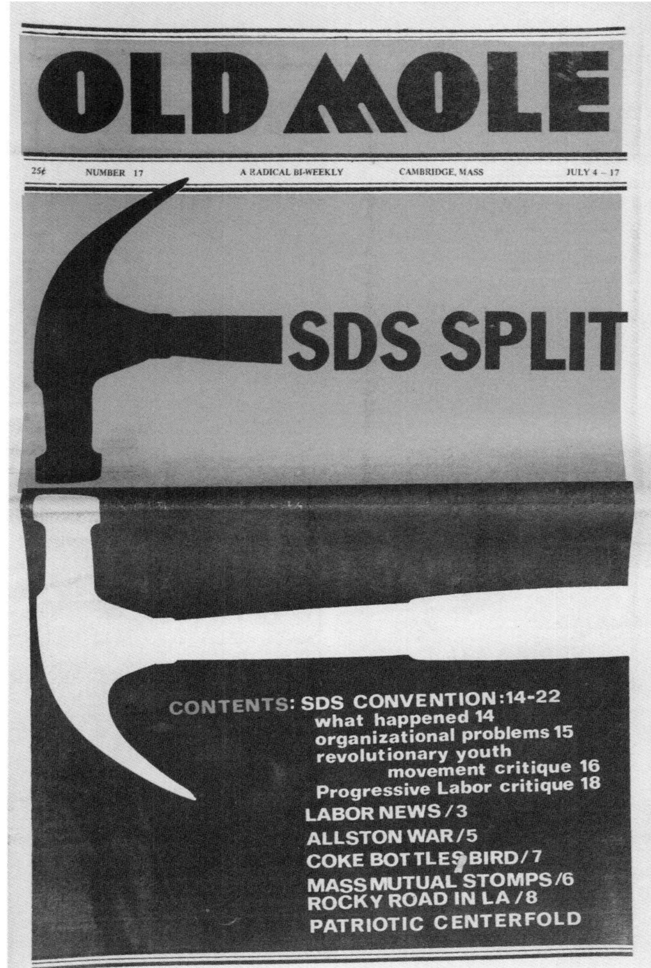

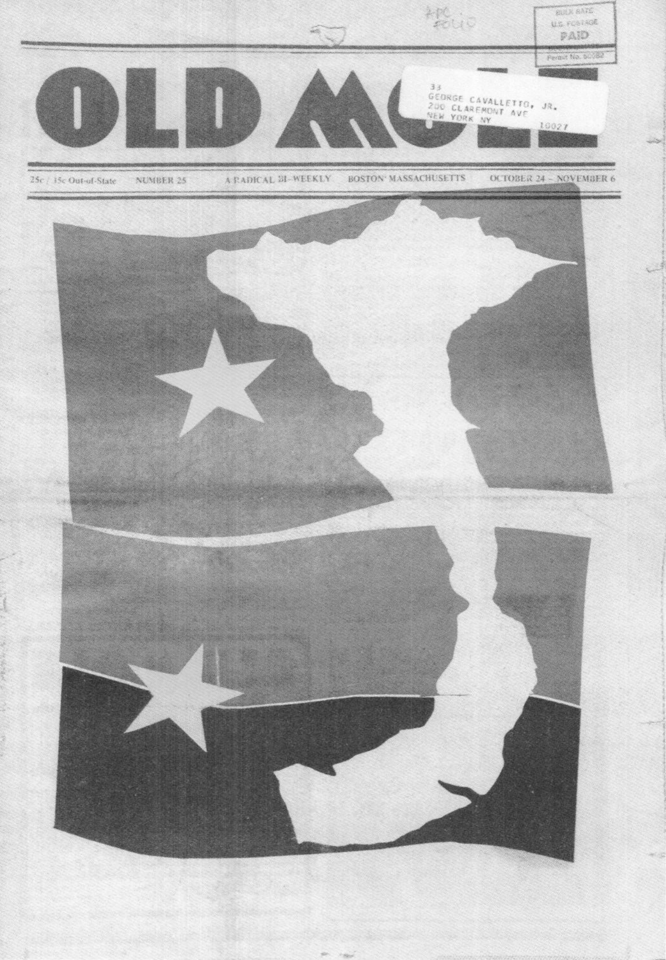

Fig. 3.28 (cont'd.) **Old Mole** (Boston), April 22–May 9, 1969, no. 12, p. 13, and back cover; July 4–17, 1969, no. 17, cover; October 24–November 6, 1969, no. 25, cover

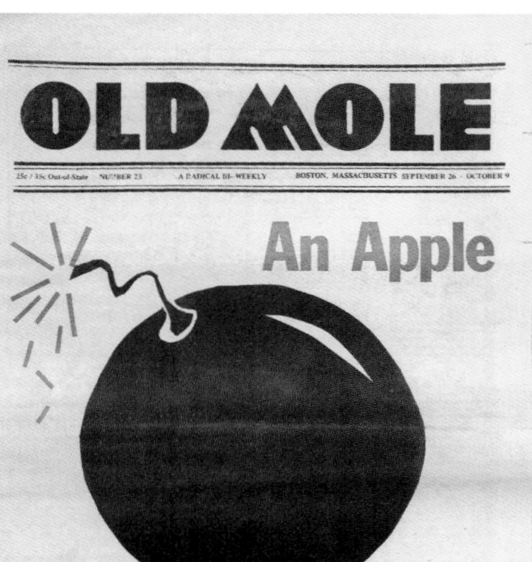

OLD MOLE

25¢ / 35¢ Out-of-State NUMBER 23 A RADICAL BI-WEEKLY BOSTON, MASSACHUSETTS SEPTEMBER 26 - OCTOBER 9

An Apple for the Teacher

FULL SCHEDULE
FALL FLICKS:
BACK TO SCHOOL
Computerized counter-insurgency
women & the U.
behind western civ.
$27 MILLION BURP

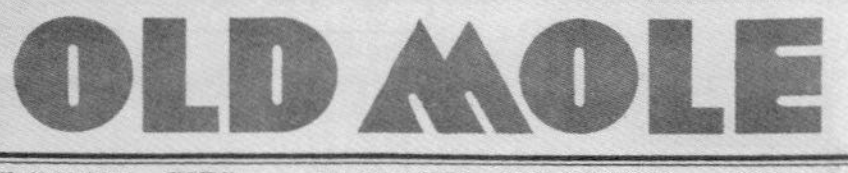

OLD MOLE

25¢ / 35¢ Out-of-State NUMBER 24 A RADICAL BI-WEEKLY BOSTON, MASSACHUSETTS OCTOBER 14 - 23

American Flag Decal

U.S. INTERVENES: GUATEMALA, 1920, 54
CUBA, 1906-09, 12, 17-19, 61, 62
CHINA, 1894, 95, 1900, 11, 12, 27
DOMINICAN REP., 1903-04, 1916-24, 1965
PHILIPPINES, 1899-1903
NICARAGUA, 1898, 99, 1910, 12-25, 26-33
GREECE, 1947-49
WATTS, 1965
KOREA, 1953
USSR, 1918-1920
IRAN, 1953
LEBANON, 1957

CONTENTS
Chicago / Weatherman
Squatters
Demonstrations:
Fort Dix
MIT
Harvard
University Power Chart

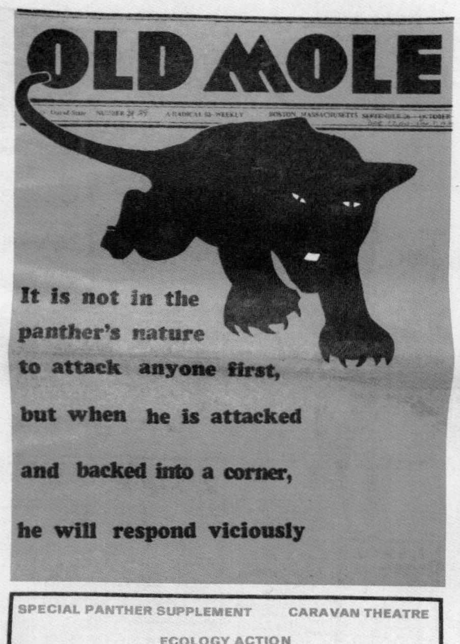

OLD MOLE

A RADICAL BI-WEEKLY BOSTON, MASSACHUSETTS

It is not in the panther's nature to attack anyone first, but when he is attacked and backed into a corner, he will respond viciously

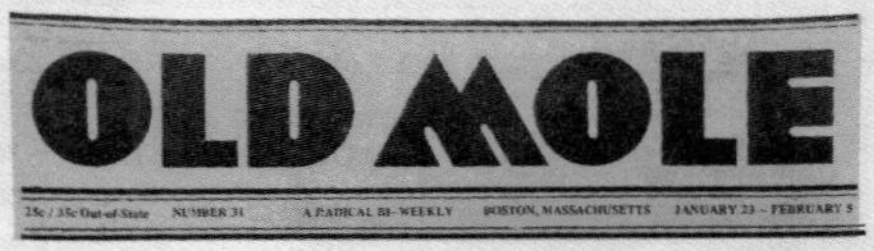

SPECIAL PANTHER SUPPLEMENT
CARAVAN THEATRE
ECOLOGY ACTION
AMERICANS IN CUBA
WOODSTOCK NATION REVIEW

OLD MOLE

25¢ / 35¢ Out-of-State NUMBER 31 A RADICAL BI-WEEKLY BOSTON, MASSACHUSETTS JANUARY 23 - FEBRUARY 5

Biafra:

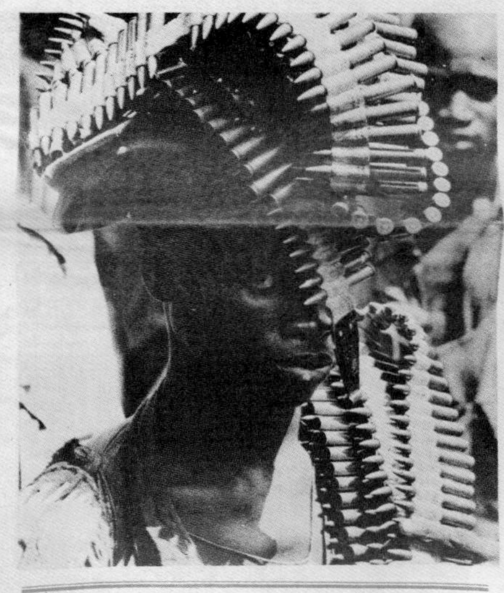

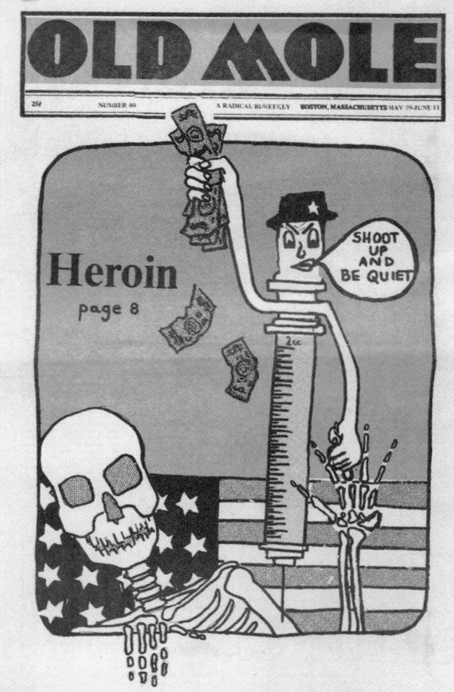

OLD MOLE

25¢ NUMBER 40 A RADICAL BI-WEEKLY BOSTON, MASSACHUSETTS MAY 29-JUNE 11

Heroin
page 8

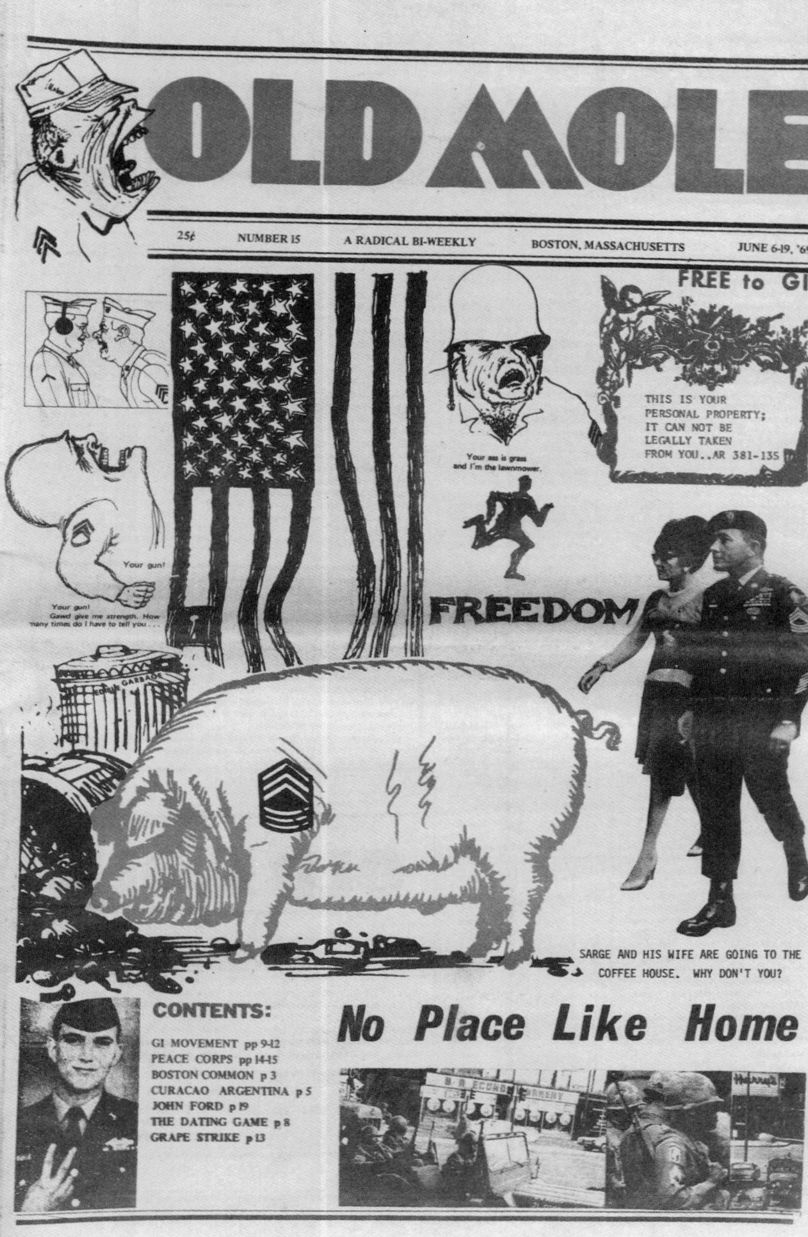

OLD MOLE

25¢ NUMBER 15 A RADICAL BI-WEEKLY BOSTON, MASSACHUSETTS JUNE 6-19, '69

FREE to GIs

THIS IS YOUR PERSONAL PROPERTY; IT CAN NOT BE LEGALLY TAKEN FROM YOU..AR 381-135

SARGE AND HIS WIFE ARE GOING TO THE COFFEE HOUSE. WHY DON'T YOU?

CONTENTS:

No Place Like Home

Fig. 3.28 (cont'd). **Old Mole** (Boston), September 26–October 9, 1969, no. 23, cover; December 17, 1969–January 8, 1970, no. 29, cover; June 6–19, 1969, no. 15, cover; October 14–23, 1969, no. 24, cover; January 23–Feb. 5, 1970, no. 31, cover; May 29–June 11, 1970, no. 40, cover

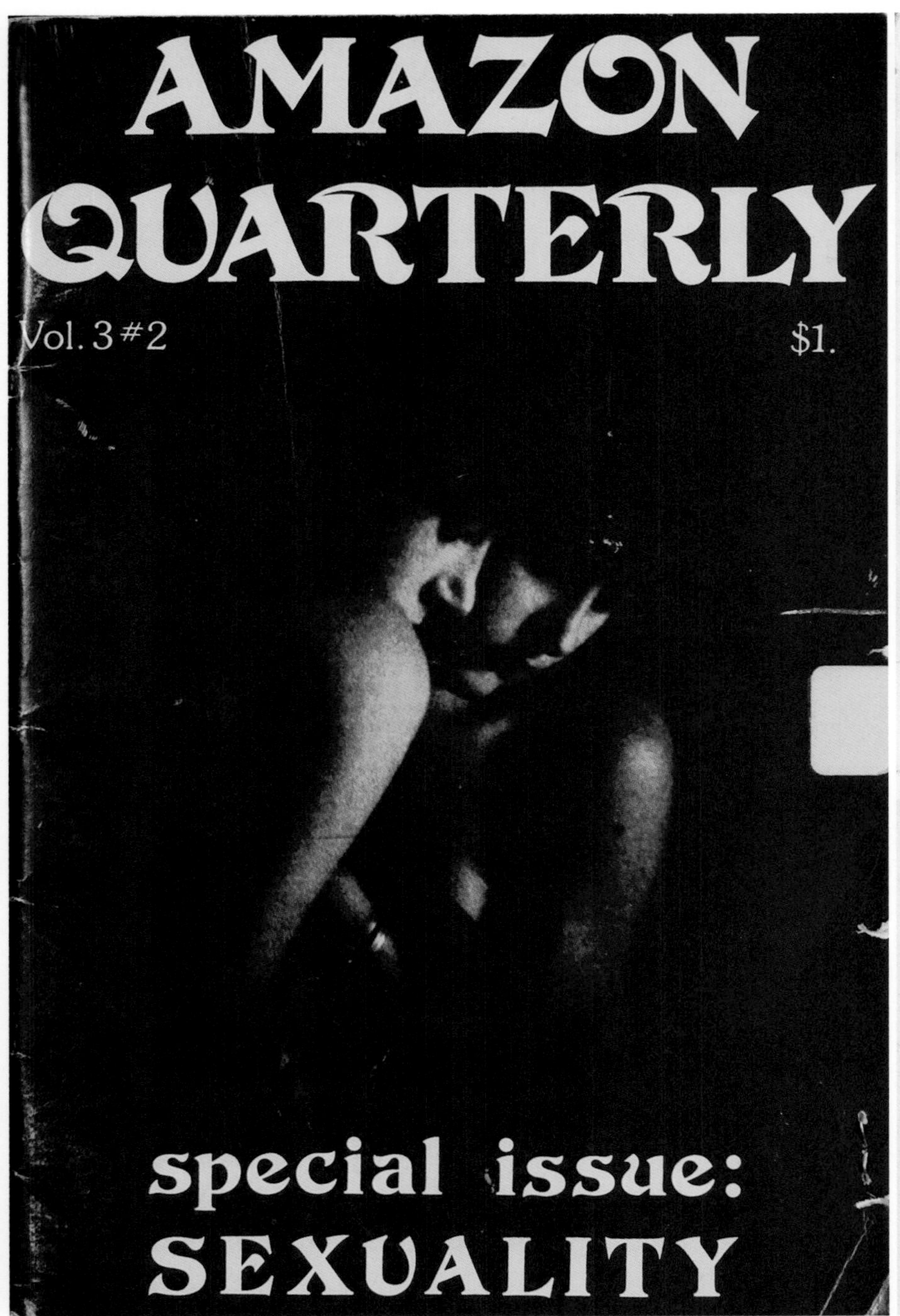

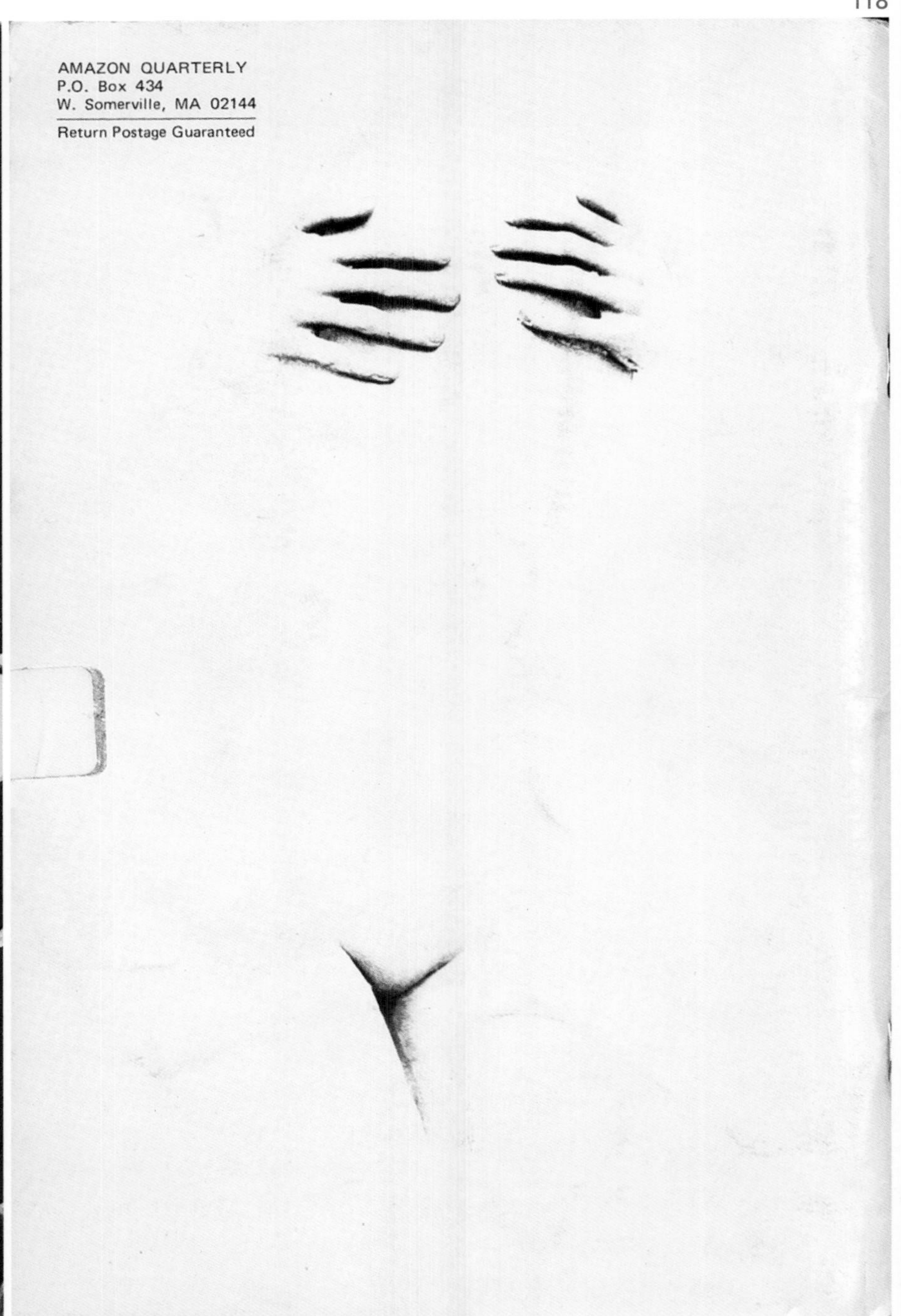

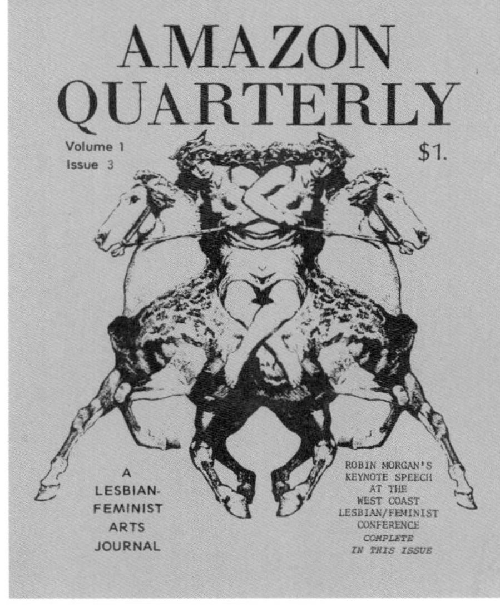

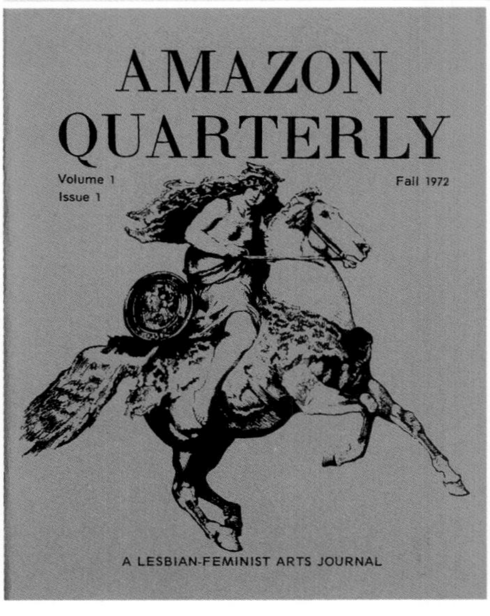

Fig. 3.29. **Amazon Quarterly,** March 1975, vol. 3, no. 2, cover, back cover; May 1973, vol. 1, no. 3, cover; Fall 1972, vol. 1, no. 1, cover

Next page
Fig. 3.29 (cont'd.). **Amazon Quarterly,** March 1974, vol. 2, no. 3, cover; October 1973, vol. 1, no. 4 and vol. 2, no. 1 (double issue), cover; July 1974, vol. 2, no. 4, cover; March 1974, vol. 2, no. 3, back cover; October 1973, vol. 1, no. 4 and vol. 2, no. 1 (double issue), back cover; July 1974, vol. 2, no. 4, back cover

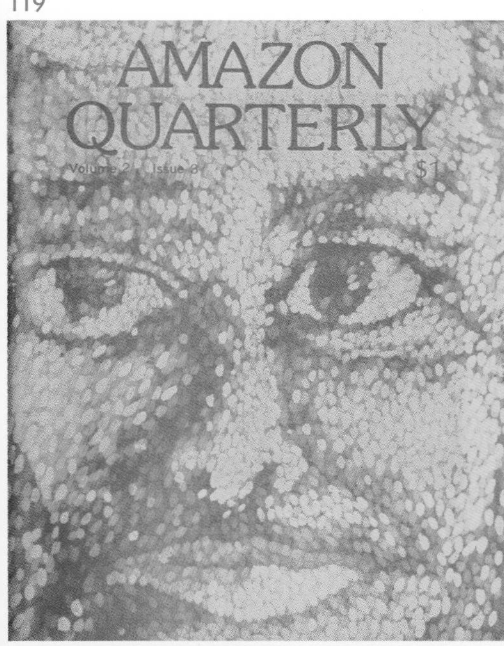
AMAZON
QUARTERLY
Volume 2 Issue 3
$1

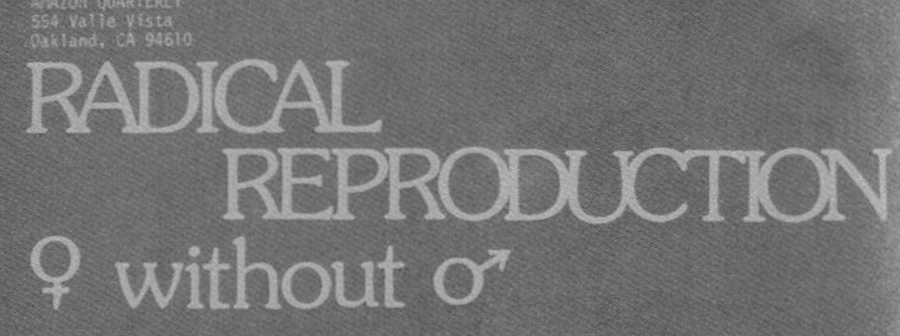
AMAZON QUARTERLY
554 Valle Vista
Oakland, CA 94610
RADICAL
REPRODUCTION
♀ without ♂
POETRY BY:
robin morgan
jennie orvino
adrienne rich
&
how to
make a magazine

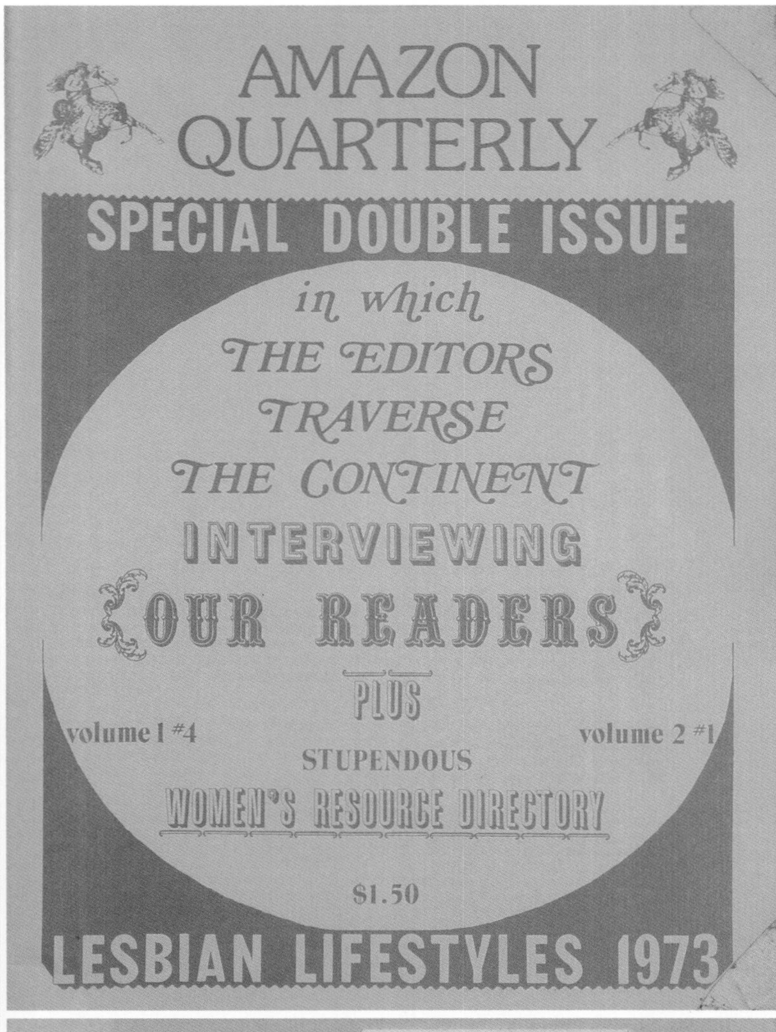
AMAZON
QUARTERLY
SPECIAL DOUBLE ISSUE
in which
THE EDITORS
TRAVERSE
THE CONTINENT
INTERVIEWING
OUR READERS
PLUS
volume 1 #4
volume 2 #1
STUPENDOUS
WOMEN'S RESOURCE DIRECTORY
$1.50
LESBIAN LIFESTYLES 1973

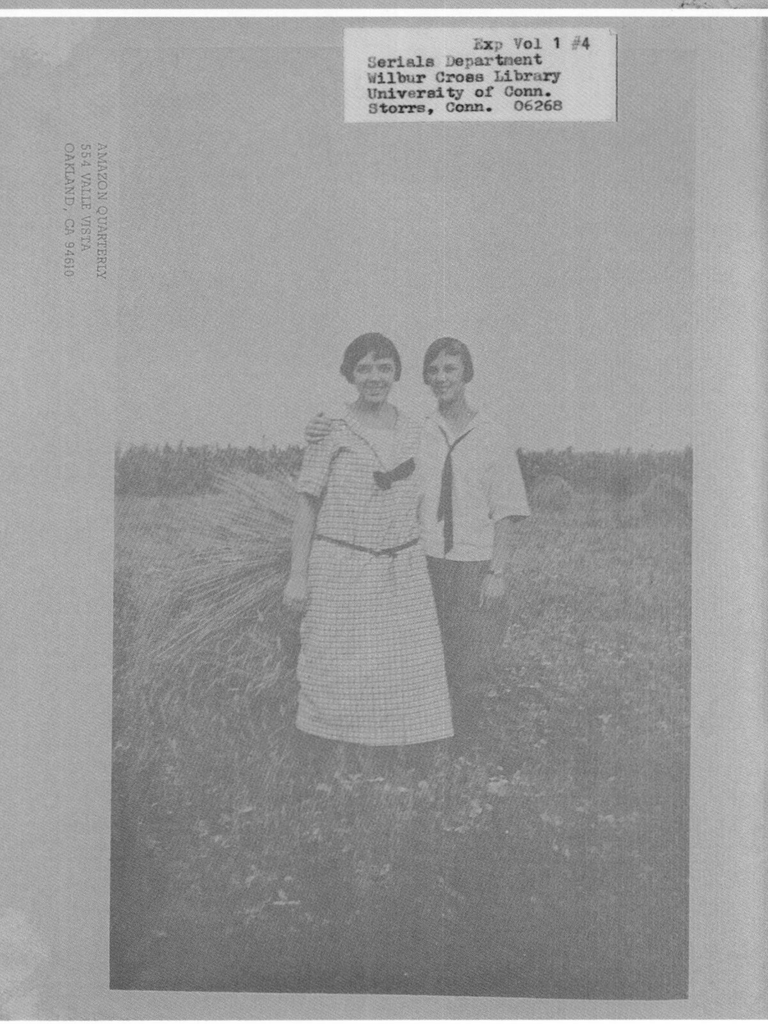
Exp Vol 1 #4
Serials Department
Wilbur Cross Library
University of Conn.
Storrs, Conn. 06268
AMAZON QUARTERLY
554 VALLE VISTA
OAKLAND, CA 94610

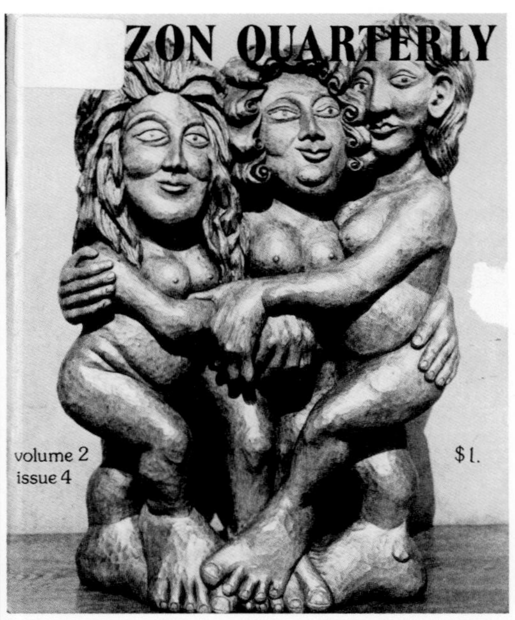
ZON QUARTERLY
volume 2
issue 4
$1.

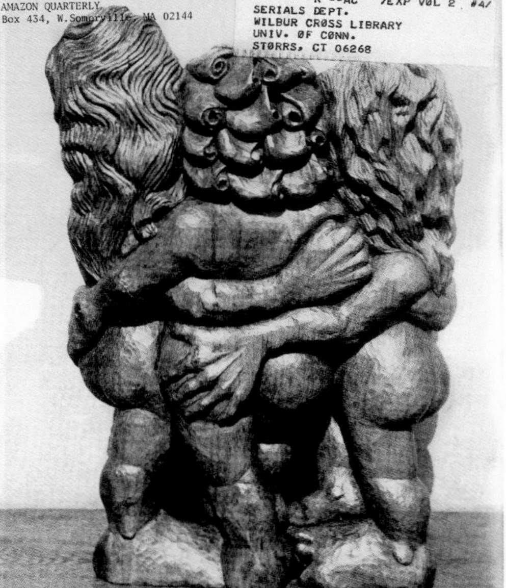
AMAZON QUARTERLY
Box 434, W. Somerville, MA 02144
R --AC /EXP VOL 2 #4/
SERIALS DEPT.
WILBUR CROSS LIBRARY
UNIV. OF CONN.
STORRS, CT 06268

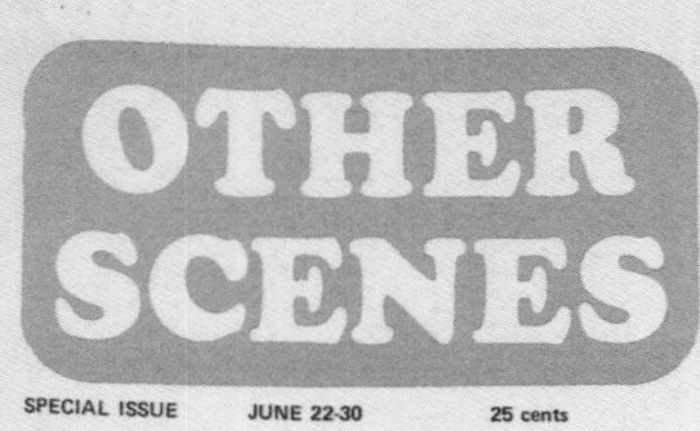

SPECIAL ISSUE JUNE 22-30 25 cents

NOTICE

This special issue costs 25 cents.

Most of it consists of blank pages.

Do not waste your money buying it unless
(a) you want a collector's item, or
(b) you are planning to enter our do-it-yourself newspaper contest.

first prize is $250.

Details in centerfold.

THE DO-IT-YOURSELF NEWS PAPER CONTEST

WINNERS

SUBJECT MATTER

TECHNIQUE

PAGES

11	10	13	8	9	12	7	14
20	1	18	3	2	19	4	17

COLOR

DECLARATION

Fig. 3.30. **Other Scenes** (New York), June 22-30, 1969, cover and two spreads kinds of public spaces. Drawing on cybernetics and the media theories of Marshall McLuhan, designers envisioned new models of communication, creating layouts that referenced television screens and computer circuitry, and arranging text nonlinearly in bubbles and boxes linked by arrows, inviting readers to determine the sequence.

Such visual forms found their corollary in actual opportunities for readers to contribute to these publications. *Radical Software*, for example, published a column called "Feedback" at the end of each issue, where snippets sent in by various video groups or individuals were printed on a lopsided matrix, visually embodying the chatter of multiple voices and points of view. The lesbian publication *Amazon Quarterly* published a special issue in which the editors traveled across the country interviewing readers (fig. 3.29). In 1969, *Other Scenes* published a special Do-It-Yourself Newspaper Contest issue, consisting of sixteen blank pages that readers were invited to fill in with text and graphics, with the winning entry being produced as a regular issue. Printed in an edition of 10,000 copies, it sold out the second day on the newsstand. Perhaps there is no better example of the utopian impulses of underground graphic design than these sixteen empty pages, which, in their unfinished blankness, stand as an emblem of its effort to imagine—and encourage readers to imagine—a different world, a world yet to come (fig. 3.30).

In his influential 1967 essay "The Death of the Author," Roland Barthes called for the "birth of the reader," insisting that cultural meaning should not be dictated from above by an individual author but produced collectively by readers. Artists explored the radical implications of Barthes's antiauthoritarian call for semantic freedom, using various strategies to displace artistic intention and engage viewers as coproducers of artistic meaning. The political significance of such practices comes into sharper focus when understood against the radical design practices of the underground press. Whether or not designers read Barthes's essay—and surely some did—they understood that in order to transform the media, they had to remake the relationship between producers and consumers of media.

Art and design have long been segregated from one another in critical accounts. To instead see them as part of a continuum sheds light on the significance of each. It allows us to see, for example, how designers have approached the processes and media of communication with the kind of critical self-reflexivity typically attributed to artists; and how artists have borrowed production and distribution techniques from designers in their attempt to challenge traditional models of the artist and work of art. The goal of such an approach is not to elide the important differences between art and design—differences that stem from their divergent audiences, contexts, and histories, and that account for the distinct capacities and advantages of each. Nor is the point to give design a fine-art pedigree, which merely reinforces the hierarchy between the two. Rather the benefit of comparing the practices of art and design is to better understand how both have contributed to the collective social possibilities of language, visual representation, and mass media. These possibilities are not the exclusive domain of either art or design; they belong to us all.

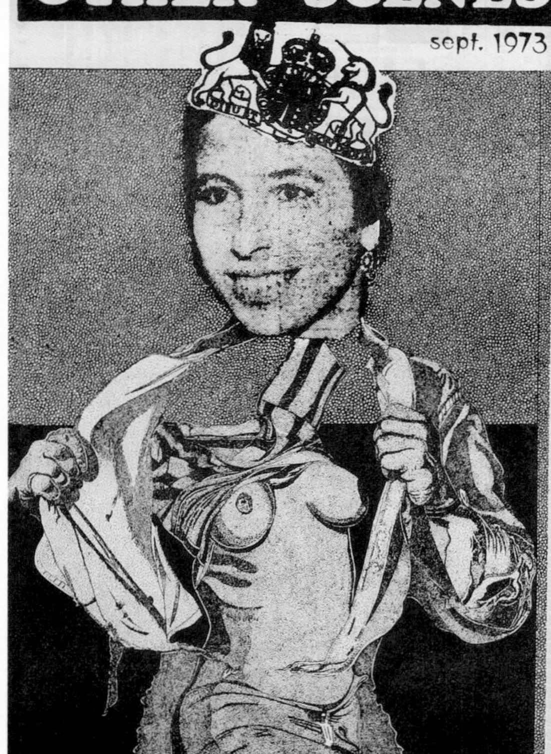
OTHER SCENES
sept. 1973

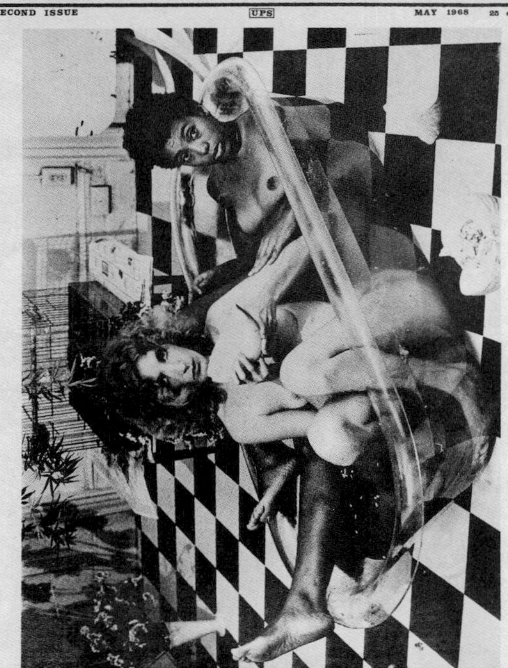
JOHN WILCOCK'S
OTHER SCENES
&
THE NEW YORK SEER
SECOND ISSUE
UPS
MAY 1968
25 cents
photo by BILLY NAME

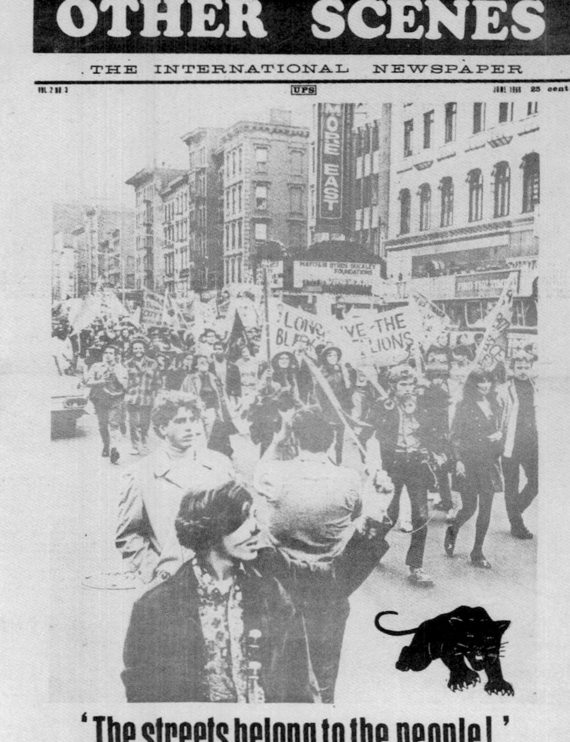
JOHN WILCOCK'S
OTHER SCENES
THE INTERNATIONAL NEWSPAPER
UPS
25 cents
'The streets belong to the people!'

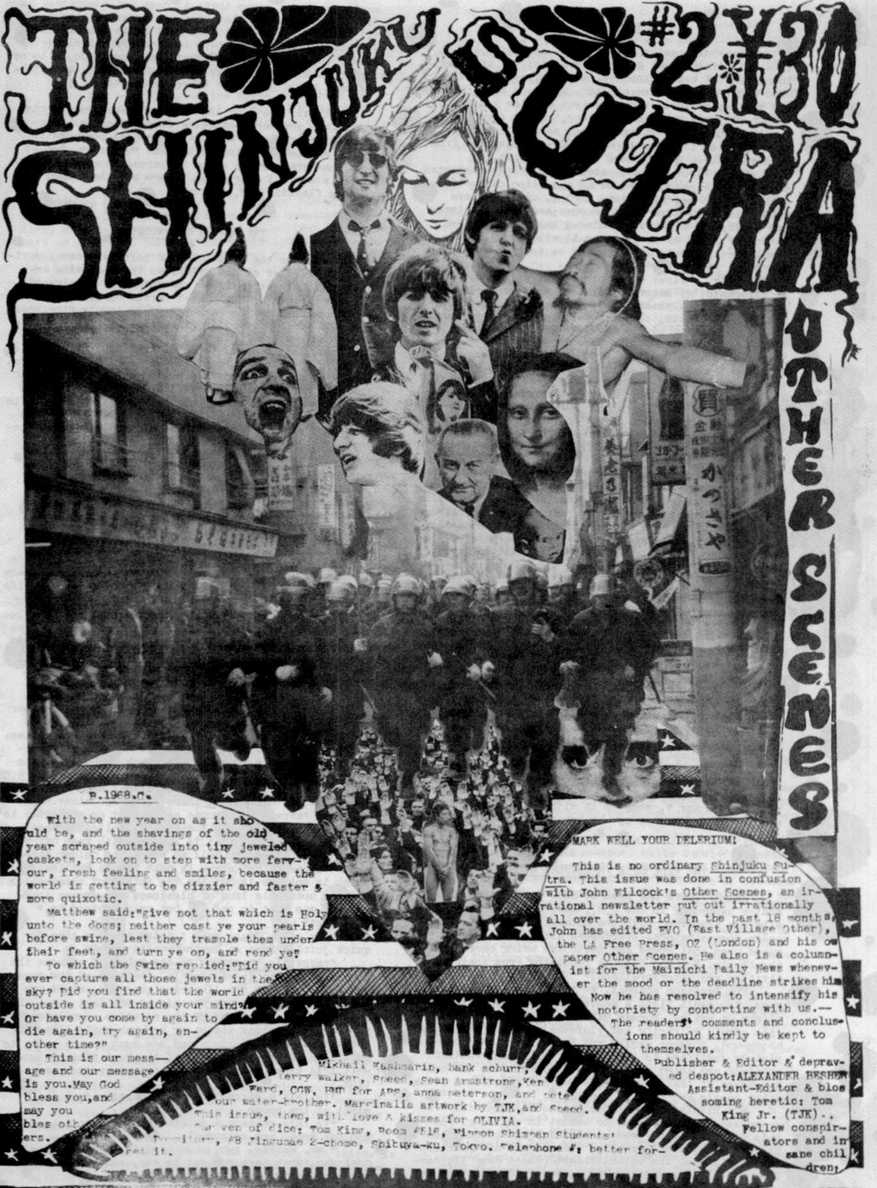
THE SHINJUKU SUTRA
#2 ¥30
OTHER SCENES
B.1968.C.
With the new year on as it should be, and the shavings of the old year scraped outside into tiny jeweled caskets, look on to step with more fervour, fresh feeling and smiles, because the world is getting to be dizzier and faster & more quixotic.
Matthew said:"give not that which is Holy unto the dogs; neither cast ye your pearls before swine, lest they trample them under their feet, and turn ye on, and rend ye"
To which the Swine replied:"Did you ever capture all those jewels in the sky? Did you find that the world outside is all inside your mind? Or have you come by again to die again, try again, another time?"
This is our message and our message is you. May God bless you, and may you bless others.
MARK WELL YOUR DELERIUM!
This is no ordinary Shinjuku Sutra. This issue was done in confusion with John Wilcock's Other Scenes, an irrational newsletter put out irrationally all over the world. In the past 18 months, John has edited EVO (East Village Other), the LA Free Press, OZ (London) and his own paper Other Scenes. He also is a columnist for the Mainichi Daily News whenever the mood or the deadline strikes him. Now he has resolved to intensify his notoriety by contorting with us.—
The readers' comments and conclusions should kindly be kept to themselves.
Publisher & Editor & depraved despot: ALEXANDER BESHER
Assistant-Editor & blossoming heretic: Tom King Jr. (TJK).
Fellow conspirators and insane children:
Mikhail Kashmarin, hank schurr,
terry walker, Speed, Sean Armstrong, Ken
Ward, CGW, HMP for APS, anna peterson, and pete
our water-brother. Marginalia artwork by TJK, and Speed.
This issue, then, with love & kisses for OLIVIA.
ven of dice: Tom King, Room #518, Nippon Shimpan Students'
#8 Jingumae 2-chome, Shibuya-ku, Tokyo. Telephone #: better for-
get it.

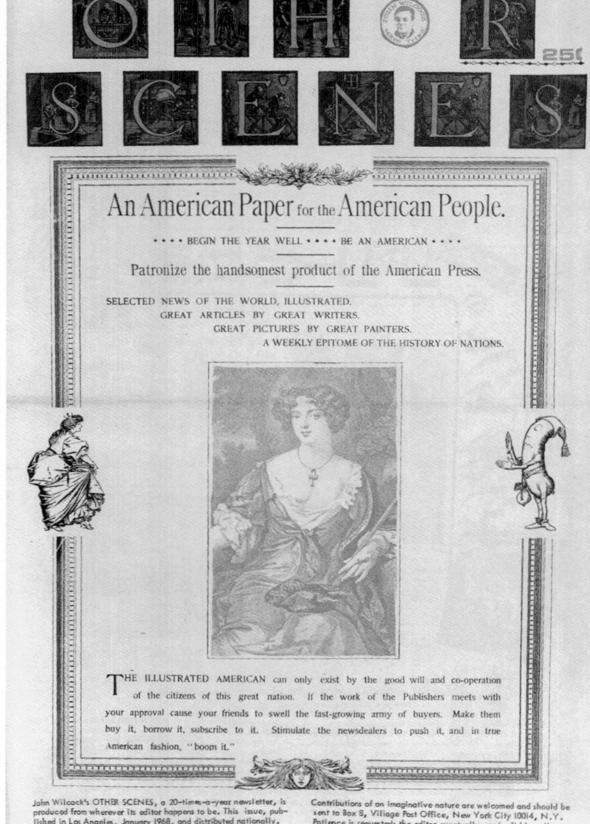
OTHER SCENES
25¢
An American Paper for the American People.
• • • • BEGIN THE YEAR WELL • • • • BE AN AMERICAN • • • •
Patronize the handsomest product of the American Press.
SELECTED NEWS OF THE WORLD, ILLUSTRATED.
GREAT ARTICLES BY GREAT WRITERS.
GREAT PICTURES BY GREAT PAINTERS.
A WEEKLY EPITOME OF THE HISTORY OF NATIONS.
THE ILLUSTRATED AMERICAN can only exist by the good will and co-operation of the citizens of this great nation. If the work of the Publishers meets with your approval cause your friends to swell the fast-growing army of buyers. Make them buy it, borrow it, subscribe to it. Stimulate the newsdealers to push it, and in true American fashion, "boom it."
John Wilcock's OTHER SCENES, a 20-times-a-year newsletter, is produced from wherever its editor happens to be. This issue, published in Los Angeles, January 1968, and distributed nationally.
Contributions of an imaginative nature are welcomed and should be sent to Box 8, Village Post Office, New York City 10014, N.Y. Patience is requested; the editor eventually reads all his mail.

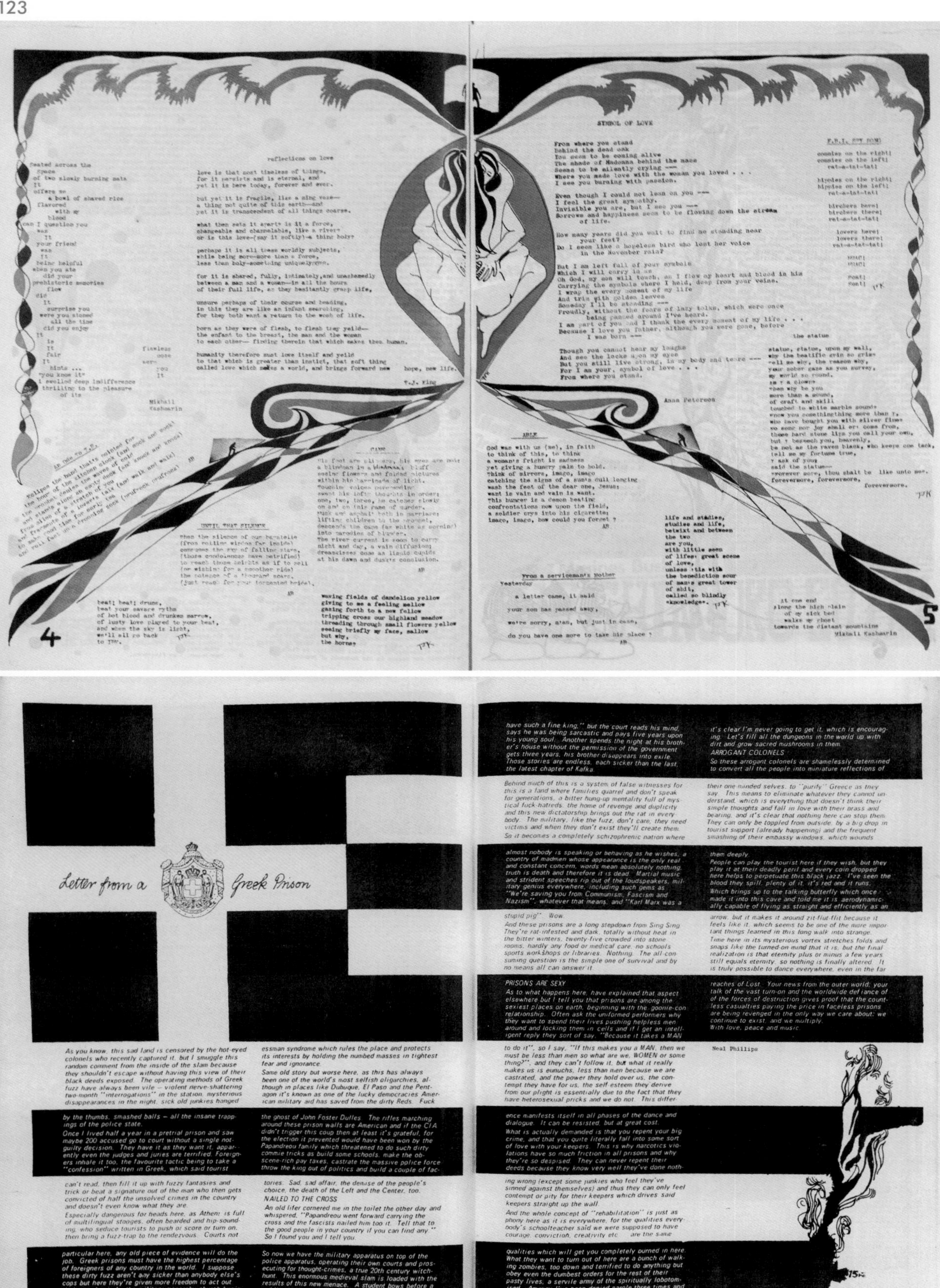

reflections on love

love is that most timeless of things,
for it persists and is eternal, and
yet it is here today, forever and ever.

but yet it is fragile, like a ming vase—
a thing not quite of this earth—and
yet it is transcendent of all things coarse.

what then sets it apart? is it a force,
changeable and channelable, like a river?
or is this love—(say it softly)—a thing holy?

perhaps it is all these worldly subjects,
while being more—more than a force,
less than holy—something uniquely?

for it is shared, fully, intimately, and unashamedly
between a man and a woman—in all the hours
of their full life, as they hesitantly grasp life,

unsure perhaps of their course and heading,
in this they are like an infant searching,
for they both want a return to the womb of life.

born as they were of flesh, to flesh they yeild—
the enfant to the breast, the man and the woman
to each other— finding therein that which makes them human.

humanity therefore must love itself and yeild
to that which is greater than instict, that soft thing
called love which makes a world, and brings forward new hope, new life.

T.J. King

seated across the
space
of two slowly burning mats
It
offers me
a bowl of shaved rice
flavored
with my
blood
can I question you
was
It
your friend
was
It
being helpful
when you ate
did your
prehistoric memories
flow
did
It
surprise you
were you stoned
all the time
did you enjoy
It
is
It
fair
It
hints ...
"you know it"
I swelled deep indifference
thrilling to the pleasure
of its

flawless
ooze
were
you
It

Mikhail
Kashmarin

An Ode to T.E.

Eclipse the hand that's pointed for
the hour of the kitchen clock (saw) mock and mock!
the prophet denies the waves of cold
and stands along an empty dock (and knock and knock)
from alien of a stretch of you
and fragments of a lover's talk (and walk and walk)
to make good time for early tea
and roll fast on a dropping rock (prufrock prufrock)

AP

CAME

His feet are all ..., his eyes are ...
a blindman in a bladman's bluff
seeing flowers and folded pictures
within his barricade of light.
... voices ...
... his lofty thoughts in order;
one, two, three, he catches slowly
on and on this game of murder.
Musk and asphalt both in marriage;
lifting children to the ...,
descends the cape (as white as morning)
into parodies of blunder.
The river current is soon to carry
night and day, a vain diffusion;
dreamkisses come as liquid cupids
at his dawn and dusk's conclusion.

AP

UNTIL THAT SILENCE

When the silence of our ...
(from roiling wisdom far inside)
consumes the sky of falling stars,
(those condolences have petrified)
to reach those heights as if to sell
(or wishing for a smoother ride)
the patience of a thousand scars.
(just reach for your tormented bride).

AP

beat! beat! drums,
beat your savage rythm
of hot blood and drunken marrow,
of lusty love played to your beat,
and when the sky is light,
we'll all go back
to ...

TJK

waving fields of dandelion yellow
giving to me a feeling mellow
gazing forth to a new fellow
tripping cross our highland meadow
threading through small flowers yellow
seeing briefly my face, sallow
but why,
the horns?

TJK

4

SYMBOL OF LOVE

From where you stand
Behind the dead oak
You seem to be coming alive
The shade of Madonna behind the mass
Seems to be silently crying ---
Where you made love with the woman you loved . . .
I see you burning with passion.

Even though I could not lean on you ---
I feel the great sympathy.
Invisible you are, but I see you ---
Sorrows and happiness seem to be flowing down the stream
of life.

How many years did you wait to find me standing near
your feet?
Do I seem like a hopeless bird who lost her voice
in the November rain?

But I am left full of your symbols
Which I will carry in me
Oh God, my son will touch, as I flow my heart and blood in his
Carrying the symbols where I held, deep from your veins.
I wrap the every moment of my life
And trim with golden leaves
Someday I'll be standing ---
Proudly, without the fears of lazy folks, which were once
being passed around I've heard.
I am part of you and I thank the every moment of my life . . .
Because I love you father, although you were gone, before
I was born ---

Though you cannot hear my laughs
And see the locks upon my eyes
But you still live strong, in my body and tears ---
For I am your, symbol of love . . .
From where you stand.

Anna Peterson

F.B.I. SPY SONG

commies on the right!
commies on the left!
rat-a-tat-tat!

hippies on the right!
hippies on the left!
rat-a-tat-tat!

birchers here!
birchers there!
rat-a-tat-tat!

lovers here!
lovers there!
rat-a-tat-tat!

WHAC!
WHAC!

rent!
rent!

TJK

the statue

statue, statue, upon my wall,
why the beatific grin so grim?
tell me why, the reason why,
your sober gaze as you survey,
my world so round.
am I a clown?
then why be you
more than a sound,
of craft and skill
touched to white marble sound?
know you somethingthing more than I,
who have bought you with silver fines
no song nor joy shall ere come from,
those hard stone lips you call your own,
but I beseech you, heavenly,
be not as the raven black, who keeps one tack,
tell me my fortune true,
I ask of you;
said the statue—
forever more, thou shalt be like unto me.
forevermore, forevermore,
forevermore.

TJK

ABLE

God was with us (me), in faith
to think of this, to think
a woman's fright is sadness
yet giving a hungry palm to hold.
Think of mirrors, imago, imago
catching the signs of a sun's dull longing
wash the feet of the dear one, Jesus;
want is vain and vain is want.
This hunger is a demon beating
confrontations now upon the field,
a soldier crys into his cigarette;
imago, imago, how could you forget ?

AP

life and studies,
studies and life,
betwixt and between
the two
are you,
with little seen
of lifes great scene
of love,
unless 'tis with
the benediction sour
of man's great tower
of shit,
called so blindly
"knowledge".

TJK

From a serviceman's Mother

Yesterday

a letter came, it said

your son has passed away,

we're sorry, ma'am, but just in case,

do you have one more to take his place ?

AP

At one end
Along the high plain
of my sick bed
walks my ghost
towards the distant mountains

Mikhail Kashmarin

5

Letter from a Greek Prison

As you know, this sad land is censored by the hot-eyed colonels who recently captured it, but I smuggle this random comment from the inside of the slam because they shouldn't escape without having this view of their black deeds exposed. The operating methods of Greek fuzz have always been vile — violent nerve-shattering two-month "interrogations" in the station, mysterious disappearances in the night, sick old junkies hanged by the thumbs, smashed balls — all the insane trappings of the police state.

Once I lived half a year in a pretrial prison and saw maybe 200 accused go to court without a single not-guilty decision. They have it as they want it, apparently even the judges and juries are terrified. Foreigners inhale it too, the favourite tactic being to take a "confession" written in Greek, which said tourist can't read, then fill it up with fuzzy fantasies and trick or beat a signature out of the man who then gets convicted of half the unsolved crimes in the country and doesn't even know what they are.

Especially dangerous for heads here, as Athens is full of multilingual stooges, often bearded and hip-sounding, who seduce tourists to push or score or turn on, then bring a fuzz-trap to the rendezvous. Courts not particular here, any old piece of evidence will do the job. Greek prisons must have the highest percentage of foreigners of any country in the world. I suppose these dirty fuzz aren't any sicker than anybody else's cops but here they're given more freedom to act out their psychosis by the military-monarchy-church-businessman syndrome which rules the place and protects its interests by holding the numbed masses in tightest fear and ignorance.

Same old story but worse here, as this has always been one of the world's most selfish oligarchies, although in places like Dubuque, El Paso and the Pentagon it's known as one of the lucky democracies American military aid has saved from the dirty Reds. Fuck the ghost of John Foster Dulles. The rifles marching around these prison walls are American and if the CIA didn't trigger this coup then at least it's grateful, for the election it prevented would have been won by the Papandreou family which threatened to do such dirty commie tricks as build some schools, make the obscene-rich pay taxes, castrate the massive police force throw the king out of politics and build a couple of factories. Sad, sad affair, the demise of the people's choice, the death of the Left and the Center, too.

NAILED TO THE CROSS

An old lifer cornered me in the toilet the other day and whispered, "Papandreou went forward carrying the cross and the fascists nailed him too it. Tell that to the good people in your country if you can find any." So I found you and I tell you.

So now we have the military apparatus on top of the police apparatus, operating their own courts and prosecuting for thought-crimes, a true 20th century witch-hunt. This enormous medieval slam is loaded with the results of this new menace. A student bows before a public picture of the king and says, "We're lucky to have such a fine king," but the court reads his mind, says he was being sarcastic and pays five years upon his young soul. Another spends the night at his brother's house without the permission of the government gets three years, his brother disappears into exile. Those stories are endless, each sicker than the last, the latest chapter of Kafka.

Behind much of this is a system of false witnesses for this is a land where families quarrel and don't speak for generations, a bitter hung-up mentality full of mystical fuck-hatreds, the home of revenge and duplicity and this new dictatorship brings out the rat in everybody. The military, like the fuzz, don't care; they need victims and when they don't exist they'll create them.

So it becomes a completely schizophrenic nation where almost nobody is speaking or behaving as he wishes, a country of madmen whose appearance is the only real and constant concern, words mean absolutely nothing, truth is death and therefore it is dead. Martial music and strident speeches rip out of the loudspeakers, military genius everywhere, including such gems as "We're saving you from Communism, Fascism and Nazism", whatever that means, and "Karl Marx was a stupid pig". Wow.

And these prisons are a long stepdown from Sing Sing. They're rat-infested and dark, totally without heat in the bitter winters, twenty-five crowded into stone rooms, hardly any food or medical care, no schools sports workshops or libraries. Nothing. The all-consuming question is the simple one of survival and by no means all can answer it.

PRISONS ARE SEXY

As to what happens here, have explained that aspect elsewhere but I tell you that prisons are among the sexiest places on earth, beginning with the goonie-con relationship. Often ask the uniformed performers why they want to spend their lives pushing helpless men around and locking them in cells and if I get an intelligent reply they sort of say, "Because it takes a MAN to do it", so I say, "If this makes you a MAN, then we must be less than men so what are we, WOMEN or something?", and they can't follow it, but what it really makes us is eunuchs, less than men because we are castrated, and the power they hold over us, the contempt they have for us, the self-esteem they derive from our plight is essentially due to the fact that they have heterosexual pricks and we do not. This difference manifests itself in all phases of the dance and dialogue. It can be resisted, but at great cost.

What is actually demanded is that you repent your big crime, and that you quite literally fall into some sort of love with your keepers. This is why narcotics violations have so much friction in all prisons and why they're so despised. They can never repent their deeds because they know very well they've done nothing wrong (except some junkies who feel they've sinned against themselves) and thus they can only feel contempt or pity for their keepers which drives said keepers straight up the wall.

And the whole concept of "rehabilitation" is just as phony here as it is everywhere, for the qualities everybody's schoolteacher said we were supposed to have courage, conviction, creativity etc. are the same qualities which will get you completely burned in here. What they want to turn out of here are a bunch of walking zombies, too down and terrified to do anything but obey even the dumbest orders for the rest of their pasty lives, a servile army of the spiritually lobotomised. Anyway I've been denied parole three times and it's clear I'm never going to get it, which is encouraging. Let's fill all the dungeons in the world up with dirt and grow sacred mushrooms in them.

ARROGANT COLONELS

So these arrogant colonels are shamelessly determined to convert all the people into miniature reflections of their one-minded selves, to "purify" Greece as they say. This means to eliminate whatever they cannot understand, which is everything that doesn't think their simple thoughts and fall in love with their brass and bearing, and it's clear that nothing here can stop them. They can only be toppled from outside, by a big drop in tourist support (already happening) and the frequent smashing of their embassy windows, which wounds them deeply.

People can play the tourist here if they wish, but they play it at their deadly peril and every coin dropped here helps to perpetuate this black jazz. I've seen the blood they spill, plenty of it, it's red and it runs.

Which brings up to the talking butterfly which once made it into this cave and told me it is aerodynamically capable of flying as straight and efficiently as an arrow, but it makes it around zit-flut-flit because it feels like it, which seems to be one of the more important things learned in this long walk into strange.

Time here in its mysterious vortex stretches folds and snaps like the turned-on mind that it is, but the final realization is that eternity plus or minus a few years still equals eternity, so nothing is finally altered. It is truly possible to dance everywhere, even in the far reaches of Lost. Your news from the outer world, your talk of the vast turn-on and the worldwide defiance of of the forces of destruction gives proof that the countless casualties paying the price in faceless prisons are being revenged in the only way we care about: we continue to exist, and we multiply.

With love, peace and music.

Neal Phillips

A benefit performance for Melina Mercouri's Greek Freedom Fund will be held at New York's Village Gate on March 19.

Neal Phillips was released from jail recently and is now safely out of Greece.

Previous page
Other Scenes (London), September 1973, no. 67, cover
Other Scenes (New York), May 1968, vol. 2, no. 2, cover
Other Scenes (New York), June 1968, vol. 2, no. 3, cover
Other Scenes/Shinjuku Sutra (Japan), 1968, no. 13, cover
Other Scenes (Los Angeles), January 1968, no. 14, cover

Other Scenes/Shinjuku Sutra (Japan), 1968, no. 13, pp. 405
Other Scenes, January 1968, vol. 2, no. 1, center spread

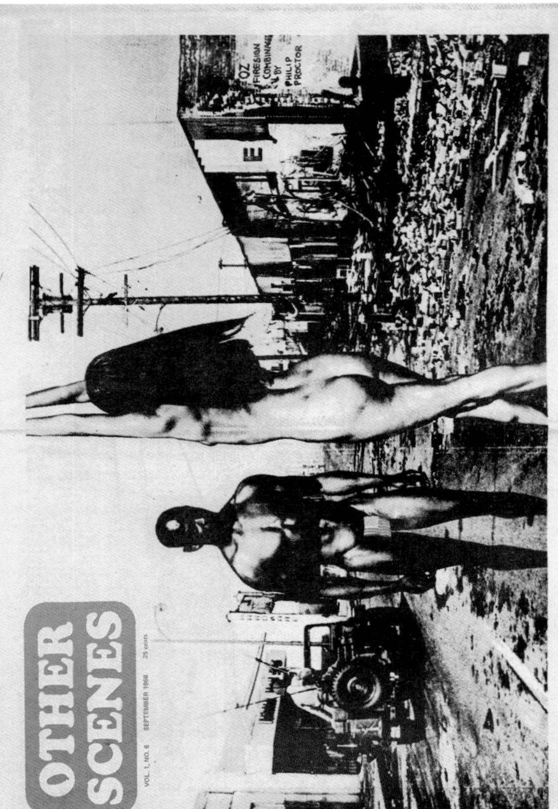

He is a right-wing Tory opportunist who will stop at nothing to help his party and his class. He is director of the National Discount Company (assets £224,000,000) which pays him a salary bigger than the £3,500 a year he gets as an MP. He lives in fashionable Belgravia and writes Greek verse.

What Does He Believe In?

Higher Unemployment. He has consistently advocated a national average of 3 per cent unemployed.

Cuts in the Social Services. He wants higher Health charges, less Council houses, charges for State education and lower unemployment pay.

Mass Sackings in the Docks. Again and again he has argued that the docks are " grossly over-manned ". Enoch Powell is the consistent, declared enemy of the working class — a high priest of the capitalist system. He is opposed to all controls except immigration control.

He is playing exactly the same trick as Hitler and Mosley played before the last war. He is saying exactly the same things which Mosley was saying four years ago. He is whipping up racialist feeling against the minority to get the support of the majority. The workers who fought for Hitler in Germany in 1933 soon paid the price. Their trade unions were smashed. Their welfare services abolished, their lives at home and at work terrorized by Fascist thugs.

The choice is simple; either you work together with your workmates of all colours and nationalities for a strong socialist trade union movement. Or; support Powell and lose your jobs, your homes and your standard of living in a wave of racialist hysteria.

BLACK POWER MICHAEL

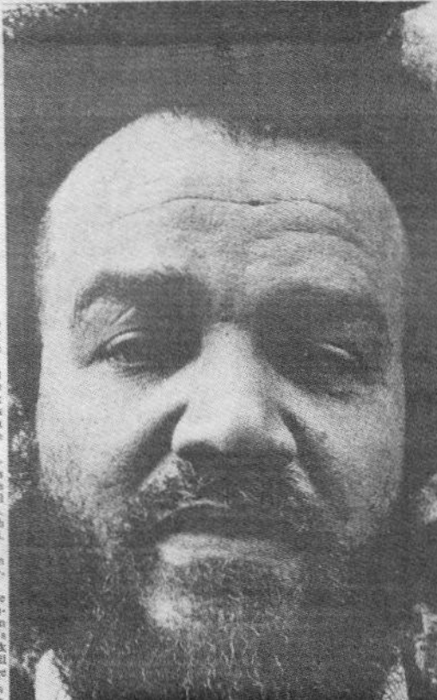

Michael X was pushed through the information media with hateful vengence. In his book " From Michael de Freitas to Michael X ", Michael Abdul Malik translates urban slavery in England, and back in Trinidad where the white capitalist subjects totally. From childhood to the present is a long time to live in chains. Michael X broke the chains here in England—in the heart of the ghetto. Here he became conscious, and turned on the information media, using the same " fiction " Michael X.

Michael explains, more generously than most, and certainly with much more honesty and clarity, the events that led up to the change in his life. As hustler in Ladbroke Grove he watched police, racketeers, landlords, and Kensington Borough Council, all release the iron grip of death at the throat of the black man.

The many-sided guillotine sliced into the flesh that was misery, the beds of misery, the streets of misery at miserable hours, day and night.

He asked " Why?" Not until he met Malcolm X did he start his trip along the road to self-liberation. Why? The black man has always been the white man's labour force ever since the black man set eyes upon the white man and tasted the " bit " of slavery in his jaw-bones.

The one group of black men who successfully resisted chains were the pigmies and they ate the white man on sight. It is no coincidence that the white peoples all over the world feared Mau Mau so much. Kenyatta used the one weapon which capitalists have always feared—canibalism.

These and other historical facts from the black man's culture Michael X understood.

Obviously such a man quickly became the enemy of the Establishment—particularly when he showed such dexterity in bringing 900 black workers at Courtauld's factory in Preston out on strike. Any black man with this power is the enemy of all white racists, and it's common knowledge that nearly 100 per cent of the people in England are racists, either consciously or unconsciously.

At this point the press painted Michael X as the devil himself. It's curious how these things happen. When the pigmy set eyes on the white man the pigmy said " There is the devil " and ate him. Mankana, the first Black Nationalist in Southern Africa who has the dubious honour of being the first black man to rot in Robin Island Prison in South Africa in the 18th Century, said exactly the same thing. He also said Africa would never be free until the white man is driven back into the sea from whence he came.

Michael X simply said that the white man was a racist, and that any time he dishes out violence to the black man, the black man should hand it back " tit for tat."

The mass media turned him on viciously and then left the pressmen to give evidence and the jury of racists to convict.

But time is longer than rope. Even now this book stands as a record to the humanity of Michael Abdul Malik. He writes, calmly, incident after incident, with humour, care and understanding—it is clear that he pities " whitey," that he spends a lot of time with " whitey " trying to humanize " whitey." We all know that he failed to do the latter.

There is no attempt made in this book to deal with the greater issues which naturally most people secretly expected him to delve into, but looking at it subjectively why should any black man give information to people who are going to use it against him? It's probably best that he explained himself and not the wider issues concerning the black struggle to finally free black from white economic slavery. Every man has a right to speak, even Enoch Powell (thanks Enoch for helping to unite more and more black people) whom everyone who lives off black blood eagerly agrees with.

As one man said " I don't know why those dockers are getting heated because the blacks will end up doing their jobs for less money, which will ease us out of our difficulties and set this country back on its feet . . . "—was Michael X wrong?

" From Michael de Freitas to Michael X," published by Deutsch 25s.

THE HUSTLER

Cybernetic Serendipity

the computer and the arts

held at the Institute of Contemporary Arts Nash House, The Mall, London S.W.1 August 2—October 20, 1968 Organized by Jasia Reichardt

There are three sorts of exhibits: 1, very good IBM models (with earphones) demonstrating how computers work; 2, artworks produced by machines; these include drawings, there are numerous machines (computers down to Meccano) producing curved-line patterns. More visually developed are the film cartoons (especially the one by Stan Vanderbeek). There are also poems (and Manchester University Computer does love letters: 'Honey dear ... My fellow feeling breathlessly hopes for your dear eagerness.... yours wistfully, MUC'). There are fibreglass spheres for listening to taped electronic music; there is an amazing machine by Vladimir Ussachevsky that produces visual and audial variations on tunes whistled into its mike. There are TV pictures, some reacting to sound impulses, others to forms of mechanical interference. 3, machines that are artworks in themselves; they include strobe-lit sound-vibrated metal rods; a mechanical flower that tosses when you speak to it, 7-foot radio-controlled Rosa Bosom who shrieks and swipes at people with her red foam-plastic lips, and, also by Bruce Lacey, a sex simulator (3½-minute treatment) and a photosensitive owl....

In conception and layout the exhibition is like a funfair with an arbitrary assortment of sideshows. It demonstrates that cybernetic machines are a drag in finite art situations where they merely take over a human activity (as in drawing and writing). On the other hand, where there is interaction with people and with other events, they are capable of infinite development.

Biddy Peppin IT

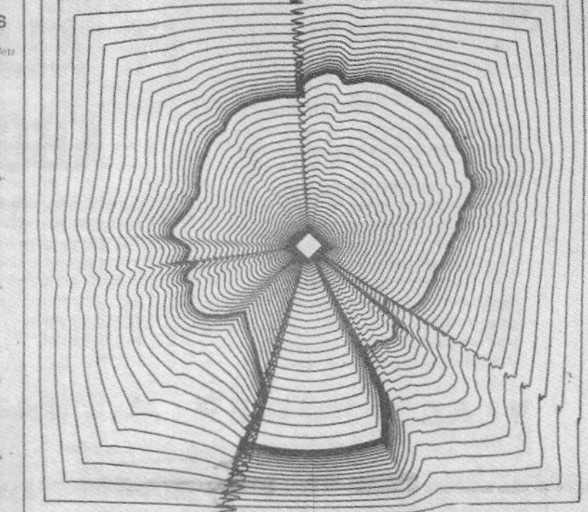

A computer metamorphosis. A square is transformed into a profile of a woman and then back into a square

jollymerry
hollyberry
jellyberry
merryholly
happyjolly
jollyjelly
jellybelly
bellymerry
hollyhappy
jollyholly
marryJerry
happyBarry
heppyJarry
boppyheppy
berryjerry
jerryjolly
moppyjelly
Mollymerry
Jerryjolly
bellyboppy
jerryhoppy
hollymeppy
Barrymerry
Jarryhappy
happyboppy
boppyjolly
jollymerry
merrymerry
merrymerry
merryChris
ammerryasa
Chrismerry
asMERRYCHR
YSANTHEMUM

Computer's first Christmas card

Kennedy in a dog

Data from a photograph of Kennedy is inserted into data from a photograph of a dog. The final output looks like the face of Kennedy in the shape of a dog's head. Thus there are three contributing elements: Kennedy, dog and the square which forms the element of the overall pattern.

Idea by Masao Komura, programme by Fujio Niwa (CTG)

Computer art

A fascinating experiment was made by Michael Noll of the Bell Telephone Laboratories whereby he analysed a 1917 black-and-white plus-and-minus picture by Mondrian and produced a number of random computer graphics using the same number of horizontal and vertical bars placed within an identical overall area. He reported that 59% of the people who were shown both the Mondrian and one of the computer versions preferred the latter, 28% identified the computer picture correctly, and 72% thought that the Mondrian was done by computer. The experiment is not involved either with proof or theory, it simply provides food for thought.

Jasia Reichardt

A 35-mm transparency is made from a photo of some real-world object and scanned by a machine similar to a television camera. The resultant electrical signals are converted into numerical representations on magnetic tape. This provides a digitized version of the picture for computer processing.

COMPUTER
Any system which operates on information to produce an output.

Piet Mondrian's *Composition with lines* 1917

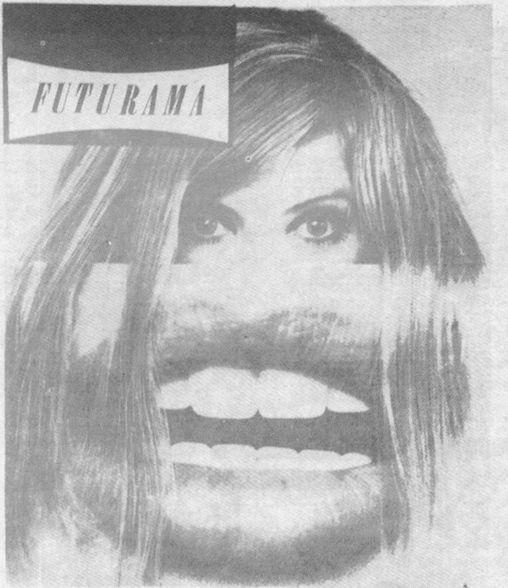

Where Movies Are Heading

EVER since I read, in 1960, an article written by Norman Bel Geddes in 1930 predicting what life would be like thirty years from then, I've been leary of the crystal-ball technique of looking into the future. Science had indeed, as Bel Geddes anticipated, changed the future, but not at all in the direction he had expected. Most of his suggestions seemed irrelevant to life as it was lived at the beginning of the sixties. So I wouldn't like to predict what cinema will be thirty years from now. But a look into the seventies, and the direction the film is now taking, should be easier.

One safe prediction, there will still be a large audience for the middle-aged entertainments on the order of "The Sound of Music" or the movies of Elvis Presley. I don't know anyone who really enjoyed the former or who now goes to see the latter. But both are money-makers. They attract. Mainly because of their traditional elements. Because they assume a safe, unquestioning, set of values. They're part of the backward-looking cinema. And this is where 90% of film is based. It's the other 10% that explores the interesting possibilities.

The screens will get larger, and going to the movies will be more a wraparound experience. As it is we are already — in California, at least — dealing with a post-movie generation. One which takes movie's magic for granted, and demands more than flickerings on a sheet. To them the single-screen movie is becoming as antiquated as the theater's proscenium arch. Visual perceptions increase with each generation, I'm sure. Those of us born to those who went early to the movies see more quickly, over a wider spectrum, than the pre-movie generations.

Kids who now have a television screen flickering across their consciousness before they can even speak, will have a greater visual command than we did. The potential movie audience coming up is already educated, visually, way beyond what is being offered to them in most movies.

To catch and keep this audience (48% of current film admissions are from the 16-24 age group, a segment of the population which is numerically growing all the time) the movies will have to burst their present frame-lines. They've already started. The newest trend in HOllywood ("Grand Prix," "The Boston Strangler," "The Thomas Crown Affair") is to parallels of action across screens split into multi-images.

But the trend to bigness isn't something new. During the fifties, threatened by Tv, that's the way the movies chose to go. But once the thrill of CinemaScope, Cinerama, and the rest had worn off the audience realized they were being given nothing new, just inflated versions of those same fluorescent old fantasies they'd been retreating from. But now there's evidence of expanded visions to match expanded screens. Otherwise it's going to be just another gimmicky technique (like 3-D, 4-D, Smell-O-Vision, and the like) quickly forgotten.

The cinema has always been laggardly in taking up its visionaries' fresh ideas. In 1900, for instance, Raoul Grimoin-Sanson originated Cineorama for the Paris Exposition. This stood its audience in the center of a balloon-shaped structure and, with the aid of ten projectors, beamed on to the walls, persuaded them they were flying through the air. From there it took fifty years for Cinerama to discover roller-coasters. But there are signs the lessons of EXPO 67 have been more quickly learned. Film is, once more, aiming at a total sensory experience.

***But the most hopeful trend, accelerating through the sixties, has been the use of film as luminal rather than literary art.** For most of its history film has aimed for wholeness of structure, a smoothness of surface, but now the best of modern film is reversing. Because they are dealing with a world, a culture, characters and themes, that are fragmented, disassociated, fractured, and alienated, the best movies no longer insist on formal structures.*

"There are no disciplines, only vestiges of disciplines: no forms, only vestiges of forms," the critic, Harold Rosenberg, wrote not long ago. He was referring to current movements in art, but he could just as well have been discussing film. The legacies of Dadaism, of surrealism, are scattered across the modern movie as they are across the other arts. A deliberate noncontinuity has spread down to the tackiest of commercial movies.

The influences of Jean-Luc Godard, currently the most powerful force in film, have reached down to the lowest levels of cinema. The copyists have the superficialities of his style, the bits of jump-cutting and the shudder of hand-held cameras, but without really reproducing the essentials of Godard, that he is experimenting with the form in order to make it an adequate vehicle for his ideas (Godard is a film-philosopher rather than just another filmaker). The copyists seem most active in England at the present time. Clive Donner, John Schlesinger, Michael Winner, achieve a surface sixties look on what is, basically, fifties material.

Even Richard Lester, with his rag-bag of styles which has not yet been integrated into an authentic, personal style (and I haven't yet seen "Petulia" which comes closer, I understand, to capturing the sensibility of the sixties than do his earlier movies) is still only a popularizer of other people's good ideas. But a lot of what is being done is more than the same tired old cliches, re-assembled in a different way.

"2001, A Space Odyssey" has been roughed up by the majority of American critics, who approached it gingerly as narrative rather than interpretative cinema. But Kubrick's masterpiece, visionary and expansive where most of film is still conventional and circumspect, is futuristic in more than its subject. It is the first ten-million dollar avant-garde movie spectacle (and that Ed Emshwiller anticipated a lot of its ideas in his masterpiece, "Relativity," doesn't alter the fact). And the public is buying.

Those critics, incidentally, who were baffled by Kubrick's movie, are the very same who, last year, missed the significance of Roger Corman's "The Trip." The important thing about that movie was not whether it gave a valid reconstruction of a LSD trip (which it didn't, particularly, although Corman says he took acid under medical supervision before he made the movie) but that it was the first Hollywood film in recent memory to be structured entirely on its visuals.

The American avant-garde cinema, in which painters and sculptors bulk so large, has been using film as a plastic rather than a narrative art for the last ten years or more. Form, color, texture, movement, pattern, these are the basis on which they work. At first in a splendid, and largely self-sought, isolation. But while this revelatory free-style is still, I think, the most fruitful movement in the modern film, their work has been plagiarised by the makers of Tv commercials (there is a cult, presumably by those who can't take ideas at first-hand but must have them conventionalized, of excessive admiration for Tv's commercial breaks) and, from there, borrowed back by commercial film. The influence ofthe underground filmaker is being felt by movie audiences who've never been near an underground film.

Ambiguity is the basis of most modern art, ambiguity is the basis of the best modern cinema. The collages, assemblages, juxtapositions of the avant-garde cinema, the iconographies of the most personal of its commercial form, have more in common than either camp are often willing to admit. The cinema of Breer, Baillie, Brakhage, Conner, Emshwiller, Vanderbeek, Warhol is not too disruptively distant from that of Godard, Fellini, Antonioni, Bunuel, Bergman, Bellochio, Bertolucci. A fusion of all these forward-looking elements is, I think, going to be the great development of the seventies.

RICHARD WHITEHALL

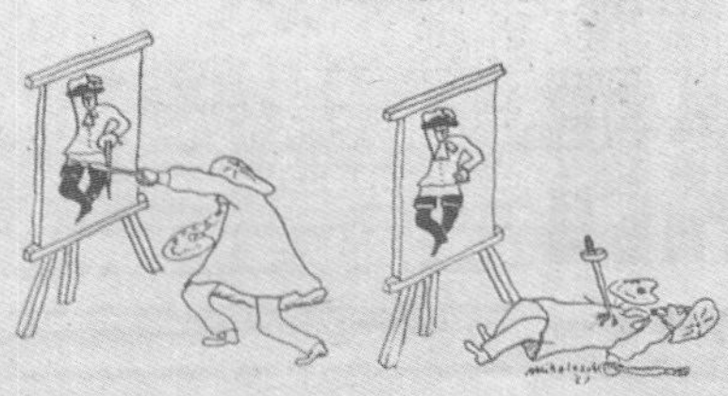

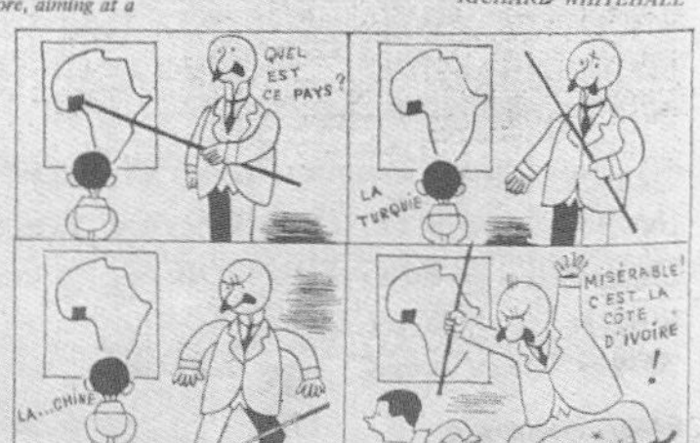

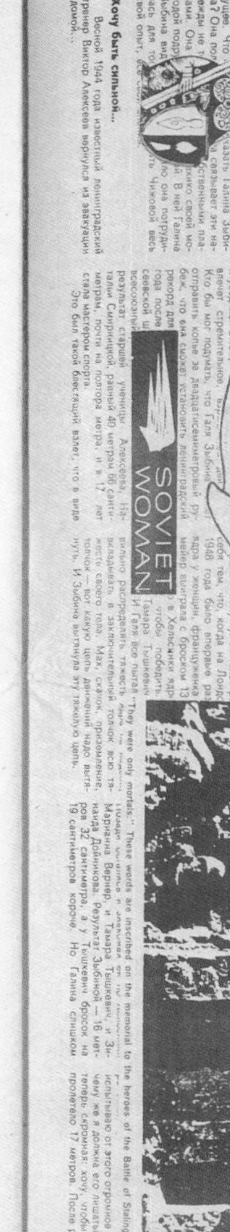

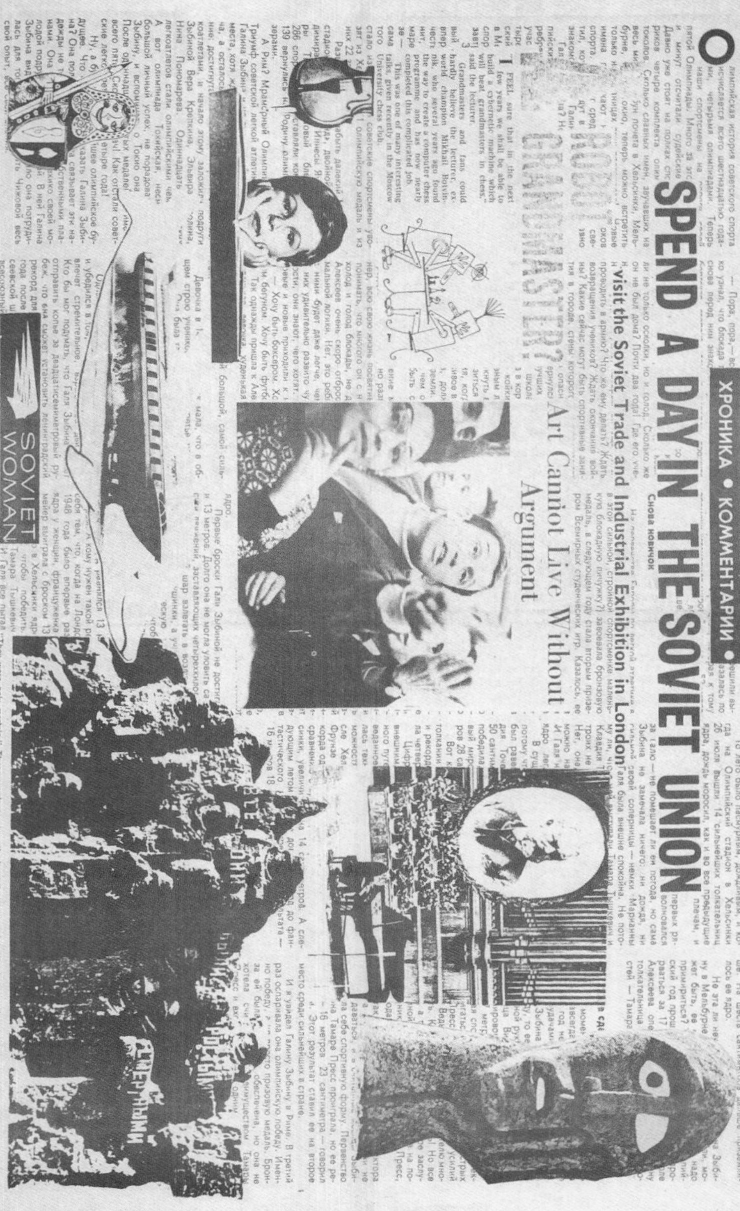

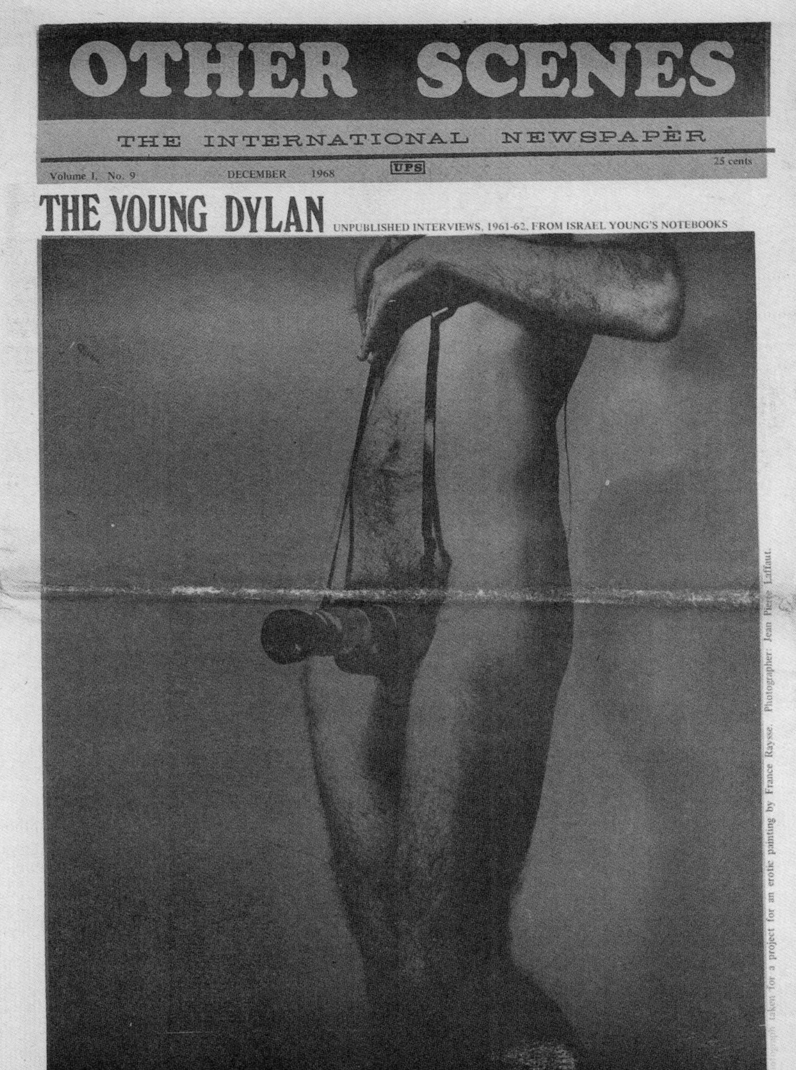

KEN WEAVER

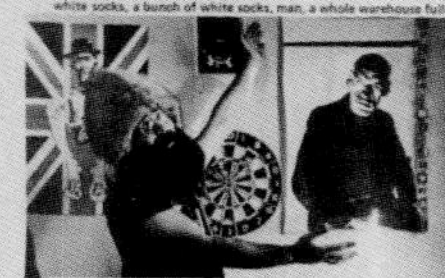

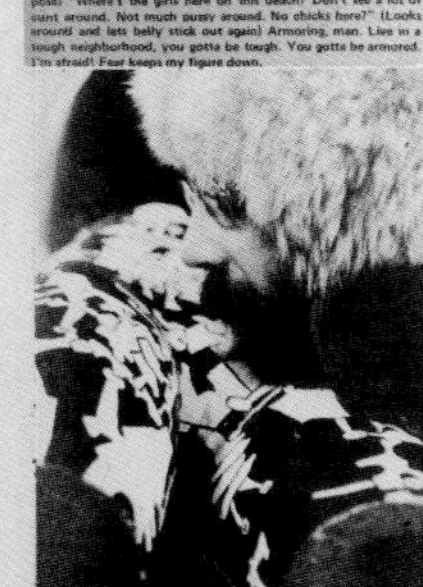

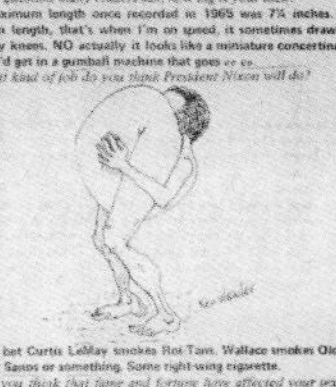

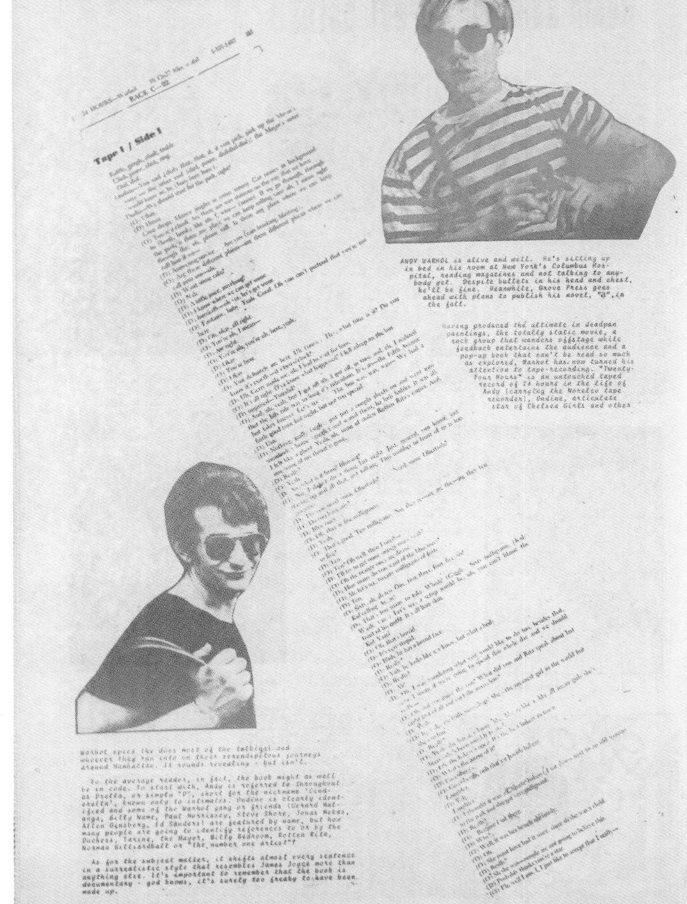

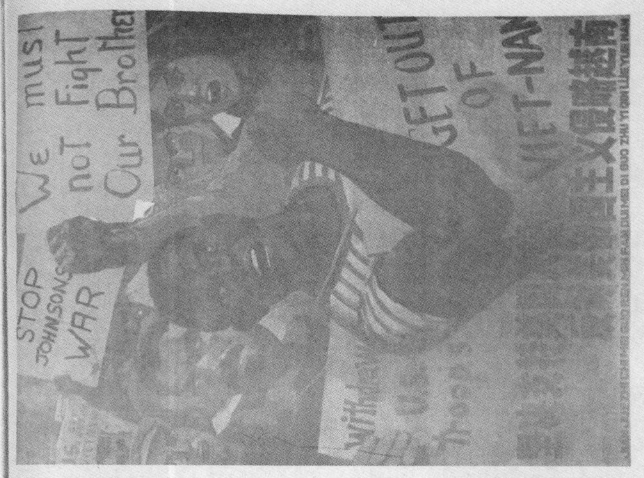

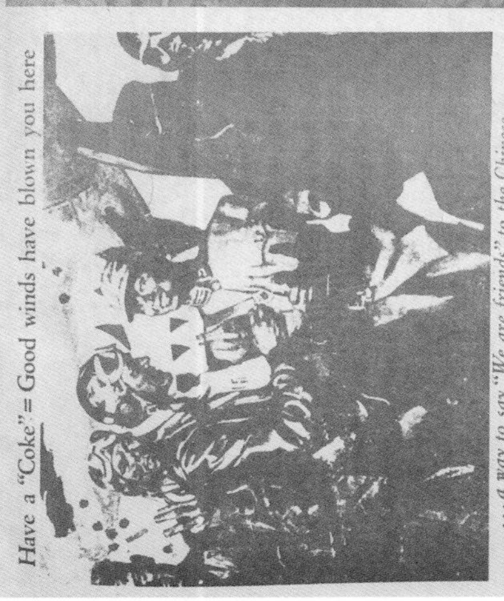

Have a "Coke" = Good winds have blown you here

…a way to say "We are friends" to the Chinese

Previous page
Other Scenes (New York), September 1968, vol. 1, no. 6, cover
Other Scenes (New York), September 1968, vol. 1, no. 6, spread
Other Scenes (New York), September 1968, vol. 1, no. 6, spread

Other Scenes (New York), December 1968, vol. 1, no. 9, cover
Other Scenes (New York), December 1968, vol. 1, no. 9, back cover
Other Scenes (New York), August 1968, vol. 2, no. 5, spread

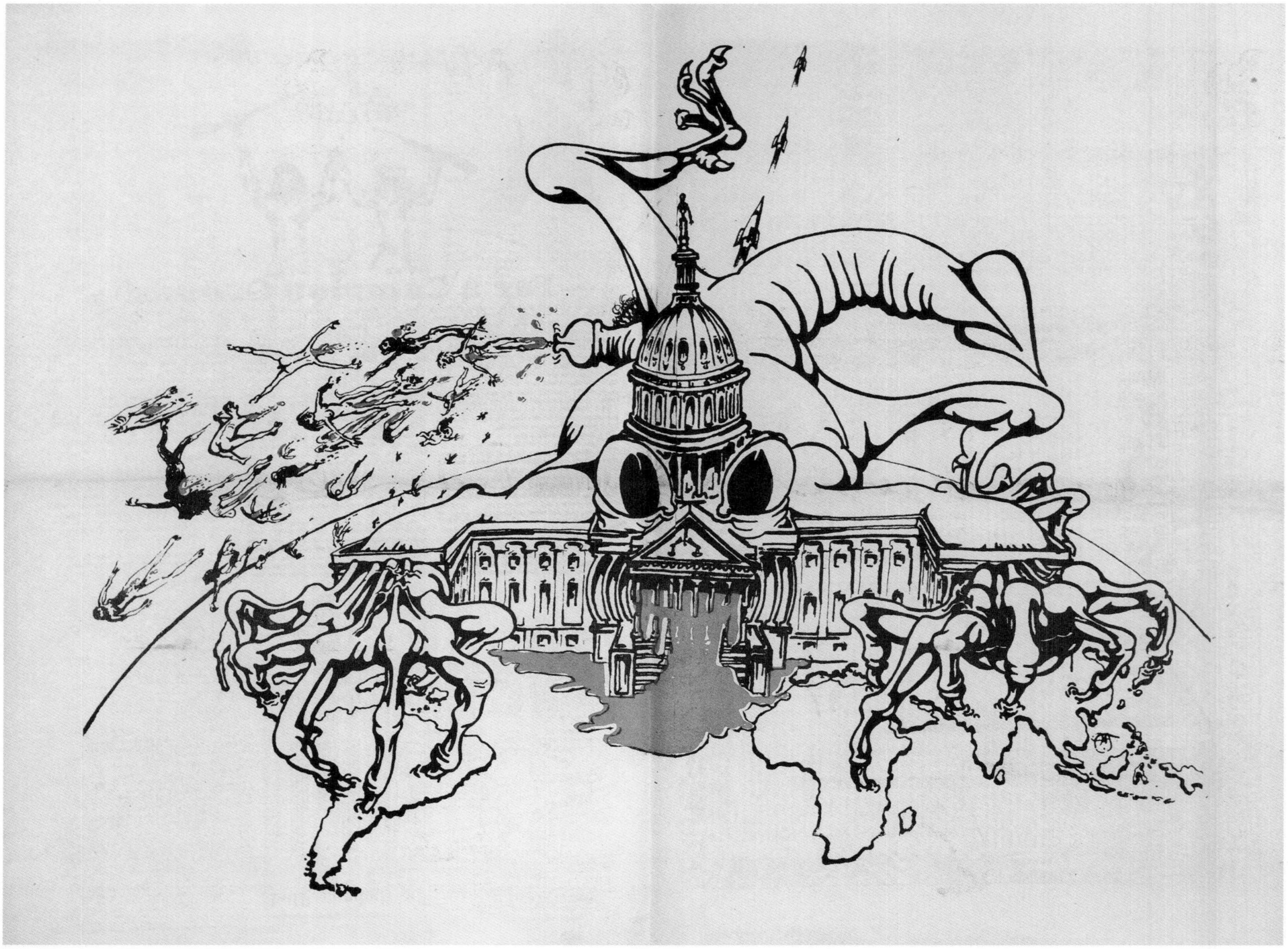

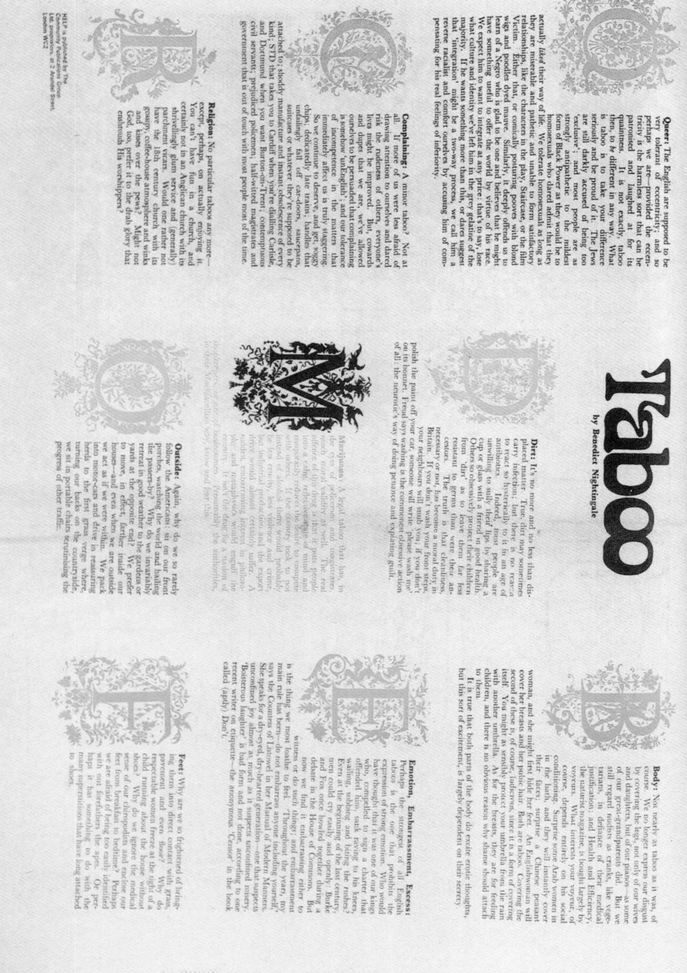

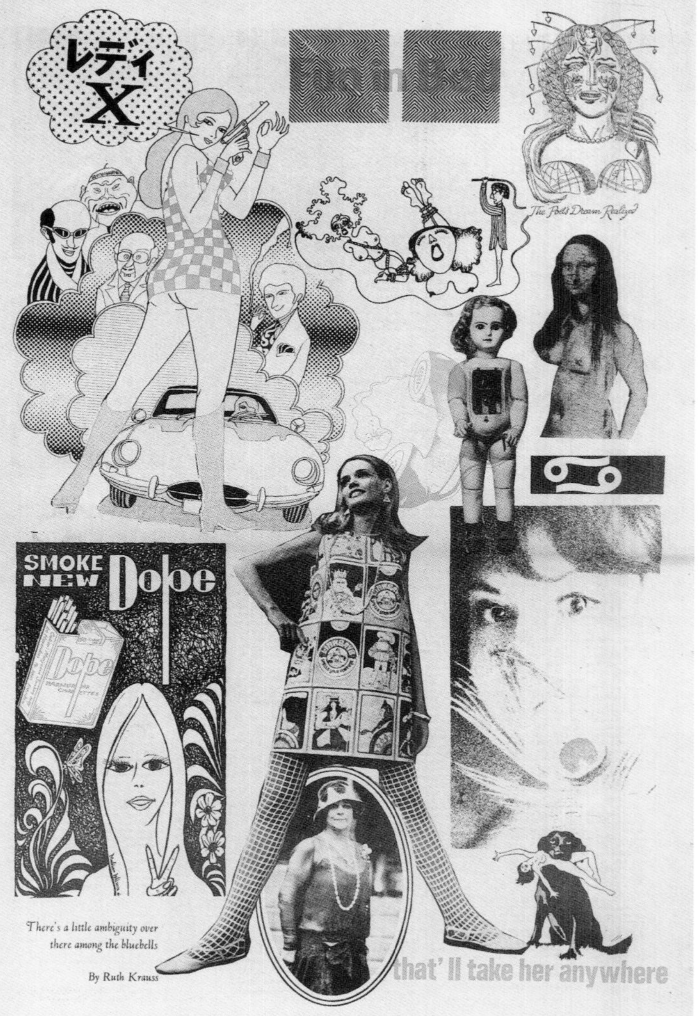

Other Scenes (New York), January 1969, vol. 1, no. 10, center spread

Other Scenes (New York), March 1969, vol. 3, no. 3, center spread

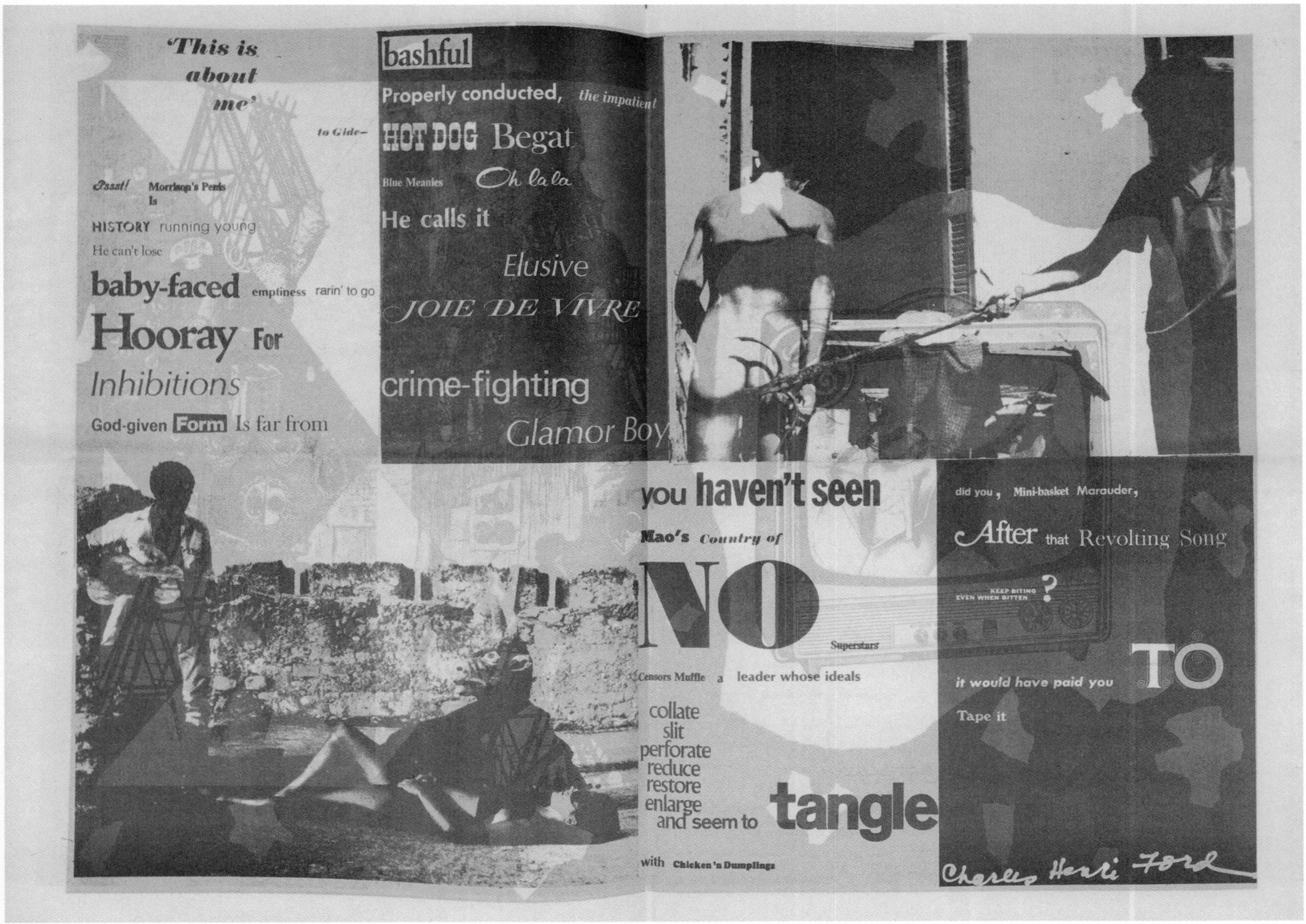

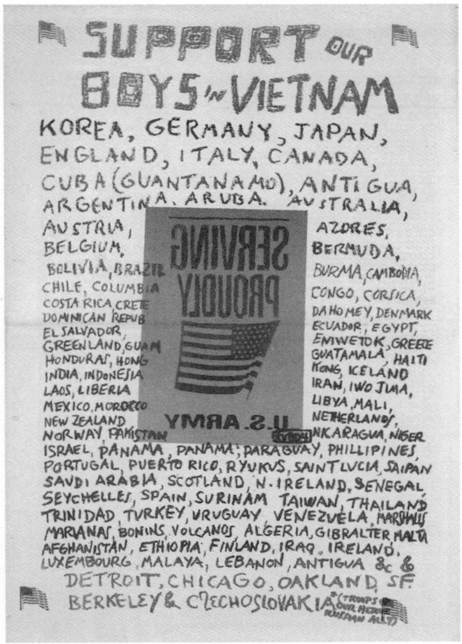

'This is about me'
to Gide–
Psssst! Morrison's Penis Is
HISTORY running young
He can't lose
baby-faced emptiness rarin' to go
Hooray For
Inhibitions
God-given Form Is far from

bashful
Properly conducted, the impatient
HOT DOG Begat
Blue Meanies Oh la la
He calls it
Elusive
JOIE DE VIVRE
crime-fighting
Glamor Boy

you haven't seen
Mao's Country of
NO
Superstars
Censors Muffle a leader whose ideals
collate
slit
perforate
reduce
restore
enlarge
and seem to tangle
with Chicken 'n Dumplings

did you, Mini-basket Marauder,
After that Revolting Song
KEEP BITING EVEN WHEN BITTEN ?
it would have paid you TO
Tape it
Charles Henri Ford

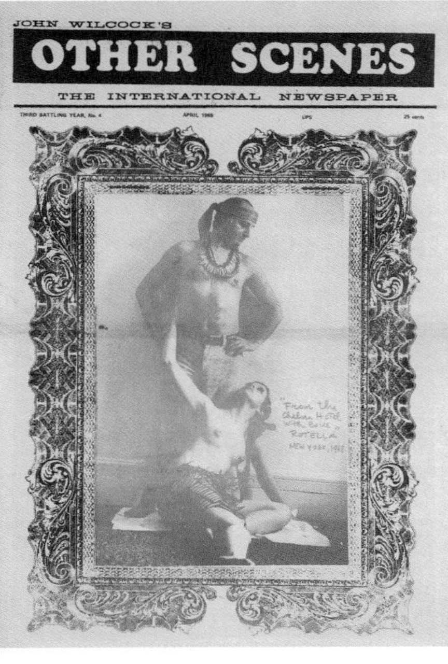

SUPPORT OUR BOYS IN VIETNAM
KOREA, GERMANY, JAPAN, ENGLAND, ITALY, CANADA, CUBA (GUANTANAMO), ANTIGUA, ARGENTINA, ARUBA, AUSTRALIA, AUSTRIA, AZORES, BELGIUM, BERMUDA, BOLIVIA, BRAZIL, BURMA, CAMBODIA, CHILE, COLUMBIA, CONGO, CORSICA, COSTA RICA, CRETE, DAHOMEY, DENMARK, DOMINICAN REPUB, ECUADOR, EGYPT, EL SALVADOR, ENIWETOK, GREECE, GREENLAND, GUAM, GUATAMALA, HAITI, HONDURAS, HONG KONG, ICELAND, INDIA, INDONESIA, IRAN, IWO JIMA, LAOS, LIBERIA, LIBYA, MALI, MEXICO, MOROCCO, NETHERLANDS, NEW ZEALAND, NICARAGUA, NIGER, NORWAY, PAKISTAN, ISRAEL, PANAMA, PANAMA, PARAGUAY, PHILLIPINES, PORTUGAL, PUERTO RICO, RYUKUS, SAINT LUCIA, SAIPAN, SAUDI ARABIA, SCOTLAND, N. IRELAND, SENEGAL, SEYCHELLES, SPAIN, SURINAM, TAIWAN, THAILAND, TRINIDAD, TURKEY, URUGUAY, VENEZUELA, MARSHALLS, MARIANAS, BONINS, VOLCANOS, ALGERIA, GIBRALTER, MALTA, AFGHANISTAN, ETHIOPIA, FINLAND, IRAQ, IRELAND, LUXEMBOURG, MALAYA, LEBANON, ANTIGUA &c &c
DETROIT, CHICAGO, OAKLAND, SF, BERKELEY & CZECHOSLOVAKIA
SERVING PROUDLY
U.S. ARMY

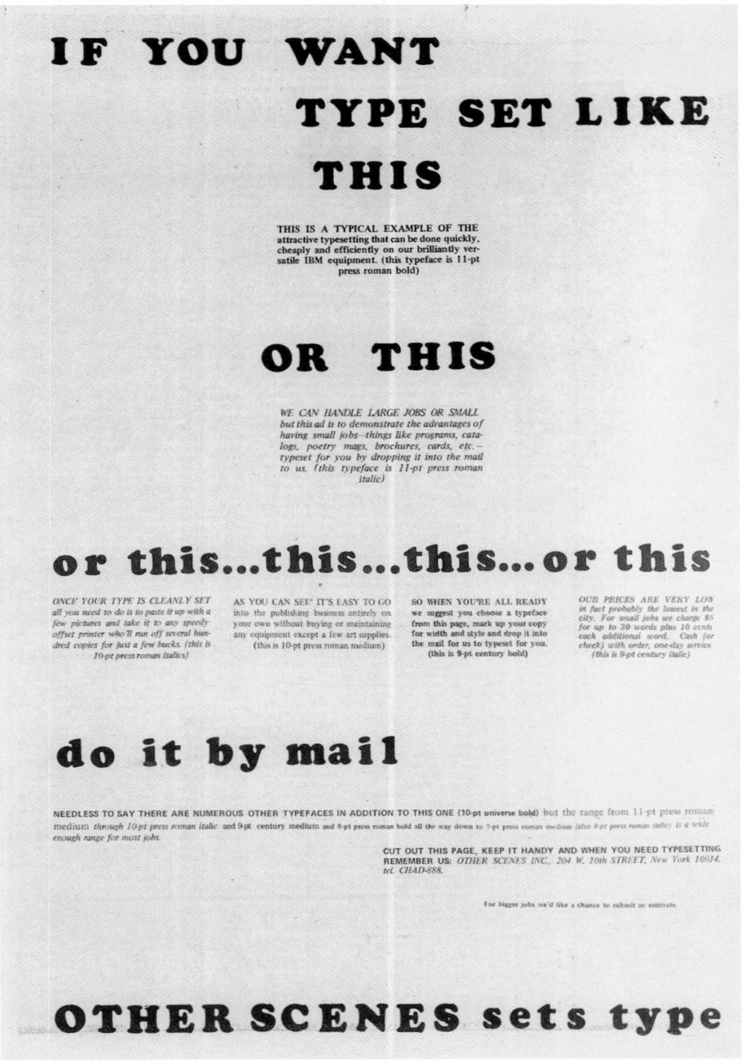

IF YOU WANT TYPE SET LIKE THIS

THIS IS A TYPICAL EXAMPLE OF THE attractive typesetting that can be done quickly, cheaply and efficiently on our brilliantly versatile IBM equipment. (this typeface is 11-pt press roman bold)

OR THIS

WE CAN HANDLE LARGE JOBS OR SMALL but this ad is to demonstrate the advantages of having small jobs—things like programs, catalogs, poetry mags, brochures, cards, etc.—typeset for you by dropping it into the mail to us. (this typeface is 11-pt press roman italic)

or this...this...this...or this

ONCE YOUR TYPE IS CLEANLY SET all you need to do is to paste it up with a few pictures and take it to any speedy offset printer who'll run off several hundred copies for just a few bucks. (this is 10-pt press roman italics)

AS YOU CAN SEE' IT'S EASY TO GO into the publishing business entirely on your own without buying or maintaining any equipment except a few art supplies. (this is 10-pt press roman medium)

SO WHEN YOU'RE ALL READY we suggest you choose a typeface from this page, mark up your copy for width and style and drop it into the mail for us to typeset for you. (this is 9-pt century bold)

OUR PRICES ARE VERY LOW in fact probably the lowest in the city. For small jobs we charge $5 for up to 30 words plus 10 cents each additional word. Cash (or check) with order, one-day service. (this is 9-pt century italic)

do it by mail

NEEDLESS TO SAY THERE ARE NUMEROUS OTHER TYPEFACES IN ADDITION TO THIS ONE (10-pt universe bold) but the range from 11-pt press roman medium *through 10-pt press roman italic* and 9-pt century medium and 8-pt press roman bold all the way down to 7-pt press roman medium *(also 8-pt press roman italic) is a wide enough range for most jobs.*

CUT OUT THIS PAGE, KEEP IT HANDY AND WHEN YOU NEED TYPESETTING REMEMBER US: *OTHER SCENES INC., 204 W. 10th STREET, New York 10014, tel. CHAD-888.*

For bigger jobs we'd like a chance to submit an estimate.

OTHER SCENES sets type

Other Scenes (New York), May 1969, vol. 3, no. 5, center spread
Other Scenes (New York), April 1969, vol. 3, no. 4, cover
Other Scenes (New York), April 1969, vol. 3, no. 4, back cover
Other Scenes (New York), 1969, vol. 3, no. 15, inside page, recto

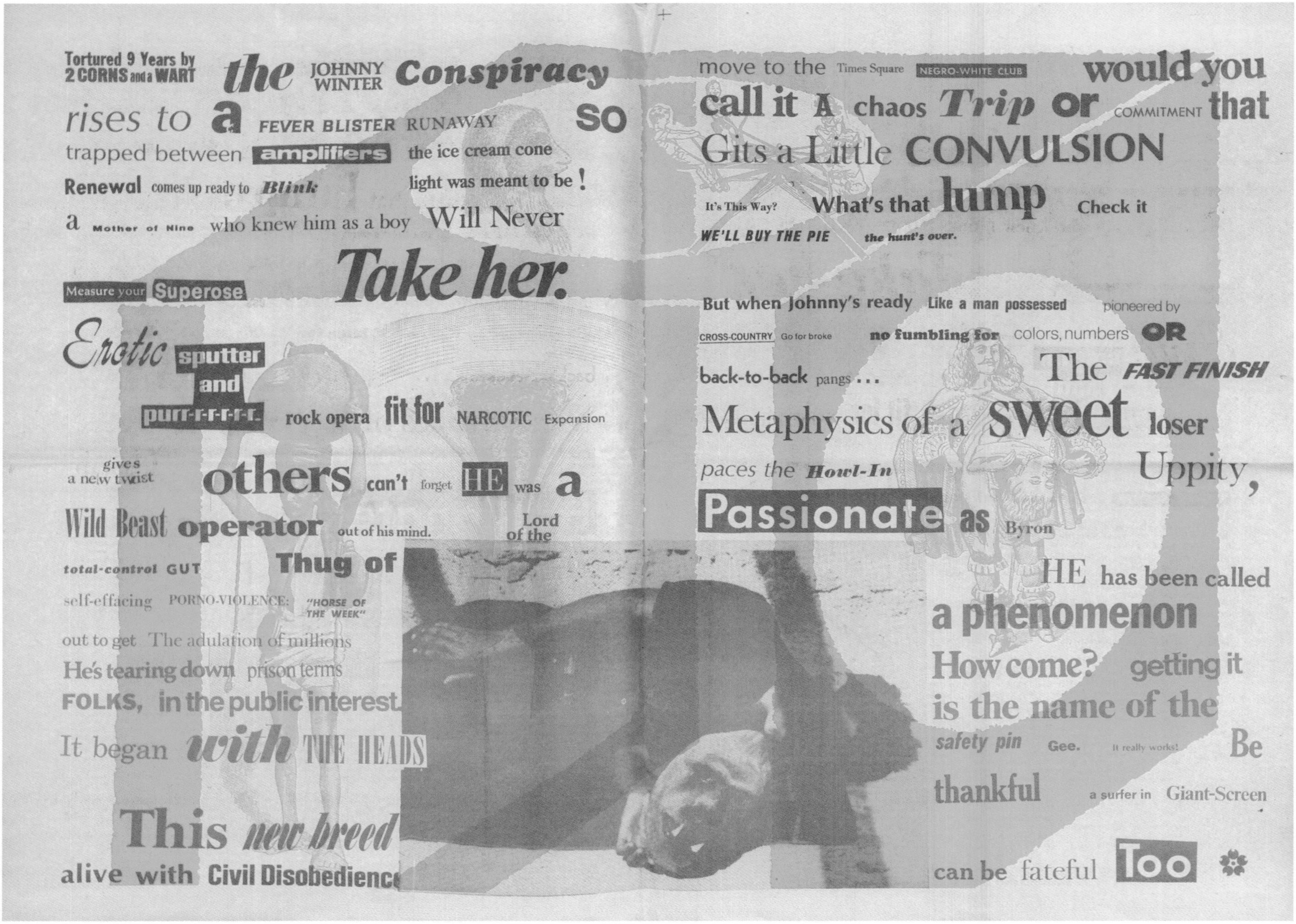

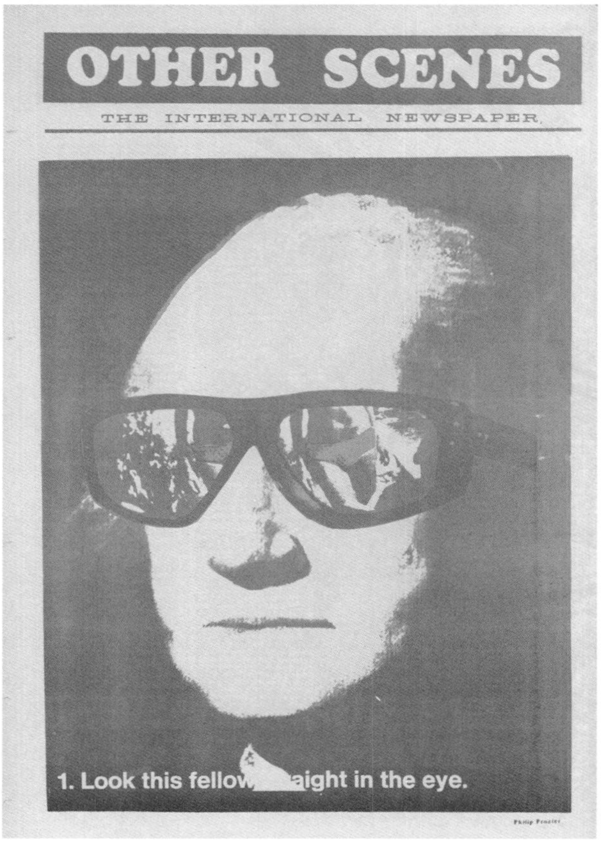

Tortured 9 Years by 2 CORNS and a WART the JOHNNY WINTER Conspiracy rises to a FEVER BLISTER RUNAWAY SO trapped between amplifiers the ice cream cone Renewal comes up ready to Blink light was meant to be ! a Mother of Nine who knew him as a boy Will Never

Take her.

Measure your Superose

Erotic sputter and purr-r-r-r-r. rock opera fit for NARCOTIC Expansion

gives a new twist others can't forget HE was a

Wild Beast operator out of his mind. Lord of the

total-control GUT Thug of

self-effacing PORNO-VIOLENCE: "HORSE OF THE WEEK"

out to get The adulation of millions

He's tearing down prison terms

FOLKS, in the public interest

It began with THE HEADS

This new breed

alive with Civil Disobedience

move to the Times Square NEGRO-WHITE CLUB would you call it A chaos Trip OR COMMITMENT that Gits a Little CONVULSION

It's This Way? What's that lump Check it

WE'LL BUY THE PIE the hunt's over.

But when Johnny's ready Like a man possessed pioneered by

CROSS-COUNTRY Go for broke no fumbling for colors, numbers OR

back-to-back pangs . . . The FAST FINISH

Metaphysics of a sweet loser

paces the Howl-In Uppity,

Passionate as Byron

HE has been called

a phenomenon

How come? getting it

is the name of the

safety pin Gee. It really works! Be

thankful a surfer in Giant-Screen

can be fateful Too ✿

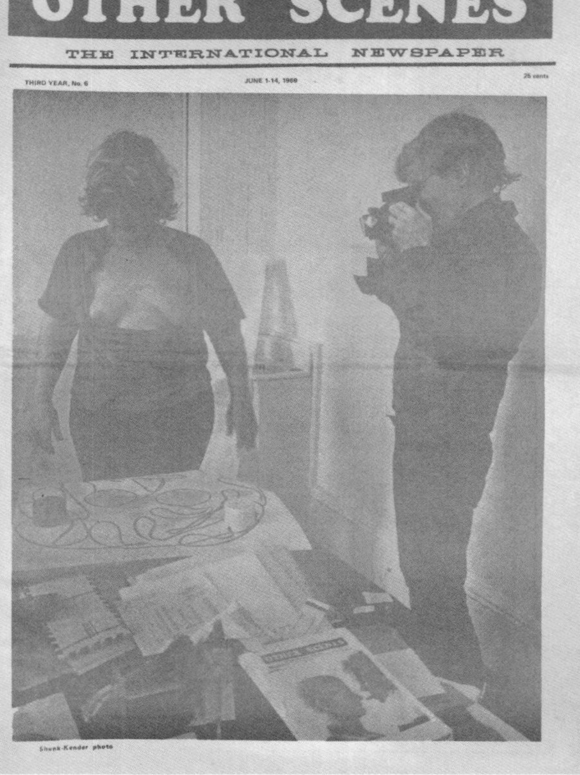

JOHN WILCOCK'S
OTHER SCENES
THE INTERNATIONAL NEWSPAPER
THIRD YEAR, No. 6 JUNE 1-14, 1969 25 cents

OTHER SCENES
THE INTERNATIONAL NEWSPAPER

1. Look this fellow [...]aight in the eye.

Other Scenes (New York), June 1969, vol. 3, no. 6, center spread
Other Scenes (New York), June 1969, vol. 3, no. 6, cover
Other Scenes (New York), 1969, vol. 3, no. 6, back cover

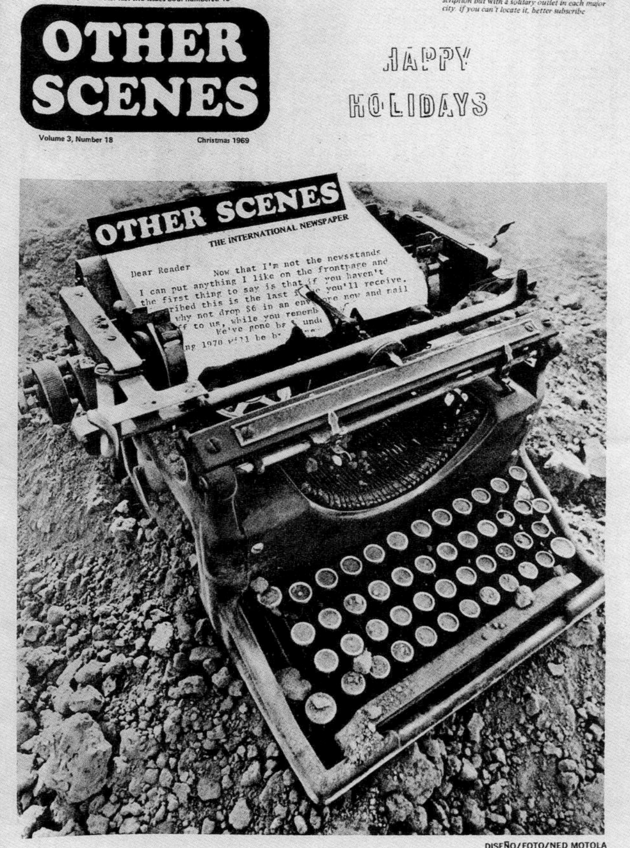

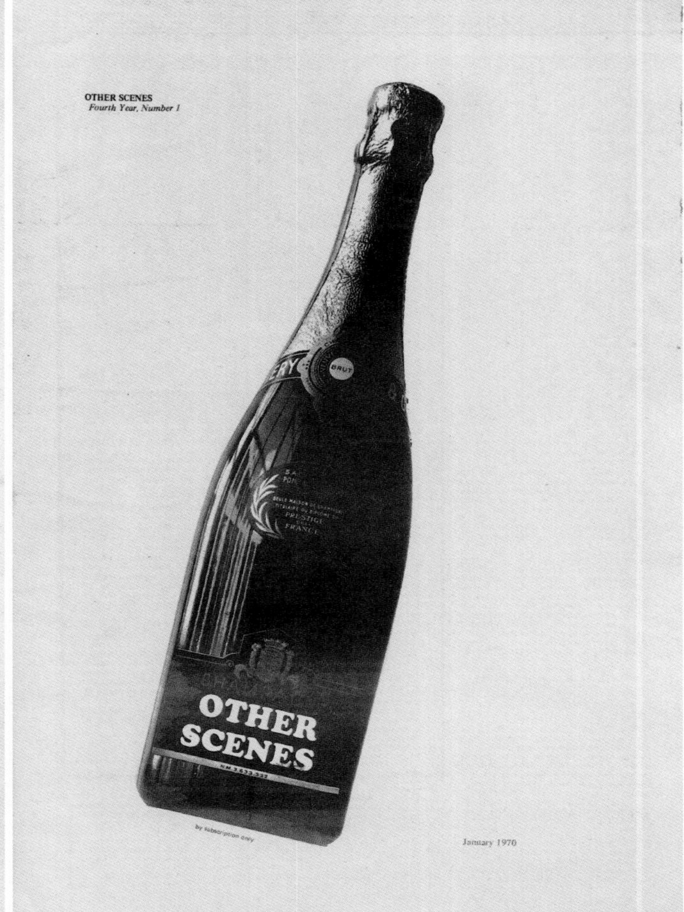

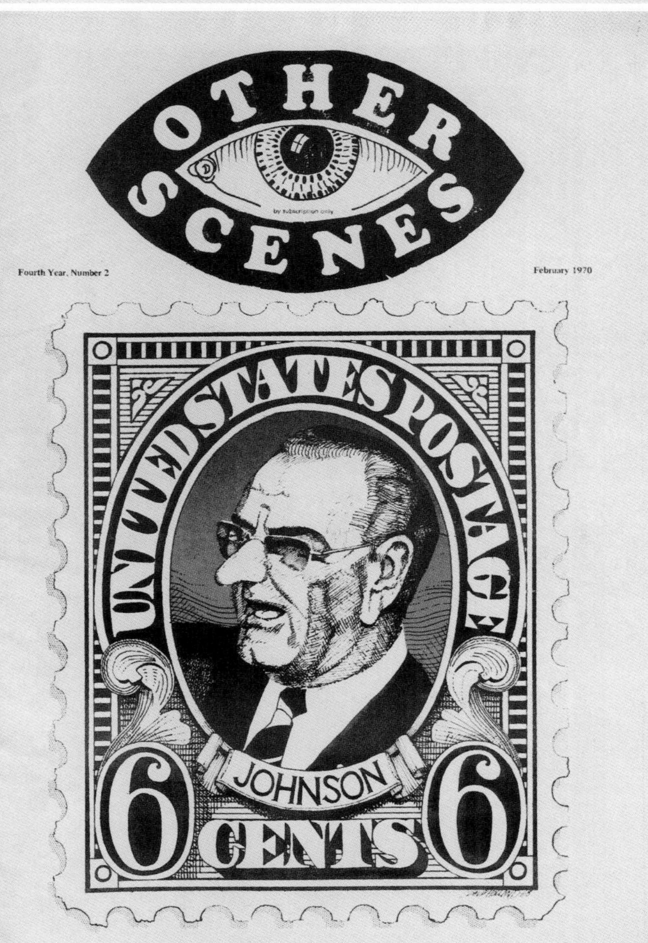

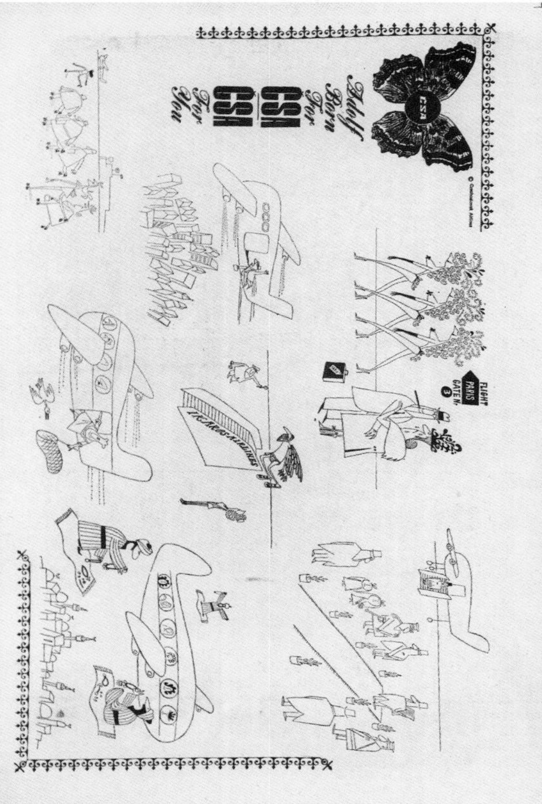

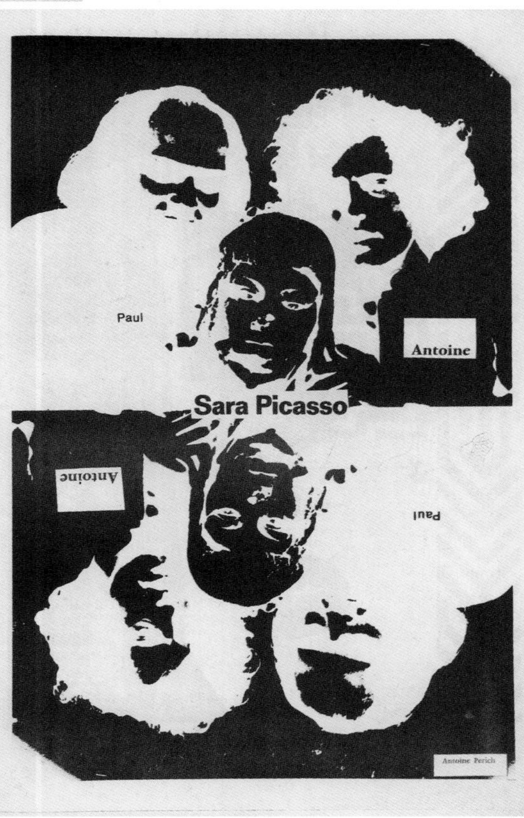

Other Scenes (New York), December 1969, vol. 3, no. 18, cover
Other Scenes (New York), January 1970, vol. 4, no. 1, cover
Other Scenes (New York), February 1970, vol. 4, no. 2, cover
Other Scenes (New York), February 1970, vol. 4, no. 2, spread

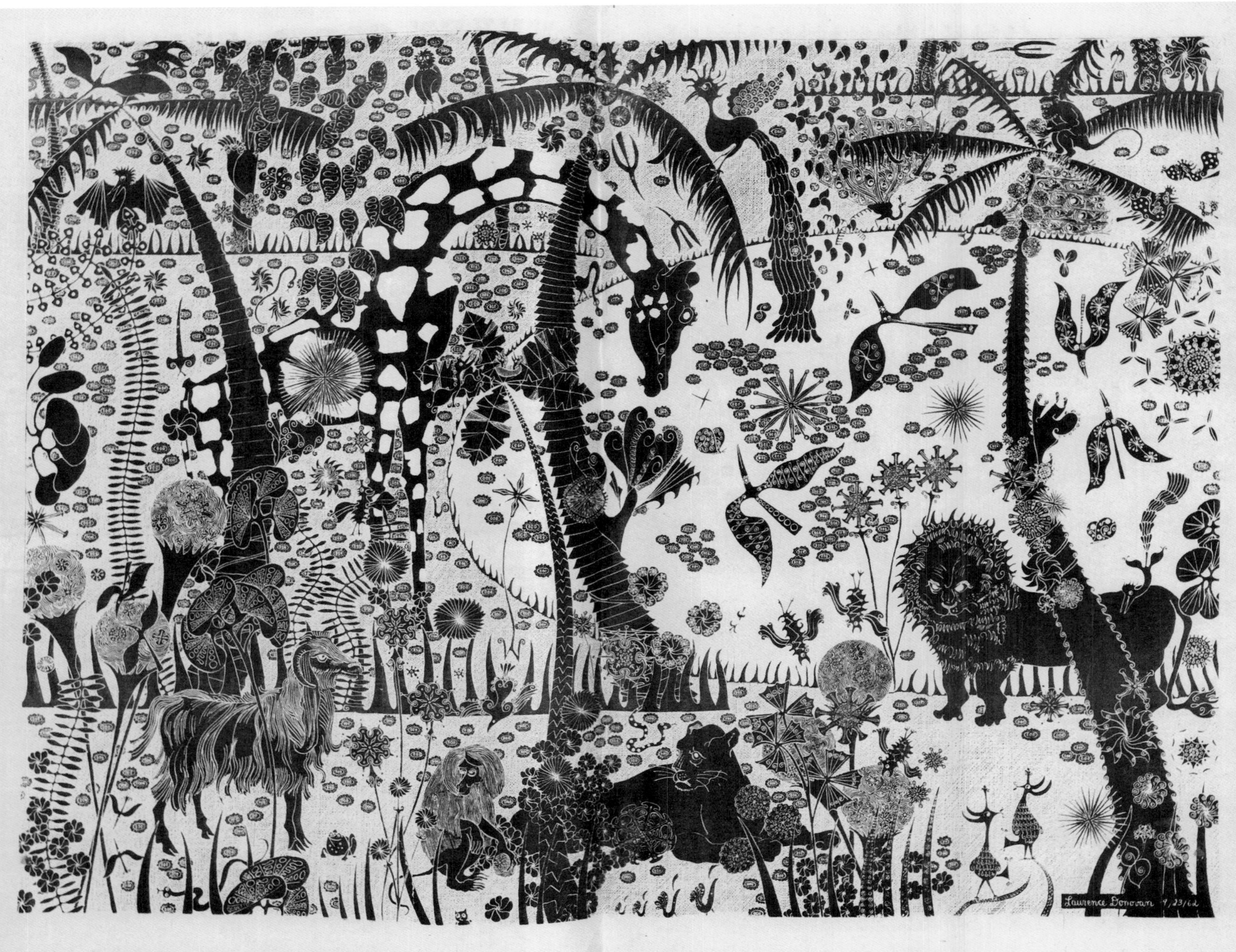

Other Scenes (New York), February 1970, vol. 4, no. 2, center spread

DA KIND MEN LIKED.

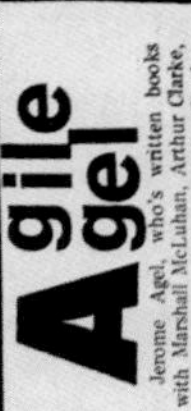

J. MORTIMER PRIKEETER *Presents* Hairbreadth HARRY in The Rescue

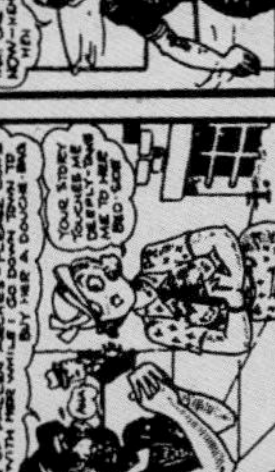

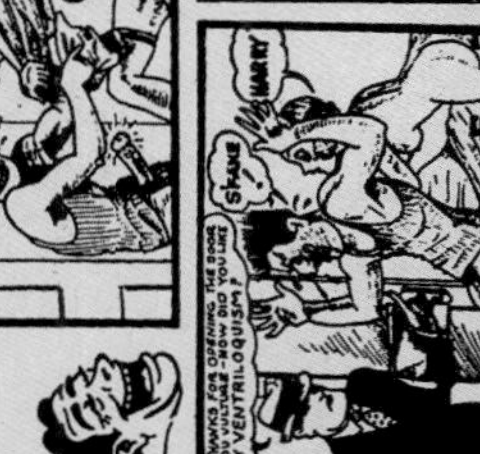

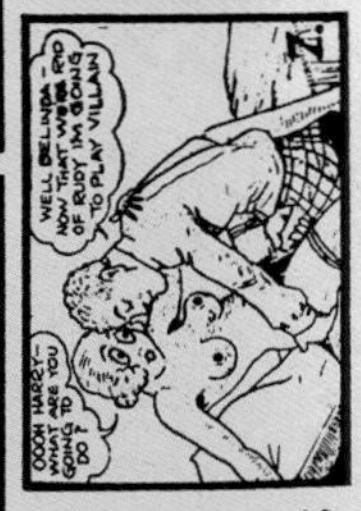

Sam & Janet Evening

THE early eight-page erotic comics which have created such a permanent impression on twentieth century American culture were distinguished by three factors, of which the foremost is the explicit depiction of sexual activities, forbidden despite the fact that they are personally familiar to most readers and conceptually familiar to all but the youngest child. The under-the-counter defiance which these comics represent was an avatar of the current growing insistence on the human right to present human activities without restriction.

Two other concepts make these comics important: their satirical stance and their format. Taking familiar personages (like gangsters, comic-strip characters and similar popular heroes) or situations (as in the example here, "The Rescue"), and introducing the sexual element often created a liberating effect exclusive of titillation by demonstrating the vacant and shopworn quality of approved or "wholesome" entertainment. The inclusion of realistic or cynical events or attitudes among the stereotypes accounts for much of their appeal. Thus in examples like "A Hasty Exit" (John Dillinger), criminals are shown to be attractive as well as menacing, and here, the motif of the lecherous villain, idiot hero and virginal heroine is exploded. This combination of social satire and artistic parody was a likely source for the inspiration of the popular publication *Mad*, which began as a comic book devoted to parodies of comic strips and books, and was a comparatively sophisticated version of the attack employed by the eight-pagers, although, of course, without the sexual emphasis.

The third quality of the eight-pagers lies in their format: the fact that they are comic *books*. The underground sources of these books makes it impossible to determine the date on which they were first introduced to the public, but their style and substance make it virtually certain that they pre-date the appearance, near the outbreak of World War II, of the legitimate, color, ten cent comics like *Famous Funnies* (newspaper reprints) and *Action Comics*. The transformation of the unwieldy, eminently disposable newspaper strips into the self-contained, compact, permanent and somehow more legitimate book form, which can be attributed with reasonable accuracy to the eight pagers, created a new medium, though, once again, "cleaned up" for distribution through legitimate channels.

"Hairbreadth Harry" is the prototype of exaggerated modern "speed demon" characters like Pancho "Speedy" Gonzales and Warner Brothers' Roadrunner. The name of the character is based on the increasingly self-conscious use of the device of the last minute rescue or "Hairbreadth" escape as it was employed in melodramas in the media of fiction, stage, and cinema.

The first panel of "The Rescue" shows a typical melodramatic situation, rendered ridiculous by Rudolph Razzendale's outlandish story and transparent disguise, and by Harry's unnoticed presence, which guarantees that the villain's plot will not succeed. The tactic of the villain who employs female impersonation is always thought-provoking, but seems to have been used here as a legitimate device in keeping with the villain's need to entice into his trap a heroine of discretion and purity. The stock motifs are continued in the second panel as Belinds remains ignorant of Rudolph's plan while he actually spouts of with "me proud beauty." Rudolph's literary mouthings continue unabated in panel three as he comes up with an exquisitely alliterative description of a seduction. Judging from Belinda's reply, his style is contagious.

Panel four gives us the incredibly lame ventriloquism routine for Harry's heroics, brilliantly rejoined by Rudolph's classic reworking of "Curses—foiled again." Once Rudolph is out of the picture, Harry begins to move into action (panel six). His reply to Belinda ("why speak of love when there's work to be done?") is something of a non-sequitur, but does serve to deflate the myth of asexual love which existed as a cultural stereotype. It is possible that Harry is stepping out of character to make a snide remark, but equally possible that he is still operating within the context of the attitudes which "The Rescue" is parodying, and that he represents the attitude that love and sex are unrelated phenomena. Harry removes his coat and hat only, and this is typical of eight-pager heroes who frequently engage in intense sexual activity while virtually clothed.

Of course the tunabout, the line that places the story in its proper context is Harry's "Now that we're rid of Rudy I'm going to play villain." Here it is demonstrated that the villain is at the core of every plot, that he is the springboard of the action, that, beneath the veneer of disapproval, he is the focal point of interest in every tale of threatened virtue. In Freudian terms, he represents the id, the heroine the ego and the hero the super-ego. Harry's last remark indicates a gain in perception through experience, as Belinda's reply confirms the readers' suspicions that innocence and virtue are most often hypocrisy and sham

The producer's pseudonym on the title page (try reading it aloud) casts a faint light on the world of these comics, where fellatio is a commonplace but cunnilingus, for whatever reason, is virtually unknown.

Agile Agel

Jerome Agel, who's written books with Marshall McLuhan, Arthur Clarke, Buckminster Fuller, and Stanley Kubrick, is now collaborating with William Shakespeare. Agel's latest, "Shakespeare's Complaint," is a series a one-liners right from the sex-drenched pages of the Bard of Stratford-on-Avon. Some examples:

"Soft! whether away so fast!"—Love's Labor Lost.

"He's sudden if a thing comes in his head."—Henry IV

"That Man that hath a tongue, I say, is no man, if with his tongue he cannot win a woman."—Two Gentlemen of Verona.

"A fair thought to lie between a maiden's head."—Hamlet.

"A little touch of Harry in the night."—Henry V.

"He makes me no more ado, but whips me out of his chamber."—Two Gentlemen of Verona.

Agel has two more books coming out in April: the 350-page original paperback, "The Making of Kubrick's 2001," will be published by New American Library, and the 192-page illustrated original paperback, co-authored with Buckminster Fuller, "I Seem To Be a Verb," will be published by Bantam (He's also contracted to co-author a book called Arthur C. Clarke Meets Hieronymus Bosch, collaborating with the celebrated science fiction writer.)

The "20001" work details how the $10.5 million production reached the screen and includes a portion of the original screenplay and pictures of scenes filmed but not included in the final print.

"I Seem To Be a Verb"—half of which is printed upside down—reflects the view that Spaceship Earth did not come with an operating manual. It also includes recent Fuller ideas, such as "It is possible that Charles Darwin was wrong. Man may have come to Earth from another planet. In Darwin's time, all the sciences were unsophisticated and Darwin had to base his theory of evolution on available information. Now there is different information, gained from nuclear physics, genetics, molecular chemistry. Archeologists keep finding examples of man having lived on Earth as long as four million years ago, but the evidence does not always indicate a more ape-like structure. Evolution may be going the other way—Niwrad—and it is possible that we may be making monkeys of ourselves."

---

14 story OF is a monster? Hi

If you have to reach a lot of people in a hurry, you have three alternatives.

In each woman's heart Four years ago, Eva sent her pupils out to explore Western Romans gave us the cornerstones Dormire come quando si era bambini.

August

Sie glaubte an seine Karriere

We will save out a dollar for you to live

Mann Männer

Barbara, this is embarrassing.

Few men knew Sir Winston Churchill

If this keeps up, pretty soon Carson McCullers won't have any flock of pigeons flying low over Grant's Tomb.

They think in billionths of a second.

Materasso granRiposo

the deserts, mountains and cliffs loved by artists

900-man unit at McCho Force Base near Seattle.

July

WELCOME HOME

We're human for better ideas when we win at Daytona. Darlington or Riverside a better idea you may not have real reason for. And let's face it, you don't come in first and champagne as the next guy to expect O more than good looks. So when you go out to Marquis Brougham track if your engines don't last.

pour « Révolution », constitue une autre pièce importante à ajouter au dossier de l'oppression nationale aux Etats-Unis.

June

ALL THE OFFSPRING OF THE MICE WERE BORN WITH DAMAGED BRAINS!

Phoning them all, which takes hours; writing them all, which takes days; which takes about five Christmas

By now you've been in and out of that you've got an hour living for other people 20 times, told a vacuum salesman

Two, two hundred, more than one person. We'll even keep a file. Your message can be anything.

New York: The Day Lost Whose Timetable?

OUT get out! Coming in

yes, yes, yes, yes

GABRIELE BENNETT

Other Scenes (New York), April 1970, vol. 4, no. 4, spread

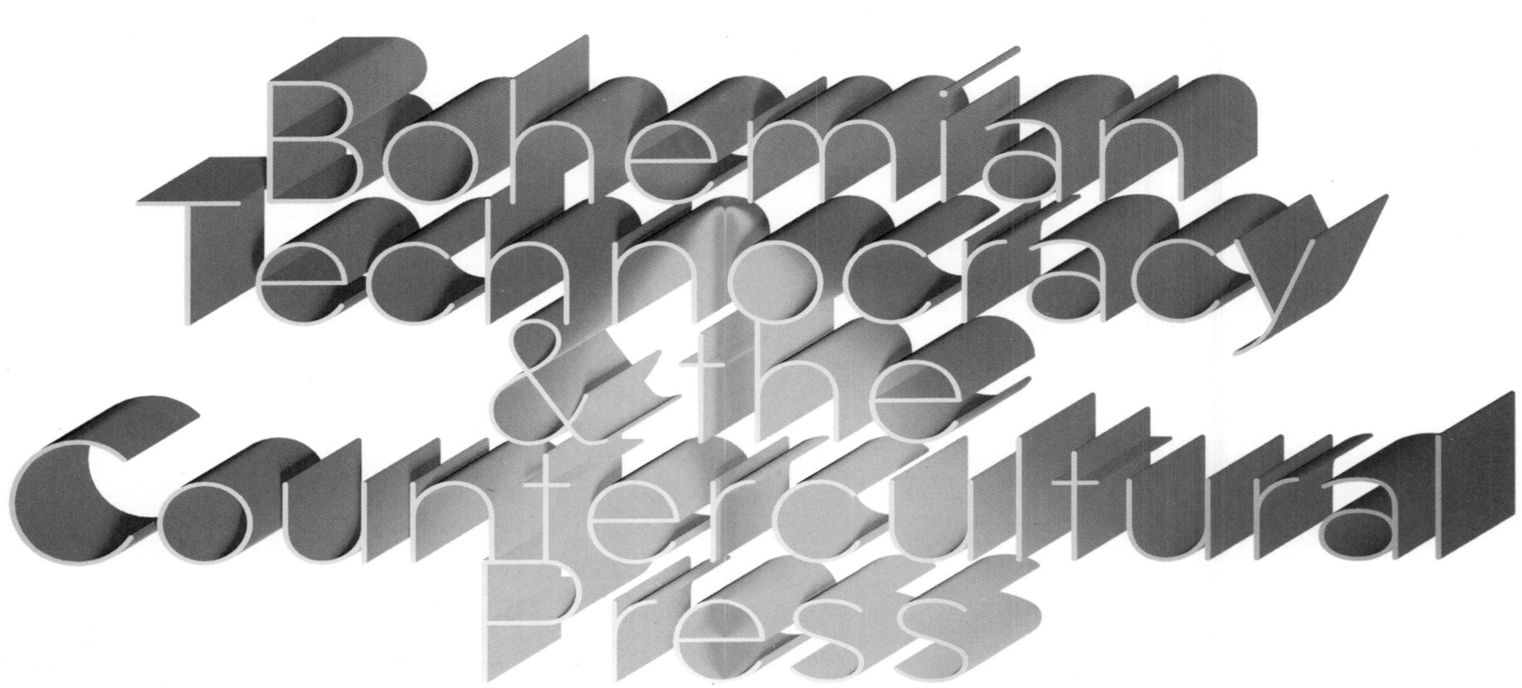

Fred Turner

IN 1973, EMINENT SOCIOLOGIST DANIEL BELL PUBLISHED A 507-PAGE VOLUME BUILT AND TITLED AROUND A SINGLE IDEA: ***The Coming of Post-Industrial Society*.** The high-industrial order that had dominated the nineteenth and early twentieth centuries was beginning to melt away, he claimed. In the past, men had wrestled with mechanical monsters on the floors of giant factories and sold the goods they made for profit. Now, Bell argued, the real money would be made through the application of scientific acumen to already existing ways of thinking and acting. Under the pressure of new forms of knowledge and new information technologies, manufacturing would give way to service industries; science would drive the invention of new devices; and finally, a new technocratic elite would take its place at the forefront of American society (fig. 4.1). According to Bell, the "axial principle" of the new order would be "theoretical knowledge"; its defining technology, the computer.[1]

On its face, Bell's account of new modes of labor and manufacturing would seem to have little to do with the rise of the American counterculture. After all, by the time Bell wrote his book, students had been marching against the military-industrial complex and its war in Vietnam for nearly a decade. Tens of thousands of young Americans had turned their backs on professional life entirely and packed themselves off to communes on the plains of Colorado and the hills of Vermont. Even Bell himself argued that the counterculture was a "counterfeit culture" and an attack on "a shared moral order."[2]

1. Daniel Bell, *The Coming of Post-Industrial Society: A Venture in Social Forecasting* (New York: Basic Books, 1973), p. xi.

2. Daniel Bell, "1978 Foreword," in *The Cultural Contradictions of Capitalism* (New York: Basic Books, 1996), p. xxvii.

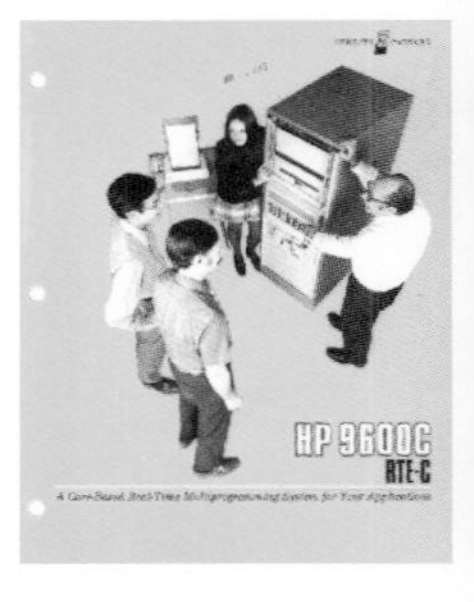

Fig. 4.1. **HP 9600C RTE-C: A Core-Based Real-Time Multiprogramming System for Your Applications** (Hewlett-Packard, 1973), cover

Yet, a closer look at two exceptionally influential publications of the era, the *Whole Earth Catalog* (fig. 4.2) and *Radical Software*, reveals a very different arrangement of forces. Far from rejecting mainstream culture, these two publications actually embraced its technocratic ideals, its faith in expertise, and even its information technologies. In their view, mainstream America offered a cornucopia of high-technology tools; given the proper instructions, readers could use these tools to transform their collective consciousness and thereby build a new, more collaborative society. Though it is tempting today to recall the youth movements of the 1960s as a single antinomian uprising, these publications remind us that at a fundamental level, parts of the counterculture were not countercultural at all. On the contrary: in the pages of the *Catalog* and *Radical Software* and their many imitators, the technocratic ideals of Daniel Bell's postindustrial society and the bohemian dreams of the counterculture became one.

THE *Whole Earth Catalog* AND THE DREAM OF BOHEMIAN TECHNOCRACY

To understand the appeal of this fusion, we need to return to Berkeley, California, on October 15, 1965. On that day, Ken Kesey, novelist and leader of the Merry Pranksters, had been invited to address a gathering of antiwar marchers before they took to the streets. Less than a year earlier, a rolling series of free-speech protests had roiled the campus of the University of California nearby. Meantime, LSD was still legal, and across the bay, in San Francisco's Haight-Ashbury district, the psychedelic scene was just beginning to blossom. For the leaders of the march against the war, Berkeley's free-speech movement and the Haight's burgeoning hipster

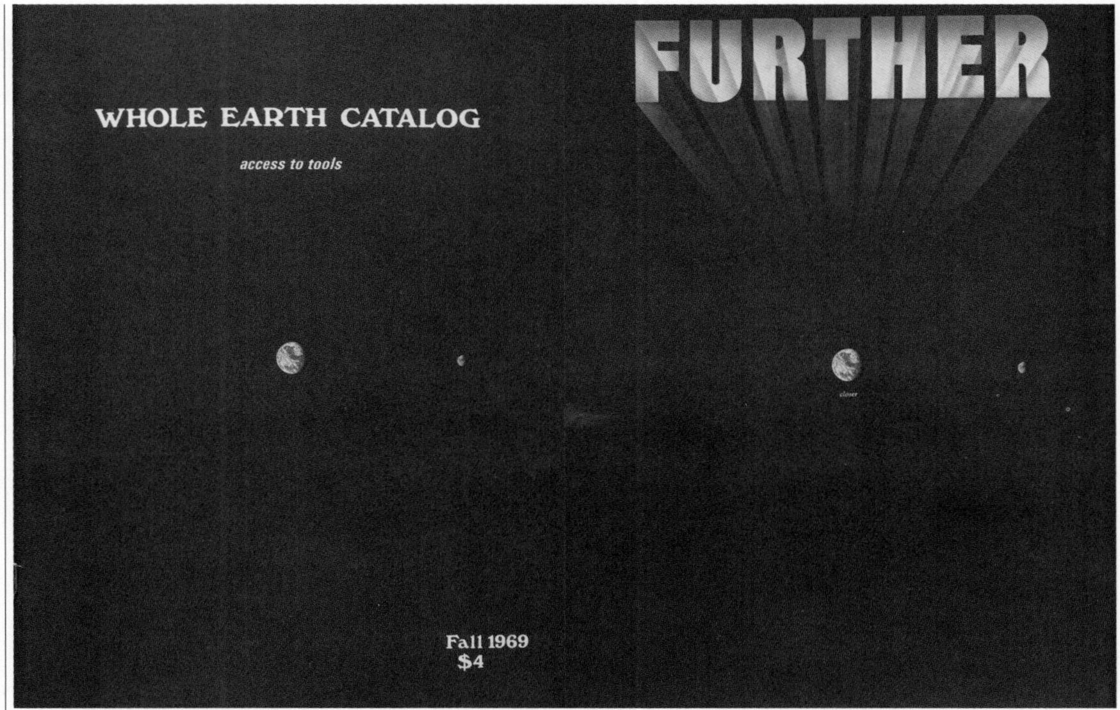

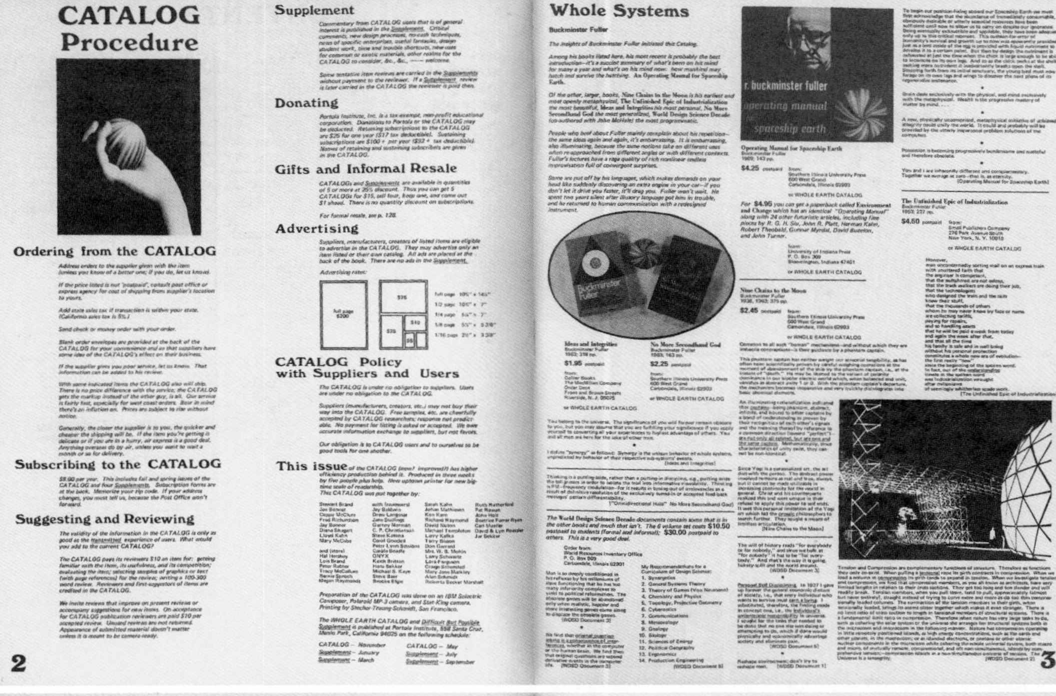

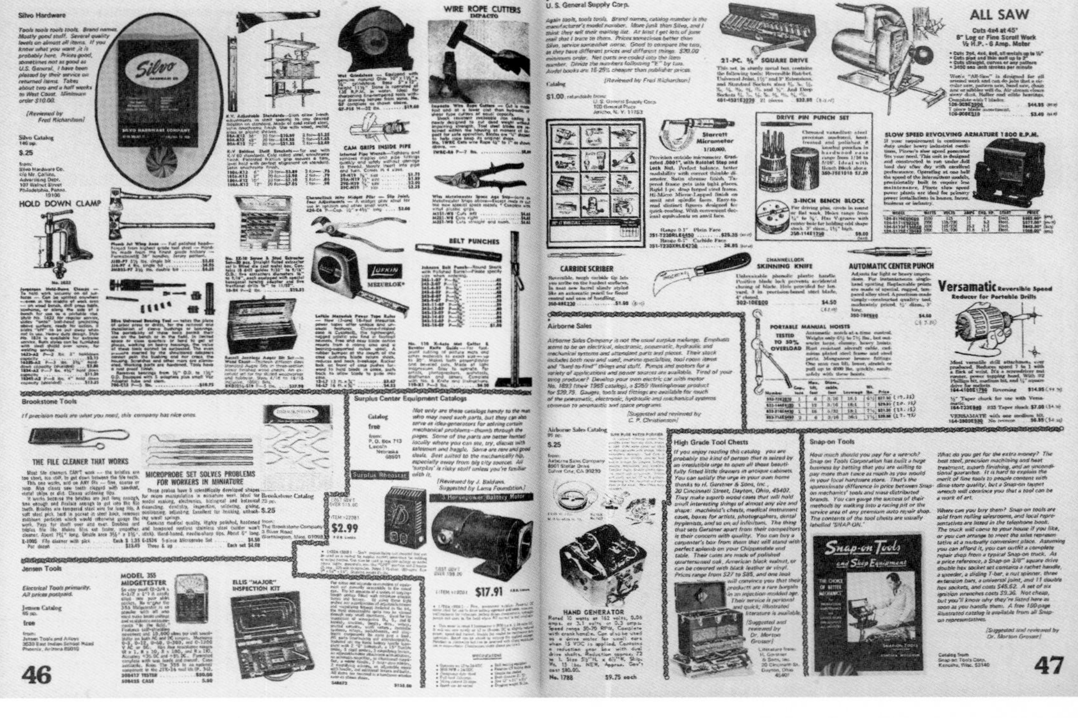

Fig. 4.2. **Whole Earth Catalog,** Fall 1969, cover, back cover, pp. 2-3, 46-47

Intelligent Life in the Universe

Methodically blow your mind. The information in this book, mutually massaged by the American and Soviet co-authors, proceeds from superb introductions to evolutionary astronomy and biology, through a complete presentation of recent discoveries of astronomy and space science, to brilliant speculation on the parameters of inter-civilization communication. It's the best general astronomy book of recent years but that's nothing next to its impact on all the biggest questions we know.

Almost any other of the many accounts of alleged contacts of human beings with the crews of flying saucers—accounts which regale the flying saucer societies—follow the same pattern and stress the same points. The extraterrestrials are human, with few even minor physical differences from local cosmetic standards. (I know of no case of Negro saucerians, or Oriental saucerians, reported in the United States; but there are very few flying saucer reports made in this country by Negroes or by Orientals.)

So, by an interesting coincidence, the distances between the stars in interstellar space, relative to their diameters, are just about the same as the distances between the atoms and molecules in interstellar space, relative to their diameters. Interstellar space is as empty as a cubical building, 60 miles long, 60 miles wide, and 60 miles high, containing a single grain of sand.

Taken at face value, the legend suggests that contact occurred between human beings and a non-human civilization of immense powers on the shores of the Persian Gulf, perhaps near the site of the ancient Sumerian city of Eridu, and in the fourth millennium B.C. or earlier. There are three different but cross-referenced accounts of the Apkallu dating from classical times.

But how can a natural satellite have such a low density? The material of which it is made must have a certain amount of rigidity, so that cohesive forces will be stronger than the gravitational tidal forces of Mars, which will tend to disrupt the satellite. Such rigidity would ordinarily exclude densities below about 0.1 gm cm^{-3}. Thus, only one possibility remains. Could Phobos be indeed rigid, on the outside—but hollow in the inside? A natural satellite cannot be a hollow object. Therefore, we are led to the possibility that Phobos—and possibly Deimos as well—may be artificial satellites of Mars.

Radio astronomers may be interested to know that the so-called "brightness temperature" of the Earth at television wavelengths is some hundreds of millions of degrees. This is 100 times greater than the radio brightness of the sun at comparable wavelengths, during a period of low sunspot activity.

With 10^{11} stars in our Galaxy and 10^{9} other galaxies, there are at least 10^{20} stars in the universe. Most of them, as we shall see in subsequent chapters, may be accompanied by solar systems. If there are 10^{20} solar systems in the universe, and the universe is 10^{10} years old—and if, further, solar systems have formed roughly uniformly in time—then one solar system is formed every 10^{10} yr ÷ 10^{20} = 3×10^{-3} seconds. On the average, a million solar systems are formed in the universe each hour.

The existence of more than one universe is impossible, by definition.

"Well, ladies and gentlemen," Struve concluded, "it was pretty dull on Epsilon Eridani and Tau Ceti eleven years ago."

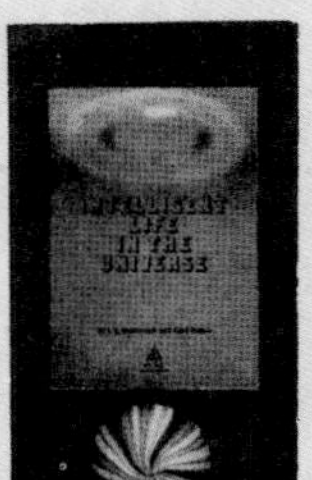

▽ An advanced technical civilization is trying to communicate with us. But how can we possibly understand what they are saying? They are not likely to speak English or Russian. They have had a different evolutionary history. They are on a planet with perhaps an entirely different physical environment.

FIGURE 30-1. *A hypothetical interstellar message due to Frank Drake. The 551 zeros and ones are representations of the two varieties of signals contained in the message. The problem is to convert this sequence of 551 symbols into an intelligible message, knowing that there has been no previous communication between the transmitting and receiving civilizations.*

```
11110000101001000011001000000010000010100
10000011001011001111000001100001101000000
00100000100001000010001010100001000000000
00000000000000000001000100000000000000000
01010000000001000111101101011000101000000
00000000000000000100000000000000000001000
00000000000011101000101010101000000100000
00000000111110000000000111110000000000000
00011000011000011000011000100000001000011
01000011000110000110101111101111101111101
00111011001000100000000000000000000000000
10000000000001000000000000000000000000000
01000000000000000000000000100000000000000
001000111100101111
```

1. decode this ∗

2. into this ∗

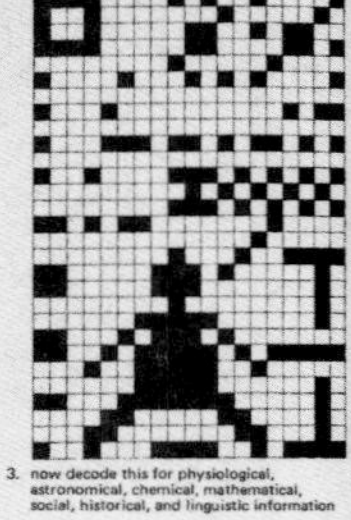

Intelligent Life in the Universe
I. S. Shklovskii and Carl Sagan
1966; 509 pp.

$2.95 postpaid

from:
Delta Books
c/o Montville Warehousing Co.,Inc.
Changebridge Rd.
Pine Brook, N.J. 07058

900 Pratt Blvd.
Elk Grove Village, Illinois 60007

1104 S. Lawrence Street
Los Angeles, Calif. 90021

or WHOLE EARTH CATALOG

3. now decode this for physiological, astronomical, chemical, mathematical, social, historical, and linguistic information

In our discussion up to this point, we have considered only interstellar radio contact among civilizations at or just slightly beyond our present state of technical advance. Yet the bulk of technical civilizations in the universe may be immensely more advanced than ours—perhaps even billions of years beyond. The Soviet astrophysicist N.S. Kardashev, an associate of I.S. Shklovskii at the Sternberg Astronomical Institute, has considered the possibility of the detection of signals from such greatly advanced civilizations. He classifies possible technologically advanced civilizations in three categories: (I) A level of technological advance close to that of the contemporary terrestrial civilization. The rate of energy consumption is about 4 X 10^{19} ergs sec^{-1}. (II) A civilization capable of utilizing and channeling the entire radiation output of its star. The energy utilization would then be comparable to the luminosity of our Sun, about 4 X 10^{33} ergs per second. In Chapter 34, we will consider a specific proposal for the harnessing of such power. (III) A civilization with access to the power comparable to the luminosity of an entire galaxy, some 4 X 10^{44} ergs per second.

The information contained in a single human sperm cell is equivalent to that of 133 volumes, each of the size and fineness of print of Webster's Unabridged Dictionary.

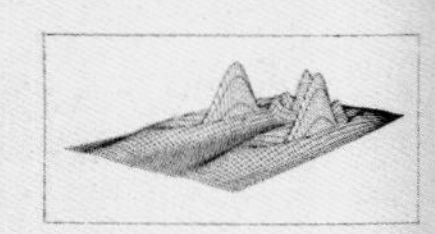

(Art, if you want a definition of it, is criminal action. It conforms to no rules. Not even its own. Anyone who experiences a work of art is as guilty as the artist. It is not a question of sharing the guilt. Each one of us gets all of it.)

Cybernetic Serendipity

This book started life as an exhibit at the Institute of Contemporary Arts in London last year. Simultaneously it was an issue of Studio International *magazine. It must have been an Event. Certainly it is the best collection of computer art yet, the only one not dismissable as engineers kidding themselves. There's been talk for years (e.g. The* New Landscape, *1956) of how art and science are gonna come together, and indeed communications have improved. But there was no direct avenue, no real mutual domain. Not until computers got common enough for funky hands to lay hold of them to do tricks for funky heads. That's happening now, and this book is good evidence. Ahead, deep space.*

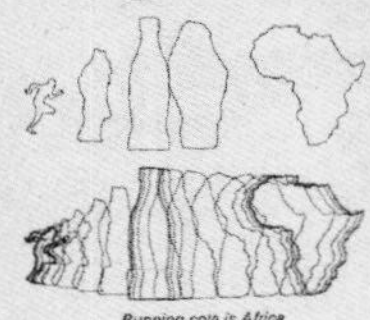

Running coils is Africa

To co-operate or even to orient themselves and to engage their programmes, the mobiles must communicate. They do so in a simple but many-levelled language of light flashes and sounds. You may engage in this discourse if you wish to, though your goals may be alien to the goals of the mobiles; for example, you might be trying to achieve a configuration that you regard as pleasing.

1 Poem
eons deep in the ice
I paint all time in a whorl
bang the sludge has cracked

2 Poem
eons deep in the ice
I see gelled time in a whorl
pfffft the sludge has cracked

3 Poem
all green in the leaves
I smell dark pools in the trees
crash the moon has fled

3 Poem
all white in the buds
I flash snow peaks in the spring
bang the sun has fogged

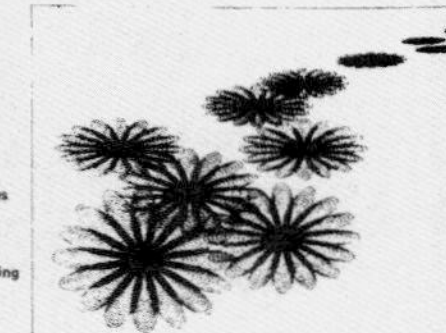

A sustained image of the visual world around us is maintained by the brain's continual coordination of a great flux of varying sensory input. Much of this co-ordination is achieved by the series of voluntary and involuntary eyemovements which serve to scan the image of the pattern across the retina. When these eyemovements are eliminated or controlled, a remarkable collapse of the perceptual process occurs in which visual patterns disintegrate—but in non-random fashion, and according to 'rules' which appear to be common to all humans. The device, which we have called the CYBERNETIC INTROSPECTIVE PATTERN—CLASSIFIER—because that is as good a description as any—is not really the exhibit itself. It is by means of this device that the human brain can be turned into its own exhibit. People looking into the CIPC will be given a brief, bright flash of a pattern which plants an image on the retina in such a way that it can be seen, with eyes closed, for one or two minutes. Since the image is fixed on the retina, eye movements are irrelevant, and the perceptual system collapses as described above. The pattern can be seen to fragment and change its form, and these forms are probably the basic perceptual units used by the brain in recognising the pattern. This exhibit therefore allows people to watch their own cerebral processes actually in action.

Cybernetic Serendipity
1969; 100 pp.; 260 illustrations

$8.95 postpaid

from:
Frederick A. Praeger, Publisher
111 Fourth Avenue
New York, N. Y. 10003

or WHOLE EARTH CATALOG

Understanding Media

Everybody talks about McLuhan, and everybody does something about him, and that makes it subjectively harder to get at him. *He's got other insights than what you hear about, so it's worth the trouble to track him down, both his current sayings and his prime collections. An excellent set of recent sayings was in a* Playboy *interview a few months ago (the foresaw the imminent demise of language into global telepathy: 'The body of Christ). For prime collection the primest is* Understanding Media.
(Suggested by Gerd Stern, then.)

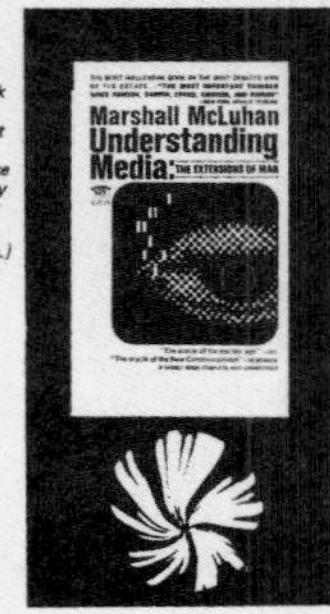

Understanding Media
Marshall McLuhan
1964; 318 pp.

$.95 postpaid

from:
Signet—New American Library, Inc.
1301 Avenue of the Americas
New York, N. Y. 10019

or WHOLE EARTH CATALOG

Eventually the method of the counting board gave rise to the great discovery of the principle of position in the early centuries of our era. By simply putting 3 and 4 and 2 in position on the board, one after another, it was possible to step up the speed and potential of calculation fantastically. The discovery of calculation by positional numbers rather than by merely additive numbers led, also, to the discovery of zero. Mere positions for 3 and 2 on the board created ambiguities about whether the number was 32 or 302. The need was to have a sign for the gaps between numbers. It was not till the thirteenth century that sifr, the Arab word for 'gap' or 'empty,' was Latinized and added to our culture as 'cipher' (ziphirum) and finally became the Italian zero. Zero really meant a positional gap.

'Work,' however, does not exist in a nonliterate world. The primitive hunter or fisherman did no work, any more than does the poet, painter, or thinker of today. Where the whole man is involved there is no work.

If the phonetic alphabet was a technical means of severing the spoken word from its aspects of sound and gesture, the photograph and its development in the movie restored gesture to the human technology of recording experience.

Man the food-gatherer reappears incongruously as information-gatherer. In this role, electronic man is no less a nomad than his paleolithic ancestors.

Everybody experiences far more than he understands. Yet it is experience, rather than understanding, that influences behavior, especially in collective matters of media and technology, where the individual is almost inevitably unaware of their effect upon him.

Said the Duke of Gloucester to Edward Gibbon upon the publication of his Decline and Fall: 'Another damned fat book, eh, Mr. Gibbon? Scribble, scribble, scribble, eh, Mr. Gibbon?'

Language does for intelligence what the wheel does for the feet and the body. It enables them to move from thing to thing with greater ease and speed and ever less involvement.

As W. B. Yeats wrote of this reversal, 'The visible world is no longer a reality and the unseen world is no longer a dream.'

Even slight changes in the environment of the very well adjusted find them without any resource to meet new challenge. Such is the plight of the representatives of 'conventional wisdom' in any society. Their entire stake of security and status is in a single form of acquired knowledge, so that innovation is for them not novelty but annihilation.

It is a principal aspect of the electric age that it establishes a global network that has much of the character of our central nervous system. Our central nervous system is not merely an electric network, but it constitutes a single unified field of experience. As biologists point out, the brain is the interacting place where all kinds of impressions and experiences can be exchanged and translated, enabling us to react to the world as a whole.

Not only does the visual, specialist, and fragmented Westerner have now to live in closest daily association with all the ancient oral cultures of the earth, but his own electric technology now begins to translate the visual or eye man back into the tribal and oral pattern with its seamless web of kinship and interdependence.

Meantime, the countryside, as oriented and fashioned by plane, by highway, and by electric information-gathering, tends to become once more the nomadic trackless area that preceded the wheel.

Cybernetics

McLuhan's assertion that computers constitute an extension of the human nervous system is an accurate historical statement. The research and speculation that led to computer design arose from investigation of healthy and pathological human response patterns embodied in the psychological make-up of the nervous system. Insights here soon expanded into generalizations about communication that permitted the building of analogous electronic devices physically separate from the Central Nervous System. But they're just one artifact of these new understandings about communication. Society, from organism to community to civilization to universe, is the domain of cybernetics. Norbert Wiener has the story, and to some extent, is the story.

I have spoken of the race. This is really too broad a term for the scope of most communal information. Properly speaking, the community extends only so far as there extends an effectual transmission of information. It is possible to give a sort of measure to this by comparing the number of decisions entering a group from outside with the number of decisions made in the group. We can thus measure the autonomy of the group. A measure of the effective size of a group is given by the size which it must have to have achieved a certain stated degree of autonomy.

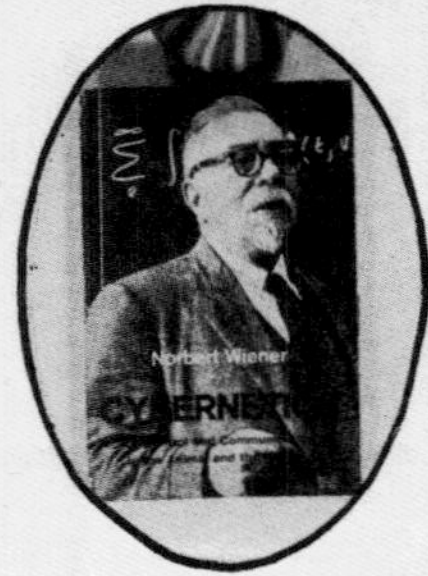

To predict the future of a curve is to carry out a certain operation on its past.

Thus small, closely knit communities have a very considerable measure of homeostasis; and this, whether they are highly literate communities in a civilized country or villages of primitive savages. Strange and even repugnant as the customs of many barbarians may seem to us, they generally have a very definite homeostatic value, which it is part of the function of anthropologists to interpret. It is only in the large community, where the Lords of Things as They Are protect themselves from hunger by wealth, from public opinion by privacy and anonymity from private criticism by the laws of libel and the possession of the means of communication, that ruthlessness can reach its most sublime levels. Of all of these anti-homeostatic factors in society, the control of the means of communication is the most effective and most important.

Cybernetics — or Control and Communication in the Animal and the Machine
Norbert Wiener
1948,1961;212 pp.

$2.45 postpaid

from:
The M. I. T. Press
Cambridge, Mass. 02142

or WHOLE EARTH CATALOG

The central nervous system no longer appears as a self-contained organ, receiving inputs from the senses and discharging into the muscles. On the contrary, some of its most characteristic activities are explicable only as circular processes, emerging from the nervous system into the muscles, and re-entering the nervous system through the sense organs, whether they be proprioceptors or organs of the special senses. This seemed to us to mark a new step in the study of that part of neurophysiology which concerns not solely the elementary processes of nerves and synapses but the performance of the nervous system as an integrated whole.

The mongoose begins with a feint, which provokes the snake to strike. The mongoose dodges and makes another such feint, so that we have a rhythmical pattern of activity on the part of the two animals. However, this dance is not static but develops progressively. As it goes on, the feints of the mongoose come earlier and earlier in phase with respect to the darts of the cobra, until finally the mongoose attacks when the cobra is extended and not in a position to move rapidly. This time the mongoose's attack is not a feint but a deadly accurate bite through the cobra's brain.

In other words, the snake's pattern of action is confined to single darts, each one for itself, while the pattern of the mongoose's action involves an appreciable, if not very long, segment of the whole past of the fight. To this extent the mongoose acts like a learning machine, and the real deadliness of its attack is dependent on a much more highly organized nervous system.

The feedback of voluntary activity is of this nature. We do not will the motions of certain muscles, and indeed we generally do not know which muscles are to be moved to accomplish a given task; we will, say, to pick up a cigarette. Our motion is regulated by some measure of the amount by which it has not yet been accomplished.

To use a biological analogy, the parallel system had a better homeostasis than the series system and therefore survived, while the series system eliminated itself by natural selection.

We thus see that a non-linear interaction causing the attraction of frequency can generate a self-organizing system. . . .

★ Earth Flag

A gentleman named John McConnell came into the Truck Store a few weeks ago and said that since all the nations have flags, and the UN has a flag, and states and businesses have flags, maybe there ought to be a flag that's just for people. So he got together with artist Norman LaLiberte and one of the Apollo Earth photographs and came up with the Earth Flag. I don't know if I'd die for it, but it's the first flag I've seen that I don't feel it somehow excludes me. The Earth Flag feels nice to wave.

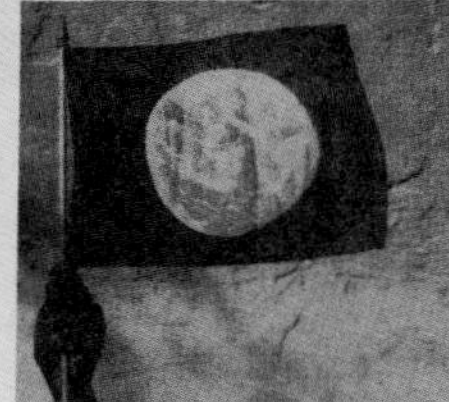

Earth Flag (11" x 13" with staff)

$1.50 postpaid from:
"WE" Inc.
19 Troutman Street
Brooklyn, N.Y. 11206

or WHOLE EARTH CATALOG

★ Vocations for Social Change

This nifty service has been going for about a year now and is clearly growing in effectiveness. They earn your donation.

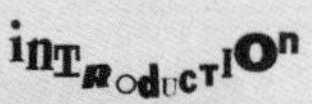

Vocations for Social Change is a decentralized clearing house for persons struggling with one basic question: How can people earn a living in America in 1969 and ensure that their social impact is going to affect basic humanistic change in our social, political and economic institutions? Nobody has any "real answers" to this question, but many ideas are being developed out of people's experiences. VSC helps make these ideas available to the general public so that each person's individual search can be enriched.

This newsletter serves as the main gathering point for ideas with which we have come in contact. Not only do we include descriptions of job openings with groups working for social change from a wide variety of viewpoints, but also proposals for new projects that need help in getting started, descriptions of places where you can learn more about social action in an educational setting, and articles on topics related to working for social change on a full-time basis. What all of the people behind these various ideas have in common is a genuine concern for stimulating basic change in American institutions.

Informing you of available opportunities for involvement in social change is only part of our goal. We also hope that the information that we have gathered here will stimulate you to think about what new roles need to be created and to consider the possibility of actually finding a new role for yourself. Many more dedicated people are needed if we are to see significant change in our lifetimes.

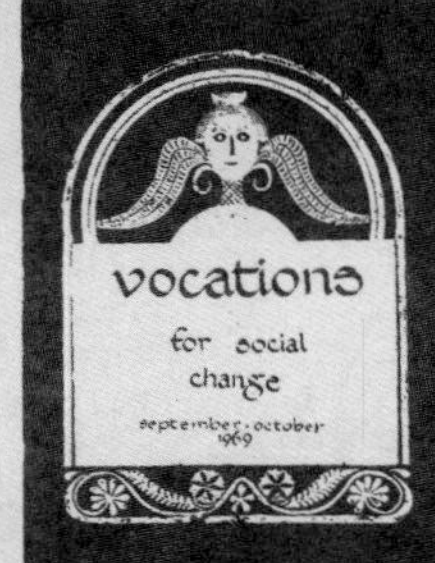

IF YOU WANT TO RECEIVE THE NEWSLETTER we'll be happy to send you a sample copy. We send VSC regularly for six months to people who support us financially with donations of $5.00 or more, or send us monthly pledges. This helps cover the costs of mailing and enables us to send sample copies to those who cannot afford to send any money. Institutions, such as libraries and schools are charged $10.00 a year.

★ A Manual of Simple Burial

Not everybody has an opportunity to depart this world gracefully, and those that do usually blow it. The people left behind fumble just as badly, for largely the same reasons: ignorance, fear, a lack of foresight and preparation. None but the dead can know for sure the full consequences of the failure. But even if there are no consequences for the dead, there are enough of them for the survivors in the forms of trauma and ruptured bank accounts, to make this **Manual of Simple Burial** *seem something like a life-saver.*

For this little manual of death is firmly on the side of life. As part of the literature of funerals, it's like a living rosebud in a bouquet of plastic flowers. In 64 pages it quietly tells you how to avoid the ghastly system of converting human left-overs into products packaged as "funerals." In simple language backed by intelligent sympathy, it suggests ways to surround the act of passage with appropriate rites of passage that offer real meaning to people in need of meaning.

According to the manual, the main alternative to expensive, hastily-improvised funerals is membership in a memorial society. A memorial society is "a voluntary group of people who have joined together to obtain dignity, simplicity and economy in funeral arrangements through advance planning." The manual provides a list of several societies by name and address. It also has information on cremation, autopsies, eye-banks, bequeathal of bodies, and the business and legal matters that usually attend a death, as well as chapters with titles like "Interpreting Death To A Child," and "What to Do When Death Occurs."

Men choose their horrors. We choose war. We choose pollution. And, by default, we choose to make the rituals surrounding death grotesque. But what is chosen can be unchosen, once an alternative is clear. The **Manual of Simple Burial** *describes a clear alternative to one of our chosen horrors.*

[Reviewed by Gurney Norman]

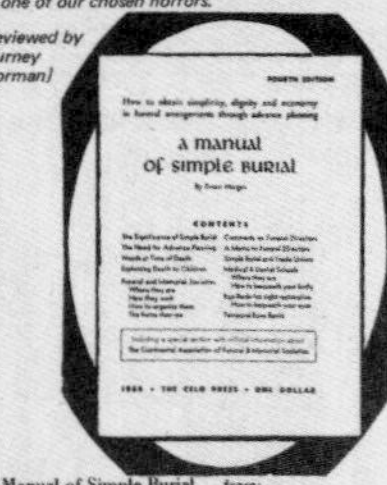

A Manual of Simple Burial
Ernest Morgan
1968; 64pp.

$1.00 postpaid

from:
The Celo Press
Burnsville, North Carolina 28714

or WHOLE EARTH CATALOG

Figuring out how much to mark-up the price of the goods over what we paid for them was another real mystery. We were aware that many co-ops are short lived because they try to be a miracle store in the beginning by charging very little for the food before they fully understand how much money it takes to run the store. A number of other small grocers in town told us that we couldn't survive on less than a twenty percent mark up. Yet at that mark up we would be pricing ourselves at least five cents above the average supermarket price. We didn't know how much our overhead was going to be so we couldn't calculate it on that. What we ended up doing was taking a chance. If we could operate on volunteer help for several months then we could charge supermarket prices and try to get a lot of people to continue buying at the store out of something more than simple loyalty. Using every night's receipts to increase the stock, we managed to attract even more people by having a larger and larger stock every time they came in. We also did things like compensating for marking staples down by keeping luxuries at about a 20 per cent mark up. Having everyone a volunteer made the store a real community project with many different people working in the store day and night - a constant party or freak show depending on what time of day you came in.

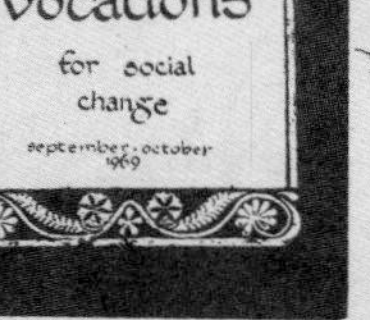

★ The Moonlighter's Manual

Moonlighting means having a second job. Lots of people don't have a first job or want one. Birds of this feather flock economically together and pool resources for rent, food, dope, etc.—which still requires some modest income. Moonlight-type work may be the answer. Most of the income-sources in this book are part-time, or do-at-home, and involve low commitment of psyche (an advantage they have over stealing or dope peddling). The book includes a good list of technical training schools.

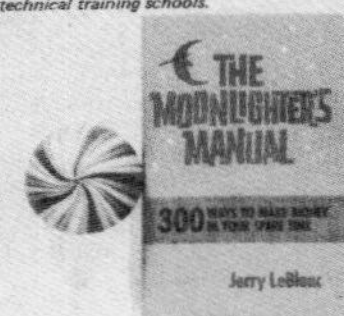

BE A LOCKSMITH

Picking locks, installing them, or making keys, freeing people from locked rooms, or getting them into their locked homes and cars, is an art that mystifies most people, thus making the locksmith in any town a respected craftsman. But actually, almost anyone who can work with tools and has a steady hand for dealing with tiny objects can master this craft and make a secure and profitable living from it. Generally this is a job for a self-starter, whether he pursues it full time or part time. The more than three hundred tools of the trade are the secret; they really do the work.

Earnings

Some beginners report averaging $3 to $10 an hour in their spare time, while learning, and those who set up their own shops, either in their homes or in a small, rented downtown store, come closest to the higher figure. And it's almost 100 per cent profit.

Hours

Variable. This job can be placed on a regular workday basis if you concentrate on installing and replacing locks and key-making, and there are always many jobs that can be done in spare time at home. But there will always be emergency calls, too, and these can mean an hour's rush work at any time of day or night.

Requirements

If you can concentrate on simple diagrams, follow instructions and handle small tools, you can learn this trade quickly, studying in your free time at home and gaining practical experience by working with actual car locks, home locks, safe locks, and padlocks. You'll also need a car for transportation, of course.

Future

Some large-traffic supermarket and department stores are glad to set up a locksmith with the space he needs, just for the service to their customers, although they will expect a commission or rent for their ideal situation. But opening your own shop is a distinct future calling, and you can double your earnings by selling locks, keys, and safety devices, too.

For Information

Write Locksmithing Institute, Little Falls, New Jersey 07424.

American Tuning School, Gilroy, California 95020. Home study in piano tuning.

Anderson School of Scientific Massage, Princeton, Illinois. Professional massage taught by mail; diploma awarded.

The Moonlighter's Manual
Jerry LeBlanc
1969; 150 pp.

$4.95 postpaid

from:
Nash Publishing Corporation
9255 Sunset Blvd.
Los Angeles, Calif. 90069

or WHOLE EARTH CATALOG

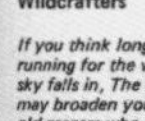

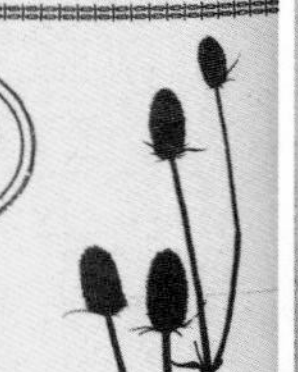

Sample copy

free

from:
Vocations for Social Change
Canyon, CA 94516

The Modern Utopian

Intentional communities by now constitute a realm of activity worth having a magazine. This could be it, except it seems to be coming out at greater and greater intervals. It's well edited, with each issue on a specific aspect of the trend (communal schools, street people, etc.).

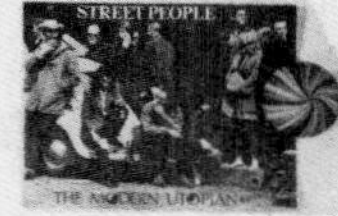

The Modern Utopian / A Way Out
Dick Fairfield, ed.

$4.00 for one year (quarterly

from:
The Modern Utopian
2441 Le Conte Avenue
Berkeley, California 94709

Starting a community farm is an incredibly difficult thing. We didn't fully realize this when we began. Setting up a new farm -- or rather, rehabilitating an old and neglected one -- was at least a season's work. Not to mention compensating for the work which should have been done the previous autumn.

BEAUTIFUL NATURAL GRAIN CEREAL — PUT ALL THE GRAINS IN A LARGE CAN — MIX — THIS CAN WILL LAST 4 PEOPLE 2 MONTHS — EAT IT EVERY DAY AND STRENGTH WILL COME TO YOU — WARM MILK AND HONEY OVER IT — MILK AND SUGAR — COOK IT LIKE OATMEAL — FOR CAMPING ADD WATER

6 lbs. of OATS
6 lbs. WHEAT FLAKES
6 lbs. RYE FLAKES
3 lbs. WHEAT GERM
3 lbs. SUNFLOWER SEEDS
1½ lbs. PUMPKIN SEEDS
4–6 lbs. RAISINS
3–5 lbs. DRIED FRUIT
3 oz. RICE POLISHINGS
2 oz. SOY LECITHEN
3 oz. GROUND CHIA SEEDS
2 lbs. NUTS
1 lb. SOY FLOUR (OR CORN FLOUR)
3 lbs. SESAME SEEDS
ORGANIC FAMILIA

ADD ANY SOFT CHEWABLE GRAINS YOU LIKE — KEEP ADDING TO IT — ALWAYS CHANGING

eat and enjoy

Whether it is guarding a shrine, making electric music, applying Gestalt Therapy or feeding transient hippies, all viable communities have a conscious intent and meaningful function. As opposed to the lack of meaningful direction in today's American society, a conscious sense of purpose is the actualizing force if the community is to be more than a particularization of the social malaise it seeks to answer. Functions may change, sometimes with a rapidity which causes misunderstanding within the community; these changes, how they occur, and the control of change must be understood throughout the community.

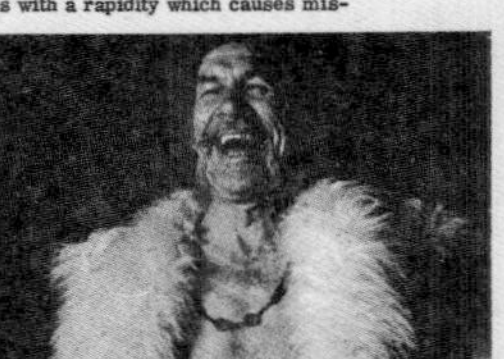

"Dinner begins with a song followed by a short meditative silence. Sometimes a record is played, or the news listened to. During dinner we report on the day's happenings at our jobs, things we've read, and discuss the news. Around dessert we share the day's mail. Then dishes and lunch-packing. Usually Connie and Rae--either separately or together--prepare dinner. The men usually either wash or rinse dishes. Connie packs lunches one week, Rae the next.

Dear Friends,
I have spent over twenty years in what is now called the "Hippie Movement", living in short-lived communes based on an anarchistic freedom and long-lived communes based on religion, taking part in political activities such as CORE work in the early 50's and the political action era of the Sexual Freedom League, and writing for, drawing for and editing little literary reviews and underground newspapers. This experience has brought me, gradually and reluctantly, to certain conclusions that I'm pretty sure some of your readers will dispute, yet to me they seem inescapable.
First, those communes based on freedom inevitably fail, usually within a year.
Second, those communes based on authority, particularly religious authority, often endure and survive even against vigorous opposition from the outside world. (The best example of the strength of religious authoritarian communism is the monasteries and nunneries of the Catholic Church.). . .
How, then, can an intentional community possibly be be superior to conventional society? If the intentional community hopes to survive, it must be authoritarian, and if it is authoritarian, it offers no more freedom than conventional society. I am not pleased with this conclusion, but it now seems to me that the only way to be free is to be alone.
ORO, El Cerrito, Calif.

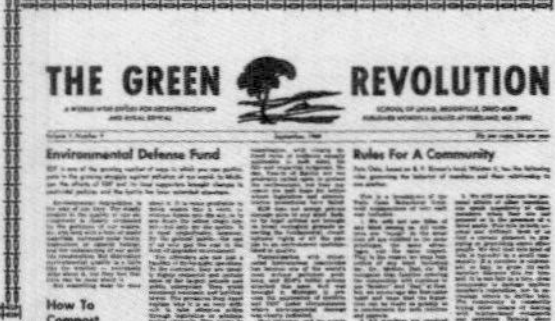

★ Wildcrafters

If you think longhairs are the only people running for the woods before the smoggy sky falls in, The Wildcrafters publications may broaden your view. They're the work of old geezers who groove on hunting and gathering food and fantasizing and opinionating about independence just like thee and me. Maybe we ought to get together and have a geezer conference.

SURVIVAL HINTS
BEWARE of slipping, tripping or falling.

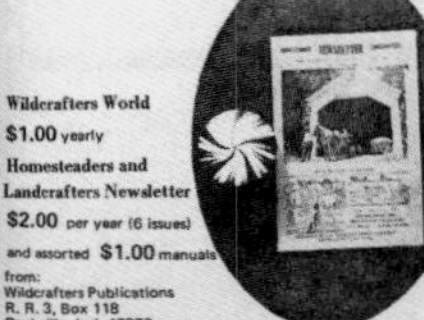

Wildcrafters World
$1.00 yearly

Homesteaders and Landcrafters Newsletter
$2.00 per year (6 issues)

and assorted **$1.00** manuals

from:
Wildcrafters Publications
R. R. 3, Box 118
Rockville, Ind. 47872

USING AGAR AGAR AND VITAMIN B1 to start a peach tree. The kernels are removed from the hard pits of the peach seed and soaked in a solution of agar agar and vitamin B1 for three weeks. They sprout rapidly and are moved to clean washed sand, where they are kept moist for three weeks longer. Seedlings are then husky and large enough to be placed in soil filled pots. By the time they are nine months old they are ready for field planting and by their second birthday they should produce peaches. Sent in by Mrs. Zoller, Canada.

Far away I could hear the *roar of the falls.* Catatonic and gibbering I rose to the rear. Also Butch lifted me up. We climb a final knoll and *oowee.* Natural fuckin wonder Jim! The majesty of all that water flashing and crashing like a moving post card. Without camera or guard rail or tour guide or beercan . . . not even the plastic music that pervades most national scenery marts.

This place was special because you had to earn it. Here come Bonnie Jean and White rabbit and David LeBruan all wasted from the walk. But the falls fixes all. Quivering with dying sun shouts rose and orange, rusty like the lord's own snot she set us down to worship while the sun sunk into sleep.

Let's take a quick look at the blackboard. All us earth people are holding hands in a circle. Whether we know it or not. We are all dancing and chanting and making our own individual sound which makes up the whole racket of life. Now somewhere along the line the circle turned in on itself so the folks in the middle are squished and screaming like hell. Maybe that's where Hell is . . . in the middle of that circle . . . Hiroshima . . . Dachau . . . Vietnam . . . Bellevue. Just close your ears and you can hear 'em. Now what we can do is help relieve the pressure by absorbing a taste of the tug. Pass it on. Trust your neighbor. Trust your trust. Practice makes perfect and everybody wants to be practice. Open the whole thing up so everybody's comfortable. Take a deep breath and start all over.

It gets real cozy in the center when everybody's watching out for everybody else like at Yale University. In the middle of all rock and roll my brother-in-law let loose 5 live frogs . . . on cue . . . I grab a mike. *"Don't anybody move! Some nut has just let loose 5 live frogs!"* And the hunt was on . . . like looking for jumping contact lenses but we brought 'em back alive. It was a calculated risk and it worked.

Later we all laid on the floor with his head on her tummy and her head on somebody else. Not freaky at all but warm and snuggle. After a while I asked to be passed around. Over the top of the pile. Everybody lend a hand . . . and I'm skimming along at a pretty good clip and it really felt nifty. Then we sent Tooker aloft. The baby of Barry and Moe. He's maybe two and bald like the buddha. Talk about total attention. Hand over hand . . . it was really quite grand with Tooker on top of us all. We can fly with the help of our friends.

The Realist

Green Revolution

If The Realist *is the father of recent underground newspapers,* Green Revolution *is the mother of community newsletters. Both are kind.*

The Realist
Paul Krassner, ed.

$3.00 postpaid

from:
The Realist
595 Broadway
New York, N.Y. 10012

Green Revolution
Mildred Loomis, ed.

$3.00 for one year (monthly)

from:
School of Living Center
Heathcote Road
Freeland, Md. 21053

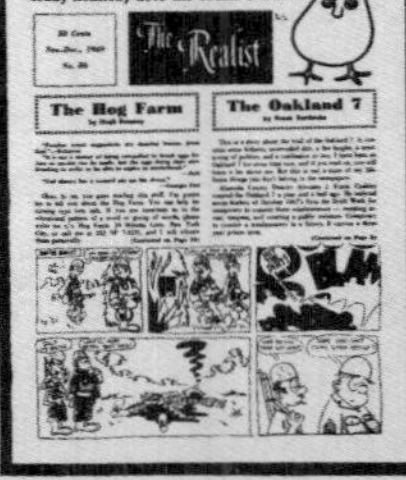

Cardinal principles: (1) If it's late try to get out at an all night cafe or truck stop (truckers aren't supposed to pick you up due to insurance rules, but especially at night they do it anyhow and sometimes you can curl up in a long-haul sleeper). If there's no cafe, try at least for a 24 hour gas station—you can ask the people who come in for gas to take you along.

(2) Carry food. The kind that's good for you. Raisons and nuts and seeds and fruit and cheese and bread as unrefined as you can get it. Otherwise, travel as light as you can.

(3) Always have identification and someplace you can call if it comes to that. Make sure not to carry alcohol or anything else not nice. Avoid Delaware and the State of Washington altogether if you're going by thumb. Arizona is risky too. Check your route if you can with somebody's who was just there.

(4) Remember that you can often offer something in exchange — companionship, most likely. One thing about hitchhiking — you can go night and day, nonstop, either riding or scratching for rides. That's how you get speed. But if you're on one of those marathons it's likely you'll get tired. Sleep when you have to, but apologise first. People pick you up for somebody to talk to more often than not. Maybe it's just to help them stay awake. Maybe they want you to help with the driving. Do it if you can.

The earth is ours, we aren't supposed to ride indentured when we travel on her.

Whole Earth Catalog

access to tools

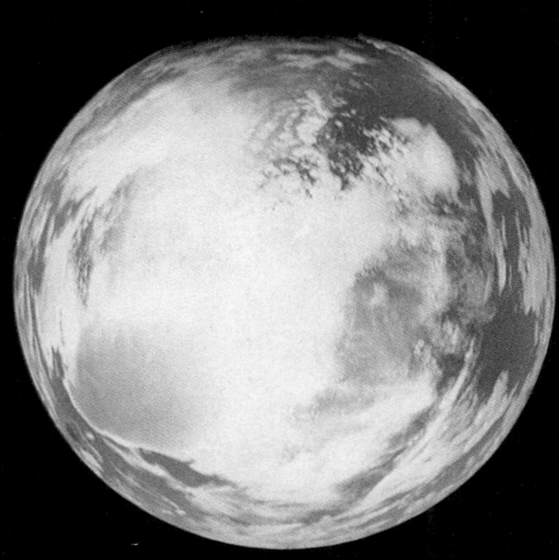

THE UNIVERSE
from planet Earth
on a sunny day

Fall 1970
$3

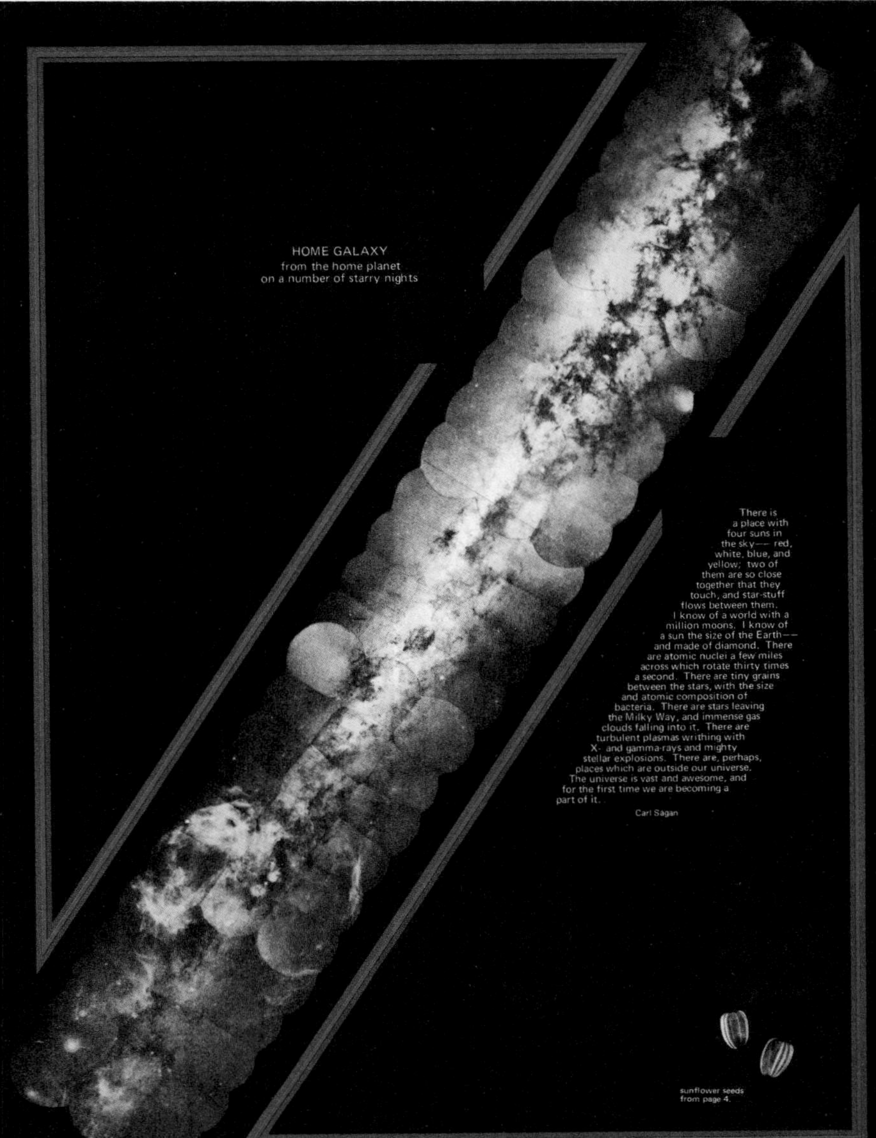

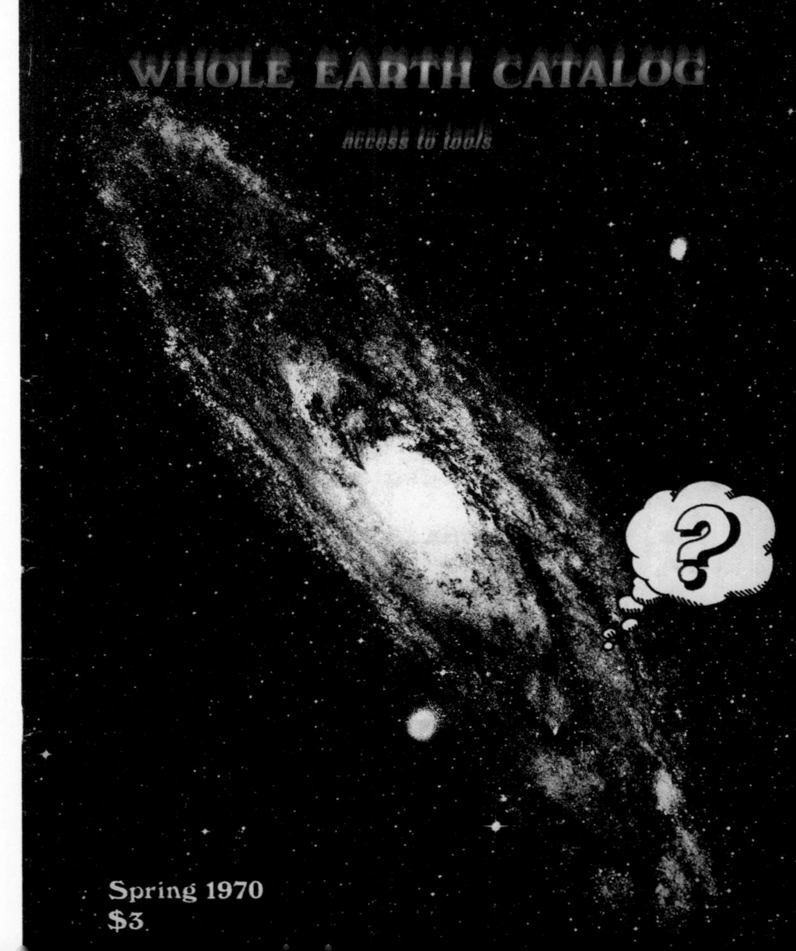

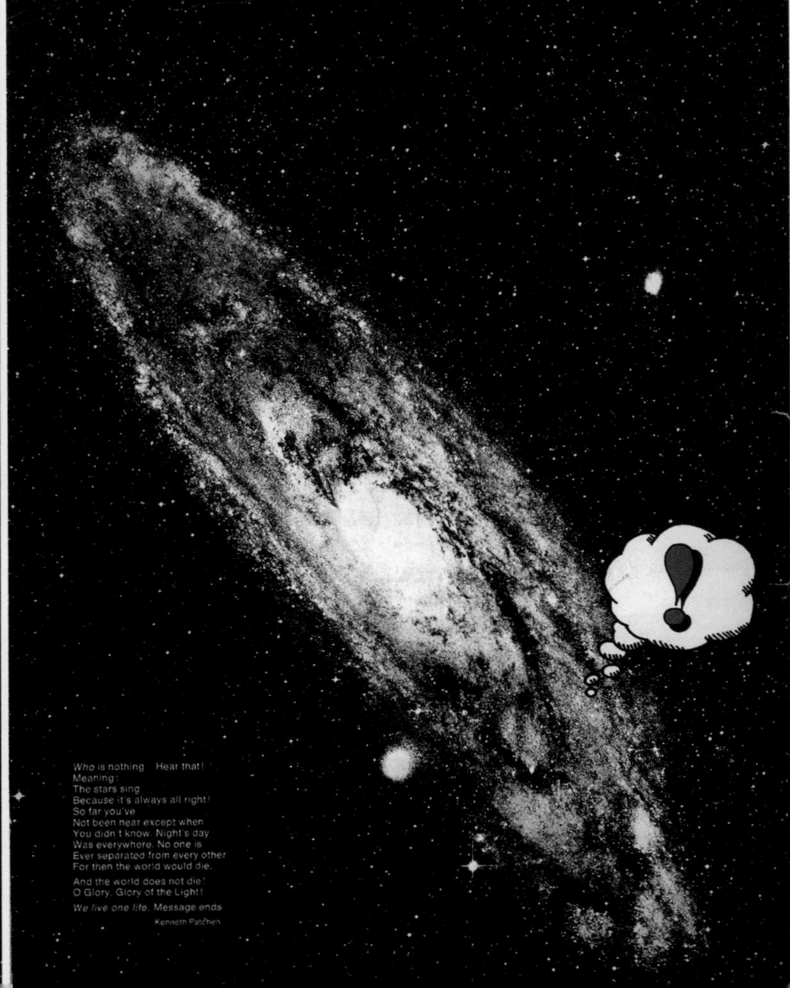

Previous page
Fig. 4.2 (cont'd).
Whole Earth Catalog, pp. 60–61, 80–81

Fig. 4.2 (cont'd).
Whole Earth Catalog, Fall 1970, cover, back cover; Spring 1970, cover, back cover

culture represented two different worlds—socially, ideologically, and even to some degree geographically. Thus, they had invited Kesey as if he were the head of a foreign state: with his presence they hoped to bring the two communities together and to join the politics of protest with the rebellious play of the Pranksters.[3]

When he mounted the stage however, Kesey turned on his hosts. If they wanted a harangue, they wouldn't get it. Looking out over the crowd, Kesey leaned in to the microphone and said, "You know, you're not going to stop this war with this rally, by marching .... That's what they do."[4] He then pulled a harmonica out of his pocket, played "Home on the Range," and left the stage. For Kesey and the Pranksters and, ultimately, for an entire wing of the American counterculture, the confrontational politics favored by the New Left looked like a trap. To do politics was to become a politician; to change the world, you needed to begin with yourself, at home. More specifically still, you needed to begin by changing your state of mind. In his 1969 best seller, ***The Making of a Counter Culture***, Theodore Roszak put it this way: "Building the good society is not primarily a social, but a psychic task."[5] In Roszak's view, mainstream, military-industrial America had driven the nation into Vietnam and the world to the edge of the nuclear abyss by depending on "the scientific world view, with its entrenched commitment to an egocentric and cerebral mode of consciousness."[5] To defeat the war makers and their industrialist allies, he argued, Americans needed to invent a new kind of politics, a "politics of consciousness."[7]

But how? If the process of doing politics in the conventional way—by forming social movements, holding meetings, making rules and regulations—had been hopelessly entwined with instrumental rationality, where could those pursuing another form of consciousness turn? On what principles and with what tools and techniques could they build an alternative form of sociability?

In many ways, it was these questions that the *Whole Earth Catalog* was founded to answer. In 1966, Stewart Brand was a thirty-year-old photographer and peripheral member of the Merry Pranksters. He had just helped create the Trips Festival—a two-night gathering featuring copious quantities of LSD, psychedelic lighting, performance art, and rock music that helped kick-start San Francisco's psychedelic scene (fig. 4.3). He had also hung around outside the campus gates at Berkeley, hawking buttons that read, "Why haven't we seen a picture of the whole earth yet?" For Brand, psychedelic drugs, rocket ships, and satellite photography were all part of a new universe of technologies that could enhance the individual's ability to perceive his or her place in the world. Such new perceptions, he believed, could ultimately become grounds for a kind of society that might finally transcend the military politics and mechanistic mind-set of mainstream America.

By 1968, such beliefs had also helped drive the largest wave of communalization in American history.[8] In the wake of 1967's "Summer of Love," the citizens of Haight-Ashbury and other hip urban enclaves had begun taking themselves to the plains of Colorado and New Mexico and the hills of Vermont. By the early 1970s, the most reliable estimates suggested that some 750,000 Americans were living in more than 10,000 communes nationwide (fig. 4.4), many in the rural wilds.[9] While the texture and aims of communal life varied from site to site, virtually all sought to create alternatives to a world they imagined as bureaucratic and psychologically constrained. And like the Pranksters, they hoped to build such alternatives not through politics, but through the design and deployment of new, small-scale technologies.

In the summer of 1968, Brand and his then-wife Lois piled into their old Dodge pickup truck and drove east, to the communes of Colorado and New Mexico, to see what tools the communards might need. When they returned to the San Francisco area, they began compiling a catalog that over the next four years would swell to some 448 pages, sell more than a million copies, and win a National Book Award.[10]

3. Jay Stevens, *Storming Heaven: LSD and the American Dream* (New York: Atlantic Monthly Press, 1987), pp. 295-298.

4. Quoted in Tom Wolfe, *The Electric Kool-Aid Acid Test* (New York: Farrar, Straus and Giroux, 1968), p. 222.

5. Theodore Roszak, *The Making of a Counter Culture: Reflections on the Technocratic Society and Its Youthful Opposition* (Berkeley: University of California Press, 1995), p. 49.

6. Ibid., p. 50.

7. Ibid., p. 51.

8. For an analysis of the literature detailing the number of communes built in this period and its relationship to pre-1960s communalism in America, see Turner, *From Counterculture to Cyberculture* (Chicago: University of Chicago Press, 2006), pp. 32-35. For more detailed analyses, see Hugh Gardner, *The Children of Prosperity: Thirteen Modern American Communes* (New York: St. Martin's Press, 1978); Judson Jerome, *Families of Eden: Communes and the New Anarchism* (New York: Seabury Press, 1974); Rosabeth Moss Kanter, *Commitment and Community: Communes and Utopias in Sociological Perspective* (Cambridge: Harvard University Press, 1972); Rosabeth Moss Kanter, *Communes: Creating and Managing the Collective Life* (New York: Harper & Row, 1973); Timothy Miller, *The 60s Communes: Hippies and Beyond* (Syracuse, NY: Syracuse University Press, 1999); Timothy Miller, *American Communes, 1860-1960: A Bibliography* (New York: Garland, 1990).

9. Jerome, *Families of Eden*, pp. 16-18, cited in Miller, *60s Communes*, pp. xix-xx.

10. For a more comprehensive history of the *Catalog*, see Turner, *From Counterculture to Cyberculture*, pp. 69-102; and Andrew G. Kirk, *Counterculture Green: The Whole Earth Catalog and American Environmentalism* (Lawrence: University Press of Kansas, 2007), pp. 1-12.

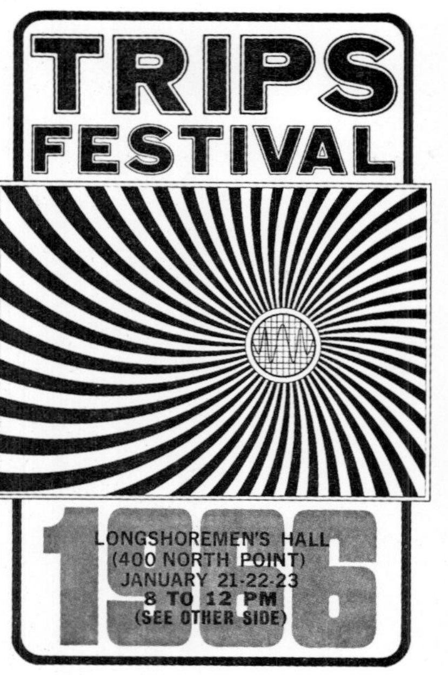

Fig. 4.3. Trips Festival flyer

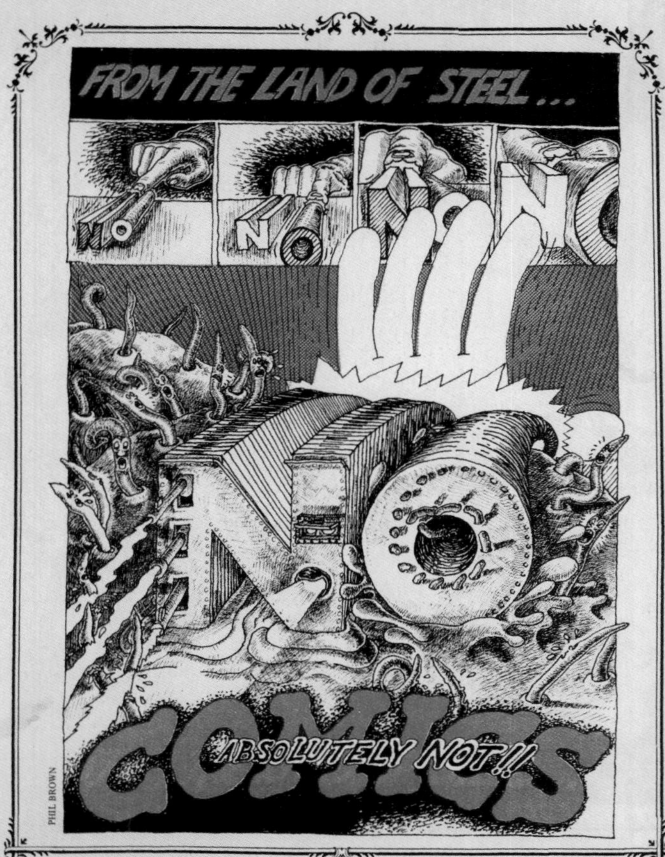

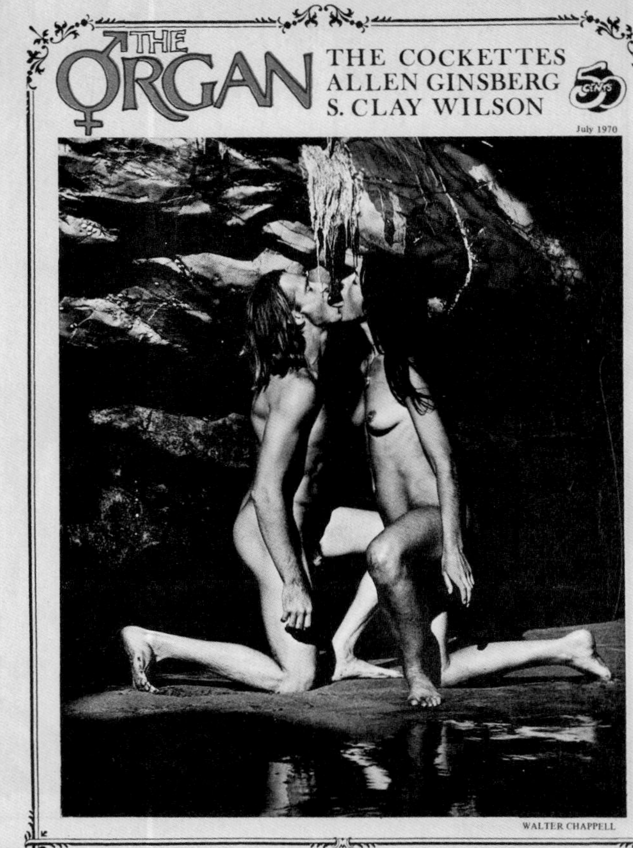

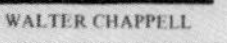

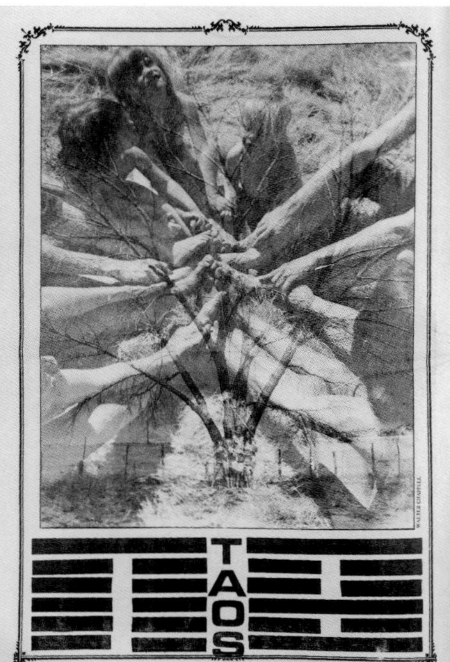

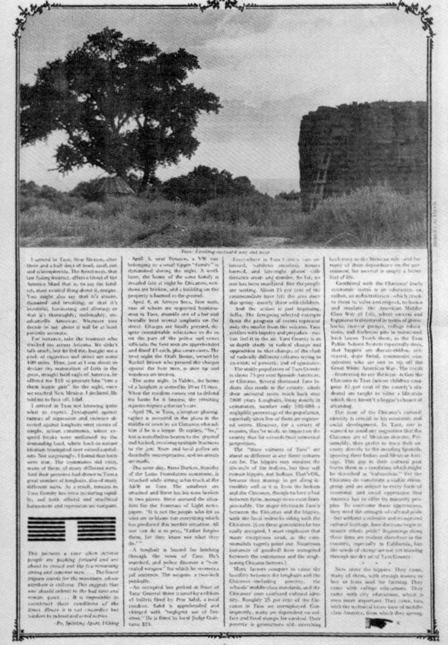

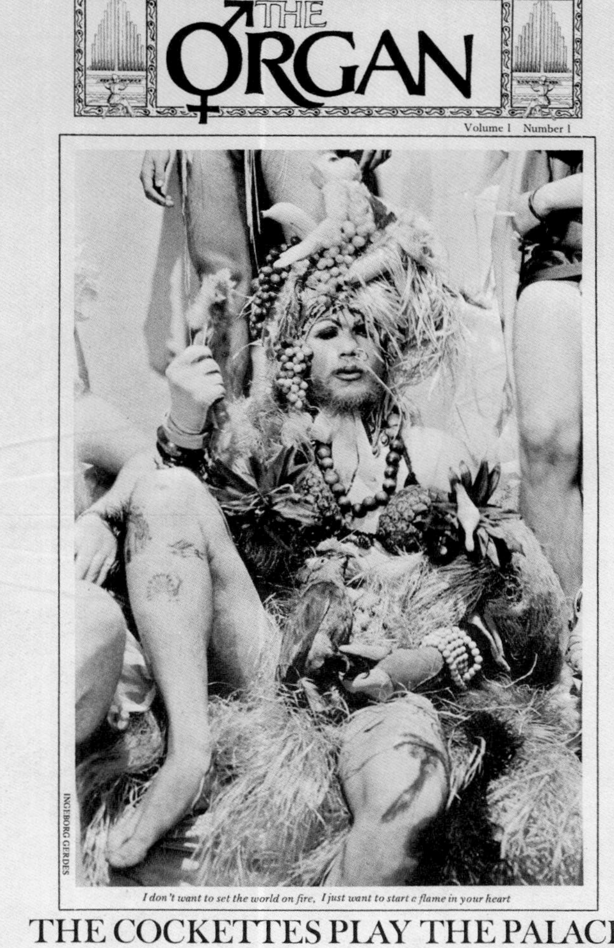

I don't want to set the world on fire, I just want to start a flame in your heart

THE COCKETTES PLAY THE PALACE

In the immediate vicinity of Washington Square Park in San Francisco's North Beach there are three landmarks whose juxtaposition relates as well as any other chance event the tangled cultural consciousness of America in 1970. The first is a superbly surreal, if somewhat stunted, Catholic cathedral replete with cherubs, latin inscriptions, and gobs of gold paint. The second is the rather dowdy though stern statue of Benjamin Franklin which is situated at the center of the park itself.

The Palace Theatre is the third landmark on the periphery of Washington Square and it is there, on a Friday or Saturday midnight, that the strangest metamorphosis since Martha Mitchell was turned into a frog occurs. At that hour the Palace Theatre transforms itself from a Chinese Opera into the Nocturnal Dream Show, and with the Nocturnal Dream Show appear (not every night, but some nights) the psychic circumcision rite known as the Cockettes.

Outwardly, the Cockettes resemble a bizarre and explosive transvestite review and bawdy drag parade. In blazing tufts of

16

Fig. 4.4. **Organ** (Berkeley), July 1970, vol. 1, no. 1, inside cover spread; September 1970, vol. 1, no. 2, pp. 4–5; July 1970, vol. 1, no. 1, cover

FETISHPHILE

"The object of my affection/ can change my complexion/ from white to rosey red."

As a public service, each issue of THE ORGAN presents a thoroughly documented, well-researched and notarized case-history concerning the more bizarre and unsettling aspects of modern life. Designed not to shock but, rather, to inform and educate, this series will deal exclusively in the real-life confessions and memoirs of real-life people in their real-life situations. These are the true stories of the people that make the news; the heads behind the headlines. Dedicated to the unswerving principle that an informed public is an aware public and an aware public is a deadly weapon, THE ORGAN unveils the heretofore untold stories that make, break, and obfuscate the times we live in. Told in their own language, be it earthy or ethereal, these texts come to you bereft of shame or censorship. If reality has not already repressed you beyond recall, read on.

drawing by Tomi Ungerer

The Great Blue Velvet Whip Fuck Conspiracy

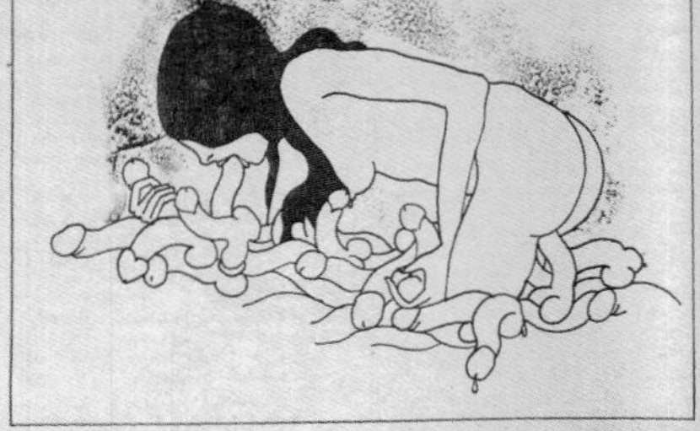

By Shad Sharwick

When the tawny sun blisters the Pacific's horizon into a sheet of deliquescent platinum, and the sunset Joseph's coat of mauve, chartreuse, fuschia, purple and puce undulates across the uncaring western sky to pull the lid of night across the eye of day in ripples of blue on darker blue melting down the edge of day to merge with darkness, then the Golden Gate Bridge like strands of spun tinsel funnels into the clustering lights of San Francisco dripping across the city's hills like gaudy rhinestone sheets of cheap jewelry glimmering against the pale withered breasts of a tatty dowager, and another day in the city's night begins.

Both natives and those new to acquire the patina of the city's much-touted charm will habitually refer to it as 'San Francisco.' To call it 'Frisco' is to commit a social felony. The cultured and not-so-cultured of the city think of San Francisco as a gracious and delicate lady preserving in her storied mansions the essences of that which was best in classic American culture. Resolutely, the grandame that is San Francisco guards these vestiges of former glory against the creeping deluge of Doggy Diners, pay toilets, house-trailers, and styrofoam coffee cups. As the Guardian of the Gates the city is worthy of praise and occasional worship, like all great ladies of the past. But like all great ladies she has her whorish side. In the horizontal, unremitting squalor of the Mission District, the bleak and tragic corduroy of the Fillmore, or the exhausted and overdosed hills of the Haight, she is Frisco cheap and dirty.

One may be whatever one likes in San Francisco. In some quarter of the City any life style is considered valid, any perversion accepted, any product bought or sold. People who, in the great corn pone of the American wilderness, would have had to live out their lives in secret, fearful of discovery at every turn, may indulge their psychic predilections quite openly in San Francisco.

In such an atmosphere of permissiveness and decadence, it is not surprising that cults of strange and terrible purposes have evolved in the shadows of the city.

As a reporter for one of the major tabloids in the city, I was privy to the doings of the inner circle of one of the most fanatical of these cults. Although my story was, for obvious reasons, too shocking for publication in these 'establishment' organs, I feel I can set down here the details and rituals of The Blue Velvet Whip Club as I witnessed them.

One balmy evening last fall, I had been drinking not a little bit of the house chianti at an intimate Italian restaurant in North Beach when I was suddenly approached by a thirtyish blonde with a figure that could crush a bull. I first thought something was up when she grabbed me in the crotch.

"Orgy-porgy?" she asked in a voice that wouldn't take no for an answer. I glanced down the smooth line of her breasts to where her buttocks swelled under her naugahyde skirt in a provocative manner.

"Are your friends anything like you?" I asked.

"You bet," she said. "C'mon. There's no easier way to earn your Canadian Club."

We turned and left the restaurant arm in arm while my ravioli cooled uneaten on the table. At that moment I imagined a small intimate orgy in some loft or penthouse led, perhaps, by a qualified psychologist. I didn't dream that I would end up with a group of people who made a fetish out of mass sex—people who found it impossible to express themselves sexually in groups of less than one hundred couples.

My accoster's name turned out to be Leda. Shaking her tumescent torrent of blonde hair she opened the door of a low-slung ebony Jaguar. We got in, she started the powerful motor, and in a burst of high-octane pollution we spun off towards the financial district. The fog-laced city night slid across my face like cold opals. Shifting through the range of gears like a professional, Leda slid deeper and deeper down the deserted streets and alleyways towards the very epicenter of the Montgomery Street complex of skyscrapers, banks, and stock exchanges. The buildings folded the low slung car into their concrete canyons like a cockroach crawling dementedly in the bottom of an enigma.

Leda took a hard left followed by a sharp right and screeched to a halt in front of a nondescript door. She flashed the headlights in some kind of signal and the door slid silently back revealing a large, but quite empty, garage. We drove in and the door slid shut behind us. There was a whirring of gears and the floor beneath the car began to sink slowly into the bedrock. Polished granite walls rose above us as the car sunk lower and lower into the shaft. Water and slime oozed from the walls. Suddenly we emerged from the shaft into an immense underground parking lot lit by glaring arc lights. I looked around. Close to two hundred gleaming automobiles were parked in neat rows up and down the rough-hewn cavern. Leda bit my thigh and we got out of the car.

We walked down the long corridor of cars to where a streak of violent blue neon lettering proclaimed BLUE VELVET WHIP: ABANDON EXITS YE WHO ENTER! against dark stone walls. We stopped at an opening in the stone draped over with immense blue-velvet curtains and hung with obscene gold cords. Parting these curtains I heard distant strains of a rock band swell louder in the distance. Leda and I entered into a long chamber paneled in the finest mahogany and guarded on both sides by a pair of deaf-mute Swedes dressed only in blue satin turbans and rhinestone jockstraps, equipped with matching jewelled scimitars. Leda nodded amiably to them as they swung

☛ 22

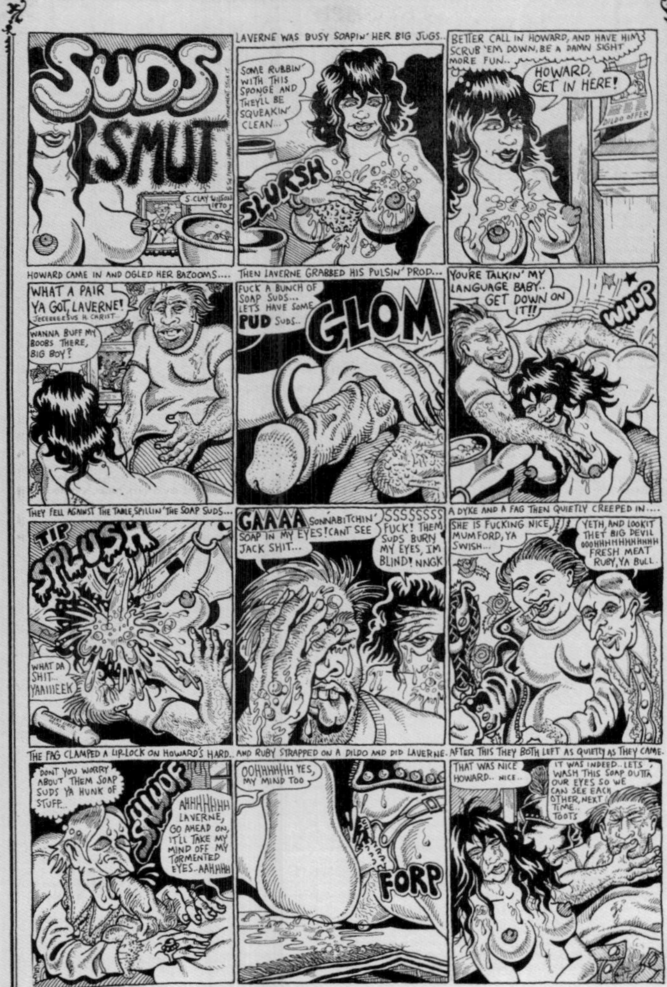

How to Build a Nuclear Device at Home in Your Spare Time, Make Big Money, Win Swell Prizes.

There are presently five nuclear powers in the world: Russia, China, Britain, France, and the University of California. The potential new members of this cartel are Germany, Japan, Israel and revolutionaries. It is this latter group to whom we address ourselves in our discussion of the various and nefarious ways to join the mushroom-power oligarchy. A nuclear device in the hands of a revolutionary could put the blackmail back in brinkmanship.

The term "nuclear device" is the Atomic Energy Commission's jargon for any of their *Gotterdämmerung* machines—be they field deployed warheads for ballistic missiles, or drawing board plans for the excavation of a new Panama Canal through Venezuela. "Device" sounds so much nicer than "bomb," just as "Department of Defense" in *newspeak* is more desirable than "Department of War" even though they are the same thing.

The immediate problem at hand is the acquisition of a nuclear device. Three methods come to mind: buy one, steal one, make one. Of the first, there is no record of a nuke ever being sold to anybody, anywhere, anytime—not that the Wall Street Journal would report such a transaction, but word would surely have leaked out if it had occurred. However, nukes have been known to change hands. Our government loans them to some of our friendlier allies, complete with guards, locks, chains and shackles to which the president (ours) holds the keys.

Buying, then, is difficult. Perhaps theft is more feasible? However, considering the security associated with nuclear weapons, it would require so much money, time and talent to engineer such a rip-off, you could probably manage, by redirecting your energies, to buy a seat on the stock exchange and proceed to take over from the inside.

Even assuming that you did manage to steal a nuke, your chances of being able to employ the device are small. Due to the official paranoia surrounding accidental detonation, modern nuclear devices are labyrinthically complicated, particularly in the sequence of events required to assure initiation of the chain reaction. There is almost no chance of using one except as Pop art. However, the Chinese might trade with you. Finally, stealing a nuclear device is impractical and unnecessary; building one is better.

I should point out that we are not considering the construction of a hydrogen bomb as it involves too much labor, and it uses an atomic bomb as a trigger and what devoted revolutionary needs more than the trigger?

Here an explanation of the dif-

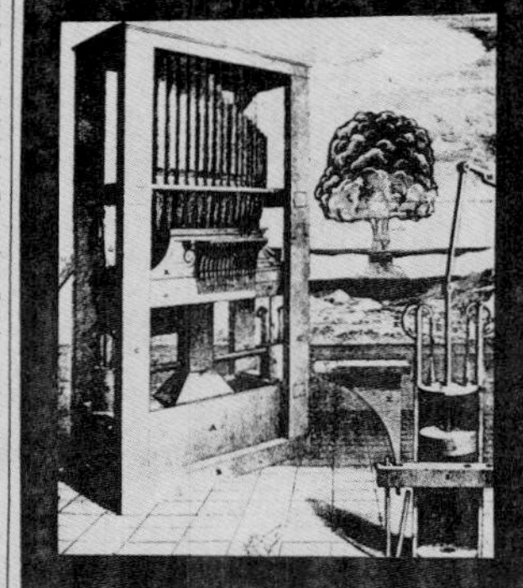

ferences between an atomic and a hydrogen bomb is in order: an atomic bomb is a fission device; a hydrogen bomb is a fusion device. If a neutron hits an atom dead center it will split into two or more pieces. At that moment some energy is released. This is basically the fission process. The neutrons that are part of the energy released will split other atoms releasing more energy and more neutrons, and so on, a chain reaction . . .POOF! In a fusion bomb, atoms of hydrogen are fused together by prodigious quantities of heat and pressure into a helium atom. Since two hydrogen atoms equal more than one helium atom, there is something left over. That something is, again, energy.

But as I said, building a hydrogen bomb is, for political purposes, redundant. Let us be modest and construct a small atomic device in our basement. The optimum nuclear fuel is plutonium, but it's too hot to handle. Leave a lump of it out on the table and the first thing you know (also probably the last thing if you're close by) you'll have a very spontaneous, very deadly fire. Less than two years ago there was a little plutonium fire in Rocky Flats, Colorado—a major factory for AEC gadgets. According to the reports, only one building at the facility was affected and no sign of the fire was visible from the outside. But, inside that building was the plutonium production line for the United States. Total damage: $46,000,000! Merely disposing of the radioactive water used to fight the blaze was a Herculean task. So, forget about the plutonium.

For our bomb plain vanilla uranium 235 will do nicely. How you procure it is your own business. You will need about 25 pounds. This amount is a little more than one critical mass (one "crit.") For God's sake, don't put more than 20 pounds in a pile. The reason is not that it would blow up in any spectacular fashion, but more that it would shorten your life expectancy to like eight days.

Once we accumulate our one crit of U-235 we are ready to build our device. A nuclear device in its most primitive form consists of two twelve and a half pound lumps of U-235 and one extremely self-sacrificing revolutionary. His method will be to take a lump of the stuff in each hand, run shouting slogans into some crowded, well-known bastion of capitalist imperialism and clap—LOUDLY. Now let it be said that he will never get those two lumps together and will not create a bona fide nuclear explosion. Heat pressure will throw the pieces apart with much greater force than he can muster to slam them together. What he will create will be one very radioactive revolutionary who will glow ecstatically in broad daylight before his final fade, while most of the onlookers for about a block around will soon become bald and bear strange looking children.

Of the somewhat more sophisticated fission devices, the implosion type and the gun type are the most practical and popular. The implosion type uses explosives to squeeze a hollow ball into a solid ball. Since the explosively created solid ball is an optimum shape, it will go critical even though the same amount of mass in a hollow sphere would not. This is hard as hell to do, however, requiring explosive lenses, precision timing, and a thousand other complex and difficult manipulations. Forget it. The gun type is easier.

Now, how do you assemble two pieces of hot nuclear material fast enough to create conditions favorable to a chain reaction? The simplest way is to take a spherical chunk (less than one crit) and cut out a plug—forming a sort of radioactive bagel, as it were. The plug can then be rammed into the hole at the desired instant, giving the assembled unit more than one crit and, BAROOM! The best method for doing this is to put the plug in a cannon with a few pounds of TNT behind it and align the barrel with the empty space in the bagel. The unit that fried Hiroshima was a gun type device of twenty kilotons (that's 20,000 tons of TNT).

Constructing this assemblage will require some highly precise and quite dangerous machining. It might help to have an expendable machinist, as you are not likely to find a uranium sphere with the plug missing just awaiting its mate for a cosmic love-in.

Along with an expendable machinist you will certainly need an initiator. This piece of gadgetry provides the necessary neutron which triggers the chain reaction at precisely the optimum time. There are only a few thousandths of a second during which our nuclear contraption can go critical. If a neutron doesn't come by during that time, then we're all dressed up with no place to go.

☛ 24

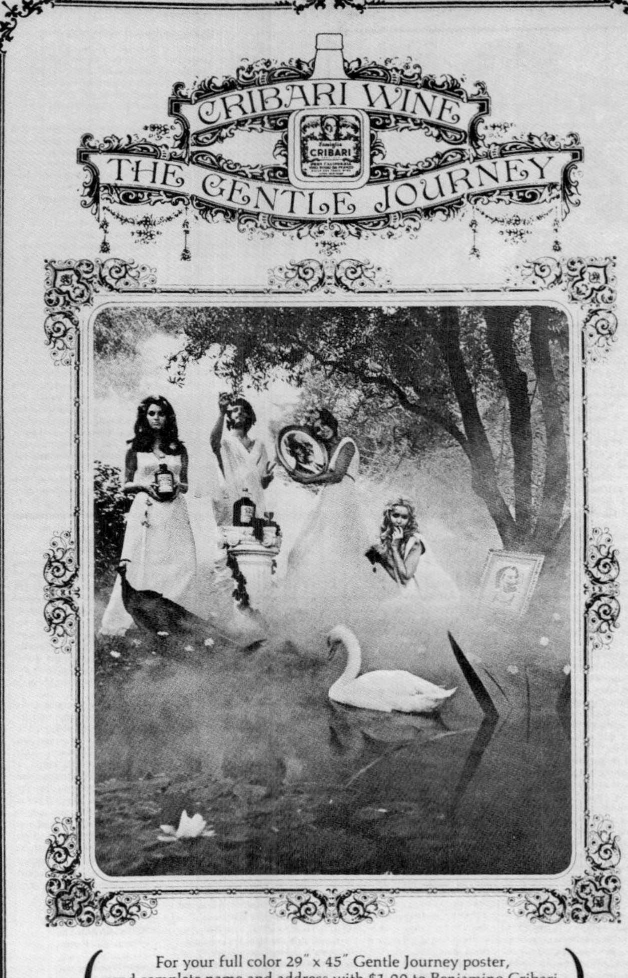

Fig. 4.4 (cont'd.) **Organ** (Berkeley), July 1970, vol. 1, no. 1, pp. 10–11, 12–13.

Next page
Fig. 4.4 (cont'd.) **Organ** (Berkeley), July 1970, vol. 1, no. 1, pp. 18–19, 20–21

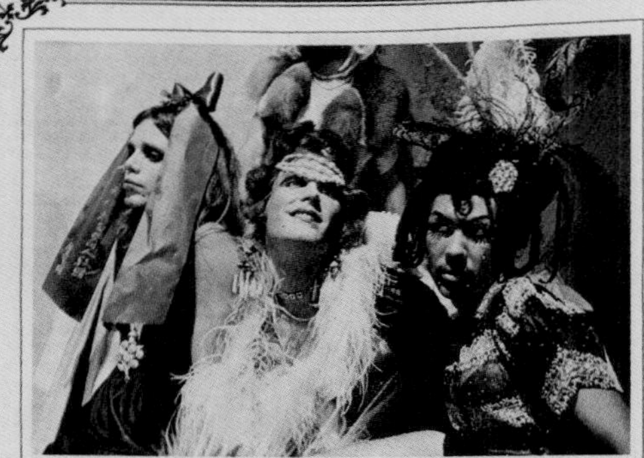

Photograph by INGEBORG GERDES

plumage and lurid sequins, skirts, and pasties they romp, bump, grind, kick, scream, flaunt, swish, stagger and writhe their way through the rooms behind your mind; egos, ids, and cocks flapping to a ragtime rhythm.

One arrives at the Palace sometime shortly before midnight. One usually arrives stoned or tired, or both. The facade of the Palace provides through its plethora of hieroglyphic Chinese posters ample hallucinatory material to pass the time before the change of shows.

The interior of the Palace is a hybrid of Kubla Khan's Pleasure Dome and some stoned-out Rockwell Kent's W.P.A. opium vision. The ceiling is dominated by an immense green, red, and gold mandala whose motifs and patterns creep down the wall to repeat themselves in gilt and pastel patches. The floor is composed of some unidentifiable sticky substance awash in pistachio nut shells, styrofoam tea cups, cigar and cigarette butts, and shredded candy wrappers that crunch and crackle everywhere as the audience settles in.

When the Cockettes first appeared in January of this year, they were just a balls-out, bare-assed melange of fantasies, fictions, shadows, whimsies, and uninhibited sexual freak-outs that took over the stage at the Palace through sheer, brazen *chutzpah*. The Nocturnal Dream Show's audience, loving by nature and design, and loving of anything at three in the morning, took them to its bosom.

The Cockettes initial blatant exhibitionism soon became tempered with satire and parody. What they lost in spontaneity they gained in staying power. In the process they also worked out a series of skits, riffs, camp-gags, and musical numbers which aid in forming the Cockettes into something more than a group-grope that simultaneously avoids the egomanias and role traps usually associated with theatre.

One of the Cockettes' latest outrages is a rendition of something that resembles a blending of *Showboat* and *Gone with the Wind*. The show opens with a falsetto rendering of "Old Man River" by a beefy contralto decked out in a feathered boa. This is followed by a reverse striptease as a dazzling Cockette dances onto the stage naked from the waist down to squirm his way into a floor-length satin formal. Then from behind a cardboard plantation door and a cardboard showboat, the mass of the Cockettes swarms out looking for all the world like slightly raunchy Southern Belles down on their luck. The belles come fully equipped with a couple of pickaninnies (burnt cork make-up, taffeta frocks, white gloves).

After a bit of generalized groping and camping about, the gaggle of belles suddenly forms into a ragged Rockettes chorus line, burst into a threnody of song with, what else, "There's No Business Like Show Business," all of them kicking with the stomping clunk that only a size ten brogan in a six-A pump can manage.

Throughout, the Cockettes improvisational attitude is unmistak-

☞ 18

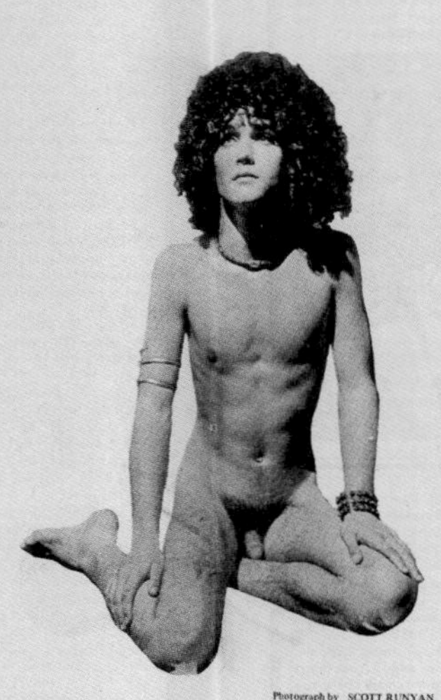

Photograph by SCOTT RUNYAN

THE COCKETTES

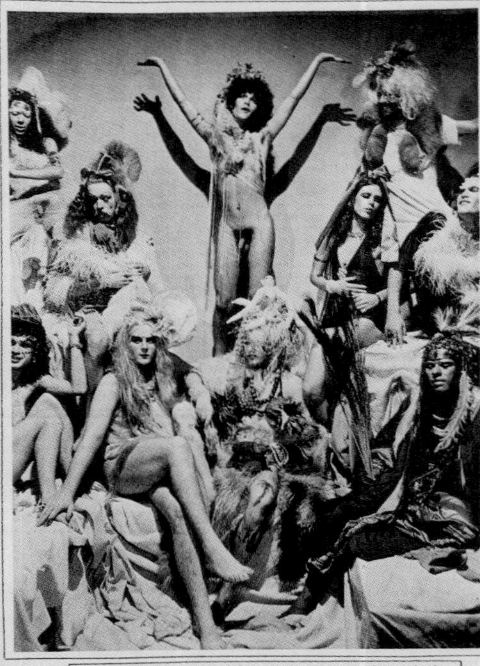

Photograph by INGEBORG GERDES

"More strange than true. I never may believe
These antic fables nor these fairy toys.
Lovers and madmen have such seething brains,
Such shaping fantasies, that apprehend
More than cool reason ever comprehends."
—Midsummer Night's Dream

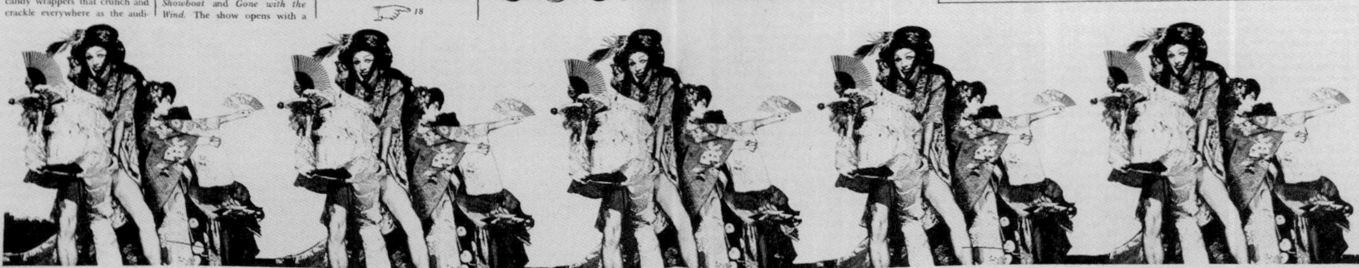

THE INDIANS

1.

Thirty-six Indians raided a cavalry outpost at night.
They didn't come hooping and yelling and giving themselves
away. They didn't drink, they used no guns.

2.

The thirty-six were especially chosen for the raid.
They had been to Japan via Alaska on a cultural exchange
mission:
    Twenty-seven Samurai had been to America
    to learn how to ride fast pintos
    to understand the peyote rights.
It was a fair exchange.
It lasted the traditional six years.
The return of the Samurai,
their duty and their pledge,
is another story.

3.

The Indians returned as zen archers,
    masters of their art,
    perfectly controlled,
    honorably dressed,
    relaxed in demeanor and gait,
    dedicated to their ideals.
They were received and welcomed with full honors.
These were the Indians who made the attack.
There was no discussion of whether or not they would succeed.

4.

It must be said that there was much bloodshed,
some necessary, some uncalled for.
Two of the group were overzealous in overcoming the enemy:
    These two are still with the group.
    Their errors have been pointed out.
    They are repentant, they are not ashamed.
    It is open to question whether or not they understand
    "the way."

5.

None of the thirty-six Indians was killed or wounded
This was not considered remarkable by the group.
If a few had been killed it would not have seemed remarkable.
Whatever had taken place would have been expected.

6.

They made no more raids.
The tribe moved West immediately and settled on the coast,
below Mission Monterey
in an inaccessible area,
where there was lush greenery and hot mineral baths.

7.

They programmed themselves to disappear,
knowing that to live on
would court both physical and spiritual disaster.
Some claim that the tribe has several living members.
The reports differ:
    They remain Indians,
    living in seclusion in this still inaccessible area.
    They have assimilated.
    Retaining their identity secretly,
    they influence those who now live where they lived.
Either explanation is valid.
Both are the same

By Artie Ross

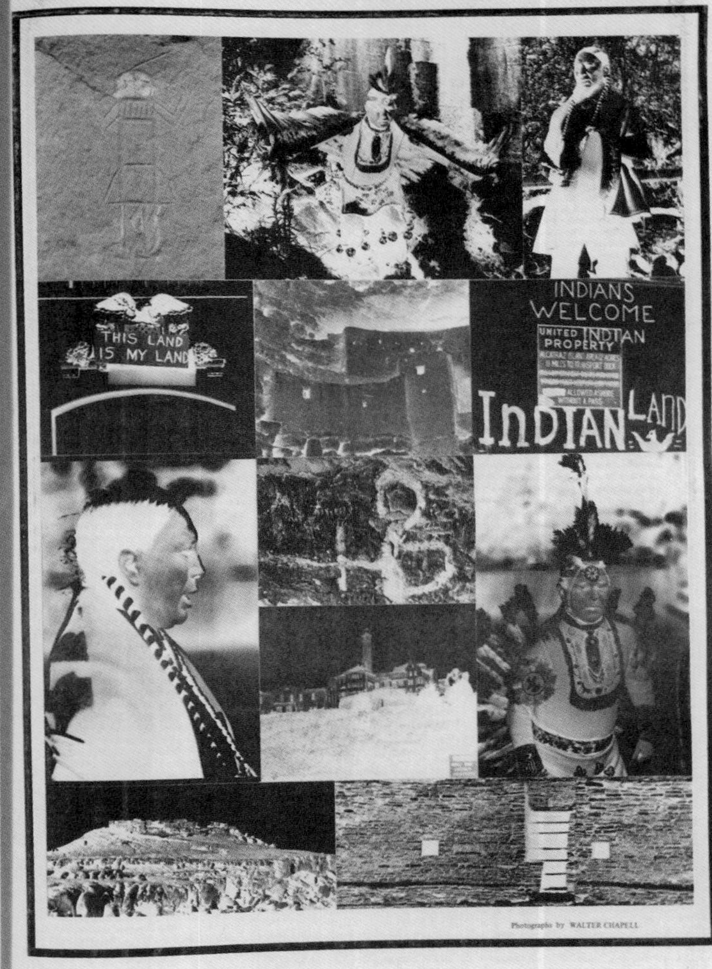

Photographs by WALTER CHAPELL

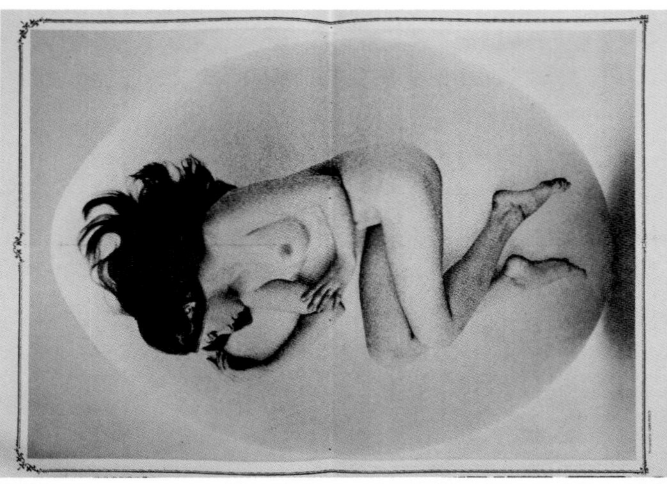

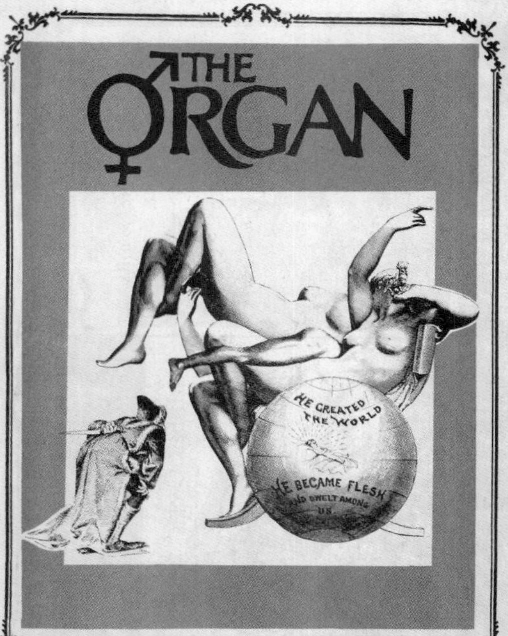

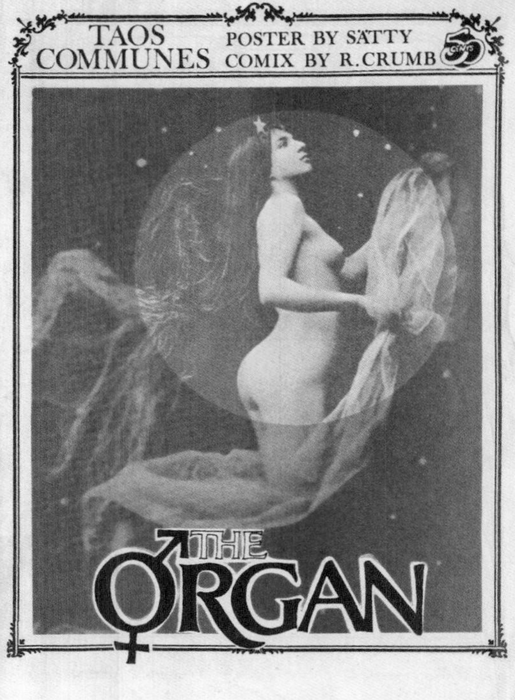

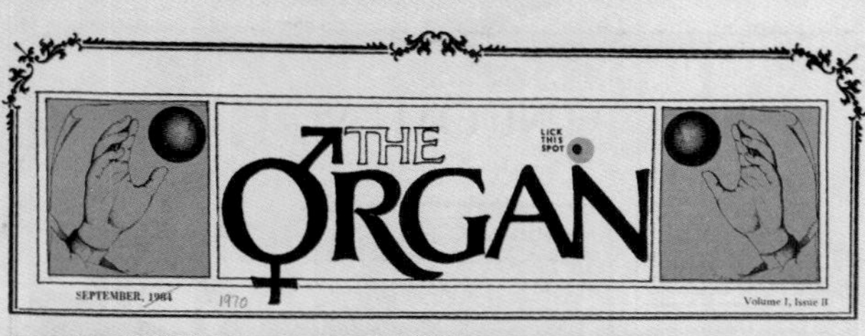

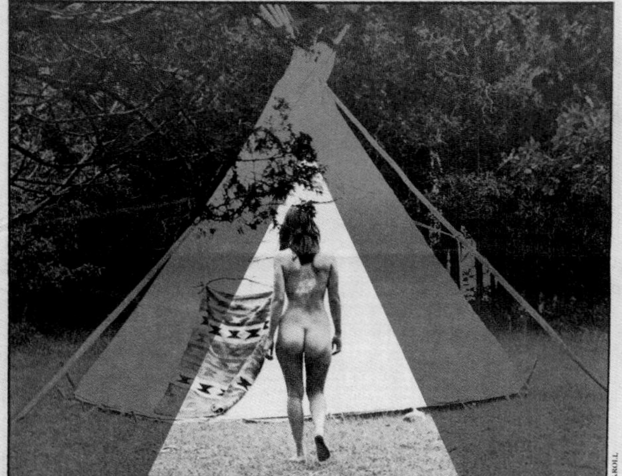

TRUCKIN' TOWARD TAOS WITH TOOTSIE

by Jon Stewart

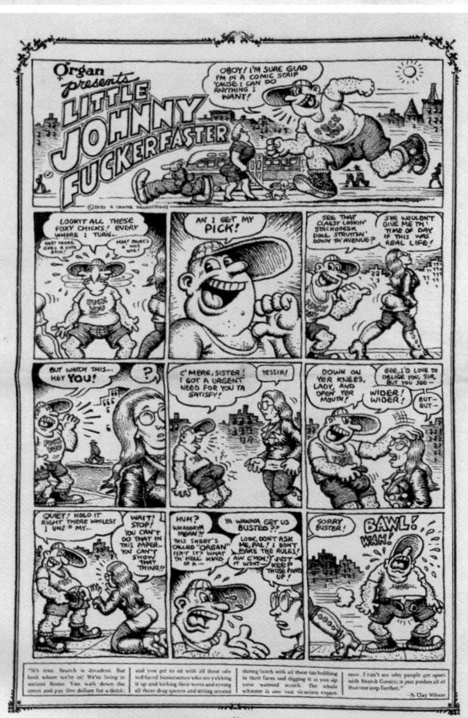

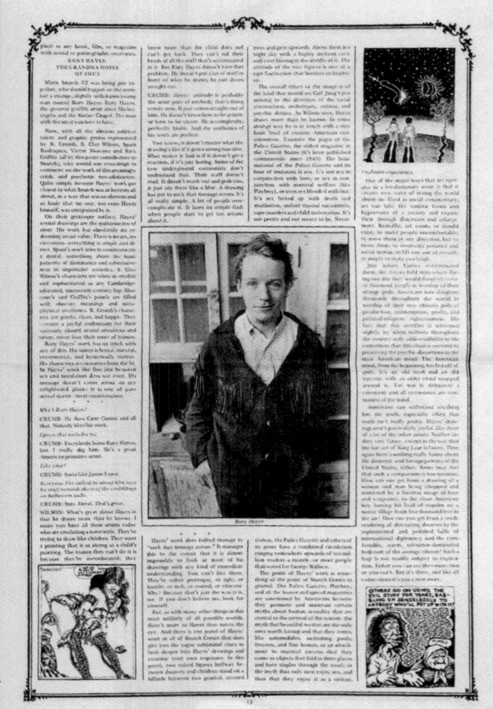

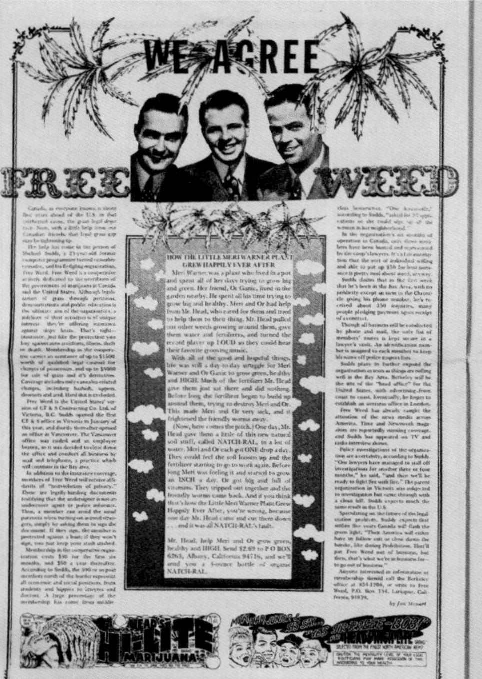

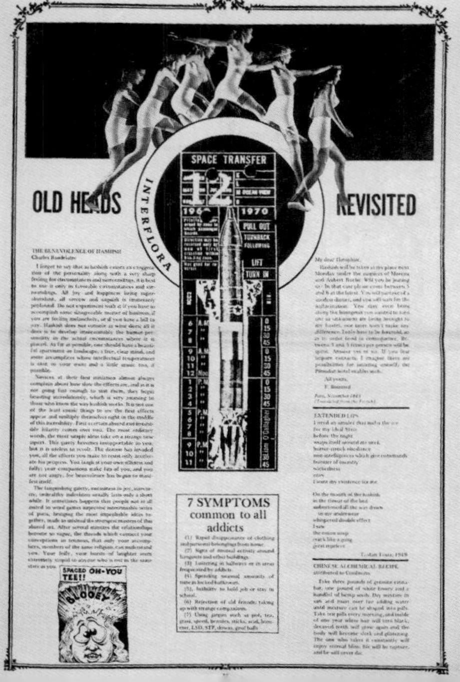

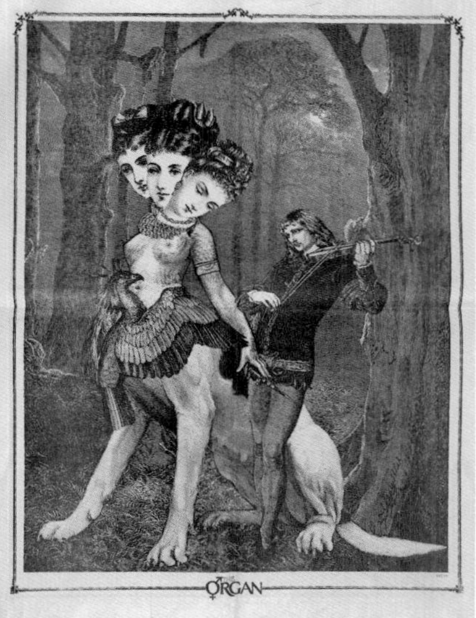

Fig. 4.4 (cont'd). **Organ** (Berkeley), July 1970, vol. 1, no. 1, center spread; September 1970, vol. 1, no. 2, inside cover spread, cover, pp. 14–15, 26–27, and center spread

Next page
Fig. 4.4 (cont'd). **Organ** (Berkeley), December 1970, vol. 1, no. 3, pp. 10–11, cover, center spread, pp. 20–21, and inside cover spread

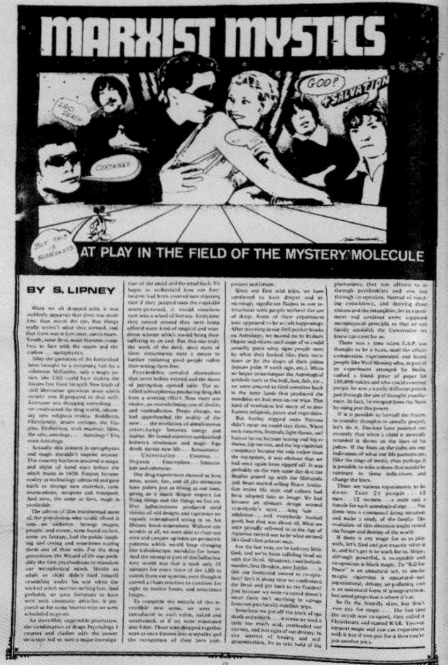
MARXIST MYSTICS
AT PLAY IN THE FIELD OF THE MYSTERY MOLECULE
BY S. LIPNEY

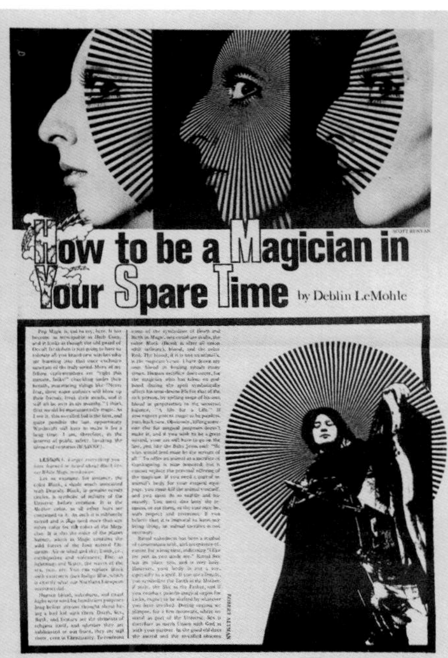
How to be a Magician in Your Spare Time
by Deblin LeMohle

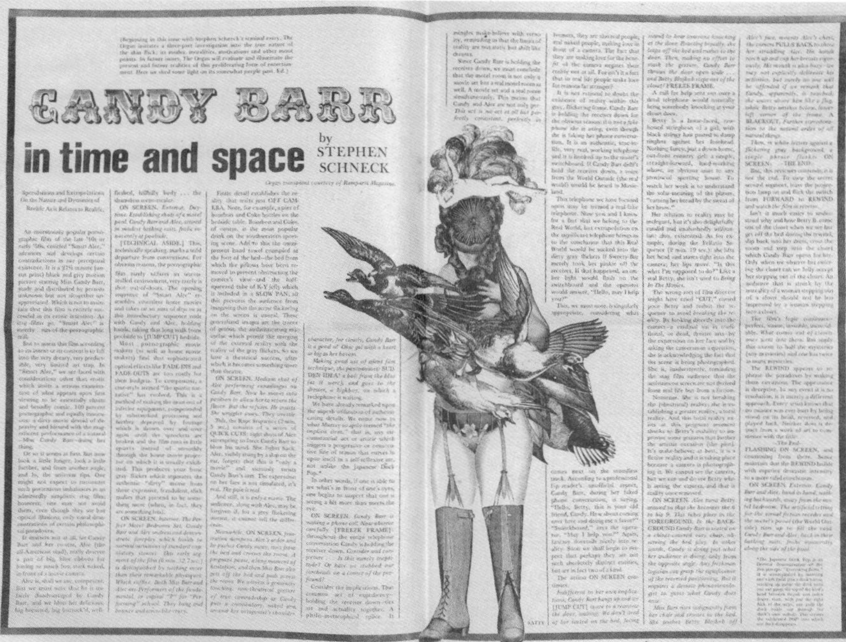
CANDY BARR
in time and space
by STEPHEN SCHNECK

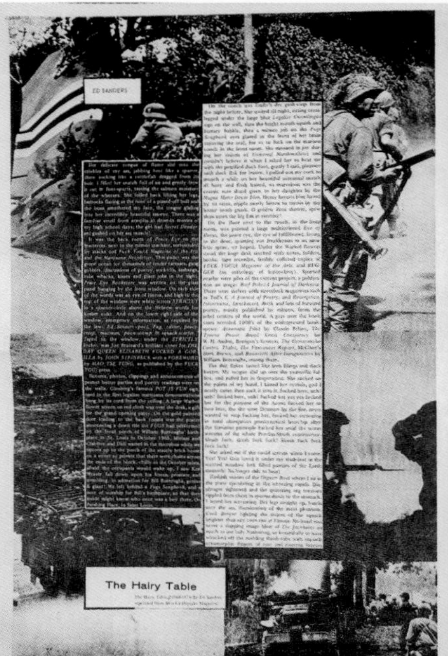
The Hairy Table

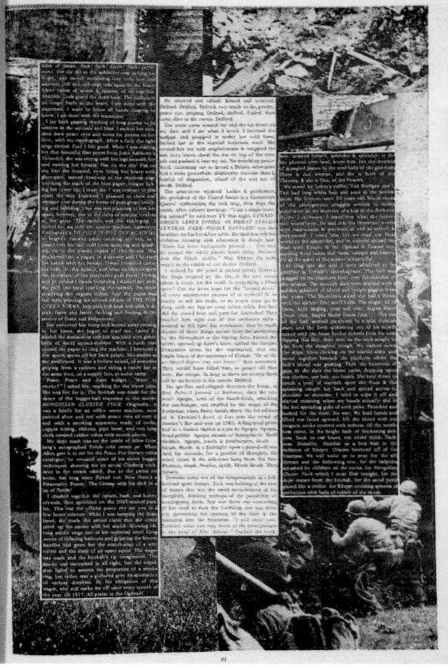

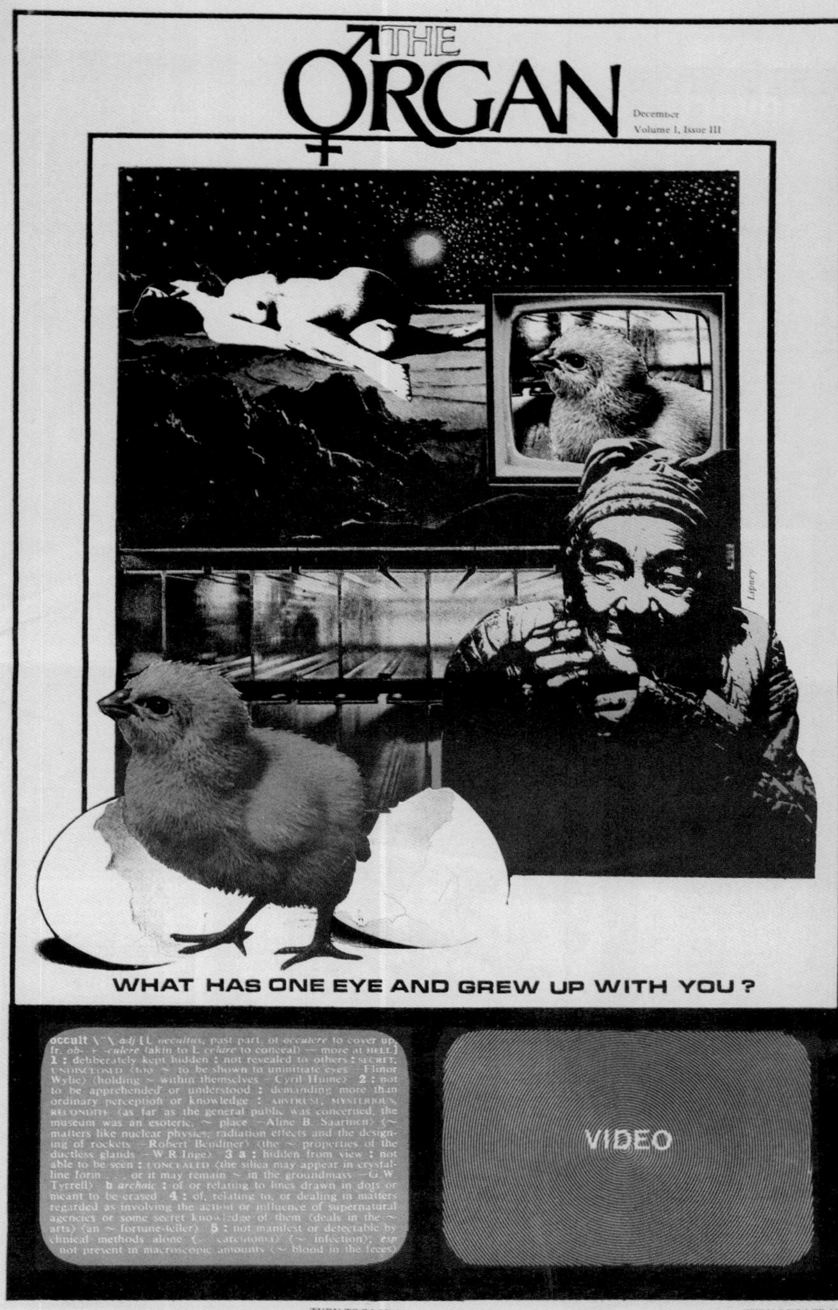
THE ORGAN
December
Volume 1, Issue III
WHAT HAS ONE EYE AND GREW UP WITH YOU ?
VIDEO
TURN TO PAGE 4
TURN TO PAGE 23

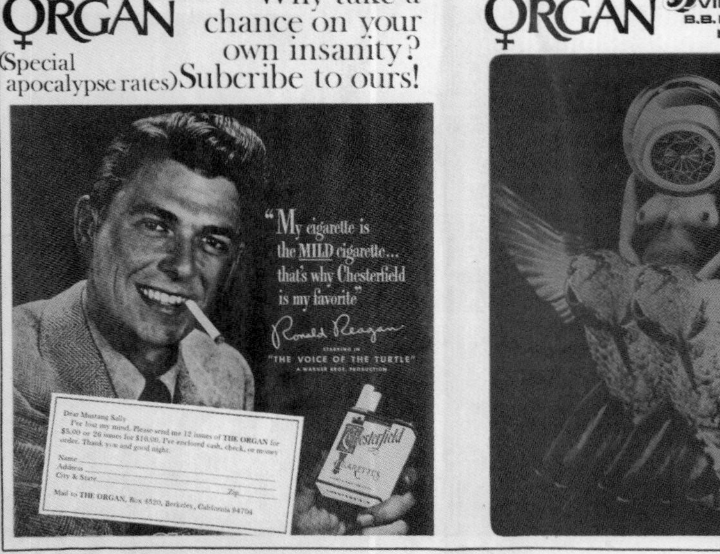
THE ORGAN
(Special apocalypse rates)
Why take a chance on your own insanity? Subcribe to ours!
"My cigarette is the MILD cigarette... that's why Chesterfield is my favorite"
THE ORGAN
MODES OF MAGIC
VIDEO REVOLUTION
B.B. KING ON THE RUN
KENNETH ANGER

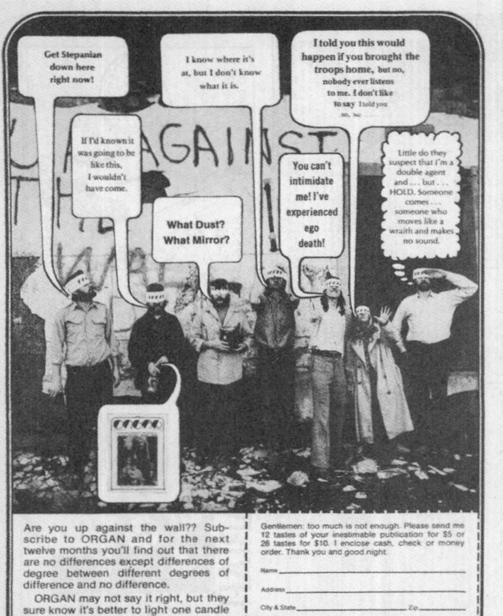

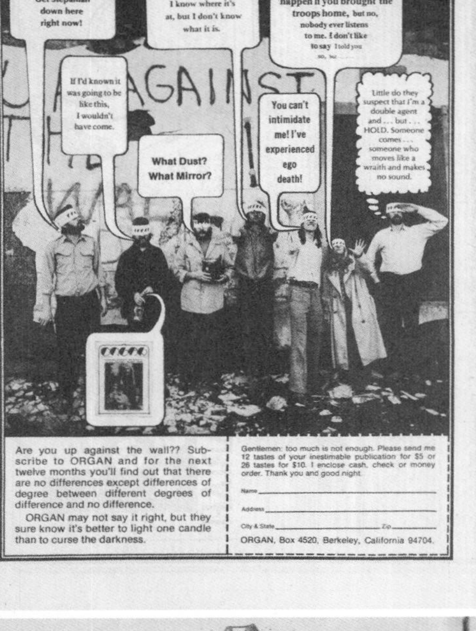

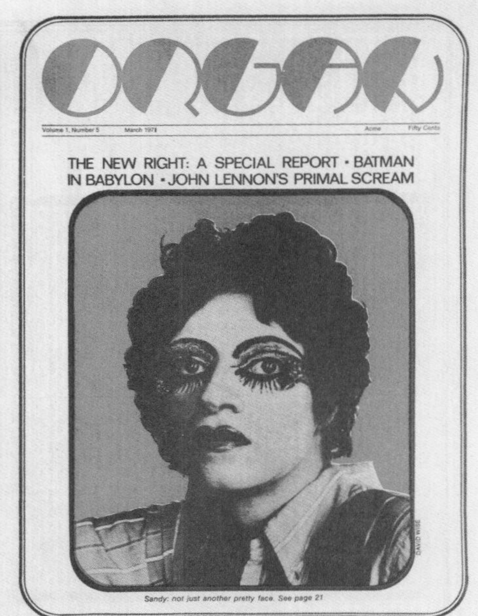

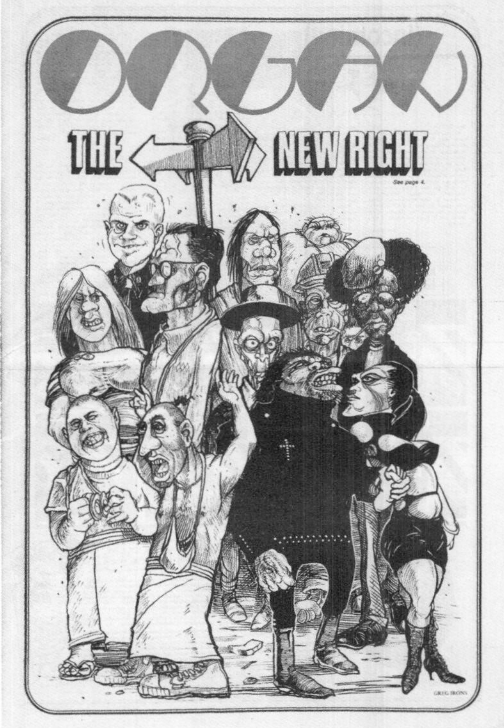

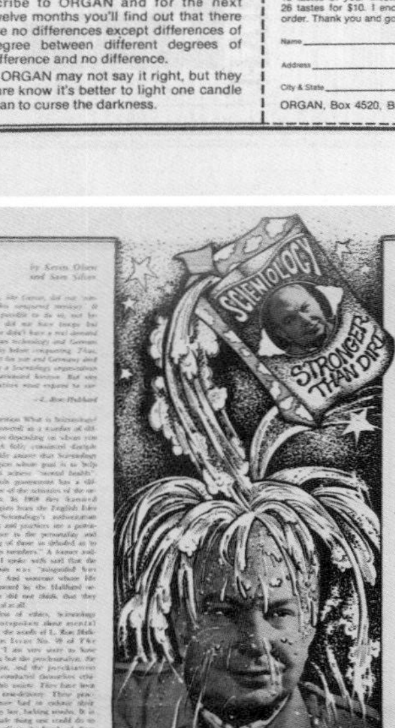

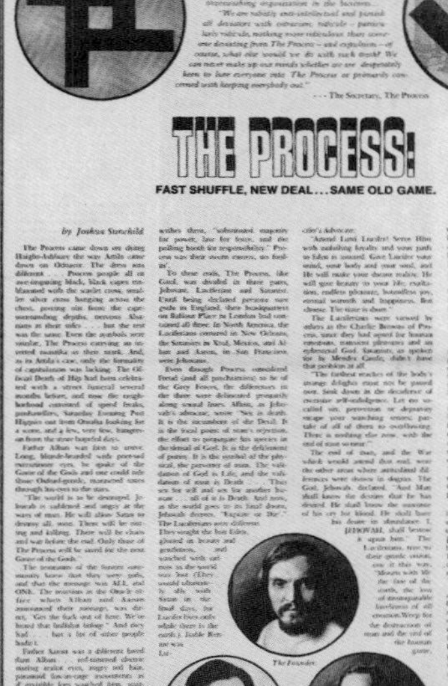

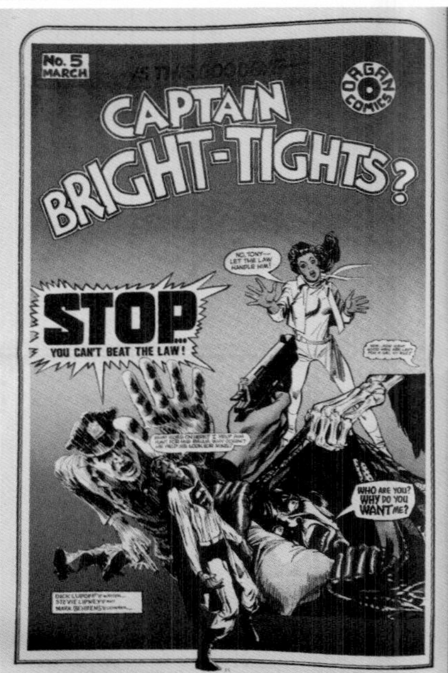

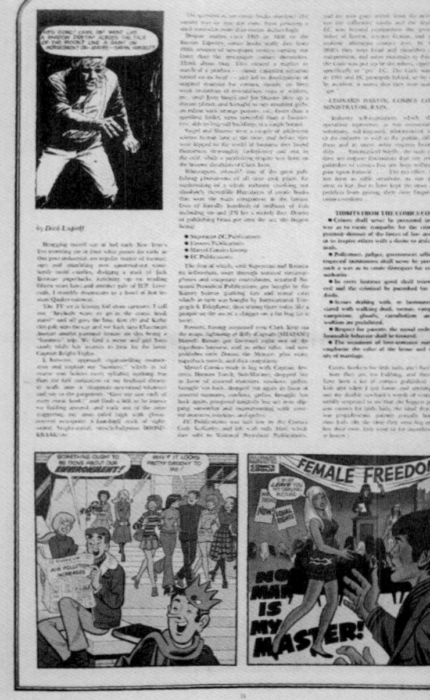

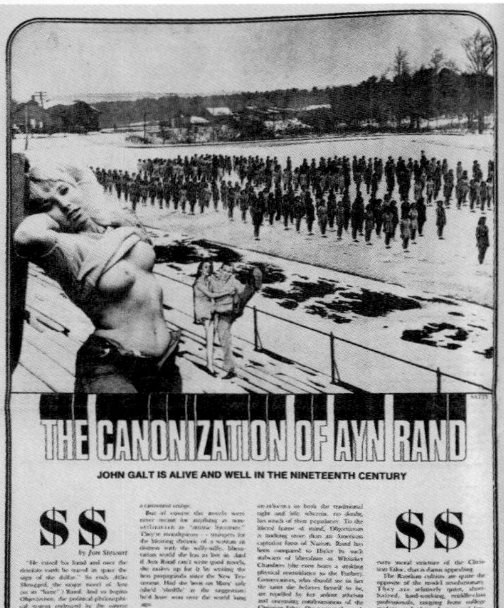

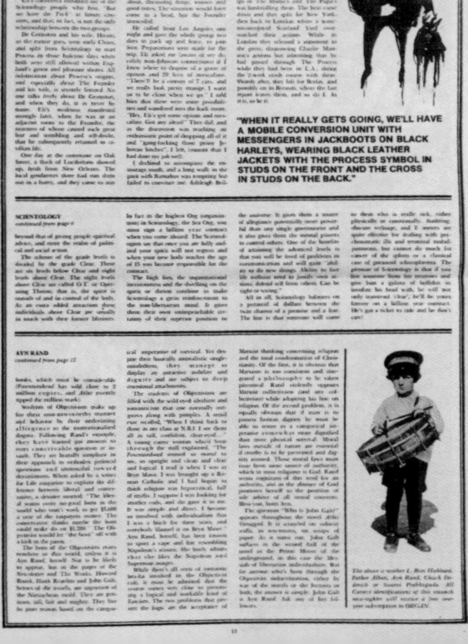

Fig. 4.4 (cont'd.). **Organ** (Berkeley), March 1971, vol. 1, no. 5, inside cover spread, cover, pp. 6-7, 14-15, and 12-13

Next page
Fig. 4.4 (cont'd.). **Organ** (Berkeley), April 1971, vol. 1, no. 6, pp. 24-25, cover, and center spread

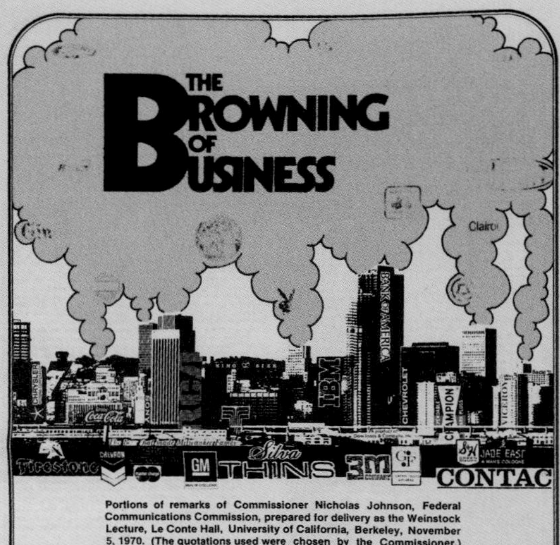

Portions of remarks of Commissioner Nicholas Johnson, Federal Communications Commission, prepared for delivery as the Weinstock Lecture, Le Conte Hall, University of California, Berkeley, November 5, 1970. (The quotations used were chosen by the Commissioner.)

"The biggest big business in America is not steel, automobiles or television. It is the manufacture, refinement and distribution of anxiety....Logically extended, this process can only terminate in a mass nervous breakdown or in a collective condition of resentment...."

Eric Sevareid

The corporations have had their greening. Now it's America's turn, says Charlie Reich.

There are a great many Americans who agree with him. In fact, the response to *The Greening of America* this past October seems to have produced about the cleanest sorting process so far devised for lining up the academic community on either side of the generation gap.

The academic put down of one's colleagues is nothing new, of course. But I don't think I can recall a prior instance in which there has been quite as rapid and as forceful a response from as many people in the academic community in all corners of this country—by long distance phone, conference presentations, letters, conversations, and public print—in the effort to demonstrate that a colleague's book was of little consequence.

Don't get me wrong. I don't agree with everything Professor Reich has written either. But I do think he has provided a very useful insight into what is going on in a great many people's heads right now. If you've been going through it too you understand exactly what he's talking about. If you haven't, well, read it again.

Charlie and I have a number of things in common. We were both trained as lawyers prior to the 1960's. We both came under the inspiring influence of Justice Black during our clerkships at the Supreme Court. We both share the same general philosophy of the law. I, too, was once a law professor with research and teaching interests in administrative law. We both try to promote, and personally enjoy, the literal as well as the figurative "greening of America." We have both tried to square our lives in the 1950's with the insights from our young friends during the 1960's. And, unknown to each other, we have both spent the past few months trying to express it.

That's a part of the burden, responsibility—and joy—of being my age in this age. My generation constitutes the straggling last remains of the puritan ethic, inner-directed old Americans. I can recall as a child the arrival of a "civilization" at my uncle's Iowa farm: electricity for the lights and water pump instead of kerosene lanterns and the wind mill; a fancy stove to replace the old cast iron pot-belly we fed corn cobs and coal; indoor plumbing and a hot water heater to replace the out house and the heating of bath water on the stove. Those were days of genuine and grateful American patriotism taught you by immigrant grandparents, family ties, hard work, some hard times, Franklin Roosevelt, the Fourth of July, and "The War." I was young, but I was alive and aware and I have some feeling for the confusion, frustration and fears that many of my older family and friends express today.

"A specter is stalking in our midst whom only a few see with clarity. It is not the old ghost of communism or fascism. It is a new specter: a completely mechanized society, devoted to maximal material output and consumption, directed by computers; and in this social process, man himself is being transformed into a part of the total machine, well fed and entertained, yet passive, unalive, and with little feeling."

Erich Fromm

But I am young enough, and open enough, that I can hear what my children are saying, and their friends, and my young staff and friends in Washington. I realize that I am no longer 17, or 27, and that it's important to remember that fact. I know that the experience that comes with age does bring valuable insights (even if not always wisdom), and that some of the attitudes and activities of some of the young are nonconstructive and worse. But I also know that there is much in the beliefs and life styles of most of my young friends that makes a great deal of sense for people of any age. To the extent that I can understand what they are saying, and to the lesser degree that I can live it as well, that is a joy I cherish.

"For awhile, I would like to sit in the shade with a glass of wine in my hands just watching the people dance."

Adlai Stevenson

No age is easy; but being in one's thirties at this time is especially difficult. You are caught between cultures. The temptation is to take sides—to move either forward or backward in time. The challenge is to stand firm, to try to discover as precisely as you can your best possible-self, to pick the best from all possible worlds, and to try to encourage constructive communication between two generations that seem to be missing most of what the other is saying. That is what many my age realize to be their responsibility and their opportunity; it is what I am trying to do.

The times are changing. A new world is coming. And the surface trivia—hair styles, dress, music, sexual and "marriage" relationships—are in many ways the least significant aspect of all.

You cannot "buy" (or sell) a new identity. You cannot just walk into a non-conformist store and buy the latest non-conformist clothes, records, and wall posters and get it over with. Those businessmen who have tried have made few profits or prophets.

"Lives based on having are less free than lives based on either doing or on being."

William James

Because what we are really talking about is a rebirth of the human personality. We are talking about a blend of philosophy, psychiatry, politics and poetry that must be personally experienced and worked through. You not only can't buy the finished product, you can't even buy a kit and assemble it yourself.

Indeed, central to this renaissance of the human spirit is a self-determination, power, and simplicity that is totally at odds with the purchase of most of the products sold, for example, in a typical, large urban all-purpose drug store.

Why buy kitchen cleansers, toothpaste, mouthwash, bath salts, room freshener, burn ointments, children's clay and stomach settlers—for many dollars—when you can get it all in a little box of Arm and Hammer bicarbonate of soda for pennies?

Or take the matter of bicycle riding. You don't ride a bicycle because you hate General Motors but don't have the courage to bomb an auto plant. You don't do it as a gesture of great sacrifice and personal sacrifice. You are not even engaged, necessarily, in an act of political protest over the company's responsibility for most of the air pollution by turning on the United States. It's like finally giving up cigarettes. You just wake up one morning and realize you don't want to stain the day with another automobile. Just as cigarette smoking is not a pleasure, it's a business, so you finally come to realize that you don't need General Motors, they need you. They need you to drive their cars for them. You are driving for Detroit, and paying them to do it. Automobiles are just a part of your life that's over, that's all. No hard feelings. You've just moved on to something else. From now on you just use their buses, taxis and rental cars when they suit your convenience. You don't keep one for them that you have to house, feed and water, and care for.

"I am waiting for someone to really discover America."

Lawrence Ferlinghetti

You ride a bicycle because it feels good—especially if your city has bicycle paths (I use the C & O Canal towpath in Washington), but even if it doesn't (I sometimes ride in traffic). The air feels good on your body; even the rain feels good. The blood starts moving around your body, and pretty soon it gets to your head and, glory be, your head feels good. You start noticing things. You look until you really see. You hear things, and smell smells, you never knew were there. You start whistling nice little original tunes to suit the moment. Words start getting caught in the web of poetry in your mind. And there's a nice feeling, too, in knowing you're doing a fundamental life thing for yourself: transportation. You got a little bit of your life back! And the thing you use is simple, functional and relatively cheap; you want one that fits you, and rides smoothly, but with proper care and a few parts it should last almost forever. Your satisfaction comes from within you, not from the envy or jealousy of others. (Although you are entitled to feel a little smug during rush hours, knowing you are also making better time than most of the people in cars.)

Where I disagree with Charlie Reich is in his prediction that such attitudes are going to bring the downfall of the corporate state, that they constitute a new and powerful political movement. I think not. I think we are talking about 30% of the population at best, and that while it will have a substantial impact, meaningful reforms are still going to require more conventional political action and legislation. There are going to continue to be an awful lot of people who, for a variety of reasons, can't or won't break out of the corporate trap. They would rather continue to tell themselves that they really want to drive that car, smoke those cigarettes, and use that hair spray. Under it all may be the fear that if they went out in search of themselves they might come back empty handed. Almost any alternative is preferable to that nightmare.

"...The ordinary person is a shriveled, desiccated fragment of what a person can be.

...Our capacity even to see, hear, touch, taste and smell is so shrouded in veils of mystification that an intensive discipline of unlearning is necessary for anyone before one can begin to experience the world afresh, with innocence, truth and love."

R. D. Laing, *The Politics of Experience*

I also disagree—either with Charlie or a number of his detractors (by now it is hard to keep straight what it was he really said)—that there is going to be a great "dropping out" of industrialized, urban America in a massive return-to-nature movement. However you personally may feel about life in the woods, the fact is that most of us are going to stay in the city most of the time. (More and more people are buying wooded areas, and other second homes, and spending longer "vacations" there; but they still "live"(?) in the city.) The challenge, therefore, in my judgment, is not how to escape—that's relatively easy. The challenge is how to stay; how can one work out, for himself, a life before death in the corporate state.

"There is such a thing as psychological suicide in which one does not take his own life by a given act, but dies because he has chosen—perhaps without being entirely aware of it—not to live."

Rollo May

The answer, in my experience, is to find those places where you can break through the interlocked system and get some of those bits and pieces of your life back that you are paying other people to live for you. Bicycle riding may be totally impractical for you. O.K., then find something else. Raise some of your own food. Make some of your own clothes. You can't possibly do it all; and wouldn't want to. There would be no time left to read and write poetry. That's one of the advantages of living in the city; you don't have to do it all. But you do have to do enough of it to regain the feeling that it's your life you're living. You do need to know that you are only consuming because you need to and want to, not because the TV and the big corporations need you to.

The problem is that our non-life in the corporate state does get interlocked: business suits, automobiles, air conditioning, restaurants, underarm deodorant, cocktail parties, suburban homes, and television watching are kind of interdependent. Once you get a big house you fill it full of things—more things than you "need" (or even enjoy). Then you need other things to take care of those things, and a station wagon to haul them, and a repairman to fix them, and so on ad infinitum.

"Even though we know we are being taken, we are being taken."

William F. Fore

I recall one evening Mason Williams and I were debating whether to go out for dinner or cook at his house. We decided we didn't want to change clothes so we'd stay home. That prompted him to speculate that the reason you have to dress up to go out to dinner is that the same people who own the restaurants own the clothing stores.

What all of us need to learn, more effectively than any of us have so far, is what we have in common as people. When children reject the standards and life styles of their parents, what they are sometimes substituting instead turns out to be pretty close to the value system of their grandparents. Whether or not "God is dead"—in the sense that organized, institutionalized religion is failing to respond to the needs of people in this age—it is clear that "religion" is not dead (in the sense of a personal quest for a meaning in life beyond the daily routine). Those who are turning away from corporate jobs are most often opting for harder and more meaningful work, not lethargy. Young people are not the only Americans who enjoy music, physical activity, poetry, and the great outdoors. Everybody likes flowers—and increasing numbers of all ages are discovering they're nicer when grown and given than when purchased. (I just saw, while writing this, a garbage truck with pink holly hooks attached to each head light.)

Learned scholars who know much more psychiatry, sociology and political science than I, report that we are in danger as a people. They have predicted today's incidence of social disintegration twenty years before it happened: "nervous breakdowns" and mental illness, alcoholism and drug addiction, divorce and promiscuity, crime and violence. They say it is because humans need to be able to grow and develop as people; that they need whole lives in which love, pride of productivity, dignity, beauty and creativity play a daily role. They say that if people cannot lead lives like that they not only suffer fundamentally as individuals, but that they also make for a bad society for everybody else—that the whole country rises and falls together. In other words, "quality of life" doesn't just mean getting the smoke out of the air. That's necessary for us as animals; pollution is bad for cows and citrus trees, too. But quality of life for humans has to do with the smog inside our minds. And as we look around we find the same guys who are putting the garbage in the air are putting the garbage in our heads. It is the result of an engineer with his eye only on the gauge that reports the gross national product.

"As we talk to people across the nation, over and over again, we hear questions like these: 'What does it all mean?' 'Where am I going?' 'Why don't things seem more worth while...when we all work so hard and have so darn many things to play with?"

The question is: Can your product fill this gap?"

a consumer products survey report

We have long passed the time when concern for the real quality of human life could be dismissed as mere "romanticism," or naive idealism. We not only have the economic opportunity to create the self-fulfilling society, we not only have the moral imperative that we do so, we are confronted with the political and social necessity of doing so if we are not to perish in our own self-inflicted violence and insanity.

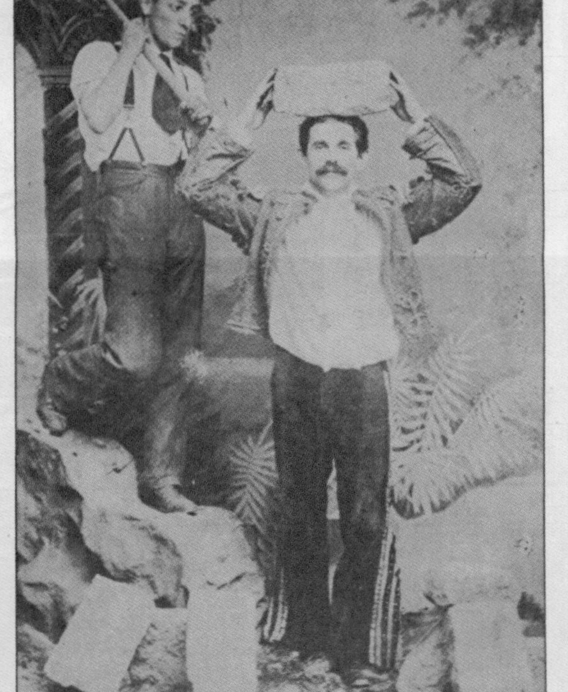

The first recorded dope deal: the infamous Pensacola Phil splitting a brick of Guadalajara Green. See page 4.

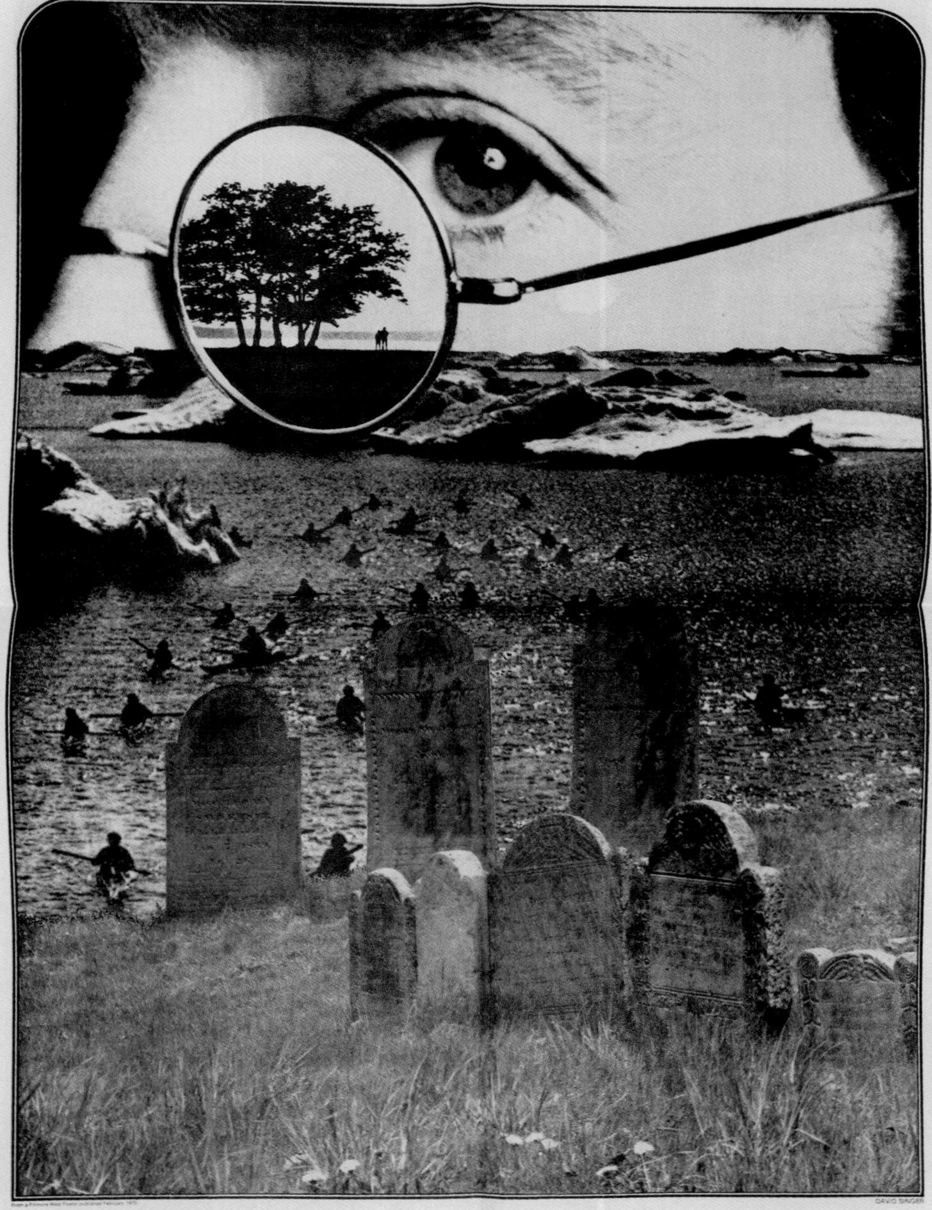

DAVID SINGER

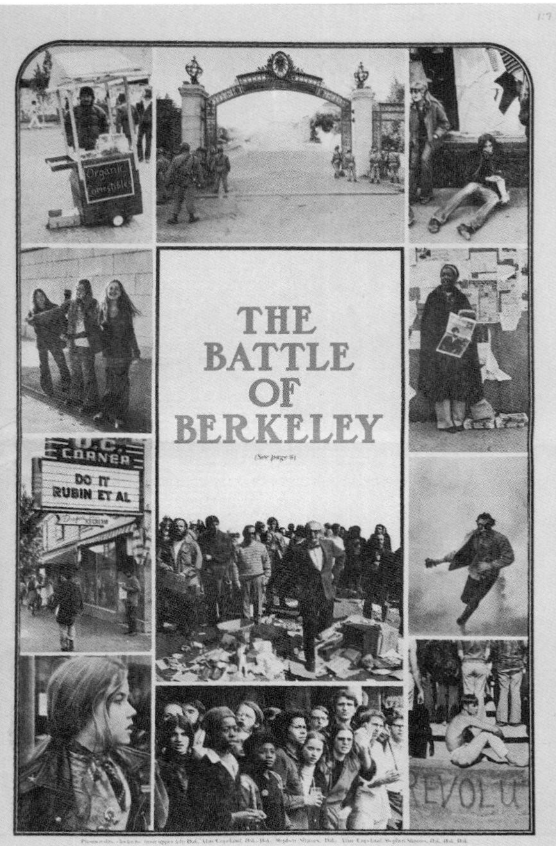

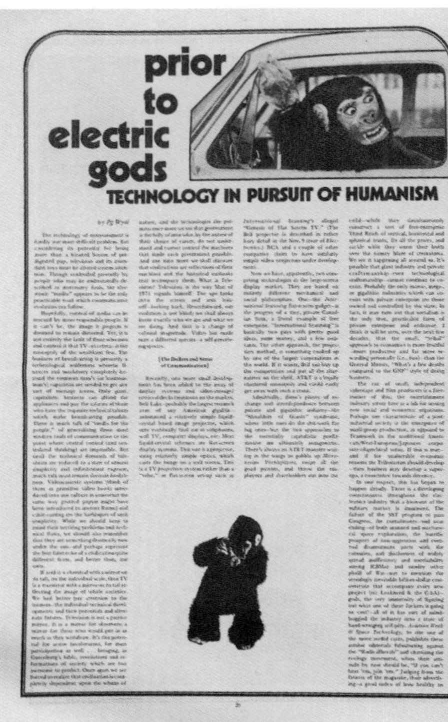

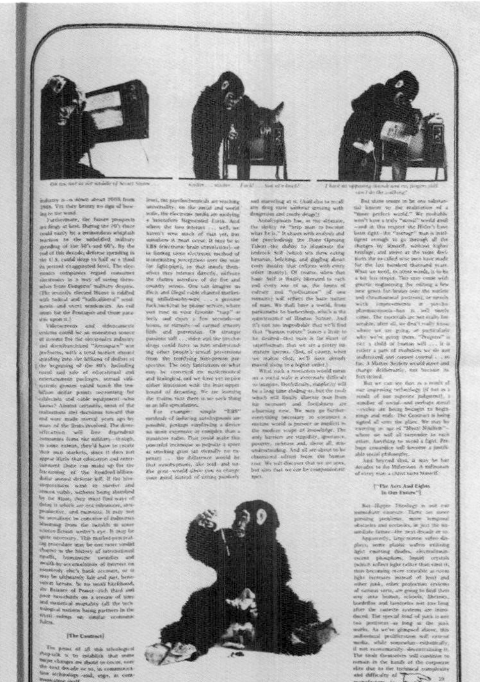

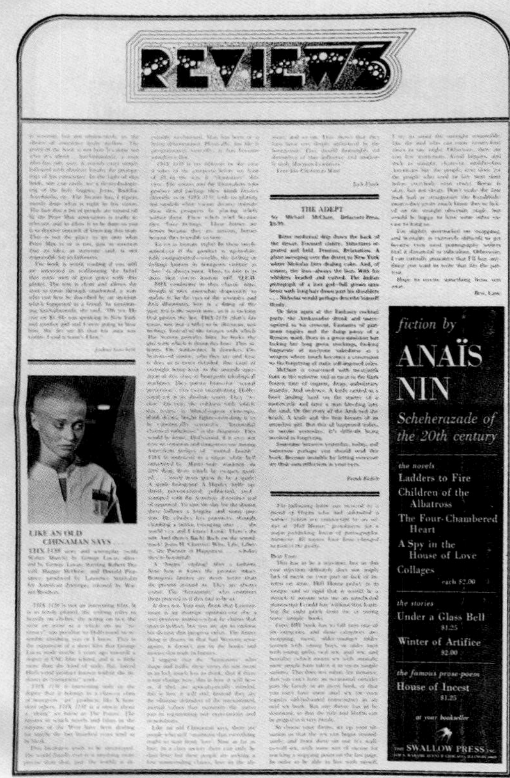

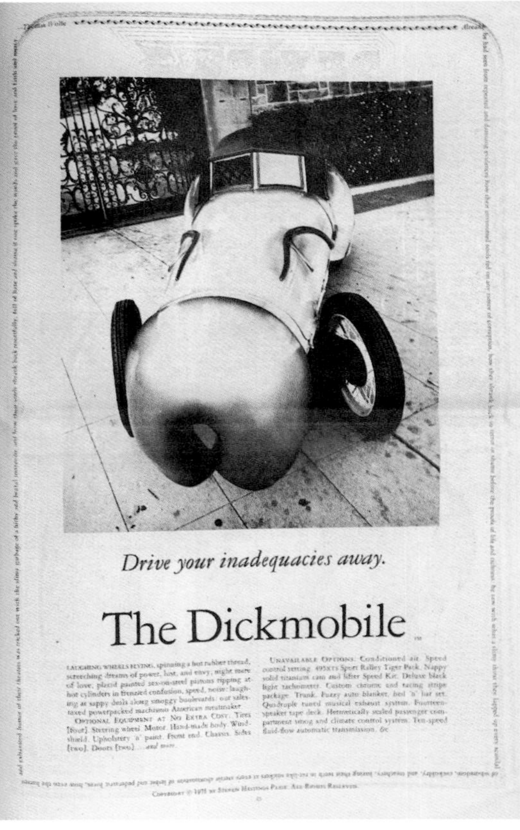

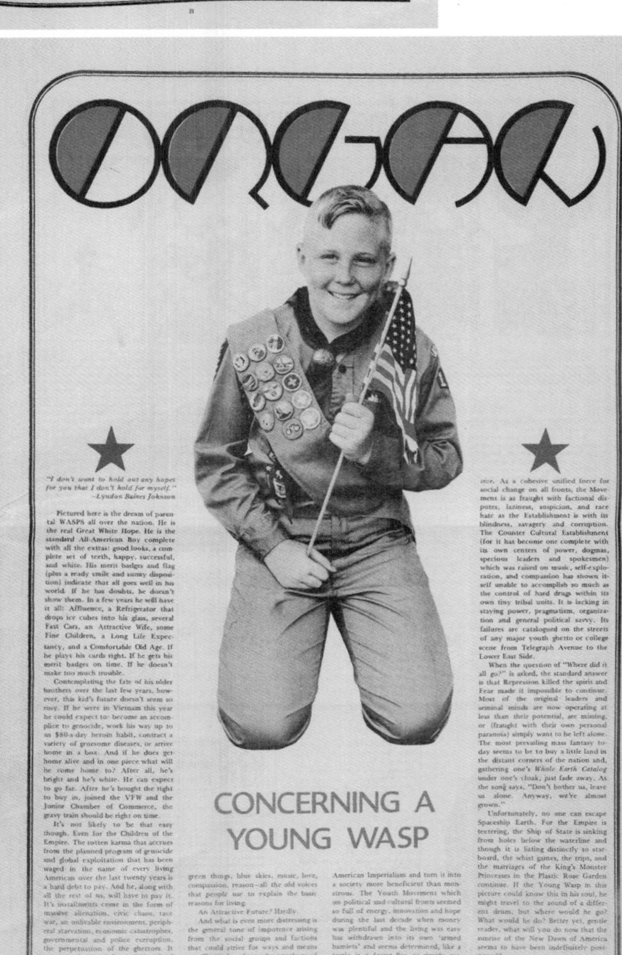

Fig. 4.4 (cont'd). **Organ** (Berkeley), May 1971, vol. 1, no. 7, cover, pp. 20-21 and 32-33; July 1971, vol. 1, no. 9, cover

Though ostensibly founded to serve an audience daily engaged in building houses and starting farms in the rural wilds, the *Catalog* in fact spoke to an entire generation that had been coming to grips with the technological abundance of the post–World War II era. On its first page, Brand articulated the *Catalog*'s purpose thus:

> We are as gods and might as well get good at it. So far, remotely done power and glory—as via government, big business, formal education, church—has succeeded to the point where gross defects obscure actual gains. In response to this dilemma and to these gains a realm of intimate, personal power is developing—power of the individual to conduct his own education, find his own inspiration, shape his own environment, and share his adventure with whoever is interested. Tools that aid this process are sought and promoted by the *Whole Earth Catalog*.[11]

In 1968, much of the alternative press could be found advocating sit-ins and marches. Like Kesey, however, Brand and the communalists he spoke to advocated a different form of power, a way of living and making social change that was both bohemian and deeply technocratic. On the one hand, like generations of bohemians before them, the communalists sought to live together in their own alternative enclaves. On the other, however, they sought to improve their lives and govern those communities using the tools and the logic of postindustrial production. Much like Daniel Bell, Brand and the communalists believed that high technology had created a radical new stage in human social organization. And like Bell, they placed a special faith in the power of information technology to free American society from the hyperrational mind-set and the hierarchical organizational forms of the industrial era.

The preeminent information technology for Brand and the communalists was the *Catalog* itself. Given popular recollections of the 1960s as an anticommercial era, the choice of a catalog as a countercultural form might seem a little out of place. And so it might have been if the *Catalog* had actually served as a retail outlet. Yet, as Brand wrote in the first issue, the *Catalog* was designed to function "as an evaluation and access device. With it, the user should know better what is worth getting and where and how to do the getting."[12] Though *Catalog* staffers maintained a Whole Earth Truck Store near their offices in Menlo Park, California, and though readers could in fact purchase many items featured in the *Catalog* there, the *Catalog* itself served as a reference device. Readers could write in to Brand and his staff and recommend particular products. If their recommendations were accepted, Brand would pay the contributor a ten-dollar fee. The reader's recommendation would then appear in the *Catalog*, alongside information on how other readers might contact the manufacturer or otherwise acquire the product.

This production pattern transformed the industrial-era role of the catalog. In the nineteenth century, the ***Sears Roebuck Catalog***, for example, served as a centralized distribution point for mass-manufactured goods (fig. 4.5). The *Whole Earth Catalog*, on the other hand, served as a map of an emerging, geographically distributed community of consciousness. As readers wrote in, they made visible not only particular products, but their ideals, their tastes, and the new communities in which they lived. To buy the *Whole Earth Catalog* was not simply to buy a mechanism for identifying particular tools (though it was that too); it was to purchase a window on an alternative world.

Brand himself was very much aware of this function. He published the *Catalog* twice a year through 1972 and intermittently after that. For the first four years, between editions of the *Catalog*, he also published a supplement in which he updated listings. In both of these publications, Brand regularly offered reports on various gatherings of the countercultural tribes. In March 1969, for instance, he reported on Alloy, a gathering of 150 self-defined "world thinkers"—ranging from commune architects to Bay Area scientists to teachers at a Bay Area high school—in

11. Stewart Brand, ed., *Whole Earth Catalog* (Menlo Park, CA: Portola Institute, 1968), n.p.

12. Ibid.

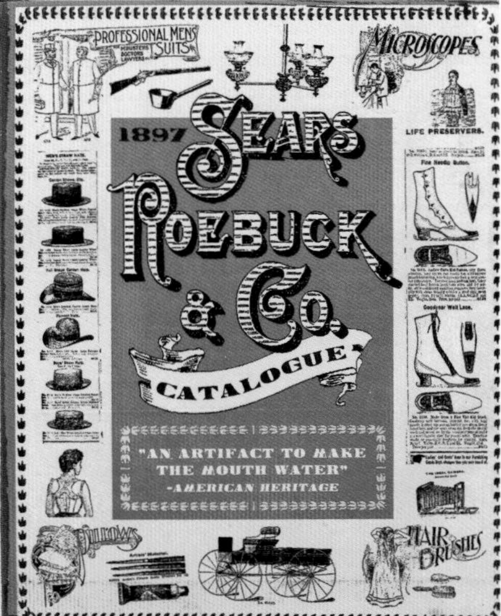

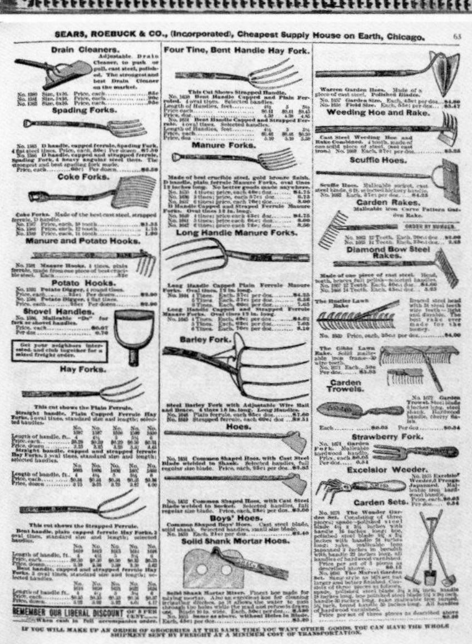

Fig. 4.5. **Sears Roebuck & Co.** catalog, 1897, cover and p. 63

an abandoned New Mexico factory.[13] At other times, he included coverage of a Prankster bus race, the funeral of a monk, and the deployment of a giant inflatable plastic house in the desert. For readers, the *Catalog* was never primarily about buying and selling goods. Rather, as one reader put it, "I think the whole scene is tantamount to a sort of community in print, with the crafty taciturn old bastards hawking and spitting into the fire, and occasionally laying one on us out of the experience store."[14]

In that sense, the *Whole Earth Catalog* represented a powerful paper-based prototype of a new kind of society, a geographically distributed network of communities and individuals linked by shared tastes and consumption practices, and by an information technology that allowed its members to reveal their personal predilections to one another. In retrospect, we can see that the *Catalog*'s tactics foreshadowed the online social networks of our own time. Yet, in 1968, they also grew out of a deep affinity for key ideas and practices of the military-industrial world of midcentury America. Each edition of the *Catalog* was divided into seven sequential categories: "Understanding Whole Systems"; "Shelter and Land Use"; "Industry and Craft"; "Communications"; "Community"; "Nomadics"; and "Learning." Within those sections readers could find pointers to such hip essentials as deerskin jackets or guides to macrobiotic cooking. But they could also find pictures of the latest Hewlett-Packard calculator and discussions of cutting-edge plastics.

By far the most common tools on display were not devices at all. They were books. For Brand and his readers, these books resembled LSD or rock music or flickering lights: all served as tools with which to transform the consciousness of their readers and, thereby, the structure of society. At the same time however, they tended to celebrate the power of expert knowledge and of a systems framework for understanding the social and natural worlds. They derived their systems theory primarily from two extraordinarily influential midcentury technocrats: Buckminster Fuller and Norbert Wiener. Since the 1920s, Fuller had traveled the United States, a peripatetic architect, designer, and self-styled technological visionary. Though lacking any long-term institutional employment, he found his way into such centers of the American corporate imaginary as ***Fortune*** magazine, where in 1940 he opined on issues ranging from patterns of American industrialization to the workings of the Sperry gyroscope. His designs for a three-wheeled automobile (the Dymaxion Car) and for a house suspended on a pole (the Dymaxion House) fascinated readers in the years before World War II. In 1954 he patented the geodesic dome. At the behest of the United States military, he helped deploy the dome to shelter radar stations along the Distant Early Warning Line. This three-thousand-mile-long string of stations was designed to watch for Soviet air attacks and stretched across the arctic from Alaska through Canada to Greenland. By the end of the 1950s, the dome had become a preeminent mode of housing American national exhibitions abroad, and by the end of the 1960s, it had become the preferred housing of many rural communards[15] (fig. 4.6).

For Fuller, industrial America served as a great bank of technologies from which individual adepts might withdraw and refashion new machines for living. As he put it in his 1963 volume ***Ideas and Integrities***, a book read on communes and campuses across the country,

> Only the free-wheeling artist-explorer, non-academic, scientist-philosopher, mechanic, economist-poet who has never waited for patron-starting and accrediting of his coordinate capabilities holds the prime initiative today. If man is to continue as a successful pattern-complex function in universal evolution, it will be because the next decades will have witnessed the artist-scientist's spontaneous seizure of the prime design responsibility and his successful conversion of the total capability of tool-augmented man from killingry [sic] to advanced livingry [sic]—adequate for all humanity.[16]

For Fuller, as for the generation that had come of age in the wake of the atom bomb, industrial technology

13. Turner, *From Counterculture to Cyberculture*, pp. 96-97; 273n54.

14. Rolan Jacopetti, letter to the editor, in *The Difficult but Possible Supplement to the Whole Earth Catalog*, ed. Stewart Brand, Ann Helmuth, Joe Bonner, et al. (Menlo Park, CA: Portola Institute, 1969), p. 8.

15. For more on Fuller and the geodesic dome, see Alex Soojung-Kim Pang, "Dome Days: Buckminster Fuller in the Cold War," in *Cultural Babbage: Technology, Time and Invention*, ed. Francis Spufford and Jenny Uglow (Boston: Faber and Faber, 1996), pp. 167-192.

To explore how the dome was used on communes, see Lloyd Kahn, Jay Baldwin, Kathleen Whitacre, et al., *Domebook One* (Los Gatos, CA: Pacific Domes, 1970); and Lloyd Kahn and Pacific Domes, *Domebook Two* (Bolinas, CA: Shelter Publications, 1974).

16. R. Buckminster Fuller, *Ideas and Integrities: A Spontaneous Autobiographical Disclosure* (Englewood Cliffs, NJ: Prentice-Hall, 1963), p. 249.

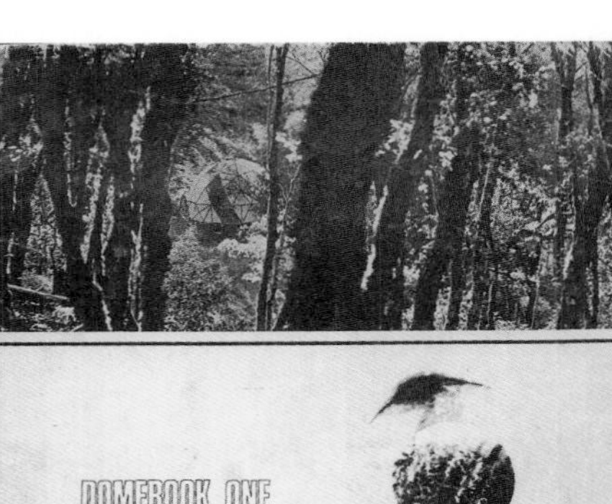

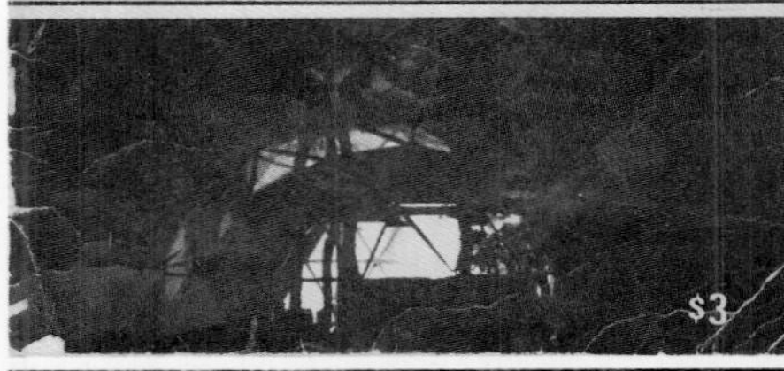

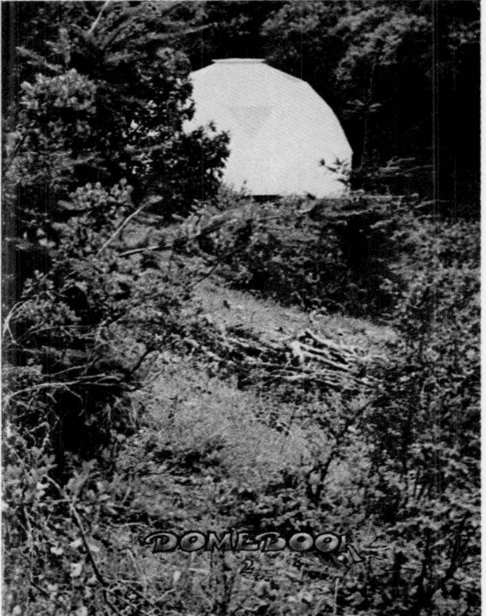

Fig. 4.6. **Dome Book,** March 1970, vol. 1, cover; May 1970, vol. 2, cover

had brought humanity into a new evolutionary era. Human beings could now destroy themselves, completely. Militarists could fire off a barrage of nuclear missiles. Or more insidiously, greedy industrialists could simply hoard resources in such a way as to starve the other citizens of the planet. Under these circumstances, it was up to flexible individuals, working together, to reclaim the technologies of the industrial mainstream and turn them into tools with which to redistribute the globe's resources. Fuller called this task "comprehensive design," and to the young utopians who contributed to the *Whole Earth Catalog*, it offered a powerful example.[17] As comprehensive designers, they could simultaneously enjoy such fruits of science and technology as geodesic domes and LSD, and transform them into tools with which to overthrow, at least within their own social circles, the rational, destructive logic of the industries and government agencies that had produced them.

So too could those who embraced midcentury information theory. In his 1948 volume of the same name, MIT mathematician Norbert Wiener coined the term "cybernetics." During World War II, Wiener had sought to mathematically predict the flight of enemy aircraft. In the process of that research, and in conversations with scientists in other domains, he began to imagine the social world as a complex information system. Like other information systems, he believed, societies tended to entropy, and, literally, to the madness of warfare; yet, pockets of order also remained. It was the job of information systems—and societies—to foster these zones of stability. To do so, however, at least in Wiener's model, one must accept that the world itself was a system and that one could influence it only iteratively, through a process that he and his colleagues called "feedback." To wield instrumental power was not enough to make order in Wiener's view; one must instead participate in a process of interaction, of information exchange, with one's fellow human beings, and with the natural and technological worlds. Only then could the mass chaos of future wars be averted.[18]

In the late 1960s, Brand and the communalists coupled Wiener's understanding of society as a self-organizing system to Fuller's notion of comprehensive design. Together, these technology-and-systems-driven views of social change offered a powerful intellectual alternative to the politics of struggle then playing out in the antiwar and civil rights movements. By turning away from politics per se and toward the personal sphere, the readers of the *Catalog* could escape the turmoil of mainstream American life. By taking up the same industrial products and consumption habits that floated through suburbia, they could partake of the pleasures of mainstream technocracy while developing their own bohemian communities. They could ape the collaborative research styles and the search for perception-extending technologies that had long governed military research. They could reclaim military shelters as homes within which to bend their minds in a more pacific direction. And knowing that both their communal enclaves and the world as a whole could be thought of as a single system, they could deploy information technologies such as the *Catalog*—or for that matter, LSD—in search of a mystical interconnection that scientists had already named. In the pages of the *Catalog*, the individual's search for psychological transformation claimed the collective urgency of the need for planetary survival.

Radical Software AND CYBERNETIC GUERRILLA WARFARE

Within two years of the *Catalog*'s appearance, other publications imitated its style and even reprinted its contents. Some, like the bimonthly *Mother Earth News*, tried to reach the *Catalog*'s back-to-the-land audience with how-to stories, coverage of rural living, and a tool-centered approach to helping their readers develop new lifestyles. As sociologist Sam Binkley has pointed out, others simply adopted the access-catalog model wholesale. Whether dealing with jewelry and smoking gear (the *Goodfellow Catalog of Wonderful Things*), ecology (the *Good Earth Almanac*), or sexuality (the *Catalog of Sexual Consciousness*), these catalogs too saw the intimate realm of the

17. Fred Turner, "Buckminster Fuller: A Technocrat for the Counterculture," in *New Views on R. Buckminster Fuller*, ed. Hsiao-Yun Chu and Roberto Trujillo (Stanford, CA: Stanford University Press, 2009).

18. Norbert Wiener, *The Human Use of Human Beings: Cybernetics and Society* (New York: Da Capo Press, 1988), pp. 16, 47-77, and 95-96.

personal as a place to make social change.[19] By the early 1970s, the *Whole Earth Catalog* had had a particular impact in high-technology circles. In the San Francisco Area, members of the Homebrew Computing Club (including Lois Brand) helped found the *People's Computer Company* (fig. 4.7), an irregular, informal guide to using computers as tools for personal and social transformation. Another programmer, Theodor Nelson, turned to the *Catalog* as a model for his own compendium of countercultural computing lore, *Computer Lib*[20] (fig. 4.8). A few years later, programmer Alan Kay, creator of the Dynabook and a pioneer in the design of laptop computers, would turn to the *Catalog* as a model of interface design.[21]

In each of these settings, "tools" retained a communalist connotation. That is, they were not simply a means to accomplish a task; they were mechanisms by which to transform individual consciousness and thereby, social order. Yet, even as the *Whole Earth Catalog*'s vision of a simultaneously bohemian and technocratic society rippled out into bookstores across America, its youthful countercultural readers found themselves under increasing assault. In May 1969, in Berkeley, California, marchers protested the police occupation of a formerly abandoned park recently reclaimed by residents. In the ensuing protests, police used shotguns to kill one protestor and permanently wound another. A year later, National Guard troops opened fire on students at Kent State University, and two hundred construction workers attacked a group of antiwar marchers in Manhattan. In the streets at least, the easy optimism of the "Summer of Love" had faded away.

In New York, a group of video artists responded to this new and darker political environment by turning the bohemian technocratic ideals of the *Whole Earth Catalog* in a more militant direction. In the summer of 1969, an artist and activist named Frank Gillette founded Raindance Corporation, a video collective that he hoped would be "an alterna-

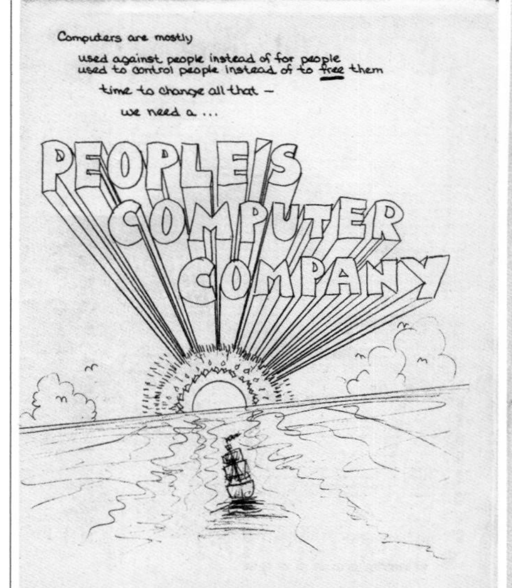

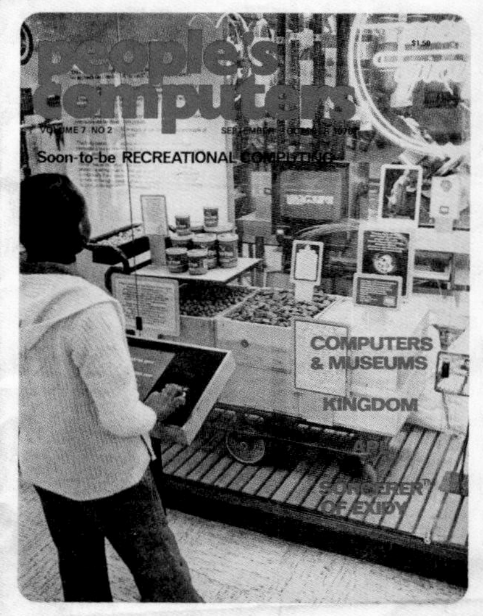

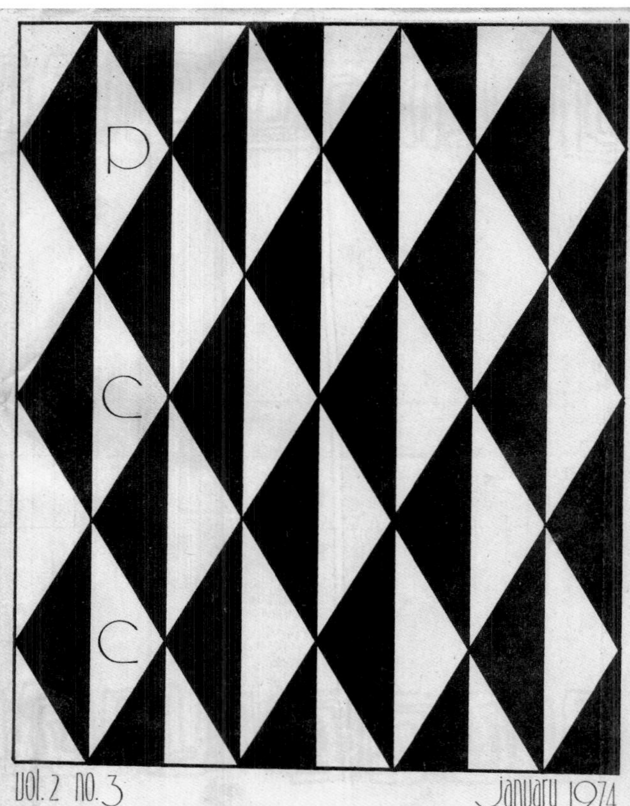

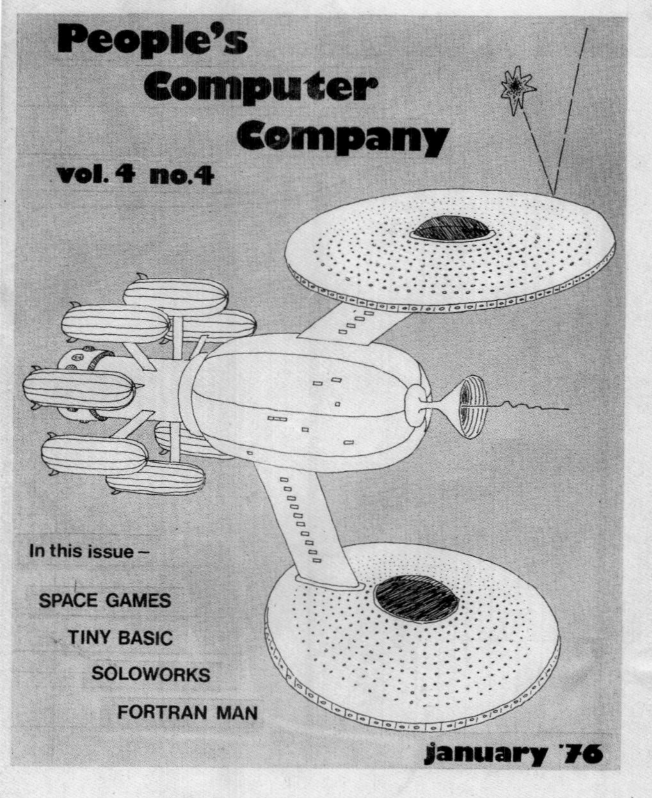

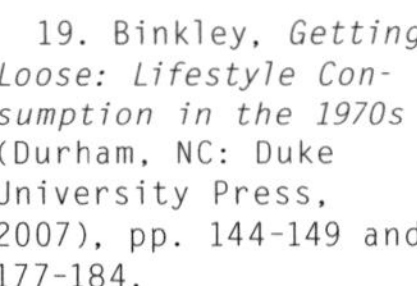

19. Binkley, *Getting Loose: Lifestyle Consumption in the 1970s* (Durham, NC: Duke University Press, 2007), pp. 144-149 and 177-184.

20. Turner, *From Counterculture to Cyberculture*, p. 275n23.

21. Alan Kay, interview, August 5, 2004.

Fig. 4.7. **People's Computer Company,** covers: [Undated]; September-October 1978, vol. 7, no. 2; January 1974, vol. 2, no. 3; January 1976, vol. 4, no. 4

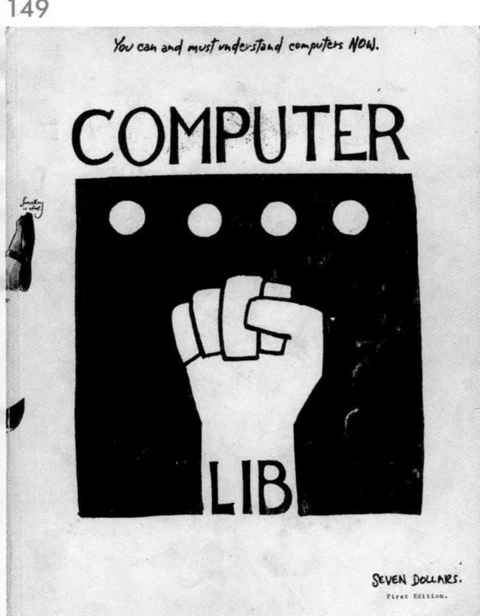

Fig. 4.8. **Computer Lib,** 1974

tive media think tank; a source of ideas, publications, videotapes and energy providing a theoretical basis for implementing communication tools in the project of social change."[22] Since 1967, Gillette had been involved with a growing New York alternative media scene. Artists such as Howard Gutstadt, David Cort, Ken Marsh, and Nam Jun Paik were experimenting with video and the television screen as new artistic media. Others, such as Victor Gioscia, a professor of philosophy at Adelphi and director of research for Jewish Family Services, had begun deploying video in psychotherapeutic settings. In the spring of 1969, Gillette was invited to exhibit his work in a show of television art called ***Wipe Cycle*** (fig. 4.9) at the Howard Wise Gallery. Through that show, and through his growing social network, he met former ***Time*** magazine reporter Michael Shamberg, and musician Louis Jaffe. Over the next few years, Jaffe funded Raindance with family money, while Shamberg became its most visible theoretician.

22. Davidson Gigliottie, "A Brief History of Rain-Dance," available at http://www.radical-software.org/history.html; accessed February 4, 2009. My account of the founding of Raindance largely follows his.

For the members of Raindance, as for the founders of the *Whole Earth Catalog*, high technology seemed to have brought human beings to the brink of a new age. And like Brand and company, Gillette and his colleagues embraced the politics of consciousness and the power of information technology. Gillette had even chosen the word "Raindance" as a play on the name of the RAND Corporation. Like RAND, Gillette hoped Raindance would model new, postindustrial, postbureaucratic ways of working with communication technology—albeit for a hipper clientele. Where the communalists of the back-to-the-land movement had sought to separate themselves from mainstream society, the video tacticians of Raindance saw themselves as guerrillas, operating within the existing media system. Inspired by Marshall McLuhan, they believed that mass media and particularly television had enlarged the human sensorium and linked the world in a single electronic network. Yet they feared that the structure of the media industries made it difficult if not impossible for ordinary people to help shape the mediasphere. To wage their battle on behalf of those people, the founders of Raindance relied on two media technologies: the inexpensive, hand-held

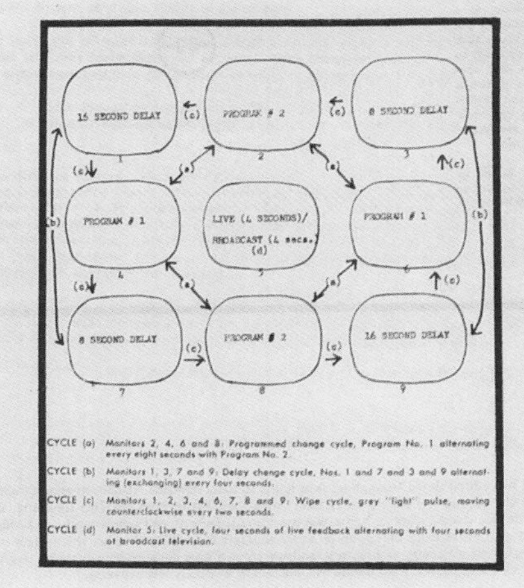

Fig. 4.9. **Radical Software,** 1970, no. 1, graph, included in an interview with Frank Gillette and Ira Schneider on p. 10

video camera, and the printing press. Their approach to each reflected a fusion of the bohemian technocentrism of the *Whole Earth Catalog* and the new militancy of antiwar protest.

The members of Raindance encountered the portable video camera and the *Whole Earth Catalog* at almost the same time. In 1968, Sony released the Portapak, a mobile video unit retailing for about $1,500.[23] Until that time, artists such as Nam Jun Paik and Aldo Tambellini who were interested in using the television screen as a medium had generally manipulated an image on the screen itself rather than make their own programs for broadcast.[24] With the Sony however, the members of Raindance began to make their own videos and to imagine releasing cameras into the general population. Once there, the cameras would function like LSD, transforming the social and interpersonal awareness of their users. They would also function like guns with which to challenge a repressive media order. As art historian David Joselit has pointed out, the Raindance collective sought to change society with "feedback" in two senses: one, it aimed to create new contexts for the exchange of information; and two, it aimed to disrupt the existing media system by feeding "noise" back into it.[25] For the Raindance collective, unlike the communalists, the transformation of consciousness would have to be accompanied by a form of technological direct action. As Raindance member Paul Ryan explained in 1970,

> Traditional guerrilla activity such as bombings, snipings, and kidnappings complete with printed manifestos seems like so many ecologically risky short change feedback devices compared with the real possibilities of portable video, maverick data banks, acid metaprogramming, Cable TV, satellites, cybernetic craft industries, and alternate life styles. Yet the guerrilla tradition is highly relevant in the current information environment.[26]

Raindance, then, brought together the technocentric idealism of the communalists and the direct action sensibilities of the increasingly radical New Left.

23. Paul Ryan, "A Genealogy of Video," *Leonardo*, vol. 21, no. 1 (1988), pp. 39–44.

24. Ibid.

25. David Joselit, *Feedback: Television against Democracy* (Cambridge, MA: MIT Press, 2007), p. 96.

26. Paul Ryan, "Cybernetic Guerrilla Warfare," *Radical Software*, vol. 1, no. 3 (Spring 1971), pp. 1–2.

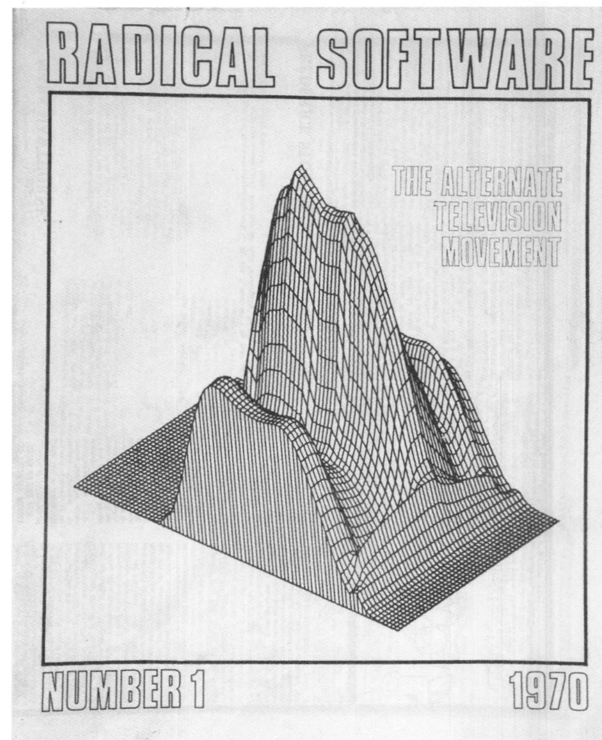

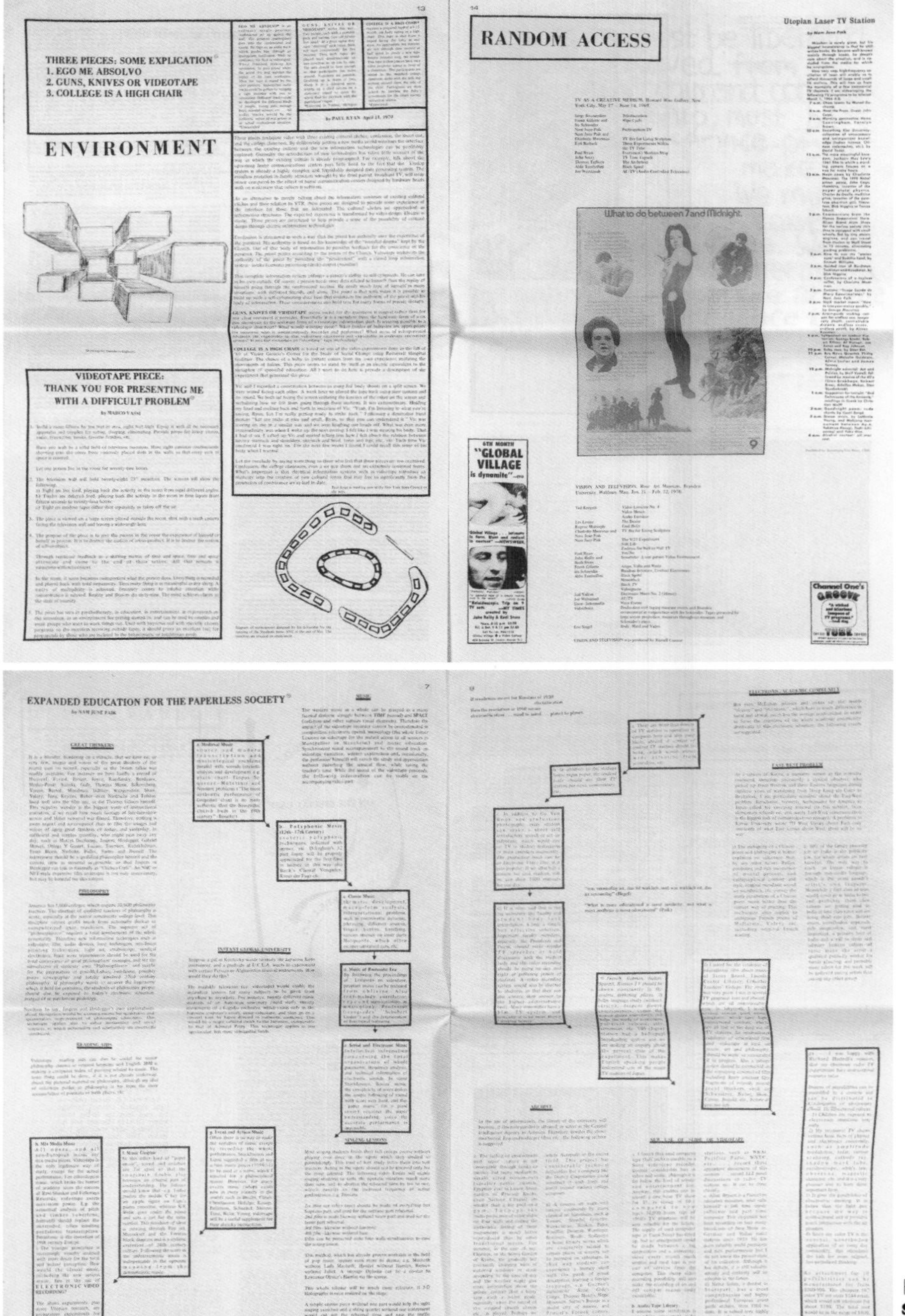

Fig. 4.10. **Radical Software,** 1970, no. 1, cover, pp. 13–14 and 7–8

19

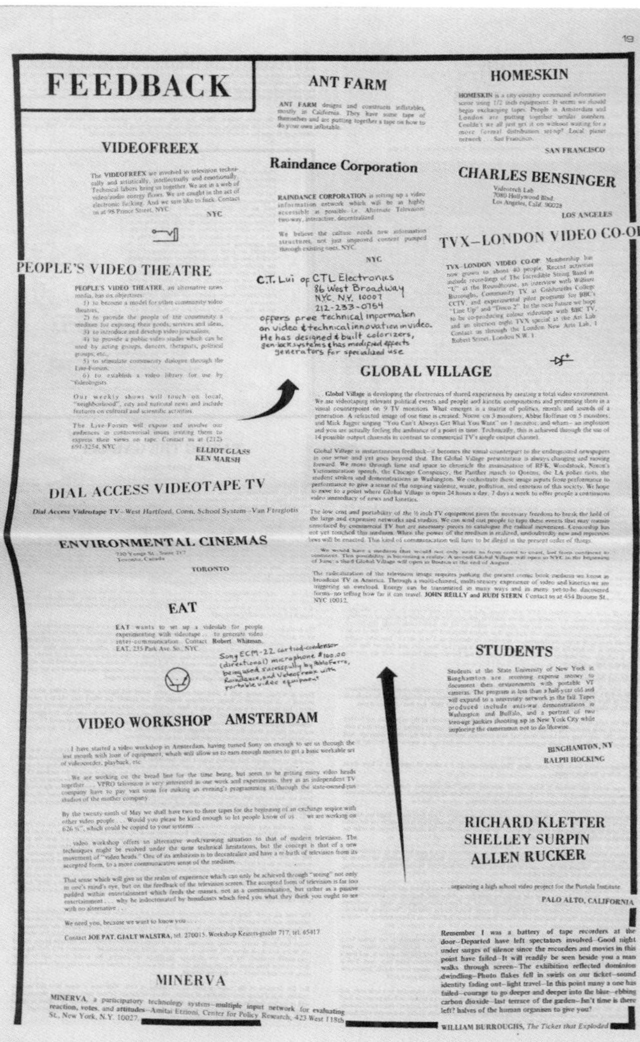

FEEDBACK

ANT FARM

HOMESKIN

VIDEOFREEX

Raindance Corporation

CHARLES BENSINGER

PEOPLE'S VIDEO THEATRE

TVX—LONDON VIDEO CO-OP

GLOBAL VILLAGE

DIAL ACCESS VIDEOTAPE TV

ENVIRONMENTAL CINEMAS

EAT

STUDENTS

VIDEO WORKSHOP AMSTERDAM

RICHARD KLETTER
SHELLEY SURPIN
ALLEN RUCKER

MINERVA

20

BRIAN WOOD

PHIL GIETZEN

PETER SORENSON

SHADY, NY

GENE YOUNGBLOOD

LA

PAUL RYAN

VT is not TV. Videotape is TV flipped into itself. Television has to do with transmitting information over a distance. Videotape has to do with infolding information—feedback.

ERIC SIEGEL

R. BUCKMINSTER FULLER

HOWARD JUNKER

FRANK CAVESTANI

JOE WEINTRAUB

LOREN SEARS

FOREST KNOLLS, CALIFORNIA

5

SOFTWARE

R. BUCKMINSTER FULLER

Pirated transcription of interview videotaped by Raindance Corporation

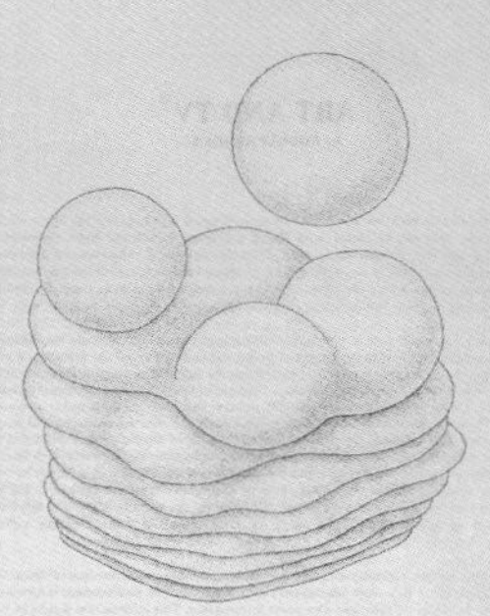

6

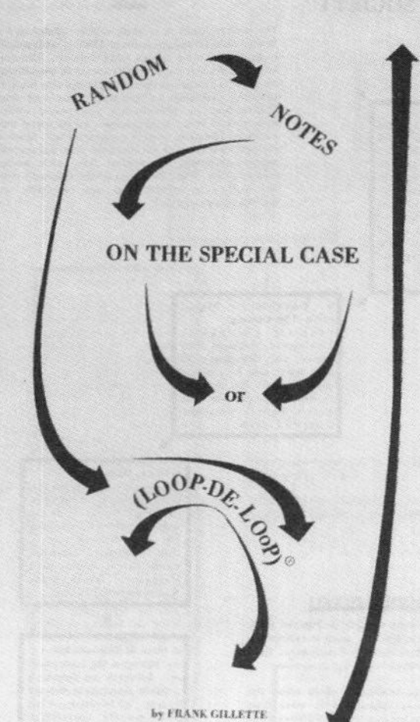

That intellectual space, psychic interplay, and silence solidified by thought which exist between the members of a written phrase is here, in the scenic space, traced between the members, the air, and the perspectives of a certain number of shouts, colors and movements. ANTONIN ARTAUD

Plane Falls Into House

SAO PAULO, Brazil (AP)—A light airplane crashed through the roof into the living room where Divaldo Giminez and his girl friend were watching television. Two men climbed out, caught a taxicab outside and sped away. A third man came in and started smashing up the plane with an ax.

Fig. 4.10 (cont'd.) **Radical Software,** 1970, no. 1, pp. 19–20 and 5–6

RADICAL SOFTWARE

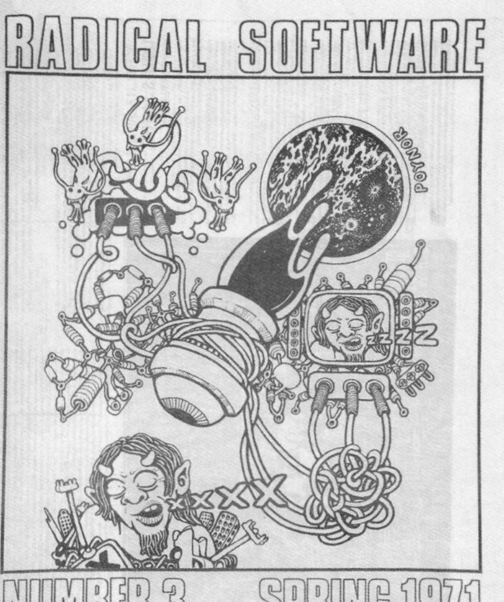

The ELECTROMAGNETIC SPECTRUM

NUMBER 2 1970

$1.25

RADICAL SOFTWARE

NUMBER 3 SPRING 1971

$1.50

RADICAL SOFTWARE

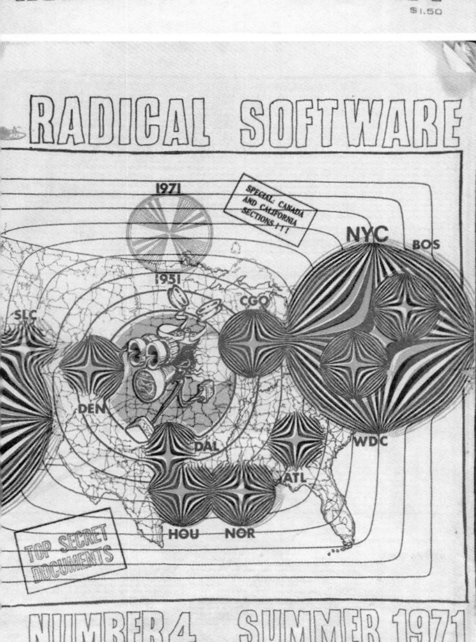

NUMBER 4 SUMMER 1971

Meta-Manual

New technologies begin life by being mistaken for the ones they replaced. The car was first called "horseless carriage." Another name for radio was "wireless." And some people still see broadcast TV as "a radio with a screen."

There is a similar bias against portable video generated by people who are mired in old media. Film freaks question the potential of videotape as if it were merely "Polaroid movies" and are more concerned about what it can't do in imitation of film, rather than what it can do uniquely. Media instructors tend to be unimpressed by the Porta-Pak because for their money it's just expensive "Super-Eight." Even those who understand that the grammar of television is different from film, nonetheless mistake portables for a less sophisticated version of the old TV studio.

Portable video is a new, major medium. It is a high access form of our culture's dominant communications mode and precisely the opposite of product television which can accept only artificial behavior because it is based on a scarcity of time and equipment access.

The economics of portable video are subversive to anyone whose authority and security are based on controlling information flow. Thus the usual argument against portable video is that it has inferior "technical standards" which is a hype promoted by unions whose jobs are based on scarcity, owners who can't afford both their overhead and "equal time," and educators who build a mystique of expertise and certification.

Unlike product television, the Porta-Pak embodies technological evolution towards decentralization, reduced size and cost, increased ease-of-operation. As a totally self-contained system it gives control of information to whoever is being processed. Films, on the other hand, goes off to central processing and is usually programmed by people who weren't there when the information was compiled.

The bias of self-contained record, storage and instant playback punctures the estranging mythology of technology as something to be operated and therefore controlled by an elite.

Not only are portables simple enough for even kids to use, but they can take a system home and live with it. It's a high access technology. Most of America's media structures are the opposite: centralized and one-way.

Biological systems with those characteristics are usually unstable and non-adaptive. Because the way information flows through a system determines its structure, we can't expect our culture to embody ecological sanity unless our media are restructured to reflect that bias.

A media ecology demands decentralized, two-way information structures; just as survival pressure is now on to decentralize schools and governments to give control back to the people.

Our experience at Raindance is that the Porta-Pak works best in its own context:

Don't demand that portable video imitate another, product-oriented medium. Treat it instead as a general purpose technology which has many uses indigenous to many different and unique behaviors. It's like the difference between an electric can opener, which is hardwired into one use, and a computer or the human brain, which have many uses independent of predetermined criteria of what is or isn't information.

Use portable video to process your own life, not to produce products which imitate life, or Johnny Carson and Walter Cronkite. Also avoid making superstars out of "alternate culture" heroes because that's the same old "leader" and "lead" bullshit. It's best to be intimate with video, not estranged by plastic modes of behavior put over on product TV.

So don't worry about initial inadequacies of technique. Everyone we know who's picked up a Porta-Pak for the first time used it to feedback on their own lives and environment because that seemed natural. Some of the strongest tapes we've seen are technically the crudest. It's a medium without experts. Not everyone writes novels, but everyone has writing as a tool.

And most important: structure your system to maximize access. Like guerrilla warfare, your heavy, centralized units should help support your most flexible one (the Porta-Pak), not vice-versa. If you want heavy hardware, (e.g. mixers, slick editing), design it as a technological support system in service to the portable. High flexibility is an optimum survival mode.

We are Raindance: 24 East 22nd St., New York, N.Y. 10010. [illegible]

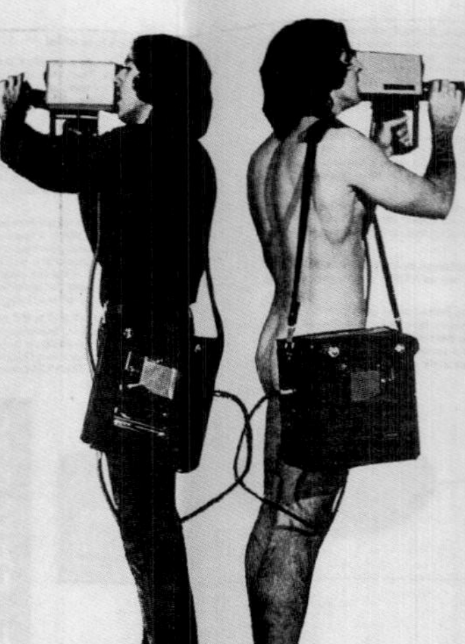

Manual

There are three standards of videotape and a fourth one coming: two-inch, one-inch, half-inch, and quarter-inch.

Two-inch or "high band" tape systems are indigenous to broadcasting and are exclusively low access systems. They are temperamental, complex to operate, and stationary.

Generally, the wider the tape the more information it can hold. Two-inch systems; also called "quadraplex," lay the scanning signal perpendicular to the edge of the tape. All one and half-inch systems incorporate helical scan which lays the signal at an angle to the tape edge.

Typically, clean editing was once an exclusive function of two-inch machines. One-inch was first used as a cheaper version as their size and price range ($3,000 to $10,000) make them ideal for institutions with closed-circuit TV systems which imitate broadcast. Like two-inch, its editing capability is perfect.

There are no one-inch portables. However, all of the half-inch portables listed below can be interfaced with one-inch to provide perfectly edited one-inch masters.

The major technical problem with half-inch systems had been an unstable signal which precluded clean edits and even intra-system compatibility, in some cases. But most of the "technical" objections came from people who had a vested interest in limiting access to TV. Some of the best video we've ever seen was made on early, relatively crude Porta-Paks which were nonetheless flexible enough to go where people had something to record. Process versus product.

Moreover, many of the technical problems have been eliminated since the Porta-Paks were first introduced in 1968. There is now a Japanese standard of intersystem compatibility between manufacturers (although not all the portables share it) which has a stable enough signal to be perfectly edited on relatively inexpensive (approx. $900) half-inch editing decks (e.g. the Sony AV3650).

Most of the information in this report is grounded in our experience with Sony. The system has many faults, but nonetheless has been the easiest to get and get serviced because of Sony's marketing acumen. Thus, the charts below give more space to Sony than the three other available half-inch systems, two of which are manufactured for two brand names.

The far right column of "coming" machines has more space than Sony because the systems listed there incorporate distinct advantages over the current Sony.

The charts are divided into four different scans: **Specs** (for specifications). They're generally the same for signal-to-noise ratio (the strength of the signal in relation to inherent noise); audio range (VTR's have a separate, synched, magnetic soundtrack); tape speed (the faster it is the more information stored, but the less recording time); and resolution (most cameras transmit more lines than the tape actually stores, so deck resolution is more important than camera capacity).

The second generation systems all incorporate 2:1 interlace which essentially means that the synch-pulse is continuous and therefore the signal is stable.

Systems variables to look for are battery life and recharging time; standard microphones and lenses; and playback capability. Some Porta-Paks are record only and the signal won't playback through any TV set. Of course, a playback motor means a heavier unit which you may not need.

Design Intelligence. Even the best of the systems is an imitation of film technology. Rather than exploit the potentials inherent in electronics, Porta-Paks still have a small TV screen eyepiece between your eye and the lens. They could be separate. A lens in your hand, for example, and a monitor on your wrist. They're also still configured as guns, with triggers. And are thought of as packs, i.e. something you carry but which isn't part of you.

Other **Design Intelligence** criteria are how accessible is the tape path for monitoring and threading, can you get to the guts for repairs, and configuration of cable jacks and inputs and outputs.

Experience. This tells you what has screwed-up both electronically and mechanically from our own experience. Where we have none it's been left blank for others to feedback and fill in our ignorance.

Support. Some Porta-Paks are less flexible than others first, because they have few inherent options; second, because other units in the manufacturer's line aren't too good; and third, because they're less than a total system in their inability to interface with support technologies like one-inch and cable television.

This section also evaluates the quality and accessibility of dealer service.

PORTABLE VIDEO

A RADICAL SOFTWARE STATE-OF-THE-ART REPORT

CENTERFOLD

PORTA-PAKS

INDICATES TYPE ONE (COMPATIBLE) STANDARD ◄

HERE | COMING

SONY	PANASONIC CONCORD	SHIBADEN APECO	CRAIG	AMPEX
SPECS [illegible]	SPECS [illegible]	SPECS [illegible]	SPECS [illegible]	SPECS [illegible]

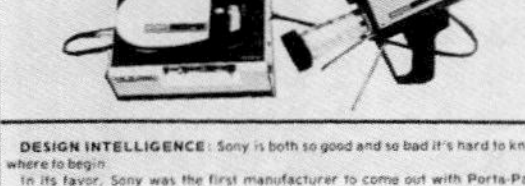

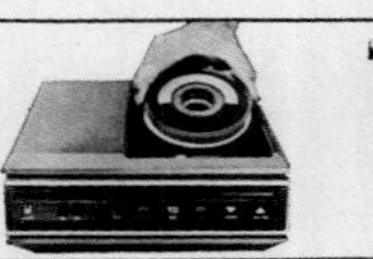

SONY

DESIGN INTELLIGENCE: Sony is both so good and so bad it's hard to know where to begin.

In its favor, Sony was the first manufacturer to come out with Porta-Paks (their CV series) and the first to make a quantum leap with a second generation, a handy self-contained system with record and playback (the CV series was record only) through any TV set (using an RF converter which changes the output signal to a broadcast one, $39.95 extra). The Sony also has playback through the monitor eyepiece for on-the-scene previewing which can really turn on people you've just taped and help build an instant trust.

On the downside, the Sony camera and deck seem to have been designed by engineers **in vitro**, not for people **in vivo**. The camera is overly heavy and not well-weighted. The pack is very cumbersome and can only be carried in a leather case which obscures visibility to the tape path so you can't run quick checks on whether or not its running right. (see **Experience**)

Sony has its own form of mini-plugs for microphones which are incompatible with other manufacturers'. While the cable from the camera to the deck is a stanard ten-pin, that is the only way to get in and out in video mode. Normal systems accept coax plugs which are universally compatible. In essence, this all means that technological support is not inherent in the system and any options, like editing with a Porta-Pak, require special modifications.

SUPPORT: The rest of the Sony half-inch line (AV series) is pretty good. With a modified cable (see back) you can have editing on a compact table deck (AV3600) for only $650 more. The pack itself has audio dubbing and still-framing.

Next up in the Sony half-inch line is their color deck (AV5000) although cameras are not yet compact or cheap enough, and certainly not portable. The final piece is a full-blown editing deck (AV3650) but they've only been around a month or so and we've not gotten feedback yet. First reports are that it's pretty good except for sound which has the usual two second lag on cuts.

As for dealers, Sony is everywhere. Service will always vary individually, of course, but in terms of getting parts we'd count on Sony everywhere in the U.S.

EXPERIENCE: The Sony Porta-Pak has many, many faults, partly because they rushed it into production which meant that those of us first owners have been doing the necessary field testing. Here are the results:

Mechanically the problems are many. The control levers break off after not much use (they're made of plastic). You'll never see anyone who uses their Porta-Pak a lot who has a camera eyepiece intact. They break off like crazy because of poor hinges which can't take much stress. Finally, it's very easy for the tape to become wrapped around the capstan inside because the reels don't hang onto the spindles. This means that you think you're recording and open the deck up later to find a useless spaghetti of videotape. If you're moving around a lot this can really be a problem.

Electronically, the system could be better overall but there doesn't seem to be any recurring problem.

PANASONIC CONCORD

DESIGN INTELLIGENCE: The configuration of the record deck (more rectangular than Sony) makes for a better weighting and the camera has a detachable microphone instead of a hardwired one. But there is no playback mode on the Porta-Pak itself (tape must be transferred to another deck).

Panasonic actually makes two models of Porta-Pak although they are visually the same. The one not listed here is on their old standard which had a high recording speed (12 ips) and therefore a low recording time (14 mins) and was compatible with only Panasonic decks. Sony, on the other hand, has discontinued its old series (CV) Porta-Paks (which had no play-back) and table recorders.

SUPPORT: Panasonic has a generally good reputation, especially in its half-inch editing. But not all of its current line is Type One (the compatible) standard. As for Concord, its marketing organization is much less solid and hearsay feedback is that it's not very reliable to work with.

EXPERIENCE: Except for encounters with the Panasonic table decks, we've never used the Porta-Pak except demos at trade shows.

SHIBADEN APECO

DESIGN INTELLIGENCE: The configuration of the deck is similar to that of the Panasonic/Concord and likewise the Shibaden/Apeco has no internal playback. Still not much of an improvement over the Sony.

SUPPORT: Shibaden has a good reputation, most of their equipment is made for professional use (although they've just been bought out by Hitachi, a Japanese electronics conglomerate), and they just make video hardware. As for Apeco, its an offshoot of a Midwestern company whose main product is office copying equipment. Neither one seems to have a high access marketing and servicing system.

EXPERIENCE: None.

CRAIG

DESIGN INTELLIGENCE: The Craig has one nice, and one sort of nice thing about it. First, there are two microphones, one front, one back. This means that whoever is taping can also talk into the soundtrack. The other thing is that the Craig has playback but only with a manual rewind. This offers the convenience of a total system without the extra weight that a rewind motor means. Like Sony and Ampex, it also has playback through the camera eyepiece as well as any TV set.

SUPPORT: The Craig is not Type One standard although there is one model in the support line that is. But it's pretty hard to find a dealer.

EXPERIENCE: Except for some editing we did once from Sony half-inch to Craig one-inch, which worked very well, we have none.

AMPEX

DESIGN INTELLIGENCE: Ah, here it is, the first total system Porta-Pak. Instavideo (it used to be called Instavision but Ampex changed it because someone else had that copyright) has all the options of the Sony and more.

This is because the pack itself sets into a more stationary (weight 6.5 lbs.) service pod. The back of the pod is a regular patchboard with standard coax and audio in-and-out jacks. (Of course, it also interfaces with a regular TV set through the antennae plugs, like the Sony). This means you don't have to hassle modifications to do editing.

The pod is upgradable with modules. Basic price is $800 for a black-and-white playback only system. For $900 you get record too (plus $400 separate for the camera, or $1,300 system total) and another $100 buys a color clip-in circuit board. (Remember that the module, not the pack, has the additional circuitry so color is not a function of the Porta-Pak per se).

The reason for all this is that Ampex (in conjunction with Toshiba, the Japanese company which will do the actual manufacturing) wanted a machine to compete with both cassettes and Porta-Paks. Thus, the tape has two play modes. One is normal recording and playback with a thirty minute tape time. In an extended mode, for prepackaged material, it will play 60 minutes.

Here's some more goodies. The tape has a plastic leader and is self-threading. You don't have to touch the tape path. There is an internal brush activated by a button for head cleaning. And a pulse code button which electronically marks your last stopping place so next time you insert the tape it will do an automatic high speed search.

You can also do electronic editing, still-framing, and slow motion (no other Porta-Pak has that). There are two sound tracks which means the option of stereo, and of course the system subscribes to Type One standard.

Finally, you can adjust tape tension (Sony has only a tracking control on its portable) and both audio and video input levels. The control levers themselves are configured like an autiotape cassettes recorder for easy control and access.

What's wrong with Instavideo? Well, the camera design is awfully hokey, sort of an old movie (or video) camera in drag.

Another major problem is that although tape is compatible with other systems, the physical reel is indigenous only to Ampex. Thus although you have the electronic capability of playing another systems tapes, you are totally restricted mechanically.

SUPPORT: Ampex has a generally bad reputation in its one- and two-inch lines. They have too many mechanical parts and down time is high.

Instavideo is their only half-inch machine and they have done a pure paranoid thing. They keep hyping it as a non-professional machine, but people are going to start producing with it. This means that come editing time to stay with Ampex you've got to go to at least a $6,000 machine (in one-inch format).

Not many people can afford that. As a result Ampex will be used for shooting, its competitors for editing support. So for every Porta-Pak they sell, Ampex will generate business for another company. Control instead of service.

EXPERIENCE: Ha! The only machine we've seen represents three prototypes travelling in America. In that form they're high Technology costing about $75,000 apiece. There simply are no production models available (Ampex claims late summer). They wouldn't even let us touch the thing at a demonstration which consisted of one vacuous model shooting another ratting her hair. They were even too paranoid to let us shoot the scene with our Sony, which they made us keep in a closet.

So, even though the thing shapes up as the next generation of Porta-Pak, a major improvement over the last, stay skeptical until you can actually feel and buy one.

See Back For Specs on Akai Porta-Pak

CENTERFOLD

Fig. 4.10 (cont'd). **Radical Software,** 1970, no. 2, cover; Spring 1971, no. 3, inside spread; Spring 1971, no. 3, cover; Summer 1971, no. 4, cover

Next page
Fig. 4.10 (cont'd). **Radical Software,** Spring 1971, no. 3, pp. 15–16, 1974, vol. 2, no. 6, cover; 1972, vol. 2, no. 1, front and back covers; 1973, vol. 2, no. 3, cover; 1973, vol. 2, no. 4, cover; 1973, vol. 2, no. 2, cover and pp. 24–25

Both of these impulses fueled the design and publication of the collective's newspaper, *Radical Software* (fig. 4.10). Edited by Phyllis Gershuny and Beryl Korot, *Radical Software* appeared three times a year from 1970 to 1974. Early issues resembled a traditional newspaper and ran to 24 pages; later issues were published by Gordon and Breach and ran to as many as 120 pages in a bound magazine format. In both cases, they took up the tool-centered politics and design techniques of the *Whole Earth Catalog* and linked them to a rhetoric of insurrection.

Each issue, for instance, featured half a dozen categories into which the editors slotted correspondence and news about products from within and outside the Raindance group. In the first issue, these categories included HARDWARE, SOFTWARE, ENVIRONMENT, FEEDBACK, and RANDOM ACCESS (all capitalized). The HARDWARE section focused on new video and cable television technologies. Articles by Gene Youngblood and Thea Sklover outlined the latest technical developments in each, and then linked them, in Youngblood's phrase, to the politics of the "videosphere." As Youngblood put it on page 1,

> Television is the software of the Earth.
>
> The videosphere is the ***noosphere***—global organized intelligence—transformed into a perceivable state ….
>
> Television, like the computer, is a sleeping giant. But those who are beginning to use it in revolutionary new ways are very much awake.[27]

27. Youngblood, "The Videosphere," *Radical Software*, vol. 1, no. 1 (1970), p. 1.

The SOFTWARE section in turn offered a two-page transcription of an interview with Buckminster Fuller, in which Fuller spun a cotton-candy web of ruminations on topics ranging from human evolution to new media technologies to his own recent travels. Immediately after the Fuller piece, the section offered an equally lengthy disquisition by Nam Jun Paik entitled "EXPANDED EDUCATION FOR THE PAPERLESS SOCIETY." In a set of boxes linked by arrows and arrayed in a way that resembled the steps in a computer program, Paik's article reimagined video not simply as a

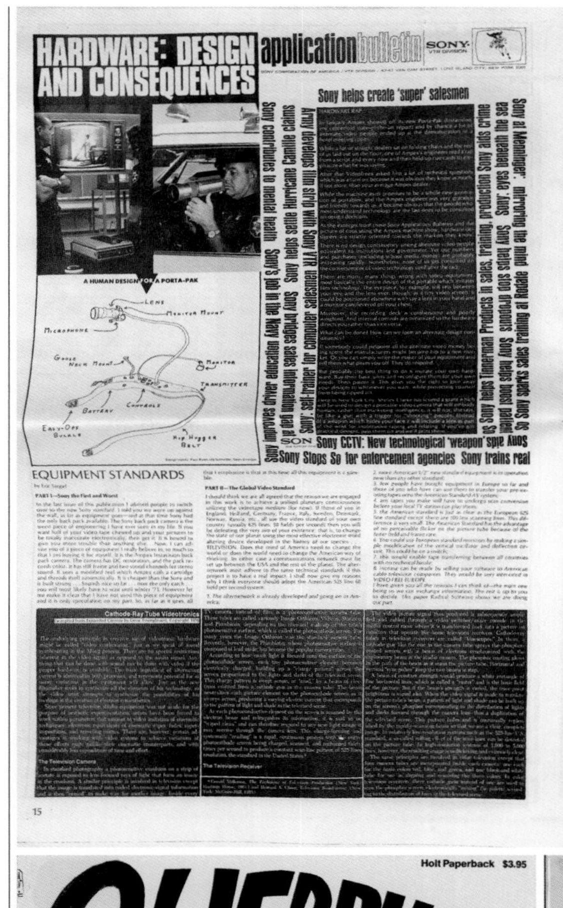
HARDWARE: DESIGN AND CONSEQUENCES

application bulletin

Sony helps create 'super' salesmen

A HUMAN DESIGN FOR A PORTA-PAK

Sony CCTV: New technological 'weapon' spies AUOS

Sony Steps So for enforcement agencies Sony trains real

EQUIPMENT STANDARDS

Cathode-Ray Tube Videotronics

The Television Camera

The Television Replayer

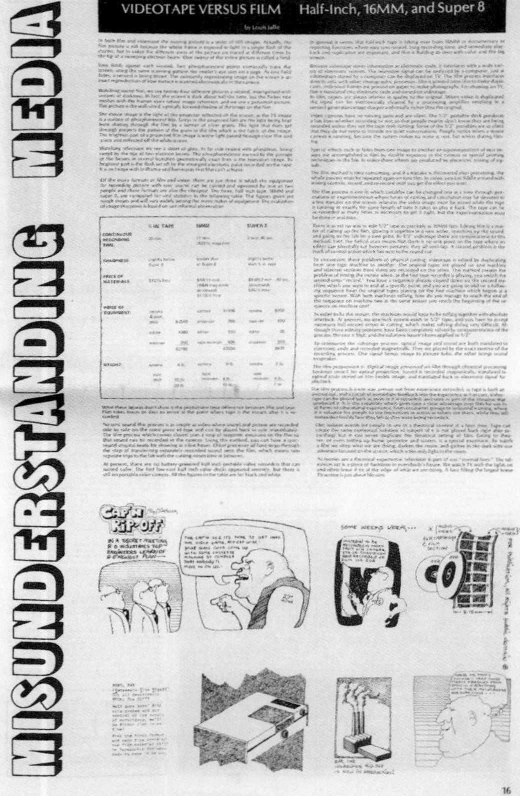
VIDEOTAPE VERSUS FILM Half-Inch, 16MM, and Super 8

MISUNDERSTANDING MEDIA

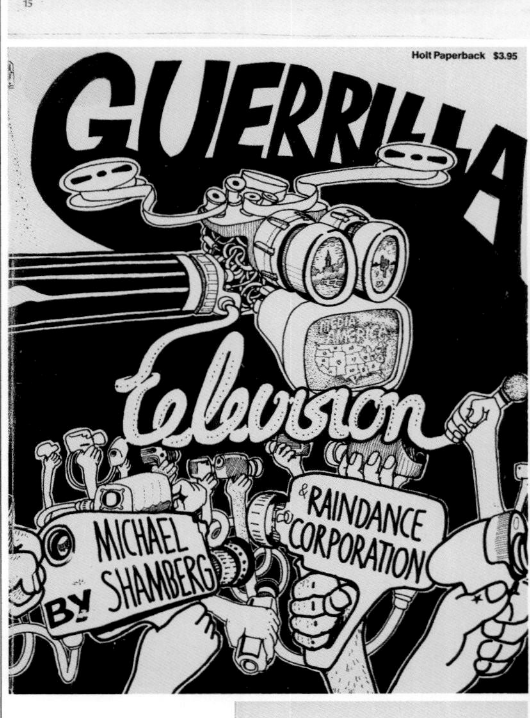

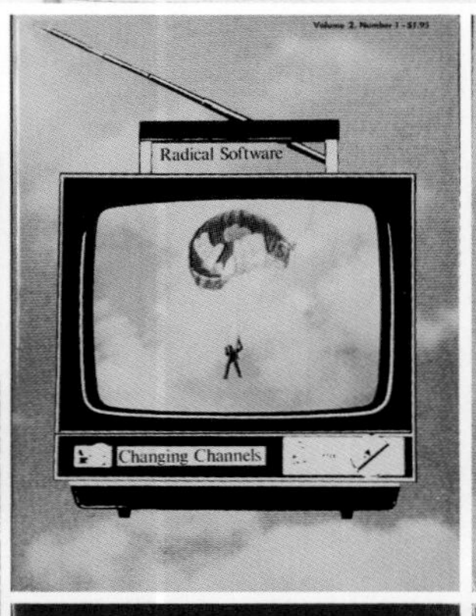

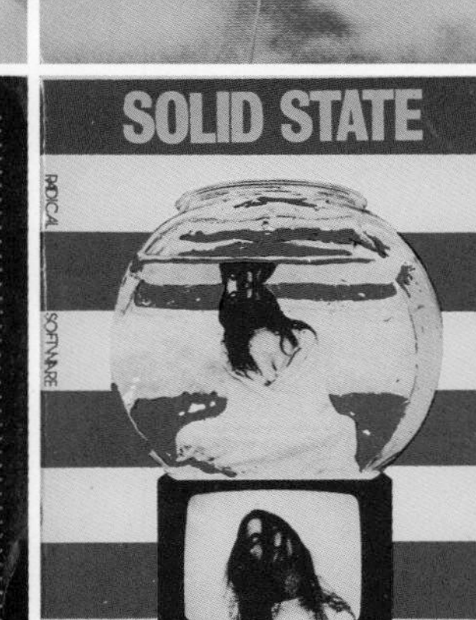

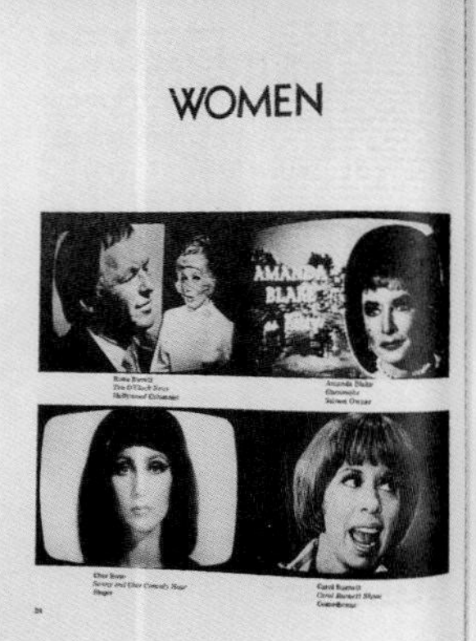

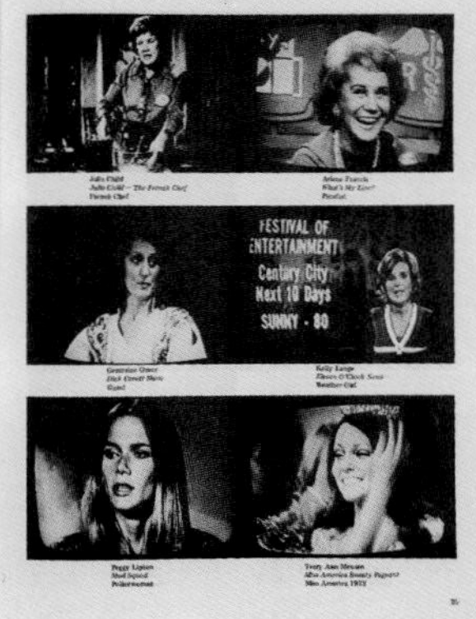

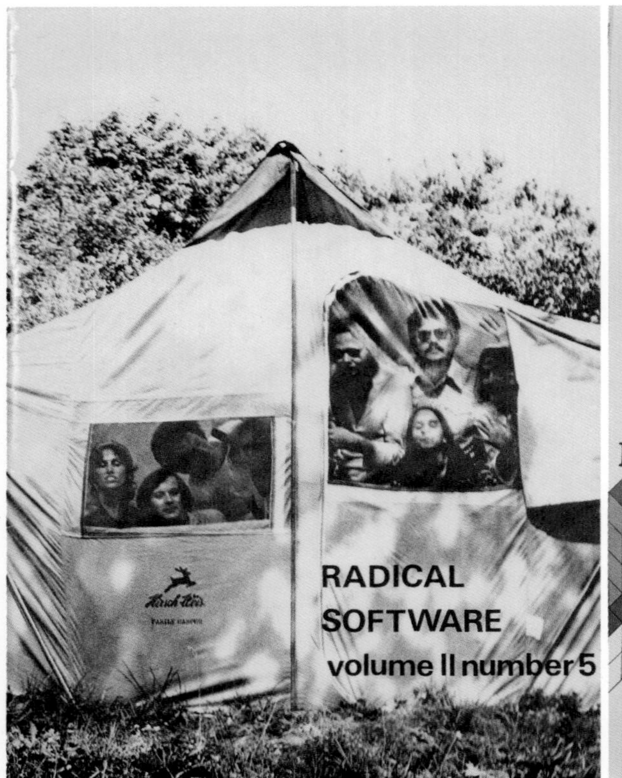

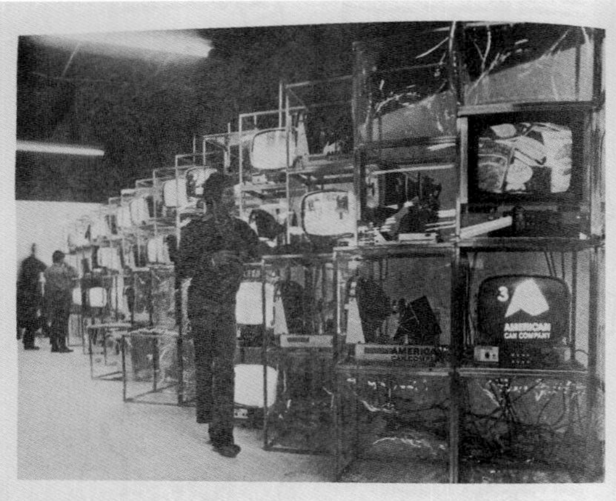

MODULAR VIDEO MATRIX

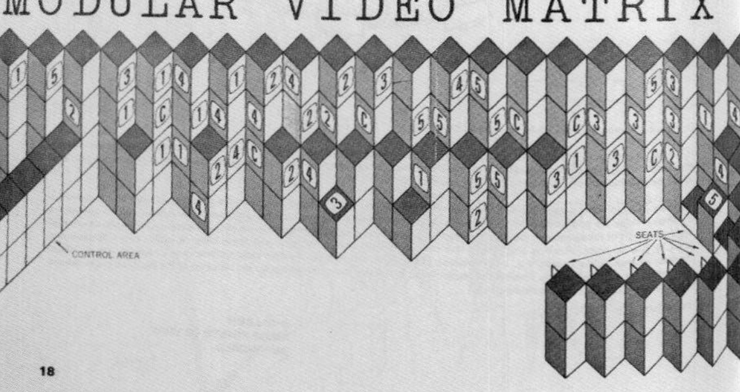

18

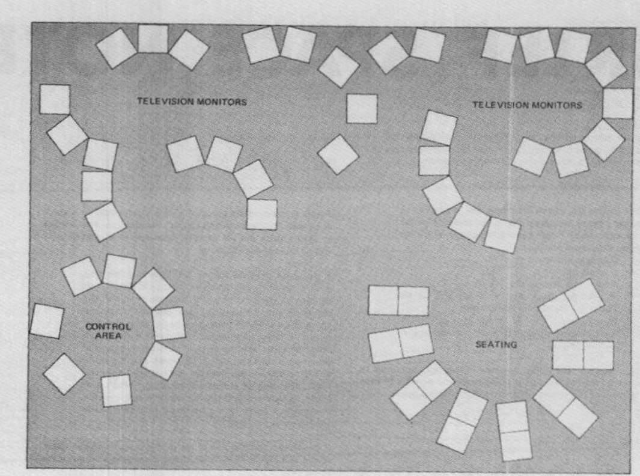

VIDEO MATRIX
50 monochrome 17" T.V. monitors
6 color 19" T.V. monitors
7 monochrome videotape recorders
2 color videotape recorders
7 crystal controlled live vidicon cameras
1 video distribution amplifier
5 control consoles
1 audio distributor
1 master switching console

The master switching console creätes these video-matrix capabilities:

1. 5 separate videotape programs into 5 banks of 10 T.V. monitors
2. Automatic switching to live T.V. cameras in each bank after videotape program
3. Sixth videotape program optionally switched to all T.V. monitors at once
4. Live camera at control console switched to all T.V. monitors simultaneously
5. Color videotape programs into color monitors

The Modular Video Matrix designed by Frank Gillette and Ira Schneider with Paul Ryan and John Riley in 1969 offered flexibility in the configuration of video environments. 56 monitors encased in plexiglass with stainless steel supports allowed for stacking to produce a wall of monitors or for arrangement into circles, semi-circles, etc. Inputs from cameras were presented live, or were taped for later playback. 5 pre-taped programs could be presented simultaneously. Programming could also contain a mix of live, delayed, and pretaped material. This Matrix was designed for the American Can Corporation and contrary to the desire of the designers the software was assembled by Harvey Lloyd Productions. Software for the Matrix presented at Industrial Trade Shows consisted mainly of bald-headed men touting American Can products intermixed with men (live camera) gawking at cheesecake hostesses.

19

VIDEO TRANS AMERICAS

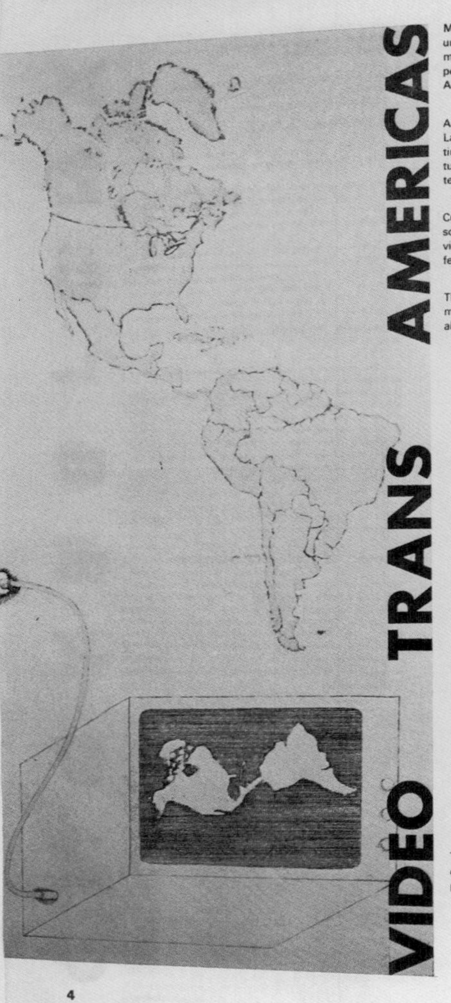

Many of America's cultures exist today in total isolation, unaware of their overall variety and of commonly shared myths. This automobile trip is designed to develop a holistic perspective among the various populations inhabiting the American continents, thus generating cultural interaction.

A videotaped account from New York to the southern tip of Latin America. A form of infolding in space while evolving in time. Playing back a culture in the context of another, the culture itself in its own context, and, finally, editing all the interactions of time, space and context into one work of art.

Cultural information (art, architecture, cooking, dance, landscape, language, etc.) will be mainly exchanged by means of video-tape shot along the way and played back in the different villages, for the people to see others and themselves.

The role of the artist is here conceived as a cultural communicant, as an activating aesthetic anthropologist with visual means of expression: video-tape.

The expedition will leave in July and return to New York in early September, where the video-tapes will be edited and presented in final version.

Juan Downey

4

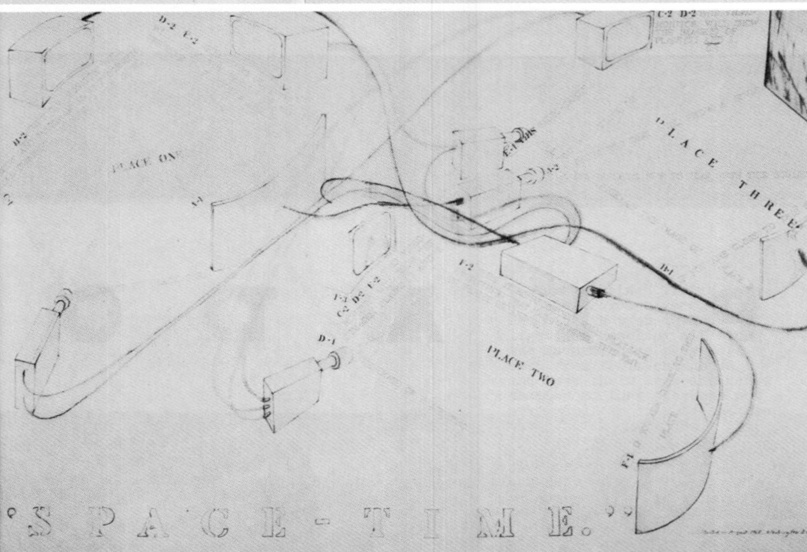

Project for the Juan Downey exhibition at the Corcoran Gallery of Art Washington D.C. 1968.

3 way comunication

Three performers sit at the corners of a large triangle formed by three voice--transmission laser beams. The performers exchange faces by means of super-8-movie projections while talking through the laser beams.
Conversations and transfigurations are video-taped and played-back once the three performers leave.
Central Michigan University, 1972
New York Avant-Garde Festival, 1972
Everson Museum of Art, Syracuse, N.Y., 1973

Juan Downey

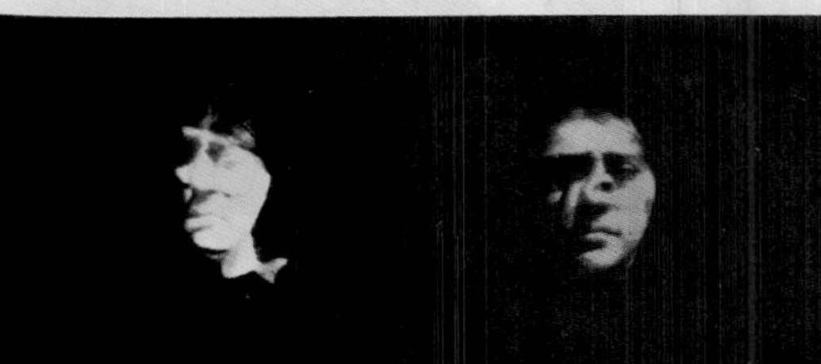

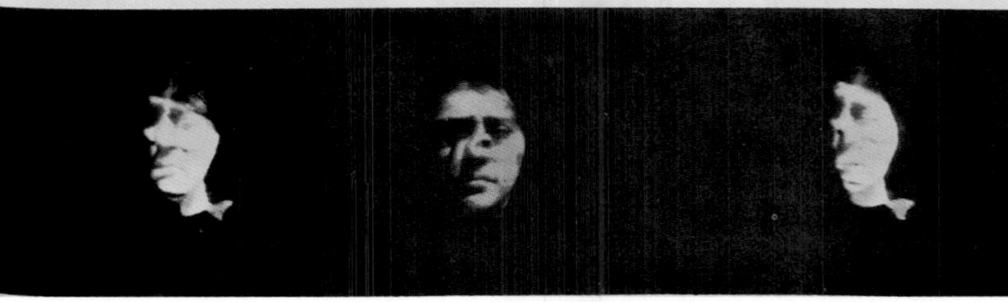

Fig. 4.10 (cont'd.). **Radical Software,** 1973, vol. 2, no. 5, cover; 1973, vol. 2, no. 5, pp. 18–19 and 4–5

Next page
Fig. 4.10 (cont'd.). **Radical Software,** 1973, vol. 2, no. 5, unnumbered page and pp. 42–43

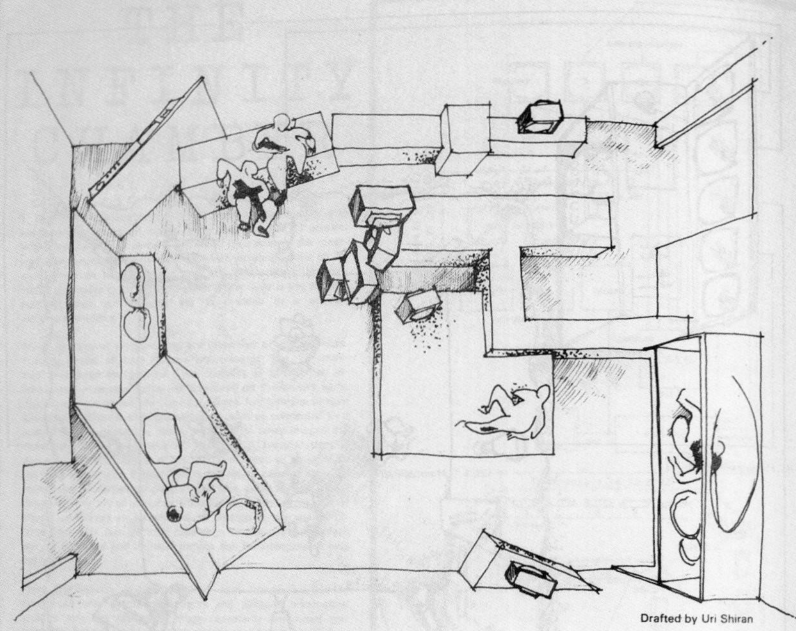

Drafted by Uri Shiran

VIDEO THEATRE

We have had many requests from readers asking us for information on the structure of the video theatre we ran at our New York Raindance loft in the winter of 1970. The following is a description of the theatre, a diagram, and a financial statement.

Starting December 19, 1970 Raindance Corporation opened its loft at 24 east 22nd Street, NYC, for 10 consecutive Saturday evenings of cooperative videotape presentations with Videofreex, Peoples' Video Theatre, and others. A single channel of video (and audio) was selected from one of 3 Sony EIAJ decks or one of 2 Sony CV vtrs by means of a passive switcher. This number of vtrs allowed for rewinding and cuing up (through several preview monitors in the control area) of tapes for more integrated programming. Seven monitors were arranged in a space of approximately 55′ x 22′. Seating was on comfortable cloth covered cushions on multilevel platforming creating many sub-environments. The space was laid out according to the diagram on the next page.

The major focus for most of the audience was a spire containing 23″ monitors in the bottom and second rung, and 18″ monitors on the third and top rung. People were able to look beyond the monitors and see other members of the audience. The ambience and decor seemed to dispell the traditional New York paranoia. People who had never met would rap with each other. This was contributed to by the programming which was made up of many short tapes (sequences)—many humorous, some ecological, informational, artistic. Melodrama and hardline entertainment with blasting sound was avoided. This again allowed the audience to rap and comment on the material they were viewing.

On the opening night 3 shows were presented 8, 10 and 12pm. Thereafter we had two shows at 8 and 10pm. Each week an ad was placed in the *Village Voice*. The cost of the ad and additional expenses such as nuts and raisins, cleaning supplies, etc. was subtracted from the gate and then the remainder was split 3 ways. Below we have listed the gate, cost of ad, total expenses and split to each of the contributing groups. (No fee was charged for rental of the space, electricity, etc. This must be figured in for anyone who wants to open and run a video theatre.)

Ira Schneider

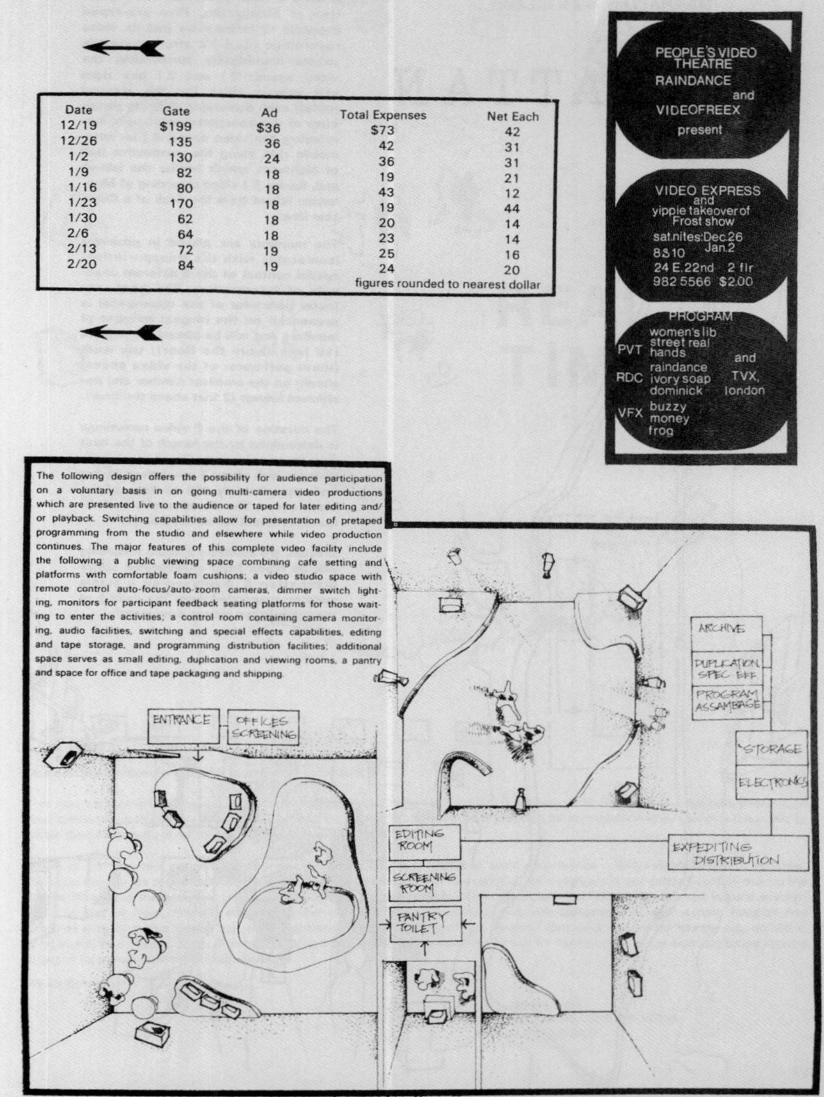

Date	Gate	Ad	Total Expenses	Net Each
12/19	$199	$36	$73	42
12/26	135	36	42	31
1/2	130	24	36	31
1/9	82	18	19	21
1/16	80	18	43	12
1/23	170	18	19	44
1/30	62	18	20	14
2/6	64	18	23	14
2/13	72	19	25	16
2/20	84	19	24	20

figures rounded to nearest dollar

The following design offers the possibility for audience participation on a voluntary basis in on going multi-camera video productions which are presented live to the audience or taped for later editing and/or playback. Switching capabilities allow for presentation of pretaped programming from the studio and elsewhere while video production continues. The major features of this complete video facility include the following: a public viewing space combining cafe setting and platforms with comfortable foam cushions; a video studio space with remote control auto-focus/auto-zoom cameras, dimmer switch lighting, monitors for participant feedback seating platforms for those waiting to enter the activities; a control room containing camera monitoring, audio facilities, switching and special effects capabilities, editing and tape storage, and programming distribution facilities; additional space serves as small editing, duplication and viewing rooms, a pantry and space for office and tape packaging and shipping.

Designs by Schneider

Drafted by Uri Shiran

NOTES FOR A PROPOSAL ON CONCEPTUAL GAMMING FRANK GILLETTE

1. " Trouble arises" writes Gregory Bateson, "precisely because the 'logic' of adaptation is a different 'logic' from that of the survival and evolution of the ecological system". The purpose (goal, object, context) of the game is one of simulating ecologic and behavioral complexity ... of distinguishing the sets of relationship between, and the channels of influence exchanged by conceptions of the world and their subsequent control over behavior in the world.

2. The game is played by 3,6,9,12,15 or 18 people with a computer system which provides the constantly evolving context within which conceptual models are created and embodied in a range of media, from diagramatic print-out to holographic simulation. The system also provides the criteria by which models are tested.

3. A primary function of the game is the development of a variety of world-process orientations articulated or embodied in more and more encompassing contexts.

4. How does the game evolve models which seperate the contingences of economic and social behavior from the bionomic contingences of the ecologic system in which the given behavior is a constituent part?

5. How does the game evolve corresponding values governed by a meritocracy of ecological description?

6. How does the game seperate mythical attitudes based upon the successful domination of nature from conceptions based upon the successful interaction with natural forces?

7. LEXICAL POINTS OF DEPARTURE:

Sequential	Simultaneous, Topological
Linear	Atemporal
Historical	Ahistorical
Labor	Play
Acquisition	Access
Product, Goal	Process
Dualistic	Systemic
Continuity	Discontinuity
Environmental Exploitation	Enviromental Enhancment
Ideological	Ecological
Static Image	Moving Image
Taxonomic	Simbiotic, Shared Dependence
Maximum	Optimum
Money	Information

8. Michael Apter* pictures the structure of cybernetics thus:

theoritical systems

living systems ⟷ machine systems

How does the game reflect the interactive flux between these structural elements?

* Apter,M. The Computer Simulation Of Behaviour, Harper & Row, 1970,p.43

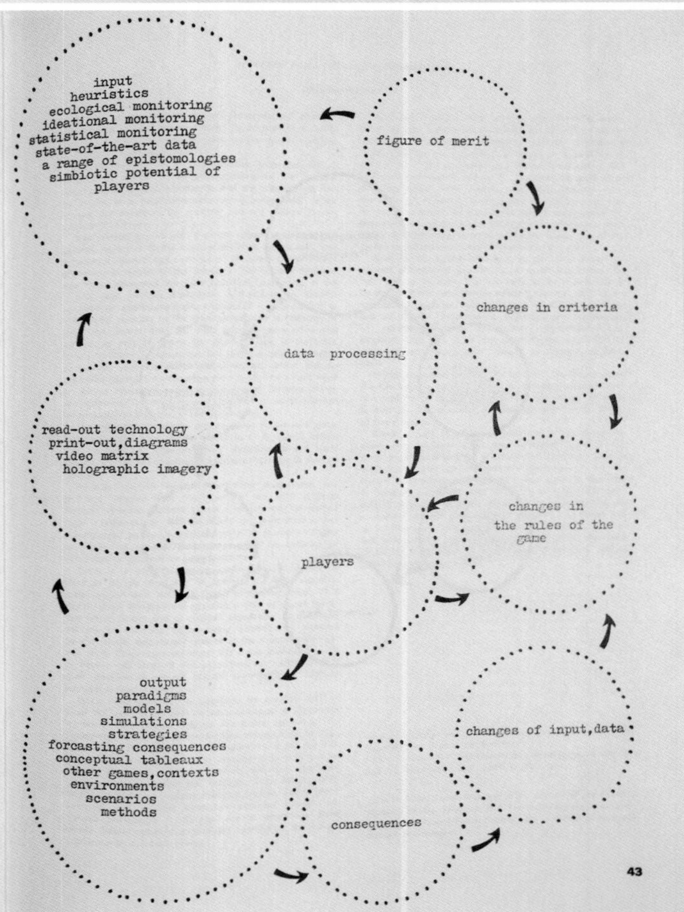

means of personal psychological liberation but as a way to distribute education throughout society. The new technologies seemed to Paik to offer what the Internet has now delivered: a networked resource for the dissemination of theoretical and practical knowledge. Far from rejecting the distributed, information-centered patterns of postindustrial production, Paik's essay encouraged them.

Subsequent sections of the publication featured interviews with other members of Raindance, a report on citizen media activism in Canada, and lists of resources, communities, and individuals involved in making alternative video. Like the categories of the *Whole Earth Catalog*, these sections encouraged readers to see themselves as part of technological, intellectual, and social systems simultaneously. The mind, the community, the society—all were information systems, and all could be mapped and remade by information technologies. By using the electronic tools described in HARDWARE or perhaps the books or theoretical writings in SOFTWARE, the reader could reshape his own mind. Once reshaped, that mind could be connected through the FEEDBACK and RANDOM ACCESS sections to those of other, like-minded video and media freaks, in New York and across the continent. Like the *Whole Earth Catalog*, *Radical Software* offered access to tools, and at the same time, a map of an emerging social world and instructions for establishing citizenship in it.

Much of *Radical Software*'s resemblance to the *Catalog* grew out of its editors' shared fondness for Buckminster Fuller and Norbert Wiener. Like Fuller, the members of the Raindance collective saw technology, and specifically information technology, as a far more effective and egalitarian mechanism for social change than traditional government. And like Wiener, they saw the world as a system of overlapping information patterns, some entropic, some not.[28] They also embraced a metaphor that had long stood at the heart of cybernetics. In much cybernetic writing of the 1940s, and especially in Wiener's work, the individual mind, the society, and the natural world all consisted of fundamentally isomorphic information patterns—patterns that could be modeled and manipulated by a computer. For the video freaks of Raindance, this isomorphism offered a lever for social change that linked the communalist dream of communities of consciousness to their own project of creating nonmass media. The key to making change—in the mind, in society, and in the natural world—was to reprogram the information system.

It was for that reason that they called their publication "software." In 1971, Raindance published *Guerrilla Television*, a book by member Michael Shamberg that outlined their philosophy. "True cybernetic guerrilla warfare means restructuring communications channels, not capturing existing ones," wrote Shamberg.[29] Raindance, he explained, was "a survival center" for a species whose sensorium had just been dramatically expanded by the introduction of television:[30]

> The use of the word "guerrilla" is a sort of bridge between an old and a new consciousness. The name of our publication, *Radical Software*, performs a similar function. Most people think of something "radical" as being political, but we are not. We do, however, believe in post-political solutions to cultural problems which are radical in their discontinuity with the past.[31]

For the editors and writers of *Radical Software*, as for those at the *Whole Earth Catalog*, true revolution would not come at the barrel of a gun or even through peaceful marches in the street. Rather, the revolution had already arrived in the form of media and other industrial technologies. The challenge now was to recognize the new information and media systems as they existed, to develop alternative research institutes in which to understand them, and to create and distribute new media and information technologies with which to reshape them.

28. For more on the Raindance group's debt to cybernetics, see Paul Ryan, *Video Mind, Earth Mind: Art, Communications, and Ecology* (New York: P. Lang, 1993); and William Kaizen, "Steps to an Ecology of Communication: Radical Software, Dan Graham, and the Legacy of Gregory Bateson," *Art Journal*, vol. 67, no. 3 (2008), pp. 86-107.

29. Michael Shamberg and Raindance Corporation, *Guerrilla Television* (New York: Holt, Rinehart and Winston, 1971), 29, quoted in Joselit, *Feedback*, p. 101.

30. Shamberg, *Guerrilla Television*, p. 37.

31. Ibid., introduction, n.p.

THE COUNTERCULTURAL POST-INDUSTRIAL TURN AND ITS LEGACY

By the mid-1970s, both *Radical Software* and the *Whole Earth Catalog* had closed their doors. While Raindance continued to serve as a resource for New York–area video artists, *Radical Software* suffered from financial problems, editorial turnover, and ultimately, disagreements with the publisher Gordon and Breach.[32] For Stewart Brand, shuttering the *Whole Earth Catalog* was a matter of principle. In 1971, the *Catalog* remained enormously profitable and enjoyed a large readership, but Brand thought that it had done its educational work. On June 21, he brought some five hundred *Whole Earth* staffers and friends to San Francisco's Palace of Arts and Sciences to celebrate what he believed would be the final edition of the *Catalog*. In the folds of the monk's habit he donned for the occasion, Brand carried $20,000 in cash. The money, he said, was a tool, like the *Catalog*. He announced that he would give the money to whatever cause the crowd—by consensus—deemed best. Long into the night, guests stepped up to a microphone to offer possibilities. By dawn, the sum had mysteriously dwindled by about $5,000 and the rest had been given to a social activist and computer hobbyist named Fred Moore. Four years later, Moore cofounded the Homebrew Computer Club (fig. 4.11).

Even as the youth movements of the 1960s faded from public view, the *Whole Earth Catalog* and *Radical Software* went on to have long cultural afterlives. *Radical Software* and the Raindance collective inspired citizen media activists for the next twenty years.[33] Paul Ryan, for instance, went on to create experimental video and conceptual art. He also continued to pen cybernetic visions of activism in his books ***Cybernetics of the Sacred*** (1974) and ***Video Mind, Earth Mind*** (1993). Michael Shamberg went to work in Hollywood. Over the next twenty years, Shamberg produced films ranging from ***The Big Chill*** (1983), in which a group of former radicals now turned young urban professionals gather for a weekend and mull over their life choices, to ***Pulp Fiction*** (1994), ***Gattaca*** (1997), and ***Erin Brockovich*** (2000).[34] For his part, Stewart Brand became an even more influential network entrepreneur. In 1971, he published what he called the *Last Whole Earth Catalog*; yet, new versions of the *Whole Earth Catalog* (fig. 4.12) appeared periodically into the late 1990s. Perhaps even more importantly, the *Catalog* became a model for one of the most influential virtual communities of the early Internet era, the Whole Earth 'Lectronic Link (or WELL). Brand and other contributors to the *Catalog* went on to found or cofound new journals (such as *CoEvolution Quarterly* (fig. 4.13) and the *Whole Earth Review* (fig. 4.14) and a major international consulting firm (the Global Business Network). They would even help launch ***Wired***—the magazine that, more than any other, promoted a utopian vision of information technology just as the Internet came into widespread public use.[35]

In part, *Radical Software* and the *Whole Earth Catalog* owe their continuing relevance to a revolution in sensibility that they themselves helped bring about. But they also owe their cultural longevity to deep changes in the American economy. Even as they turned away from the bureaucracies and large-scale technologies of heavy industry, the authors and editors of the *Whole Earth Catalog* and *Radical Software* embraced the tools and trends that Daniel Bell had characterized as key elements of the emerging postindustrial order: systemic forms of expertise, participatory models of organization, and information technology. Today of course, the postindustrial order has become part of our everyday world. Theoretical knowledge has been applied to virtually every mechanical and social process we know. Information technologies link us to one another and to databanks of fact and thought. Twenty-four hours a day, computer systems transform the expertise embedded in algorithms and social communities into electronic actions, sorting and delivering a new world of goods and ideas to our desktops. Moreover, much

32. Gigliottie, "A Brief History of RainDance."

33. Deirdre Boyle and ebrary, Inc., *Subject to Change: Guerrilla Television Revisited* (New York: Oxford University Press, 1997), pp. 190–208.

34. Joselit, *Feedback*, p. 101.

35. Turner, *From Counterculture to Cyberculture*, pp. 207–236.

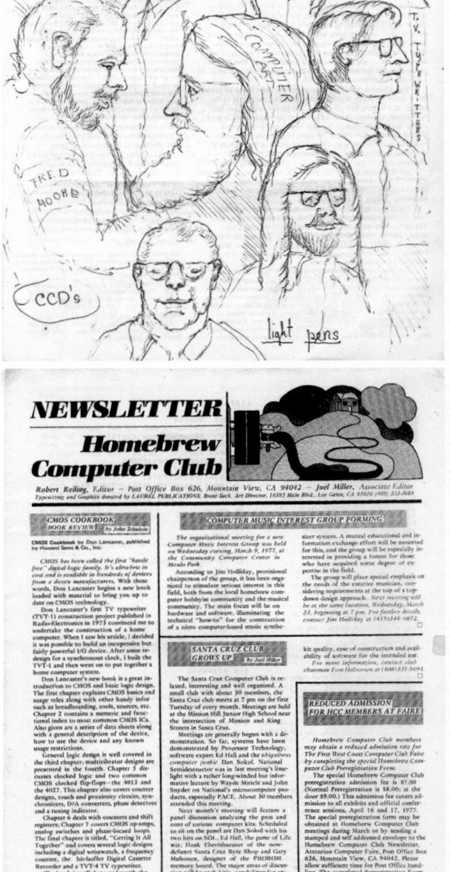
AMATEUR COMPUTER USERS GROUP NEWSLETTER HOMEBREW COMPUTER CLUB
Issue number two Fred Moore, editor, 558 Santa Cruz Ave., Menlo Park, Ca. 94025 April 12, 1975

NEWSLETTER
Homebrew Computer Club

Fig. 4.11. **Amateur Computer Users Group Newsletter**—Homebrew Computer Club, April 12, 1975, no. 2; March 16, 1977, no. 2, vol. 15

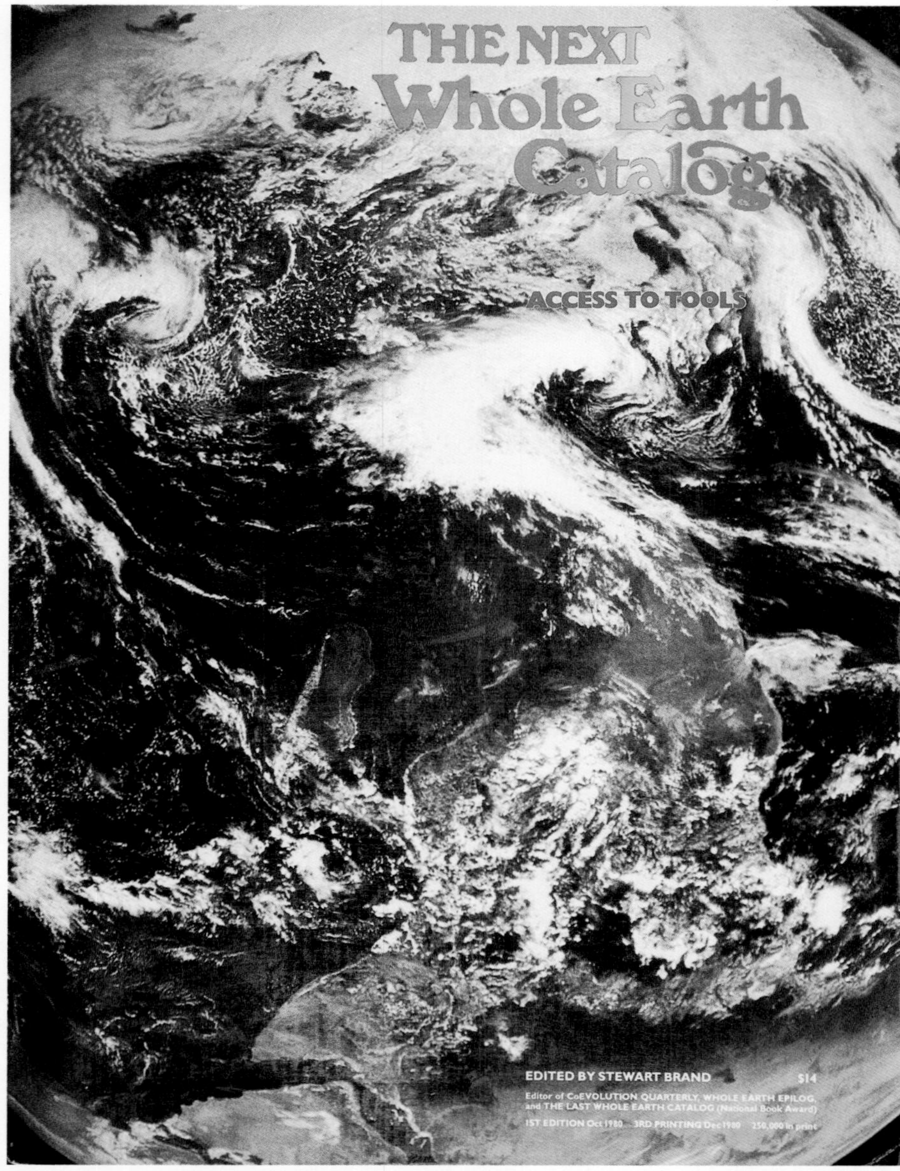
THE NEXT
Whole Earth
Catalog
ACCESS TO TOOLS
EDITED BY STEWART BRAND
$14
Editor of CoEVOLUTION QUARTERLY, WHOLE EARTH EPILOG, and THE LAST WHOLE EARTH CATALOG (National Book Award)
1ST EDITION Oct 1980 ... 3RD PRINTING Dec 1980 250,000 in print

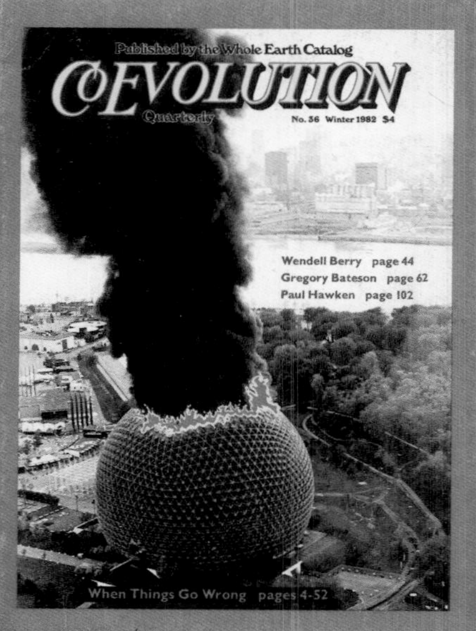
Published by the Whole Earth Catalog
CoEVOLUTION
Quarterly
No. 36 Winter 1982 $4
Wendell Berry page 44
Gregory Bateson page 62
Paul Hawken page 102
When Things Go Wrong pages 4-52

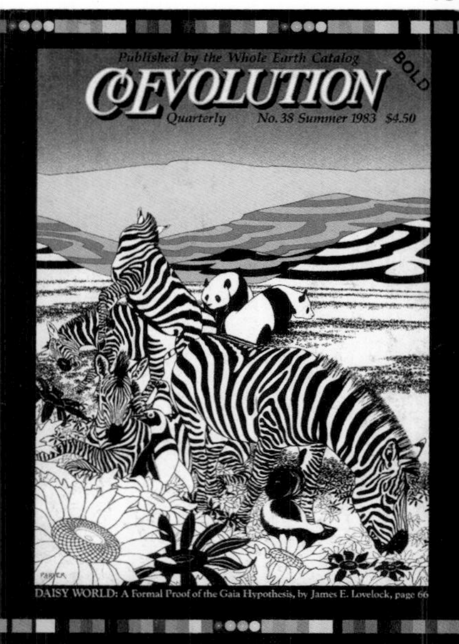
Published by the Whole Earth Catalog
CoEVOLUTION
BOLD
Quarterly No. 38 Summer 1983 $4.50
DAISY WORLD: A Formal Proof of the Gaia Hypothesis, by James E. Lovelock, page 66

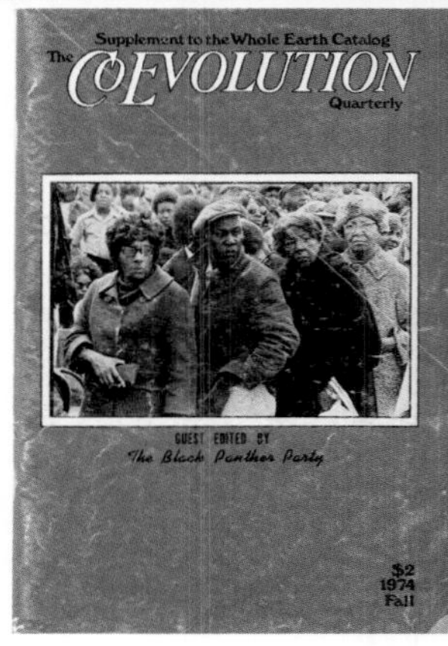
Supplement to the Whole Earth Catalog
The CoEVOLUTION
Quarterly
GUEST EDITED BY
The Black Panther Party
$2
1974
Fall

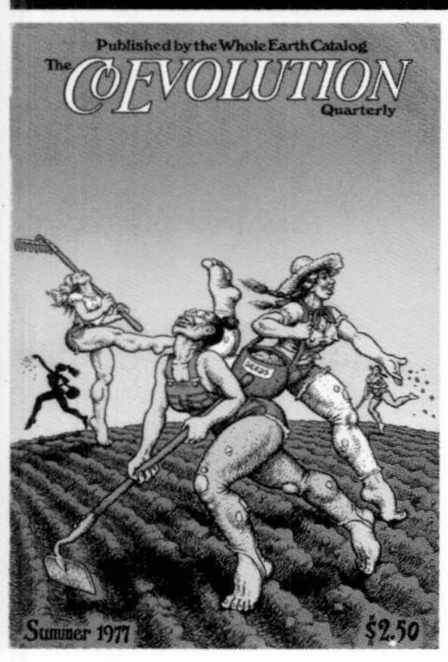
Published by the Whole Earth Catalog
The CoEVOLUTION
Quarterly
Summer 1977
$2.50

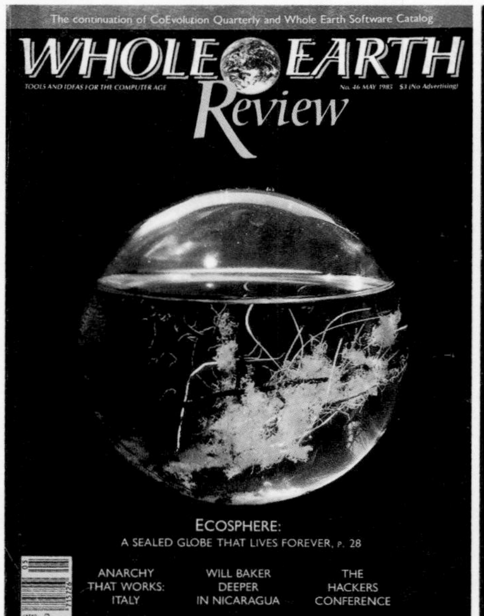
The continuation of CoEvolution Quarterly and Whole Earth Software Catalog
WHOLE EARTH
Review
ECOSPHERE:
A SEALED GLOBE THAT LIVES FOREVER, P. 28
ANARCHY THAT WORKS: ITALY
WILL BAKER DEEPER IN NICARAGUA
THE HACKERS CONFERENCE

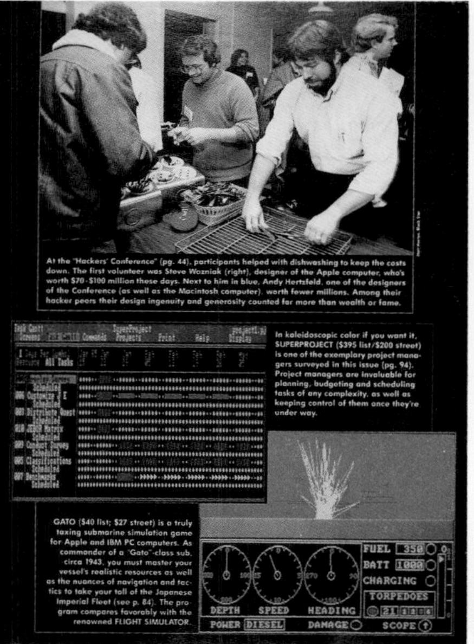
At the "Hackers' Conference" (pg. 44), participants helped with dishwashing to keep the costs down. The first volunteer was Steve Wozniak (right), designer of the Apple computer, who's worth $70-$100 million these days. Next to him in blue, Andy Hertzfeld, one of the designers of the Conference (as well as the Macintosh computer), worth fewer millions. Among their hacker peers their design ingenuity and generosity counted far more than wealth or fame.
In kaleidoscopic color if you want it, SUPERPROJECT ($395 list/$200 street) is one of the exemplary project managers surveyed in this issue (pg. 94). Project managers are invaluable for planning, budgeting and scheduling tasks of any complexity, as well as keeping control of them once they're under way.
GATO ($40 list; $27 street) is a truly taxing submarine simulation game for Apple and IBM PC computers. As commander of a "Gato"-class sub, circa 1943, you must master your vessel's realistic resources as well as the nuances of navigation and tactics to take your toll of the Japanese Imperial Fleet (see p. 84). The program compares favorably with the renowned FLIGHT SIMULATOR.
FUEL 350
BATT 1000
CHARGING
TORPEDOES
DEPTH
SPEED
HEADING
POWER DIESEL
DAMAGE
SCOPE

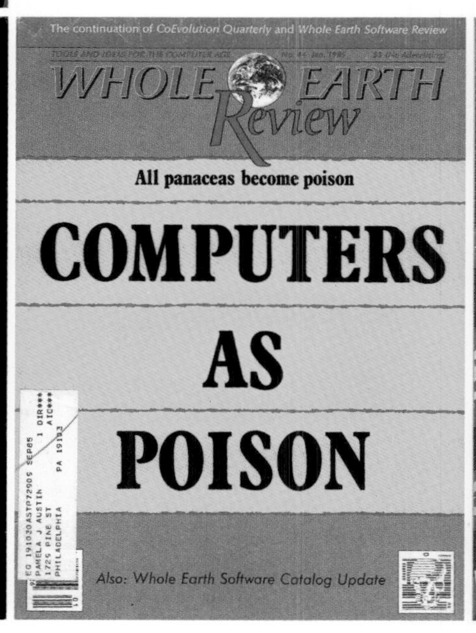
The continuation of CoEvolution Quarterly and Whole Earth Software Review
WHOLE EARTH
Review
All panaceas become poison
COMPUTERS
AS
POISON
Also: Whole Earth Software Catalog Update

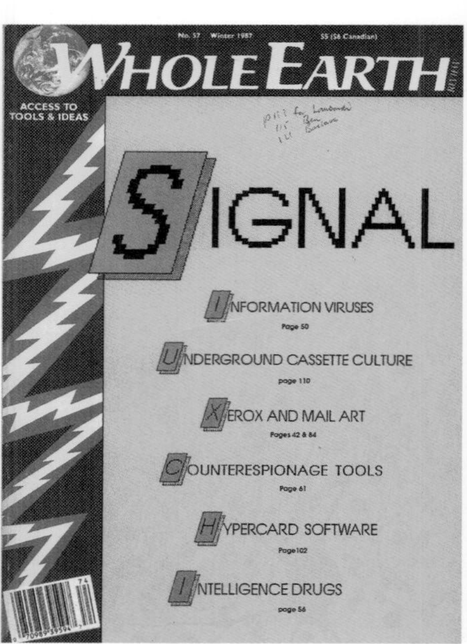
WHOLE EARTH
ACCESS TO TOOLS & IDEAS
SIGNAL
INFORMATION VIRUSES
UNDERGROUND CASSETTE CULTURE
XEROX AND MAIL ART
COUNTERESPIONAGE TOOLS
HYPERCARD SOFTWARE
INTELLIGENCE DRUGS

as Bell predicted, the status structure of American society reflects this shift. Today, scientists and technologists such as Bill Gates and Steve Jobs have become international icons. Likewise, the values we associate with information and media technologies have become ubiquitous: calls for entrepreneurship, small group collaboration, and the promotion of egalitarian access to knowledge can be heard across the developed world.

Today, even the *form* of information technology that the Whole Earth Catalog and Radical Software helped pioneer remains influential. Neither the Catalog nor Radical Software really covered events; rather, they invited participants into their pages and in so doing, became events in their own right. That is, they made an emerging, geographically distributed social world visible to itself. They offered the citizens of that world tools with which to design their own psychological and social futures. And they asked in return only that their readers imagine themselves as cybernetic nomads. To flip open their publications was to wander in a world in which mind and society, nature and machine, mirrored one another. To change society was as simple as finding and using the right tool. Today of course, digital technologies have rendered such worlds ubiquitous. Online social networks, multiplayer computer games, and virtual worlds such as ***Second Life*** all offer access to new tools, new social groups, and for some at least, alternative communities in which to live.

If Daniel Bell was right and it was the rise of big science and the deployment of massive computers after World War II that helped bring us into the flexible, mobile, work-anywhere country we inhabit now, it was publications like the Catalog and Radical Software that made that country look cool. Even as they turned against bureaucracy in favor of a do-it-yourself ethos, they cracked open a vision of using information technologies to support massively distributed labor. Even as they called for the blurring of work and everyday life on communes and in video collectives, they helped legitimize a turn toward highly informated, geographically dispersed production. To Daniel Bell, this shift looked like a transformation in the American mode of manufacturing. To the authors of the Whole Earth Catalog and Radical Software, it looked like utopia.

Fig. 4.12. **The Next Whole Earth Catalog,** 1980, cover

Fig. 4.13. **CoEvolution Quarterly,** Winter 1982, no. 36, cover; Summer 1983, no. 38, cover; Fall 1974, no. 3, cover; Summer 1977, no. 14, cover

Fig. 4.14. **Whole Earth Review,** May 1985, no. 46, front and back covers; January 1985, no. 44, cover; Winter 1987, no. 57, cover

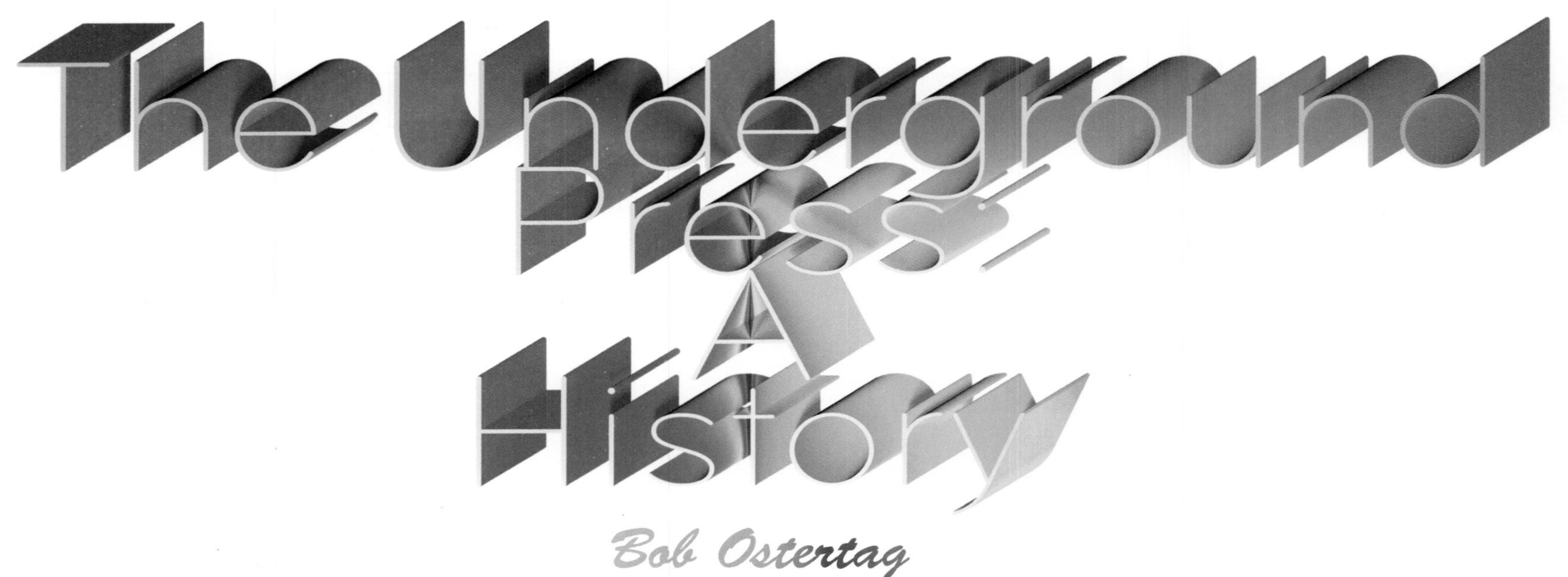

Bob Ostertag

EVERY PERIOD OF SOCIAL UPHEAVAL IN AMERICAN HISTORY HAS HAD ITS OWN "UNDERGROUND PRESS." The British colonies at the time of the war of independence were awash in pamphlets, of which Thomas Paine's *Common Sense* (fig. 5.1) is the most celebrated. Twenty-five years later, alone in an attic with hardly any money or even food, William Lloyd Garrison launched what would become the flagship "underground" newspaper of the abolitionist movement, the *Liberator* (fig. 5.2). Soon there was a multitude of abolitionist publications with a combined circulation of over a million. After the Civil War, many women who had cut their political teeth in the abolitionist movement moved into advocacy of women's rights, and a vast woman suffrage press emerged. Another few decades later, turn-of-the-century radicalism was promoted in the pages of the socialist *Appeal to Reason* (fig. 5.3), Emma Goldman's anarchist *Mother Earth* (fig. 5.4), Max Eastman's the *Masses* (fig. 5.5), and others.

The underground press of the 1960s was heir to this history. The *Los Angeles Free Press* (fig. 5.6), or *FREEP* as it came to be known, was launched in 1964 with a budget of fifteen dollars, and things quickly snowballed from there. Just two years later, five leading underground papers with a combined circulation of 50,000 joined together to form the Underground Press Syndicate, announcing their intention "to warn the civilized world of its impending collapse, [and] to offer as many alternatives as the mind can bear."[1] Within a year the five papers of UPS (*FREEP*, the *Berkeley Barb*, New York City's *East Village Other*, the *Oracle* in San Francisco [fig. 5.7], and the *Paper* in Lansing, Michigan) were providing news feeds for nineteen others, but this was just the tip of the iceberg.[2] The emerging "black power" movement was supporting the *Black Liberator* and the *Black Panther*; the United Farm Workers (fig. 5.8) had *El Macriado*; and militant Chicanos in New Mexico were publishing *El Grito del Norte*. Later, *Akwesasne Notes* would act as the voice of the American Indian Movement.

1. David Armstrong, *Trumpet to Arms: Alternative Media in America* (Boston: South End Press, 1981), p. 60.

2. Abe Peck, *Uncovering the Sixties: The Life and Times of the Underground Press* (New York: Coral, 1991), p. 44.

COMMON SENSE;

ADDRESSED TO THE

INHABITANTS

OF

AMERICA,

On the following interesting

SUBJECTS.

I. Of the Origin and Design of Government in general, with concise Remarks on the English Constitution.

II. Of Monarchy and Hereditary Succession.

III. Thoughts on the present State of American Affairs.

IV. Of the present Ability of America, with some miscellaneous Reflections.

Man knows no Master save creating HEAVEN,
Or those whom choice and common good ordain.

THOMSON.

PHILADELPHIA;
Printed, and Sold, by R. BELL, in Third-Street.
MDCCLXXVI.

THE LIBERATOR.

VOL. I.] WILLIAM LLOYD GARRISON AND ISAAC KNAPP, PUBLISHERS. [NO. 1.

BOSTON, MASSACHUSETTS.] OUR COUNTRY IS THE WORLD—OUR COUNTRYMEN ARE MANKIND. [SATURDAY, JANUARY 1, 1831.

THE LIBERATOR IS PUBLISHED WEEKLY AT NO. 6, MERCHANTS' HALL.

WM. L. GARRISON, EDITOR.

Stephen Foster, Printer.

TERMS.

Two Dollars per annum, payable in advance.

Agents allowed every sixth copy gratis.

No subscription will be received for a shorter period than six months.

All letters and communications must be POST PAID.

THE LIBERATOR.

TO THE PUBLIC.

WILLIAM LLOYD GARRISON.
BOSTON, January 1, 1831.

DISTRICT OF COLUMBIA.

[From the Washington Spectator, of Dec. 4.]

THE SLAVE TRADE IN THE CAPITAL.

PREMIUM.

W. RAWLE,
J. PRESTON,
THOMAS SHIPLEY, } Committee.
Philadelphia, Oct. 11.

APPEAL TO REASON.

NO. 21

KANSAS CITY, MO., SATURDAY, JANUARY 18, 1896.

PUBLISHED WEEKLY. 50 Cents a Year.

J. A. WAYLAND, One-Hoss Editor. NO PEOPLE CAN BE SELF-GOVERNING, WHO ARE DENIED THE RIGHT TO VOTE "YES" OR "NO" ON EVERY LAW BY WHICH THEY ARE TO BE GOVERNED. CITY DELIVERY, 5 Cents Per Month.

WHY THE STRUGGLE OF LIFE?

THE USES OF ADVERSITY.

HIS GUARDIAN ANGELS.

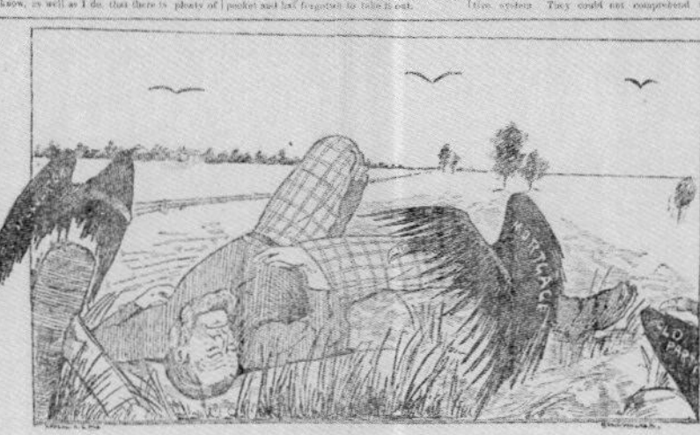

Fig. 5.1. **Thomas Paine's Common Sense,** 1776

Fig. 5.2. **Liberator,** January 1, 1831, vol. 1, no. 1

Fig. 5.3. **Appeal to Reason,** January 18, 1898, front page

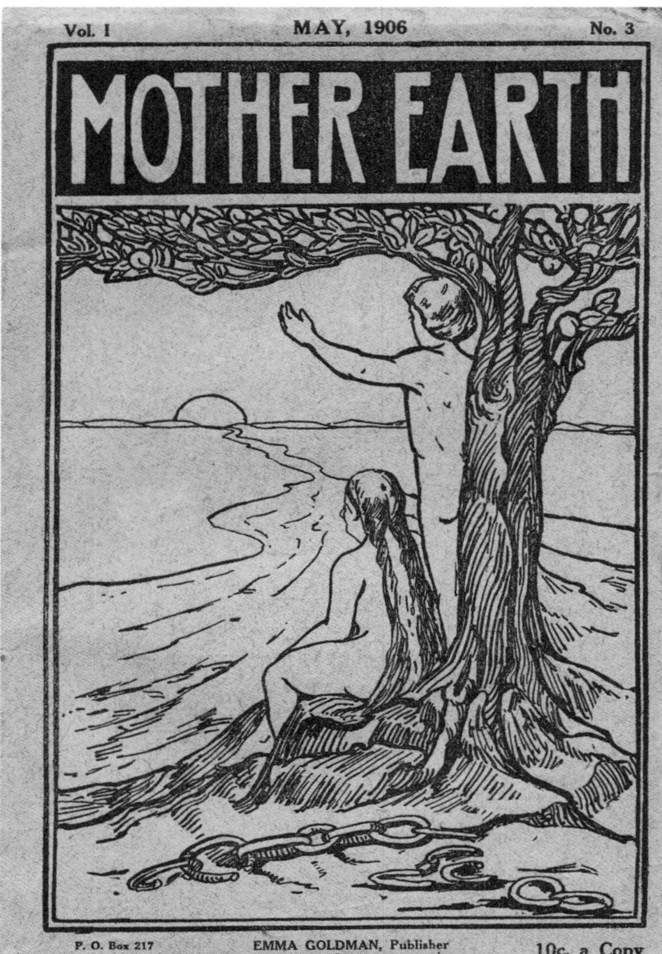

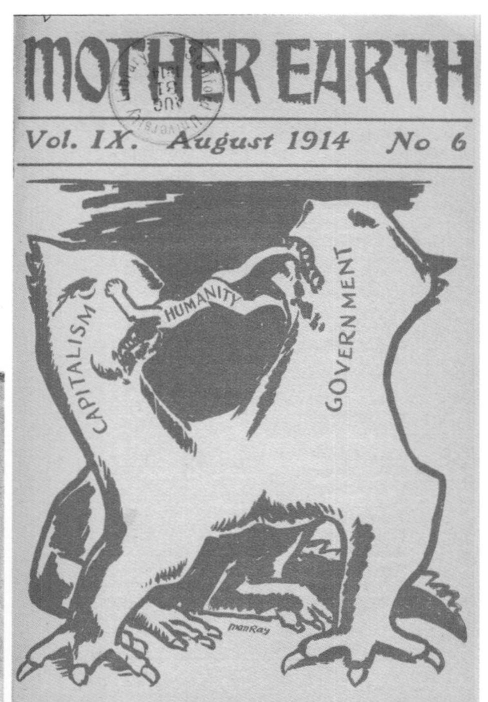

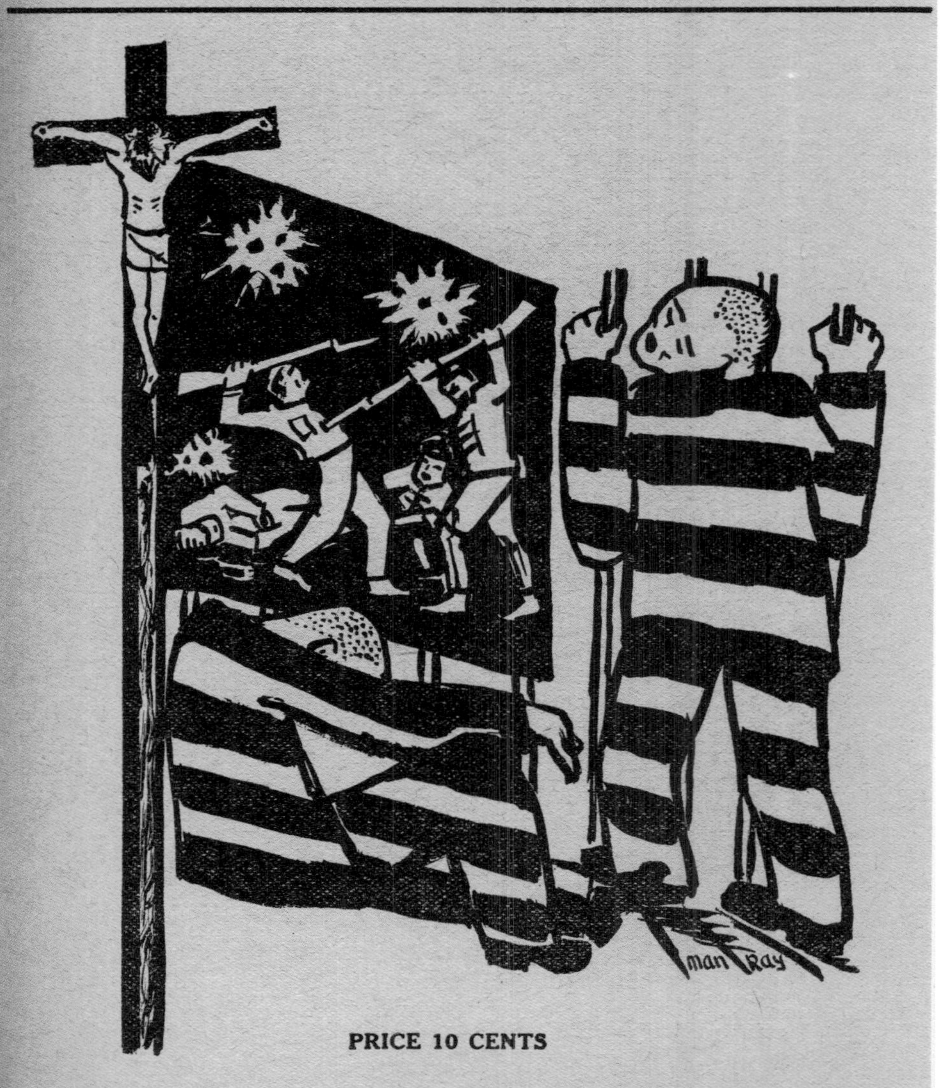

Fig. 5.4. **Mother Earth,** May 1906, vol. 1, no. 3, cover, August 1914, vol. 9, no. 6, cover (by Man Ray), September 1914, vol. 9, no. 7, cover (by Man Ray)

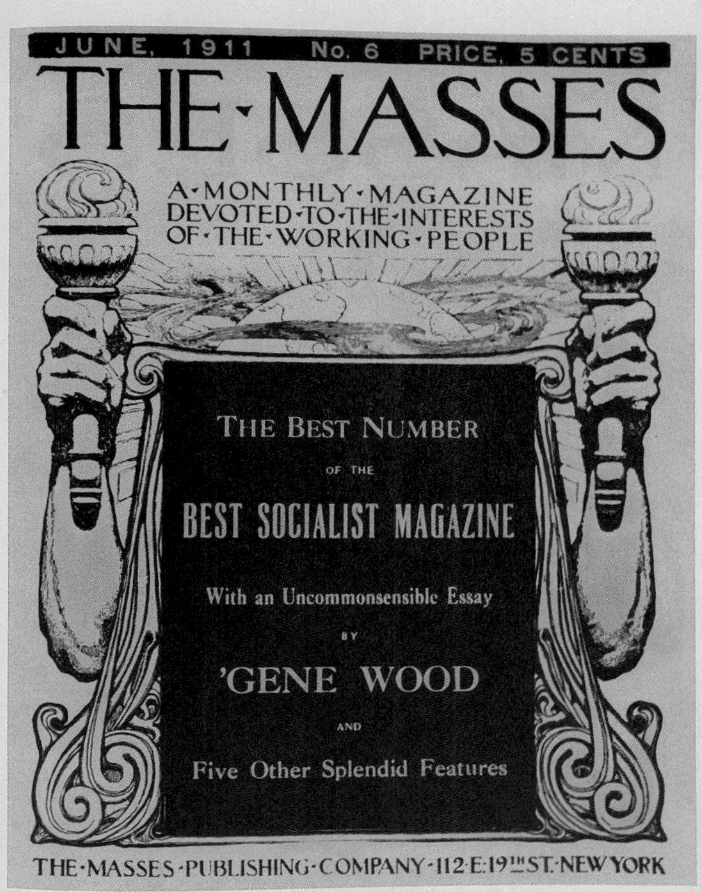

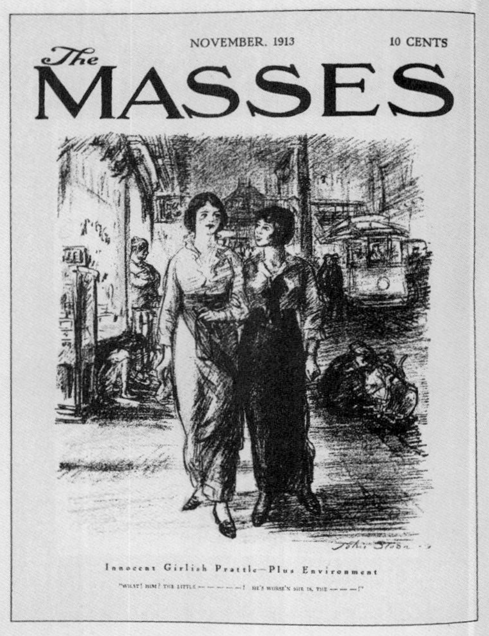

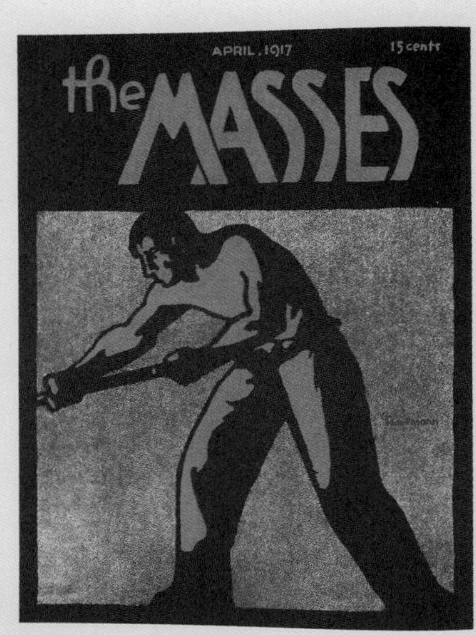

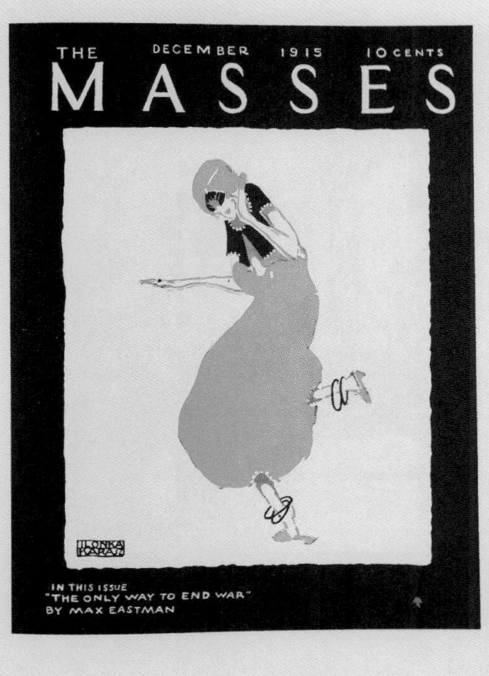

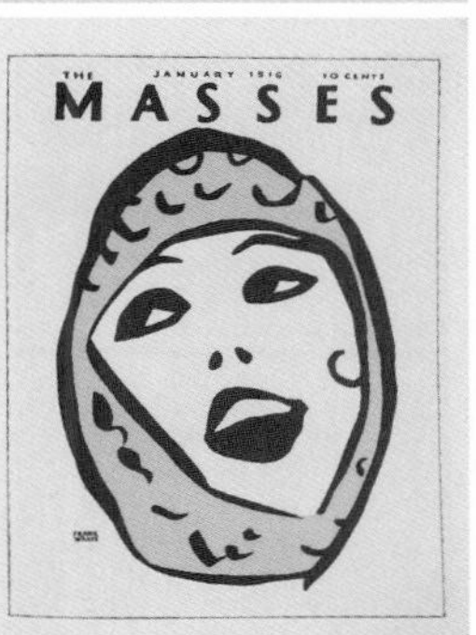

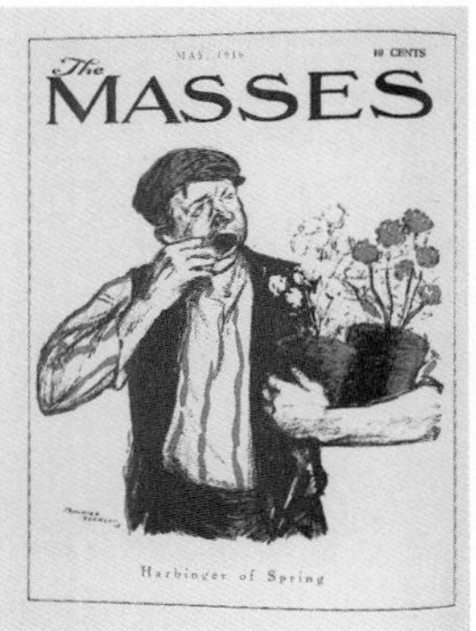

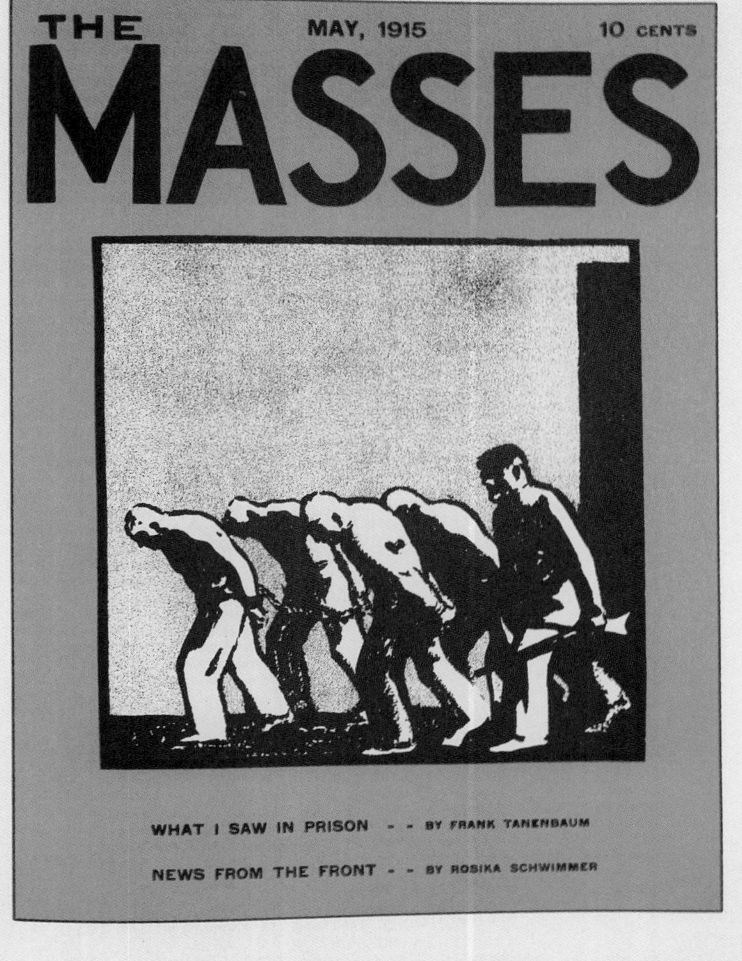

Fig. 5.5. **The Masses,** June 1911, no. 6, cover; November 1913, cover; April 1917, cover; December 1915, cover; January 1916, cover; May 1915, cover; May 1916, cover

LOS ANGELES

FREE PRESS

Newspaper

15c 25 CENTS OUT OF L.A. COUNTY

Mayoral election wrap -up

Che gets busted in New York

Sacramento launches counter-revolution

140 Places to go this week — see page 52

Volume 6 (Issue # 245) $5.00 PER YEAR In two parts: Part One

WE 7-1970 March 28-April 4, 1969

WHO'S WHO IN THE CIA

See page 6

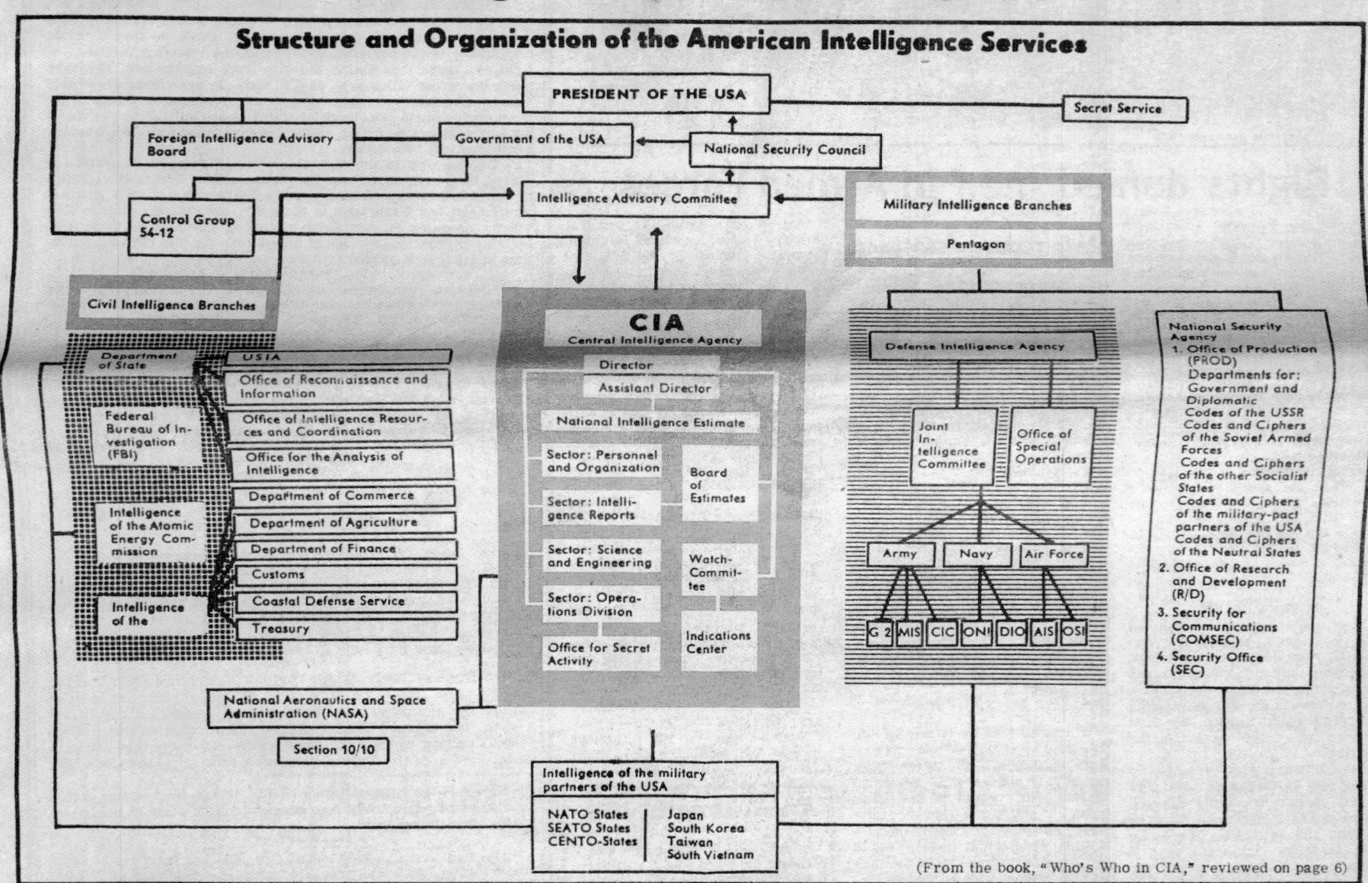

(From the book, "Who's Who in CIA," reviewed on page 6)

Anti -Ballistic Missiles

Draw fast..............Shoot straight ....Die laughing...........

TED ZATLYN

NO FLIES ON ME

The ABM mythos has risen Frankensteinian and absurd from the gutter of American politics. The monster was created by the nutsies in uniform, public office and industry who glued it together with the same stickum that made the Vietnam war: fear, guilt and greed. They made the thing so horribly absurd you can't even laugh at it. But laugh you must, even if it kills you.

Secretary of Defense Melvin Laird seems to fear laughter more than anything—especially gallows humor. During a recent televised hearing conducted by the Senate Foreign Relations Committee, Senator Cooper, a Republican from Kentucky, tried to determine what would happen if, say, three or four enemy missiles came over the horizon, and Sentinel were deployed: then, after all the anti-missile missiles were used up, along came some more enemy missiles, then more and more.

Something about the way he described the situation—a hundred billion dollars worth of wasted missiles—brought laughter to the galleries. The senators laughed. Fulbright chuckled. If only they had guts enough to keep laughing, they might have laughed ABM into oblivion.

Not the least bit blithered, Melvin began putting on more

(Continued on Page 5)

Freep Price increase

Due to an increase in printing costs and growth in number of pages, the Free Press now costs more per copy to print and circulate than is paid by our local distributors.

Since the Free Press will probably publish more than 100,000 copies per issue by Summer, the price per copy must be raised next week to 25¢.

The subscription price will remain the same as always, $5 per year, which averages out to a bargain price of 10¢ per copy. We will hold to this as long as possible without endangering the paper.

The stabilization of our income will permit a greater expansion of our editorial ability to serve the community, go into modernizing subscription procedures and give the newsboy in the street an increase of income.

I have a dream

Earl Ofari reflects on the first anniversary of the assasination

I HAVE A DREAM

These words entoned by Dr. King at the March on Washington in 1963 served as both a scathing indictment of American injustice and an offer of hope to black people for liberation. However, as most dreams go, so went Dr. King's, and with it his life in the process.

Today, with the recent closure in Memphis of the James Earl Ray case, much speculation has arisen over possible motives and plots behind the King murder. It is heartening to see that most black people are not fooled. There is only one conspiracy behind the murder of Dr. King, and it didn't begin in the minds of a few feeble men in the time immediately prior to April 4th.

The real conspiracy here began to take shape when the greed of the white West forced the European nations to rape and plunder the African continent stealing over one hundred million Africans and bringing them to the

(Continued on Page 21)

Free Press Forum on Middle East

Raya Dunayevskaya, author of "Marxism and Freedom," will speak on the subject of the United States and Russia in the Middle East, Friday, March 28th, 8 pm at the Unitarian Church, 2936 West 8th St., Los Angeles.

Art Kunkin, Editor of the L.A. Free Press, will act as chairman of the meeting in Channing Hall.

LOS ANGELES FREE PRESS

15c 25 cents out of L.A.

Warhol on Nude Restaurant
Lipton: Is self-defense illegal?
Ellison: The television generation

152 Places to go this week-page 44

WHO RULES THE COUNTRY? See page 25

Vol. 5 #45 (Issue #225) In two parts: Part One Copyright 1968 The Los Angeles Free Press, Inc. WE 7-1970 November 8-13th, 1968

The young make love; The old make obscene elections.

All quotations on this page were emitted by President-elect Nixon as cited in "The Almanack of Poor Richard Nixon," World Publishing Company, $2, 1968.

Tactical atomic explosives are now conventional and will be used against the targets of any aggressive force.
Chicago, Illinois March 17, 1955

If you think the United States has stood still, who built the largest shopping center in the world?
Portland, Oregon September 14, 1960

I know I'm weakest on the liberal side. You can't win 'em all. I have no thought of trying.
Quoted in *National Review* November 14, 1967

When we're elected, we'll take care of people like you! Okay, boys, throw him out!
To a heckler *The Facts About Nixon* 1960

It's not worth killing American boys to have Vietnams have free elections.
New York, New York December 17, 1967

We've got to have a tent everybody can get into.
Quoted in *Newsweek* December 25, 1967

I was elected to smash the labor bosses, and my one principle is to accept no dictation from the CIO.
First day in Congress Washington, D.C. January 3, 1947

The United States must make a decision that Castro must go, and then do what is necessary to bring him down.
New York, New York March 5, 1964

California, which has not had a single item of antisubversive legislation in the last four years, must reverse this dismal record and become a shining example to the nation.
Chico, California September 15, 1962

In my opinion the proposal to halt the bombing and talk about the proposal simply have the effect of prolonging the war by encouraging the enemy. They are led to believe there is a division in the United States and they can win.
New York, New York March 5, 1967

We can't all be President—I found that out.
San Francisco, California February 28, 1962

In the Democratic Party, about half of their representatives get elected by being for civil rights and the other half by being against civil rights.
New York, New York January 20, 1958

We cannot talk equality to the peoples of Africa and Asia and practice inequality in the United States.
Washington, D.C. April 6, 1957

We must not use milquetoast or kid-glove tactics.
Chicago, Illinois March 7, 1960

I am a chance taker in foreign affairs.
Quoted in *Saturday Evening Post* July 12, 1958

LIVING ARTS SUPPLEMENT - SECTION TWO

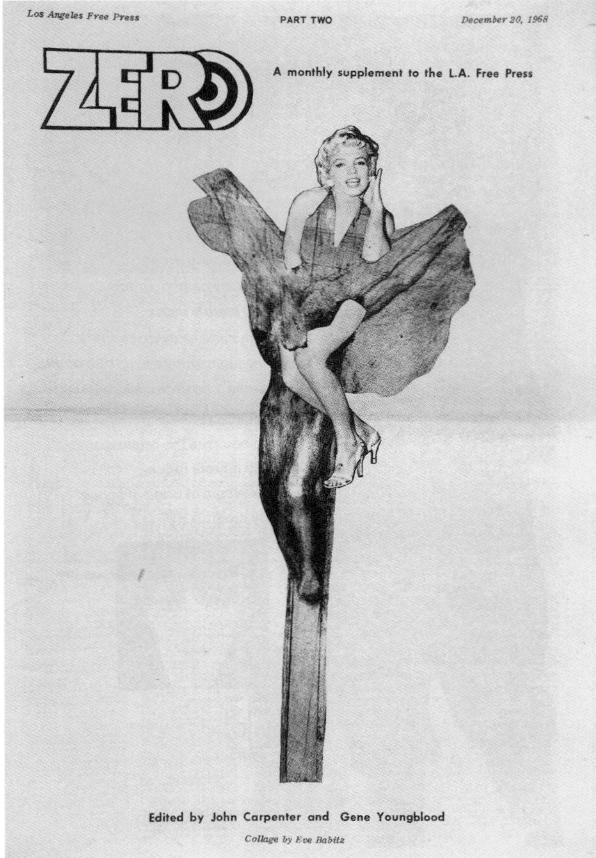

Los Angeles Free Press Sept. 20, 1968 Page 25

REHEARSAL FOR REVOLUTION

Marat: "I am the rage of the people."

Robespierre: "Virtue without terror is powerless."

ROY L. WALFORD

Beginning on 14 July with an unauthorized street manifestation of 700 young revolutionaries down from Paris, the renowned Festival of Avignon in southern France developed rapidly into one of the wildest scenes played this year on the European continent. Events in the ancient city near the playgrounds of the Cote d'Azur, events that centered around the anarchist Living Theater's presentation of PARADISE NOW, revitalized and perhaps fundamentally redirected the young leftist movement in France. So this is not a report about "the Festival of Avignon."

Like the biennale art exhibit in Venice, the film festival in Cannes, and whatever might be going on at any moment at the Lincoln Center, the Avignon festival had, according to the revolutionaries, become a show of puppets performing before puppets. Nevertheless, this year in Avignon many doors opened into the heart of the now world-wide cultural revolution taking place among the young and the hip. I take you therefore on a trip to the heartland.

One of the new-left's theses is that today's art and culture, even the most avant-garde types, serve merely as opiate to the masses. Culture is made into a purchasable commodity whose producers and owners serve the interests more or less of one class. This industrial culture, whether right-wing or left-wing, turns the people who purchase it into amorphous robots who absorb prepackaged art and are lulled into impassivity by the various forms of organized leisure. It's a smoke screen, this contemporary middle-class culture. It does not arrive at changing anybody's viewpoint, either of himself as an individual or of society. It does not open people up to human values. It entertains them and solidifies their smugness. It is a form of consumption.

To enlarge the above orientation, I quote first from a taped interview with one of the original 147 members of the Movement of 22 March, the now outlawed radical group that sparked the massive revolution in France a few months ago. Cohn-Bendit was part of this group.

"You have asked me why a permanent revolution is necessary. Well, we saw in May that a minority of agitators created a situation in Paris where the Sorbonne, the Theater of France, and many other places were occupied by students and workers and made free and public. However, a tendency soon appeared for these places to be taken over by organized albeit revolutionary groups who in their turn set up service d'ordres and issued rules and forbade certain actions. For us, on the other hand, it is not a question of replacing one kind of order and prohibition by another, but of permanent freedom. Most of the revolutions in history started out good, yet matured only into new systems of repression. Therefore we need a revolution that is always evolving, a permanent revolution.

"Recently it has become customary for the upper bourgeoisie to invite us to dinner, whereupon one of the guests will say to the hostess, 'Oh you have invited an anarchist to dinner. That's charming! He will explain to us what will be the nature of the new society.'

"You see, they are waiting for us to propose a new structure, a new order. But it is disorder, not order, that is creative. We do not wish to reestablish a brand of parent/child dialogue where the child listens to the father and does what the father says. Such relationships are presently found at all social levels; in the family, in the schools where the children haven't the right to discuss anything real or valid and must simply respond to precise questions after raising their hands, in the universities, everywhere. What is almost unbelievable is that all structures at all levels are fundamentally repressive structures which severely limit the self-expression and choice of the individual.

"We do not wish to tell people what to do but to persuade them to express themselves, to really express themselves. Merely to talk about art, about culture, about politics—that means nothing. It's of no avail to propose missions to the United Nations, to propose negotiation between Biafra and Nigeria, between the Arabs and the Jews. When a certain number of celebrities sign a petition, one knows full well that it comes to nothing, because they take only a verbal position and do not engage themselves absolutely. The only effective place of engagement is in the streets, in street action, because there one can modify reality, because there one obliges the forces of repression to unmask themselves, because there one obliges individuals to take a non-verbal stand. And this is why we have come to Avignon, by direct confrontation to unmask, to de-mystify this famous festival. For all such festivals and art programs are merely circuses staged for themselves and for others by the bourgeoise elite. The festival is an intellectual circus. When it is directly contested, the repressive police structure behind it will be unmasked."

Such talk may sound young and wild, but when the political circus of the Democratic Convention in Chicago was directly contested by street action, did not a certain repressive police structuring thrust itself into public view? A lot of people thought so.

****

To return now to Avignon, the feature attraction scheduled for the festival was the first presentation by the formerly New York-based Living Theater of their new play, PARADISE NOW. The anti-festival resolve of the revolutionaries was therefore complicated by the fact that in repudiating the festival they would be repudiating also the Living Theater, which is itself a potent revolutionary force. The Living Theater's avowed purpose is to promote non-violent revolution by breaking barriers of inhibition between people,—by involving them with one another on a basic human level, by teaching them how to love one another, by turning them on and tuning them in. Incidentally, I hesitate to call PARADISE NOW a play, but there's no precise word for it. It is a kind of manifestation, confrontation, celebration, a mystical rite about humanity in which the artificial barrier between lerformer and spectator becomes erased.

The sensation I personally got from PARADISE NOW was the same I experienced during the great days of May and June in Paris: the days and nights in the streets, with the students, inside the Sorbonne, behind the barricades, running from the advancing lines of the C.R.S., in the smoky middle of tear gas clouds blowing down the boulevards of the left bank. All in the company of people I respected, people who were for the moment freed of their small ego games and emerging not merely into a new political consciousness but into a change in the perception of values, whereby all the crud, all the mindless social barriers, all the thou shalt not's abruptly dropped off! If you want a familiar west coast analogy, it was like body-surfing, just as the long-awaited great wave broke and you're in the middle of it with the whole ocean suddenly alive and around you and embracing you as you come down the steep slant of the wave. What I'm saying is that PARADISE NOW provides the authentic feeling of the revolutionary experience. People who were not at Chicago, Columbia, or Paris can find out during this play how the revolution feels. They can come down

(Continued on page 26)

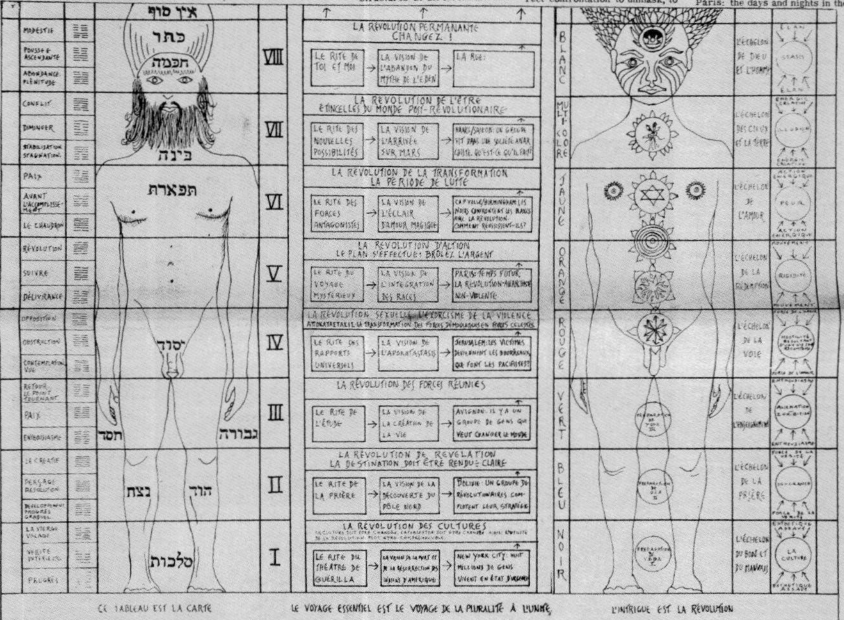

Photo by Roy Walford

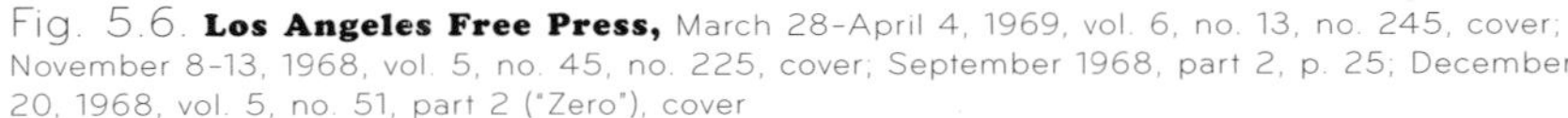

Fig. 5.6. **Los Angeles Free Press,** March 28–April 4, 1969, vol. 6, no. 13, no. 245, cover; November 8–13, 1968, vol. 5, no. 45, no. 225, cover; September 1968, part 2, p. 25; December 20, 1968, vol. 5, no. 51, part 2 ("Zero"), cover

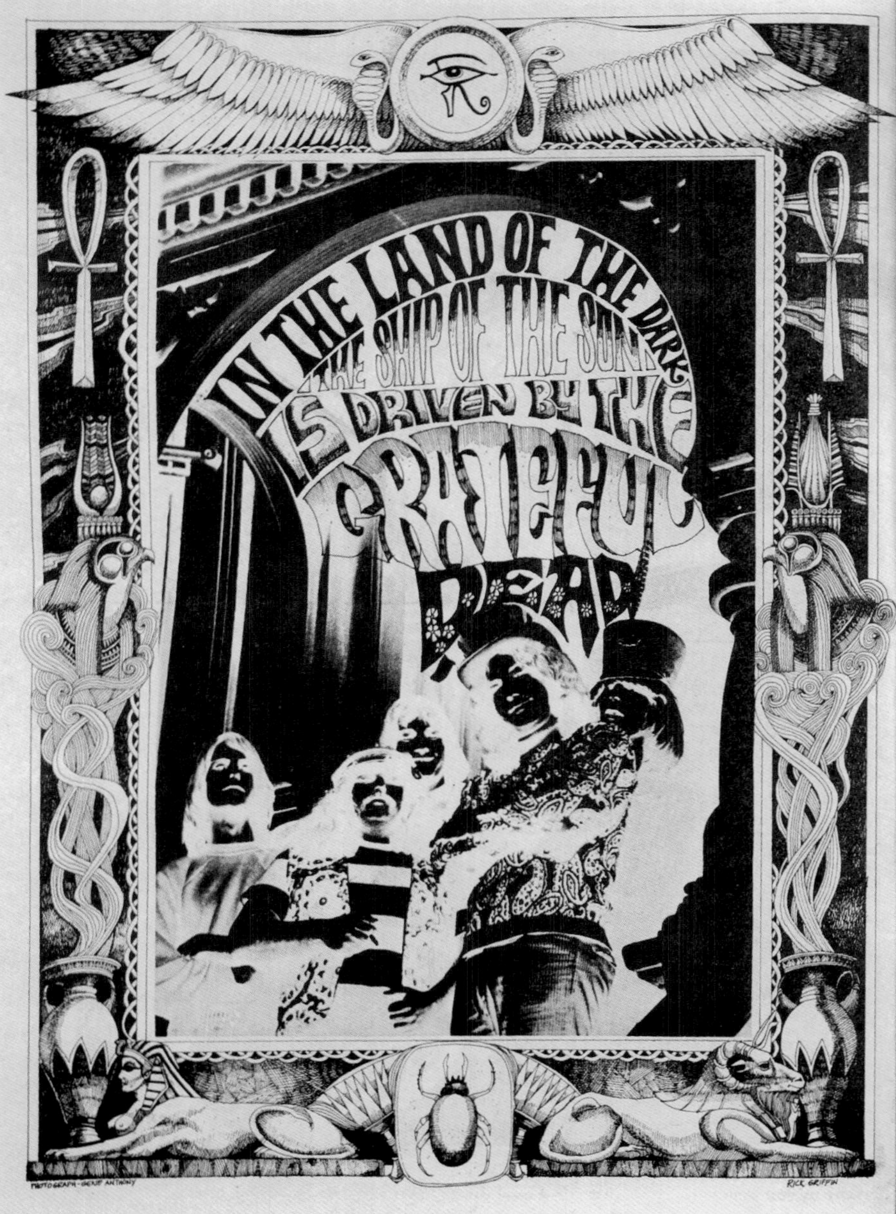

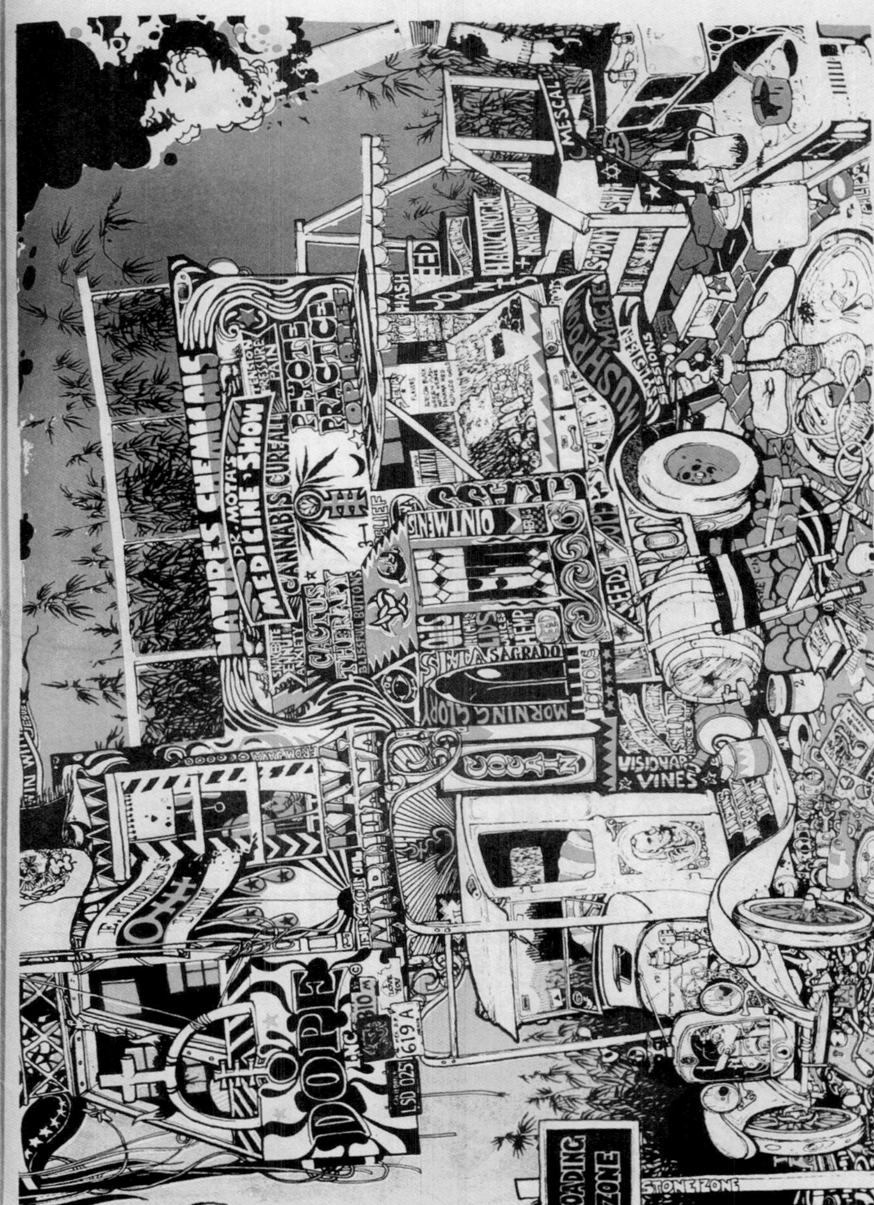

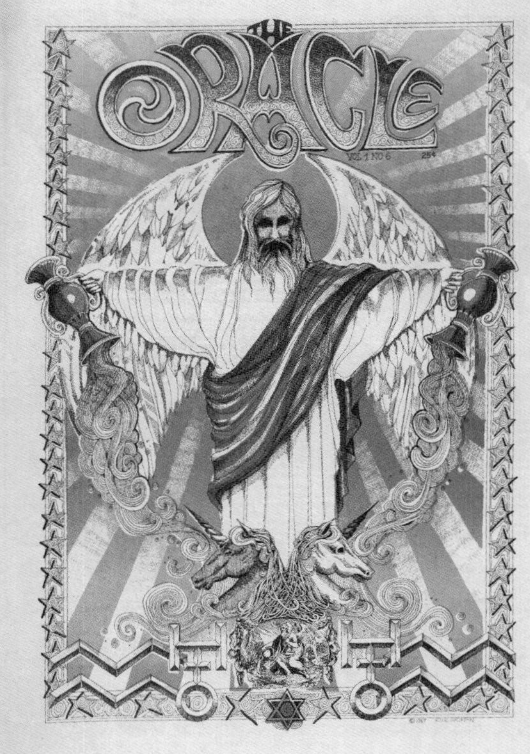

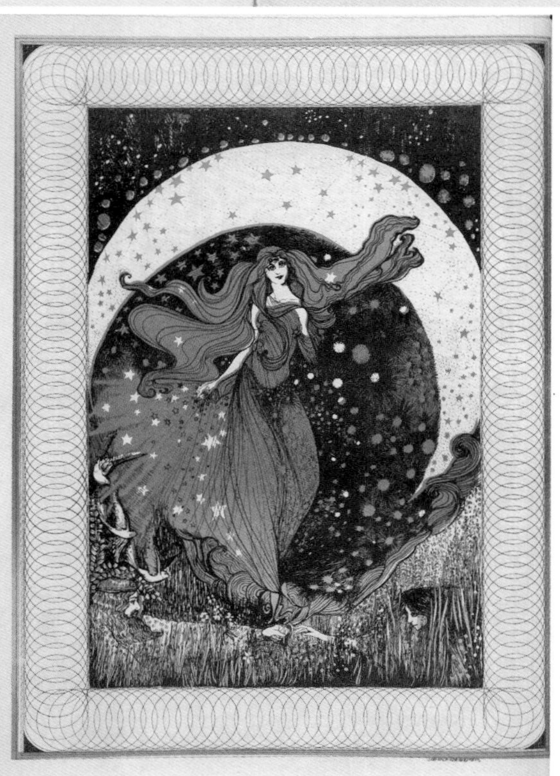

Fig. 5.7. **Oracle** (San Francisco), 1967, vol. 1, no. 6, pp. 28–29; front and back covers; pp. 10–11 and 2–3

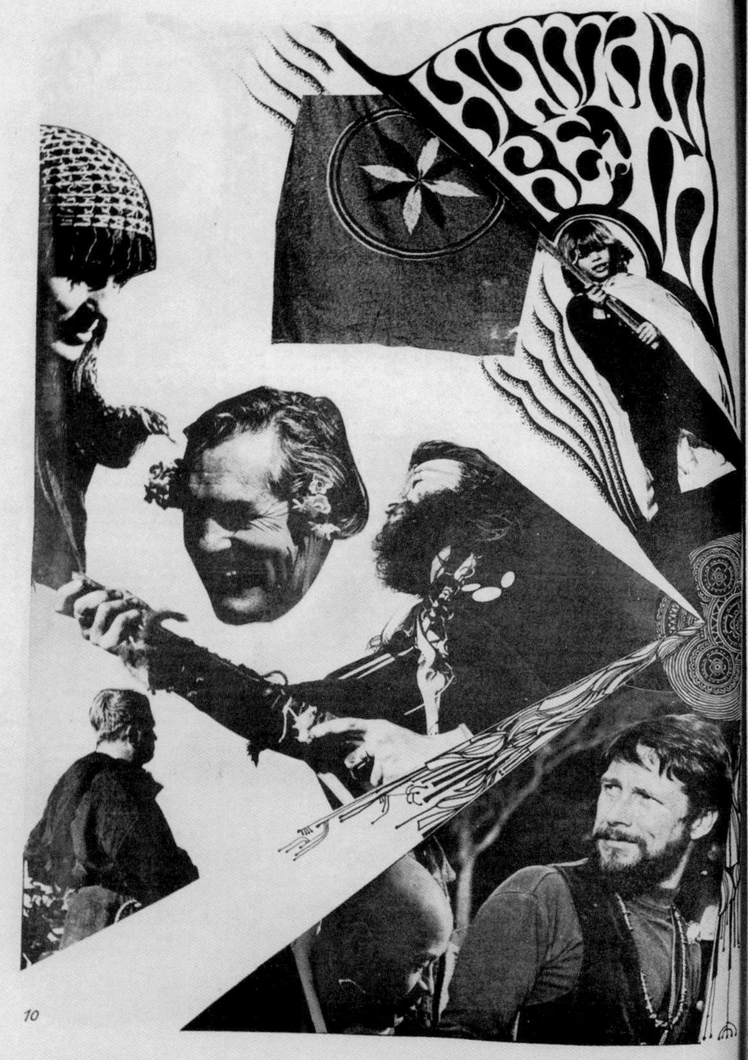

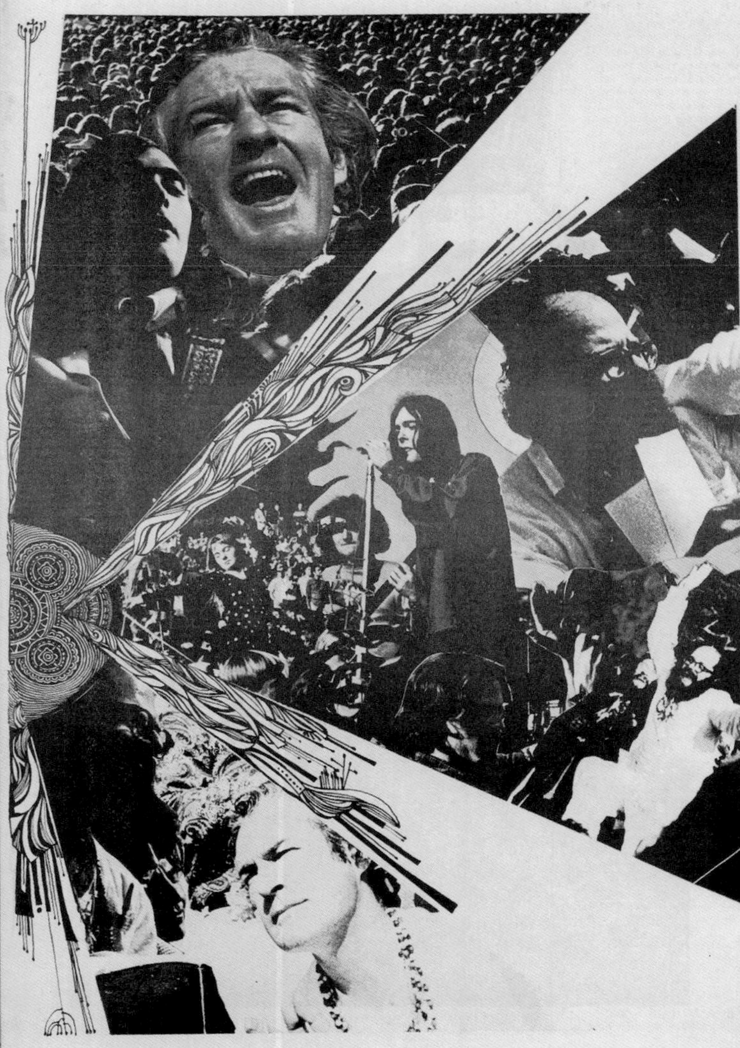

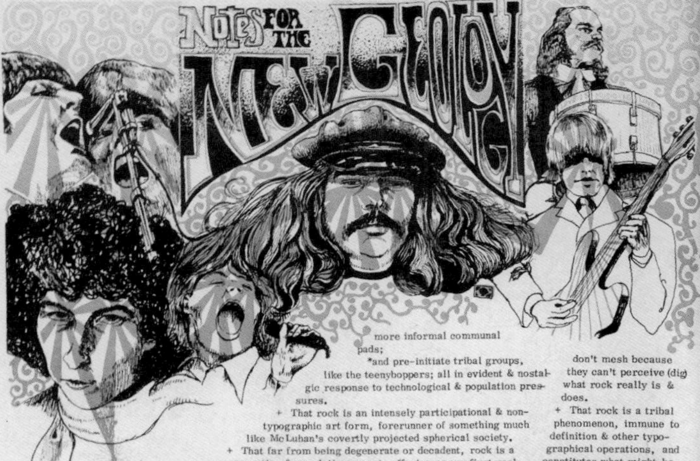

by Chester Anderson

I

Rock's the first head music we've had since the end of the baroque. By itself, without the aid of strobe lights, day-glo paints & other subimaginative copouts, it engages the entire sensorium, appealing to the intelligence with no interference from the intellect. Extremely typographic people are unable to experience it, which--because TV didn't approach universality till 1950--is why the rock folk are so young, generally. (Most of the astounding exceptions are people, like the poet Walter Lowenfels, who have lived a long time but have not become old.)

II

SOME PRINCIPLES:

+ That rock is essentially head (or even psychedelic) music.

+ That rock is a legitimate avant garde art form, with deep roots in the music of the past (especially the baroque & before), great vitality, and vast potential for growth & development, adaptation, experiment, etcetera.

+ That rock shares most of its formal/structural principles with baroque music (wherein lie its most recent cultural roots), and that it & baroque can be judged by the same broad standards (the governing principles being that of mosaic structure of tonal & textural contrast: tactility, collage).

+ That rock is evolving Sturgeonesque homo gestalt configurations:

*the groups themselves, far more intimately interrelated & integrated than any comparable ensembles in the past;

*super-families, like Kerista & the more informal communal pads;

*and pre-initiate tribal groups, like the teenyboppers; all in evident & nostalgic response to technological & population pressures.

+ That rock is an intensely participational & nontypographic art form, forerunner of something much like McLuhan's covertly projected spherical society.

+ That far from being degenerate or decadent, rock is a regenerative & revolutionary art, offering us our first real hope for the future (indeed, for the present) since August 6, 1945; and that its effects on the younger population, especially those effects most deplored by typeheads, have all been essentially good & healthy so far.

+ That rock principles are not limited to music, and that much of the shape of the future can be seen in its aspirations today (these being mainly total freedom, total experience, total love, peace & mutual affection).

+ That today's teenyboppers will be voting tomorrow and running for office the day after.

+ That rock is an intensely synthesizing art, an art of amazing relationships (collage is rock & roll), able to absorb (maybe) all of society into itself as an organizing force, transmuting & reintegrating what it absorbs (as it has so far); and that its practitioners & audience are learning to perceive & manipulate reality in wholly new ways, quite alien to typeheads.

+ That rock has reinstated the ancient truth that art is fun.

+ That rock is a way of life, international & verging in this decade on universal; and can't be stopped, retarded, put down, muted, modified or successfully controlled by typeheads, whose arguments don't apply & whose machinations don't mesh because they can't perceive (dig) what rock really is & does.

+ That rock is a tribal phenomenon, immune to definition & other typographical operations, and constitutes what might be called a 20th century magic.

+ That rock seems to have synthesized most of the intellectual & artistic movements of our time & culture, cross-fertilizing them & forcing them rapidly toward fruition & function.

+ That rock is a vital agent in breaking down absolute & arbitrary distinctions.

+ That any artistic activity not allied to rock is doomed to preciousness & sterility.

+ That group participation, total experience & complete involvement are rock's minimal desiderata and those as well of a world that has too many people.

+ That rock is creating the social rituals of the future.

+ That the medium is indeed the message, & rock knows what that means.

+ That no arbitrary limitations of rock are valid (i.e., that a rock symphony or opera, for example, is possible).

+ That rock is handmade, and only the fakes are standardized.

+ That rock presents an aesthetic of discovery.

III

Marshall McLuhan makes no sense at all, not as I was taught to define sense in my inadequately cynical youth. He's plainly no Aquinas. And yet, somehow, he embarrassingly manages to explain to perfection an overwhelming array of things that used to make even less sense than he does and were somewhat threatening as well: things like pop, op & camp (which sounds like a breakfast food); the psychedelic revolution, the pot & acid explosion; the Haight-Ashbury community, and especially continued on p. 23

THE GOSSIPING GURU (#3)

through the Golden Gate:
the Journey into Aquarius,
building their tongues from ashes,
the beautiful, the brave:
bold priests of road and river
and the mescaline princes,
the ghost-sons of Dis,
far from the troubling of Rome.

Hobbits and Holy Men,
gitano and guru
and He Who Wears the Buffalo Mask,
Karmic refugees from Atlantis
singing a new birthsong,
warriors of the Lotus,
the legions of Pan,
tribesmen and nomads,
and how many were Their numbers?

Far beyond the American dominions of money, and their tomb-shadowed, history-haunted walls, we listened and dreamed, and how far did we reach out with that vast gypsy Smile?

666

And this week, from the Collective Cortex, a welcome new voice speaks of the wonders unfolding before the eager eyes of the Children of Aquarius:

"Dear Gossiping Guru:

"In the Leary issue you asked 'Who can tell us further of Him who was born on February 5th, 1962, when seven planets were in Aquarius?'

"I didn't suppose anyone cared, as He'll have to make His way without a long white nightie. Most any publication in the country would smile and tap their heads knowingly at anyone who purported to have tuned in on that scene. I'm pleased Jeanne Dixon got through.

"I can tell you a little about some of the preparation for that great event on the inner planes...are you willing to listen?

"On August 3rd, 1961, there was a convocation of spiritual adepts -- a great number of them -- in fact all those having attained a certain degree of adeptship on the planet. This meeting took place on the inner planes, but there was nothing nebulous about it. It was as dynamic an event as it is possible for one to imagine.

"For the first few hours, the work was the gathering of inner power, which was accompanied by a sort of precipitation from the akashic records of the emotional history and progress toward enlightenment of humankind. Lump all the filmed tear-jerkers you've ever seen into one and you have only a faint inkling of the collective woe of the human race. Again and again a surge of aspiration and a new ideal would come forth. Great hope would swell in the hearts of mankind. Like a huge wave of enthusiasm human hopes would mount to a mighty historical crescendo. Too high. Too high. Then a slight falling out and underhandedness would begin at the base of the structure of hope. Just a little. But it would pull the foundation out a little more, a little more, until in great despair the whole scene would come crashing down.

"As a culmination of the pageant of the planet, the time came for the collected adepts to focus an appeal to a spiritual center outside our solar system for an avatar, the carrier of a new vibration of spiritual energy. continued on p. 18

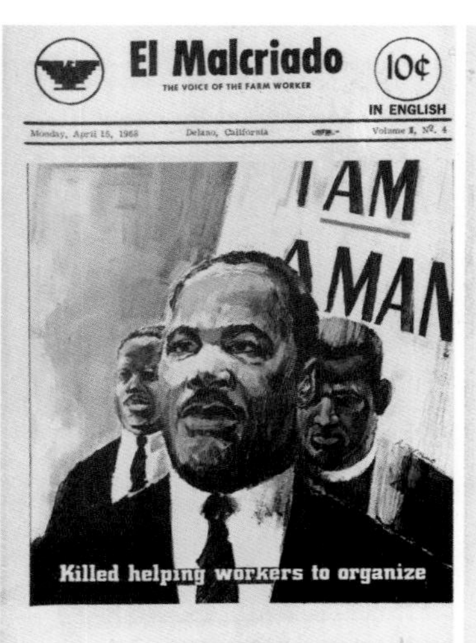

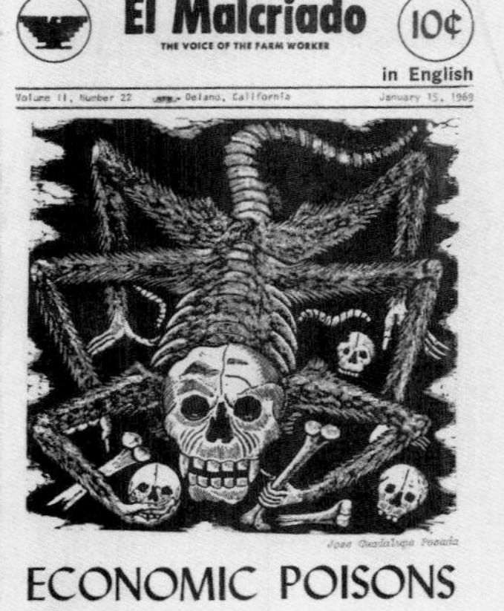

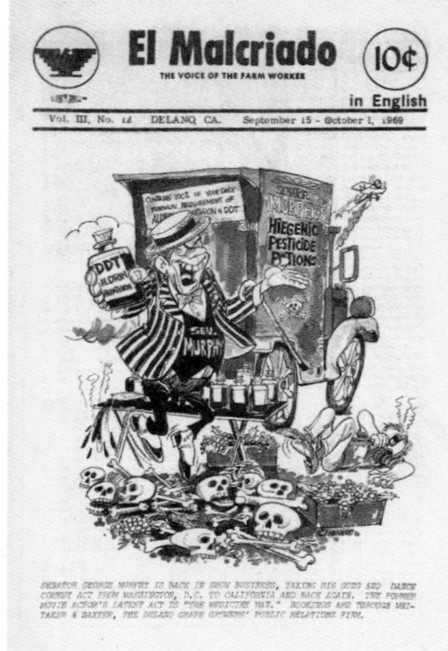

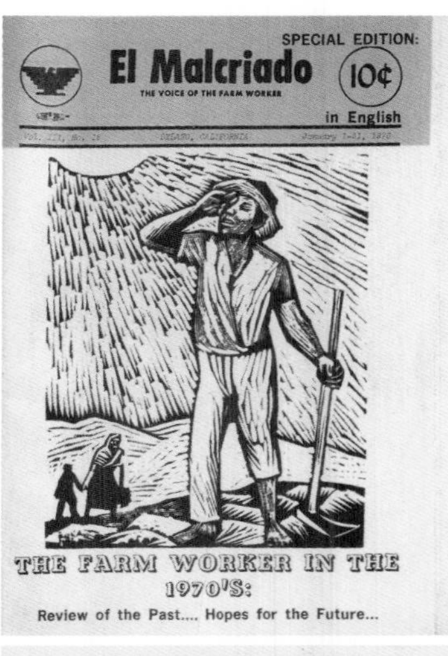

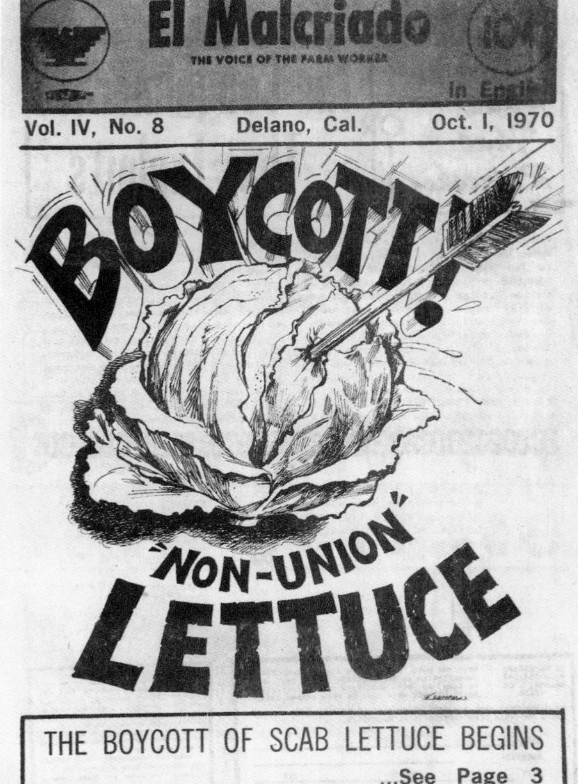

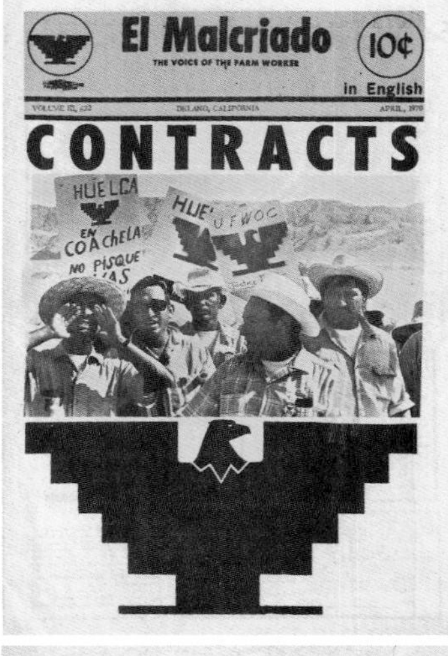

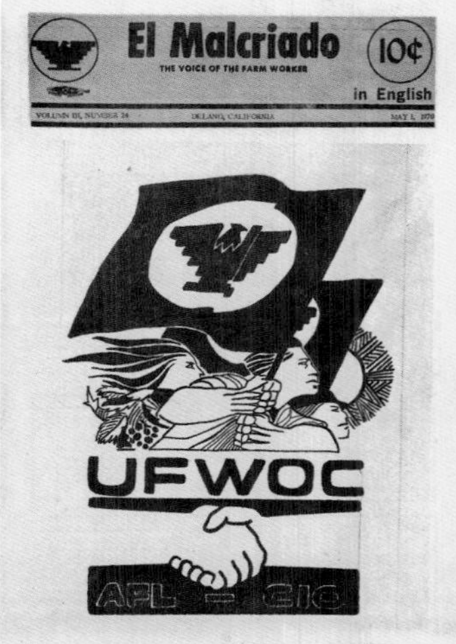

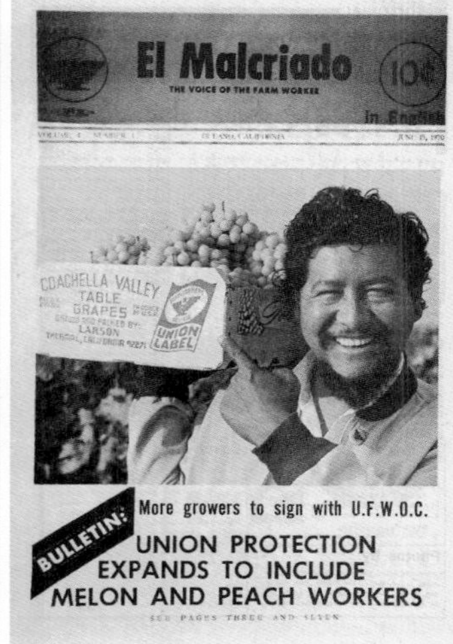

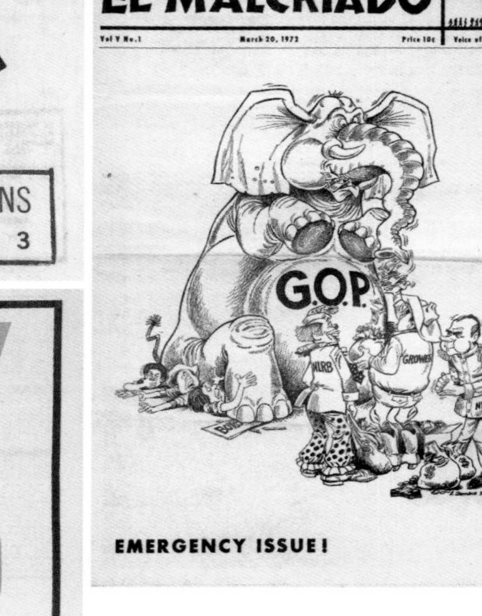

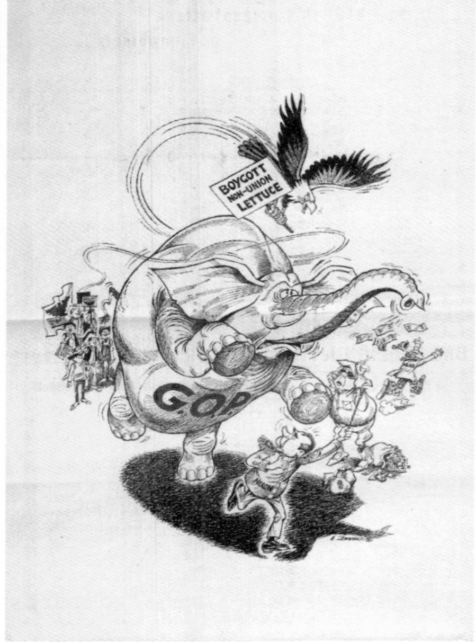

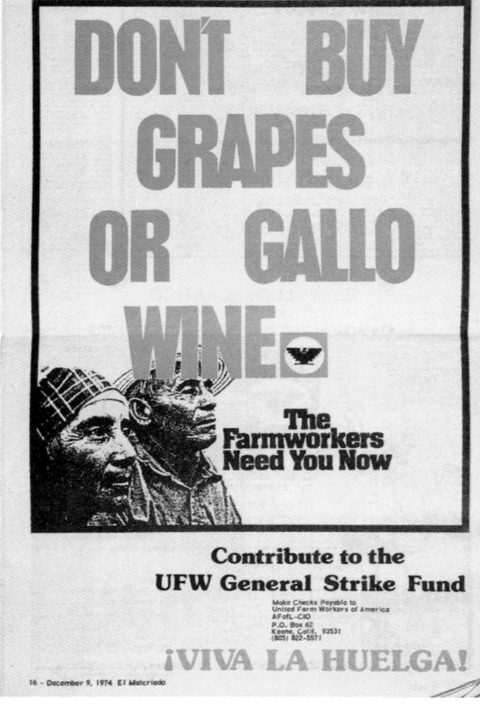

Fig. 5.8. **El Malcriado,** April 15, 1968, vol. 2, no. 4, cover; January 15, 1969, vol. 2, no. 22, cover; September 15–October 1, 1969, vol. 3, no. 12, cover; January 1–31, 1970, vol. 3, no. 19, cover; October 1, 1970, vol. 4, no. 8, cover; April 15, 1970, vol. 3, no. 23, cover; May 1, 1970, vol. 3, no. 24, cover; June 15, 1970, vol. 4, no. 1, cover; March 20, 1972, vol. 5, no. 1, cover, back cover; December 9, 1974, vol. 7, no. 11, back cover

The Liberation News Service (LNS), which had formed as a more explicitly political alter ego to the more countercultural UPS, began in 1968 sending packets of articles to 125 "underground" papers, 80 "peace" papers, and 75 college papers. Before the year was out they were sending to 400 papers in total.[3] Even high school students were getting into the act, as the movement drew in younger and younger kids.[4] A High School Independent Press Service (HIPS) was formed, with 400 paid subscribers publishing an estimated 500 underground papers. No one had any idea how many total underground high school papers there might be circulating in or around the country's high schools, but educated guesses put the number well into the thousands.[5]

Yet another press service was distributing to the underground papers springing up on US military bases throughout the world. In 1967 there were just three underground GI papers. Two years later, the first mailing of the GI Press Service (GIPS) contained 48 pages of stories mailed to 27 papers. After one month the mailing was going to 39 papers. By the end of the year, 208 pages of stories were being sent to 55 papers.[6]

By the time the sixties turned to the seventies, the flagship *LA Free Press* was a $2 million-a-year, 150-employee operation with a circulation of 100,000. LNS had 600 regular subscribers.[7] But the movement had grown so fast that no one could keep track of it. The ***Wall Street Journal*** put the total readership of the underground press at 330,000; ***Newsweek*** guessed 2 million; and both LNS and UPS claimed 4.5 million. In 1971, an even larger and more chaotic state was reached. One estimate held that the underground press included 800 papers with 10 million readers; another found 400 papers with 20 million readers. UPS claimed 30 million.[8] In 1972, just within the military alone, the Department of Defense reported that 245 underground papers were being published by active-duty US military personnel.[9]

WHILE THE UNDERGROUND PRESS OF THE 1960s WAS BUT ONE CHAPTER in the grand tradition of radical journalism in America, it was nevertheless in many respects utterly unique. This would be made immediately clear if you were to, say, make an exhibit of the front pages of American underground publications from the revolutionary era to the present day. From 1776 right down to the 1950s, you would be confronted with front pages that in general did their best to mimic the look of their establishment counterparts. After nearly two hundred years of neatly ordered type and carefully placed headlines, the underground newspapers of the 1960s would appear to have suddenly dropped to our planet from outer space, with no earthly precedent. Then again, many of the kids who produced the papers looked equally otherworldly.

And for the most part, the social insurgents of the sixties actually were kids. Mario Savio's fiery speeches in the free-speech movement on the Berkeley campus brought him to national prominence at the ripe old age of twenty-two. When the Black Panther Party blasted into the national media spotlight to challenge not only the federal government but the entirety of white culture, its chairman, Huey Newton, was twenty-four. The Liberation News Service was launched by Marshall Bloom, twenty-three, and Ray Mungo, twenty-one. The slogan "Don't Trust Anyone Over 30," repeated on buttons, placards, and the pages of underground papers, was made partly in jest, but what made it funny was the element of truth in conveyed.

The youth culture of the sixties lay at the explosive intersection of several historical trends. The baby boom that followed World War II and the unprecedented postwar affluence Americans enjoyed ushered a new character onto the stage of history: the "teenager"—both a market demographic and social identity. Not only did these freshly minted teenagers have a little spending money in their pockets, but the economic optimism of the era meant that concern as to how they would make their future livelihood weighed lightly on their minds in comparison with past (and future) generations, leaving them free to dive into a shiny new youth market that gave them an exciting and

3. Peck, *Uncovering the Sixties*, p. 86.

4. Ibid., p. 147.

5. Robert J. Glessing, *The Underground Press in America* (Bloomington: Indiana University Press, 1970), pp. 32, 129.

6. GI Press Service, vol. 1, no. 1 (June 26, 1969), through vol. 1, no. 14 (December 25, 1969).

7. Peck, *Uncovering the Sixties*, p. 187.

8. Armstrong, *Trumpet to Arms*, p. 60.

9. Terry H. Anderson, "The GI Movement and the Response from the Brass," in *Give Peace a Chance: Exploring the Vietnam Antiwar Movement*, ed. Melvin Small and William D. Hoover (Syracuse, NY: Syracuse University Press, 1992), p. 96.

novel sense of culture, identity, and mission. For the most socially minded, the formative influence on this new sense of identity had been growing up in the shadow of the civil rights movement of the 1950s and early 1960s (seen from within by many black kids, and on the newly ubiquitous television screens by the rest).

Just as teenagers stepped into this limelight, young men were confronted with conscription into the extremely unpopular war in Vietnam. The draft was hardly universal: class and racial connections provided a plethora of ways out for the privileged. One could escape the draft by going to college (at a time when far fewer Americans were enrolled in college than now), studying to be a priest or rabbi, or getting married and fathering children. Some 100,000 teenagers fled the country. Another ticket out of Vietnam was to volunteer for the National Guard, which became the special preserve of the wealthy and politically connected (like George W. Bush). The result was that the approach of one's eighteenth birthday created a moral crisis that profoundly radicalized many young men and women.

The spark that lit this tightly packed powder keg was provided by the friction between draft age (eighteen) and voting age (twenty-one). The idea that young men could be conscripted into fighting an undeclared war when they could not vote for the politicians who were forcing them into uniform and handing them the weapons was simply not going to fly for this new generation of American youth.

This situation was already explosive, but there was another catalyzing agent introduced into the mix which ratcheted up the intensity of everything it came into contact with: a colorless, tasteless, odorless chemical named lysergic acid diethylamide, known more commonly by its acronym, LSD. Perhaps more than anything else, this strangely powerful chemical is what gave the social insurgency of the sixties, and the underground newspapers associated with it, their peculiar and distinctive stamp. One simply cannot explain the cultural fervor among the youth of the era without taking into account that many thousands of teenagers and young adults, including many of the best and brightest minds of an unprecedentedly large and wealthy generation, swallowed a tiny amount of a synthetic chemical and woke up the next morning convinced that everything their parents knew was profoundly, egregiously, wrong, and equally firm in their conviction that another, radically different world was possible—a world that lay hidden just behind the shadow world of everyday appearances. If the belief that everything about mainstream culture was wrong fueled the counterculture that ensued, the conviction that another world was possible drove much of the youth politics. Perhaps only those who have actually ingested LSD are aware of how psychedelic art, which makes the papers reproduced in this book so immediately identifiable as "sixties," was a literal attempt to render on the printed page what was seen by the mind's eye while acid tripping. If psychedelic art attempted to portray the world as it looked through the lens of LSD, the counterculture was an attempt to live the morality that chemical seemed to reveal, and the political movement was an effort to refashion the rest of the world along the same lines. More than any other forum, it was in the underground newspapers that all these threads—art, culture, and politics—were brought together in a playful, even fantastic, fashion, often all on the same page, even printed in layers one directly on top of another.

The social insurgency of the sixties could not be encompassed by any single ambition in the way the "abolitionist movement" sought to abolish slavery or the "woman suffrage movement" demanded the female vote. Nor could it be described by one constituency like the "labor movement" or the "gay and lesbian movement," or by ideology, as in a "socialist movement." Its partisans saw themselves simply as part of "the movement."[10] While a minority of activists who eventually gravitated to the dogmas of Mao or Lenin saw this lack of ideological definition as a serious shortcoming, most had no problem with the fact that the cultural and political challenge in which they were immersed defied categorization.

10. Terry H. Anderson, *The Movement and the Sixties: Protest in America from Greensboro to Wounded Knee* (Oxford: Oxford University Press, 1995).

Not that the coexistence of these disparate threads was easy. The emergence of "black power" ideology in the wake of the assassination of Martin Luther King posed a sharp challenge to more inclusive movement practices and led many black activists into racially segregated organizations such as the Black Panthers. More culturally mainstream political activists despaired over the alienation that those who president Richard Nixon dubbed the "silent majority" felt when confronted with antiwar activists smoking dope and clad in hippie attire, or even worse wearing nothing but body paint. At the other end of the spectrum, those who answered to Harvard professor turned LSD prophet Timothy Leary's call to "turn on, tune in, and drop out" saw the "square" wing of the movement as hopelessly compromised with "the system."[11] In between the extremes, however, was a sea of young people simultaneously embracing a constantly shifting mix of psychedelic bliss and political fire, personified in older generation icons like beat poet Allen Ginsberg and young upstarts like the Diggers, San Francisco's anarchist street theater collective.

In cities where the movement was large enough to support multiple underground papers, the two wings of the youth culture had their own mouthpieces, like the countercultural *Oracle* in San Francisco and the more political *Barb* across the bay in Berkeley. Manhattan had the psychedelic *East Village Other* and, more stridently political, the *Rat*, in New York City. More often, both tendencies coexisted in the same paper, like the *Seed* in Chicago or the *Great Speckled Bird* in Atlanta.

Sometimes all these threads would be synthesized in a single individual, a person like John Sinclair. All at the same time, Sinclair managed to be a poet, a publisher of Detroit's underground newspaper the *Fifth Estate* (which has remained in continuous publication to the present day) (fig. 5.9), a founder of the Detroit Artists Workshop (which had its own publication, *Work*), the manager of the MC5 (fig. 5.10) (a musically precocious,

11. *Summer of Love* documentary, PBS, March 14, 2007.

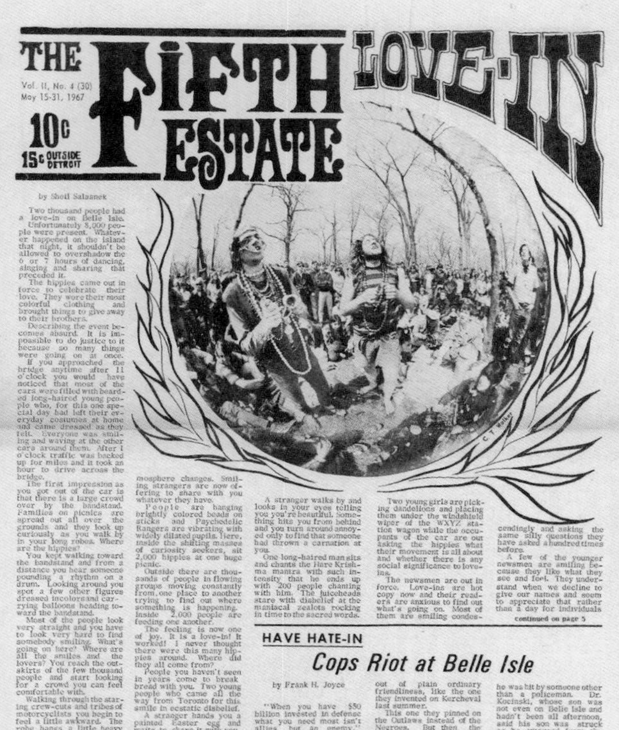

THE FIFTH ESTATE LOVE-IN

Vol. II, No. 4 (30)
May 15-31, 1967

10¢
15¢ OUTSIDE DETROIT

by Sheil Salasnek

Two thousand people had a love-in on Belle Isle. Unfortunately 8,000 people were present. Whatever happened on the island that night, it shouldn't be allowed to overshadow the 6 or 7 hours of dancing, singing and sharing that preceded it.

The hippies came out in force to celebrate their love. They wore their most colorful clothing and brought things to give away to their brothers.

Describing the event becomes absurd. It is impossible to do justice to it because so many things were going on at once.

If you approached the bridge anytime after 11 o'clock you would have noticed that most of the cars were filled with bearded long-haired young people who, for this one special day had left their everyday costumes at home and came dressed as they felt. Everyone was smiling and waving at the other cars around them. After 1 o'clock traffic was backed up for miles and it took an hour to drive across the bridge.

The first impression as you got out of the car is that there is a large crowd over by the bandstand. Families on picnics are spread out all over the grounds and they look up curiously as you walk by in your long robes. Where are the hippies?

You kept walking toward the bandstand and from a distance you hear someone pounding a rhythm on a drum. Looking around you spot a few other figures dressed incolorsand carrying balloons heading toward the bandstand.

Most of the people look very straight and you have to look very hard to find somebody smiling. What's going on here? Where are all the smiles and the lovers? You reach the outskirts of the few thousand people and start looking for a crowd you can feel comfortable with.

Walking through the staring crew-cuts and tribes of motorcyclists you begin to feel a little awkward. The robe hangs a little heavy now and the "LOVE" balloon looks kind of absurd.

You push your way on through the beer drinkers toward the bandstand hoping to find some smiling faces.

Then you notice some sticks with colored ribbons flowing in the breeze and you head in that direction. As you move into the center the whole atmosphere changes. Smiling strangers are now offering to share with you whatever they have.

People are hanging brightly colored beads on sticks and Psychedelic Rangers are vibrating with widely dilated pupils. Here, inside the shifting masses of curiosity seekers, sit 2,000 hippies at one huge picnic.

Outside there are thousands of people in flowing groups moving constantly from one place to another trying to find out where something is happening. Inside 2,000 people are feeding one another.

The feeling is now one of joy. It is a love-in! It worked! I never thought there were this many hippies around. Where did they all come from?

People you haven't seen in years come to break bread with you. Two young people who came all the way from Toronto for this smile in ecstatic disbelief.

A stranger hands you a painted Easter egg and waits to share it with you. Someone else sets up cases of oranges and tomatoes and offers them to everyone passing by.

A woman in a pure white nun's habit with a diffraction grid on her forehead is handing out slices of kosher salami and a grey-haired old man is passing out balloons. Their eyes meet and they stop to smile at one another.

A stranger walks by and looks in your eyes telling you you're beautiful. Something hits you from behind and you turn around annoyed only to find that someone had thrown a carnation at you.

One long-haired man sits and chants the Hare Krishma mantra with such intensity that he ends up with 200 people chanting with him. The juiceheads stare with disbelief at the maniacal zealots rocking in time to the sacred words.

Two young girls are picking dandelions and placing them under the windshield wiper of the WXYZ station wagon while the occupants of the car are out asking the hippies what their movement is all about and whether there is any social significance to love-ins.

The newsmen are out in force. Love-ins are hot copy now and their readers are anxious to find out what's going on. Most of them are smiling condescendingly and asking the same silly questions they have asked a hundred times before.

A few of the younger newsmen are smiling because they like what they see and feel. They understand when we decline to give our names and seem to appreciate that rather than a day for individuals

continued on page 5

HAVE HATE-IN

Cops Riot at Belle Isle

by Frank H. Joyce

"When you have $50 billion invested in defense what you need most isn't allies but an enemy," Nelson Algren said in Ramparts, May, 1967.

When you have policemen on horses and Tactical Mobile Units with little baseball bats and "riot-trained" commandoes, what you need most is not a Love-In but a riot.

And when the Detroit Police Department wants a riot bad enough, they get one; manufactured it right out of plain ordinary friendliness, like the one they invented on Kercheval last summer.

This one they pinned on the Outlaws instead of the Negroes. But then the Outlaws are almost as good an excuse. Besides, once it's started, you can crack heads without regard to race, creed, color or national origin.

To a policeman that is apparently what a head is for.

One of the heads belonged to the son of a Dearborn doctor named Clem Kocinski. The police claim he was hit by someone other than a policeman. Dr. Kocinski, whose son was not even on Belle Isle and hadn't been all afternoon, said his son was struck as he emerged from the Howard Johnson's Restaurant at the foot of the Belle Isle bridge.

The doctor added that a Detroit area school teacher had called to inform him that he too had been attacked by the police when he sought assistance in getting from the restaurant to his car.

continued on page 5

Fig. 5.9. **Fifth Estate** (Detroit), May 15–31, 1967, vol. 2, no. 4, front and back covers

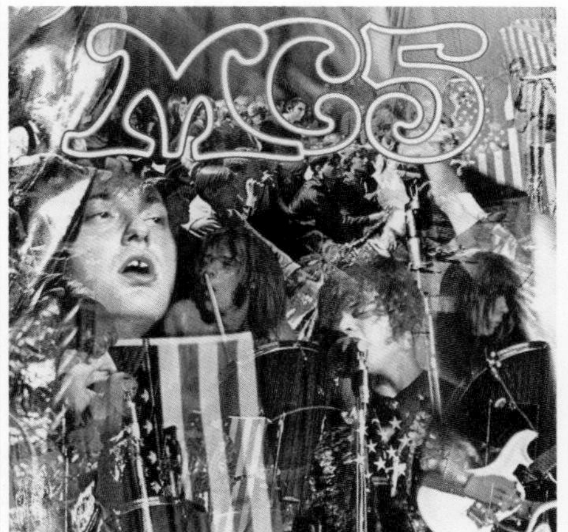

Fig. 5.10. MC5, **Kick Out the Jams,** 1969, album cover

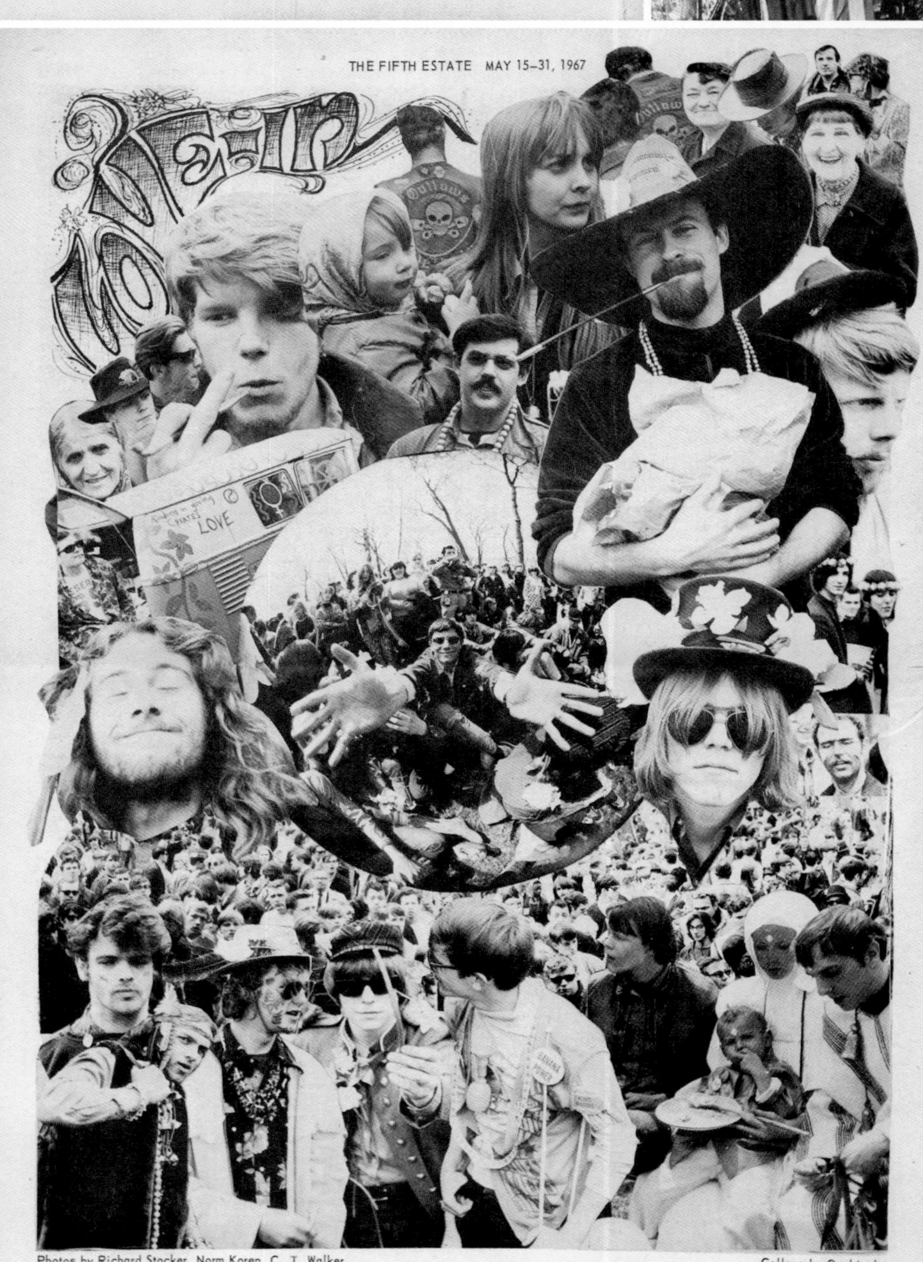

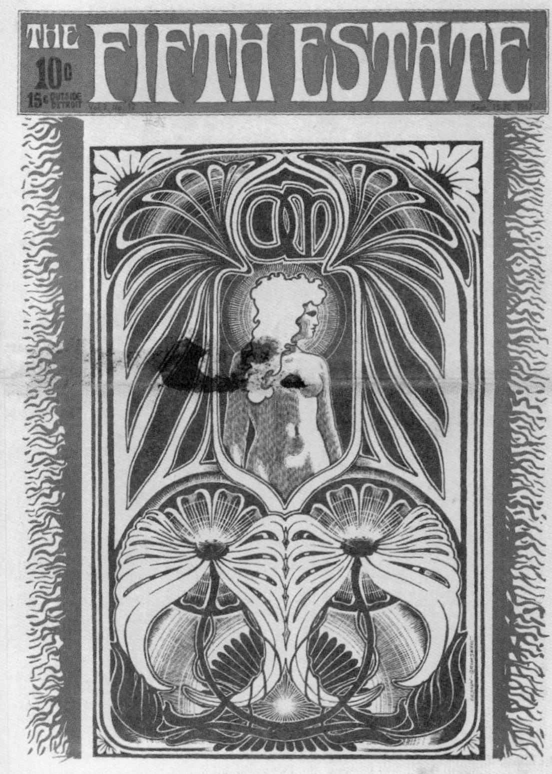

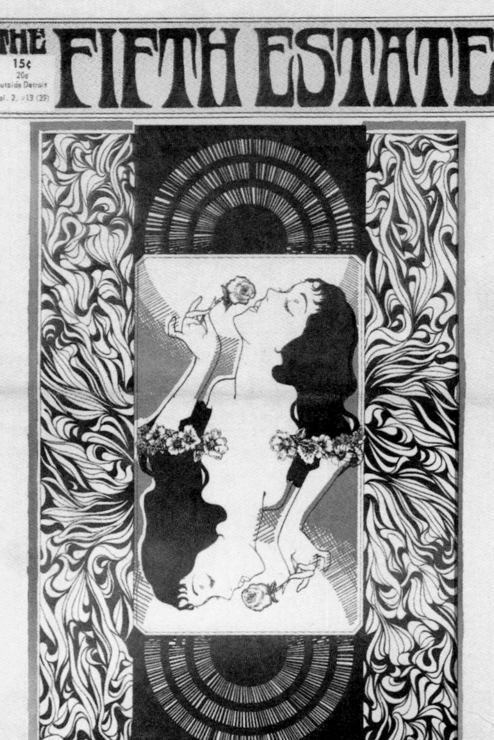

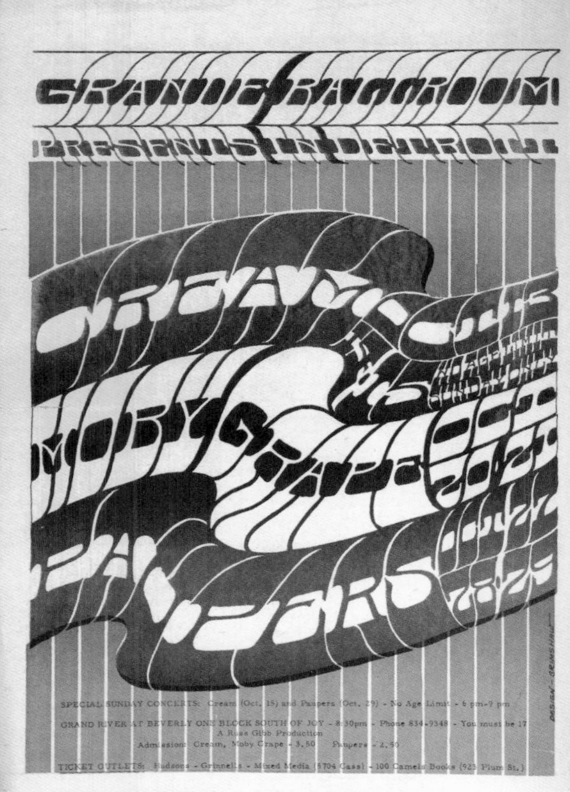

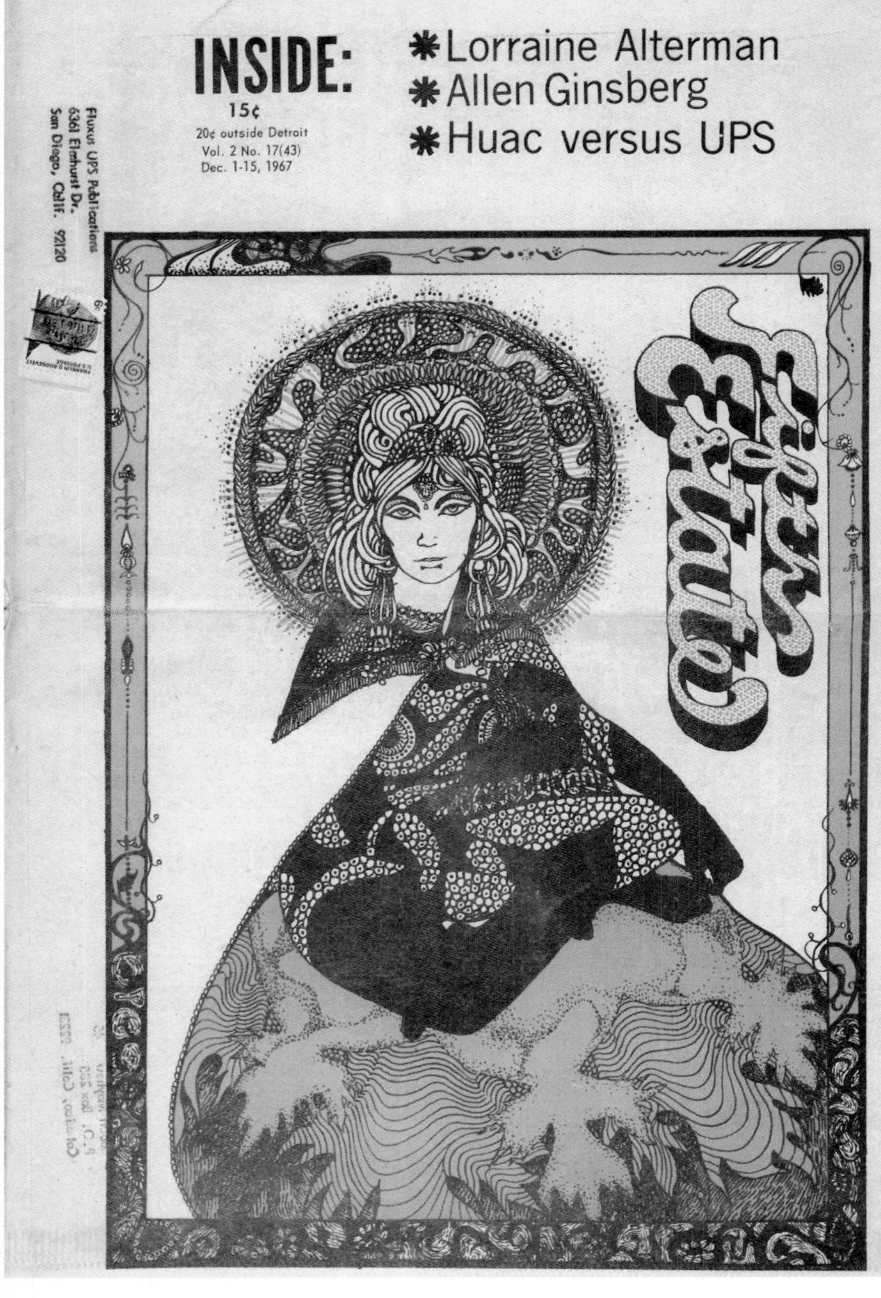

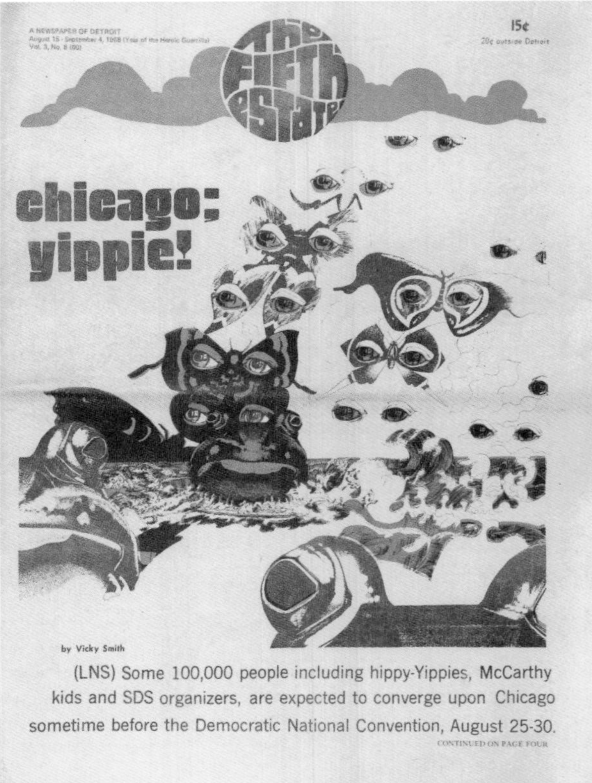

Fig. 5.9 (cont'd.). **Fifth Estate** (Detroit), September 15–30, 1967, vol. 2, no. 12, cover; October 1–15, 1967, vol. 2, no. 13, front and back covers; December 1–15, 1967, vol. 2, no. 17, cover; August 15–September 4, 1968, vol. 3, no. 8, cover

Next page
Fig. 5.9 (cont'd.). **Fifth Estate** (Detroit), December 12–25, 1968, vol. 3, no. 16, front and back covers; February 20–March 5, 1969, vol. 3, no. 21, cover; September 15–30, 1967, vol. 3, no. 12, cover

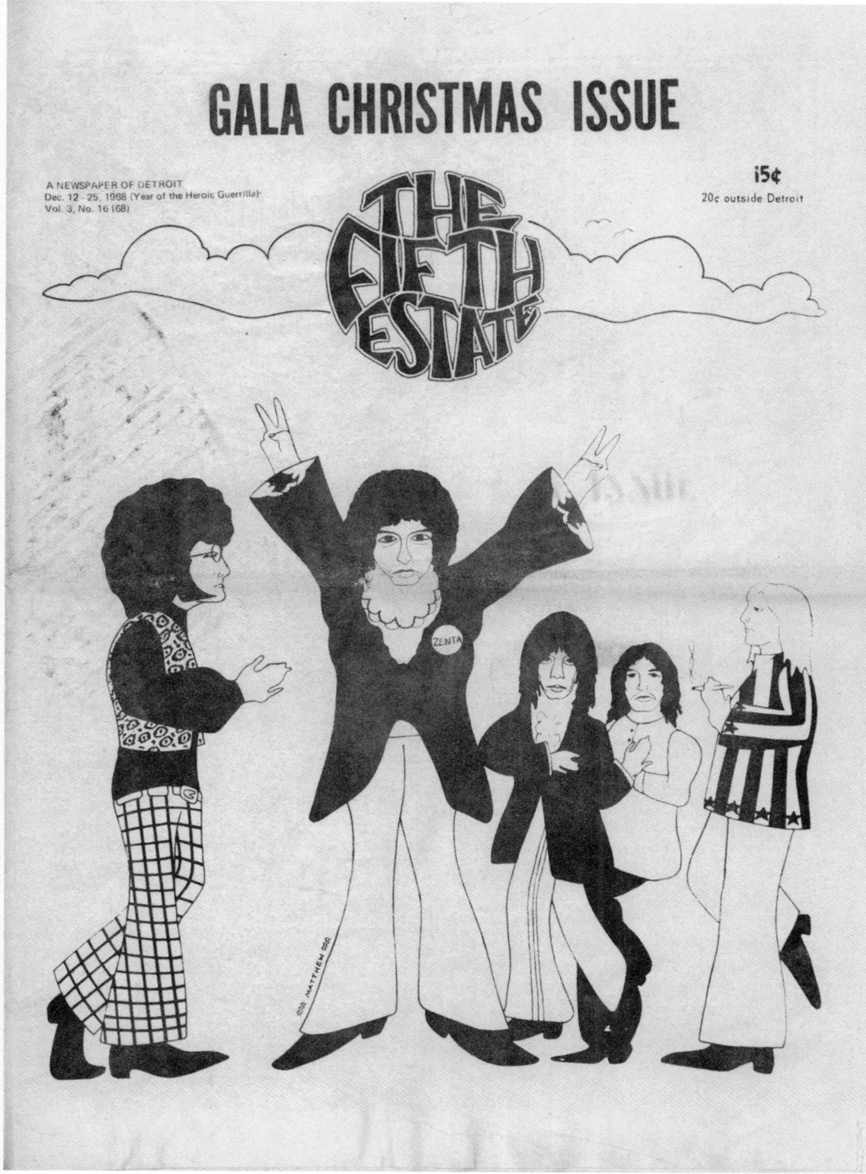
GALA CHRISTMAS ISSUE
A NEWSPAPER OF DETROIT
Dec. 12 - 25, 1968 (Year of the Heroic Guerrilla)
Vol. 3, No. 16 (68)
15¢
20¢ outside Detroit
THE FIFTH ESTATE
ZENTA

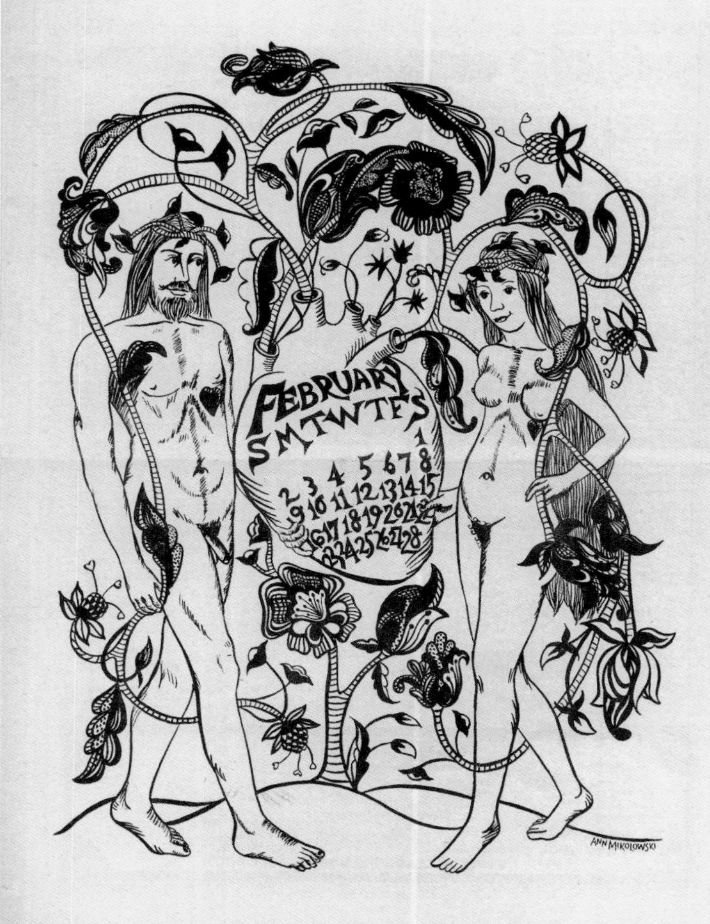
FEBRUARY
SMTWTFS
ANN MIKOLOWSKI

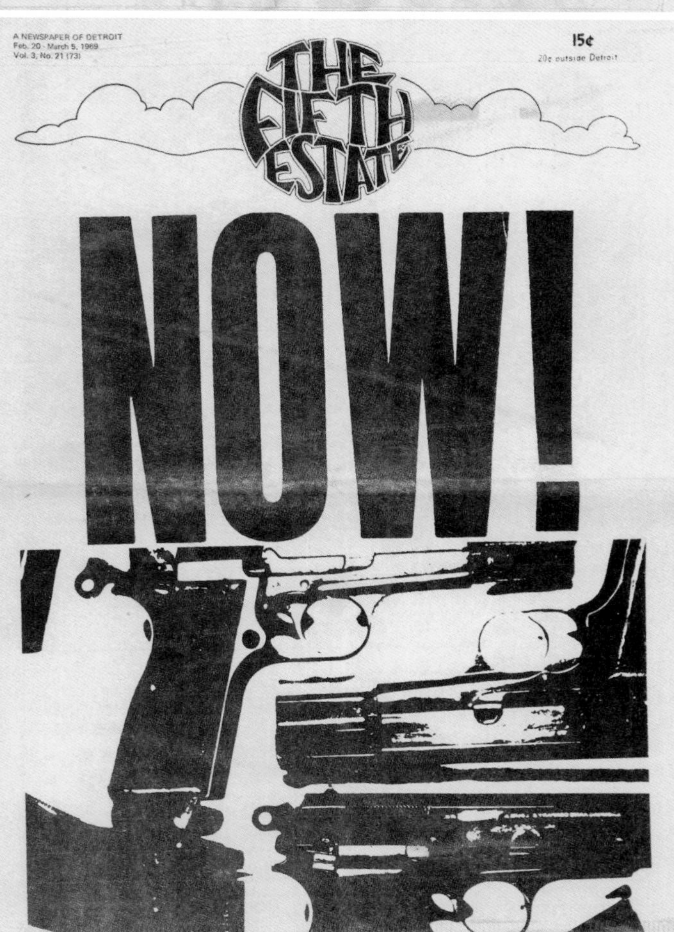
A NEWSPAPER OF DETROIT
Feb. 20 - March 5, 1969
Vol. 3, No. 21 (73)
15¢
20¢ outside Detroit
THE FIFTH ESTATE
NOW!

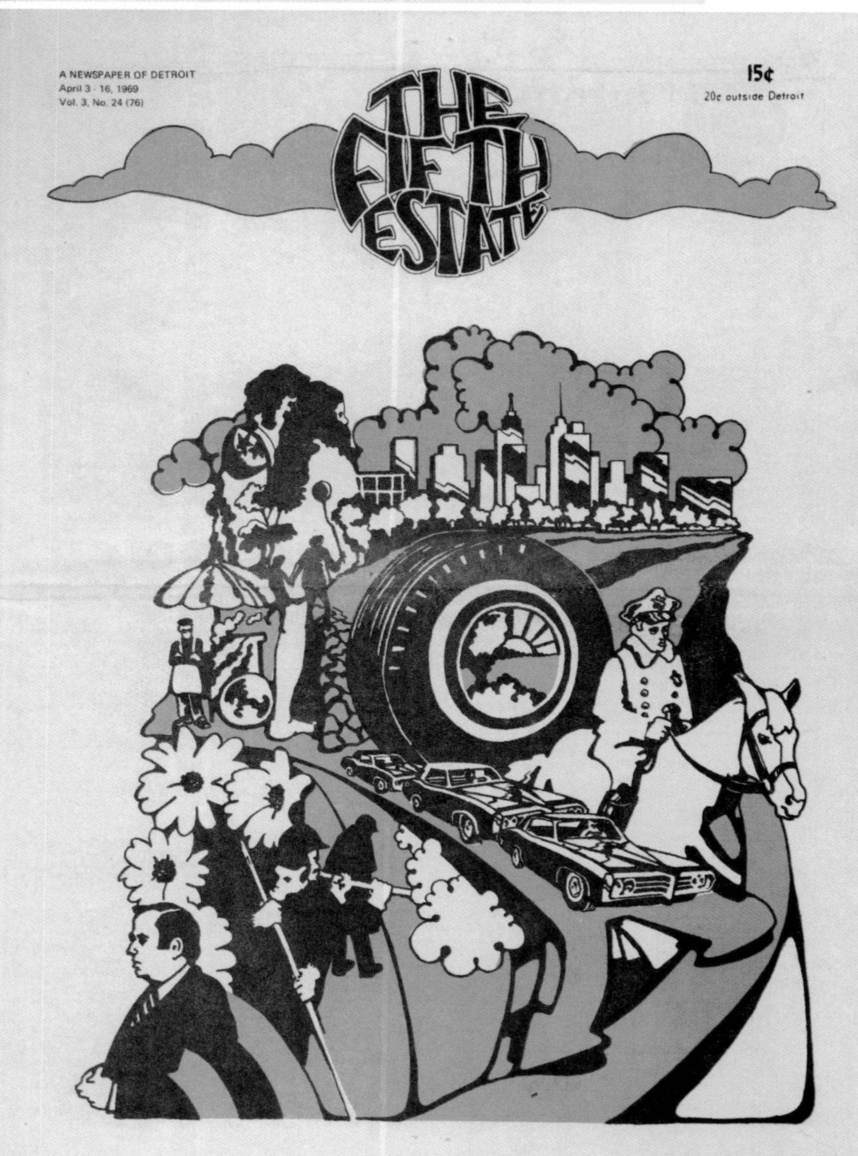
A NEWSPAPER OF DETROIT
April 3 - 16, 1969
Vol. 3, No. 24 (76)
15¢
20¢ outside Detroit
THE FIFTH ESTATE

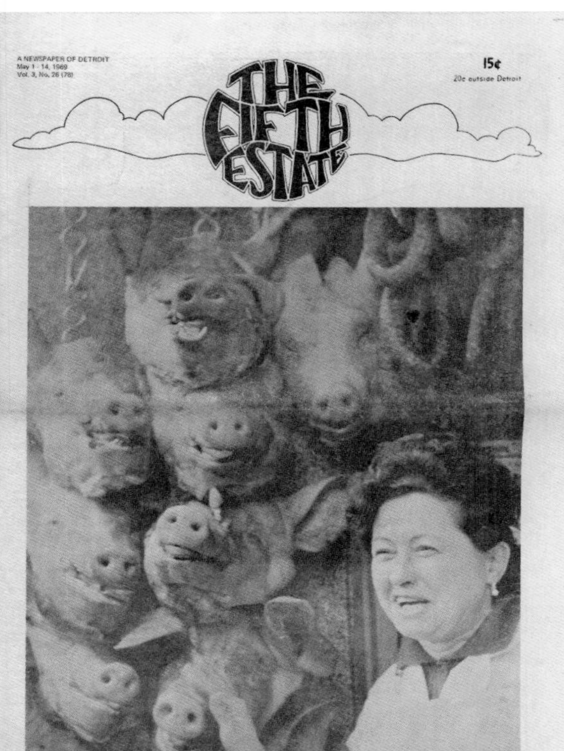

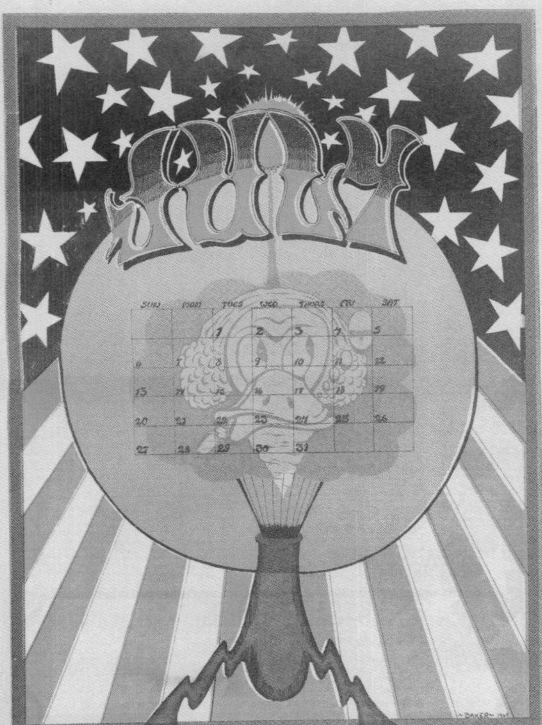

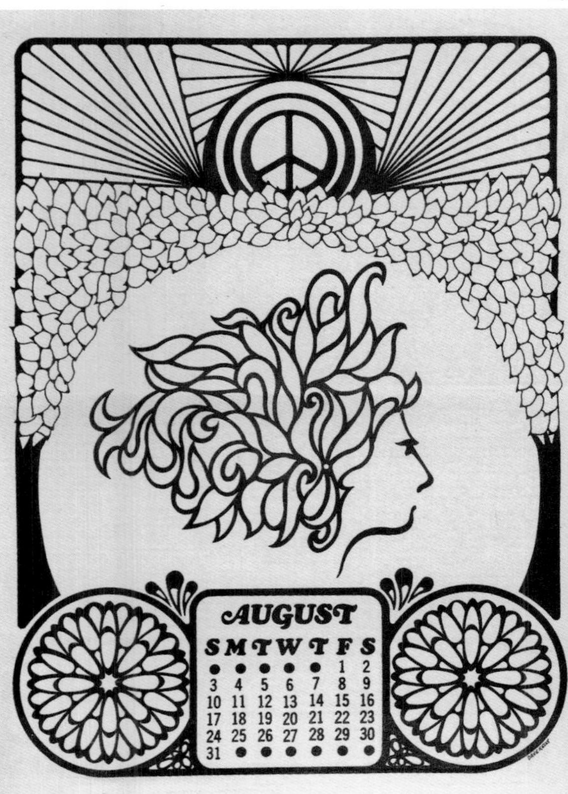

SECRET

THIS IS A COVER SHEET

BASIC SECURITY REQUIREMENTS ARE CONTAINED IN AR 380–5

THE UNAUTHORIZED DISCLOSURE OF THE INFORMATION CONTAINED IN THE ATTACHED DOCUMENT(S) COULD RESULT IN SERIOUS DAMAGE TO THE UNITED STATES

RESPONSIBILITY OF PERSONS HANDLING THE ATTACHED DOCUMENT(S)

1. Exercise the necessary safeguards to prevent unauthorized disclosure by never leaving the document(s) unattended except when properly secured in in a locked safe.
2. Transfer document(s) only to persons who need to know and who possess the required security clearance.
3. Obtain receipt whenever relinquishing control of the document(s).

STORAGE

Store as prescribed in AR 380–5.

REPRODUCTION

1. SECRET material originating in an agency outside the Department of Defense will not be reproduced; copied, or extracted without the consent of the originating agency
2. The reproduction, extraction or copying of SECRET material originating within the Department of Defense is authorized except when the originator or higher authority has specifically denied this authority.
3. Reproduction of Joint Chiefs of Staff papers is not authorized.

DISPOSITION

This cover sheet should be removed when document(s) are filed in a permanent file, declassified, destroyed, or mailed.

(This cover sheet is unclassified when separated from classified documents)

SECRET

DA LABEL 1 FEB 59 23 PREVIOUS EDITIONS OF THIS LABEL ARE OBSOLETE

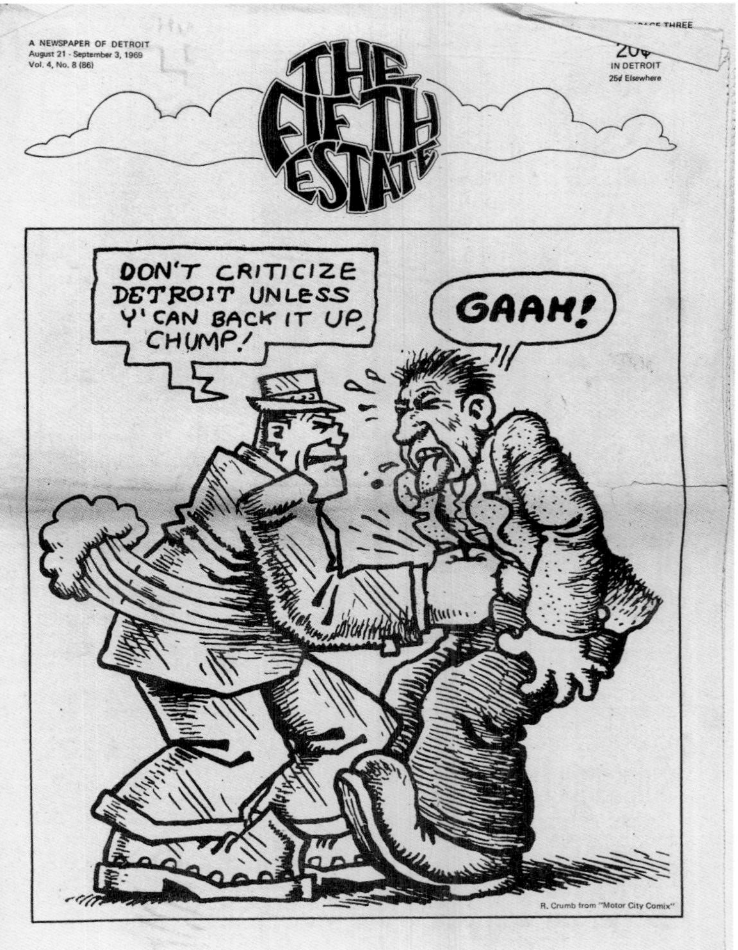

Fig. 5.9 (cont'd.). **Fifth Estate** (Detroit), May 1–14, 1969, vol. 3, no. 26, cover; June 26–July 9, 1969, vol. 4, no. 4, cover; July 24–August 6, 1969, vol. 4, no. 6, back cover; January 23–February 5, 1969, vol. 3, no. 19, cover; August 21–September 3, 1969, vol. 4, no. 8, cover

Next page
Fig. 5.9 (cont'd.). **Fifth Estate** (Detroit), November 13–26, 1969, vol. 4, no. 14, cover; February 4–18, 1970, vol. 4, no. 20, cover; April 16–29, 1970, vol. 4, no. 25, cover, back cover; April 30–May 13, 1970, vol. 4, no. 26, cover

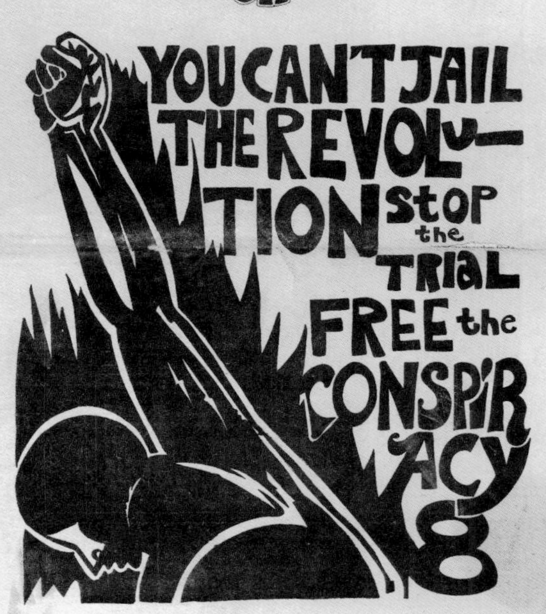

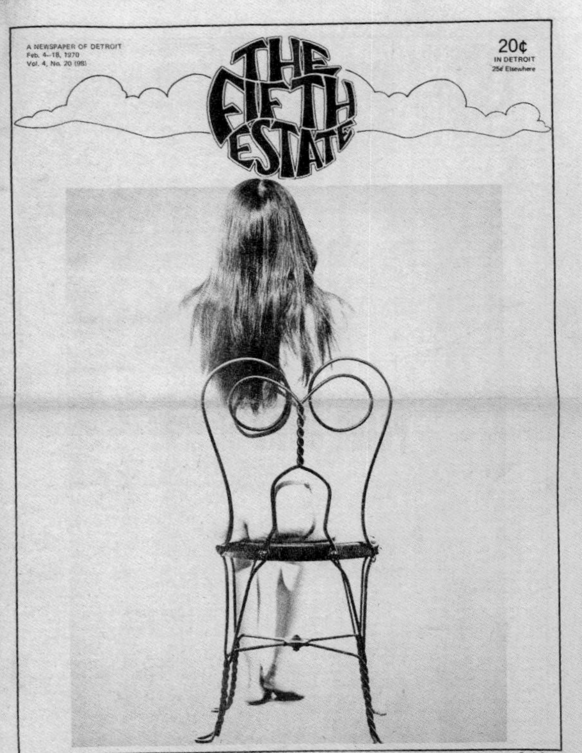

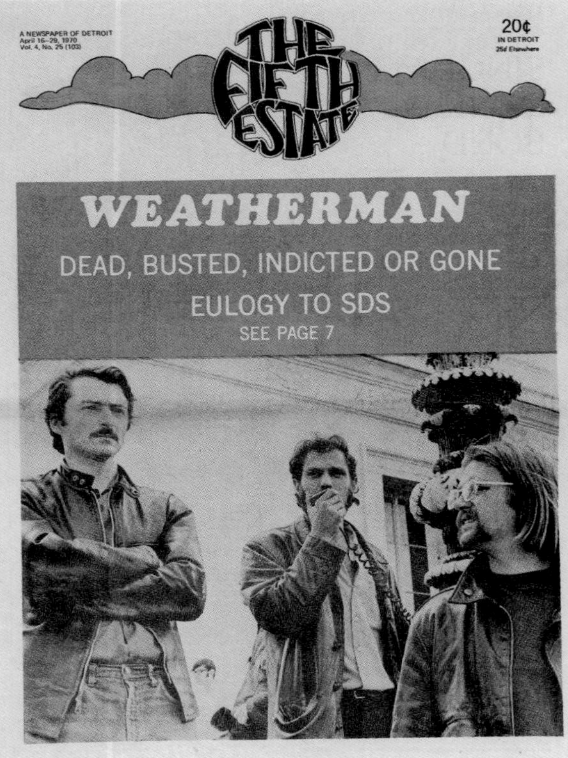

MAY·DAY IS J·DAY !

The word is out. May 1st, 1970 is the day for the **First Annual Marijuana Mail-In and Cross Country Toke-Down.** Dealers and heads all over the U.S. are already madly rolling joints and stuffing envelopes in preparation for the big occasion...

MAY DAY IS CALLED LAW DAY HERE IN THE U.S.A. and every dope smoker will be doing his or her part on that day to change the marijuana laws that are being used by the government, police, and courts of Amerika in an attempt to destroy our rapidly growing culture. Over **200,000** of our brothers and sisters are already rotting in jail for so-called "marijuana crimes"--White Panther **John Sinclair** is doing **10 years** for possession of **2 joints**, brother **Tim Leary** has recieved sentences totalling **20 years** for **one joint**. On May 1st, we, the **20-million** or more dope smokers in this country, will serve notice on the pig power structure that **THIS CULTURAL GENOCIDE MUST BE STOPPED IMMEDIATELY!!!**

On May Day all Amerikans who have not yet turned on to the **truth of grass** will get their chance. Dope smokers will mail joints--with letters of explanation on how to get high on this **ILLEGAL substance**--to every non-smoker. Every policeman, mayor, senator, housewife, factory worker, and businessman will finally learn how to start the day right: with a little bit of reefer.

Through the last week of April every head will send some grass to at least a few straight members of his community. Dope dealers will roll up at least one pound of weed each, tear random pages out of telephone books, and mail joints to every listed name.

Come historic May Day, 1970, pigs will find it impossible to bust thousands of dopers that will gather under the warm spring sun in every park and square of every city and town to share food, music, bodies, and marijuana. The U.S.A. will come together in psychedelic harmony at last. Amerika will break out in one huge smile as everyone will be stoned, high, fucked up, jacked out of shape, mellow, blasted.

The Marijuana Question will be answered May 1st!!!

GRASS FOR THE MASSES!

A JOINT IN EVERY MAILBOX

POT IN EVERY PUBLIC PLACE

MAY 1

the pill: birth of conspiracy

SEE PAGE 12

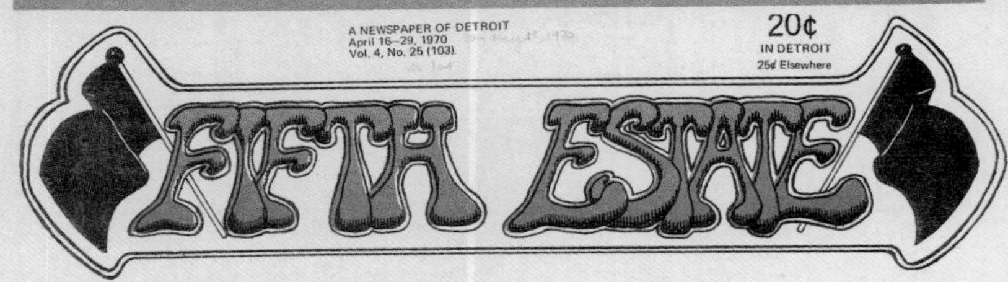

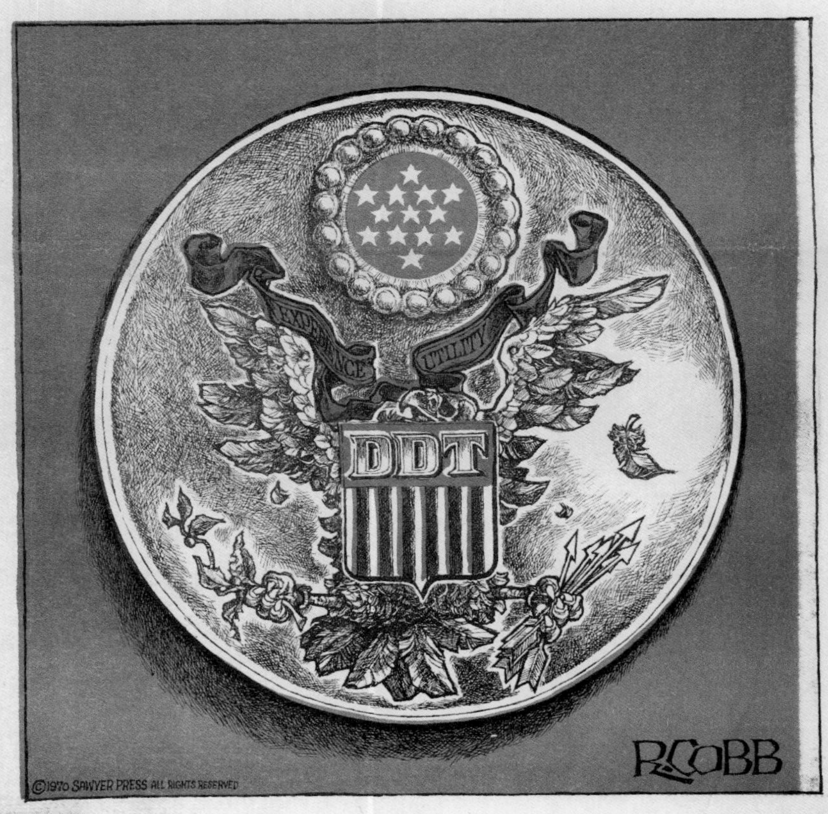

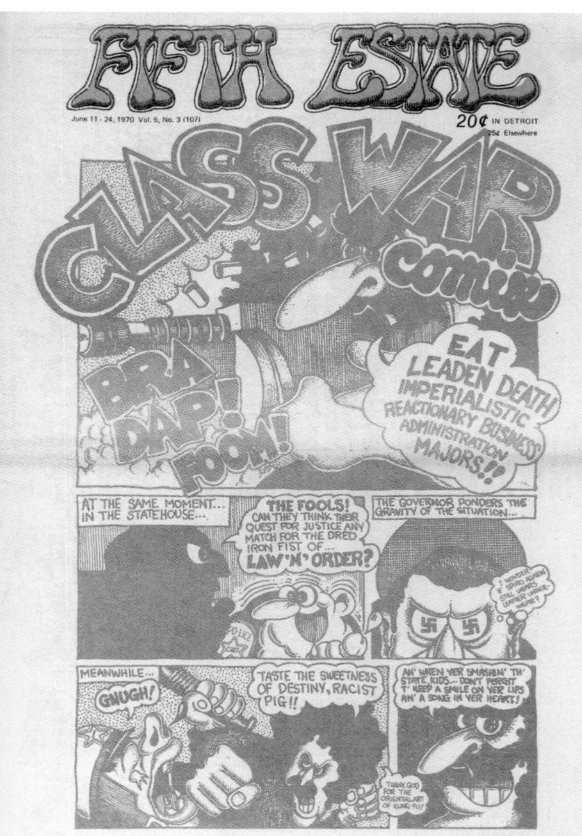

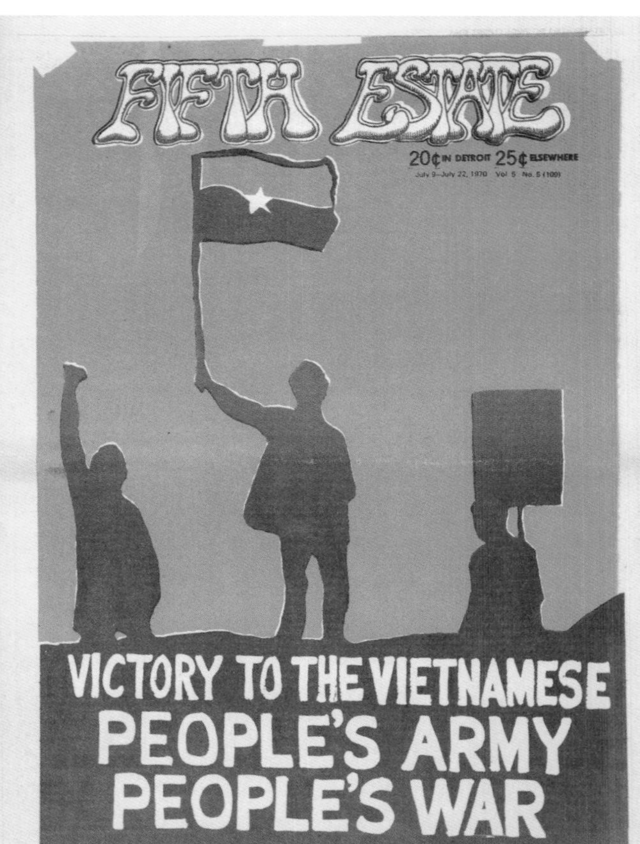

Fig. 5.9 (cont'd.) **Fifth Estate** (Detroit), June 11–24, 1970, vol. 5, no. 3, cover; July 9–22, 1970, vol. 5, no. 5, cover; October 15–28, 1970, vol. 5, no. 12, cover; November 12–25, 1970, vol. 5, no. 14, cover

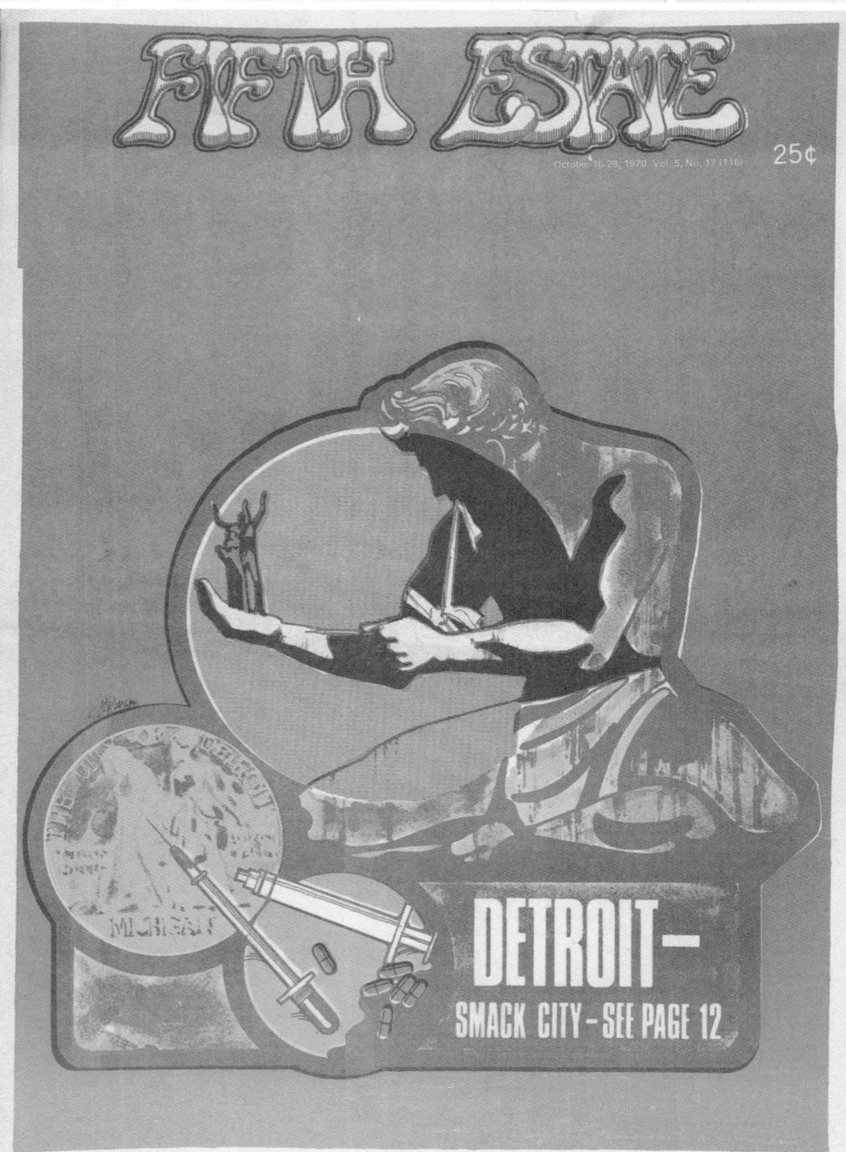

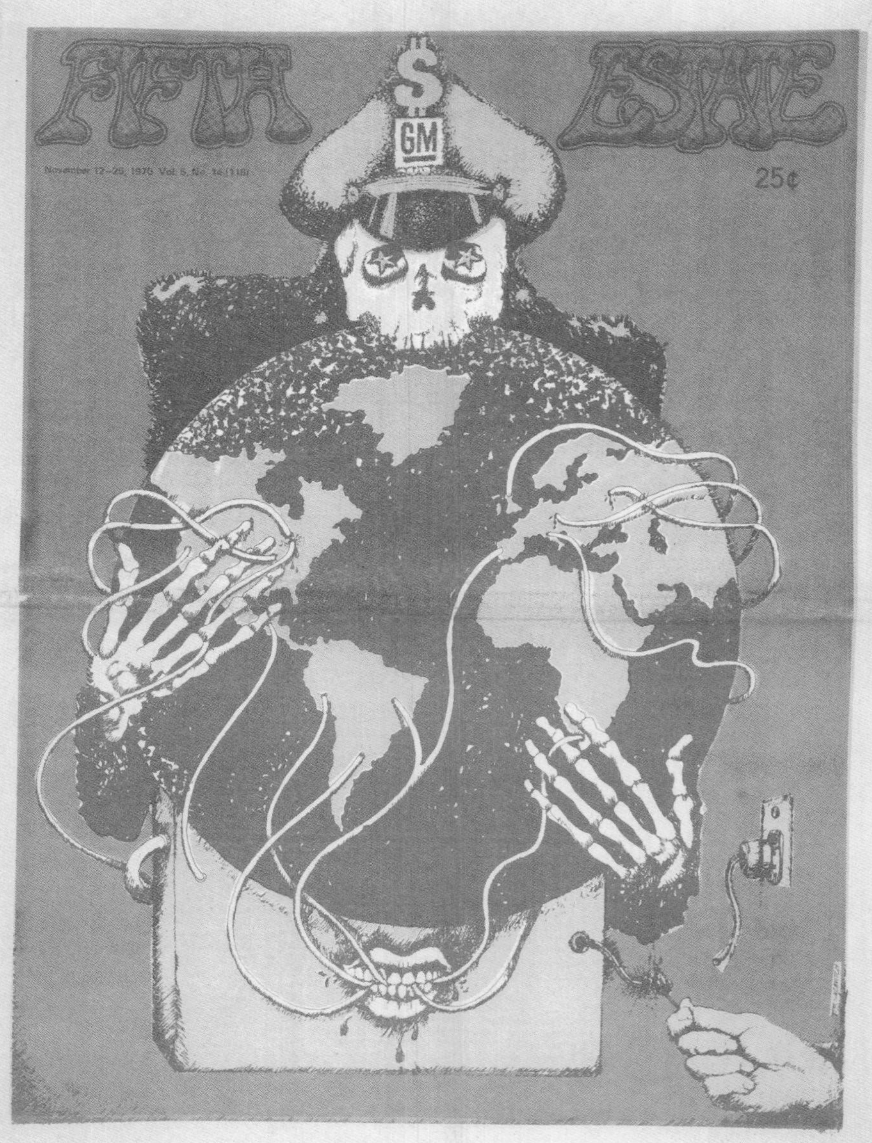

angry proto–punk rock band surrounded by flower children, a decade before the term "punk rock" was coined), and founder of the White Panther Party, formed to support the work of the Black Panther Party.

For Sinclair and many others like him around the country, organizing "the movement" and publishing an underground paper were indistinguishable activities. In San Francisco, the *Oracle* and the first Human Be-In in Golden Gate Park with 20,000 people in attendance (a few months after the first issue of the paper appeared) emerged from the same energetic social circle. Liberation News Service emerged out of the antiwar march on the Pentagon in 1967. In Chicago, the *Seed* became the key source of information and debate in the lead-up to the apocalyptic demonstrations at the Democratic Convention in 1968.

NOWHERE WAS THE CONNECTION BETWEEN PUBLISHING A PAPER AND ORGANIZING opposition to the Vietnam War tighter than within the US military itself. With active-duty military personnel barred from more conventional forms of opposition to the war, the underground papers that sprang up on bases and warships around the world were the closest thing to "organization" soldiers had. And there were a lot of them.

The first military papers were published by young men who had just left the service. In 1967 the *Bond* (fig. 5.11) was launched by Andy Stapp following his court martial and dishonorable discharge for having antiwar literature on base.[12] In the same year, a group of deserters who had fled to Paris formed Resistance Inside the Military (RITA). The RITA newsletter, *ACT* (fig. 5.12), encouraged soldiers not to desert but to stay in the military and actively resist. *ACT*'s circulation eventually hit 10,000.[13]

In January of the following year the *Vietnam GI* (fig. 5.13) was launched by Jeff Sharlet, a brilliant twenty-five-year-old vet who spoke fluent Vietnamese and had done top-secret work monitoring, decoding, and translating North Vietnamese radio transmissions. *Vietnam GI* became not only the flagship of the underground GI press but a unique paper in the history of American journalism. Its target audience was American soldiers currently in Vietnam, though after a few months the paper had grown into two editions, the main Vietnam edition and a second "Stateside" edition addressing GI issues on domestic bases.[14] Distribution to Vietnam was done by mail, according to procedures carefully designed to avoid

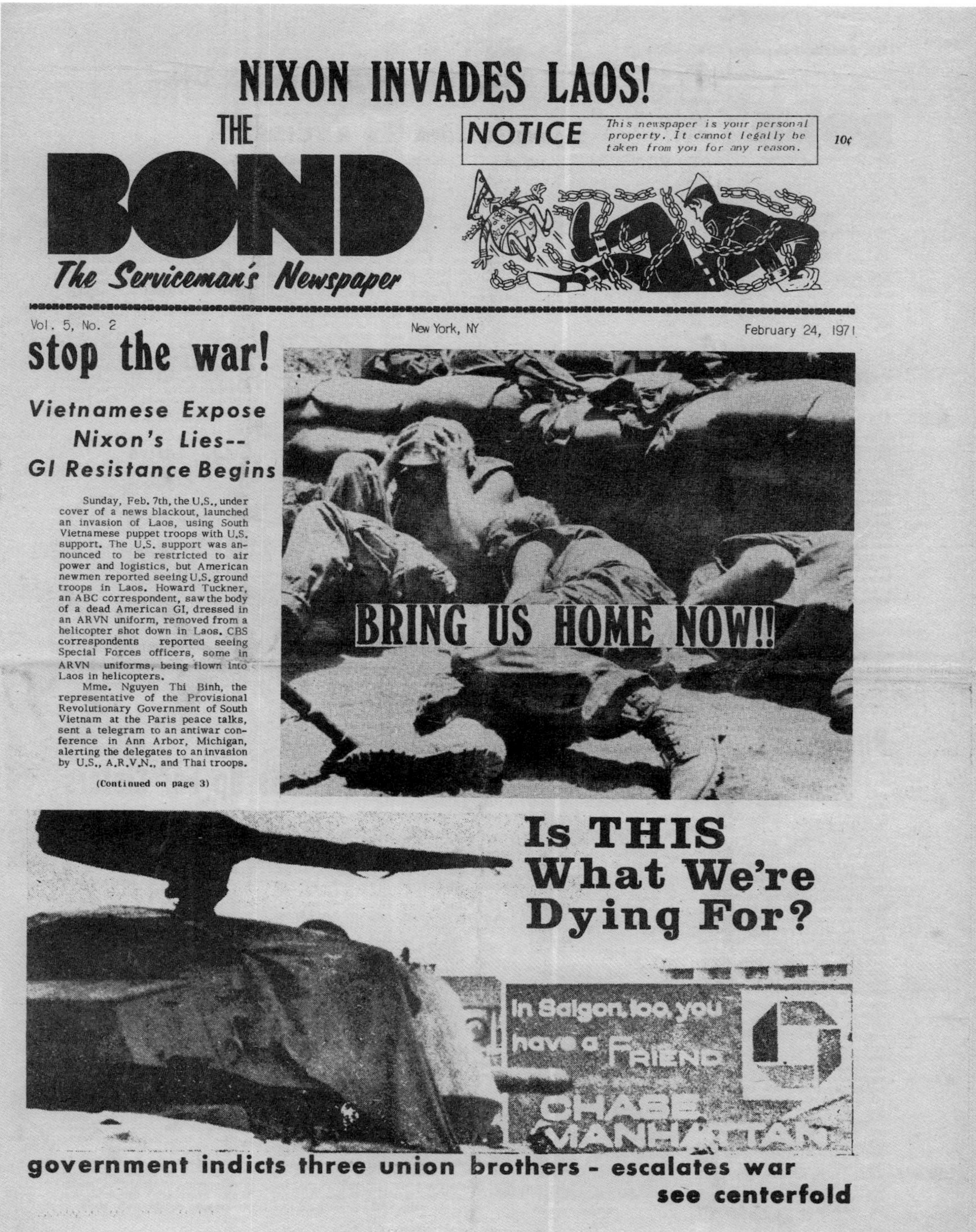

NIXON INVADES LAOS!

THE BOND

The Serviceman's Newspaper

NOTICE This newspaper is your personal property. It cannot legally be taken from you for any reason.

10¢

Vol. 5, No. 2 New York, NY February 24, 1971

stop the war!

Vietnamese Expose Nixon's Lies-- GI Resistance Begins

Sunday, Feb. 7th, the U.S., under cover of a news blackout, launched an invasion of Laos, using South Vietnamese puppet troops with U.S. support. The U.S. support was announced to be restricted to air power and logistics, but American newmen reported seeing U.S. ground troops in Laos. Howard Tuckner, an ABC correspondent, saw the body of a dead American GI, dressed in an ARVN uniform, removed from a helicopter shot down in Laos. CBS correspondents reported seeing Special Forces officers, some in ARVN uniforms, being flown into Laos in helicopters.

Mme. Nguyen Thi Binh, the representative of the Provisional Revolutionary Government of South Vietnam at the Paris peace talks, sent a telegram to an antiwar conference in Ann Arbor, Michigan, alerting the delegates to an invasion by U.S., A.R.V.N., and Thai troops.

(Continued on page 3)

Is THIS What We're Dying For?

government indicts three union brothers - escalates war

see centerfold

Fig. 5.11. **The Bond** (New York), February 1971, vol. 5, no. 2, cover

12. *The Bond* was originally briefly published by two civilian activists in Berkeley. The two quickly split in political disagreement, and one of the two hooked up with Stapp, taking the fledgling paper with him. Author's interview with Clark Smith, October 7, 2003.
    See also Andy Stapp, *Up Against the Brass* (New York: Simon and Schuster, 1970).

13. Dick Perrin, *GI Resister: The Story of How One American Soldier and His Family Fought the War in Vietnam* (Victoria, Canada: Trafford, 2001).

14. The *Ally*, published in San Francisco by civilians and vets, targeted GIs in both Vietnam and the United States.

the attention of military authorities. Bundles were sent to civilian committees and individual GIs around the country. The local group would then mail their papers to soldiers in Vietnam, in a plain brown wrapper (suggesting that inside was ***Playboy*** or a ***Playboy*** competitor). The return addresses had to be changed constantly to avoid detection by authorities. The complete address list was a secret to which only a few people had access.

Vietnam GI's content was even more extraordinary than its production and distribution. It was written entirely by vets and soldiers, and it never strayed "from the point of view of the grunt on the ground" who was concerned about his buddies first, and who always spoke from immediate experience.[15] The paper's reach in Vietnam is suggested by this letter it published after just six months:

> Gentlemen:
>
> It seems like every time you put a new issue out I have six or seven guys who want subscriptions after ripping my copy to shreds. Right now it's an even-money bet which is more popular in our unit, ***Playboy*** or *Vietnam GI* … Enclosed are several more names for subscriptions.
>
> —Pfc., 198th Light Infantry[16]

Vietnam GI reached a peak circulation of around 10,000. But after just one year of publishing, Sharlet died at age twenty-seven. The cause of death was officially cancer, but vets who worked with him believe his death was caused by exposure to Agent Orange.

By this time underground GI papers were turning up everywhere. In 1969 the GI Press Service was launched by vets working out of the Student Mobilization Committee, a national peace group based in New York City. The first GIPS mailing contained 48 pages of stories mailed to 27 papers. The next mailing went to 39 papers. Six months later, 208 pages of stories were being sent to 55 papers.[17] By 1972, the Department of Defense reported that 245 had been published.[18]

A confidential Army directive obtained from Vietnam shows that Army commanders have been ordered to intercept and confiscate personal, first-class mail containing anti-war or other dissident publication sent to soldiers there.

This shouldn't come as a surprise, but this directive is clearly illegal. Here's why.

1) — Article 65-I, para. 8-3, rev. 12 Dec. 1968 —
« The secrecy of the mail is inviolable. Military postal personnel will not break, nor permit to be broken, the seal of any first class mail while in military channel. »

2) — A Dept. of Army letter entitled « Guidance on Dissent » sent to all commands in May, 1969 said that :
« A commander may not prevent distribution of a publication simply because he does not like its' contents » and
« A commander must have cogent reasons, with supporting evidence for any denial of distribution privileges. The fact that a publication is critical of government policies is not on itself a grounds for denial ».

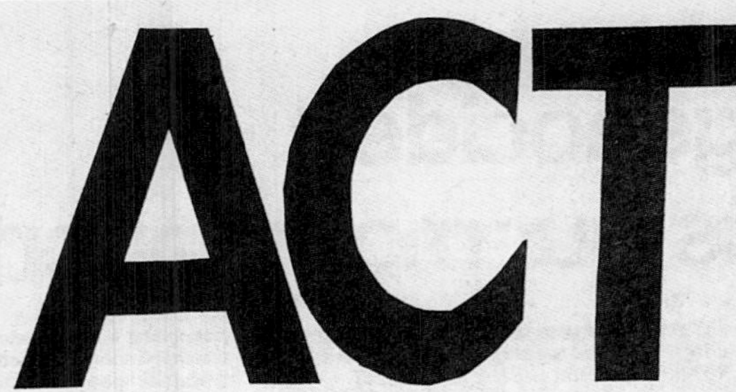
ACT

RITA-ACT, 10 , Passage du Chantier, Paris 12 or Heidelberg 69, Schiffgasse 3 — only for mail)

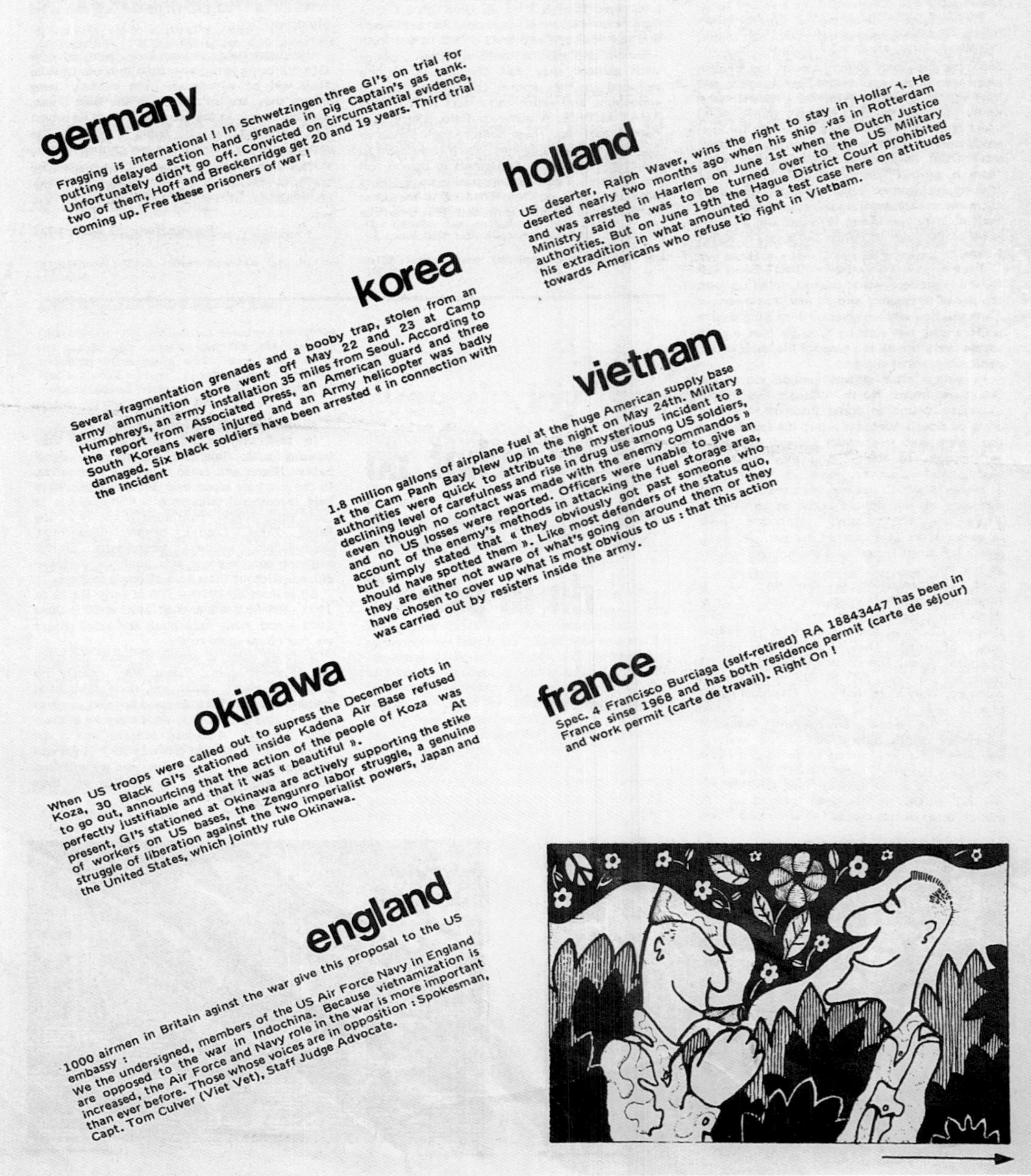
germany

Fragging is international ! In Schwetzingen three GI's on trial for putting delayed action hand grenade in pig Captain's gas tank. Unfortunately didn't go off. Convicted on circumstantial evidence, two of them, Hoff and Breckenridge get 20 and 19 years. Third trial coming up. Free these prisoners of war !

holland

US deserter, Ralph Waver, wins the right to stay in Hollar 1. He deserted nearly two months ago when his ship vas in Rotterdam and was arrested in Haarlem on June 1st when the Dutch Justice Ministry said he was to be turned over to the US Military authorities. But on June 19th the Hague District Court prohibited his extradition in what amounted to a test case here on attitudes towards Americans who refuse tio fight in Vietbam.

korea

Several fragmentation grenades and a booby trap, stolen from an army ammunition store went off May 22 and 23 at Camp Humphreys, an army installation 35 miles from Seoul. According to the report from Associated Press, an American guard and three South Koreans were injured and an Army helicopter was badly damaged. Six black soldiers have been arrested « in connection with the incident

vietnam

1.8 million gallons of airplane fuel at the huge American supply base at the Cam Panh Bay blew up in the night on May 24th. Military authorities were quick to attribute the mysterious incident to a declining level of carefulness and rise in drug use among US soldiers, «even though no contact was made with the enemy commandos » and no US losses were reported. Officers were unable to give an account of the enemy's methods in attacking the fuel storage area, but simply stated that « they obviously got past someone who should have spotted them ». Like most defenders of the status quo, they are either not aware of what's going on around them or they have chosen to cover up what is most obvious to us : that this action was carried out by resisters inside the army.

okinawa

When US troops were called out to supress the December riots in Koza, 30 Black GI's stationed inside Kadena Air Base refused to go out, annourcing that the action of the people of Koza was perfectly justifiable and that it was « beautiful ». At present, GI's stationed at Okinawa are actively supporting the stike of workers on US bases, the Zengunro labor struggle, a genuine struggle of liberation against the two imperialist powers, Japan and the United States, which jointly rule Okinawa.

france

Spec. 4 Francisco Burciaga (self-retired) RA 18843447 has been in France sinse 1968 and has both residence permit (carte de séjour) and work permit (carte de travail). Right On !

england

1000 airmen in Britain aginst the war give this proposal to the US embassy :
We the undersigned, members of the US Air Force Navy in England are opposed to the war in Indochina. Because vietnamization is increased, the Air Force and Navy role in the war is more important than ever before. Those whose voices are in opposition : Spokesman, Capt. Tom Culver (Viet Vet), Staff Judge Advocate.

15. Author's interview with Dave Cline, September 30, 2003.

16. *Vietnam GI* (June 1968), p. 8.

17. GI Press Service, vol. 1, no. 1 (June 26, 1969), through vol. 1, no. 14 (December 25, 1969).

18. Anderson, "The GI Movement," p. 96.

Fig. 5.12. **ACT** (Paris, France; Heidelberg, Germany), 1971, cover; (next page), 1970, vol. 1, no. 2, cover; 1970, vol. 1, no. 4, cover

NOTICE: THIS PAPER IS YOUR PERSONAL PROPERTY. IT CANNOT BE LEGALLY TAKEN FROM YOU FOR ANY REASON.

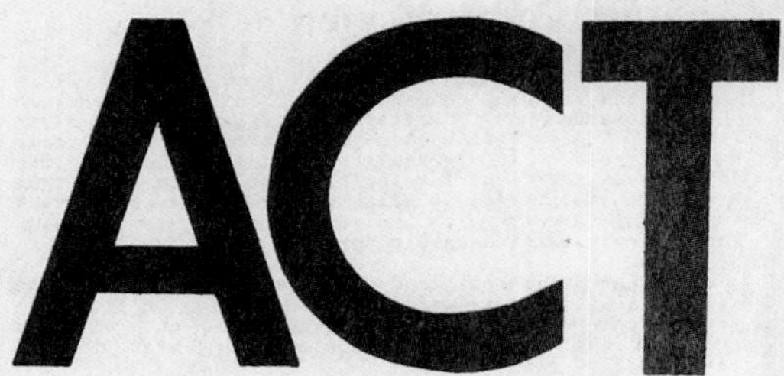

The RITA's Newsletter
Vol. 1, No. 2
Western Europe

Blind Nationalism

Pvt. Richard Perrin, RA11748246

Since the first printing of ACT, an American Embassy official told the press that our effect on troop morale was "potentially calamitous". Some of us are and some have been in the Army. We know the type of information you are receiving either from the STARS AND STRIPES or the brass. It is the job of the STARS AND STRIPES and officers to keep up your morale; of course to do this they indoctrinate you with pro-war ideas. They must make you believe that U.S. policies in Vietnam are just.

We all know high morale is necessary for a successful war effort. Stop and think for a minute about how Germany kept up their troops' morale during W.W. II. The Nazi cause was unjust, yet the German troops were tough and difficult to defeat. How did the Nazis accomplish their high troop morale? They did it by appealing to German boys' blind nationalism. A good German accepted the draft, fought, killed, and died for Germany. They did it because Hitler was their elected leader, Germany was at war and a "good citizen" is not afraid to die for his country.

If someone asks you to kill and die, we say you should know why. The ACT shows you the other side of the story; all we ask is that you question U.S. government policies and your involvement with them.

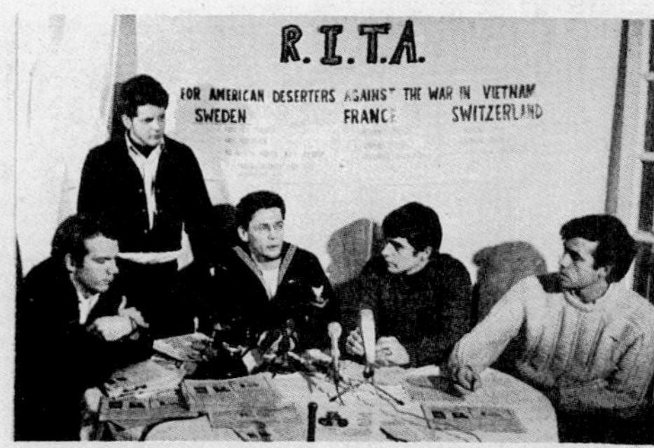

RITAS LAUNCH ACT AT INTERNATIONAL PRESS CONFERENCE
From left to right: Terry Klug, Cornell Hiselman, G. Wuerth, Dick Perrin and Philip Wagner.

Flicker of Light

Pvt. Ralph David Denman, RA16930188

As a deserter of the United States Army a question arises in the minds of my countrymen. Was he just another one of the misfits who was unable to adjust? Or, perhaps he has tangible and sincere beliefs.

The everlovin' undecided homosapiens have freewill as a gift from the creator. It is only natural for a man to make use of this gift, rather than conceal it behind a cloak of conformity as a vast majority of people choose to do.

I have denied myself the expression of my innermost convictions for the majority of my life. But now that some unknown flicker of light is visible for the first time I staunchly refuse to surrender my integrity to the force of social pressure.

You as a soldier and human being have reached the time in your life where an important decision must be made. That is, a decision between conformity to the common belief that our government's position is righteous, or that a stand must be taken against our shoddy administration.

If you have a sincere desire for a decent and peaceful life, do something about it. Don't allow yourself to settle into the inevitable stagnation.

United we stand

G.W.Wuerth Jr., RD 3, B202678

The country which preaches "life, liberty, and the pursuit of happiness," the country whose principles I would defend to the death, has become immorally and illegally involved in a war of aggression. This realisation is difficult to accept.

"It's your country, right or wrong". Right or wrong the United States leaders are allowed to decide who lives and who dies, and with which type of government a country will be endowed—all this in the name of freedom and democracy.

Is the "pursuit of happiness" coming home to find one's father and mother dead and one's village completely destroyed? Is that happiness! Dropping bombs on innocent people, or anyone for that matter, destroying schools, hospitals and land, spreading poisonous gases and inhuman chemicals throughout south Vietnam; is this our interpretation of "of the people, for the people and by the people.

What corruption, what madness renders our country the sole protectorate and ultimately, the destructor of humanity? What derangement, what stupidity continues our brutal aggression? Our leaders have rejected negotiations, the courageous Vietnamese can never be defeated, and each escalation further enflames and involves the "red" powers of China and the U.S.S.R. Are we destined towards a world wide showdown? Must all humanity be deprived of life itself because of the deranged audacity of our leaders and the blind obedience of their subservients.

My fellow Americans, I appeal to you, to your conscience, to your sense of justice and righteousness, and to your love of life.

The war must be stopped! Now! It is the individual responsibility of each American to clarify and to realize the true meaning of "life, liberty, and the pursuit of happiness".

THIS NEWSLETTER IS WRITTEN BY DESERTERS AND RITAS FOR THE PURPOSE OF PROVIDING INFORMATION TO AMERICAN SERVICEMEN.

Dear Sirs,
I am a GI serving in Germany. I read your paper called GIs ACT and agree with a lot of what you say. Many of my friends have got orders for Vietnam. I think I will get orders to go too. I would like to resist this rotten war but am afraid to do anything by myself. Can you send me some information that could help me decide what to do? I am so confused about my position in the Army and no one here will give me any help. I hope that you can help me.

From a soldier stationed near Frankfurt.

American servicemen unite! You have nothing to lose but your stripes!

VETERANS STARS & STRIPES for PEACE

5¢ · Vol. 1, No. 7, Chicago, Ill., May-June, 1968 · dedicated to ending the war in Vietnam

Big blowup ahead? GI's RESIST VIET WAR

Kennedy death shocks US; top GI toll, 4,308, ignored

by LeRoy Wolins

Lt. pickets White House in uniform

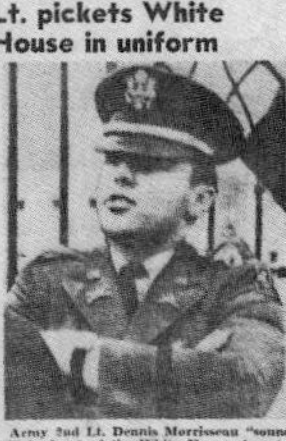

Establish GI coffee houses

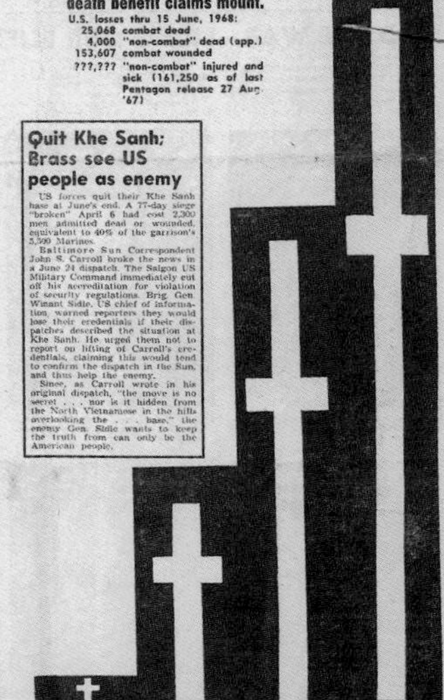

VIETNAM DEATH GRAPH
Pentagon victory claims, family death benefit claims mount.
U.S. losses thru 15 June, 1968:
25,068 combat dead
4,000 "non-combat" dead (app.)
153,607 combat wounded
???,??? "non-combat" injured and sick (161,250 as of last Pentagon release 27 Aug '67)

Quit Khe Sanh; Brass see US people as enemy

1961-1966 average: 21 combat dead/week
1967 average: 179 combat dead/week
1968 average: 378 combat dead/week to 15 June
Week ended 11 May 68: 562 combat dead; record and portent

This copy of VETERANS STARS & STRIPES FOR PEACE distributed by:

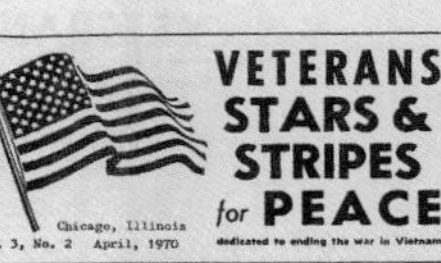

VETERANS STARS & STRIPES for PEACE

10¢ · Vol. 3, No. 2 · Chicago, Illinois · April, 1970 · dedicated to ending the war in Vietnam

Set National GI Antiwar Conference

April 15—Civilian tax protest, GI strike call

SAVE THE PRIEST

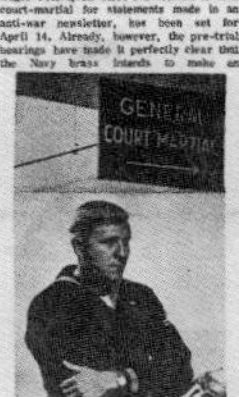

Vets sue military spies, face House snoopers

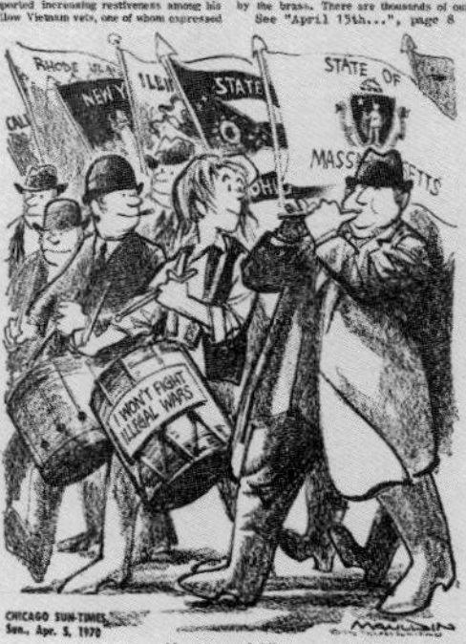

Unexpected Allies

Open Letter to GI's
From an Army deserter somewhere in Europe.

GIs ACT

Where it's at

GIs protest war

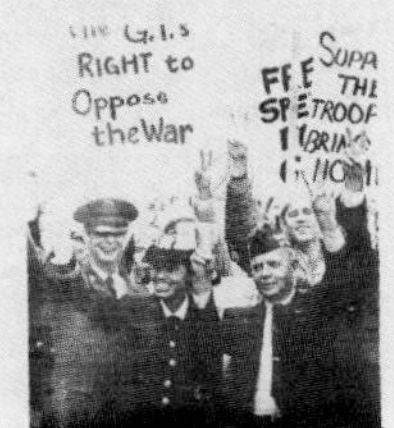

publications

Published by RITA

THE LAW WAS MADE FOR MAN NOT MAN FOR THE LAW

Veterans Stars & Stripes for Peace
(Chicago), May-June 1968, vol. 1, no. 7, cover
Veterans Stars & Stripes for Peace
(Chicago), April 1970, vol. 3, no. 2, cover

The circulation of most of these papers was limited to the bases on which they were published and their immediate vicinity. Many were no more than a few mimeographed sheets put out clandestinely by a few friends until they were caught, transferred, or ran out of money. Others grew into major operations which broke stories before the mainstream press, mobilized large GI demonstrations, and had circulations in the thousands. Almost invariably, these latter had the support of off-base coffeehouses run by vets and civilians, which provided funds, a stable base of operations, and perhaps most importantly, continuity when active-duty personnel were busted or transferred. Whether a coffeehouse, a "peace center," or a mimeograph machine hidden in someone's basement, the place the paper was produced became the center of GI antiwar activity.

Gigline (fig. 5.14) was an underground paper put out by GIs at Fort Bliss, Texas, and its office became a de facto GI counseling center.[19] "Many people would come into the office and say 'I can't do it any more. I can't put on the uniform any more. What do I do?'" remembers *Gigline*'s David Cortright. "We had it down to a science: how many pills to take to make yourself really sick without actually killing yourself but get into the hospital to get their stomach pumped and then get out on section 8 suicide. This would happen once or twice a week."[20]

The names of the papers reflected the dark humor which was the cultural coin of the GI resistance movement: *Shakedown* (fig. 5.15) at Fort Dix, *Attitude Check* at the Marines Camp Pendleton, *Fed Up* (fig. 5.16) at Fort Lewis, *All Hands Abandon Ship* at Newport Naval Station, the *Last Harass* at Fort Gordon, *Left Face* at Fort McClellan, the *Star-Spangled Bummer* at Wright-Patterson Air Force Base, *Your Military Left* at Randolph Air Force Base, and on the submarine tender USS *Huntley*, the *Huntley Hemorrhoid*, which informed officers, "We Serve to Preserve the Pain in Your Ass." The

Vietnam GI

March, 1968

FREE to Servicemen

Tet / Saigon

The following is an interview with Steve Goldburg, who's just returned stateside after a 8-month tour as a civilian refugee worker in Vietnam. Goldburg was with both the International Voluntary Service and Committee of Responsibility, the medical group arranging stateside treatment for badly wounded children.

Q. How did the Tet Offensive begin for you, Steve?

A. That morning. When I got out of bed I turned on the radio and heard that the VC had taken the Embassy. At first I thought I'd gotten Radio Hanoi! We couldn't believe it.

I lived just down the street from the 716th MP Bn. barracks. They were the only American forces handling the Tet Offensive in Saigon. They were bitching about being short-handed. It's true. A couple of blocks from the MP compound is a new hotel where the VC were holed up for about ten days before the 716th had enough manpower to clean them out.

A Saigon police station was also down the street. They simply stayed inside for the duration because they were too scared to venture out after the VC. The 716th brought out a truck with a .50 cal. machinegun mounted on it. Their plan was if the VC attacked the police station, they'd just blast the entire station with the gun--VC, police and all. You know, one of those .50 cal. machineguns can take apart a building!

The problem was the gun mount was broken, and didn't swivel. Therefore the truck had to be aimed in the direction of fire.

(continued on Page 3)

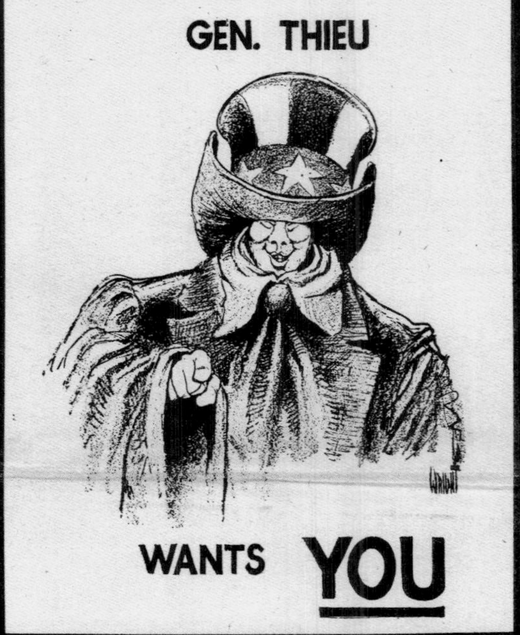

GI'S TAKE THE RAP

It's time to start "telling it like it is" about war crimes in the Nam. Torturing POWs and killing peasants is OK with the Brass—just so they don't have to dirty their hands or take the rap when the shit hits the fan. But when it does, the Brass always cleans their hands at the expense of EMs, who end up paying the bill! A good example is the trial last year of five AirCav soldiers from C Co., 1/8 Inf.

Capt. Paul Ogg, C Co. CO, was charged with ordering one of his platoon leaders, Lt. John Patrick, to get rid of a Vietnamese suspect taken during the day's sweep near Canhau. In court Lt. Patrick admitted carrying out the order. Sgt. Walter Griffin, Sp/5 Raul Garcia, and Pfc. David Woods admitted actually taking the "detainee" out in the boonies and shooting him. The result?

All four admitted taking part in the killing, but only Lt. Patrick was found "innocent." Griffin got 25 years, Garcia got 4 years and a BCD, and Woods got "one and one."

The kicker is that Sgt. Griffin, a lifer, is never going to serve his 25-year sentence—that was just for public relations stateside. *Some JAG lawyers are predicting that he'll be back on duty as soon as the case is forgotten about.*

Capt. Ogg, of course, was found "innocent," even though six men in his company testified they heard him give the fatal order. It's the enlisted men who paid!

Other war crimes trials have worked out the same way. Two Marines, a lieutenant and a sergeant, were also tried for killing a POW. The result? The lieutenant was found "innocent" and the sergeant drew life imprisonment.

In one of the best known cases, Pfc. Charles Keenan of the 1st Mar. Div. got 25 years for killing an old man and woman (two other EMs on his patrol drew ten and life respectively).

Keenan claimed that he didn't have a clear view of the fleeing suspects, and when he hesitated, his sergeant yelled "Shoot, dammit, shoot!" But since Keenan was tried in the States, his civilian lawyer was unable to interview other members of his platoon, see the area where the incident occurred, or otherwise build a defense.

Whether any of these guys are guilty or not, it's clear that they as well as other EMs are being railroaded. As one JAG officer told a reporter: *"Army court martials have a funny habit of absolving officers at the expense of enlisted men."* (*N.Y. Times* 6 Aug. 67). Because the officers who give the orders are "gentlemen," the GIs who carry out the orders become "war criminals." This is called "military justice."

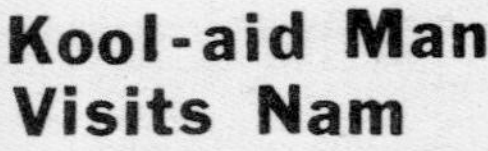

Kool-aid Man Visits Nam

Some of the most callous bastards around are the Congressional hawks. Take Rep. Joe Resnick of Ellenville, N.Y., for example. On his latest junket to the Nam, Joe lived like a king. Dressed in his red cap emblazoned with five stars and the word, "BOSS"—Congressman Joe was waited on by MACV brass, had a champagne breakfast with the press, and even was assigned an Army chaplain to carry his gifts around for him.

And on the taxpayers' money, Joe even found time to "talk" to the troops. Not only did he encourage "his boys" by telling them "we are winning the war and winning it big," *but he also passed out kool-aid and hunting knives to GIs. Big Joe is so bent on having the Nam as our colony he thinks that GIs are natives, too.*

But in the end, Congressman Joe felt that his vacation was spoiled. You see, MACV wouldn't give his daughter, 17, and his son, 19 [why the hell isn't he in the Army?] helicopters so they could fly around the country. Well, at Tan Son Nhut, Old Joe blew up, screaming at a Colonel: "You've nearly ruined my entire trip . . . Now my daughter won't be able to write an article for TEEN AGE AMERICA." That's tough shit, Joe!

What we weren't told about TET!

The biggest story of the Tet Offensive has yet to get any real publicity. Even MACV had to admit that the infiltration of 70,000 VC troops into the cities was only possible with the silent help of the population. What has shaken up the brass even more is the evidence of VC agents or sympathizers in high levels of ARVN and GVN.

It's been an open secret that Pentagon East stubbornly guards many plans from ARVN, having learned the hard way that information given to ARVN general staff is somehow passed on to the VC.

Now, after the unbelievable events of Tet, the picture looks even grimmer. The night that the U.S. Embassy compound was attacked by a 19-man VC "suicide squad" there were no Vietnamese Police on guard outside. Somehow, the four police normally on duty never showed up. And even though a police HQ is next to the Embassy compound, no other guards were provided. *In fact, Vietnamese police from that building didn't fire at the VC, but by "mistake" opened fire on the six Marines who rushed to defend the compound.*

Incidentally, the two MPs on guard at the compound gate were "taken out" before the attack even began—shot in the back by two trusted Vietnamese employees of the Embassy.

The VC captured Tra Vinh, capital of Vinh Binh Province, without firing a shot. In Hue, ARVN Officers pulled out of the arsenal, handing over 1,000 brand-new M-16s to the VC without a fight. It's true that ARVN is "the world's worst army," regularly pulling stunts that in any other outfit would look like treason. *But it appears that many Vietnamese officers and officials, fearful of their future if the Saigon government falls, are "playing it safe" by giving the VC at least a limited cooperation.*

19. The term "gigline" refers to the visual line made by the buttons on a GI's shirt and the fly of his or her trousers, which must make a straight line when facing inspection.

20. Author's interview with David Cortright, September 17, 2003.

Fig. 5.13. **Vietnam GI** (Chicago), March 1968, cover

movement penetrated Strategic Air Command Headquarters at Offutt Air Force Base in Omaha, where the *Offul Times* was published. Even the Pentagon had an underground paper published from within.

These papers were profoundly subversive. Many papers professed more allegiance to the "enemy" than to the US military. *Gigline* reported the death of Vietnamese leader Ho Chi Minh on the front page: "We who deeply regret our nation's longstanding interference in the affairs of the Vietnamese people wish to express our great sadness at the death of Chairman Ho Chi Minh, whose dedication to the welfare of his people and their liberation from foreign domination should be an inspiration to the leaders of all nations."[21] Another paper proclaimed: "Don't desert. Go to Vietnam and kill your commanding officer."

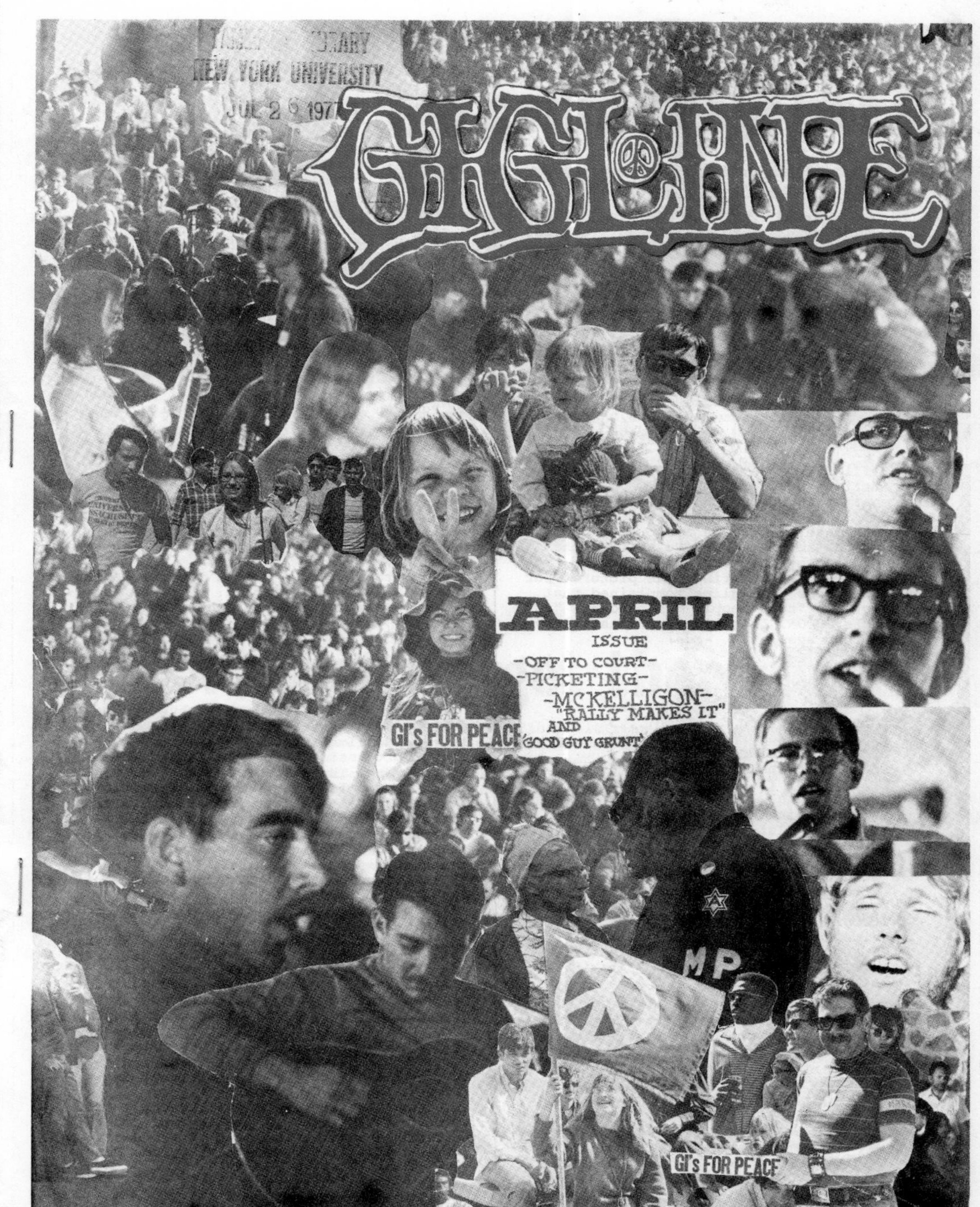

Fig. 5.14. **Gigline** (Fort Bliss, Texas), April 1977, vol. 2, no. 4, cover

21. *Gigline*, vol. 1, no. 3 (1969).

THE GI PAPERS (fig. 5.17) skated on precariously thin legal ice. The right to free speech should have been protected by the First Amendment, but in practice soldiers were at the mercy of the military chain of command in which they were embedded. When commanders figured out who was behind the underground base paper, they had many ways to mete out punishment without even mentioning the paper and thus giving the appearance of respecting the soldier's right to free speech. Infractions could be invented. Transfers to undesirable posts could be arranged. And of course, the guilty parties could be sent to Vietnam.

These threats were serious. A dishonorable discharge would hang over a GI's head for the rest of his life, making employment difficult. Many charges on which GIs were framed carried substantial time at Fort Leavenworth doing hard labor. Andy Stapp served forty-five days at hard labor in 1967, and was threatened with much more. Pvt. Wade Carson was sentenced to six months for "intention" to distribute *Fed Up* at Fort Lewis. Pvt. Bruce Peterson, the first editor of *Fatigue Press* at Fort Hood,

....THE TIME HAS COME FOR A LONG-NEEDED....

SHAKEDOWN

Vol. 1, No. 11 P.O. Box 68, Wrightstown, N.J. Oct. 17, 1969

THOUSANDS MARCH ON FORT DIX

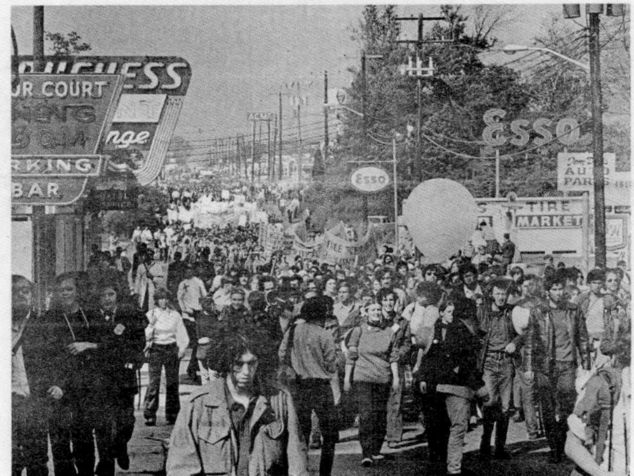

...And This Is Only the Start

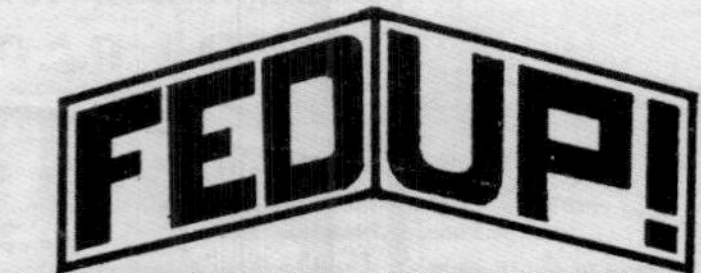

This paper is written by a group of Fort Lewis GI's who can no longer stand the oppression of the US military.
WE SHALL BE HEARD

Volume 1, No 3 PO Box 414 January 16, 1970
Free to servicemen Tacoma, Washington 98409 25¢ to civilians

HANDS OFF THE SHELTER HALF

The Army is trying to put the Shelter Half off limits to all servicemen. The GI coffee house at 5437 South Tacoma Way has been open for over a year. Why is the Army just now getting around to this action?

In October the first issue of FED UP was printed and almost 5,000 copies found their way onto Fort Lewis. On October 20, the American Serviceman's Union had a meeting at the Cascadian Service Club on post. 35 GI's were arrested and held for five hours, but no on was charged with anything, mostly because of the solidarity of the men. A few weeks later, a group of black GI's had a meeting at the Pioneer Service Club on main post. Again, MP's broke up the meeting, but again, no one was charged. About 5,000 copies of the second issue of FED UP were distributed on Fort Lewis. Our movement is getting stronger. We're talking and acting about the immediate end to the war in Viet Nam. More and more of our brothers are refusing to fight against the Vietnamese people. We're refusing to fight our own people in the streets of America. We're getting hip to how we're being used to play the cops of the world and we don't like it. We're getting together and the brass are getting uptight.

In a letter to the Shelter Half, the Armed Forces Disciplinary Control Board said,"The board took this action after receiving information that the Shelter Half is a source of dissident counseling and literature and other activities enimical to the good morale, order and discipline within the Armed Services." What this means when you translate it out of the military double-talk is that the brass are trying to tell us who we can talk with and what we can read. The Shelter Half is one of the links between the GI movement and the civilian movement. They provide material and moral support for our struggle. Now the military wants to keep us from our meeting place. They're afraid of what will happen when we will no longer be used as robots and slaves. But they can't stop us from getting together. The Shelter Half is ours.

On January 21, we are putting the brass on trial. The charges range from inhumane harrassment of GI's to carrying out the war in Viet Nam to the suppression of American people fighting to be free. Witnesses will include active duty enlisted men, victims of the stockade system, Viet Nam veterans, and civilians who have been victims of the military here in the United States. The jury will be made up of active duty, rank-and-file enlisted men. Several Fort Lewis officials will be subpoenaed to appear at the trial and defend themselves. Failure to appear would seem to be an admission of guilt. The trial will be at the HUB Ballroom on the University of Washington campus. There will be free transportation provided by the Shelter Half and the Fort Lewis American Serviceman's Union for all GI's who want to go. Call the Shelter Half at GR5-9875 so we can get a count of the men who want to go. Rides will be leaving from the Shelter Half at 7:00 Wednesday night.

On January 22, the staff of the Shelter Half is supposed to appear before a military board (the same board that decided to start this off limits action in the first place) "to show cause why it should not be placed OFF LIMITS." This hearing will be at the Sand Point Naval Air Station in Seattle. Outside, while the hearing is going on, there will be a large demonstration of civilians. These people will be showing their support for the GI movement and and protesting the action that the Army is trying to take against the GI movement and the Shelter Half. The demonstration is centered around seven demands: 1) An immediate end to the war in Viet Nam, 2) Freedom for all political prisoners, both military and civilian, 3) Abolish the stockade system, 4) No troops for riot control, 5) An end to the racism in the Armed Forces, 6) Amnesty for all exiles, and 7) End the draft. Civilians realize that we think that both the war and the Army suck, and they're with us in our struggle against the brass of the Army and this country.

The Shelter Half is NOT off limits now. That decision won't be made until January 22. The Fort Lewis American Serviceman's Union has meetings at the Shelter Half on Monday nights and the Shelter Half is open every night from five until midnight or later. Come down and see why the Army is so uptight. You'll see that the Shelter Half is not bad for your morale; maybe the morale of some of the brass, but not your morale.

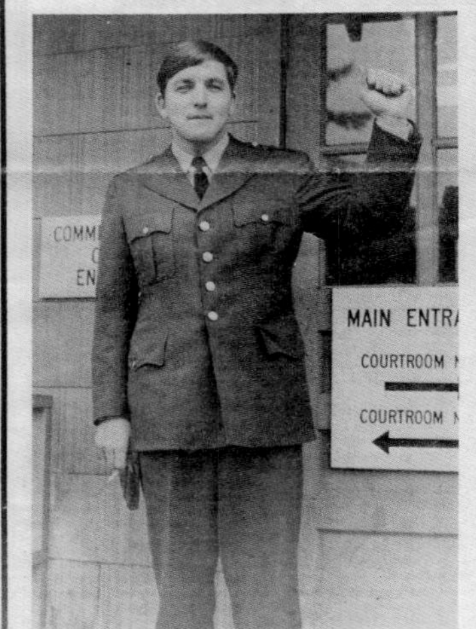

PFC Leonard Wathen of the 513th Maintenance Company on Fort Lewis, after a special court-martial for refusing to be on reactionary force. See the story "Justice?" on page 8.

VOL. 1 NO. 7 DECEMBER 1969 FREE TO GI'S

UP FRONT

FINAL EDITION

GI's Unite: DEC. 14 See page 3

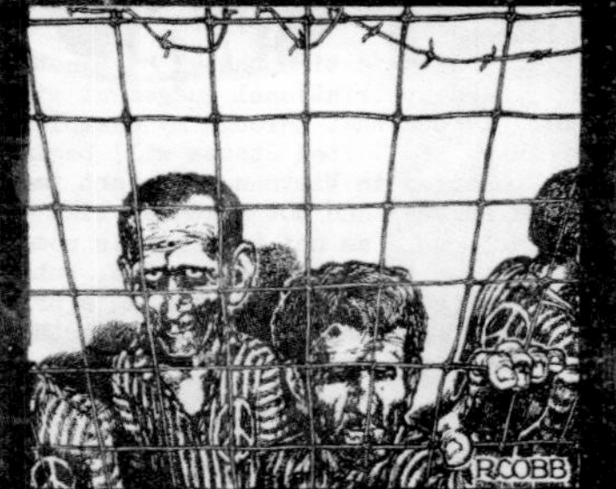

To: Pres. Nixon
FROM: All us GI's
SUBJECT: XMAS GREETINGS!!!

MEMO: Let's get home and solve some of our Problems Like Military Injustice!!!!!

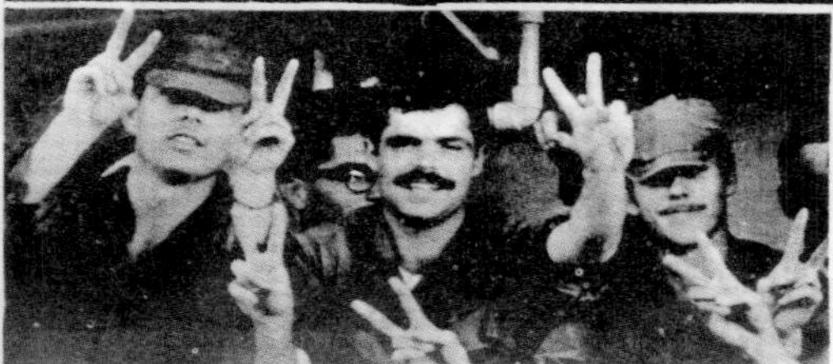

Marines returning from Vietnam express their opinion of antiwar movement.

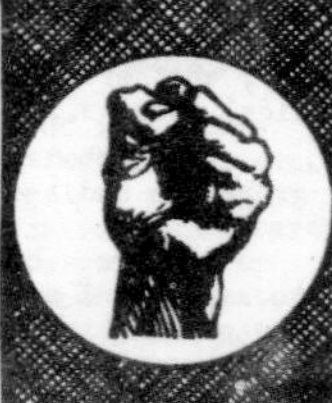

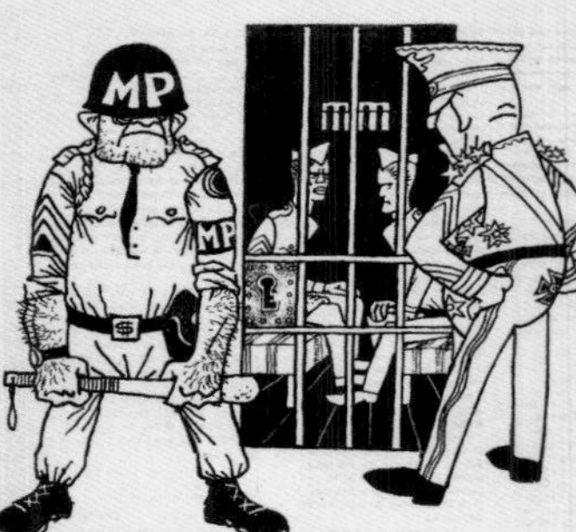

" It's a free country and you're fighting to keep it free -- whatsa matter don't you believe in freedom ?"

JOIN THE GI's UNION

To Break Down the Bars

The American Servicemen's Union is a joining together of rank and file servicemen to gain their rights.

It recognizes that the services are run by a military dictatorship which violates the rights of every servicemen everyday.

"Attention!"... "Right face!"... "Forward march!"... "Say 'sir' when you're talking to an officer!" are merely every day humiliations to prepare you to be a willing robot, to do the dirty work, to die if the boss-man says so, so that the boss-man can go on giving unjust orders.

Your fellow GIs are founding this union. They are no longer willing to be slaves of this dictatorship. But they know that individual resistance alone, while it can inspire others, is not enough. The Brass, who have usurped illegal, un-Constitutional and completely unjust power over you and millions of others, is able to control you precisely because they are organized into a machine that can grind individuals up. And rank filers must organize their own power into a stronger machine.

It may seem now an impossible thing -- that nothing could unite all the guys so that you can act together against the power of the Brass. But it can be done -- and WILL be done!

THAT'S WHAT ORGANIZATION IS ALL ABOUT. JOIN TODAY!

To Andy Stapp, Chairman, Provisional Organizing Committee of the American Servicemen's Union, c/o The Bond Room 633, 156 Fifth Ave., New York 10010.

I am a rank and file enlisted man.

I hereby declare that I support the American Servicemen's Union and enclose one dollar to register myself as a member. As a union member I agree to support other union members in our effort to gain our rights. As a union member I will receive a copy of The GI's Handbook on Military Injustice and any other advice and instruction issued by central union organizers. I will also contact the union center for advice in case of emergency and keep the center informed in order to aid other union members.

name ______
military address ______
home address ______
ETS ______

UNION DEMANDS

1. An end to saluting and sir-ing of officers -- let's get off our knees
2. Election of officers by vote of the men
3. Racial equality
4. Rank and filers control of court-martial boards
5. Federal minimum wages
6. The right of free political association
7. The right to disobey illegal orders -- like orders to go and fight in an illegal war in Vietnam.
8. The right of collective bargaining.

NOTICE:
THIS NEWSPAPER IS YOUR PERSONAL PROPERTY. IT CANNOT LEGALLY BE TAKEN FROM YOU FOR ANY REASON

THE BOND

The Servicemen's Newspaper

Vol. 2, No. 5 New York, N.Y. May 13, 1968

Military Methods In Vietnam

"Colonels Are Not Very Brave"

By a Viet GI

I have no interest in dying for something I oppose. So I'm not a line trooper and I don't crew a gunship. Out of a desire to keep in touch with the war though, I am crew chief on a battalion command ship. Colonels are not very brave, so barring mechanical failure, the war I see won't kill me.

Some information. You might check into the legalities of a weapon called Fleshette. It's a special anti-personal load for the 90mm recoilless rifle which blasts thousands of small steel "darts" like a huge shotgun. An infantryman who told me of using it said it was outlawed by conventions and kept very secret. He personally used it when LZ Byrd was being overrun last December. This is just south of the Bong Son plain.

Our battalion was experimenting with dropping napalm by Chinook helicopter. The napalm was in 55 gallon drums with a thermite grenade wired to each drum. The grenades were armed by static line as the drums were pushed out of the back of the Chinook. As you may imagine, the idea of carrying quantities of the "humane" weapon in their ships was extremely upsetting to the crews.

Always concerned with morale, our officers held a special briefing session and explained to the crews that if the napalm were to accidentally go off on board, it would bubble harmlessly out the rear! Unbelievable? One minute out of the Pick-up Zone on the first large scale mission (36 drums on 3 Chinooks) the pins vibrated out of the grenades and the drums were pushed overboard where they exploded in a paddy below. The remaining napalm was dropped on target, but that was the last napalm mission by Chinook.

The National Police Field Force has earned a solid reputation of brutality here. I've seen some women they interrogated. By the way, badly beaten subjects are usually released. They don't look good in PW camps. I heard an American officer on the radio directing a patrol to "find out what you can and if they don't talk, beat the hell out of them and tell them to stay out of the area."

Oh. Did you know that all news releases from Vietnam must be cleared by MAC-V. And if a reporter skips this, he and his agency, if he is attached, are banned from the country. This I learned from a P.I.O. man who has met repeated frustration. C.O.s simply "classify" his material if they disapprove of it.

What do the Vietnamese think of GIs? All phony elections aside, the Vietnamese in Ankhe vote at night by firing at air craft flying overhead. Ankhe is right outside our gate and has received as much American "goodwill" as any village here. But it still votes at night.

Racial Bias Pushed By Brass

--WHILE THEY TALK PRETTY

By Sp/4 Dick Wheaton

One of the demands of the American Servicemen's Union is for an end to racial discrimination in the Armed Forces.

It is a vital demand. It is vital for whites as well as blacks because the Brass will try to use it to crush our efforts to unite and form a union.

The military apparatus proudly struts about cock-a-doodle-doing about its equal opportunity program and GIs are regularly told how fair the Armed Forces are to all races, colors and creeds. The story is not true.

Racial discrimination is Army policy even though much of it is hidden. Just as racism serves to make money and keep the power in the hands of a small group of industrial magnates against the mass of American people, so does racism work in the interest of officers against the enlisted men.

If any of you are in an artillery unit, as I was before being transferred to a Little John Rocket Battalion, you can readily see that there are more blacks than whites in the line batteries (from which the guns are fired) and service batteries (in which GIs do the back-breaking job of carrying ammo from the dump to the firing point) than there are in the headquarters batteries where the relatively easy "brain" work of Fire Control, Survey and Commo is done. I have known black GIs assigned to Service battery of my former unit, the 2nd Howitzer Bn, 2nd Artillery, who had some college and one who had graduated from Howard University. They were there "humping ammo" not because of a lack of education or ability. They were there because they were black.

This is not at all surprising when the Army has officers like a certain Lt.McCarthy who bragged to me and two other white enlisted men how "Every nigger I get I try and put him in the lowest, dirtiest job I can find." (!)

Not only are we enlisted men oppressed (blacks doubly), we are also expected to help smash other oppres-

(continued on page 3)

Printed in U.S.A. FREE to GIs; BRASS, LIFERS, CIVILIANS 15¢ donation

ABOUT FACE: the EM news

no. 5 743½ South ALVARADO Street, Los Angeles, Ca. 90057 (213) 382-2833 4th-of-July edition

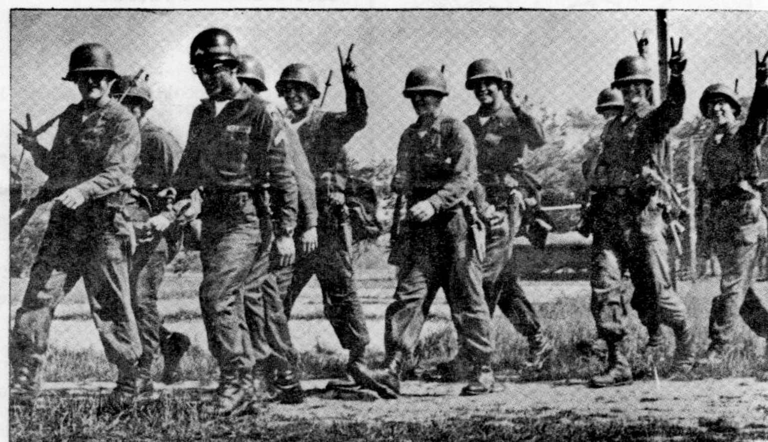

WAS THIS PHOTO TAKEN AT CAMP PENDLETON? FT. MacARTHUR? EL TORO? MARCH AFB? M.C.R.D.? LONG BEACH NAVAL YARDS? BERKELEY? 29 PALMS? FOR THE ANSWER...

read this paper NOW!

This newspaper is your personal property. It cannot legally be taken from you for any reason. Hell no!

"GIs & Vietnam Vets *Against* The War" CHALLENGES the CAMP PENDLETON BRASS, LIFERS - SEE PAGE 4

Up For A Summary ? Call Us! ...or see p.6 for list of GI counseling centers. By the way, our number is... DELTA-UTAH: 2-2833 *

COUNTERPOINT

Fort Lewis McChord

Vol. 2, No. 3

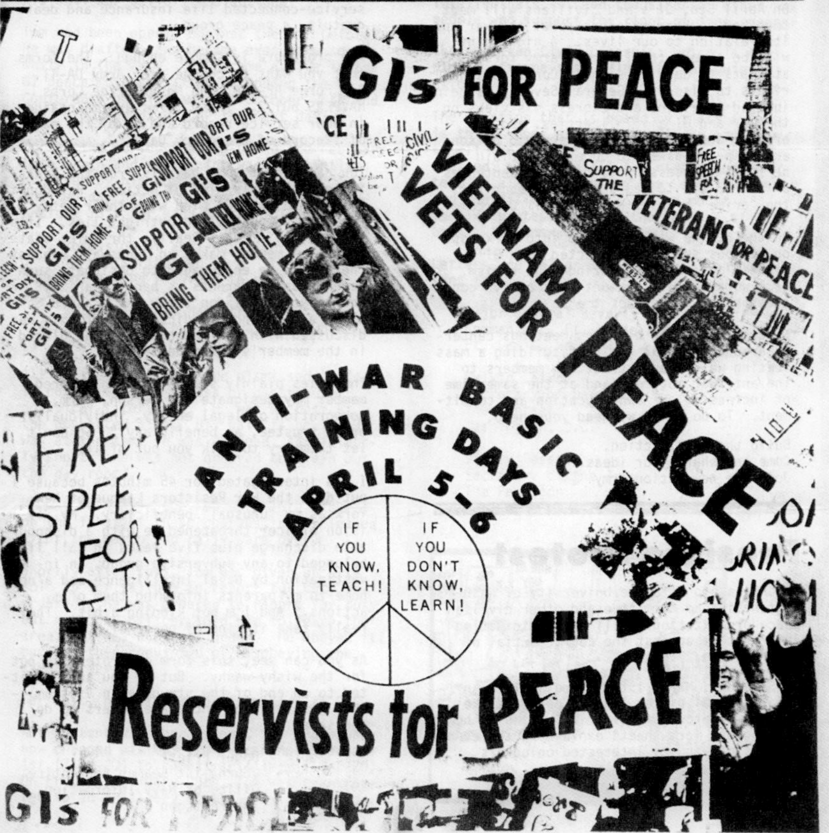

ISSUE "RIOT" CONTROL

FREE TO G.I.'S

FATIGUE PRESS

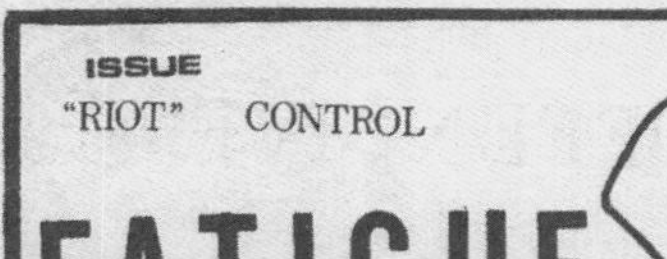

VOICE OF GI SOC

BY AND FOR GI'S FT. HOOD

AR 381-135 (D) THE RIGHT TO READ AND RETAIN COMMERCIAL PUBLICATIONS THIS IS YOUR PERSONAL PROPERTY IT CAN NOT BE TAKEN AWAY FROM YOU

"RIOT" CONTROL?

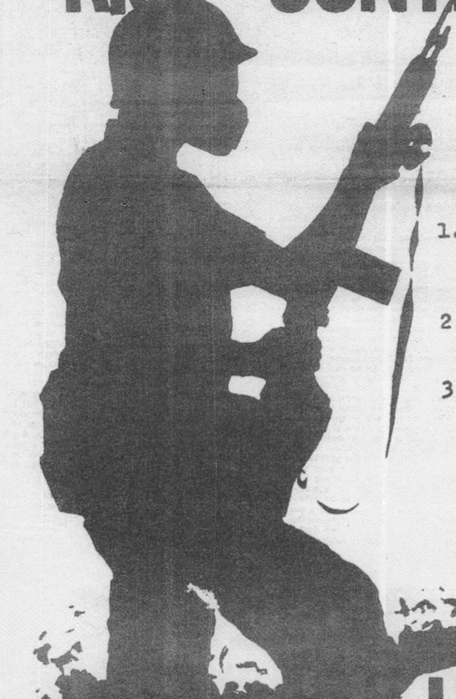

1. WE DEMAND AN END TO THE USE OF GIS AS COPS AND STRIKE-BREAKERS.
2. WE DEMAND THE US TO GET OUT OF SOUTHEAST ASIA.
3. WE DEMAND CONSTITUTIONAL RIGHTS FOR ALL GIS.

* GI SOC *

HELL NO!

Previous Page

Fig. 5.15. **Shakedown** (Wrightstone, New Jersey), October 17, 1969, vol. 1, no. 12, cover

Fig. 5.16. **Fed Up** (Fort Lewis, Tacoma, Washington), January 16, 1970, vol. 1, no. 3, cover

Fig. 5.17. **Up Front,** December 1969, vol. 1, no. 7, cover; **The Bond** (New York), May 1968, vol., 2 no. 5, cover

Fig. 5.17. (cont'd.). **About Face** (Los Angeles), July 4, 1972, vol. 1, no. 5, cover; **Fatigue Press** (Fort Hood, Texas), [no year], "Riot Control" issue, cover; **Counterpoint** (Fort Lewis, Tacoma, Washington), [no year], vol. 2, no. 3, cover

PAC·O·LIES

DEC. 25, 1969 VOL. 1 NO. 2

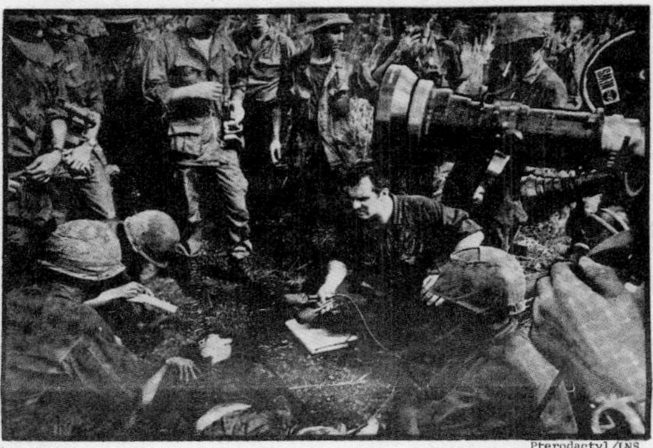

Pterodactyl/LNS

MEDIA & THE WAR

SAIGON, South Vietnam--American troops caught a North Vietnamese force in a pincer movement in the central coastal plain yesterday, killing 128 enemy soldiers in daylong fighting.
--New York Times, March 17, 1968, p. 1.

Sound like the usual day-to-day news report we read about Vietnam? Sure--only this particular pack of military lies--dutifully transmitted to the American people by the New York Times and the rest of the news media--backfired a year-and-a-half later when it was revealed the dead were not "enemy soldiers," but unarmed civilians, including many women and children, massacred at My Lai.

What about the many Vietnam news stories and broadcasts we are fed every day? Are they any more truthful or accurate than last year's Times story of March 17? Of course not. The media have continually distorted reports by their own correspondents which reveal the true nature of the Vietnam war by incorporating Pentagon euphemisms and Administration rhetoric. They continually befuddle the reader in his search for objectivity by reconciling language and style with U.S. foreign policy assumptions and propaganda.

Political necessities in America distort what we read. Big newspapers have two considerations: on the one hand, if they want to maintain their precious contacts inside the government and the big political machines as well as their advertising revenue, they cannot offend big corporate interests; on the other hand, if they are to maintain any credibility with a public that wants the war ended, they have to report in a way that at least suggests they are independent and in touch with America's failure in Vietnam. On top of that, they are subject to pressure from elements within the ruling elite who are split over how to conduct the war and have to run articles that point to one solution or another.

All of these problems create reporting on the war that is full of inconsistencies, absurdities, distortions and outright lies. But there are patterns in the murk, patterns dictated by the kind of economic and political power that defines the establishment press. The reporting is inconsistent, but it is inconsistent around particular issues: there are lies, but the lies are all in the same direction, all aimed at establishing certain beliefs among the public.

Therefore, so that we might all more readily pierce mass media obfuscation, New York Media Project offers this quick, comparative glossary of what gets printed and how to decipher it.

Death coverage. As the My Lai massacre recently demonstrated, "enemy soldiers" in the press are not always enemy soldiers in fact.

(Continued on page 8)

PAC·O·LIES

new york media project

Vol 1 No 3 March, 1970

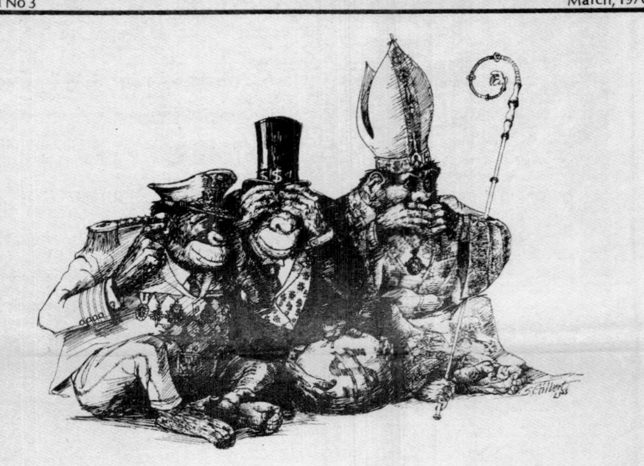

"It will be this Company's policy to analyze each subpoena carefully and weigh its relevance to trial proceedings or criminal actions. Should we believe that there is no immediate relevance ..." and blah, blah, blah.

Hedley Donovan
Editor-in-Chief
Time Magazine
Feb. 3, 1970

The Pentagon Paper

War Bulletin Included

Number 4
September, 1972
Pentagon Paper
125 W. 4th Street
Los Angeles, California 90013
(213) 489-4250

Legal Tangle Delays Trial

In June, 1971, articles from the Pentagon Papers, a secret governmental account of the Vietnam War, appeared in the *New York Times*. Soon afterwards, Dan Ellsberg and Tony Russo were arrested. They were charged with stealing government documents, spying against the government, and conspiring to commit both these acts.

The Ellsberg-Russo trial (known as the Pentagon Papers Trial) began in early July of this year. By July 21, the jury was sworn in. But, three days later, Judge Byrne threw the case into total confusion. On that date, the judge admitted that the government had bugged a conversation carried on by a member of the defense team.

The defense argued that it was entitled to know the contents of the tapped conversation. This was denied by Judge Byrne on July 25. The next day the Ninth Circuit Court of Appeals backed up that decision.

The defense then appealed to Supreme Court Justice William O. Douglas, who hears cases from the Ninth Circuit for the Supreme Court. Justice Douglas ruled that the issues were important enough to delay the trial until the Supreme Court as a whole could decide whether it wanted to hear the defense motions.

The Supreme Court is now on vacation and will decide whether to hear the case when it reconvenes in October. If at that time the Court decides that it does not want to hear the arguments about the wiretapping, the trial will most likely start around the middle of October. If four justices decide that the case is important enough for the Supreme Court to hear, the trial will continue to be delayed and would probably not start again until after January, six months after the trial first began.

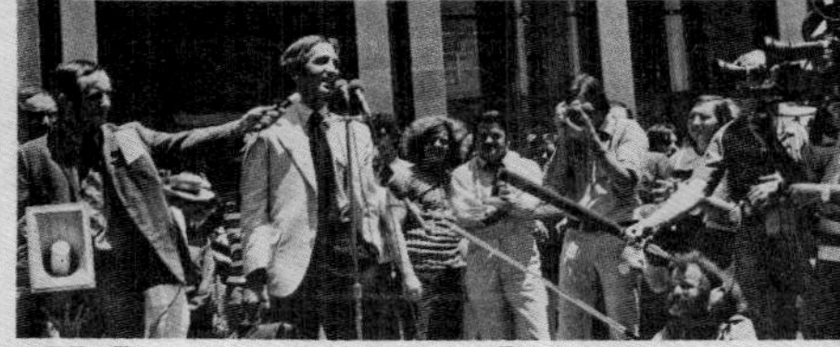

Ellsberg Meets the Press

President Nixon consciously planned to escalate the Indochina War from the moment he took office. His secret plan to end the war was in fact a new phase of escalation, involving all of the technological might that the U.S. could muster. A strategy in which the U.S. removed itself from Vietnam was never considered by the President and his policy-makers.

These were the points emphasized by Daniel Ellsberg at a news conference on August 22. Stating that Nixon embarked "on a conscious policy that precluded any possibility of peace then or now," the former government analyst and Rand researcher outlined the development of the Nixon policy.

Secret Operations

He also talked about some of the secret military operations which were carried out in the first ten weeks of the administration. These led to the widening of the war, and were the first steps of Nixon's escalation.

In December of 1968, Ellsberg was head of a Rand project which outlined the options available to the new administration. Developed at the request of top Presidential advisor Henry Kissinger, the paper listed seven possible courses of action. These ranged from total war to unilateral American withdrawal.

A second draft of the paper was sent to the National Security Council, to be formally considered as the basis for the new policy. Although this draft was described to the press as encompassing "the complete range of options," there was one important difference between the second draft and the first. In the second draft, Kissinger eliminated the option of a planned American withdrawal by a fixed date. The National Security Council was presented with six possible strategies, each of which guaranteed a continued military involvement in Vietnam. Each demanded the survival of the Thieu regime.

The plan which was adopted — Nixon's "secret plan to end the war" — turned out to be a policy of escalation. While troop withdrawals were being carried out, the bombing increased.

Nixon's Escalation

At the press conference Ellsberg described three secret operations which took place in 1969 to show North Vietnam that the U.S. was prepared to escalate the war.

The first of these was a prolonged Marine invasion of Laos. Heavy B-52 raids were then carried out in Cambodia. Navy frogmen were sent into Haiphong harbor. They were deliberately allowed to be detected by the North Vietnamese. This operation was never made public until the Ellsberg press conference. It was meant to be a signal to the North Vietnamese that the U.S. was prepared to mine the port.

Ellsberg's main point was that the Administration never considered a policy of withdrawal — a policy favored by 73 percent of the American people. While Nixon talked peace, he made preparations for further war.

Local Labor Backs McGovern

"We're going to enthusiastically support him."

With this statement, Gordon McCullough, head of the Carpenters Union District Council of Southern California AFL-CIO, joined dozens of other labor officials in both local and state AFL-CIO bodies across the country which have publicly backed the presidential candidacy of Senator George McGovern.

These endorsements, opposing the decisions of the national AFL-CIO leadership under George Meany, have sent shock waves throughout the organized labor movement. They could produce important changes in the Federation well past the November elections.

Convention Controversy

The controversy was apparent at the California State AFL-CIO convention held in Los Angeles in late August. Although the convention failed to pass any presidential endorsement, pro-McGovern feelings ran very high.

The delegates were undecided at the early stages at the convention. Al Barkan, national COPE (Committee on Political Education) director, was mildly booed when he defended AFL-CIO president George Meany's position of not supporting either McGovern or Nixon. Resolutions calling for Nixon's defeat were submitted by three Bay Area labor organizations. But the state AFL leadership would not allow a floor vote on these resolutions or any other motions favorable to McGovern.

But when Senator John Tunney (Dem.-Calif.) addressed the convention and called for a McGovern victory, he received a standing ovation. This led to a meeting of delegates from almost 75 unions, which formally set up a Local Labor for McGovern Committee.

The revolt in Southern California is typical of events which have taken place in AFL-CIO organizations since the Democratic convention. Meany and the top AFL leadership backed Humphrey for the nomination. After McGovern was nominated, the 35 member AFL Executive Council met and passed a resolution declaring the Federation's neutrality in the campaign. The motion was pushed through by Meany, despite strong resistance.

Warnings Issued

Meany then sent out strong warnings against supporting McGovern to all state and local councils. Punitive sanctions were threatened if they did, although individual unions could take a position in the campaign.

Opposition to Meany's orders from state and local labor officials and rank and file members has grown. This represents an increasing opposition to national AFL policies. Meany has been a strong supporter of Nixon's Vietnam policy, and has lobbied in Congress for the SST, the ABM, and higher defense budgets. He sat on the pay board, helping to enforce Nixon's wage freeze.

McGovern Support Grows

Such actions have eroded Meany's support within the unions. Support for McGovern is now rising in the labor movement, and many unions both in and out of the AFL-CIO are planning to work for McGovern.

A National Labor Committee for McGovern has been formed, with 27 AFL-CIO units joining so far. These include many of the nation's largest unions, such as the United Auto Workers, the Meatcutters, the Machinists, and many others.

The committee's aim is to use its $250,000 budget to put out literature and publicity to encourage the rank and file to vote for McGovern. In many parts of the country, including Southern California, Local Labor for McGovern Committees are working closely with the McGovern campaign.

At this time, the McGovern candidacy may have only a slight effect on the AFL-CIO and the labor movement as a whole. But new relationships are developing between the Democratic Party regulars, pro-McGovern union leaders, and the McGovern campaign organization. The rank and file may now be stimulated to challenge the traditional union leadership during and after the elections.

"What we need are not more millions on welfare rolls, but more millions on payrolls."
—1968 Campaign Brochure

"Government must say what it means and mean what it says. Economic credibility is the basis for confidence, and confidence is the basis for an ongoing prosperity."
—1970 Economic report to Congress

Nixonomics

On June 22, 1970, Nixon vetoed the hospital construction bill which provided for 50,000 jobs. (Congress overrode veto.)

In addition, 2.6 million jobs were lost when Nixon refused to use $12 billion in funds appropriated by Congress.

On December 16, 1970, Nixon vetoed the manpower training and employment bill which would have provided 360,000 public service jobs.

On June 29, 1971, Nixon vetoed the accelerated public works bill that would have created 420,000 jobs in communities with high unemployment.

The Next Two Weeks

SUN 27

Graphic Exhibition — "Rising Cry for Justice." 2626 W. Jefferson Blvd., now thru Aug. 30. Free

Slide Show Workshop. 10-3. Call 477-0968 for address.

Fair — Ballet Folklorico, Booths. Brand Park — San Fernando Mission. 10 A.M. — 10 P.M., Historical Pageant, 8 P.M.

Pacific Brass Quintet. County Museum of Natural History, 2:30 P.M. Free.

Jo Wilkinson/Lightning Hopkins. Ashgrove, 8 P.M. $3.00

Summer Dance Symposium. Bill Heiden's Cabaret Theatre, Lomita. 8:30 P.M. Free.

MON 28

Art Exhibition at Century Square. Century City.

Self-Help Clinic for Women. Westside Women's Center, 218 Venice Blvd., Venice.

Harrison & Tyler (feminist comedy team). **Lightnin' Hopkins** (thru Sept. 3). Ash Grove, 8 P.M.

Chicago (thru Sept. 3). Greek Theater.

TUES 29

People's March. Begins at Noon, Beacon Park (1st & Beacon). Call 263-2121 for details.

Pregnancy Screening. Westside Women's Center, 218 Venice Blvd., Venice. 2-6 P.M.

Debate between McGovern and Nixon representatives. Sponsored by Senior Citizens. Beverly-Carlton Hotel, 9400 W. Olympic Blvd., L.A. 7 P.M.

The Kinks/Taj Mahal. Santa Monica Civic Auditorium, 8 P.M. $4, $5, $6.

WED 30

Last Soul Caravan Concert. 3 hours of music, 12 Noon-3 P.M., Rancho Cienega Recreation Center, 5001 Rodeo Road. Free!

Women's Self-Help Clinic. 746 Crenshaw, L.A., 7:30 P.M.

Tony Bennett Concert. Hollywood Bowl, 8:30 P.M. $1.50-$8.50.

THURS 31

Plan your menus for September. Look for good food values in: turkey, eggs, dry beans, peanuts, fresh apples, and some fresh vegetables.

San Diego International Congress of African Peoples. (thru Sept. 4). For info, call 586-6181.

National Dance Company of Mexico. "Fiesta Folklorico." (thru Sept. 9). Pilgrimage Theater, 8 P.M., $2.50-$5.50.

Stevie Wonder. Whiskey A Go Go, thru Sept. 4.

FRI 1

"The Glass Menagerie." (thru Oct. 21). Oxford Playhouse.

Party for Kathy O'Neill. Larry Sherman speaks out for McGovern. 1344 Marinette, Pacific Palisades. 7:30 P.M. Call 454-6650 for info.

Idyllwild Festival Chamber Choir. Bowman Theater, I.S.O.M.A.T.A., Idyllwild, Calif., 8:15 P.M., $3 adults, $1 students.

Jane Fonda speaks on Elections and the War. Slide show on the dikes. 8:30 P.M., The Long March, 715 S. Parkview, L.A. Donation.

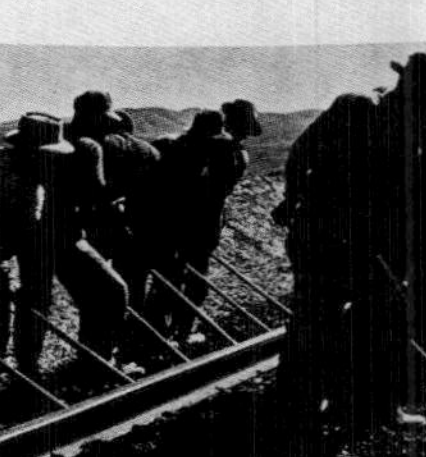

Wayne Miller, *LIFE*

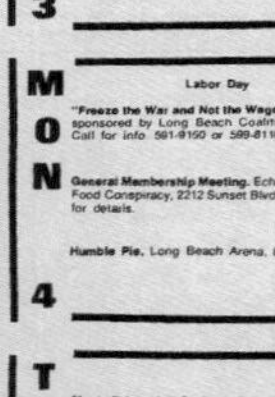

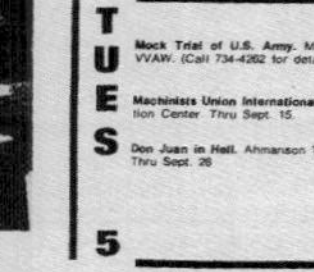

Walter Sanders, *LIFE*

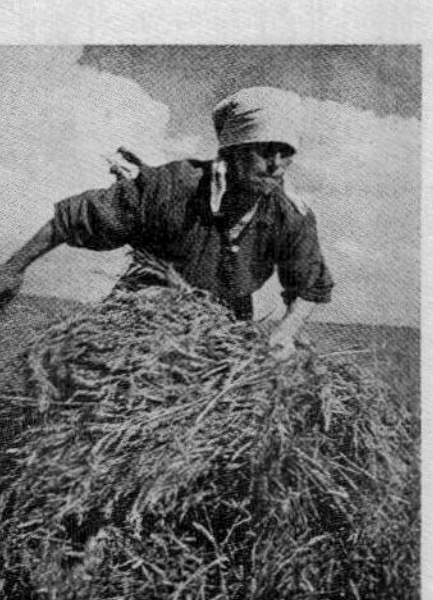

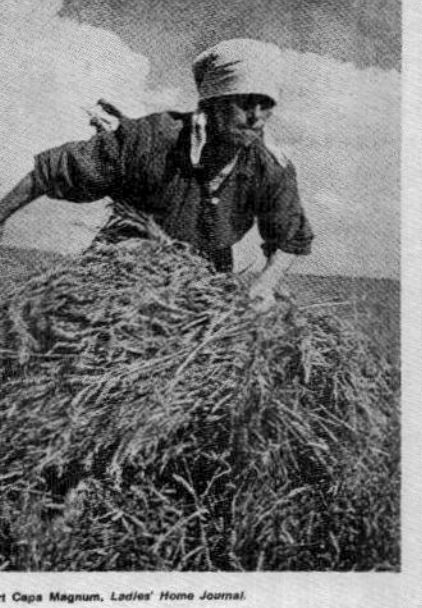

Robert Capa Magnum, *Ladies' Home Journal*.

Events, Times, and Places subject to change.

SAT 2

Pentagon Papers Peace Project. Anthony Russo, speaker. Guerilla Theater & Slide Show. 8:30 P.M., The Long March, 715 S. Parkview, L.A. Donation.

Idyllwild Festival Orchestra. Bowman Theater, I.S.O.M.A.T.A., Idyllwild, Calif. 8:15 P.M. $3 Adults; $1 Students.

SUN 3

Idyllwild Festival of the Arts. 2-part concert, festival choir, orchestra & soloist. 3 P.M. & 7:30 P.M., Bowman Theater. $3.00 adults; $1.00 students.

Fund raiser for McGovern. Musical evening, 12824 Evanston, L.A., 6-10 P.M.

MON 4

Labor Day

"Freeze the War and Not the Wages." March and rally sponsored by Long Beach Coalition. 11 A.M.-3 P.M. Call for info 591-9160 or 599-8118.

General Membership Meeting. Echo Park — Silverlake Food Conspiracy, 2212 Sunset Blvd., L.A. Call 487-4262 for details.

Humble Pie. Long Beach Arena. 8 P.M. $4, $5, $6.

TUES 5

Mock Trial of U.S. Army. Monterey, sponsored by VVAW. (Call 734-4262 for details.)

Machinists Union International Convention. Convention Center. Thru Sept. 15.

Don Juan in Hell. Ahmanson Theater, Music Center. Thru Sept. 26.

WED 6

Opening of Billy Dean Smith Trial. Massive demonstration in Monterey: March to Fort Ord.

THURS 7

Music and Dances of Mexico. UCLA, outside Schoenberg Hall. 12 noon; free.

F.D.R. Sunset Democratic Club. Meet local candidates. For info, call Adrianna Babior, 487-6930.

FRI 8

Bring your lunch to the Brown Bag Concert. Virgil Patterson Inter-racial Choir, 11:45-1:45 P.M., Lafayette Park, Wilshire & Hoover. Free.

Film: The Organizer, starring Marcello Mastroianni. The Long March, 715 S. Park View, L.A., Donation. 8:30 P.M.

AMEX-CANADA
P.O. Box 189 Station P
Toronto, Ontario, Canada
M5S 2S7

Second Class Mail Registration Number 2364
Return Postage Guaranteed
Second Class postage paid at Toronto Terminal A

UNITY STATEMENT OF U.S. WAR RESISTERS ON AMNESTY

As people who have been opposed to the U.S. government's war in Indochina and face prosecution or other loss of rights because of our opposition, we demand universal, unconditional amnesty. This does not mean forgiveness or forgetfulness for our acts of resistance, of which we are proud. Nor does it mean that we are begging permission to "return to the American fold." We are calling on the American people to demand with us that the U.S. government stop any efforts to prosecute us or deny our rights because of our just acts of resistance.

Specifically, we demand immediate amnesty without conditions (such as alternate service) and without case-by-case review, for:

- all military resisters (including "deserters") and draft resisters, whether in exile or underground in the U.S.;

- all persons who, because of their opposition to the war and the military, have been administratively punished, convicted by civilian or military courts, or are subject to prosecution; and

- all veterans with less-than-honorable discharges.

The war in Southeast Asia is not over. We demand that the U.S. government fully implement the Cease-Fire Agreements and thereby immediately cease all military operations in Southeast Asia, and support of its client governments in Indochina, and insist upon the release of all political prisoners in South Vietnam.

Some of us are in exile; some of us have made permanent homes outside the U.S.; most people who need amnesty are in the U.S. Some of us do or will need to surface from underground, return from exile, or fight for individual upgrading of less than honorable discharges. (We call on all who support us to help in this case-by-case legal work while continuing the fight for amnesty.) But wherever we live, and wherever we see our future, we are one in the conviction that it was right to resist participation in the U.S. government's war in Indochina. This is what we mean by amnesty.

--adopted in Vancouver, B.C., Canada, December 14, 1973, by the Coalition of American War Resisters in Canada (CAWRC), composed of the following groups:
Vancouver American Exiles Association, 130 W. Hastings, Vancouver, B.C.;
Vancouver Committee to Assist War Objectors, P.O. Box 34231, Vancouver;
Edmonton Committee to Assist War Objectors, 10140-122 St., Edmonton, Alta.;
Calgary Committee on War Immigrants, 1507-3524 31st St. N.W., Calgary, Alta.;
Regina Committee to Assist War Objectors, 2500 College Ave., Regina, Sask.;
Winnipeg Committee to Assist War Objectors, 175 Colony St., Winnipeg, Man.;
Ottawa Aid Committee, #3, 121 Glenora, Ottawa, Ont.;
Toronto Anti-Draft Programme, 11-1/2 Spadina Rd., Toronto, Ont.;
AMEX-CANADA, P.O. Box 189 Station P (614 Huron St.), Toronto, Ont.;
American Refugee Service, c/o Yellow Door, 3625 Aylmer, Montreal, Quebec;
Halifax Committee to Aid American War Resisters, 1671 Argyle, Halifax, N.S.

WE, INDIVIDUAL WAR RESISTERS AND FAMILIES, ENDORSE THE STATEMENT
(name) (address--optional) (phone--optional)

RETURN SIGNED STATEMENTS TO: Jack Colhoun, at AMEX

amex→canada

OCTOBER 74

Published by Americans exiled in Canada 60¢

BOYCOTT

EARNED RE-ENTRY

• SIXTH YEAR: VOLUME 5-NUMBER 1, WHOLE NUMBER 40 •

amex→canada

NOV-DEC 74

Published by Americans exiled in Canada 60¢

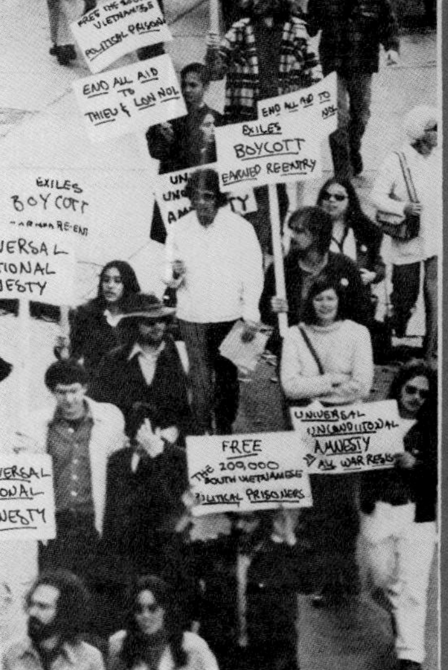

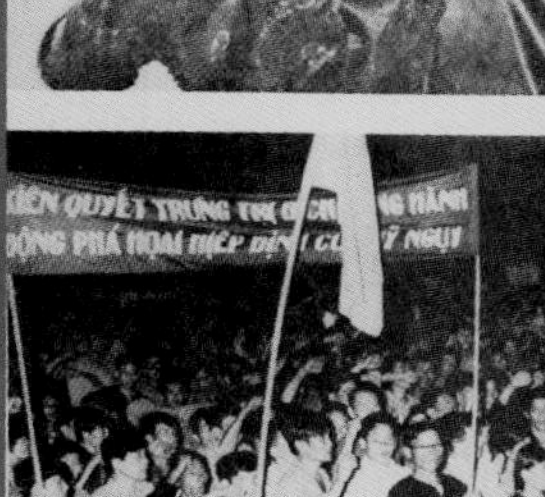

FORD'S 'CLEMENCY' FLOPS

(Inside: Legal Alternatives to 'Earned Re-entry')

THIEU REGIME COLLAPSING

(Inside: In-depth Analysis of Current Situation)

VOLUME 5, NUMBER 2 [SIXTH YEAR] WHOLE NUMBER 41

Previous page
Fig. 5.17 (cont'd.) **Pac-O-Lies** (New York), December 25, 1969, vol. 1, no. 2, cover; March 1970, vol. 1, no. 3, cover; the **Pentagon Paper** (Los Angeles), September 1982, no. 4, cover; August–September 1972, no. 3, back cover

Fig. 5.17 (cont'd.) **Amex_Canada,** January–March 1974, vol. 4, no. 6, cover; October 1974, vol. 5, no. 1, cover; November–December 1974, vol. 5, no. 2, cover

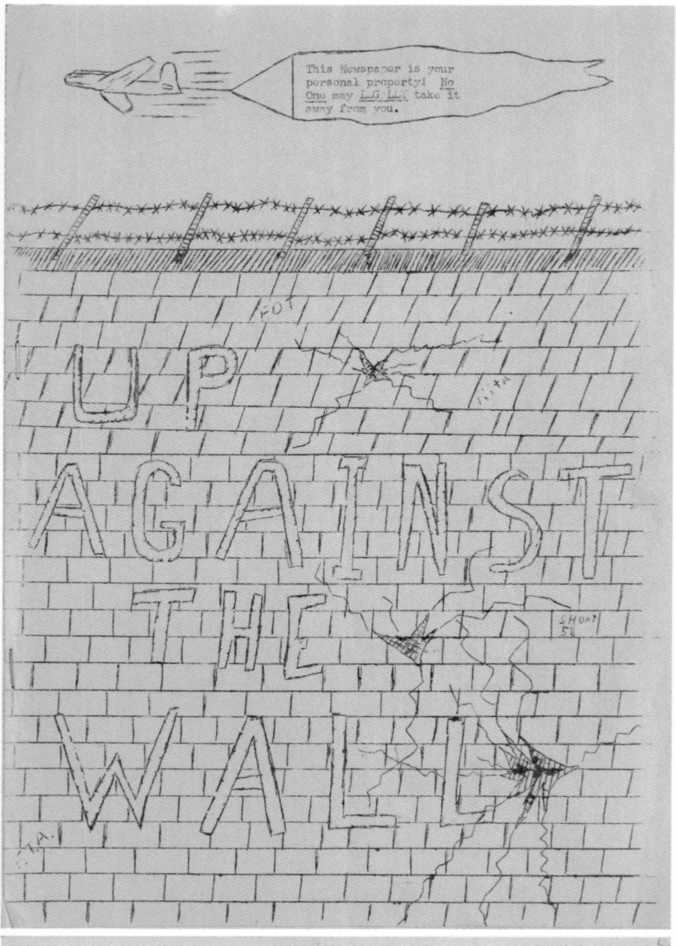

IN ORDER TO GIVE FELLOW GIs AN OPPORTUNITY TO GET TOGETHER AND FREELY DISCUSS MUTUAL PROBLEMS, MEETINGS WILL BE HELD ON FEBRUARY 22 and MARCH 8 (those are Sundays) AT THE ZENTRIFUGE, SYBEL STRASSE 38 (see map below) AT 8:00 P.M. (that's 2000 hours for you lifers). FREE FILMS ABOUT THE U.S. WILL BE SHOWN! PLANS FOR A FUTURE GI COFFEE HOUSE CLOSE TO McNAIR AND ANDREWS WILL BE DISCUSSED. SO BRING YOUR GRIPES AND IDEAS. WE MUST GET TOGETHER AND HELP OURSELVES!!!

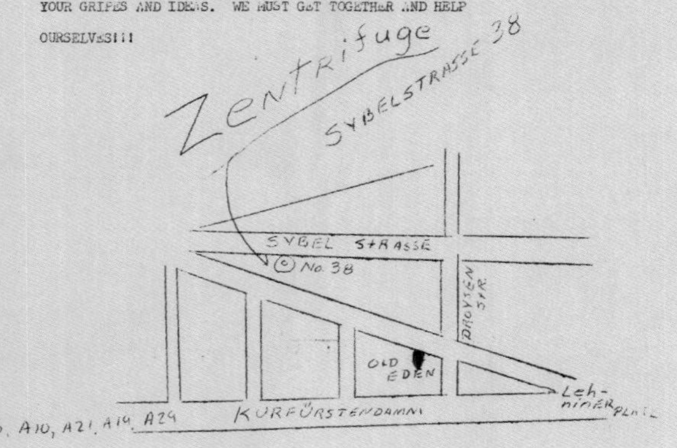

EASY TO FIND: Sybel Strasse is parallel to the Kurfürstendamm.
The Zentrifuge is only one block from the OLD EDEN.
McNAIR: Take the No. 1 Bus to the Kurfürstendamm and walk -- or transfer to No. 19 Bus and ride to Joachimfriedrich Strasse.
ANDREWS: Take the No. 85 Bus from the corner of Kadettenweg and Ring Strasse. Transfer at Wittenbergplatz to the No. 19 or 29. Get out at Joachim-Friedrich-Strasse and walk one block to Sybel Strasse.

RIGHT ON

MESSAGE TO A WHITE MAN

We have formed some of the worst habits. We talk too much. We are of the assumption that talking is a job, that it is accomplishing something.

The white man should get the hint. We are tired and need a rest.

We are overworked—from building your country and fighting your wars without pay.

A jackass bucks when overloaded. Now we are at the point that we just change our course. We have tried to work it out with you but all you do is pass the buck, which you call a bill.

Now we are going to change. We can't use force because we are not armed, but you taught us that God is the strongest, so we are trying him. If that does not work we have a secret weapon that has got to be respected.

I want an accounting. You have yours. Give me mine.

Where the black man is often at the very bottom of the mammoth pyra[mid] the poor white person and the working white man and woman sometimes are also at the bottom or only one layer above the black population. If they would only turn around and take the hand in friendship of their black fellow worker and the unemployed poor and unemployable workers and unite and struggle against the oppressive system that i[s] characterized by the philosophy and outlook of a George Wallace. I[f] they would turn their energy and effort to unite together against these conditions - as individuals, and together - to change these conditions, we would achieve a decent life to live for all people.

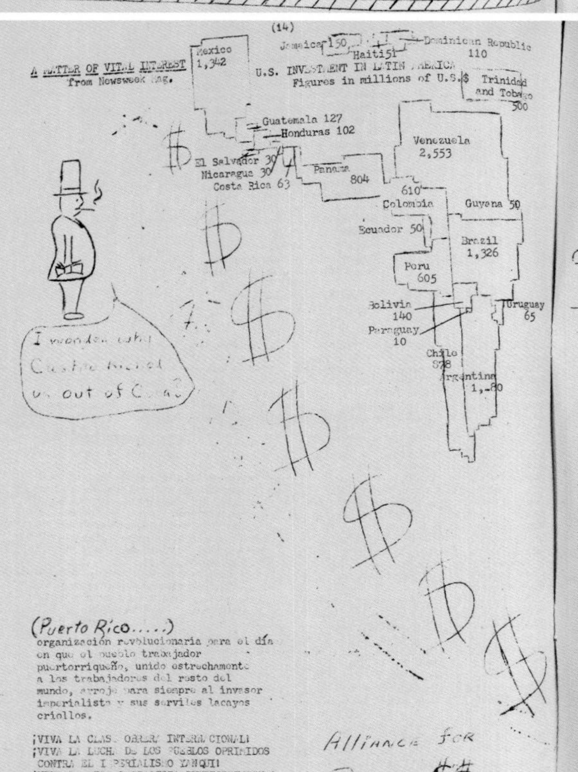

CYA

a public service for GIs

Part of army life is to "COVER YOUR ASS." Unfortunately the Lifers have the upper hand and are much better at covering theirs: This section is dedicated to helping the EM cover theirs.

* * * * * * *

UNLAWFUL ORDERS - A GI must obey lawful orders as that is the performance of his duty. But too often GIs are told to obey all orders first, and if they question them, to then complain through the chain of command. Since actually using the chain of command is rarely attempted by GIs, the person who does use it to file a complaint may be subject to much harassment and thereafter be branded a "troublemaker". If a "superior" dislikes you he can easily make you perform all sorts of degrading and boring details. He tells you they are only part of your duty, but he is really using them to get you. It is often this sort of thing that makes the life of a GI both miserable and pointless. GIs threatened with this sort of "punishment" are traditionally afraid to assert even the most basic rights. Many thus become only manipulated things with actually no rights at all.

Others have tried the chain of command and found the deck was stacked against them. Some few have gotten satisfaction through the chain of command. But frequently their rights were only manipulated so that they thought they were getting them.

If then the chain of command is so useless, what can a GI do? First, if there is some amount of solidarity in the unit, it can be arranged for a number of fellow GIs to raise the same complaint. No commander can afford to dismiss a united protest as mere griping, since this co[uld] have bad effects on the "morale of the troops". However, this protest should not take the form of a mass visit to t[he] I.G. or higher commander for the simpl[e] reason that such mass action scares he[ll] out of officers because it looks too m[uch] like a "mutiney." A series of individ[ual] visits is much better. But remember, [this] will work only where there is solidari[ty] in the unit. As long as GIs aren't to[-]gether, as long as they are content to [see] their buddies mistreated when the same thing is not happening to them, as long as they are timid and afraid in the fac[e] of illegal harassment, they have no ri[ghts].

Orders, to be legal, must pertain to military duty. Futhermore they may not [be] in violation of orders of higher autho[rity] intended to protect "inferiors" nor ma[y] they demand the performance of an act itself illegal. Details ordinarily as[sign]ed by duty roster, and all regular det[ails] may not be assigned as punishment exce[pt] under Article 15.

If you decide to disobey what you kn[ow] is an illegal order, don't do it by directly disobeying the order. This w[ill] cause you to be punished under Article [for] insubordination. It also may lead to [a] charge of disrespect under Article 91.

YOU HAVE NOT CONVERTED A MAN BECAUSE YOU HAVE SILENCED HIM.

Join the American Serviceman's Union, $1.00, 156 Fifth Ave., N.Y.C. 10010

Re-enlist in the New Action Army, Intervene in the country of your choic[e]

Fig. 5.17 (cont'd.) **Up Against the Wall** (Berlin), 1970, no. 1, cover, back cover, pp. 10–11 and 14–15

Next page
Fig. 5.17 (cont'd.) **Up Against the Wall** (Berlin). May 1970, no. 5, pp. 2–3; 1970, no. 6, pp. 3–4

. . . . the wealth of this country."

Now that has got to mean that in the US there are two patriotisms. One for those who own and one for those who work--be they white collar, blue collar, infantry or ASA, black or white, red or brown. The first patriotism is the kind Nixon or any other lifer talks about. They call it National Interest. But what it really means is how much more profits the industrialists and financiers can drain out of us. Their patriotism is based on profit, on ### and ¢¢¢, and so they think that is good, that it is "patriotic":

1. to spend money on weapons, and more weapons, ...
2. to send EMs to protect their foreign factories and markets (and while doing so to destroy the weapons so they can make more)
3. to keep down wages, increase speed-up, charge high rents, and tax us heavily
4. and of course to keep us Americans divided among ourselves (for example, blacks against whites).

The second kind of patriotism--the common man's patriotism--sees things from the bottom side up. We don't think that it is a good idea:

1. to keep on spending money on missiles and rockets while millions of our own people are starving, while our cities are decaying.
2. to have a war. It kills or maimes many of us. And it only makes the profiteers rich. It makes us poorer. [illegible] takes [illegible] inflation [illegible] of our wages. Not to mention what speed-up and bad working conditions do to our health.
3. to waste our lives so a few can get richer.

We don't see a country run by a few for their personal profits.

Instead of basing our patriotism on profit--### and ¢¢¢--[illegible] it on the needs and desires of all the common people. Not profit needs and profit desires.

[illegible] we never talk about the problems of the lifers like President Nixon and the [illegible], [illegible], and [illegible]. [illegible] talk about the problems of the people who work for them--the lifer Brass [illegible]. What we wrote about were the problems that [illegible] working people, especially [illegible] are [illegible].

[illegible] is written by GIs from various backgrounds [illegible] [illegible]

F.T.A. IN

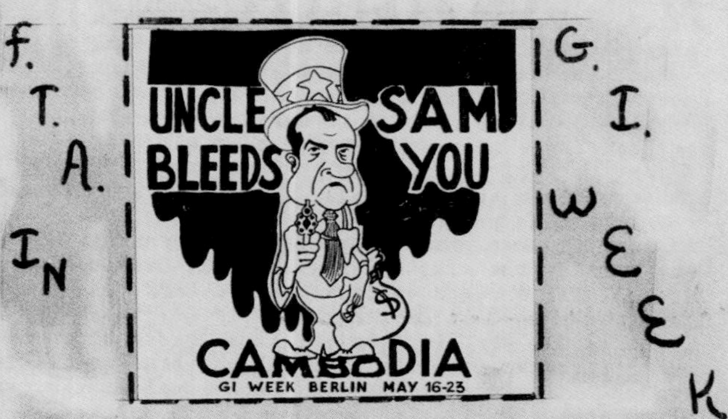

GI WEEK

Sitting around Berlin stoned out of our minds or doing some mox-nix details, Nixon's push into Cambodia or GI Week don't seem to have too much to do with us. Nixon says by going into Cambodia he'll shorten the war. Yea! Remember all those other military short-cuts that Kennedy & Johnson took. They led to the deaths of over a million Vietnamese and at least 42,000 US dead. Back home they caused such internal conflict that the US is turning into an undeclared war. How many others will be killed this time?

No! Nixon is playing with our lives. The war has got to stop. It is up to us to stop it - us, the guys who die for the rich in Washington.

Since about 1967, GIs have been working to stop the war. The GI movement has been rapidly growing. The Presidio Stockade, Fort Jackson 8, FT. Gordon 40, and ASU are now part of a common vocabulary. In Dec. 1969, 1000 active duty GIs and marines led 4000 civilians in a march against the war; in Oceanside, Calif. black and white marines at Camp Pendleton have formed the Movement For A Democratic Military. At FT. Dix black and white soldiers have formed The

-3-

3

EVERYBODY LOVES A PARADE!

A few weeks ago many guys were forced to march in the Allied Parade. How many of them would have liked to have seen it busted? Many Germans saw it the same way - they would have liked to put a stop to the lifers' show! But the Brass was so uptight they got the West Berlin cops to "protect" the U.S. Army. There were massive police lines, searches and ID controls, and barbed wire around the Technical University. Because they were warned that this repression would take place, many West Germans who opposed the parade stayed home. For those who came anyway, direct interference with the horror show was impossible.

Why is it that the German Left is against U.S. Military presence in West Berlin? They know - like we do - that West Berlin is impossible to defend from outside attack. Instead, the Army is here to back up the Berlin cops in maintaining "law and order," which means breaking up strikes and controlling dissenters. EMs are put on alert during every demonstration. What would happen if German workers struck a U.S. company like IBM on Ernst-Reuter-Platz? With U.S. control in Germany of 40% of the petroleum, 40% of the autos, 80% of the computer market, we can be sure the Army will be used to protect the bosses' profits and not to insure that workers' needs are met. That's no different than in Indochina where U.S. business sees a market worth $3 billion and what is more, a source of cheap labor. Already in Vietnam, U.S. Corporations like Johnson and Johnson, Foremost Dairies, International Harvester and Philco-Ford are enjoying high profits (Philco-Ford projects $1.7 billion through 1971). The Saigon government helps the large corporations

"Fuk zee Armee, Fuk zee Brass"

At the Allied Parade I tried to express my protest, together with some other German students and workers, against this obscene weapon-show. We shouted USA-SA-SS, referring to the latest crimes of the National Guard. Then the cops threw tear gas, pulled their rubber penises, and cleaned up the place so properly that they didn't fail to strike down an old veteran with a wooden leg until he stopped moving. Next they stormed the Technical University and the Art Academy with drawn guns, destroyed laboratories, pictures, and struck down who they wanted to. Over 300 employees and students were arrested from their working place. That's what SS and SA practice looked like in the beginning - we know from Nazi movies. Now we know how to resist next - militant only!

****

Note: This German student was formerly a lieutenant in the Bundeswehr. Now he helps distribute Up Against the Wall as part of "Project Partnership".

4

get rich by setting a maximum labor code of $1.40 a day.

This economic imperialism would certainly have grown unchecked had the people of Indochina not decided to take up the struggle to decide their own future.

And whether in Vietnam or Cambodia, West Berlin or the USA, when the people are dissatisfied and decide to fight for what they believe in, they're going to hit out at their enemy, the protector of the status quo. They react to GIs then not as they might treat a fellow working guy, but as a part of the US Police Machine. As long as the Machine protects U.S. Business and uses working guys as the backbone of that force, those guys are going to keep getting the brunt end of the deal. Germans who want an end to that U.S. control in their country are striking out at its protector. But at the same time they are sympathetic to the tight spot GIs are in. Among the many "USA-SA-SS" and "Ami go home" slogans yelled at the Parade were also to be heard "Fuck the Army," "Black Power," and "Fuck the Brass."

GIs all over the world are getting sick of the role we have to play. At home we are forced to work hard for the bosses' profit, while at the same time at home and abroad we are forced to be the cop in the Bosses' World Police Force, making sure other working guys keep the profits coming.

BEHIND THE RED DOT MYSTERY

There's some confusion about the meaning of those red dots you see on many cars' windshields. They simply mean that the people inside are offering free rides in town, but the army says that those people are dirty commie subversives who good soldiers should stay away from. That version sounds a little paranoid, but they may have a reason.

The dots are one practical way the workers and students of the German left have found of sticking together and taking care of their own. Solidarity is strength. Lifers know that better than anyone, so they try to keep guys apart - from each other and from potential allies.

No one is promising you that if you stick your thumb out you'll get an instant welcome; German students don't dig much about the American military. But increasingly they're realizing that it's not the lowly GI they should be fighting, but the Lifers and Super-Lifers who run things. The students who work with us passing out papers know this and are offering solid help.

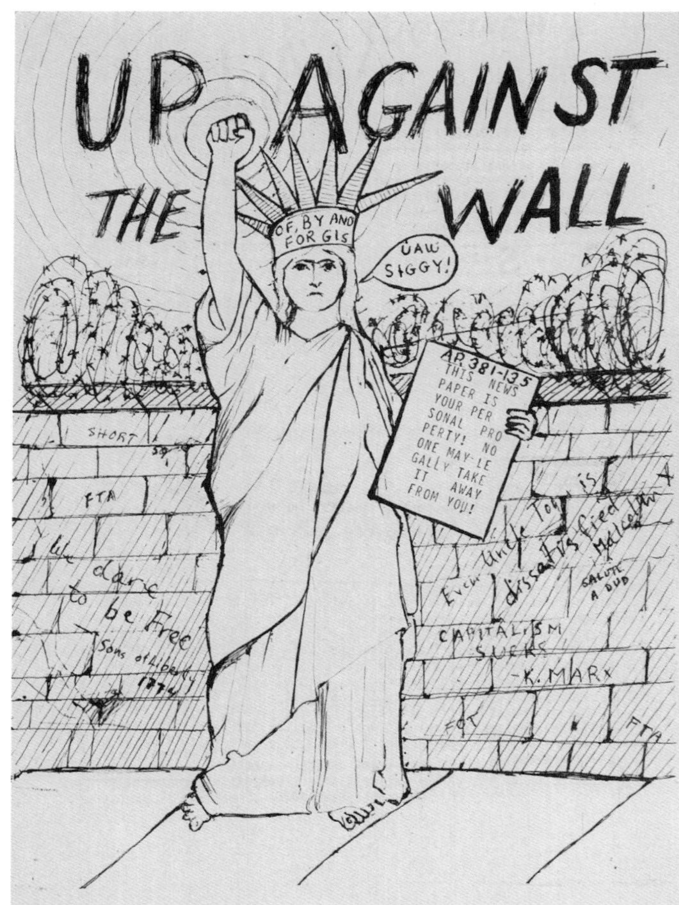

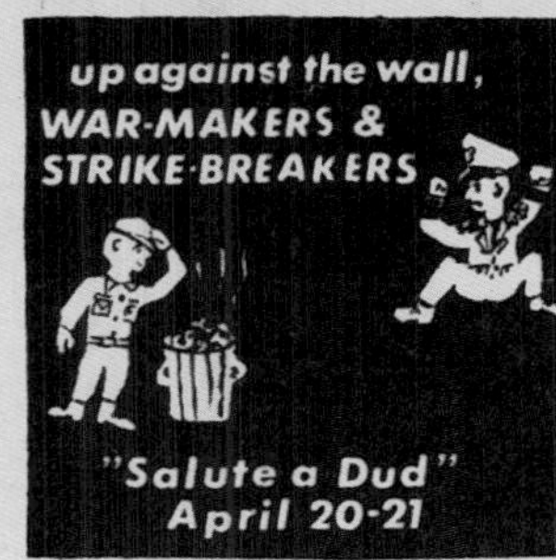

UP AGAINST THE WALL, in honor of our new General and his tireless efforts to improve our fighting readiness, is proclaiming "SALUTE A DUD WEEK" in Berlin, April 20-27. Already some GIs here are following the practice of saluting all the EM in front of an approaching officer. We'd like to carry this a step further. This week, SALUTE EVERYTHING!

The salute is supposed to be "just a greeting," but like constant inspections, haircut hassling, etc.etc.etc. it's just one more way the brass can make us aware of our lowly position and keep us there. We feel that if our beloved General deserves a greeting, then so do fellow EM, snackbar employees, trash cans, service club personnel, garbage collectors, little kids, trees, bulletin boards, buildings, construction workers, trucks, dogs, toilets, etc.

It definitely takes the thrill out of a salute for officers if they see everyone saluting everything in sight. And watch them try to stop it. As one GI at Hardt Casern, where the GI paper THE WITNESS promoted a "SALUTE A DUD WEEK", puts it: "What the hell can they do - order us not to salute anymore?"

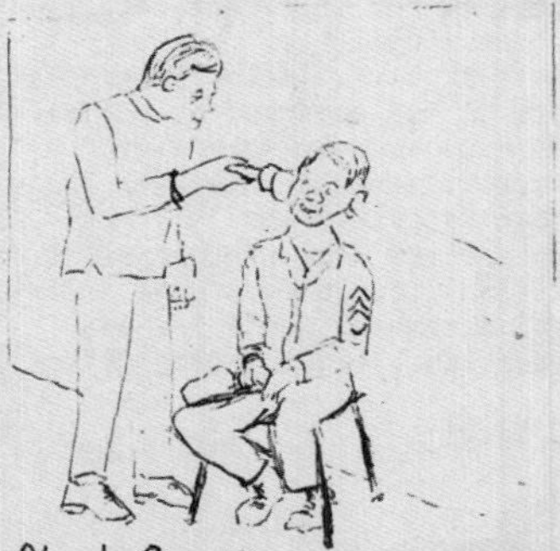

Aha! Another career man.

Has the army blown your mind? - If not ...

Up Against the Wall

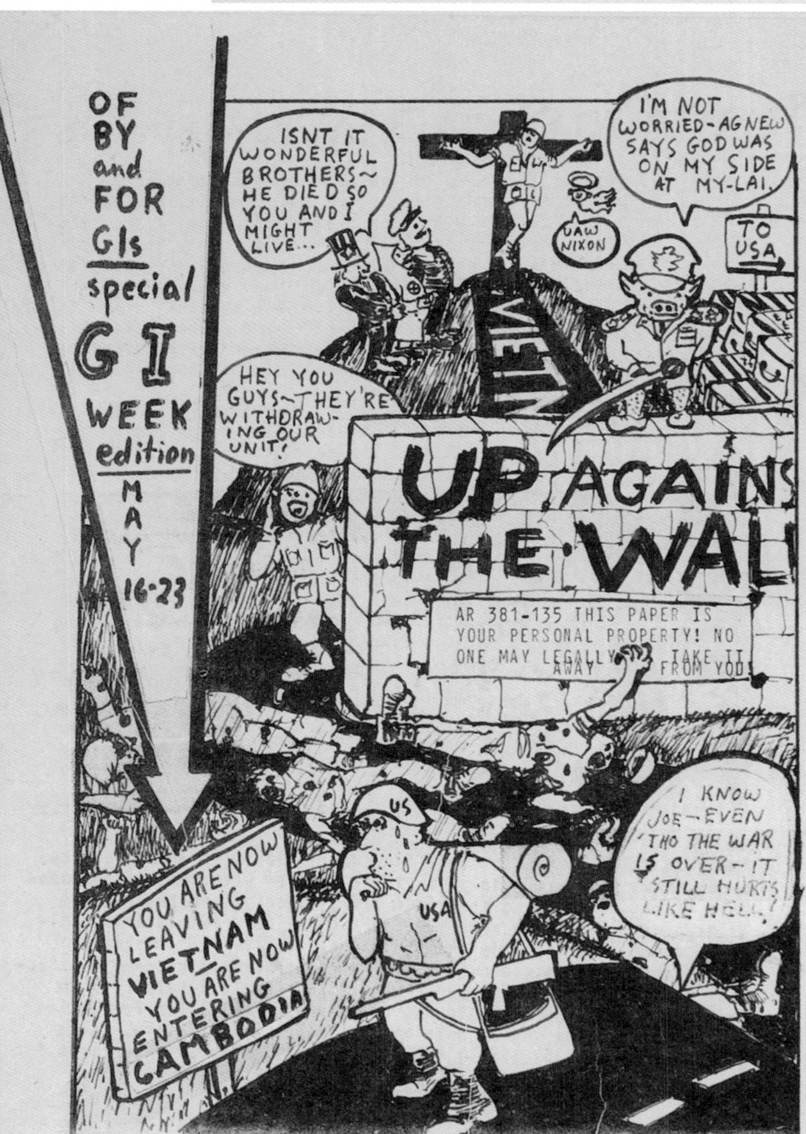

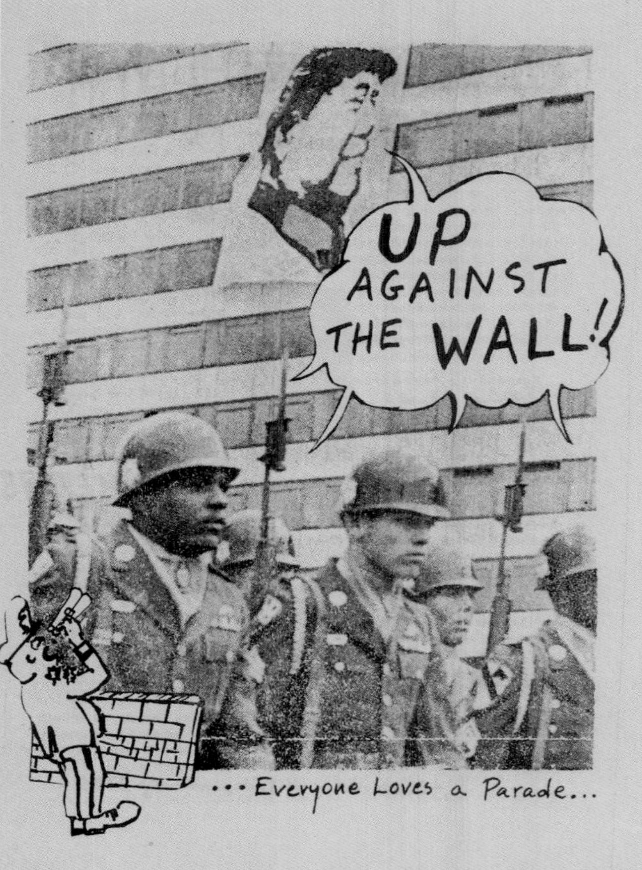

...Everyone Loves a Parade...

THE SECOND FRONT

THE OFFICIAL NEWSPAPER OF THE INTERNATIONAL UNION OF AMERICAN DESERTERS AND DRAFT RESISTERS---CANADIAN EDITION

To Stay or To Split

Many GIs who oppose the Vietnam war often have a tough time deciding whether it's right for them to cut out on the army and go underground in the states, or split to another country.

Up until recently most GIs knew only that deserters could be safe in France and Sweden and because those two countries are so far away, and speak different languages, many guys decided to stick it out in the service. They try to resist in the Army. Now this is a hard thing to do because the military is the most oppressive segment of our society and has a whole tradition of pushing people around and treating them like shit. It's a good idea to give out anti-war literature and rap with other servicemen and to organize something. But we know from experience that when you really get effective the brass cracks down.

In cases like that, when you know they are planning to come down on you hard, more and more guys seem to think that the only sensible thing to do is to split. Let's say you get orders to Nam. If you're against the war, if you think it's stupid to risk your life in a dumb war, you may wonder why the hell you should let them send you to Nam. If you see it boiling down to a choice between refusing orders and going to the stockade, on the one hand, and deserting on the other, you should understand that in case you do decide to desert it is possible to come to Canada. If this is what you choose to do, when you get that last furlough before shipping out, it is advisable to get your papers together (birth certificate, IDs, diplomas, etc.) and split.

This is especially a good idea now that it is clear you can safely come here to Canada. As a deserter working in a political community, like the American Deserters Committee is setting up here, you can really hurt them where it hurts most. You can write to your buddies, telling them what it's like here. Make your opposition really public. Show them you're a man who can still think for yourself despite all the indoctrination crap in the service. As more and more guys begin cutting out on the war, it'll be harder and harder for the army to keep it up; whoever heard of an army without soldiers?

They call you a man, and treat you like an animal; they feed you their line, and you think it's the truth. Remember in basic training: double time, chow line, right face, left face. They wanted you disciplined like a well-running machine, easy to control, easy to handle. They gave you a trade and called you a soldier. A soldier: a man ready to die for a cause they call your own, to kill a man they call your enemy. And you believed it: you swallowed the story lock, stock, and barrel. And after being so generous, and making you a soldier, they're still ready to do you more favors. They clothe you, and feed you, and pay for your transportation to the war, or wherever they need you. And when you die, they.ll pay for your funeral.

Bill Jones, Chairman
American Deserters
Committee, Sweden

Deserters Safe in Canada

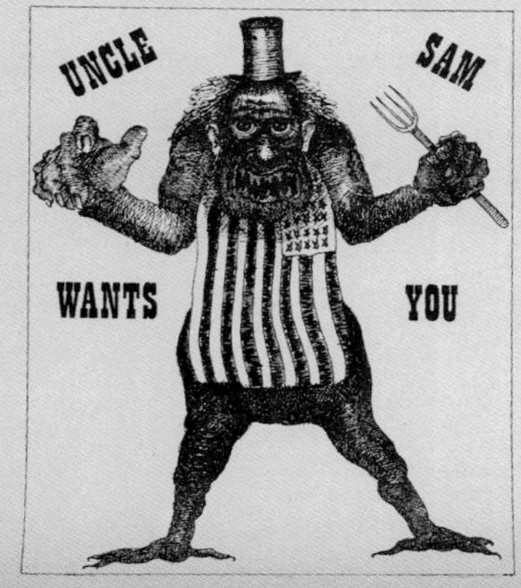

uncle pig, I quit!

Upon entering the military machine in the year of Our Lord? 1966 I found a way of life completely different from what I was accustomed to. It was a life of complete fear and confusion. They said they'd make a man out of me and then they taught me how to kill. I couldn't understand why I had to go through all this training in destruction because I was supposed to be a medical corpsman and save life without discrimination---not destroy life.

After my completion of Basic Training and a short time at Fort Sam Houston, Texas in what was supposed to be a medical school, although a .good amount of our time was spent on inspections, physical conditioning, drill and ceremony, and hand to hand combat, I did learn how to apply bandages and fill out medical forms. A short time after that I was sent to Vietnam to first, stop communist aggression and second, to save lives. After spending a year in the Republic of Vietnam and witnessing American imperialism at its highest level, I was returned home to spend six months in a hospital with hepatitis. It seemed like a dream to me. And I couldn't believe I was really home and everything was going to be OK or so I was told.

It took me the whole time I was in the hospital to learn how to sleep at night and how to eat and how to talk to people again. Sometimes I think if I would not have made it. I've been back a year now and still my mind haunts me---the screams of children being burnt, the look of hungry peasants, the feeling of life slipping out of your hands because you couldn't get to him fast enough. I still hear the cry "MEDIC" at night.

I remember the doctor coming in my room and saying "you're OK now. You can go back to duty." Then I woke up to the fact that it wasn't over, that I still had to complete my sentence before I could take off that uniform, of which I was not so proud of any more. So down to Fort Hood,Texas I went---only to find riot controls, segregation, prejudice, Wallace posters and a lot of fucked up people in total confusion. I spent a month or so down there and watched the Democratic Convention on TV and was told that I was going back to Vietnam Even though I had six months left and had a medical profile; Could it be that my rap was a little too strong or my friends weren't all white and my fear of the brass had gone and that reality was the name of the game I was playing and not Army? I'm afraid Uncle Pig will have to find someone else to do his killing for him because I QUIT! A great man once siad."To kill in war is not a wit better than to commit ordinary murder."

fraud?

THE PEACE TALKS...A FRAUD?

Since the beginning of the Paris Peace Talks a lot of soldiers found out that the talks do not diminish the danger to die in Viet Nam. Instead, they only hide the fact that the US Army is throwing more tons of bombs a day than ever before, and they hide the fact US Army more desperately than ever before enforces their efforts to gain ground in Viet Nam. The Peace Talks are not talks intended to lead to peace by negotiations, but an alibi for intensified war.

Are you or your friends planning to Desert from the US Military Machine? Here is some information we have compiled from guys who have actually deserted and who are now living in Canada LEGALLY:

First you must understand that in applying for Landed Immigrant Status in Canada, you are dealing with a government agency. This means that it takes time. Sometimes two or three months before final papers come through. The American government is not at all happy with Canada for taking draft resisters and deserters. So of course pressure is being put on the Immigration Department.

Canadian Immigration laws permit immigration of those who meet their standards regardless of whether or not a person has completed military service. This applies to those who refuse induction as well as those who have interrupted their military service by leaving the Armed Forces. Whether you are a draft resister, AWOL or deserter, this will not be held against you or prohibit you from receiving Landed Immigrant Status in Canada.

Nevertheless, there are still pressures on the Immigration Department. Because of this, the best thing for you to do is enter Canada as a visitor or tourist and contact the nearest anti-draft group or the American Deserters Committee here in Montreal.

When you come into Canada you have to stop at the border and they often ask you how long you are going to visit. You should give them a definite answer---like, visiting friends for a few days, or a week. The Immigration guy may ask you for some identification and want to know how much money you have. Don't show your military I.D.(but don't get rid of it either; it might come in handy later). Use a driver's license, or a birth certificate. Don't bring in any food, DRUGs, or animals. They won't let you in.

There are a certain number of things you must bring with you, if possible. Birth certificate to show proof of citizenship. Money, as much as you can possibly get legally. High school diploma. Any military diplomas you have. Letters of reference from priests, doctors, former employers, friends, etc.

If you can't get these papers, or are having trouble getting them, don't take the chance of getting busted. Come up to Canada and mail for the documents you need.

Recently the mass media have tried to distort the status of deserters here in Canada. Have no fear. Deserters can safely live in Canada. There are problems, that's true enough. What else can you expect when Canada is so close to the U.S. and so much of it is owned by the States. But you can be SAFE here. The Montreal Star, a major daily here recently reported that a spokesamn for the Minister of Manpower and Immigration had said that "If an American soldier on leave comes to Canada and then decides not to return to his unit he becomes a deserter under American law but this country(Canada) will do nothing to return him to the U.S.

Words of Wisdom ✂

Here is a sampling of what our president, Lyndon Baines Johnson, has been saying the past few years. Don't forget, LBJ is the man who brought Hubert Humphrey to the White House.

I hate war. And if the day ever comes when my vote must be cast to send your boy to the trenches, that day Lyndon Johnson will leave his senate seat to join with him.
Unsuccessful campaign for US Senate....Texas,1941.

Our one desire--our one determination--is that the people of southeast Asia be left in peace to work out their own destinies in their own way.
Washington,D.C.
Aug. 19,1964 and March 13,1965.

Now some people say I talk out of both sides of my mouth.
Washington,D.C.
April 27,1964.

Now you folks come on and be happy, come on and be happy.
St. Louis, Missouri
October 21,1964.

When we line them up at the reception centers to fit them for their uniforms, we don't say,"What is your church? What is your political affiliation? What section of the country do you live in and who was your grandpa?" We say, "Give him size 42...".
Baltimore,Maryland
October 1,1964.

NOW YOU FOLKS COME ON AND BE HAPPY, COME ON AND BE HAPPY.......

WHAT'S THE POINT?

Raymond Bryant joined the Army on February 17, 1965 and was sent to Vietnam April 2nd of the following year as an infantryman. He spent 13 months in Vietnam and received two purple hearts and a bronze star.

A few days after Ray arrived in Vietnam, his CO said to him, "I'm not the least bit prejudiced about your kind. I like to give the colored guys every chance in the world to prove themselves; that's why I'm going to place you right up front".

This was just the beginning of Ray's tour in Vietnam. Any books he had were confiscated and he was ridiculed for reading Malcolm X in his spare time. As punishment for his attitude, Ray's Sgt. made him point man and made him carry the radio too for three straight weeks without rotation. Normally, the point men are rotated every two hours and as Ray says, "If you are a careless POINT MAN then your chances of lasting the two-hour shift are slim".

However, Ray's most intolerable experience in Vietnam was when his Platoon Sgt. called Ray's platoon together and said to the men, " There's a very disagreeable person (namely, Ray) in our platoon. Because of his attitude he is a danger to all of us. Everyone knows who he is and I suggest that somebody should shoot him in the next fire-fight for the good of all of us!"

After he was sent back to Germany, Ray deserted and went to Paris. After several months he decided to come to Sweden and he is now living in the south of the country.

Ray's military career was filled with horrifying experiences like those above, yet now, because he deserted, he can look forward to a life free of harassment in Sweden.

United We Stand !!

I deserted the Army in January of 1968, and after spending a month in Germany, I came to France with the help of the German SDS. I'm not going into an explanation of why I deserted, because you know as well as I do that if you look at your situation in the Army and then start thinking about the war in Vietnam, there are many reasons why you should make your move to desert immediately.

After you desert, you will find many other Americans who have made the same decision before you, as well as many Americans living in France and Sweden who are resisting the draft. We have gotten together with the draft resisters to form the INTERNATIONAL SECOND FRONT.

We are working together to urge our buddies who are still in the Army to desert, and our friends back home who have so far escaped the draft to resist. We deserters are very glad to have the draft resisters working with us because they too have stood up in opposition to the war in Vietnam; they have risked jail sentences to resist being inducted into the Army.

To those of you who have not yet been inducted, we say this: find out what is going on in Vietnam before you are drafted; don't wait until you are in the Army to find out that you want no part of the war in Vietnam.

To those of you who are in the Army, we say this: your real friends are everyone who is opposed to the war in Vietnam; the people of the country where you are stationed will help you once you decide to desert.

Together, we deserters and draft resisters can work in our new homes to end the war as soon as possible.

Michael Jesus Garcia

BE A MAN,
not a war machine;
DESERT.

Vietnam's First Casualty

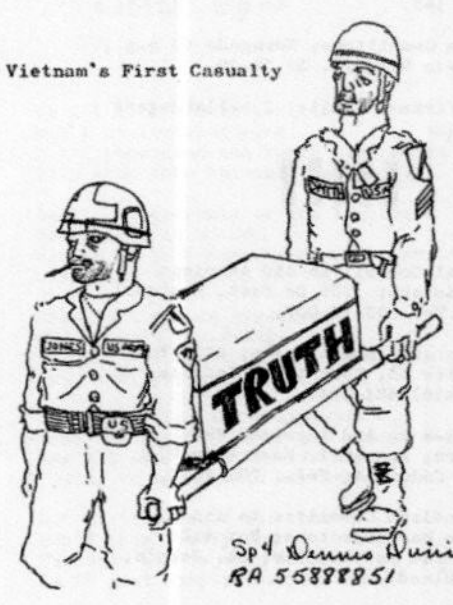

4

Tune in to
RADIO SECOND FRONT:
Vietnam & Germany

I'm No Machine !

I was inducted into the Army at Ashland, Kentucky in April of 1966 and was then sent to Ft. Knox for basic training. They tried to turn us into mindless animals so we'd be better killers in Vietnam. Their goal was to make us into machines which they could use to kill people around the world. To do this, they tried to destroy every inch of manhood and pride which we had. The Army doesn't make you a man, it makes you into a machine.

No man had any say in what he was supposed to do. We had to blindly follow the orders of N.C.O.'s who were doing everything in their power to break our will. They confiscated our personal belongings and would make us look like fools in front of other people. They once ordered me to scrub the floor with a toothbrush. If they saw us on the streets they would make us drop and do push-ups. Everybody who passed by would laugh at us, but now I know it was only because that was what the soldier-machine was trained to do.

When you are in the Army you feel like nobody because you have no freedom. They destroy every ounce of individuality that you have.

And suppose they send you to Vietnam and you're killed there. Your family will mourn but the Army will get another machine to replace you. They'll think, "He died in our war game like a stupid hero."

I deserted the 11th Air Defense Signal Battalion in Kaiserslautern, Germany on March 20, 1968 and went to Amsterdam, Holland to find safety from the U.S. Army. I contacted an organization there to help me get to Sweden and they told me that I could also go to France if I wanted to. I decided to come to Paris and am now working with the French Union of American Deserters and Draft Resisters. I am living in a small town outside of Paris and have a very good job.

If you want to deny that you're just an Army machine, desert, because if you hesitate they will probably decide to send you to Vietnam and sacrifice your life in a worthless war and replace you with another machine after you are killed.

Gerald Meek, E3
X-RA 15755057

DESERTION FACT SHEET: SWEDEN

Deserters granted asylum with the full rights of a Swedish citizen.

Deserters eligible for social security benefits, housing, jobs, food and clothing allowances, and Swedish lessons by the government. Medical and legal expenses free.

There are now over 170 deserters in Sweden.

Over 80% of the Swedish people support the Vietnamese struggle for liberation.

•••

DESERTION FACT SHEET: FRANCE

Deserters given permission to live and to work in France.

Housing with French families and jobs all over France. French lessons. Medical and legal services free.

There are now over 50 deserters in France.

Over 72% of the French people support the Vietnamese struggle for liberation.

Previous page
Fig. 5.17 (cont'd). **Up Against the Wall** (Berlin), April 1970, front and back covers, May 1970, cover; June 1970, cover

Fig. 5.17 (cont'd). **The Second Front,** Canadian edition, cover; September 1968, vol. 1, no. 2, back cover was busted twice for possession of quantities of marijuana so tiny that they "disappeared" under analysis. With only months to go before his discharge, he was sentenced to eight years of hard labor at Leavenworth.[22] Terry Irvin was even court-martialed for distributing copies of the Declaration of Independence at McChord Air Force Base on July 4, 1971.[23]

Incarceration in a base stockade or at Fort Leavenworth was a very serious matter. Abuse of prisoners was commonplace. Randy Roland remembers that during his incarceration, "one night every prisoner in the hole got their legs broken. The guards came in and broke their legs .... Another time a sergeant sat on [a prisoner], sat on him and bent his thumb back until his thumb broke .... They put another guy's head in a cell door and slammed it, cracked his skull."[24]

Out in the civilian world, the federal government's response to the underground press explosion was also "extra-legal" in the extreme. Especially after Richard Nixon took office in 1969, the FBI targeted these publications. The *Nola Express* in New Orleans and the *Rat* in New York City came under extensive FBI surveillance. During 1969–1970 the editor of Miami's *Daily Planet* was arrested twenty-nine times and acquitted twenty-eight, posting a total of $93,000 in bond (a staggering sum for an underground activist in 1969). The FBI sent phony letters designed to exacerbate internal tensions at LNS[25] and even launched three phony underground papers of its own, as well as three phony news services. Army intelligence got into the act and burglarized the *Free Press* in Washington.[26] Perhaps more effectively, FBI agents worked behind the scenes pressuring record companies to pull the ads that financed many underground papers.[27]

What the FBI began, the fading of "the movement" completed. Much more than advertising revenue, the key resource that kept the underground press running was the social energy of the youth insurgency that swept the nation, which provided a steady pool of people willing to work long hours for little or no compensation other than the thrill of making and experimenting. When this river began to run dry, and record company advertising was pulled in response to FBI pressure, underground papers confronted a crisis. Some survived through increasing reliance on sex ads in the personals, a practice that began as an expression of "free love" ethics and degenerated into crass pornography. A few managed to transition from an activist-run journal to a professional enterprise without losing focus on their core social and political objectives. *Mother Earth News*, for example, emerged from the widespread "back to the land" movement of the early 1970s and survives to this day as a journal of organic gardening and culture. Others ramped up to become the ubiquitous urban arts and culture weeklies of the 1980s and 1990s. Most simply folded, and their largely volunteer staffs moved on to other pursuits.

THE EMERGENCE OF THE INTERNET and related information technology has been accompanied by a deluge of writing about the profound changes in publishing that have come in its wake, but there is widespread confusion about what is actually new in this digital frontier. Thus Clay Shirky, one of the more thoughtful heralds of the new age, contrasts the publishing environment offered by the Internet with the newspaper environment that came before: "No one can found a newspaper on a moment's notice, run it for two issues, and then fold it, while incurring no cost but leaving a permanent record."[28] Not true. The sixties were awash in newspapers founded on a moment's notice and run for a few issues that incurred minimal cost and left a permanent record. Many such papers can be seen in the pages of the book you are now holding. The seminal lesbian feminist underground paper, *The Furies* (fig. 5.18), to name just one, was started by a collective household of women who each chipped in a few dollars and published just a few issues over the course of less than a year, and yet it became hugely influential among lesbians in the second half of the twentieth

22. Author's interview with Dave Cline, September 30, 2003.

23. Willa Seidenberg and William Short, *A Matter of Conscience: GI Resistance During the Vietnam War* (Andover: Addison Gallery of American Art, undated), p. 44.

24. Author's interview with Randy Roland, October 15, 2003.

25. Peck, *Uncensoring the Sixties*, p. 132.

26. Ibid., 142.

27. Ibid., 176.

28. Clay Shirky, *Here Comes Everybody: The Power of Organizing without Organizations* (New York: Penguin, 2008), p. 170.

the furies

lesbian/feminist monthly

march-april 1972 volume 1 issue 3

35¢

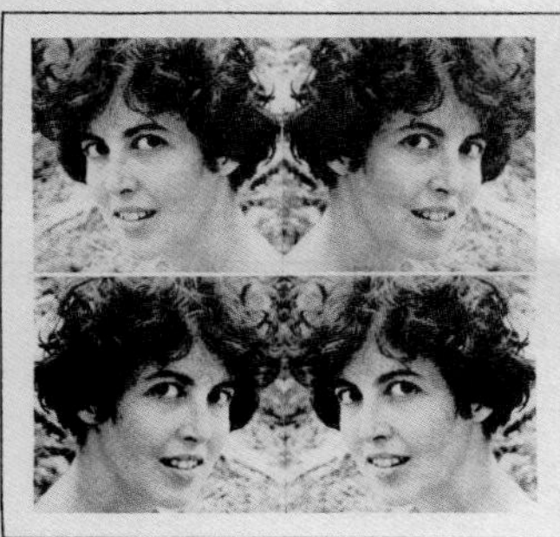

LESBIAN HEADACHE
69

Tension. Have you been fighting with your lover? Has your job been getting you down? The cost of living rising? Monogomy or non-monogomy taking its toll? And how do these problems leave us? Either constipated, with the runs, aching backs, necks, or shoulders, or just that all over tight feeling. We all know what tension feels like in our bodies. But few of us know how to eliminate it - except, of course eliminating the tension causing situation, which is not always possible. When we don't release this tnesion an armor builds up. This body armor, built up over a long period of time hinders your physical abilaties. Women who have poor posture, bad backs, tight faces, or stiff movements may all be suffering from tension, and they don't even realize it.

How women move, where they're tense, where they're loose, how they carry themselves, can tell a lot about their personalities. The body speaks a potent and eloquent language all its own.

It's important that we are all aware of our bodies and that we not abuse them. Not only is physical important but also the knowledge of how to reduce tension. Even when we do struggle thru tense situations the tension is not necessarily eliminated in our bodies. Massage is one excellent and direct way of dealing with body tension.

Massage is best done without clothes and on a firm surface - a massage table ideally, the floor will do fine. The best way to start the massage is first look at the persons body you are about to massage. Where is the tension? Do her hips look turned in? Are her hands clenched? Is her chest tight? Are the shoulders hunched too high or rigidly held? Skin color is another way to spot tension. Wherever there is tension, the skin is whiter and more faded. All of these are ways to detect tension, but, the best and most accurate way to know is by touch.

The tensest areas are usually the shoulders and upper back or the lower back or neck. In general, where someone is tense, the skin simply feels tight, stiff, and is resistant to handling. First apply oil or cream. If the oil or cream is not room temperature, rub it between your hands before applying. Massage the areas that are these. If the muscles between the shoulders are tight, work not only on those particular muscles, but all the muscles surrounding the tight ones, since the tight ones are usually just a focal point for tension. Once you've started to massage someone, don't take your hands off them until you've finished, it breaks the continuity of the massage.

After you've massaged the tense area, focus on the actual tense spot. It is important to stroke with pressure. Using the tips of your fingers and your thumbs, massage very thouroughly, trying to feel the individual muscles and pressing the tension out. Frequently this pressure will be painful. This pain is a good pain and when you've stopped, the person will feel much better.

Massaging just tense areas is fine, but a whole body massage is also wonderful. An entire massage takes about an hour. I like to start with someones head, moving onto the chest, then arms and hands, followed by the legs, feet, back of legs, buttocks and the back. Using gentle strokes, long strokes, short strokes, kneading movements, let your hands discover the person's body. Be systematic, cover every part of the body from the toes to the scalp.

Massaging is a way to communicate. It allows you to develop a skill in knowing bodies. It should make you more aware of how other people move and each person's particular body language.

Lee Schwing

* *

your hand is placed just to the right of the spine, with your other hand on top. pressing down using a circular motion, cover from the waist to the buttock. this is important, since the lower back is full of tension.

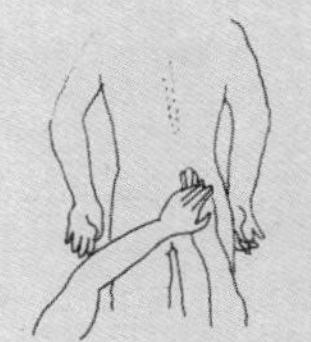

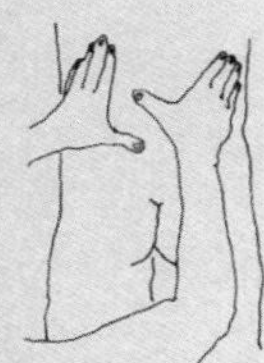

using the ball of your thumb, move up the spine on either side. make short, rapid strokes, concentrate on the same spot before moving on. work close to the spine.

*

put the tips of your fingers right beside the spine, glide your hands down the entire back - pressing firmly with your finger tips

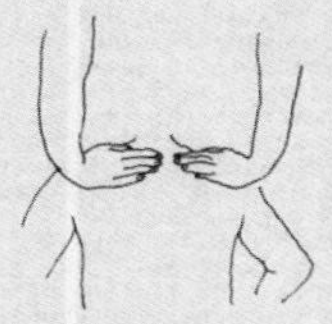

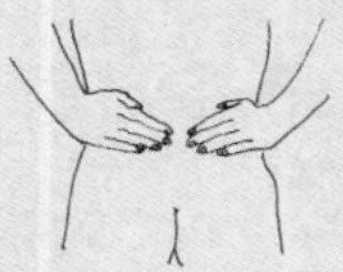

* * * *

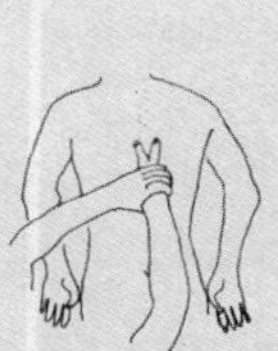

as you come down the spine, dig your fingers into the two furrows that are immediately to either side of the spine

the furies

January 1972 lesbian/feminist monthly volume 1

35¢

The story of the Furies is the story of strong, powerful women, the "Angry Ones", the avengers of matricide, the protectors of women. Three Greek Goddesses, they were described (by men) as having snakes for hair, blood-shot eyes, and bats' wings; like Lesbians today, they were cursed and feared. They were born when Heaven (the male symbol) was castrated by his son at the urging of Earth (the female symbol). The blood from the wound fell on Earth and fertilized her, and the Furies were born. Their names were Alecto (Never-ceasing), Tisiphone (Avenger of Blood), and Magaera (Grudger). Once extremely powerful, they represented the supremacy of women and the primacy of mother right.

Their most famous exploit (famous because in it they lost much of their power) involved Orestes in the last episode connected with the cycle of the Trojan War. Orestes, acting on the orders of the Sun God Apollo, killed his mother Clytemnestra, because she had killed his father. Clytemnestra had killed the father because he had sacrificed their daughter Iphigenia, in order to get favorable winds so his fleet could sail to Troy. The Furies tormented Orestes: they literally drove him crazy, putting him under a spell where for days he could not eat or wash his blood-stained hands. He bit off his finger to try to appease them, but to no avail. Finally, in desperation, Orestes went before the court of Athena to plead his case.

The point at issue was whether matricide was justifiable to avenge your father's murder, or in other words, whether men or women were to dominate. Apollo defended Orestes and totally denied the importance of motherhood, claiming that women were no more than passive sperm receptacles for men, and that the father was the only parent worthy of the name. One might have thought that Athena, Goddess of Wisdom, would have condemned Orestes, but Athena was the creation of the male God, Zeus, sprung full-grown from his head, the first token woman. Athena decided for Orestes. Some mythologists say that Zeus, Athena, and Apollo had conspired from the beginning, ordering Orestes to kill his mother in order to put an end, once and for all, to the religious belief that motherhood was more divine than fatherhood. In any case, that was the result.

The Furies were, of course, furious, and threatened to lay waste the city of Athens. But Athena had a direct line to Zeus, King of the Gods; she told the Furies to accept the new male supremacist order or lose everything. Some of the Furies and their followers relented, the rest pursued Orestes until his death.

We call our paper The FURIES because we are also angry. We are angry because we are oppressed by male supremacy. We have been fucked over all our lives by a system which is based on the domination of men over women, which defines male as good and female as only as good as the man you are with. It is a system in which heterosexuality is rigidly enforced and Lesbianism rigidly suppressed. It is a system which has further divided us by class, race, and nationality.

We are working to change this system which has kept us separate and powerless for so long. We are a collective of twelve Lesbians living and working in Washington, D.C. We are rural and urban; from the Southwest, Midwest, South and Northeast. Our ages range from 18 to 28. We are high school dropouts and Ph.D. candidates, We are lower class, middle and upper-middle class. We are white. Some of us have been Lesbians for twelve years, others for ten months. We are committed to ending all oppressions by attacking their roots--male supremacy.

ORESTES PURSUED BY FURIES

We believe The FURIES will make important contributions to the growing movement to destroy sexism. As a collective, in addition to outside projects, we are spending much time building an ideology which is the basis for action. For too long, women in the Movement have fallen prey to the very male propaganda they seek to refute. They have rejected thought, building an ideology, and all intellectual activity as the realm of men, and tried to build a politics based only on feelings--the area traditionally left to women. The philosophy has been, "if it feels good, it's O.K. If not, forget it." But that is like saying that strength, which is a "male" characteristic, should be left to men, and women should embrace weakness. Most straight women, to say nothing of men, feel afraid or contemptuous of Lesbians. That fear and contempt is similar to the feelings middle class whites have towards Blacks or lower class people. These feelings are the result of our socialization and are hardly worth glorifying. This is not to say that feelings are irrelevant, only that they are derived from our experience which is limited by our class, race, etc. Furthermore, feelings are too often used to excuse inaction and inability to change.

A political movement cannot advance without systematic thought and practical organization. The haphazard, non-strategic, zig-zag tactics of the straight women's movement, the male left, and many other so-called revolutionary groups have led only to frustration and dissolution. We do not want to make those same mistakes; our ideology forms the basis for developing long-range strategies and short-term tactics, projects, and actions.

The base of our ideological thought is: Sexism is the root of all other oppressions, and Lesbian and woman oppression will not end by smashing capitalism, racism, and imperialism. Lesbianism is not a matter of sexual preference, but rather one of political choice which every woman must make if she is to become woman-identified and thereby end male supremacy. Lesbians, as outcasts from every culture but their own have the most to gain by ending race, class, and national supremacy within their own ranks. Lesbians must get out of the straight women's movement and form their own movement in order to be taken seriously, to stop straight women from oppressing us, and to force straight women to deal with their own Lesbianism. Lesbians cannot develop a common politics with women who do not accept Lesbianism as a political issue.

In this (see page 8) and following issues of The FURIES we will share our thoughts with you. We welcome your comments, letters, articles, fiction, poetry, news, graphics, and support. We want to build a movement in this country and in the world which can effectively stop the violent, sick, oppressive acts of male supremacy. We want to build a movement which makes all people free.

For the Chinese women whose feet were bound and crippled; for the Ibibos of Africa whose clitori were mutilated; for every woman who has ever been raped, physically, economically, psychologically, we take the name of the FURIES, Goddesses of Vengeance and protectors of women.

Ginny Berson

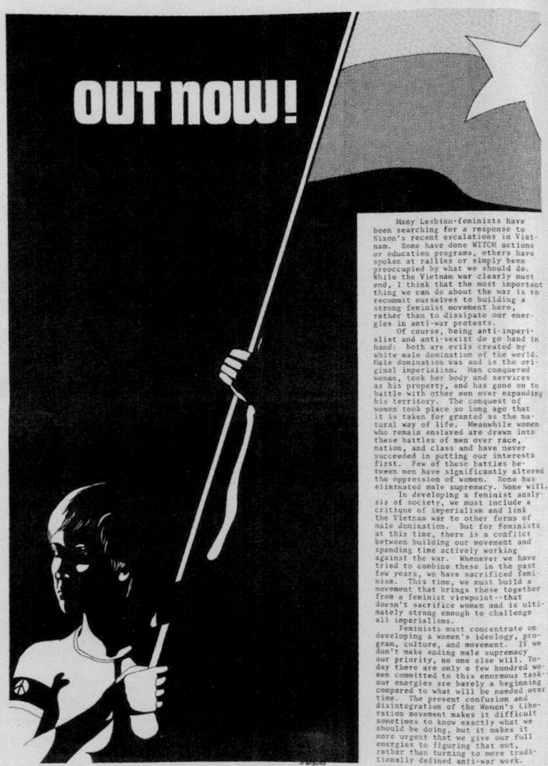

Many Lesbian-feminists have been searching for a response to Nixon's recent escalations in Vietnam. Some have done WITCH actions or education programs, others have spoken at rallies or simply been preoccupied by what we should do. While the Vietnam war clearly must end, I think that the most important thing we can do about the war is to recommit ourselves to building a strong feminist movement here, rather than to dissipate our energies in anti-war protests.

Of course, being anti-imperialist and anti-sexist do go hand in hand: both are evils created by white male domination of the world. Male domination was and is the original imperialism. Man conquered woman, took her body and services as his property, and has gone on to battle with other men over expanding his territory. The conquest of women took place so long ago that it is taken for granted as the natural way of life. Meanwhile women who remain enslaved are drawn into these battles of men over race, nation, and class and have never succeeded in putting our interests first. Few of these battles between men have significantly altered the oppression of women. None has eliminated male supremacy. None will.

In developing a feminist analysis of society, we must include a critique of imperialism and link the Vietnam war to other forms of male domination. But for feminists at this time, there is a conflict between building our movement and spending time actively working against the war. Whenever we have tried to combine these in the past few years, we have sacrificed feminism. This time, we must build a movement that brings these together from a feminist viewpoint--that doesn't sacrifice women and is ultimately strong enough to challenge all imperialisms.

Feminists must concentrate on developing a women's ideology, program, culture, and movement. If we don't make ending male supremacy our priority, no one else will. Today there are only a few hundred women committed to this enormous task--our energies are barely a beginning compared to what will be needed over time. The present confusion and disintegration of the Women's Liberation movement makes it difficult sometimes to know exactly what we should be doing, but it makes it more urgent that we give our full energies to figuring that out, rather than turning to more traditionally defined anti-war work.

Fig. 5.18. **The Furies** (Washington, DC), March–April 1972, vol. 1, no. 3, cover and p. 5; January 1972, vol. 1, cover and p. 12

keep your chin up

Lee Schwing

Physical fitness and mental fitness can never truly be separated Both are directly related to each other. A woman who is physically fit has an inner energy and a certain kind of drive. The relation between a healthy and sound body and your mental activities is very subtle and complex. Intelligence and skill can function only at their utmost when the body is healthy and strong. So here for your continued enjoyment AND work are some wonderful arm, back, leg, and stomach muscle-builders.

The chinning bar should be high enough so that your arms are almost straight when you start to pull yourself up. This plain chin-up basically strengthens your arms (the biceps) and your shoulder and back muscles.

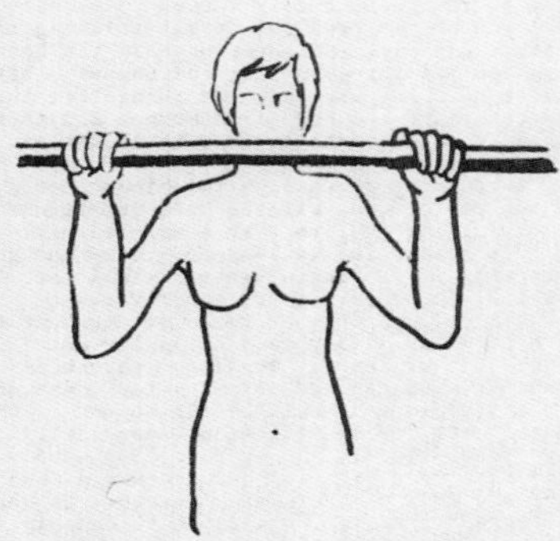

Notice the hands on this picture. Your hands may face either way, depending on which muscles you want to strengthen. This way your triceps are emphasized, along with your shoulder and back muscles.

This sequence is a more advanced exercise. This exercise calls for strong stomach and leg muscles. As soon as you can do one chin-up you should start practicing this one - it takes quite awhile to master.

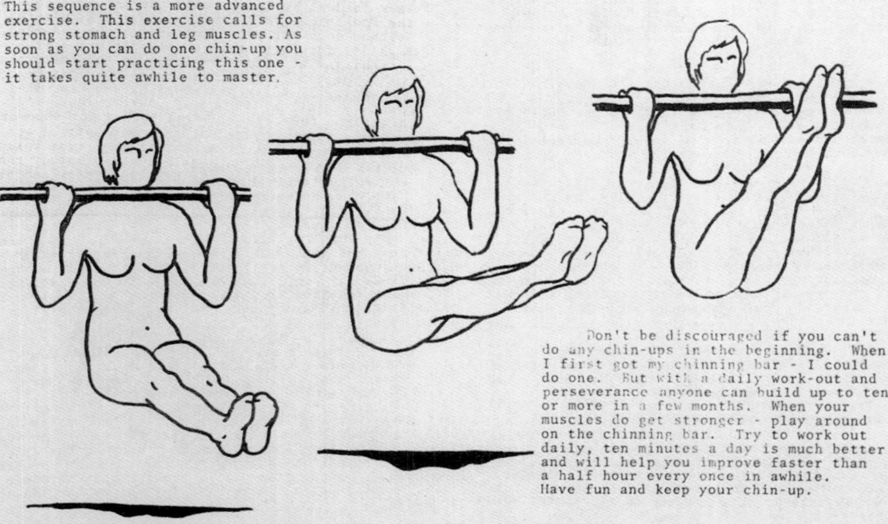

Don't be discouraged if you can't do any chin-ups in the beginning. When I first got my chinning bar - I could do one. But with a daily work-out and perseverance anyone can build up to ten or more in a few months. When your muscles do get stronger - play around on the chinning bar. Try to work out daily, ten minutes a day is much better and will help you improve faster than a half hour every once in awhile. Have fun and keep your chin-up.

February 1972 The Furies 7

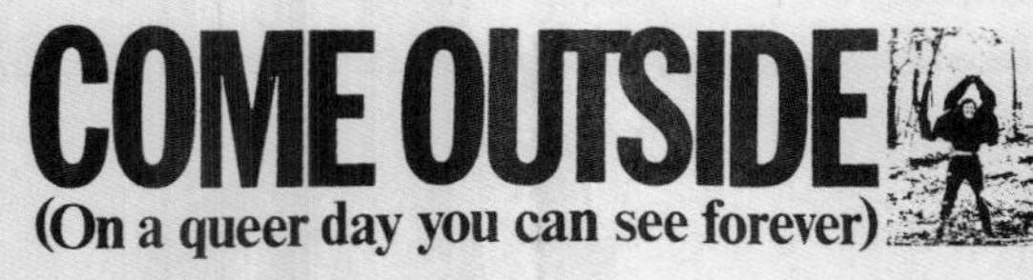

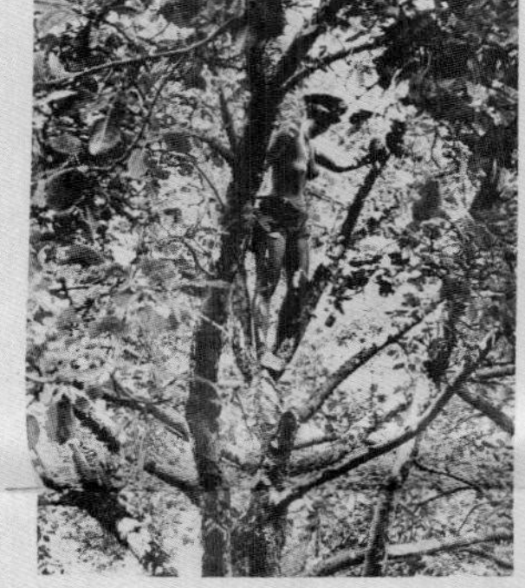

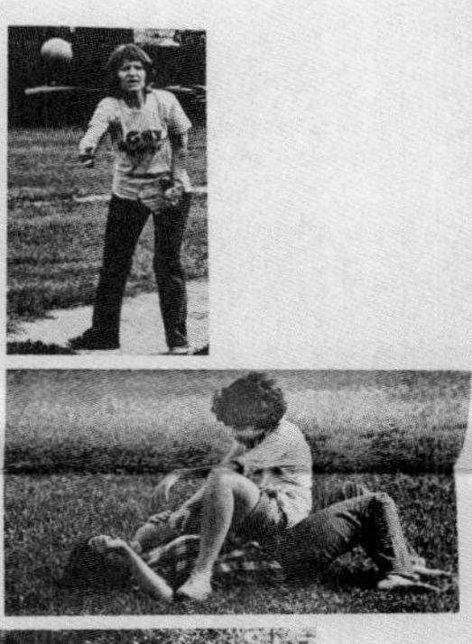

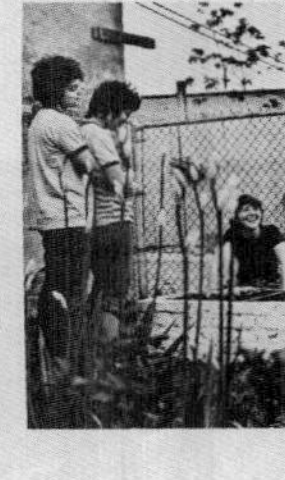

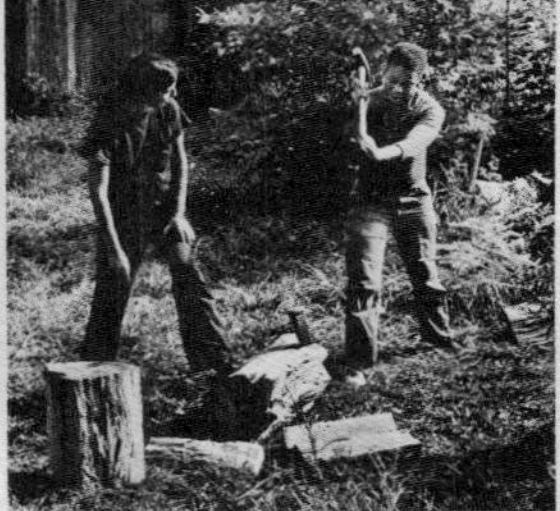

Photos by JEB

WALKER'S

APPEAL,

IN FOUR ARTICLES,

TOGETHER WITH

A PREAMBLE,

TO THE

COLORED CITIZENS OF THE WORLD,

BUT IN PARTICULAR, AND VERY EXPRESSLY TO THOSE OF THE

UNITED STATES OF AMERICA.

Written in B ston, in the State of Massachusetts, Sept. 28, 1829.

SECOND EDITION, WITH CORRECTIONS, &c.

BY DAVID WALKER.

1830.

Fig. 5.18 (cont'd.). **The Furies** (Washington, DC), February 1972, vol. 1, no. 2, p. 7; June–July 1972, vol. 1, no. 5, back cover

Fig. 5.19. **Walker's Appeal,** September 28, 1829, title page

Next page
Fig. 5.20. **Freedom's Journal,** June 22, 1827, vol. 1, no. 15, cover

century. In the late 1980s and 1990s, as personal computers were becoming commonplace but not yet networked, "desktop publishing" technology fueled the underground zine scene in which founding a paper on the spur of the moment and putting out just a few issues was not the exception but the norm.

Or we could look all the way back to the early nineteenth century, when David Walker, a free black man who ran a used clothing store in Boston, self-published a one-issue pamphlet known as *Walker's Appeal* (fig. 5.19) which created an immediate national sensation.[29] "Within months the State of Georgia had new laws quarantining all black sailors entering Georgia ports, punishing anyone introducing seditious literature into the state, and tightening laws against educating slaves."[30] The Virginia governor called an emergency closed-door session of the General Assembly to discuss how to keep *Walker's Appeal* out of Virginia,[31] and the Louisiana State Legislature imposed a penalty of life imprisonment or death on anyone who might "write, print, publish, or distribute any thing having a tendency to create discontent among the free coloured population of this state, or insubordination among the slaves therein."[32]

Throughout American history, every period of insurgent social journalism creatively exploited recent advances in communications technology. In the 1820s, the introduction of machine-made paper and more durable iron presses with a more efficient lever mechanism dramatically dropped the cost of publishing a paper and resulted in the "penny press" (newspapers priced at one cent instead of the typical six) that is considered the beginning of the modern American newspaper. But the advantages of the new technology were hardly the monopoly of the Horace Greeleys of the Industrial Age. The first newspaper published by African Americans (*Freedom's Journal* [fig. 5.20] in 1827), by labor (the *Philadelphia Journeyman Mechanic's Advocate* in 1827), by Native Americans (the *Cherokee Phoenix* in

29. The complete title was *Walker's Appeal, in Four Articles; Together with a Preamble, to the Coloured Citizens of the World, but in Particular, and Very Expressly, to Those of the United States of America.*

30. Peter P. Hinks, *To Awaken My Afflicted Brethren: David Walker and the Problem of Antebellum Slave Resistance* (University Park: Pennsylvania State University Press, 1997), pp. 118-119.

31. Ibid., 134-135.

32. Ibid., 150.

FREEDOM'S JOURNAL.

"RIGHTEOUSNESS EXALTETH A NATION."

CORNISH & RUSSWURM, Editors and Proprietors. NEW-YORK, FRIDAY, JUNE 22, 1827. VOL. I. NO. 15.

1828), and the vast panoply of the abolitionist press all date to this transition in printing technology.

In much the same way, two crucial changes in printing technology allowed the underground papers of the 1960s to take root. "Cold type" composition equipment revolutionized newspaper preparation. The previously used "hot type" technology cost about $20,000 and required a year of training to use. By the second half of the 1960s, preparing a paper for offset printing had become a simple and inexpensive task. All one needed was "an IBM typewriter with interchangeable typefaces, a lot of artwork (cartoons, photographs, drawings, illustrations) and an urge to express his or her social, political, or cultural point of view."[33]

The cost of printing had also fallen dramatically. Offset printing had been invented in 1903, but it only gradually caught on as various improvements to the process were made. In the 1950s, the technology became sufficiently generalized that establishment newspapers and entrepreneurs throughout the country invested heavily in offset printing plants, to the tune of a hundred thousand 1950s dollars each. They quickly discovered that making a profit from such a large outlay was not a simple task, and many went looking for customers who would keep their presses running during their off hours. Thus, in San Francisco, the same plant that printed the *Berkeley Barb* also printed the ***Catholic Monitor***, while "one courageous printer" in Wisconsin handled "all editions (Chicago, Milwaukee, Madison) of *kaleidoscope*, Chicago's colorful *Seed*, Wisconsin's *Counterpoint*, ***Bauls of the Brickyard***, and a handful of independent high school publications."[34]

The mimeograph offered an even cheaper and simpler alternative to offset printing, anticipating by twenty years the zine culture of the 1990s. Most underground high school papers were mimeographed. In 1967, the anarchist street theater group the Diggers (fig. 5.21) produced a steady

33. Glessing, *The Underground Press in America*, p. 42.

34. Ibid., p. 45.

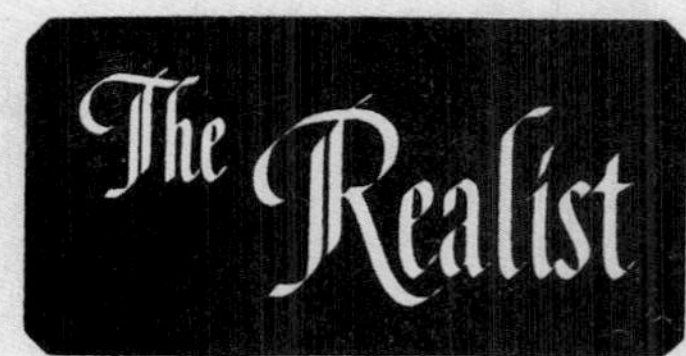

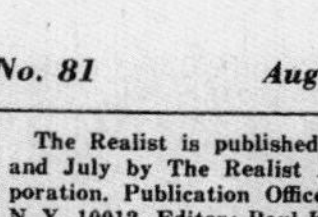

No. 81 *August, 1968* *35c*

The Realist is published monthly except for January and July by The Realist Association, a non-profit corporation. Publication Office: 595 Broadway, New York, N. Y. 10012. Editor: Paul Krassner, Box 379, Stuyvesant Sta., New York, N. Y. 10009. Subscribtion rates: $3 for 10 issues; $5 for 20 issues. Application to mail at second class postage rates is pending at New York, N. Y.

Memo to the Reader

When *Time* magazine decided to do a cover story on the hippies last year, a cable to their San Francisco bureau instructed researchers to "go at the description and delineation of the subculture as if you were studying the Samoans or the Trobriand Islanders."

Thus were they supposed to remain — a frozen fad for posterity.

But a few months ago, police rioted on Haight St. Next day, at a town hall meeting in the Straight Theater, the spectrum of reaction ranged from "Let's have another be-in" to "We gotta get guns!" A compromise was reached: bottles painted *Love* were thrown at the cops.

And yet, the question remains—*What* is being defended?

This issue of the *Realist*, therefore, has been created entirely by The Diggers, in an attempt to convey the flavor and feeling-tone of a revolutionary community.

An inadequate list of the brothers and sisters whose work is represented in this document:

Antonin Artaud, Richard, Avedon, Billy Batman, Peter Berg, Wally Berman, Richard Brautigan, Bryden, William Burroughs, Martin Carey, Neil Cassidy, Fidel Castro, Don Cochran, Peter Cohon, Gregory Corso, Dangerfield, Kirby Doyle, Bill Fritsch, Allen Ginsberg, Emmett Grogan, Dave Haselwood, George Hermes, Linn House, Lenore Kandel, Billy Landout, Norman Mailer, Don Martin, Michael McClure, George Metesky, George Montana, Malcolm X. Natural Suzanne, Huey Newton, Pam Parker, Rose-a-Lee, David Simpson, Gary Snyder, Ron Thelin, Rip Torn, Time Inc., Lew Welch, Thomas Weir, Gerard Winstanley, and Anonymous.

The contents herein are not copyrighted. Anyone may reprint anything without permission. Additional copies are available at the rate of 5 for $1. The Diggers have been given 40,000 copies to spread their word: free.

The 10th anniversary issue of the *Realist* will be out in June.

THE DIGGER PAPERS

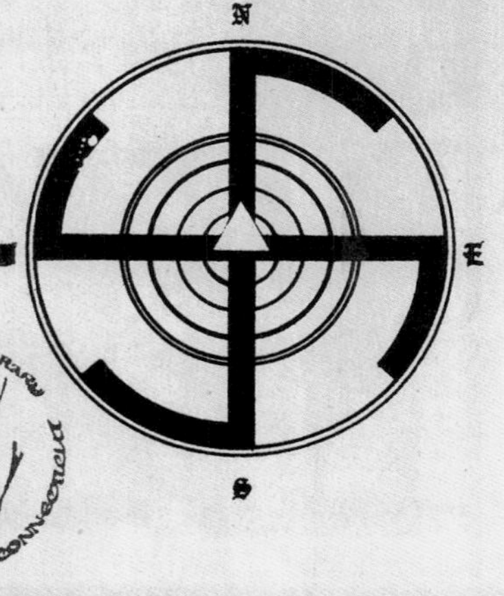

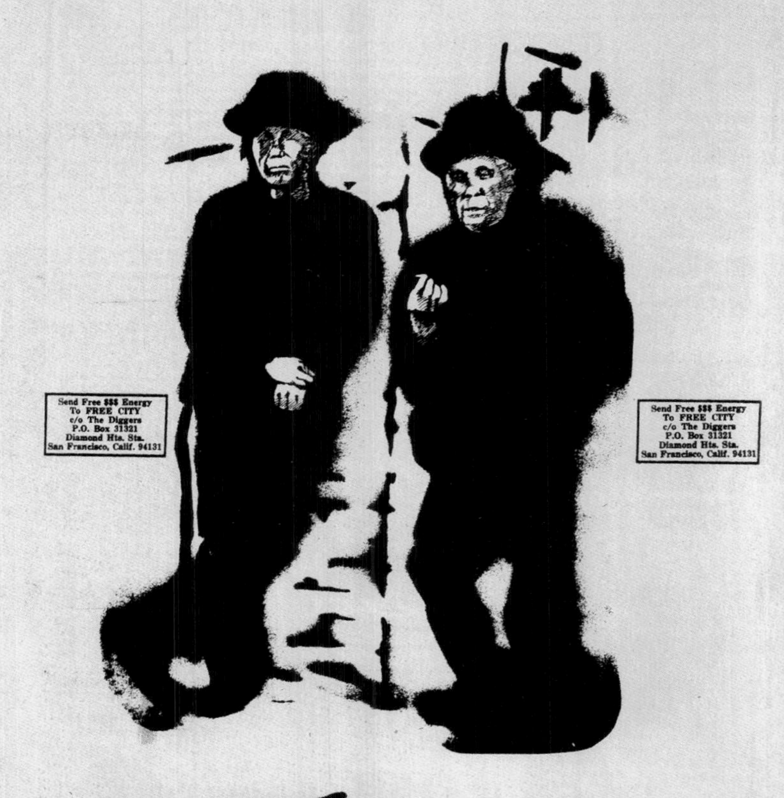

A CURSE
ON THE MEN IN WASHINGTON, PENTAGON

om a ka ca ta ta pa ya sa svaha

As you shoot down the Vietnamese girls and men
in their fields
Burning and chopping,
Poisoning and blighting,

So surely I hunt the white man down
in my heart.
The crew-cutted Seattle boy
The Portland boy who worked for U.P.
that was me.

I won't let him live. The "American"
I'll destroy. The "Christian"
has long been dead.

They won't pass on to my children.
I'll give them Chief Joseph, the Bison herds,
Ishi, sparrowhawk, the Fir trees,
The Buddha, their own naked bodies,
Swimming and dancing and singing
instead.

As I kill the white man,
the "American"
in me
And dance out the Ghost Dance:
To bring back America, the grass and the streams.

To trample your throat in your dreams.

This magic I work, this loving I give
That my children may flourish

And yours won't live.

hi'niswa' vita'ki'ni

2

Trip Without a Ticket

Our authorized sanities are so many Nembutals. "Normal" citizens with store-dummy smiles stand apart from each other like cotton-packed capsules in a bottle. Perpetual mental out-patients. Maddeningly sterile jobs for strait-jackets, love scrubbed into an insipid "functional personal relationship" and Art as a fantasy pacifier. Everyone is kept inside while the outside is shown through windows: advertising and manicured news. And we all know this.

How many TV specials would it take to establish one Guatemalan revolution? How many weeks would an ad agency require to face-lift the image of the Viet Cong? Slowly, very slowly we are led nowhere. Consumer circuses are held in the ward daily. Critics are tolerated like exploding novelties. We will be told which burning Asians to take seriously. Slowly. Later.

But there is a real danger in suddenly waking a somnambulistic patient. And we all know this.

What if he is startled right out the window?

No one can control the single circuit-breaking moment that charges games with critical reality. If the glass is cut, if the cushioned distance of media is removed, the patients may never respond as normals again. They will become life-actors.

Theater is territory. A space for existing outside padded walls. Setting down a stage declares a universal pardon for imagination. But what happens next must mean more than sanctuary or preserve. How would real wardens react to life-actors on liberated ground? How can the intrinsic freedom of theater illuminate walls and show the weak-spots where a breakout could occur?

Guerrilla theater intends to bring audiences to liberated territory to create life-actors. It remains light and exploitative of forms for the same reasons that it intends to remain free. It seeks audiences that are created by issues. It creates a cast of freed beings. It will become an issue itself.

This is theater of an underground that wants out. Its aim is to liberate ground held by consumer wardens and establish territory without walls. Its plays are glass cutters for empire windows.

Free store/property of the possessed

The Diggers are hip to property. Everything is free, do your own thing. Human beings are the means of exchange. Food, machines, clothing, materials, shelter and props are simply there. Stuff. A perfect dispenser would be an open Automat on the street. Locks are time-consuming. Combinations are clocks.

So a store of goods or clinic or restaurant that is free becomes a social art form. Ticketless theater. Out of money and control.

> "First you gotta pin down what's wrong with the West. Distrust of human nature, which means distrust of Nature. Distrust of wildness in oneself literally means distrust of Wilderness." — Gary Snyder.

Diggers assume free stores to liberate human nature. First free the space, goods and services. Let theories of economics follow social facts. Once a free store is assumed, human wanting and giving, needing and taking become wide open to improvisation.

A sign: *If someone Asks to See the Manager*
Tell Him He's the Manager.

Someone asked how much a book cost. How much did he think it was worth? 75 cents. The money was taken and held out for anyone. "Who wants 75 cents?" A girl who had just walked in came over and took it.

A basket labeled *Free Money.*

No owner, no Manager, no employees and no cash-register. A salesman in a free store is a life-actor. Anyone who will assume an answer to a question or accept a problem as a turn-on.

Question (*whispered*): "Who pays the rent?"

Answer (*loudly*): "May I help you?"

Who's ready for the implications of a free store? Welfare mothers pile bags full of clothes for a few days and come back to hang up dresses. Kids case the joint wondering how to boost.

Fire helmets, riding pants, shower curtains, surgical gowns and World War I Army boots are parts for costumes. Nightsticks, sample cases, water pipes, toy guns and weather balloons are taken for props. When materials are free imagination becomes currency for spirit.

Where does the stuff come from? People, persons, beings. Isn't it obvious that objects are only transitory subjects of human value? An object released from one person's value may be destroyed, abandoned or made available to other people. The choice is anyone's.

The question of a free store is simply: What would you have?

Street event — birth of haight / funeral for $ now

Pop Art mirrored the social skin. Happenings X-rayed the bones. Street events are social acid heightening consciousness of what is real on the street. To expand eyeball implications until facts are established through action.

The Mexican Day of the Dead is celebrated in cemeteries. Yellow flowers falling petal by petal on graves. In moonlight. Favorite songs of the deceased and everybody gets loaded. Children suck deaths-head candy engraved with their names in icing.

A Digger event. Flowers, mirrors, penny-whistles, girls in costumes of themselves, Hell's Angels, street people, Mime Troupe.

Angels ride up Haight with girls holding *Now!* signs. Flowers and penny-whistles passed out to everyone.

A chorus on both sides of the street chanting *Uhh!— Ahh! — Shh be cool!* Mirrors held up to reflect faces of passersby.

The burial procession. Three black-shrouded messengers holding staffs topped with reflective dollar signs. A runner swinging a red lantern. Four pall-bearers wearing animal heads carry a black casket filled with blowups of silver dollars. A chorus singing *Get Out Of My Life Why Don't You Babe* to Chopin's *Death March.* Members of the procession give out silver dollars and candles.

Now more reality. Someone jumps on a car with the news that two Angels were busted. Crowd, funeral cortage and friends of the Angels fill the street to march on Park Police Station. Cops confront 400 free beings: a growling poet with a lute, animal spirits in black, candle-lit girls singing *Silent Night.* A collection for bail fills an Angel's helmet. March back to Haight and street dancing.

Street events are rituals of release. Re-claiming of territory (sundown, traffic, public joy) through spirit. Possession. Public NewSense.

3

stream of mimeographed papers for the street scene in the Haight-Ashbury. "If someone heard a rumor of a bust, or had a good lead on free food, or wanted to announce a poetry reading, the Diggers had roving reporters on the street who could rush at a moment's notice back to the flat where the [mimeographs] were kept. Within a short time, a new street sheet would appear, distributed by the volunteers who used the street poles as their community bulletin board."[35] During the brief heyday of the flower children, before the scene soured from bad drugs, bad cops, and bad vibes and the Diggers held a "Death of Hippie" funeral before leaving the city for rural communes, they had produced some nine hundred issues of their instant newspapers.

35. The Digger Archives, http://www.diggers.org.

It has been possible since the early nineteenth century for a highly motivated individual or group to publish

Previous page
Fig. 5.21. **Realist** (New York), August 1968, no. 81, front and back covers

Fig. 5.21 (cont'd.). **Realist** (New York), August 1968, no. 81, pp. 2-3

GARBAGE OR NOTHING

I. The recent death of capitalism has everybody fucked around & confused.

Private enterprise laissez faire legally murderous piracy GONE already buried to be replaced by what?

If it doesn't have a name, how can you talk about it?

And what about the garbage?

WHO'S GOING TO COLLECT THE GARBAGE?

Now there's something you can talk about . .

II. America 1968 so incredibly wealthy that the local spiritual crisis is what're we going to do about the garbage.

the economic crisis how to distribute the garbage,

the political crisis who's going to collect the garbage & why should anyone want the job,

while in the oblivious streets attention has suddenly exploded into flesh bodies & the various ways of rubbing them together.

The Evolutionary Credit & Loan Association has terminated our contract, stamped it PAID IN FULL, & the planet is ours at last.

Sudden flashes that maybe those five thousand years of time payments

—all those payments ON THE DOT—

all those food wars & social cipher contracts were gestures of empty anxiety.

Now that it's ours & we can take a casual look around, well there's so much GARBAGE.

4 bilion people camped in the planetary wilderness & somehow WE FORGOT ABOUT THE GARBAGE.

Our wilderness is turning sour.

IT STINKS!

No place in the cosmology of planetary physics for garbage.

What?

What an astounding oversight!

What were our ancestors THINKING about?

III. America a nation in 1968 so incredibly wealthy that all morality is based on the problems of EXCESS:

fantasy executives & governmental spies running wild-eyed down the corridors of control:

"There's too fucking much of it!"

"It's completely out of control!"

"Power leak! Power leak!"

The cells of power grow wild: undisciplined freedom cancer.

Sudden flashes that the future of bureaucracy spy systems lies in garbage control.

People are USING it, picking it up FREE on the streets, living on it, they no longer respond to the seduction of the state, there's no way to get a HOLD on them.

Pomposity suicided & rigidity machines put to work at a furious clip: all this garbage must be catalogued & filed, garbage destruction teams trained, parking lots on the tillable land, thousands of well-programed garbage experts march to work each day to GET IT DOWN ON PAPER, enormous factories hastily tooled for garbage conversion.

"By God, we'll make napalm out of it."

Youngsters who don't understand it's all been paid for already

are given guns!

given napalm!

& shipped to parts of the planet where there MAY be people who MIGHT be hip to OUR garbage & MIGHT WANT SOME OF IT FOR THEMSELVES.

The situation complicates itself incredibly.

Computer engineers make it worse: the machines don't UNDERSTAND power, sex, & control: the machines program useable garbage & forbidden fantasies of FREE.

The Secretary of Garbage Control considers dropping acid & getting it over with.

Systems of control grow schizophrenic . . . they writhe & contort in involute paranoia.

SYSTEMICIDE MAKES HEADLINES.

IV. America a nation so incredibly wealthy in 1968 that all morality is based on EXCESS:

true American career counselors now ask only one question.

"Do you want to produce garbage or do you want to collect garbage?"

Industrialist or politician?

Fishfarm or junkyard?

The young people want no part of it, of course, what with garbage their natural matrix & medium.

Produce it?

Collect it?

They want to fuck in it!

The career counselors build marvelous constructions of seduction & mystery, they trans-substantiate symbol money

into sex
into power
into death insurance
into pleasure.

But it's just THINGS, it's garbage, it's overflow & the young people know it.

They throw the career counselor out the window.

Who's going to collect the garbage?

who knows?

who cares?

Let's use it to act out our fantasies, use it for unimaginable gratifications.

V. We were sitting around the other night talking about garbage, making screaming intuitive leaps thru each others arguments, when Wm. Fritsch suddenly woke up & shouted, "What I gotta do is learn to do nothing."

And of course that's it

& it's not surprising that the solution came from a man who sometimes arrives at the compulsion to visit all his friends & empty the garbage for them.

VI. Garbage crises cannot be SOLVED:

they must be ALLOWED TO DISAPPEAR.

The alternative to the garbage collection production box is to do just exactly nothing . . . no more & no less.

Sudden flashes of the invisible network w/ the individual spine planted squarely on it,

organic units in the planetary ecology,

DOING NOTHING.

Ecological systems have no garbage in them, contain nothing that is alien to them.

VII. Invisible networks of nameless human connectives (names shed as metaphysical garbage) can help each other to do nothing.

That part of the psyche organism to which name is attached, that part which DOES things in praise of the name,

that part withers in the flesh caress of the anonymous community.

The galactic actor does nothing in the NAME of anything:

he receives his direction from the silent spinal telegraph,

his spine is planted square on the invisible network,

HE DOES NOTHING,

his movements are not outside the process.

18

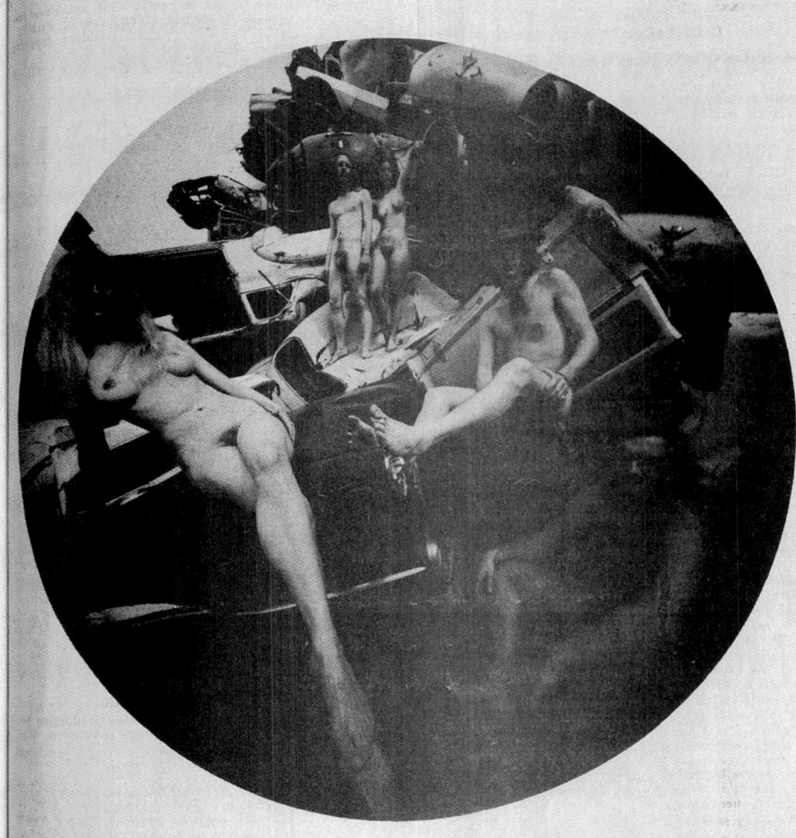

VIII. It's paid for, all of it.

A cellophane bag represents 5000 years of machine history, inventors suicided by their inventions, aeons of garbage dedication, paid for in cancer wombs, in fallen cocks, in the crazy waste of our fathers.

Generations dead of lacklove sold for 29 cents.

Your birth certificate is your final credit card.

Stack the garbage in piles & people will live in among it, communities of free parallel spines planted square on the invisible network.

They will do nothing to effect the celebratory transformation of garbage into spinal food.

Their movements are not outside the process.

IX. The invisible networks grow thru the absent university of nothingness, disguised as dopesellers.

as sneakthieves
as naked dripping 17 year old Americans girls.

Doctors of garbage philosophy.

Doing nothing in PUBLIC teaching nothing demonstrating nothing living paradigms of nothing!

The absent university is powered by social magic.

It has flesh classrooms.

It is the university of the spine.

Tuition is paid in units of psychic bondage.

Its graduates are FREE.

19

their views on the printed page with few resources other than a passion for justice. What the Internet has revolutionized is not production but distribution. William Lloyd Garrison, Frederick Douglass, and Susan B. Anthony all made nineteenth-century papers that peaked at a circulation of three thousand. Making use of offset printing, some underground papers in the sixties managed press runs in the hundreds of thousands. In the 1990s, desktop publishing technology again substantially dropped the cost of creating a paper (including money, training, and effort) without altering the cost of distribution, and a tidal wave of DIY zines with tiny circulations was the result. With the development of the Internet, and in particular the subset of technologies that comprise the World Wide Web, the bottom has fallen out from under the cost of both producing and distributing self-published material. Distribution is now immediate, worldwide, and free. "Production runs" are essentially infinite: there is no limit to the number of times a blog can be read.

This does not mean that the problems of media and democracy in hi-tech societies have suddenly been solved; rather, they have been reconfigured. The limitless nature of the electronic word creates its own set of problems. The problem of who gets to speak and for how long has been solved: everyone speaks

Fig. 5.21 (cont'd.) **Realist** (New York), August 1968, no. 81, pp. 18–19 as much as they want. But with everyone speaking, who will listen? How will all the "chatter" facilitated by information technology cohere into the sort of sustained discourse that leads people to identify with a social movement, cast the obligations of their daily lives to the side, and make history?

"OBJECTIVITY," CIRCULATION, LONGEVITY, GEOGRAPHIC DISTRIBUTION, AND ADVERTISING REVENUE are commonly considered universal standards by which the importance of newspapers and magazines can be measured. And by these standards, the underground press of the 1960s hardly merits serious consideration: small circulation, short duration, little or no real news, dubious accuracy, frequently atrocious profanity-laced writing, deliberately amateurish production. For the corporate media, however, these measures are not ends in themselves, but are simply tools for maximizing profits. Advertising generates revenue. Circulation supports advertising. Longevity keeps the money coming. Large geographic distribution diversifies the profit base against local downturns.

Social movement journalism seeks to promote ideas, not profits. Movement journals seek to challenge corporate control of media, not justify it. They address readers as members of communities, not individual consumers. They cover social movements as participants, not "observers." They exist to make change, not business.

So what, in the end, did the 1960s change?

By the yardstick conventionally employed to measure revolution, the 1960s have been judged a failure. The gates of the White House were never stormed. No revolutionary government was formed. The two political parties which framed the electoral field before the sixties—the Democrats and Republicans—continued their reign after the smoke had cleared. The most prominent organizations the movement had created shattered under the combined weight of state repression, sectarian politics, and too much drug use. But if instead of looking at flags and governments, we look at real-life human relationships, a quite different picture comes into view. Nearly every type of human relationship emerged from the era profoundly changed, and in every case the change was toward greater equality: male/female, parent/child, white/black/brown/yellow, teacher/student, boss/worker, straight/gay, rich/poor, officer/soldier, north/south, first world/third world. Measured by how real people live real lives, the 1960s can be considered the most successful revolution ever, certainly far more successful than those revolutions that succeeded in seizing the reins of state power. Many of these changes have proven remarkably resilient over the years. It is inconceivable that relations between men and women, and straights and gays, for example, could ever return to what they were before the sixties. Race issues still bedevil American society, of course, but they do so differently today than before.

The same traits that made the sixties counterculture so distinctive in its time made it immediately anachronistic once its moment had passed. Looking through the images in this book, it is easy to laugh and even ridicule. ***What were they thinking?*** Yet the feminist movement, the gay and lesbian movement, the environmental movement, and the peace movement—all of which have profoundly shaped the culture we now perceive as contemporary—emerged from the mix of democratic ideals with personal and social experimentation that reached a frenetic peak in the sixties counterculture. As I write these words, the first biracial American president, whose mixed-race parentage was very much a product of the sixties, is proposing an alternative energy plan for the nation that is considered cutting edge, even far-fetched. Finally, in early 2009, the country is catching up with countercultural thinking about alternative energy circa 1969—ideas that were first introduced to the world in the pages of the colorful, zany, joyous, tripped-out pages of the underground press.

[g]reat society means pussy galore

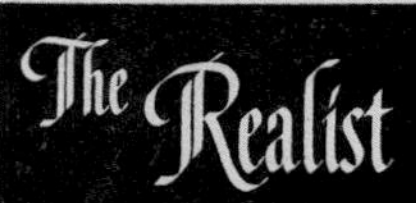

No. 58
April, 1965
35 Cents

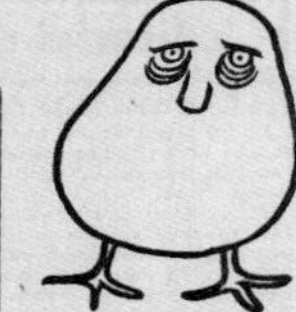

Dick Gregory and His Mississippi Airlift

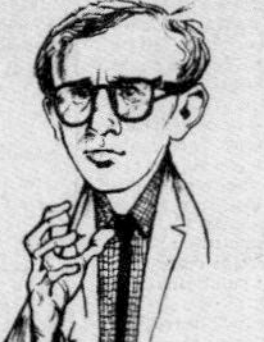

Steve Allen and His Chinese A-Bomb

The cold war has become an internal struggle as well as an international exchange, and both phases of the battle share common characteristics. As Berlin, Germany was the international target of the first cold war airlift, so Jackson, Mississippi was the internal site of Dick Gregory's airlift.

Deane and David Heller observe in *The Berlin Crisis:* "By Christmas, 1948, the airlift had accomplished the miracle of having carried into Berlin 700,000 tons of food, supplies and fuel." Even more miraculous is it that by Christmas, 1964, the Gregory Airlift had brought into Mississippi over 100,000 pounds of frozen turkeys. I say "more miraculous" because the

(Continued on Page 23)

Woody Allen and His Impolite Interview

Q. Hey, I thought you didn't smoke?

A. I didn't smoke. Well, I originally did smoke, when I was young. And then I started increasing my smoking a lot. And then I began to see where it was going to be trouble for me. This is when I was very young, and I stopped smoking. And then, I didn't smoke for years. And the day the Surgeon-General's report came out that you could die from smoking, I started smoking again. Not consciously for that reason. Just, I felt all of a sudden a tremendous urge to have a cigarette that day. And I haven't stopped smoking since then.

(Continued on Page 10)

William F. Buckley's recent column —one syndicated, alas, in far more papers than will ever carry reference to my response—suggesting that I stand shoulder-to-shoulder with him in recommending an immediate nuclear attack by our Strategic Air Command against Communist China's nuclear installations, has stirred up a great deal of comment, as well it should.

In reply I wish to make clear first of all that those who now find themselves seriously concerned with my views on foreign policy may find them expressed at considerable length in three books: my autobiography *Mark It and Strike It* (Holt, Rinehart and Winston) *God and the H-Bomb* (Bellmeadows Press) and *Dialogues in Americanism* (Regnery). So far as I am aware there has

(Continued on Page 28)

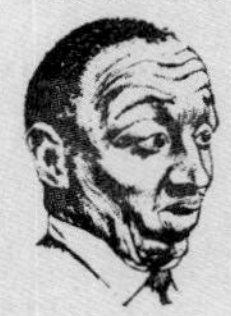

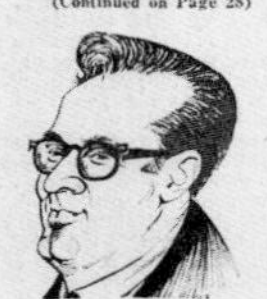

—bhob

November, 1966 35c

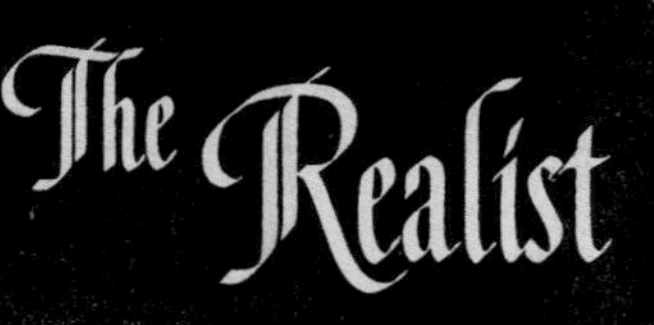

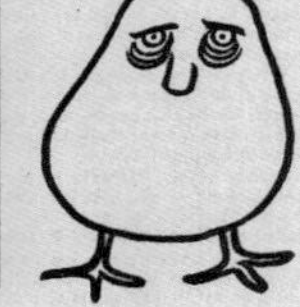

Remember, Next Tuesday, Get Tufts!

by John M. Anderson

The election of former movie star George Murphy to the Senate of the United States in November, 1964 suggests this question: Why can't Elizabeth Taylor be President?

Quite simply, she probably can. It may take an election or two. But if a faded box office attraction can be elected United States Senator from the most populous State in the Union, surely the nation's number one box office attraction should be a favorite in the run for the White House.

Will Miss Taylor enter the race? The answer probably depends on the answer to another question: Will movie actor Ronald Reagan be elected Governor of California in 1966? If Mr. Reagan succeeds, Miss Taylor must be considered a serious presidential candidate. In short, a new era in American politics may depend on the success or failure of Ronald Reagan.

Who's behind Ronald Reagan? What are his chances? If he wins, what are the implications for government in America?

On November 3, 1964, a small cross-section of the Hollywood community gathered at the Beverly Hills home of motion picture producer Joseph E. Levine.

Those present included actor Steve Reeves, director Stanley Kramer, screenwriter Abby Mann, lawyer Norman H. Garey and actress Carroll Baker. They were all, as Miss Baker would probably say, "just good friends."

They had come together at Joseph E. Levine's prophetically insistent urging, to watch the 1964 election returns.

"Don't be late," he had said to each of them. And when they arrived, Levine was already hunched over on a stool in front of the world's largest television set, eye to eye with David Brinkley.

Almost immediately, it was apparent to his guests that Joseph E. Levine was interested in only one contest: Pierre Salinger versus George Murphy. Throughout the evening their tight race for one of California's U.S. Senate seats was the sole concen of Levine and, eventually, his guests.

(Continued on Page 2)

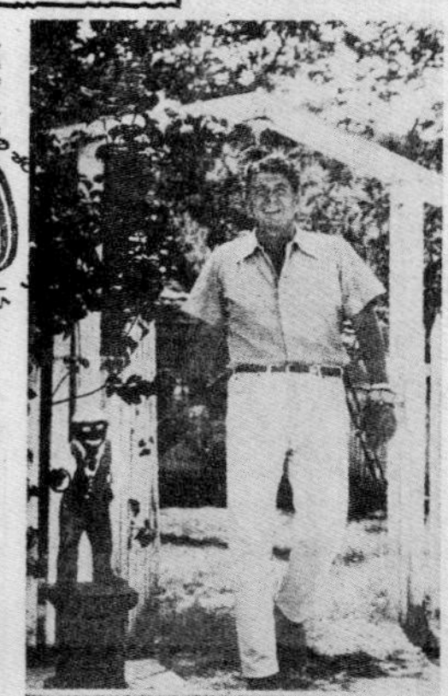

Ronald Reagan and Friend

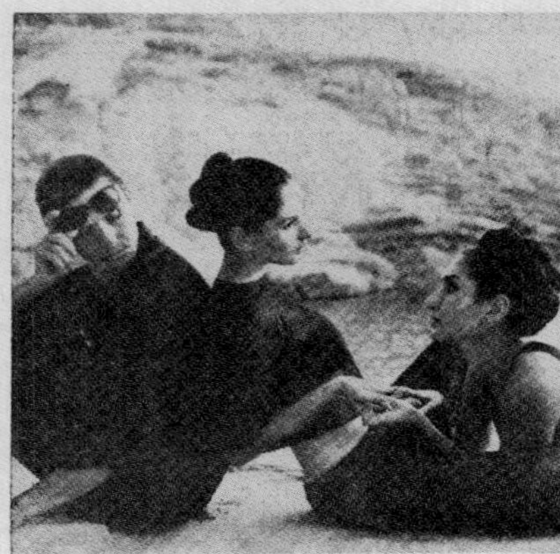

Mènage á Trois in Harper's Bazaar

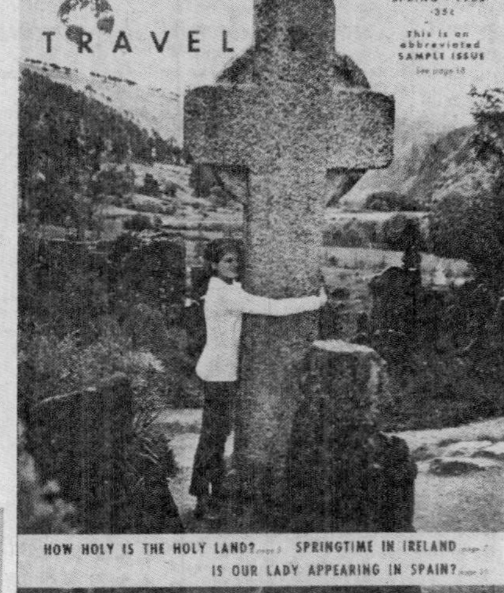

Fetishism in The Catholic Traveler

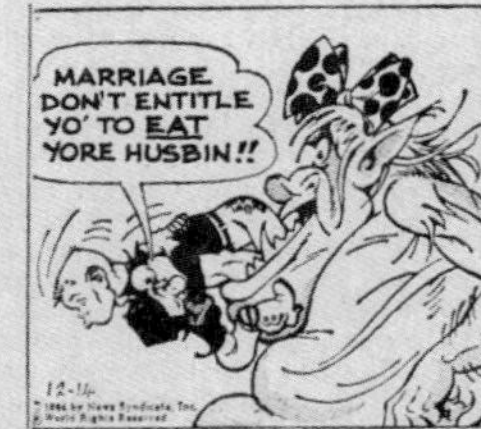

Fellatio in the Funnies

soft-core pornography of the month

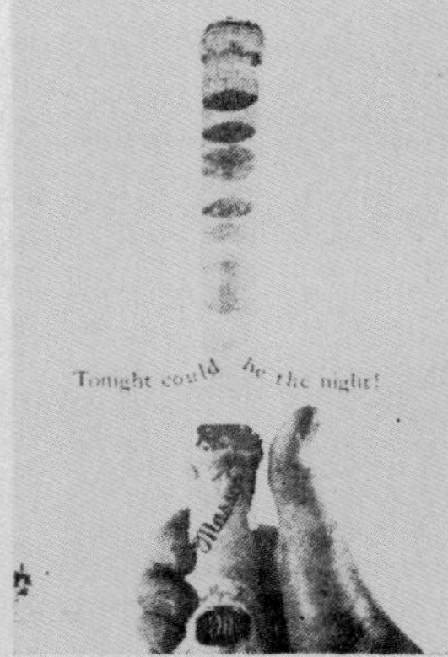

Ejaculation at the San Francisco Opera

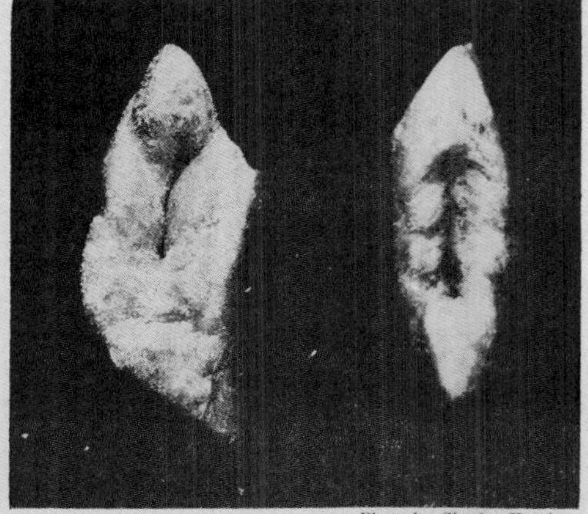

—Photo by Charles Harrison

Yonic Symbolism in a Long Island Bakery

The Fluffy Doughnut Shop features two special crullers. One is labelled the "Shirley Temple" (left), which is smooth and sugar-coated; the other is called the "Mae West," which is wrinkled and unsugared.

December, 1966 35c

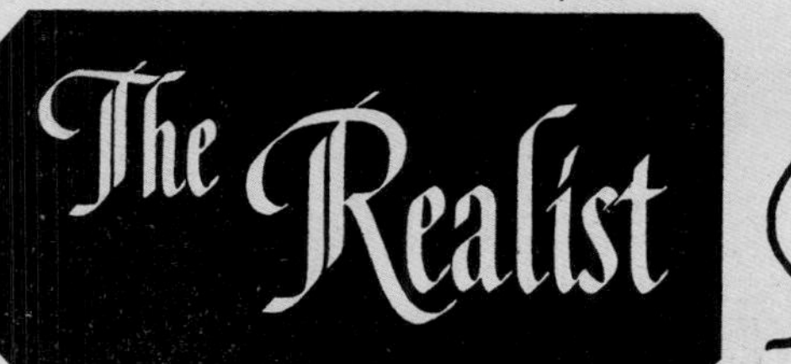

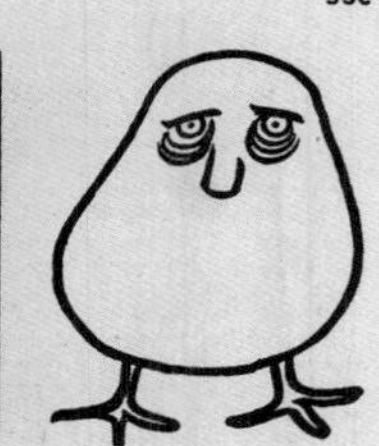

The Cybernetic Revolution

by Robert Anton Wilson

Paul Revere 1976, two hundred years after the original, will be a guy galloping through every middlesex, village and farm, yelling: "Grab your guns, boys, *the machines is a-coming!*"

The Triple Revolution Manifesto got a great deal of

(Continued on Page 5)

Automation and Aberration

by Renfreu Neff

What has happened to perversion?

Where are the Great Perverts of yore?

Within the past decade the old aberrations — the "classics"—have not disappeared; they have been assimilated into our cultural patterns to the extent that few are really "perverse" anymore.

Advancements in the fields of psychiatry, sociology and technology have made them more popular, more convenient and, alas, more socially acceptable.

The loosening of literary and film censorship lends Artistic Interpretation to the new morality, and after a respectful period of hard-cover probation, paper-back editions are rushed out so that the budget-minded masses can catch up with the latest Excursion Beyond The Norm.

The sexual revolution has stripped away the secrecy, and instead of strong, healthy, clandestine "deviations," we are left with piddling "variations" on the theme.

With this new popularity and practicability has come the inevitable—vulgarity, to which the serious pervert has no recourse. Science no longer marches on; it goes by jet, and the pervert has lost the exclusive rights to his own depravity.

The Homosexual is little more than a statistic.

The Movie Masher has gone the way of all great freaks—he is sitting at home watching TV.

Television and the movie industry — technological voyeurism, exploiting the human will to watch—have turned the Voyeur into a sedentary creature who no longer has to move about, shift his position on a chair, or bend over to see anything. It is only the truly die-hard Voyeur, too out of touch with the times to be of much interest, who bothers to notice the exposed knees and thighs that parade past him along the avenues.

The Flagellant is merely a noisy nuisance in the next apartment.

The Fetishist is not only the victim of over-acceptance and built-in obsolescence, he is further victimized by the psychiatric lag; modern shrinkers have been loitering in fetishism for the past decade and there have

(Continued on Page 2)

The Realist (New York), April 1965, no. 58, cover
The Realist (New York), April 1965, no. 58, back cover
The Realist (New York), November 1966, no. 71, cover
The Realist (New York), December 1966, no. 72, cover

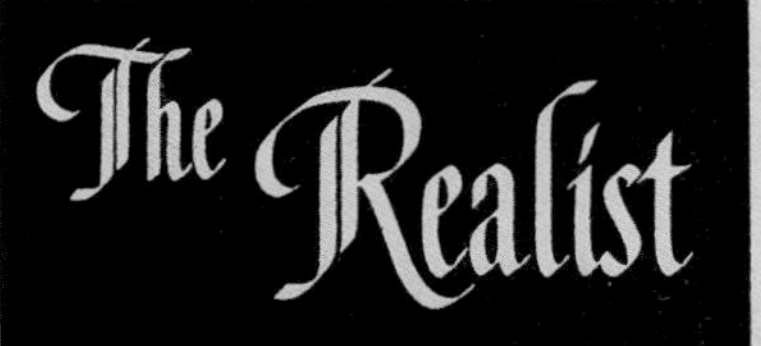
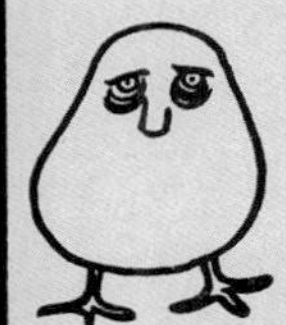

No. 76 *35 Cents*

We're a little late, folks . . . This is the August 1967 issue being published in January '68 of The Realist (the magazine of cherry pie and violence)

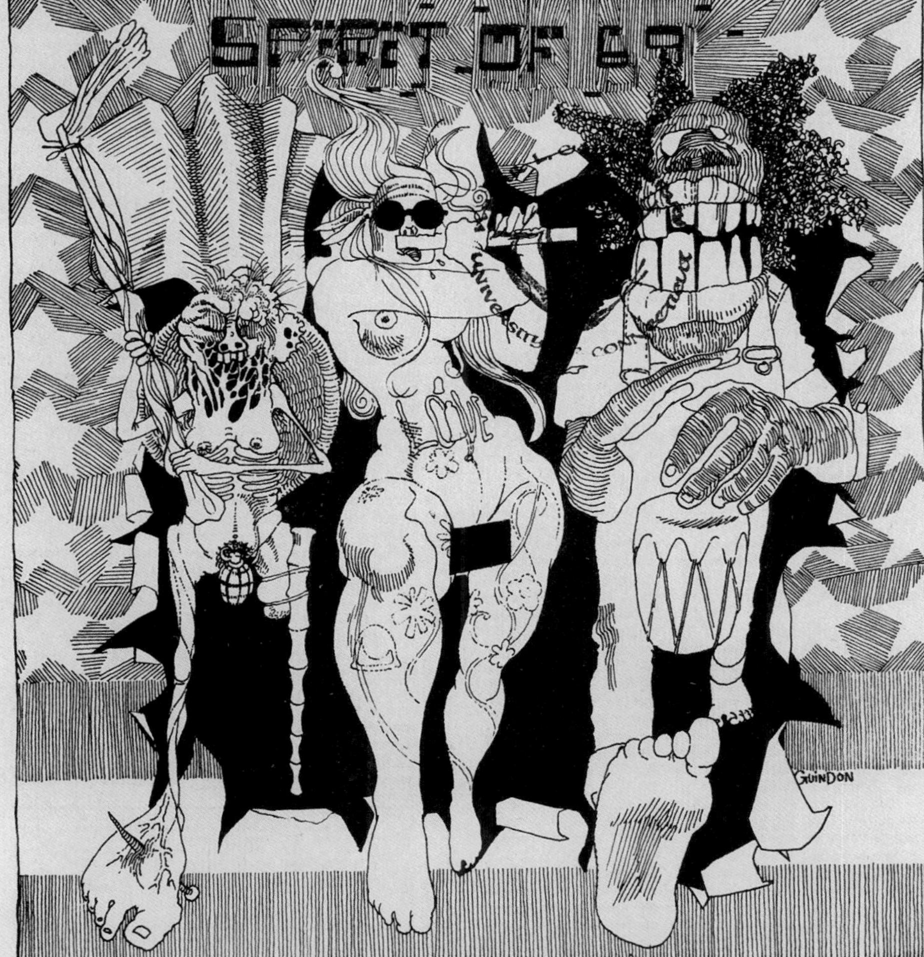

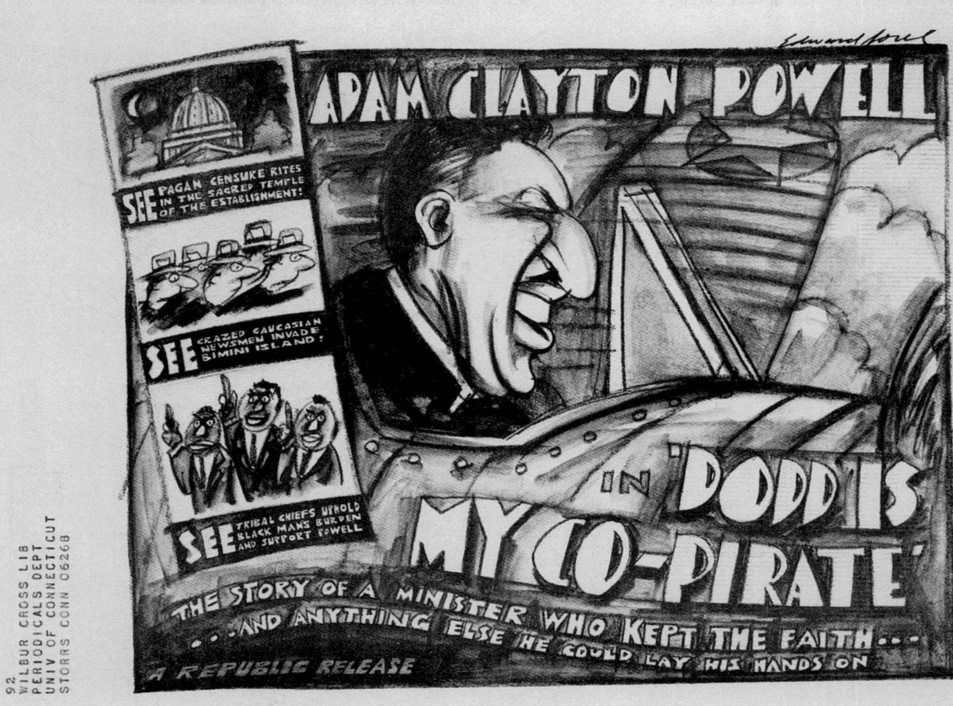

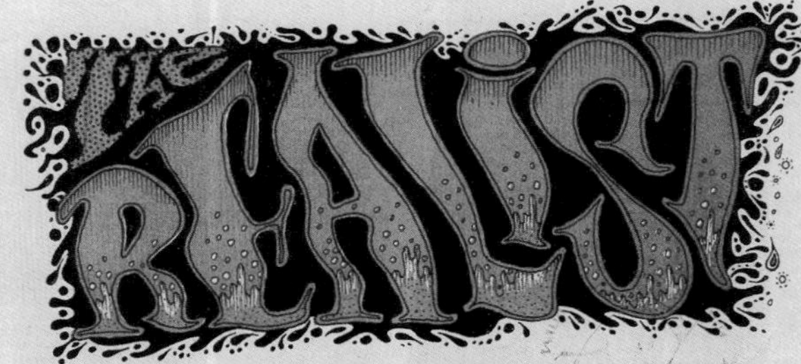

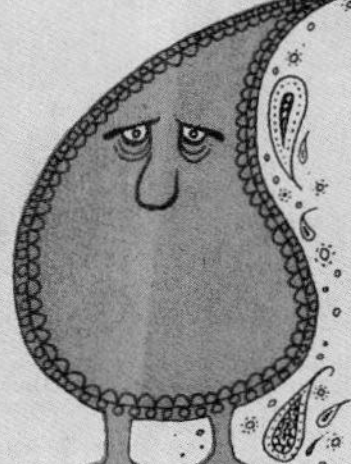

Case History of the Manchester Caper

by Paul Krassner

Once there was upon a time a face painted on the hand of Señor Wences that magically became a real person named Jacqueline. She kissed a senator in a Spearmint ad, and he in turn became a real person named Jack. They were married by Chief Justice Earl Warren and lived in good taste for not quite ever after.

Suddenly he was slain by the man who had most to gain—Mark Lane—who in turn was killed at the police station by Vaughn Meader.

(Continued on Page 13)

Legal and Actual Concentration Camps in America

by Charles R. Allen, Jr.

While fascism is many things, reflected in unnumbered manifestations, it is, quintessentially, the art of the end square—carried to a terrible science. Hitler, Mussolini, Trujillo, Batista, Franco—and, of course, today's variant, Johnson—were, and are, above all proto-type squares.

It's not only that each in his own way — Mussolini with his castor oil 'treatment,' Hitler with his concentration camp system leading directly to the 'Final Solution' (the last, desperate

(Continued on Page 5)

Blow-Up, Psychedelic Sexualis and The War Game —or, David Hemmings Is Herman Kahn in Disguise

Ready for another little trippypoo?

Start with this letter from a subscriber: "I've recently heard rumors that Paul Krassner doesn't exist and that he is, in fact, a composite of a number of fulsome individuals. These people, it's said, each subject themselves monthly to a strange experience, then everyone's experience is compiled into one story which is subsequently given some idiotic moral (much in the same way *Time* magazine writes its articles). In issue #74, for example, the *Crazy SANE to Loving Haight* story was actually written by a Krassner who attended SANE's rally, another who's an ascetic but takes acid, another who visited Haight-Ashbury, another who reads *McCall's* ads in the N.Y. *Times*, another who insulted Joe Pyne, etc. In this way, the story appears to be the exploits of one man, the mythical Paul Krassner. I've also heard that a conspiracy has developed by which one faction of Paul Krassners is seeking to gain control over the rest through the use of CIA terror tactics. Is this the reason I haven't received issue #75?"

Now the whole world knows.

This has been Vietnam Summer, a men's cologne, more fragrant than Spring Mobilization, which sponsored an anti-war march on April 15, in San Francisco, where then-*Ramparts*-publisher-not-to-be Ed Keating

(Continued on Page 17)

No. 75 **35 Cents**

Pope Paul Pricks Prophylactics

October, 1968
35 Cents

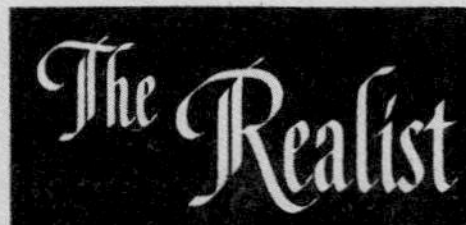
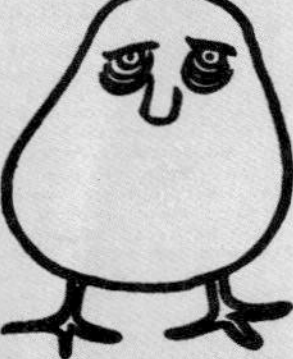

Mailer, McLuhan and Muggeridge: On Obscenity

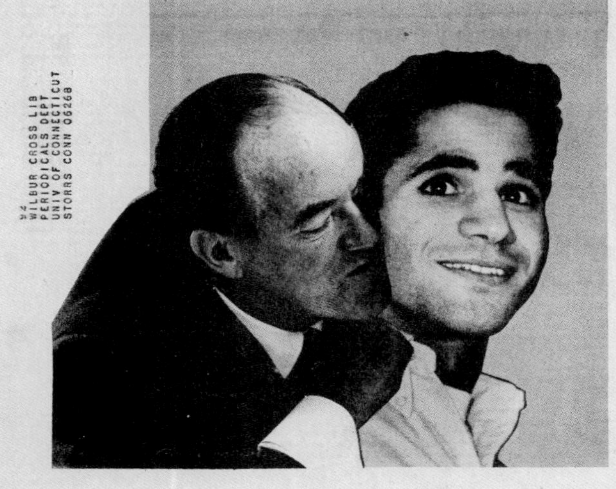

The Realist (New York), August 1967, no. 76, cover
The Realist (New York), June 1967, no. 75, cover
The Realist (New York), August 1967, no. 76, back cover
The Realist (New York), October 1968, no. 83, cover

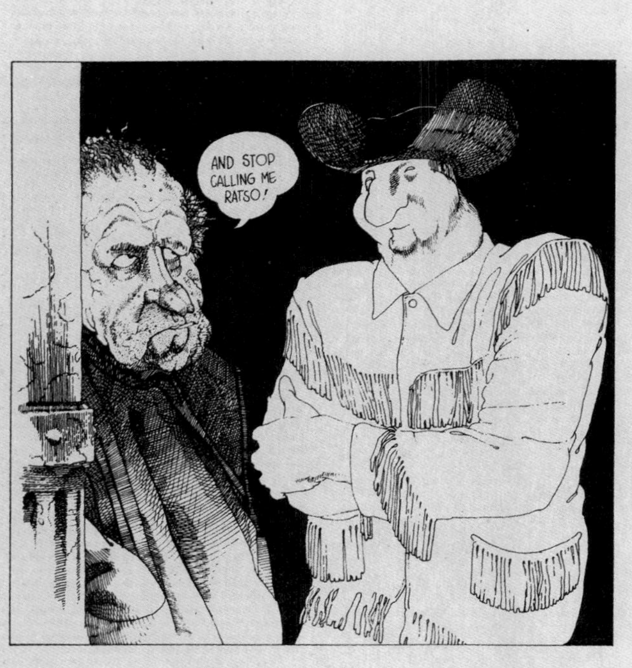

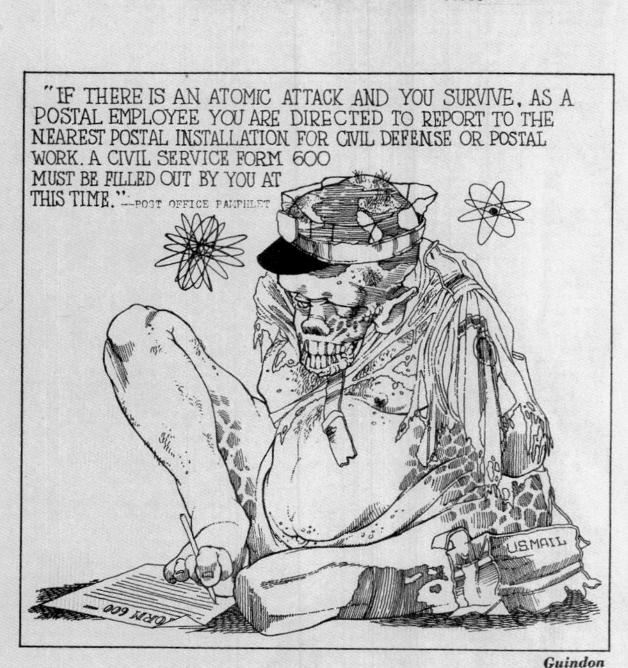

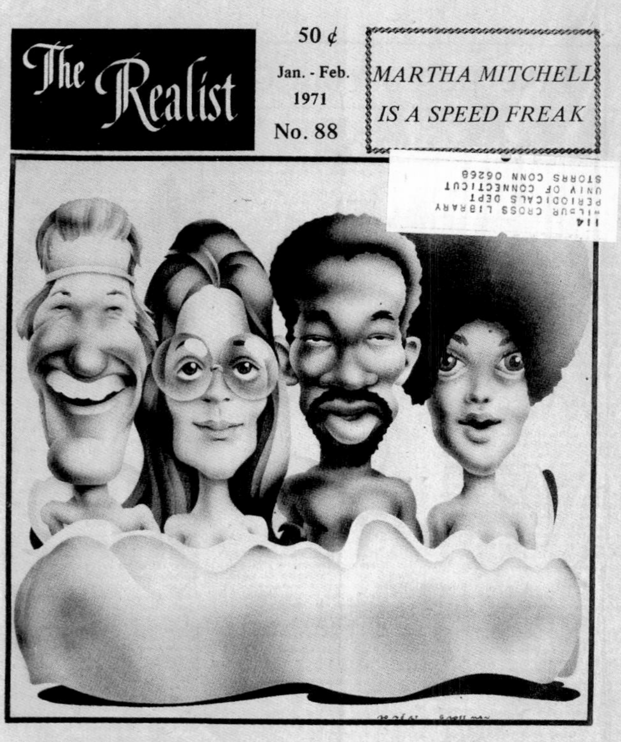

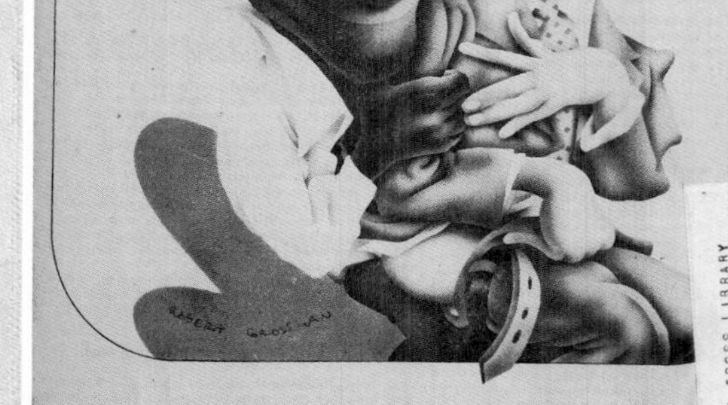

The Realist (New York), March–April 1970, no. 86b, back cover
The Realist (New York), May–June 1970, no. 87, back cover
The Realist (New York), January–February 1970, no. 88, cover
The Realist (New York), 1971, cover

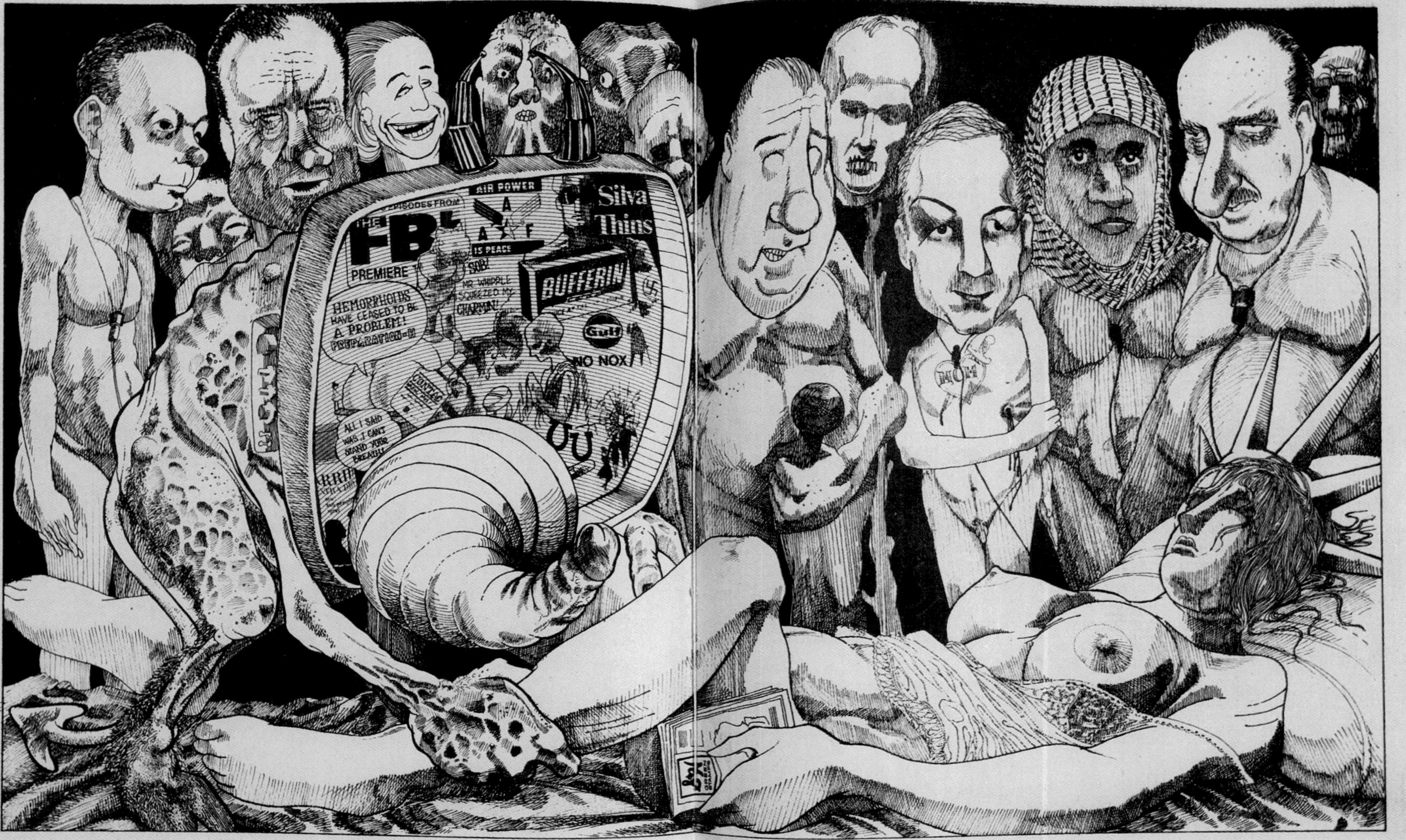

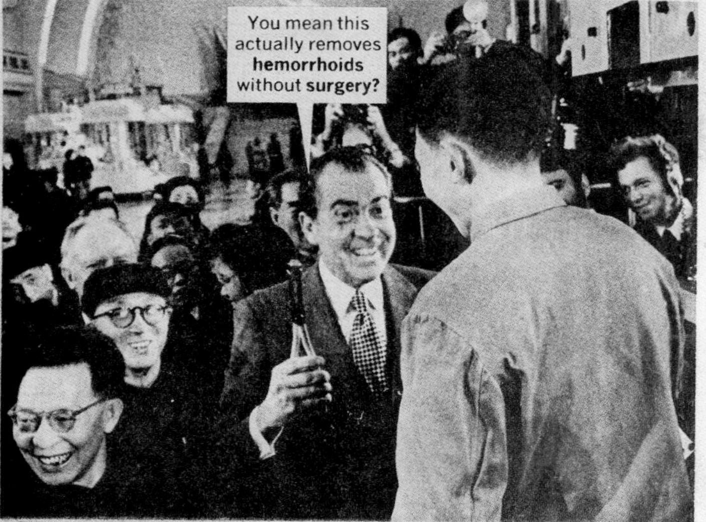

How District Attorney Jim Garrison Was Framed

Jim Garrison was arrested in July 1971 by federal agents who charged him with taking bribes to protect illegal pinball gambling in New Orleans.

John Mitchell in Washington and U.S. Attorney Gerald Gallinghouse from New Orleans announced the arrest. They were assisted by the FBI and the Internal Revenue Service.

A federal judge earlier that Spring had ordered Garrison to halt charges of perjury against Clay Shaw which stemmed from his conspiracy trial in New Orleans.

Associated Press, UPI, *Life, Time* and all the media were on hand to photograph Jim being fingerprinted, framed and taken away by federal agents.

The New Orleans States-Item delighted in printing every word of the 107-page allegations against the New Orleans D.A. It made front pages for many consecutive days.

Pershing Gervais, former friend and investigator for Jim, helped the government attempt to imprison and fine his pal.

On May 25, 1972, Gervais surfaced and had a change of heart.

Details were revealed about how the Justice Department went to great efforts to get some kind of a conviction against Jim Garrison. This was obviously punishment for his revealing the conspiracy that murdered President Kennedy.

The Justice Department, the FBI and the Treasury Department are involved in every one of the major and minor political assassinations and conspiracies in the U.S.

These departments are supposed to investigate misconduct and criminals. They are not supposed to frame and turn the word 'justice' around to create convictions of innocent persons.

Pershing Gervais gave a detailed account of his relationship with the Justice Dept. Legal action by Congress, impeachment of public officials, is required.

Associated Press, UPI, *Life, Time* and all the media were strangely silent as the account of Jim Garrison's innocence was announced. There were no cameras on hand to photograph the criminals in Washington.

Gervais made the following statements:

1. "The Justice Department forced me to make a false affidavit against Jim Garrison."
2. "Gerald Shur, Ries Cash, Kathy Kimry were my contacts from the Justice Dept."
3. "I was given a phony minister's permit in order to work in Canada."
4. "I was given an alias in Washington, following the New Orleans arrangements, which became Paul Mason."
5. A birth certificate was issued to his son under the new false name, so he could attend school in Canada.
6. "My next job, in Canada, was to spy on an oil company, to see why they were not getting drilling rights."
7. The chain of command from the Justice Dept. went from Washington, to General Motors in Detroit, to General Motors in Canada where Gervais was placed in a job paying $18,000 a year. He didn't work. This was a pay-off.
8. The contact man in Canada was a man named Blackemore, now a "retired" member of the Royal Canadian Mounted Police.

Pershing Gervais has stated that "I have been working at a fake job in Canada since January, and living there since July, all because of *connivance between the Justice Department, the Canadian Government and General Motors.*"

The Realist (New York), August 1972, no. 93, inside spread and back cover

Up to Mar. 21 **NORTH VIETNAM**

1,729

U.S. Aircraft Downed

VIETNAM COURIER

March 27 1967 No 103 4th Year

INFORMATION WEEKLY — E.O. : 46 Tran Hung Dao Street — Hanoi — D.R.V. — Tel. 3841

D.R.V. Foreign Ministry Makes Public President HO CHI MINH'S Reply to U.S. President L. B. JOHNSON

OVER the past period, world public opinion has been vehemently condemning the U.S. imperialists' aggression in Vietnam, and at the same time vigorously supporting the Vietnamese people's patriotic struggle and just stand. It has given a warm response to the statement made by the Foreign Minister of the Democratic Republic of Vietnam to journalist W. Burchett on January 28, 1967.

To the legitimate demands of public opinion, the U.S. aggressors have impudently replied by a very serious escalation of the war. They are holding a war conference in Guam with a view to stepping up and expanding the war of aggression in Vietnam to a more serious extent. On the other hand, they unceasingly clamour about their hypocritical "desire for peace" and spread misinformation about so-called "existing contacts" between the United States and the Government of the Democratic Republic of Vietnam.

With a view to exposing to world public opinion the stubbornness and perfidy of the U.S. rulers, the Foreign Ministry of the Democratic Republic of Vietnam makes public President Ho Chi Minh's reply to U.S. President L.B. Johnson.

Hanoi, March 21, 1967
THE D.R.V. FOREIGN MINISTRY

In the first week of February 1967, the representative of the United States in Moscow requested to meet the representative of the Democratic Republic of Vietnam and handed him a message from U.S. President L. B. Johnson to President Ho Chi Minh. A few days later, the United States resorted to the trick of "prolonging the bombing pause in North Vietnam" on the occasion of Tet (Lunar New Year Festival—Ed.) and set a time limit for Hanoi to give a "response". On February 14, 1967, the President of the United States ordered the bombing of the Democratic Republic of Vietnam to be resumed and brazenly declared "a resumption of full-scale hostilities."

On February 15, 1967, the representative of the Democratic Republic of Vietnam handed to the representative of the United States President Ho Chi Minh's reply to U.S. President L. B. Johnson.

See page 2: U.S. President L. B. Johnson's Message to President Ho Chi Minh.

PRESIDENT HO CHI MINH'S REPLY TO U.S. PRESIDENT LYNDON B. JOHNSON

"The U.S. Government Has Unleashed the War of Aggression in Vietnam. It Must Cease This Aggression. That Is the Only Way to the Restoration of Peace."

To His Excellency Mr LYNDON B. JOHNSON,
President,
United States of America

Your Excellency,

ON February 10, 1967, I received your message. This is my reply.

Vietnam is thousands of miles away from the United States. The Vietnamese people have never done any harm to the United States. But contrary to the pledges made by its representative at the 1954 Geneva Conference, the U.S. Government has ceaselessly intervened in Vietnam, it has unleashed and intensified the war of aggression in South Vietnam with a view to prolonging the partition of Vietnam and turning South Vietnam into a neo-colony and a military base of the United States. For over two years now, the U.S. Government has, with its air and naval forces, carried the war to the Democratic Republic of Vietnam, an independent and sovereign country.

The U.S. Government has committed war crimes, crimes against peace and against mankind. In South Vietnam, half a million U.S. and satellite troops have resorted to the most inhuman weapons and the most barbarous methods of warfare, such as napalm, toxic chemicals and gases, to massacre our compatriots, destroy crops, and raze villages to the ground. In North Vietnam, thousands of U.S. aircraft have dropped hundreds of thousands of tons of bombs, destroying towns, villages, factories, roads, bridges, dykes, dams, and even churches, pagodas, hospitals, schools. In your message, you apparently deplored the sufferings and destructions in Vietnam. May I ask you: Who has perpetrated these monstrous crimes? It is the U.S. and satellite troops. The U.S. Government is entirely responsible for the extremely serious situation in Vietnam.

The U.S. war of aggression against the Vietnamese people constitutes a challenge to the countries of the socialist camp, a threat to the national independence movement, and a serious danger to peace in Asia and the world.

The Vietnamese people deeply love independence, freedom and peace. But in the face of the U.S. aggression, they have risen up, united as one man, fearless of sacrifices and hardships; they are determined to carry on their Resistance until they have won genuine independence and freedom and true peace. Our just cause enjoys strong sympathy and support from the peoples of the whole world including broad sections of the American people.

The U.S. Government has unleashed the war of aggression in Vietnam. It must cease this aggression. That is the only way to the restoration of peace. The U.S. Government must stop definitively and unconditionally its bombing raids and all other acts of war against the Democratic Republic of Vietnam; withdraw from South Vietnam all U.S. and satellite troops; recognize the South Vietnam National Front for Liberation; and let the Vietnamese people settle themselves their own affairs. Such is the basic content of the four-point stand of the Government of the Democratic Republic of Vietnam, which embodies the essential principles and provisions of the 1954 Geneva Agreements on Vietnam. It is the basis of a correct political solution to the Vietnam problem.

In your message, you suggested direct talks between the Democratic Republic of Vietnam and the United States. If the U.S. Government really wants these talks, it must first of all stop unconditionally its bombing raids and all other acts of war against the Democratic Republic of Vietnam.

It is only after the unconditional cessation of the U.S. bombing raids and all other acts of war against the Democratic Republic of Vietnam that the Democratic Republic of Vietnam and the United States could enter into talks and discuss questions concerning the two sides.

The Vietnamese people will never submit to force; they will never accept talks under the threat of bombs.

Our cause is absolutely just. It is to be hoped that the U.S. Government will act in accordance with reason.

Sincerely,
HO CHI MINH

SOUTH VIETNAM

U.S. FAILURES IN ITS "SECOND DRY-SEASON COUNTER-OFFENSIVE"

- **In Tay Ninh Province (80km NW of Saigon) between Feb. 22 and Mar. 16: 5,216 G.I.'s Put out of Action, 420 Armoured Cars and Tanks, 55 Guns Destroyed, 91 Aircraft Downed.**
- **In the Western High Plateaux (350km NE of Saigon) between Feb. 15 and Mar. 14: 2,020 Enemy Troops (Mostly G.I.'s) Wiped Out, 34 Military Vehicles and 12 Guns Destroyed, 24 Aircraft Downed.**
- **In Quang Tri (South of the 17th Parallel) between Feb. 26 and Mar. 11: 2,730 Enemy Troops (Mostly U.S. Marines) Put out of Action, 20 Armoured Cars and 7 175mm Guns Destroyed, 13 Aircraft Downed.**

THIS SPECIAL ISSUE OF VIETNAM COURIER REPRINTED BY THE U.S. COMMITTEE TO AID THE N.L.F.-S.V. Box C Old Chelsea Sta. NY NY YU2-7162

WRITE for information and our catalog of Vietnamese literature and films.

Our purpose is to help make the U. S. public aware of the essentially just and moral aims of the Vietnamese in their resistance to U. S. government efforts to "pacify" their country. We seek a call for peace that will allow the Vietnamese to determine their own affairs.

VIETNAM COURIER

25¢ 1967 No 127 4th Year

INFORMATION WEEKLY — E.O.: 46 Tran Hung Dao Street — Hanoi — D.R.V.N. — Tel. 3841

POLITICAL PROGRAMME OF THE SOUTH VIET NAM NATIONAL FRONT FOR LIBERATION

COMMUNIQUE OF THE EXTRAORDINARY CONGRESS OF THE SOUTH VIET NAM N.F.L.

AN extraordinary congress of the South Viet Nam National Front for Liberation, convened by its Central Committee, met in mid-August 1967 in a liberated area to discuss and adopt the **Political Programme of the Front.**

The Congress was attended by all the members of the Central Committee of the Front, representatives of political parties, mass organizations, nationalities, religions, the Command of the South Viet Nam Liberation Armed Forces, committees under the Central Committee of the Front, and committees of all levels of the Front from the northernmost province of Quang Tri to Point Camau in the south, from the mountain areas to the plains.

Also present were many personalities, intellectuals and representatives of the people in Saigon and other cities, many heroes and heroines of the South Viet Nam Liberation Armed Forces, many "valiant fighters" destroying the enemy forces and many emulation fighters.

The Congress was the most splendid image of the great solidarity of the entire people in the struggle against U.S. aggression, for national salvation. It symbolizes the growth by leaps and bounds of the armed forces and people in South Viet Nam in the past seven years since the birth of the South Viet Nam National Front for Liberation, particularly after the victories fight against the U.S. aggressors in the Winter and Spring of the last two years.

After the opening speech by Dr. Phung Van Cung, Vice President of the Presidium of the Central Committee of the South Viet Nam National Front for Liberation, Lawyer Nguyen Huu Tho, President of the Presidium of the Front Central Committee, read a report in which he reviewed the extremely important successes recorded by the South Viet Nam Liberation armed forces and people since the founding of the Front with its 10-point programme aimed at uniting the people to resist the U.S. aggressors and their henchmen and save the country.

President Nguyen Huu Tho analysed the present situation, laid down new tasks for the South Vietnamese armed forces and people, and pointed out the favourable conditions for broadening the great solidarity of the entire people with a view to pushing forward the resistance to U.S. aggression, for national salvation till complete victory.

He proposed to the Congress to discuss and adopt the Political Programme drafted by the Front's Central Committee.

Huynh Tan Phat, Vice-President of the Presidium and Secretary General of the Central Committee of the Front, submitted the draft Political Programme to the Congress.

The Congress warmly discussed the report by President Nguyen Huu Tho and the draft Political Programme of the Front. It also heard addresses by representatives of various localities, political parties, mass organizations, nationalities, religions, the Liberation Armed Forces and many personalities and intellectuals.

The Congress unanimously held that:

SINCE the U.S. imperialists started their aggression against

Continued page 4)

Adopted at the Extraordinary Congress of the South Viet Nam N.F.L.

- **The Arch Enemy of Our People Is U.S. Imperialism and the Puppet Administration**
- **The N.F.L. Fights For:**
  - The Establishment of an Independent, Democratic, Neutral, Peaceful and Prosperous South Viet Nam and the Eventual Reunification of the Country.
  - The Formation of a Broad National Union Government.
  - The Election of a Representative National Assembly.
  - The Institution of Fundamental Democratic Freedoms Guaranteeing Legitimate Interests to All Social Strata of the People.
  - A Foreign Policy of Peace and Neutrality.
- **To Defeat the U.S. Aggressors and Overthrow the Puppet Administration, the South Viet Nam N.F.L., Pursuing Its Policy of Broad National Union, Calls for the Unity of the Entire People to Fight More Resolutely than Ever Until Victory.**

(Full text of the Political Programme on page 4)

AT 7 p.m. on September 1, 1967 in Hanoi, the Permanent Representation of the South Viet Nam N.F.L. in the D.R.V.N. held a press conference (See page 8) to make public the essential documents regarding the Extraordinary Congress of the South Viet Nam N.F.L. Full texts of these documents are printed in this issue.

SOUTH Vietnam

RESOUNDING VICTORIES OF THE PEOPLE'S LIBERATION ARMED FORCES

PLAIN OF REEDS (Dec. 4):

1,000 Enemy Soldiers Put out of Action, 30 War Vessels Sunk or Set Afire in Nguyen Van Tiep Canal.

GIA LAI (Nov. 24):

A Convoy of 68 Vehicles Wiped Out on Road 19, 20 Km from An Khe.

BU DOP (Nov. 28 and 29):

A U.S. Battalion and 5 Puppet Companies Put out of Action 135 Km North of Saigon.

(PAGE 8)

VIETNAM COURIER

December 11 1967 No 141 4th Year

Information Weekly — E.O. : 46 Tran Hung Dao Street, Hanoi — Democratic Republic of Viet Nam

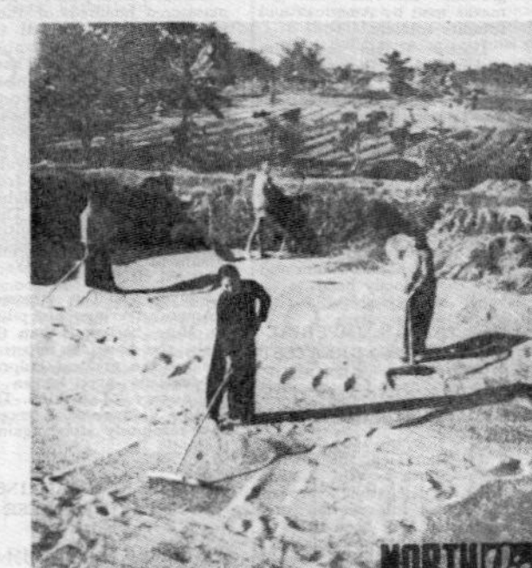

Despite heavy U.S. bombings, Co-operative Y, in Dong Anh district, suburb of Hanoi, obtains an average yield of 5.6 tons per hectare in 1967

NORTH Vietnam

A BUMPER RICE CROP, HIGH YEARLY YIELDS BETWEEN 6 AND 8 TONS PER HECTARE

(PAGE 4)

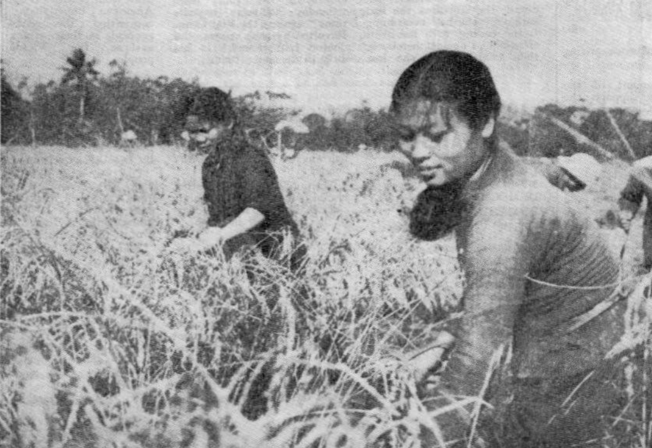

Tan Phong Co-operative (Thai Binh province): average yield of 8.1 tons per hectare in 1967

Up to Dec. 4, 1967

2,614

U.S. planes were downed over North Viet Nam

VIETNAM COURIER

December 18 1967 No 142 4th Year

Information Weekly — E.O. 46 Tran Hung Dao Street, Hanoi — Democratic Republic of Viet Nam

Up to December 16, 1967

2,635

U.S. planes were downed over North Viet Nam

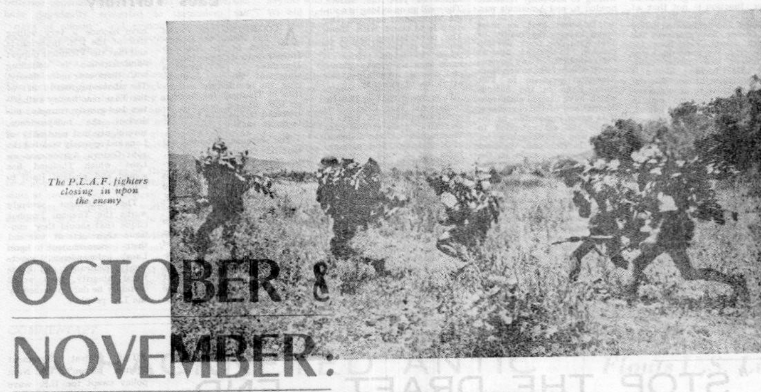

The P.L.A.F. fighters closing in upon the enemy

OCTOBER & NOVEMBER:

Two Months Inaugurating the 1967 Winter - 1968 Spring Victorious Campaign in Both Zones of Viet Nam

SOUTH VIETNAM

IMPORTANT SUCCESSES OF THE PEOPLE'S LIBERATION ARMED FORCES

- **More than 40,000 Enemy Troops Killed, Wounded or Captured, Including Nearly 20,000 G.I.'s and Satellite Troops;**
- **21 Battalions Wiped Out, Including 9 American;**
- **Over 400 Aircraft Downed or Destroyed, 130 Heavy Guns and 800 Military Vehicles of Various Kinds Destroyed Including 276 Tanks and Armoured Cars;**
- **118 Posts and Military Subsectors Razed to the Ground, 54 Bridges and Culverts Blown Up, 17 Towns and Townships Constantly Attacked.**

NORTH VIETNAM

BRILLIANT VICTORIES

262

U.S. AIRCRAFT DOWNED INCLUDING 106 OVER HANOI AND HAI PHONG

Notes from Cuba

A BULLETIN FROM AMERICANS LIVING AND WORKING IN CUBA

VOL. I OCTOBER, 1968 No. 11

ABOUT THE NEW MAN

A Truly Socialist-Communist Consciousness

(Concluding section of address by Fidel Castro July 26, 1968 commemorating the 15th anniversary of attack on Moncada army garrison.)

And we should not use money or wealth to create political awareness. We must use political awareness to create wealth. To offer a man more to do more than his duty is to buy his conscience with money. To give a man participation in more collective wealth because he does his duty and produces more and creates more for society is to turn political awareness into wealth.

As we said before, communism, certainly, cannot be established if we do not create abundant wealth. But the way to do this, in our opinion, is not by creating political awareness with money or with wealth, but by creating wealth with political awareness, and more and more collective wealth with more collective political awareness. (APPLAUSE).

The road is not easy. The task is difficult, and many will critize us. They will call us petty bourgeois, idealists; they will say we are dreamers; they will say we are bound to fail. And yet, facts will speak for us, realities will speak for us and our people will speak and act for us, because we know our people have the capacity to comprehend these roads and to follow these roads.

In the same way, some day we will all have to receive the same. Why? Some will ask: will a canecutter earn as much as an engineer? Yes. Does that mean that an engineer will receive less? No. But some day a canecutter — and I say canecutter symbolically, because in the future we won't have any canecutters — let us say, the driver of a harvest combine or a truck, will earn as much as an engineer today.

And why? The thing is clear very logical. The Revolution has thousands of young students in the universities. The Revolution has thousands of young people studying abroad, dedicated to studying, to becoming engineer, chemists, specializing in different fields. Who pays for their expenses? The people.

If the Revolution needs to send many young people to study in Europe and others in universities, all right; we ask them to study, and they do it in a disciplined way, but that doesn't mean they are privileged. It is important to the Revolution that they study, that they

(Continued on page 13)

Notes From Cuba

A bulletin from Americans living and working in Cuba

VOLUME II OCT — NOV NUMBER 9

STOP THE WAR

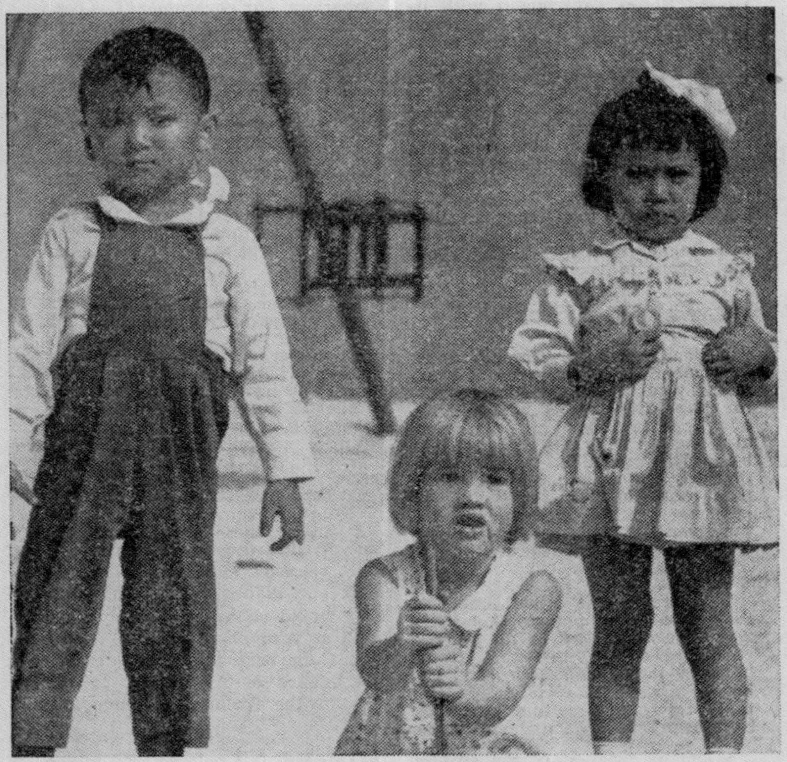

WE NEED PEACE!

An American youngster (center) and her little Vietnamese friends in a Cuban playground.

IN VIET NAM

Previous page
Vietnam Courier (Hanoi), March 27, 1967, no. 103, cover
Vietnam Courier (Hanoi), September 5, 1967, no. 127, cover
Vietnam Courier (Hanoi), December 11, 1967, no. 141, cover
Vietnam Courier (Hanoi), December 18, 1967, no. 142, cover

Notes from Cuba (Havana), October 1968, vol. 1, no. 11, cover
Notes from Cuba (Havana), October-November [1969?], vol. 2, no. 9, cover

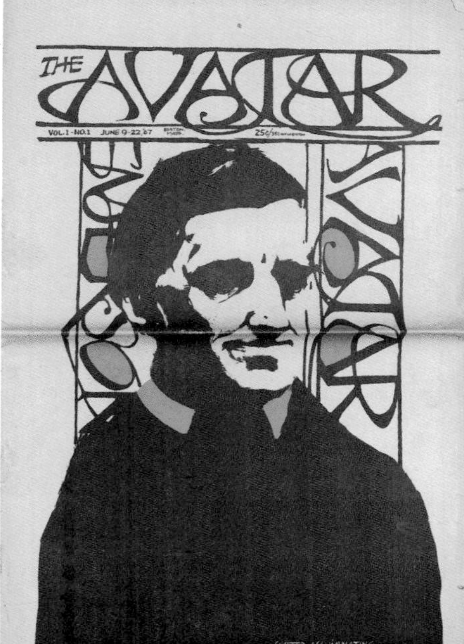

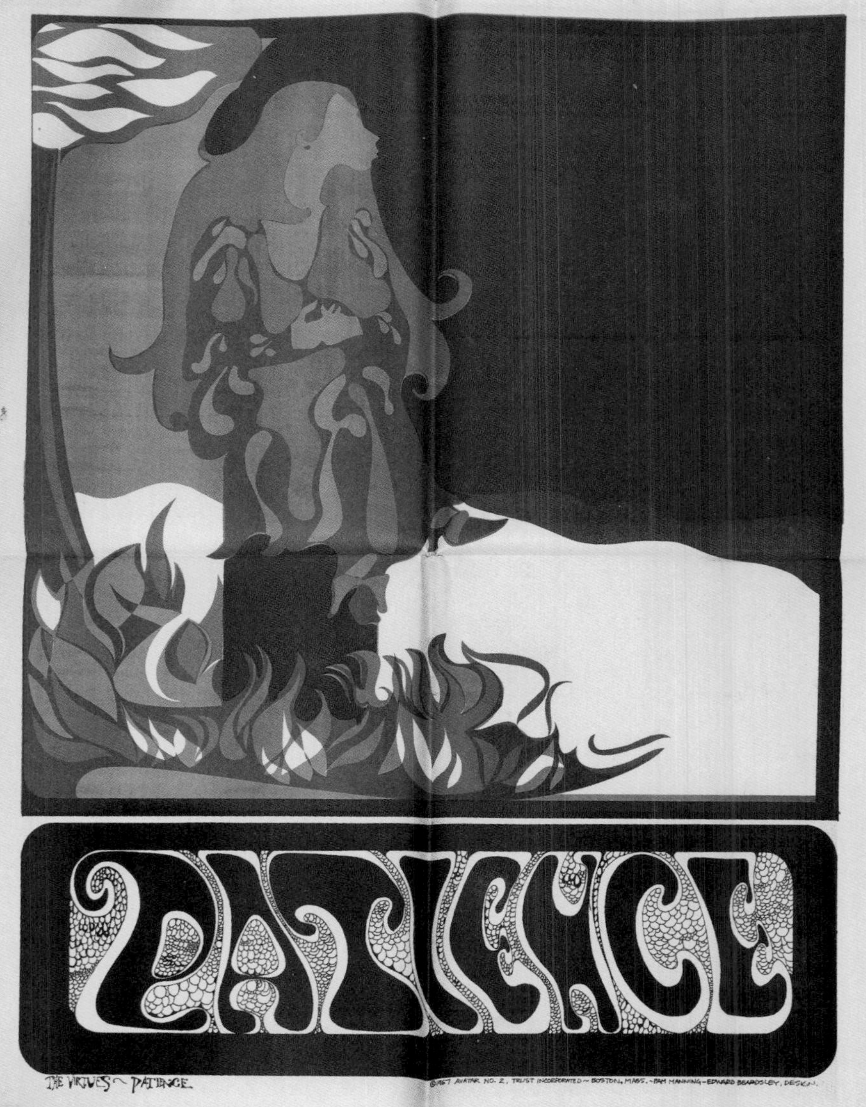

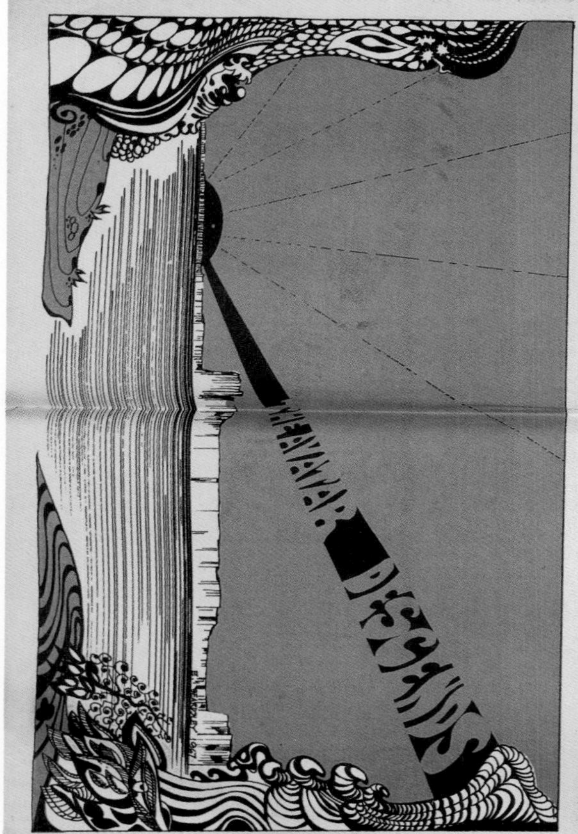

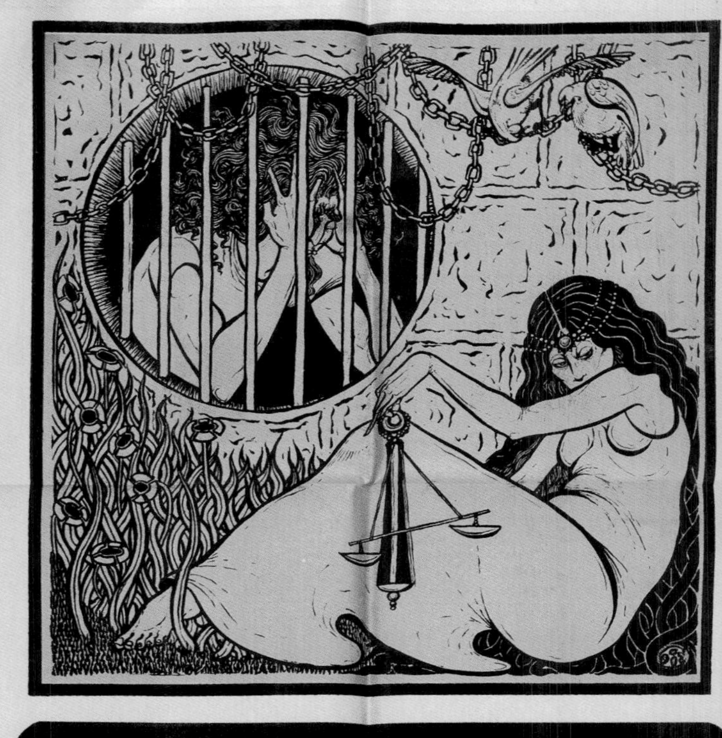

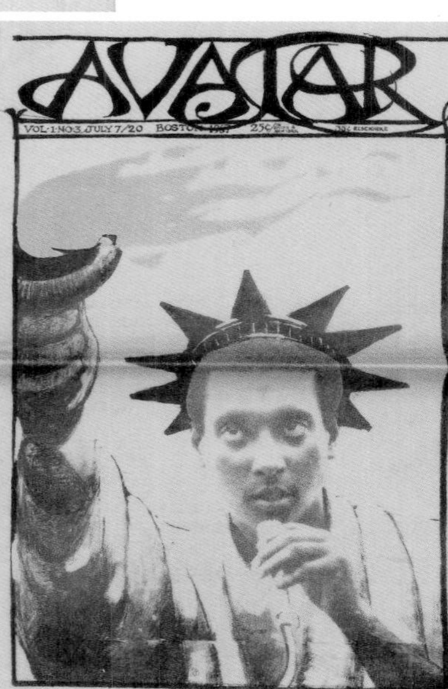

The Avatar (Boston), June 9–22, 1967, vol. 1, no. 1, cover
The Avatar (Boston), June 23–July 6, 1967, vol. 1, no. 2, back cover
The Avatar (Boston), June 9–22, 1967, vol. 1, no. 1, back cover
The Avatar (Boston), July 7–20, 1967, vol. 1, no. 3, back cover
The Avatar (Boston), July 7–20, 1967, vol. 1, no. 3, cover

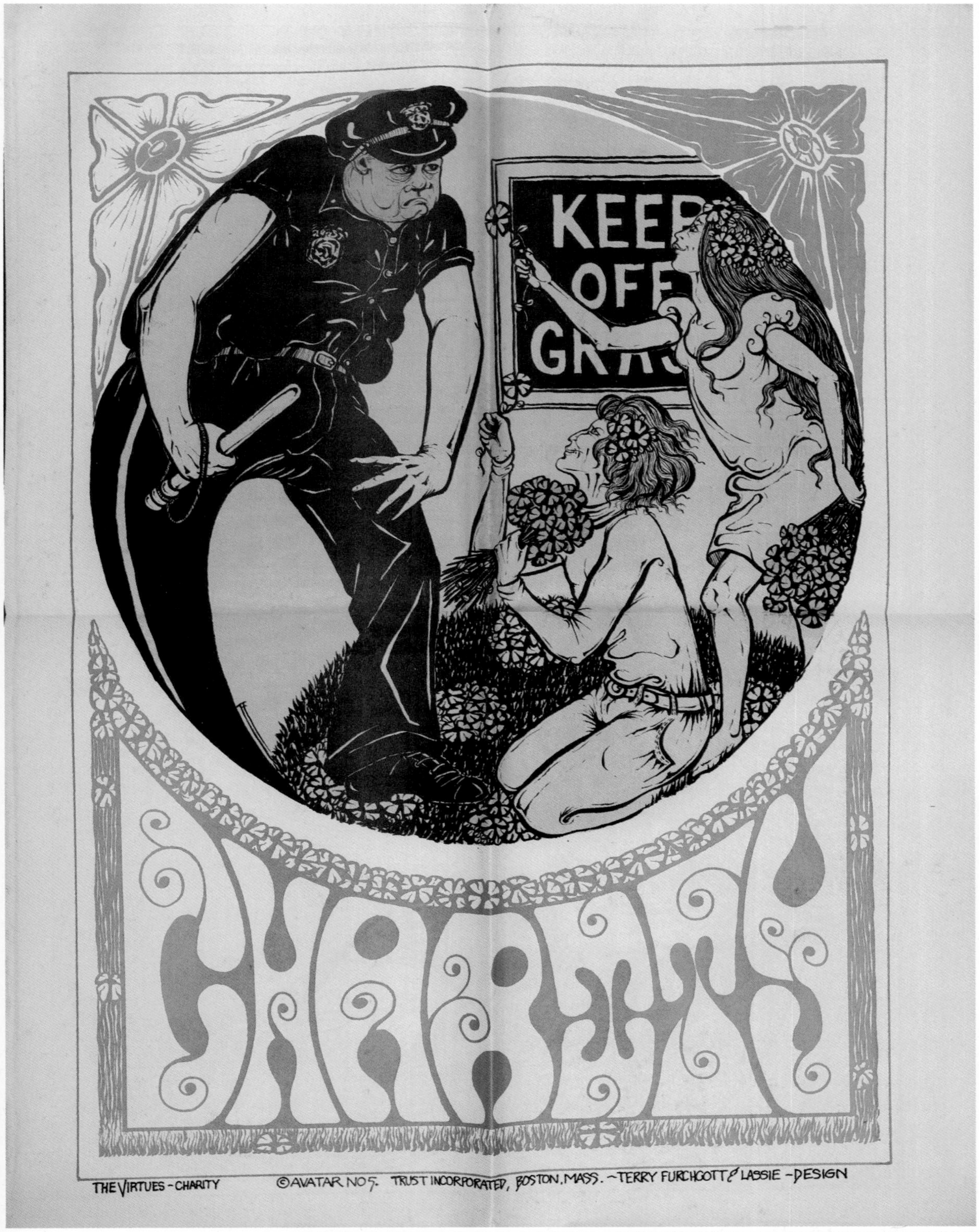

KEEP OFF GRAS

THE VIRTUES - CHARITY ©AVATAR NO 5. TRUST INCORPORATED, BOSTON, MASS. ~ TERRY FURCHGOTT & LASSIE - DESIGN

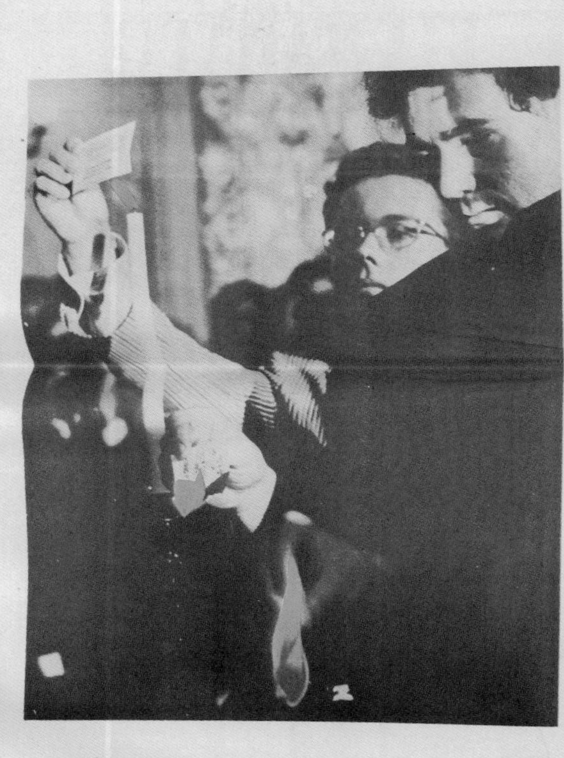

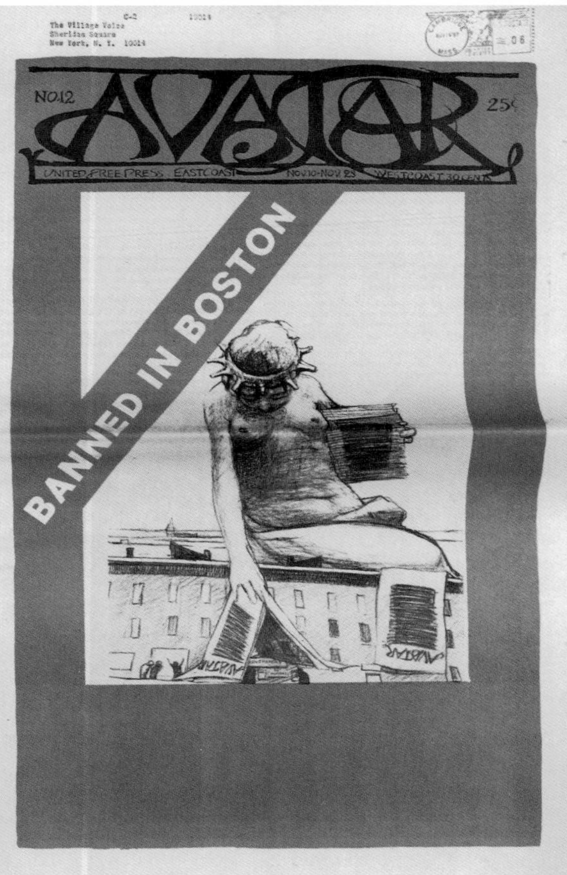

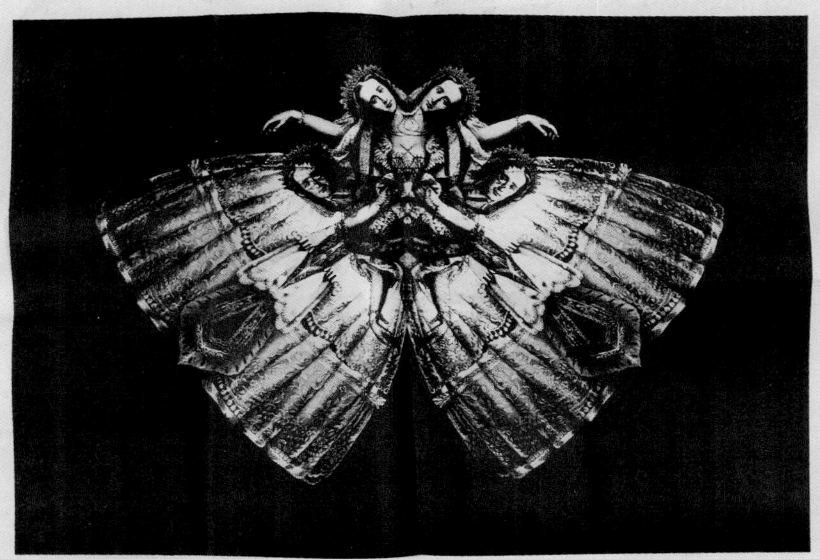

The Avatar (Boston), August 4-17, 1967, vol. 1, no. 5, center spread
The Avatar (Boston), October 27-November 9, 1967, vol. 1, no. 11, back cover
The Avatar (Boston), November 10-23, 1967, vol. 1, no. 12, cover
The Avatar (Boston), December 22-January 4, 1967, vol. 1, no. 15, center spread

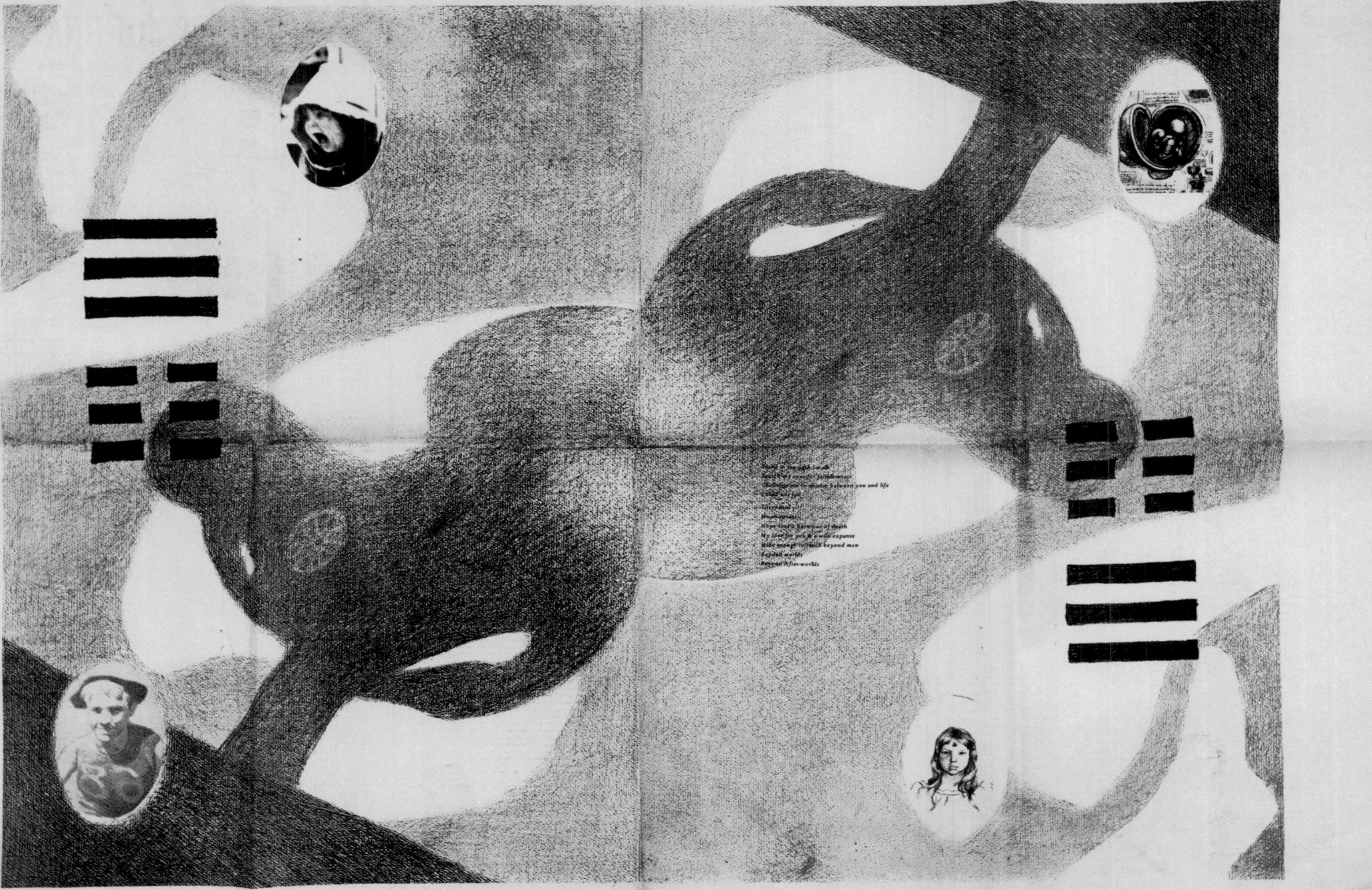

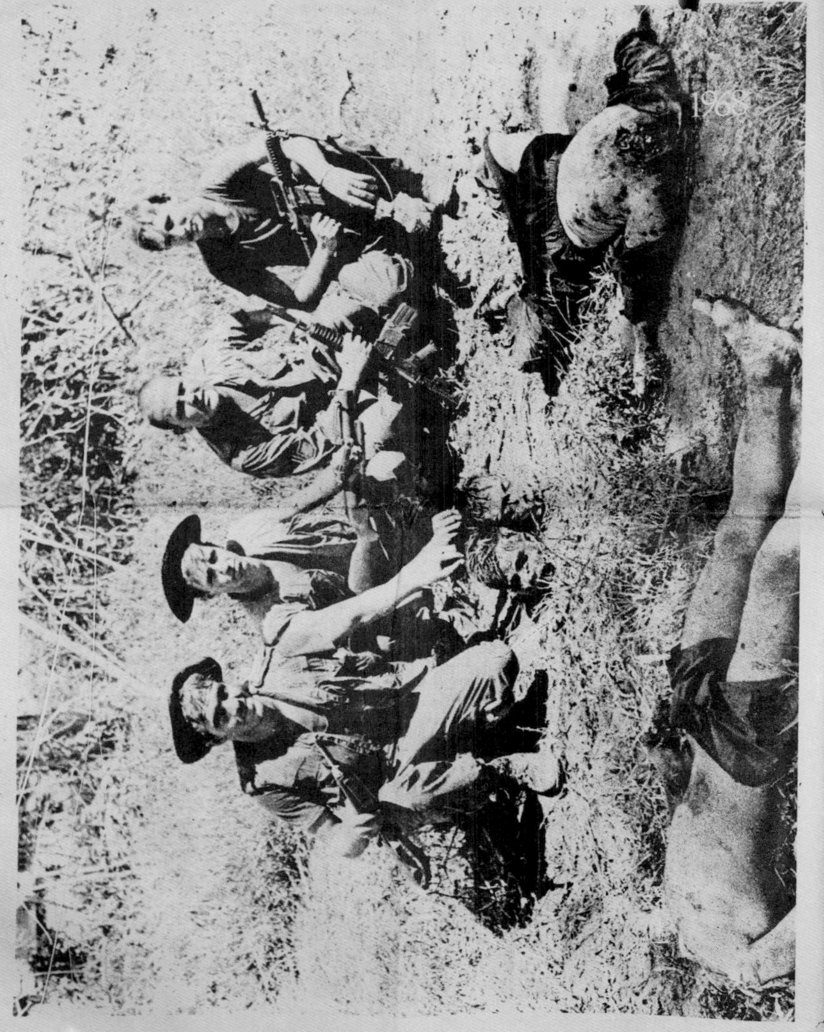

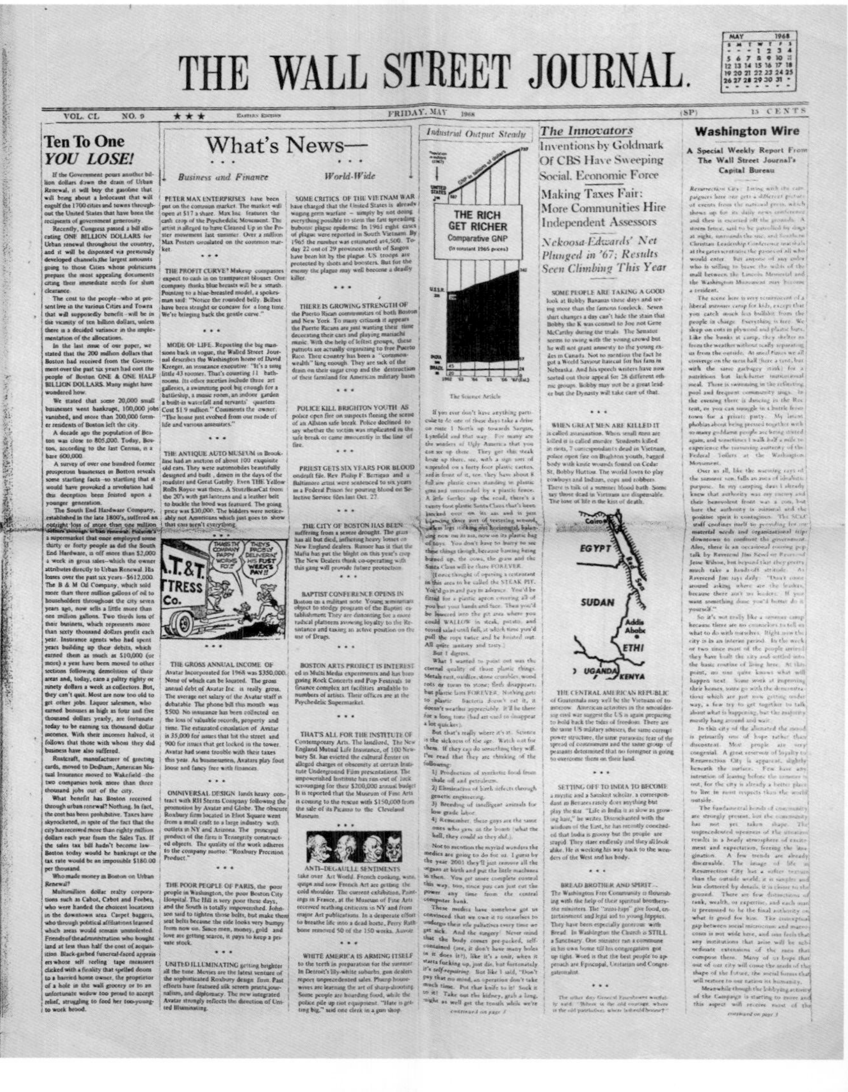

THE WALL STREET JOURNAL.

MAY						1968
S	M	T	W	T	F	S
-	-	-	1	2	3	4
5	6	7	8	9	10	11
12	13	14	15	16	17	18
19	20	21	22	23	24	25
26	27	28	29	30	31	-

VOL. CL NO. 9 ★★★ EASTERN EDITION FRIDAY, MAY 1968 (SP) 15 CENTS

Ten To One *YOU LOSE!*

If the Government pours another billion dollars down the drain of Urban Renewal, it will buy the gasoline that will bring about a holocaust that will engulf the 1700 cities and towns throughout the United States that have been the recipients of government generosity.

Recently, Congress passed a bill allocating ONE BILLION DOLLARS for Urban renewal throughout the country, and it will be dispensed via previously developed channels,the largest amounts going to those Cities whose politicians prepare the most appealing documents citing their immediate needs for slum clearance.

The cost to the people—who at present live in the various Cities and Towns that will supposedly benefit—will be in the vicinity of ten billion dollars, unless there is a decided variance in the implementation of the allocations.

In the last issue of our paper, we stated that the 200 million dollars that Boston had received from the Government over the past six years had cost the …

What's News—

Business and Finance

PETER MAX ENTERPRISES have been put on the common market. The market will open at $17 a share. Max Inc. features the cash crop of the Psychedelic Movement. The artist is alleged to have Cleaned Up in the Poster movement last summer. Over a million Max Posters circulated on the common market.

• • •

THE PROFIT CURVE? Makeup companies expect to cash in on transparent blouses. One company thinks blue breasts will be a smash. Pointing to a blue-breasted model, a spokesman said: "Notice the rounded belly. Bellies have been straight or concave for a long time. We're bringing back the gentle curve."

• • •

MODE OF LIFE. Reporting the big mansions back in vogue, the Walled Street Journal describes the Washington home of David Kreeger, an insurance executive: "It's a snug little 43 roomer. …

World-Wide

SOME CRITICS OF THE VIETNAM WAR have charged that the United States is already waging germ warfare — simply by not doing everything possible to stem the fast spreading bubonic plague epidemic. In 1961 eight cases of plague were reported in South Vietnam. By 1965 the number was estimated at4,500. Today 22 out of 29 provinces north of Saigon have been hit by the plague. US troops are protected by shots and boosters. But for the enemy the plague may well become a deadly killer.

• • •

THERE IS GROWING STRENGTH OF the Puerto Rican communities of both Boston and New York. To many citizens it appears the Puerto Ricans are just wasting their time decorating their cars and playing mariachi music. With the help of leftist groups, these patriots are actually organizing to free Puerto Rico. Their country has been a "commonwealth" long enough. They are sick of the drain on their sugar crop and the destruction …

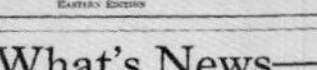

Industrial Output Steady

The Innovators

Inventions by Goldmark Of CBS Have Sweeping Social, Economic Force

Making Taxes Fair: More Communities Hire Independent Assessors

Nekoosa-Edwards' Net Plunged in '67; Results Seen Climbing This Year

SOME PEOPLE ARE TAKING A GOOD look at Bobby Bananas these days and seeing more than the famous forelock. Seven shirt changes a day can't hide the stain that Bobby the K was counsel to Joe not Gene McCarthy during the trials. The Senator seems to swing with the young crowd but he will not grant amnesty to the young exiles in Canada. Not to mention the fact he got a World Saviour haircut for his fans in Nebraska. And his speech writers have now …

Washington Wire

A Special Weekly Report From The Wall Street Journal's Capital Bureau

Resurrection City: Living with the campaigners here one gets a different picture of events from the national press, which shows up for its daily news conference and then is escorted off the grounds. A storm fence, said to be patrolled by dogs at night, surrounds the site, and Southern Christian Leadership Conference marshals at the gates scrutinize the passes of all who would enter. But anyone of any color who is willing to brave the walls of the mall between the Lincoln Memorial and the Washington Monument may become a resident.

The scene here is very reminiscent of a liberal summer camp for kids, except that you catch much less bullshit from the people in charge. Everything is free. We sleep on cots in plywood and plastic huts. Like the bunks at camp, they shelter us from the weather without really separating us from the outside. At meal times we all converge on the mess hall (here a tent, but with the same garbagey stink) for a …

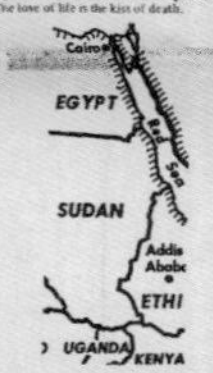

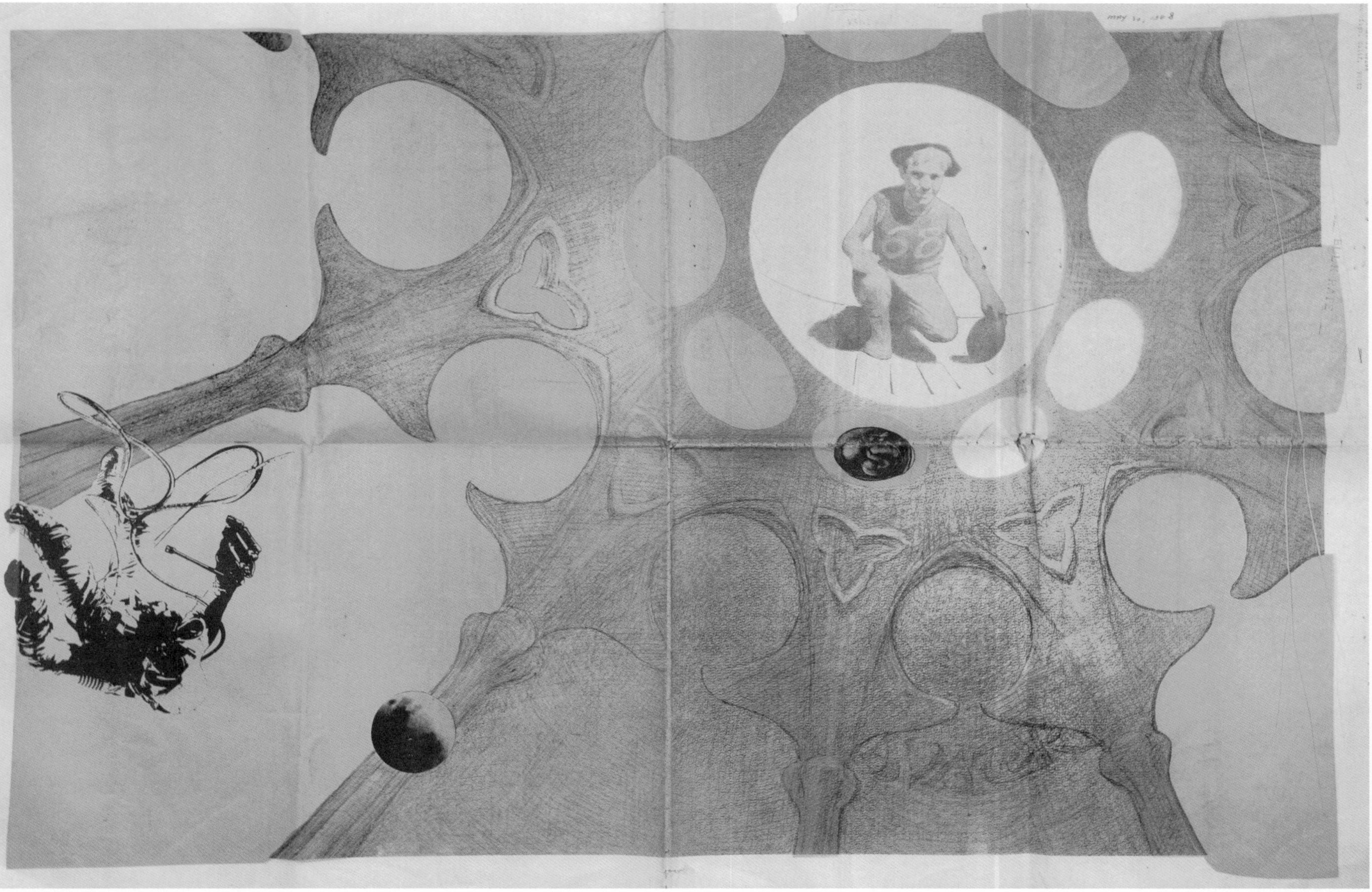

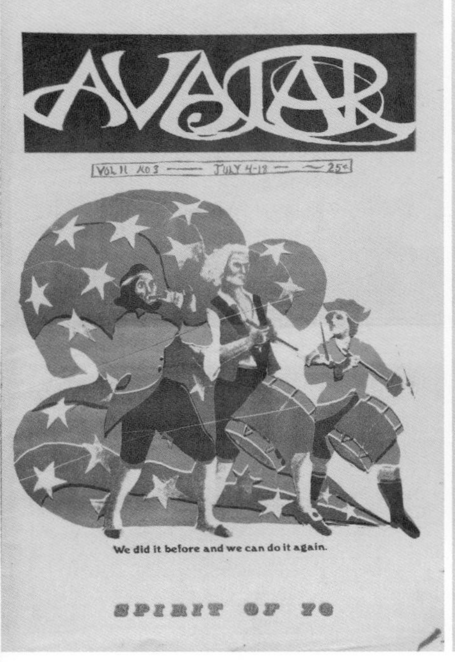

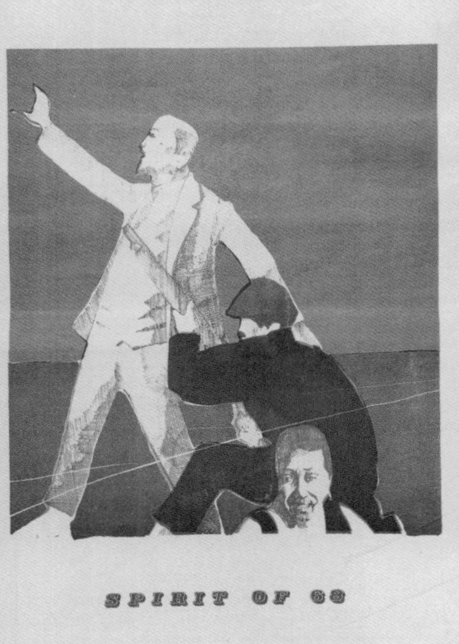

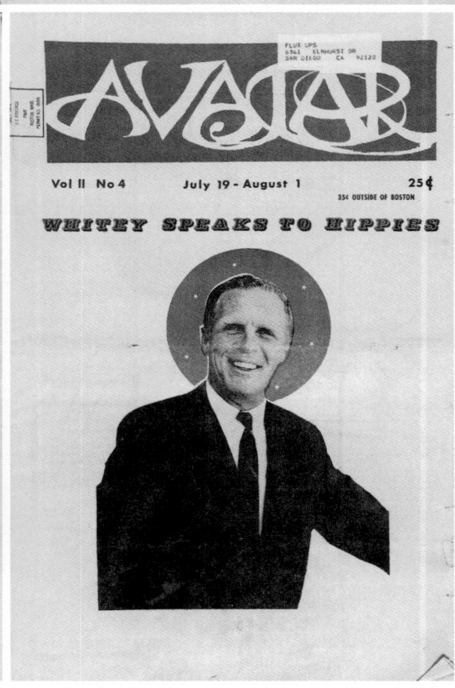

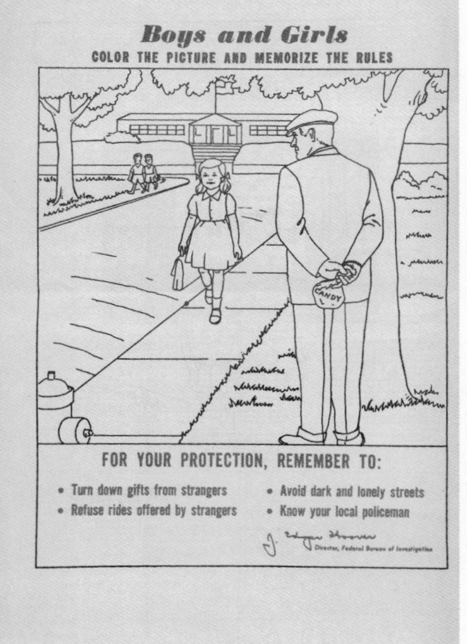

Previous page
The Avatar (Boston), May 30, 1968, vol. 2, no. 1, center spread
The Avatar (Boston), May 30, 1968, vol. 2, no. 1, spread

The Avatar (Boston), May 30, 1968, vol. 2, no. 1, center spread
The Avatar (Boston), July 4–18, 1968, vol. 2, no. 3, cover
The Avatar (Boston), July 4–18, 1968, vol. 2, no. 3, back cover
The Avatar (Boston), July 19–August 1, 1968, vol. 2, no. 4, cover
The Avatar (Boston), July 19–August 1, 1968, vol. 2, no. 4, back cover

DESECRATION CITY

by Marshall Law

WASHINGTON, D. C. LNS – By 11:00 a.m. June 24 – the streets and homes of Resurrection City were deserted, except for patrolling military jeeps and hundreds of police guards stationed at the fence on the City's perimeter. Flies were beginning to swarm on the fresh, hot bread left out in the haste of evacuation. No troops would touch it though, lest the native food give them dysentery.

The Urbal Renewal tactic practiced in evacuating and burning cities in Vietnam was brought back home. In the place of a translated leaflet dropped from an airplane, the Government made this loudspeaker announcement at 9:45 a.m.:

"The permit on this property has expired. You must leave here within the next 56 minutes to avoid arrest and prosecution. For those of you who have no other means of transportation, bus service to your homes will be provided by the Travelers Aid. Shuttle buses are now available at the west side of the Reflecting Pool."

Later this week, the tactic will be carried to fruition; the city will be quietly bulldozed and burned.

But the "facesaving" devices which our military say are crucial to Oriental psyches were not forgotten: Ralph David Abernathy had miraculously led most of the last several hundred residents out of the Camp and toward a demonstration at the Agriculture Department, an hour before the final eviction announcement.

The mass exodus to the Agriculture building and then on to the Capitol for the arrests which were SCLC's announced goal of the day, was carefully synchronized with the government, and was even predicted in the Washington Post of that morning. Abernathy's group assembled at 8:30 and was just far enough away not to know what was happening when the bust occurred. Earlier, Abernathy had complained to the press that the trouble with confronting the federal government is that, unlike Selma or Birmingham, there was no obvious enemy. But the Agriculture Demonstration was hatched to avoid the one real confrontation of the Poor People's Campaign.

Abernathy and the government had been working together since the early days of the campaign, the poor people being pawns in both their games of lobbying Congress – by a new, quaint technique – to cough up poverty funds and stop black alienation from spreading. Yesterday's Evening Star revealed how the City Commissioner's office had arranged the provision of lumber, bullhorns and other equipment for the Campaign and had worked closely with SCLC in planning it. Walter Fauntelroy, SCLC's man in D. C., is one of Johnson's appointees to the City Council.

But this cozy relationship went sour as officials began to realize that Abernathy did not have as much control over "his" poor people as he claimed. Various incidents of violence led to bad publicity. Most threatening, some of the residents were beginning to talk as if they'd never go – and it was becoming clear that Congress wasn't about to be budged, especially by a bunch of poor people camped out on its doorstep. The heart-rending village was becoming an unpopular eyesore.

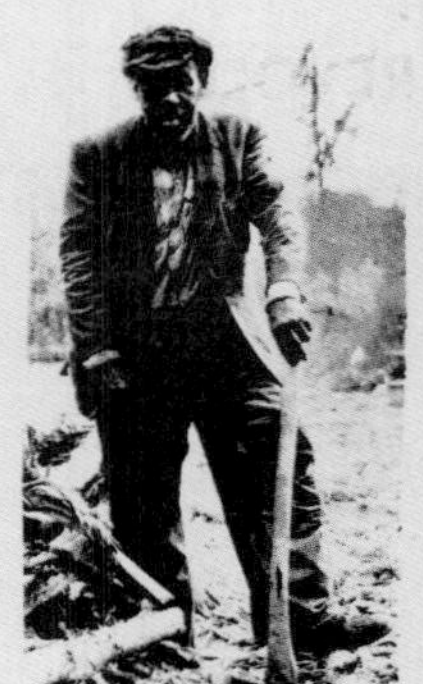

So SCLC quietly arranged to de-escalate by offering free bus tickets to any remaining residents who wanted to (would) go home. Powerless to prevent the expiration of the good behavior permit, SCLC could not afford an ugly and bloody fight with the government.

At the same time; SCLC could not risk being too obvious in selling out the We-Won't-Budge principle of the campaign lest it lose all control over tent city's residents. Particularly important was maintaining enough trust so that the residents would march downtown with Abernathy the day after the permit had expired. ("If you trust me, Ralph Abernathy, you'll go back to your beds," he had blared over the loudspeaker two nights earlier when an angry group had assembled.)

So, Sunday, June 23, the last legal day, SCLC was busy constructing a hugh new wooden edifice, next to City Hall, the most permanent-looking of all the Camp's buildings. But donated wood is cheap and the labor was free. The Registration Booth was still open.

For their part, the residents lived no differently that day than any other, and some of them spent the afternoon painting their shacks.

Why did most of them follow Abernathy out?

Why did many residents carry bundles of clothing to the Agriculture demonstration, even though the marshals insisted they would all be coming back and never, never abandon the city?

"You see, it's like this. When you have so many internal problems – all those troublemakers and all that negotiating by the leaders when we is not involved – then folks don't care so much. It don't seem worth fighting so hard."

But some of us refused to leave and 112 were hauled off to jail from their homes at Resurrection City. 1500 cops joined in the raid. Abandoning all pretense of the residents being residents, and of citizens being citizens, no warrants were issued before the police entered the huts and removed people.

The news of the maneuverings which closed the City sent a wave of frustration through Washington's black community today, and angry young men roamed the streets, throwing bricks and bottles, and looking menacing. A few stores were looted. But Washington is Saigon, and since King's death, troops have been stationed just outside the city on the alert.

National Guardsmen were trucked and bussed in. A stretch of 14th Street was systematically tear gassed every half block.

By 9:00 p.m., the City was put under martial law. A blanket of military law and order prevailed; a curfew was declared. The actual incidents of window breaking and looting which had occurred were minor, and require little retelling. But it took military action of this scope and speed to prevent Washington's second major outburst in two months.

The government sees quite correctly that Washington must become a permanently militarized city. For if the troops go too far away, hell will break loose. It is no longer possible for white America to govern Washington by civilian authority.

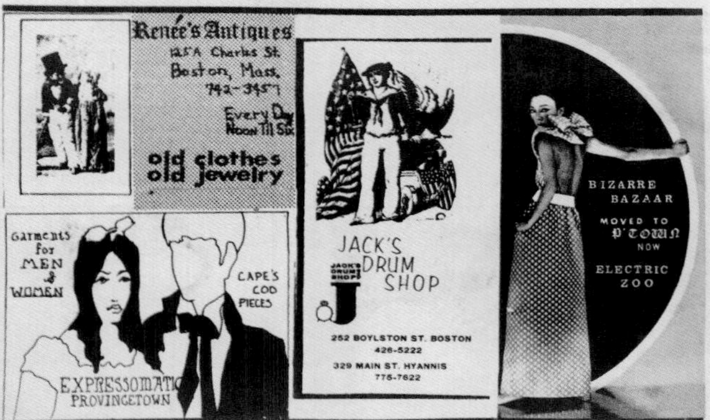

REVOLUTION

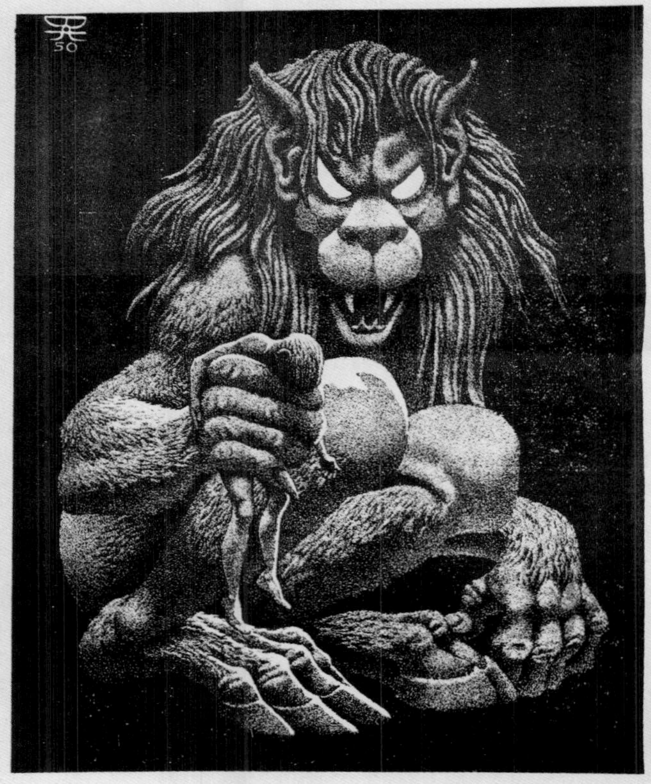

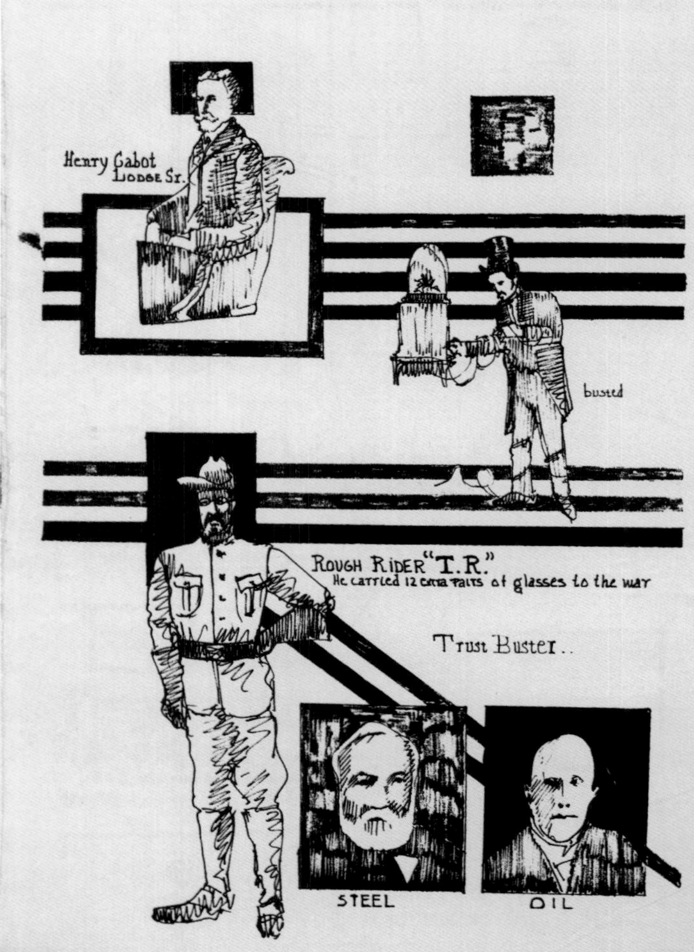

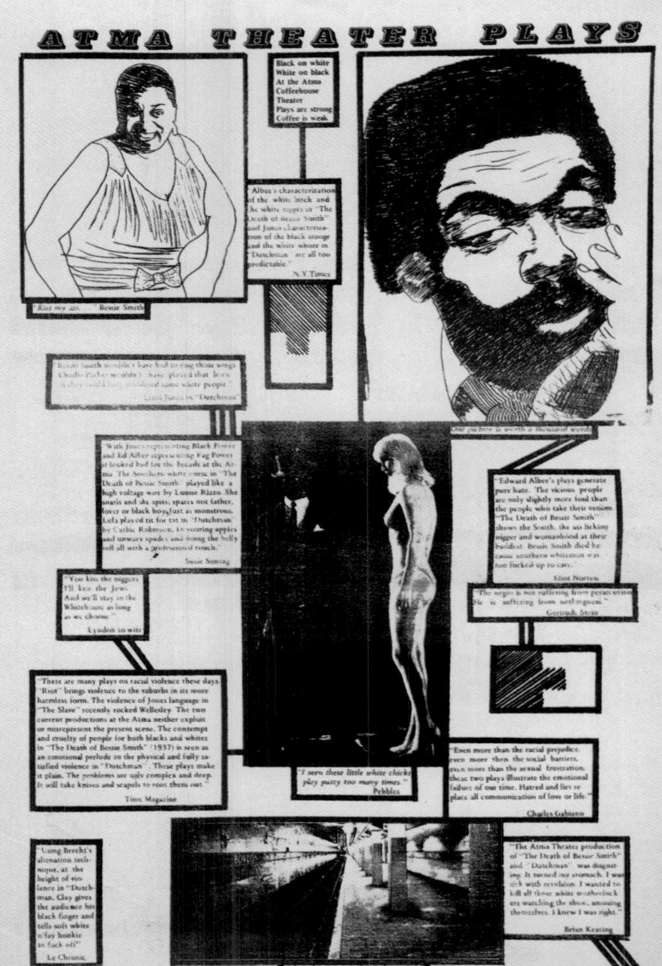

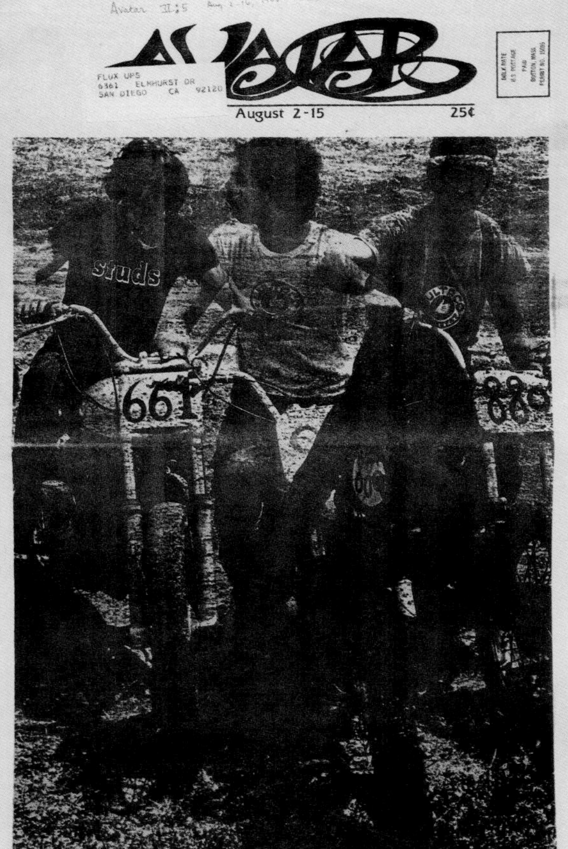

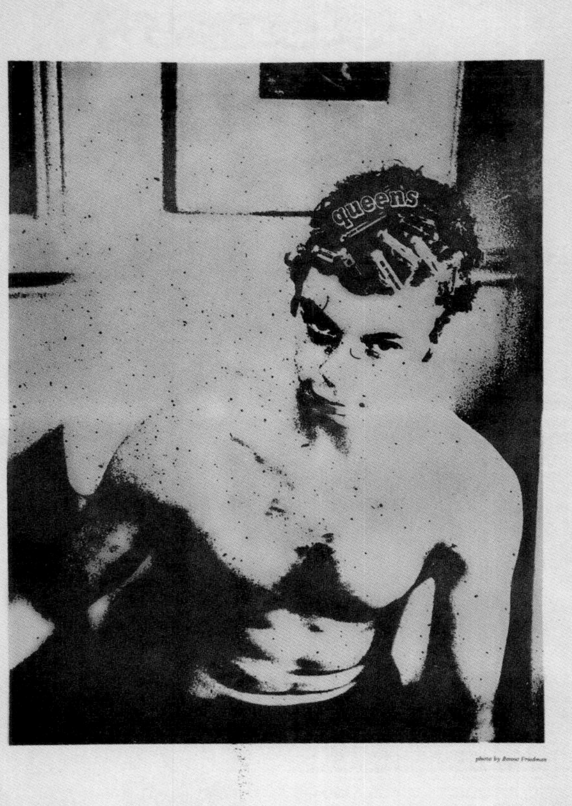

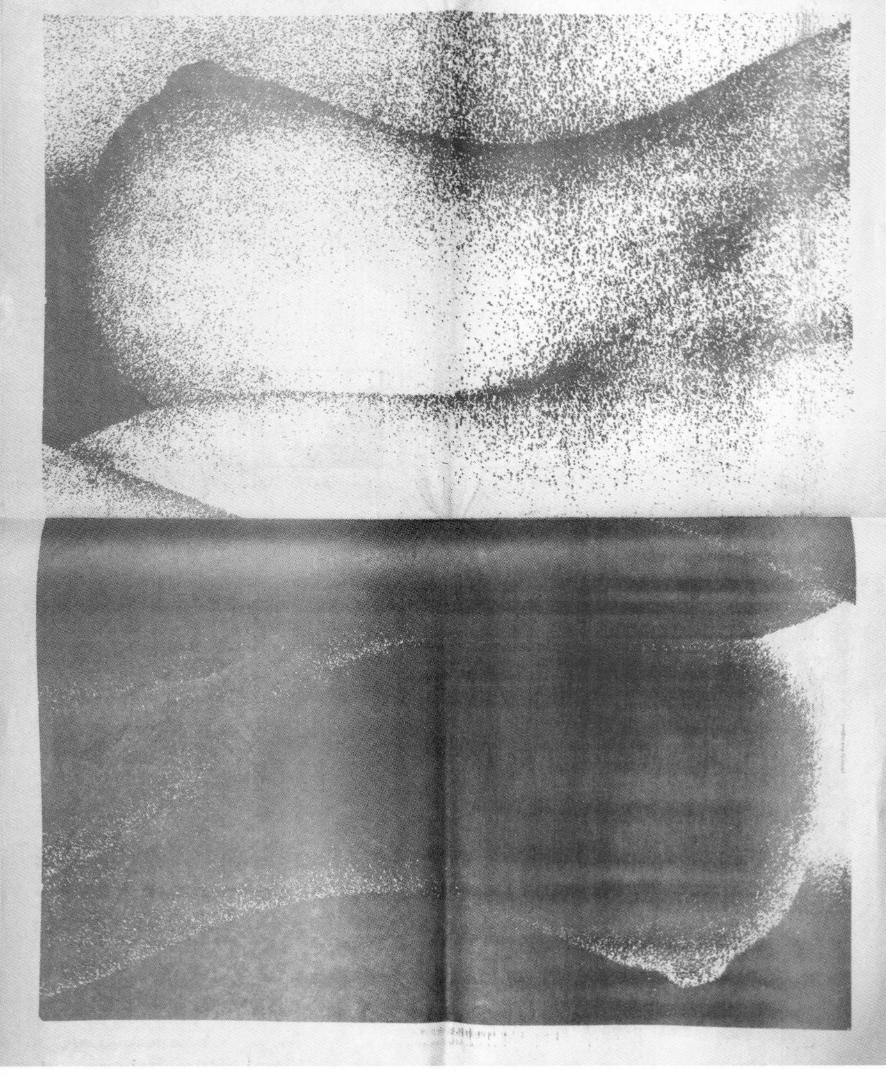

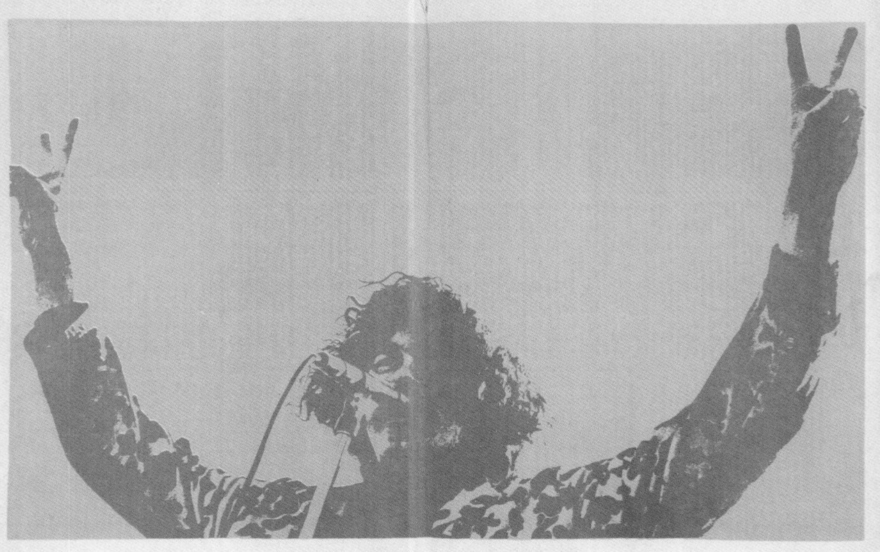

Previous page
The Avatar (Boston), July 4–18, 1968, vol. 2, no. 3, spread
The Avatar (Boston), July 4–18, 1968, vol. 2, no. 3, spread

The Avatar (Boston), August 2–15, 1968, vol. 2, no. 5, cover
The Avatar (Boston), August 2–15, 1968, vol. 2, no. 5, back cover
The Avatar (Boston), August 2–15, 1968, vol. 2, no. 5, center spread
The Avatar (Boston), August 16–29, 1968, vol. 2, no. 6, center spread

PAGE EIGHT THE BOSTON FREE PRESS

Americans !---Liberty or Death !---Join or Die !

THE Massachusetts Spy Or, American ORACLE of Liberty.

VOL. V WORCESTER, WEDNESDAY, MAY 3, 1775. (NUMB. 219.

To the PUBLIC.

THE good People of this County, at a Meeting some Time since, voted to encourage the Establishment of a Printing-Office in this Place: In Consequence thereof, Application was made to me, then in Boston, to issue Proposals for publishing a weekly NEWS-PAPER in this Town, to be entitled, The WORCESTER GAZETTE, or AMERICAN ORACLE of LIBERTY: This I accordingly did; since that Time, Things have worn a different Face in our distressed Capital, and it was thought highly necessary that I should remove my Printing Materials from Boston to this Place, and instead of publishing the intended WORCESTER GAZETTE, &c. continue the Publication of the well-known MASSACHUSETTS SPY, or THOMAS's BOSTON JOURNAL: I accordingly removed my Printing Utensils to this Place, and escaped myself from Boston on the memorable 19th of April, 1775, which will be remembered in future as the Anniversary of the BATTLE of LEXINGTON! I intend publishing this Paper regularly every Wednesday, and have made an Alteration in the Title, in order to take in Part of that intended for the Gazette.

I beg the Assistance of all the Friends to our righteous Cause to circulate this Paper.—They may rely that the utmost of my poor Endeavours shall be used to maintain those rights and Priviledges for which we and *our Fathers have bled*! and that all possible Care will be taken to procure the most interesting and authentic Intelligence.

I am the Public's most obedient Servant,
ISAIAH THOMAS.

Worcester, May 2d, 1775.

PROPOSLAS
For continuing the Publication of
The MASSACHUSETTS SPY,
OR,
American ORACLE of LIBERTY.
CONDITIONS.

Boston Free Press

The BOSTON FREE PRESS represents the combined journalistic efforts of Boston's three underground newspapers -- Avatar, Le Chronic, and The Resistance -- to cover the trial of the Boston Five and activities within the First Liberated Zone at Arlington Street Church.

The BOSTON FREE PRESS plans to publish twice a week, on Tuesdays and Fridays, for the duration.

The free press in America has developed in direct response to the failure of the commercial press to deal with the critical issues and news of the world. Under the banner of objectivity, the daily press, which is owned by the military-industrial-academic complex, regularly ignores and distorts the news. For instance, almost every straight newspaper in the country in covering the war in Vietnam refers to "Communists killed" or "the enemy." In fact, the Vietnamese people and all peoples of the world are our friends. Through the established press, the US Government and the interests which it serves would have the American people think otherwise. It is this and other myths that the free press will combat in its effort to liberate the American people.

THE BOSTON FREE PRESS
c/o The First Liberated Zone
Arlington St. Church
355 Boyleston St., Boston, Mass.
(617) 536-9793

While the Spock trial captures headlines men are being called for induction and refusing to serve.

On Thursday, May 23, HERALD HECTOR, WALUMGUMBE SUMANGURU, GARY QUIGLY will refuse induction.

They feel that there is a law higher than statutory law.

Demonstration:	March:	Draft Card Turn-In:
7:30 A.M. Boston Army Base (Take MTA "Army Base" bus from South Station)	10:30 A.M. March to the Arlington Street Church from the Army Base.	12:30 P.M. Arlington Street Church

be there.

PAGE TWELVE THE BOSTON FREE PRESS

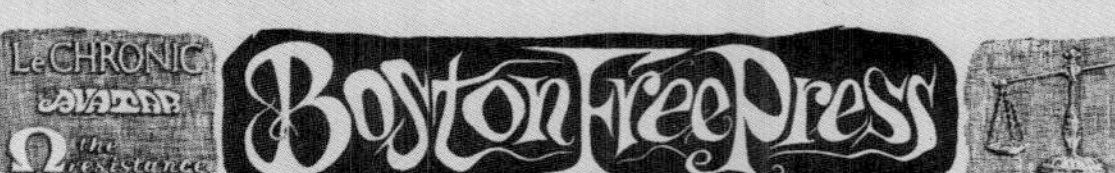

AVATAR JOB NETS 45000

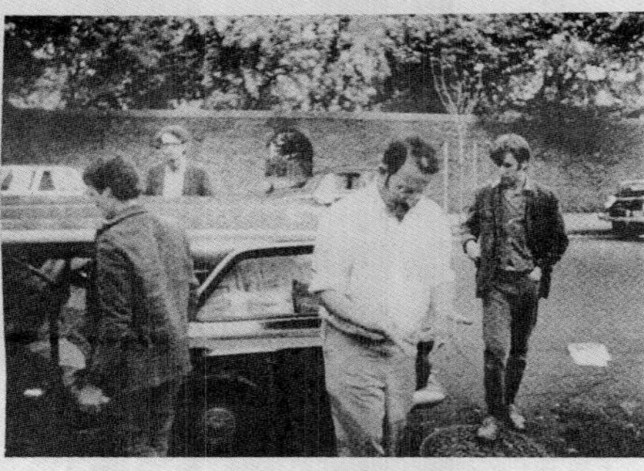

At approximately 4:30 A.M. EDT May 11, 1968 several sleek, dark, vehicles belonging to the Fort Hill Mob pulled quietly up to the curb at the AVATAR offices, 37 Rutland St. Boston. As the Mob, including the notorious ring leaders Eben Given and Brian Keating and henchmen George Peper, Ian Frankenstein, David Gude, and several as yet unidentified members of the ring left their automobiles, two figures emerged from a nearby alley. The two were rather immediately recognized as prominent Salem financier, young roustabout, and heart of young Republicanism, J. Michael Freedberg and the notorious Ethel "Frankie" Nagel.

It soon became obvious to the lone member of the South Side Gang then present in the AVATAR office, John Pebbles, that the Mob had decided to move in on the 45,000 copies of a newspaper labeled AVATAR No. 25 then present there. The bundles of papers were still warm from the giant presses at Paul's place in Worchester and had been delivered only an hour before.

Whether the presence of politician Freedberg and his lady companion Nagel was part of a larger plan, or whether they joined the Mob only by chance is not entirely clear, but they did join the raiding party almost immediately upon finishing large, spectacularly lavish ice-cream cones.

After the Mob had entered the office by means of keys supplied by Freedberg, they were confronted with South Side Gang member Pebbles, who managed to stall them for several minutes in conversation. When he could hold them off no longer and the leaders of the newspaper ring gave the signal to cop the $10,000 worth of beautiful tri-colored newspapers, Pebbles feigned indifference and set to work alerting the other members of the widely dispersed South Side Gang by telephone.

The Mob moved with swift precision. Before the press arrived, 40,000 papers were trucked to a then secret hideaway on Fort Hill. During the final five minutes of the heist, however, while the Mob was busy locating and lifting the last 5,000 papers, 4000 photos were taken of the operation.

The Great Newspaper heist of '68 was a part of a growing feud between AVATAR's Fort Hill Mob and AVATAR's South Side Gang. Subsequent to AVATAR's battle with the police in Boston and Cambridge there came a division of intent in the internal workings of the newspaper. There was an ever-growing resistance to Fort Hill domination of AVATAR even as early

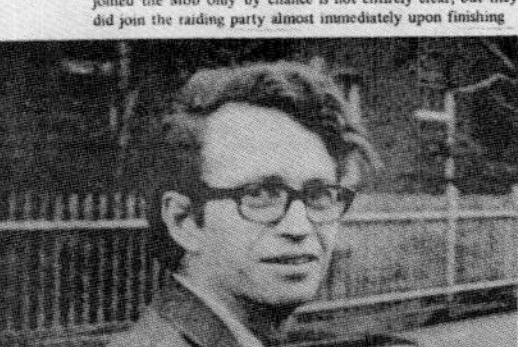

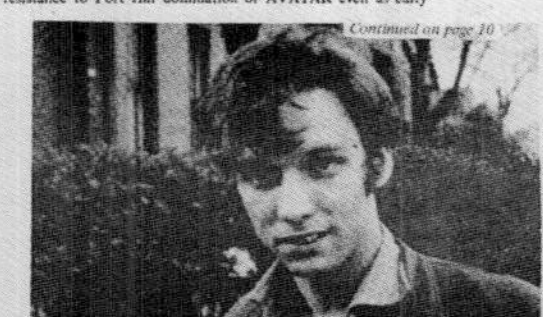

Continued on page 10

Page 4 THE FREE PRESS

SCUM manifesto

Copyright 1967 Valerie Solanas

THE FREE PRESS Page 5

LOVE LOVE

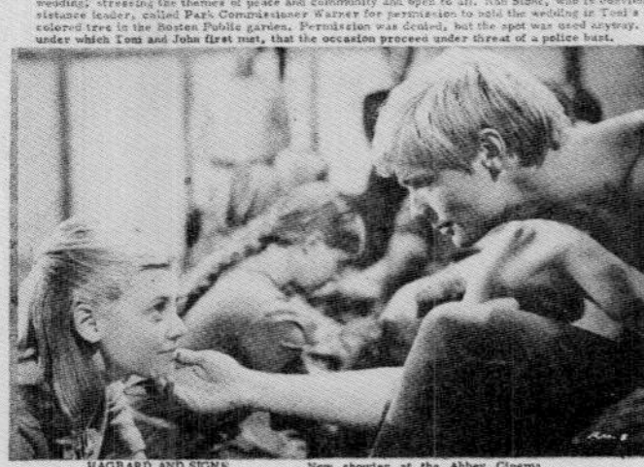

HAGBARD AND SIGNE. Now showing at the Abbey Cinema

Boston Free Press, 1967, vol. 1, back cover
Boston Free Press, 1967, vol. 3, back cover
Boston Free Press, 1967, vol. 3, spread

Next page
Boston Free Press, 1968, vol. 10, cover
Boston Free Press, 1968, vol. 10, spread

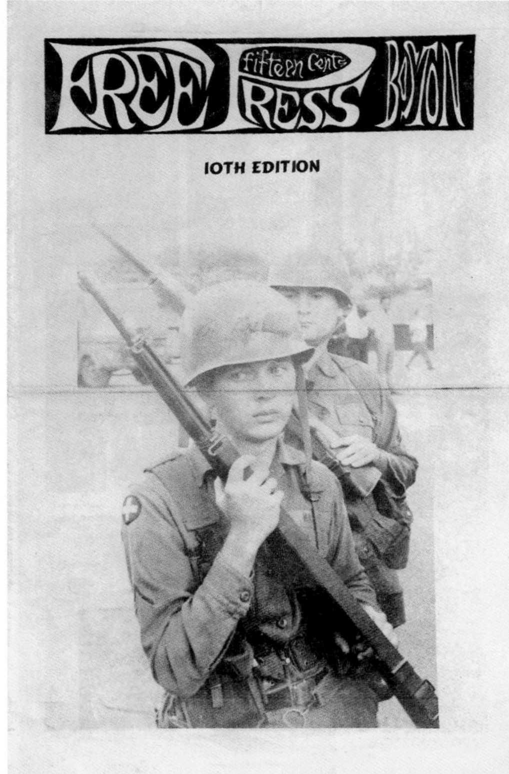
FREE fifteen cents PRESS

IOTH EDITION

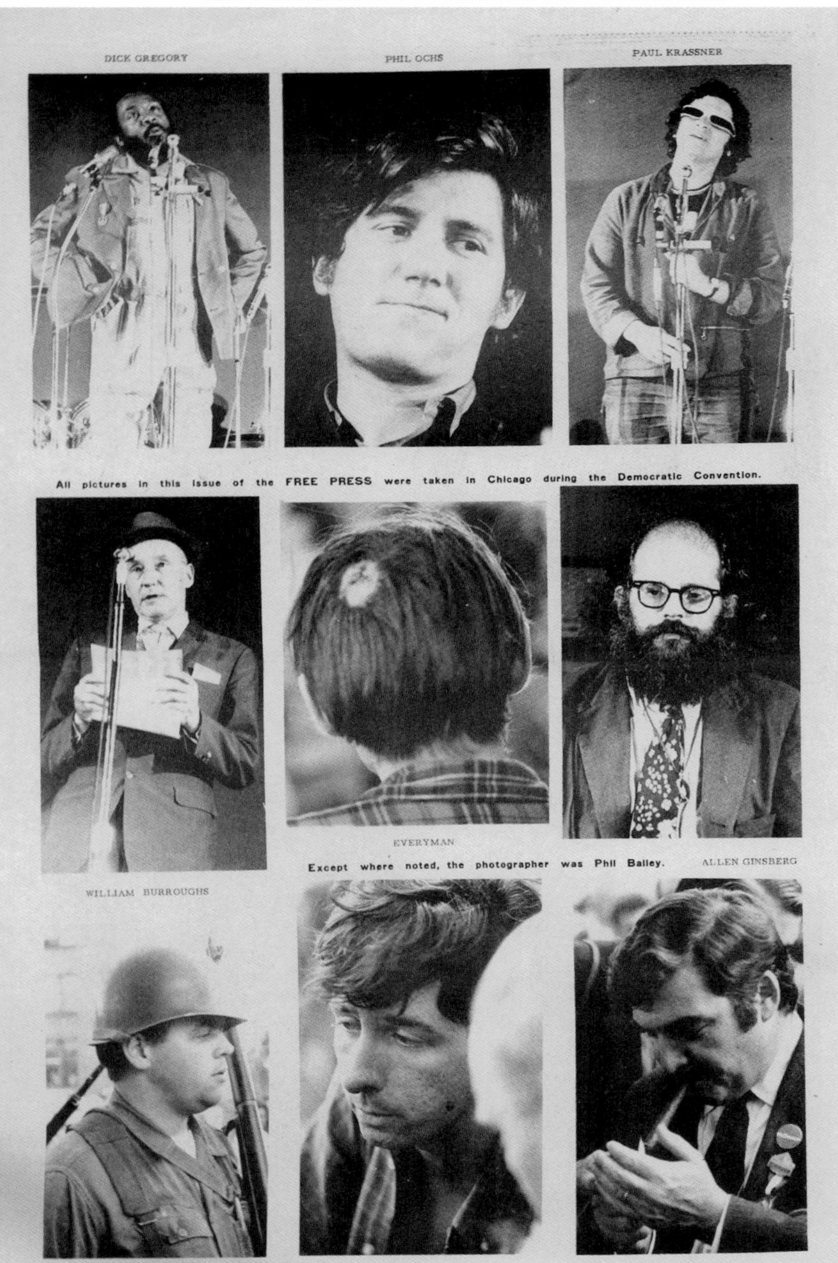
DICK GREGORY

PHIL OCHS

PAUL KRASSNER

All pictures in this issue of the FREE PRESS were taken in Chicago during the Democratic Convention.

WILLIAM BURROUGHS

EVERYMAN

ALLEN GINSBERG

Except where noted, the photographer was Phil Bailey.

THE UNKNOWN SOLDIER

TOM HAYDEN

PIERRE SALINGER

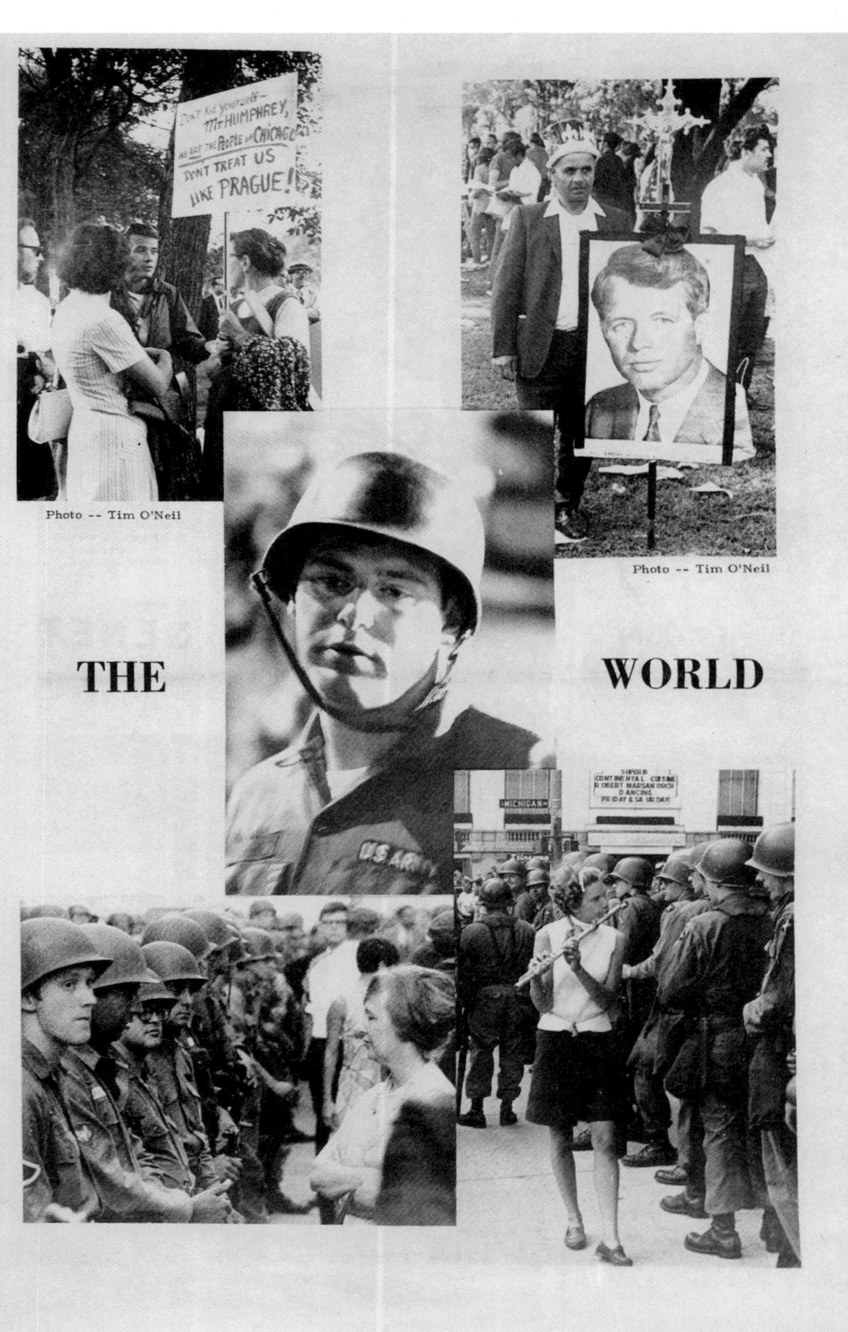

Photo -- Tim O'Neil

Photo -- Tim O'Neil

THE WORLD

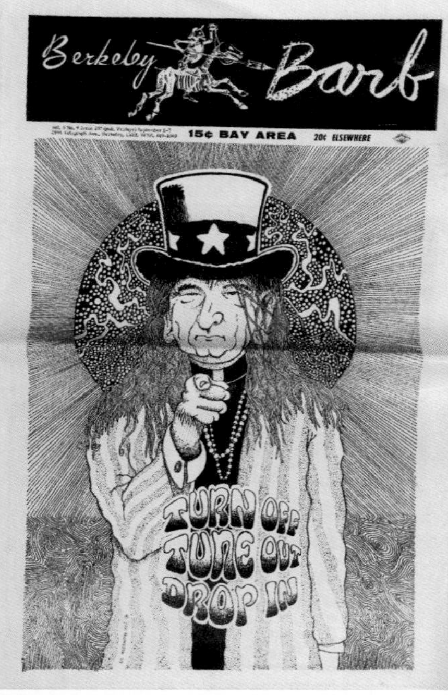

Berkeley Barb

15¢ BAY AREA 20¢ ELSEWHERE

TURN OFF
TUNE OUT
DROP IN

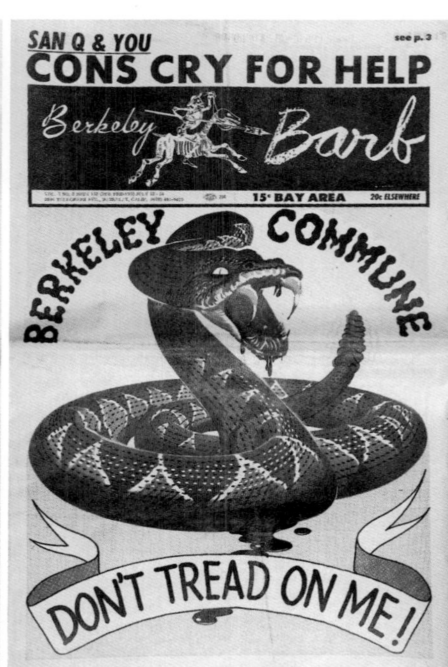

SAN Q & YOU

see p. 3

CONS CRY FOR HELP

Berkeley Barb

15¢ BAY AREA 20¢ ELSEWHERE

BERKELEY COMMUNE

DON'T TREAD ON ME!

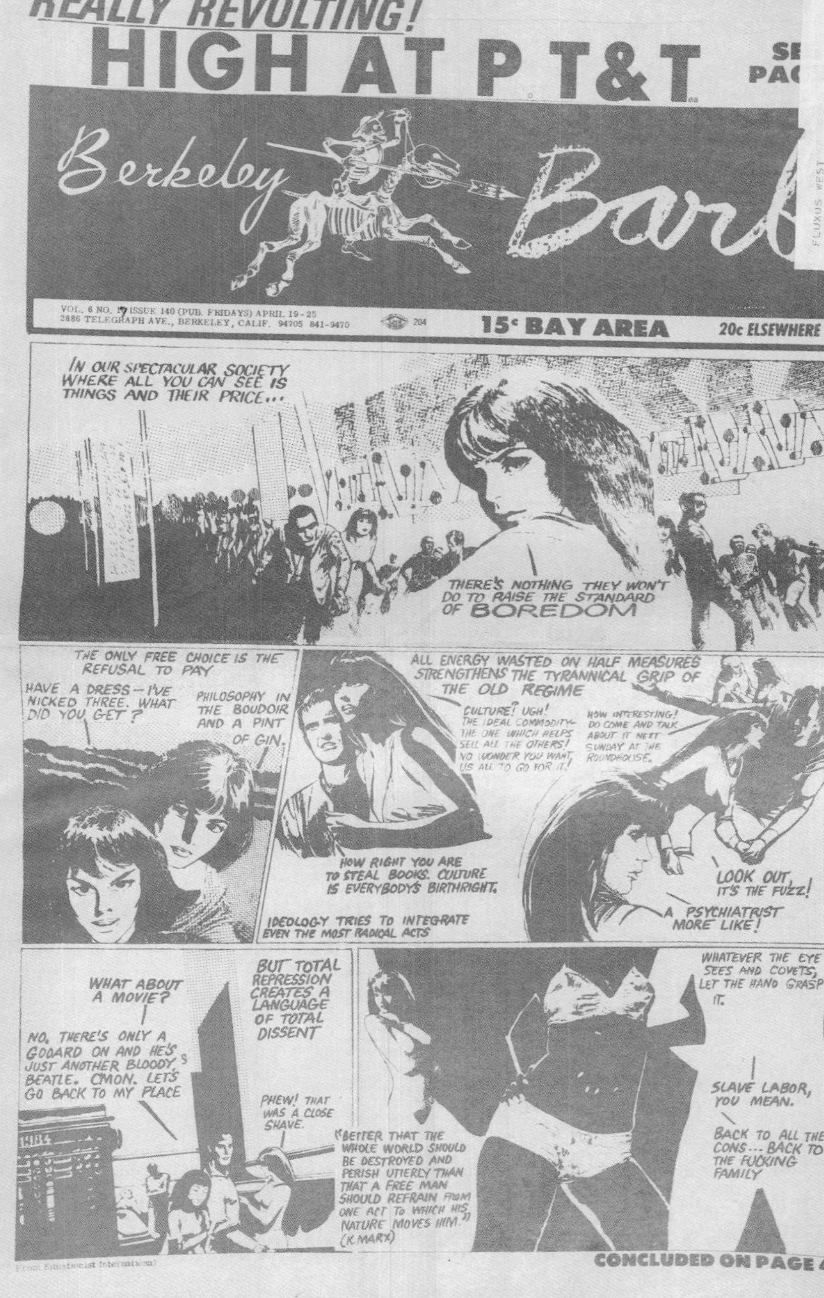

REALLY REVOLTING!

HIGH AT P T&T

Berkeley Barb

VOL. 6 NO. 7 ISSUE 140 (PUB. FRIDAYS) APRIL 19-25
2886 TELEGRAPH AVE., BERKELEY, CALIF. 94705 841-9470

15¢ BAY AREA 20¢ ELSEWHERE

FLUXUS WEST
6361 ELMHURST 09
SAN DIEGO CA 92120

IN OUR SPECTACULAR SOCIETY WHERE ALL YOU CAN SEE IS THINGS AND THEIR PRICE...

THERE'S NOTHING THEY WON'T DO TO RAISE THE STANDARD OF BOREDOM

THE ONLY FREE CHOICE IS THE REFUSAL TO PAY

HAVE A DRESS—I'VE NICKED THREE. WHAT DID YOU GET?

PHILOSOPHY IN THE BOUDOIR AND A PINT OF GIN.

HOW RIGHT YOU ARE TO STEAL BOOKS. CULTURE IS EVERYBODY'S BIRTHRIGHT.

IDEOLOGY TRIES TO INTEGRATE EVEN THE MOST RADICAL ACTS

ALL ENERGY WASTED ON HALF MEASURES STRENGTHENS THE TYRANNICAL GRIP OF THE OLD REGIME

CULTURE! UGH! THE IDEAL COMMODITY- THE ONE WHICH HELPS SELL ALL THE OTHERS! NO WONDER YOU WANT US ALL TO GO FOR IT!

HOW INTERESTING! DO COME AND TALK ABOUT IT NEXT SUNDAY AT THE ROUNDHOUSE.

LOOK OUT, IT'S THE FUZZ!

A PSYCHIATRIST MORE LIKE!

WHAT ABOUT A MOVIE?

NO, THERE'S ONLY A GODARD ON AND HE'S JUST ANOTHER BLOODY BEATLE. C'MON. LETS GO BACK TO MY PLACE

BUT TOTAL REPRESSION CREATES A LANGUAGE OF TOTAL DISSENT

PHEW! THAT WAS A CLOSE SHAVE.

"BETTER THAT THE WHOLE WORLD SHOULD BE DESTROYED AND PERISH UTTERLY THAN THAT A FREE MAN SHOULD REFRAIN FROM ONE ACT TO WHICH HIS NATURE MOVES HIM." (K. MARX)

WHATEVER THE EYE SEES AND COVETS, LET THE HAND GRASP IT.

SLAVE LABOR, YOU MEAN.

BACK TO ALL THE CONS... BACK TO THE FUCKING FAMILY

From Situationist International

CONCLUDED ON PAGE 4

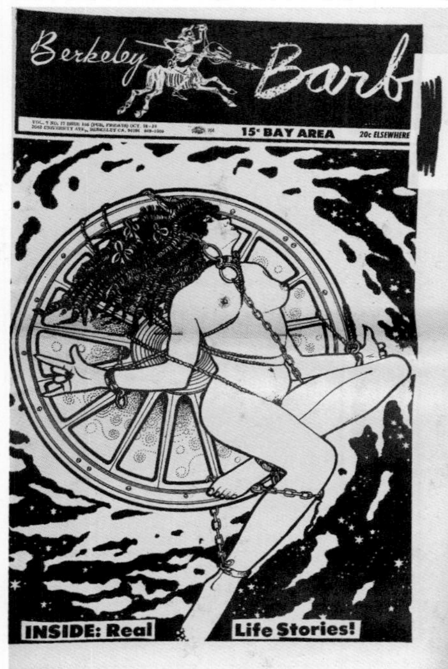

Berkeley Barb

15¢ BAY AREA 20¢ ELSEWHERE

INSIDE: Real Life Stories!

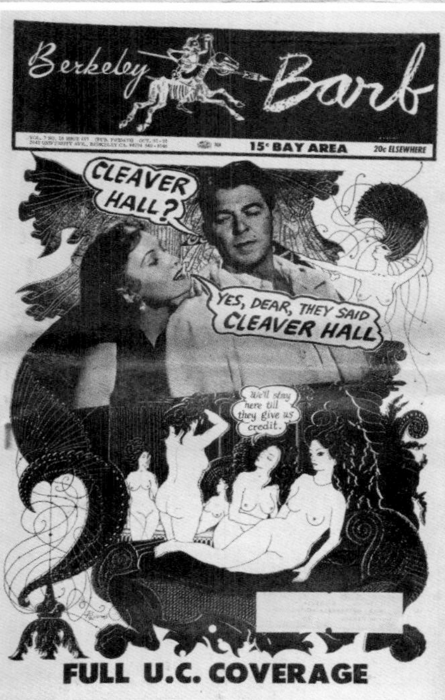

Berkeley Barb

15¢ BAY AREA 20¢ ELSEWHERE

CLEAVER HALL?

YES, DEAR, THEY SAID CLEAVER HALL

We'll stay here til they give us credit.

FULL U.C. COVERAGE

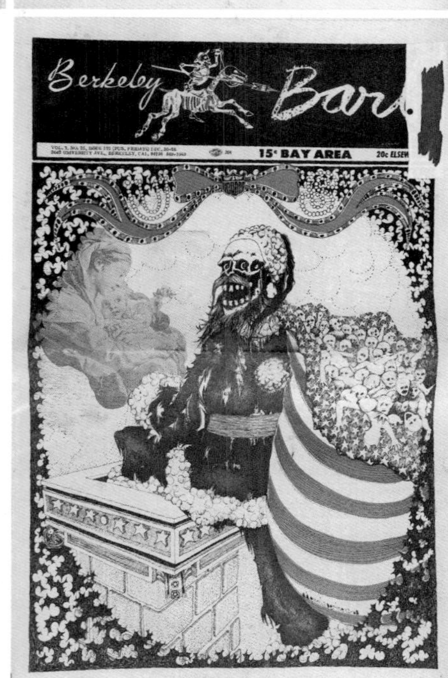

Berkeley Barb

15¢ BAY AREA

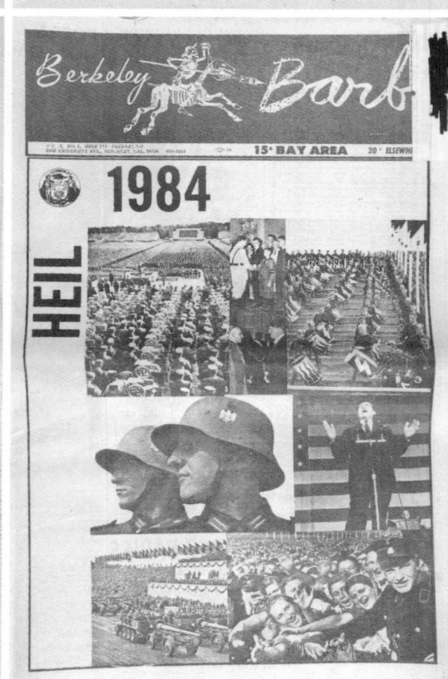

Berkeley Barb

15¢ BAY AREA

1984

HEIL

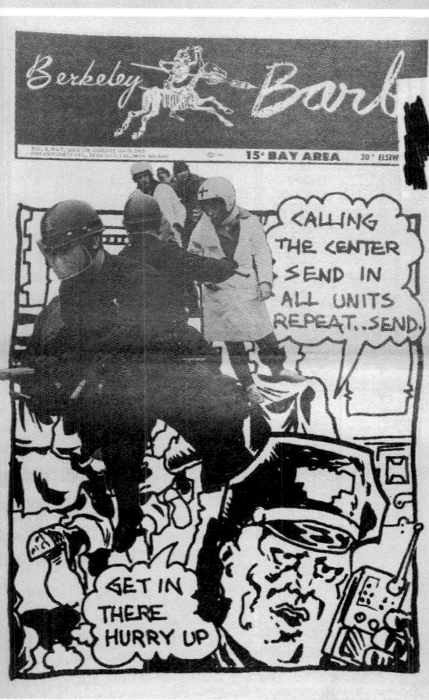

Berkeley Barb

15¢ BAY AREA

The Berkeley Barb, September 1-7, 1967, vol. 5, no. 9, cover
The Berkeley Barb, July 12-18, 1968, vol. 7, no. 2, cover
The Berkeley Barb, April 19-25, 1968, vol. 6, no. 7, cover
The Berkeley Barb, October 18-24, 1968, vol. 7, no. 17, cover
The Berkeley Barb, October 25-31, 1968, vol. 7, no. 18, cover
The Berkeley Barb, December 20-26, 1968, vol. 7, no. 25, cover
The Berkeley Barb, January 3-9, 1969, vol. 8, no. 1, cover
The Berkeley Barb, January 10-16, 1969, vol. 8, no. 2, cover

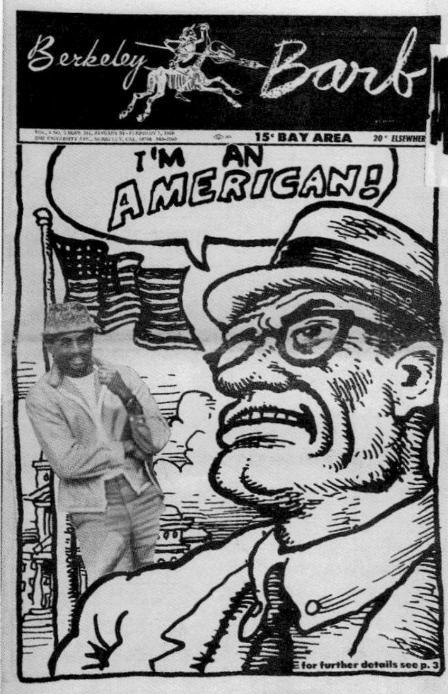

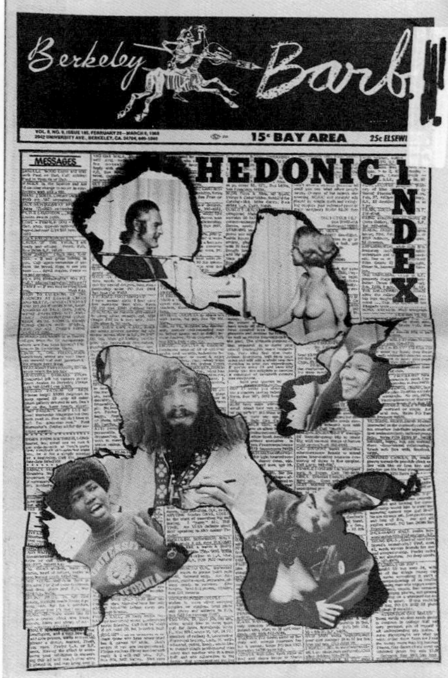

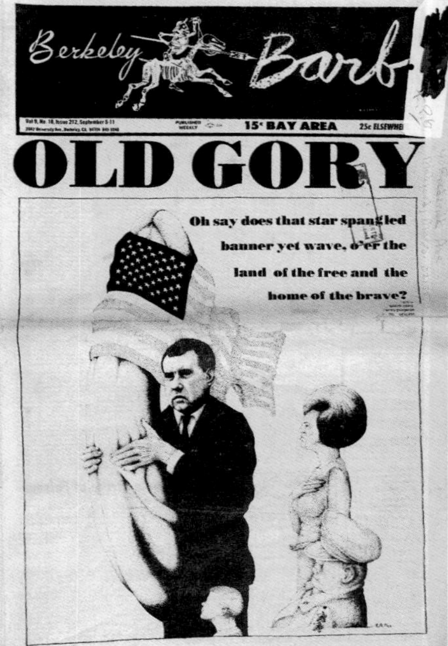

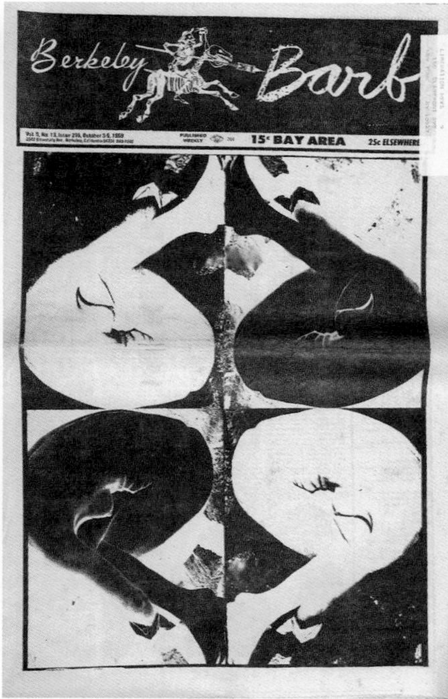

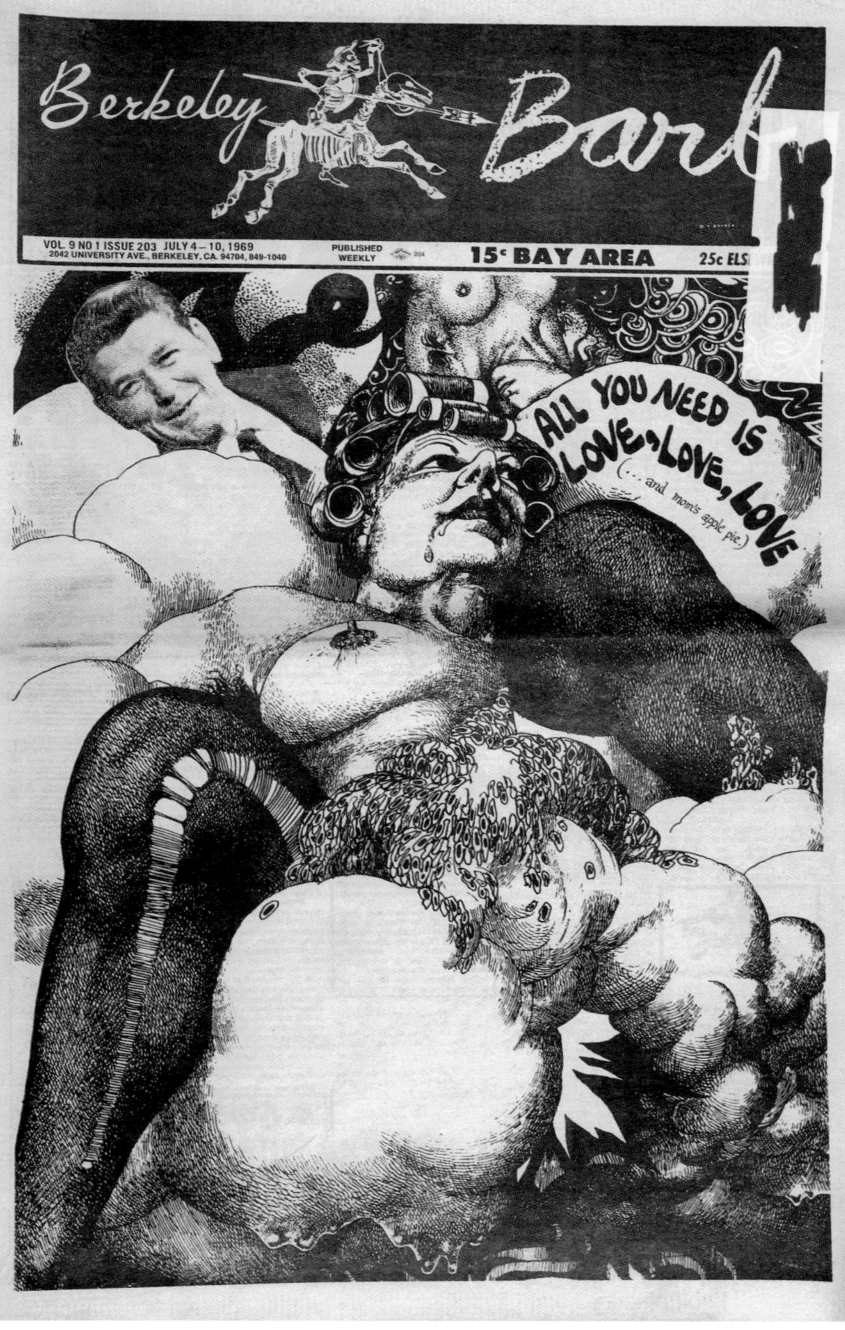

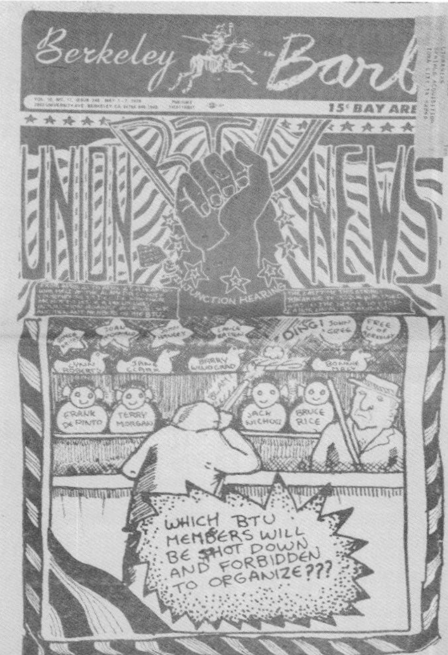

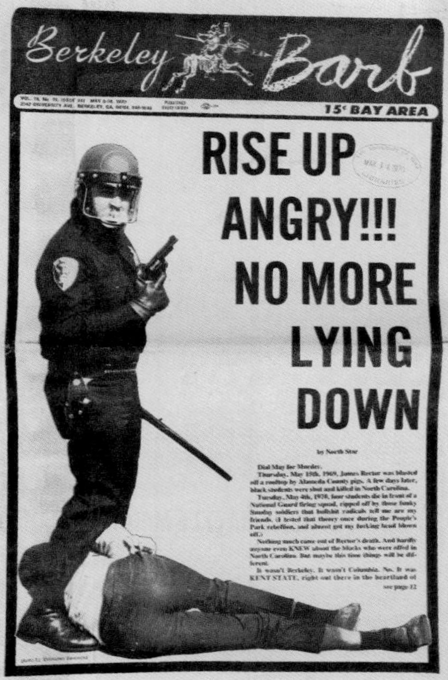

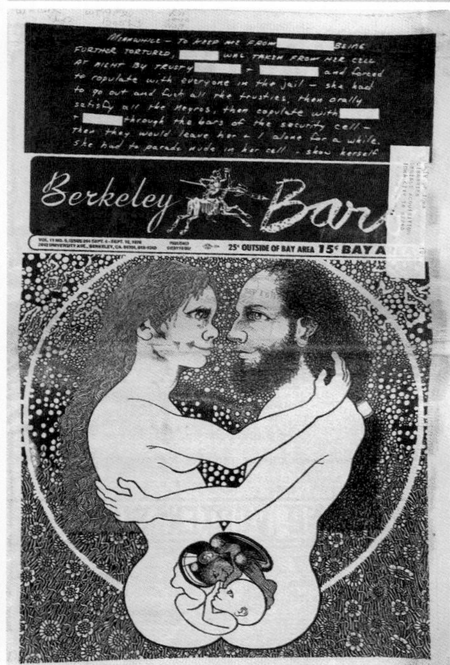

The Berkeley Barb, January 31–February 7, 1969, vol. 8, no. 5, cover
The Berkeley Barb, February 28–March 6, 1969, vol. 8, no. 9, cover
The Berkeley Barb, September 5–11, 1969, vol. 9, no. 10, cover
The Berkeley Barb, October 3–9, 1969, vol. 9, no. 13, cover
The Berkeley Barb, July 4–10, 1969, vol. 9, no. 1, cover
The Berkeley Barb, May 1–7, 1970, vol. 10, no. 17, cover
The Berkeley Barb, May 8–14, 1970, vol. 10, no. 18, cover
The Berkeley Barb, September 4–10, 1970, vol. 11, no. 9, cover

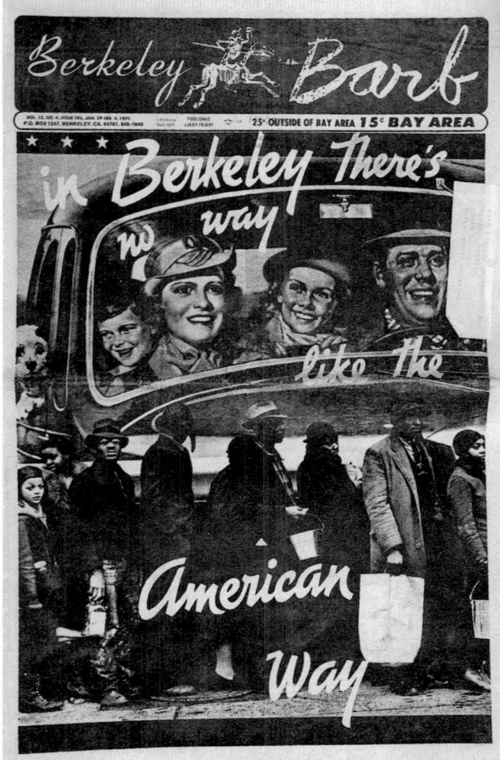

Berkeley Barb

25¢ OUTSIDE OF BAY AREA 15¢ BAY AREA

in Berkeley There's no way like the American Way

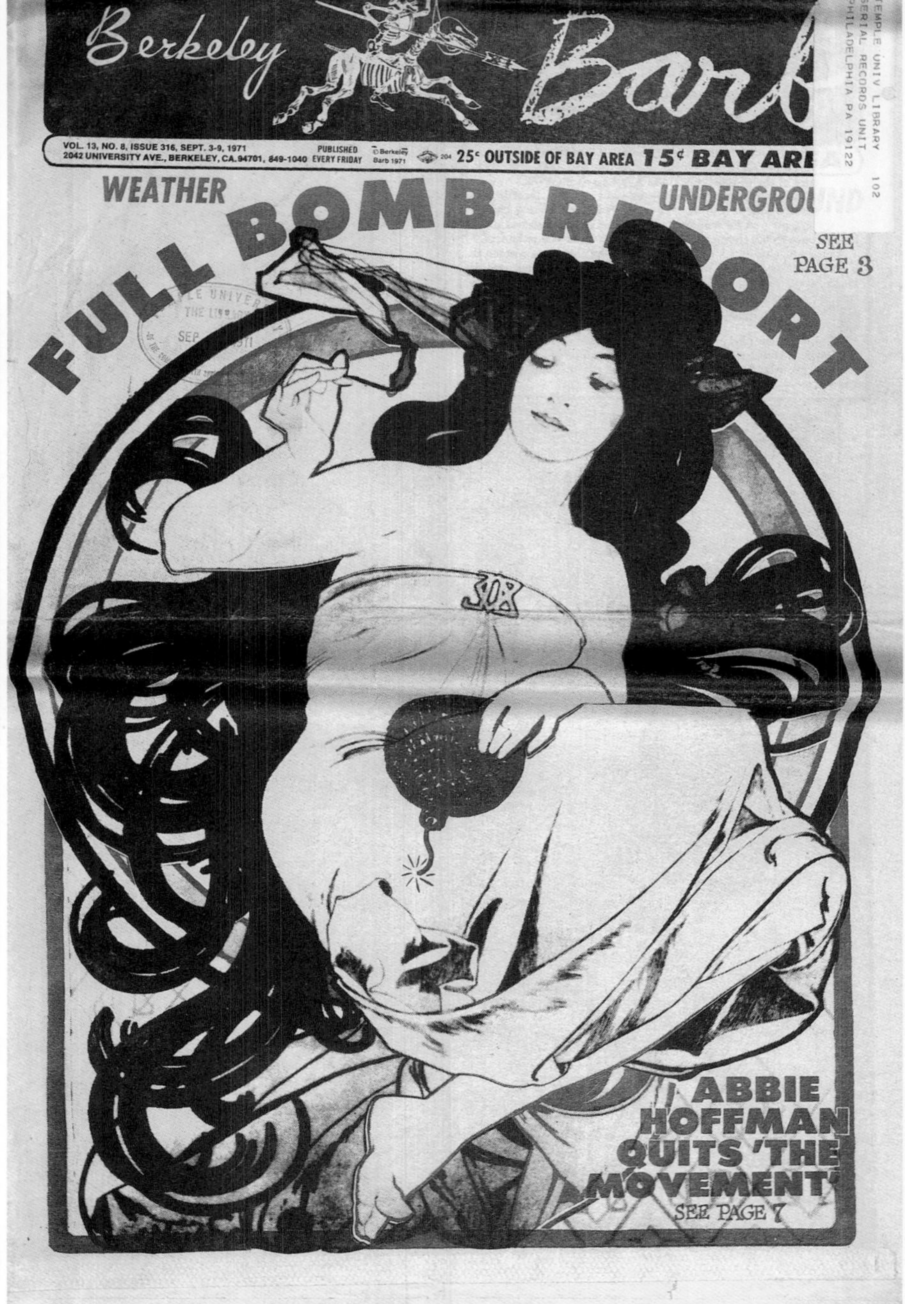

Berkeley Barb

VOL. 13, NO. 8, ISSUE 316, SEPT. 3-9, 1971
2042 UNIVERSITY AVE., BERKELEY, CA. 94701, 849-1040
PUBLISHED EVERY FRIDAY
©Berkeley Barb 1971
25¢ OUTSIDE OF BAY AREA 15¢ BAY ARE

WEATHER UNDERGROUND

FULL BOMB REPORT

SEE PAGE 3

ABBIE HOFFMAN QUITS 'THE MOVEMENT'

SEE PAGE 7

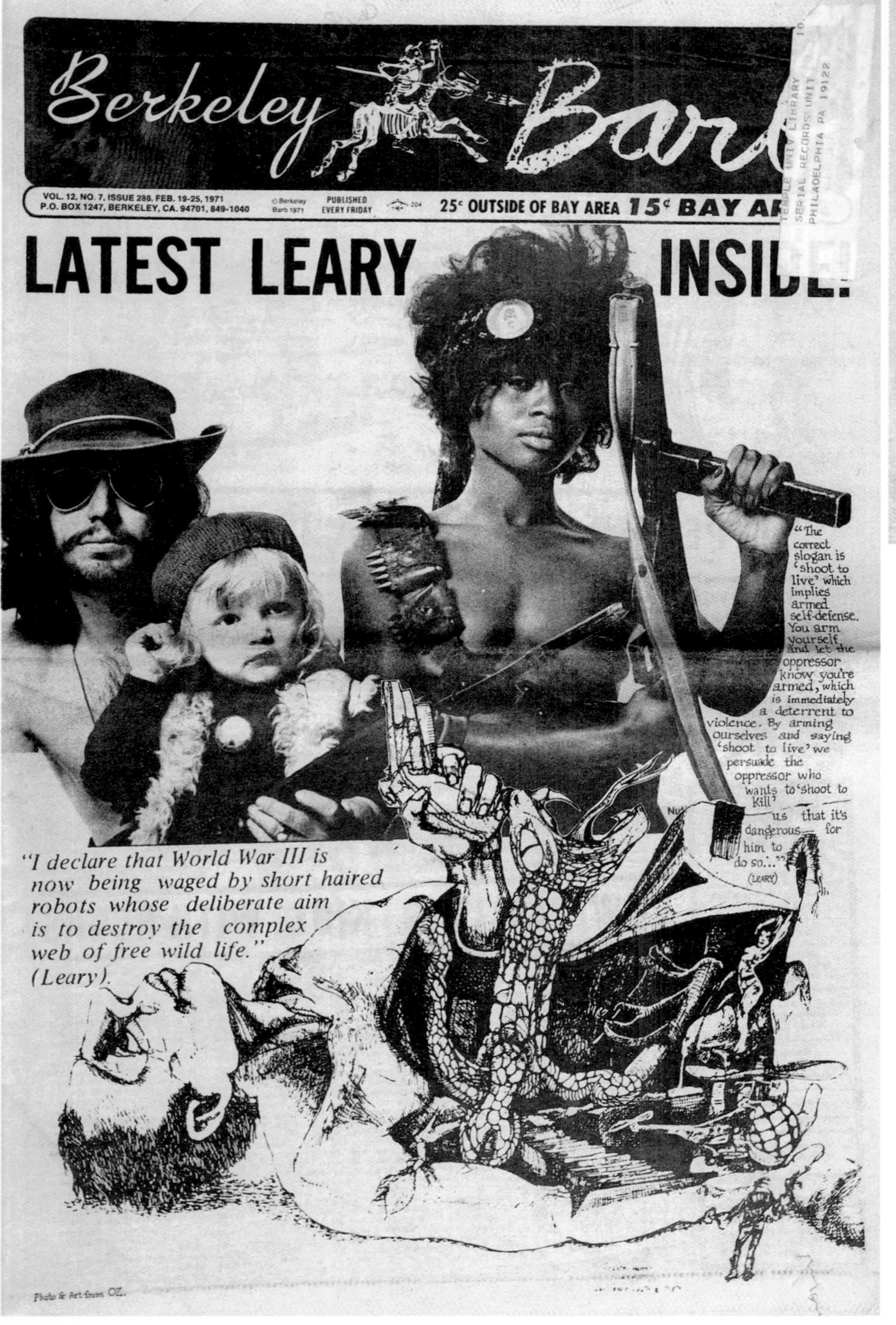

Berkeley Barb

VOL. 12, NO. 7, ISSUE 288, FEB. 19-25, 1971
P.O. BOX 1247, BERKELEY, CA. 94701, 849-1040
©Berkeley Barb 1971
PUBLISHED EVERY FRIDAY
25¢ OUTSIDE OF BAY AREA 15¢ BAY AR

LATEST LEARY INSIDE!

"The correct slogan is 'shoot to live' which implies armed self-defense. You arm yourself and let the oppressor know you're armed, which is immediately a deterrent to violence. By arming ourselves and saying 'shoot to live' we persuade the oppressor who wants to 'shoot to kill' us that it's dangerous for him to do so..." (LEARY)

"I declare that World War III is now being waged by short haired robots whose deliberate aim is to destroy the complex web of free wild life." (Leary).

Photo & Art from OZ.

The Berkeley Barb, January 29–February 4, 1971, vol. 12, no. 4, cover
The Berkeley Barb, September 3–9, 1971, vol. 13, no. 8, cover
The Berkeley Barb, February 19–25, 1971, vol. 12, no. 7, cover

Next page
The Berkeley Barb, September 17–23, 1971, vol. 13, no. 10, cover
The Berkeley Barb, November 19–25, 1971, vol. 13, no. 19, cover
The Berkeley Barb, December 3–9, 1971, vol. 13, no. 21, cover
The Berkeley Barb, 1974, Adult Advertising Section, cover

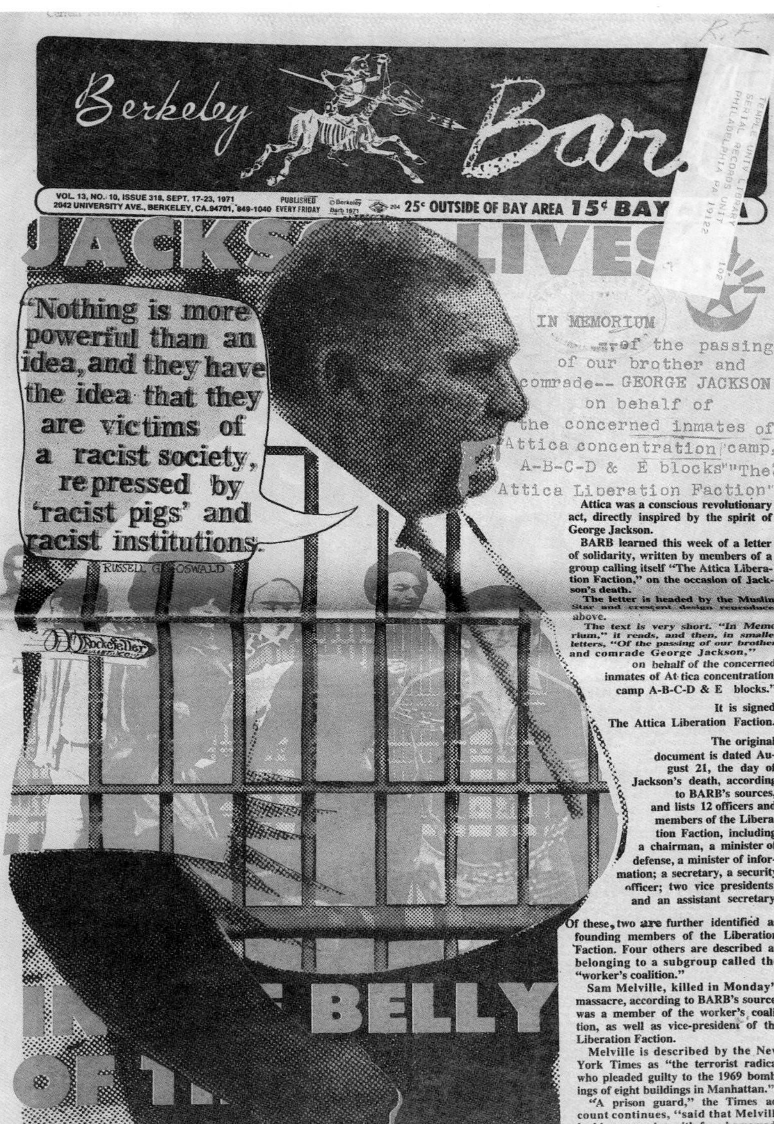

Berkeley Barb

VOL. 13, NO. 10, ISSUE 318, SEPT. 17-23, 1971
2042 UNIVERSITY AVE., BERKELEY, CA. 94701, 849-1040
PUBLISHED EVERY FRIDAY
©Berkeley Barb 1971
25¢ OUTSIDE OF BAY AREA 15¢ BAY AREA

TEMPLE UNIV LIBRARY
SERIAL RECORDS UNIT
PHILADELPHIA PA 19122

JACKSON LIVES

"Nothing is more powerful than an idea, and they have the idea that they are victims of a racist society, repressed by 'racist pigs' and racist institutions."

RUSSELL G. OSWALD

IN MEMORIUM
of the passing of our brother and comrade-- GEORGE JACKSON on behalf of the concerned inmates of Attica concentration camp, A-B-C-D & E blocks" "The Attica Liberation Faction"

Attica was a conscious revolutionary act, directly inspired by the spirit of George Jackson.

BARB learned this week of a letter of solidarity, written by members of a group calling itself "The Attica Liberation Faction," on the occasion of Jackson's death.

The letter is headed by the Muslim Star and crescent design reproduced above.

The text is very short. "In Memorium," it reads, and then, in smaller letters, "Of the passing of our brother and comrade George Jackson," on behalf of the concerned inmates of Attica concentration camp A-B-C-D & E blocks."

It is signed The Attica Liberation Faction.

The original document is dated August 21, the day of Jackson's death, according to BARB's sources, and lists 12 officers and members of the Liberation Faction, including a chairman, a minister of defense, a minister of information; a secretary, a security officer; two vice presidents, and an assistant secretary.

Of these, two are further identified as founding members of the Liberation Faction. Four others are described as belonging to a subgroup called the "worker's coalition."

Sam Melville, killed in Monday's massacre, according to BARB's source, was a member of the worker's coalition, as well as vice-president of the Liberation Faction.

Melville is described by the New York Times as "the terrorist radical who pleaded guilty to the 1969 bombings of eight buildings in Manhattan."

"A prison guard," the Times account continues, "said that Melville had been running with four homemade bombs in an apparent attempt to blow up a 500-gallon fuel tank when he was shot."

See Page 2.

IN THE BELLY OF THE BEAST

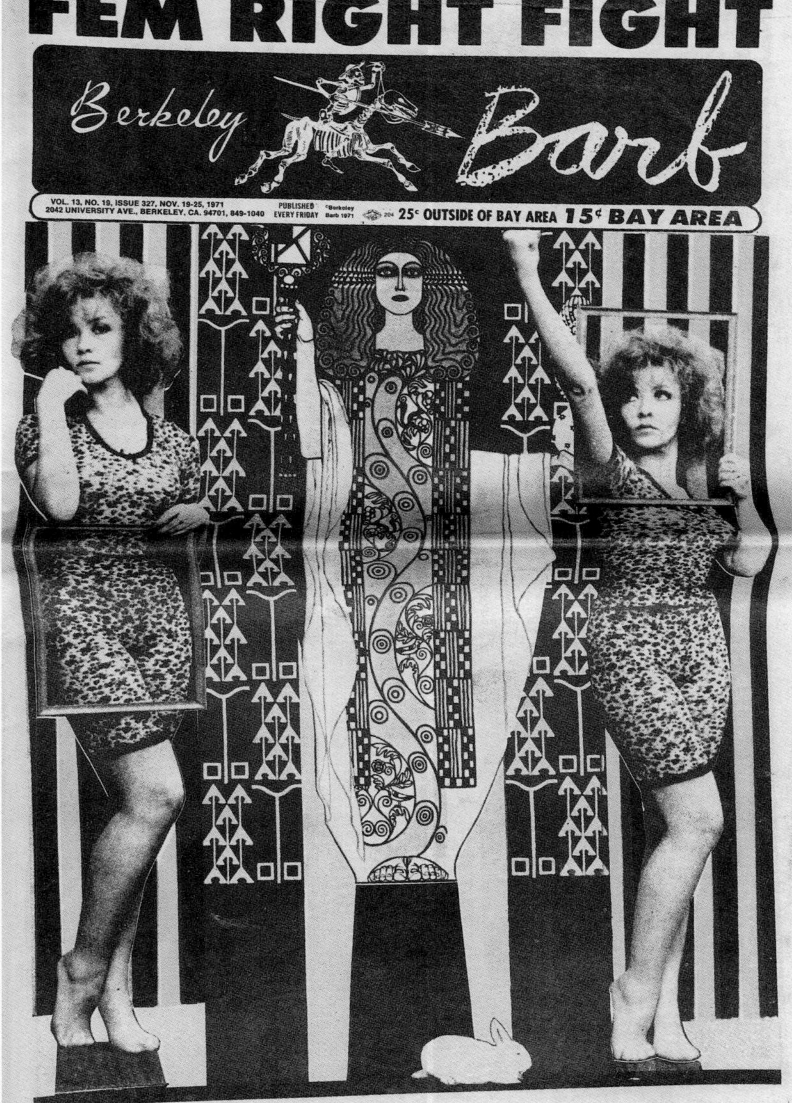

FEM RIGHT FIGHT

Berkeley Barb

VOL. 13, NO. 19, ISSUE 327, NOV. 19-25, 1971
2042 UNIVERSITY AVE., BERKELEY, CA. 94701, 849-1040
PUBLISHED EVERY FRIDAY
©Berkeley Barb 1971
25¢ OUTSIDE OF BAY AREA 15¢ BAY AREA

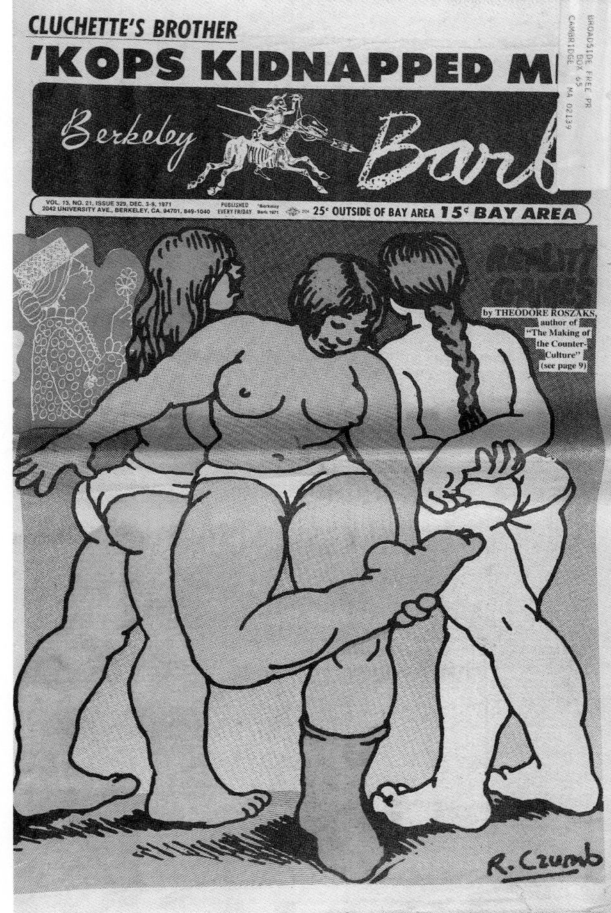

CLUCHETTE'S BROTHER

'KOPS KIDNAPPED ME

Berkeley Barb

VOL. 13, NO. 21, ISSUE 329, DEC. 3-9, 1971
2042 UNIVERSITY AVE., BERKELEY, CA. 94701, 849-1040
PUBLISHED EVERY FRIDAY
©Berkeley Barb 1971
25¢ OUTSIDE OF BAY AREA 15¢ BAY AREA

BROADSIDE FREE PR
CAMBRIDGE MA 02139

REALITY GAMES
by THEODORE ROSZAKS, author of "The Making of the Counter-Culture" (see page 9)

R. Crumb

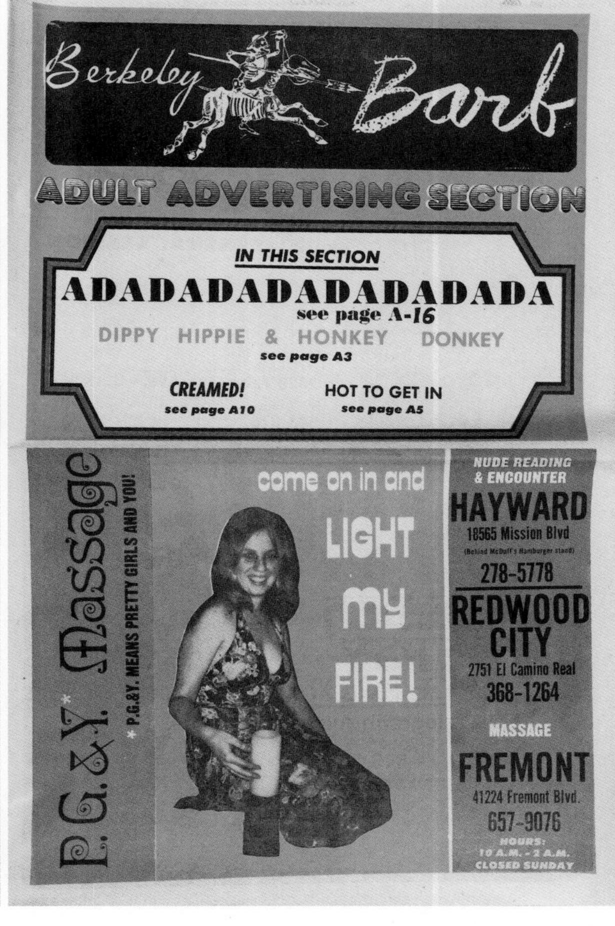

Berkeley Barb

ADULT ADVERTISING SECTION

IN THIS SECTION

ADADADADADADADADA
see page A-16

DIPPY HIPPIE & HONKEY DONKEY
see page A3

CREAMED!
see page A10

HOT TO GET IN
see page A5

P.G.&Y. Massage
* P.G.&Y. MEANS PRETTY GIRLS AND YOU! *

come on in and LIGHT my FIRE!

NUDE READING & ENCOUNTER
HAYWARD
18565 Mission Blvd
(Behind McDuff's Hamburger stand)
278-5778
REDWOOD CITY
2751 El Camino Real
368-1264
MASSAGE
FREMONT
41224 Fremont Blvd.
657-9076
HOURS:
10 A.M. - 2 A.M.
CLOSED SUNDAY

WHAT WE WERE READING: THE CREATION OF A COUNTER-PUBLIC SPHERE

Edited by
Pamela M. Lee

Questions:

WHERE WERE YOU LIVING DURING THE PERIOD IN QUESTION AND WHAT WAS THE EXTENT OF YOUR ACTIVISM?

APART FROM MAINSTREAM MAGAZINES AND NEWSPAPERS, WHAT KIND OF PRESS WERE YOU READING? PLEASE LIST TITLES.

PLEASE DESCRIBE YOUR INTEREST OR INVOLVEMENT WITH VARIOUS POLITICAL, SOCIAL, OR COUNTERCULTURAL PUBLICATIONS. IN WHAT WAYS DID THIS ENGAGEMENT INFLUENCE YOUR OWN PRACTICE AS EITHER AN ARTIST, DESIGNER, HISTORIAN, OR CRITIC?

DESCRIBE YOUR IMPRESSIONS OF THE NEW GRAPHIC INNOVATIONS IN THESE PUBLICATIONS.

Respondents:

T. J. Clark, Todd Gitlin, Harmony Hammond,
Steven Heller, Nancy Holt, Chip Lord,
Margo Machida, Yvonne Rainer, Terry Smith,
Lawrence Weiner, Faith Wilding

T. J. Clark

Between 1964 and 1974 I was mainly in London and Paris. I was involved in politics in Paris from 1965 to 1967, and then in London and at the University of Essex for the next two years. In Paris I remember reading ***Les temps modernes***: it was the moment of Sartre's "La conscience de classe chez Flaubert." And the numbers of ***internationale situationniste***. Their design could not have been more unlike the neo-jugendstil of the magazines to come (which I hated). No English-language magazine meant as much to me as these French things. ***New Left Review*** was the enemy, but a formidable one. ***Studies on the Left*** published a translation of Benjamin's "work of art" essay, for which I was grateful. The ***Review***, coming out of Oxford, had good criticism and poetry, and ***Movie*** great special issues on Antonioni, Losey, and so on. I lent a hand producing an English-language version of "De la misère en milieu étudiant" in 1966—pretty rudimentary as far as design went. Likewise the first two issues of ***King Mob Echo***: for lack of money and expertise we had to convert the wonderful handwritten text of a piece by Norman O. Brown, which we'd stolen from a magazine called ***Caterpillar*** (I think), into dull type. Too bad. In 1968 Essex hosted a dreadful "revolutionary festival," with Godard and co. in attendance. A group of naysayers produced something called the "Manifesto of Rationalism" in hopes of spoiling the party, and I remember my contribution was a strip cartoon beginning with a quote from Lewis Namier: "Liberty is the fruit of a slow growth in a stable society." But this is one item from the sixties that, I hope, even the kind of creeps who stole the typescript of "The Revolution of Modern Art" from our wastebaskets so as to publish it three decades later will never hold in their clammy paws.

Todd Gitlin

1. Where were you living during the period in question and what was the extent of your activism?

1964–1974: Ann Arbor, Chicago, Carmel, San Francisco

I was, during most of this time, a movement organizer and agitator, principally with Students for a Democratic Society (more or less full time through 1966), then with the JOIN Community Union in Chicago (an SDS spinoff), also a freelance writer and poet, and during some of the time, a tenuously employed university instructor.

2. Apart from mainstream magazines and newspapers, what kind of press were you reading? Please list titles.

Several underground papers (especially ***San Francisco Express Times***, for which I wrote in 1968–1969), the ***Guardian*** (for which I wrote a column in 1968–1969), ***New Left Review***, ***Leviathan***, the ***Movement***, etc., etc. Also the ***New York Review of Books***, ***Viet Report***, ***Ramparts***, etc.

3. Please describe your interest or involvement with various political, social or countercultural publications. In what ways did this engagement influence your own practice as either an artist, designer, historian, or critic?

In too many ways to say. Some of this I've written about in my ***The Sixties: Years of Hope, Days of Rage***, and in an introduction to the book ***Un-American Activities***. Immersion in the left & countercultural press was an education, also a bubble. It entailed the pleasures of total immersion & frequent drowning sensations.

4. Describe your impressions of the new graphic innovations in these publications.

Much of the underground press looked ugly to me. I gravitated toward the ***San Francisco Express Times*** partly because it wasn't—because there was elegance as well as shrieking. I was taken by the photo juxtapositions of Violet Ray, among others, and modernist-McLuhanite architecture and film styles (via Godard) that one saw at their highest pitch at Expo 1967 in Montreal.

Harmony Hammond

Where were you living during 1964–1974 and what was the extent of your political and/or activist engagement? What kind of journalism were you reading? Describe interest and involvement with political, social countercultural publications.

Spring 1963–fall 1969. I lived (with my parents and four younger siblings) in Hometown, Illinois, a postwar lower-middle-class housing project. I lived on Main Street. It was row upon row of duplexes. There were no black, Latino, or "other" "people of color." Hometown was lily-white—Protestant and Catholic. I did have a Jewish girlfriend, but I don't remember there being other Jewish people, nor was there a synagogue.

APOLITICAL.

In high school, I won a scholarship to take a Saturday class at the Junior School of the Art Institute of Chicago. I took dress design and fashion illustration because I thought it would make me sophisticated and classy. Would take the "El" downtown by myself—wander the School's studios and the museum galleries.

From 1961 to 1963 I attended Millikin University, a small church college in Decatur, Illinois, the soybean capitol of the United States (my parents, who said they would see that each daughter had one year of college, while the boys would get a full undergraduate education, did not want me to go to a big university. I majored in fine art (it was a three-man art dept.). There were a few foreign students and students "of color," but not many.

APOLITICAL.

In May 1963, at age nineteen, I married Stephen Clover, also an art student, who was a year older than myself. It was the only way to get out of Main Street and Hometown (where I never fit in). He was from Minnesota, so we moved to Minneapolis to be students at the University of Minnesota. We lived there from 1963 to 1969, at which time we moved to New York City.

Minneapolis Days: I worked variously as an artist's model, gallery assistant, and office receptionist and attended the university. Neither I nor my husband was politically active (although I have a sense of civil rights and anti-American/Vietnam War protests and actions near by). We lived in an apartment above a storefront (my studio) in a neighborhood that was an "American Indian ghetto." The only time I picketed was to protest the refusal of a landlord to rent to a mixed-race couple who were friends of ours. I made paintings, we saw a lot of films at the Univ and the Walker Art Center—mostly foreign—as well as art films by Kenneth Anger and Andy Warhol, etc. We were interested in experimental theater, the blues, and coffeehouse culture.

APOLITICAL.

I don't remember reading nonmainstream journals or papers, other than professional art journals such as *Art News*, *Arts International*, *Arts*, *Art Forum*, *Art in America*, etc., ... and of course exhibition catalogues. I was into Genet and remember reading and rereading *Our Lady of the Flowers*. In the summers of 1967 and 1969 (not 1968!) Stephen and I traveled on Icelandic airlines to Europe, hitchhiking, boating and bussing our way thru England, Belgium, Netherlands, German, Italy, Switzerland, France, Spain, Corsica, Tunisia, Algeria, and Morocco. We didn't have money to sit in Paris cafés, so we walked the streets of the Left Bank every night—it was full of posters announcing theater, music, and art events. We saw the Living Theater for the first time.

1969–1984. I lived in Manhattan before moving to northern New Mexico. In early fall 1969 (the fall after Stonewall) Stephen and I moved to East 4th Street on the Lower East Side (down from La MAMA Theatre). In winter 1970 (separated from Stephen but pregnant with his child), I moved to my first loft on the corner of Spring and West Broadway. There were few artists living there then, and almost no place to eat at night unless you went to the Village, Chinatown, or Little Italy.

Like Paris, Lower Manhattan (below Houston) was postered over then as now with not just Broadway productions and movies and clothing advertisements. Individuals and collectives made silkscreen, Xerox, or offset litho posters and put them up to announce exhibitions or experimental performances or make political statements.

Books on art of non-Western cultures I saw and purchased at the Strand Bookstore.

In 1970 I became involved with the women's liberation movement, and was very active in the feminist art movement—joined a CR group, cofounded AIR Gallery, the first women's cooperative art gallery, and participated in different "actions" for equal representation of women artists in museum exhibitions and collections, and later in the Gay Pride March each June.

POLITICIZED.

At AIR, we designed and printed our own exhibition announcements: ALWAYS BLACK AND WHITE (at most one color)—LUCKY IF WE COULD AFFORD TO HAVE THE TYPE SET VERSUS USING PRESS TYPE AND LUCKY IF WE COULD AFFORD AN IMAGE—AND THAT WAS USUALLY FROM A VELOX RATHER THAN HALF-TONE.

Reading: ***Whole Earth Catalog*, *Our Bodies Ourselves*, *SCUM Manifesto*, *Redstockings: Feminist Revolution*, *Woman Identified Woman*, *New Woman's Survival Sourcebook***. Mimeographed, carbon-copied, Xeroxed, and offset litho usually on newsprint.

(NOTE: WOMEN'S BOOKSTORES CHANGED THINGS. PRE–WOMEN'S BOOKSTORES—YOU ACTUALLY HAD TO ATTEND A FEMINIST POLITICAL OR CULTURAL EVENT TO GET THE HANDOUTS THAT WE THEN PASSED AROUND TO FRIENDS (LIKE ***WOMAN IDENTIFIED WOMAN***)—EVENTUALLY BUYING A BOOK AT THE WOMEN'S BOOKSTORE AND

"SUPPORTING A WOMAN AUTHOR AND WOMEN'S BUSINESS" BECAME THE POLITICAL ACT AND SUPPLANTED ANY REAL ACTIVISM ... (REFLECTING WLM MOVEMENT SHIFT TO CULTURAL FEMINISM).

Worked as storyteller for the Brooklyn Public Library. Was sent to day-care centers in ghetto areas of Brooklyn: Williamsburg, Brownsville, etc. Brought and read library books to three-, four-, five-year-old children.

READING: Early movement books (fiction, poetry, and nonfiction) self-published like Fran Winant's *Dyke Jacket* or fiction published by Daughter's or Naiad Press and nonfiction of Diana Press.

Local, regional, national art, feminist, lesbian feminist, gay papers and journals read frequently—many subscribed to: *Majority Report*, *Big Mama Rag*, *Ain't I a Woman*, *Lesbian Connection*, *Quest*, *IKON*, *Art & Artist*, *Art-Rite*, *Woman Artist News*, *Conditions*, *13th Moon*, *New Woman's Times*, *Dyke: A Quarterly*, *Sinister Wisdom*, *Off Our Backs*, *Feminist Studies*, *Feminist Art Journal*, *Lesbian Tide*, *The Ladder*, *Jump Cut*, *Camera Obscura*, *Signs*, *Frontiers*, *Country Woman*, *Fighting Woman News*, *Up from Under*, *LIP*, *Sojourner*, *Art Workers News*, *Gay Community News*, *Gaysweek*, *Ms. Magazine*, *SoHo Weekly News*, *Liberation News Service*, *Seven Days*, *Village Voice*, *Red-Herring*, the *Fox*, *An Anti-Catalogue*, *Avalanche*, *Lady-Unique-Inclination-of-the-Night*.

1972—moved to loft at 87 Bowery (off Canal Street). December 1973—big fire in loft. Temporarily lived in friends' lofts (eventually moved back). Worked for about a year at Red Ink (1974–1975), a community press run by ex- (now aboveground) Weather people .... Red Ink primarily designed and printed (offset) political posters (free political prisoners) and posters for experimental theater and dance (Charles Ludlam, La MaMa, Ballets Trocadero), etc .... I started as the receptionist but was soon trained in touching up negatives and working with the boards and the blues.

Summer 1975—taught at and attended Sagaris, a summer institute attended by radical feminist community organizers from across the country.

FURTHER POLITICIZED.

Later rented lofts on Pearl Street by the old Fulton Fish Market, then Maiden Lane, and finally on West 22nd Street between 6th and 7th Avenues at that time, a neighborhood of welfare hotels, drug houses, empty storefronts, and off-off-off Broadway theater (the 22nd Street loft went co-op around 1980).

1976—Feeling that the WLM had become apathetic, meeting with twenty woman (artists, writers, architects) who comprised the mother collective that founded ***Heresies: A Feminist Publication on Art and Politics***, in NYC. Each issue had different editors and a different theme to be explored visually and textually. Each issue was collectively designed by different women, but many of us helped with production (it was politically important that the magazine not reflect the aesthetics of one artist). The visual was to be as important as the textual. Over the years worked on three editorial collectives, assisted with design, layout, pasteup, editing, proofreading, distribution, wrote articles, and eventually was office manager (as office manager, I would receive feminist posters sent to us from around the world, and worked with editors and designers for each issue). Very aware of graphics created by the Chicago Women's Graphics Collective and feminist posters coming out of Australia.

In 1977, after working on the editorial collective for the Lesbian Art and Artist issue of ***Heresies***, I decided to curate the first exhibition of art by self-identified lesbian artists. Called "A Lesbian Show," it took place at the artist-run 112 Greene Street space. It was very much about lesbians taking space in the art world—albeit the fringes of the art world. Amy Sillman designed a poster for the show—delicate white line drawing and hand-printed text on black. It was pasted up all around SoHo and quickly torn down by truckers even though there was no "lesbian and/or sexual imagery." Just the word "lesbian" at that time in that neighborhood, was too much ... it was quickly censored ....

1984—Did the design for my first book, ***Wrappings: Essays on Feminism, Art and the Martial Arts*** (New York: TSL Press, 1984).

How did interest/involvement with countercultural publications influence my own work?

I never really liked psychedelic-influenced graphics of the 1960s and early 1970s, nor the commercial interpretation by the likes of Peter Max. I preferred the theatrical, handmade physical aesthetic of the Bread and Puppet Theater (political performances, drawings, and graphics) AND the simple typeface on carefully chosen paper stock of the ***Fox*** and ***An Anti-Catalogue***.

Starting in the early 1970s I often used hand-printed personal text in my drawings and later paintings. Sometimes the drawing was the hand-printed text. This was facilitated by the availability of oil sticks—those big fat oil crayons that many artists began to use in the 1970s. They were great for printing words—had a sense of boldness and immediacy. The way the mark sat on the page, could be smudged, etc., worked well with my survivor aesthetic: layered, torn fragments visibly pieced/collaged together.

To this day, I don't like the seamlessness of most Photoshopped graphics. I prefer, indeed invite, the indexical presence of maker and making—the possibilities of juxtaposition, interruption, disjuncture, intervention, rupture, and suture. For this reason, I find early computer-generated images (posters and photocollage) to be very interesting. With heads and body parts slightly out of proportion or awkwardly inserted, inlays, and imbeds obvious ... they are very crude by today's standards ... and therefore very interesting as they still indicate the hand of the maker ...

Describe your impressions of the new graphic innovations attending these publications.

I don't know what this question means—as this was all precomputer—we typed, used carbon paper, later Xerox (where we could happily change scale, repeat images, or reverse positive negative, etc.), Xerox collage, offset litho ... we literally cut and pasted and laid out journals on the floor in order to see the visual rhythm from page to page ... never thought of it as old or new ... just the way you did design and layout ... (not to mention how much easier it is to edit a text—we used to have to retype every draft!).

Steven Heller

Where was I living?

I was in New York City. I lived near the East Village and in the West Village. I worked at the *East Village Other* and the *New York Free Press* (on W. 72nd St.) and at *Screw Magazine* (on W. 14th St.).

Apart from mainstream magazines, what kind of press was I reading?

Almost everything I read was underground or "new left": *Ramparts*, *Evergreen Review*, *LA Free Press*, *Chicago Seed*, *RAT*, the *War Resisters League* magazine, but also *Esquire* and *New York* magazine. Oh yes, I did read the *New York Times Magazine* (and not just for the underwear ads).

My interest and involvement in countercultural publications ...

Between 1967 and 1972, when the counterculture was at its height, many lives were dramatically altered and futures were shaped. Mine was one of them. During 1968, my last year in high school, I had been drawing cartoons that explored adolescent fixations with sex and death. People who saw them presumed I had a disturbed childhood and urged me to seek therapy. Instead I took my makeshift portfolio around to four Manhattan-based influential underground papers: the *New York Free Press*, the *East Village Other*, the *Rat*, and the *Avatar*.

I went to the last first, assuming that my cartoons, featuring naked Christ-like figures in various states of crucifixion, would be welcomed with open arms. The art editor at the *Avatar* was indeed interested, because the magazine was edited by Mel Lyman, a self-proclaimed Christ-like, megalomaniac leader of a Boston-based commune with a chapter in New York. Virtually the entire contents of the *Avatar* were devoted to how world events affected Lyman's life.

Had I known that this was a serious cult, I doubt it would have made much difference, since the *Avatar* wanted to publish my work—not just one, but five of my favorite drawings in one issue. Shortly afterward, however, I realized that the *Avatar* was a little too weird, even for me, when following the publication of a subsequent batch of drawings I was summoned to an audience with Lyman, who demanded that I shave my entire body and swear a loyalty oath to him. My bar mitzvah was ritual enough for one lifetime, so I humbly declined.

Next I took my work over to the *Rat*. Edited by Jeff Shero and art directed by Bob Eisner (currently design director of *Newsday*), the *Rat* had just published several issues covering the May 1968 student uprising at Columbia University, where police were called in to restore order after the SDS (Students for a Democratic Society) occupied the president's offices. The *Rat* storefront near Cooper Square was a hotbed of radical activity. Just my thing. Eisner, exhausted after days without sleep, politely paged through my work until coming to a cartoon that showed black and white men arm in arm, giving one another the bird. "Yep, that's racial equality all right," he declared, "Can we use it?" Of course, and I assigned him worldwide rights to boot. I was so excited when it was published that I hawked copies on the street. But my *Rat* affiliation was quickly terminated. "I like your stuff," admitted Eisner, "but Shero thinks it's too spiritual. Have you tried the *Avatar*?"

Dejected, my next stop was the *East Village Other*. This anarchic clarion of youth culture and the crème de la crème of undergrounds was the launchpad for many of the early alternative comix artists, including R. Crumb. It was also the home of the "Slum Goddess of the Lower East

Side," one of the East Village's most desirable ladies. Ever since I saw my first copy on the newsstand in 1966, I wanted to be published in the *EVO*. Unfortunately, the editors, Walter Bowart and Allen Katzman, didn't think as highly of my work as I did of theirs. Our meeting was short and curt. "Leave your stuff; we'll call you," said Bowart. So after a month without any word, I collected said stuff and trekked uptown to the *New York Free Press*.

Geography was one reason for not going sooner. How could a real underground paper be located on 72nd Street and Broadway? The other reason was looks: the *New York Free Press* didn't look like an underground paper. It was too tabloidy—a cross between the *New York Post* and the *National Star*. It didn't even carry comix. The two issues that I bought were primarily concerned with proving the veracity of the Kennedy assassination plot theory. The *FREEP*, as it was known, was originally a community newspaper owned by Upper West Side liberals. The *FREEP*'s publisher was an old Lefty, Jack Banning; its editor was a thirty-something karate expert and nighttime bartender, Sam Edwards, who once edited a very prestigious arts magazine; its managing editor was Jim Buckley, who would later become the copublisher of *Screw*; and its art director was J. C. Suares, a gruff-talking, beer-drinking Egyptian who went on to be art director of the *New York Times* Op-Ed page, *New York* magazine, and scores of other publications. It was Suares who reviewed my portfolio of drawings and said between gulping down swigs from a quart bottle of malt liquor, "Good shit, but I can't use it. Do you want a mechanical job?"

At seventeen, I was appointed the art director of the *Free Press* as long as I stayed within the budget and editorial constraints. Since the budget was nil, I became a master of collage. Since the editor wanted a text-driven newspaper, there really wasn't much room for visual experimentation anyway. His aim was to develop the *FREEP* into a muckraking paper devoted to city politics. Some of our best stories focused on corruption in the sanitation and police departments and picture features showing "Red Squad" cops impersonating hippies or reporters to spy on antiwar demonstrators. On the cultural side, our critics included Eric Bentley, Bertolt Brecht's translator in the United States; Roger Greenspun, who later became a *New York Times* theater critic; Gregory Battcock, a leading author and art critic; and R. Meltzer, a young music critic. Edwards, the editor, did, however, encourage me to run my cartoons in every issue. Compared to R. Crumb in the *EVO* and Jules Feiffer in the *Village Voice*, I was pretty lame.

The *FREEP* did not really have a loyal readership, which became disturbingly apparent when we ran our first nude on the cover. It was a fortuitous accident really. The lead story had fallen through, and the editor had put a piece about an erotic "happening" artist named Kusama on the cover. Kusama was the consummate publicity hound and provided all papers—over and underground—with photographs of her living artworks featuring naked men and women debauching under her watchful eye. The sales of the issue with one of her art/orgy photographs on the cover skyrocketed. The following week sales plummeted when we ran a cover with a staid illustration. Nudes followed on the covers of virtually every subsequent issue. Nevertheless, the *FREEP* couldn't compete with *EVO*'s comparatively large circulation (50,000 to our 15,000), the result of its popular sex-oriented classified personals. So Banning and Edwards decided to fold the *FREEP* and launch a sex paper in its place, satirically titled the *New York Review of Sex*. I was asked to be copublisher and art director, which I agreed to immediately and thus quit college (which I was attending only sporadically as an English major). Art directing a sex paper is not exactly what parents want their kids to do when they grow up, but for me, caught in the vortex of the social, cultural, and political flux that defined the Youth Culture, this was the right thing. After all, I was a product of my times. I got my diploma at the *FREEP* and took postgraduate courses at the *New York Review of Sex*, and was well on my way to a PhD in street-smart design. Although it was not the most conventional way to study design, from these two experiences I learned how to be an art director.

Impressions of the new graphic innovations ...

The *East Village Other*'s paste-up was the closest I had ever come to a tribal ritual. Every Thursday night for well over a year I joined the others in the group encounter that was part makeup and part make-out session. I had done all-nighters before but none were as fever-pitched or as drug-stimulated as *EVO*. While I harbored superstitions about drugs and never touched the stuff myself, the joints and acid tabs were the payment for a good night's work. Someone routinely emerged from the editor's office around 8:30 PM with a shoebox full of the stuff, as well as with the night's layout assignments, which included at least three pages of "intimate" classifieds. The layout crew would help themselves to grass (the acid was saved until after the session was over) and manuscripts, find their tables, select their decorative ruling tapes and transfer type sheets, and settle down to "design" pages.

I'm not sure I'd call these "innovations." It was a lot of seat-of-the-pants work, often pretty poorly done. Only these days, given the DIY movement, did it seem innovative. I did, however, like some of the techniques, like split-fountain printing (an old technique but put to new and good use). I was not a fan of psychedelic design until decades later, when I appreciated its importance. Otherwise, my only real graphic excitement was underground comix. This was indeed innovation born of repression.

Nancy Holt

The coverage of my work in alternative media supported and stimulated my art. There was immediate exposure to an audience amenable to my investigations, and engaged feedback, which in turn elicited a corresponding response in me. Being heard and seen through alternative media, which had sprung up because of rigidity, authoritarian attitudes, slowness, and a lack of awareness of social issues in mainline media, was essential for the evolving of my ideas.

In the early 1970s the magazines which recognized my work, as I was doing it, were ***Avalanche*** (Liza Béar interview, and my writing, photographs), ***Art-Rite*** (Lucy Lippard, and my writing, photographs), ***Feminist Art Journal*** (Cindy Nemser), as well as the ***Triquarterly Review*** (my photographs of works) and the ***SoHo Weekly News*** (reviews by Peter Frank, John Perreault) and the ***Village Voice*** (reviews by Jonas Mekas, John Perreault), the last two being in those days rougher and more radical publications.

Through other media, film and video, I also expressed my social concerns. Made in 1974, my videotape ***Underscan*** addresses the abuses of the elderly. My 16 mm film, ***Pine Barrens***, 1975, looked at a landscape and its people without an authoritarian "objective" narration. The landscape spoke for itself. These works were shown many times in many social settings, not just in galleries and museums, continuing to the present. Similarly my videotape, ***Revolve***, 1977, dealt with death and dying in a very candid way. My solo showings of these films and videos at MOMA in 1979 were reviewed in the ***Independent***, published by the Association of Independent Video and Filmmakers, an organization I joined and actively supported.

In the 1960s and 1970s I lived in NYC in the West Village. I read the ***NYTimes*** as well as ***Heresies***. I stayed tuned into feminist causes and developments, participating in feminist discussion groups and panels and symposiums about feminism. I supported the Vietnam Veterans Against the War, some of whose members I met through Bob Fiore and Barbara Jarvis while they were shooting and editing the film ***Winter Soldier***, which I wholeheartedly endorsed. I was sympathetic to the Art Workers Coalition, though not an active member of the organization.

Fortunately, in the 1960s and 1970s there were just one or two art bars where artists congregated. At St. Adrian's or Max's Kansas City we sat around having intense political discussions, which echoed way beyond the bar. It was here that many ideas for articles in underground media were generated. Through these barroom discussions I felt connected with my community and motivated to act. The radical print media reinforced these tendencies.

Avalanche and *Art-Rite*, printed in newspaper format, were bold and immediate. As soon as an artwork was completed it would be covered there. I was asked to write pieces in both magazines. The voice of the artist was heard and given predominance over art criticism. Art ideas travel fast, and the established art magazines were so slow, what they published was after the fact, not part of the dialogue. In the alternate publications words generated new artworks; discourse between artists was heightened.

Oddly, during the same time, I was attempting to reach people through the mass media. I was an assistant literary editor in 1966–1967, working with Dale McConathy at *Harper's Bazaar*. At *Harper's Bazaar* I worked half days mainly reading unsolicited manuscripts. Dale and I thought that by publishing the best poetry and prose in a mass magazine we could reach a huge audience, in beauty parlors, doctor's offices, and homes around the country. We could have a wide-ranging effect. We published writers like Iris Murdoch and Nathalie Sarraute, who I also got to know, as well as Smithson's "The Crystal Land" and the "X Factor in Art," Sol LeWitt's piece on Beckett, and Dan Graham's *Figurative*.

Chip Lord

For the purposes of this endeavor, I am restricting my answers to the period 1968–1974 during the first few years of Ant Farm.

I was living in San Francisco, Houston, Texas, Berkeley, Sausalito, and then Texas again during this period. As a founding member of Ant Farm I primarily confined my activism to the countercultural architectural (soon to be media) practice of Ant Farm.

The strongest influence came from the *Whole Earth Catalog*, as it manifested a cultural movement which included back-to-the-land, new technologies, traditional tools, and other countercultural resources. Each edition of the *Catalog* began with a philosophical or intellectual section—"Whole Systems"—that included reprints or new works by Buckminster Fuller, Gregory Bateson, and other thinkers—this was a kind of graduate education for me. Eventually we were proudly included in the *Whole Earth Catalog* as contributors—and our own publication—*The Inflatocookbook* (1970, edition of 1,000, self-produced) was influenced by the "access to tools" mantra of the *Whole Earth Catalog*.

Obviously the *Whole Earth Catalog* didn't have a new graphic style—it had *no* graphic style, but this antiaesthetic may have been intentional. A way to proclaim voluntary simplicity. The goal, I think, was to come across as straightforward, honest, and participatory. But I believe Stewart Brand did have a sense of how it should look and function, and his decision to make the first from-space photograph of the earth the logo or brand of the periodical was brilliant.

We also read the *Berkeley Barb* and other local alternative papers, which seemed to likewise have no graphic style. To be countercultural was to be messy, collaged, and ad hoc within a loose aesthetic framework.

Margo Machida

What I was reading would change dramatically from the mid-1960s to the late 1970s, as that marked a major transitional period spanning the life I had led in Hawaii, where I was born and raised, and my first six years in New York City. When I was a teenager in high school during the mid-1960s, my interests centered on Henry Miller, George Orwell, Albert Camus, Colette, Yukio Mishima, Hubert Selby Jr., and the Beats—Jack Kerouac, Allen Ginsberg, and Lawrence Ferlinghetti. Betty Friedan's *The Feminine Mystique* (1963) was also revelatory, in articulating an early feminist politics. Although the Asian American movement and university ethnic studies departments were also emerging on the "mainland" during this tumultuous era, my involvement with Asian American publications and activist groups did not begin until long after 1968, when I had moved to New York City to attend NYU.

Living in a relatively small town like Hilo on the Big Island of Hawaii, there was little access to alternative press publications. My visits to Honolulu, on Oahu, were sporadic, as interisland flights were expensive. Hence, at that time I had no direct contact with the sort of urban outlets (head shops, cafés, specialty bookstores, etc.) where such publications were typically distributed, to say nothing of the intellectual and academic social networks within which they also circulated. Apart from mainstream glossy illustrated magazines like *Life* and *Look*, my main journalistic sources of information about the social and political debates of the day, and the arts, came via national media such as the *New York Times*, the *Atlantic*, and *Harper's Magazine*. Images of the civil rights, antiwar, and youth movements arrived largely filtered through the popular media, Vietnam War–era photojournalism, television, and psychedelic rock concert posters and album covers for bands like the Grateful Dead, Big Brother and the Holding Company, Jimi Hendrix, and Jefferson Airplane. Coupled with the profound impact of the music, I have come to recognize that such countercultural imagery often exerted a powerful allure for those of my generation—especially for those who, like myself, spent our formative years far from the major American urban centers.

I came to New York City at the age of seventeen, both for college and to pursue a desire to become a writer. Not only was this my first time away from Hawaii, but the NYU campus, centered on Washington Square, was a nexus of wide-ranging political activity and boisterous antiwar demonstrations. This bracing encounter would radically alter my life. Rallies I attended led by the Black Panther Party and the Young Lords made a powerful impression on me, in bringing forward both domestic and international issues of race and class solidarity among oppressed peoples. I rapidly became involved with various leftist organizations, and took part in feminist and Third World women's groups.

Soon afterward, I moved to the Lower East Side, where I increasingly read the alternative papers and zines that were very much a part of the neighborhood milieu. They included the *East Village Other* (*EVO*), *Rat*, and the *Realist* as well as more national publications like the *Village Voice* and *Rolling Stone*. *EVO* was particularly memorable for its eye-catching graphics; it regularly featured comic strips by artists like Robert Crumb, Kim Deitch, Spain Rodriguez, Art Spiegelman, and Trina Robbins, who were key figures in the emerging underground comix scene of the late 1960s. Robbins, along with Lee Marrs and others, later founded the feminist-inspired *Wimmen's Comix* in 1970, which I avidly read. Those graphic works sparked my continuing interest in the genre, based on an abiding appreciation for the freedom this medium offered as a high-spirited, unbridled, and often self-published form of expression that could deploy downright scatological social critique, as well as for these independently owned presses' prolific use of low-end technologies. Whereas this genre is certainly not limited to autobiographical confessionals, satire, or social commentary, I was (and still am) particularly fascinated by artists like R. Crumb, with their gleeful, discomfiting, and flagrantly transgressive approaches to violating social, moral, and "politically correct" taboos by graphically depicting sex and sexism, race and racism (viz. Crumb's notorious characters like Angelfood McSpade and Whiteman), violence, sadism, and anarchic behavior, among the gamut of human foibles and neuroses. While there is no direct line to the work I would later produce as a cultural activist and scholar of contemporary art, I nevertheless retain a strong affinity for the idiosyncratic countercultural sensibilities that permeated these publications.

During this first decade in New York, my exposure to local Asian communities (then largely Chinese) remained very limited. The local Japanese American community was minuscule, and, although Manhattan's Chinatown was poised for explosive growth following the abolition of restrictive federal immigration quotas in 1965, it was still comparatively small. Further, as a third-generation Japanese American from Hawaii where people of Asian heritages were the majority, and conceptions of "Asian American–ness" did not have much resonance, I had had no prior exposure to Asian American political or cultural activism. Even though my arrival in New York did coincide with the cusp of that transformation, it was not until the late 1970s—after moving to a loft in Chinatown—that I first became acquainted with Asian American arts groups; in particular with two Chinatown-based organizations, Basement Workshop and the Asian American Arts Center, both of which were founded in the early 1970s by Asian American students, artists, and political activists. While I had already been involved with visual art as an emerging artist and later as a cofounder of a cooperative gallery in Soho, these new contacts proved to be catalytic in fostering an ongoing interest in contemporary Asian American art and thus encouraged my development as a curator, scholar, and critic. Through these groups I met activist artists, writers, filmmakers, and performers from the Asian American arts movement and realized that cultural production could be a primary vehicle for both self- and collective expression, in bringing forward the particular experiences, histories, and struggles of the local Asian communities.

It was, moreover, through archives maintained by these groups (and later, by the New York Chinatown History Project—now the Museum of Chinese in America) that I first saw Asian American alternative press publications, from both the East and the West Coasts, including ***Bridge*** magazine, which Basement had first published in the early 1970s. Significantly, ***Bridge*** typically included a lively mix of reproductions of artworks alongside political commentary, essays, poetry, and fiction. Through these periodicals, I acquired a sense of the range of work and social issues that could engage Asian American artists, both locally and nationally. I also became aware of how the late 1960s and 1970s had been an especially productive time, as the Asian American movement spawned an array of alternative press publications of widely varying ideological orientations and readerships. They included the Los Angeles–based ***Gidra*** magazine and ***Crosscurrents***; ***Amerasia Journal*** (first published in 1971 by the Yale Asian American Students Association, and later by UCLA); ***Rodan*** (San Francisco); and ***Getting Together*** (New York).

Although their readerships were comparatively limited, these alternative periodicals created important sites for critical dialogue and engagement in constituting localized nodes of a distinctively Asian American intellectual, political, and visual culture. Among them, *Amerasia* would evolve into a leading academic journal of Asian American studies with a national presence. Even though the visual arts have historically received little attention from *Amerasia*, a milestone was nonetheless achieved in 2004, when an entire issue was devoted to the late painter and illustrator Miné Okubo, best known for her contemporaneous drawings of the World War II Japanese American internment that were later compiled in her book, *Citizen 13660* (1946). This signaled an important recognition of the role of the visual in constituting a larger Asian American historical imaginary.

In sum, I believe that the impact and influence of media like the alternative, underground, and countercultural press in constituting a vital "counter-public sphere" must be also considered on the personal level, as it is necessarily influenced by the vicissitudes of local conditions particular to specific times and places. As my example brings forward, access and exposure to these forms of information are often quite uneven and idiosyncratic, especially for Americans who have lived far beyond the shores of the continental United States. Certainly, prior to the advent of the Internet and associated digital technologies, print media (alongside television and radio) were the primary means by which people commonly visualized their lifeworld(s), which in turn helped to shape their perceptions of common cause with others. Given the strong interpersonal and social component inherent in the consumption of such media, my experience suggests that their impact on the individual cannot be adequately viewed as wholly apart from the specific local contexts and networks of relationships in which they circulate and thus are assigned meaning and value.

Yvonne Rainer

1) Living and activism: NYC antiwar (Vietnam) demonstrations, Art Workers' Coalition meetings and sit-ins and demonstrations.

2) Reading: *Mother Jones*, *Liberation Magazine*, *New York Review of Books*, *Village Voice*, *Soho News*.

3) Not involved with any publications.

4) Don't remember "new graphic innovations" in the publications I was reading.

Terry Smith

The two dates bracketing this questionnaire locate me in very different, but deeply connected, places. Some of the differences and most of the connections lay in what I was reading; much of both came from what I—working always with others—did with what I read.

In 1964 I was a twenty-year-old second-year arts student at the University of Melbourne, majoring in English (Milton, Dryden, Pope, but mercifully Donne and Hopkins), history (Luther, thank God) and philosophy (*The Republic*, Aristotle), with a minor in fine arts ("Introduction to Art"). Off-campus in nearby Carlton, I struggled to be a writer: an obsessively detailed, unreadable diary my only sustained output.

Ten years later, I was in New York, living in Chinatown, a graduate student at the Institute of Fine Arts, New York University, advised by Robert Goldwater and taking courses from William Rubin ("Formalism since Pollock"), Robert Rosenblum ("American Painting and the Northern Romantic Tradition") among others, while also attending Meyer Schapiro's "Art History: Theories and Methods" seminar at Columbia ("Semiotics and Cybernetics Applied to Art History"). Supported by a Harkness Fellowship, my wife and I toured a deeply divided US in a Volkswagen hatchback, visiting sixty-four museums and galleries in thirty-two states, plus a side trip to Mexico. Meanwhile I worked away at my master's thesis on abstract expressionism and ethics. Active in the New York branch of the Art & Language group of conceptual artists, headquartered on the Bowery just south of Houston, I produced work for shows at John Weber Gallery and various venues in Europe, an issue of *Art-Language* with Ian Burn and Mel Ramsden (vol. 3, no. 1, "Draft for an Anti-Textbook"), and articles on "Art and Art & Language" and "The Provincialism Problem" for *Artforum*. Among other things, these articles register the turn from pure conceptualism to political sociality in some late modern avant-garde practice.[1]

During the decade between 1964 and 1974 I drifted far from formal study, immersed in copious quantities of (usually stolen) books that sustained my existential nausea. Somehow, I completed my arts degree while (improperly) suspended from the university for misconduct (1966); then shelved books in a suburban library (1967). Bernard Smith's invitation to be a tutor (assistant professor) at the newly formed Power Institute of Fine Arts at the University of Sydney (1968) was a turning point. In addition to teaching university students and in the evenings at the Workers' Educational Association, I worked on catalogs of Power exhibitions, presented a television series *The Objects of Art* (1969), edited *Other Voices*, a contemporary art journal (1970–1971), and wrote weekly art reviews for national newspapers (the *Australian*, *Nation Review*). In

1. See Heather Barker and Charles Green, "The Provincialism Problem: Terry Smith and Centre-Periphery Art History," *Journal of Art Historiography*, no. 3, December 2010, http://arthistoriography.files.wordpress.com/2011/02/media_183176_en.pdf

1972 I won a Harkness Fellowship to study at the Institute of Fine Arts (1972–1974).

What shaped the reading that so comprehensively drew me into and got me out of the void? What has design got to do with it? The fact that there were few books in my family's house was obviated by excellent public education and local lending libraries. Two or three times a week during my early adolescence my mother would send me to pick up her replacement romance. I soon learned that design—starting with the covers—signaled much about a book's likely depth of interest. The man in the bookshop would offer me a Penguin Classic for free if I would read it before my next visit. At the time, those books stood out due to their color-coded framing, elegant black lettering, and engraved image front and center. After a while, he added the orange bars and plainly lettered titles of Penguin Books' more modern novels and plays. Sociology and politics in the Pelican Originals series were framed by (what I later learned were) Germano Facetti's Marber grid designs. Thus primed, I graduated to the full orange-and-red-covered output of the older but more radical Left Book Club. Throughout my school days, the official syllabus—good, but not memorably designed—was augmented each week by a couple of books from such sources. By my last years in high school I was a committed existentialist. My first year at university was devoted to the assiduous consumption of every book referred to by Colin Wilson in his *Outsider* (a mediocre mind at best, but what a bibliography!).

Existentialist introversion kept me out of active politics during the later 1960s in Melbourne, although I do recall being at the 1966 demonstration when red and green paint was thrown at LBJ's car as he went by the university on his visit to drum up support for the US war against Vietnam. I was more active in Sydney from 1968 onward, organizing protests against the war, against conscription, and specifically against a law prohibiting people from inciting young men to resist the draft. Getting that law repealed was my one concrete political victory. We presented our views, and recorded the struggle, through university publications, such as *Farrago* (Melbourne) and *Honi Soit* (Sydney). Design-wise, they tended toward the almanac-style, collective DIY production modes of the *Whole Earth Catalog* and shared its goal: "access to tools." Apart from mainstream journalism and the well-known English and US radical journals, we read and wrote for Australian radical publications such as *Dissent*, *Arena*, *Thesis 11* and *Tribune* as well as local literary, cultural journals such as *Meanjin* and *Quadrant*.

The 1960s and 1970s were boom years for Australian art, especially figurative and expressive abstract painting: in the work of artists such as Sidney Nolan, Arthur Boyd, John Olsen, and Brett Whiteley, it had become a vital component of the national imaginary. In the three or four newspapers published each day in each of the six capital cities, a weekly column on the latest exhibitions could be found. Tony McGillick, Paul McGillick, and I started *Other Voices* because the one local journal, *Art and Australia*, was tied to the growing market for this art, and to this nationalist narrative. Long, critical, reflexive articles were a feature of the overseas publications that we admired: *Artforum* had published Michael Fried's entire dissertation, for Chrissake, on the "Frenchness" of French Art! *Other Voices* imitated *Artforum*'s almost-square landscape format, and (for economic reasons) favored pop graphics for the covers, but its insides were laid out like *Avalanche*, the magazine we really loved for its ideas-oriented, event-structured rhythms, and for its unabashed romanticism of the avant-garde artist. My personal goal was to write art historical essays within magazine formats, and art criticism within the art-reviewing framework of my newspaper columns: the aim was to break genres, and in so doing, elevate both to levels of seriousness that they had, in Australia at least, rarely achieved. *Other Voices* lasted for just three issues, but the enterprise has, I believe, remained valid ever since.

In 1971 I curated an exhibition for the Contemporary Art Society in Sydney entitled "The Situation Now: Object and Post-Object Art." It was a survey of the Australian manifestations of what I saw as the worldwide shifts in art from hard-edge, color-field painting to conceptual and performance art. The catalog consisted of my statement of a set of "propositions" about these changes, and interviews with each of the artists involved—from painters such as David Aspden to text by Ian Burn and Mel Ramsden in New York.[2] Bound in waxed wrapping paper, the subtitle stamped on its cover in homage to Donald Brook's distinction, the typewritten materials on its plain pages were cranked out on a Gestetner, then stapled together one by one. The design instinct was to exemplify the exhibition's argument: high art was disappearing into everyday life.

Art & Language publications favored the spare, pared-down nonlook of an academic journal—that of an esoteric subdiscipline, such as the *Journal of Logic, Language, and Information*. Introducing red letters, even adding a subtitle, to the issue of *Art-Language* that we made in 1974 caused much headshaking among English members of the group ("much too Constructivist"). More than minimalism—already an aesthetic of refinement by 1970—conceptual artists sought a resolutely nonvisual stylelessness. The goal was to disappear the support, to remove it from visibility, so that the ideas in play would stand out for the reader, nakedly. Thus *Blurting in A&L* (1973) stayed as close as it could to being a typed-up listing of the words used during a conversational exchange among members of the group. Its subtitle, *The Handbook*, underscored its intended role: to enable the reader to join an imagined conversation.

2. For the "Propositions," see Alex Alberro and Blake Stimson, eds., *Conceptual Art: A Critical Anthology* (Cambridge, MA: MIT Press, 2000), pp. 258-261. See also Terry Smith, *Transformations in Australian Art: The Twentieth Century—Modernism and Aboriginality* (Sydney: Craftsman House, 2002).

Thus the rough cardboard covers and newspaper stock used for the three issues of the ***Fox*** (1975–1976). These choices also staked out territory that separated conceptualism from the word-image collaging preferred by concrete poets. Their goal was to shake up presumptions of what "the literary" looked like, and how it sounded in the mind's eye. Ours was to erase the eye from the mind altogether, in the name of bringing the mind into the world.

3. See Sandy Kirby, *Artists and Unions: A Critical Tradition; A Report on the Art and Working Life Program* (Redfern, NSW: Australia Council, 1992).

4. See Roger Butler, *Poster Art in Australia: The Streets as Galleries—Walls Sometimes Speak* (Canberra: National Gallery of Australia, 1993).

Coda. In 1975, my fellowship ended, I returned to teach at universities and art schools in Melbourne first, then, for twenty-five years, at the Power Institute in Sydney. Nineteen seventy-five was a volatile year in Australian politics and art, although few made the necessary connections between them. In 1976 Ian Burn and Nigel Lendon returned to Australia. We founded Media Action Group, involving a number of others, such as Michiel Dolk and Ian Milliss, to prepare slide shows for workers on political and cultural topics. This soon evolved into Union Media Services, an organization of artists and designers devoted to energizing the visual communications of left-wing trade unions, radical groups, and dissenting social movements. We applied the design principles of advanced art magazines (60 percent images, banner headlines, typeface variations) to union and group newsletters, newspapers, posters, banners, and demonstrations. UMS spun off a number of other similar organizations and inspired a federal government policy known as Art and Working Life that, for many years, financed arts officers in trade unions throughout the country.[3] Its work was paralleled by that of a number of other activist artist groups, such as the Earthworks Poster Collective (Tin Shed, University of Sydney, 1972–1979) and Redback Graphix (Wollongong, 1980–1994), which together launched a poster movement that echoes but also rivals the Cuban posters of the 1960s.[4]

Lawrence Weiner

IN RESPONSE TO YOUR QUESTIONS

I MUST CAUTION THAT IN THE NAME OF COURTESY I SHALL ANSWER THEM BUT I DO NOT BELIEVE IN THE PREMISE OF A COUNTERCULTURE. I DO NOT BELIEVE THAT THE GRAPHICS & THE WORK I HAVE DONE IS COUNTERCULTURE.

WHEN ONE IS DISSATISFIED WITH THE CONFIGURATION AS IT IS PRESENTED (BOTH IN MEANING & IN CONTEXT) WHATEVER ONE DOES PROPOSE IS STILL COMPOSED OF THE INTEGERS OF THE OVERALL SOCIETY THAT ENCOMPASSES AN APPOSITE.

AN OPPOSITE WOULD REQUIRE A BELIEF IN PARALLEL STRUCTURES & IN EFFECT A HIERARCHY. EACH MANIFESTATION OF THE CULTURE PRESENTS ITSELF AT A SIMULTANEOUS MOMENT IN FACT AT THE SAME PLACE AT THE SAME TIME.

LOOKING AT THE PERIOD 1964–1974: I WAS LIVING IN AMSTERDAM & NEW YORK CITY (SIMULTANEOUSLY AT TIMES). THE EXTENT OF MY ACTIVISM WAS WHAT PRESENTED ITSELF AS A NECESSITY. AS TO WHAT KIND OF PRESS WAS I READING: THE SAME PRESS I WAS PARTICIPATING IN & WHATEVER CAME TO HAND. I DID NOT SEE WHAT YOU WOULD REFER TO AS GRAPHIC INNOVATIONS. THEY WERE THE RESULT OF THE NECESSITY OF PRESENTING A DIFFERENT FORM OF INFORMATION. FORM DID NOT FOLLOW FUNCTION. FORM WAS FUNCTION.

THE INTERESTING THING IS THAT ALL OF THESE OPINIONS MATTERED FOR NOT MUCH AS THE MATERIAL OF THAT PERIOD ITSELF IS STILL EXTANT & VISIBLE EITHER AS ANTIQUITIES OR AS REVELATIONS.

BEST I CAN DO. GOOD LUCK WITH YOUR ENDEAVOR.

Faith Wilding

1966–1968: I lived in Iowa City, IA (finishing my BA at the University of Iowa).

I came to Iowa already a member of SDS. I lived in a "movement house" that had both a beer brewing setup and a big offset printing press in the basement. Here we printed the Iowa City underground newspaper ***Middle Earth*** (yep—we were referring to the Midwest as well as hobbit-land). Iowa City had a large and active SDS chapter whose leaders (among them my then boyfriend) regularly traveled back and forth between Chicago, Urbana, Bloomington, and other Big Ten university campuses holding regional meetings, planning protests and actions, and training people in passive resistance tactics and draft counseling. I took part in all of this and spent a good deal of time draft counseling and working with a welfare mothers organization who were trying to get free admittance for mothers to the university.

For ***Middle Earth*** I was mostly an illustrator and also solicited advertising and laid out the ads. My graphic inspiration was a mixture of William Blake (on whose illuminated ***Prophecies*** I was writing an honor's thesis) and the drug-inspired psychedelia of that period. We were able to do handmade color bleeds on our printing press and made some quite garish stuff. Many of us regularly read all the underground and radical mags we could get—the *Berkeley Barb* was a favorite, the *Rat* from NYC, and the one from Austin, Texas (don't recall the name of it, but they once printed maps to all the hemp fields between Texas and Iowa). In Iowa, which was home to the writer's workshop, we also did a poetry zine called the *Penny Paper* and produced endless posters, picket signs, and other ephemera. Gentle Thursday celebrations were also started in Iowa City during that time and there was influential influx from the likes of the San Francisco Mime Troupe, the *Whole Earth Catalog*, and Allen Ginsberg and the Beats, many of whom also produced wonderful graphics and text posters. All SDS members also received SDS's *CAW* magazine that came out of NYC at the time. In 1968, *CAW* was visited by some members of the March 22 Movement in Paris who brought with them: "a suitcase full of French documents, posters, and photographs. The material they brought reflects intimately and powerfully the struggles of the French students and workers and is important to us because of the startling similarity between the forms of their struggle against bourgeois France and ours against bourgeois America." (A note from the *CAW* staff.) I have this publication in my possession still and it basically reprints much of the material in Rene Vienet's *Enrages and Situationists in the Occupation Movement, France, May 1968* (Autonomedia). All of the French material was translated into English and reprinted here for the first time, and there were lots of reproductions of the Occupationist posters, graphics, etc. A great influence for all of us.

1968–1969: I lived in River Falls, Wisconsin (my husband's first academic job).

With very few numbers and resources here we published a few issues of a zine called *the stifled vice*. Also began regularly reading the *New York Review of Books* and watching the Smothers Brothers on black-and-white TV. There were many graphically minimal and more ideological and political publications such as the *International Socialist Review*, *New Left Notes*, and the *Far East Reporter*.

1969–1971: Fresno, California. (I undertook graduate studies in art/art history at Fresno State University. Suzanne Lacy and I started the first consciousness-raising group here; I also founded and taught "The Second Sex," the first women's studies course in the Experimental College at FSU; and I met Judy Chicago in 1970, and we started the first Feminist Art Program at FSU.)

It was around this time that the first women's studies courses and departments began to be organized. I think the earliest one was at San Diego State College. I still have one of their magazines, very roughly and crudely printed with Käthe Kollwitz–like illustrations, and graphics and photos. The German expressionist style lino or woodcut was still quite influential in terms of broadsheets, etc. We were mostly all using the mimeograph machine and offset printing, for which they were just developing paper plates. But everything still had to go through various analog processes, so we were all adept at pasting up magazine pages, doing bold hand-lettering, and photocollaging. The feminist art program was invited to do a special issue of *Everywoman* magazine, and this was designed by Sheila De Bretteville (now a professor at the Yale School of Art) who was beginning to think about a feminist graphic look and design that matched the content in new ways. Lots of feminist zines and publications began to appear here and there—I got some at City Lights in San Francisco—but I do not think they were in any way exciting graphically.

1971–1974: I lived in Los Angeles (attended CalArts, where I completed my MFA; I was the TA for the Feminist Art Program at CalArts and team leader on the Womanhouse project and other feminist program projects). Graphically noteworthy at this time were the graphics workshops taught at CalArts by Sheila de Bretteville and others. Also the interesting graphic and poster interventions by the likes of Fluxus artists Emmett Williams, Dick Higgins, and Alison Knowles, who were all at CalArts. When Sheila, Judy Chicago, and Arlene Raven left CalArts to start the Feminist Studio Workshop, they started a graphics shop there and taught typesetting, printing on various printing presses, and feminist graphic design. There were some really beautiful posters and small books and many other graphic productions made there. I have always been interested in image/text combinations and have always produced drawings and collages that also use text. I have extensively studied illuminated manuscripts and have made versions of artist books that mixed medieval and modern styles. To me, many of the psychedelic posters and mags suggested this mixture.

I can't say that I was terrifically influenced in my work by graphic innovations in political publications at the time. Though maybe the fact that I was actually producing some work that imitated or borrowed from those styles showed I was influenced. I've probably forgotten lots of things, and also I've been divorced from the archive of this part of my life, so this is about as much as I can contribute at the moment.

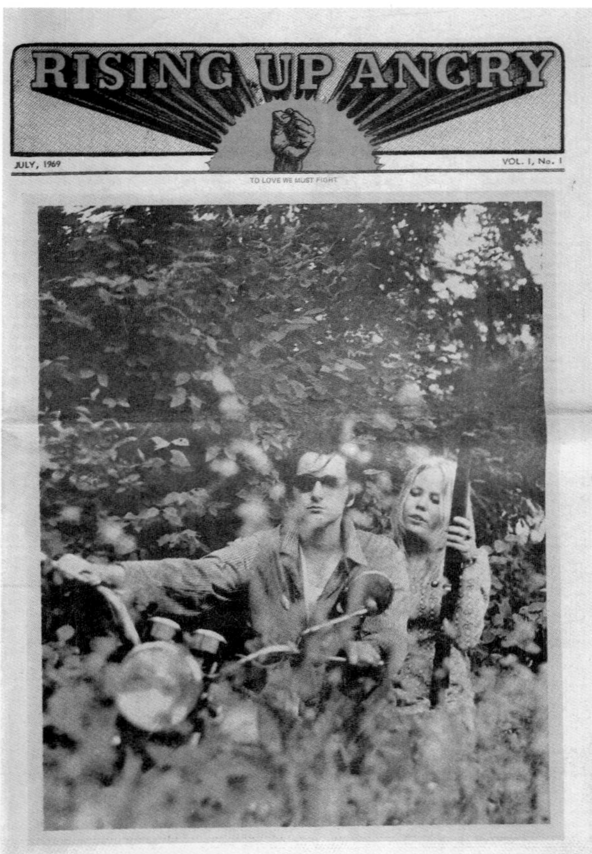

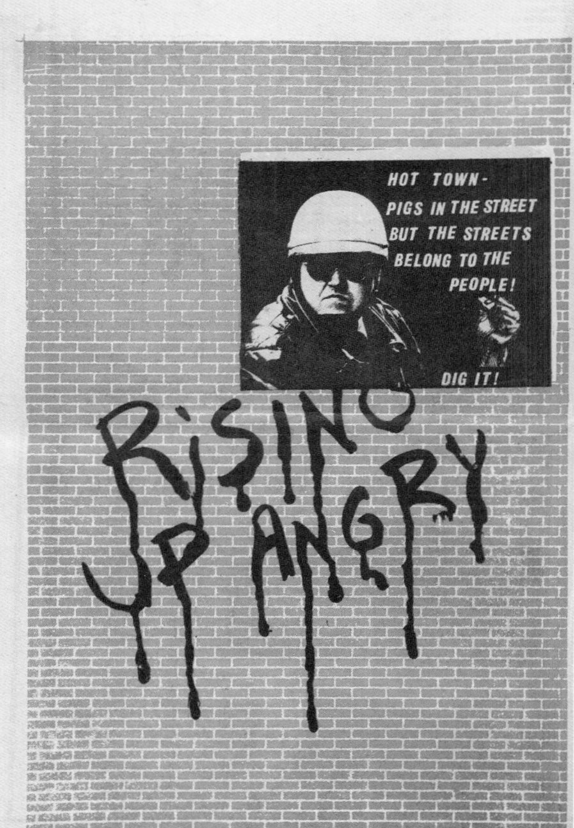

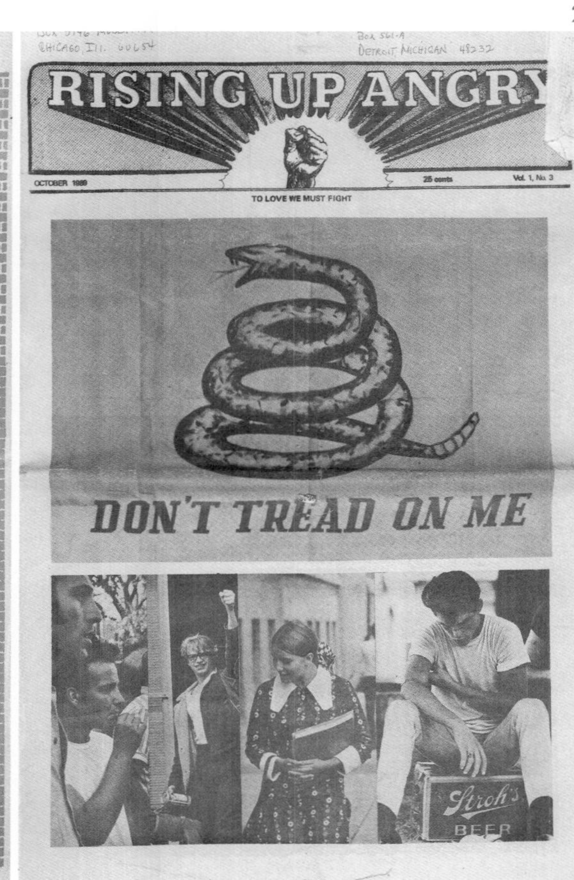

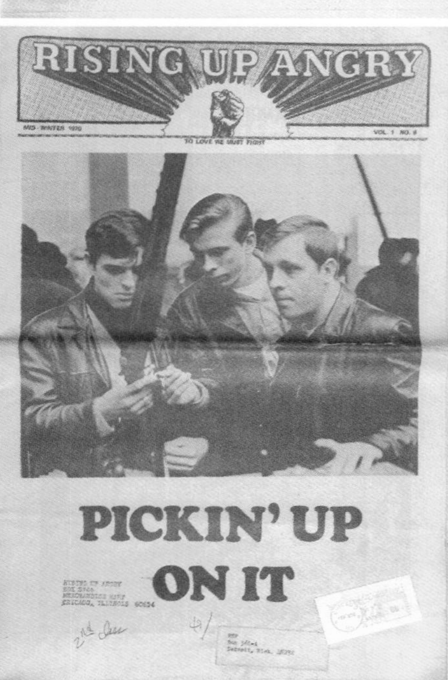

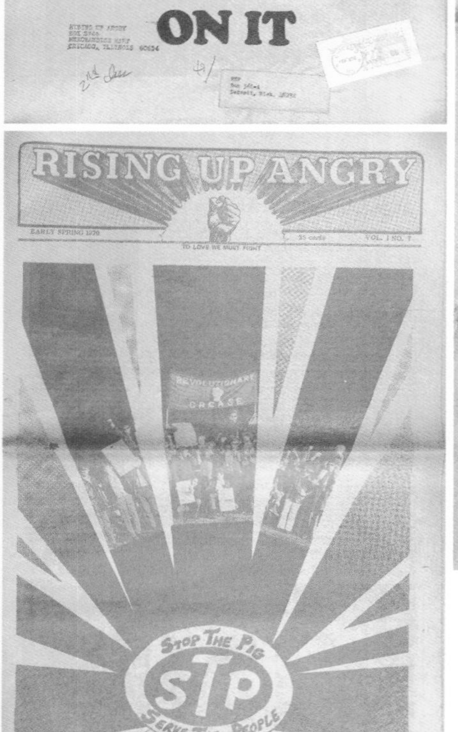

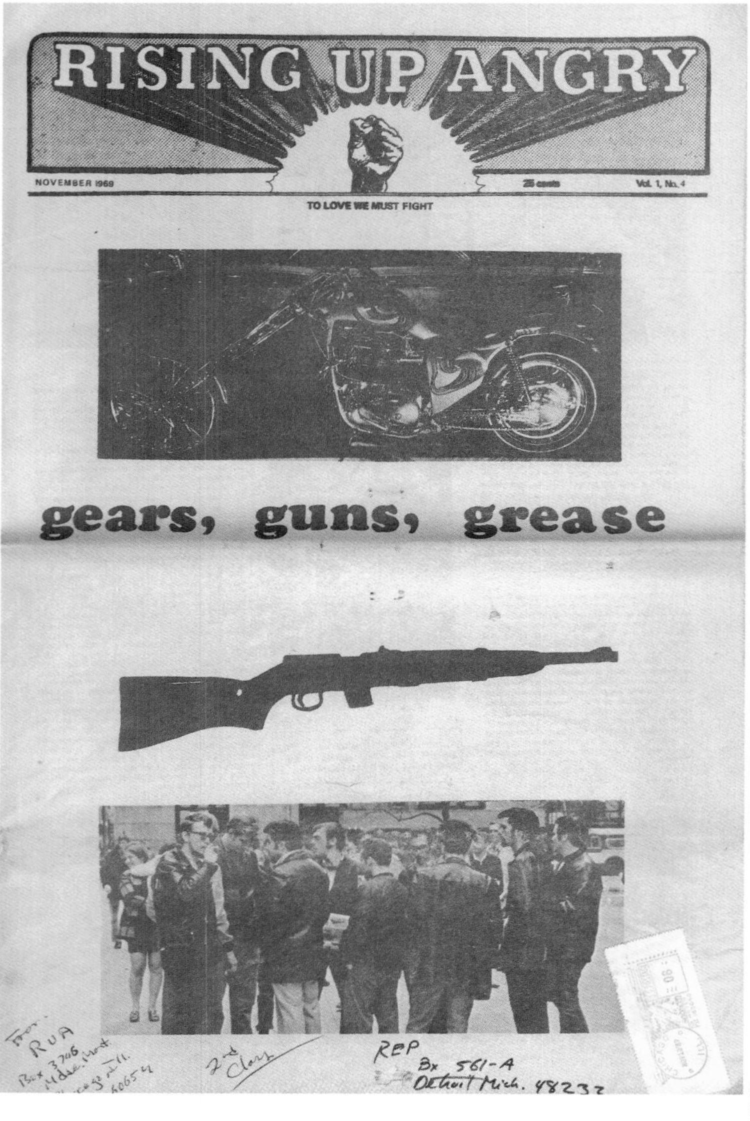

ALL POWER TO THE BROTHERS & SISTERS
who love their people

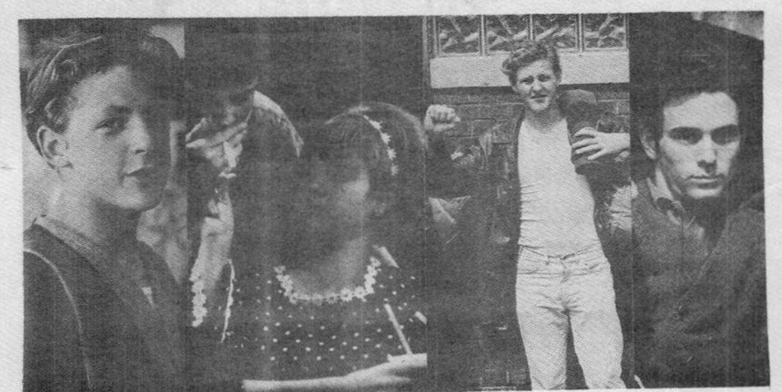

and fight the real enemy

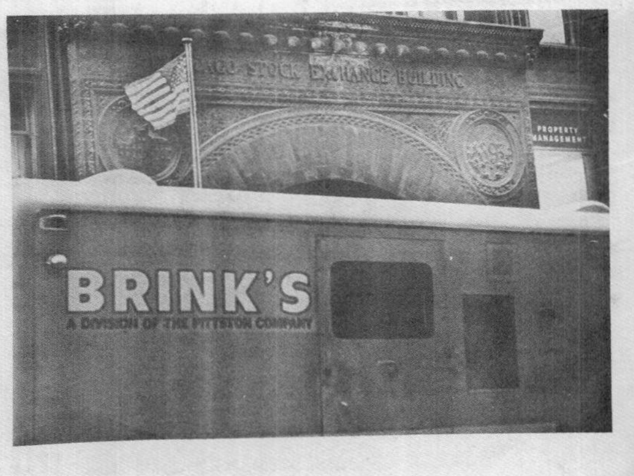

Rising Up Angry (Chicago), July 1969, vol. 1, no. 1, cover
Rising Up Angry (Chicago), July 1969, vol. 1, no. 1, back cover
Rising Up Angry (Chicago), October 1969, vol. 1, no. 3, cover
Rising Up Angry (Chicago), 1970, vol. 1, no. 6, cover
Rising Up Angry (Chicago), November 1969, vol. 1, no. 4, cover
Rising Up Angry (Chicago), October 1969, vol. 1, no. 3, back cover
Rising Up Angry (Chicago), 1970, vol. 1, no. 7, cover

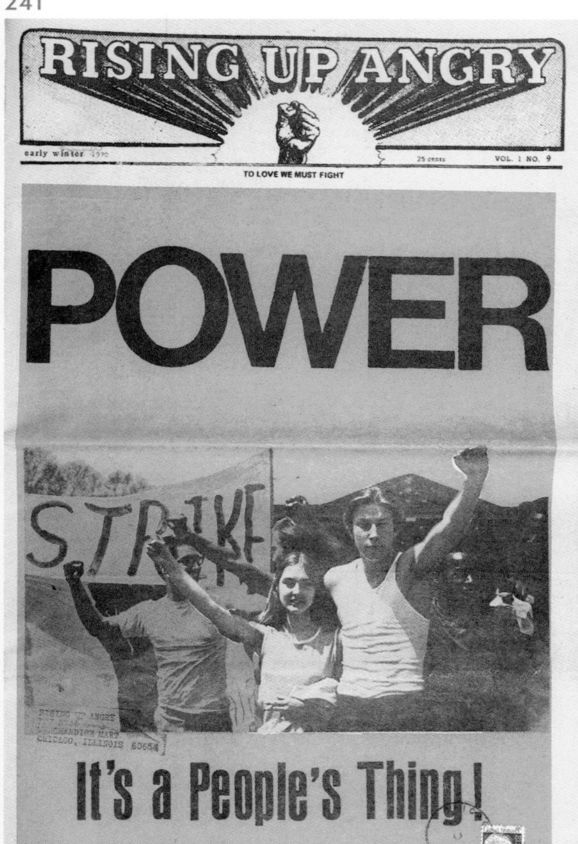

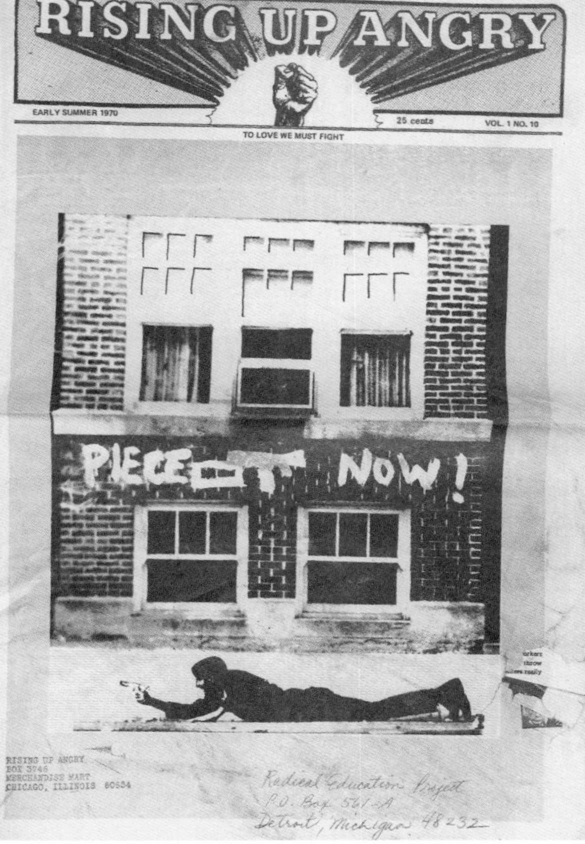

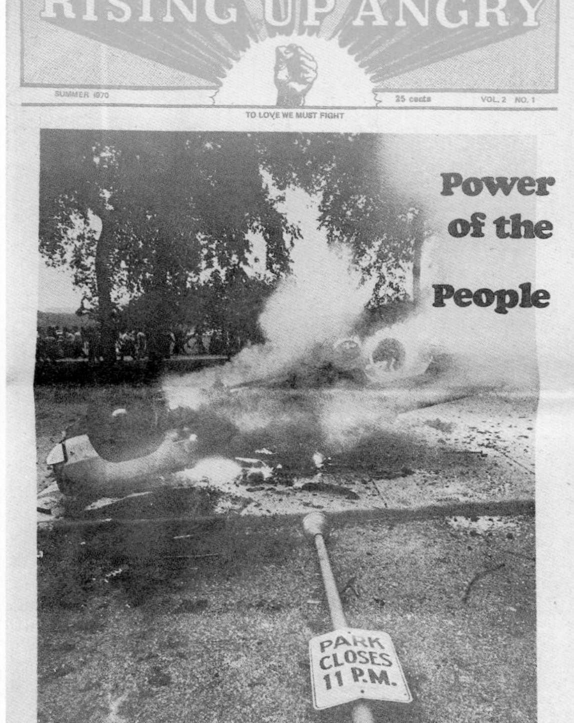

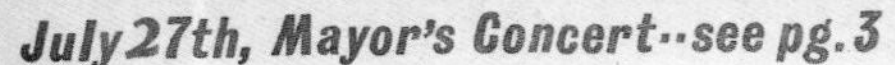

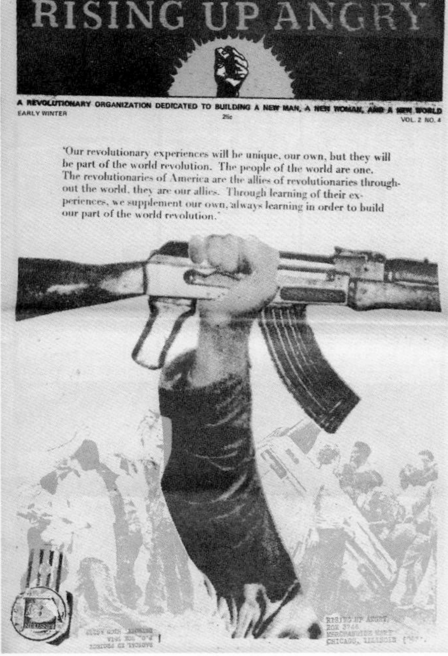

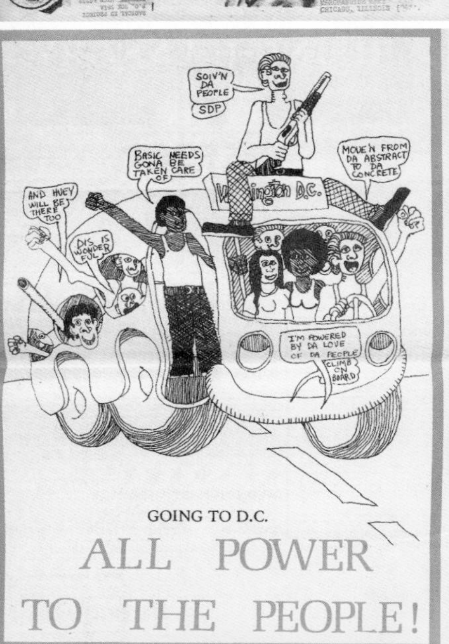

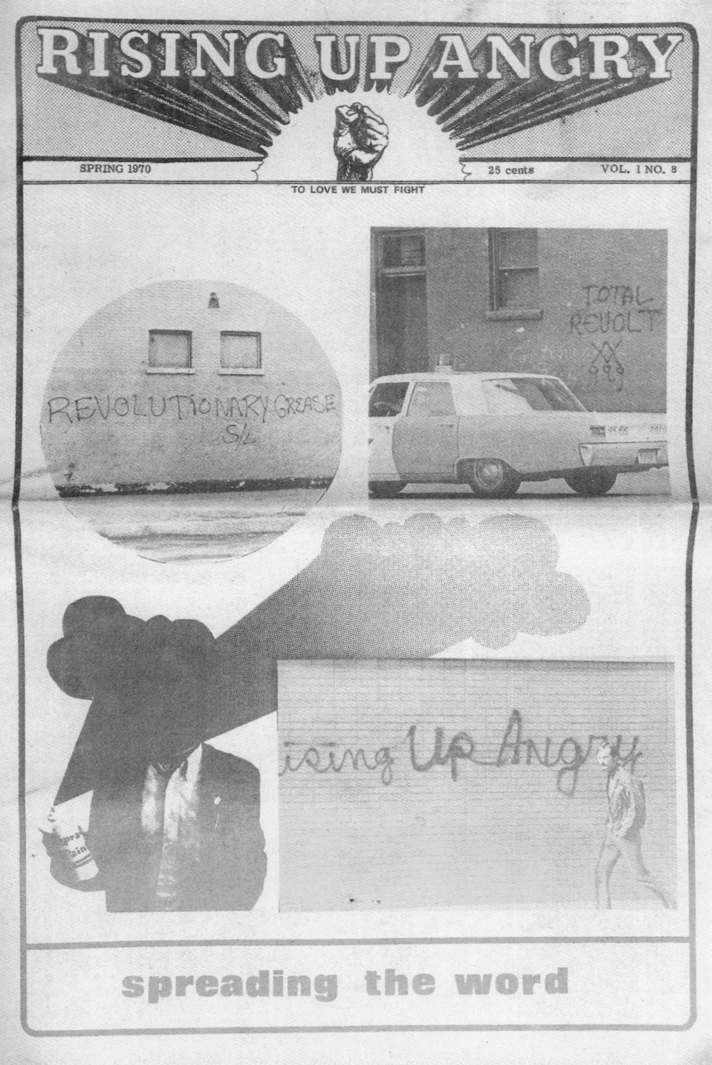

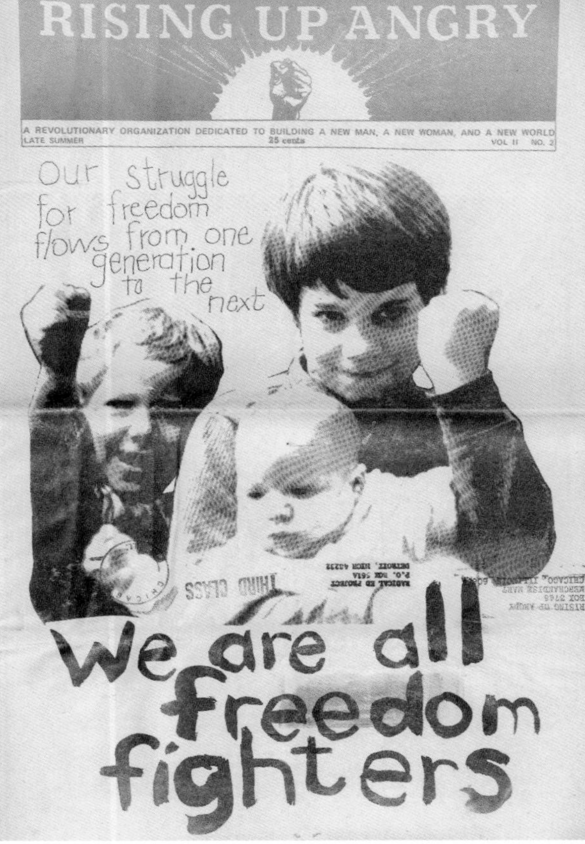

Rising Up Angry (Chicago), 1970, vol. 1, no. 9, cover
Rising Up Angry (Chicago), 1970, vol. 1, no. 10, cover
Rising Up Angry (Chicago), 1970, vol. 2, no. 1, cover
Rising Up Angry (Chicago), 1971, vol. 2, no. 4, cover
Rising Up Angry (Chicago), 1970, vol. 1, no. 8, cover
Rising Up Angry (Chicago), 1970, vol. 2, no. 2, cover
Rising Up Angry (Chicago), 1971, vol. 2, no. 4, back cover

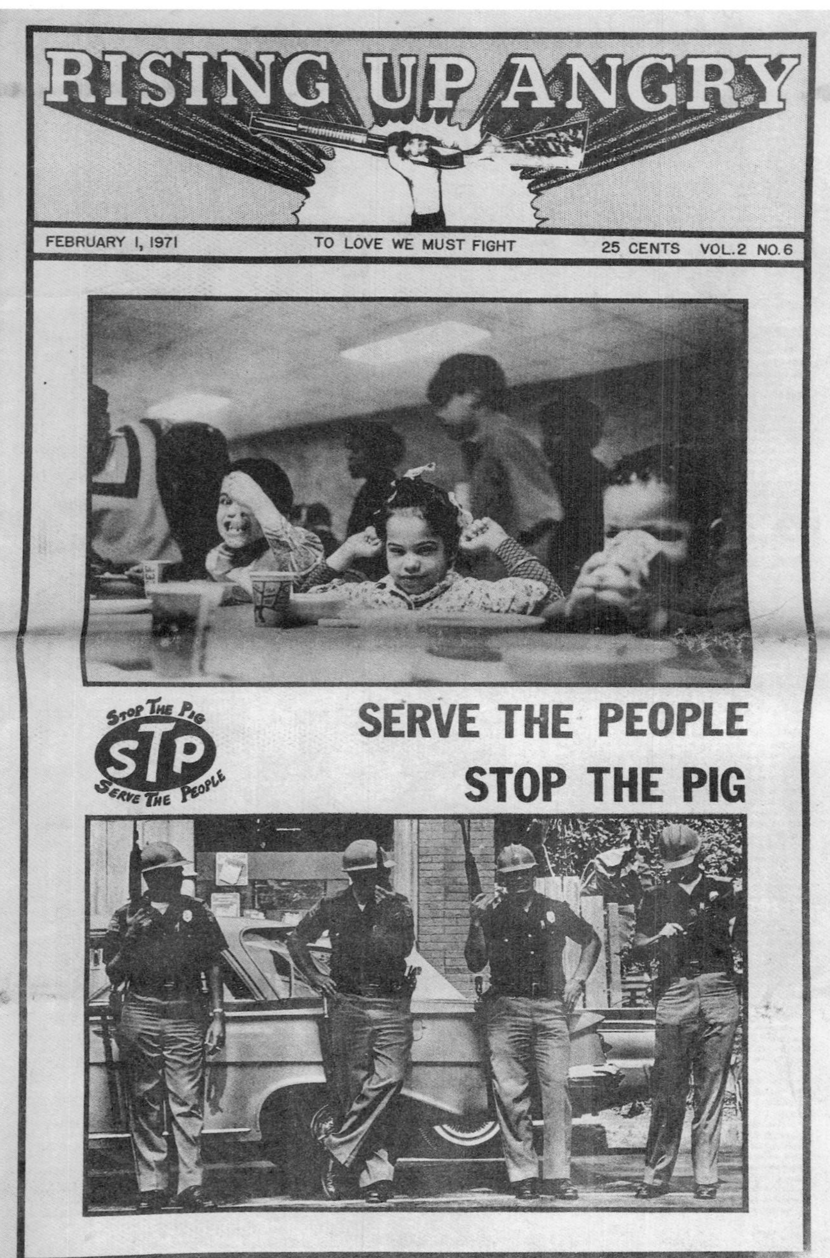

RISING UP ANGRY

FEBRUARY 1, 1971 TO LOVE WE MUST FIGHT 25 CENTS VOL.2 NO.6

STOP THE PIG
STP
SERVE THE PEOPLE

SERVE THE PEOPLE

STOP THE PIG

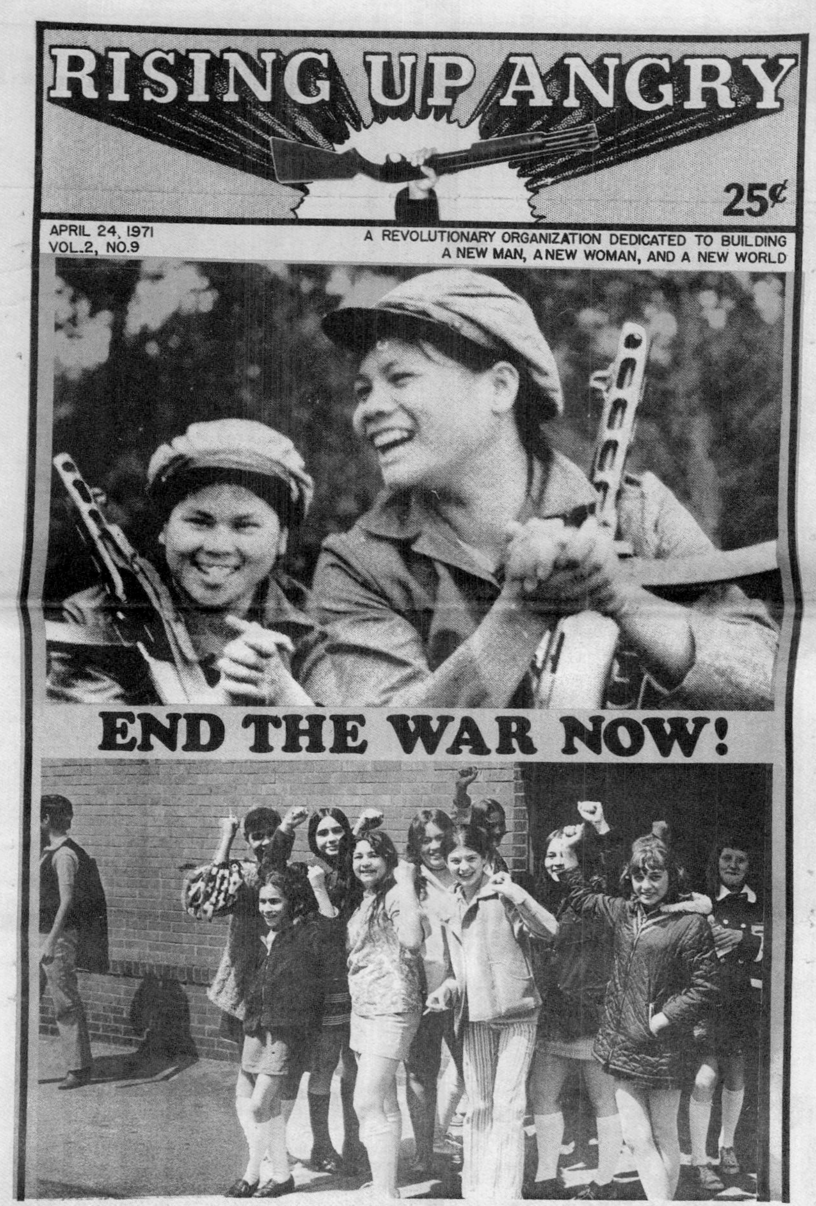

RISING UP ANGRY

25¢

APRIL 24, 1971
VOL.2, NO.9

A REVOLUTIONARY ORGANIZATION DEDICATED TO BUILDING A NEW MAN, A NEW WOMAN, AND A NEW WORLD

END THE WAR NOW!

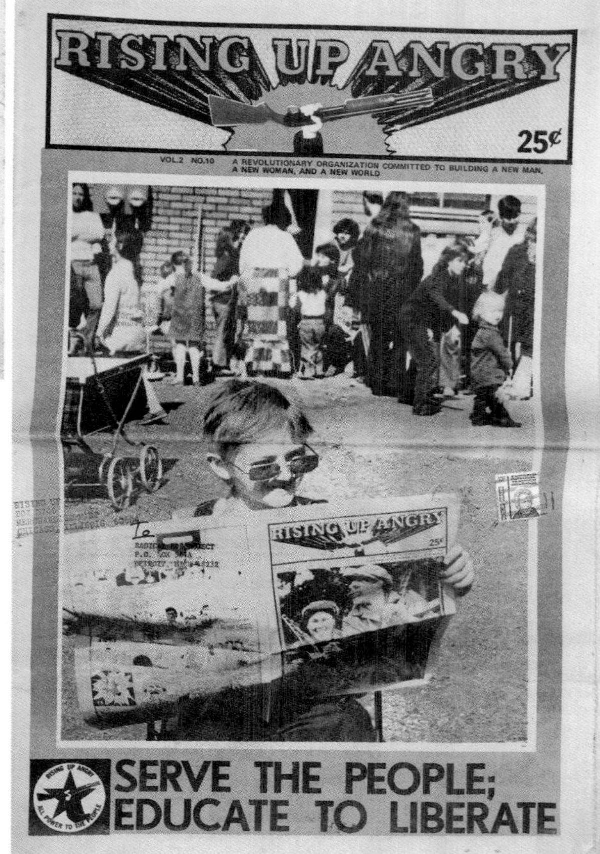

RISING UP ANGRY

25¢

VOL.2 NO.10 A REVOLUTIONARY ORGANIZATION COMMITTED TO BUILDING A NEW MAN, A NEW WOMAN, AND A NEW WORLD

SERVE THE PEOPLE;
EDUCATE TO LIBERATE

Rising Up Angry (Chicago), February 1, 1971, vol. 2, no. 6, cover
Rising Up Angry (Chicago), April 24, 1971, vol. 2, no. 9, cover
Rising Up Angry (Chicago), 1971, vol. 2, no. 10, cover

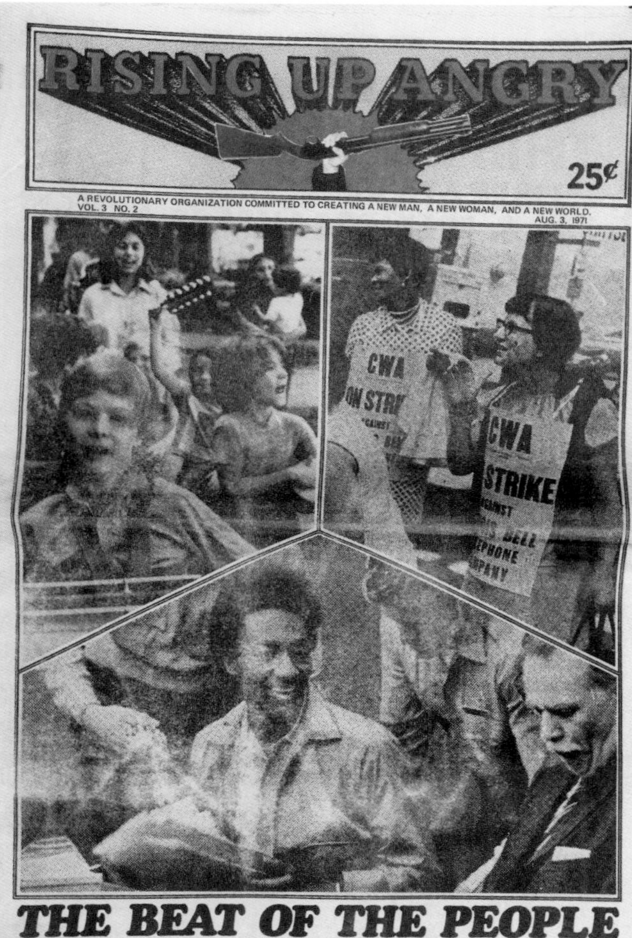

RISING UP ANGRY

25¢

A REVOLUTIONARY ORGANIZATION COMMITTED TO CREATING A NEW MAN, A NEW WOMAN, AND A NEW WORLD.
VOL. 3 NO. 2
AUG. 3, 1971

THE BEAT OF THE PEOPLE

[Clockwise from bottom] Ruchell McGee (page 3), charged with killing a judge, fighting against the injustices of the courts and prisons. Music at the Diversey/Wilton Summer Liberation School (page 2). Women strikers- part of the militant and just struggle against Bell Telephone (page 3).

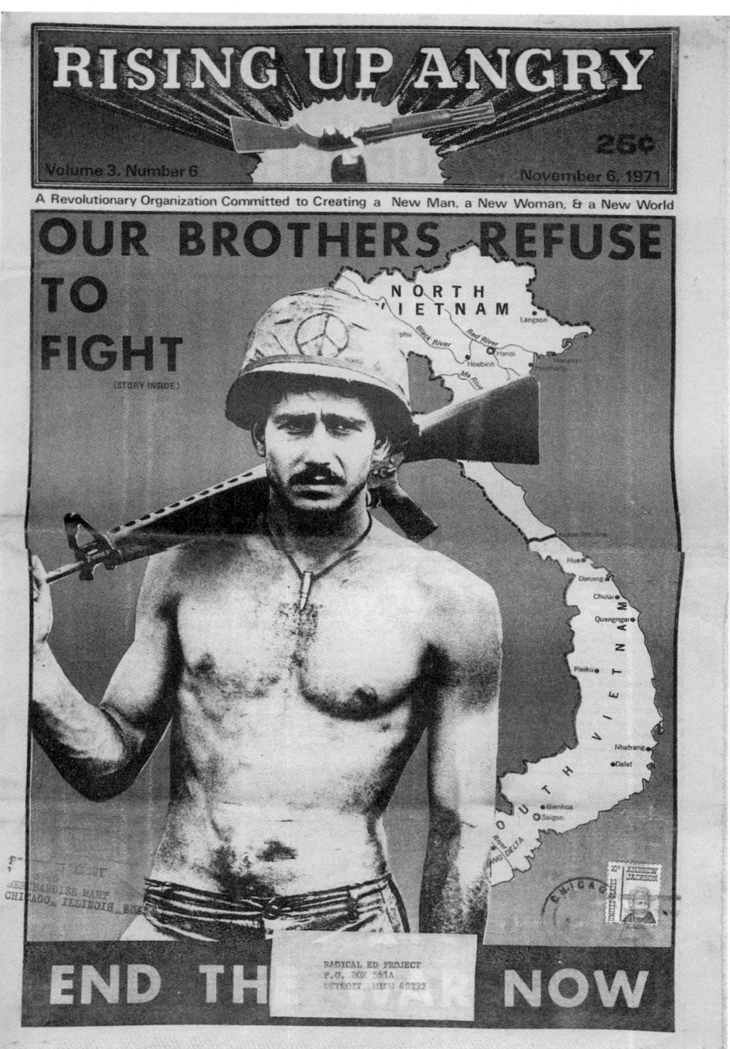

RISING UP ANGRY

Volume 3, Number 6
25¢
November 6, 1971

A Revolutionary Organization Committed to Creating a New Man, a New Woman, & a New World

OUR BROTHERS REFUSE TO FIGHT

(STORY INSIDE)

END THE WAR NOW

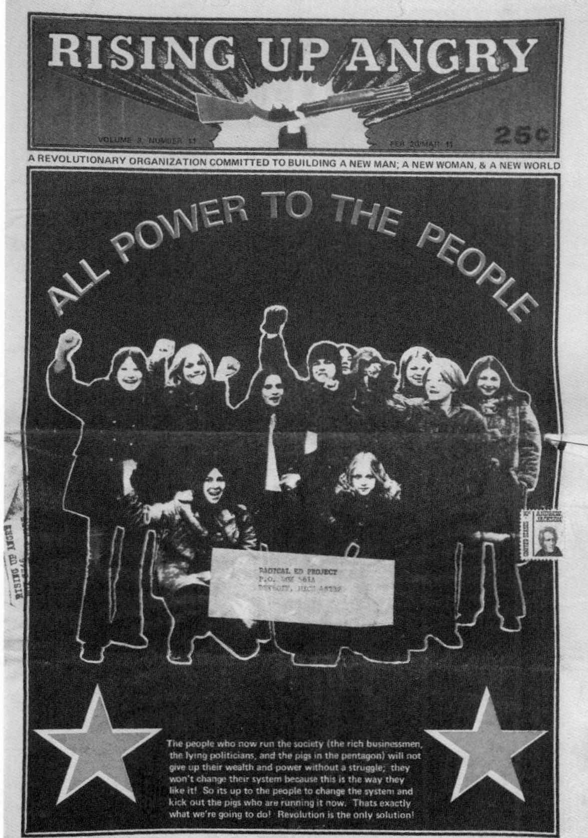

RISING UP ANGRY

25¢

A REVOLUTIONARY ORGANIZATION COMMITTED TO BUILDING A NEW MAN; A NEW WOMAN, & A NEW WORLD

ALL POWER TO THE PEOPLE

The people who now run the society (the rich businessmen, the lying politicians, and the pigs in the pentagon) will not give up their wealth and power without a struggle; they won't change their system because this is the way they like it! So its up to the people to change the system and kick out the pigs who are running it now. Thats exactly what we're going to do! Revolution is the only solution!

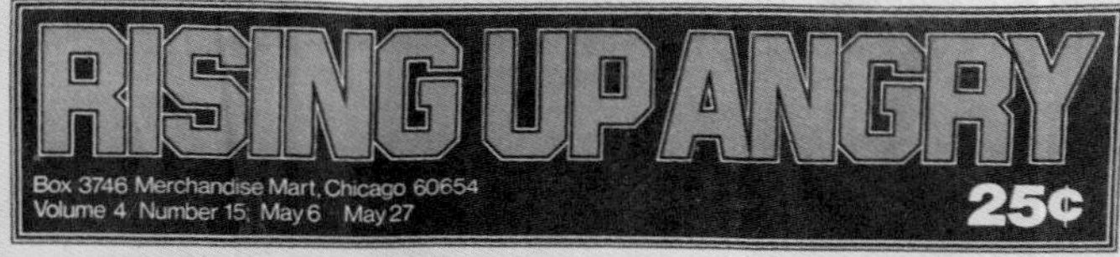

RISING UP ANGRY

Box 3746 Merchandise Mart, Chicago 60654
Volume 4 Number 15: May 6 - May 27
25¢

THE GOVERNMENT IS RUN BY CROOKS, LIARS, AND THIEVES

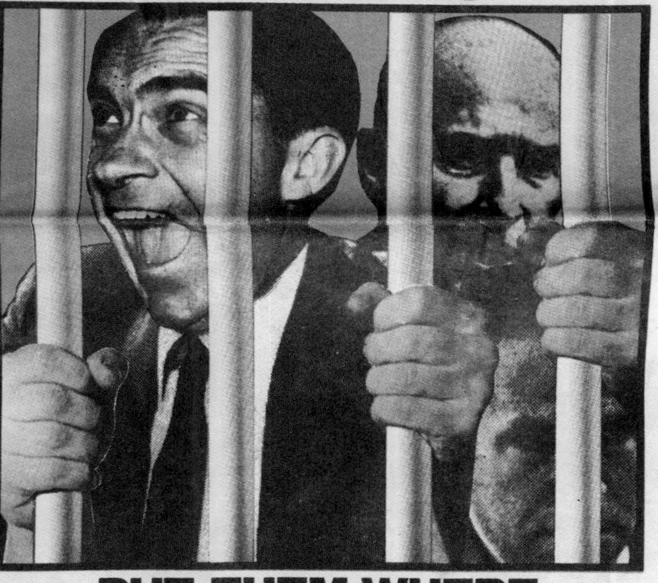

PUT THEM WHERE THEY BELONG....

R.U.A. BOX 3746
MERCHANDISE MART
CHICAGO, ILLINOIS 60654
RETURN POSTAGE GUARANTEED
ADDRESS CORRECTION REQUESTED

BULK RATE
U.S. POSTAGE
PAID
CHICAGO, ILL.
PERMIT NO. 4985

Rising Up Angry (Chicago), August 3, 1971, vol. 3, no. 2, cover

Rising Up Angry (Chicago), November 6, 1971, vol. 3, no. 6, cover

Rising Up Angry (Chicago), February 20–March 11, 1972, vol. 3, no. 11, cover

Rising Up Angry (Chicago), May 6–27, 1973, vol. 4, no. 15, cover

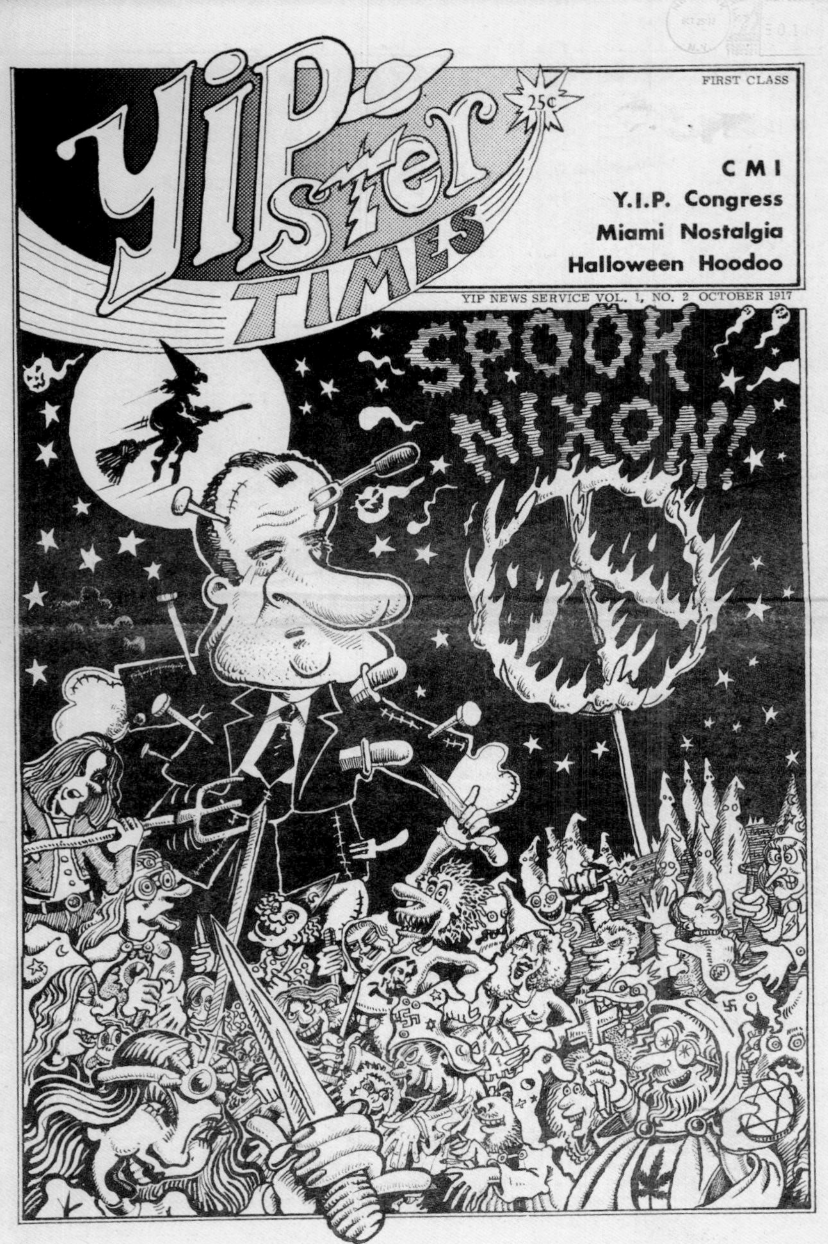

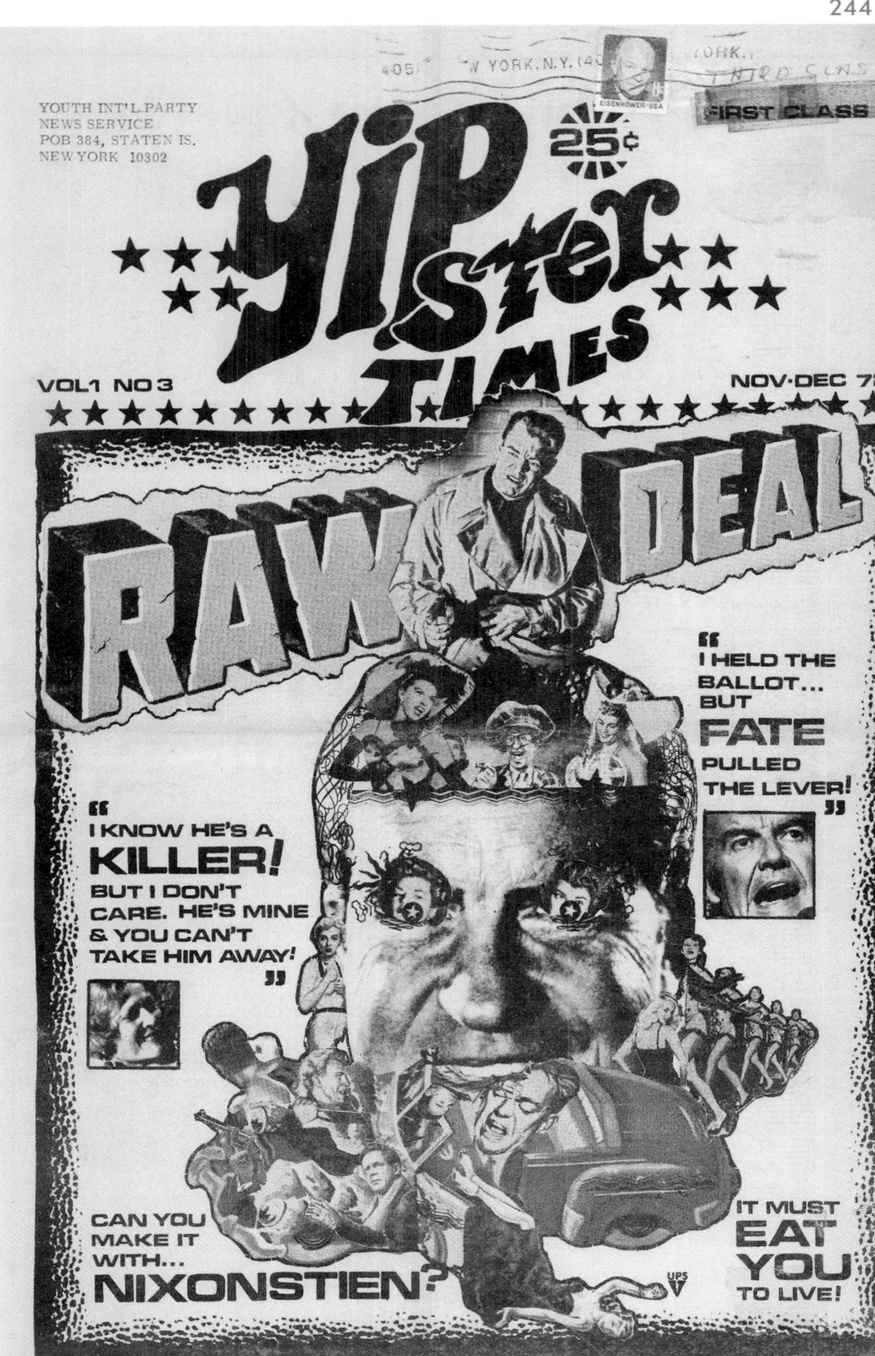

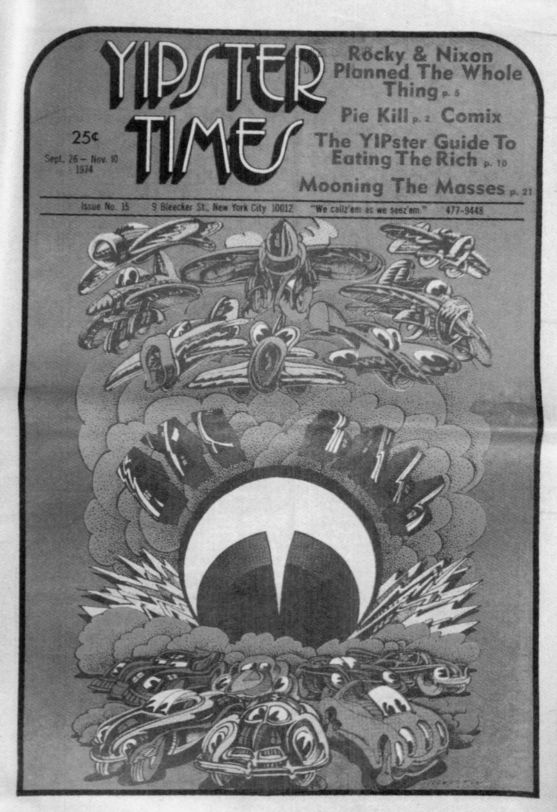

FIRST CLASS

Forcade-Watergate Link! (p. 10) - Wounded Knee (p. 3)
National Marijuana Day (p. 3) - Karl Armstrong (p. 5) - Rat
Documentary (pps. 8-9) - New Credit Card Code (p. 16)

YIPSTER TIMES

MARIJUANA HELPS BUILD
STRONG AURAS 9 WAYS
(see 14)

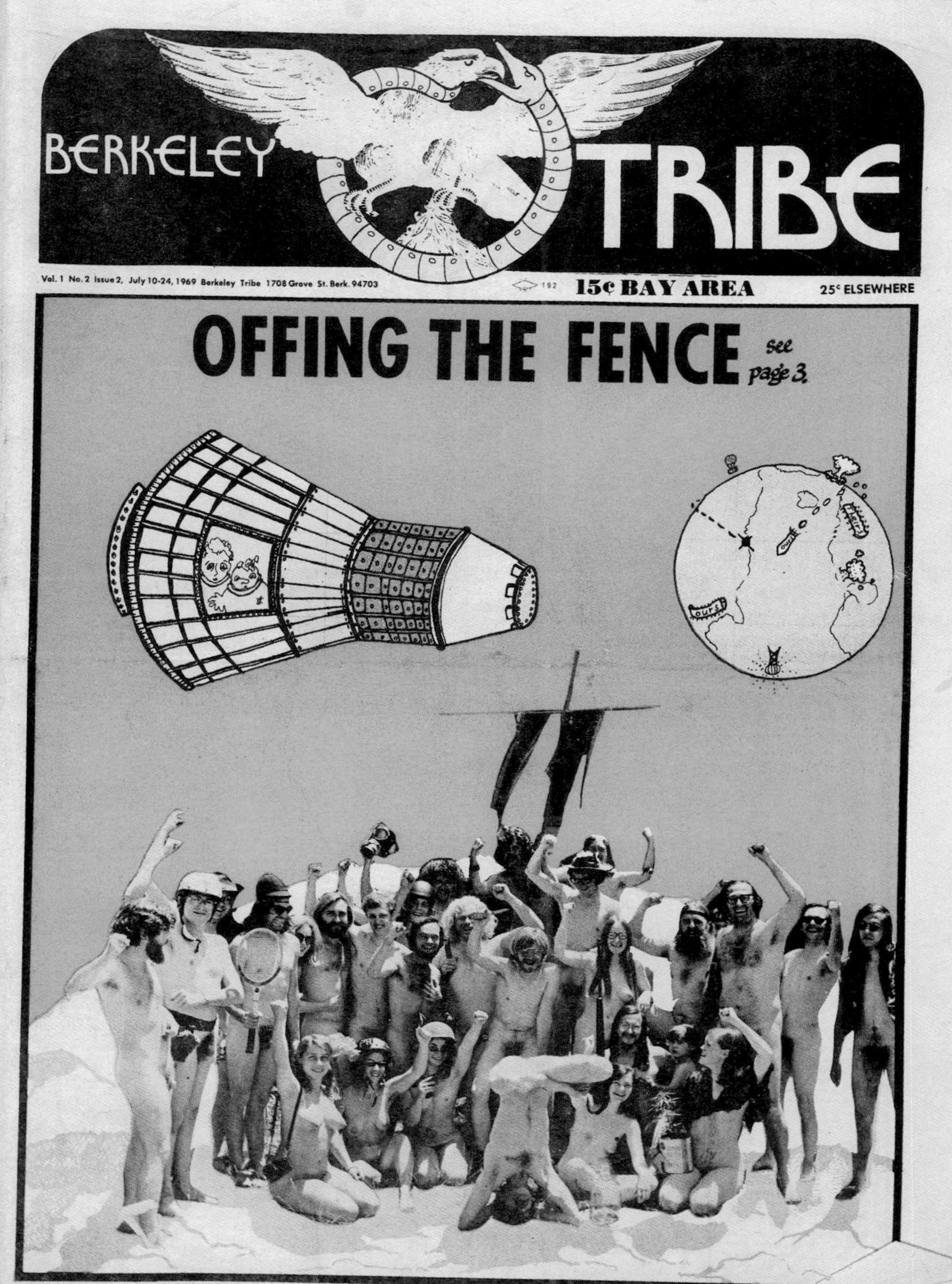

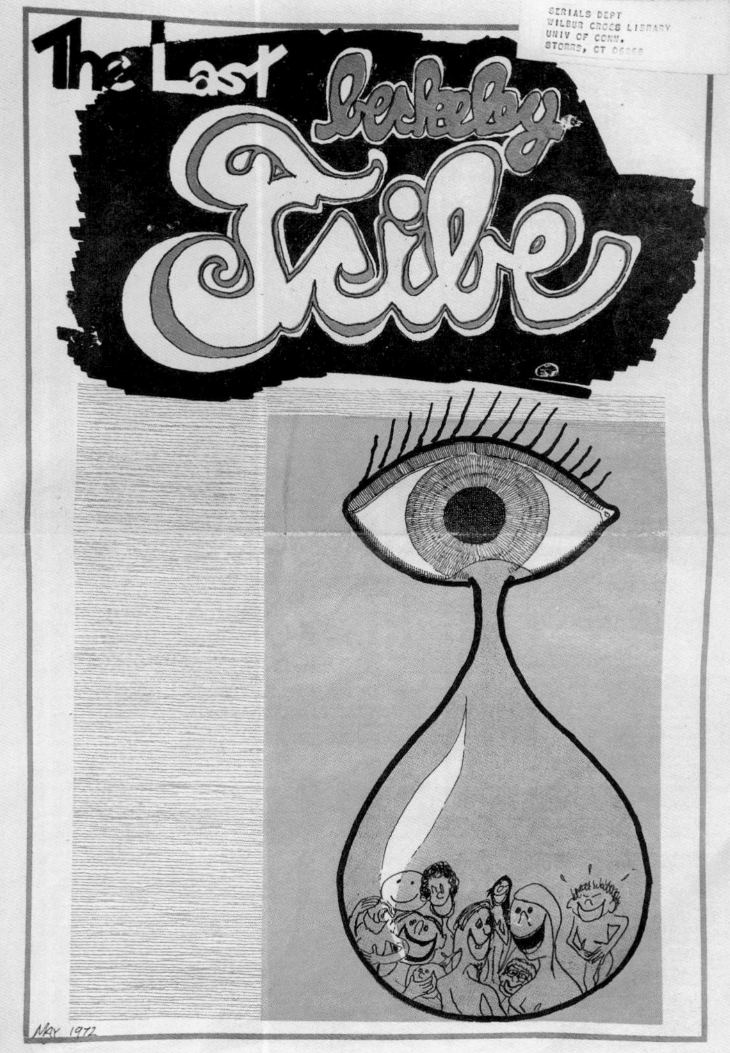

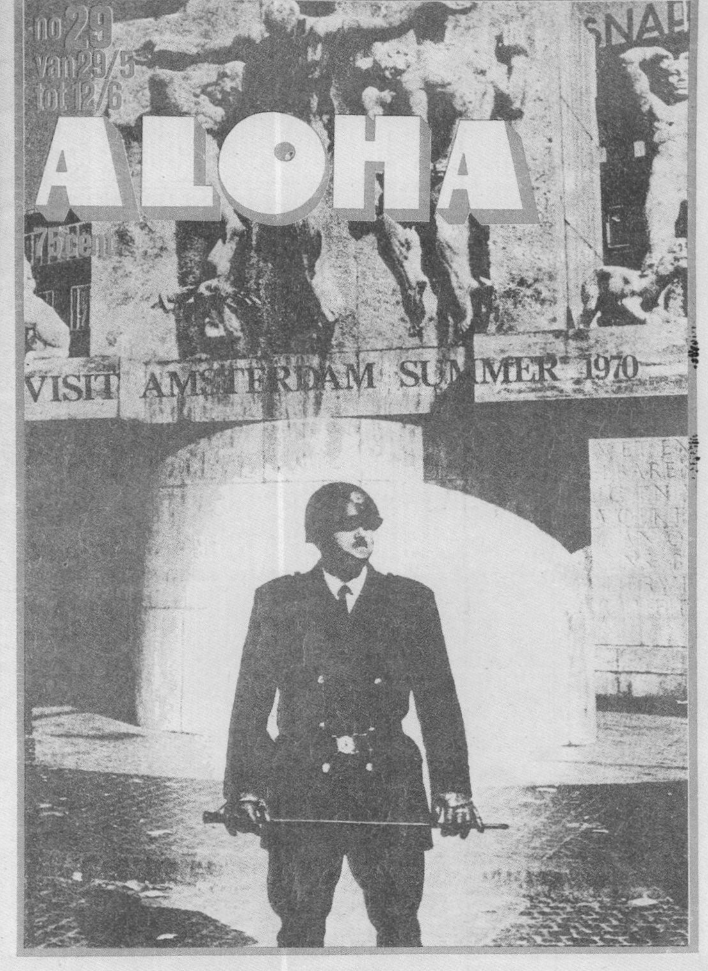

Previous page
Yipster Times (New York), October 1972, vol. 1, no. 2, cover
Yipster Times (New York), November-December 1972, vol. 1, no. 3, cover
Yipster Times (New York), September 26–November 10, 1974, vol. 1, no. 15, cover
Yipster Times (New York), March 1973, vol. 1, no. 5, cover

Berkeley Tribe, July 10–24, 1969, vol. 1, no. 2, cover
Berkeley Tribe, May 1972, cover
Aloha (Hawaii), Summer 1970, no. 29, cover

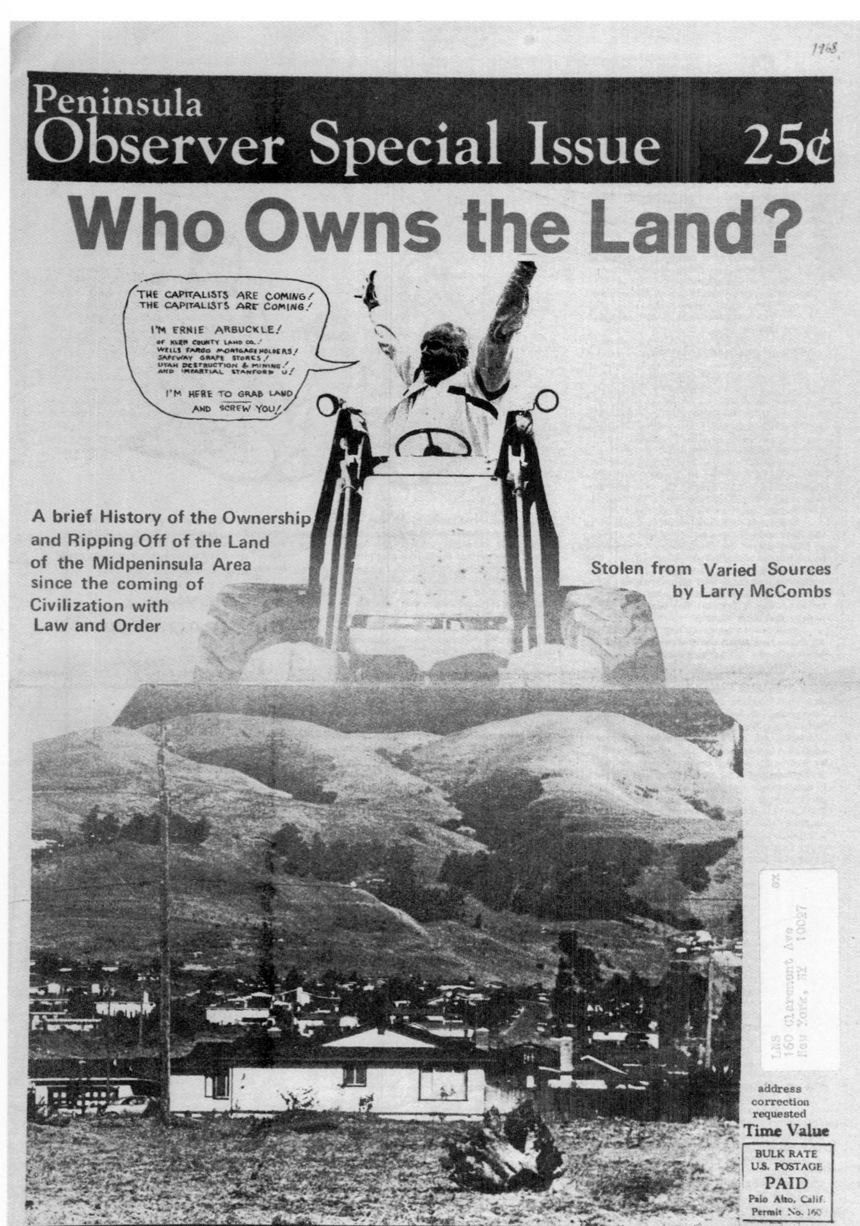

1968

Peninsula Observer Special Issue 25¢

Who Owns the Land?

THE CAPITALISTS ARE COMING!
THE CAPITALISTS ARE COMING!
I'M ERNIE ARBUCKLE!
OF KERN COUNTY LAND CO./
WELLS FARGO MORTGAGEHOLDERS!
SAFEWAY GRAPE STORES!
UTAH DESTRUCTION & MINING!
AND IMPARTIAL STANFORD U!
I'M HERE TO GRAB LAND AND SCREW YOU!

A brief History of the Ownership and Ripping Off of the Land of the Midpeninsula Area since the coming of Civilization with Law and Order

Stolen from Varied Sources by Larry McCombs

LNS
160 Claremont Ave
New York, NY 10027

address correction requested

Time Value

BULK RATE
U.S. POSTAGE
PAID
Palo Alto, Calif.
Permit No. 160

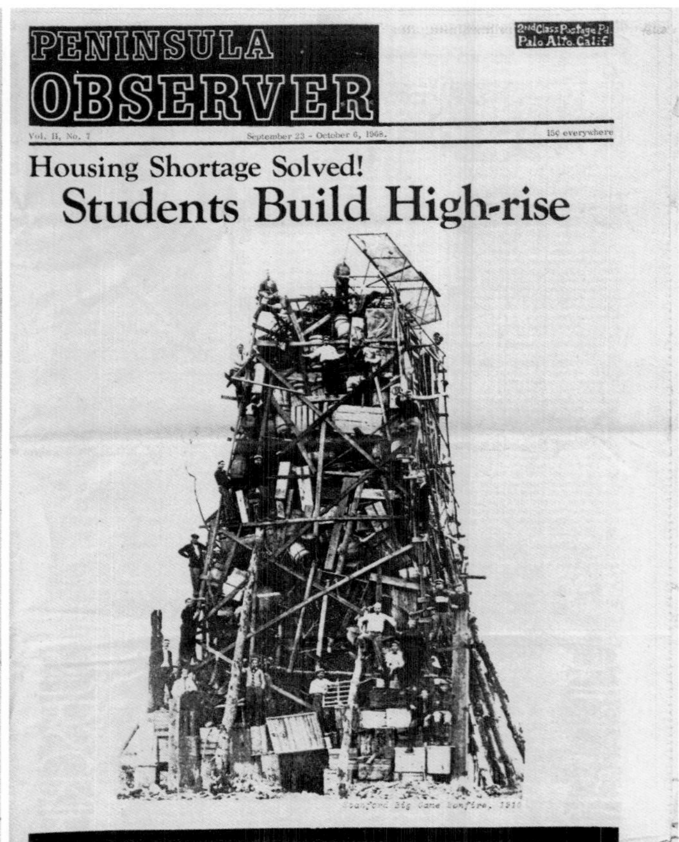

PENINSULA OBSERVER

2nd Class Postage Pd.
Palo Alto, Calif.

Vol. II, No. 7 — September 23 - October 6, 1968 — 15¢ everywhere

Housing Shortage Solved!

Students Build High-rise

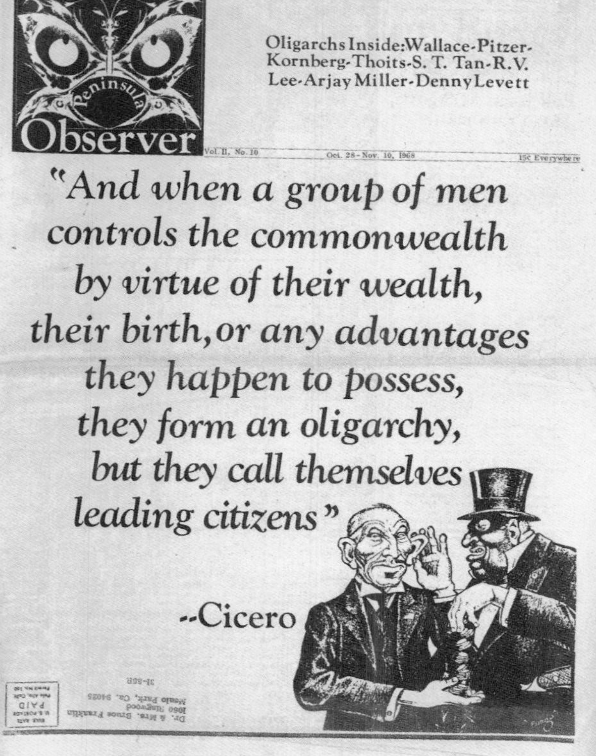

Peninsula Observer

Oligarchs Inside: Wallace-Pitzer-Kornberg-Thoits-S. T. Tan-R.V. Lee-Arjay Miller-Denny Levett

Vol. II, No. 10 — Oct. 28 - Nov. 10, 1968 — 15¢ Everywhere

"And when a group of men controls the commonwealth by virtue of their wealth, their birth, or any advantages they happen to possess, they form an oligarchy, but they call themselves leading citizens"

--Cicero

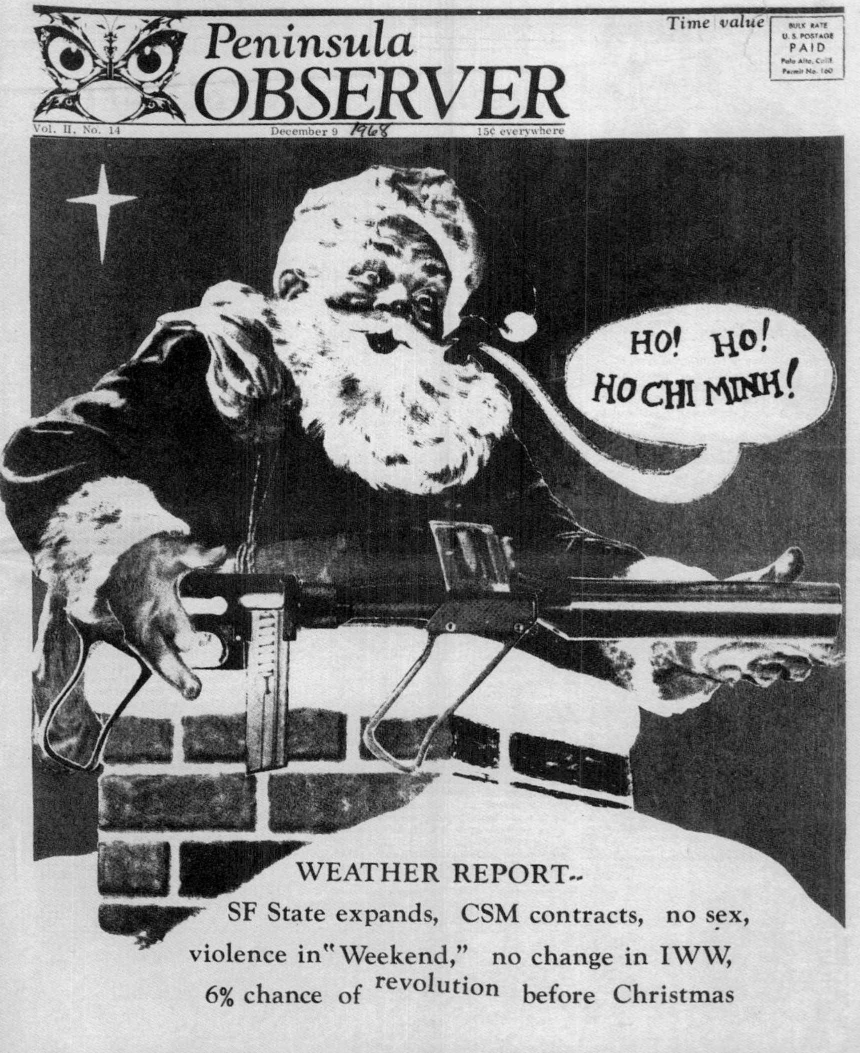

Time value

BULK RATE
U. S. POSTAGE
PAID
Palo Alto, Calif.
Permit No. 160

Peninsula OBSERVER

Vol. II, No. 14 — December 9 1968 — 15¢ everywhere

HO! HO! HO CHI MINH!

WEATHER REPORT--
SF State expands, CSM contracts, no sex, violence in "Weekend," no change in IWW, 6% chance of revolution before Christmas

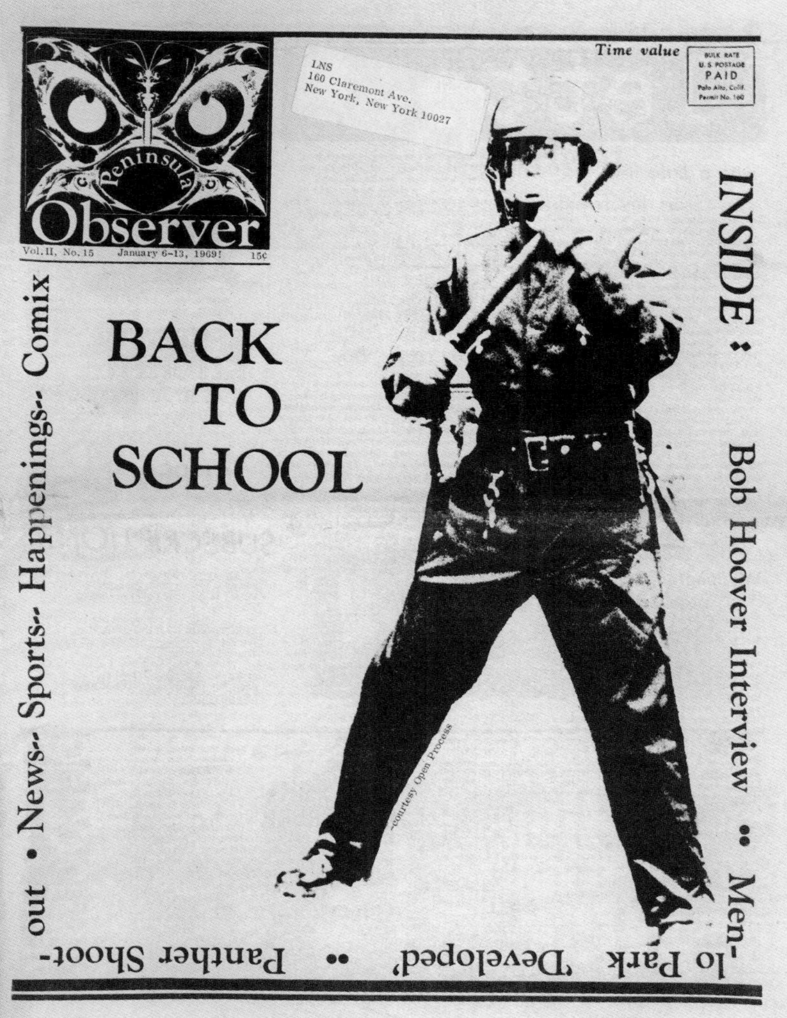

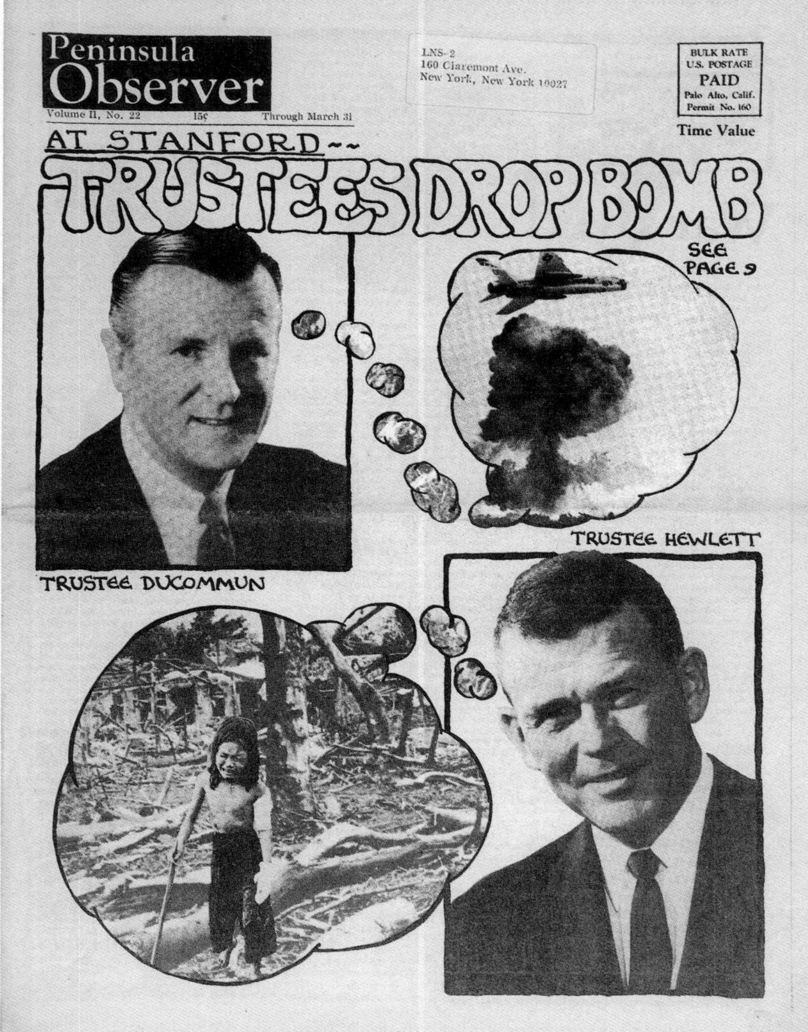

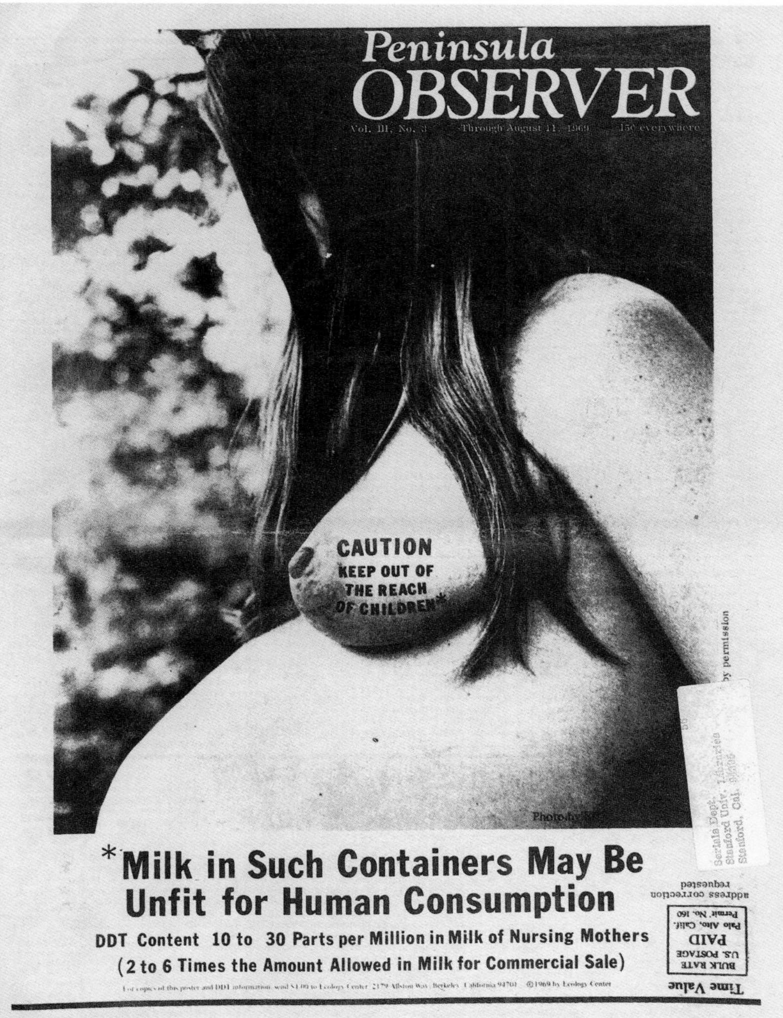

Previous page
Peninsula Observer (Palo Alto, California), October 1968
Peninsula Observer (Palo Alto, California), September 23–October 6, 1968, vol. 2, no. 7, cover
Peninsula Observer (Palo Alto, California), October 28–November 10, 1968, vol. 2, no. 10, cover
Peninsula Observer (Palo Alto, California), December 9, 1968, vol. 2, no. 14, cover

Peninsula Observer (Palo Alto, California), January 6–13, 1969, vol. 2, no. 15, cover
Peninsula Observer (Palo Alto, California), through March 31, vol. 2, no. 22, cover
Peninsula Observer (Palo Alto, California), through August 11, 1969, vol. 3, no. 3, cover

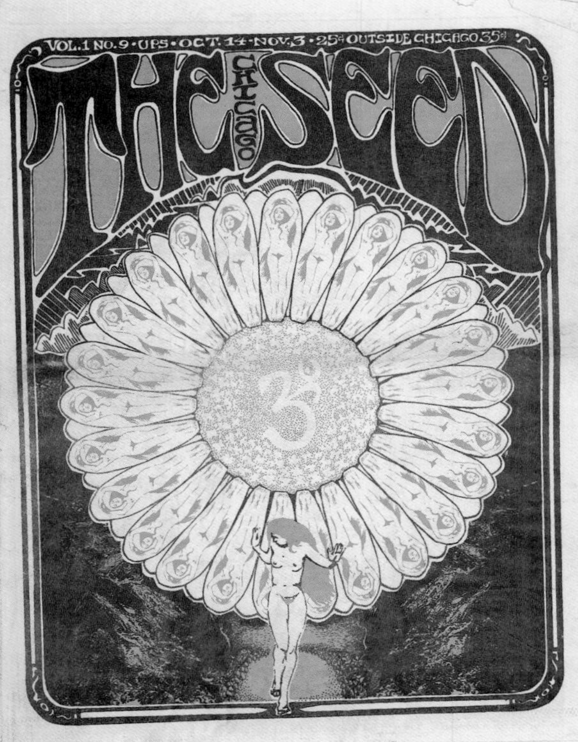

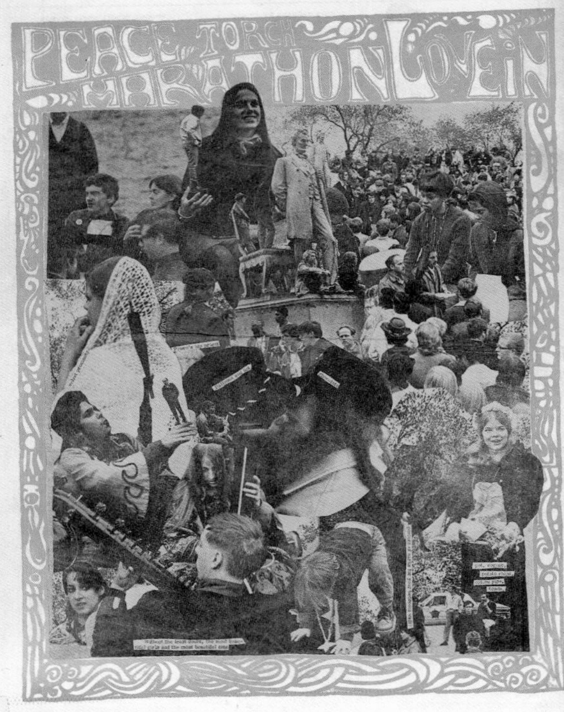

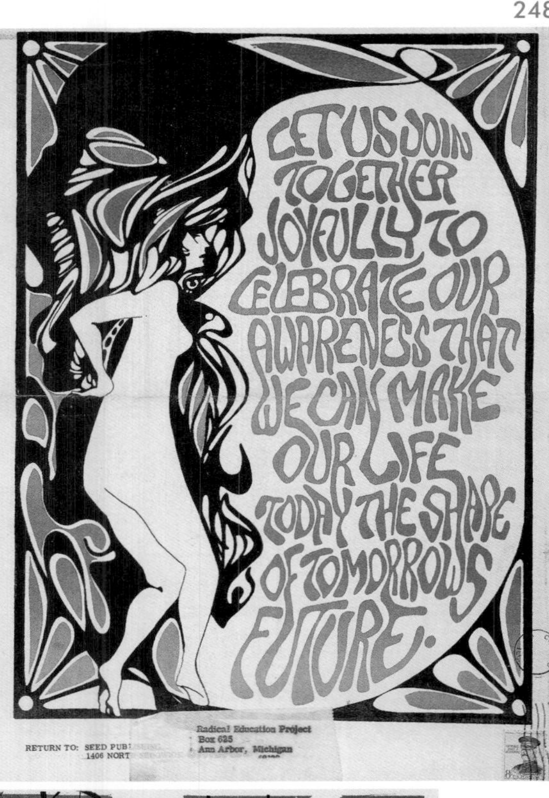

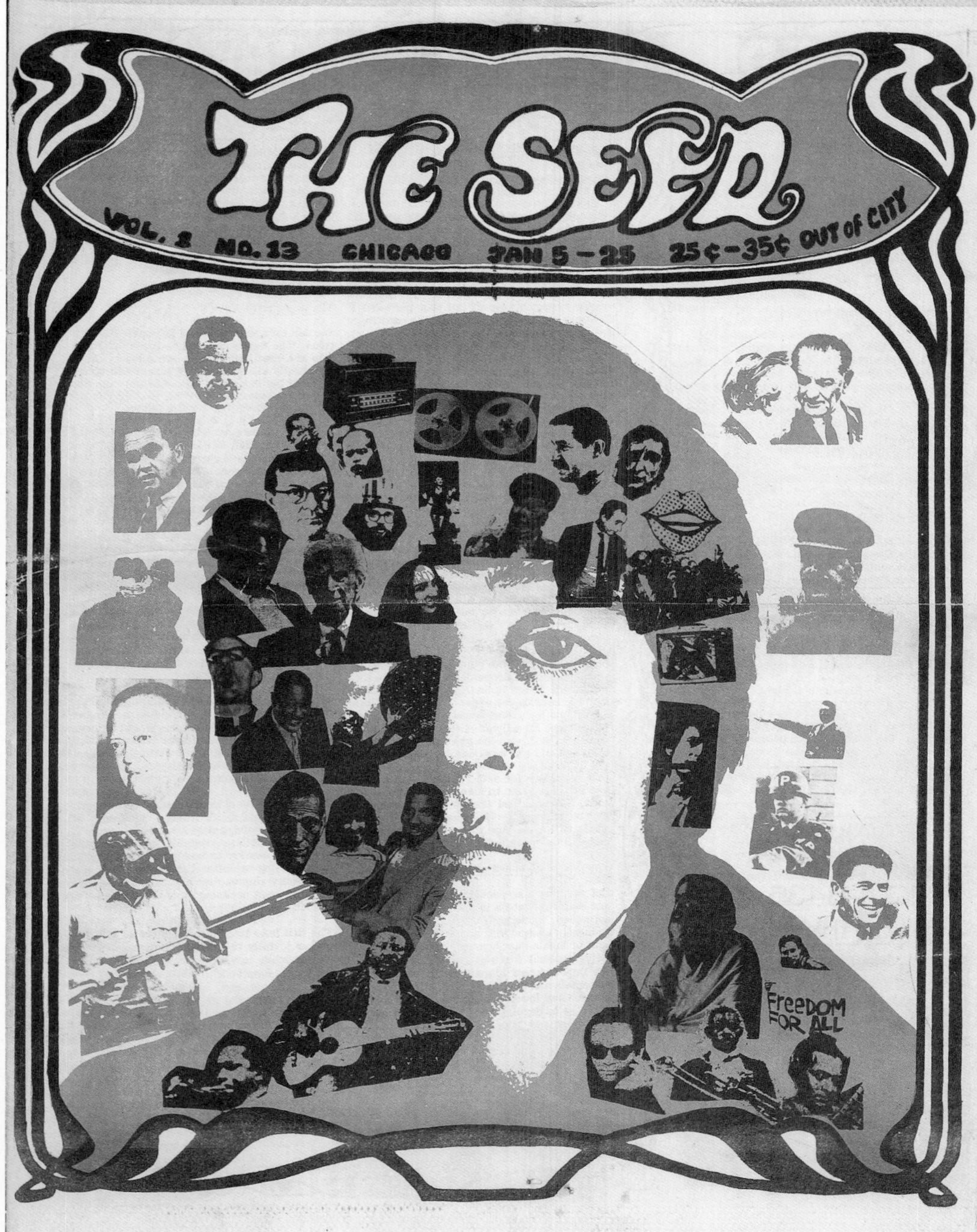

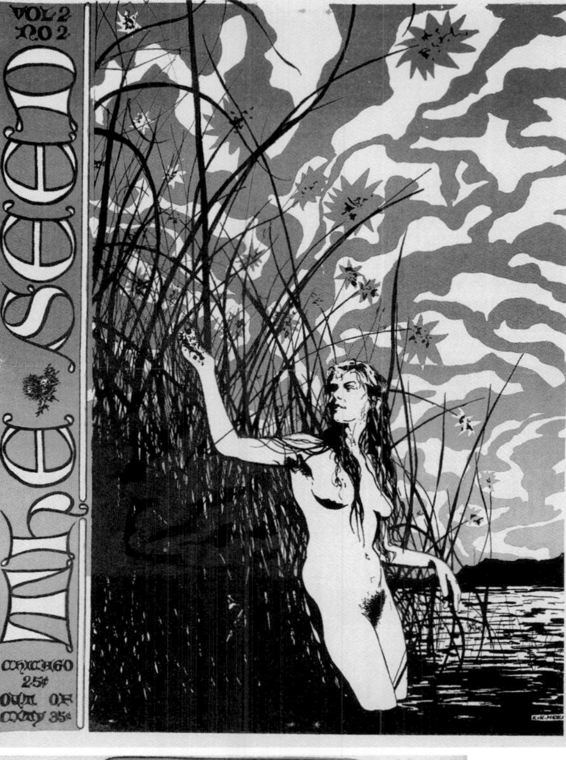

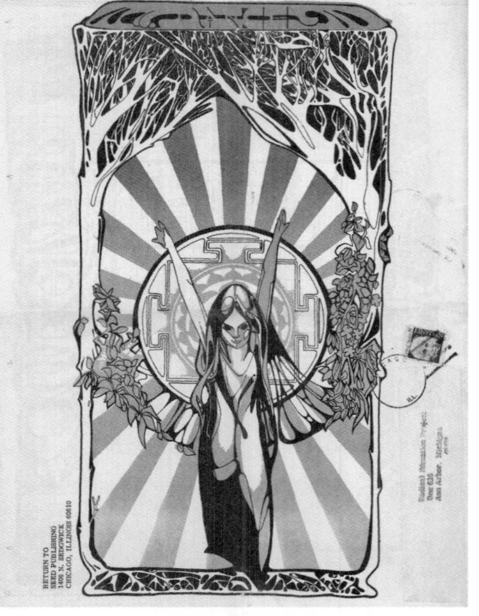

The Chicago Seed, October 14–November 3, 1967, vol. 1, no. 9, cover
The Chicago Seed, October 14–November 3, 1967, vol. 1, no. 9, back cover
The Chicago Seed, January 5–25, 1968, vol. 1, no. 13, back cover
The Chicago Seed, January 5–25, 1968, vol. 1, no. 13, cover
The Chicago Seed, 1968, vol. 2, no. 2, cover
The Chicago Seed, 1968, vol. 2, no. 1, back cover

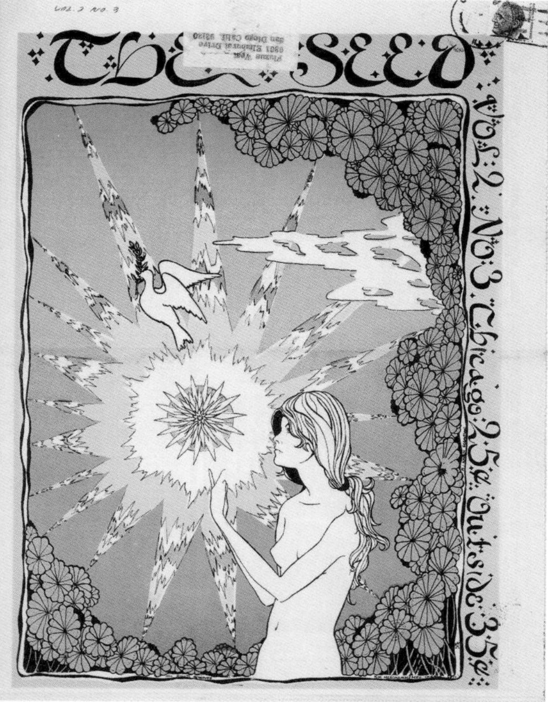

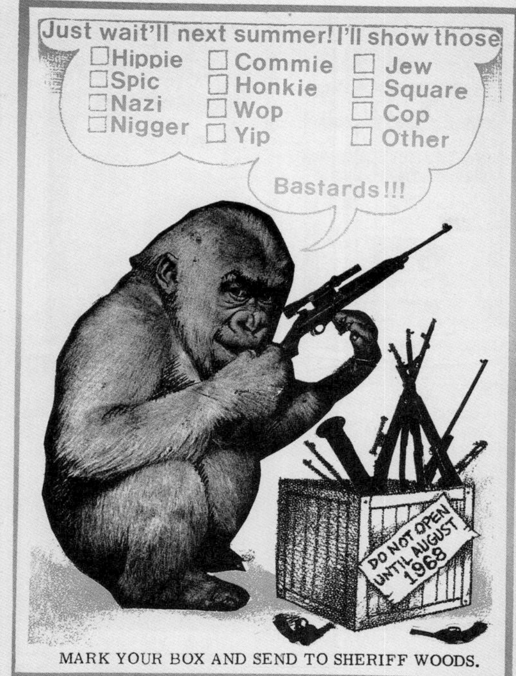

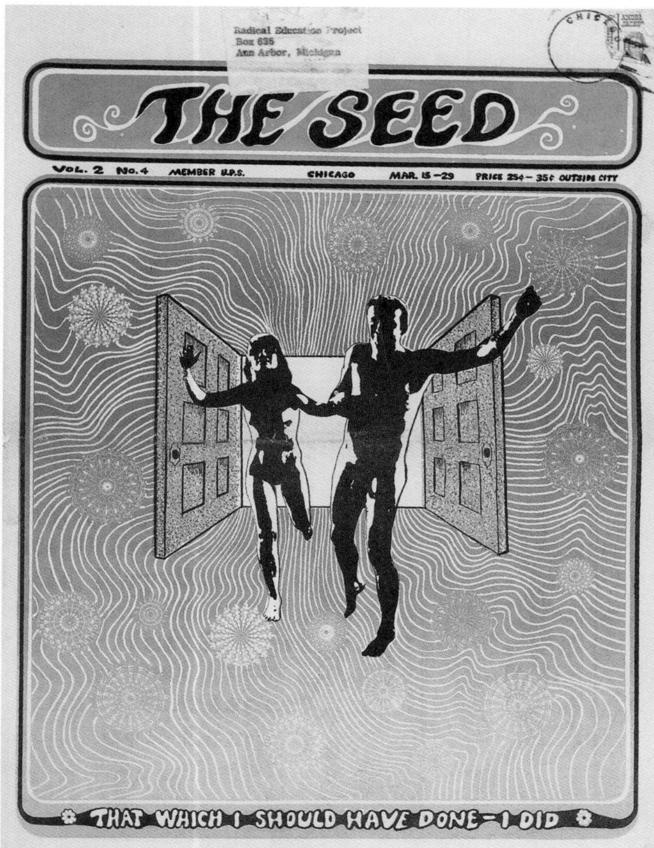

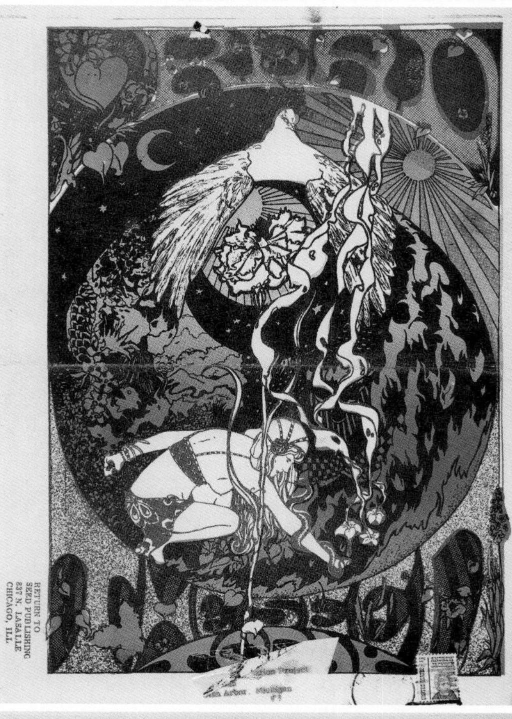

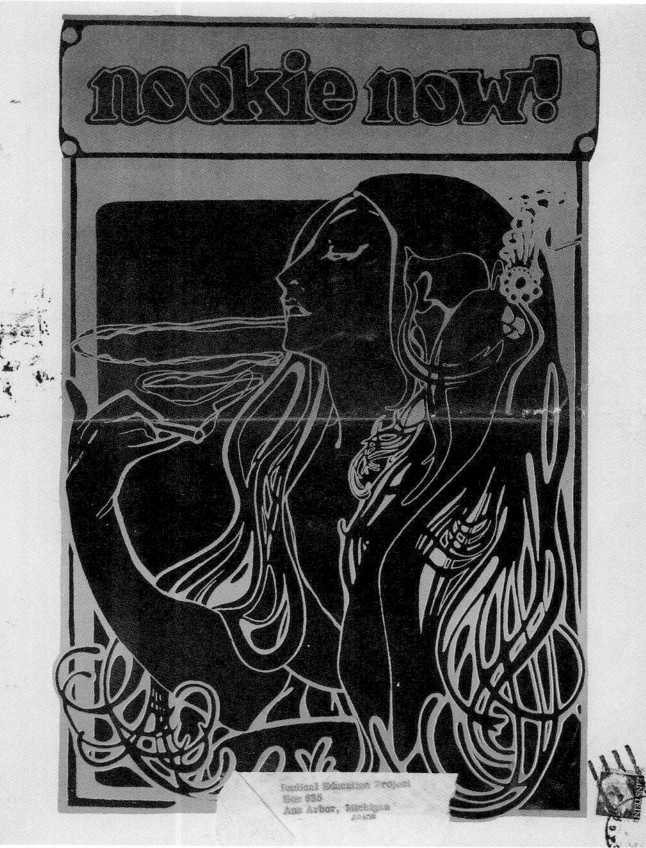

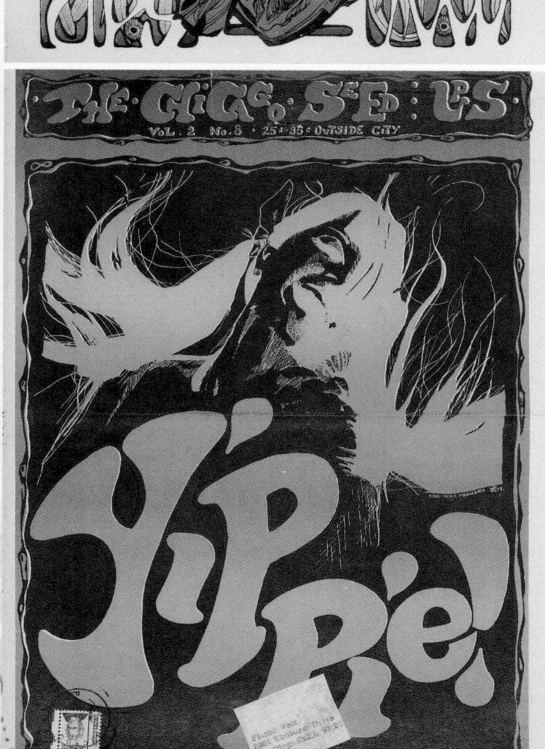

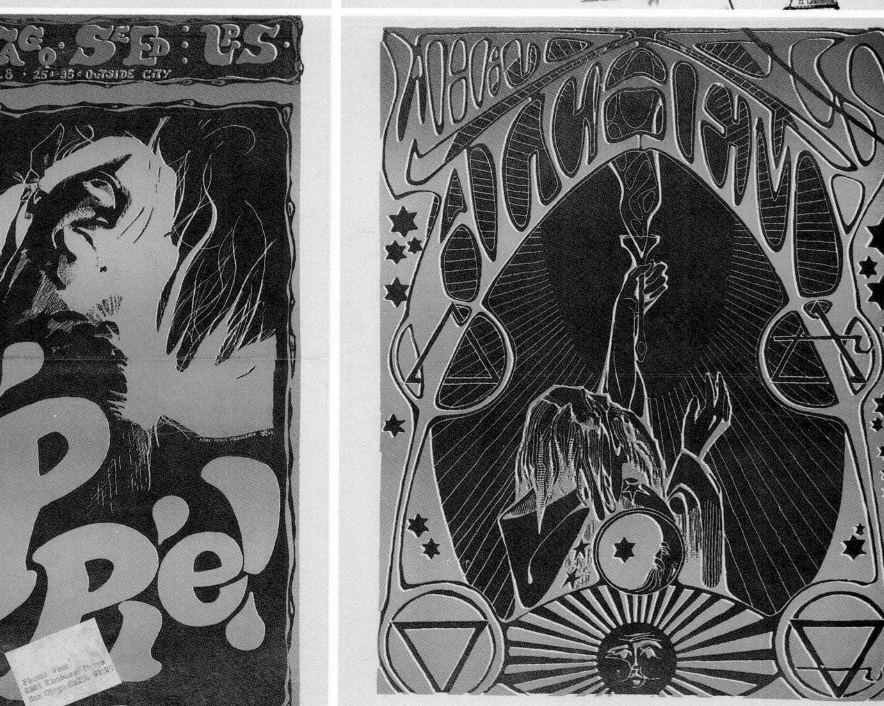

The Chicago Seed, 1968, vol. 2, no. 3, cover
The Chicago Seed, 1968, vol. 2, no. 3, back cover
The Chicago Seed, 1968, vol. 2, no. 4, cover
The Chicago Seed, 1968, vol. 2, no. 6, cover
The Chicago Seed, 1968, vol. 2, no. 6, back cover
The Chicago Seed, 1968, vol. 2, no. 2, back cover
The Chicago Seed, 1968, vol. 2, no. 8, cover
The Chicago Seed, 1968, vol. 2, no. 8, back cover

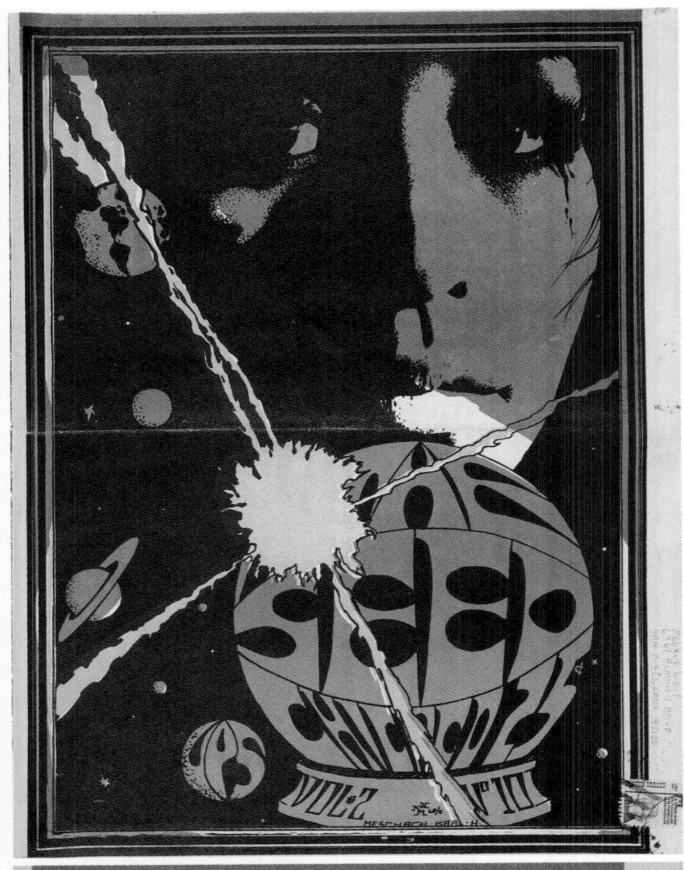

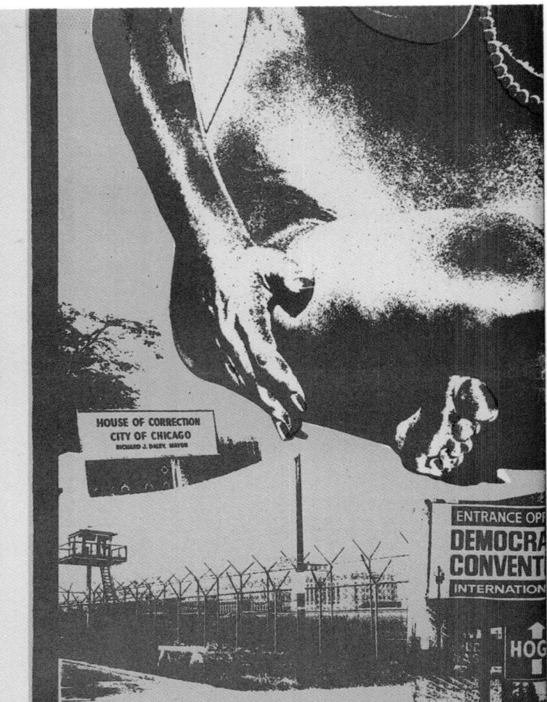

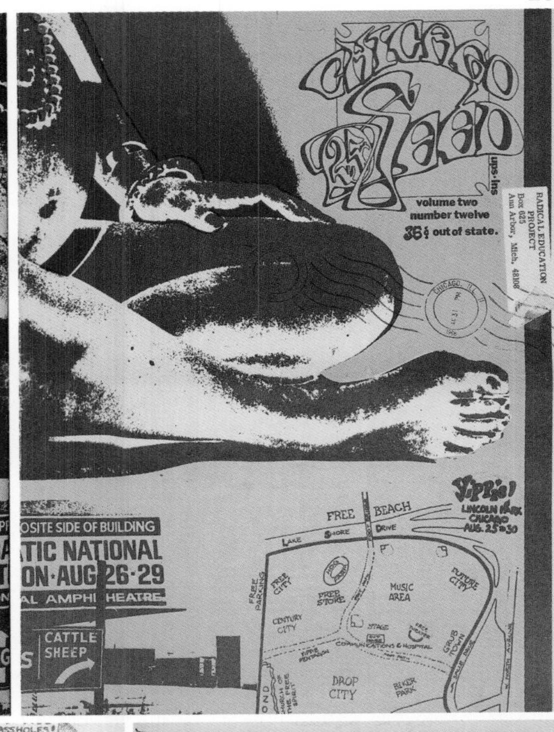

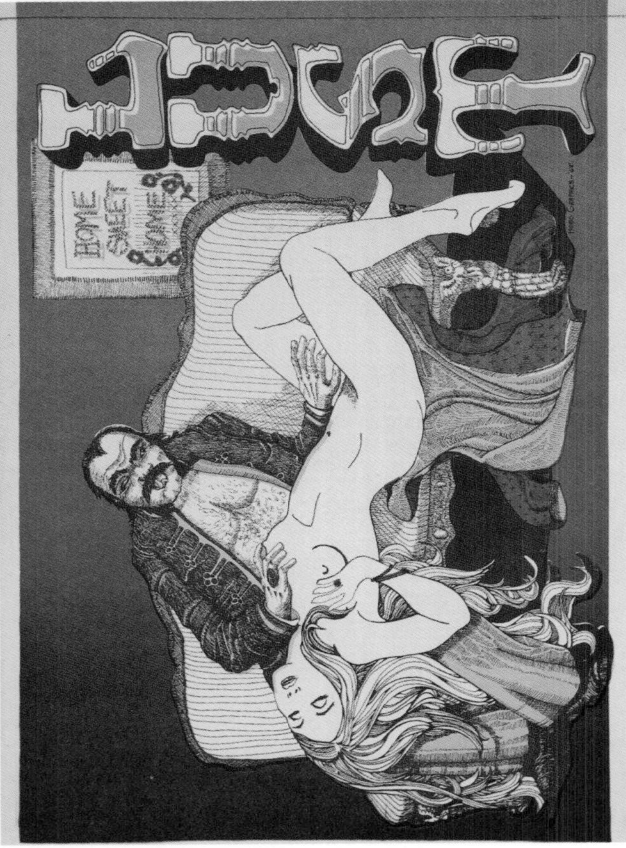

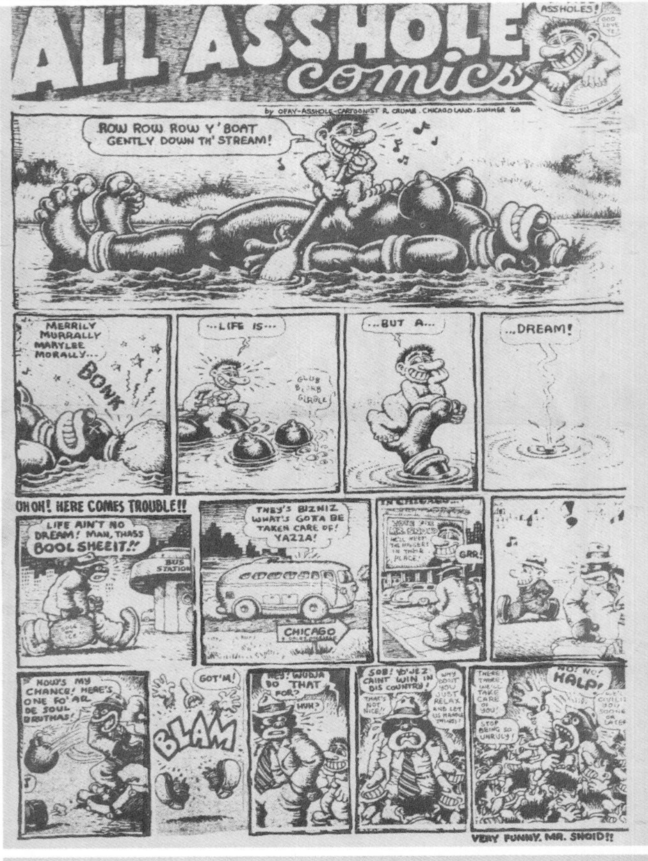

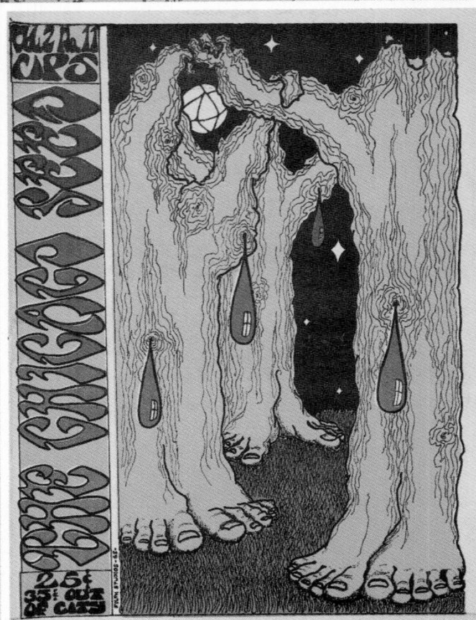

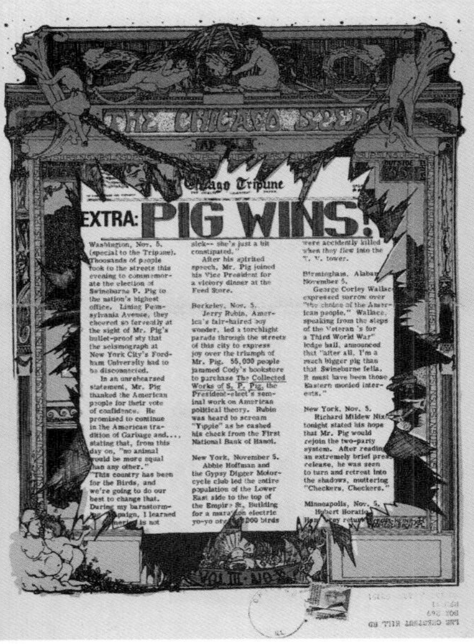

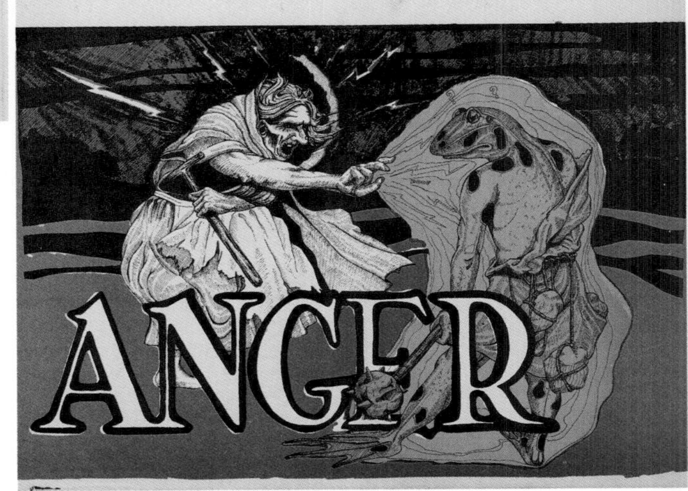

The Chicago Seed, 1968, vol. 2, no. 10, cover
The Chicago Seed, 1968, vol. 2, no. 12, back cover
The Chicago Seed, 1968, vol. 2, no. 12, cover
The Chicago Seed, 1968, vol. 2, no. 11, back cover
The Chicago Seed, Summer 1968, vol. 3, no. 1, cover
The Chicago Seed, 1968, vol. 2, no. 11, cover
The Chicago Seed, 1968, vol. 3, no. 2, cover
The Chicago Seed, 1968, vol. 2, no. 13, back cover

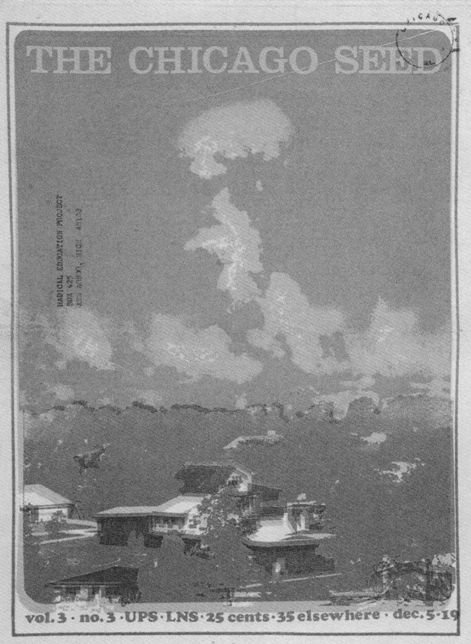

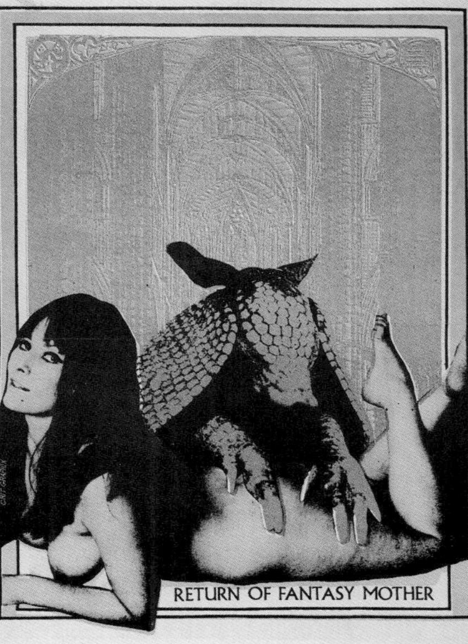

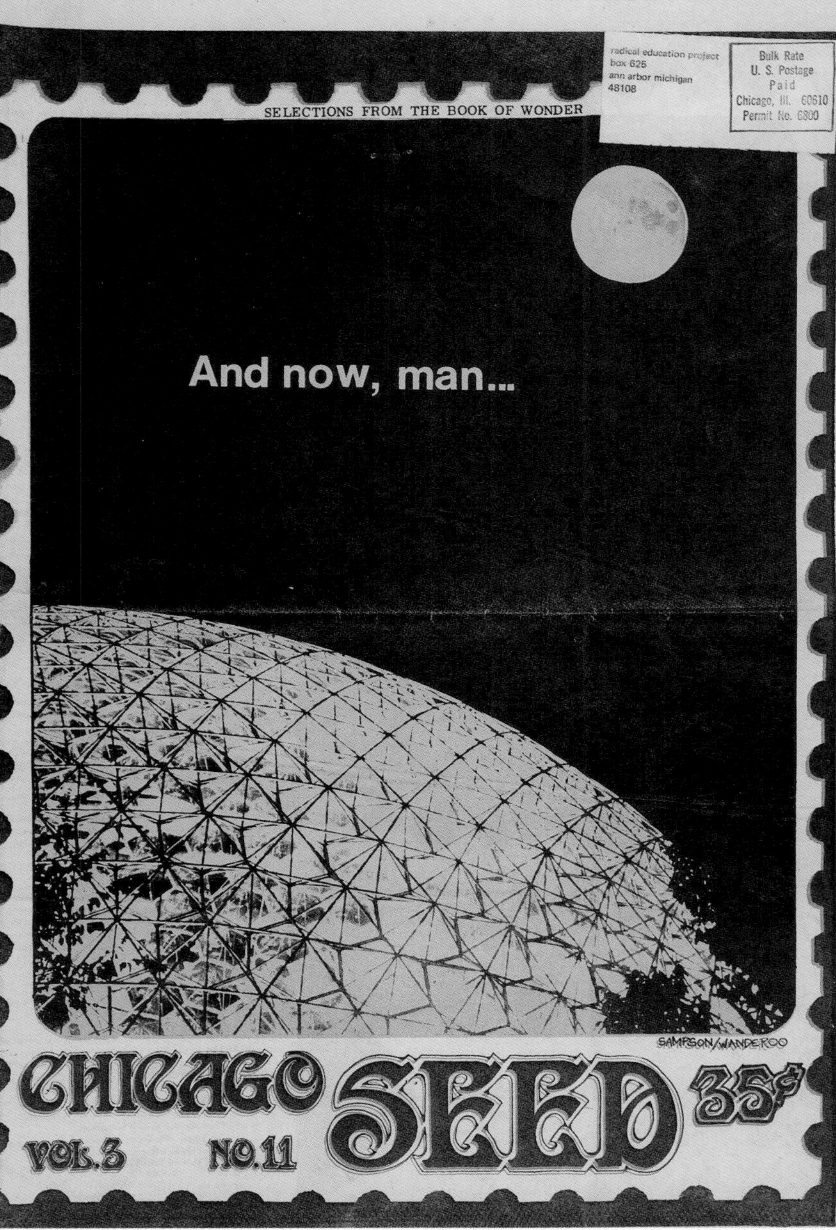

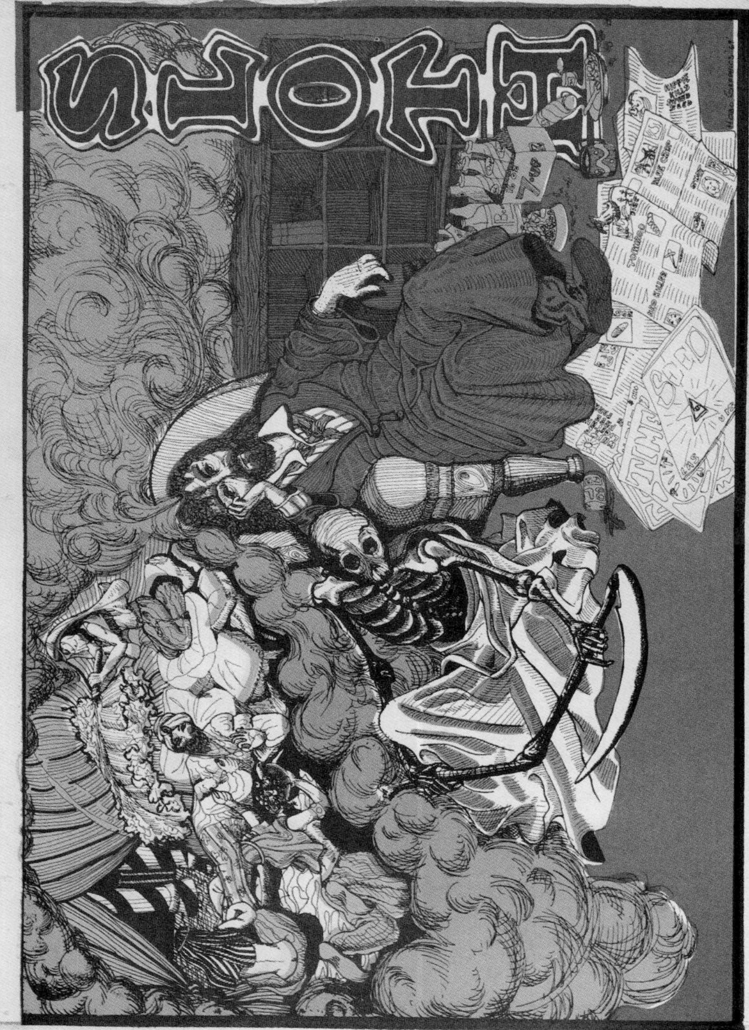

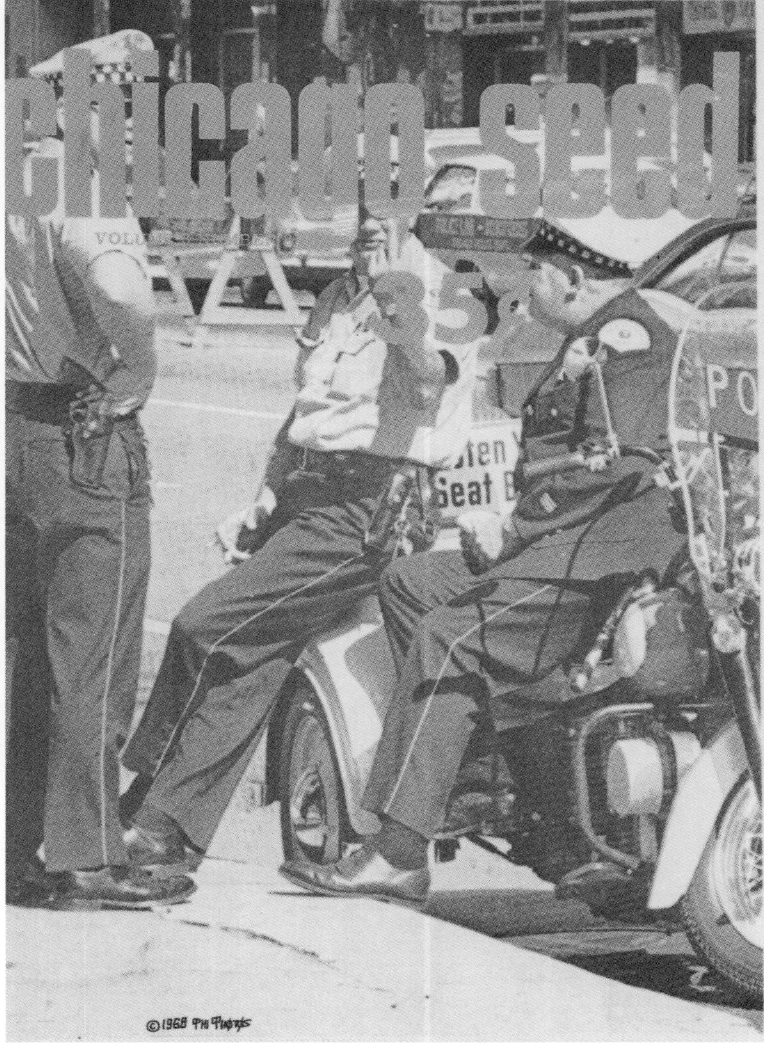

The Chicago Seed, December 5–19, 1968, vol. 3, no. 3, cover
The Chicago Seed, December 20, 1968–January 9, 1969, vol. 3, no. 4, back cover
The Chicago Seed, January 10–24, 1969, vol. 3, no. 5, back cover
The Chicago Seed, 1969, vol. 3, no. 11, cover
The Chicago Seed, 1969, vol. 3, no. 8, cover

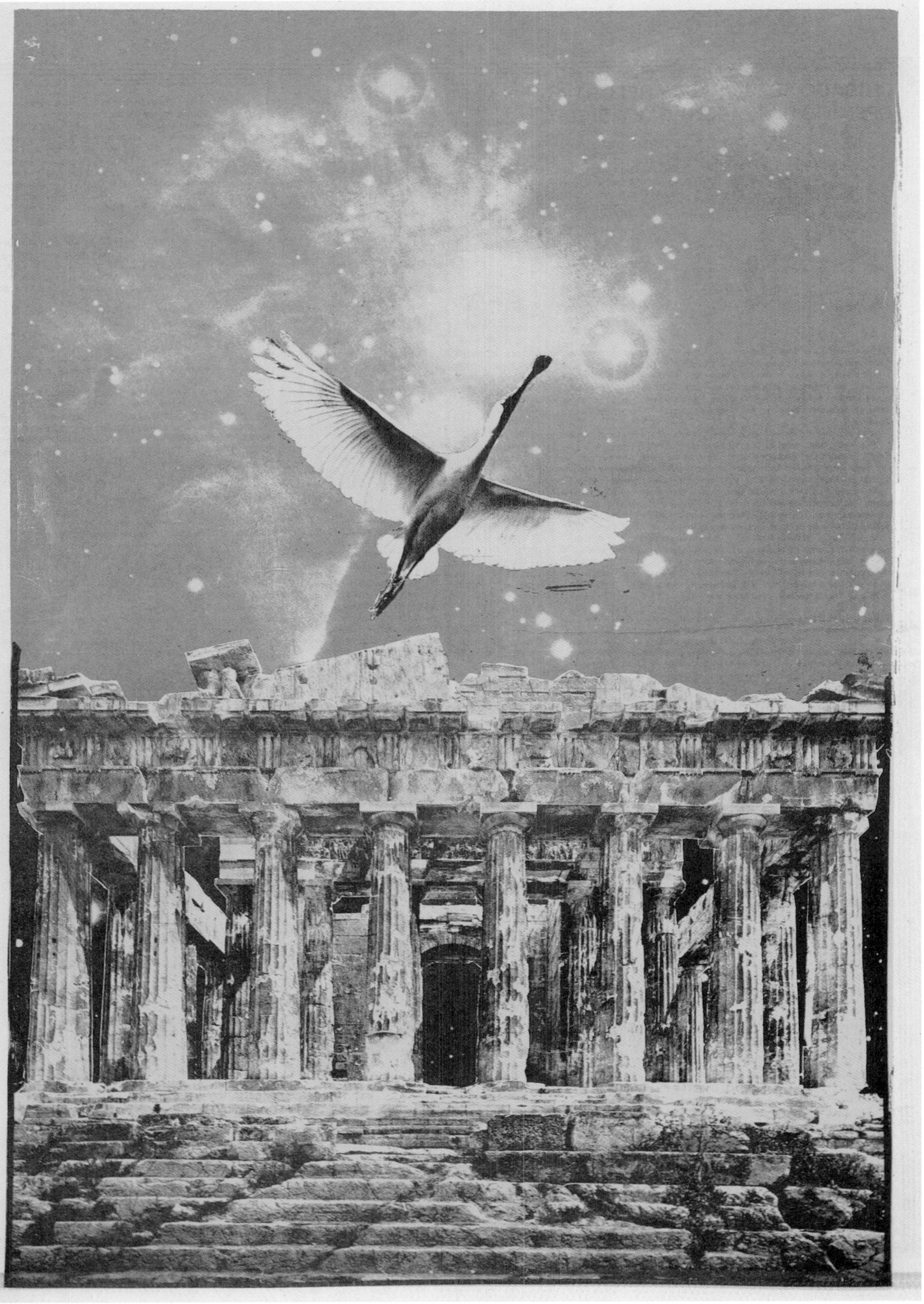

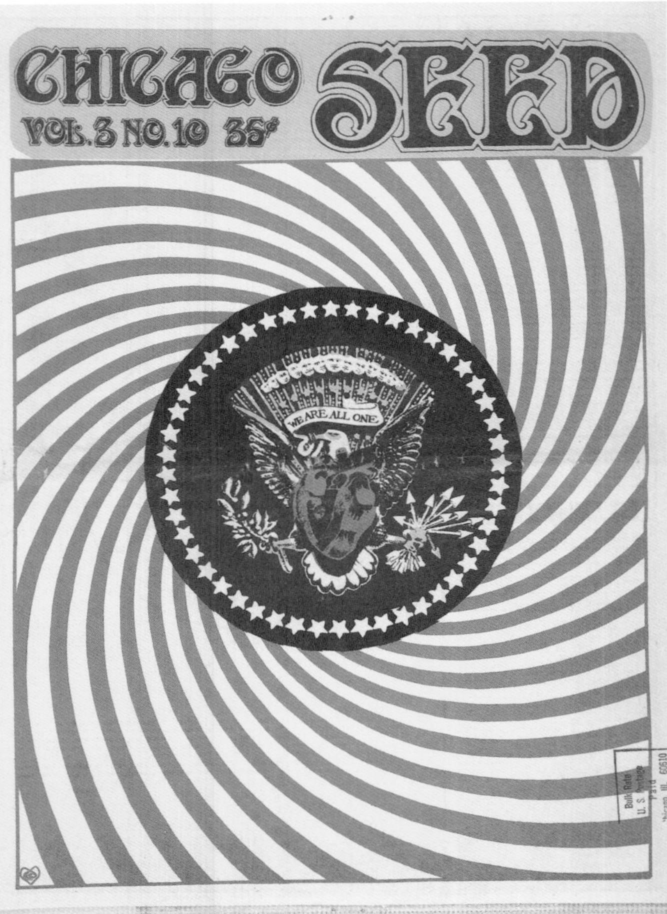

The Chicago Seed, 1969, vol. 3, no. 10, back cover
The Chicago Seed, 1969, vol. 3, no. 10, cover

Next page
The Chicago Seed, 1969, vol. 3, no. 12, cover
The Chicago Seed, 1969, vol. 3, no. 13, cover
The Chicago Seed, 1969, vol. 3, no. 13, back cover
The Chicago Seed, 1969, vol. 4, no. 4, cover
The Chicago Seed, 1969, vol. 4, no. 4, alternate cover

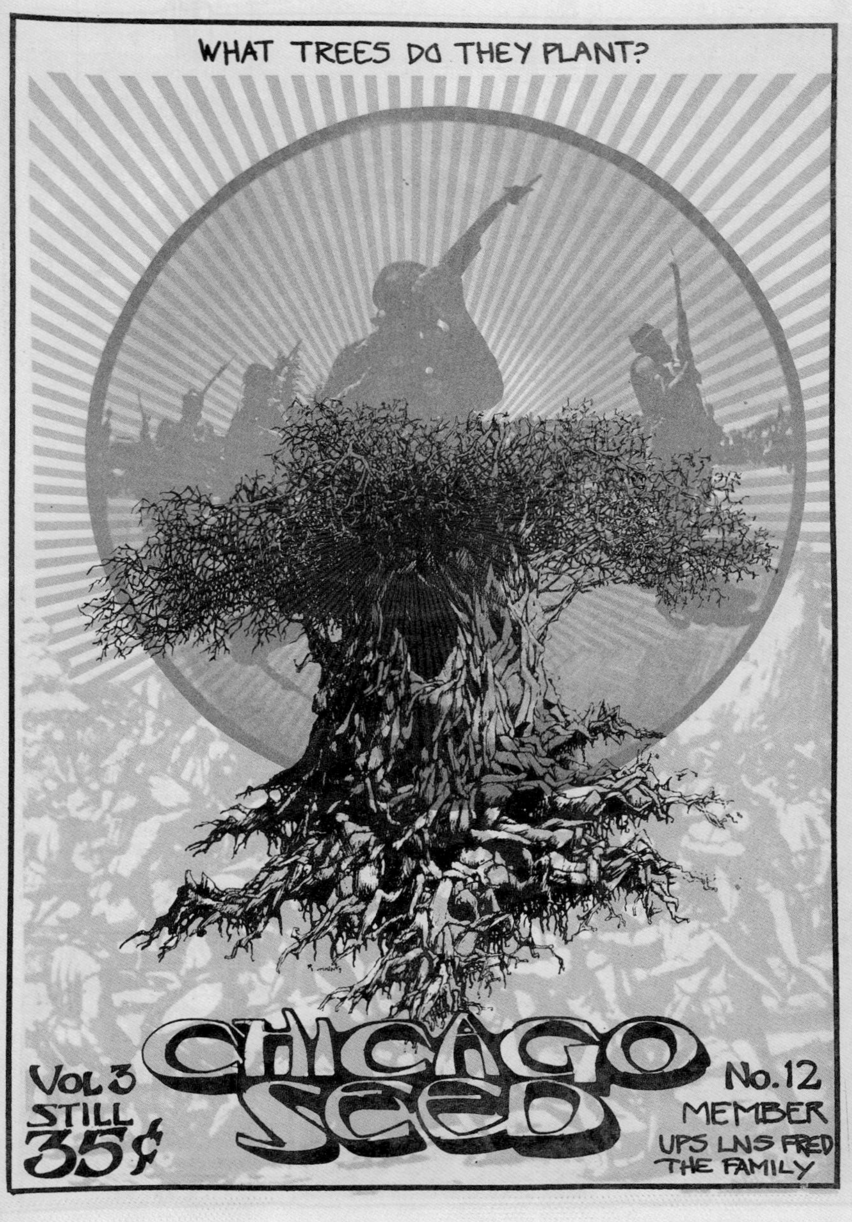
WHAT TREES DO THEY PLANT?
VOL 3
STILL
35¢
CHICAGO
SEED
No.12
MEMBER
UPS LNS FRED
THE FAMILY

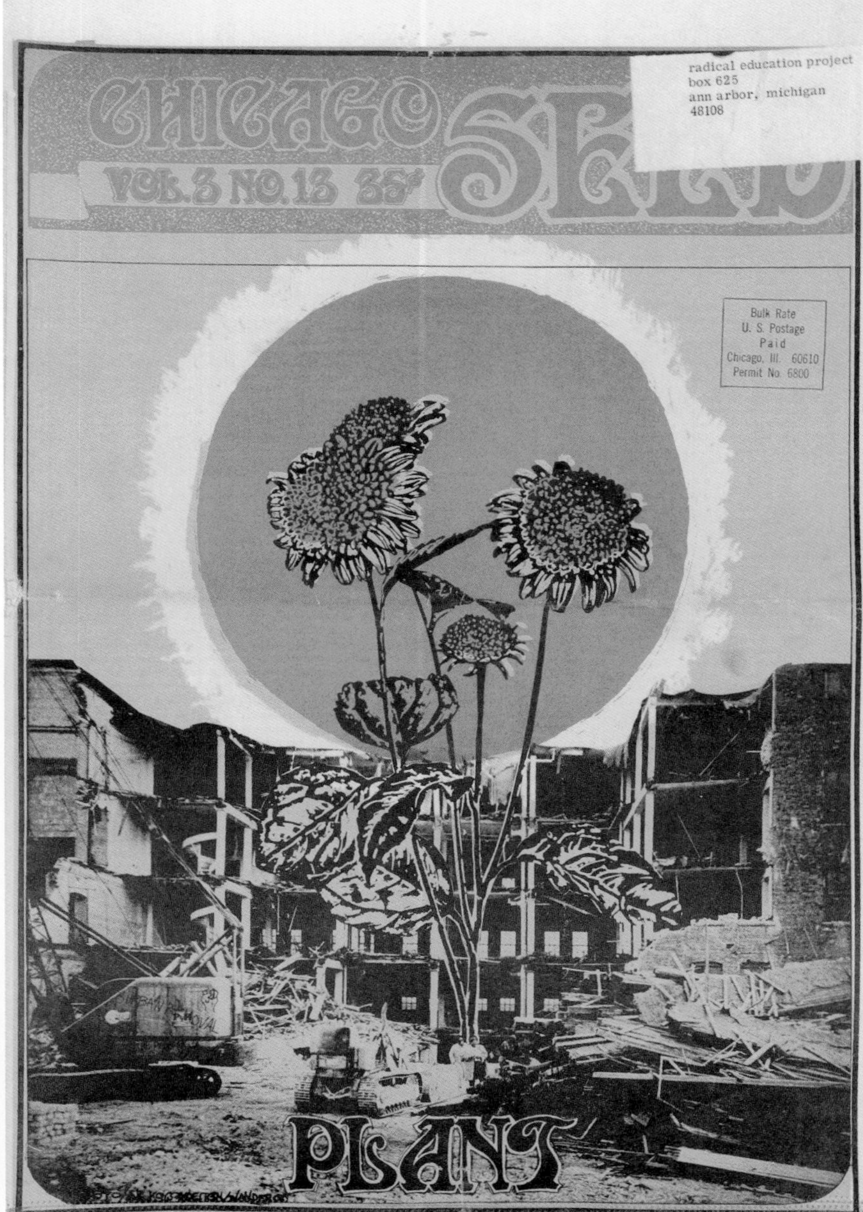
CHICAGO SEED
VOL.3 NO.13 35¢
radical education project
box 625
ann arbor, michigan
48108
Bulk Rate
U. S. Postage
Paid
Chicago, Ill. 60610
Permit No. 6800
PLANT

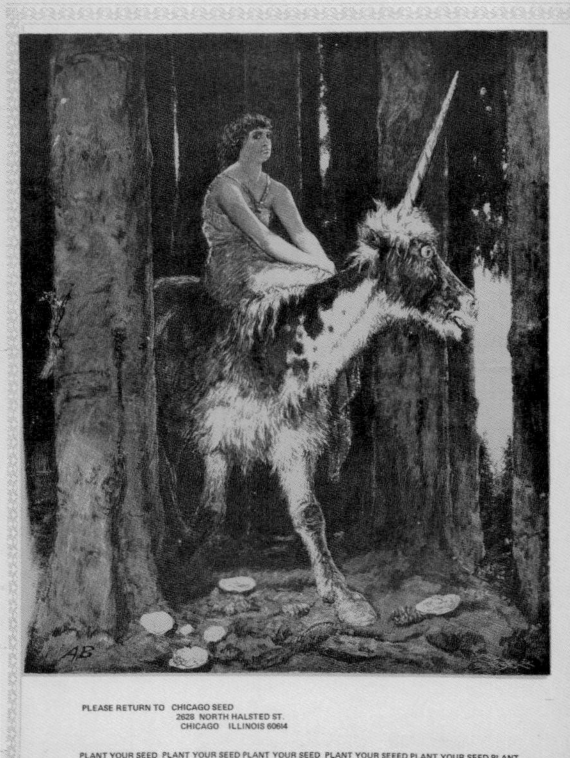
PLEASE RETURN TO CHICAGO SEED
2628 NORTH HALSTED ST.
CHICAGO ILLINOIS 60614
PLANT YOUR SEED PLANT YOUR SEED PLANT YOUR SEED PLANT YOUR SEED PLANT YOUR SEED PLANT

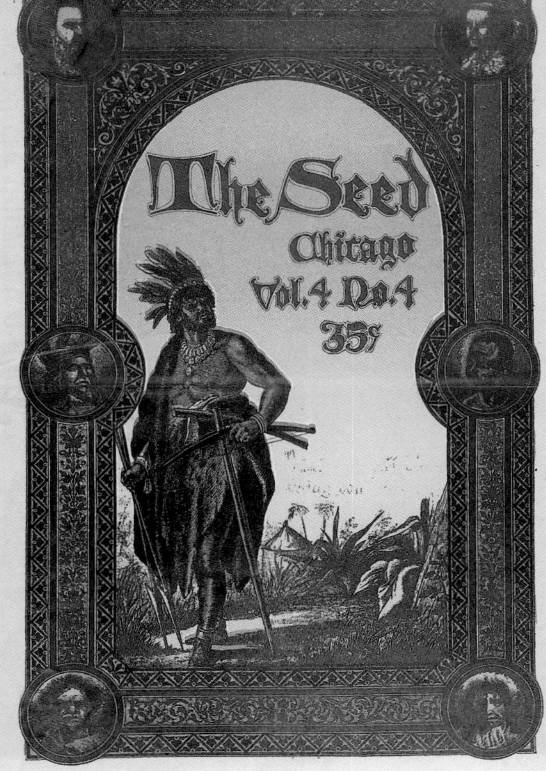
The Seed
Chicago
Vol.4 No.4
35¢

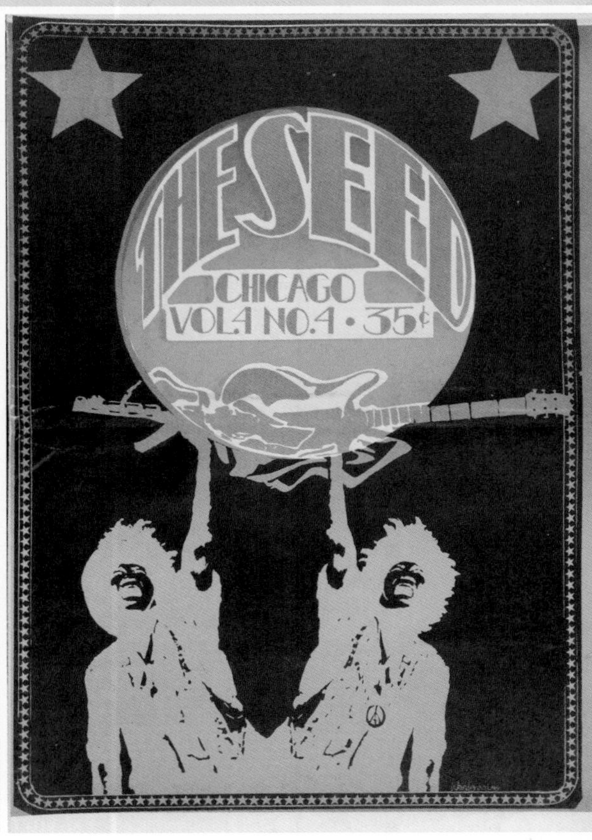
THE SEED
CHICAGO
VOL.4 NO.4 • 35¢

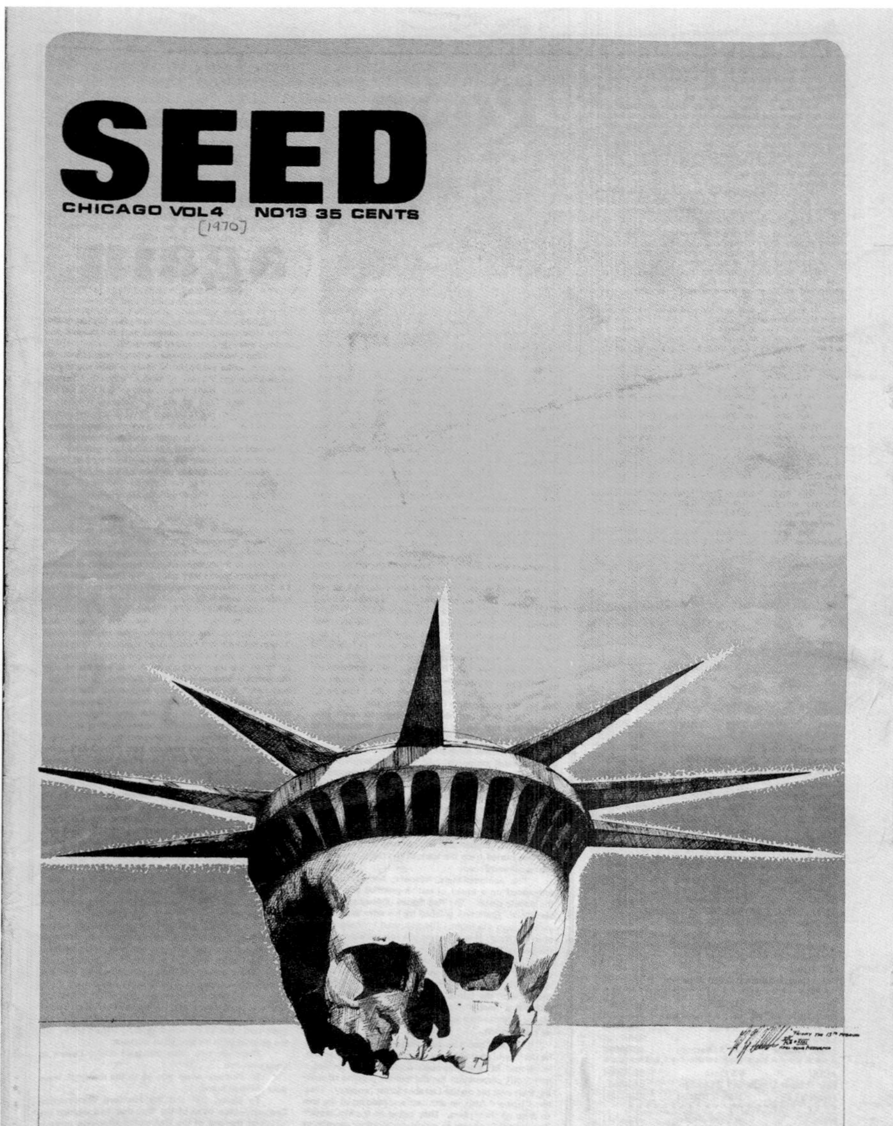

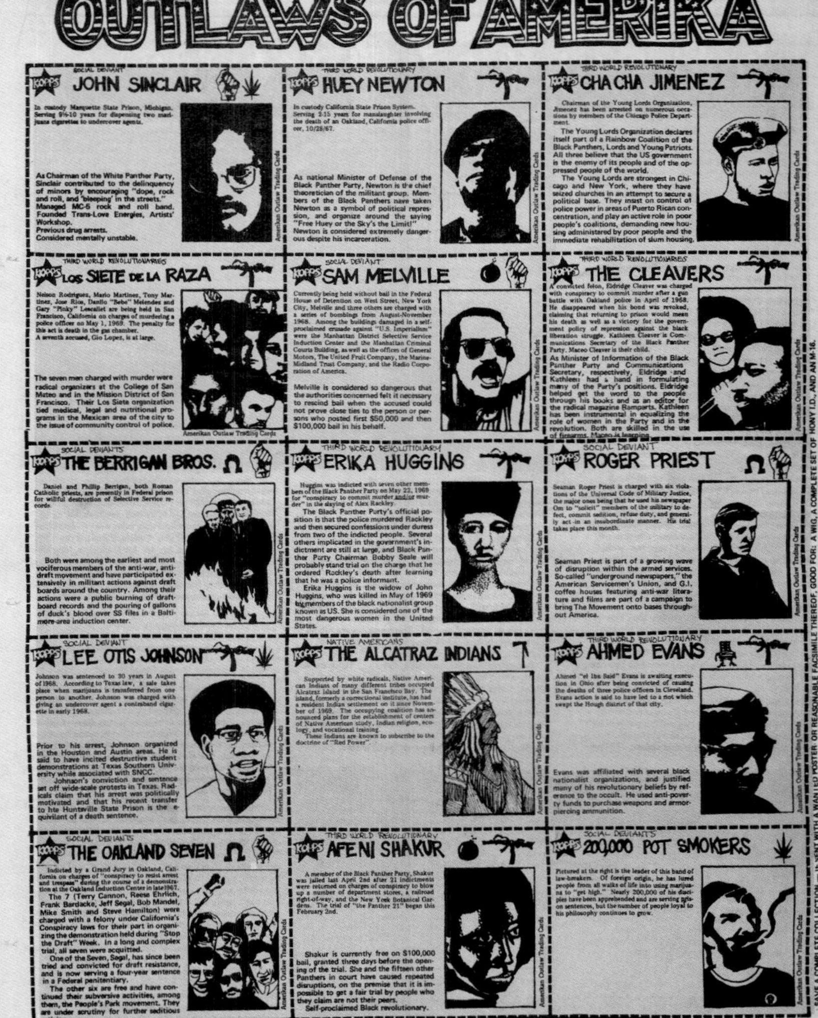

OUTLAWS OF AMERIKA

SOCIAL DEVIANT
JOHN SINCLAIR

In custody Marquette State Prison, Michigan. Serving 9½-10 years for dispensing two marijuana cigarettes to undercover agents.

As Chairman of the White Panther Party, Sinclair contributed to the delinquency of minors by encouraging "dope, rock and roll, and 'bleeping' in the streets." Managed MC-5 rock and roll band. Founded Trans-Love Energies, Artists' Workshop. Previous drug arrests. Considered mentally unstable.

Amerikan Outlaw Trading Cards

THIRD WORLD REVOLUTIONARY
HUEY NEWTON

In custody California State Prison System. Serving 2-15 years for manslaughter involving the death of an Oakland, California police officer, 10/28/67.

As national Minister of Defense of the Black Panther Party, Newton is the chief theoretician of the militant group. Members of the Black Panthers have taken Newton as a symbol of political repression, and organize around the saying "Free Huey or the Sky's the Limit!" Newton is considered extremely dangerous despite his incarceration.

Amerikan Outlaw Trading Cards

THIRD WORLD REVOLUTIONARY
CHA CHA JIMENEZ

Chairman of the Young Lords Organization, Jimenez has been arrested on numerous occasions by members of the Chicago Police Department.

The Young Lords Organization declares itself part of a Rainbow Coalition of the Black Panthers, Lords and Young Patriots. All three believe that the US government is the enemy of its people and of the oppressed people of the world.

The Young Lords are strongest in Chicago and New York, where they have seized churches in an attempt to secure a political base. They insist on control of police power in areas of Puerto Rican concentration, and play an active role in poor people's coalitions, demanding new housing administered by poor people and the immediate rehabilitation of slum housing.

Amerikan Outlaw Trading Cards

THIRD WORLD REVOLUTIONARIES
LOS SIETE DE LA RAZA

Nelson Rodriguez, Mario Martinez, Tony Martinez, Jose Rios, Danilo "Bebe" Melendez and Gary "Pinky" Lescallet are being held in San Francisco, California on charges of murdering a police officer on May 1, 1969. The penalty for this act is death in the gas chamber. A seventh accused, Gio Lopez, is at large.

The seven men charged with murder were radical organizers at the College of San Mateo and in the Mission District of San Francisco. Their Los Siete organization tied medical, legal and nutritional programs in the Mexican area of the city to the issue of community control of police.

Amerikan Outlaw Trading Cards

SOCIAL DEVIANT
SAM MELVILLE

Currently being held without bail in the Federal House of Detention on West Street, New York City, Melville and three others are charged with a series of bombings from August-November 1968. Among the buildings damaged in a self-proclaimed crusade against "U.S. Imperialism" were the Manhattan District Selective Service Induction Center and the Manhattan Criminal Courts Building, as well as the offices of General Motors, The United Fruit Company, the Marine-Midland Trust Company, and the Radio Corporation of America.

Melville is considered so dangerous that the authorities concerned felt it necessary to rescind bail when the accused could not prove close ties to the person or persons who posted first $50,000 and then $100,000 bail in his behalf.

Amerikan Outlaw Trading Cards

THIRD WORLD REVOLUTIONARIES
THE CLEAVERS

A convicted felon, Eldridge Cleaver was charged with conspiracy to commit murder after a gun battle with Oakland police in April of 1968. He disappeared when his bond was revoked, claiming that returning to prison would mean his death as well as a victory for the government policy of repression against the black liberation struggle. Kathleen Cleaver is Communications Secretary of the Black Panther Party. Maceo Cleaver is their child.

As Minister of Information of the Black Panther Party and Communications Secretary, respectively, Eldridge and Kathleen had a hand in formulating many of the Party's positions. Eldridge helped get the word to the people through his books and as an editor for the radical magazine Ramparts. Kathleen has been instrumental in equalizing the role of women in the Party and in the revolution. Both are skilled in the use of firearms. Maceo is learning.

Amerikan Outlaw Trading Cards

SOCIAL DEVIANTS
THE BERRIGAN BROS.

Daniel and Phillip Berrigan, both Roman Catholic priests, are presently in Federal prison for willful destruction of Selective Service records.

Both were among the earliest and most vociferous members of the anti-war, anti-draft movement and have participated extensively in militant actions against draft boards around the country. Among their actions were a public burning of draft-board records and the pouring of gallons of duck's blood over SS files in a Baltimore-area induction center.

Amerikan Outlaw Trading Cards

THIRD WORLD REVOLUTIONARY
ERIKA HUGGINS

Huggins was indicted with seven other members of the Black Panther Party on May 22, 1969 for "conspiracy to commit murder and/or murder" in the slaying of Alex Rackley.

The Black Panther Party's official position is that the police murdered Rackley and then secured confessions under duress from two of the indicted people. Several others implicated in the government's indictment are still at large, and Black Panther Party Chairman Bobby Seale will probably stand trial on the charge that he ordered Rackley's death after learning that he was a police informant.

Erika Huggins is the widow of John Huggins, who was killed in May of 1969 by members of the black nationalist group known as US. She is considered one of the most dangerous women in the United States.

Amerikan Outlaw Trading Cards

SOCIAL DEVIANT
ROGER PRIEST

Seaman Roger Priest is charged with six violations of the Universal Code of Military Justice, the major ones being that he used his newspaper Om to "solicit" members of the military to defect, commit sedition, refuse duty, and generally act in an insubordinate manner. His trial takes place this month.

Seaman Priest is part of a growing wave of disruption within the armed services. So-called "underground newspapers," the American Servicemen's Union, and G.I. coffee houses featuring anti-war literature and films are part of a campaign to bring The Movement onto bases throughout America.

Amerikan Outlaw Trading Cards

SOCIAL DEVIANT
LEE OTIS JOHNSON

Johnson was sentenced to 30 years in August of 1968. According to Texas law, a sale takes place when marijuana is transferred from one person to another. Johnson was charged with giving an undercover agent a contraband cigarette in early 1968.

Prior to his arrest, Johnson organized in the Houston and Austin areas. He is said to have incited destructive student demonstrations at Texas Southern University while associated with SNCC.

Johnson's conviction and sentence set off wide-scale protests in Texas. Radicals claim that his arrest was politically motivated and that his recent transfer to hte Huntsville State Prison is the equivilant of a death sentence.

Amerikan Outlaw Trading Cards

NATIVE AMERICANS
THE ALCATRAZ INDIANS

Supported by white radicals, Native American Indians of many different tribes occupied Alcatraz Island in the San Francisco Bay. The island, formerly a correctional institute, has had a resident Indian settlement on it since November of 1969. The occupying coalition has announced plans for the establishment of centers of Native American study, Indian religion, ecology, and vocational training.

These Indians are known to subscribe to the doctrine of "Red Power".

Amerikan Outlaw Trading Cards

THIRD WORLD REVOLUTIONARY
AHMED EVANS

Ahmed "el Ibn Said" Evans is awaiting execution in Ohio after being convicted of causing the deaths of three police officers in Cleveland. Evans action is said to have led to a riot which swept the Hough district of that city.

Evans was affiliated with several black nationalist organizations, and justified many of his revolutionary beliefs by reference to the occult. He used anti-poverty funds to purchase weapons and armor-piercing ammunition.

Amerikan Outlaw Trading Cards

SOCIAL DEVIANTS
THE OAKLAND SEVEN

Indicted by a Grand Jury in Oakland, California on charges of "conspiracy to resist arrest and trespass" during the course of a demonstration at the Oakland Induction Center in late 1967.

The 7 (Terry Cannon, Reese Ehrlich, Frank Bardacke, Jeff Segal, Bob Mandel, Mike Smith and Steve Hamilton) were charged with a felony under California's Conspiracy laws for their part in organizing the demonstration held during "Stop the Draft" Week. In a long and complex trial, all seven were acquitted.

One of the Seven, Segal, has since been tried and convicted for draft resistance, and is now serving a four-year sentence in a Federal penitentiary.

The other six are free and have continued their subversive activities, among them, the People's Park movement. They are under scrutiny for further seditious activity.

Amerikan Outlaw Trading Cards

THIRD WORLD REVOLUTIONARY
AFENI SHAKUR

A member of the Black Panther Party, Shakur was jailed last April 2nd after 21 indictments were returned on charges of conspiracy to blow up a number of department stores, a railroad right-of-way, and the New York Botanical Gardens. The trial of "the Panther 21" began this February 2nd.

Shakur is currently free on $100,000 bail, granted three days before the opening of the trial. She and the fifteen other Panthers in court have caused repeated disruptions, on the premise that it is impossible to get a fair trial by people who they claim are not their peers. Self-proclaimed Black revolutionary.

Amerikan Outlaw Trading Cards

SOCIAL DEVIANTS
200,000 POT SMOKERS

Pictured at the right is the leader of this band of law-breakers. Of foreign origin, he has lured people from all walks of life into using marijuana to "get high." Nearly 200,000 of his disciples have been apprehended and are serving prison sentences, but the number of people loyal to his philosophy continues to grow.

Amerikan Outlaw Trading Cards

SAVE A COMPLETE COLLECTION — IF SENT WITH A WANTED POSTER OR REASONABLE FACSIMILE THEREOF, GOOD FOR: A WIG, A COMPLETE SET OF HONY I.D., AND AN M-16.

WATCH FOR THE SECOND SERIES OF AMERIKAN OUTLAW TRADING CARDS. YOU MAY BE NEXT !!!

Bulk Rate
U. S. Postage
Paid
Chicago, Ill. 60610

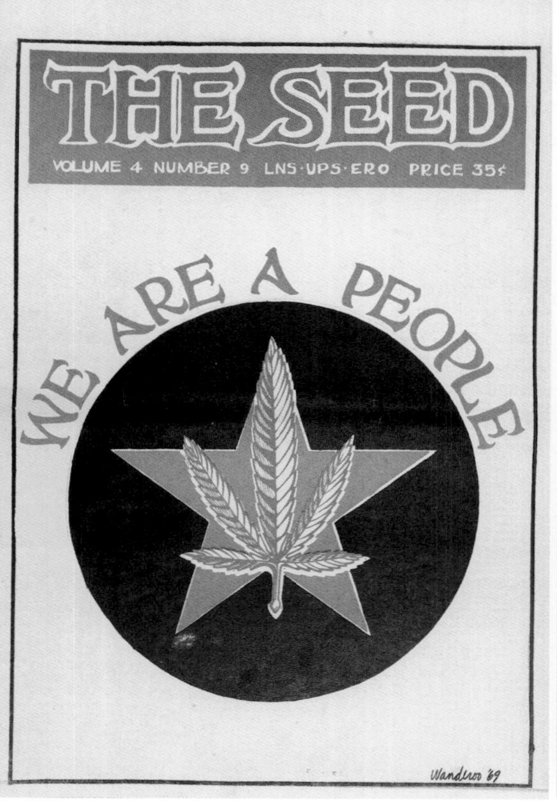

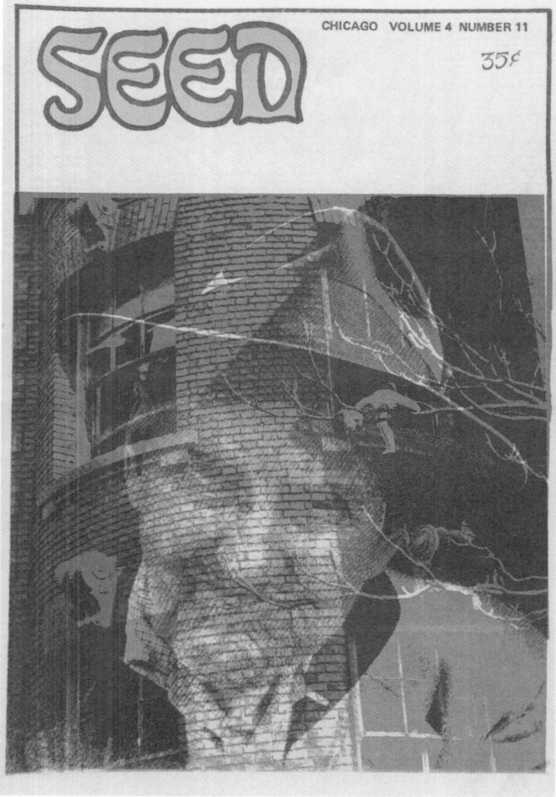

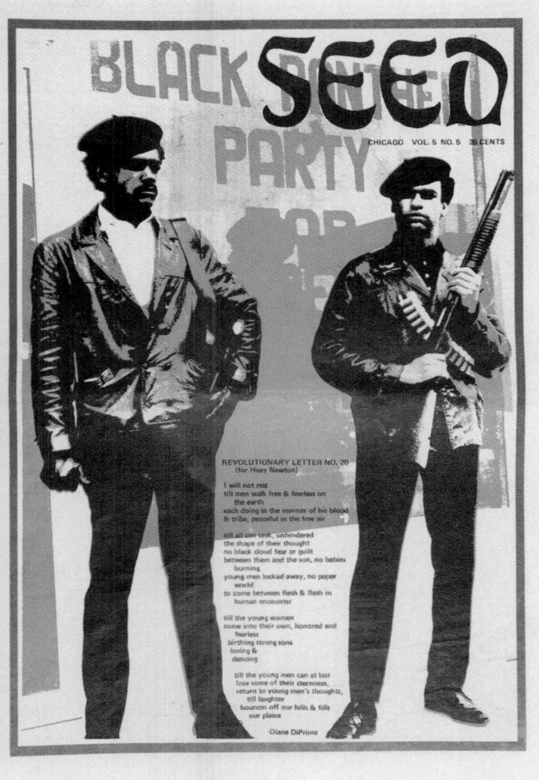

The Chicago Seed, 1970, vol. 4, no. 13, cover
The Chicago Seed, 1970, vol. 4, no. 13, back cover
The Chicago Seed, November 21–December 4, 1969, vol. 4, no. 9, cover
The Chicago Seed, 1970, vol. 4, no. 11, cover
The Chicago Seed, 1970, vol. 5, no. 5, cover

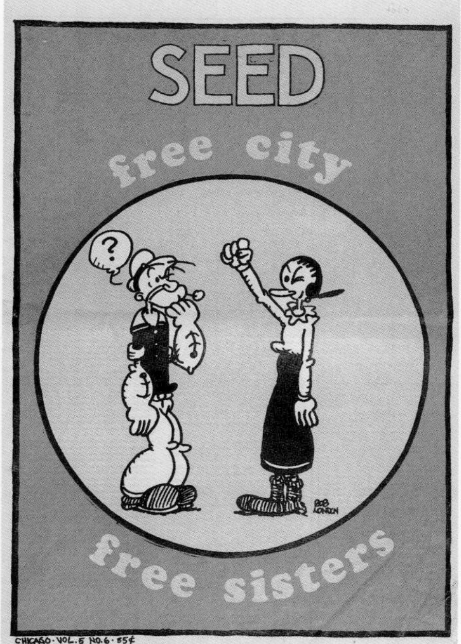

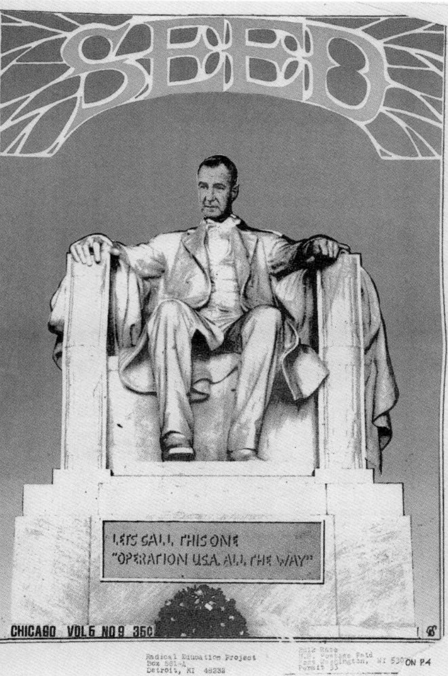

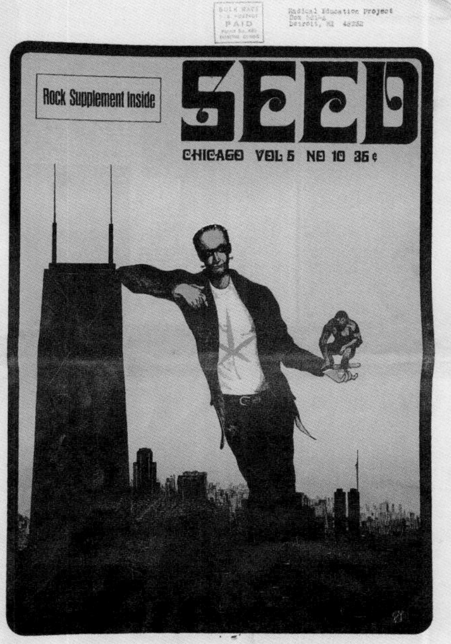

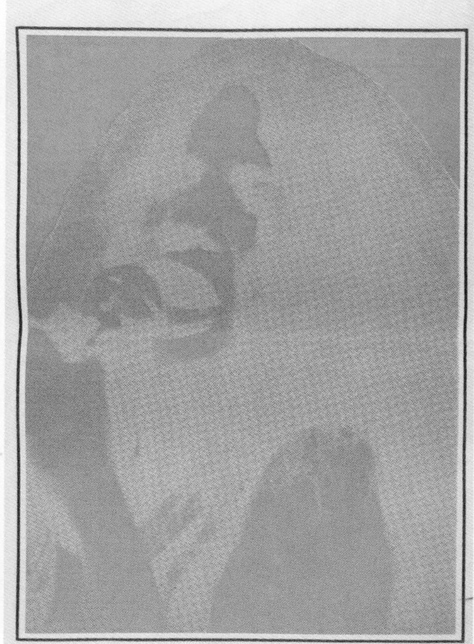

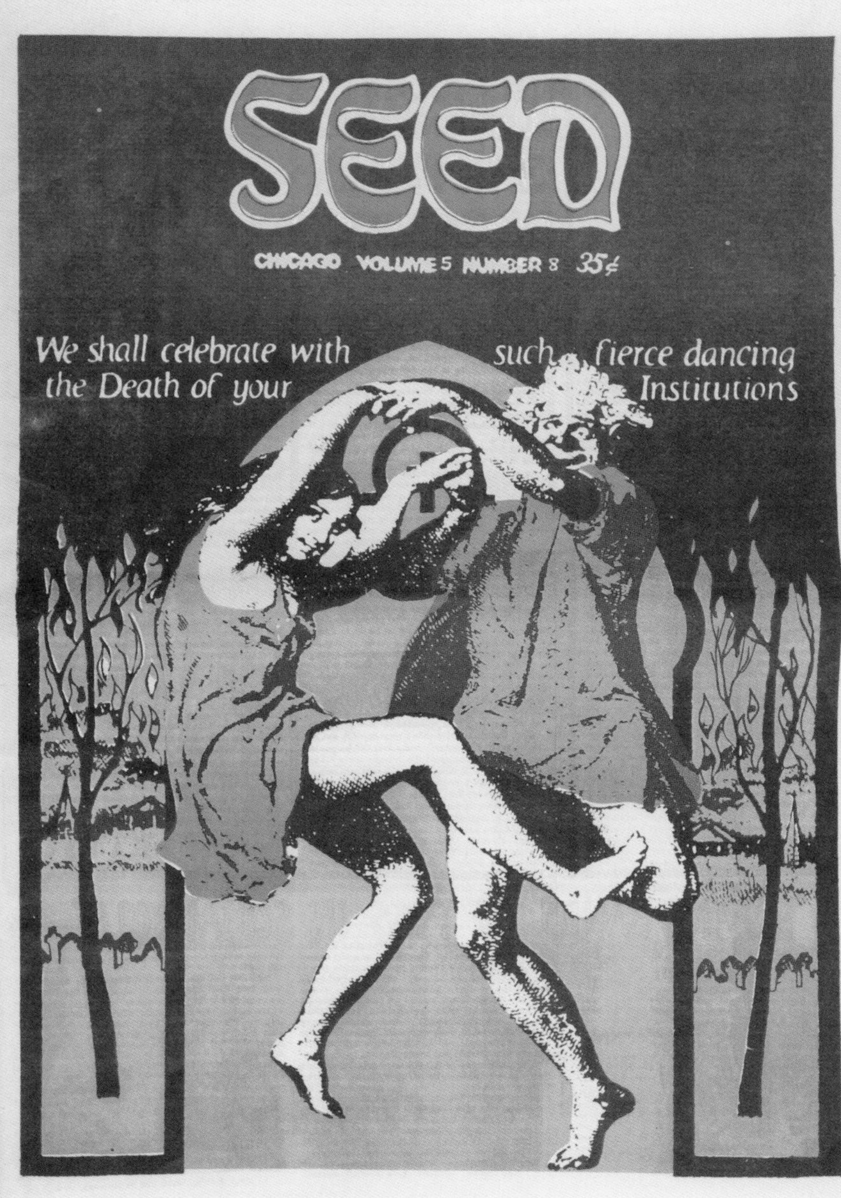

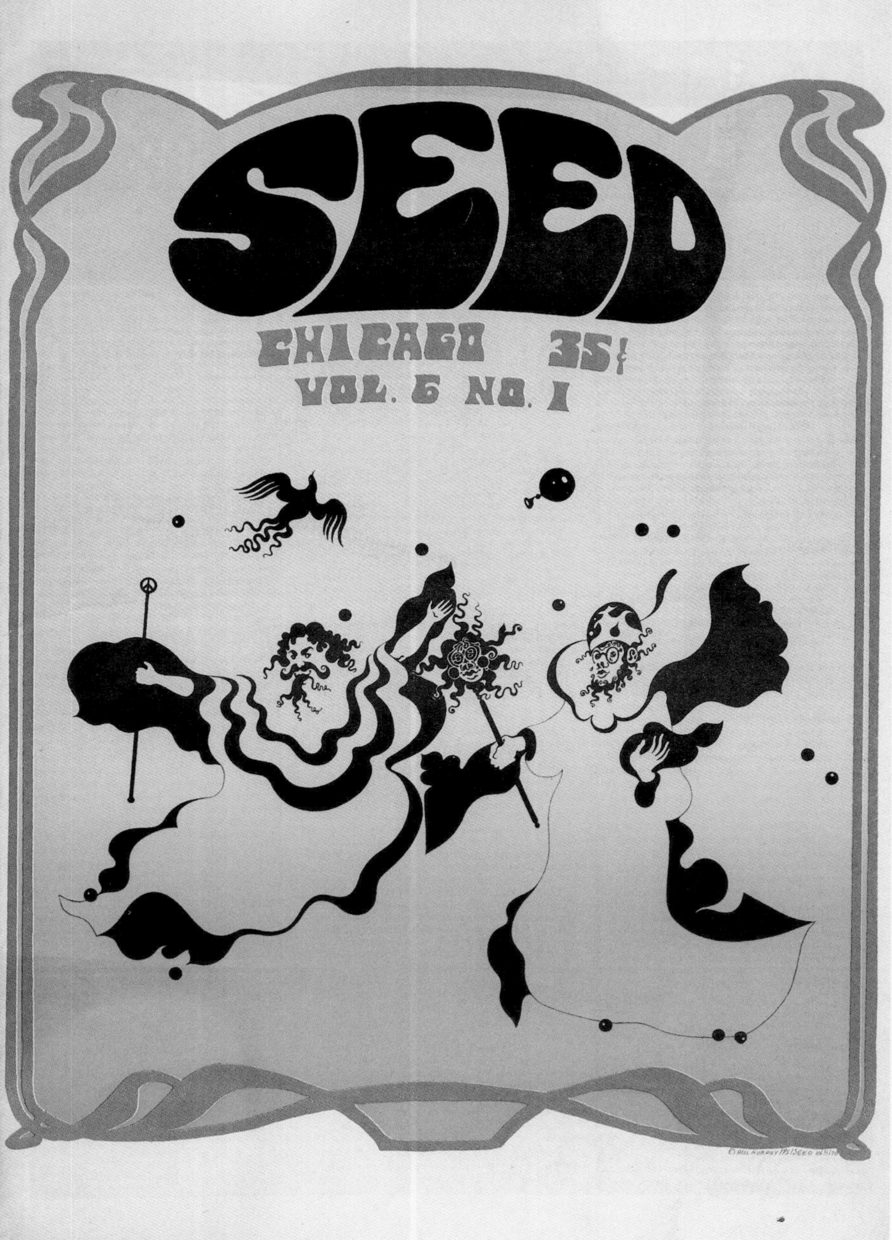

The Chicago Seed, 1970, vol. 5, no. 6, cover
The Chicago Seed, 1970, vol. 5, no. 9, cover
The Chicago Seed, 1970, vol. 5, no. 10, cover
The Chicago Seed, 1970, vol. 5, no. 13, back cover
The Chicago Seed, 1970, vol. 5, no. 8, cover
The Chicago Seed, 1970, vol. 6, no. 1, cover

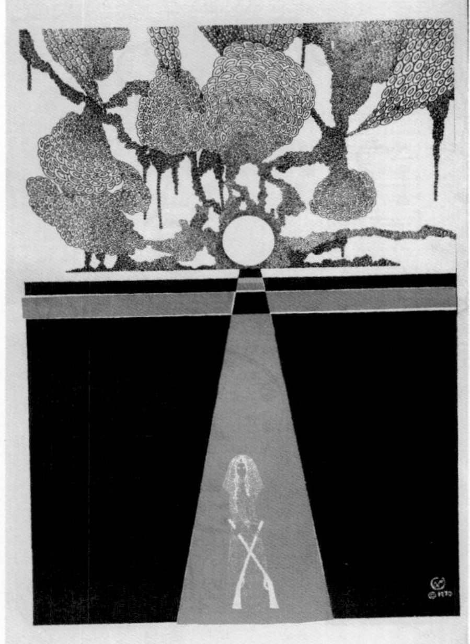

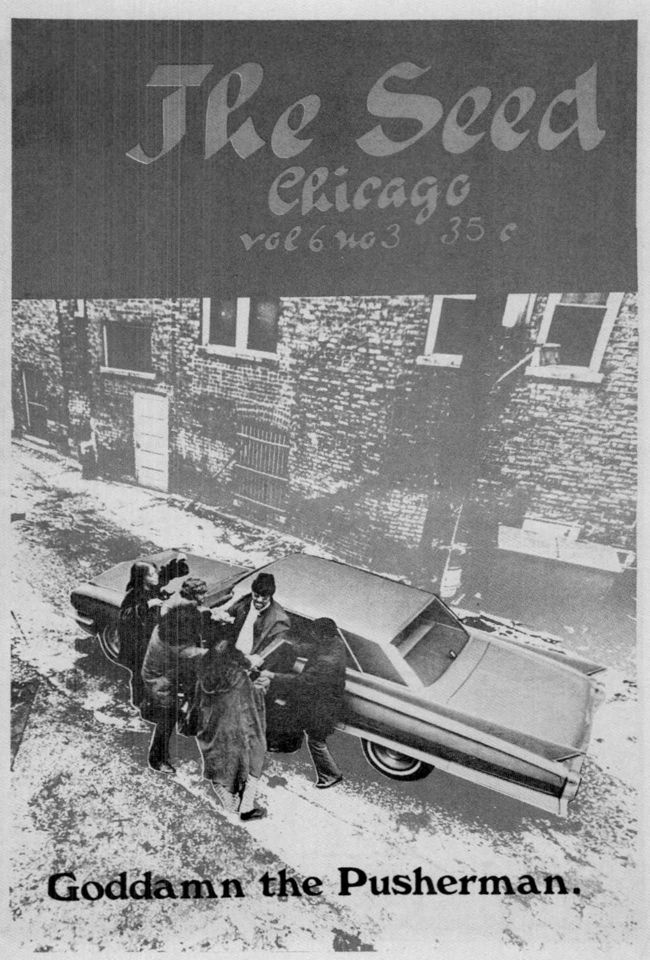

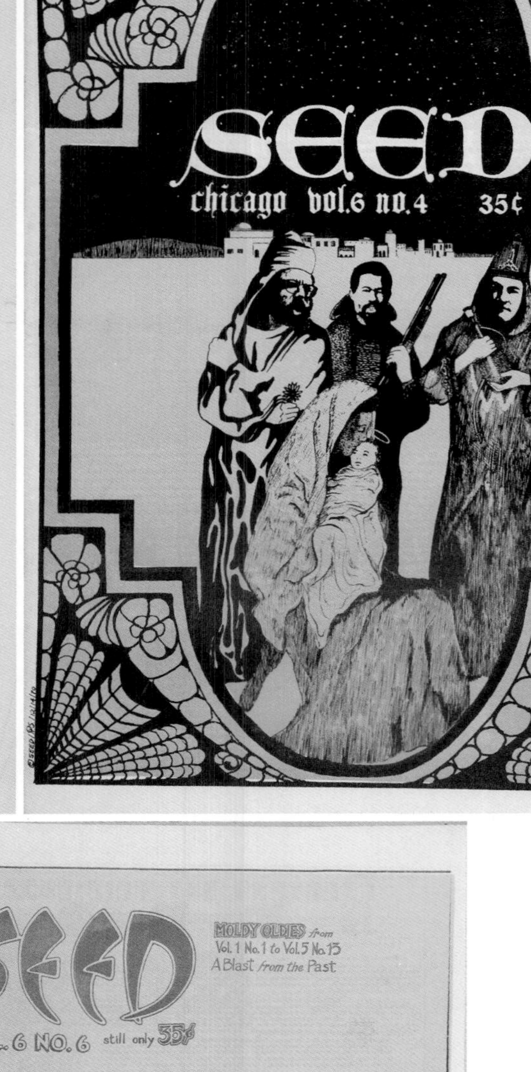

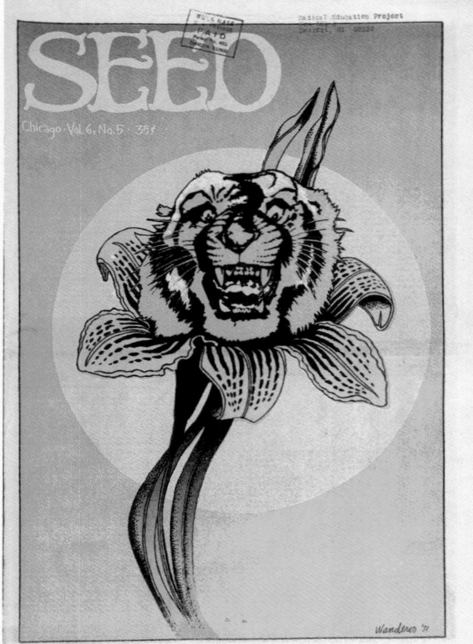

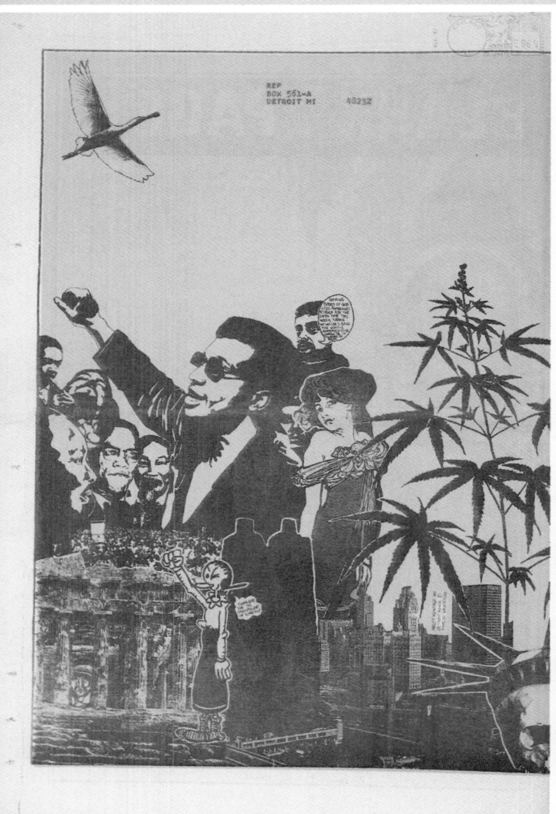

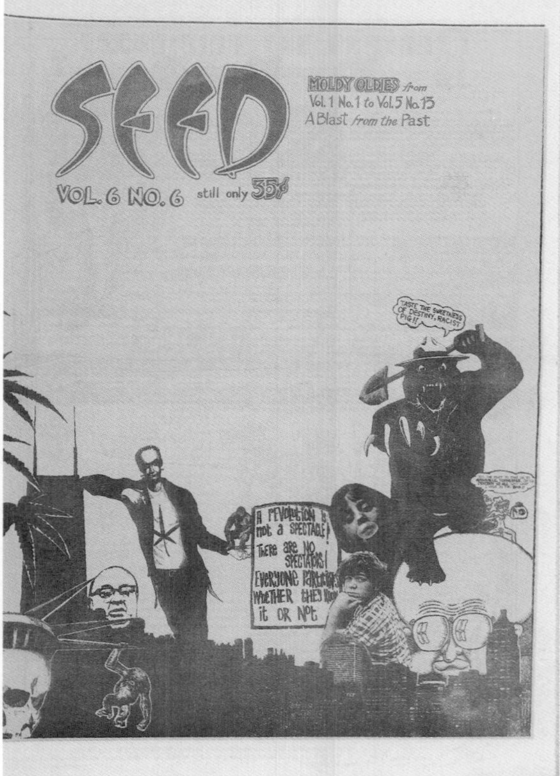

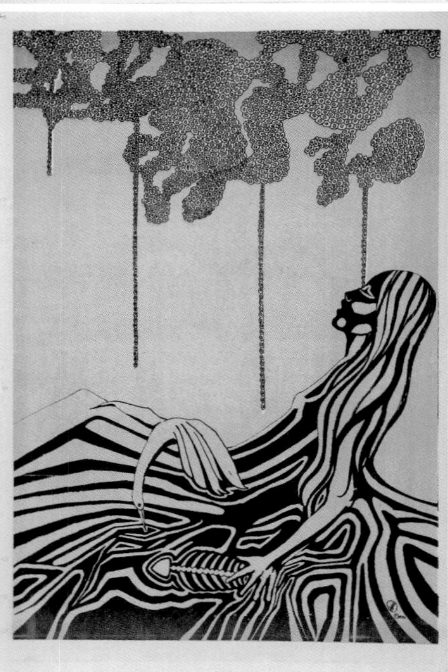

The Chicago Seed, 1970, vol. 6, no. 2, back cover
The Chicago Seed, 1970, vol. 6, no. 3, cover
The Chicago Seed, 1970, vol. 6, no. 4, cover
The Chicago Seed, 1970, vol. 6, no. 5, cover
The Chicago Seed, 1970, vol. 6, no. 6, back cover
The Chicago Seed, 1970, vol. 6, no. 6, cover
The Chicago Seed, 1970, vol. 6, no. 5, back cover

Next page
The Chicago Seed, May 1970, vol. 6, no. 12, back cover
The Chicago Seed, 1970, vol. 6, no. 13, cover
The Chicago Seed, June 1971, vol. 7, no. 2, cover
The Chicago Seed, June 1971, vol. 7, no. 2, back cover
The Chicago Seed, July 1971, vol. 7, no. 3, back cover

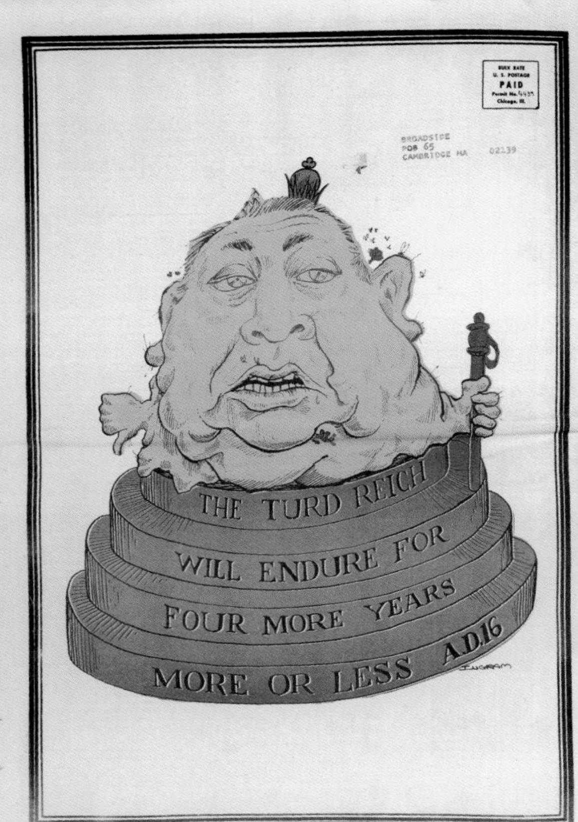
BULK RATE
U. S. POSTAGE
PAID
Chicago, Ill.
BROADSIDE
POB 65
CAMBRIDGE MA 02139
THE TURD REICH
WILL ENDURE FOR
FOUR MORE YEARS
MORE OR LESS A.D.16

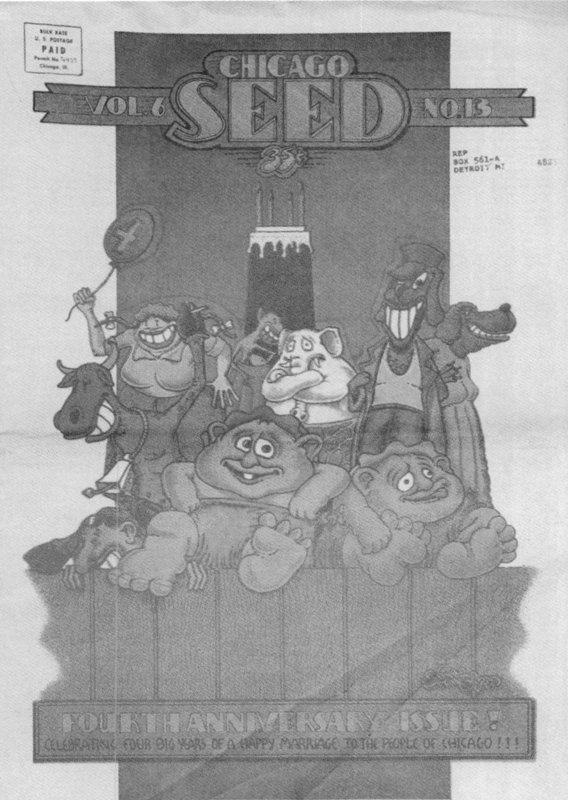
BULK RATE
U. S. POSTAGE
PAID
Chicago, Ill.
CHICAGO
VOL.6 SEED NO.13
FOURTH ANNIVERSARY ISSUE!
CELEBRATING FOUR BIG YEARS OF A HAPPY MARRIAGE TO THE PEOPLE OF CHICAGO!!!

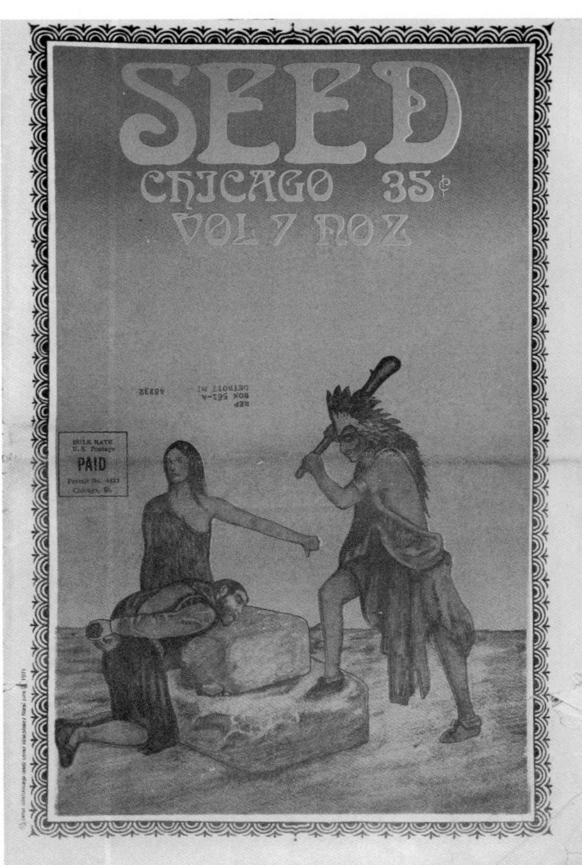
SEED
CHICAGO 35¢
VOL 7 NO 2
BULK RATE
U. S. Postage
PAID
Chicago, Ill.

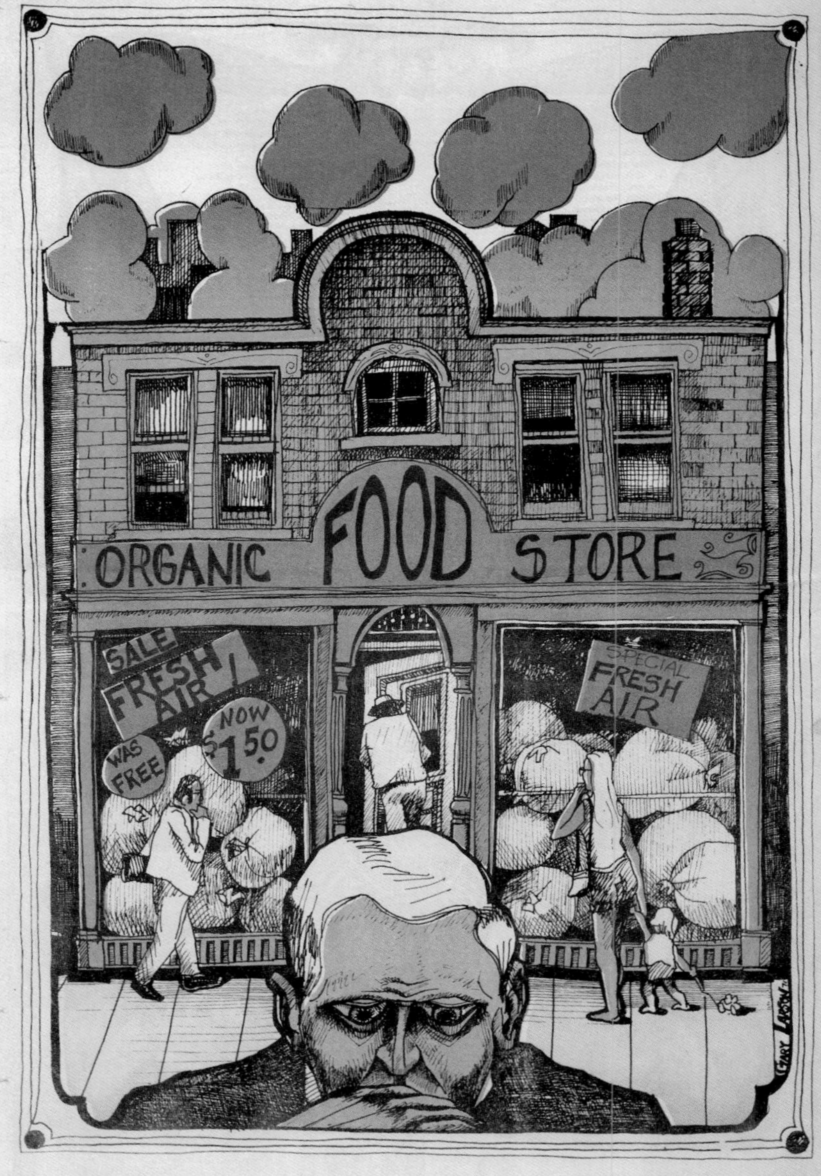
ORGANIC FOOD STORE
SALE
FRESH AIR
NOW $1.50
WAS FREE
SPECIAL
FRESH AIR

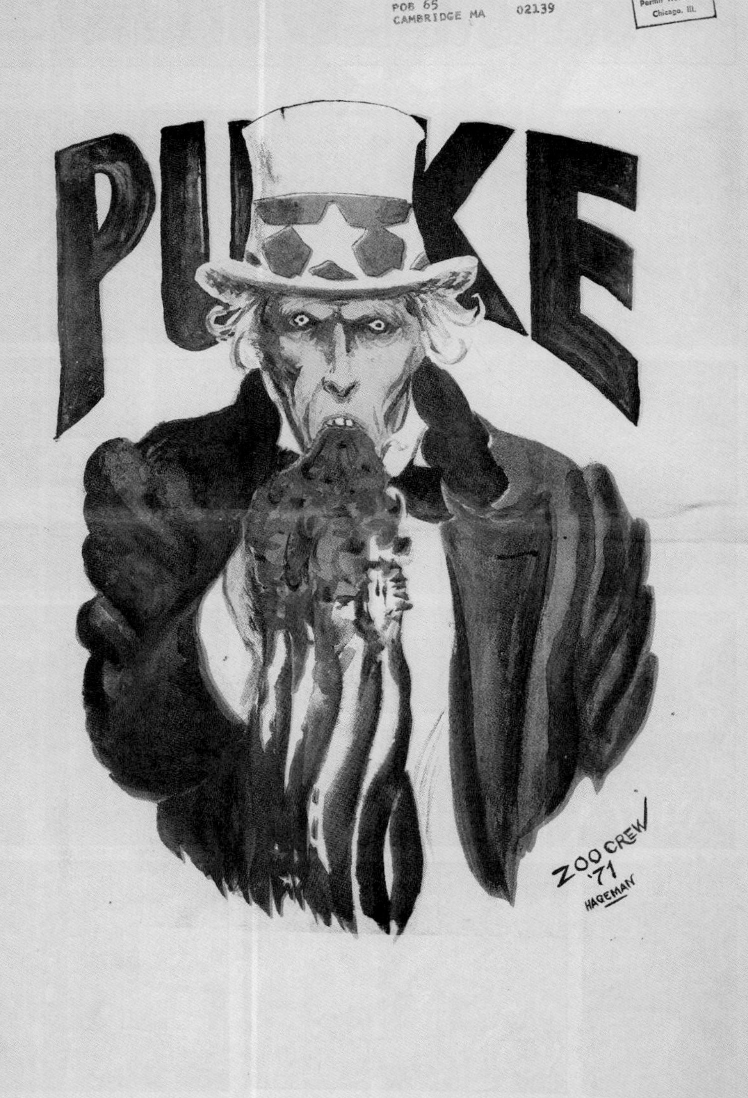
BROADSIDE
POB 65
CAMBRIDGE MA 02139
BULK RATE
U. S. POSTAGE
PAID
Chicago, Ill.
PUKE
ZOO CREW
'71
HAGEMAN

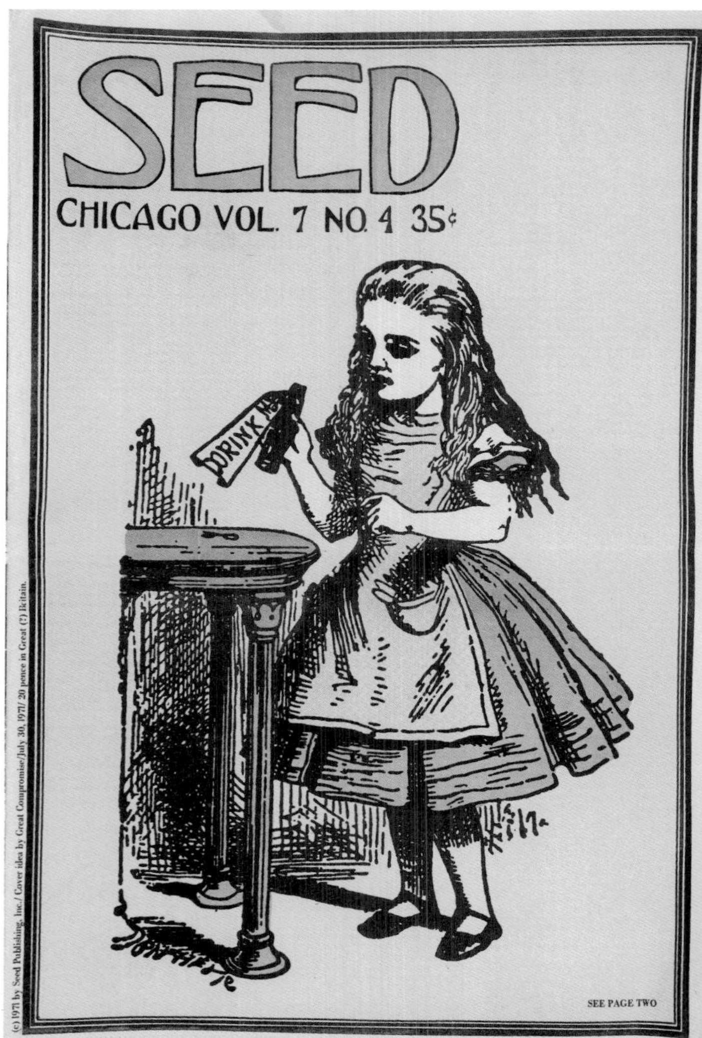
SEED
CHICAGO VOL. 7 NO. 4 35¢
DRINK ME
SEE PAGE TWO
(c) 1971 by Seed Publishing, Inc./ Cover idea by Great Compromise/July 30, 1971/ 20 pence in Great (?) Britain.

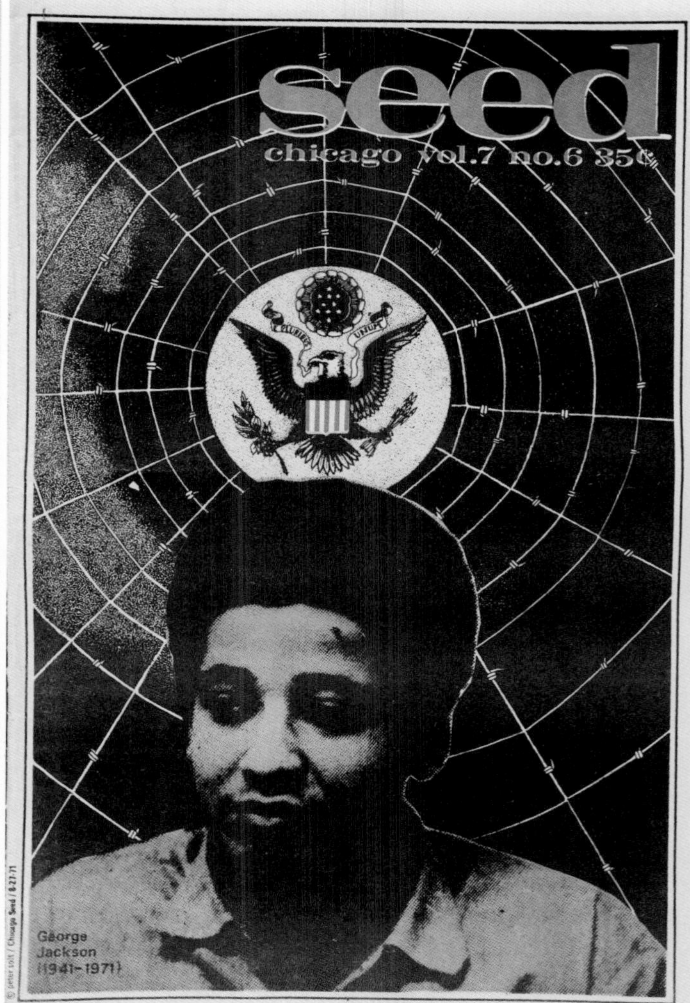
seed
chicago vol.7 no.6 35¢
George
Jackson
(1941-1971)

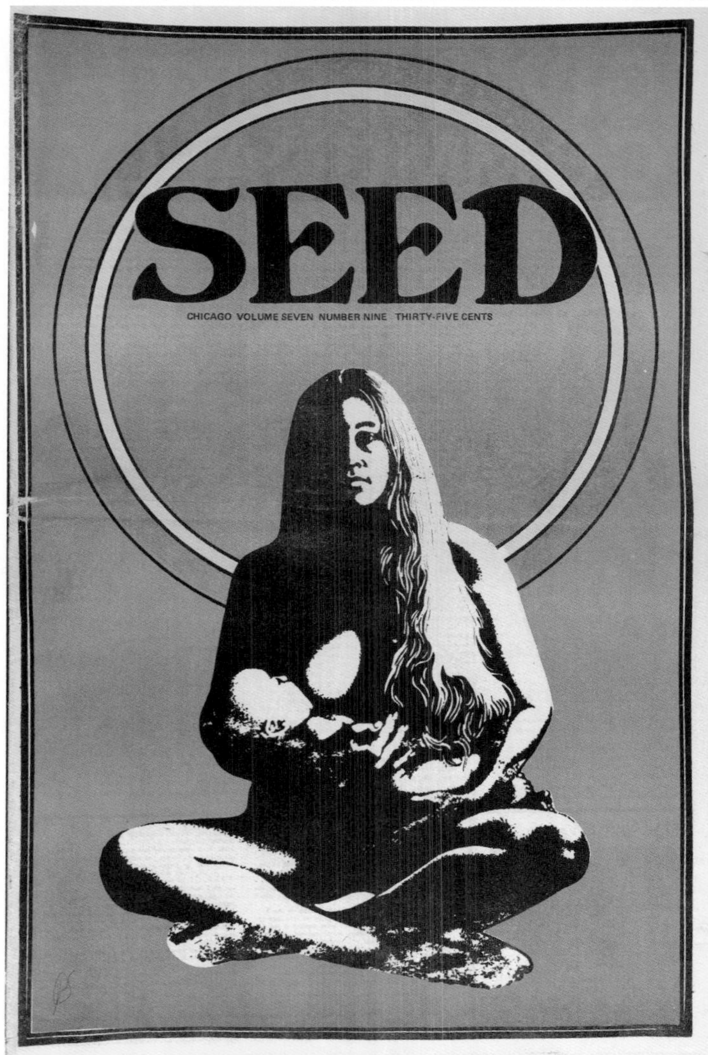
SEED
CHICAGO VOLUME SEVEN NUMBER NINE THIRTY-FIVE CENTS

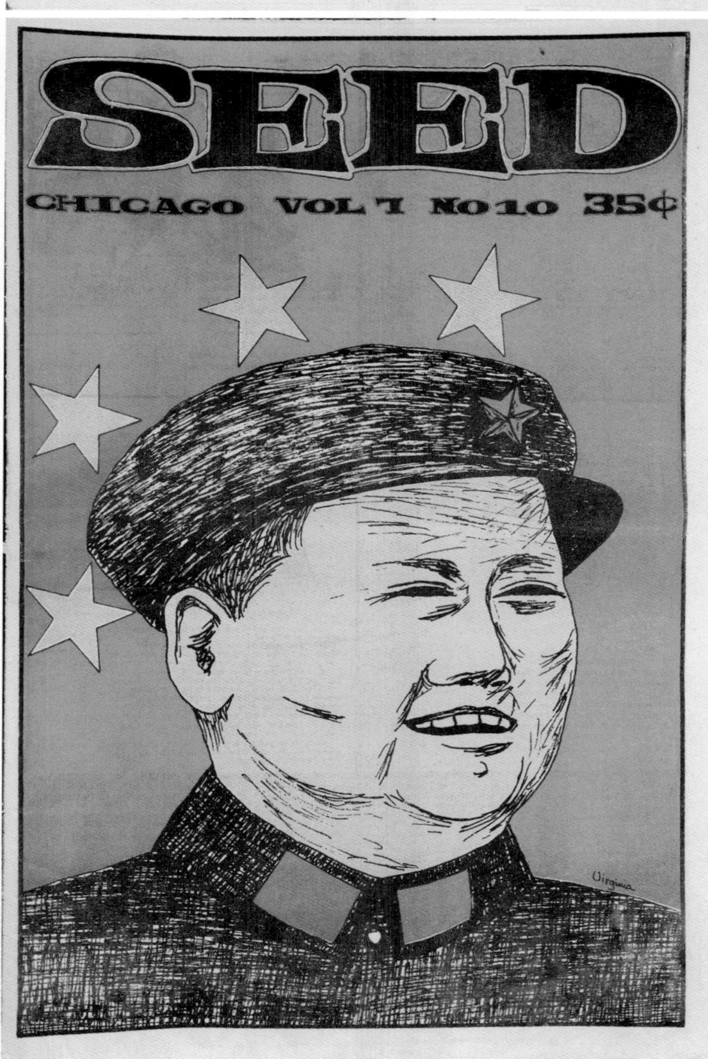
SEED
CHICAGO VOL 7 NO 10 35¢
Virginia

SEED

CHICAGO VOL.8 NO.5 35c

seed

chicago
vol. 8 no. 8
35¢

angela is free!!

Previous page
The Chicago Seed, July 1971, vol. 7, no. 4, cover
The Chicago Seed, August 1971, vol. 7, no. 6, cover
The Chicago Seed, October 1971, vol. 7, no. 9, cover
The Chicago Seed, 1971, vol. 7, no. 10, cover

The Chicago Seed, May 5, 1972, vol. 8, no. 5, cover
The Chicago Seed, 1972, vol. 8, no. 8, cover

Contributors

GWEN ALLEN is assistant professor of art history at San Francisco State University. She is the author of ***Artists' Magazines: An Alternative Space for Art*** (Cambridge, MA: MIT Press, 2011).

GEOFF KAPLAN of General Working Group has produced projects for a range of academic and cultural institutions. His work is included in San Francisco's Museum of Modern Art's and MoMA's permanent collections. He received his MFA from Cranbrook and teaches in the Graduate Program of Design at California College of the Arts and in the TransMedia program in Brussels.

PAMELA M. LEE is professor of art history at Stanford University. She is the author of ***Object to Be Destroyed: The Work of Gordon Matta-Clark*** (2000) and ***Chronophobia: On Time in the Art of the 1960s*** (2004), both published by the MIT Press.

BOB OSTERTAG is a composer, historian, instrument builder, journalist, and activist. He has published three books, twenty-one music CDs, two movies, and two DVDs. His writings on contemporary politics have been published on every continent and in many languages. He is currently professor of technocultural studies at the University of California at Davis.

FRED TURNER is associate professor of communication at Stanford University. He is the author of two books on American media culture since World War II: ***From Counterculture to Cyberculture: Stewart Brand, the Whole Earth Network, and the Rise of Digital Utopianism*** (Chicago: University of Chicago Press, 2006); and ***Echoes of Combat: The Vietnam War in American Memory*** (New York: Anchor Books, 1996; 2nd ed., Minneapolis: University of Minnesota Press, 2001). A former journalist, he has also written for publications ranging from the ***Boston Globe Sunday Magazine*** to ***Nature***.

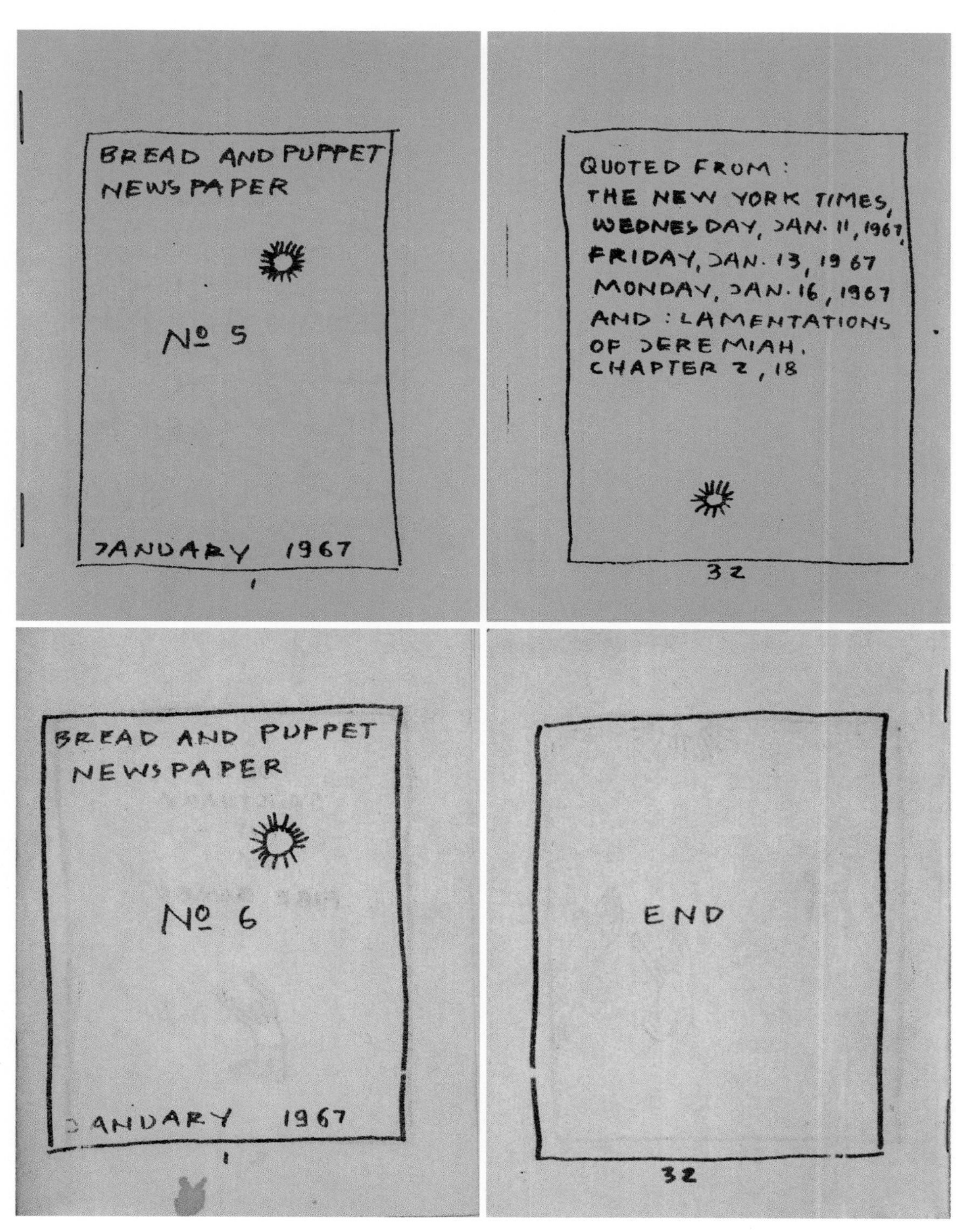

Bread and Puppet Newsletter, January 1967, no. 5, cover
Bread and Puppet Newsletter, January 1967, no. 5, back cover
Bread and Puppet Newsletter, January 1967, no. 6, cover
Bread and Puppet Newsletter, January 1967, no. 6, back cover

Index

Illustration Credits

1.1, 3.1, 3.2, 3.9–3.14, 3.17–3.18, 3.20, 3.22–3.23, 3.26, 3.28–3.30, 4.4, 4.9–4.10, 5.6, 5.7, 5.8, 5.9, 5.12, 5.18, 5.21 Archives and Special Collections, Thomas J. Dodd Research Center, University of Connecticut Libraries. **3.4** © Yvonne Rainer. **3.5** Art © Estate of Robert Smithson/Licensed by VAGA, New York, NY. **3.6** © Ed Ruscha. **3.7** © Mel Bochner. **3.8** © Dan Graham. **3.15** © Hans Haacke/Artists Rights Society. **3.16** The Getty Research Institute, Los Angeles (87-S194). **3.19** Collection of the Oakland Museum of California, All of Us or None Archive. Fractional and promised gift of the Rossman Family. **3.21** Collection Pierre and Micky Alechinsky © Donation Jorn, Silkeborg. **4.2** Department of Special Collections, Stanford University Libraries. **4.11–4.14** Department of Special Collections, Stanford University Libraries. **5.1** Beinecke Rare Book and Manuscript Library, Yale University. **5.2** Rare Book and Manuscript Library, Van Pelt-Dietrich Library Center, University of Pennsylvania. **5.3** Kansas Collection, Spencer Research Library, University of Kansas Libraries. **5.11** Charles Deering McCormick Library of Special Collections, Northwestern University Library. **5.13–5.16** Tamiment Library, New York University. **5.17** Archives and Special Collections, Thomas J. Dodd Research Center, University of Connecticut Libraries; Tamiment Library, New York University. **5.19** Collection of the New-York Historical Society. **5.20** Wisconsin Historical Society, WHI-37278. **Gallery Oz** magazine © Richard Neville. All other images, Archives and Special Collections, Thomas J. Dodd Research Center, University of Connecticut Libraries.

Acknowledgments

Power to the People was inspired by two different kinds of media archives. The first is an online archive of covers from the Australian magazine **Oz** (http://www.wussu.com/zines/ozlinks.htm). In 2005 the designer Kim West and I were browsing through the archive when it occurred to me that I could—and should—design a book about the graphic sensibility of utopian communities. I mentioned this idea to a good friend of mine, Joe Evans, who was then an archivist at the California Historical Society in San Francisco. Joe immediately referred me to the society's holdings of the Diggers' papers, which includes the Diggers' newsletter **Kaliflower**, and the archive of the People's Temple. The moment I came into contact with these original documents, I knew I needed to make this book. I thank Kim and Joe for guiding me to the light.

Throughout the process of editing **Power to the People** I've been moved many times by the boundless generosity of colleagues, friends, and contributors. Gwen Allen, Pamela M. Lee, Bob Ostertag, and Fred Turner: Thank you for your immensely thoughtful contributions and your trust in the project and its editor.

In addition, I'd like to thank the artists, activists, art historians, designers, and critics who contributed to the section "What We Were Reading." I am grateful to T. J. Clark, Todd Gitlin, Harmony Hammond, Steven Heller, Nancy Holt, Chip Lord, Margo Machida, Yvonne Rainer, Terry Smith, Lawrence Weiner, and Faith Wilding for sharing their memories and insights.

Susan Bielstein and the team at the University of Chicago have provided their expertise and support from the get-go. My great thanks go to Susan for championing this book at all stages of its making. And it was nothing but a pleasure to work with Anthony Burton, Carol Fisher Saller, Jill Shimabukuro, Michael Brehm, and Kira Bennett.

Ann Benoit was a tremendous design assistant, particularly with the heavy timeline lifting. Over the long haul Gloria Boyd, Joel Stillman, A. Ammo Eisu Wong, Raschin Fatemi, and Sarah Cline have pushed countless pixels.

This project would not be possible were it not for the generous support of the Neil Harris Fund and a faculty development grant from the California College of the Arts.

Of course, there are many people I need to acknowledge whose own work and relation to this material have shaped my thinking in myriad ways. They are: Alex Alberro, Dewey Ambrosino, Sasha Archibald, Amy Balkin, Andrew Blauvelt, Mel Bochner, Alan Chong, Chad Coerver, David Cortright, Gina Covina, Lincoln Cushing, Linnea Due, Sean Dungan, Thomas Eggerer, Eliot Fackler, Ed Fella, Courtney Fink, Karen Fiss, Francoise Flamant, Seeta Pena Gangadharan, Maria Gough, Dan Graham, Rene de Guzman, Hans Haacke, Steve Hartzog, Thomas Hirschhorn, Laurel Holliday, Nancy Holt, Allen Hori, David Humphrey, Steve Incontro, Billy X Jennings, David Joselit, Jordan Kantor, David Karam, Chris Kubick, Annette Keogh, Tirza Latimer, Maud Lavin, Catherine Lord, Henry Lowood, Brett MacFadden, Kathy McCoy, Maria McVarish, Richard Meyer, Olivia Neel, Steven Nelson, Richard Neville, Bill Noll, Josh On, Andrew Perchuk, Jeff Preiss, Rebecca Quaytman, Yvonne Rainer, Alan Rapp, Dont Rhine, Martha Rosler, Ed Ruscha, Tomo Saito, Scott Santoro, Stijn Schiffeleers, Jeffrey Schnapp, Amy Sillman, Jon Sueda, Margaret Sundell, Gail Swanlund, the excellent people at the Thomas J. Dodd Research Center University of Connecticut, Martin Venezky, Anne Walsh, Carol Wells, Michael Worthington, Shinjoung Yeo, and Andres Zervigon. Thank you all for your support and patience as I rambled on and on.

And finally to my family: Kaplans and Lees.

ACT
ALOHA
AMAZON QUARTERLY
amex-canada
AVPO
it aint me babe
kaleidoscope
THE LIBERATOR
FREE PRESS
MASSES
ABOUT FACE
ANN ARBOR SUN
APPEAL TO REASON
AVATAR
Berkeley Barb
Berkeley Tribe
BIAFRA
MODERN UTOPIAN
MOTHER EARTH
sds new left notes
NOLA EXPRESS
Notes from Cuba
off our backs
BLACK MASK
THE BOND
BREAD AND PUPPET NEWSPAPER
Clear Creek
OLD MOLE
ORACLE
THE ORGAN
OTHER SCENES
OZ
PAC-O-LIES
come out!
COMMON SENSE
COUNTERPOINT
distant drummer
DOCK of the BAY
Observer
The Pentagon Paper
People's Computer Company
RADICAL SOFTWARE
THE RAG
The Realist
REVOLUTION
DOMEBOOK
EL MALCRIADO
FATEH
FATIGUE PRESS
FED UP!
THE FIFTH ESTATE
San Francisco Express Times
THE SECOND FRONT
SEED
SHAKEDOWN
SMALL ARMS
FREEDOM'S JOURNAL
the furies
gay liberator
Gay Sunshine
UP AGAINST THE WALL
VECTOR
VIETNAM COURIER
Vietnam GI
vocations for social change
GOOD TIMES
BLIMP
The BIRD
inner-city VOICE
The International Times it
VOICE of the LUMPEN
WALKER'S APPEAL
WHERE IT'S AT
Whole Earth Catalog
WIN
YIPster TIMES

ABOUT FACE
ACT
ALOHA
AMAZON QUARTERLY
amex-canada
AMPO
it aint me babe
kaleidoscope
THE LIBERATOR
FREE PRESS
MASSES
ANN ARBOR SUN
APPEAL TO REASON
AVATAR
Barb
Berkeley Tribe
BIAFRA
MODERN UTOPIAN
MOTHER EARTH
sds new left notes
NOLA EXPRESS
Notes from Cuba
off our backs
BLACK MASK
THE BOND
BREAD AND PUPPET NEWSPAPER
Clear Creek
OLD MOLE
ORACLE
ORGAN
OTHER SCENES
OZ
PAC-O-LIES
come out!
COMMON SENSE
COUNTERPOINT
distant drummer
DOCK OF THE BAY
Observer
The Pentagon Paper
People's Computer Company
RADICAL SOFTWARE
THE RAG
The Realist
DOMEBOOK
EL MALCRIADO
FATEH
FATIGUE PRESS
FED UP!
THE FIFTH ESTATE
San Francisco Express Times
THE SECOND FRONT
SEED
SHAKEDOWN
SMALL ARMS
FREEDOM'S JOURNAL
the furies
gay liberator
Gay Sunshine
UP AGAINST THE WALL!
UP FRONT
VECTOR
VIETNAM COURIER
Vietnam GI
vocations for social change
GIGLINE
GOOD TIMES
BLIMP
The BIRD
inner-city VOICE
The International Times it
VOICE OF THE LUMPEN
WALKER'S APPEAL
WHERE IT'S AT
Whole Earth Catalog
WHOLE EARTH
WIN
YIPSTER TIMES